CCENT/ CCNA

ICND1 100-105

Official Cert Guide

WENDELL ODOM, CCIE No. 1624

Cisco Press
800 East 96th Street
Indianapolis, IN 46240 USA

CCENT/CCNA ICND1 100-105 Official Cert Guide

Wendell Odom

Copyright© 2016 Cisco Systems, Inc.

Published by:
Cisco Press
800 East 96th Street
Indianapolis, IN 46240 USA

Printed in the United States of America

4   16

Library of Congress Control Number: 2016933699

ISBN-13: 978-1-58720-580-4

ISBN-10: 1-58720-580-7

Warning and Disclaimer

This book is designed to provide information about the Cisco ICND1 100-105 exam for CCENT certification. Every effort has been made to make this book as complete and as accurate as possible, but no warranty or fitness is implied.

The information is provided on an "as is" basis. The authors, Cisco Press, and Cisco Systems, Inc. shall have neither liability nor responsibility to any person or entity with respect to any loss or damages arising from the information contained in this book or from the use of the discs or programs that may accompany it.

The opinions expressed in this book belong to the author and are not necessarily those of Cisco Systems, Inc.

Trademark Acknowledgments

All terms mentioned in this book that are known to be trademarks or service marks have been appropriately capitalized. Cisco Press or Cisco Systems, Inc., cannot attest to the accuracy of this information. Use of a term in this book should not be regarded as affecting the validity of any trademark or service mark.

Special Sales

For information about buying this title in bulk quantities, or for special sales opportunities (which may include electronic versions; custom cover designs; and content particular to your business, training goals, marketing focus, or branding interests), please contact our corporate sales department at corpsales@pearsoned.com or (800) 382-3419.

For government sales inquiries, please contact governmentsales@pearsoned.com.

For questions about sales outside the U.S., please contact intlcs@pearson.com.

Feedback Information

At Cisco Press, our goal is to create in-depth technical books of the highest quality and value. Each book is crafted with care and precision, undergoing rigorous development that involves the unique expertise of members from the professional technical community.

Readers' feedback is a natural continuation of this process. If you have any comments regarding how we could improve the quality of this book, or otherwise alter it to better suit your needs, you can contact us through email at feedback@ciscopress.com. Please make sure to include the book title and ISBN in your message.

We greatly appreciate your assistance.

Publisher	Paul Boger
Associate Publisher	Dave Dusthimer
Business Operation Manager, Cisco Press	Jan Cornelssen
Executive Editor	Brett Bartow
Managing Editor	Sandra Schroeder
Senior Development Editor	Christopher Cleveland
Senior Project Editor	Tonya Simpson
Copy Editors	Keith Cline, Chuck Hutchinson
Technical Editors	Aubrey Adams, Elan Beer
Editorial Assistant	Vanessa Evans
Cover Designer	Mark Shirar
Composition	Studio Galou
Senior Indexer	Erika Millen
Proofreaders	Kathy Ruiz, Paula Lowell

Americas Headquarters
Cisco Systems, Inc.
San Jose, CA

Asia Pacific Headquarters
Cisco Systems (USA) Pte. Ltd.
Singapore

Europe Headquarters
Cisco Systems International BV
Amsterdam, The Netherlands

Cisco has more than 200 offices worldwide. Addresses, phone numbers, and fax numbers are listed on the Cisco Website at www.cisco.com/go/offices.

About the Author

Wendell Odom, CCIE No. 1624 (Emeritus), has been in the networking industry since 1981. He has worked as a network engineer, consultant, systems engineer, instructor, and course developer; he currently works writing and creating certification study tools. This book is his 27th edition of some product for Pearson, and he is the author of all editions of the CCNA R&S and CCENT Cert Guides from Cisco Press. He has written books about topics from networking basics, certification guides throughout the years for CCENT, CCNA R&S, CCNA DC, CCNP ROUTE, CCNP QoS, and CCIE R&S. He helped develop the popular Pearson Network Simulator. He maintains study tools, links to his blogs, and other resources at www.certskills.com.

About the Technical Reviewers

Aubrey Adams is a Cisco Networking Academy instructor in Perth, Western Australia. With a background in telecommunications design, Aubrey has qualifications in electronic engineering and management; graduate diplomas in computing and education; and associated industry certifications. He has taught across a broad range of both related vocational and education training areas and university courses. Since 2007, Aubrey has technically reviewed several Pearson Education and Cisco Press publications, including video, simulation, and online products.

Elan Beer, CCIE No. 1837, is a senior consultant and Cisco instructor specializing in data center architecture and multiprotocol network design. For the past 27 years, Elan has designed networks and trained thousands of industry experts in data center architecture, routing, and switching. Elan has been instrumental in large-scale professional service efforts designing and troubleshooting internetworks, performing data center and network audits, and assisting clients with their short- and long-term design objectives. Elan has a global perspective of network architectures via his international clientele. Elan has used his expertise to design and troubleshoot data centers and internetworks in Malaysia, North America, Europe, Australia, Africa, China, and the Middle East. Most recently, Elan has been focused on data center design, configuration, and troubleshooting as well as service provider technologies. In 1993, Elan was among the first to obtain the Cisco Certified System Instructor (CCSI) certification, and in 1996, he was among the first to attain the Cisco System highest technical certification, the Cisco Certified Internetworking Expert. Since then, Elan has been involved in numerous large-scale data center and telecommunications networking projects worldwide.

Dedications

For Hannah Grace Odom, my wonderful daughter:

Tomato softball, equiangular equilateral quadrilaterals, being Jesus's hands and feet, wasabi, smart brain and a bigger heart, movies while other kids are at school, Underdog stories, math homework—hooray!, singing scat. Love you, precious girl.

Acknowledgments

Brett Bartow again served as executive editor on the book. We've worked together on probably 20+ titles now. Besides the usual wisdom and good decision making to guide the project, he was the driving force behind adding all the new apps to the DVD/web. As always, a pleasure to work with, and an important part of deciding what the entire Official Cert Guide series direction should be.

As part of writing these books, we work in concert with Cisco. A special thanks goes out to various people on the Cisco team who work with Pearson to create Cisco Press books. In particular, Greg Cote, Joe Stralo, and Phil Vancil were a great help while we worked on these titles.

Chris Cleveland did the development editing for the very first Cisco Press exam certification guide way back in 1998, and he's been involved with the series ever since. It's always great to work with Chris, even though I'm jealous of his office setup. This book has more moving parts than most, and Chris's part of the work happened on a challenging timeline. Thanks, Chris, for the many late-night hours working through the different elements, and especially for keeping us on track with the new features.

As for technical editors, ho hum, Elan Beer did his usual amazing job. It is truly abnormal to find one person who can do all aspects of technical editing in the same pass, with excellence. From finding small technical errors, to noticing phrasing that might mislead, to suggesting where an extra thought or two rounds out a topic, Elan does it all. Fantastic job as usual; thanks, Elan.

Aubrey Adams tech edited the book, his first time tech editing one of my books, and he also provided some excellent feedback. Aubrey's experience teaching the material was a big help in particular, because he knows of the common mistakes that students make when learning these same topics. Diligent, objective, useful comments all around; thanks, Aubrey!

Welcome and thanks to a new team member, Lisa Matthews, new at least in terms of someone I interact with during the writing process. Lisa handled all the practice app development: taking various appendixes, learning some subnetting (fun, huh Lisa?), and building apps to make the practice experience more interactive. Thanks for guiding us through the process, Lisa!

I love the magic wand that is production. Presto, word docs with gobs of queries and comments feed into the machine, and out pops these beautiful books. Thanks to Sandra Schroeder, Tonya Simpson, Mandie Frank, for jumping into the fray to keep the schedule moving, and all the production team for making the magic happen. From fixing all my grammar, crummy word choices, passive-voice sentences, and then pulling the design and layout together, they do it all; thanks for putting it all together and making it look easy. And Tonya, once again getting the "opportunity" to manage two books with many elements at the same timeline, once again, the juggling act continues, and done well. Thanks for managing the whole production process again.

Mike Tanamachi, illustrator and mind reader, did a great job on the figures again. I use a different process with the figures than most authors, with Mike drawing new figures as soon as I outline a new section or chapter. It means more edits when I change my mind, and lots of mind reading of what Wendell really wanted versus what I drew poorly on my Wacom tablet. Mike came through again with some beautiful finished products. And a thanks goes out to Laura Robbins for working on helping make sure all the figures follow our color standards—standards she helped develop over several other editions of other books.

I could not have made the timeline for this book without Chris Burns of Certskills Professional. Chris owns the mind map process now, owns big parts of the lab development process for the associated labs added to my blogs, does various tasks related to specific chapters, and then catches anything I need to toss over my shoulder so I can focus on the books. Chris, you are the man!

Sean Wilkins played the largest role he's played so far with one of my books. A long-time co-collaborator with Pearson's CCNA Simulator, Sean did a lot of technology work behind the scenes. No way the books are out on time without Sean's efforts; thanks for the great job, Sean!

A special thanks you to you readers who write in with suggestions and possible errors, and especially those of you who post online at the Cisco Learning Network. Without question, the comments I receive directly and overhear by participating at CLN made this edition a better book.

Thanks to my wonderful wife, Kris, who helps make this sometimes challenging work lifestyle a breeze. I love walking this journey with you, doll. Thanks to my daughter Hannah (see dedication). And thanks to Jesus Christ, Lord of everything in my life.

Contents at a Glance

Contents

Reader Services

To access additional content for this book, simply register your product. To start the registration process, go to www.ciscopress.com/register and log in or create an account*. Enter the product ISBN 9781587205804 and click Submit. After the process is complete, you will find any available bonus content under Registered Products.

*Be sure to check the box that you would like to hear from us to receive exclusive discounts on future editions of this product.

Icons Used in This Book

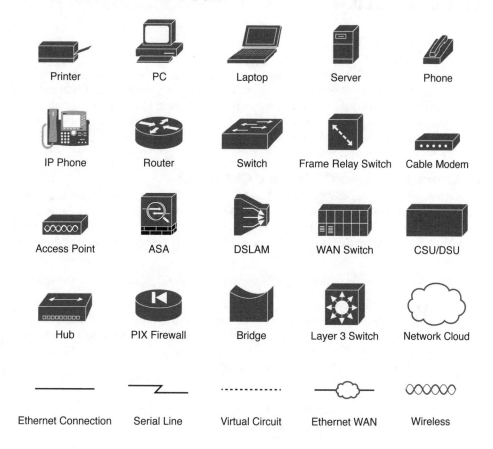

Printer   PC   Laptop   Server   Phone

IP Phone   Router   Switch   Frame Relay Switch   Cable Modem

Access Point   ASA   DSLAM   WAN Switch   CSU/DSU

Hub   PIX Firewall   Bridge   Layer 3 Switch   Network Cloud

Ethernet Connection   Serial Line   Virtual Circuit   Ethernet WAN   Wireless

Command Syntax Conventions

The conventions used to present command syntax in this book are the same conventions used in the IOS Command Reference. The Command Reference describes these conventions as follows:

- **Boldface** indicates commands and keywords that are entered literally as shown. In actual configuration examples and output (not general command syntax), boldface indicates commands that are manually input by the user (such as a **show** command).
- *Italic* indicates arguments for which you supply actual values.
- Vertical bars (|) separate alternative, mutually exclusive elements.
- Square brackets ([ ]) indicate an optional element.
- Braces ({ }) indicate a required choice.
- Braces within brackets ([{ }]) indicate a required choice within an optional element.

Introduction

About the Exams

Congratulations! If you're reading far enough to look at this book's Introduction, you've probably already decided to go for your Cisco certification. If you want to succeed as a technical person in the networking industry at all, you need to know Cisco. Cisco has a ridiculously high market share in the router and switch marketplace, with more than 80 percent market share in some markets. In many geographies and markets around the world, networking equals Cisco. If you want to be taken seriously as a network engineer, Cisco certification makes perfect sense.

The Exams to Achieve CCENT and CCNA R&S

Cisco announced changes to the CCENT and CCNA Routing and Switching certifications, and the related 100-105 ICND1, 200-105 ICND2, and 200-125 CCNA exams, early in the year 2016. Most everyone new to Cisco certifications begins with either CCENT or CCNA Routing and Switching (CCNA R&S). However, the paths to certification are not quite obvious at first.

The CCENT certification requires a single step: pass the ICND1 exam. Simple enough.

Cisco gives you two options to achieve CCNA R&S certification, as shown in Figure I-1: pass both the ICND1 and ICND2 exams, or just pass the CCNA exam. Both paths cover the same exam topics, but the two-exam path does so spread over two exams rather than one. You also pick up the CCENT certification by going through the two-exam path, but you do not when working through the single-exam option.

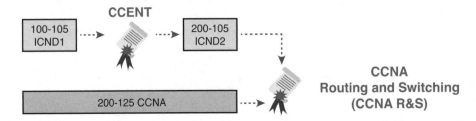

Figure I-1   *Cisco Entry-Level Certifications and Exams*

Note that Cisco has begun referencing some exams with a version number on some of their web pages. If that form holds true, the exams in Figure I-1 will likely be called version 3 (or v3 for short). Historically, the 200-125 CCNA R&S exam is the seventh separate version of the exam (which warrants a different exam number), dating back to 1998. To make sure you reference the correct exam, when looking for information, using forums, and registering for the test, just make sure to use the correct exam number as shown in the figure.

Types of Questions on the Exams

The ICND1, ICND2, and CCNA exams all follow the same general format. At the testing center, you sit in a quiet room with a PC. Before the exam timer begins, you have a chance to do a few other tasks on the PC; for instance, you can take a sample quiz just to get accustomed to the PC and the testing engine. Anyone who has user-level skills in getting around a PC should have no problems with the testing environment. The question types are

- Multiple-choice, single-answer
- Multiple-choice, multiple-answer
- Testlet (one scenario with multiple multi-choice questions)
- Drag-and-drop
- Simulated lab (sim)
- Simlet

Before taking the test, learn the exam user interface by using the Cisco Exam Tutorial. To find the Cisco Certification Exam Tutorial, search for "exam tutorial" at www.cisco.com. This tool walks through each type of question Cisco may ask on the exam.

Although the first four types of questions in the list should be somewhat familiar from other tests in school, the last two are more common to IT tests and Cisco exams in particular. Both use a network simulator to ask questions, so that you control and use simulated Cisco devices. In particular:

Sim questions: You see a network topology, a lab scenario, and can access the devices. Your job is to fix a problem with the configuration.

Simlet questions: This style combines sim and testlet question formats. Like a sim question, you see a network topology, a lab scenario, and can access the devices. However, like a testlet, you also see multiple multiple-choice questions. Instead of changing/fixing the configuration, you answer questions about the current state of the network.

These two question styles with the simulator give Cisco the ability to test your configuration skills with sim questions, and your verification and troubleshooting skills with simlet questions.

What's on the CCNA Exams—And What's in the Book?

Ever since I was in grade school, whenever the teacher announced that we were having a test soon, someone would always ask, "What's on the test?" Even in college, people would try to get more information about what would be on the exams. At heart, the goal is to know what to study hard, what to study a little, and what to not study at all.

You can find out more about what's on the exam from two primary sources: this book and from the Cisco website.

The Cisco Published Exam Topics

First, Cisco tells the world the specific topics on each of their exams. Cisco wants the public to know both the variety of topics, and an idea about the kinds of knowledge and skills required for each topic, for every Cisco certification exam. Just go to www.cisco.com/go/certifications, look for the CCENT and CCNA Routing and Switching pages, and navigate until you see the exam topics in Appendix R, "Exam Topic Cross Reference." This PDF appendix lists two cross references: one with a list of the exam topics and the chapters that include something about each topic, as well as the reverse: a list of chapters, with the exam topics included in each chapter.

Cisco does more than just list the topic (for example, IPv4 addressing), but they also list the depth to which you must master the topic. The primary exam topics each list one or more verbs that describe the skill level required. For example, consider the following exam topic, which describes one of the most important topics in both CCENT and CCNA R&S:

Configure, verify, and troubleshoot IPv4 addressing and subnetting

Note that this one exam topic has three verbs (configure, verify, and troubleshoot). So, you should be able to not only configure IPv4 addresses and subnets, but you should understand them well enough to verify that the configuration works, and to troubleshoot problems when it is not working. And if to do that, you need to understand concepts, and you need to have other knowledge, those details are implied. The exam questions will attempt to assess whether you can configure, verify, and troubleshoot.

Note that the list of exam topics provides a certain level of depth. For example, the ICND1 100-105 exam topic list has 41 primary exam topics (topics with verbs), plus additional subtopics that further define that technology area.

You should take the time to not only read the exam topics, but read the short material above the exam topics as listed at the Cisco web page for each certification and exam. Look for notices about the use of unscored items, and the fact that Cisco intends the exam topics to be a set of general guidelines for the exams.

This Book: About the Exam Topics

This book provides a complete study system for the Cisco published exam topics for the ICND1 100-105 exam. All the topics in this book either directly relate to some ICND1 exam topic or provide more basic background knowledge for some exam topic. The scope of the book is based on the exam topics.

For those of you thinking more specifically about the CCNA R&S certification and the CCNA 200-125 single-exam path to CCNA, this book covers about one-half of the CCNA exam topics. The ICND1 book (and ICND1 100-105 exam topics) covers about half of the topics listed for the CCNA 200-125 exam, and the ICND2 book (and the ICND2 200-105 exam topics) cover the other half. In short, for content, CCNA = ICND1 + ICND2.

Book Features

This book, and the similar *CCNA Routing and Switching ICND2 200-105 Official Cert Guide*, go beyond what you would find in a simple technology book. These books give you a study system designed to help you not only learn facts but also to develop the skills need to pass the exams. To do that, in the technology chapters of the book, about three-quarters of the chapter is about the technology, and about one-quarter is for the related study features.

The "Foundation Topics" section of each chapter contains rich content to explain the topics on the exam and to show many examples. This section makes extensive use of figures, with lists and tables for comparisons. It also highlights the most important topics in each chapter as key topics, so you know what to master first in your study.

Most of the book's features tie in some way to the need to study beyond simply reading the "Foundation Topics" section of each chapter. The rest of this section works through these book features. And because the book organizes your study by chapter, and then by part (a part contains multiple chapters), and then a final review at the end of the book, this Introduction discusses the book features introduced by chapter, part, and for final review.

Chapter Features and How to Use Each Chapter

Each chapter of this book is a self-contained short course about one small topic area, organized for reading and study, as follows:

"Do I Know This Already?" quizzes: Each chapter begins with a prechapter quiz.

Foundation Topics: This is the heading for the core content section of the chapter.

Chapter Review: This section includes a list of study tasks useful to help you remember concepts, connect ideas, and practice skills-based content in the chapter.

Figure I-2 shows how each chapter uses these three key elements. You start with the DIKTA quiz. You can use the score to determine whether you already know a lot, or not so much, and determine how to approach reading the Foundation Topics (that is, the technology content in the chapter). When finished, use the chapter review tasks to start working on mastering your memory of the facts and skills with configuration, verification, and troubleshooting.

Figure I-2   *Three Primary Tasks for a First Pass Through Each Chapter*

In addition to these three main chapter features, each "Chapter Review" section uses a variety of other book features, including the following:

- **Review Key Topics:** Inside the "Foundation Topics" section, the Key Topic icon appears next to the most important items, for the purpose of later review and mastery. While all content matters, some is, of course, more important to learn, or needs more review to master, so these items are noted as key topics. The chapter review lists the key topics in a table; scan the chapter for these items to review them.

- **Complete Tables from Memory:** Instead of just rereading an important table of information, some tables have been marked as memory tables. These tables exist in the Memory Table app that is available on the DVD and from the companion website. The app shows the table with some content removed, and then reveals the completed table, so you can work on memorizing the content.

- **Key Terms You Should Know:** You do not need to be able to write a formal definition of all terms from scratch. However, you do need to understand each term well enough to understand exam questions and answers. The chapter review lists the key terminology from the chapter. Make sure you have a good understanding of each term, and use the DVD Glossary to cross-check your own mental definitions.

- **Labs:** Many exam topics use verbs list "configure," "verify," and "troubleshoot"; all these refer to skills you should practice at the user interface (CLI) of a router or switch. The chapter review refers you to these other tools. The Introduction's upcoming section titled "About Building Hands-On Skills" discusses your options.

- **Command References:** Some book chapters cover a large amount of router and switch commands. The chapter review includes reference tables for the command used in that chapter, along with an explanation. Use these tables for reference, but also use them for study—just cover one column of the table, and see how much you can remember and complete mentally.

- **Review DIKTA Questions:** Although you have already seen the DIKTA questions from the chapters in a part, re-answering those questions can prove a useful way to review facts. The part review suggests that you repeat the DIKTA questions, but using the Pearson IT Certification Practice Test (PCPT) exam software that comes with the book, for extra practice in answering multiple choice questions on a computer.

- **Subnetting and Other Process Exercises:** Many chapters in the ICND1 book ask you to perform various tasks that use math or use a particular process. The chapter review asks you to do additional practice problems as found in DVD-only PDF appendixes.

Part Features and How to Use Part Review

The book organizes the chapters into parts. Each part contains a number of related chapters. Figure I-3 lists the titles of the parts and the chapters in those parts (by chapter number).

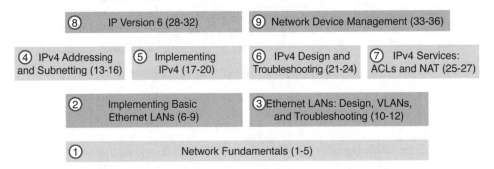

Figure I-3   *The Book Parts (by Title), and Chapter Numbers in Each Part*

Each book part ends with a "Part Review" section that contains a list of activities for study and review, much like the "Chapter Review" section at the end of each chapter. However, because the part review takes place after completing a number of chapters, the part review includes some tasks meant to help pull the ideas together from this larger body of work. The following list explains the types of tasks added to part review beyond the types mentioned for chapter review:

- **Answer Part Review Questions:** The books comes with exam software and databases on questions. One database holds questions written specifically for part review. These questions tend to connect multiple ideas together, to help you think about topics from multiple chapters, and to build the skills needed for the more challenging analysis questions on the exams.

- **Mind Maps:** Mind maps are graphical organizing tools that many people find useful when learning and processing how concepts fit together. The process of creating mind maps helps you build mental connections. The part review elements make use of mind maps in several ways: to connect concepts and the related configuration commands, to connect **show** commands and the related networking concepts, and even to connect terminology. (For more information about mind maps, see the section "About Mind Maps.")

- **Labs:** The "Part Review" section will direct you to the kinds of lab exercises you should do with your chosen lab product, labs that would be more appropriate for this stage of study and review. (Check out the section "About Building Hands-On Skills" for information about lab options.)

In addition to these tasks, many "Part Review" sections have you perform other tasks with book features mentioned in the "Chapter Review" section: repeating DIKTA quiz questions, reviewing key topics, and doing more lab exercises.

Final Review

The "Final Review" chapter at the end of this book lists a series of preparation tasks that you can best use for your final preparation before taking the exam. The "Final Review" chapter focuses on a three-part approach to helping you pass: practicing your skills, practicing answering exam questions, and uncovering your weak spots. To that end, the "Final Review" chapter uses the same familiar book features discussed for the chapter review and part review elements, along with a much larger set of practice questions.

Other Features

In addition to the features in each of the core chapters, this book, as a whole, has additional study resources, including the following:

- **DVD-based practice exam:** The companion DVD contains the powerful Pearson IT Certification Practice Test (PCPT) exam engine. You can take simulated ICND1 exams with the DVD and activation code included in this book. (You can take simulated ICND2 and CCNA R&S exams with the DVD in the *CCNA Routing and Switching ICND2 200-105 Official Cert Guide*.)

- **CCENT ICND1 100-105 Network Simulator Lite:** This lite version of the best-selling CCNA Network Simulator from Pearson provides you with a means, right now, to experience the Cisco command-line interface (CLI). No need to go buy real gear or buy a full simulator to start learning the CLI. Just install it from the DVD in the back of this book.

- **eBook:** If you are interested in obtaining an eBook version of this title, we have included a special offer on a coupon card inserted in the DVD sleeve in the back of the book. This offer enables you to purchase the *CCENT/CCNA ICND1 100-105 Official Cert Guide Premium Edition eBook and Practice Test* at a 70 percent discount off the list price. In addition to three versions of the eBook, PDF (for reading on your computer), EPUB (for reading on your tablet, mobile device, or Nook or other eReader), and Mobi (the native Kindle version), you also receive additional practice test questions and enhanced practice test features.

- **Subnetting videos:** The companion DVD contains a series of videos that show you how to calculate various facts about IP addressing and subnetting (in particular, using the shortcuts described in this book).

- **Subnetting practice:** The companion DVD contains five appendixes (D–H) with a set of subnetting practice problems and answers. This is a great resource to practice building subnetting skills. You can also do these same practice problems with applications that you can access from the DVD or the companion web site.

- **Other practice:** The companion DVD contains four other appendixes (I–K) that each contain other practice problems related to a particular chapter from the book. Use these for more practice on the particulars with some of the math- and process-oriented activities in the chapters. You can also do these same practice problems with applications that you can access from the DVD or the companion website.

- **Mentoring videos:** The DVD included with this book includes four other instructional videos, about the following topics: switch basics, CLI navigation, router configuration, and VLANs.

- **Companion website:** The website www.ciscopress.com/title/9781587205804 posts up-to-the-minute materials that further clarify complex exam topics. Check this site regularly for new and updated postings written by the author that provide further insight into the more troublesome topics on the exam.

- **PearsonITCertification.com:** The website www.pearsonitcertification.com is a great resource for all things IT-certification related. Check out the great CCNA articles, videos, blogs, and other certification preparation tools from the industry's best authors and trainers.

- **CCNA Simulator:** If you are looking for more hands-on practice, you might want to consider purchasing the CCNA Network Simulator. You can purchase a copy of this software from Pearson at http://pearsonitcertification.com/networksimulator or other retail outlets. To help you with your studies, I have created a mapping guide that maps each of the labs in the simulator to the specific sections in these CCNA cert guides. You can get this mapping guide for free on the Extras tab of the companion website.

- **Author's website and blogs:** The author maintains a website that hosts tools and links useful when studying for CCENT and CCNA. The site lists information to help you build your own lab, study pages that correspond to each chapter of this book and the ICND1 book, and links to the author's CCENT Skills blog and CCNA Skills blog. Start at www.certskills.com; look to blog.certskills.com for a page about the blogs in particular, with links to the pages with the labs related to this book.

A Big New Feature: Review Applications

One of the single biggest additions to this edition of the book is the addition of study apps for many of the chapter review activities. In the past, all chapter review activities use the book chapter, or the chapter plus a DVD-only appendix. Readers tell us they find that content useful, but the content is static.

This book (and the *CCNA Routing and Switching ICND2 200-105 Official Cert Guide*) are the first Cisco Press Cert Guides with extensive interactive applications. Basically, most every activity that can be done at chapter review can now be done with an application. The applications can be found both on the DVD that comes with the book and on the book's companion website.

The advantages of using these apps are as follows:

- **Easier to use:** Instead of having to print out copies of the appendixes and do the work on paper, these new apps provide you with an easy to use, interactive experience that you can easily run over and over.

- **Convenient:** When you have a spare 5–10 minutes, go to the book's website, and review content from one of your recently finished chapters.

- **Untethered from Book/DVD:** Because these apps are available on the book's companion web page in addition to the DVD, you can access your review activities from anywhere—no need to have the book or DVD with you.

- **Good for tactile learners:** Sometimes looking at a static page after reading a chapter lets your mind wander. Tactile learners may do better by at least typing answers into an app, or clicking inside an app to navigate, to help keep you focused on the activity.

Our in-depth reader surveys show that readers who use the chapter review tools like them, but that not everyone uses the "Chapter Review" sections consistently. So, we want to increase the number of people using the review tools, and make them both more useful and more interesting. Table I-1 summarizes these new applications and the traditional book features that cover the same content.

Table I-1 Book Features with Both Traditional and App Options

Feature	Traditional	App
Key Topic	Table with list; flip pages to find	Key Topics Table app
Config Checklist	Just one of many types of key topics	Config Checklist app
Memory Table	Two static PDF appendixes (one with sparse tables for you to complete, one with completed tables)	Memory Table app
Key Terms	Listed in each "Chapter Review" section, with the Glossary in the back of the book	Glossary Flash Cards app
Subnetting Practice	Appendixes D–H, with practice problems and answers	A variety of apps, one per problem type
Other Practice	Appendixes I–K with practice problems and answers	A variety of apps, one per problem type

How to Get the Electronic Elements of This Book

Traditionally, all chapter review activities use the book chapter plus appendixes, with the appendixes often being located on the DVD. But most of that content is static: useful, but static.

If you buy the print book, and have a DVD drive, you have all the content on the DVD. Just spin the DVD and use the disk menu that should automatically start to explore all content.

If you buy the print book but do not have a DVD drive, you can get the DVD files by registering your book on the Cisco Press website. To do so, simply go to www.ciscopress.com/register and enter the ISBN of the print book: 9781587205804. After you have registered your book, go to your account page and click the **Registered Products** tab. From there, click the **Access Bonus Content** link to get access to the book's companion website.

If you buy the Premium Edition eBook and Practice Test from Cisco Press, your book will automatically be registered on your account page. Simply go to your account page, click the **Registered Products** tab, and select **Access Bonus Content** to access the book's companion website.

If you buy the eBook from some other bookseller, the very last page of your eBook file will contain instructions for how to register the book and access the companion website. The steps are the same as noted earlier for those who buy the print book but do not have a DVD drive.

Book Organization, Chapters, and Appendixes

This book contains 36 core chapters, Chapters 1 through 36, with Chapter 37 as the "Final Review" chapter. Each core chapter covers a subset of the topics on the ICND1 exam. The core chapters are organized into sections. The core chapters cover the following topics:

- Part I: Networking Fundamentals
  - Chapter 1, "Introduction to TCP/IP Networking," introduces the central ideas and terms used by TCP/IP, and contrasts the TCP/IP networking model with the OSI model.
  - Chapter 2, "Fundamentals of Ethernet LANs," introduces the concepts and terms used when building Ethernet LANs.
  - Chapter 3, "Fundamentals of WANs," covers the concepts and terms used for the data link layer for WANs, including HDLC.
  - Chapter 4, "Fundamentals of IPv4 Addressing and Routing": IP is the main network layer protocol for TCP/IP. This chapter introduces the basics of IPv4, including IPv4 addressing and routing.
  - Chapter 5, "Fundamentals of TCP/IP Transport and Applications": This chapter completes most of the detailed discussion of the upper two layers of the TCP/IP model (transport and application), focusing on TCP and applications.
- Part II: Implementing Basic Ethernet LANs
  - Chapter 6, "Using the Command-Line Interface," explains how to access the text-based user interface of Cisco Catalyst LAN switches.
  - Chapter 7, "Analyzing Ethernet LAN Switching," shows how to use the Cisco CLI to verify the current status of an Ethernet LAN and how it switches Ethernet frames.
  - Chapter 8, "Configuring Basic Switch Management," explains how to configure Cisco switches for basic management features, such as remote access using Telnet and SSH.
  - Chapter 9, "Configuring Switch Interfaces," shows how to configure a variety of switch features that apply to interfaces, including duplex/speed and port security.
- Part III: Ethernet LANs: Design, VLANs, and Troubleshooting
  - Chapter 10, "Analyzing Ethernet LAN Designs," examines various ways to design Ethernet LANs, discussing the pros and cons, and explains common design terminology.
  - Chapter 11, "Implementing Ethernet Virtual LANs": This chapter explains the concepts and configuration surrounding virtual LANs, including VLAN trunking.
  - Chapter 12, "Troubleshooting Ethernet LANs," focuses on how to tell whether the switch is doing what it is supposed to be doing, mainly through the use of show commands.

- Part IV: IP Version 4 Addressing and Subnetting

  - Chapter 13, "Perspectives on IPv4 Subnetting," walks you through the entire concept of subnetting, from starting with a Class A, B, or C network to a completed subnetting design as implemented in an enterprise IPv4 network.

  - Chapter 14, "Analyzing Classful IPv4 Networks": IPv4 addresses originally fell into several classes, with unicast IP addresses being in Class A, B, and C. This chapter explores all things related to address classes and the IP network concept created by those classes.

  - Chapter 15, "Analyzing Subnet Masks," shows how an engineer can analyze the key facts about a subnetting design based on the subnet mask. This chapter shows how to look at the mask and IP network to determine the size of each subnet and the number of subnets.

  - Chapter 16, "Analyzing Existing Subnets": Most troubleshooting of IP connectivity problems starts with an IP address and mask. This chapter shows how to take those two facts and find key facts about the IP subnet in which that host resides.

- Part V: Implementing IPv4

  - Chapter 17, "Operating Cisco Routers," is like Chapter 8, focusing on basic device management, but it focuses on routers instead of switches.

  - Chapter 18, "Configuring IPv4 Addresses and Static Routes," discusses how to add IPv4 address configuration to router interfaces and how to configure static IPv4 routes.

  - Chapter 19, "Learning IPv4 Routes with RIPv2," explains how routers work together to find all the best routes to each subnet using a routing protocol. This chapter also shows how to configure the RIPv2 routing protocol for use with IPv4.

  - Chapter 20, "DHCP and IP Networking on Hosts," discusses how hosts can be configured with their IPv4 settings, and how they can learn those settings with DHCP.

- Part VI: IPv4 Design and Troubleshooting

  - Chapter 21, "Subnet Design," takes a design approach to subnetting. This chapter begins with a classful IPv4 network, and asks why a particular mask might be chosen, and if chosen, what subnet IDs exist.

  - Chapter 22, "Variable-Length Subnet Masks," moves away from the assumption of one subnet mask per network to multiple subnet masks per network—which makes subnetting math and processes much more challenging. This chapter explains those challenges.

  - Chapter 23, "IPv4 Troubleshooting Tools," focuses on how to use two key troubleshooting tools to find routing problems: the ping and traceroute commands.

  - Chapter 24, "Troubleshooting IPv4 Routing," looks at the most common IPv4 problems and how to find the root causes of those problems when troubleshooting.

- Part VII: IPv4 Services: ACLs and NAT

  - Chapter 25, "Basic IPv4 Access Control Lists": This chapter examines how standard IP ACLs can filter packets based on the source IP address so that a router will not forward the packet.

- Part XII: DVD Appendixes

The following appendixes are available in digital format on the DVD that accompanies this book:

- Appendix C, "Answers to the 'Do I Know This Already?' Quizzes," includes the explanations to all the questions from Chapters 1 through 36.

- Appendix D, "Practice for Chapter 14: Analyzing Classful IPv4 Networks"

- Appendix E, "Practice for Chapter 15: Analyzing Subnet Masks"

- Appendix F, "Practice for Chapter 16: Analyzing Existing Subnets"

- Appendix G, "Practice for Chapter 21: Subnet Design"

- Appendix H, "Practice for Chapter 22: Variable-Length Subnet Masks"

- Appendix I, "Practice for Chapter 25: Basic IPv4 Access Control Lists"

- Appendix J, "Practice for Chapter 28: Fundamentals of IP Version 6"

- Appendix K, "Practice for Chapter 30: Implementing IPv6 Addressing on Routers"

- Appendix L, "Mind Map Solutions," shows an image of sample answers for all the part-ending mind map exercises.

- Appendix M, "Study Planner," is a spreadsheet with major study milestones, where you can track your progress through your study.

- Appendix N, "Classless Inter-domain Routing," is an extra chapter for anyone interested in reading more about the concepts, terminology, and math related to CIDR.

- Appendix O, "Route Summarization," is a copy of a chapter that was in the previous edition of this book, but was removed for this edition. It is included here for anyone who has interest, and for instructors who may need the chapter for their existing course.

- Appendix P, "Implementing Point-to-Point WANs," is a copy of the ICND2 book's chapter about serial WANs. In a lab environment, you may want to use serial WAN links, and you may not have a copy of the ICND2 book. I included this chapter for reference if you need a little more depth about serial links.

- Appendix Q, "Topics from Previous Editions," is a collection of information about topics that have appeared on previous versions of the CCNA exams. While no longer within this exam's topics, the concepts are still of interest to someone with the CCENT or CCNA certification.

- Appendix R, "Exam Topics Cross Reference," provides some tables to help you find where each exam objectives is covered in the book.

Reference Information

This short section contains a few topics available for reference elsewhere in the book. You may read these when you first use the book, but you may also skip these topics and refer back to them later. In particular, make sure to note the final page of this introduction, which lists several contact details, including how to get in touch with Cisco Press.

Install the Pearson IT Certification Practice Test Engine and Questions

This book, like many other Cisco Press books, includes the rights to use the Pearson IT Certification Practice Test (PCPT) software, along with rights to use some exam questions related to this book. PCPT allows has many options, including the option to answer questions in study mode, so you can see the answers and explanations for each question as you go along, or to take a simulated exam that mimics real exam conditions, or to view questions in flash card mode, where all the answers are stripped out, challenging you to answer questions from memory.

You should install PCPT so it is ready to use even for the earliest chapters. This book's Part Review sections ask you specifically to use PCPT, and you can even take the DIKTA chapter pre-quizzes using PCPT.

NOTE   The right to use the exams associated with this book is based on an activation code. For those with a print book, the code is in the DVD sleeve at the back of the book. For those who purchase the Premium Edition eBook and Practice Test directly from the Cisco Press website, the code will be populated on your account page after purchase. For those who purchase a Kindle edition, the access code will be supplied directly from Amazon. Note that if you purchase an eBook version from any other source, the practice test is not included, as other vendors are not able to vend the required unique access code. *Do not lose the activation code.*

NOTE   Also on this same piece of paper, on the opposite side from the exam activation code, you will find a one-time-use coupon code that gives you 70 percent off the purchase of the *CCENT/CCNA ICND1 100-105 Official Cert Guide, Premium Edition eBook and Practice Test.*

PCPT Exam Databases with This Book

This book includes an activation code that allows you to load a set of practice questions. The questions come in different exams or exam databases. When you install the PCPT software and type in the activation code, the PCPT software downloads the latest version of all these exam databases. And with the ICND1 book alone, you get four different "exams," or four different sets of questions, as listed in Figure I-4.

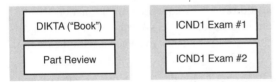

Figure I-4   *PCPT Exams/Exam Databases and When to Use Them*

You can choose to use any of these exam databases at any time, both in study mode and practice exam mode. However, many people find it best to save some of the exams until exam review time, after you have finished reading the entire book. Figure I-4 begins to suggest a plan, spelled out here:

- During part review, use PCPT to review the DIKTA questions for that part, using study mode.

- During part review, use the questions built specifically for part review (the part review questions) for that part of the book, using study mode.

- Save the remaining exams to use with the "Final Review" chapter at the end of the book.

The two modes inside PCPT give you better options for study versus practicing a timed exam event. In study mode, you can see the answers immediately, so you can study the topics more easily. Also, you can choose a subset of the questions in an exam database; for instance, you can view questions from only the chapters in one part of the book.

PCPT practice mode lets you practice an exam event somewhat like the actual exam. It gives you a preset number of questions, from all chapters, with a timed event. Practice exam mode also gives you a score for that timed event.

How to View Only DIKTA Questions by Chapter or Part

Most chapters begin with a "Do I Know This Already?" (DIKTA) quiz. You can take the quiz to start a chapter, take it again during chapter review for more practice, and the "Part Review" sections even suggest that you repeat the questions from all chapters in that part.

You can use the DIKTA quiz as printed in the book, or use the PCPT software. The book lists the questions, with the letter answers on the page following the quiz. Appendix C, on the DVD, lists the answers along with an explanation; you might want to keep that PDF handy.

Using PCPT for these questions has some advantages. It gives you a little more practice in how to read questions from testing software. Also, the explanations to the questions are conveniently located in the PCPT software.

To view these DIKTA questions inside the PCPT software, you need to select **Book Questions**, which is the way PCPT references questions found inside the printed book. Then you have to deselect all chapters (with a single click), and then select one or more chapters, as follows:

Step 1.   Start the PCPT software.

Step 2.   From the main (home) menu, select the item for this product, with a name like *CCENT/CCNA ICND1 100-105 Official Cert Guide*, and click **Open Exam**.

Step 3.   The top of the next window that appears should list some exams; check the **ICND1 Book Questions** box, and uncheck the other boxes. This selects the "book" questions (that is, the DIKTA questions from the beginning of each chapter).

Step 4.   On this same window, click at the bottom of the screen to deselect all objectives (chapters). Then select the box beside each chapter in the part of the book you are reviewing.

Step 5.   Select any other options on the right side of the window.

Step 6.   Click **Start** to start reviewing the questions.

How to View Part Review Questions

The exam databases you get with this book include a database of questions created solely for study during the part review process. DIKTA questions focus more on facts, to help you determine whether you know the facts contained within the chapter. The part review questions instead focus more on application of those facts to typical real scenarios, and look more like real exam questions.

To view these questions, follow the same process as you did with DIKTA/book questions, but select the Part Review database rather than the book database. PCPT has a clear name for this database: Part Review Questions.

About Mind Maps

Mind maps are a type of visual organization tool that you can use for many purposes. For instance, you can use mind maps as an alternative way to take notes.

You can also use mind maps to improve how your brain organizes concepts. Mind maps improve your brain's connections and relationships between ideas. When you spend time thinking about an area of study, and organize your ideas into a mind map, you strengthen existing mental connections and create new connections, all into your own frame of reference.

In short, mind maps help you internalize what you learn.

Each mind map begins with a blank piece of paper or blank window in a mind mapping application. You then add a large central idea, with branches that move out in any direction. The branches contain smaller concepts, ideas, commands, pictures, whatever idea needs to be represented. Any concepts that can be grouped should be put near each other. As need be, you can create deeper and deeper branches, although for this book's purposes, most mind maps will not go beyond a couple of levels.

NOTE   Many books have been written about mind maps, but Tony Buzan often gets credit for formalizing and popularizing mind maps. You can learn more about mind maps at his website, www.thinkbuzan.com.

For example, Figure I-5 shows a sample mind map that begins to output some of the IPv6 content from Part VIII of the ICND1 book. You might create this kind of mind map when reviewing IPv6 addressing concepts, starting with the big topic of "IPv6 addressing," and then writing down random terms and ideas. As you start to organize them mentally, you draw lines connecting the ideas, reorganize them, and eventually reach the point where you believe the organization of ideas makes sense to you.

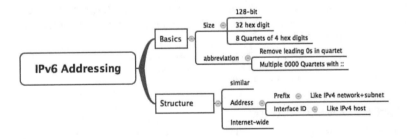

Figure I-5   *Sample Mind Map*

Mind maps may be the least popular but most effective study tool suggested in this book. I personally find a huge improvement in learning new areas of study when I mind map; I hope you will make the effort to try these tools and see if they work well for you too.

Finally, for mind mapping tools, you can just draw them on a blank piece of paper, or find and download a mind map application. I have used Mind Node Pro on a Mac, and we build the sample mind maps with XMIND, which has free versions for Windows, Linux, and OS X.

About Building Hands-On Skills

You need skills in using Cisco routers and switches, specifically the Cisco command-line interface (CLI). The Cisco CLI is a text-based command-and-response user interface; you type a command, and the device (a router or switch) displays messages in response. To answer sim and simlet questions on the exams, you need to know a lot of commands, and you need to be able to navigate to the right place in the CLI to use those commands.

This next section walks through the options of what is included in the book, with a brief description of lab options outside the book.

Config Lab Exercises

Some router and switch features require multiple configuration commands. Part of the skill you need to learn is to remember which configuration commands work together, which ones are required, and which ones are optional. So, the challenge level goes beyond just picking the right parameters on one command. You have to choose which commands to use, in which combination, typically on multiple devices. And getting good at that kind of task requires practice.

The Config Labs feature, introduced as a new feature in this edition of the book, helps provide that practice. Each lab presents a sample lab topology, with some requirements, and you have to decide what to configure on each device. The answer then shows a sample configuration. Your job is to create the configuration, and then check your answer versus the supplied answer.

Also for the first time, this edition places the content not only outside the book but also onto the author's blog site. To reach my blog sites for ICND1 content or for ICND2 content (two different blogs), you can start at my blog launch site (blog.certskills.com), and click from there.

> **blog.certskills.com/ccent/** Wendell's CCENT (ICND1): In the menus, navigate to Hands On... Config Lab
>
> **blog.certskills.com/ccna/** Wendell's CCNA (ICND2): In the menus, navigate to Hands On... Config Lab

Both blogs are geared toward helping you pass the exams, so feel free to look around. Note that the Config Lab posts should show an image like this in the summary:

Figure I-6 *Config Lab Logo in the Author's Blogs*

These Config Labs have several benefits, including the following:

Untethered and responsive: Do them from anywhere, from any web browser, from your phone or tablet, untethered from the book or DVD.

Designed for idle moments: Each lab is designed as a 5- to 10-minute exercise if all you are doing is typing in a text editor or writing your answer on paper.

Two outcomes, both good: Practice getting better and faster with basic configuration, or if you get lost, you have discovered a topic that you can now go back and reread to complete your knowledge. Either way, you are a step closer to being ready for the exam!

Blog format: Allows easy adds and changes by me, and easy comments by you.

Self-assessment: As part of final review, you should be able to do all the Config Labs, without help, and with confidence.

Note that the blog organizes these Config Lab posts by book chapter, so you can easily use these at both chapter review and part review. See the "Your Study Plan" element that follows the Introduction for more details about those review sections.

A Quick Start with Pearson Network Simulator Lite

The decision of how to get hands-on skills can be a little scary at first. The good news: You have a free and simple first step to experience the CLI: Install and use the Pearson NetSim Lite that comes with this book.

This book comes with a lite version of the best-selling CCNA Network Simulator from Pearson, which provides you with a means, right now, to experience the Cisco CLI. No need to go buy real gear or buy a full simulator to start learning the CLI. Just install it from the DVD in the back of this book.

The labs with this latest version of NetSim Lite includes labs associated with Part II of this book. Part I includes concepts only, with Part II being the first part with commands. So, make sure and use the NetSim Lite to learn the basics of the CLI to get a good start.

Of course, one reason that NetSim Lite comes on the DVD is that the publisher hopes you will buy the full product. However, even if you do not use the full product, you can still learn from the labs that come with NetSim Lite while deciding about what options to pursue.

NOTE The ICND1 and ICND2 books each contain a different version of the Sim Lite product, each with labs that match the book content. If you bought both books, make sure you install both Sim Lite products.

The Pearson Network Simulator

The Config Labs and the Pearson Network Simulator Lite both fill specific needs, and they both come with the book. However, you need more than those two tools.

The single best option for lab work to do along with this book is the paid version of the Pearson Network Simulator. This simulator product simulates Cisco routers and switches so that you can learn for the CCENT and CCNA R&S certifications. But more importantly, it focuses on learning for the exam by providing a large number of useful lab exercises. Reader surveys tell us that those people who use the Simulator along with the book love the learning process, and rave about how the book and Simulator work well together.

Of course, you need to make a decision for yourself, and consider all the options. Thankfully, you can get a great idea of how the full Simulator product works by using the Pearson Network Simulator Lite product include with the book. Both have the same base code and same user interface, and the same types of labs. Try the Lite version, and check out the full product. There is a full product for CCENT only, and another for CCNA R&S (which includes all the labs in the CCENT product, plus others for the ICND2 parts of the content).

Note that the Simulator and the books work on a different release schedule. For a time in 2016, the Simulator will be the Simulator created for the previous versions of the exams (ICND1 100-101, ICND2 200-101, and CCNA 200-120). That product includes approximately 80 percent of the CLI topics in the ICND1 100-105 and 200-105 books. So during that time, the Simulator is still very useful.

On a practical note, when you want to do labs when reading a chapter or doing part review, the Simulator organizes the labs to match the book. Just look for "Sort by Chapter" tab in the Simulator's user interface. However, during the months in 2016 for which the Simulator is the older edition listing the older exams in the title, you will need to refer to a PDF that lists those labs versus this book's organization. You can find that PDF on the book product page under the Downloads tab here: www.ciscopress.com/title/9781587205804.

More Lab Options

If you decide against using the full Pearson Network Simulator, you still need hands-on experience. You should plan to use some lab environment to practice as much CLI as possible.

First, you can use real Cisco routers and switches. You can buy them, new or used, or borrow them at work. You can rent them for a fee. If you have the right mix of gear, you could even do the Config Lab exercises from my blog on that gear, or try and re-create examples from the book.

Cisco offers a virtualization product that lets you run router and switch operating system (OS) images in a virtual environment. This tool, the Virtual Internet Routing Lab (VIRL; http://virl.cisco.com), lets you create a lab topology, start the topology, and connect to real router and switch OS images. Check out http://virl.cisco.com for more information.

You can even rent virtual Cisco router and switch lab pods from Cisco, in an offering called Cisco Learning Labs (www.cisco.com/go/learninglabs).

All these previously mentioned options cost some money, but the next two are generally free to the user, but with a different catch for each. First, GNS3 works somewhat like VIRL, creating a virtual environment running real Cisco IOS. However, GNS3 is not a Cisco product, and cannot provide you with the IOS images for legal reasons.

Cisco also makes a simulator that works very well as a learning tool: Cisco Packet Tracer. However, Cisco intends Packet Tracer for use by people currently enrolled in Cisco Networking Academy courses, and not for the general public. So, if you are part of a Cisco Academy, definitely use Packet Tracer.

This book does not tell you what option to use, but you should plan on getting some hands-on practice somehow. The important thing to know is that most people need to practice using the Cisco CLI to be ready to pass these exams.

For More Information

If you have any comments about the book, submit them via www.ciscopress.com. Just go to the website, select **Contact Us**, and type your message.

Cisco might make changes that affect the CCNA certification from time to time. You should always check www.cisco.com/go/ccna and www.cisco.com/go/ccent for the latest details.

The *CCENT/CCNA ICND1 100-105 Official Cert Guide* helps you attain CCENT and CCNA Routing and Switching certification. This is the CCNA ICND1 certification book from the only Cisco-authorized publisher. We at Cisco Press believe that this book certainly can help you achieve CCNA certification, but the real work is up to you! I trust that your time will be well spent.

Your Study Plan

You just got this book. You have probably already read (or quickly skimmed) the Introduction. You are probably now wondering whether to start reading here or skip ahead to Chapter 1, "Introduction to TCP/IP Networking."

Stop to read this section about how to create your own study plan for the exam(s) you plan to take (ICND1 100-105, ICND2 200-105, and/or CCNA 200-125). Your study will go much better if you take time (maybe 15 minutes) to think about a few key points about how to study before starting on this journey. That is what this section will help you do.

A Brief Perspective on Cisco Certification Exams

Cisco sets the bar pretty high for passing the ICND1, ICND2, and CCNA R&S exams. Most anyone can study and pass these exams, but it takes more than just a quick read through the book and the cash to pay for the exam.

The challenge of these exams comes from many angles. Each of these exams covers a lot of concepts and many commands specific to Cisco devices. Beyond knowledge, these Cisco exams also require deep skills. You must be able to analyze and predict what really happens in a network. You must be able to configure Cisco devices to work correctly in those networks. And you must be ready to troubleshoot problems when the network does not work correctly.

The more challenging questions on these exams work a lot like a jigsaw puzzle, but with four out of every five puzzle pieces not even in the room. To solve the puzzle, you have to mentally re-create the missing pieces. To do that, you must know each networking concept and remember how the concepts work together.

For instance, the ICND1 exam includes many troubleshooting topics. A simple question might ask you why a host cannot communicate with some server. The question would supply some of the information, like some pieces of the jigsaw puzzle, as represented with the white pieces in Figure 1. You have to apply your knowledge of IPv4 routing, IP addressing, and Ethernet LAN switching to the scenario in the question to come up with some of the other pieces of the puzzle. For a given question, some pieces of the puzzle may remain a mystery, but with enough of the puzzle filled in, you should be able to answer the question. And some pieces will just remain unknown for a given question.

These skills require that you prepare by doing more than just reading and memorizing what you read. Of course, you need to read many pages in this book to learn many individual facts and how these facts relate to each other. But a big part of this book lists exercises beyond reading, exercises that help you build the skills to solve these networking puzzles.

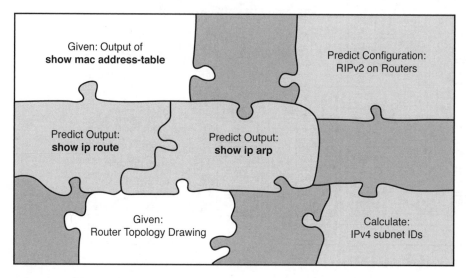

Figure 1 *Filling In Puzzle Pieces with Your Analysis Skills*

Five Study Plan Steps

These exams are challenging, but many people pass them every day. So, what do you need to do to be ready to pass, beyond reading and remembering all the facts? You need to develop skills. You need to mentally link each idea with other related ideas. Doing that requires additional work. To help you along the way, the next few pages give you five key planning steps to take so that you can more effectively build those skills and make those connections, before you dive into this exciting but challenging world of learning networking on Cisco gear.

Step 1: Think in Terms of Parts and Chapters

The first step in your study plan is to get the right mindset about the size and nature of the task you have set out to accomplish. This is a large book. So you cannot think about the book as one huge task or you might get discouraged. Besides, you never sit down to read 900 pages in one study session. So break the task down into smaller tasks.

The good news here is that the book is designed with obvious breakpoints and built-in extensive review activities. In short, the book is more of a study system than a book.

So the first step in your study plan is to visualize the book not as one large book, but as 9 parts. Then, within each part, visualize an average of 4 chapters. Your study plan has you working through the chapters in each part, and then reviewing the material in that part before moving on, as shown in Figure 2.

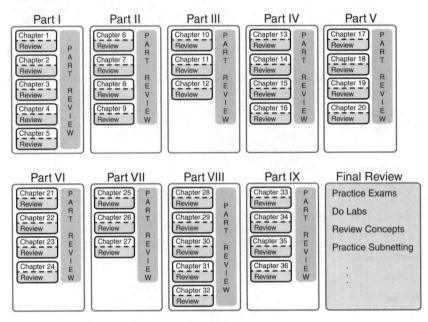

Figure 2   *9 Parts, with an Average of 4 Chapters Each, with Part Reviews*

Now your plan has the following:

1 large task: Read and master all content in the book.

9 medium tasks/book: Read and master a part.

4 small tasks/part: Read and master a chapter.

Step 2: Build Your Study Habits Around the Chapter

For your second step, possibly the most important step, approach each chapter with the same process: read it, and then study the chapter before moving on.

Each chapter follows the same design with three parts, as shown in Figure 3. The chapter pre-quiz (called a DIKTA quiz, or Do I Know This Already? quiz) helps you decide how much time to spend reading versus skimming the core of the chapter, called the Foundation Topics. The Chapter Review section then gives you instructions about how to study and review what you just read.

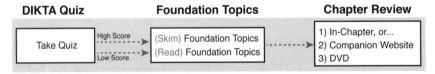

Figure 3   *Suggested Approach to Each Chapter*

The book has no long chapters, on purpose. They average just over 20 pages for the Foundation Topics. By keeping the size reasonable, you can complete all of a chapter in one or two short study sessions. Go into each study session that begins a new chapter thinking that you have a chance to complete the chapter, or at least make a great start on it. And if you do not have enough time, look for the major headings inside the chapter—each chapter has two to three major headings, and those make a great place to stop reading when you need to wait to complete the reading in the next study sessions.

The Chapter Review tasks are very important to your exam-day success. Doing these tasks after you've read the chapter really does help you get ready. Do not put off using these tasks until later! The chapter-ending review tasks help you with the first phase of deepening your knowledge and skills of the key topics, remembering terms, and linking the concepts together in your brain so that you can remember how it all fits together. The following list describes most of the activities you will find in the "Chapter Review" sections:

- Review key topics
- Review key terms
- Repeat the DIKTA questions
- Review memory tables
- Re-create config checklists
- Review command tables
- Do lab exercises
- Do subnetting exercises

Check out the upcoming section titled "Find Review Activities on the Web and DVD?" later in this planning section for more details.

Step 3: Use Book Parts for Major Milestones

Studies show that to master a concept and/or skill, you should plan to go through multiple study sessions to review the concept and to practice the skill. The "Chapter Review" section at the end of each chapter is the first such review, while the Part Review, at the end of each part, acts as that second review.

Plan time to do the Part Review task at the end of each part, using the Part Review elements found at the end of each Part. You should expect to spend about as much time on one Part Review as you would on one entire chapter, or maybe a little more for some parts. So in terms of planning your time, think of the Part Review itself as another chapter.

Figure 4 lists the names of the parts in this book, with some color coding. Note that Parts II and III are related (Ethernet), and Parts IV through VII are also related (IP version 4). Each part ends with a Part Review section of 2 to 4 pages, with notes about what tools and activities to use.

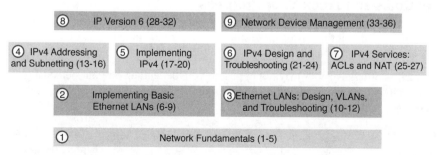

Figure 4 *Parts as Major Milestones*

Chapter Review and Part Review differ in some ways. Chapter Review tasks tend to provide a lot of context, so you can focus on mentally adding a specific piece of knowledge, or practicing a specific skill. Part Review activities instead remove a lot of the context, more like real life and the real exams. Removing that context means that you have to exercise your own knowledge and skills. The result: You uncover your weaknesses. The better you become at uncovering weaknesses, and then learning what you are missing in that area, the better prepared you will be for the exam.

The Part Review sections use the following kinds of tools in additional to some of the same tools used for Chapter Review:

- Mind maps
- Part Review questions with PCPT
- Labs

Also, consider setting a goal date for finishing each part of the book (and a reward, as well). Plan a break, some family time, some time out exercising, eating some good food, whatever helps you get refreshed and motivated for the next part.

Step 4: Use the Final Review Chapter to Refine Skills and Uncover Weaknesses

Your fourth step has one overall task: Follow the details outlined in Chapter 37, "Final Review," at the end of this book for what to do between finishing the book and taking the exam.

The "Final Review" chapter has two major goals. First, it helps you further develop the analytical skills you need to answer the more complicated questions on the exam. Many questions require that you connect ideas about concepts, configuration, verification, and troubleshooting. The closer you get to taking the exam, the less reading you should do, and the more you should do other learning activities; this chapter's tasks give you activities to further develop these skills.

The tasks in the "Final Review" chapter also help you uncover your weak areas. This final element gives you repetition with high-challenge exam questions, uncovering any gaps in your knowledge. Many of the questions are purposefully designed to test your knowledge of the most common mistakes and misconceptions, helping you avoid some of the common pitfalls people experience with the actual exam.

Step 5: Set Goals and Track Your Progress

Your fifth study plan step spans the entire timeline of your study effort. Before you start reading the book and doing the rest of these study tasks, take the time to make a plan, set some goals, and be ready to track your progress.

While making lists of tasks may or may not appeal to you, depending on your personality, goal setting can help everyone studying for these exams. And to do the goal setting, you need to know what tasks you plan to do.

NOTE   If you read this, and decide that you want to try to do better with goal setting beyond your exam study, check out a blog series I wrote about planning your networking career here: http://blog.certskills.com/ccna/tag/development-plan/.

As for the list of tasks to do when studying, you do not have to use a detailed task list. (You could list every single task in every chapter-ending Chapter Review section, every task in the Part Reviews, and every task in the "Final Review" chapter.) However, listing the major tasks can be enough.

You should track at least two tasks for each typical chapter: reading the "Foundation Topics" section and doing the Chapter Review at the end of the chapter. And, of course, do not forget to list tasks for Part Reviews and Final Review. Table 1 shows a sample for Part I of this book.

Table 1   Sample Excerpt from a Planning Table

Element	Task	Goal Date	First Date Completed	Second Date Completed (Optional)
Chapter 1	Read Foundation Topics			
Chapter 1	Do Chapter Review tasks			
Chapter 2	Read Foundation Topics			
Chapter 2	Do Chapter Review tasks			
Chapter 3	Read Foundation Topics			
Chapter 3	Do Chapter Review tasks			
Part I Review	Do Part Review activities			

NOTE   Appendix M, "Study Planner," on the DVD that comes with this book, contains a complete planning checklist like Table 1 for the tasks in this book. This spreadsheet allows you to update and save the file to note your goal dates and the tasks you have completed.

Use your goal dates as a way to manage your study, and not as a way to get discouraged if you miss a date. Pick reasonable dates that you can meet. When setting your goals, think about how fast you read and the length of each chapter's "Foundation Topics" section, as listed in the table of contents. Then, when you finish a task sooner than planned, move up the next few goal dates.

If you miss a few dates, do *not* start skipping the tasks listed at the ends of the chapters! Instead, think about what is impacting your schedule—real life, commitment, and so on— and either adjust your goals or work a little harder on your study.

Things to Do Before Starting the First Chapter

Now that you understand the big ideas behind a good study plan for the book, take a few more minutes for a few overhead actions that will help. Before leaving this section, look at some other tasks you should do either now, or around the time you are reading the first few chapters, to help make a good start in the book.

Find Review Activities on the Web and DVD

The earlier editions of the book have used review activities that relied on the chapter, plus PDF appendixes found on the DVD. Some activities also rely on the PCPT testing software.

This edition is the first Cisco Press certification guide to offer a large set of apps to use instead of the traditional study features. The Introduction's section titled "A Big New Feature: Review Applications" detailed some of the reasons.

I encourage you to go ahead and access the book's companion website to find the review apps and explore. Also, spin the DVD, and find the review apps there. Both methods organize the review activities by chapter and by part.

Note that this book includes the traditional methods of review as well, with instructions in the book, and matching PDF appendixes in some cases. For instance, all the subnetting exercises can be done in an app, but those same exercises exist in DVD-only appendixes—you choose which works better for you.

Should I Plan to Use the Two-Exam Path or One-Exam Path?

You do not have to make this choice today, but you can be mulling the decision while you study.

To get a CCNA Routing and Switching certification, you choose either a one-exam or two-exam path. Which should you use? The following is my opinion, but it's based on chatter and opinions from readers from many years. You can consider the one-exam path if

- You already know about half the topics well, through prior experience or study.
- You have already proven that you are excellent at learning through self-study.

Otherwise, in my opinion, you would be better off taking the two-exam path. First, there is no cost savings for most people with the one-exam path. Check the exam prices in your country, for ICND1, ICND2, and CCNA, and then make some comparisons. Assume you pass the tests on the first try: traditionally, the cost is identical for both the ICND1 + ICND2 path and the CCNA path. Or, assume that you fail each exam once: again, the costs are identical.

Next, consider the number of topics. From a content perspective, CCNA = ICND1 + ICND2. So, both paths require learning the same content.

Next, which would you rather have done in school: take a final exam over a single semester's material, or a final exam covering the whole year? It is just harder to prepare for an exam that covers more material, so the two-exam path gain has an advantage.

Finally, the most compelling reason for the two-exam path is that you probably have no experience with Cisco exams yet. I hope you have a chance to pass many Cisco exams during your career. The two-exam path gets you to that first exam attempt sooner, and the exam experience teaches you things about the exam and yourself that no study tool can teach you.

Thankfully, you do not have to decide now. In fact, you can study the entire ICND1 book and all the while ponder whether to use the one-exam or two-exam path to CCNA R&S. At that point, you can make a better decision about which path works better for you.

Study Options for Those Taking the 200-125 CCNA Exam

Studying for the two-exam path has an obvious approach: just use the ICND1 book for the ICND1 exam, and the ICND2 book for the ICND2 exam. Simple enough.

If you do plan to take the 200-125 CCNA R&S exam, you have a couple of study options. First, to be clear: The 200-125 CCNA exam covers the topics in the combined ICND1 and ICND2 books. So, using both the ICND1 and ICND2 books covers everything for the 200-125 CCNA R&S exam. The only question is when to read each part of the two books. You have two reasonable options when going with the one-exam option:

- Complete all the ICND1 book, then move on to the ICND2 book.
- Move back and forth between the ICND1 and ICND2 books, by part, based on topics, as shown in Figure 5.

The first option is pretty obvious, but the second one is less obvious. Figure 5 shows a study plan in which you complete the Ethernet parts in the ICND1, then the Ethernet part in ICND2. Similarly, you complete the IPv4 parts in ICND1, then ICND2, and then the IPv6 part in both books, and then the final part in both books.

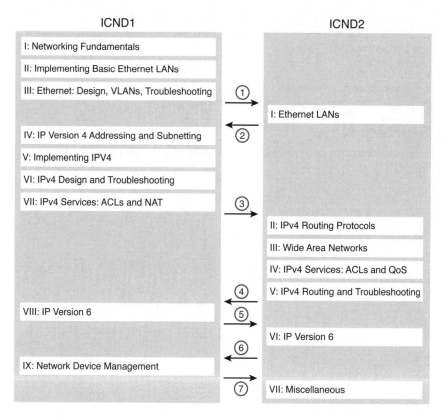

Figure 5 *Alternate Reading Plan for CCNA: Moving Between Books by Part*

Personally, I am a fan of completing the ICND1 book completely, and then moving on to the ICND2 book. However, for those of you with a large amount of experience already, this alternate reading plan may work well.

Other Small Tasks Before Getting Started

You need to do a few overhead tasks to install software, find some PDFs, and so on. You can do these tasks now or do them in your spare moments when you need a study break during the first few chapters of the book. But do these early. That way, if you do stumble upon an installation problem, you have time to work through it before you need a particular tool.

Register (for free) at the Cisco Learning Network (CLN, http://learningnetwork.cisco.com) and join the CCENT/CCNA R&S study group. This group allows you to both lurk and participate in discussions about topics related to the ICND1 exam, ICND2 exam, and CCNA R&S exam. Register (for free), join the groups, and set up an email filter to redirect the messages to a separate folder. Even if you do not spend time reading all the posts yet, later, when you have time to read, you can browse through the posts to find interesting topics (or just search the posts from the CLN website).

Explore the electronic elements of this book, as detailed in the Introduction's section titled "How to Get the Electronic Elements of This Book." That includes the installation of the PCPT and Sim Lite software.

Also find my blog site as listed in the Introduction, and bookmark the pages that list the config labs, to have those handy for later study. (The URL is http://blog.certskills.com/ccent/category/hands-on/config-lab.)

Getting Started: Now

Now dive in to your first of many short, manageable tasks: reading the relatively short Chapter 1. Enjoy!

This first part of the book introduces the most important topics in TCP/IP networking. Chapter 1 provides a broad look at TCP/IP, introducing the common terms, big concepts, and major protocols for TCP/IP. Chapters 2 through 5 each look more deeply at a single portion of TCP/IP, as follows:

Chapter 2 focuses on links between nearby devices (local-area networks, or LANs).

Chapter 3 focuses on links between far-away devices (wide-area networks, or WANs).

Chapter 4 focuses on the rules of IP routing, which pulls the LAN and WAN links of Chapters 2 and 3 together by forwarding data all the way from one user device to another.

Chapter 5 focuses on what happens on the endpoint devices in the network, with how they transmit data and how the applications interface to the network.

Of these chapters, note that this book explores the topics from Chapter 2 (LANs) and Chapter 4 (IP routing) in much more detail.

Part I

Networking Fundamentals

Introduction to TCP/IP Networking

This chapter covers the following exam topics:

1.0 Network Fundamentals

1.1 Compare and contrast OSI and TCP/IP models

1.2 Compare and contrast TCP and UDP protocols

Welcome to the first chapter in your study for CCENT and CCNA! This chapter begins Part I, which focuses on the basics of networking. Because networks require all the devices to follow the rules, this part starts with a discussion of networking models, which gives you a big-picture view of the networking rules.

You can think of a networking model as you think of a set of architectural plans for building a house. A lot of different people work on building your house, such as framers, electricians, bricklayers, painters, and so on. The blueprint helps ensure that all the different pieces of the house work together as a whole. Similarly, the people who make networking products, and the people who use those products to build their own computer networks, follow a particular networking model. That networking model defines rules about how each part of the network should work, as well as how the parts should work together, so that the entire network functions correctly.

The CCNA exams include detailed coverage of one networking model: Transmission Control Protocol/Internet Protocol (TCP/IP). TCP/IP is the most pervasively used networking model in the history of networking. You can find support for TCP/IP on practically every computer operating system (OS) in existence today, from mobile phones to mainframe computers. Every network built using Cisco products today supports TCP/IP. And not surprisingly, the CCNA Routing and Switching exams focus heavily on TCP/IP.

The exams also compare TCP/IP to a second networking model, called the Open Systems Interconnection (OSI) reference model. Historically, OSI was the first large effort to create a vendor-neutral networking model. Because of that timing, many of the terms used in networking today come from the OSI model, so this chapter's section on OSI discusses OSI and the related terminology.

"Do I Know This Already?" Quiz

Take the quiz (either here, or use the PCPT software) if you want to use the score to help you decide how much time to spend on this chapter. The answers are at the bottom of the page following the quiz, and the explanations are in DVD Appendix C and in the PCPT software.

Table 1-1 "Do I Know This Already?" Foundation Topics Section-to-Question Mapping

Foundation Topics Section	Questions
Perspectives on Networking	None
TCP/IP Networking Model	1–6
OSI Networking Model	7–8

1. Which of the following protocols are examples of TCP/IP transport layer protocols? (Choose two answers.)

   a. Ethernet

   b. HTTP

   c. IP

   d. UDP

   e. SMTP

   f. TCP

2. Which of the following protocols are examples of TCP/IP data link layer protocols? (Choose two answers.)

   a. Ethernet

   b. HTTP

   c. IP

   d. UDP

   e. SMTP

   f. TCP

   g. PPP

3. The process of HTTP asking TCP to send some data and making sure that it is received correctly is an example of what?

   a. Same-layer interaction

   b. Adjacent-layer interaction

   c. OSI model

   d. All of these answers are correct.

4. The process of TCP on one computer marking a TCP segment as segment 1, and the receiving computer then acknowledging the receipt of TCP segment 1 is an example of what?

   a. Data encapsulation

   b. Same-layer interaction

   c. Adjacent-layer interaction

   d. OSI model

   e. All of these answers are correct.

5. The process of a web server adding a TCP header to the contents of a web page, followed by adding an IP header and then adding a data link header and trailer, is an example of what?

   a. Data encapsulation

   b. Same-layer interaction

   c. OSI model

   d. All of these answers are correct.

6. Which of the following terms is used specifically to identify the entity created when encapsulating data inside data link layer headers and trailers?

   a. Data

   b. Chunk

   c. Segment

   d. Frame

   e. Packet

7. Which OSI layer defines the functions of logical network-wide addressing and routing?

   a. Layer 1

   b. Layer 2

   c. Layer 3

   d. Layer 4

   e. Layer 5, 6, or 7

8. Which OSI layer defines the standards for cabling and connectors?

   a. Layer 1

   b. Layer 2

   c. Layer 3

   d. Layer 4

   e. Layer 5, 6, or 7

Foundation Topics

This chapter introduces some of the most basic ideas about computer networking, while also defining the structure of two networking models: TCP/IP and OSI. The chapter begins with a brief introduction of how most people view a network, which hopefully connects with where you are to start your CCNA journey. The middle of this chapter introduces networking by explaining some of the key features of TCP/IP. The chapter closes with some additional concepts and terminology related to the OSI model.

Perspectives on Networking

So, you are new to networking. Like many people, your perspective about networks might be that of a user of the network, as opposed to the network engineer who builds networks. For some, your view of networking might be based on how you use the Internet, from home, using a high-speed Internet connection like digital subscriber line (DSL) or cable TV, as shown in Figure 1-1.

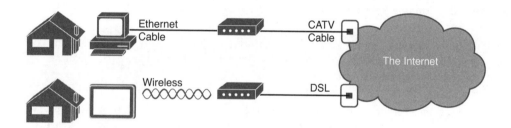

Figure 1-1 *End-User Perspective on High-Speed Internet Connections*

The top part of the figure shows a typical high-speed cable Internet user. The PC connects to a cable modem using an Ethernet cable. The cable modem then connects to a cable TV (CATV) outlet in the wall using a round coaxial cable—the same kind of cable used to connect your TV to the CATV wall outlet. Because cable Internet services provide service continuously, the user can just sit down at the PC and start sending email, browsing websites, making Internet phone calls, and using other tools and applications.

The lower part of the figure uses two different technologies. First, the tablet computer uses wireless technology that goes by the name wireless local-area network (wireless LAN), or Wi-Fi, instead of using an Ethernet cable. In this example, the router uses a different technology, DSL, to communicate with the Internet.

Both home-based networks and networks built for use by a company make use of similar networking technologies. The Information Technology (IT) world refers to a network created by one corporation, or enterprise, for the purpose of allowing its employees to communicate, as an *enterprise network*. The smaller networks at home, when used for business purposes, often go by the name small office/home office (SOHO) networks.

Answers to the "Do I Know This Already?" quiz:

1 D and F **2** A and G **3** B **4** B **5** A **6** D **7** C **8** A

Users of enterprise networks have some idea about the enterprise network at their company or school. People realize that they use a network for many tasks. PC users might realize that their PC connects through an Ethernet cable to a matching wall outlet, as shown at the top of Figure 1-2. Those same users might use wireless LANs with their laptop when going to a meeting in the conference room as well. Figure 1-2 shows these two end-user perspectives on an enterprise network.

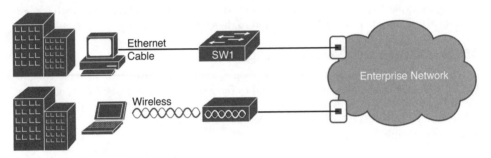

Figure 1-2 *Example Representation of an Enterprise Network*

NOTE   In networking diagrams, a cloud represents a part of a network whose details are not important to the purpose of the diagram. In this case, Figure 1-2 ignores the details of how to create an enterprise network.

Some users might not even have a concept of the network at all. Instead, these users just enjoy the functions of the network—the ability to post messages to social media sites, make phone calls, search for information on the Internet, listen to music, and download countless apps to their phones—without caring about how it works or how their favorite device connects to the network.

Regardless of how much you already know about how networks work, this book and the related certifications help you learn how networks do their job. That job is simply this: moving data from one device to another. The rest of this chapter, and the rest of this first part of the book, reveals the basics of how to build both SOHO and enterprise networks so that they can deliver data between two devices.

In the building business, much work happens before you nail the first boards together. The process starts with some planning, an understanding of how to build a house, and some architectural blueprints of how to build that specific house. Similarly, the journey toward building any computer network does not begin by installing devices and cables, but instead by looking at the architectural plans for those modern networks: the TCP/IP model.

TCP/IP Networking Model

A *networking model*, sometimes also called either a *networking architecture* or *networking blueprint*, refers to a comprehensive set of documents. Individually, each document describes one small function required for a network; collectively, these documents define everything that should happen for a computer network to work. Some documents define a *protocol*, which is a set of logical rules that devices must follow to communicate. Other documents define some physical requirements for networking. For example, a document could define the voltage and current levels used on a particular cable when transmitting data.

You can think of a networking model as you think of an architectural blueprint for building a house. Sure, you can build a house without the blueprint. However, the blueprint can ensure that the house has the right foundation and structure so that it will not fall down, and it has the correct hidden spaces to accommodate the plumbing, electrical, gas, and so on. Also, the many different people that build the house using the blueprint—such as framers, electricians, bricklayers, painters, and so on—know that if they follow the blueprint, their part of the work should not cause problems for the other workers.

Similarly, you could build your own network—write your own software, build your own networking cards, and so on—to create a network. However, it is much easier to simply buy and use products that already conform to some well-known networking model or blueprint. Because the networking product vendors build their products with some networking model in mind, their products should work well together.

History Leading to TCP/IP

Today, the world of computer networking uses one networking model: TCP/IP. However, the world has not always been so simple. Once upon a time, networking protocols didn't exist, including TCP/IP. Vendors created the first networking protocols; these protocols supported only that vendor's computers. For example, IBM published its Systems Network Architecture (SNA) networking model in 1974. Other vendors also created their own proprietary networking models. As a result, if your company bought computers from three vendors, network engineers often had to create three different networks based on the networking models created by each company, and then somehow connect those networks, making the combined networks much more complex. The left side of Figure 1-3 shows the general idea of what a company's enterprise network might have looked like back in the 1980s, before TCP/IP became common in enterprise internetworks.

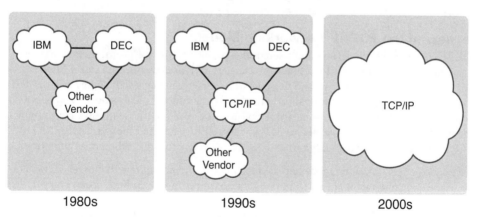

Figure 1-3   *Historical Progression: Proprietary Models to the Open TCP/IP Model*

Although vendor-defined proprietary networking models often worked well, having an open, vendor-neutral networking model would aid competition and reduce complexity. The International Organization for Standardization (ISO) took on the task to create such a model, starting as early as the late 1970s, beginning work on what would become known as the Open Systems Interconnection (OSI) networking model. ISO had a noble goal for the OSI model: to standardize data networking protocols to allow communication among all computers across the entire planet. ISO worked toward this ambitious and noble goal, with participants from most of the technologically developed nations on Earth participating in the process.

A second, less-formal effort to create an open, vendor-neutral, public networking model sprouted forth from a U.S. Department of Defense (DoD) contract. Researchers at various universities volunteered to help further develop the protocols surrounding the original DoD work. These efforts resulted in a competing open networking model called TCP/IP.

During the 1990s, companies began adding OSI, TCP/IP, or both to their enterprise networks. However, by the end of the 1990s, TCP/IP had become the common choice, and OSI fell away. The center part of Figure 1-3 shows the general idea behind enterprise networks in that decade—still with networks built upon multiple networking models but including TCP/IP.

Here in the twenty-first century, TCP/IP dominates. Proprietary networking models still exist, but they have mostly been discarded in favor of TCP/IP. The OSI model, whose development suffered in part because of a slower formal standardization process as compared with TCP/IP, never succeeded in the marketplace. And TCP/IP, the networking model originally created almost entirely by a bunch of volunteers, has become the most prolific network model ever, as shown on the right side of Figure 1-3.

In this chapter, you will read about some of the basics of TCP/IP. Although you will learn some interesting facts about TCP/IP, the true goal of this chapter is to help you understand what a networking model or networking architecture really is and how it works.

Also in this chapter, you will learn about some of the jargon used with OSI. Will any of you ever work on a computer that is using the full OSI protocols instead of TCP/IP? Probably not. However, you will often use terms relating to OSI.

Overview of the TCP/IP Networking Model

The TCP/IP model both defines and references a large collection of protocols that allow computers to communicate. To define a protocol, TCP/IP uses documents called Requests For Comments (RFC). (You can find these RFCs using any online search engine.) The TCP/IP model also avoids repeating work already done by some other standards body or vendor consortium by simply referring to standards or protocols created by those groups. For example, the Institute of Electrical and Electronic Engineers (IEEE) defines Ethernet LANs; the TCP/IP model does not define Ethernet in RFCs, but refers to IEEE Ethernet as an option.

An easy comparison can be made between telephones and computers that use TCP/IP. You go to the store and buy a phone from one of a dozen different vendors. When you get home and plug in the phone to the same cable in which your old phone was connected, the new phone works. The phone vendors know the standards for phones in their country and build their phones to match those standards.

Similarly, when you buy a new computer today, it implements the TCP/IP model to the point that you can usually take the computer out of the box, plug in all the right cables, turn it on, and it connects to the network. You can use a web browser to connect to your favorite website. How? Well, the OS on the computer implements parts of the TCP/IP model. The Ethernet card, or wireless LAN card, built in to the computer implements some LAN standards referenced by the TCP/IP model. In short, the vendors that created the hardware and software implemented TCP/IP.

To help people understand a networking model, each model breaks the functions into a small number of categories called *layers*. Each layer includes protocols and standards that relate to that category of functions. TCP/IP actually has two alternative models, as shown in Figure 1-4.

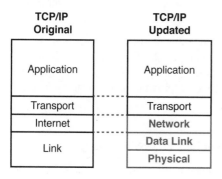

Figure 1-4 *Two TCP/IP Networking Models*

The model on the left shows the original TCP/IP model listed in RFC 1122, which breaks TCP/IP into four layers. The top two layers focus more on the applications that need to send and receive data. The bottom layer focuses on how to transmit bits over each individual link, with the Internet layer focusing on delivering data over the entire path from the original sending computer to the final destination computer.

The TCP/IP model on the right shows the more common terms and layers used when people talk about TCP/IP today. It expands the original model's link layer into two separate layers: data link and physical (similar to the lower two layers of the OSI model). Also, many people commonly use the word "Network" instead of "Internet" for one layer.

> **NOTE** The original TCP/IP model's link layer has also been referred to as the *network access* and *network interface* layer.

Many of you will have already heard of several TCP/IP protocols, like the examples listed in Table 1-2. Most of the protocols and standards in this table will be explained in more detail as you work through this book. Following the table, this section takes a closer look at the layers of the TCP/IP model.

Table 1-2 TCP/IP Architectural Model and Example Protocols

TCP/IP Architecture Layer	Example Protocols
Application	HTTP, POP3, SMTP
Transport	TCP, UDP
Internet	IP
Link	Ethernet, Point-to-Point Protocol (PPP), T1

TCP/IP Application Layer

TCP/IP application layer protocols provide services to the application software running on a computer. The application layer does not define the application itself, but it defines services that applications need. For example, application protocol HTTP defines how web browsers can pull the contents of a web page from a web server. In short, the application layer provides an interface between software running on a computer and the network itself.

Arguably, the most popular TCP/IP application today is the web browser. Many major software vendors either have already changed or are changing their application software to support access from a web browser. And thankfully, using a web browser is easy: You start a web browser on your computer and select a website by typing the name of the website, and the web page appears.

HTTP Overview

What really happens to allow that web page to appear on your web browser?

Imagine that Bob opens his browser. His browser has been configured to automatically ask for web server Larry's default web page, or *home page*. The general logic looks like Figure 1-5.

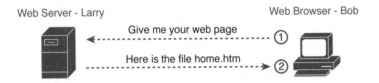

Figure 1-5   *Basic Application Logic to Get a Web Page*

So, what really happened? Bob's initial request actually asks Larry to send his home page back to Bob. Larry's web server software has been configured to know that the default web page is contained in a file called home.htm. Bob receives the file from Larry and displays the contents of the file in Bob's web browser window.

HTTP Protocol Mechanisms

Taking a closer look, this example shows how applications on each endpoint computer—specifically, the web browser application and web server application—use a TCP/IP application layer protocol. To make the request for a web page and return the contents of the web page, the applications use the Hypertext Transfer Protocol (HTTP).

HTTP did not exist until Tim Berners-Lee created the first web browser and web server in the early 1990s. Berners-Lee gave HTTP functionality to ask for the contents of web pages, specifically by giving the web browser the ability to request files from the server and giving the server a way to return the content of those files. The overall logic matches what was shown in Figure 1-5; Figure 1-6 shows the same idea, but with details specific to HTTP.

NOTE   The full version of most web addresses—also called Uniform Resource Locators (URL) or Universal Resource Identifiers (URI)—begins with the letters *http*, which means that HTTP is used to transfer the web pages.

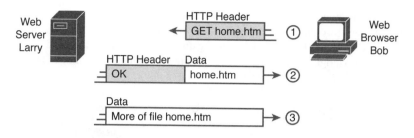

Figure 1-6 *HTTP GET Request, HTTP Reply, and One Data-Only Message*

To get the web page from Larry, at Step 1, Bob sends a message with an HTTP header. Generally, protocols use headers as a place to put information used by that protocol. This HTTP header includes the request to "get" a file. The request typically contains the name of the file (home.htm, in this case), or if no filename is mentioned, the web server assumes that Bob wants the default web page.

Step 2 in Figure 1-6 shows the response from web server Larry. The message begins with an HTTP header, with a return code (200), which means something as simple as "OK" returned in the header. HTTP also defines other return codes so that the server can tell the browser whether the request worked. (Here is another example: If you ever looked for a web page that was not found, and then received an HTTP 404 "not found" error, you received an HTTP return code of 404.) The second message also includes the first part of the requested file.

Step 3 in Figure 1-6 shows another message from web server Larry to web browser Bob, but this time without an HTTP header. HTTP transfers the data by sending multiple messages, each with a part of the file. Rather than wasting space by sending repeated HTTP headers that list the same information, these additional messages simply omit the header.

TCP/IP Transport Layer

Although many TCP/IP application layer protocols exist, the TCP/IP transport layer includes a smaller number of protocols. The two most commonly used transport layer protocols are the Transmission Control Protocol (TCP) and the User Datagram Protocol (UDP).

Transport layer protocols provide services to the application layer protocols that reside one layer higher in the TCP/IP model. How does a transport layer protocol provide a service to a higher-layer protocol? This section introduces that general concept by focusing on a single service provided by TCP: error recovery. Later chapters examine the transport layer in more detail and discuss more functions of the transport layer.

TCP Error Recovery Basics

To appreciate what the transport layer protocols do, you must think about the layer above the transport layer, the application layer. Why? Well, each layer provides a service to the layer above it, like the error-recovery service provided to application layer protocols by TCP.

For example, in Figure 1-5, Bob and Larry used HTTP to transfer the home page from web server Larry to Bob's web browser. But what would have happened if Bob's HTTP GET request had been lost in transit through the TCP/IP network? Or, what would have happened if Larry's response, which included the contents of the home page, had been lost? Well, as you might expect, in either case, the page would not have shown up in Bob's browser.

TCP/IP needs a mechanism to guarantee delivery of data across a network. Because many application layer protocols probably want a way to guarantee delivery of data across a network, the creators of TCP included an error-recovery feature. To recover from errors, TCP uses the concept of acknowledgments. Figure 1-7 outlines the basic idea behind how TCP notices lost data and asks the sender to try again.

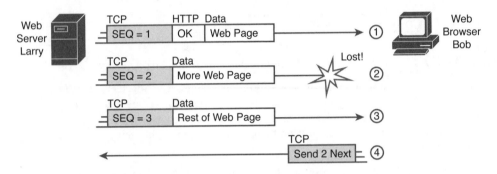

Figure 1-7 *TCP Error-Recovery Services as Provided to HTTP*

Figure 1-7 shows web server Larry sending a web page to web browser Bob, using three separate messages. Note that this figure shows the same HTTP headers as Figure 1-6, but it also shows a TCP header. The TCP header shows a sequence number (SEQ) with each message. In this example, the network has a problem, and the network fails to deliver the TCP message (called a segment) with sequence number 2. When Bob receives messages with sequence numbers 1 and 3, but does not receive a message with sequence number 2, Bob realizes that message 2 was lost. That realization by Bob's TCP logic causes Bob to send a TCP segment back to Larry, asking Larry to send message 2 again.

Same-Layer and Adjacent-Layer Interactions

The example in Figure 1-7 also demonstrates a function called *adjacent-layer interaction*, which refers to the concepts of how adjacent layers in a networking model, on the same computer, work together. In this example, the higher-layer protocol (HTTP) wants error recovery, and the higher layer uses the next lower-layer protocol (TCP) to perform the service of error recovery; the lower layer provides a service to the layer above it.

Figure 1-7 also shows an example of a similar function called *same-layer interaction*. When a particular layer on one computer wants to communicate with the same layer on another computer, the two computers use headers to hold the information that they want to communicate. For example, in Figure 1-7, Larry set the sequence numbers to 1, 2, and 3 so that Bob could notice when some of the data did not arrive. Larry's TCP process created that TCP header with the sequence number; Bob's TCP process received and reacted to the TCP segments.

Table 1-3 summarizes the key points about how adjacent layers work together on a single computer and how one layer on one computer works with the same networking layer on another computer.

Table 1-3   Summary: Same-Layer and Adjacent-Layer Interactions

Concept	Description
Same-layer interaction on different computers	The two computers use a protocol (an agreed-to set of rules) to communicate with the same layer on another computer. The protocol defined by each layer uses a header that is transmitted between the computers to communicate what each computer wants to do. Header information added by a layer of the sending computer is processed by the same layer of the receiving computer.
Adjacent-layer interaction on the same computer	On a single computer, one layer provides a service to a higher layer. The software or hardware that implements the higher layer requests that the next lower layer perform the needed function.

TCP/IP Network Layer

The application layer includes many protocols. The transport layer includes fewer protocols, most notably, TCP and UDP. The TCP/IP network layer includes a small number of protocols, but only one major protocol: the Internet Protocol (IP). In fact, the name TCP/IP is simply the names of the two most common protocols (TCP and IP) separated by a /.

IP provides several features, most importantly, addressing and routing. This section begins by comparing IP's addressing and routing with another commonly known system that uses addressing and routing: the postal service. Following that, this section introduces IP addressing and routing. (More details follow in Chapter 4, "Fundamentals of IPv4 Addressing and Routing.")

Internet Protocol and the Postal Service

Imagine that you just wrote two letters: one to a friend on the other side of the country and one to a friend on the other side of town. You addressed the envelopes and put on the stamps, so both are ready to give to the postal service. Is there much difference in how you treat each letter? Not really. Typically, you would just put them in the same mailbox and expect the postal service to deliver both letters.

The postal service, however, must think about each letter separately, and then make a decision of where to send each letter so that it is delivered. For the letter sent across town, the people in the local post office probably just need to put the letter on another truck.

For the letter that needs to go across the country, the postal service sends the letter to another post office, then another, and so on, until the letter gets delivered across the country. At each post office, the postal service must process the letter and choose where to send it next.

To make it all work, the postal service has regular routes for small trucks, large trucks, planes, boats, and so on, to move letters between postal service sites. The service must be able to receive and forward the letters, and it must make good decisions about where to send each letter next, as shown in Figure 1-8.

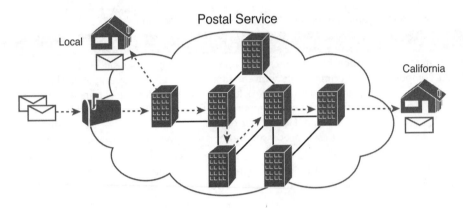

Figure 1-8 *Postal Service Forwarding (Routing) Letters*

Still thinking about the postal service, consider the difference between the person sending the letter and the work that the postal service does. The person sending the letters expects that the postal service will deliver the letter most of the time. However, the person sending the letter does not need to know the details of exactly what path the letters take. In contrast, the postal service does not create the letter, but it accepts the letter from the customer. Then, the postal service must know the details about addresses and postal codes that group addresses into larger groups, and it must have the ability to deliver the letters.

The TCP/IP application and transport layers act like the person sending letters through the postal service. These upper layers work the same way regardless of whether the endpoint host computers are on the same LAN or are separated by the entire Internet. To send a message, these upper layers ask the layer below them, the network layer, to deliver the message.

The lower layers of the TCP/IP model act more like the postal service to deliver those messages to the correct destinations. To do so, these lower layers must understand the underlying physical network because they must choose how to best deliver the data from one host to another.

So, what does this all matter to networking? Well, the network layer of the TCP/IP networking model, primarily defined by the Internet Protocol (IP), works much like the postal service. IP defines that each host computer should have a different IP address, just as the postal service defines addressing that allows unique addresses for each house, apartment, and business. Similarly, IP defines the process of routing so that devices called routers can work like the post office, forwarding packets of data so that they are delivered to the correct destinations. Just as the postal service created the necessary infrastructure to deliver letters—post offices, sorting machines, trucks, planes, and personnel—the network layer defines the details of how a network infrastructure should be created so that the network can deliver data to all computers in the network.

NOTE   TCP/IP defines two versions of IP: IP version 4 (IPv4) and IP version 6 (IPv6). The world still mostly uses IPv4, so this introductory part of the book uses IPv4 for all references to IP. Later in this book, Part VIII, "IP Version 6," discusses this newer version of the IP protocol.

Internet Protocol Addressing Basics

IP defines addresses for several important reasons. First, each device that uses TCP/IP—each TCP/IP *host*—needs a unique address so that it can be identified in the network. IP also defines how to group addresses together, just like the postal system groups addresses based on postal codes (like ZIP codes in the United States).

To understand the basics, examine Figure 1-9, which shows the familiar web server Larry and web browser Bob; but now, instead of ignoring the network between these two computers, part of the network infrastructure is included.

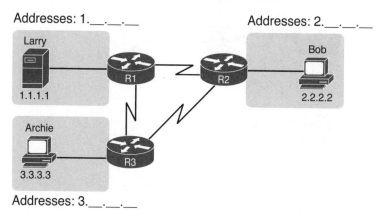

Figure 1-9 *Simple TCP/IP Network: Three Routers with IP Addresses Grouped*

First, note that Figure 1-9 shows some sample IP addresses. Each IP address has four numbers, separated by periods. In this case, Larry uses IP address 1.1.1.1, and Bob uses 2.2.2.2. This style of number is called a dotted-decimal notation (DDN).

Figure 1-9 also shows three groups of addresses. In this example, all IP addresses that begin with 1 must be on the upper left, as shown in shorthand in the figure as 1.__.__.__. All addresses that begin with 2 must be on the right, as shown in shorthand as 2.__.__.__. Finally, all IP addresses that begin with 3 must be at the bottom of the figure.

In addition, Figure 1-9 introduces icons that represent IP routers. Routers are networking devices that connect the parts of the TCP/IP network together for the purpose of routing (forwarding) IP packets to the correct destination. Routers do the equivalent of the work done by each post office site: They receive IP packets on various physical interfaces, make decisions based on the IP address included with the packet, and then physically forward the packet out some other network interface.

IP Routing Basics

The TCP/IP network layer, using the IP protocol, provides a service of forwarding IP packets from one device to another. Any device with an IP address can connect to the TCP/IP network and send packets. This section shows a basic IP routing example for perspective.

NOTE The term *IP host* refers to any device, regardless of size or power, that has an IP address and connects to any TCP/IP network.

Figure 1-10 repeats the familiar case in which web server Larry wants to send part of a web page to Bob, but now with details related to IP. On the lower left, note that server Larry has the familiar application data, HTTP header, and TCP header ready to send. In addition, the message now contains an IP header. The IP header includes a source IP address of Larry's IP address (1.1.1.1) and a destination IP address of Bob's IP address (2.2.2.2).

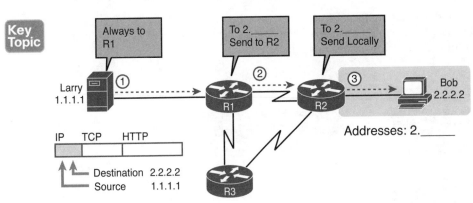

Figure 1-10 *Basic Routing Example*

Step 1, on the left of Figure 1-10, begins with Larry being ready to send an IP packet. Larry's IP process chooses to send the packet to some router—a nearby router on the same LAN—with the expectation that the router will know how to forward the packet. (This logic is much like you or me sending all our letters by putting them in a nearby mailbox.) Larry doesn't need to know anything more about the topology or the other routers.

At Step 2, Router R1 receives the IP packet, and R1's IP process makes a decision. R1 looks at the destination address (2.2.2.2), compares that address to its known IP routes, and chooses to forward the packet to Router R2. This process of forwarding the IP packet is called *IP routing* (or simply *routing*).

At Step 3, Router R2 repeats the same kind of logic used by Router R1. R2's IP process will compare the packet's destination IP address (2.2.2.2) to R2's known IP routes and make a choice to forward the packet to the right, on to Bob.

You will learn IP to more depth than any other protocol while preparing for CCENT and CCNA. Practically half the chapters in this book discuss some feature that relates to addressing, IP routing, and how routers perform routing.

TCP/IP Link Layer (Data Link Plus Physical)

The TCP/IP model's original link layer defines the protocols and hardware required to deliver data across some physical network. The term *link* refers to the physical connections, or links, between two devices and the protocols used to control those links.

Just like every layer in any networking model, the TCP/IP link layer provides services to the layer above it in the model. When a host's or router's IP process chooses to send an IP packet to another router or host, that host or router then uses link-layer details to send that packet to the next host/router.

Because each layer provides a service to the layer above it, take a moment to think about the IP logic related to Figure 1-10. In that example, host Larry's IP logic chooses to send the IP packet to a nearby router (R1), with no mention of the underlying Ethernet. The Ethernet network, which implements link-layer protocols, must then be used to deliver that packet from host Larry over to router R1. Figure 1-11 shows four steps of what occurs at the link layer to allow Larry to send the IP packet to R1.

> **NOTE**   Figure 1-11 depicts the Ethernet as a series of lines. Networking diagrams often use this convention when drawing Ethernet LANs, in cases where the actual LAN cabling and LAN devices are not important to some discussion, as is the case here. The LAN would have cables and devices, like LAN switches, which are not shown in this figure.

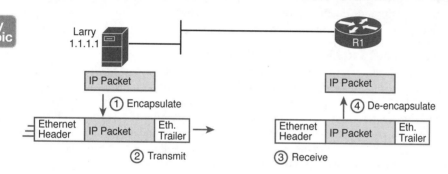

Figure 1-11   *Larry Using Ethernet to Forward an IP Packet to Router R1*

Figure 1-11 shows four steps. The first two occur on Larry, and the last two occur on Router R1, as follows:

Step 1.   Larry encapsulates the IP packet between an Ethernet header and Ethernet trailer, creating an Ethernet *frame*.

Step 2.   Larry physically transmits the bits of this Ethernet frame, using electricity flowing over the Ethernet cabling.

Step 3.   Router R1 physically receives the electrical signal over a cable, and re-creates the same bits by interpreting the meaning of the electrical signals.

Step 4.   Router R1 de-encapsulates the IP packet from the Ethernet frame by removing and discarding the Ethernet header and trailer.

By the end of this process, the link-layer processes on Larry and R1 have worked together to deliver the packet from Larry to Router R1.

> **NOTE**   Protocols define both headers and trailers for the same general reason, but headers exist at the beginning of the message and trailers exist at the end.

The link layer includes a large number of protocols and standards. For example, the link layer includes all the variations of Ethernet protocols, along with several other LAN standards that were more popular in decades past. The link layer includes wide-area network

(WAN) standards for different physical media, which differ significantly compared to LAN standards because of the longer distances involved in transmitting the data. This layer also includes the popular WAN standards that add headers and trailers as shown generally in Figure 1-11—protocols such as the Point-to-Point Protocol (PPP) and Frame Relay. Chapter 2, "Fundamentals of Ethernet LANs," and Chapter 3, "Fundamentals of WANs," further develop these topics for LANs and WANs, respectively.

In short, the TCP/IP link layer includes two distinct functions: functions related to the physical transmission of the data, plus the protocols and rules that control the use of the physical media. The five-layer TCP/IP model simply splits out the link layer into two layers (data link and physical) to match this logic.

TCP/IP Model and Terminology

Before completing this introduction to the TCP/IP model, this section examines a few remaining details of the model and some related terminology.

Comparing the Original and Modern TCP/IP Models

The original TCP/IP model defined a single layer—the link layer—below the Internet layer. The functions defined in the original link layer can be broken into two major categories: functions related directly to the physical transmission of data and those only indirectly related to the physical transmission of data. For example, in the four steps shown in Figure 1-11, Steps 2 and 3 were specific to sending the data, but Steps 1 and 4—encapsulation and de-encapsulation—were only indirectly related. This division will become clearer as you read about additional details of each protocol and standard.

Today, most documents use a more modern version of the TCP/IP model, as shown in Figure 1-12. Comparing the two, the upper layers are identical, except a name change from Internet to Network. The lower layers differ in that the single link layer in the original model is split into two layers to match the division of physical transmission details from the other functions. Figure 1-12 shows the two versions of the TCP/IP model again, with emphasis on these distinctions.

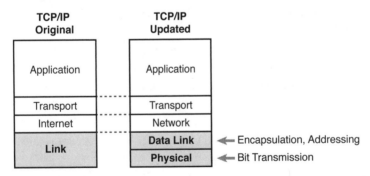

Figure 1-12 *Link Versus Data Link and Physical Layers*

Data Encapsulation Terminology

As you can see from the explanations of how HTTP, TCP, IP, and Ethernet do their jobs, each layer adds its own header (and for data-link protocols, also a trailer) to the data supplied by the higher layer. The term *encapsulation* refers to the process of putting headers (and sometimes trailers) around some data.

Many of the examples in this chapter show the encapsulation process. For example, web server Larry encapsulated the contents of the home page inside an HTTP header in Figure 1-6. The TCP layer encapsulated the HTTP headers and data inside a TCP header in Figure 1-7. IP encapsulated the TCP headers and the data inside an IP header in Figure 1-10. Finally, the Ethernet link layer encapsulated the IP packets inside both a header and a trailer in Figure 1-11.

The process by which a TCP/IP host sends data can be viewed as a five-step process. The first four steps relate to the encapsulation performed by the four TCP/IP layers, and the last step is the actual physical transmission of the data by the host. In fact, if you use the five-layer TCP/IP model, one step corresponds to the role of each layer. The steps are summarized in the following list:

Step 1.   **Create and encapsulate the application data with any required application layer headers.** For example, the HTTP OK message can be returned in an HTTP header, followed by part of the contents of a web page.

Step 2.   **Encapsulate the data supplied by the application layer inside a transport layer header.** For end-user applications, a TCP or UDP header is typically used.

Step 3.   **Encapsulate the data supplied by the transport layer inside a network layer (IP) header.** IP defines the IP addresses that uniquely identify each computer.

Step 4.   **Encapsulate the data supplied by the network layer inside a data link layer header and trailer.** This layer uses both a header and a trailer.

Step 5.   **Transmit the bits.** The physical layer encodes a signal onto the medium to transmit the frame.

The numbers in Figure 1-13 correspond to the five steps in this list, graphically showing the same concepts. Note that because the application layer often does not need to add a header, the figure does not show a specific application layer header.

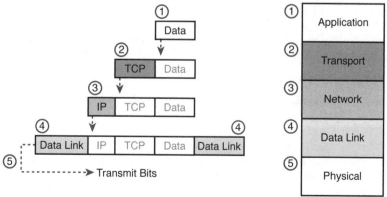

Figure 1-13   *Five Steps of Data Encapsulation: TCP/IP*

Names of TCP/IP Messages

Finally, take particular care to remember the terms *segment*, *packet*, and *frame* and the meaning of each. Each term refers to the headers (and possibly trailers) defined by a particular layer and the data encapsulated following that header. Each term, however, refers to a different layer: segment for the transport layer, packet for the network layer, and frame for the link layer. Figure 1-14 shows each layer along with the associated term.

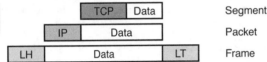

Figure 1-14   *Perspectives on Encapsulation and "Data"**

* The letters LH and LT stand for link header and link trailer, respectively, and refer to the data link layer header and trailer.

Figure 1-14 also shows the encapsulated data as simply "data." When focusing on the work done by a particular layer, the encapsulated data typically is unimportant. For example, an IP packet can indeed have a TCP header after the IP header, an HTTP header after the TCP header, and data for a web page after the HTTP header. However, when discussing IP, you probably just care about the IP header, so everything after the IP header is just called data. So, when drawing IP packets, everything after the IP header is typically shown simply as data.

OSI Networking Model

At one point in the history of the OSI model, many people thought that OSI would win the battle of the networking models discussed earlier. If that had occurred, instead of running TCP/IP on every computer in the world, those computers would be running with OSI.

However, OSI did not win that battle. In fact, OSI no longer exists as a networking model that could be used instead of TCP/IP, although some of the original protocols referenced by the OSI model still exist.

So, why is OSI even in this book? Terminology. During those years in which many people thought the OSI model would become commonplace in the world of networking (mostly in the late 1980s and early 1990s), many vendors and protocol documents started using terminology from the OSI model. That terminology remains today. So, while you will never need to work with a computer that uses OSI, to understand modern networking terminology, you need to understand something about OSI.

Comparing OSI and TCP/IP

The OSI model has many similarities to the TCP/IP model from a basic conceptual perspective. It has (seven) layers, and each layer defines a set of typical networking functions. As with TCP/IP, the OSI layers each refer to multiple protocols and standards that implement the functions specified by each layer. In other cases, just as for TCP/IP, the OSI committees did not create new protocols or standards, but instead referenced other protocols that were already defined. For example, the IEEE defines Ethernet standards, so the OSI committees did not waste time specifying a new type of Ethernet; it simply referred to the IEEE Ethernet standards.

Today, the OSI model can be used as a standard of comparison to other networking models. Figure 1-15 compares the seven-layer OSI model with both the four-layer and five-layer TCP/IP models.

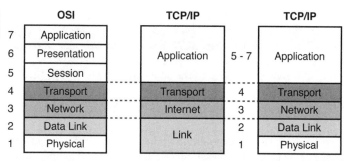

Figure 1-15 *OSI Model Compared to the Two TCP/IP Models*

Next, this section examines two ways in which we still use OSI terminology today: to describe other protocols and to describe the encapsulation process. Along the way, the text briefly examines each layer of the OSI model.

Describing Protocols by Referencing the OSI Layers

Even today, networking documents often describe TCP/IP protocols and standards by referencing OSI layers, both by layer number and layer name. For example, a common description of a LAN switch is "Layer 2 switch," with "Layer 2" referring to OSI layer 2. Because OSI did have a well-defined set of functions associated with each of its seven layers, if you know those functions, you can understand what people mean when they refer to a product or function by its OSI layer.

For another example, TCP/IP's original Internet layer, as implemented mainly by IP, equates most directly to the OSI *network* layer. So, most people say that IP is a *network layer protocol*, or a *Layer 3 protocol*, using OSI terminology and numbers for the layer. Of course, if you numbered the TCP/IP model, starting at the bottom, IP would be either Layer 2 or 3, depending on what version of the TCP/IP model you care to use. However, even though IP is a TCP/IP protocol, everyone uses the OSI model layer names and numbers when describing IP or any other protocol for that matter.

The claim that a particular TCP/IP layer is similar to a particular OSI layer is a general comparison, but not a detailed comparison. The comparison is a little like comparing a car to a truck: Both can get you from point A to point B, but they have many specific differences, like the truck having a truck bed in which to carry cargo. Similarly, both the OSI and TCP/IP network layers define logical addressing and routing. However, the addresses have a different size, and the routing logic even works differently. So the comparison of OSI layers to other protocol models is a general comparison of major goals, and not a comparison of the specific methods.

OSI Layers and Their Functions

Today, because most people happen to be much more familiar with TCP/IP functions than with OSI functions, one of the best ways to learn about the function of different OSI layers is to think about the functions in the TCP/IP model and to correlate those with the OSI model. For the purposes of learning, you can think of five of the OSI layers as doing the same kinds of things as the matching five layers in the TCP/IP model. For example, the application layer of each model defines protocols to be used directly by the applications, and the physical layer of each defines the electro-mechanical details of communicating over physical connections. Table 1-4 briefly describes each OSI layer.

Table 1-4   OSI Reference Model Layer Descriptions

Layer	Functional Description
7	**Application layer.** Provides an interface from the application to the network by supplying a protocol with actions meaningful to the application, for example, "get web page object."
6	**Presentation layer.** This layer negotiates data formats, such as ASCII text, or image types like JPEG.
5	**Session layer.** This layer provides methods to group multiple bidirectional messages into a workflow for easier management and easier backout of work that happened if the entire workflow fails.
4	**Transport layer.** In function, much like TCP/IP's transport layer. This layer focuses on data delivery between the two endpoint hosts (for example, error recovery).
3	**Network layer.** Like the TCP/IP network (Internet) layer, this layer defines logical addressing, routing (forwarding), and the routing protocols used to learn routes.
2	**Data link layer.** Like the TCP/IP data link layer, this layer defines the protocols for delivering data over a particular single type of physical network (for example, the Ethernet data link protocols).
1	**Physical layer.** This layer defines the physical characteristics of the transmission medium, including connectors, pins, use of pins, electrical currents, encoding, light modulation, and so on.

Table 1-5 lists a sampling of the devices and protocols and their comparable OSI layers. Note that many network devices must actually understand the protocols at multiple OSI layers, so the layer listed in Table 1-5 actually refers to the highest layer that the device normally thinks about when performing its core work. For example, routers need to think about Layer 3 concepts, but they must also support features at both Layers 1 and 2.

Table 1-5   OSI Reference Model: Device and Protocol Examples

Layer Name	Protocols and Specifications	Devices
Application, presentation, session (Layers 5–7)	Telnet, HTTP, FTP, SMTP, POP3, VoIP, SNMP	Hosts, firewalls
Transport (Layer 4)	TCP, UDP	Hosts, firewalls
Network (Layer 3)	IP	Router
Data link (Layer 2)	Ethernet (IEEE 802.3), HDLC	LAN switch, wireless access point, cable modem, DSL modem
Physical (Layer 1)	RJ-45, Ethernet (IEEE 802.3)	LAN hub, LAN repeater, cables

Besides remembering the basics of the features of each OSI layer (as in Table 1-4), and some protocol and device example at each layer (as in Table 1-5), you should also memorize the names of the layers. You can simply memorize them, but some people like to use a mnemonic phrase to make memorization easier. In the following three phrases, the first letter of each word is the same as the first letter of an OSI layer name, in the order specified in parentheses:

- All People Seem To Need Data Processing (Layers 7 to 1)
- Please Do Not Take Sausage Pizzas Away (Layers 1 to 7)
- Pew! Dead Ninja Turtles Smell Particularly Awful (Layers 1 to 7)

OSI Layering Concepts and Benefits

While networking models use layers to help humans categorize and understand the many functions in a network, networking models use layers for many reasons. For example, consider another postal service analogy. A person writing a letter does not have to think about how the postal service will deliver a letter across the country. The postal worker in the middle of the country does not have to worry about the contents of the letter. Likewise, networking models that divide functions into different layers enable one software package or hardware device to implement functions from one layer, and assume that other software/ hardware will perform the functions defined by the other layers.

The following list summarizes the benefits of layered protocol specifications:

- **Less complex:** Compared to not using a layered model, network models break the concepts into smaller parts.
- **Standard interfaces:** The standard interface definitions between each layer allow multiple vendors to create products that fill a particular role, with all the benefits of open competition.
- **Easier to learn:** Humans can more easily discuss and learn about the many details of a protocol specification.
- **Easier to develop:** Reduced complexity allows easier program changes and faster product development.
- **Multivendor interoperability:** Creating products to meet the same networking standards means that computers and networking gear from multiple vendors can work in the same network.
- **Modular engineering:** One vendor can write software that implements higher layers—for example, a web browser—and another vendor can write software that implements the lower layers—for example, Microsoft's built-in TCP/IP software in its operating systems.

OSI Encapsulation Terminology

Like TCP/IP, each OSI layer asks for services from the next lower layer. To provide the services, each layer makes use of a header and possibly a trailer. The lower layer encapsulates the higher layer's data behind a header.

OSI uses a more generic term to refer to messages, rather than frame, packet, and segment. OSI uses the term protocol data unit (PDU). A PDU represents the bits that include the headers and trailers for that layer, as well as the encapsulated data. For example, an IP packet, as shown in Figure 1-14, using OSI terminology, is a PDU, more specifically a *Layer 3 PDU* (abbreviated L3PDU) because IP is a Layer 3 protocol. OSI simply refers to the Layer *x* PDU (LxPDU), with *x* referring to the number of the layer being discussed, as shown in Figure 1-16.

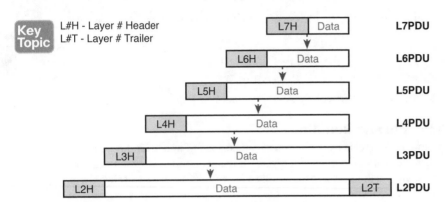

Figure 1-16   *OSI Encapsulation and Protocol Data Units*

Chapter Review

The "Your Study Plan" element, just before Chapter 1, discusses how you should study and practice the content and skills for each chapter before moving on to the next chapter. That element introduces the tools used here at the end of each chapter. If you haven't already done so, take a few minutes to read that section. Then come back here and do the useful work of reviewing the chapter to help lock into memory what you just read.

Review this chapter's material using either the tools in the book, DVD, or interactive tools for the same material found on the book's companion website. Table 1-6 outlines the key review elements and where you can find them. To better track your study progress, record when you completed these activities in the second column.

Table 1-6   Chapter Review Tracking

Review Element	Review Date(s)	Resource Used
Review key topics		Book, DVD/website
Review key terms		Book, DVD/website
Repeat DIKTA questions		Book, PCPT

Review All the Key Topics

Table 1-7   Key Topics for Chapter 1

Key Topic Elements	Description	Page Number
Table 1-3	Provides definitions of same-layer and adjacent-layer interaction	25
Figure 1-10	Shows the general concept of IP routing	28
Figure 1-11	Depicts the data link services provided to IP for the purpose of delivering IP packets from host to host	29
Figure 1-13	Five steps to encapsulate data on the sending host	31
Figure 1-14	Shows the meaning of the terms *segment*, *packet*, and *frame*	32
Figure 1-15	Compares the OSI and TCP/IP network models	33
List	Lists the benefits of using a layered networking model	35
Figure 1-16	Terminology related to encapsulation	36

Key Terms You Should Know

adjacent-layer interaction, de-encapsulation, encapsulation, frame, networking model, packet, protocol data unit (PDU), same-layer interaction, segment

CHAPTER 2

Fundamentals of Ethernet LANs

This chapter covers the following exam topics:

1.0 Network Fundamentals

1.6 Select the appropriate cabling type based on implementation requirements

2.0 LAN Switching Technologies

2.1 Describe and verify switching concepts

    2.1.a MAC learning and aging

    2.1.b Frame switching

    2.1.c Frame flooding

    2.1.d MAC address table

2.2 Interpret Ethernet frame format

Most enterprise computer networks can be separated into two general types of technology: local-area networks (LAN) and wide-area networks (WAN). LANs typically connect nearby devices: devices in the same room, in the same building, or in a campus of buildings. In contrast, WANs connect devices that are typically relatively far apart. Together, LANs and WANs create a complete enterprise computer network, working together to do the job of a computer network: delivering data from one device to another.

Many types of LANs have existed over the years, but today's networks use two general types of LANs: Ethernet LANs and wireless LANs. Ethernet LANs happen to use cables for the links between nodes, and because many types of cables use copper wires, Ethernet LANs are often called *wired LANs*. In comparison, wireless LANs do not use wires or cables, instead using radio waves for the links between nodes.

This chapter introduces Ethernet LANs, with more detailed coverage in Parts II and III of this book.

"Do I Know This Already?" Quiz

Take the quiz (either here, or use the PCPT software) if you want to use the score to help you decide how much time to spend on this chapter. The answers are at the bottom of the page following the quiz, and the explanations are in DVD Appendix C and in the PCPT software.

Table 2-1 "Do I Know This Already?" Foundation Topics Section-to-Question Mapping

Foundation Topics Section	Questions
An Overview of LANs	1–2
Building Physical Ethernet Networks	3–4
Sending Data in Ethernet Networks	5–8

1. In the LAN for a small office, some user devices connect to the LAN using a cable, while others connect using wireless technology (and no cable). Which of the following is true regarding the use of Ethernet in this LAN?

    a. Only the devices that use cables are using Ethernet.

    b. Only the devices that use wireless are using Ethernet.

    c. Both the devices using cables and those using wireless are using Ethernet.

    d. None of the devices are using Ethernet.

2. Which of the following Ethernet standards defines Gigabit Ethernet over UTP cabling?

    a. 10GBASE-T

    b. 100BASE-T

    c. 1000BASE-T

    d. None of the other answers is correct.

3. Which of the following is true about Ethernet crossover cables for Fast Ethernet?

    a. Pins 1 and 2 are reversed on the other end of the cable.

    b. Pins 1 and 2 on one end of the cable connect to pins 3 and 6 on the other end of the cable.

    c. Pins 1 and 2 on one end of the cable connect to pins 3 and 4 on the other end of the cable.

    d. The cable can be up to 1000 meters long to cross over between buildings.

    e. None of the other answers is correct.

4. Each answer lists two types of devices used in a 100BASE-T network. If these devices were connected with UTP Ethernet cables, which pairs of devices would require a straight-through cable? (Choose three answers.)

    a. PC and router

    b. PC and switch

    c. Hub and switch

    d. Router and hub

    e. Wireless access point (Ethernet port) and switch

5. Which of the following is true about the CSMA/CD algorithm?

   a. The algorithm never allows collisions to occur.

   b. Collisions can happen, but the algorithm defines how the computers should notice a collision and how to recover.

   c. The algorithm works with only two devices on the same Ethernet.

   d. None of the other answers is correct.

6. Which of the following is true about the Ethernet FCS field?

   a. Ethernet uses FCS for error recovery.

   b. It is 2 bytes long.

   c. It resides in the Ethernet trailer, not the Ethernet header.

   d. It is used for encryption.

7. Which of the following are true about the format of Ethernet addresses? (Choose three answers.)

   a. Each manufacturer puts a unique OUI code into the first 2 bytes of the address.

   b. Each manufacturer puts a unique OUI code into the first 3 bytes of the address.

   c. Each manufacturer puts a unique OUI code into the first half of the address.

   d. The part of the address that holds this manufacturer's code is called the MAC.

   e. The part of the address that holds this manufacturer's code is called the OUI.

   f. The part of the address that holds this manufacturer's code has no specific name.

8. Which of the following terms describe Ethernet addresses that can be used to send one frame that is delivered to multiple devices on the LAN? (Choose two answers.)

   a. Burned-in address

   b. Unicast address

   c. Broadcast address

   d. Multicast address

Foundation Topics

An Overview of LANs

The term *Ethernet* refers to a family of LAN standards that together define the physical and data link layers of the world's most popular wired LAN technology. The standards, defined by the Institute of Electrical and Electronics Engineers (IEEE), define the cabling, the connectors on the ends of the cables, the protocol rules, and everything else required to create an Ethernet LAN.

Typical SOHO LANs

To begin, first think about a small office/home office (SOHO) LAN today, specifically a LAN that uses only Ethernet LAN technology. First, the LAN needs a device called an Ethernet *LAN switch*, which provides many physical ports into which cables can be connected. An Ethernet uses *Ethernet cables*, which is a general reference to any cable that conforms to any of several Ethernet standards. The LAN uses Ethernet cables to connect different Ethernet devices or nodes to one of the switch's Ethernet ports.

Figure 2-1 shows a drawing of a SOHO Ethernet LAN. The figure shows a single LAN switch, five cables, and five other Ethernet nodes: three PCs, a printer, and one network device called a *router*. (The router connects the LAN to the WAN, in this case to the Internet.)

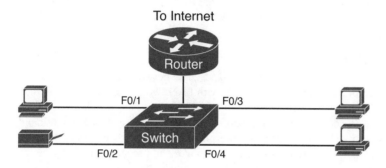

Figure 2-1   *Typical Small Ethernet-Only SOHO LAN*

Although Figure 2-1 shows a simple Ethernet LAN, many SOHO Ethernet LANs today combine the router and switch into a single device. Vendors sell consumer-grade integrated networking devices that work as a router and Ethernet switch, as well as doing other functions. These devices typically have "router" on the packaging, but many models also have four-port or eight-port Ethernet LAN switch ports built in to the device.

Typical SOHO LANs today also support wireless LAN connections. Ethernet defines wired LAN technology only; in other words, Ethernet LANs use cables. However, you can build one LAN that uses both Ethernet LAN technology as well as wireless LAN technology, which is also defined by the IEEE. Wireless LANs, defined by the IEEE using standards that begin with 802.11, use radio waves to send the bits from one node to the next.

Most wireless LANs rely on yet another networking device: a wireless LAN access point (AP). The AP acts somewhat like an Ethernet switch, in that all the wireless LAN nodes communicate with the Ethernet switch by sending and receiving data with the wireless AP. Of course, as a wireless device, the AP does not need Ethernet ports for cables, other than for a single Ethernet link to connect the AP to the Ethernet LAN, as shown in Figure 2-2.

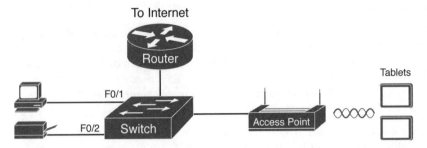

Figure 2-2 *Typical Small Wired and Wireless SOHO LAN*

Note that this drawing shows the router, Ethernet switch, and wireless LAN access point as three separate devices so that you can better understand the different roles. However, most SOHO networks today would use a single device, often labeled as a "wireless router," that does all these functions.

Typical Enterprise LANs

Enterprise networks have similar needs compared to a SOHO network, but on a much larger scale. For example, enterprise Ethernet LANs begin with LAN switches installed in a wiring closet behind a locked door on each floor of a building. The electricians install the Ethernet cabling from that wiring closet to cubicles and conference rooms where devices might need to connect to the LAN. At the same time, most enterprises also support wireless LANs in the same space, to allow people to roam around and still work and to support a growing number of devices that do not have an Ethernet LAN interface.

Figure 2-3 shows a conceptual view of a typical enterprise LAN in a three-story building. Each floor has an Ethernet LAN switch and a wireless LAN AP. To allow communication between floors, each per-floor switch connects to one centralized distribution switch. For example, PC3 can send data to PC2, but it would first flow through switch SW3 to the first floor to the distribution switch (SWD) and then back up through switch SW2 on the second floor.

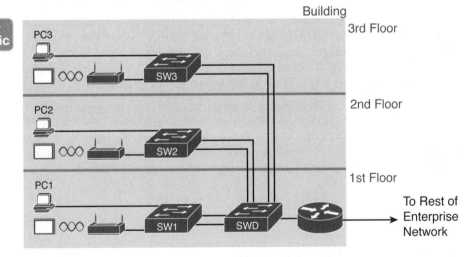

Figure 2-3 *Single-Building Enterprise Wired and Wireless LAN*

The figure also shows the typical way to connect a LAN to a WAN using a router. LAN switches and wireless access points work to create the LAN itself. Routers connect to both the LAN and the WAN. To connect to the LAN, the router simply uses an Ethernet LAN interface and an Ethernet cable, as shown on the lower right of Figure 2-3.

The rest of this chapter focuses on Ethernet in particular.

The Variety of Ethernet Physical Layer Standards

The term *Ethernet* refers to an entire family of standards. Some standards define the specifics of how to send data over a particular type of cabling, and at a particular speed. Other standards define protocols, or rules, that the Ethernet nodes must follow to be a part of an Ethernet LAN. All these Ethernet standards come from the IEEE and include the number 802.3 as the beginning part of the standard name.

Ethernet supports a large variety of options for physical Ethernet links given its long history over the last 40 or so years. Today, Ethernet includes many standards for different kinds of optical and copper cabling, and for speeds from 10 megabits per second (Mbps) up to 100 gigabits per second (Gbps). The standards also differ as far as the types of cabling and the allowed length of the cabling.

The most fundamental cabling choice has to do with the materials used inside the cable for the physical transmission of bits: either copper wires or glass fibers. The use of unshielded twisted-pair (UTP) cabling saves money compared to optical fibers, with Ethernet nodes using the wires inside the cable to send data over electrical circuits. Fiber-optic cabling, the more expensive alternative, allows Ethernet nodes to send light over glass fibers in the center of the cable. Although more expensive, optical cables typically allow longer cabling distances between nodes.

To be ready to choose the products to purchase for a new Ethernet LAN, a network engineer must know the names and features of the different Ethernet standards supported in Ethernet products. The IEEE defines Ethernet physical layer standards using a couple of naming conventions. The formal name begins with 802.3 followed by some suffix letters. The IEEE also uses more meaningful shortcut names that identify the speed, as well as a clue about whether the cabling is UTP (with a suffix that includes *T*) or fiber (with a suffix that includes *X*).

Table 2-2 lists a few Ethernet physical layer standards. First, the table lists enough names so that you get a sense of the IEEE naming conventions. It also lists the four most common standards that use UTP cabling, because this book's discussion of Ethernet focuses mainly on the UTP options.

Table 2-2   Examples of Types of Ethernet

Speed	Common Name	Informal IEEE Standard Name	Formal IEEE Standard Name	Cable Type, Maximum Length
10 Mbps	Ethernet	10BASE-T	802.3	Copper, 100 m
100 Mbps	Fast Ethernet	100BASE-T	802.3u	Copper, 100 m
1000 Mbps	Gigabit Ethernet	1000BASE-LX	802.3z	Fiber, 5000 m
1000 Mbps	Gigabit Ethernet	1000BASE-T	802.3ab	Copper, 100 m
10 Gbps	10 Gig Ethernet	10GBASE-T	802.3an	Copper, 100 m

NOTE   Fiber-optic cabling contains long thin strands of fiberglass. The attached Ethernet nodes send light over the glass fiber in the cable, encoding the bits as changes in the light.

Consistent Behavior over All Links Using the Ethernet Data Link Layer

Although Ethernet includes many physical layer standards, Ethernet acts like a single LAN technology because it uses the same data link layer standard over all types of Ethernet physical links. That standard defines a common Ethernet header and trailer. (As a reminder, the header and trailer are bytes of overhead data that Ethernet uses to do its job of sending data over a LAN.) No matter whether the data flows over a UTP cable or any kind of fiber cable, and no matter the speed, the data-link header and trailer use the same format.

While the physical layer standards focus on sending bits over a cable, the Ethernet data-link protocols focus on sending an *Ethernet frame* from source to destination Ethernet node. From a data-link perspective, nodes build and forward frames. As first defined in Chapter 1, "Introduction to TCP/IP Networking," the term *frame* specifically refers to the header and trailer of a data-link protocol, plus the data encapsulated inside that header and trailer. The various Ethernet nodes simply forward the frame, over all the required links, to deliver the frame to the correct destination.

Figure 2-4 shows an example of the process. In this case, PC1 sends an Ethernet frame to PC3. The frame travels over a UTP link to Ethernet switch SW1, then over fiber links to Ethernet switches SW2 and SW3, and finally over another UTP link to PC3. Note that the bits actually travel at four different speeds in this example: 10 Mbps, 1 Gbps, 10 Gbps, and 100 Mbps, respectively.

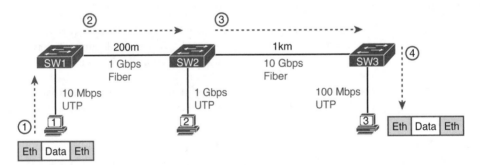

Figure 2-4   *Ethernet LAN Forwards a Data-Link Frame over Many Types of Links*

So, what is an Ethernet LAN? It is a combination of user devices, LAN switches, and different kinds of cabling. Each link can use different types of cables, at different speeds. However, they all work together to deliver Ethernet frames from the one device on the LAN to some other device.

The rest of this chapter takes these concepts a little deeper, first looking at the details of building the physical Ethernet network, followed by some discussion of the rules for forwarding frames through an Ethernet LAN.

Building Physical Ethernet Networks with UTP

For this second of three major sections of this chapter, I focus on the individual physical links between any two Ethernet nodes. Before the Ethernet network as a whole can send Ethernet frames between user devices, each node must be ready and able to send data over an individual physical link. This section looks at some of the particulars of how Ethernet sends data over these links.

This section focuses on the three most commonly used Ethernet standards: 10BASE-T (Ethernet), 100BASE-T (Fast Ethernet, or FE), and 1000BASE-T (Gigabit Ethernet, or GE). Specifically, this section looks at the details of sending data in both directions over a UTP cable. It then examines the specific wiring of the UTP cables used for 10-Mbps, 100-Mbps, and 1000-Mbps Ethernet.

Transmitting Data Using Twisted Pairs

While it is true that Ethernet sends data over UTP cables, the physical means to send the data uses electricity that flows over the wires inside the UTP cable. To better understand how Ethernet sends data using electricity, break the idea down into two parts: how to create an electrical circuit and then how to make that electrical signal communicate 1s and 0s.

First, to create one electrical circuit, Ethernet defines how to use the two wires inside a single twisted pair of wires, as shown in Figure 2-5. The figure does not show a UTP cable between two nodes, but instead shows two individual wires that are inside the UTP cable. An electrical circuit requires a complete loop, so the two nodes, using circuitry on their Ethernet ports, connect the wires in one pair to complete a loop, allowing electricity to flow.

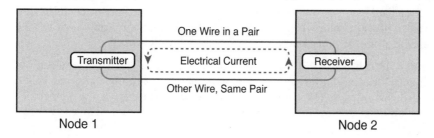

Figure 2-5 *Creating One Electrical Circuit over One Pair to Send in One Direction*

To send data, the two devices follow some rules called an *encoding scheme*. The idea works a lot like when two people talk using the same language: The speaker says some words in a particular language, and the listener, because she speaks the same language, can understand the spoken words. With an encoding scheme, the transmitting node changes the electrical signal over time, while the other node, the receiver, using the same rules, interprets those changes as either 0s or 1s. (For example, 10BASE-T uses an encoding scheme that encodes a binary 0 as a transition from higher voltage to lower voltage during the middle of a 1/10,000,000th-of-a-second interval.)

Note that in an actual UTP cable, the wires will be twisted together, instead of being parallel as shown in Figure 2-5. The twisting helps solve some important physical transmission issues. When electrical current passes over any wire, it creates electromagnetic interference (EMI) that interferes with the electrical signals in nearby wires, including the wires in the same cable. (EMI between wire pairs in the same cable is called *crosstalk*.) Twisting the wire pairs together helps cancel out most of the EMI, so most networking physical links that use copper wires use twisted pairs.

Breaking Down a UTP Ethernet Link

The term *Ethernet link* refers to any physical cable between two Ethernet nodes. To learn about how a UTP Ethernet link works, it helps to break down the physical link into those basic pieces, as shown in Figure 2-6: the cable itself, the connectors on the ends of the cable, and the matching ports on the devices into which the connectors will be inserted.

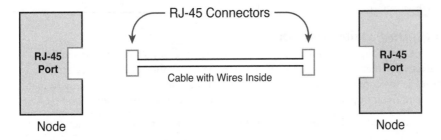

Figure 2-6   *Basic Components of an Ethernet Link*

First, think about the UTP cable itself. The cable holds some copper wires, grouped as twisted pairs. The 10BASE-T and 100BASE-T standards require two pairs of wires, while the 1000BASE-T standard requires four pairs. Each wire has a color-coded plastic coating, with the wires in a pair having a color scheme. For example, for the blue wire pair, one wire's coating is all blue, while the other wire's coating is blue-and-white striped.

Many Ethernet UTP cables use an RJ-45 connector on both ends. The RJ-45 connector has eight physical locations into which the eight wires in the cable can be inserted, called *pin positions*, or simply *pins*. These pins create a place where the ends of the copper wires can touch the electronics inside the nodes at the end of the physical link so that electricity can flow.

> **NOTE**   If available, find a nearby Ethernet UTP cable and examine the connectors closely. Look for the pin positions and the colors of the wires in the connector.

To complete the physical link, the nodes each need an RJ-45 *Ethernet port* that matches the RJ-45 connectors on the cable so that the connectors on the ends of the cable can connect to each node. PCs often include this RJ-45 Ethernet port as part of a network interface card (NIC), which can be an expansion card on the PC or can be built in to the system itself. Switches typically have many RJ-45 ports because switches give user devices a place to connect to the Ethernet LAN.

Figure 2-7 shows photos of the cables, connectors, and ports.

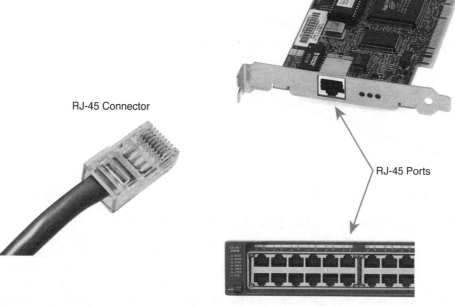

RJ-45 Connector

RJ-45 Ports

Figure 2-7 *RJ-45 Connectors and Ports (Ethernet NIC © Mark Jansen, LAN Cable ©*
Mikko Pitkänen)

NOTE   The RJ-45 connector is slightly wider, but otherwise similar, to the RJ-11 connectors commonly used for telephone cables in homes in North America.

The figure shows a connector on the left and ports on the right. The left shows the eight pin positions in the end of the RJ-45 connector. The upper right shows an Ethernet NIC that is not yet installed in a computer. The lower-right part of the figure shows the side of a Cisco 2960 switch, with multiple RJ-45 ports, allowing multiple devices to easily connect to the Ethernet network.

Finally, while RJ-45 connectors with UTP cabling can be common, Cisco LAN switches often support other types of connectors as well. When you buy one of the many models of Cisco switches, you need to think about the mix and numbers of each type of physical ports you want on the switch.

To give its customers flexibility as to the type of Ethernet links, even after the customer has bought the switch, Cisco switches include some physical ports whose port hardware (the transceiver) can be changed later, after you purchase the switch.

For example, Figure 2-8 shows a photo of a Cisco switch with one of the swappable transceivers. In this case, the figure shows an enhanced small form-factor pluggable (SFP+) transceiver, which runs at 10 Gbps, just outside two SFP+ slots on a Cisco 3560CX switch. The SFP+ itself is the silver colored part below the switch, with a black cable connected to it.

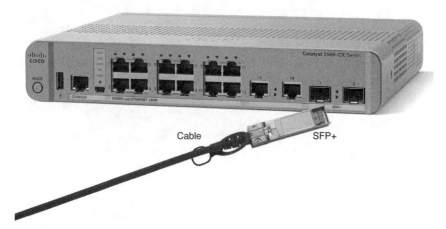

Figure 2-8   *10Gbps SFP+ with Cable Sitting Just Outside a Catalyst 3560CX Switch*

UTP Cabling Pinouts for 10BASE-T and 100BASE-T

So far in this section, you have learned about the equivalent of how to drive a truck on a 1000-acre ranch, but you do not know the equivalent of the local traffic rules. If you worked the ranch, you could drive the truck all over the ranch, any place you wanted to go, and the police would not mind. However, as soon as you get on the public roads, the police want you to behave and follow the rules. Similarly, so far this chapter has discussed the general principles of how to send data, but it has not yet detailed some important rules for Ethernet cabling: the rules of the road so that all the devices send data using the right wires inside the cable.

This next topic discusses conventions for 10BASE-T and 100BASE-T together, because they use UTP cabling in similar ways (including the use of only two wire pairs). A short comparison of the wiring for 1000BASE-T (Gigabit Ethernet), which uses four pairs, follows.

Straight-Through Cable Pinout

10BASE-T and 100BASE-T use two pairs of wires in a UTP cable, one for each direction, as shown in Figure 2-9. The figure shows four wires, all of which sit inside a single UTP cable that connects a PC and a LAN switch. In this example, the PC on the left transmits using the top pair, and the switch on the right transmits using the bottom pair.

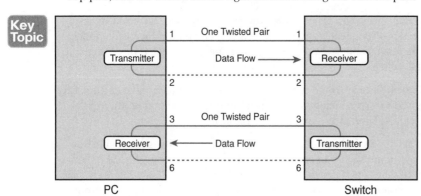

Figure 2-9   *Using One Pair for Each Transmission Direction with 10- and 100-Mbps Ethernet*

For correct transmission over the link, the wires in the UTP cable must be connected to the correct pin positions in the RJ-45 connectors. For example, in Figure 2-9, the transmitter on the PC on the left must know the pin positions of the two wires it should use to transmit. Those two wires must be connected to the correct pins in the RJ-45 connector on the switch, so that the switch's receiver logic can use the correct wires.

To understand the wiring of the cable—which wires need to be in which pin positions on both ends of the cable—you need to first understand how the NICs and switches work. As a rule, Ethernet NIC transmitters use the pair connected to pins 1 and 2; the NIC receivers use a pair of wires at pin positions 3 and 6. LAN switches, knowing those facts about what Ethernet NICs do, do the opposite: Their receivers use the wire pair at pins 1 and 2, and their transmitters use the wire pair at pins 3 and 6.

To allow a PC NIC to communicate with a switch, the UTP cable must also use a *straight-through cable pinout*. The term *pinout* refers to the wiring of which color wire is placed in each of the eight numbered pin positions in the RJ-45 connector. An Ethernet straight-through cable connects the wire at pin 1 on one end of the cable to pin 1 at the other end of the cable; the wire at pin 2 needs to connect to pin 2 on the other end of the cable; pin 3 on one end connects to pin 3 on the other, and so on. Also, it uses the wires in one wire pair at pins 1 and 2, and another pair at pins 3 and 6.

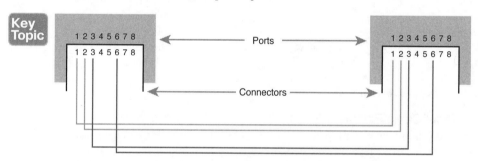

Figure 2-10   *10BASE-T and 100BASE-T Straight-Through Cable Pinout*

Figure 2-11 shows one final perspective on the straight-through cable pinout. In this case, PC Larry connects to a LAN switch. Note that the figure again does not show the UTP cable, but instead shows the wires that sit inside the cable, to emphasize the idea of wire pairs and pins.

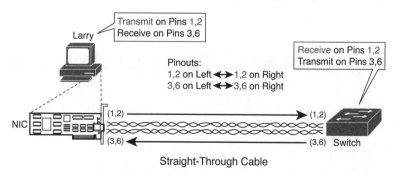

Figure 2-11   *Ethernet Straight-Through Cable Concept*

A straight-through cable works correctly when the nodes use opposite pairs for transmitting data. However, when two like devices connect to an Ethernet link, they both transmit on the same pins. In that case, you then need another type of cabling pinout called a *crossover cable*. The crossover cable pinout crosses the pair at the transmit pins on each device to the receive pins on the opposite device.

While that previous sentence is true, this concept is much clearer with a figure such as Figure 2-12. The figure shows what happens on a link between two switches. The two switches both transmit on the pair at pins 3 and 6, and they both receive on the pair at pins 1 and 2. So, the cable must connect a pair at pins 3 and 6 on each side to pins 1 and 2 on the other side, connecting to the other node's receiver logic. The top of the figure shows the literal pinouts, and the bottom half shows a conceptual diagram.

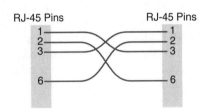

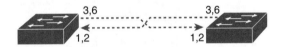

Figure 2-12   *Crossover Ethernet Cable*

Choosing the Right Cable Pinouts

For the exam, you should be well prepared to choose which type of cable (straight-through or crossover) is needed in each part of the network. The key is to know whether a device acts like a PC NIC, transmitting at pins 1 and 2, or like a switch, transmitting at pins 3 and 6. Then, just apply the following logic:

> **Crossover cable:** If the endpoints transmit on the same pin pair
>
> **Straight-through cable:** If the endpoints transmit on different pin pairs

Table 2-3 lists the devices and the pin pairs they use, assuming that they use 10BASE-T and 100BASE-T.

Table 2-3   10BASE-T and 100BASE-T Pin Pairs Used

Transmits on Pins 1,2	Transmits on Pins 3,6
PC NICs	Hubs
Routers	Switches
Wireless access point (Ethernet interface)	—

For example, Figure 2-13 shows a campus LAN in a single building. In this case, several straight-through cables are used to connect PCs to switches. In addition, the cables connecting the switches require crossover cables.

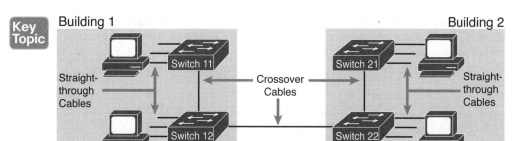

Figure 2-13 *Typical Uses for Straight-Through and Crossover Ethernet Cables*

> **NOTE** If you have some experience with installing LANs, you might be thinking that you have used the wrong cable before (straight-through or crossover) but the cable worked. Cisco switches have a feature called *auto-mdix* that notices when the wrong cable is used and automatically changes its logic to make the link work. However, for the exams, be ready to identify whether the correct cable is shown in the figures.

UTP Cabling Pinouts for 1000BASE-T

1000BASE-T (Gigabit Ethernet) differs from 10BASE-T and 100BASE-T as far as the cabling and pinouts. First, 1000BASE-T requires four wire pairs. Second, it uses more advanced electronics that allow both ends to transmit and receive simultaneously on each wire pair. However, the wiring pinouts for 1000BASE-T work almost identically to the earlier standards, adding details for the additional two pairs.

The straight-through cable connects each pin with the same numbered pin on the other side, but it does so for all eight pins—pin 1 to pin 1, pin 2 to pin 2, up through pin 8. It keeps one pair at pins 1 and 2 and another at pins 3 and 6, just like in the earlier wiring. It adds a pair at pins 4 and 5 and the final pair at pins 7 and 8 (refer to Figure 2-10).

The Gigabit Ethernet crossover cable crosses the same two-wire pairs as the crossover cable for the other types of Ethernet (the pairs at pins 1,2 and 3,6). It also crosses the two new pairs as well (the pair at pins 4,5 with the pair at pins 7,8).

Sending Data in Ethernet Networks

Although physical layer standards vary quite a bit, other parts of the Ethernet standards work the same way, regardless of the type of physical Ethernet link. Next, this final major section of this chapter looks at several protocols and rules that Ethernet uses regardless of the type of link. In particular, this section examines the details of the Ethernet data link layer protocol, plus how Ethernet nodes, switches, and hubs forward Ethernet frames through an Ethernet LAN.

Ethernet Data-Link Protocols

One of the most significant strengths of the Ethernet family of protocols is that these protocols use the same data-link standard. In fact, the core parts of the data-link standard date back to the original Ethernet standards.

The Ethernet data-link protocol defines the Ethernet frame: an Ethernet header at the front, the encapsulated data in the middle, and an Ethernet trailer at the end. Ethernet actually defines a few alternate formats for the header, with the frame format shown in Figure 2-14 being commonly used today.

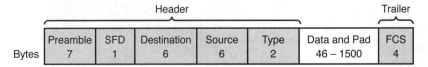

Figure 2-14   *Commonly Used Ethernet Frame Format*

While all the fields in the frame matter, some matter more to the topics discussed in this book. Table 2-4 lists the fields in the header and trailer and a brief description for reference, with the upcoming pages including more detail about a few of these fields.

Table 2-4   IEEE 802.3 Ethernet Header and Trailer Fields

Field	Bytes	Description
Preamble	7	Synchronization.
Start Frame Delimiter (SFD)	1	Signifies that the next byte begins the Destination MAC Address field.
Destination MAC Address	6	Identifies the intended recipient of this frame.
Source MAC Address	6	Identifies the sender of this frame.
Type	2	Defines the type of protocol listed inside the frame; today, most likely identifies IP version 4 (IPv4) or IP version 6 (IPv6).
Data and Pad*	46–1500	Holds data from a higher layer, typically an L3PDU (usually an IPv4 or IPv6 packet). The sender adds padding to meet the minimum length requirement for this field (46 bytes).
Frame Check Sequence (FCS)	4	Provides a method for the receiving NIC to determine whether the frame experienced transmission errors.

* The IEEE 802.3 specification limits the data portion of the 802.3 frame to a minimum of 46 and a maximum of 1500 bytes. The term *maximum transmission unit* (MTU) defines the maximum Layer 3 packet that can be sent over a medium. Because the Layer 3 packet rests inside the data portion of an Ethernet frame, 1500 bytes is the largest IP MTU allowed over an Ethernet.

Ethernet Addressing

The source and destination Ethernet address fields play a huge role in how Ethernet LANs work. The general idea for each is relatively simple: The sending node puts its own address in the source address field and the intended Ethernet destination device's address in the destination address field. The sender transmits the frame, expecting that the Ethernet LAN, as a whole, will deliver the frame to that correct destination.

Ethernet addresses, also called Media Access Control (MAC) addresses, are 6-byte-long (48-bit-long) binary numbers. For convenience, most computers list MAC addresses as 12-digit hexadecimal numbers. Cisco devices typically add some periods to the number for easier readability as well; for example, a Cisco switch might list a MAC address as 0000.0C12.3456.

Most MAC addresses represent a single NIC or other Ethernet port, so these addresses are often called a *unicast* Ethernet address. The term *unicast* is simply a formal way to refer to the fact that the address represents one interface to the Ethernet LAN. (This term also contrasts with two other types of Ethernet addresses, *broadcast* and *multicast*, which will be defined later in this section.)

The entire idea of sending data to a destination unicast MAC address works well, but it works only if all the unicast MAC addresses are unique. If two NICs tried to use the same MAC address, there could be confusion. (The problem would be like the confusion caused to the postal service if you and I both tried to use the same mailing address—would the postal service deliver mail to your house or mine?) If two PCs on the same Ethernet tried to use the same MAC address, to which PC should frames sent to that MAC address be delivered?

Ethernet solves this problem using an administrative process so that, at the time of manufacture, all Ethernet devices are assigned a universally unique MAC address. Before a manufacturer can build Ethernet products, it must ask the IEEE to assign the manufacturer a universally unique 3-byte code, called the organizationally unique identifier (OUI). The manufacturer agrees to give all NICs (and other Ethernet products) a MAC address that begins with its assigned 3-byte OUI. The manufacturer also assigns a unique value for the last 3 bytes, a number that manufacturer has never used with that OUI. As a result, the MAC address of every device in the universe is unique.

NOTE The IEEE also calls these universal MAC addresses global MAC addresses.

Figure 2-15 shows the structure of the unicast MAC address, with the OUI.

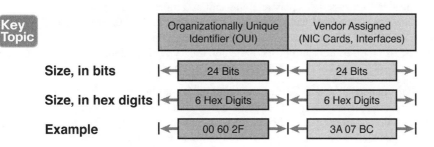

Figure 2-15 *Structure of Unicast Ethernet Addresses*

Ethernet addresses go by many names: LAN address, Ethernet address, hardware address, burned-in address, physical address, universal address, or MAC address. For example, the term burned-in address (BIA) refers to the idea that a permanent MAC address has been encoded (burned into) the ROM chip on the NIC. As another example, the IEEE uses the term *universal address* to emphasize the fact that the address assigned to a NIC by a manufacturer should be unique among all MAC addresses in the universe.

In addition to unicast addresses, Ethernet also uses group addresses. *Group addresses* identify more than one LAN interface card. A frame sent to a group address might be delivered to a small set of devices on the LAN, or even to all devices on the LAN. In fact, the IEEE defines two general categories of group addresses for Ethernet:

Broadcast address: Frames sent to this address should be delivered to all devices on the Ethernet LAN. It has a value of FFFF.FFFF.FFFF.

Multicast addresses: Frames sent to a multicast Ethernet address will be copied and forwarded to a subset of the devices on the LAN that volunteers to receive frames sent to a specific multicast address.

Table 2-5 summarizes most of the details about MAC addresses.

Table 2-5   LAN MAC Address Terminology and Features

LAN Addressing Term or Feature	Description
MAC	Media Access Control. 802.3 (Ethernet) defines the MAC sublayer of IEEE Ethernet.
Ethernet address, NIC address, LAN address	Other names often used instead of MAC address. These terms describe the 6-byte address of the LAN interface card.
Burned-in address	The 6-byte address assigned by the vendor making the card.
Unicast address	A term for a MAC address that represents a single LAN interface.
Broadcast address	An address that means "all devices that reside on this LAN right now."
Multicast address	On Ethernet, a multicast address implies some subset of all devices currently on the Ethernet LAN.

Identifying Network Layer Protocols with the Ethernet Type Field

While the Ethernet header's address fields play an important and more obvious role in Ethernet LANs, the Ethernet Type field plays a much less obvious role. The Ethernet Type field, or EtherType, sits in the Ethernet data link layer header, but its purpose is to directly help the network processing on routers and hosts. Basically, the Type field identifies the type of network layer (Layer 3) packet that sits inside the Ethernet frame.

First, think about what sits inside the data part of the Ethernet frame shown earlier in Figure 2-14. Typically, it holds the network layer packet created by the network layer protocol on some device in the network. Over the years, those protocols have included IBM Systems Network Architecture (SNA), Novell NetWare, Digital Equipment Corporation's DECnet, and Apple Computer's AppleTalk. Today, the most common network layer protocols are both from TCP/IP: IP version 4 (IPv4) and IP version 6 (IPv6).

The original host has a place to insert a value (a hexadecimal number) to identify the type of packet encapsulated inside the Ethernet frame. However, what number should the sender put in the header to identify an IPv4 packet as the type? Or an IPv6 packet? As it turns out, the IEEE manages a list of EtherType values, so that every network layer protocol that needs a unique EtherType value can have a number. The sender just has to know the list. (Anyone can view the list; just go to www.ieee.org and search for *EtherType*.)

For example, a host can send one Ethernet frame with an IPv4 packet and the next Ethernet frame with an IPv6 packet. Each frame would have a different Ethernet Type field value, using the values reserved by the IEEE, as shown in Figure 2-16.

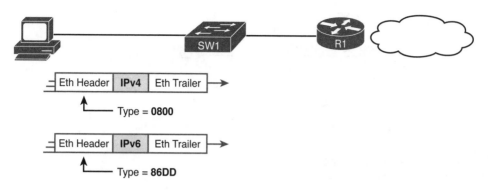

Figure 2-16 *Use of Ethernet Type Field*

Error Detection with FCS

Ethernet also defines a way for nodes to find out whether a frame's bits changed while crossing over an Ethernet link. (Usually, the bits could change because of some kind of electrical interference, or a bad NIC.) Ethernet, like most data-link protocols, uses a field in the data-link trailer for the purpose of error detection.

The Ethernet Frame Check Sequence (FCS) field in the Ethernet trailer—the only field in the Ethernet trailer—gives the receiving node a way to compare results with the sender, to discover whether errors occurred in the frame. The sender applies a complex math formula to the frame before sending it, storing the result of the formula in the FCS field. The receiver applies the same math formula to the received frame. The receiver then compares its own results with the sender's results. If the results are the same, the frame did not change; otherwise, an error occurred and the receiver discards the frame.

Note that *error detection* does not also mean *error recovery*. Ethernet defines that the errored frame should be discarded, but Ethernet does not attempt to recover the lost frame. Other protocols, notably TCP, recover the lost data by noticing that it is lost and sending the data again.

Sending Ethernet Frames with Switches and Hubs

Ethernet LANs behave slightly differently depending on whether the LAN has mostly modern devices, in particular, LAN switches instead of some older LAN devices called LAN hubs. Basically, the use of more modern switches allows the use of full-duplex logic, which is much faster and simpler than half-duplex logic, which is required when using hubs. The final topic in this chapter looks at these basic differences.

Sending in Modern Ethernet LANs Using Full Duplex

Modern Ethernet LANs use a variety of Ethernet physical standards, but with standard Ethernet frames that can flow over any of these types of physical links. Each individual link can run at a different speed, but each link allows the attached nodes to send the bits in the frame to the next node. They must work together to deliver the data from the sending Ethernet node to the destination node.

The process is relatively simple, on purpose; the simplicity lets each device send a large number of frames per second. Figure 2-17 shows an example in which PC1 sends an Ethernet frame to PC2.

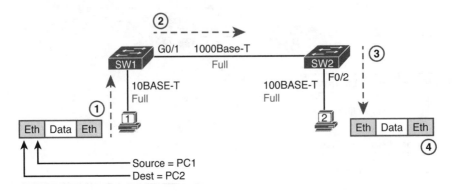

Figure 2-17   *Example of Sending Data in a Modern Ethernet LAN*

Following the steps in the figure:

1. PC1 builds and sends the original Ethernet frame, using its own MAC address as the source address and PC2's MAC address as the destination address.

2. Switch SW1 receives and forwards the Ethernet frame out its G0/1 interface (short for Gigabit interface 0/1) to SW2.

3. Switch SW2 receives and forwards the Ethernet frame out its F0/2 interface (short for Fast Ethernet interface 0/2) to PC2.

4. PC2 receives the frame, recognizes the destination MAC address as its own, and processes the frame.

The Ethernet network in Figure 2-17 uses full duplex on each link, but the concept might be difficult to see.

Full-duplex means that that the NIC or switch port has no half-duplex restrictions. So, to understand full duplex, you need to understand half duplex, as follows:

Half duplex: The device must wait to send if it is currently receiving a frame; in other words, it cannot send and receive at the same time.

Full duplex: The device does not have to wait before sending; it can send and receive at the same time.

So, with all PCs and LAN switches, and no LAN hubs, all the nodes can use full duplex. All nodes can send and receive on their port at the same instant in time. For example, in Figure 2-17, PC1 and PC2 could send frames to each other simultaneously, in both directions, without any half-duplex restrictions.

Using Half Duplex with LAN Hubs

To understand the need for half-duplex logic in some cases, you have to understand a little about an older type of networking device called a LAN hub. When the IEEE first introduced 10BASE-T in 1990, the Ethernet did not yet include LAN switches. Instead of switches, vendors created LAN hubs. The LAN hub provided a number of RJ-45 ports as a place to connect links to PCs, just like a LAN switch, but it used different rules for forwarding data.

LAN hubs forward data using physical layer standards, and are therefore considered to be Layer 1 devices. When an electrical signal comes in one hub port, the hub repeats that electrical signal out all other ports (except the incoming port). By doing so, the data reaches all the rest of the nodes connected to the hub, so the data hopefully reaches the correct destination. The hub has no concept of Ethernet frames, of addresses, and so on.

The downside of using LAN hubs is that if two or more devices transmitted a signal at the same instant, the electrical signal collides and becomes garbled. The hub repeats all received electrical signals, even if it receives multiple signals at the same time. For example, Figure 2-18 shows the idea, with PCs Archie and Bob sending an electrical signal at the same instant of time (at Steps 1A and 1B) and the hub repeating both electrical signals out toward Larry on the left (Step 2).

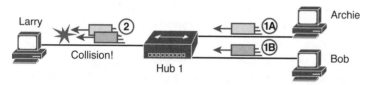

Figure 2-18 *Collision Occurring Because of LAN Hub Behavior*

> **NOTE**   For completeness, note that the hub floods each frame out all other ports (except the incoming port). So, Archie's frame goes to both Larry and Bob; Bob's frame goes to Larry and Archie.

If you replace the hub in Figure 2-18 with a LAN switch, the switch prevents the collision on the left. The switch operates as a Layer 2 device, meaning that it looks at the data-link header and trailer. A switch would look at the MAC addresses, and even if the switch needed to forward both frames to Larry on the left, the switch would send one frame and queue the other frame until the first frame was finished.

Now back to the issue created by the hub's logic: collisions. To prevent these collisions, the Ethernet nodes must use half-duplex logic instead of full-duplex logic. A problem occurs only when two or more devices send at the same time; half-duplex logic tells the nodes that if someone else is sending, wait before sending.

For example, back in Figure 2-18, imagine that Archie began sending his frame early enough so that Bob received the first bits of that frame before Bob tried to send his own frame. Bob, at Step 1B, would notice that he was receiving a frame from someone else, and using half-duplex logic, would simply wait to send the frame listed at Step 1B.

Nodes that use half-duplex logic actually use a relatively well-known algorithm called carrier sense multiple access with collision detection (CSMA/CD). The algorithm takes care of the obvious cases but also the cases caused by unfortunate timing. For example, two nodes could check for an incoming frame at the exact same instant, both realize that no other node is sending, and both send their frames at the exact same instant, causing a collision. CSMA/CD covers these cases as well, as follows:

Step 1.   A device with a frame to send listens until the Ethernet is not busy.

Step 2.   When the Ethernet is not busy, the sender begins sending the frame.

Step 3. The sender listens while sending to discover whether a collision occurs; collisions might be caused by many reasons, including unfortunate timing. If a collision occurs, all currently sending nodes do the following:

A. They send a jamming signal that tells all nodes that a collision happened.

B. They independently choose a random time to wait before trying again, to avoid unfortunate timing.

C. The next attempt starts again at Step 1.

Although most modern LANs do not often use hubs, and therefore do not need to use half duplex, enough old hubs still exist in enterprise networks so that you need to be ready to understand duplex issues. Each NIC and switch port has a duplex setting. For all links between PCs and switches, or between switches, use full duplex. However, for any link connected to a LAN hub, the connected LAN switch and NIC port should use half-duplex. Note that the hub itself does not use half-duplex logic, instead just repeating incoming signals out every other port.

Figure 2-19 shows an example, with full-duplex links on the left and a single LAN hub on the right. The hub then requires SW2's F0/2 interface to use half-duplex logic, along with the PCs connected to the hub.

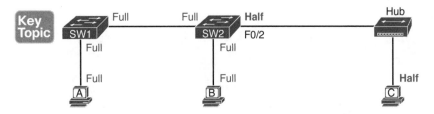

Figure 2-19 *Full and Half Duplex in an Ethernet LAN*

Chapter Review

One key to doing well on the exams is to perform repetitive spaced review sessions. Review this chapter's material using either the tools in the book, DVD, or interactive tools for the same material found on the book's companion website. Refer to the "Your Study Plan" element for more details. Table 2-6 outlines the key review elements and where you can find them. To better track your study progress, record when you completed these activities in the second column.

Table 2-6 Chapter Review Tracking

Review Element	Review Date(s)	Resource Used
Review key topics		Book, DVD/website
Review key terms		Book, DVD/website
Repeat DIKTA questions		Book, PCPT
Review memory tables		Book, DVD/website

Review All the Key Topics

Table 2-7   Key Topics for Chapter 2

Key Topic Element	Description	Page Number
Figure 2-3	Drawing of a typical wired and wireless enterprise LAN	42
Table 2-2	Several types of Ethernet LANs and some details about each	43
Figure 2-9	Conceptual drawing of transmitting in one direction each over two different electrical circuits between two Ethernet nodes	48
Figure 2-10	10- and 100-Mbps Ethernet straight-through cable pinouts	49
Figure 2-12	10- and 100-Mbps Ethernet crossover cable pinouts	50
Table 2-3	List of devices that transmit on wire pair 1,2 and pair 3,6	50
Figure 2-13	Typical uses for straight-through and crossover Ethernet cables	51
Figure 2-15	Format of Ethernet MAC addresses	53
List	Definitions of half duplex and full duplex	56
Figure 2-19	Examples of which interfaces use full duplex and which interfaces use half duplex	58

Key Terms You Should Know

Ethernet, IEEE, wired LAN, wireless LAN, Ethernet frame, 10BASE-T, 100BASE-T, 1000BASE-T, Fast Ethernet, Gigabit Ethernet, Ethernet link, RJ-45, Ethernet port, network interface card (NIC), straight-through cable, crossover cable, Ethernet address, MAC address, unicast address, broadcast address, Frame Check Sequence

CHAPTER 3

Fundamentals of WANs

This chapter covers the following exam topics:

1.0 Network Fundamentals

1.1 Compare and contrast OSI and TCP/IP models

1.6 Select the appropriate cabling type based on implementation requirements

3.0 Routing Technologies

3.1 Describe the routing concepts

   3.1.c Frame rewrite

Most Layer 1 and 2 networking technology falls into one of two primary categories: wide-area networks (WAN) and local area networks (LAN). Because both WANs and LANs match OSI Layers 1 and 2, they have many similarities: Both define cabling details, transmission speeds, encoding, and how to send data over physical links, as well as data-link frames and forwarding logic.

Of course, WANs and LANs have many differences as well, most notably the distances between nodes and the business model for paying for the network. First, in terms of the distance, the terms *local* and *wide* give us a small hint: LANs typically include nearby devices, whereas WANs connect devices that can be far apart, potentially hundreds or thousands of miles apart.

The other big difference between the two is this: You pay for and own LANs, but you lease WANs. With LANs, you buy the cables and LAN switches and install them in spaces you control. WANs physically pass through other people's property, and you do not have the right to put your cables and devices there. So, a few companies, like a telephone company or cable company, install and own their own devices and cables, creating their own networks, and lease the right to send data over their networks.

This chapter introduces WANs in three major sections. The first introduces leased line WANs, a type of WAN link that has been part of enterprise networks since the 1960s. The second part shows how Ethernet can be used to create WAN services by taking advantage of the longer cable length possibilities of modern fiber-optic Ethernet standards. The last part of the chapter takes a survey of common WAN technology used to access the Internet.

"Do I Know This Already?" Quiz

Take the quiz (either here, or use the PCPT software) if you want to use the score to help you decide how much time to spend on this chapter. The answers are at the bottom of the page following the quiz, and the explanations are in DVD Appendix C and in the PCPT software.

Table 3-1 "Do I Know This Already?" Foundation Topics Section-to-Question Mapping

Foundation Topics Section	Questions
Leased Line WANs	1–3
Ethernet as a WAN Technology	4
Accessing the Internet	5–6

1. In the cabling for a leased line, which of the following typically connects to a four-wire line provided by a telco?

   a. Router serial interface without internal CSU/DSU

   b. CSU/DSU

   c. Router serial interface with internal transceiver

   d. Switch serial interface

2. Which of the following is an accurate speed at which a leased line can operate in the United States?

   a. 100 Mbps

   b. 100 Kbps

   c. 256 Kbps

   d. 6.4 Mbps

3. Which of the following fields in the HDLC header used by Cisco routers does Cisco add, beyond the ISO standard HDLC?

   a. Flag

   b. Type

   c. Address

   d. FCS

4. Two routers, R1 and R2, connect using an Ethernet over MPLS service. The service provides point-to-point service between these two routers only, as a Layer 2 Ethernet service. Which of the following are the most likely to be true about this WAN? (Choose two answers.)

   a. R1 will connect to a physical Ethernet link, with the other end of the cable connected to R2.

   b. R1 will connect to a physical Ethernet link, with the other end of the cable connected to a device at the WAN service provider point of presence.

   c. R1 will forward data-link frames to R2 using an HDLC header/trailer.

   d. R1 will forward data-link frames to R2 using an Ethernet header/trailer.

5. Which of the following Internet access technologies, used to connect a site to an ISP, offers asymmetric speeds? (Choose two answers.)

   a. Leased lines

   b. DSL

   c. Cable Internet

   d. BGP

6. Fred has just added DSL service at his home, with a separate DSL modem and consumer-grade router with four Ethernet ports. Fred wants to use the same old phone he was using before the installation of DSL. Which is most likely true about the phone cabling and phone used with his new DSL installation?

   a. He uses the old phone, cabled to one of the router/switch device's Ethernet ports.

   b. He uses the old phone, cabled to the DSL modem's ports.

   c. He uses the old phone, cabled to an existing telephone port and not to any new device.

   d. The old phone must be replaced with a digital phone.

Foundation Topics

Leased-Line WANs

Imagine that you are the primary network engineer for an enterprise TCP/IP internetwork. Your company is building a new building at a site 100 miles away from your corporate head-quarters. You will of course install a LAN throughout the new building, but you also need to connect that new remote LAN to the rest of the existing enterprise TCP/IP network.

To connect the new building's LAN to the rest of the existing corporate network, you need some kind of a WAN. At a minimum, that WAN must be able to send data from the remote LAN back to the rest of the existing network and vice versa. Leased line WANs do exactly that, forwarding data between two routers.

From a basic point of view, a leased line WAN works a lot like an Ethernet crossover cable connecting two routers, but with few distance limitations. Each router can send at any time (full duplex) over the leased line, for tens, hundreds, or even thousands of miles.

This section begins by giving some perspective about where leased lines fit with LANs and routers, because one main goal for a WAN is to move data between LANs. The rest of this first section explains the physical details about leased lines, followed with information about data-link protocols.

Positioning Leased Lines with LANs and Routers

The vast majority of end-user devices in an enterprise or small office/home office (SOHO) network connect directly into a LAN. Many PCs use an Ethernet network interface card (NIC) that connects to a switch. More and more, devices use 802.11 wireless LANs, with some devices like phones and tablets supporting only wireless LAN connections.

Now think about a typical company that has many different locations. From a human resources perspective, it might have lots of employees that work at many locations. From a facilities perspective, the company might have a few large sites, with hundreds or even thousands of individual branch offices, stores, or other small locations. However, from a networking perspective, think of each site as being one or more LANs that need to communicate with each other, and to communicate, those LANs need to be connected to each other using a WAN.

To connect LANs using a WAN, the internetwork uses a router connected to each LAN, with a WAN link between the routers. First, the enterprise's network engineer would order some kind of WAN link. A router at each site connects to both the WAN link and the LAN, as shown in Figure 3-1. Note that a crooked line between the routers is the common way to represent a leased line when the drawing does not need to show any of the physical details of the line.

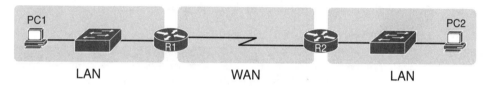

Figure 3-1 *Small Enterprise Network with One Leased Line*

The world of WAN technologies includes many different options in addition to the leased line shown in the figure. WAN technology includes a large number of options for physical links, as well as the data-link protocols that control those links. By comparison, the wired LAN world basically has one major option today—Ethernet—because Ethernet won the wired LAN battle in the marketplace back in the 1980s and 1990s.

Physical Details of Leased Lines

The leased line service delivers bits in both directions, at a predetermined speed, using full-duplex logic. In fact, conceptually it acts as if you had a full-duplex crossover Ethernet link between two routers, as shown in Figure 3-2. The leased line uses two pairs of wires, one pair for each direction of sending data, which allows full-duplex operation.

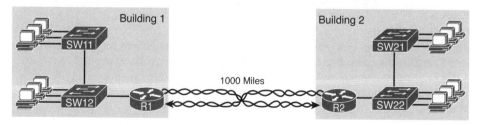

Figure 3-2 *Conceptual View of the Leased-Line Service*

Answers to the "Do I Know This Already?" quiz:

1 B **2** C **3** B **4** B and D **5** B and C **6** C

Of course, leased lines have many differences compared to an Ethernet crossover cable. To create such possibly long links, or circuits, a leased line does not actually exist as a single long cable between the two sites. Instead, the telco installs a large network of cables and specialized switching devices to create its own computer network. The telco network creates a service that acts like a crossover cable between two points, but the physical reality is hidden from the customer.

Leased lines come with their own set of terminology as well. First, the term *leased line* refers to the fact that the company using the leased line does not own the line, but instead pays a monthly lease fee to use it. However, many people today use the generic term *service provider* to refer to a company that provides any form of WAN connectivity, including Internet services.

Given their long history, leased lines have had many names. Table 3-2 lists some of those names, mainly so that in a networking job, you have a chance to translate from the terms each person uses with a basic description as to the meaning of the name.

Table 3-2 Different Names for a Leased Line

Name	Meaning or Reference
Leased circuit, Circuit	The words *line* and *circuit* are often used as synonyms in telco terminology; *circuit* makes reference to the electrical circuit between the two endpoints.
Serial link, Serial line	The words *link* and *line* are also often used as synonyms. *Serial* in this case refers to the fact that the bits flow serially, and that routers use serial interfaces.
Point-to-point link, Point-to-point line	Refers to the fact that the topology stretches between two points, and two points only. (Some older leased lines allowed more than two devices.)
T1	A specific type of leased line that transmits data at 1.544 megabits per second (1.544 Mbps).
WAN link, Link	Both these terms are very general, with no reference to any specific technology.
Private line	Refers to the fact that the data sent over the line cannot be copied by other telco customers, so the data is private.

Leased-Line Cabling

To create a leased line, some physical path must exist between the two routers on the ends of the link. The physical cabling must leave the buildings where each router sits. However, the telco does not simply install one cable between the two buildings. Instead, it uses what is typically a large and complex network that creates the appearance of a cable between the two routers.

Figure 3-3 gives a little insight into the cabling that could exist inside the telco for a short leased line. Telcos put their equipment in buildings called central offices (CO). The telco installs cables from the CO to most every other building in the city, expecting to sell services to the people in those buildings one day. The telco would then configure its switches to use some of the capacity on each cable to send data in both directions, creating the equivalent of a crossover cable between the two routers.

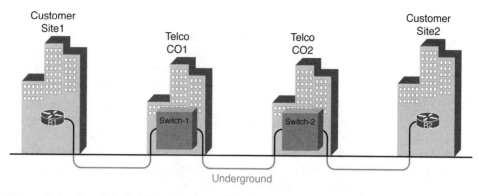

Figure 3-3 *Possible Cabling Inside a Telco for a Short Leased Line*

Although what happens inside the telco is completely hidden from the telco customer, enterprise engineers do need to know about the parts of the link that exist inside the customer's building at the router.

First, each site has customer premises equipment (CPE), which includes the router, serial interface card, and CSU/DSU. Each router uses a serial interface card that acts somewhat like an Ethernet NIC, sending and receiving data over the physical link. The physical link requires a function called a channel service unit/data service unit (CSU/DSU). The CSU/DSU can either be integrated into the serial interface card in the router or sit outside the router as an external device. Figure 3-4 shows the CPE devices, along with the cabling.

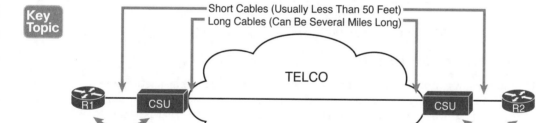

Figure 3-4 *Point-to-Point Leased Line: Components and Terminology*

The cabling includes a short serial cable (only if an external CSU/DSU is used) plus the cable installed by the telco for the leased line itself. The serial cable connects the router serial interface to the external CSU/DSU. (Many cable options exist; the cable just needs to match the connector of the serial interface on one end and the CSU/DSU on the other end.) The four-wire cable from the telco plugs in to the CSU/DSU, typically using an RJ-48 connector that has the same size and shape as an RJ-45 connector (as shown in Figure 2-7 in Chapter 2, "Fundamentals of Ethernet LANs").

Telcos offer a wide variety of speeds for leased lines. However, you cannot pick the exact speed you want; instead, you must pick from a long list of predefined speeds. Slower-speed links run at multiples of 64 kbps (kilobits per second), while faster links run at multiples of about 1.5 Mbps (megabits per second).

Building a WAN Link in a Lab

On a practical note, to prepare for the CCENT and CCNA Routing and Switching exams, you can choose to buy some used router and switch hardware for hands-on practice. If you do, you can create the equivalent of a leased line without a real leased line from a telco, and without CSU/DSUs, just using a cabling trick. This short topic tells you enough information to create a WAN link in your home lab.

First, the serial cables normally used between a router and an external CSU/DSU are called *data terminal equipment (DTE) cables*. To create a physical WAN link in a lab, you need two serial cables: one serial DTE cable, plus a similar but slightly different matching *data communications equipment (DCE) cable*. The DCE cable has a female connector, while the DTE cable has a male connector, which allows the two cables to be attached directly. The DCE cable also does the equivalent task of an Ethernet crossover cable by swapping the transmit and receive wire pairs, as shown in Figure 3-5.

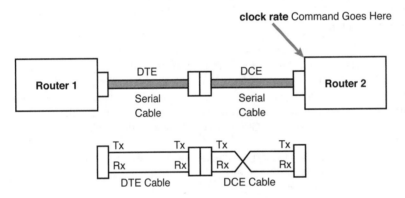

Figure 3-5   *Serial Cabling Uses a DTE Cable and a DCE Cable*

The figure shows the cable details at the top, with the wiring details inside the cable at the bottom. In particular, at the bottom of the figure, note that the DCE cable swaps the transmit and receive pairs, whereas the DTE serial cable does not, acting as a straight-through cable.

Finally, to make the link work, the router with the DCE cable installed must do one function normally done by the CSU/DSU. The CSU/DSU normally provides a function called *clocking*, in which it tells the router exactly when to send each bit through signaling over the serial cable. A router serial interface can provide clocking, and the more recent router software versions automatically supply clocking when the router senses a DCE cable is plugged into the serial port. Regardless of whether a router has an older or newer software version, you will want to know how to configure serial clocking using the **clock rate** command. The section "Bandwidth and Clock Rate on Serial Interfaces," in Chapter 17, "Operating Cisco Routers," shows a sample configuration.

Data-Link Details of Leased Lines

A leased line provides a Layer 1 service. In other words, it promises to deliver bits between the devices connected to the leased line. However, the leased line itself does not define a data link layer protocol to be used on the leased line.

Because leased lines define only the Layer 1 transmission service, many companies and standards organizations have created data-link protocols to control and use leased lines. Today, the two most popular data link layer protocols used for leased lines between two routers are High-Level Data Link Control (HDLC) and Point-to-Point Protocol (PPP). This next topic takes a brief look at HDLC, just to show one example, plus a few comments about how routers use WAN data-link protocols.

HDLC Basics

All data-link protocols perform a similar role: to control the correct delivery of data over a physical link of a particular type. For example, the Ethernet data-link protocol uses a destination address field to identify the correct device that should receive the data, and an FCS field that allows the receiving device to determine whether the data arrived correctly. HDLC provides similar functions.

HDLC has less work to do because of the simple point-to-point topology of a point-to-point leased line. When one router sends an HDLC frame, it can go only one place: to the other end of the link. So, while HDLC has an address field, the destination is implied. The idea is sort of like when I have lunch with my friend Gary, and only Gary. I do not need to start every sentence with "Hey Gary"—he knows I am talking to him.

NOTE   In case you wonder why HDLC has an address field at all, in years past, the telcos offered multidrop circuits. These circuits included more than two devices, so there was more than one possible destination, requiring an address field to identify the correct destination.

HDLC has other fields and functions similar to Ethernet as well. Table 3-3 lists the HDLC fields, with the similar Ethernet header/trailer field, just for the sake of learning HDLC based on something you have already learned about (Ethernet).

Table 3-3   Comparing HDLC Header Fields to Ethernet

HDLC Field	Ethernet Equivalent	Description
Flag	Preamble, SFD	Lists a recognizable bit pattern so that the receiving nodes realize that a new frame is arriving.
Address	Destination Address	Identifies the destination device.
Control	N/A	Mostly used for purposes no longer in use today for links between routers.
Type	Type	Identifies the type of Layer 3 packet encapsulated inside the frame.
FCS	FCS	A field used by the error detection process. (It is the only trailer field in this table.)

HDLC exists today as a standard of the International Organization for Standardization (ISO), the same organization that brought us the OSI model. However, ISO standard HDLC does not have a Type field, and routers need to know the type of packet inside the frame. So, Cisco routers use a Cisco-proprietary variation of HDLC that adds a Type field, as shown in Figure 3-6.

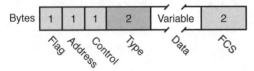

Proprietary Cisco HDLC (Adds Type Field)

Figure 3-6 *HDLC Framing*

How Routers Use a WAN Data Link

Today, most leased lines connect to routers, and routers focus on delivering packets to a destination host. However, routers physically connect to both LANs and WANs, with those LANs and WANs requiring that data be sent inside data-link frames. So, now that you know a little about HDLC, it helps to think about how routers use the HDLC protocol when sending data.

First, the TCP/IP network layer focuses on forwarding IP packets from the sending host to the destination host. The underlying LANs and WANs just act as a way to move the packets to the next router or end-user device. Figure 3-7 shows that network layer perspective.

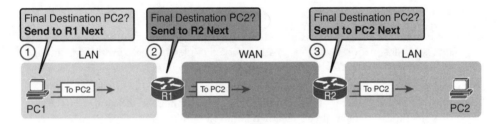

Figure 3-7 *IP Routing Logic over LANs and WANs*

Following the steps in the figure, for a packet sent by PC1 to PC2's IP address:

1. PC1's network layer (IP) logic tells it to send the packet to a nearby router (R1).

2. Router R1's network layer logic tells it to forward (route) the packet out the leased line to Router R2 next.

3. Router R2's network layer logic tells it to forward (route) the packet out the LAN link to PC2 next.

While Figure 3-7 shows the network layer logic, the PCs and routers must rely on the LANs and WANs in the figure to actually move the bits in the packet. Figure 3-8 shows the same figure, with the same packet, but this time showing some of the data link layer logic used by the hosts and routers. Basically, three separate data link layer steps encapsulate the packet, inside a data-link frame, over three hops through the internetwork: from PC1 to R1, from R1 to R2, and from R2 to PC2.

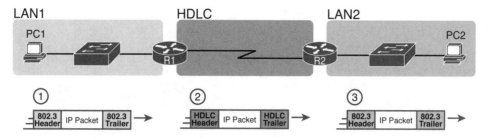

Figure 3-8 *General Concept of Routers De-encapsulating and Re-encapsulating IP Packets*

Following the steps in the figure, again for a packet sent by PC1 to PC2's IP address:

1. To send the IP packet to Router R1 next, PC1 encapsulates the IP packet in an Ethernet frame that has the destination MAC address of R1.

2. Router R1 de-encapsulates (removes) the IP packet from the Ethernet frame, encapsulates the packet into an HDLC frame using an HDLC header and trailer, and forwards the HDLC frame to Router R2 next.

3. Router R2 de-encapsulates (removes) the IP packet from the HDLC frame, encapsulates the packet into an Ethernet frame that has the destination MAC address of PC2, and forwards the Ethernet frame to PC2.

In summary, a leased line with HDLC creates a WAN link between two routers so that they can forward packets for the devices on the attached LANs. The leased line itself provides the physical means to transmit the bits, in both directions. The HDLC frames provide the means to encapsulate the network layer packet correctly so that it crosses the link between routers.

Leased lines have many benefits that have led to their relatively long life in the WAN marketplace. These lines are simple for the customer, are widely available, are of high quality, and are private. However, they do have some negatives as well compared to newer WAN technologies, including a higher cost and typically longer lead times to get the service installed. The next section looks at an alternative WAN technology used in some examples in this book: Ethernet.

Ethernet as a WAN Technology

For the first several decades of the existence of Ethernet, Ethernet was only appropriate for LANs. The restrictions on cable lengths and devices might allow a LAN that stretched a kilometer or two, to support a campus LAN, but that was the limit.

As time passed, the IEEE improved Ethernet standards in ways that made Ethernet a reasonable WAN technology. For example, the 1000BASE-LX standard uses single-mode fiber cabling, with support for a 5-km cable length; the 1000BASE-ZX standard supports an even longer 70-km cable length. As time went by, and as the IEEE improved cabling distances for fiber Ethernet links, Ethernet became a reasonable WAN technology.

Today, in this second decade of the twenty-first century, many WAN service providers (SP) offer WAN services that take advantage of Ethernet. SPs offer a wide variety of these Ethernet WAN services, with many different names. But all of them use a similar model, with Ethernet used between the customer site and the SP's network, as shown in Figure 3-9.

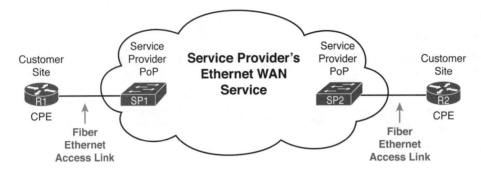

Figure 3-9   *Fiber Ethernet Link to Connect a CPE Router to a Service Provider's WAN*

The model shown in Figure 3-9 has many of the same ideas of how a telco creates a leased line, as shown earlier in Figure 3-3, but now with Ethernet links and devices. The customer connects to an Ethernet link using a router interface. The (fiber) Ethernet link leaves the customer building and connects to some nearby SP location called a point of presence (PoP). Instead of a telco switch as shown in Figure 3-3, the SP uses an Ethernet switch. Inside the SP's network, the SP uses any technology that it wants to create the specific Ethernet WAN services.

Ethernet WANs that Create a Layer 2 Service

The WAN services implied by Figure 3-9 include a broad number of services, with a lot of complex networking concepts needed to understand those services. Yet, we sit here at the third chapter of what is probably your first Cisco certification book, so clearly, getting into depth on these WAN services makes little sense. So, this book focuses on one specific Ethernet WAN service that can be easily understood if you understand how Ethernet LANs work.

> **NOTE**   For perspective about the broad world of the service provider network shown in Figure 3-9, look for more information about the Cisco CCNA, CCNP, and CCIE Service Provider certifications. See www.cisco.com/go/certifications for more details.

The one Ethernet WAN service goes by two names: Ethernet emulation and Ethernet over MPLS (EoMPLS). Ethernet emulation is a general term, meaning that the service acts like one Ethernet link. EoMPLS refers to Multiprotocol Label Switching (MPLS), which is one technology that can be used inside the SP's cloud. This book will refer to this specific service either as Ethernet emulation or EoMPLS.

The type of EoMPLS service discussed in this book gives the customer an Ethernet link between two sites. In other words, the EoMPLS service provides

- A point-to-point connection between two customer devices
- Behavior as if a fiber Ethernet link existed between the two devices

So, if you can imagine two routers, with a single Ethernet link between the two routers, you understand what this particular EoMPLS service does.

Figure 3-10 shows the idea. In this case, the two routers, R1 and R2, connect with an EoMPLS service instead of a serial link. The routers use Ethernet interfaces, and they can send data in both directions at the same time. Physically, each router actually connects to some SP PoP, as shown earlier in Figure 3-9, but logically, the two routers can send Ethernet frames to each other over the link.

 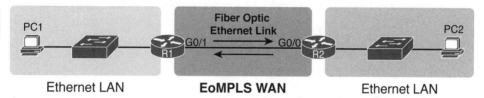

Figure 3-10 *EoMPLS Acting Like a Simple Ethernet Link Between Two Routers*

How Routers Route IP Packets Using Ethernet Emulation

WANs, by their very nature, give IP routers a way to forward IP packets from a LAN at one site, over the WAN, and to another LAN at another site. Routing over an EoMPLS WAN link still uses the WAN like a WAN, as a way to forward IP packets from one site to another. However, the WAN link happens to use the same Ethernet protocols as the Ethernet LAN links at each site.

The EoMPLS link uses Ethernet for both Layer 1 and Layer 2 functions. That means the link uses the same familiar Ethernet header and trailer, as shown in the middle of Figure 3-11.

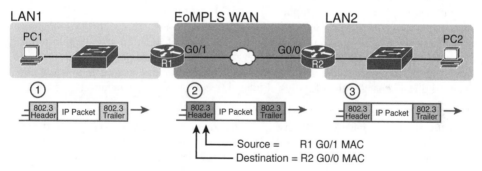

Figure 3-11 *Routing over an EoMPLS Link*

> **NOTE** This book shows EoMPLS connections as a familiar single black line, like other Ethernet links, but with a small cloud overlaid to note that this particular Ethernet link is through an Ethernet WAN service.

The figure shows the same three routing steps as shown with the serial link in the earlier Figure 3-8. In this case, all three routing steps use the same Ethernet (802.3) protocol. However, note that each frame's data-link header and trailer are different. Each router discards the old data-link header/trailer and adds a new set, as described in these steps. Focus mainly on Step 2, because compared to the similar example shown in Figure 3-8, Steps 1 and 3 are unchanged:

1. To send the IP packet to Router R1 next, PC1 encapsulates the IP packet in an Ethernet frame that has the destination MAC address of R1.

2. Router R1 de-encapsulates (removes) the IP packet from the Ethernet frame and encapsulates the packet into a new Ethernet frame, with a new Ethernet header and trailer. The destination MAC address is R2's G0/0 MAC address, and the source MAC address is R1's G0/1 MAC address. R1 forwards this frame over the EoMPLS service to R2 next.

3. Router R2 de-encapsulates (removes) the IP packet from the Ethernet frame, encapsulates the packet into an Ethernet frame that has the destination MAC address of PC2, and forwards the Ethernet frame to PC2.

Accessing the Internet

Many people begin their CCENT and CCNA Routing and Switching study never having heard of leased lines, but many people have heard of two other WAN technologies used to gain access to the Internet: digital subscriber line (DSL) and cable. These two WAN technologies do not replace leased lines in all cases, but they do play an important role in the specific case of creating a WAN connection between a home or office and the Internet.

This last major section of the chapter begins by introducing the basic networking concepts behind the Internet, followed by some specifics of how DSL and cable provide a way to send data to/from the Internet.

The Internet as a Large WAN

The Internet is an amazing cultural phenomenon. Most of us use it every day. We post messages on social media sites, we search for information using a search engine like Google, and we send emails. We use apps on our phones to pull down information, like weather reports, maps, and movie reviews. We use the Internet to purchase physical products and to buy and download digital products like music and videos. The Internet has created completely new things to do and changed the old ways of living life compared to a generation ago.

However, if you instead focus on the networking technology that creates the Internet, the Internet is simply one huge TCP/IP network. In fact, the name "Internet" comes from the core network layer protocol: Internet Protocol. The Internet includes many LANs, and because the Internet spans the globe, it of course needs WAN links to connect different sites.

As a network of networks, the Internet is actually owned by countless companies and people. The Internet includes most every enterprise TCP/IP network and a huge number of home-based networks, as well as a huge number of individuals from their phones and other wireless devices, as shown in Figure 3-12.

The middle of the Internet, called the *Internet core*, exists as LANs and WANs owned and operated by Internet service providers (ISP). (Figure 3-12 shows the Internet core as a cloud, because network diagrams show a cloud when hiding the details of a part of the network.) ISPs cooperate to create a mesh of links between each other in the Internet core, so that no matter through which ISP a particular company or person connects, some path exists to every device.

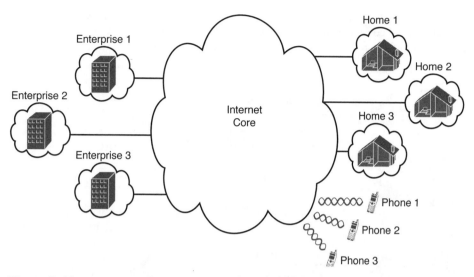

Figure 3-12   *Internet with Enterprise, Home, and Phone Subscribers*

Figure 3-13 shows a slightly different version of Figure 3-12, in this case showing the concept of the Internet core: ISP networks that connect to both their customers as well as each other, so that IP packets can flow from every customer of every ISP to every other customer of every other ISP.

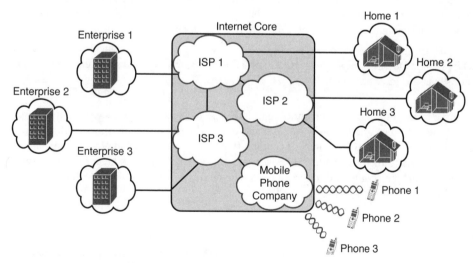

Figure 3-13   *Internet Core with Multiple ISPs and Telcos*

Internet Access (WAN) Links

The Internet also happens to use a huge number of WAN links. All of those lines connecting an enterprise or home to one of the ISPs in Figure 3-13 represent some kind of WAN link that uses a cable, while the phones create their WAN link using wireless technology. These links usually go by the name *Internet access link*.

Historically, businesses tend to use one set of WAN technologies as Internet access links, while home-based consumers use others. Businesses often use leased lines, connecting a router at the business to a router at the ISP. The top of Figure 3-14 shows just such an example.

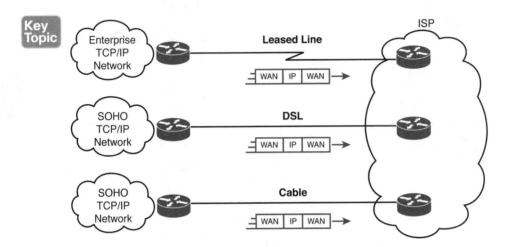

Figure 3-14 *Three Examples of Internet Access Links*

Consumers often use technologies like DSL and cable for Internet access links. These technologies use cabling that is already installed in most homes, making these services somewhat inexpensive for home users. DSL uses the analog phone lines that are already installed in homes, while cable Internet uses the cable TV (CATV) cable.

NOTE While DSL and cable are popular with consumers, many businesses use these technologies for Internet access.

All three of the Internet access technologies in Figure 3-14 happen to use a pair of routers: one at the customer side of the WAN link and one at the ISP side. The routers will continue to think about network layer logic, of sending IP packets to their destination by forwarding the packets to the next router. However, the physical and data link layer details on the WAN link differ as compared to leased lines. The next few pages examine both DSL and cable Internet to show some of those differences.

Digital Subscriber Line

Digital subscriber line (DSL) creates a relatively short (miles long, not tens of miles) high-speed link WAN between a telco customer and an ISP. To do so, it uses the same single-pair telephone line used for a typical home phone line. DSL, as a technology, does not try to replace leased lines, which run between any two sites, for potentially very long distances. DSL instead just provides a short physical link from a home to the telco's network, allowing access to the Internet. First, to get an idea about the cabling, think about typical home telephone service in the United States, before adding DSL service. Each home has one phone line that runs from a nearby telco CO to the home. As shown on the left side of Figure 3-15, the telephone wiring splits out and terminates at several wall plates, often with RJ-11 ports that are a slightly skinnier cousin of the RJ-45 connector.

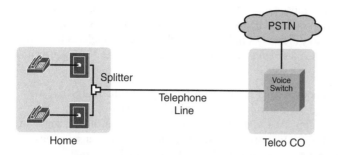

Figure 3-15 *Typical Voice Cabling Concepts in the United States*

Next, think about the telephone line and the equipment at the CO. Sometime in the past, the telco installed all the telephone lines from its local CO to each neighborhood, apartment, and so on. At the CO, each line connects to a port on a telco switch. This switch supports the ability to set up voice calls, take them down, and forward the voice through the worldwide voice network, called the public switched telephone network, or PSTN.

To add DSL service at the home in Figure 3-15, two changes need to be made. First, you need to add DSL-capable devices at the home. Second, the telco has to add DSL equipment at the CO. Together, the DSL equipment at each side of the local telephone line can send data while still supporting the same voice traffic.

The left side of Figure 3-16 shows the changes. A new *DSL modem* now connects to a spare phone outlet. The DSL modem follows the DSL physical and data link layer standards to send data to/from the telco. The home now has a small LAN, implemented with a consumer-grade router, which often includes an Ethernet switch and possibly a wireless LAN access point. (Note that the telephones may now also need a short extra cable with a filter in it, installed at the wall jack, to filter out the sounds of the higher electrical frequencies used for DSL.)

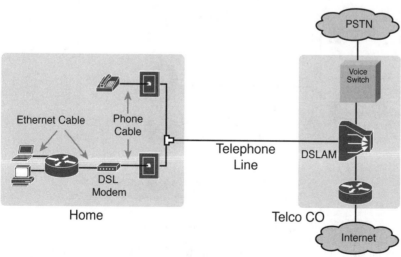

Figure 3-16 *Wiring and Devices for a Home DSL Link*

The home-based router on the left must be able to send data to/from the Internet. To make that happen, the telco CO uses a product called a DSL access multiplexer (DSLAM). The DSLAM splits out the data over to the router on the lower right, which completes the connection to the Internet. The DSLAM also splits out the voice signals over to the voice switch on the upper right.

DSL gives telcos a useful high-speed Internet service to offer their customers. Telcos have had other offerings that happen to use the same telephone line for data, but these options ran much slower than DSL. DSL supports asymmetric speeds, meaning that the transmission speed from the ISP toward the home (downstream) is much faster than the transmissions toward the ISP (upstream). Asymmetric speeds work better for consumer Internet access from the home, because clicking a web page sends only a few hundred bytes upstream into the Internet, but can trigger many megabytes of data to be delivered downstream to the home.

Cable Internet

Cable Internet creates an Internet access service which, when viewed generally rather than specifically, has many similarities to DSL. Like DSL, cable Internet takes full advantage of existing cabling, using the existing cable TV (CATV) cable to send data. Like DSL, cable Internet uses asymmetric speeds, sending data faster downstream than upstream, which works better than symmetric speeds for most consumer locations. And like DSL, cable Internet does not attempt to replace long leased lines between any two sites, instead focusing on the short WAN links from a customer to an ISP.

Cable Internet also uses the same basic in-home cabling concepts as does DSL. Figure 3-17 shows a figure based on the earlier DSL Figure 3-16, but with the DSL details replaced with cable Internet details. The telephone line has been replaced with coaxial cable from the CATV company, and the DSL modem has been replaced by a cable modem. Otherwise, the details in the home follow the same overall plan.

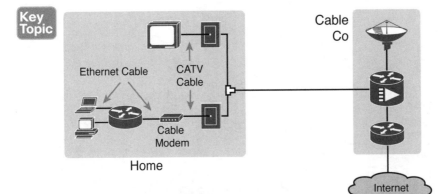

Figure 3-17 *Wiring and Devices for a Home Cable Internet Link*

On the CATV company side of the cable Internet service, the CATV company has to split out the data and video, as shown on the right side of the figure. Data flows to the lower right, through a router, while video comes in from video dishes for distribution out to the TVs in people's homes.

Cable Internet service and DSL directly compete for consumer and small-business Internet access. Generally speaking, while both offer high speeds, cable Internet typically runs at faster speeds than DSL, with DSL providers keeping their prices a little lower to compete. Both support asymmetric speeds, and both provide an "always on" service, in that you can communicate with the Internet without the need to first take some action to start the Internet connection.

Chapter Review

One key to doing well on the exams is to perform repetitive spaced review sessions. Review this chapter's material using either the tools in the book, DVD, or interactive tools for the same material found on the book's companion website. Refer to the "Your Study Plan" element section titled "Step 2: Build Your Study Habits Around the Chapter" for more details. Table 3-4 outlines the key review elements and where you can find them. To better track your study progress, record when you completed these activities in the second column.

Table 3-4   Chapter Review Tracking

Review Element	Review Date(s)	Resource Used
Review key topics		Book, DVD/website
Review key terms		Book, DVD/website
Repeat DIKTA questions		Book, PCPT
Review memory tables		Book, DVD/website

Review All the Key Topics

Table 3-5   Key Topics for Chapter 3

Key Topic Element	Description	Page Number
Figure 3-4	Typical cabling diagram of CPE for a leased line	65
Figure 3-10	Ethernet over MPLS—physical connections	71
Figure 3-14	Common Internet access links	74
Figure 3-16	Typical DSL cabling at home	75
Figure 3-17	Typical cable Internet cabling at home	76

Key Terms You Should Know

leased line, wide-area network (WAN), telco, serial interface, HDLC, DSL, cable Internet, Ethernet over MPLS

CHAPTER 4

Fundamentals of IPv4 Addressing and Routing

This chapter covers the following exam topics:

3.0 Routing Technologies

3.1 Describe the routing concepts

    3.1.a Packet handling along the path through a network

    3.1.b Forwarding decision based on route lookup

    3.1.c Frame rewrite

The TCP/IP network layer (Layer 3) defines how to deliver IP packets over the entire trip, from the original device that creates the packet to the device that needs to receive the packet. That process requires cooperation among several different jobs and concepts on a number of devices. This chapter begins with an overview of all these cooperating functions, and then it dives into more detail about each area, as follows:

IP routing: The process of hosts and routers forwarding IP packets (Layer 3 protocol data units [PDU]), while relying on the underlying LANs and WANs to forward the bits.

IP addressing: Addresses used to identify a packet's source and destination host computer. Addressing rules also organize addresses into groups, which greatly assists the routing process.

IP routing protocol: A protocol that aids routers by dynamically learning about the IP address groups so that a router knows where to route IP packets so that they go to the right destination host.

Other utilities: The network layer also relies on other utilities. For TCP/IP, these utilities include Domain Name System (DNS), Address Resolution Protocol (ARP), and ping.

Note that all these functions have variations both for the well-established IP version 4 (IPv4) and for the emerging newer IP version 6 (IPv6). This chapter focuses on IPv4 and the related protocols. Part VIII of this book looks at the same kinds of functions for IPv6.

"Do I Know This Already?" Quiz

Take the quiz (either here, or use the PCPT software) if you want to use the score to help you decide how much time to spend on this chapter. The answers are at the bottom of the page following the quiz, and the explanations are in DVD Appendix C and in the PCPT software.

Table 4-1 "Do I Know This Already?" Foundation Topics Section-to-Question Mapping

Foundation Topics Section	Questions
Overview of Network Layer Functions	1
IPv4 Addressing	2–4
IPv4 Routing	5–7
IPv4 Routing Protocols	8
Network Layer Utilities	9

1. Which of the following are functions of OSI Layer 3 protocols? (Choose two answers.)

   a. Logical addressing

   b. Physical addressing

   c. Path selection

   d. Arbitration

   e. Error recovery

2. Which of the following is a valid Class C IP address that can be assigned to a host?

   a. 1.1.1.1

   b. 200.1.1.1

   c. 128.128.128.128

   d. 224.1.1.1

3. What is the assignable range of values for the first octet for Class A IP networks?

   a. 0 to 127

   b. 0 to 126

   c. 1 to 127

   d. 1 to 126

   e. 128 to 191

   f. 128 to 192

4. PC1 and PC2 are on two different Ethernet LANs that are separated by an IP router. PC1's IP address is 10.1.1.1, and no subnetting is used. Which of the following addresses could be used for PC2? (Choose two answers.)

   a. 10.1.1.2

   b. 10.2.2.2

   c. 10.200.200.1

   d. 9.1.1.1

   e. 225.1.1.1

   f. 1.1.1.1

5. Imagine a network with two routers that are connected with a point-to-point HDLC serial link. Each router has an Ethernet, with PC1 sharing the Ethernet with Router1 and PC2 sharing the Ethernet with Router2. When PC1 sends data to PC2, which of the following is true?

   a. Router1 strips the Ethernet header and trailer off the frame received from PC1, never to be used again.

   b. Router1 encapsulates the Ethernet frame inside an HDLC header and sends the frame to Router2, which extracts the Ethernet frame for forwarding to PC2.

   c. Router1 strips the Ethernet header and trailer off the frame received from PC1, which is exactly re-created by Router2 before forwarding data to PC2.

   d. Router1 removes the Ethernet, IP, and TCP headers and rebuilds the appropriate headers before forwarding the packet to Router2.

6. Which of the following does a router normally use when making a decision about routing TCP/IP packets?

   a. Destination MAC address

   b. Source MAC address

   c. Destination IP address

   d. Source IP address

   e. Destination MAC and IP addresses

7. Which of the following are true about a LAN-connected TCP/IP host and its IP routing (forwarding) choices? (Choose two answers.)

   a. The host always sends packets to its default gateway.

   b. The host sends packets to its default gateway if the destination IP address is in a different class of IP network than the host.

   c. The host sends packets to its default gateway if the destination IP address is in a different subnet than the host.

   d. The host sends packets to its default gateway if the destination IP address is in the same subnet as the host.

8. Which of the following are functions of a routing protocol? (Choose two answers.)

   a. Advertising known routes to neighboring routers

   b. Learning routes for subnets directly connected to the router

   c. Learning routes, and putting those routes into the routing table, for routes advertised to the router by its neighboring routers

   d. Forwarding IP packets based on a packet's destination IP address

9. A company implements a TCP/IP network, with PC1 sitting on an Ethernet LAN. Which of the following protocols and features requires PC1 to learn information from some other server device?

   a. ARP

   b. ping

   c. DNS

   d. None of these answers is correct.

Foundation Topics

Overview of Network Layer Functions

Many protocol models have existed over the years, but today the TCP/IP model dominates. And at the network layer of TCP/IP, two options exist for the main protocol around which all other network layer functions revolve: IP version 4 (IPv4) and IP version 6 (IPv6). Both IPv4 and IPv6 define the same kinds of network layer functions, but with different details. This chapter introduces these network layer functions for IPv4, leaving the IPv6 details until Part VIII of this book.

NOTE   All references to IP in this chapter refer to the older and more established IPv4.

IP focuses on the job of routing data, in the form of IP packets, from the source host to the destination host. IP does not concern itself with the physical transmission of data, instead relying on the lower TCP/IP layers to do the physical transmission of the data. Instead, IP concerns itself with the logical details, rather than physical details, of delivering data. In particular, the network layer specifies how packets travel end to end over a TCP/IP network, even when the packet crosses many different types of LAN and WAN links.

This first section of the chapter begins a broad discussion of the TCP/IP network layer by looking at IP routing and addressing. The two topics work together, because IP routing relies on the structure and meaning of IP addresses, and IP addressing was designed with IP routing in mind. Following that, this overview section looks at routing protocols, which let routers learn the information they need to know to do routing correctly.

Network Layer Routing (Forwarding) Logic

Routers and end-user computers (called *hosts* in a TCP/IP network) work together to perform IP routing. The host operating system (OS) has TCP/IP software, including the software that implements the network layer. Hosts use that software to choose where to send IP packets, often to a nearby router. Those routers make choices of where to send the IP packet next. Together, the hosts and routers deliver the IP packet to the correct destination, as shown in the example in Figure 4-1.

Answers to the "Do I Know This Already?" quiz:

1 A and C **2** B **3** D **4** D and F **5** A **6** C **7** B and C **8** A and C **9** C

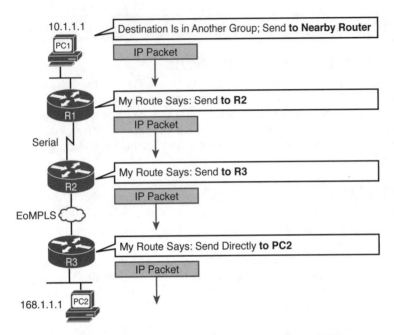

Figure 4-1   *Routing Logic: PC1 Sending an IP Packet to PC2*

The IP packet, created by PC1, goes from the top of the figure all the way to PC2 at the bottom of the figure. The next few pages discuss the network layer routing logic used by each device along the path.

NOTE   The term *path selection* is sometimes used to refer to the routing process shown in Figure 4-1. At other times, it refers to routing protocols, specifically how routing protocols select the best route among the competing routes to the same destination.

Host Forwarding Logic: Send the Packet to the Default Router

In this example, PC1 does some basic analysis, and then chooses to send the IP packet to the router so that the router will forward the packet. PC1 analyzes the destination address and realizes that PC2's address (168.1.1.1) is not on the same LAN as PC1. So PC1's logic tells it to send the packet to a device whose job it is to know where to route data: a nearby router, on the same LAN, called PC1's default router.

To send the IP packet to the default router, the sender sends a data-link frame across the medium to the nearby router; this frame includes the packet in the data portion of the frame. That frame uses data link layer (Layer 2) addressing in the data-link header to ensure that the nearby router receives the frame.

> **NOTE**   The *default router* is also referred to as the *default gateway*.

R1 and R2's Logic: Routing Data Across the Network

All routers use the same general process to route the packet. Each router keeps an *IP routing table*. This table lists IP address *groupings*, called *IP networks* and *IP subnets*. When a router receives a packet, it compares the packet's destination IP address to the entries in the routing table and makes a match. This matching entry also lists directions that tell the router where to forward the packet next.

In Figure 4-1, R1 would have matched the destination address (168.1.1.1) to a routing table entry, which in turn told R1 to send the packet to R2 next. Similarly, R2 would have matched a routing table entry that told R2 to send the packet, over an Ethernet over MPLS (EoMPLS) link, to R3 next.

The routing concept works a little like driving down the freeway when approaching a big interchange. You look up and see signs for nearby towns, telling you which exits to take to go to each town. Similarly, the router looks at the IP routing table (the equivalent of the road signs) and directs each packet over the correct next LAN or WAN link (the equivalent of a road).

R3's Logic: Delivering Data to the End Destination

The final router in the path, R3, uses almost the same logic as R1 and R2, but with one minor difference. R3 needs to forward the packet directly to PC2, not to some other router. On the surface, that difference seems insignificant. In the next section, when you read about how the network layer uses LANs and WANs, the significance of the difference will become obvious.

How Network Layer Routing Uses LANs and WANs

While the network layer routing logic ignores the physical transmission details, the bits still have to be transmitted. To do that work, the network layer logic in a host or router must hand off the packet to the data link layer protocols, which, in turn, ask the physical layer to actually send the data. And as was described in Chapter 2, "Fundamentals of Ethernet LANs," the data link layer adds the appropriate header and trailer to the packet, creating a frame, before sending the frames over each physical network.

The routing process forwards the network layer packet from end to end through the network, while each data-link frame only takes a smaller part of the trip. Each successive data link layer frame moves the packet to the next device that thinks about network layer logic. In short, the network layer thinks about the bigger view of the goal, like "Send this packet to the specified next device...," while the data link layer thinks about the specifics, like "Encapsulate the packet in a data-link frame and transmit it." Figure 4-2 points out the key encapsulation logic on each device, using the same examples as shown in Figure 4-1.

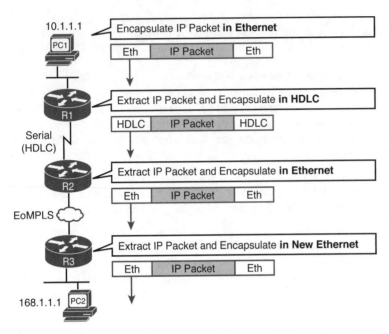

Figure 4-2 *Network Layer and Data Link Layer Encapsulation*

Because the routers build new data-link headers and trailers, and because the new headers contain data-link addresses, the PCs and routers must have some way to decide what data-link addresses to use. An example of how the router determines which data-link address to use is the IP Address Resolution Protocol (ARP). *ARP dynamically learns the data-link address of an IP host connected to a LAN.* For example, at the last step, at the bottom of Figure 4-2, Router R3 would use ARP once to learn PC2's MAC address before sending any packets to PC2.

Routing as covered so far has two main concepts:

■ The process of routing forwards Layer 3 packets, also called *Layer 3 protocol data units (L3 PDU)*, based on the destination Layer 3 address in the packet.

■ The routing process uses the data link layer to encapsulate the Layer 3 packets into Layer 2 frames for transmission across each successive data link.

IP Addressing and How Addressing Helps IP Routing

IP defines network layer addresses that identify any host or router interface that connects to a TCP/IP network. The idea basically works like a postal address: Any interface that expects to receive IP packets needs an IP address, just like you need a postal address before receiving mail from the postal service.

TCP/IP groups IP addresses together so that IP addresses used on the same physical network are part of the same group. IP calls these address groups an *IP network* or an *IP subnet*. Using that same postal service analogy, each IP network and IP subnet works like a postal code (or in the United States, a ZIP code). All nearby postal addresses are in the same postal code (ZIP code), while all nearby IP addresses must be in the same IP network or IP subnet.

> **NOTE**   IP defines the word *network* to mean a very specific concept. To avoid confusion when writing about IP addressing, this book (and others) often avoids using the term *network* for other uses. In particular, this book uses the term *internetwork* to refer more generally to a network made up of routers, switches, cables, and other equipment.

IP defines specific rules about which IP address should be in the same IP network or IP subnet. Numerically, the addresses in the same group have the same value in the first part of the addresses. For example, Figures 4-1 and 4-2 could have used the following conventions:

- Hosts on the top Ethernet: Addresses start with 10
- Hosts on the R1-R2 serial link: Addresses start with 168.10
- Hosts on the R2-R3 EoMPLS link: Addresses start with 168.11
- Hosts on the bottom Ethernet: Addresses start with 168.1

It's similar to the USPS ZIP code system and how it requires local governments to assign addresses to new buildings. It would be ridiculous to have two houses next door to each other, whose addresses had different ZIP codes. Similarly, it would be silly to have people who live on opposite sides of the country to have addresses with the same ZIP code.

Similarly, to make routing more efficient, network layer protocols group addresses, both by their location and by the actual address values. A router can list one routing table entry for each IP network or subnet, instead of one entry for every single IP address.

The routing process also makes use of the IPv4 header, as shown in Figure 4-3. The header lists a 32-bit source IP address, as well as a 32-bit destination IP address. The header of course has other fields, a few of which matter for other discussions in this book. The book will refer to this figure as needed, but otherwise, be aware of the 20-byte IP header and the existence of the source and destination IP address fields.

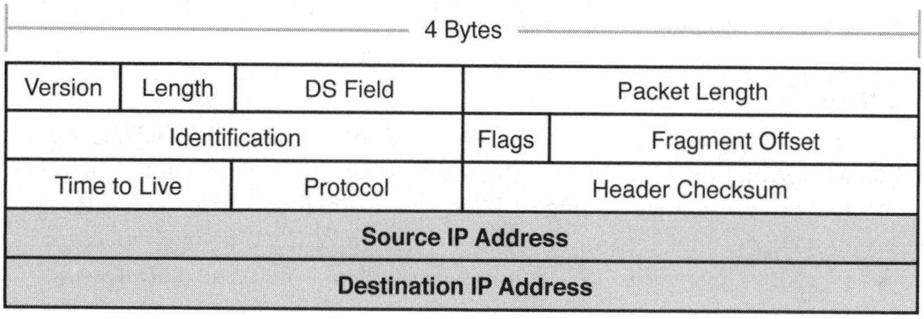

← 4 Bytes →			
Version	Length	DS Field	Packet Length
Identification		Flags	Fragment Offset
Time to Live		Protocol	Header Checksum
Source IP Address			
Destination IP Address			

Figure 4-3   *IPv4 Header, Organized as Four Bytes Wide for a Total of 20 Bytes*

Routing Protocols

For routing logic to work on both hosts and routers, each needs to know something about the TCP/IP internetwork. Hosts need to know the IP address of their default router so that hosts can send packets to remote destinations. Routers, however, need to know routes so that routers know how to forward packets to each and every IP network and IP subnet.

Although a network engineer could configure (type) all the required routes, on every router, most network engineers instead simply enable a routing protocol on all routers. If you enable the same routing protocol on all the routers in a TCP/IP internetwork, with the cor-rect settings, the routers will send routing protocol messages to each other. As a result, all the routers will learn routes for all the IP networks and subnets in the TCP/IP internetwork.

Figure 4-4 shows an example, using the same diagram as in Figures 4-1 and 4-2. In this case, IP network 168.1.0.0, which consists of all addresses that begin with 168.1, sits on the Ethernet at the bottom of the figure. R3, knowing this fact, sends a routing protocol mes-sage to R2 (Step 1). R2 learns a route for network 168.1.0.0 as a result, as shown on the left. At Step 2, R2 turns around and sends a routing protocol message to R1 so that R1 now has a route for that same IP network (168.1.0.0).

R1 Routing Table

Subnet	Interface	Next Hop
168.1.0.0	Serial0	R2

R2 Routing Table

Subnet	Interface	Next Hop
168.1.0.0	F0/0	R3

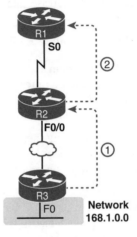

Figure 4-4 *Example of How Routing Protocols Advertise About Networks and Subnets*

This concludes the overview of how the TCP/IP network layer works. The rest of this chapter re-examines the key components in more depth.

IPv4 Addressing

IPv4 addressing may be the single most important topic for the CCENT and CCNA Routing and Switching exams. By the time you have finished reading this book, you should be com-fortable and confident in your understanding of IP addresses, their formats, the grouping concepts, how to subdivide groups into subnets, how to interpret the documentation for existing networks' IP addressing, and so on. Simply put, you had better know addressing and subnetting!

This section introduces IP addressing and subnetting and also covers the concepts behind the structure of an IP address, including how it relates to IP routing. In Parts III and V of this book, you will read more about the concepts and math behind IPv4 addressing and subnetting.

Rules for IP Addresses

If a device wants to communicate using TCP/IP, it needs an IP address. When the device has an IP address and the appropriate software and hardware, it can send and receive IP packets. Any device that has at least one interface with an IP address can send and receive IP packets and is called an *IP host*.

IP addresses consist of a 32-bit number, usually written in dotted-decimal notation (DDN). The "decimal" part of the term comes from the fact that each byte (8 bits) of the 32-bit IP address is shown as its decimal equivalent. The four resulting decimal numbers are written in sequence, with "dots," or decimal points, separating the numbers—hence the name *dotted-decimal*. For example, 168.1.1.1 is an IP address written in dotted-decimal form; the actual binary version is 10101000 00000001 00000001 00000001. (You almost never need to write down the binary version, but you can use the conversion chart in Appendix A, "Numeric Reference Tables," to easily convert from DDN to binary or vice versa.)

Each DDN has four decimal *octets*, separated by periods. The term *octet* is just a vendor-neutral term for *byte*. Because each octet represents an 8-bit binary number, the range of decimal numbers in each octet is between 0 and 255, inclusive. For example, the IP address of 168.1.1.1 has a first octet of 168, the second octet of 1, and so on.

Finally, note that each network interface uses a unique IP address. Most people tend to think that their computer has an IP address, but actually their computer's network card has an IP address. For example, if your laptop has both an Ethernet network interface card (NIC) and a wireless NIC, with both working at the same time, both will have an IP address. Similarly, routers, which typically have many network interfaces that forward IP packets, have an IP address for each interface.

Rules for Grouping IP Addresses

The original specifications for TCP/IP grouped IP addresses into sets of consecutive addresses called *IP networks*. The addresses in a single IP network have the same numeric value in the first part of all addresses in the network. Figure 4-5 shows a simple internetwork that has three separate IP networks.

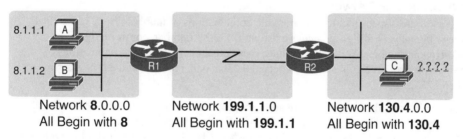

Figure 4-5 *Sample TCP/IP Internetwork Using IPv4 Network Numbers*

The figure lists a network identifier (network ID) for each network, as well as a text description of the DDN values in each network. For example, the hosts in the Ethernet LAN on the far left use IP addresses that begin with a first octet of 8; the network ID happens to be 8.0.0.0. As another example, the serial link between R1 and R2 consists of only two interfaces—a serial interface on each router—and uses an IP address that begins with the three octets 199.1.1.

Figure 4-5 also provides a good figure with which to discuss two important facts about how IPv4 groups IP addresses:

- All IP addresses in the same group must not be separated from each other by a router.
- IP addresses separated from each other by a router must be in different groups.

Take the first of the two rules, and look at hosts A and B on the left. Hosts A and B are in the same IP network and have IP addresses that begin with 8. Per the first rule, hosts A and B cannot be separated from each other by a router (and they are indeed not separated from each other by a router).

Next, take the second of the two rules and add host C to the discussion. Host C is separated from host A by at least one router, so host C cannot be in the same IP network as host A. Host C's address cannot begin with 8.

NOTE   This example assumes the use of IP networks only, and no subnets, simply because the discussion has not yet dealt with the details of subnetting.

As mentioned earlier in this chapter, IP address grouping behaves similarly to ZIP codes. Everyone in my ZIP code lives in a little town in Ohio. If some addresses in my ZIP code were in California, some mail might be delivered to the wrong local post office, because the postal service delivers the letters based on the postal (ZIP) codes. The post system relies on all addresses in one postal code being near to each other.

Likewise, IP routing relies on all addresses in one IP network or IP subnet being in the same location, specifically on a single instance of a LAN or WAN data link. Otherwise, the routers might deliver IP packets to the wrong locations.

For any TCP/IP internetwork, each LAN and WAN link will use either an IP network or an IP subnet. Next, this chapter looks more closely at the concepts behind IP networks, followed by IP subnets.

Class A, B, and C IP Networks

The IPv4 address space includes all possible combinations of numbers for a 32-bit IPv4 address. Literally 2^{32} different values exist with a 32-bit number, for more than 4 billion different numbers. With DDN values, these numbers include all combinations of the values 0 through 255 in all four octets: 0.0.0.0, 0.0.0.1, 0.0.0.2, and all the way up to 255.255.255.255.

IP standards first subdivide the entire address space into classes, as identified by the value of the first octet. Class A gets roughly half of the IPv4 address space, with all DDN numbers that begin with 1–126, as shown in Figure 4-6. Class B gets one-fourth of the address space, with all DDN numbers that begin with 128–191 inclusive, and Class C gets one-eighth of the address space, with all numbers that begin with 192–223.

Figure 4-6 also notes the purpose for the five address classes. Classes A, B, and C define unicast IP addresses, meaning that the address identifies a single host interface. Class D defines multicast addresses, used to send one packet to multiple hosts. Class E originally defined experimental addresses. (Class E addresses are no longer defined as experimental, and are simply reserved for future use.)

IPv4 standards also subdivide the Class A, B, and C unicast classes into predefined IP networks. Each IP network makes up a subset of the DDN values inside the class.

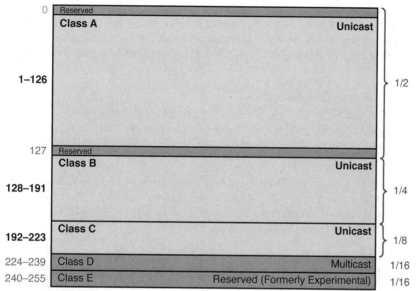

Figure 4-6   *Division of the Entire IPv4 Address Space by Class*

IPv4 uses three classes of unicast addresses so that the IP networks in each class can be different sizes, and therefore meet different needs. Class A networks each support a very large number of IP addresses (more than 16 million host addresses per IP network). However, because each Class A network is so large, Class A holds only 126 Class A networks. Class B defines IP networks that have 65,534 addresses per network, but with space for more than 16,000 such networks. Class C defines much smaller IP networks, with 254 addresses each, as shown in Figure 4-7.

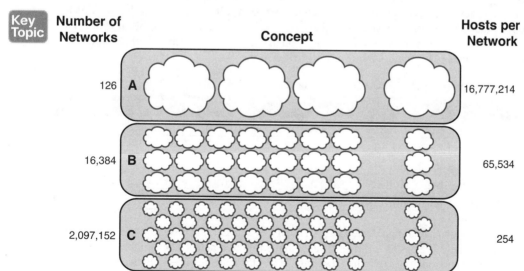

Figure 4-7   *Size of Network and Host Parts of Class A, B, and C Addresses*

Figure 4-7 shows a visual perspective, as well as the literal numbers, for all the Class A, B, and C IPv4 networks in the entire world. The figure shows clouds for IP networks. It, of course, does not show one cloud for every possible network, but shows the general idea, with a small number of large clouds for Class A and a large number of small clouds for Class C.

The Actual Class A, B, and C IP Networks

Figure 4-7 shows the number of Class A, B, and C IP networks in the entire world. Eventually, you need to actually pick and use some of these IP networks to build a working TCP/IP internetwork, so you need to be able to answer the question: What are the specific IP networks?

First, you must be able to identify each network briefly using a network identifier (network ID). The network ID is just one reserved DDN value per network that identifies the IP network. (The network ID cannot be used by a host as an IP address.) For example, Table 4-2 shows the network IDs that match the earlier Figure 4-5.

Table 4-2   Network IDs Used in Figure 4-5

Concept	Class	Network ID
All addresses that begin with 8	A	8.0.0.0
All addresses that begin with 130.4	B	130.4.0.0
All addresses that begin with 199.1.1	C	199.1.1.0

NOTE   Many people use the term *network ID*, but others use the terms *network number* and *network address*. Be ready to use all three terms.

So, what are the actual Class A, B, and C IP networks, and what are their network IDs? First, consider the Class A networks. Per Figure 4-7, only 126 Class A networks exist. As it turns out, they consist of all addresses that begin with 1, all addresses that begin with 2, all addresses that begin with 3, and so on, up through the 126th such network of "all addresses that begin with 126." Table 4-3 lists a few of these networks.

Table 4-3   Sampling of IPv4 Class A Networks

Concept	Class	Network ID
All addresses that begin with 8	A	8.0.0.0
All addresses that begin with 13	A	13.0.0.0
All addresses that begin with 24	A	24.0.0.0
All addresses that begin with 125	A	125.0.0.0
All addresses that begin with 126	A	126.0.0.0

Class B networks have a first octet value between 128 and 191, inclusive, but in a single Class B network, the addresses have the same value in the first two octets. For example, Figure 4-5 uses Class B network 130.4.0.0. The DDN value 130.4.0.0 must be in Class B, because the first octet is between 128 and 191, inclusive. However, the first two octets define the addresses in a single Class B network. Table 4-4 lists some sample IPv4 Class B networks.

Table 4-4   Sampling of IPv4 Class B Networks

Concept	Class	Network ID
All addresses that begin with 128.1	B	128.1.0.0
All addresses that begin with 172.20	B	172.20.0.0
All addresses that begin with 191.191	B	191.191.0.0
All addresses that begin with 150.1	B	150.1.0.0

Class C networks can also be easily identified, with a first octet value between 192 and 223, inclusive. With Class C networks and addresses, the first three octets define the group, with addresses in one Class C network having the same value in the first three octets. Table 4-5 shows some samples.

Table 4-5   Sampling of IPv4 Class C Networks

Concept	Class	Network ID
All addresses that begin with 199.1.1	C	199.1.1.0
All addresses that begin with 200.1.200	C	200.1.200.0
All addresses that begin with 223.1.10	C	223.1.10.0
All addresses that begin with 209.209.1	C	209.209.1.0

Listing all the Class A, B, and C networks would of course take too much space. For study review, Table 4-6 summarizes the first octet values that identify the class and summarizes the range of Class A, B, and C network numbers available in the entire IPv4 address space.

Table 4-6   All Possible Valid Network Numbers

Class	First Octet Range	Valid Network Numbers
A	1 to 126	1.0.0.0 to 126.0.0.0
B	128 to 191	128.0.0.0 to 191.255.0.0
C	192 to 223	192.0.0.0 to 223.255.255.0

NOTE   The term *classful IP network* refers to any Class A, B, or C network, because it is defined by Class A, B, and C rules.

IP Subnetting

Like IP addressing, IP subnetting is also one of the most important topics for the CCENT and CCNA R&S certifications. You need to know how subnetting works and how to "do the math" to figure out issues when subnetting is in use, both in real life and on the exam. Parts IV and VI of this book cover the details of subnetting concepts, motivation, and math, but you should have a basic understanding of the concepts while reading the Ethernet topics between here and Part IV.

Subnetting defines methods of further subdividing the IPv4 address space into groups that are smaller than a single IP network. IP subnetting defines a flexible way for anyone to take a single Class A, B, or C IP network and further subdivide it into even smaller groups of consecutive IP addresses. In fact, the name *subnet* is just shorthand for *subdivided network*.

Then, in each location where you used to use an entire Class A, B, or C network, you can use a smaller subnet, wasting fewer IP addresses.

To make it clear how an internetwork can use both classful IPv4 networks as well as subnets of classful IPv4 networks, the next two figures show the same internetwork, one with classful networks only and one with subnets only. Figure 4-8 shows the first such example, which uses five Class B networks with no subnetting.

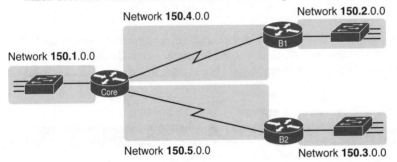

Figure 4-8   *Example That Uses Five Class B Networks*

The design in Figure 4-8 requires five groups of IP addresses, each of which is a Class B network in this example. Specifically, the three LANs each use a single Class B network, and the two serial links each use a Class B network.

Figure 4-8 wastes many IP addresses, because each Class B network has $2^{16} - 2$ host addresses—far more than you will ever need for each LAN and WAN link. For example, the Ethernet on the left uses an entire Class B network, which supports 65,534 IP addresses that begin with 150.1. However, a single LAN seldom grows past a few hundred devices, so many of the IP addresses in Class B network 150.1.0.0 would be wasted. Even more waste occurs on the point-to-point serial links, which need only two IP addresses.

Figure 4-9 illustrates a more common design today, one that uses basic subnetting. As in the previous figure, this figure needs five groups of addresses. However, in this case, the figure uses five subnets of Class B network 150.9.0.0.

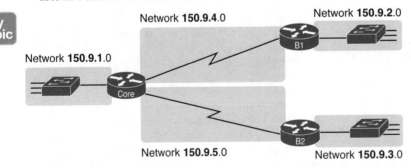

Figure 4-9   *Using Subnets for the Same Design as the Previous Figure*

Subnetting allows the network engineer for the TCP/IP internetwork to choose to use a longer part of the addresses that must have the same value. Subnetting allows quite a bit of flexibility, but Figure 4-9 shows one of the simplest forms of subnetting. In this case, each subnet includes the addresses that begin with the same value in the first three octets, as follows:

- One group of the 254 addresses that begin with 150.9.1
- One group of the 254 addresses that begin with 150.9.2
- One group of the 254 addresses that begin with 150.9.3
- One group of the 254 addresses that begin with 150.9.4
- One group of the 254 addresses that begin with 150.9.5

As a result of using subnetting, the network engineer has saved many IP addresses. First, only a small part of Class B network 150.9.0.0 has been used so far. Each subnet has 254 addresses, which should be plenty of addresses for each LAN, and more than enough for the WAN links.

In summary, you now know some of the details of IP addressing, with a focus on how it relates to routing. Each host and router interface will have an IP address. However, the IP addresses will not be randomly chosen but will instead be grouped together to aid the routing process. The groups of addresses can be an entire Class A, B, or C network number or it can be a subnet.

IPv4 Routing

In the first section of this chapter ("Overview of Network Layer Functions"), you read about the basics of IPv4 routing using a network with three routers and two PCs. Armed with more knowledge of IP addressing, you now can take a closer look at the process of routing IP. This section begins with the simple two-part routing logic on the originating host, and then moves on to discuss how routers choose where to route or forward packets to the final destination.

IPv4 Host Routing

Hosts actually use some simple routing logic when choosing where to send a packet. If you assume that the design uses subnets (which is typical), this two-step logic is as follows:

Step 1. If the destination IP address is in the same IP subnet as I am, send the packet directly to that destination host.

Step 2. Otherwise, send the packet to my *default gateway*, also known as a *default router*. (This router has an interface on the same subnet as the host.)

For example, consider Figure 4-10 and focus on the Ethernet LAN on the left. When PC1 sends an IP packet to PC11 (150.9.1.11), PC1 first considers some math related to subnetting. PC1 concludes that PC11's IP address is in the same subnet as PC1, so PC1 ignores its default router (Core, 150.9.1.1), sending the packet directly to PC11, as shown in Step 1 of the figure.

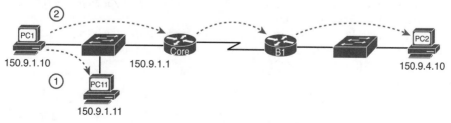

Figure 4-10 *Host Routing: Forwarding to a Host on the Same Subnet*

Alternatively, when PC1 sends a packet to PC2 (150.9.4.10), PC1 does the same kind of subnetting math, and realizes that PC2 is not on the same subnet as PC1. So, PC1 forwards the packet (Step 2) to its default gateway, 150.9.1.1, which then routes the packet to PC2.

Router Forwarding Decisions and the IP Routing Table

Earlier in this chapter, Figure 4-1 shows the network layer concepts of routing, while Figure 4-2 shows the data-link encapsulation logic related to routing. This next topic dives a little deeper into that same process, using an example with three routers forwarding (routing) one packet. But before looking at the example, the text first summarizes how a router thinks about forwarding a packet.

A Summary of Router Forwarding Logic

First, when a router receives a data-link frame addressed to that router's data-link address, the router needs to think about processing the contents of the frame. When such a frame arrives, the router uses the following logic on the data-link frame:

Step 1.   Use the data-link Frame Check Sequence (FCS) field to ensure that the frame had no errors; if errors occurred, discard the frame.

Step 2.   Assuming that the frame was not discarded at Step 1, discard the old data-link header and trailer, leaving the IP packet.

Step 3.   Compare the IP packet's destination IP address to the routing table, and find the route that best matches the destination address. This route identifies the outgoing interface of the router, and possibly the next-hop router IP address.

Step 4.   Encapsulate the IP packet inside a new data-link header and trailer, appropriate for the outgoing interface, and forward the frame.

With these steps, each router forwards the packet to the next location, inside a data-link frame. With each router repeating this process, the packet reaches its final destination.

While the router does all the steps in the list, Step 3 is the main routing or forwarding step. The packet has a destination IP address in the header, whereas the routing table lists slightly different numbers, typically a list of networks and subnets. To match a routing table entry, the router thinks like this:

> Network numbers and subnet numbers represent a group of addresses that begin with the same prefix. Think about those numbers as groups of addresses. In which of the groups does this packet's destination address reside?

The next example shows specific examples of matching the routing table.

A Detailed Routing Example

The routing example uses Figure 4-11. In this example, all routers happen to use the Open Shortest Path First (OSPF) routing protocol, and all routers know routes for all subnets. In particular, PC2, at the bottom, sits in subnet 150.150.4.0, which consists of all addresses that begin with 150.150.4. In the example, PC1 sends an IP packet to 150.150.4.10, PC2's IP address.

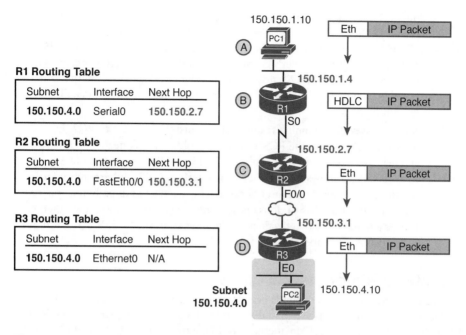

Figure 4-11 *Simple Routing Example, with IP Subnets*

> **NOTE**   Note that the routers all know in this case that "subnet 150.150.4.0" means "all addresses that begin with 150.150.4."

The following list explains the forwarding logic at each step in the figure. (Note that the text refers to Steps 1, 2, 3, and 4 of the routing logic shown in the previous section.)

Step A.   **PC1 sends the packet to its default router.** PC1 first builds the IP packet, with a destination address of PC2's IP address (150.150.4.10). PC1 needs to send the packet to R1 (PC1's default router) because the destination address is on a different subnet. PC1 places the IP packet into an Ethernet frame, with a destination Ethernet address of R1's Ethernet address. PC1 sends the frame on to the Ethernet. (Note that the figure omits the data-link trailers.)

Step B.   **R1 processes the incoming frame and forwards the packet to R2.** Because the incoming Ethernet frame has a destination MAC of R1's Ethernet MAC, R1 copies the frame off the Ethernet for processing. R1 checks the frame's FCS, and no errors have occurred (Step 1). R1 then discards the Ethernet header and trailer (Step 2). Next, R1 compares the packet's destination address (150.150.4.10) to the routing table and finds the entry for subnet 150.150.4.0—which includes addresses 150.150.4.0 through 150.150.4.255 (Step 3). Because the destination address is in this group, R1 forwards the packet out interface Serial0 to next-hop Router R2 (150.150.2.7) after encapsulating the packet in a High-Level Data Link Control (HDLC) frame (Step 4).

Step C.   **R2 processes the incoming frame and forwards the packet to R3.** R2 repeats the same general process as R1 when R2 receives the HDLC frame. R2 checks the FCS field and finds that no errors occurred (Step 1). R2 then discards the HDLC header and trailer (Step 2). Next, R2 finds its route for subnet 150.150.4.0—which includes the address range 150.150.4.0–150.150.4.255— and realizes that the packet's destination address 150.150.4.10 matches that route (Step 3). Finally, R2 sends the packet out interface Fast Ethernet 0/0 to next-hop router 150.150.3.1 (R3) after encapsulating the packet in an Ethernet header (Step 4).

Step D.   **R3 processes the incoming frame and forwards the packet to PC2.** Like R1 and R2, R3 checks the FCS, discards the old data-link header and trailer, and matches its own route for subnet 150.150.4.0. R3's routing table entry for 150.150.4.0 shows that the outgoing interface is R3's Ethernet interface, but there is no next-hop router because R3 is connected directly to subnet 150.150.4.0. All R3 has to do is encapsulate the packet inside a new Ethernet header and trailer, with a destination Ethernet address of PC2's MAC address, and forward the frame.

IPv4 Routing Protocols

The routing (forwarding) process depends heavily on having an accurate and up-to-date IP routing table on each router. This section takes another look at routing protocols, considering the goals of a routing protocol, the methods routing protocols use to teach and learn routes, and an example.

First, consider the goals of a routing protocol, regardless of how the routing protocol works:

- To dynamically learn and fill the routing table with a route to each subnet in the internetwork.

- If more than one route to a subnet is available, to place the best route in the routing table.

- To notice when routes in the table are no longer valid, and to remove them from the routing table.

- If a route is removed from the routing table and another route through another neighboring router is available, to add the route to the routing table. (Many people view this goal and the preceding one as a single goal.)

- To work quickly when adding new routes or replacing lost routes. (The time between losing the route and finding a working replacement route is called *convergence* time.)

- To prevent routing loops.

Routing protocols all use some similar ideas to allow routers to learn routing information from each other. Of course, each routing protocol works differently; otherwise, you would not need more than one routing protocol. However, many routing protocols use the same general steps for learning routes:

Step 1.   Each router, independent of the routing protocol, adds a route to its routing table for each subnet directly connected to the router.

Step 2.   Each router's routing protocol tells its neighbors about the routes in its routing table, including the directly connected routes and routes learned from other routers.

Step 3.   After learning a new route from a neighbor, the router's routing protocol adds a route to its IP routing table, with the next-hop router of that route typically being the neighbor from which the route was learned.

For example, Figure 4-12 shows the same sample network as in Figure 4-11, but now with a focus on how the three routers each learned about subnet 150.150.4.0. Note that routing protocols do more work than is implied in the figure; this figure just focuses on how the routers learn about subnet 150.150.4.0.

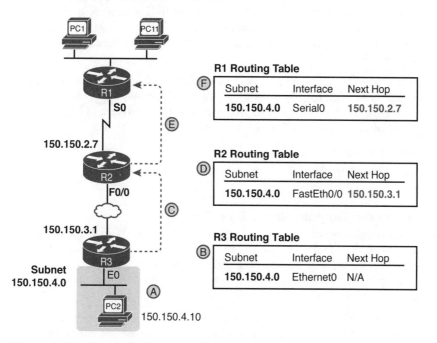

R1 Routing Table

Subnet	Interface	Next Hop
150.150.4.0	Serial0	**150.150.2.7**

R2 Routing Table

Subnet	Interface	Next Hop
150.150.4.0	FastEth0/0	150.150.3.1

R3 Routing Table

Subnet	Interface	Next Hop
150.150.4.0	Ethernet0	N/A

Figure 4-12   *Router R1 Learning About Subnet 150.150.4.0*

Follow items A through F shown in the figure to see how each router learns its route to 150.150.4.0. All references to Steps 1, 2, and 3 refer to the list just before Figure 4-12.

Step A.   Subnet 150.150.4.0 exists as a subnet at the bottom of the figure, connected to Router R3.

Step B.   R3 adds a connected route for 150.150.4.0 to its IP routing table (Step 1); this happens without help from the routing protocol.

Step C.   R3 sends a routing protocol message, called a *routing update*, to R2, causing R2 to learn about subnet 150.150.4.0 (Step 2).

Step D.   R2 adds a route for subnet 150.150.4.0 to its routing table (Step 3).

Step E.   R2 sends a similar routing update to R1, causing R1 to learn about subnet 150.150.4.0 (Step 2).

Step F.   R1 adds a route for subnet 150.150.4.0 to its routing table (Step 3). The route lists R1's own Serial0 as the outgoing interface and R2 as the next-hop router IP address (150.150.2.7).

Chapter 19, "Learning IPv4 Routes with RIPv2," covers routing protocols in more detail. Next, the final major section of this chapter introduces several additional functions related to how the network layer forwards packets from source to destination through an internetwork.

Other Network Layer Features

The TCP/IP network layer defines many functions beyond the function defined by the IPv4 protocol. Sure, IPv4 plays a huge role in networking today, defining IP addressing and IP routing. However, other protocols and standards, defined in other Requests For Comments (RFC), play an important role for network layer functions as well. For example, routing protocols like Open Shortest Path First (OSPF) exist as separate protocols, defined in separate RFCs.

This last short section of the chapter introduces three other network layer features that should be helpful to you when reading through the rest of this book. These last three topics just help fill in a few holes, helping to give you some perspective, and helping you make sense of later discussions as well. The three topics are

■ Domain Name System (DNS)

■ Address Resolution Protocol (ARP)

■ Ping

Using Names and the Domain Name System

Can you imagine a world in which every time you used an application, you had to think about the other computer and refer to it by IP address? Instead of using easy names like google.com or facebook.com, you would have to remember and type IP addresses, like 74.125.225.5. Certainly, that would not be user friendly and could drive some people away from using computers at all.

Thankfully, TCP/IP defines a way to use *hostnames* to identify other computers. The user either never thinks about the other computer or refers to the other computer by name. Then, protocols dynamically discover all the necessary information to allow communications based on that name.

For example, when you open a web browser and type in the hostname **www.google.com**, your computer does not send an IP packet with destination IP address www.google.com; it sends an IP packet to an IP address used by the web server for Google. TCP/IP needs a way to let a computer find the IP address used by the listed hostname, and that method uses the Domain Name System (DNS).

Enterprises use the DNS process to resolve names into the matching IP address, as shown in the example in Figure 4-13. In this case, PC11, on the left, needs to connect to a server named Server1. At some point, the user either types in the name Server1 or some application on PC11 refers to that server by name. At Step 1, PC11 sends a DNS message—a DNS query—to the DNS server. At Step 2, the DNS server sends back a DNS reply that lists Server1's IP address. At Step 3, PC11 can now send an IP packet to destination address 10.1.2.3, the address used by Server1.

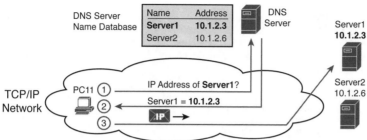

Figure 4-13 *Basic DNS Name Resolution Request*

Note that the example in Figure 4-13 shows a cloud for the TCP/IP network because the details of the network, including routers, do not matter to the name resolution process. Routers treat the DNS messages just like any other IP packet, routing them based on the destination IP address. For example, at Step 1 in the figure, the DNS query will list the DNS server's IP address as the destination address, which any routers will use to forward the packet.

Finally, DNS defines much more than just a few messages. DNS defines protocols, as well as standards for the text names used throughout the world, and a worldwide set of distributed DNS servers. The domain names that people use every day when web browsing, which look like www.example.com, follow the DNS naming standards. Also, no single DNS server knows all the names and matching IP addresses, but the information is distributed across many DNS servers. So, the DNS servers of the world work together, forwarding queries to each other, until the server that knows the answer supplies the desired IP address information.

The Address Resolution Protocol

IP routing logic requires that hosts and routers encapsulate IP packets inside data link layer frames. In fact, Figure 4-11 shows how every router de-encapsulates each IP packet and encapsulates the IP packet inside a new data-link frame.

On Ethernet LANs, whenever a host or router needs to encapsulate an IP packet in a new Ethernet frame, the host or router knows all the important facts to build that header—except for the destination MAC address. The host knows the IP address of the next device, either another host IP address or the default router IP address. A router knows the IP route used for forwarding the IP packet, which lists the next router's IP address. However, the hosts and routers do not know those neighboring devices' MAC addresses beforehand.

TCP/IP defines the Address Resolution Protocol (ARP) as the method by which any host or router on a LAN can dynamically learn the MAC address of another IP host or router on the same LAN. ARP defines a protocol that includes the *ARP Request*, which is a message that asks the simple request "if this is your IP address, please reply with your MAC address." ARP also defines the *ARP Reply* message, which indeed lists both the original IP address and the matching MAC address.

Figure 4-14 shows an example that uses the same router and host from the bottom part of the earlier Figure 4-11. The figure shows the ARP Request on the left as a LAN broadcast, so all hosts receive the frame. On the right, at Step 2, host PC2 sends back an ARP Reply, identifying PC2's MAC address. The text beside each message shows the contents inside the ARP message itself, which lets PC2 learn R3's IP address and matching MAC address, and R3 learn PC2's IP address and matching MAC address.

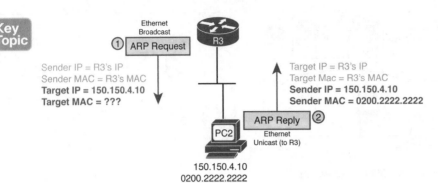

Figure 4-14   *Sample ARP Process*

Note that hosts remember the ARP results, keeping the information in their *ARP cache* or *ARP table*. A host or router only needs to use ARP occasionally, to build the ARP cache the first time. Each time a host or router needs to send a packet encapsulated in an Ethernet frame, it first checks its ARP cache for the correct IP address and matching MAC address. Hosts and routers will let ARP cache entries time out to clean up the table, so occasional ARP Requests can be seen.

> **NOTE**   You can see the contents of the ARP cache on most PC operating systems by using the **arp -a** command from a command prompt.

ICMP Echo and the ping Command

After you have implemented a TCP/IP internetwork, you need a way to test basic IP connectivity without relying on any applications to be working. The primary tool for testing basic network connectivity is the **ping** command.

Ping (Packet Internet Groper) uses the Internet Control Message Protocol (ICMP), sending a message called an *ICMP echo request* to another IP address. The computer with that IP address should reply with an *ICMP echo reply*. If that works, you successfully have tested the IP network. In other words, you know that the network can deliver a packet from one host to the other and back. ICMP does not rely on any application, so it really just tests basic IP connectivity—Layers 1, 2, and 3 of the OSI model. Figure 4-15 outlines the basic process.

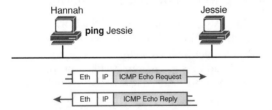

Figure 4-15   *Sample Network, ping Command*

Note that while the **ping** command uses ICMP, ICMP does much more. ICMP defines many messages that devices can use to help manage and control the IP network. Chapter 20, "DHCP and IP Networking on Hosts," gives you more information about and examples of **ping** and ICMP.

Chapter Review

The "Your Study Plan" element, just before Chapter 1, discusses how you should study and practice the content and skills for each chapter before moving on to the next chapter. That element introduces the tools used here at the end of each chapter. If you haven't already done so, take a few minutes to read that section. Then come back here and do the useful work of reviewing the chapter to help lock into memory what you just read.

Review this chapter's material using either the tools in the book, DVD, or interactive tools for the same material found on the book's companion website. Table 4-7 outlines the key review elements and where you can find them. To better track your study progress, record when you completed these activities in the second column.

Table 4-7   Chapter Review Tracking

Review Element	Review Date(s)	Resource Used
Review key topics		Book, DVD/website
Review key terms		Book, DVD/website
Repeat DIKTA questions		Book, PCPT
Review memory table		Book, DVD/website

Review All the Key Topics

Table 4-8   Key Topics for Chapter 4

Key Topic Element	Description	Page Number
List	Two statements about how IP expects IP addresses to be grouped into networks or subnets	87
Figure 4-6	Breakdown of IPv4 address space	89
Figure 4-7	Sizes of Class A, B, and C networks	89
Table 4-6	List of the three types of unicast IP networks and the size of the network and host parts of each type of network	91
Figure 4-9	Conceptual view of how subnetting works	92
List	Two-step process of how hosts route (forward) packets	93
List	Four-step process of how routers route (forward) packets	94
List	Goals of IP routing protocols	96
Figure 4-13	Example that shows the purpose and process of DNS name resolution	99
Figure 4-14	Example of the purpose and process of ARP	100

Key Terms You Should Know

default router (default gateway), routing table, IP network, IP subnet, IP packet, routing protocol, dotted-decimal notation (DDN), IPv4 address, unicast IP address, subnetting, hostname, DNS, ARP, ping

CHAPTER 5

Fundamentals of TCP/IP Transport and Applications

This chapter covers the following exam topics:

1.0 Network Fundamentals

1.2 Compare and contrast TCP and UDP protocols

4.0 Infrastructure Services

4.1 Describe DNS lookup operation

The CCENT and CCNA Routing and Switching exams focus mostly on functions at the lower layers of TCP/IP, which define how IP networks can send IP packets from host to host using LANs and WANs. This chapter explains the basics of a few topics that receive less attention on the exams: the TCP/IP transport layer and the TCP/IP application layer. The functions of these higher layers play a big role in real TCP/IP networks, so it helps to have some basic understanding before moving into the rest of the book, where you go deeper into LANs and IP routing.

This chapter begins by examining the functions of two transport layer protocols: Transmission Control Protocol (TCP) and User Datagram Protocol (UDP). The second major section of the chapter examines the TCP/IP application layer, including some discussion of how Domain Name System (DNS) name resolution works.

"Do I Know This Already?" Quiz

Take the quiz (either here, or use the PCPT software) if you want to use the score to help you decide how much time to spend on this chapter. The answers are at the bottom of the page following the quiz, and the explanations are in DVD Appendix C and in the PCPT software.

Table 5-1 "Do I Know This Already?" Foundation Topics Section-to-Question Mapping

Foundation Topics Section	Questions
TCP/IP Layer 4 Protocols: TCP and UDP	1–4
TCP/IP Applications	5–6

1. Which of the following header fields identify which TCP/IP application gets data received by the computer? (Choose two answers.)

   a. Ethernet Type

   b. SNAP Protocol Type

   c. IP Protocol

   d. TCP Port Number

   e. UDP Port Number

2. Which of the following are typical functions of TCP? (Choose four answers.)

   a. Flow control (windowing)

   b. Error recovery

   c. Multiplexing using port numbers

   d. Routing

   e. Encryption

   f. Ordered data transfer

3. Which of the following functions is performed by both TCP and UDP?

   a. Windowing

   b. Error recovery

   c. Multiplexing using port numbers

   d. Routing

   e. Encryption

   f. Ordered data transfer

4. What do you call data that includes the Layer 4 protocol header, and data given to Layer 4 by the upper layers, not including any headers and trailers from Layers 1 to 3? (Choose two answers.)

   a. L3PDU

   b. Chunk

   c. Segment

   d. Packet

   e. Frame

   f. L4PDU

5. In the URI http://www.certskills.com/ICND1, which part identifies the web server?

   a. http

   b. www.certskills.com

   c. certskills.com

   d. http://www.certskills.com

   e. The file name.html includes the hostname.

   6. Fred opens a web browser and connects to the www.certskills.com website. Which of
   the following are typically true about what happens between Fred's web browser and
   the web server? (Choose two answers.)

   a. Messages flowing toward the server use UDP destination port 80.

   b. Messages flowing from the server typically use RTP.

   c. Messages flowing to the client typically use a source TCP port number of 80.

   d. Messages flowing to the server typically use TCP.

Foundation Topics

TCP/IP Layer 4 Protocols: TCP and UDP

The OSI transport layer (Layer 4) defines several functions, the most important of which are
error recovery and flow control. Likewise, the TCP/IP transport layer protocols also implement these same types of features. Note that both the OSI model and the TCP/IP model
call this layer the transport layer. But as usual, when referring to the TCP/IP model, the
layer name and number are based on OSI, so any TCP/IP transport layer protocols are considered Layer 4 protocols.

The key difference between TCP and UDP is that TCP provides a wide variety of services
to applications, whereas UDP does not. For example, routers discard packets for many reasons, including bit errors, congestion, and instances in which no correct routes are known.
As you have read already, most data-link protocols notice errors (a process called *error
detection*) but then discard frames that have errors. TCP provides retransmission (error
recovery) and helps to avoid congestion (flow control), whereas UDP does not. As a result,
many application protocols choose to use TCP.

However, do not let UDP's lack of services make you think that UDP is worse than TCP. By
providing fewer services, UDP needs fewer bytes in its header compared to TCP, resulting
in fewer bytes of overhead in the network. UDP software does not slow down data transfer
in cases where TCP can purposefully slow down. Also, some applications, notably today
Voice over IP (VoIP) and video over IP, do not need error recovery, so they use UDP. So,
UDP also has an important place in TCP/IP networks today.

Table 5-2 lists the main features supported by TCP/UDP. Note that only the first item listed
in the table is supported by UDP, whereas all items in the table are supported by TCP.

Table 5-2   TCP/IP Transport Layer Features

Function	Description
Multiplexing using ports	Function that allows receiving hosts to choose the correct application for which the data is destined, based on the port number
Error recovery (reliability)	Process of numbering and acknowledging data with Sequence and Acknowledgment header fields
Flow control using windowing	Process that uses window sizes to protect buffer space and routing devices from being overloaded with traffic

Function	Description
Connection establishment and termination	Process used to initialize port numbers and Sequence and Acknowledgment fields
Ordered data transfer and data segmentation	Continuous stream of bytes from an upper-layer process that is "segmented" for transmission and delivered to upper-layer processes at the receiving device, with the bytes in the same order

Next, this section describes the features of TCP, followed by a brief comparison to UDP.

Transmission Control Protocol

Each TCP/IP application typically chooses to use either TCP or UDP based on the application's requirements. For example, TCP provides error recovery, but to do so, it consumes more bandwidth and uses more processing cycles. UDP does not perform error recovery, but it takes less bandwidth and uses fewer processing cycles. Regardless of which of these two TCP/IP transport layer protocols the application chooses to use, you should understand the basics of how each of these transport layer protocols works.

TCP, as defined in Request For Comments (RFC) 793, accomplishes the functions listed in Table 5-2 through mechanisms at the endpoint computers. TCP relies on IP for end-to-end delivery of the data, including routing issues. In other words, TCP performs only part of the functions necessary to deliver the data between applications. Also, the role that it plays is directed toward providing services for the applications that sit at the endpoint computers. Regardless of whether two computers are on the same Ethernet, or are separated by the entire Internet, TCP performs its functions the same way.

Figure 5-1 shows the fields in the TCP header. Although you don't need to memorize the names of the fields or their locations, the rest of this section refers to several of the fields, so the entire header is included here for reference.

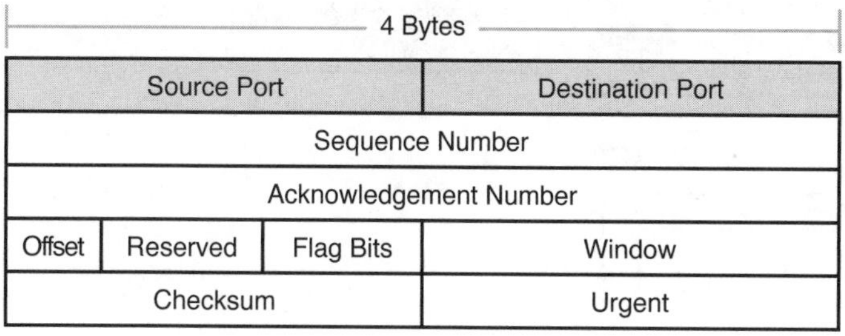
4 Bytes
Source Port
Destination Port
Sequence Number
Acknowledgement Number
Offset
Reserved
Flag Bits
Window
Checksum
Urgent

Figure 5-1 *TCP Header Fields*

Answers to the "Do I Know This Already?" quiz:

1 D, E **2** A, B, C, F **3** C **4** C, F **5** B **6** C, D

The message created by TCP that begins with the TCP header, followed by any application data, is called a *TCP segment*. Alternatively, the more generic term *Layer 4 PDU*, or *L4PDU*, can also be used.

Multiplexing Using TCP Port Numbers

TCP and UDP both use a concept called *multiplexing*. Therefore, this section begins with an explanation of multiplexing with TCP and UDP. Afterward, the unique features of TCP are explored.

Multiplexing by TCP and UDP involves the process of how a computer thinks when receiving data. The computer might be running many applications, such as a web browser, an email package, or an Internet VoIP application (for example, Skype). TCP and UDP multiplexing tells the receiving computer to which application to give the received data.

Some examples will help make the need for multiplexing obvious. The sample network consists of two PCs, labeled Hannah and Jessie. Hannah uses an application that she wrote to send advertisements that appear on Jessie's screen. The application sends a new ad to Jessie every 10 seconds. Hannah uses a second application, a wire-transfer application, to send Jessie some money. Finally, Hannah uses a web browser to access the web server that runs on Jessie's PC. The ad application and wire-transfer application are imaginary, just for this example. The web application works just like it would in real life.

Figure 5-2 shows the sample network, with Jessie running three applications:

■ A UDP-based advertisement application

■ A TCP-based wire-transfer application

■ A TCP web server application

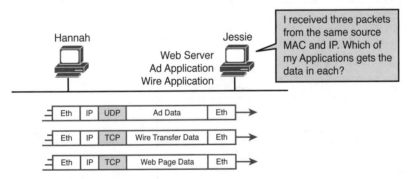

Figure 5-2   *Hannah Sending Packets to Jessie, with Three Applications*

Jessie needs to know which application to give the data to, but *all three packets are from the same Ethernet and IP address.* You might think that Jessie could look at whether the packet contains a UDP or TCP header, but as you see in the figure, two applications (wire transfer and web) are using TCP.

TCP and UDP solve this problem by using a port number field in the TCP or UDP header, respectively. Each of Hannah's TCP and UDP segments uses a different *destination port number* so that Jessie knows which application to give the data to. Figure 5-3 shows an example.

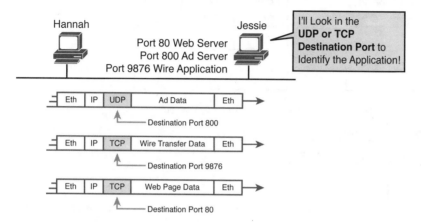

Figure 5-3 *Hannah Sending Packets to Jessie, with Three Applications Using Port Numbers to Multiplex*

Multiplexing relies on a concept called a *socket*. A socket consists of three things:

- An IP address
- A transport protocol
- A port number

So, for a web server application on Jessie, the socket would be (10.1.1.2, TCP, port 80) because, by default, web servers use the well-known port 80. When Hannah's web browser connects to the web server, Hannah uses a socket as well—possibly one like this: (10.1.1.1, TCP, 1030). Why 1030? Well, Hannah just needs a port number that is unique on Hannah, so Hannah sees that port 1030 is available and uses it. In fact, hosts typically allocate *dynamic port numbers* starting at 1024 because the ports below 1024 are reserved for well-known applications.

In Figure 5-3, Hannah and Jessie use three applications at the same time—hence, three socket connections are open. Because a socket on a single computer should be unique, a connection between two sockets should identify a unique connection between two computers. This uniqueness means that you can use multiple applications at the same time, talking to applications running on the same or different computers. Multiplexing, based on sockets, ensures that the data is delivered to the correct applications. Figure 5-4 shows the three socket connections between Hannah and Jessie.

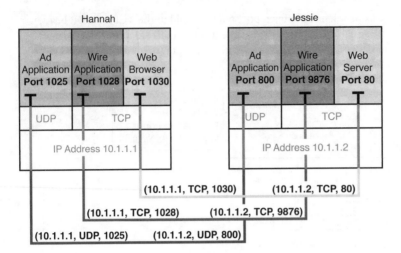

Figure 5-4 *Connections Between Sockets*

Port numbers are a vital part of the socket concept. Well-known port numbers are used by servers; other port numbers are used by clients. Applications that provide a service, such as FTP, Telnet, and web servers, open a socket using a well-known port and listen for connection requests. Because these connection requests from clients are required to include both the source and destination port numbers, the port numbers used by the servers must be well-known. Therefore, each service uses a specific well-known port number. The well-known ports are listed at www.iana.org/assignments/service-names-port-numbers/service-names-port-numbers.txt.

On client machines, where the requests originate, any locally unused port number can be allocated. The result is that each client on the same host uses a different port number, but a server uses the same port number for all connections. For example, 100 web browsers on the same host computer could each connect to a web server, but the web server with 100 clients connected to it would have only one socket and, therefore, only one port number (port 80, in this case). The server can tell which packets are sent from which of the 100 clients by looking at the source port of received TCP segments. The server can send data to the correct web client (browser) by sending data to that same port number listed as a destination port. The combination of source and destination sockets allows all participating hosts to distinguish between the data's source and destination. Although the example explains the concept using 100 TCP connections, the same port-numbering concept applies to UDP sessions in the same way.

> **NOTE** You can find all RFCs online at www.rfc-editor.org/rfc/rfc*xxxx*.txt, where *xxxx* is the number of the RFC. If you do not know the number of the RFC, you can try searching by topic at www.rfc-editor.org.

Popular TCP/IP Applications

Throughout your preparation for the CCNA Routing and Switching exams, you will come across a variety of TCP/IP applications. You should at least be aware of some of the applications that can be used to help manage and control a network.

The World Wide Web (WWW) application exists through web browsers accessing the content available on web servers. Although it is often thought of as an end-user application, you can actually use WWW to manage a router or switch. You enable a web server function in the router or switch and use a browser to access the router or switch.

The Domain Name System (DNS) allows users to use names to refer to computers, with DNS being used to find the corresponding IP addresses. DNS also uses a client/server model, with DNS servers being controlled by networking personnel and DNS client functions being part of most any device that uses TCP/IP today. The client simply asks the DNS server to supply the IP address that corresponds to a given name.

Simple Network Management Protocol (SNMP) is an application layer protocol used specifically for network device management. For example, Cisco supplies a large variety of network management products, many of them in the Cisco Prime network management software product family. They can be used to query, compile, store, and display information about a network's operation. To query the network devices, Cisco Prime software mainly uses SNMP protocols.

Traditionally, to move files to and from a router or switch, Cisco used Trivial File Transfer Protocol (TFTP). TFTP defines a protocol for basic file transfer—hence the word *trivial*. Alternatively, routers and switches can use File Transfer Protocol (FTP), which is a much more functional protocol, to transfer files. Both work well for moving files into and out of Cisco devices. FTP allows many more features, making it a good choice for the general end-user population. TFTP client and server applications are very simple, making them good tools as embedded parts of networking devices.

Some of these applications use TCP, and some use UDP. For example, Simple Mail Transfer Protocol (SMTP) and Post Office Protocol version 3 (POP3), both used for transferring mail, require guaranteed delivery, so they use TCP.

Regardless of which transport layer protocol is used, applications use a well-known port number so that clients know which port to attempt to connect to. Table 5-3 lists several popular applications and their well-known port numbers.

Table 5-3   Popular Applications and Their Well-Known Port Numbers

Port Number	Protocol	Application
20	TCP	FTP data
21	TCP	FTP control
22	TCP	SSH
23	TCP	Telnet
25	TCP	SMTP
53	UDP, TCP[1]	DNS
67	UDP	DHCP Server
68	UDP	DHCP Client
69	UDP	TFTP
80	TCP	HTTP (WWW)
110	TCP	POP3
161	UDP	SNMP

Port Number	Protocol	Application
443	TCP	SSL
514	UDP	Syslog

[1] DNS uses both UDP and TCP in different instances. It uses port 53 for both TCP and UDP.

Connection Establishment and Termination

TCP connection establishment occurs before any of the other TCP features can begin their work. Connection establishment refers to the process of initializing Sequence and Acknowledgment fields and agreeing on the port numbers used. Figure 5-5 shows an example of connection establishment flow.

Figure 5-5 *TCP Connection Establishment*

This three-way connection establishment flow (also called a three-way handshake) must complete before data transfer can begin. The connection exists between the two sockets, although the TCP header has no single socket field. Of the three parts of a socket, the IP addresses are implied based on the source and destination IP addresses in the IP header. TCP is implied because a TCP header is in use, as specified by the protocol field value in the IP header. Therefore, the only parts of the socket that need to be encoded in the TCP header are the port numbers.

TCP signals connection establishment using 2 bits inside the flag fields of the TCP header. Called the SYN and ACK flags, these bits have a particularly interesting meaning. SYN means "synchronize the sequence numbers," which is one necessary component in initialization for TCP.

Figure 5-6 shows TCP connection termination. This four-way termination sequence is straightforward and uses an additional flag, called the *FIN bit*. (FIN is short for "finished," as you might guess.) One interesting note: Before the device on the right sends the third TCP segment in the sequence, it notifies the application that the connection is coming down. It then waits on an acknowledgment from the application before sending the third segment in the figure. Just in case the application takes some time to reply, the PC on the right sends the second flow in the figure, acknowledging that the other PC wants to take down the connection. Otherwise, the PC on the left might resend the first segment repeatedly.

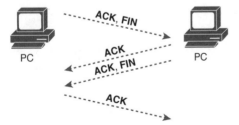

Figure 5-6 *TCP Connection Termination*

TCP establishes and terminates connections between the endpoints, whereas UDP does not. Many protocols operate under these same concepts, so the terms *connection-oriented* and *connectionless* are used to refer to the general idea of each. More formally, these terms can be defined as follows:

- **Connection-oriented protocol:** A protocol that requires an exchange of messages before data transfer begins, or that has a required pre-established correlation between two endpoints.

- **Connectionless protocol:** A protocol that does not require an exchange of messages and that does not require a pre-established correlation between two endpoints.

Error Recovery and Reliability

TCP provides for reliable data transfer, which is also called *reliability* or *error recovery*, depending on what document you read. To accomplish reliability, TCP numbers data bytes using the Sequence and Acknowledgment fields in the TCP header. TCP achieves reliability in both directions, using the Sequence Number field of one direction combined with the Acknowledgment field in the opposite direction.

Figure 5-7 shows an example of how the TCP sequence and acknowledgment fields allow the PC to send 3000 bytes of data to the server, with the server acknowledging receipt of the data. The TCP segments in the figure occur in order, from top to bottom. For simplicity's sake, all messages happen to have 1000 bytes of data in the data portion of the TCP segment. The first Sequence number is a nice round number (1000), again for simplicity's sake. The top of the figure shows three segments, with each sequence number being 1000 more than the previous, identifying the first of the 1000 bytes in the message. (That is, in this example, the first segment holds bytes 1000–1999; the second holds bytes 2000–2999; and the third holds bytes 3000–3999.)

Figure 5-7 *TCP Acknowledgment Without Errors*

The fourth TCP segment in the figure—the only one flowing back from the server to the web browser—acknowledges the receipt of all three segments. How? The acknowledgment value of 4000 means "I received all data with sequence numbers up through one less than 4000, so I am ready to receive your byte 4000 next." (Note that this convention of acknowledging by listing the next expected byte, rather than the number of the last byte received, is called *forward acknowledgment*.)

This first example does not recover from any errors, however; it simply shows the basics of how the sending host uses the sequence number field to identify the data, with the receiving host using forward acknowledgments to acknowledge the data. The more interesting discussion revolves around how to use these same tools to do error recovery. TCP uses the sequence and acknowledgment fields so that the receiving host can notice lost data, ask the sending host to resend, and then acknowledge that the re-sent data arrived.

Many variations exist for how TCP does error recovery. Figure 5-8 shows just one such example, with similar details compared to the previous figure. The web browser again sends three TCP segments, again 1000 bytes each, again with easy-to-remember sequence numbers. However, in this example, the second TCP segment fails to cross the network.

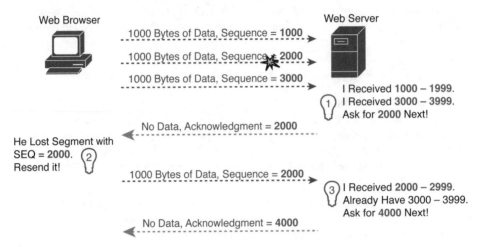

Figure 5-8   *TCP Acknowledgment with Errors*

The figure points out three sets of ideas behind how the two hosts think. First, on the right, the server realizes that it did not receive all the data. The two received TCP segments contain bytes numbered 1000–1999 and 3000–3999. Clearly, the server did not receive the bytes numbered in between. The server then decides to acknowledge all the data up to the lost data—that is, to send back a segment with the acknowledgment field equal to 2000.

The receipt of an acknowledgment that does not acknowledge all the data sent so far tells the sending host to resend the data. The PC on the left may wait a few moments to make sure no other acknowledgments arrive (using a timer called the retransmission timer), but will soon decide that the server means "I really do need 2000 next—resend it." The PC on the left does so, as shown in the fifth of the six TCP segments in the figure.

Finally, note that the server can acknowledge not only the re-sent data, but any earlier data that had been received correctly. In this case, the server received the re-sent second TCP segment (the data with sequence numbers 2000–2999), but the server had already received the third TCP segment (the data numbered 3000–3999). The server's next acknowledgment field acknowledges the data in both those segments, with an acknowledgment field of 4000.

Flow Control Using Windowing

TCP implements flow control by using a window concept that is applied to the amount of data that can be outstanding and awaiting acknowledgment at any one point in time. The window concept lets the receiving host tell the sender how much data it can receive right now, giving the receiving host a way to make the sending host slow down or speed up. The receiver can slide the window size up and down—called a *sliding window* or *dynamic window*—to change how much data the sending host can send.

The sliding window mechanism makes much more sense with an example. The example, shown in Figure 5-9, uses the same basic rules as the examples in the previous few figures.

In this case, none of the TCP segments have errors, and the discussion begins one TCP segment earlier than in the previous two figures.

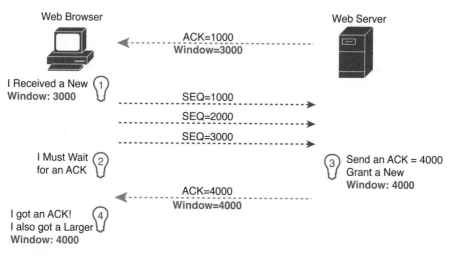

Figure 5-9 *TCP Windowing*

Begin with the first segment, sent by the server to the PC. The Acknowledgment field should be familiar by now: it tells the PC that the server expects a segment with sequence number 1000 next. The new field, the window field, is set to 3000. Because the segment flows to the PC, this value tells the PC that the PC can send no more than 3000 bytes over this connection before receiving an acknowledgment. So, as shown on the left, the PC realizes it can send only 3000 bytes, and it stops sending, waiting on an acknowledgment, after sending three 1000-byte TCP segments.

Continuing the example, the server not only acknowledges receiving the data (without any loss), but the server decides to slide the window size a little higher. Note that second message flowing right-to-left in the figure, this time with a window of 4000. Once the PC receives this TCP segment, the PC realizes it can send another 4000 bytes (a slightly larger window than the previous value).

Note that while the last few figures show examples for the purpose of explaining how the mechanisms work, the examples might give you the impression that TCP makes the hosts sit there and wait for acknowledgments a lot. TCP does not want to make the sending host have to wait to send data. For instance, if an acknowledgment is received before the window is exhausted, a new window begins, and the sender continues sending data until the current window is exhausted. Often times, in a network that has few problems, few lost segments, and little congestion, the TCP windows stay relatively large with hosts seldom waiting to send.

User Datagram Protocol

UDP provides a service for applications to exchange messages. Unlike TCP, UDP is connectionless and provides no reliability, no windowing, no reordering of the received data, and no segmentation of large chunks of data into the right size for transmission. However, UDP provides some functions of TCP, such as data transfer and multiplexing using port numbers, and it does so with fewer bytes of overhead and less processing required than TCP.

UDP data transfer differs from TCP data transfer in that no reordering or recovery is accomplished. Applications that use UDP are tolerant of the lost data, or they have some application mechanism to recover lost data. For example, VoIP uses UDP because if a voice packet is lost, by the time the loss could be noticed and the packet retransmitted, too much delay would have occurred, and the voice would be unintelligible. Also, DNS requests use UDP because the user will retry an operation if the DNS resolution fails. As another example, the Network File System (NFS), a remote file system application, performs recovery with application layer code, so UDP features are acceptable to NFS.

Figure 5-10 shows the UDP header format. Most importantly, note that the header includes source and destination port fields, for the same purpose as TCP. However, the UDP has only 8 bytes, in comparison to the 20-byte TCP header shown in Figure 5-1. UDP needs a shorter header than TCP simply because UDP has less work to do.

4 Bytes	
Source Port	Destination Port
Length	Checksum

Figure 5-10 *UDP Header*

TCP/IP Applications

The whole goal of building an enterprise network, or connecting a small home or office network to the Internet, is to use applications such as web browsing, text messaging, email, file downloads, voice, and video. This section examines one particular application—web browsing using Hypertext Transfer Protocol (HTTP).

The World Wide Web (WWW) consists of all the Internet-connected web servers in the world, plus all Internet-connected hosts with web browsers. *Web servers*, which consist of web server software running on a computer, store information (in the form of *web pages*) that might be useful to different people. A *web browser*, which is software installed on an end user's computer, provides the means to connect to a web server and display the web pages stored on the web server.

NOTE Although most people use the term *web browser*, or simply *browser*, web browsers are also called *web clients*, because they obtain a service from a web server.

For this process to work, several specific application layer functions must occur. The user must somehow identify the server, the specific web page, and the protocol used to get the data from the server. The client must find the server's IP address, based on the server's name, typically using DNS. The client must request the web page, which actually consists of multiple separate files, and the server must send the files to the web browser. Finally, for electronic commerce (e-commerce) applications, the transfer of data, particularly sensitive financial data, needs to be secure. The following sections address each of these functions.

Uniform Resource Identifiers

For a browser to display a web page, the browser must identify the server that has the web page, plus other information that identifies the particular web page. Most web servers have many web pages. For example, if you use a web browser to browse www.cisco.com and you click around that web page, you'll see another web page. Click again, and you'll see another web page. In each case, the clicking action identifies the server's IP address as well as the specific web page, with the details mostly hidden from you. (These clickable items on a web page, which in turn bring you to another web page, are called *links*.)

The browser user can identify a web page when you click something on a web page or when you enter a Uniform Resource Identifier (URI) in the browser's address area. Both options—clicking a link and typing a URI—refer to a URI, because when you click a link on a web page, that link actually refers to a URI.

> **NOTE**   Most browsers support some way to view the hidden URI referenced by a link. In several browsers, hover the mouse pointer over a link, right-click, and select **Properties**. The pop-up window should display the URI to which the browser would be directed if you clicked that link.

In common speech, many people use the terms *web address* or the similar related term *Universal Resource Locator* (URL) instead of URI, but URI is indeed the correct formal term. In fact, URL had been more commonly used than URI for more than a few years. However, the IETF (the group that defines TCP/IP), along with the W3C consortium (W3.org, a consortium that develops web standards) has made a concerted effort to standardize the use of URI as the general term. See RFC 7595 for some commentary to that effect.

From a practical perspective, the URIs used to connect to a web server include three key components, as noted in Figure 5-11. The figure shows the formal names of the URI fields. More importantly to this discussion, note that the text before the :// identifies the protocol used to connect to the server, the text between the // and / identifies the server by name, and the text after the / identifies the web page.

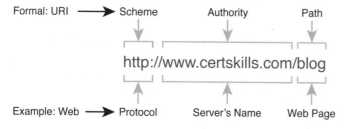

Figure 5-11   *Structure of a URI Used to Retrieve a Web Page*

In this case, the protocol is Hypertext Transfer Protocol (HTTP), the hostname is www.certskills.com, and the name of the web page is blog.

Finding the Web Server Using DNS

As mentioned in Chapter 4, "Fundamentals of IPv4 Addressing and Routing," a host can use DNS to discover the IP address that corresponds to a particular hostname. URIs typically list the name of the server—a name that can be used to dynamically learn the IP address used by that same server. The web browser cannot send an IP packet to a destination name, but it can send a packet to a destination IP address. So, before the browser can send a packet to the web server, the browser typically needs to resolve the name inside the URI to that name's corresponding IP address.

To pull together several concepts, Figure 5-12 shows the DNS process as initiated by a web browser, as well as some other related information. From a basic perspective, the user enters the URI (in this case, http://www.cisco.com/go/learningnetwork), resolves the www.cisco.com name into the correct IP address, and starts sending packets to the web server.

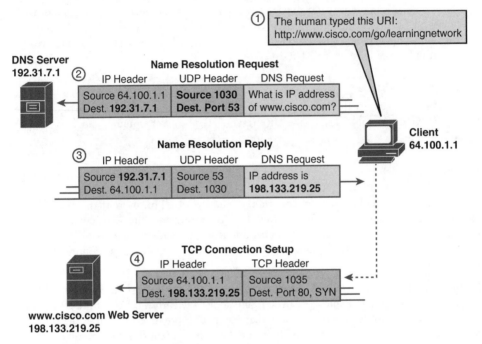

Figure 5-12 *DNS Resolution and Requesting a Web Page*

The steps shown in the figure are as follows:

1. The user enters the URI, http://www.cisco.com/go/learningnetwork, into the browser's address area.

2. The client sends a DNS request to the DNS server. Typically, the client learns the DNS server's IP address through DHCP. Note that the DNS request uses a UDP header, with a destination port of the DNS well-known port of 53. (See Table 5-3, earlier in this chapter, for a list of popular well-known ports.)

3. The DNS server sends a reply, listing IP address 198.133.219.25 as www.cisco.com's IP address. Note also that the reply shows a destination IP address of 64.100.1.1, the client's IP address. It also shows a UDP header, with source port 53; the source port is 53 because the data is sourced, or sent by, the DNS server.

4. The client begins the process of establishing a new TCP connection to the web server. Note that the destination IP address is the just-learned IP address of the web server. The packet includes a TCP header, because HTTP uses TCP. Also note that the destination TCP port is 80, the well-known port for HTTP. Finally, the SYN bit is shown, as a reminder that the TCP connection establishment process begins with a TCP segment with the SYN bit turned on (binary 1).

At this point in the process, the web browser is almost finished setting up a TCP connection to the web server. The next section picks up the story at that point, examining how the web browser then gets the files that comprise the desired web page.

Transferring Files with HTTP

After a web client (browser) has created a TCP connection to a web server, the client can begin requesting the web page from the server. Most often, the protocol used to transfer the web page is HTTP. The HTTP application layer protocol, defined in RFC 7230, defines how files can be transferred between two computers. HTTP was specifically created for the purpose of transferring files between web servers and web clients.

HTTP defines several commands and responses, with the most frequently used being the HTTP GET request. To get a file from a web server, the client sends an HTTP GET request to the server, listing the filename. If the server decides to send the file, the server sends an HTTP GET response, with a return code of 200 (meaning OK), along with the file's contents.

NOTE   Many return codes exist for HTTP requests. For example, when the server does not have the requested file, it issues a return code of 404, which means "file not found." Most web browsers do not show the specific numeric HTTP return codes, instead displaying a response such as "page not found" in reaction to receiving a return code of 404.

Web pages typically consist of multiple files, called *objects*. Most web pages contain text as well as several graphical images, animated advertisements, and possibly voice or video. Each of these components is stored as a different object (file) on the web server. To get them all, the web browser gets the first file. This file can (and typically does) include references to other URIs, so the browser then also requests the other objects. Figure 5-13 shows the general idea, with the browser getting the first file and then two others.

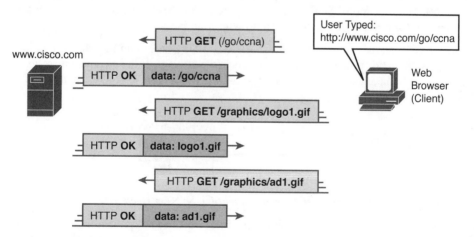

Figure 5-13   *Multiple HTTP Get Requests/Responses*

In this case, after the web browser gets the first file—the one called "/go/ccna" in the URI—the browser reads and interprets that file. Besides containing parts of the web page, the file refers to two other files, so the browser issues two additional HTTP get requests. Note that, even though it isn't shown in the figure, all these commands flow over one (or possibly more) TCP connection between the client and the server. This means that TCP would provide error recovery, ensuring that the data was delivered.

How the Receiving Host Identifies the Correct Receiving Application

This chapter closes with a discussion that pulls several concepts together from several chapters in Part I of this book. The concept revolves around the process by which a host, when receiving any message over any network, can decide which of its many application programs should process the received data.

As an example, consider host A shown on the left side of Figure 5-14. The host happens to have three different web browser windows open, each using a unique TCP port. Host A also has an email client and a chat window open, both of which use TCP. Both the email and chat applications use a unique TCP port number on host A as well (1027 and 1028) as shown in the figure.

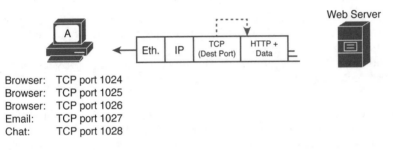

Browser: TCP port 1024
Browser: TCP port 1025
Browser: TCP port 1026
Email: TCP port 1027
Chat: TCP port 1028

Figure 5-14 *Dilemma: How Host A Chooses the App That Should Receive This Data*

This chapter has shown several examples of how Transport layer protocols use the destination port number field in the TCP or UDP header to identify the receiving application. For instance, if the destination TCP port value in Figure 5-15 is 1024, host A will know that the data is meant for the first of the three web browser windows.

Before a receiving host can even examine the TCP or UDP header, and find the destination port field, it must first process the outer headers in the message. If the incoming message is an Ethernet frame, that encapsulates an IPv4 packet, the headers look like the details in Figure 5-15.

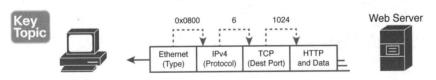

Figure 5-15 *Three Key Fields with Which to Identify the Next Header*

The receiving host needs to look at multiple fields, one per header, to identify the next header or field in the received message. For instance, host A uses an Ethernet NIC to connect to the network, so the received message is an Ethernet frame. As first shown back in Figure 2-16 in Chapter 2, "Fundamentals of Ethernet LANs," the Ethernet Type field identifies the type of header that follows the Ethernet header—in this case, with a value of hex 0800, an IPv4 header.

The IPv4 header has a similar field called the IP Protocol field. The IPv4 Protocol field has a standard list of values that identify the next header, with decimal 6 used for TCP and decimal 17 used for UDP. In this case, the value of 6 identifies the TCP header that follows the IPv4 header. Once the receiving host realizes a TCP header exists, it can process the destination port field to determine which local application process should receive the data.

Chapter Review

One key to doing well on the exams is to perform repetitive spaced review sessions. Review this chapter's material using either the tools in the book, DVD, or interactive tools for the same material found on the book's companion website. Refer to the "Your Study Plan" element section titled "Step 2: Build Your Study Habits Around the Chapter" for more details. Table 5-4 outlines the key review elements and where you can find them. To better track your study progress, record when you completed these activities in the second column.

Table 5-4   Chapter Review Tracking

Review Element	Review Date(s)	Resource Used
Review key topics		Book, DVD/website
Review key terms		Book, DVD/website
Repeat DIKTA questions		Book, PCPT
Review memory tables		Book, DVD/website

Review All the Key Topics

Table 5-5   Key Topics for Chapter 5

Key Topic Element	Description	Page Number
Table 5-2	Functions of TCP and UDP	104
Table 5-3	Well-known TCP and UDP port numbers	109
Figure 5-5	Example of TCP connection establishment	110
List	Definitions of connection-oriented and connectionless	111
Figure 5-15	Header fields that identify the next header	118

Key Terms You Should Know

connection establishment, error detection, error recovery, flow control, forward acknowledgment, HTTP, ordered data transfer, port, segment, sliding windows, URI, web server

Part I Review

Keep track of your part review progress with the checklist shown in Table P1-1. Details on each task follow the table.

Table P1-1 Part I Review Checklist

Activity	1st Date Completed	2nd Date Completed
Repeat All DIKTA Questions		
Answer Part Review Questions		
Review Key Topics		
Create Terminology Mind Maps		

Repeat All DIKTA Questions

For this task, answer the "Do I Know This Already?" questions again for the chapters in this part of the book, using the PCPT software. Refer to the Introduction to this book, section "How to View Only DIKTA Questions by Chapter or Part," for help with how to make the PCPT software show you DIKTA questions for this part only.

Answer Part Review Questions

For this task, answer the Part Review questions for this part of the book, using the PCPT software. Refer to the Introduction to this book, section "How to View Part Review Questions," for help with how to make the PCPT software show you Part Review questions for this part only. (Note that if you use the questions but then even want more, get the Premium Edition of the book, as detailed in the Introduction, in the section "Other Features," under the item labeled "eBook."

Review Key Topics

Browse back through the chapters and look for the Key Topic icons. If you do not remember some details, take the time to reread those topics, or use the Key Topics application(s) found on the companion website and the DVD.

Create Terminology Mind Maps

The first part of this book introduces a large amount of terminology. The sheer number of terms can be overwhelming. But more and more, while you work through each new chapter, you will become more comfortable with the terms. And the better you can remember the core meaning of a term, the easier your reading will be going forward.

For your first mind map exercise in this book, without looking back at the chapters or your notes, you will create six mind maps. The mind maps will each list a number in the center, 1 through 6, to match the numbers shown in Figure P1-1. Your job is as follows:

- Think of every term that you can remember from Part I of the book.
- Think of each of the six mind maps as being about the item next to the number in Figure P1-1. For example, number 1 is about the user PC, number 2 is about an Ethernet cable that connects PC1 to a switch, and so on.
- Add each term that you can recall to all mind maps to which it applies. For example, *leased line* would apply to mind map number 5.
- If a term seems to apply to multiple places, add it to all those mind maps.
- After you have written every term you can remember into one of the mind maps, review the Key Terms lists at the end of Chapters 1 through 5. Add any terms you forgot to your mind maps.

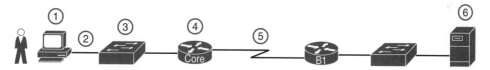

Figure P1-1 *Sample Network to Use with Mind Map Exercise*

The goal of these minds maps is to help you recall the terms with enough meaning to associate the terms with the right part of a simple network design. On your first review of Part I, do not be concerned if you cannot fully explain each term, because you will learn many of these terms more fully just by reading the rest of the book.

NOTE For more information on mind mapping, refer to the Introduction, in the section "About Mind Maps."

Create the mind maps in Table P1-2 on paper, using any mind-mapping software or even any drawing application. If you use an application, note the filename and location where you saved the file for later reference. Sample answers are listed in DVD Appendix L, "Mind Map Solutions."

Table P1-2   Configuration Mind Maps for Part I Review

Map	Description	Where You Saved It
1	Client PC	
2	Ethernet link	
3	LAN switch	
4	Router	
5	Leased line	
6	Server	

Part I provided a broad look at the fundamentals of all parts of networking. Parts II and III now drill into depth about the details of Ethernet, which was introduced back in Chapter 2, "Fundamentals of Ethernet LANs."

Part II begins that journey by discussing the basics of building a small Ethernet LAN with Cisco Catalyst switches. The journey begins by showing how to access the user interface of a Cisco switch, so that you can see evidence of what the switch is doing and to configure the switch to act in the ways you want it to act. At this point, you should start using whatever lab practice option you chose in the "Your Study Plan" section that preceded Chapter 1, "Introduction to TCP/IP Networking." (And if you have not yet finalized your plan for how to practice your hands-on skills, now is the time.)

When you complete Chapter 6 and see how to get into the command-line interface (CLI) of a switch, the next three chapters step through some important foundations of how to implement LANs—foundations used by every company that builds LANs with Cisco gear. Chapter 7 takes a close look at Ethernet switching—that is, the logic used by a switch—and how to know what a particular switch is doing. Chapter 8 shows the ways to configure a switch for remote access with Telnet and Secure Shell (SSH), along with a variety of other useful commands that will help you when you work with any real lab gear, simulator, or any other practice tools. Chapter 9, the final chapter in Part II, shows how to configure switch interfaces for several important features: port security and the inter-related features of speed, duplex, and autonegotiation.

Part II

Implementing Basic Ethernet LANs

CHAPTER 6

Using the Command-Line Interface

This chapter covers the following exam topics:

1.0 Network Fundamentals

1.6 Select the appropriate cabling type based on implementation requirements

> **NOTE** This chapter primarily explains foundational skills required before you can explore the roughly 20 exam topics that use the verbs configure, verify, and troubleshoot.

To create an Ethernet LAN, a network engineer starts by planning. They consider the requirements, create a design, buy the switches, contract to install cables, and configure the switches to use the right features.

The CCENT and CCNA Routing and Switching exams focus on skills like understanding how LANs work, configuring different switch features, verifying that those features work correctly, and finding the root cause of the problem when a feature is not working correctly. The first skill you need to learn before doing all the configuration, verification, and troubleshooting tasks is to learn how to access and use the user interface of the switch, called the command-line interface (CLI).

This chapter begins that process by showing the basics of how to access the switch's CLI. These skills include how to access the CLI and how to issue verification commands to check on the status of the LAN. This chapter also includes the processes of how to configure the switch and how to save that configuration.

Note that this chapter focuses on processes that provide a foundation for most every exam topic that includes the verbs configure, verify, and troubleshoot. Chapter 7, "Analyzing Ethernet LAN Switching," Chapter 8, "Configuring Basic Switch Management," and Chapter 9, "Configuring Switch Interfaces," then examine particular commands you can use to verify and configure different switch features.

"Do I Know This Already?" Quiz

Take the quiz (either here, or use the PCPT software) if you want to use the score to help you decide how much time to spend on this chapter. The answers are at the bottom of the page following the quiz, and the explanations are in DVD Appendix C and in the PCPT software.

Table 6-1 "Do I Know This Already?" Foundation Topics Section-to-Question Mapping

Foundation Topics Section	Questions
Accessing the Cisco Catalyst Switch CLI	1–3
Configuring Cisco IOS Software	4–6

1. In what modes can you type the command **show mac address-table** and expect to get a response with MAC table entries? (Choose two answers.)

   a. User mode

   b. Enable mode

   c. Global configuration mode

   d. Interface configuration mode

2. In which of the following modes of the CLI could you type the command **reload** and expect the switch to reboot?

   a. User mode

   b. Enable mode

   c. Global configuration mode

   d. Interface configuration mode

3. Which of the following is a difference between Telnet and SSH as supported by a Cisco switch?

   a. SSH encrypts the passwords used at login, but not other traffic; Telnet encrypts nothing.

   b. SSH encrypts all data exchange, including login passwords; Telnet encrypts nothing.

   c. Telnet is used from Microsoft operating systems, and SSH is used from UNIX and Linux operating systems.

   d. Telnet encrypts only password exchanges; SSH encrypts all data exchanges.

4. What type of switch memory is used to store the configuration used by the switch when it is up and working?

   a. RAM

   b. ROM

   c. Flash

   d. NVRAM

   e. Bubble

5. What command copies the configuration from RAM into NVRAM?

   a. copy running-config tftp

   b. copy tftp running-config

   c. copy running-config start-up-config

   d. copy start-up-config running-config

   e. copy startup-config running-config

   f. copy running-config startup-config

6. A switch user is currently in console line configuration mode. Which of the following would place the user in enable mode? (Choose two answers.)

   a. Using the **exit** command once

   b. Using the **end** command once

   c. Pressing the Ctrl+Z key sequence once

   d. Using the **quit** command

Foundation Topics

Accessing the Cisco Catalyst Switch CLI

Cisco uses the concept of a command-line interface (CLI) with its router products and most of its Catalyst LAN switch products. The CLI is a text-based interface in which the user, typically a network engineer, enters a text command and presses Enter. Pressing Enter sends the command to the switch, which tells the device to do something. The switch does what the command says, and in some cases, the switch replies with some messages stating the results of the command.

Cisco Catalyst switches also support other methods to both monitor and configure a switch. For example, a switch can provide a web interface, so that an engineer can open a web browser to connect to a web server running in the switch. Switches also can be controlled and operated using network management software.

This book discusses only Cisco Catalyst enterprise-class switches, and in particular, how to use the Cisco CLI to monitor and control these switches. This first major section of the chapter first examines these Catalyst switches in more detail, and then explains how a network engineer can get access to the CLI to issue commands.

Cisco Catalyst Switches

Within the Cisco Catalyst brand of LAN switches, Cisco produces a wide variety of switch series or families. Each switch series includes several specific models of switches that have similar features, similar price-versus-performance trade-offs, and similar internal components.

For example, at the time this book was published, the Cisco 2960-X series of switches was a current switch model series. Cisco positions the 2960-X series (family) of switches as full-featured, low-cost wiring closet switches for enterprises. That means that you would expect to use 2960-X switches as access switches in a typical campus LAN design. Chapter 10, "Analyzing Ethernet LAN Designs," discusses campus LAN design and the roles of various switches.

Figure 6-1 shows a photo of 10 different models from the 2960-X switch model series from Cisco. Each switch series includes several models, with a mix of features. For example, some of the switches have 48 RJ-45 unshielded twisted-pair (UTP) 10/100/1000 ports, meaning that these ports can autonegotiate the use of 10BASE-T (10 Mbps), 100BASE-T (100 Mbps), or 1000BASE-T (1 Gbps) Ethernet.

Figure 6-1 *Cisco 2960-X Catalyst Switch Series*

Cisco refers to a switch's physical connectors as either *interfaces* or *ports*, with an interface type and interface number. The interface type, as used in commands on the switch, is either Ethernet, Fast Ethernet, Gigabit Ethernet, and so on for faster speeds. For Ethernet interfaces that support running at multiple speeds, the permanent name for the interface refers to the fastest supported speed. For example, a 10/100/1000 interface (that is, an interface that runs at 10 Mbps, 100 Mbps, or 1000 Mbps) would be called Gigabit Ethernet no matter what speed is currently in use.

To uniquely number each different interface, some Catalyst switches use a two-digit interface number (*x/y*), while others have a three-digit number (*x/y/z*). For instance, two 10/100/1000 ports on many older Cisco Catalyst switches would be called Gigabit Ethernet 0/0 and Gigabit Ethernet 0/1, while on the newer 2960-X series, two interfaces would be Gigabit Ethernet 1/0/1 and Gigabit Ethernet 1/0/2, for example.

Accessing the Cisco IOS CLI

Like any other piece of computer hardware, Cisco switches need some kind of operating system software. Cisco calls this OS the Internetwork Operating System (IOS).

Cisco IOS Software for Catalyst switches implements and controls logic and functions performed by a Cisco switch. Besides controlling the switch's performance and behavior, Cisco IOS also defines an interface for humans called the CLI. The Cisco IOS CLI allows the user to use a terminal emulation program, which accepts text entered by the user. When the user presses Enter, the terminal emulator sends that text to the switch. The switch processes the text as if it is a command, does what the command says, and sends text back to the terminal emulator.

The switch CLI can be accessed through three popular methods—the console, Telnet, and Secure Shell (SSH). Two of these methods (Telnet and SSH) use the IP network in which the switch resides to reach the switch. The console is a physical port built specifically to allow access to the CLI. Figure 6-2 depicts the options.

Answers to the "Do I Know This Already?" quiz:

1 A, B **2** B **3** B **4** A **5** F **6** B, C

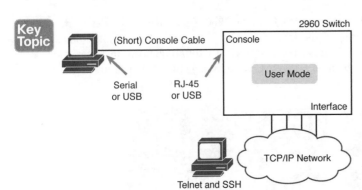

Figure 6-2   *CLI Access Options*

Console access requires both a physical connection between a PC (or other user device) and the switch's console port, as well as some software on the PC. Telnet and SSH require software on the user's device, but they rely on the existing TCP/IP network to transmit data. The next few pages detail how to connect the console and set up the software for each method to access the CLI.

Cabling the Console Connection

The physical console connection, both old and new, uses three main components: the physical console port on the switch, a physical serial port on the PC, and a cable that works with the console and serial ports. However, the physical cabling details have changed slowly over time, mainly because of advances and changes with serial interfaces on PC hardware. For this next topic, the text looks at three cases: newer connectors on both the PC and the switch, older connectors on both, and a third case with the newer (USB) connector on the PC but with an older connector on the switch.

More modern PC and switch hardware use a familiar standard USB cable for the console connection. Cisco has been including USB ports as console ports in newer routers and switches as well. All you have to do is look at the switch to make sure you have the correct style of USB cable end to match the USB console port. In the simplest form, you can use any USB port on the PC, with a USB cable, connected to the USB console port on the switch or router, as shown on the far right side of Figure 6-3.

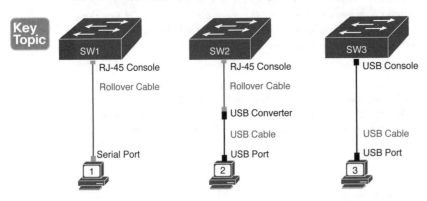

Figure 6-3   *Console Connection to a Switch*

Older console connections use a PC serial port that pre-dates USB, a UTP cable, and an RJ-45 console port on the switch, as shown on the left side of Figure 6-3. The PC serial port typically has a D-shell connector (roughly rectangular) with nine pins (often called a DB-9). The console port looks like any Ethernet RJ-45 port (but is typically colored in blue and with the word "console" beside it on the switch).

The cabling for this older-style console connection can be simple or require some effort, depending on what cable you use. You can use the purpose-built console cable that ships with new Cisco switches and routers and not think about the details. However, you can make your own cable with a standard serial cable (with a connector that matches the PC), a standard RJ-45 to DB-9 converter plug, and a UTP cable. However, the UTP cable does not use the same pinouts as Ethernet; instead, the cable uses rollover cable pinouts rather than any of the standard Ethernet cabling pinouts. The rollover pinout uses eight wires, rolling the wire at pin 1 to pin 8, pin 2 to pin 7, pin 3 to pin 6, and so on.

As it turns out, USB ports became common on PCs before Cisco began commonly using USB for its console ports. So, you also have to be ready to use a PC that has only a USB port and not an old serial port, but a router or switch that has the older RJ-45 console port (and no USB console port). The center of Figure 6-3 shows that case. To connect such a PC to a router or switch console, you need a USB converter that converts from the older console cable to a USB connector, and a rollover UTP cable, as shown in the middle of Figure 6-3.

> **NOTE** When using the USB options, you typically also need to install a software driver so that your PC's OS knows that the device on the other end of the USB connection is the console of a Cisco device. Also, you can easily find photos of these cables and components online, with searches like "cisco console cable," "cisco usb console cable," or "console cable converter."

The newer 2960-X series, for instance, supports both the older RJ-45 console port and a USB console port. Figure 6-4 points to the two console ports; you would use only one or the other. Note that the USB console port uses a mini-B port rather than the more commonly seen rectangular standard USB port.

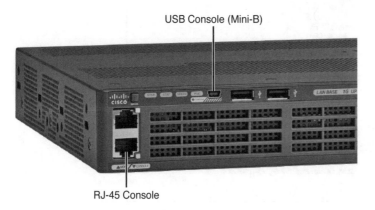

Figure 6-4 *A Part of a 2960-X Switch with Console Ports Shown*

After the PC is physically connected to the console port, a terminal emulator software package must be installed and configured on the PC. The terminal emulator software treats all data as text. It accepts the text typed by the user and sends it over the console connection to the switch. Similarly, any bits coming into the PC over the console connection are displayed as text for the user to read.

The emulator must be configured to use the PC's serial port to match the settings on the switch's console port settings. The default console port settings on a switch are as follows. Note that the last three parameters are referred to collectively as 8N1:

- 9600 bits/second
- No hardware flow control
- 8-bit ASCII
- No parity bits
- 1 stop bit

Figure 6-5 shows one such terminal emulator. The image shows the window created by the emulator software in the background, with some output of a **show** command. The foreground, in the upper left, shows a settings window that lists the default console settings as listed just before this paragraph.

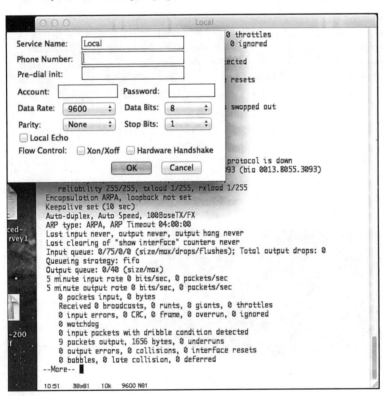

Figure 6-5 *Terminal Settings for Console Access*

Accessing the CLI with Telnet and SSH

For many years, terminal emulator applications have supported far more than the ability to communicate over a serial port to a local device (like a switch's console). Terminal emulators support a variety of TCP/IP applications as well, including Telnet and SSH. Telnet and SSH both allow the user to connect to another device's CLI, but instead of connecting through a console cable to the console port, the traffic flows over the same IP network that the networking devices are helping to create.

Telnet uses the concept of a Telnet client (the terminal application) and a Telnet server (the switch in this case). A *Telnet client*, the device that sits in front of the user, accepts keyboard input and sends those commands to the *Telnet server*. The Telnet server accepts the text, interprets the text as a command, and replies back. Telnet is a TCP-based application layer protocol that uses well-known port 23.

Cisco Catalyst switches enable a Telnet server by default, but switches need a few more configuration settings before you can successfully use Telnet to connect to a switch. Chapter 8 covers switch configuration to support Telnet and SSH in detail.

Using Telnet in a lab today makes sense, but Telnet poses a significant security risk in production networks. Telnet sends all data (including any username and password for login to the switch) as clear-text data. SSH gives us a much better option.

Think of SSH as the much more secure Telnet cousin. Outwardly, you still open a terminal emulator, connect to the switch's IP address, and see the switch CLI, no matter whether you use Telnet or SSH. The differences exist behind the scenes: SSH encrypts the contents of all messages, including the passwords, avoiding the possibility of someone capturing packets in the network and stealing the password to network devices. Like Telnet, SSH uses TCP, just using well-known port 22 instead of Telnet's 23.

User and Enable (Privileged) Modes

All three CLI access methods covered so far (console, Telnet, and SSH) place the user in an area of the CLI called *user EXEC mode*. User EXEC mode, sometimes also called *user mode*, allows the user to look around but not break anything. The "EXEC mode" part of the name refers to the fact that in this mode, when you enter a command, the switch executes the command and then displays messages that describe the command's results.

> **NOTE** If you have not used the CLI before, you might want to experiment with the CLI from the Sim Lite product, or view the video about CLI basics. You can find these resources on the DVD and on the companion website, as mentioned in the introduction.

Cisco IOS supports a more powerful EXEC mode called *enable* mode (also known as *privileged* mode or *privileged EXEC* mode). Enable mode gets its name from the **enable** command, which moves the user from user mode to enable mode, as shown in Figure 6-6. The other name for this mode, *privileged mode*, refers to the fact that powerful (or privileged) commands can be executed there. For example, you can use the **reload** command, which tells the switch to reinitialize or reboot Cisco IOS, only from enable mode.

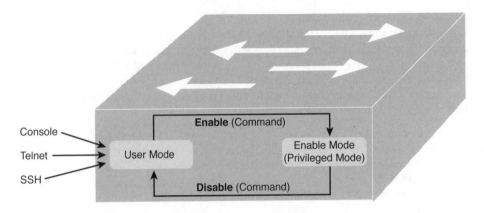

Figure 6-6   *User and Privileged Modes*

> **NOTE**   If the command prompt lists the hostname followed by a >, the user is in user mode; if it is the hostname followed by the #, the user is in enable mode.

Example 6-1 demonstrates the differences between user and enable modes. The example shows the output that you could see in a terminal emulator window, for instance, when connecting from the console. In this case, the user sits at the user mode prompt ("Certskills1>") and tries the **reload** command. The **reload** command tells the switch to reinitialize or reboot Cisco IOS, so IOS allows this powerful command to be used only from enable mode. IOS rejects the **reload** command when used in user mode. Then the user moves to enable mode—also called privileged mode—(using the **enable** EXEC command). At that point, IOS accepts the **reload** command now that the user is in enable mode.

Example 6-1   *Example of Privileged Mode Commands Being Rejected in User Mode*

```
Press RETURN to get started.


User Access Verification


Password:
Certskills1>
Certskills1> reload
Translating "reload"
% Unknown command or computer name, or unable to find computer address
Certskills1> enable
Password:
Certskills1#
Certskills1# reload


Proceed with reload? [confirm] y
00:08:42: %SYS-5-RELOAD: Reload requested by console. Reload Reason: Reload Command.
```

> **NOTE**   The commands that can be used in either user (EXEC) mode or enable (EXEC) mode are called EXEC commands.

This example is the first instance of this book showing you the output from the CLI, so it is worth noting a few conventions. The bold text represents what the user typed, and the non-bold text is what the switch sent back to the terminal emulator. Also, the typed passwords do not show up on the screen for security purposes. Finally, note that this switch has been preconfigured with a hostname of Certskills1, so the command prompt on the left shows that hostname on each line.

Password Security for CLI Access from the Console

A Cisco switch, with default settings, remains relatively secure when locked inside a wiring closet, because by default, a switch allows console access only. By default, the console requires no password at all, and no password to reach enable mode for users that happened to connect from the console. The reason is that if you have access to the physical console port of the switch, you already have pretty much complete control over the switch. You could literally get out your screwdriver and walk off with it, or you could unplug the power, or follow well-published procedures to go through password recovery to break into the CLI and then configure anything you want to configure.

However, many people go ahead and set up simple password protection for console users. Simple passwords can be configured at two points in the login process from the console: when the user connects from the console, and when any user moves to enable mode (using the **enable** EXEC command). You may have noticed that back in Example 6-1, the user saw a password prompt at both points.

Example 6-2 shows the additional configuration commands that were configured prior to collecting the output in Example 6-1. The output holds an excerpt from the EXEC command **show running-config**, which lists the current configuration in the switch.

Example 6-2   *Nondefault Basic Configuration*

```
Certskills1# show running-config
! Output has been formatted to show only the parts relevant to this discussion
hostname Certskills1
!
enable secret love
!
line console 0
 login
 password faith
! The rest of the output has been omitted
Certskills1#
```

Working from top to bottom, note that the first configuration command listed by the **show running-config** command sets the switch's hostname to Certskills1. You might have noticed that the command prompts in Example 6-1 all began with Certskills1, and that's why the command prompt begins with the hostname of the switch.

6

Next, note that the lines with a ! in them are comment lines, both in the text of this book and in the real switch CLI.

The **enable secret love** configuration command defines the password that all users must use to reach enable mode. So, no matter whether a user connects from the console, Telnet, or SSH, they would use password love when prompted for a password after typing the **enable** EXEC command.

Finally, the last three lines configure the console password. The first line (**line console 0**) is the command that identifies the console, basically meaning "these next commands apply to the console only." The **login** command tells IOS to perform simple password checking (at the console). Remember, by default, the switch does not ask for a password for console users. Finally, the **password faith** command defines the password the console user must type when prompted.

This example just scratches the surface of the kinds of security configuration you might choose to configure on a switch, but it does give you enough detail to configure switches in your lab and get started (which is the reason I put these details in this first chapter of Part II). Note that Chapter 8 shows the configuration steps to add support for Telnet and SSH (including password security), and Chapter 34, "Device Security Features," shows additional security configuration as well.

CLI Help Features

If you printed the Cisco IOS Command Reference documents, you would end up with a stack of paper several feet tall. No one should expect to memorize all the commands—and no one does. You can use several very easy, convenient tools to help remember commands and save time typing. As you progress through your Cisco certifications, the exams will cover progressively more commands. However, you should know the methods of getting command help.

Table 6-2 summarizes command-recall help options available at the CLI. Note that, in the first column, *command* represents any command. Likewise, *parm* represents a command's parameter. For example, the third row lists *command* **?**, which means that commands such as **show ?** and **copy ?** would list help for the **show** and **copy** commands, respectively.

Table 6-2   Cisco IOS Software Command Help

What You Enter	What Help You Get
?	Help for all commands available in this mode.
command **?**	With a space between the command and the **?**, the switch lists text to describe all the first parameter options for the command.
*com***?**	A list of commands that start with **com**.
*command parm***?**	Lists all parameters beginning with the **parameter typed so far**. (Notice that there is no space between *parm* and the **?**.)
command parm<Tab>	Pressing the Tab key causes IOS to spell out the rest of the word, assuming that you have typed enough of the word so there is only one option that begins with that string of characters.
command parm1 **?**	If a space is inserted before the question mark, the CLI lists all the next parameters and gives a brief explanation of each.

When you enter the ?, the Cisco IOS CLI reacts immediately; that is, you don't need to press the Enter key or any other keys. The device running Cisco IOS also redisplays what you entered before the ? to save you some keystrokes. If you press Enter immediately after the ?, Cisco IOS tries to execute the command with only the parameters you have entered so far.

The information supplied by using help depends on the CLI mode. For example, when ? is entered in user mode, the commands allowed in user mode are displayed, but commands available only in enable mode (not in user mode) are not displayed. Also, help is available in configuration mode, which is the mode used to configure the switch. In fact, configuration mode has many different subconfiguration modes, as explained in the section "Configuration Submodes and Contexts," later in this chapter. So, you can get help for the commands available in each configuration submode as well. (Note that this might be a good time to use the free NetSim Lite product on the DVD—open any lab, use the question mark, and try some commands.)

Cisco IOS stores the commands that you enter in a history buffer, storing ten commands by default. The CLI allows you to move backward and forward in the historical list of commands and then edit the command before reissuing it. These key sequences can help you use the CLI more quickly on the exams. Table 6-3 lists the commands used to manipulate previously entered commands.

Table 6-3   Key Sequences for Command Edit and Recall

Keyboard Command	What Happens
Up arrow or Ctrl+P	This displays the most recently used command. If you press it again, the next most recent command appears, until the history buffer is exhausted. (The P stands for previous.)
Down arrow or Ctrl+N	If you have gone too far back into the history buffer, these keys take you forward to the more recently entered commands. (The N stands for next.)
Left arrow or Ctrl+B	This moves the cursor backward in the currently displayed command without deleting characters. (The B stands for back.)
Right arrow or Ctrl+F	This moves the cursor forward in the currently displayed command without deleting characters. (The F stands for forward.)
Backspace	This moves the cursor backward in the currently displayed command, deleting characters.

The debug and show Commands

By far, the single most popular Cisco IOS command is the **show** command. The **show** command has a large variety of options, and with those options, you can find the status of almost every feature of Cisco IOS. Essentially, the **show** command lists the currently known facts about the switch's operational status. The only work the switch does in reaction to **show** commands is to find the current status and list the information in messages sent to the user.

For example, consider the output from the **show mac address-table dynamic** command listed in Example 6-3. This **show** command, issued from user mode, lists the table the switch uses to make forwarding decisions. A switch's MAC address table basically lists the data a switch uses to do its primary job.

Example 6-3 *Nondefault Basic Configuration*

```
Certskills1> show mac address-table dynamic
           Mac Address Table
-------------------------------------------

Vlan    Mac Address      Type        Ports
----    -----------      --------    -----
  31    0200.1111.1111   DYNAMIC     Gi0/1
  31    0200.3333.3333   DYNAMIC     Fa0/3
  31    1833.9d7b.0e9a   DYNAMIC     Gi0/1
  10    1833.9d7b.0e9a   DYNAMIC     Gi0/1
  10    30f7.0d29.8561   DYNAMIC     Gi0/1
   1    1833.9d7b.0e9a   DYNAMIC     Gi0/1
  12    1833.9d7b.0e9a   DYNAMIC     Gi0/1
Total Mac Addresses for this criterion: 7
Certskills1>
```

The **debug** command also tells the user details about the operation of the switch. However, while the **show** command lists status information at one instant of time—more like a photograph—the **debug** command acts more like a live video camera feed. Once you issue a **debug** command, IOS remembers, issuing messages that any switch user can choose to see. The console sees these messages by default. Most of the commands used throughout this book to verify operation of switches and routers are **show** commands.

Configuring Cisco IOS Software

You will want to configure every switch in an Enterprise network, even though the switches will forward traffic even with default configuration. This section covers the basic configuration processes, including the concept of a configuration file and the locations in which the configuration files can be stored. Although this section focuses on the configuration process, and not on the configuration commands themselves, you should know all the commands covered in this chapter for the exams, in addition to the configuration processes.

Configuration mode is another mode for the Cisco CLI, similar to user mode and privileged mode. User mode lets you issue non-disruptive commands and displays some information. Privileged mode supports a superset of commands compared to user mode, including commands that might disrupt switch operations. However, none of the commands in user or privileged mode changes the switch's configuration. Configuration mode accepts *configuration commands*—commands that tell the switch the details of what to do and how to do it. Figure 6-7 illustrates the relationships among configuration mode, user EXEC mode, and privileged EXEC mode.

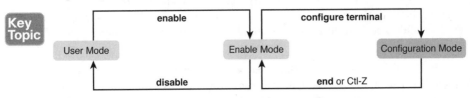

Figure 6-7 *CLI Configuration Mode Versus EXEC Modes*

Commands entered in configuration mode update the active configuration file. *These changes to the configuration occur immediately each time you press the Enter key at the end of a command.* Be careful when you enter a configuration command!

Configuration Submodes and Contexts

Configuration mode itself contains a multitude of commands. To help organize the configuration, IOS groups some kinds of configuration commands together. To do that, when using configuration mode, you move from the initial mode—global configuration mode—into subcommand modes. *Context-setting commands* move you from one configuration subcommand mode, or context, to another. These context-setting commands tell the switch the topic about which you will enter the next few configuration commands. More importantly, the context tells the switch the topic you care about right now, so when you use the **?** to get help, the switch gives you help about that topic only.

> **NOTE**   *Context-setting* is not a Cisco term. It is just a description used here to help make sense of configuration mode.

The best way to learn about configuration submodes is to use them, but first, take a look at these upcoming examples. For instance, the **interface** command is one of the most commonly used context-setting configuration commands. For example, the CLI user could enter interface configuration mode by entering the **interface FastEthernet 0/1** configuration command. Asking for help in interface configuration mode displays only commands that are useful when configuring Ethernet interfaces. Commands used in this context are called *subcommands*—or, in this specific case, *interface subcommands*. When you begin practicing with the CLI with real equipment, the navigation between modes can become natural. For now, consider Example 6-4, which shows the following:

- Movement from enable mode to global configuration mode by using the **configure terminal** EXEC command

- Using a **hostname Fred** global configuration command to configure the switch's name

- Movement from global configuration mode to console line configuration mode (using the **line console 0** command)

- Setting the console's simple password to **hope** (using the **password hope** line subcommand)

- Movement from console configuration mode to interface configuration mode (using the **interface** *type number* command)

- Setting the speed to 100 Mbps for interface Fa0/1 (using the **speed 100** interface subcommand)

- Movement from interface configuration mode back to global configuration mode (using the **exit** command)

Example 6-4   *Navigating Between Different Configuration Modes*

```
Switch# configure terminal
Switch(config)# hostname Fred
Fred(config)# line console 0
Fred(config-line)# password hope
Fred(config-line)# interface FastEthernet 0/1
```

```
Fred(config-if)# speed 100
Fred(config-if)# exit
Fred(config)#
```

The text inside parentheses in the command prompt identifies the configuration mode. For example, the first command prompt after you enter configuration mode lists (config), meaning global configuration mode. After the **line console 0** command, the text expands to (config-line), meaning line configuration mode. Each time the command prompt changes within config mode, you have moved to another configuration mode.

Table 6-4 shows the most common command prompts in configuration mode, the names of those modes, and the context-setting commands used to reach those modes.

Table 6-4   Common Switch Configuration Modes

Prompt	Name of Mode	Context-Setting Command(s) to Reach This Mode
hostname(config)#	Global	None—first mode after **configure terminal**
hostname(config-line)#	Line	**line console 0** **line vty 0 15**
hostname(config-if)#	Interface	**interface** *type number*
hostname(config-vlan)#	VLAN	**vlan** *number*

You should practice until you become comfortable moving between the different configuration modes, back to enable mode, and then back into the configuration modes. However, you can learn these skills just doing labs about the topics in later chapters of the book. For now, Figure 6-8 shows most of the navigation between global configuration mode and the four configuration submodes listed in Table 6-4.

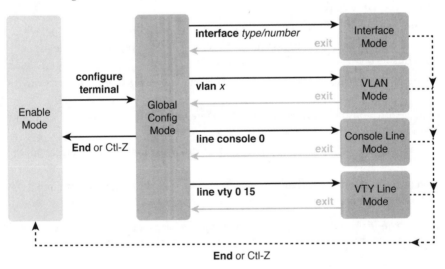

Figure 6-8   *Navigation In and Out of Switch Configuration Modes*

> **NOTE**   You can also move directly from one configuration submode to another, without first using the **exit** command to move back to global configuration mode. Just use the commands listed in bold in the center of the figure.

You really should stop and try navigating around these configuration modes. If you have not yet decided on a lab strategy, spin the DVD in the back of the book, and install the Pearson Sim Lite software. It includes the simulator and a couple of lab exercises. Start any lab, ignore the instructions, and just get into configuration mode and move around between the configuration modes shown in Figure 6-8.

No set rules exist for what commands are global commands or subcommands. Generally, however, when multiple instances of a parameter can be set in a single switch, the command used to set the parameter is likely a configuration subcommand. Items that are set once for the entire switch are likely global commands. For example, the **hostname** command is a global command because there is only one hostname per switch. Conversely, the **speed** command is an interface subcommand that applies to each switch interface that can run at different speeds, so it is a subcommand, applying to the particular interface under which it is configured.

Storing Switch Configuration Files

When you configure a switch, it needs to use the configuration. It also needs to be able to retain the configuration in case the switch loses power. Cisco switches contain random-access memory (RAM) to store data while Cisco IOS is using it, but RAM loses its contents when the switch loses power or is reloaded. To store information that must be retained when the switch loses power or is reloaded, Cisco switches use several types of more permanent memory, none of which has any moving parts. By avoiding components with moving parts (such as traditional disk drives), switches can maintain better uptime and availability.

The following list details the four main types of memory found in Cisco switches, as well as the most common use of each type:

- **RAM:** Sometimes called DRAM, for dynamic random-access memory, RAM is used by the switch just as it is used by any other computer: for working storage. The running (active) configuration file is stored here.

- **Flash memory:** Either a chip inside the switch or a removable memory card, flash memory stores fully functional Cisco IOS images and is the default location where the switch gets its Cisco IOS at boot time. Flash memory also can be used to store any other files, including backup copies of configuration files.

- **ROM:** Read-only memory (ROM) stores a bootstrap (or boothelper) program that is loaded when the switch first powers on. This bootstrap program then finds the full Cisco IOS image and manages the process of loading Cisco IOS into RAM, at which point Cisco IOS takes over operation of the switch.

- **NVRAM:** Nonvolatile RAM (NVRAM) stores the initial or startup configuration file that is used when the switch is first powered on and when the switch is reloaded.

Figure 6-9 summarizes this same information in a briefer and more convenient form for memorization and study.

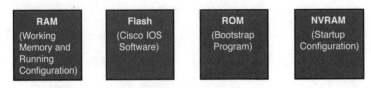

Figure 6-9 *Cisco Switch Memory Types*

Cisco IOS stores the collection of configuration commands in a *configuration file*. In fact, switches use multiple configuration files—one file for the initial configuration used when powering on, and another configuration file for the active, currently used running configuration as stored in RAM. Table 6-5 lists the names of these two files, their purpose, and their storage location.

Table 6-5   Names and Purposes of the Two Main Cisco IOS Configuration Files

Configuration Filename	Purpose	Where It Is Stored
startup-config	Stores the initial configuration used anytime the switch reloads Cisco IOS.	NVRAM
running-config	Stores the currently used configuration commands. This file changes dynamically when someone enters commands in configuration mode.	RAM

Essentially, when you use configuration mode, you change only the running-config file. This means that the configuration example earlier in this chapter (Example 6-4) updates only the running-config file. However, if the switch lost power right after that example, all that configuration would be lost. If you want to keep that configuration, you have to copy the running-config file into NVRAM, overwriting the old startup-config file.

Example 6-5 demonstrates that commands used in configuration mode change only the running configuration in RAM. The example shows the following concepts and steps:

Step 1.   The example begins with both the running and startup-config having the same hostname, per the **hostname hannah** command.

Step 2.   The hostname is changed in configuration mode using the **hostname jessie** command.

Step 3.   The **show running-config** and **show startup-config** commands show the fact that the hostnames are now different, with the **hostname jessie** command found only in the running-config.

Example 6-5 *How Configuration Mode Commands Change the Running-Config File, Not the Startup-Config File*

```
! Step 1 next (two commands)
!                (
hannah# show running-config
! (lines omitted)
hostname hannah
! (rest of lines omitted)
```

```
hannah# show startup-config
! (lines omitted)
hostname hannah
! (rest of lines omitted)
! Step 2 next. Notice that the command prompt changes immediately after
! the hostname command.

hannah# configure terminal
hannah(config)# hostname jessie
jessie(config)# exit
! Step 3 next (two commands)
!
jessie# show running-config
! (lines omitted) - just showing the part with the hostname command
hostname jessie
!
jessie# show startup-config
! (lines omitted) - just showing the part with the hostname command
hostname hannah
```

Copying and Erasing Configuration Files

The configuration process updates the running-config file, which is lost if the router loses power or is reloaded. Clearly, IOS needs to provide us a way to copy the running configuration so that it will not be lost, so it will be used the next time the switch reloads or powers on. For instance, Example 6-5 ended with a different running configuration (with the **hostname jessie** command) versus the startup configuration.

In short, the EXEC command **copy running-config startup-config** backs up the running-config to the startup-config file. This command overwrites the current startup-config file with what is currently in the running-configuration file.

In addition, in lab, you may want to just get rid of all existing configuration and start over with a clean configuration. To do that, you can erase the startup-config file using three different commands:

```
write erase
erase startup-config
erase nvram:
```

Once the startup-config file is erased, you can reload or power off/on the switch, and it will boot with the now-empty startup configuration.

Note that Cisco IOS does not have a command that erases the contents of the running-config file. To clear out the running-config file, simply erase the startup-config file, and then **reload** the switch, and the running-config will be empty at the end of the process.

> **NOTE**   Cisco uses the term *reload* to refer to what most PC operating systems call rebooting or restarting. In each case, it is a re-initialization of the software. The **reload** EXEC command causes a switch to reload.

Chapter Review

One key to doing well on the exams is to perform repetitive spaced review sessions. Review this chapter's material using either the tools in the book, DVD, or interactive tools for the same material found on the book's companion website. Refer to the "Your Study Plan" element section titled "Step 2: Build Your Study Habits Around the Chapter" for more details. Table 6-6 outlines the key review elements and where you can find them. To better track your study progress, record when you completed these activities in the second column.

Table 6-6   Chapter Review Tracking

Review Element	Review Date(s)	Resource Used
Review key topics		Book, DVD/website
Review key terms		Book, DVD/website
Repeat DIKTA questions		Book, PCPT
Review memory tables		Book, DVD/website
Review command tables		Book

Review All the Key Topics

Table 6-7   Key Topics for Chapter 6

Key Topic Element	Description	Page Number
Figure 6-2	Three methods to access a switch CLI	130
Figure 6-3	Cabling options for a console connection	130
List	A Cisco switch's default console port settings	132
Figure 6-7	Navigation between user, enable, and global config modes	138
Table 6-4	A list of configuration mode prompts, the name of the configuration mode, and the command used to reach each mode	140
Figure 6-8	Configuration mode context-setting commands	140
Table 6-5	The names and purposes of the two configuration files in a switch or router	142

Key Terms You Should Know

command-line interface (CLI), Telnet, Secure Shell (SSH), enable mode, user mode, configuration mode, startup-config file, running-config file

Command References

Tables 6-8 and 6-9 list configuration and verification commands used in this chapter, respectively. As an easy review exercise, cover the left column in a table, read the right column, and try to recall the command without looking. Then repeat the exercise, covering the right column, and try to recall what the command does.

Table 6-8   Chapter 6 Configuration Commands

Command	Mode and Purpose
line console 0	Global command that changes the context to console configuration mode.
login	Line (console and vty) configuration mode. Tells IOS to prompt for a password (no username).
password *pass-value*	Line (console and vty) configuration mode. Sets the password required on that line for login if the **login** command (with no other parameters) is also configured.
interface *type port-number*	Global command that changes the context to interface mode—for example, **interface FastEthernet 0/1**.
hostname *name*	Global command that sets this switch's hostname, which is also used as the first part of the switch's command prompt.
exit	Moves back to the next higher mode in configuration mode.
end	Exits configuration mode and goes back to enable mode from any of the configuration submodes.
Ctrl+Z	This is not a command, but rather a two-key combination (pressing the Ctrl key and the letter Z) that together do the same thing as the **end** command.

Table 6-9   Chapter 6 EXEC Command Reference

Command	Purpose
no debug all undebug all	Enable mode EXEC command to disable all currently enabled debugs.
reload	Enable mode EXEC command that reboots the switch or router.
copy running-config startup-config	Enable mode EXEC command that saves the active config, replacing the startup-config file used when the switch initializes.
copy startup-config running-config	Enable mode EXEC command that merges the startup-config file with the currently active config file in RAM.
show running-config	Lists the contents of the running-config file.
write erase erase startup-config erase nvram:	These enable mode EXEC commands erase the startup-config file.
quit	EXEC command that disconnects the user from the CLI session.
show startup-config	Lists the contents of the startup-config (initial config) file.
enable	Moves the user from user mode to enable (privileged) mode and prompts for a password if one is configured.
disable	Moves the user from enable mode to user mode.
configure terminal	Enable mode command that moves the user into configuration mode.

6

CHAPTER 7

Analyzing Ethernet LAN Switching

This chapter covers the following exam topics:

2.0 LAN Switching Technologies

2.1 Describe and verify switching concepts

2.1.a MAC learning and aging

2.1.b Frame switching

2.1.c Frame flooding

2.1.d MAC address table

When you buy a Cisco Catalyst Ethernet switch, the switch is ready to work. All you have to do is take it out of the box, power on the switch by connecting the power cable to the switch and a power outlet, and connect hosts to the switch using the correct unshielded twisted-pair (UTP) cables. You do not have to configure anything else, you do not have to connect to the console and login, or do anything: the switch just starts forwarding Ethernet frames.

In Part II of this book, you will learn how to build, configure, and verify the operation of Ethernet LANs. In Chapter 6, "Using the Command-Line Interface," you learned some skills so you know how to connect to a switch's CLI, move around in the CLI, issue commands, and configure the switch. The next step—this chapter—takes a short but important step in that journey by explaining the logic a switch uses when forwarding Ethernet frames.

This chapter has two major sections. The first reviews the concepts behind LAN switching, which were first introduced back in Chapter 2, "Fundamentals of Ethernet LANs." The second section of this chapter then uses IOS show commands to verify that Cisco switches actually learned the MAC addresses, built its MAC address table, and forwarded frames.

"Do I Know This Already?" Quiz

Take the quiz (either here, or use the PCPT software) if you want to use the score to help you decide how much time to spend on this chapter. The answers are at the bottom of the page following the quiz, and the explanations are in DVD Appendix C and in the PCPT software.

Table 7-1 "Do I Know This Already?" Foundation Topics Section-to-Question Mapping

Foundation Topics Section	Questions
LAN Switching Concepts	1–4
Verifying and Analyzing Ethernet Switching	5–6

1. Which of the following statements describes part of the process of how a switch decides to forward a frame destined for a known unicast MAC address?

   a. It compares the unicast destination address to the bridging, or MAC address, table.

   b. It compares the unicast source address to the bridging, or MAC address, table.

   c. It forwards the frame out all interfaces in the same VLAN except for the incoming interface.

   d. It compares the destination IP address to the destination MAC address.

   e. It compares the frame's incoming interface to the source MAC entry in the MAC address table.

2. Which of the following statements describes part of the process of how a LAN switch decides to forward a frame destined for a broadcast MAC address?

   a. It compares the unicast destination address to the bridging, or MAC address, table.

   b. It compares the unicast source address to the bridging, or MAC address, table.

   c. It forwards the frame out all interfaces in the same VLAN except for the incoming interface.

   d. It compares the destination IP address to the destination MAC address.

   e. It compares the frame's incoming interface to the source MAC entry in the MAC address table.

3. Which of the following statements best describes what a switch does with a frame destined for an unknown unicast address?

   a. It forwards out all interfaces in the same VLAN except for the incoming interface.

   b. It forwards the frame out the one interface identified by the matching entry in the MAC address table.

   c. It compares the destination IP address to the destination MAC address.

   d. It compares the frame's incoming interface to the source MAC entry in the MAC address table.

4. Which of the following comparisons does a switch make when deciding whether a new MAC address should be added to its MAC address table?

   a. It compares the unicast destination address to the bridging, or MAC address, table.

   b. It compares the unicast source address to the bridging, or MAC address, table.

   c. It compares the VLAN ID to the bridging, or MAC address, table.

   d. It compares the destination IP address's ARP cache entry to the bridging, or MAC address, table.

5. A Cisco Catalyst switch has 24 10/100 ports, numbered 0/1 through 0/24. Ten PCs connect to the ten lowest numbered port, with those PCs working and sending data over the network. The other ports are not connected to any device. Which of the following answers lists facts displayed by the **show interfaces status** command?

  a. Port Ethernet 0/1 is in a connected state.

  b. Port Fast Ethernet 0/11 is in a connected state.

  c. Port Fast Ethernet 0/5 is in a connected state.

  d. Port Ethernet 0/15 is in a notconnected state.

6. Consider the following output from a Cisco Catalyst switch:

```
SW1# show mac address-table dynamic
          Mac Address Table
-------------------------------------------

Vlan    Mac Address     Type        Ports
----    -----------     --------    -----
   1    02AA.AAAA.AAAA  DYNAMIC     Gi0/1
   1    02BB.BBBB.BBBB  DYNAMIC     Gi0/2
   1    02CC.CCCC.CCCC  DYNAMIC     Gi0/3
Total Mac Addresses for this criterion: 3
```

Which of the following answers are true about this switch?

  a. The output proves that port Gi0/2 connects directly to a device that uses address 02BB.BBBB.BBBB.

  b. The switch has learned three MAC addresses since the switch powered on.

  c. The three listed MAC addresses were learned based on the destination MAC address of frames forwarded by the switch.

  d. 02CC.CCCC.CCCC was learned from the source MAC address of a frame that entered port Gi0/3.

Foundation Topics

LAN Switching Concepts

A modern Ethernet LAN connects user devices as well as servers into some switches, with the switches then connecting to each other, sometimes in a design like Figure 7-1. Part of the LAN, called a campus LAN, supports the end user population as shown on the left of the figure. End user devices connect to LAN switches, which in turn connect to other switches so that a path exists to the rest of the network. The campus LAN switches sit in wiring closets close to the end users. On the right, the servers used to provide information to the users also connects to the LAN. Those servers and switches often sit in a closed room called a *data center*, with connections to the campus LAN to support traffic to/from the users.

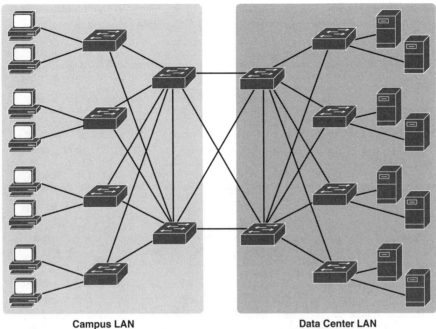

Figure 7-1   *Campus LAN and Data Center LAN, Conceptual Drawing*

To forward traffic from a user device to a server and back, each switch performs the same kind of logic, independently from each other. The first half of this chapter examines the logic: how a switch chooses to forward an Ethernet frame, when the switch chooses to not forward the frame, and so on.

Overview of Switching Logic

Ultimately, the role of a LAN switch is to forward Ethernet frames. LANs exist as a set of user devices, servers, and other devices that connect to switches, with the switches connected to each other. The LAN switch has one primary job: to forward frames to the correct destination (MAC) address. And to achieve that goal, switches use logic—logic based on the source and destination MAC address in each frame's Ethernet header.

LAN switches receive Ethernet frames and then make a switching decision: either forward the frame out some other ports or ignore the frame. To accomplish this primary mission, switches perform three actions:

1. Deciding when to forward a frame or when to filter (not forward) a frame, based on the destination MAC address

2. Preparing to forward frames by learning MAC addresses by examining the source MAC address of each frame received by the switch

3. Preparing to forward only one copy of the frame to the destination by creating a (Layer 2) loop-free environment with other switches by using Spanning Tree Protocol (STP)

The first action is the switch's primary job, whereas the other two items are overhead functions.

> **NOTE** Throughout this book's discussion of LAN switches, the terms *switch port* and *switch interface* are synonymous.

Although Chapter 2's section titled "Ethernet Data-Link Protocols" already discussed the frame format, this discussion of Ethernet switching is pretty important, so reviewing the Ethernet frame at this point might be helpful. Figure 7-2 shows one popular format for an Ethernet frame. Basically, a switch would take the frame shown in the figure, make a decision of where to forward the frame, and send the frame out that other interface.

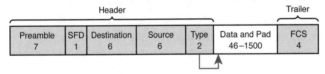

Figure 7-2 *IEEE 802.3 Ethernet Frame (One Variation)*

Most of the upcoming discussions and figures about Ethernet switching focuses on the use of the destination and source MAC address fields in the header. All Ethernet frames have both a destination and source MAC address. Both are 6-bytes long (represented as 12 hex digits in the book), and are a key part of the switching logic discussed in this section. Refer back to Chapter 2's discussion of the header in detail for more info on the rest of the Ethernet frame.

> **NOTE** The companion DVD and website include a video that explains the basics of Ethernet switching.

Now on to the details of how Ethernet switching works!

Forwarding Known Unicast Frames

To decide whether to forward a frame, a switch uses a dynamically built table that lists MAC addresses and outgoing interfaces. Switches compare the frame's destination MAC address to this table to decide whether the switch should forward a frame or simply ignore it. For example, consider the simple network shown in Figure 7-3, with Fred sending a frame to Barney.

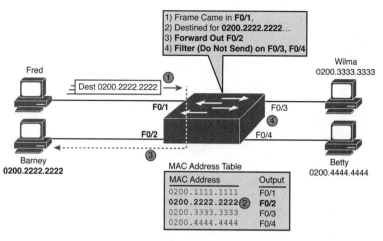

Figure 7-3   *Sample Switch Forwarding and Filtering Decision*

In this figure, Fred sends a frame with destination address 0200.2222.2222 (Barney's MAC address). The switch compares the destination MAC address (0200.2222.2222) to the MAC address table, matching the bold table entry. That matched table entry tells the switch to forward the frame out port F0/2, and only port F0/2.

NOTE   A switch's MAC address table is also called the *switching table*, or *bridging table*, or even the *Content-Addressable Memory (CAM) table*, in reference to the type of physical memory used to store the table.

A switch's MAC address table lists the location of each MAC relative to that one switch. In LANs with multiple switches, each switch makes an independent forwarding decision based on its own MAC address table. Together, they forward the frame so that it eventually arrives at the destination.

For example, Figure 7-4 shows the first switching decision in a case in which Fred sends a frame to Wilma, with destination MAC 0200.3333.3333. The topology has changed versus the previous figure, this time with two switches, and Fred and Wilma connected to two different switches. Figure 7-3 shows the first switch's logic, in reaction to Fred sending the original frame. Basically, the switch receives the frame in port F0/1, finds the destination MAC (0200.3333.3333) in the MAC address table, sees the outgoing port of G0/1, so SW1 forwards the frame out its G0/1 port.

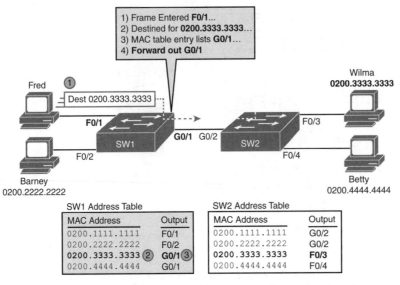

Figure 7-4 *Forwarding Decision with Two Switches: First Switch*

That same frame next arrives at switch SW2, entering SW2's G0/2 interface. As shown in Figure 7-5, SW2 uses the same logic steps, but using SW2's table. The MAC table lists the forwarding instructions for that switch only. In this case, switch SW2 forwards the frame out its F0/3 port, based on SW2's MAC address table.

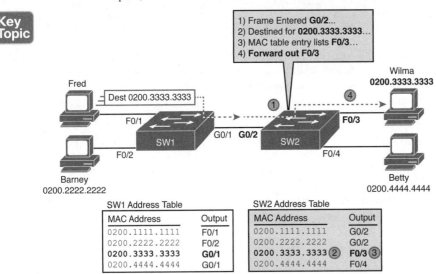

Figure 7-5 *Forwarding Decision with Two Switches: Second Switch*

NOTE The forwarding choice by a switch was formerly called a *forward-versus-filter* decision, because the switch also chooses to not forward (to filter) frames, not sending the frame out some ports.

The examples so far use switches that happen to have a MAC table with all the MAC addresses listed. As a result, the destination MAC address in the frame is known to the switch. The frames are called known unicast frames, or simply known unicasts, because the destination address is a unicast address, and the destination is known. As shown in these examples, switches forward known unicast frames out one port: the port as listed in the MAC table entry for that MAC address.

Learning MAC Addresses

Thankfully, the networking staff does not have to type in all those MAC table entries. Instead, the switches do their second main function: to learn the MAC addresses and inter-faces to put into its address table. With a complete MAC address table, the switch can make accurate forwarding and filtering decisions as just discussed.

Switches build the address table by listening to incoming frames and examining the *source MAC address* in the frame. If a frame enters the switch and the source MAC address is not in the MAC address table, the switch creates an entry in the table. That table entry lists the interface from which the frame arrived. Switch learning logic is that simple.

Figure 7-6 depicts the same single-switch topology network as Figure 7-3, but before the switch has built any address table entries. The figure shows the first two frames sent in this network—first a frame from Fred, addressed to Barney, and then Barney's response, addressed to Fred.

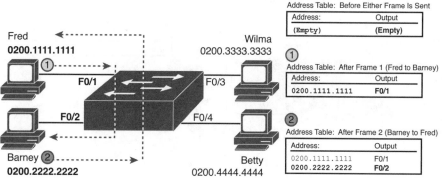

Figure 7-6 *Switch Learning: Empty Table and Adding Two Entries*

(Figure 7-6 depicts the MAC learning process only, and ignores the forwarding process and therefore ignores the destination MAC addresses.)

Focus on the learning process and how the MAC table grows at each step as shown on the right side of the figure. The switch begins with an empty MAC table, as shown in the upper right part of the figure. Then Fred sends his first frame (labeled "1") to Barney, so the switch adds an entry for 0200.1111.1111, Fred's MAC address, associated with interface F0/1. Why F0/1? The frame sent by Fred entered the switch's F0/1 port. SW1's logic runs something like this: "The source is MAC 0200.1111.1111, the frame entered F0/1, so from my perspective, 0200.1111.1111 must be reachable out my port F0/1."

Continuing the example, when Barney replies in Step 2, the switch adds a second entry, this one for 0200.2222.2222, Barney's MAC address, along with interface F0/2. Why F0/2? The frame Barney sent entered the switch's F0/2 interface. Learning always occurs by looking at the source MAC address in the frame, and adds the incoming interface as the associated port.

Flooding Unknown Unicast and Broadcast Frames

Now again turn your attention to the forwarding process, using the topology in Figure 7-5. What do you suppose the switch does with Fred's first frame, the one that occurred when there were no entries in the MAC address table? As it turns out, when there is no matching entry in the table, switches forward the frame out all interfaces (except the incoming interface) using a process called *flooding*. And the frame whose destination address is unknown to the switch is called an *unknown unicast frame*, or simply an *unknown unicast*.

Switches flood unknown unicast frames. Flooding means that the switch forwards copies of the frame out all ports, except the port on which the frame was received. The idea is simple: if you do not know where to send it, send it everywhere, to deliver the frame. And, by the way, that device will likely then send a reply—and then the switch can learn that device's MAC address, and forward future frames out one port as a known unicast frame.

Switches also flood LAN broadcast frames (frames destined to the Ethernet broadcast address of FFFF.FFFF.FFFF), because this process helps deliver a copy of the frame to all devices in the LAN.

For example, Figure 7-7 shows the same first frame sent by Fred, when the switch's MAC table is empty. At step 1, Fred sends the frame. At step 2, the switch sends a copy of the frame out all three of the other interfaces.

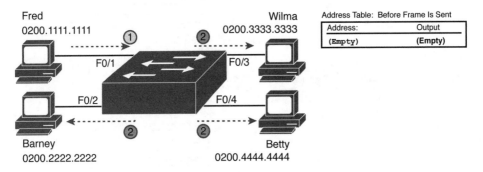

Figure 7-7 *Switch Flooding: Unknown Unicast Arrives, Floods out Other Ports*

Avoiding Loops Using Spanning Tree Protocol

The third primary feature of LAN switches is loop prevention, as implemented by Spanning Tree Protocol (STP). Without STP, any flooded frames would loop for an indefinite period of time in Ethernet networks with physically redundant links. To prevent looping frames, STP blocks some ports from forwarding frames so that only one active path exists between any pair of LAN segments.

The result of STP is good: Frames do not loop infinitely, which makes the LAN usable. However, STP has negative features as well, including the fact that it takes some work to balance traffic across the redundant alternate links.

A simple example makes the need for STP more obvious. Remember, switches flood unknown unicast frames and broadcast frames. Figure 7-8 shows an unknown unicast frame, sent by Larry to Bob, which loops forever because the network has redundancy but no STP. Note that the figure shows one direction of the looping frame only, just to reduce clutter, but a copy of the frame would also loop the other direction as well.

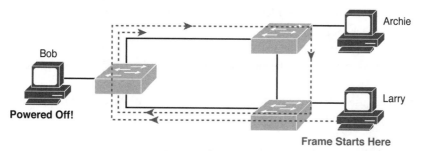

Figure 7-8   *Network with Redundant Links but Without STP: The Frame Loops Forever*

The flooding of this frame would cause the frame to rotate around the three switches, because none of the switches list Bob's MAC address in their address tables, each switch floods the frame. And while the flooding process is a good mechanism for forwarding unknown unicasts and broadcasts, the continual flooding of traffic frames as in the figure can completely congest the LAN to the point of making it unusable.

A topology like Figure 7-8, with redundant links, is good, but we need to prevent the bad effect of those looping frames. To avoid Layer 2 loops, all switches need to use STP. STP causes each interface on a switch to settle into either a blocking state or a forwarding state. *Blocking* means that the interface cannot forward or receive data frames, while *forwarding* means that the interface can send and receive data frames. If a correct subset of the interfaces is blocked, only a single currently active logical path exists between each pair of LANs.

> **NOTE**   STP behaves identically for a transparent bridge and a switch. Therefore, the terms *bridge*, *switch*, and *bridging device* all are used interchangeably when discussing STP.

The *Cisco CCNA Routing and Switching ICND2 200-105 Official Cert Guide* book covers the details of how STP prevents loops.

LAN Switching Summary

Switches use Layer 2 logic, examining the Ethernet data-link header to choose how to process frames. In particular, switches make decisions to forward and filter frames, learn MAC addresses, and use STP to avoid loops, as follows:

Step 1.   Switches forward frames based on the destination MAC address:

    A. If the destination MAC address is a broadcast, multicast, or unknown destination unicast (a unicast not listed in the MAC table), the switch floods the frame.

    B. If the destination MAC address is a known unicast address (a unicast address found in the MAC table):

        i. If the outgoing interface listed in the MAC address table is different from the interface in which the frame was received, the switch forwards the frame out the outgoing interface.

      ii. If the outgoing interface is the same as the interface in which the frame was received, the switch filters the frame, meaning that the switch simply ignores the frame and does not forward it.

Step 2.   Switches use the following logic to learn MAC address table entries:

      A. For each received frame, examine the source MAC address and note the interface from which the frame was received.

      B. If it is not already in the table, add the MAC address and interface it was learned on.

Step 3.   Switches use STP to prevent loops by causing some interfaces to block, meaning that they do not send or receive frames.

Verifying and Analyzing Ethernet Switching

A Cisco Catalyst switch comes from the factory ready to switch frames. All you have to do is connect the power cable, plug in the Ethernet cables, and the switch starts switching incoming frames. Connect multiple switches together, and they are ready to forward frames between the switches as well. And the big reason behind this default behavior has to do with the default settings on the switches.

Cisco Catalyst switches come ready to get busy switching frames because of settings like these:

- The interfaces are enabled by default, ready to start working once a cable is connected.
- All interfaces are assigned to VLAN 1.
- 10/100 and 10/100/1000 interfaces use autonegotiation by default.
- The MAC learning, forwarding, flooding logic all works by default.
- STP is enabled by default.

This second section of the chapter examines how switches will work with these default settings, showing how to verify the Ethernet learning and forwarding process.

Demonstrating MAC Learning

To see a switches MAC address table, use the **show mac address-table** command. With no additional parameters, this command lists all known MAC addresses in the MAC table, including some overhead static MAC addresses that you can ignore. To see all the dynamically learned MAC addresses only, instead use the **show mac address-table dynamic** command.

The examples in this chapter use almost no configuration, as if you just unboxed the switch when you first purchased it. For the examples, the switches have no configuration other than the **hostname** command to set a meaningful hostname. Note that to do this in lab, all I did was

- Use the **erase startup-config** EXEC command to erase the startup-config file
- Use the **delete vlan.dat** EXEC command to delete the VLAN configuration details
- Use the **reload** EXEC command to reload the switch (thereby using the empty startup-config, with no VLAN information configured)
- Configure the **hostname SW1** command to set the switch hostname

Once done, the switch starts forwarding and learning MAC address, as demonstrated in Example 7-1.

Example 7-1   show mac address-table dynamic *for Figure 7-7*

```
SW1# show mac address-table dynamic
          Mac Address Table
-------------------------------------------


Vlan    Mac Address      Type       Ports
----    -----------      --------   -----
   1    0200.1111.1111   DYNAMIC    Fa0/1
   1    0200.2222.2222   DYNAMIC    Fa0/2
   1    0200.3333.3333   DYNAMIC    Fa0/3
   1    0200.4444.4444   DYNAMIC    Fa0/4
Total Mac Addresses for this criterion: 4
SW1#
```

First, focus on two columns of the table: the Mac Address and Ports columns of the table. The values should look familiar: they match the earlier single-switch example, as repeated here as Figure 7-9. Note the four MAC addresses listed, along with their matching ports, as shown in the figure.

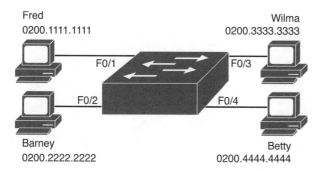

Figure 7-9   *Single Switch Topology Used in Verification Section*

Next, look at the Type field in the header. The column tells us whether the MAC address was learned by the switch as described earlier in this chapter. You can also statically pre-define MAC table entries using a couple of different features, including port security, and those would appear as Static in the Type column.

Finally, the VLAN column of the output gives us a chance to briefly discuss how VLANs impact switching logic. LAN switches forward Ethernet frames inside a VLAN. What that means is if a frame enters via a port in VLAN 1, then the switch will forward or flood that frame out other ports in VLAN 1 only, and not out any ports that happen to be assigned to another VLAN. Chapter 11, "Implementing Ethernet Virtual LANs," looks at all the details of how switches forward frames when using VLANs.

Switch Interfaces

The first example assumes that you installed the switch and cabling correctly, and that the switch interfaces work. Once you do the installation and connect to the Console, you can easily check the status of those interfaces with the **show interfaces status** command, as shown in Example 7-2.

Example 7-2   show interfaces status *on Switch SW1*

```
SW1# show interfaces status

Port        Name              Status        Vlan     Duplex  Speed Type
Fa0/1                         connected     1        a-full  a-100 10/100BaseTX
Fa0/2                         connected     1        a-full  a-100 10/100BaseTX
Fa0/3                         connected     1        a-full  a-100 10/100BaseTX
Fa0/4                         connected     1        a-full  a-100 10/100BaseTX
Fa0/5                         notconnect    1        auto    auto  10/100BaseTX
Fa0/6                         notconnect    1        auto    auto  10/100BaseTX
Fa0/7                         notconnect    1        auto    auto  10/100BaseTX
Fa0/8                         notconnect    1        auto    auto  10/100BaseTX
Fa0/9                         notconnect    1        auto    auto  10/100BaseTX
Fa0/10                        notconnect    1        auto    auto  10/100BaseTX
Fa0/11                        notconnect    1        auto    auto  10/100BaseTX
Fa0/12                        notconnect    1        auto    auto  10/100BaseTX
Fa0/13                        notconnect    1        auto    auto  10/100BaseTX
Fa0/14                        notconnect    1        auto    auto  10/100BaseTX
Fa0/15                        notconnect    1        auto    auto  10/100BaseTX
Fa0/16                        notconnect    1        auto    auto  10/100BaseTX
Fa0/17                        notconnect    1        auto    auto  10/100BaseTX
Fa0/18                        notconnect    1        auto    auto  10/100BaseTX
Fa0/19                        notconnect    1        auto    auto  10/100BaseTX
Fa0/20                        notconnect    1        auto    auto  10/100BaseTX
Fa0/21                        notconnect    1        auto    auto  10/100BaseTX
Fa0/22                        notconnect    1        auto    auto  10/100BaseTX
Fa0/23                        notconnect    1        auto    auto  10/100BaseTX
Fa0/24                        notconnect    1        auto    auto  10/100BaseTX
Gi0/1                         notconnect    1        auto    auto  10/100/1000BaseTX
Gi0/2                         notconnect    1        auto    auto  10/100/1000BaseTX
SW1#
```

Focus on the port column for a moment. As a reminder, Cisco Catalyst switches name their ports based on the fastest specification supported, so in this case, the switch has 24 interfaces named Fast Ethernet, and two named Gigabit Ethernet. Many commands abbreviate those terms, this time as Fa for Fast Ethernet and Gi for Gigabit Ethernet. (The example happens to come from a Cisco Catalyst switch that has 24 10/100 ports and two 10/100/1000 ports.)

The Status column of course tells us the status or state of the port. In this case, the lab switch had cables and devices connected to ports F0/1–F0/4 only, with no other cables connected. As a result, those first four ports have a state of connected, meaning that the ports have a cable and are functional. The notconnect state means that the port is not yet functioning. It may mean that there is no cable installed, but other problems may exist as well. (The section "Analyzing Switch Interface Status and Statistics," in Chapter 12, "Troubleshooting Ethernet LANs," works through the details of what causes a switch interface to fail.)

> **NOTE**   You can see the status for a single interface in a couple of ways. For instance, for F0/1, the command **show interfaces f0/1 status** lists the status in a single line of output as in Example 7-2. The **show interfaces f0/1** command (without the status keyword) displays a detailed set of messages about the interface.

The **show interfaces** command has a large number of options. One particular option, the **counters** option, lists statistics about incoming and outgoing frames on the interfaces. In particular, it lists the number of unicast, multicast, and broadcast frames both the in and out direction, and a total byte count for those frames. Example 7-3 shows an example, again for interface F0/1.

Example 7-3   show interfaces f0/1 counters *on Switch SW1*

```
SW1# show interfaces f0/1 counters

Port            InOctets    InUcastPkts   InMcastPkts   InBcastPkts
Fa0/1            1223303          10264           107            18


Port            OutOctets   OutUcastPkts  OutMcastPkts  OutBcastPkts
Fa0/1            3235055          13886         22940           437
```

Finding Entries in the MAC Address Table

With a single switch and only four hosts connected to them, you can just read the details of the MAC address table and find the information you want to see. However, in real networks, with lots of interconnected hosts and switches, just reading the output to find one MAC address can be hard to do. You might have hundreds of entries—page after page of output—with each MAC address looking like a random string of hex characters. (The MAC addresses used in the examples in this book are configured to make it easier to learn.)

Thankfully, Cisco IOS supplies several more options on the **show mac address-table** command to make it easier to find individual entries. First, if you know the MAC address, you can search for it—just type in the MAC address at the end of the command, as shown in Example 7-4. All you have to do is include the **address** keyword, followed by the actual MAC address. If the address exists, the output lists the address. Note that the output lists the exact same information in the exact same format, but it lists only the line for the matching MAC address.

Example 7-4   show mac address-table dynamic *with the* address *Keyword*

```
SW1# show mac address-table dynamic address 0200.1111.1111
          Mac Address Table
-------------------------------------------
```

```
Vlan    Mac Address      Type      Ports
----    -----------      --------  -----
   1    0200.1111.1111   DYNAMIC   Fa0/1
Total Mac Addresses for this criterion: 1
```

While useful, often times the engineer troubleshooting a problem does not know the MAC addresses of the devices connected to the network. Instead, the engineer has a topology diagram, knowing which switch ports connect to other switches and which connect to endpoint devices.

Sometimes you might be troubleshooting while looking at a network topology diagram, and want to look at all the MAC addresses learned off a particular port. IOS supplies that option with the **show mac address-table dynamic interface** command. Example 7-5 shows one example, for switch SW1's F0/1 interface.

Example 7-5 show mac address-table dynamic *with the* interface *Keyword*

```
SW1# show mac address-table dynamic interface fastEthernet 0/1
          Mac Address Table
-------------------------------------------

Vlan    Mac Address      Type      Ports
----    -----------      --------  -----
   1    0200.1111.1111   DYNAMIC   Fa0/1
Total Mac Addresses for this criterion: 1
```

Finally, you may also want to find the MAC address table entries for one VLAN. You guessed it—you can add the **vlan** parameter, followed by the VLAN number. Example 7-6 shows two such examples from the same switch SW1 from Figure 7-7—one for VLAN 1, where all four devices reside, and one for a non-existent VLAN 2.

Example 7-6 *The* show mac address-table vlan *command*

```
SW1# show mac address-table dynamic vlan 1
          Mac Address Table
-------------------------------------------

Vlan    Mac Address      Type      Ports
----    -----------      --------  -----
   1    0200.1111.1111   DYNAMIC   Fa0/1
   1    0200.2222.2222   DYNAMIC   Fa0/2
   1    0200.3333.3333   DYNAMIC   Fa0/3
   1    0200.4444.4444   DYNAMIC   Fa0/4
Total Mac Addresses for this criterion: 4
SW1#
SW1# show mac address-table dynamic vlan 2
          Mac Address Table
-------------------------------------------
```

```
Vlan    Mac Address      Type        Ports
----    -----------      --------    -----
SW1#
```

Managing the MAC Address Table (Aging, Clearing)

This chapter closes with a few comments about how switches manage their MAC address tables. Switches do learn MAC addresses, but those MAC addresses do not remain in the table indefinitely. The switch will remove the entries due to age, due to the table filling, and you can remove entries using a command.

First, for aging out MAC table entries, switches remove entries that have not been used for a defined number of seconds (default of 300 seconds on many switches). To do that, switches look at every incoming frame, every source MAC address, and does something related to learning. If it is a new MAC address, the switch adds the correct entry to the table of course. However, if that entry already exists, the switch still does something: it resets the inactivity timer back to 0 for that entry. Each entry's timer counts upward over time to measure how long the entry has been in the table. The switch times out (removes) any entries whose timer reaches the defined aging time.

Example 7-7 shows the aging timer setting for the entire switch. The aging time can be configured to a different time, globally and per-vlan.

Example 7-7 *The MAC Address Default Aging Timer Displayed*

```
SW1# show mac address-table aging-time
Global Aging Time:   300
Vlan     Aging Time
----     ----------
SW1#


SW1# show mac address-table count


Mac Entries for Vlan 1:
--------------------------
Dynamic Address Count  : 4
Static  Address Count  : 0
Total Mac Addresses    : 4


Total Mac Address Space Available: 7299
```

Each switch also removes the oldest table entries, even if they are younger than the aging time setting, if the table fills. The MAC address table uses content-addressable memory (CAM), a physical memory that has great table lookup capabilities. However, the size of the table depends on the size of the CAM in a particular model of switch. When a switch tries to add a new table entry, and finds the table full, the switch times out (removes) the oldest table entry to make space. For perspective, the end of Example 7-7 lists the size of a Cisco Catalyst switch's MAC table at about 8000 entries—the same four existing entries from the earlier examples, with space for 7299 more.

Finally, you can remove the dynamic entries from the MAC address table with the **clear mac address-table dynamic** command. Note that the show commands in this chapter can be executed from user and enable mode, but the clear command happens to be a privileged mode command.

MAC Address Tables with Multiple Switches

Finally, to complete the discussion, it helps to think about an example with multiple switches, just to emphasize how MAC learning, forwarding, and flooding happens independently on each LAN switch.

Consider the topology in Figure 7-10, and pay close attention to the port numbers. The ports were purposefully chosen so that neither switch used any of the same ports for this example. That is, switch SW2 does have a port F0/1 and F0/2, but I did not plug any devices into those ports when making this example. Also note that all ports are in VLAN 1, and as with the other examples in this chapter, all default configuration is used other than the hostname on the switches.

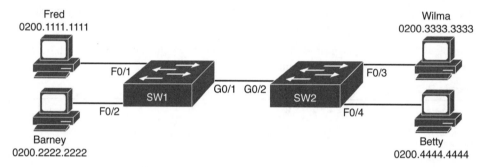

Figure 7-10   *Two-Switch Topology Example*

Think about a case in which both switches learn all four MAC addresses. For instance, that would happen if the hosts on the left communicate with the hosts on the right. SW1's MAC address table would list SW1's own port numbers (F0/1, F0/2, and G0/1), because SW1 uses that information to decide where SW1 should forward frames. Similarly, SW2's MAC table lists SW2's port numbers (F0/3, F0/4, G0/2 in this example). Example 7-8 shows the MAC address tables on both switches for that scenario.

Example 7-8   *The MAC Address Table on Two Switches*

```
SW1# show mac address-table dynamic
          Mac Address Table
-------------------------------------------

Vlan    Mac Address       Type        Ports
----    -----------       --------    -----
   1    0200.1111.1111    DYNAMIC     Fa0/1
   1    0200.2222.2222    DYNAMIC     Fa0/2
   1    0200.3333.3333    DYNAMIC     Gi0/1
   1    0200.4444.4444    DYNAMIC     Gi0/1
```

```
Total Mac Addresses for this criterion: 4
! The next output is from switch SW2
SW2# show mac address-table dynamic
    1    0200.1111.1111    DYNAMIC    Gi0/2
    1    0200.2222.2222    DYNAMIC    Gi0/2
    1    0200.3333.3333    DYNAMIC    Fa0/3
    1    0200.4444.4444    DYNAMIC    Fa0/4
Total Mac Addresses for this criterion: 4
```

Chapter Review

The "Your Study Plan" element, just before Chapter 1, "Introduction to TCP/IP Networking," discusses how you should study and practice the content and skills for each chapter before moving on to the next chapter. That element introduces the tools used here at the end of each chapter. If you haven't already done so, take a few minutes to read that section. Then come back here and do the useful work of reviewing the chapter to help lock into memory what you just read.

Review this chapter's material using either the tools in the book, DVD, or interactive tools for the same material found on the book's companion website. Table 7-2 outlines the key review elements and where you can find them. To better track your study progress, record when you completed these activities in the second column.

Table 7-2   Chapter Review Tracking

Review Element	Review Date(s)	Resource Used
Review key topics		Book, DVD/website
Review key terms		Book, DVD/website
Repeat DIKTA questions		Book, PCPT
Do labs		Book, Sim Lite, blog
Review command tables		Book

Review All the Key Topics

Table 7-3   Key Topics for Chapter 7

Key Topic Element	Description	Page Number
List	Three main functions of a LAN switch	150
Figure 7-3	Process to forward a known unicast frame	151
Figure 7-5	Process to forward a known unicast, second switch	152
Figure 7-6	Process to learn MAC addresses	153
List	Summary of switch forwarding logic	155
Example 7-1	The show mac address-table dynamic command	157

Do Labs

The Sim Lite software is a version of Pearson's full simulator learning product with a subset of the labs, included with this book for free. The subnet of labs all relate to this part. Take the time to try some of the labs.

As always, also check the author's blog site pages for configuration exercises (Config Labs) at http://blog.certskills.com/ccent/.

Key Terms You Should Know

broadcast frame, known unicast frame, Spanning Tree Protocol (STP), unknown unicast frame, MAC address table, forward, flood

Command References

Table 7-4 lists the verification commands used in this chapter; there were no configuration commands mentioned in this chapter. As an easy review exercise, cover the left column, read the right, and try to recall the command without looking. Then repeat the exercise, covering the right column, and try to recall what the command does.

Table 7-4   Chapter 7 EXEC Command Reference

Command	Mode/Purpose/Description
show mac address-table	Shows all MAC table entries of all types
show mac address-table dynamic	Shows all dynamically learned MAC table entries
show mac address-table dynamic vlan *vlan-id*	Shows all dynamically learned MAC table entries in that VLAN
show mac address-table dynamic address *MAC-address*	Shows the dynamically learned MAC table entries with that MAC address
show mac address-table dynamic interface *interface-id*	Shows all dynamically learned MAC table entries associated with that interface
show mac address-table count	Shows the number of entries in the MAC table, and the total number of remaining empty slots in the MAC table
show mac address-table aging-time	Shows the global and per-VLAN aging timeout for inactive MAC table entries
clear mac address-table dynamic	Empties the MAC table of all dynamic entries
show interfaces status	Lists one line per interface on the switch, with basic status and operating information for each

CHAPTER 8

Configuring Basic Switch Management

This chapter covers the following exam topics:

5.0 Infrastructure Management

5.4 Configure, verify, and troubleshoot basic device hardening

5.4.a Local authentication

5.4.b Secure password

5.4.c Access to device

5.4.c.2 Telnet/SSH

The work related to what a networking device does can be broken into three broad categories. The first and most obvious, called the data plane, is the work a switch does to forward frames generated by the devices connected to the switch. In other words, the data plane is the main purpose of the switch. Second, the control plane refers to the configuration and processes that control and change the choices made by the switch's data plane. The network engineer can control which interfaces are enabled and disabled, which ports run at which speeds, how Spanning Tree blocks some ports to prevent loops, and so on.

The third category, the management plane, is the topic of this chapter. The management plane deals with managing the device itself, rather than controlling what the device is doing. In particular, this chapter looks at the most basic management features that can be configured in a Cisco switch. The first section of the chapter works through the configuration of different kinds of login security. The second section shows how to configure IPv4 settings on a switch so it can be remotely managed. The last (short) section then explains a few practical matters that can make your life in lab a little easier.

"Do I Know This Already?" Quiz

Take the quiz (either here, or use the PCPT software) if you want to use the score to help you decide how much time to spend on this chapter. The answers are at the bottom of the page following the quiz, and the explanations are in DVD Appendix C and in the PCPT software.

Table 8-1 "Do I Know This Already?" Foundation Topics Section-to-Question Mapping

Foundation Topics Section	Questions
Securing the Switch CLI	1–3
Enabling IP for Remote Access	4–5
Miscellaneous Settings Useful in Lab	6

1. Imagine that you have configured the **enable secret** command, followed by the **enable password** command, from the console. You log out of the switch and log back in at the console. Which command defines the password that you had to enter to access privileged mode?

   a. **enable password**

   b. **enable secret**

   c. Neither

   d. The **password** command, if it is configured

2. An engineer wants to set up simple password protection with no usernames for some switches in a lab, for the purpose of keeping curious co-workers from logging into the lab switches from their desktop PCs. Which of the following commands would be a useful part of that configuration?

   a. A **login** vty mode subcommand

   b. A **password** *password* console subcommand

   c. A **login local** vty subcommand

   d. A **transport input ssh** vty subcommand

3. An engineer had formerly configured a Cisco 2960 switch to allow Telnet access so that the switch expected a password of **mypassword** from the Telnet user. The engineer then changed the configuration to support Secure Shell. Which of the following commands could have been part of the new configuration? (Choose two answers.)

   a. A **username** *name* **secret** *password* vty mode subcommand

   b. A **username** *name* **secret** *password* global configuration command

   c. A **login local** vty mode subcommand

   d. A **transport input ssh** global configuration command

4. An engineer's desktop PC connects to a switch at the main site. A router at the main site connects to each branch office through a serial link, with one small router and switch at each branch. Which of the following commands must be configured on the branch office switches, in the listed configuration mode, to allow the engineer to telnet to the branch office switches? (Choose three answers.)

   a. The **ip address** command in interface configuration mode

   b. The **ip address** command in global configuration mode

   c. The **ip default-gateway** command in VLAN configuration mode

   d. The **ip default-gateway** command in global configuration mode

   e. The **password** command in console line configuration mode

   f. The **password** command in vty line configuration mode

5. A Layer 2 switch configuration places all its physical ports into VLAN 2. The IP addressing plan shows that address 172.16.2.250 (with mask 255.255.255.0) is reserved for use by this new LAN switch, and that 172.16.2.254 is already configured on the router connected to that same VLAN. The switch needs to support SSH connections into the switch from any subnet in the network. Which of the following commands are part of the required configuration in this case? (Choose two answers.)

   a. The **ip address 172.16.2.250 255.255.255.0** command in interface vlan 1 configuration mode.

   b. The **ip address 172.16.2.250 255.255.255.0** command in interface vlan 2 configuration mode.

   c. The **ip default-gateway 172.16.2.254** command in global configuration mode.

   d. The switch cannot support SSH because all its ports connect to VLAN 2, and the IP address must be configured on interface VLAN 1.

6. Which of the following line subcommands tells a switch to wait until a show command's output has completed before displaying log messages on the screen?

   a. logging synchronous

   b. no ip domain-lookup

   c. exec-timeout 0 0

   d. history size 15

Foundation Topics

Securing the Switch CLI

By default, a Cisco Catalyst switch allows anyone to connect to the console port, access user mode, and then move on to enable and configuration modes without any kind of security. That default makes sense, given that if you can get to the console port of the switch, you already have control over the switch physically. However, everyone needs to operate switches remotely, and the first step in that process is to secure the switch so that only the appropriate users can access the switch command-line interface (CLI).

This first topic in the chapter examines how to configure login security for a Cisco Catalyst switch. Securing the CLI includes protecting access to enable mode, because from enable mode, an attacker could reload the switch or change the configuration. Protecting user mode is also important, because attackers can see the status of the switch, learn about the network, and find new ways to attack the network.

Note that all remote access and management protocols require that the switch IP configuration be completed and working. A switch's IPv4 configuration has nothing to do with how a Layer 2 switch forwards Ethernet frames (as discussed in Chapter 7, "Analyzing Ethernet LAN Switching"), but to Telnet and Secure Shell (SSH) to a switch, the switch needs to be configured with an IP address. This chapter also shows how to configure a switch's IPv4 settings in the upcoming section "Enabling IPv4 for Remote Access."

In particular, this section covers the following login security topics:

- Securing user mode and privileged mode with simple passwords
- Securing user mode access with local usernames
- Securing user mode access with external authentication servers
- Securing remote access with Secure Shell (SSH)

Securing User Mode and Privileged Mode with Simple Passwords

Although the default switch configuration allows a console user to move into user mode and then privileged mode with no passwords required, unsurprisingly, the default settings prevent Telnet and SSH users from even accessing user mode. And while the defaults work well to prevent unwanted access when you first install the switch, you need to add some configuration to then be able to sit at your desk and log in to all the switches in the LAN. In addition, of course, you should not allow just anyone to log in and change the configuration, so some type of secure login should be used.

The first option most people learn to secure access to user mode, one best used in a lab rather than in production, is a simple shared password. This method uses a password only—with no username—with one password for console users and a different password for Telnet users. Console users must supply the *console password*, as configured in console line configuration mode. Telnet users must supply the *Telnet password*, also called the vty password, so called because the configuration sits in vty line configuration mode. Figure 8-1 summarizes these options for using shared passwords from the perspective of the user logging into the switch.

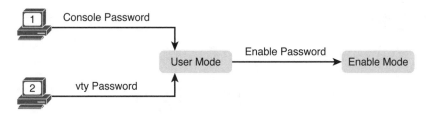

Figure 8-1   *Simple Password Security Concepts*

> **NOTE**   This section refers to several passwords as *shared* passwords. These passwords are shared in the sense that when a new worker comes to the company, others must tell them (share) what the password is. In other words, each user does not have a unique username/ password to use, but rather, all the appropriate staff knows the passwords.

In addition, Cisco switches protect enable mode (also called privileged mode) with yet another shared password called the *enable password*. From the perspective of the network engineer connecting to the CLI of the switch, once in user mode, the user types the **enable** EXEC command. This command prompts the user for this enable password; if the user types the correct password, IOS moves the user to enable mode.

Answers to the "Do I Know This Already?" quiz:

1 B **2** A **3** B, C **4** A, D, F **5** B, C **6** A

Example 8-1 shows an example of the user experience of logging into a switch from the console when the shared console password and the enable password have both been set. Note that before this example began, the user started their terminal emulator, physically connected their laptop to the console cable, and then pressed the return key to make the switch respond as shown at the top of the example.

Example 8-1   *Configuring Basic Passwords and a Hostname*

```
(User now presses enter now to start the process. This line of text does not appear.)


User Access Verification


Password: hope
Switch> enable
Password: love
Switch#
```

Note that the example shows the password text as if typed (hope and love), along with the **enable** command that moves the user from user mode to enable mode. In reality, the switch hides the passwords when typed, to prevent someone from reading over your shoulder to see the password.

To configure the shared passwords for the console, Telnet, and for enable mode, you need to configure several commands. However, the parameters of the commands can be pretty intuitive. Figure 8-2 shows the configuration of all three of these passwords.

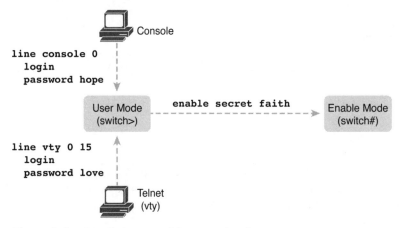

Figure 8-2   *Simple Password Security Configuration*

The configuration for these three passwords does not require a lot of work. First, the console and vty password configuration sets the password based on the context: console mode for the console (**line con 0**), and vty line configuration mode for the Telnet password (**line vty 0 15**). Then inside console mode and vty mode, respectively, the two commands in each mode are

login: Tells IOS to enable the use of a simple shared password (with no username) on this line (console or vty), so that the switch asks the user for a password

password *password-value*: Defines the actual password used on the console or vty

The configured enable password, shown on the right side of the figure, applies to all users, no matter whether they connect to user mode via the console, Telnet, or otherwise. The command to configure the enable password is a global configuration command: **enable secret** *password-value*.

> **NOTE** Older IOS versions used the command **enable password** *password-value* to set the enable password, and that command still exists in IOS. However, the **enable secret** command is much more secure. In real networks, use **enable secret**. Chapter 34, "Device Security Features," explains more about the security levels of various password mechanisms, including a comparison of the **enable secret** and **enable password** commands.

To help you follow the process, and for easier study later, use the configuration checklist before the example. The configuration checklist collects the required and optional steps to configure a feature as described in this book. The configuration checklist for shared passwords for the console, Telnet, and enable passwords is

Step 1.   Configure the enable password with the **enable secret** *password-value* command.

Step 2.   Configure the console password:

   A. Use the **line con 0** command to enter console configuration mode.

   B. Use the **login** subcommand to enable console password security using a simple password.

   C. Use the **password** *password-value* subcommand to set the value of the console password.

Step 3.   Configure the Telnet (vty) password:

   A. Use the **line vty 0 15** command to enter vty configuration mode for all 16 vty lines (numbered 0 through 15).

   B. Use the **login** subcommand to enable password security for vty sessions using a simple password.

   C. Use the **password** *password-value* subcommand to set the value of the vty password.

Example 8-2 shows the configuration process as noted in the configuration checklist, along with setting the enable secret password. Note that the lines which begin with a ! are comment lines; they are there to guide you through the configuration.

Example 8-2   *Configuring Basic Passwords*

```
! Enter global configuration mode, set the enable password, and also
! set the hostname (just because it makes sense to do so)
!
Switch# configure terminal
Switch(config)# enable secret faith
!
! At Step 2 in the checklist, enter console configuration mode, set the
! password value to "hope", and enable simple passwords for the console.
```

```
! The exit command moves the user back to global config mode.
!
Switch#(config)# line console 0
Switch#(config-line)# password hope
Switch#(config-line)# login
Switch#(config-line)# exit
!
! The next few lines do basically the same configuration, except it is
! for the vty lines. Telnet users will use "love" to login.
!
Switch#(config)# line vty 0 15
Switch#(config-line)# password love
Switch#(config-line)# login
Switch#(config-line)# end
Switch#
```

Example 8-3 shows the resulting configuration in the switch per the **show running-config** command. The gray lines highlight the new configuration. Note that many unrelated lines of output have been deleted from the output to keep focused on the password configuration.

Example 8-3   *Resulting Running-Config File (Subset) Per Example 8-2 Configuration*

```
Switch# show running-config
!
Building configuration...

Current configuration : 1333 bytes
!
version 12.2
!
enable secret 5 $1$YXRN$11zOe1Lb0Lv/nHyTquobd.
!
interface FastEthernet0/1
!
interface FastEthernet0/2
!
! Several lines have been omitted here - in particular, lines for
! FastEthernet interfaces 0/3 through 0/23.
!
interface FastEthernet0/24
!
interface GigabitEthernet0/1
!
interface GigabitEthernet0/2
!
line con 0
 password hope
```

```
 login
!
line vty 0 4
 password love
 login
!
line vty 5 15
 password love
 login
```

> **NOTE** For historical reasons, the output of the **show running-config** command, in the
> last six lines of Example 8-3, separates the first five vty lines (0 through 4) from the rest (5
> through 15).

Securing User Mode Access with Local Usernames and Passwords

Cisco switches support two other login security methods that both use per-user username/
password pairs instead of a shared password with no username. One method, referred to as
local usernames and passwords, configures the username/password pairs locally—that is, in
the switch's configuration. Switches support this local username/password option for the
console, for Telnet, and even for SSH, but do not replace the enable password used to reach
enable mode.

The configuration to migrate from using the simple shared passwords to instead use local
usernames/passwords requires only some small configuration changes, as shown in Figure 8-3.

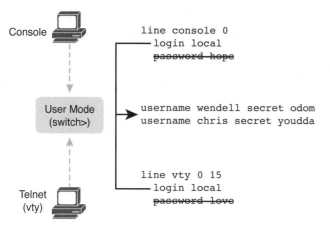

Figure 8-3 *Configuring Switches to Use Local Username Login Authentication*

Working through the configuration in the figure, first, the switch of course needs to know
the list of username/password pairs. To create these, repeatedly use the **username** *name*
secret *password* global configuration command. Then, to enable this different type of
console or Telnet security, simply enable this login security method with the **login local**
line. Basically, this command means "use the local list of usernames for login." You can
also use the **no password** command (without even typing in the password) to clean up any

remaining password subcommands from console or vty mode, because these commands are not needed when using local usernames and passwords.

The following checklist details the commands to configure local username login, mainly as a method for easier study and review:

Step 1. Use the **username** *name* **secret** *password* global configuration command to add one or more username/password pairs on the local switch.

Step 2. Configure the console to use locally configured username/password pairs:

    A. Use the **line con 0** command to enter console configuration mode.

    B. Use the **login local** subcommand to enable the console to prompt for both username and password, checked versus the list of local usernames/passwords.

    C. (Optional) Use the **no password** subcommand to remove any existing simple shared passwords, just for good housekeeping of the configuration file.

Step 3. Configure Telnet (vty) to use locally configured username/password pairs.

    A. Use the **line vty 0 15** command to enter vty configuration mode for all 16 vty lines (numbered 0 through 15).

    B. Use the **login local** subcommand to enable the switch to prompt for both username and password for all inbound Telnet users, checked versus the list of local usernames/passwords.

    C. (Optional) Use the **no password** subcommand to remove any existing simple shared passwords, just for good housekeeping of the configuration file.

When a Telnet user connects to the switch configured as shown in Figure 8-3, the user will be prompted first for a username and then for a password, as shown in Example 8-4. The username/password pair must be from the list of local usernames or the login is rejected.

Example 8-4 *Telnet Login Process After Applying Configuration in Figure 8-3*

```
SW2# telnet 10.9.9.19
Trying 10.9.9.19 ... Open


User Access Verification

Username: wendell
Password:
SW1> enable
Password:
SW1# configure terminal
Enter configuration commands, one per line.  End with CNTL/Z.
SW1(config)#^Z
SW1#
*Mar  1 02:00:56.229: %SYS-5-CONFIG_I: Configured from console by wendell on vty0
  (10.9.9.19)
```

> **NOTE**   Example 8-4 does not show the password value as having been typed because Cisco switches do not display the typed password for security reasons.

> **NOTE**   The **username secret** command has an older less-secure cousin, the **username password** command. Chapter 34 explains more about the security levels of various password mechanisms. Today, use the more secure **username secret** command.

Securing User Mode Access with External Authentication Servers

The end of Example 8-4 points out one of the many security improvements when requiring each user to log in with their own username. The end of the example shows the user entering configuration mode (**configure terminal**), and then immediately leaving (**end**). Note that when a user exits configuration mode, the switch generates a log message. If the user logged in with a username, the log message identifies that username; note the "wendell" in the log message.

However, using a username/password configured directly on the switch causes some administrative headaches. For instance, every switch and router needs the configuration for all users who might need to log in to the devices. Then, when any changes need to happen, like an occasional change to the passwords for good security practices, the configuration of all devices must be changed.

A better option would be to use tools like those used for many other IT login functions. Those tools allow for a central place to securely store all username/password pairs, with tools to make the user change their passwords regularly, tools to revoke users when they leave their current jobs, and so on.

Cisco switches allow exactly that option using an external server called an authentication, authorization, and accounting (AAA) server. These servers hold the usernames/passwords. Typically, these servers allow users to do self service and forced maintenance to their passwords. Many production networks use AAA servers for their switches and routers today.

The underlying login process requires some additional work on the part of the switch for each user login, but once set up, the username/password administration is much less. When using a AAA server for authentication, the switch (or router) simply sends a message to the AAA server asking whether the username and password are allowed, and the AAA server replies. Figure 8-4 shows an example, with the user first supplying his username/password, the switch asking the AAA server, and the server replying to the switch stating that the username/password is valid.

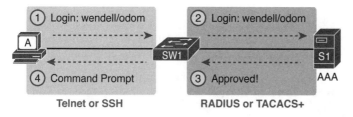

Figure 8-4   *Basic Authentication Process with an External AAA Server*

While the figure shows the general idea, note that the information flows with a couple of different protocols. On the left, the connection between the user and the switch or router uses Telnet or SSH. On the right, the switch and AAA server typically use either the RADIUS or TACACS+ protocol, both of which encrypt the passwords as they traverse the network.

Securing Remote Access with Secure Shell

So far, this chapter has focused on the console and on Telnet, mostly ignoring SSH. Telnet has one serious disadvantage: all data in the Telnet session flows as clear text, including the password exchanges. So, anyone that can capture the messages between the user and the switch (in what is called a man-in-the-middle attack) can see the passwords. SSH encrypts all data transmitted between the SSH client and server, protecting the data and passwords.

SSH can use the same local login authentication method as Telnet, with the locally configured username and password. (SSH cannot rely on a password only.) So, the configuration to support local usernames for Telnet, as shown previously in Figure 8-3, also enables local username authentication for incoming SSH connections.

Figure 8-5 shows one example configuration of what is required to support SSH. The figure repeats the local username configuration as shown earlier in Figure 8-3, as used for Telnet. Figure 8-5 shows three additional commands required to complete the configuration of SSH on the switch.

SSH-Specific Configuration

```
hostname sw1
ip domain-name example.com
! Next Command Uses FQDN "sw1.example.com"
crypto key generate rsa
```

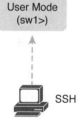

User Mode
(sw1>)

SSH

Local Username Configuration (Like Telnet)

```
username wendell secret odom
username chris secret youdda
!
line vty 0 15
  login local
```

Figure 8-5   *Adding SSH Configuration to Local Username Configuration*

IOS uses the three SSH-specific configuration commands in the figure to create the SSH encryption keys. The SSH server uses the fully qualified domain name (FQDN) of the switch as input to create that key. The term FQDN combines the hostname of a host and its domain name, in this case the hostname and domain name of the switch. Figure 8-5 begins by setting both values (just in case they are not already configured). Then the third command, the **crypto key generate rsa** command, generates the SSH encryption keys.

The configuration in Figure 8-5 relies on two default settings that the figure therefore conveniently ignored. IOS runs an SSH server by default. In addition, IOS allows SSH connections into the vty lines by default.

Seeing the configuration happen in configuration mode, step by step, can be particularly helpful with SSH configuration. Note in particular that in this example, the **crypto key** command prompts the user for the key modulus; you could also add the parameters **modulus** *modulus-value* to the end of the **crypto key** command to add this setting on the command. Example 8-5 shows the commands in Figure 8-5 being configured, with the encryption key as the final step.

Example 8-5   *SSH Configuration Process to Match Figure 8-5*

```
SW1# configure terminal
Enter configuration commands, one per line.  End with CNTL/Z.
!
! Step 1 next. The hostname is already set, but it is repeated just
! to be obvious about the steps.
!
SW1(config)# hostname SW1
SW1(config)# ip domain-name example.com
SW1(config)# crypto key generate rsa
The name for the keys will be: SW1.example.com
Choose the size of the key modulus in the range of 360 to 2048 for your
  General Purpose Keys. Choosing a key modulus greater than 512 may take
  a few minutes.

How many bits in the modulus [512]: 1024
% Generating 1024 bit RSA keys, keys will be non-exportable...
[OK] (elapsed time was 4 seconds)
SW1(config)#
!
! Optionally, set the SSH version to version 2 (only) - preferred
!
SW1(config)# ip ssh version 2
!
! Next, configure the vty lines for local username support, just like
! with Telnet
!
SW1(config)# line vty 0 15
SW1(config-line)# login local
SW1(config-line)# exit
!
! Define the local usernames, just like with Telnet
!
SW1(config)# username wendell password odom
SW1(config)# username chris password youdaman
SW1(config)# ^Z
SW1#
```

Earlier, I mentioned that one useful default was that the switch defaults to support both SSH and Telnet on the vty lines. However, because Telnet is a security risk, you could disable

Telnet to enforce a tighter security policy. (For that matter, you can disable SSH support and allow Telnet on the vty lines as well.)

To control which protocols a switch supports on its vty lines, use the **transport input** {all | none | telnet | ssh} vty subcommand in vty mode, with the following options:

transport input all or **transport input telnet ssh:** Support both Telnet and SSH

transport input none: Support neither

transport input telnet: Support only Telnet

transport input ssh: Support only SSH

To complete this section about SSH, the following configuration checklist details the steps for one method to configure a Cisco switch to support SSH using local usernames. (SSH support in IOS can be configured in several ways; this checklist shows one simple way to configure it.) The process shown here ends with a comment to configure local username support on vty lines, as was discussed earlier in the section titled "Securing User Mode Access with Local Usernames and Passwords."

Step 1. Configure the switch to generate a matched public and private key pair to use for encryption:

    A. If not already configured, use the **hostname** *name* in global configuration mode to configure a hostname for this switch.

    B. If not already configured, use the **ip domain-name** *name* in global configuration mode to configure a domain name for the switch, completing the switch's FQDN.

    C. Use the **crypto key generate rsa** command in global configuration mode (or the **crypto key generate rsa modulus** *modulus-value* command to avoid being prompted for the key modulus) to generate the keys. (Use at least a 768-bit key to support SSH version 2.)

Step 2. (Optional) Use the **ip ssh version 2** command in global configuration mode to override the default of supporting both versions 1 and 2, so that only SSHv2 connections are allowed.

Step 3. (Optional) If not already configured with the setting you want, configure the vty lines to accept SSH and whether to also allow Telnet:

    A. Use the **transport input ssh** command in vty line configuration mode to allow SSH only.

    B. Use the **transport input all** command (default) or **transport input telnet ssh** command in vty line configuration mode to allow both SSH and Telnet.

Step 4. Use various commands in vty line configuration mode to configure local username login authentication as discussed earlier in this chapter.

NOTE   Cisco routers default to **transport input none**, so that you must add the **transport input** line subcommand to enable Telnet and/or SSH into a router.

Two key commands give some information about the status of SSH on the switch. First, the **show ip ssh** command lists status information about the SSH server itself. The **show ssh** command then lists information about each SSH client currently connected into the switch. Example 8-6 shows samples of each, with user Wendell currently connected to the switch.

Example 8-6   *Displaying SSH Status*

```
SW1# show ip ssh
SSH Enabled - version 2.0
Authentication timeout: 120 secs; Authentication retries: 3

SW1# show ssh
Connection Version Mode  Encryption   Hmac          State            Username
0          2.0     IN    aes128-cbc   hmac-sha1     Session started  wendell
0          2.0     OUT   aes128-cbc   hmac-sha1     Session started  wendell
%No SSHv1 server connections running.
```

Enabling IPv4 for Remote Access

To allow Telnet or SSH access to the switch, and to allow other IP-based management protocols (for example, Simple Network Management Protocol, or SNMP) to function as intended, the switch needs an IP address, as well as a few other related settings. The IP address has nothing to do with how switches forward Ethernet frames; it simply exists to support overhead management traffic.

This next topic begins by explaining the IPv4 settings needed on a switch, followed by the configuration. Note that although switches can be configured with IPv6 addresses with commands similar to those shown in this chapter, this chapter focuses solely on IPv4. All references to IP in this chapter imply IPv4.

Host and Switch IP Settings

A switch needs the same kind of IP settings as a PC with a single Ethernet interface. For perspective, a PC has a CPU, with the operating system running on the CPU. It has an Ethernet network interface card (NIC). The OS configuration includes an IP address associated with the NIC, either configured or learned dynamically with DHCP.

A switch uses the same ideas, except that the switch needs to use a virtual NIC inside the switch. Like a PC, a switch has a real CPU, running an OS (called IOS). The switch obviously has lots of Ethernet ports, but instead of assigning its management IP address to any of those ports, the switch then uses a NIC-like concept called a switched virtual interface (SVI), or more commonly, a VLAN interface, that acts like the switch's own NIC. Then the settings on the switch look something like a host, with the switch configuration assigning IP settings, like an IP address, to this VLAN interface, as shown in Figure 8-6.

8

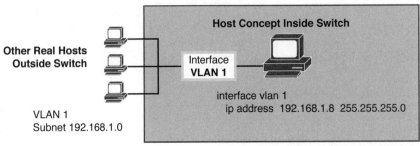

(Shaded Area is Inside the Switch)

Figure 8-6 *Switch Virtual Interface (SVI) Concept Inside a Switch*

By using interface VLAN 1 for the IP configuration, the switch can then send and receive frames on any of the ports in VLAN 1. In a Cisco switch, by default, all ports are assigned to VLAN 1.

In most networks, switches configure many VLANs, so the network engineer has a choice of where to configure the IP address. That is, the management IP address does not have to be configured on the VLAN 1 interface (as configured with the **interface vlan 1** command seen in Figure 8-6).

A Layer 2 Cisco LAN switch often uses a single VLAN interface at a time, although multiple VLAN interfaces can be configured. The switch only needs one IP address for management purposes. But you can configure VLAN interfaces and assign them IP addresses for any working VLAN.

For example, Figure 8-7 shows a Layer 2 switch with some physical ports in two different VLANs (VLANs 1 and 2). The figure also shows the subnets used on those VLANs. The network engineer could choose to create a VLAN 1 interface, a VLAN 2 interface, or both. In most cases, the engineer plans which VLAN to use when managing a group of switches, and creates a VLAN interface for that VLAN only.

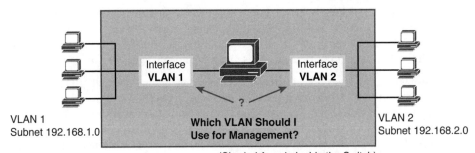

(Shaded Area is Inside the Switch)

Figure 8-7 *Choosing One VLAN on Which to Configure a Switch IP Address*

Note that you should not try to use a VLAN interface for which there are no physical ports assigned to the same VLAN. If you do, the VLAN interface will not reach an up/up state, and the switch will not have the physical ability to communicate outside the switch.

NOTE   Some Cisco switches can be configured to act as either a Layer 2 switch or a Layer 3 switch. When acting as a Layer 2 switch, a switch forwards Ethernet frames as discussed in depth in Chapter 7, "Analyzing Ethernet LAN Switching." Alternatively, a switch can also act as a *multilayer switch* or *Layer 3 switch*, which means the switch can do both Layer 2 switching and Layer 3 IP routing of IP packets, using the Layer 3 logic normally used by routers. This chapter assumes all switches are Layer 2 switches. Chapter 11, "Implementing Ethernet Virtual LANs," further defines the differences between these types of operation for LAN switches.

Configuring the IP address (and mask) on one VLAN interface allows the switch to send and receive IP packets with other hosts in a subnet that exists on that VLAN; however, the switch cannot communicate outside the local subnet without another configuration setting called the default gateway. The reason a switch needs a default gateway setting is the same reason that hosts need the same setting—because of how hosts think when sending IP packets. Specifically:

- To send IP packets to hosts in the same subnet, send them directly

- To send IP packets to hosts in a different subnet, send them to the local router; that is, the default gateway

Figure 8-8 shows the ideas. In this case, the switch (on the right) will use IP address 192.168.1.200 as configured on interface VLAN 1. However, to communicate with host A, on the far left of the figure, the switch must use Router R1 (the default gateway) to forward IP packets to host A. To make that work, the switch needs to configure a default gateway setting, pointing to Router R1's IP address (192.168.1.1 in this case). Note that the switch and router both use the same mask, 255.255.255.0, which puts the addresses in the same subnet.

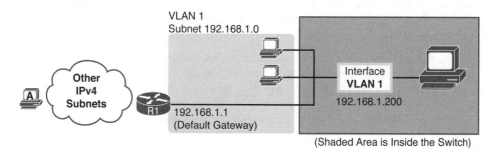

Figure 8-8   *The Need for a Default Gateway*

Configuring IPv4 on a Switch

A switch configures its IPv4 address and mask on this special NIC-like *VLAN interface*. The following steps list the commands used to configure IPv4 on a switch, assuming that the IP address is configured to be in VLAN 1, with Example 8-7 that follows showing an example configuration.

Step 1.   Use the **interface vlan 1** command in global configuration mode to enter interface VLAN 1 configuration mode.

Step 2.   Use the **ip address** *ip-address mask* command in interface configuration mode to assign an IP address and mask.

Step 3.   Use the **no shutdown** command in interface configuration mode to enable the VLAN 1 interface if it is not already enabled.

Step 4.   Add the **ip default-gateway** *ip-address* command in global configuration mode to configure the default gateway.

Step 5.   (Optional) Add the **ip name-server** *ip-address1 ip-address2 ...* command in global configuration mode to configure the switch to use Domain Name System (DNS) to resolve names into their matching IP address.

Example 8-7   *Switch Static IP Address Configuration*

```
Emma# configure terminal
Emma(config)# interface vlan 1
Emma(config-if)# ip address 192.168.1.200 255.255.255.0
Emma(config-if)# no shutdown
00:25:07: %LINK-3-UPDOWN: Interface Vlan1, changed state to up
00:25:08: %LINEPROTO-5-UPDOWN: Line protocol on Interface Vlan1, changed
  state to up
Emma(config-if)# exit
Emma(config)# ip default-gateway 192.168.1.1
```

On a side note, this example shows a particularly important and common command: the **[no] shutdown** command. To administratively enable an interface on a switch, use the **no shutdown** interface subcommand; to disable an interface, use the **shutdown** interface subcommand. This command can be used on the physical Ethernet interfaces that the switch uses to switch Ethernet messages in addition to the VLAN interface shown here in this example.

Also, pause long enough to look at the messages that appear just below the **no shutdown** command in Example 8-7. Those messages are syslog messages generated by the switch stating that the switch did indeed enable the interface. Switches (and routers) generate syslog messages in response to a variety of events, and by default, those messages appear at the console. Chapter 33, "Device Management Protocols," discusses syslog messages in more detail.

Configuring a Switch to Learn Its IP Address with DHCP

The switch can also use Dynamic Host Configuration Protocol (DHCP) to dynamically learn its IPv4 settings. Basically, all you have to do is tell the switch to use DHCP on the interface, and enable the interface. Assuming that DHCP works in this network, the switch will learn all its settings. The following list details the steps, again assuming the use of interface VLAN 1, with Example 8-8 that follows showing an example:

Step 1.   Enter VLAN 1 configuration mode using the **interface vlan 1** global configuration command, and enable the interface using the **no shutdown** command as necessary.

Step 2.   Assign an IP address and mask using the **ip address dhcp** interface subcommand.

Example 8-8 *Switch Dynamic IP Address Configuration with DHCP*

```
Emma# configure terminal
Enter configuration commands, one per line.  End with CNTL/Z.
Emma(config)# interface vlan 1
Emma(config-if)# ip address dhcp
Emma(config-if)# no shutdown
Emma(config-if)# ^Z
Emma#
00:38:20: %LINK-3-UPDOWN: Interface Vlan1, changed state to up
00:38:21: %LINEPROTO-5-UPDOWN: Line protocol on Interface Vlan1, changed state to up
```

Verifying IPv4 on a Switch

The switch IPv4 configuration can be checked in several places. First, you can always look at the current configuration using the **show running-config** command. Second, you can look at the IP address and mask information using the **show interfaces vlan** *x* command, which shows detailed status information about the VLAN interface in VLAN *x*. Finally, if using DHCP, use the **show dhcp lease** command to see the (temporarily) leased IP address and other parameters. (Note that the switch does not store the DHCP-learned IP configuration in the running-config file.) Example 8-9 shows sample output from these commands to match the configuration in Example 8-8.

Example 8-9 *Verifying DHCP-Learned Information on a Switch*

```
Emma# show dhcp lease
Temp IP addr: 192.168.1.101  for peer on Interface: Vlan1
Temp  sub net mask: 255.255.255.0
   DHCP Lease server: 192.168.1.1, state: 3 Bound
   DHCP transaction id: 1966
   Lease: 86400 secs,  Renewal: 43200 secs,  Rebind: 75600 secs
Temp default-gateway addr: 192.168.1.1
   Next timer fires after: 11:59:45
   Retry count: 0   Client-ID: cisco-0019.e86a.6fc0-Vl1
   Hostname: Emma
Emma# show interfaces vlan 1
Vlan1 is up, line protocol is up
  Hardware is EtherSVI, address is 0019.e86a.6fc0 (bia 0019.e86a.6fc0)
  Internet address is 192.168.1.101/24
  MTU 1500 bytes, BW 1000000 Kbit, DLY 10 usec,
     reliability 255/255, txload 1/255, rxload 1/255
! lines omitted for brevity
Emma# show ip default-gateway
192.168.1.1
```

The output of the **show interfaces vlan 1** command lists two very important details related to switch IP addressing. First, this **show** command lists the interface status of the VLAN 1 interface—in this case, "up and up." If the VLAN 1 interface is not up, the switch cannot use its IP address to send and receive management traffic. Notably, if you forget to issue the **no shutdown** command, the VLAN 1 interface remains in its default shutdown state and is listed as "administratively down" in the **show** command output.

Second, note that the output lists the interface's IP address on the third line. If you statically configure the IP address, as in Example 8-7, the IP address will always be listed; however, if you use DHCP and DHCP fails, the **show interfaces vlan** *x* command will not list an IP address here. When DHCP works, you can see the IP address with the **show interfaces vlan 1** command, but that output does not remind you whether the address is either statically configured or DHCP leased. So it does take a little extra effort to make sure you know whether the address is statically configured or DHCP-learned on the VLAN interface.

Miscellaneous Settings Useful in Lab

This last short section of the chapter touches on a couple of commands that can help you be a little more productive when practicing in a lab.

History Buffer Commands

When you enter commands from the CLI, the switch saves the last several commands in the history buffer. Then, as mentioned in Chapter 6, "Using the Command-Line Interface," you can use the up-arrow key or press Ctrl+P to move back in the history buffer to retrieve a command you entered a few commands ago. This feature makes it very easy and fast to use a set of commands repeatedly. Table 8-2 lists some of the key commands related to the history buffer.

Table 8-2 Commands Related to the History Buffer

Command	Description
show history	An EXEC command that lists the commands currently held in the history buffer.
terminal history size *x*	From EXEC mode, this command allows a single user to set, just for this one login session, the size of his or her history buffer.
history size *x*	A configuration command that from console or vty line configuration mode, sets the default number of commands saved in the history buffer for the users of the console or vty lines, respectively.

The logging synchronous, exec-timeout, and no ip domain-lookup Commands

These next three configuration commands have little in common, other than the fact that they can be useful settings to reduce your frustration when using the console of a switch or router.

The console automatically receives copies of all unsolicited syslog messages on a switch. The idea is that if the switch needs to tell the network administrator some important and possibly urgent information, the administrator might be at the console and might notice the message.

Unfortunately, IOS (by default) displays these syslog messages on the console's screen at any time—including right in the middle of a command you are entering, or in the middle of the output of a **show** command. Having a bunch of text show up unexpectedly can be a bit annoying.

You could simply disable the feature that sends these messages to the console, and then re-enable the feature later, using the **no logging console** and **logging console** global commands. For example, when working from the console, if you want to temporarily not be bothered by log messages, you can disable the display of these messages with the **no logging console** global configuration command, and then when finished, enable them again.

However, IOS supplies a reasonable compromise, telling the switch to display syslog messages only at more convenient times, such as at the end of output from a **show** command. To do so, just configure the **logging synchronous** console line subcommand, which basically tells IOS to synchronize the syslog message display with the messages requested using **show** commands.

Another way to improve the user experience at the console is to control timeouts of the login session from the console or when using Telnet or SSH. By default, the switch automatically disconnects console and vty (Telnet and SSH) users after 5 minutes of inactivity. The **exec-timeout** *minutes seconds* line subcommand enables you to set the length of that inactivity timer. In lab (but not in production), you might want to use the special value of 0 minutes and 0 seconds meaning "never time out."

Finally, IOS has an interesting combination of features that can make you wait for a minute or so when you mistype a command. First, IOS tries to use DNS name resolution on IP hostnames—a generally useful feature. If you mistype a command, however, IOS thinks you want to Telnet to a host by that name. With all default settings in the switch, the switch tries to resolve the hostname, cannot find a DNS server, and takes about a minute to timeout and give you control of the CLI again.

To avoid this problem, configure the **no ip domain-lookup** global configuration command, which disables IOS's attempt to resolve the hostname into an IP address.

Example 8-10 collects all these commands into a single example, as a template for some good settings to add in a lab switch to make you more productive.

Example 8-10 *Commands Often Used in Lab to Increase Productivity*

```
no ip domain-lookup
!
line console 0
 exec-timeout 0 0
 logging synchronous
 history size 20
!
line vty 0 15
 exec-timeout 0 0
 logging synchronous
 history size 20
```

8

Chapter Review

One key to doing well on the exams is to perform repetitive spaced review sessions. Review this chapter's material using either the tools in the book, DVD, or interactive tools for the same material found on the book's companion website. Refer to the "Your Study Plan" element section titled "Step 2: Build Your Study Habits Around the Chapter" for more details. Table 8-3 outlines the key review elements and where you can find them. To better track your study progress, record when you completed these activities in the second column.

Table 8-3 Chapter Review Tracking

Review Element	Review Date(s)	Resource Used
Review key topics		Book, DVD/website
Review key terms		Book, DVD/website
Repeat DIKTA questions		Book, PCPT
Review config checklists		Book, DVD/website
Do labs		Sim Lite, blog
Review command tables		Book

Review All the Key Topics

Table 8-4 Key Topics for Chapter 8

Key Topic Element	Description	Page Number
Example 8-2	Example of configuring password login security (no usernames)	171
Figure 8-5	SSH configuration commands with related username login security	176

Key Terms You Should Know

Telnet, Secure Shell (SSH), local username, AAA, AAA server, enable mode, default gateway, VLAN interface, history buffer, DNS, name resolution, log message

Do Labs

The Sim Lite software is a version of Pearson's full simulator learning product with a subset of the labs, included with this book for free. The subnet of labs all relate to this part. Take the time to try some of the labs. As always, also check the author's blog site pages for configuration exercises (Config Labs) at http://blog.certskills.com/ccent/.

Command References

Tables 8-5, 8-6, 8-7, and 8-8 list configuration and verification commands used in this chapter. As an easy review exercise, cover the left column in a table, read the right column, and try to recall the command without looking. Then repeat the exercise, covering the right column, and try to recall what the command does.

Table 8-5   Login Security Commands

Command	Mode/Purpose/Description
line console 0	Changes the context to console configuration mode.
line vty *1st-vty last-vty*	Changes the context to vty configuration mode for the range of vty lines listed in the command.
login	Console and vty configuration mode. Tells IOS to prompt for a password.
password *pass-value*	Console and vty configuration mode. Lists the password required if the **login** command (with no other parameters) is configured.
login local	Console and vty configuration mode. Tells IOS to prompt for a username and password, to be checked against locally configured **username** global configuration commands on this switch or router.
username *name* secret *pass-value*	Global command. Defines one of possibly multiple usernames and associated passwords, used for user authentication. Used when the **login local** line configuration command has been used.
crypto key generate rsa [modulus *360..2048*]	Global command. Creates and stores (in a hidden location in flash memory) the keys required by SSH.
transport input {telnet | ssh | all | none}	vty line configuration mode. Defines whether Telnet/SSH access is allowed into this switch. Both values can be configured on one command to allow both Telnet and SSH access (the default).

Table 8-6   Switch IPv4 Configuration

Command	Mode/Purpose/Description
interface vlan *number*	Changes the context to VLAN interface mode. For VLAN 1, allows the configuration of the switch's IP address.
ip address *ip-address subnet-mask*	VLAN interface mode. Statically configures the switch's IP address and mask.
ip address dhcp	VLAN interface mode. Configures the switch as a DHCP client to discover its IPv4 address, mask, and default gateway.
ip default-gateway *address*	Global command. Configures the switch's default gateway IPv4 address. Not required if the switch uses DHCP.
ip name-server *server-ip-1 server-ip-2 ...*	Global command. Configures the IPv4 addresses of DNS servers, so any commands when logged in to the switch will use the DNS for name resolution.

8

Table 8-7   Other Switch Configuration

Command	Mode/Purpose/Description
hostname *name*	Global command. Sets this switch's hostname, which is also used as the first part of the switch's command prompt.
enable secret *pass-value*	Global command. Sets this switch's password that is required for any user to reach enable mode.
history size *length*	Line config mode. Defines the number of commands held in the history buffer, for later recall, for users of those lines.
logging synchronous	Console or vty mode. Tells IOS to send log messages to the user at natural break points between commands rather than in the middle of a line of output.
[no] logging console	Global command that disables or enables the display of log messages to the console.
exec-timeout *minutes* [*seconds*]	Console or vty mode. Sets the inactivity timeout, so that after the defined period of no action, IOS closes the current user login session.

Table 8-8   Chapter 8 EXEC Command Reference

Command	Purpose
show running-config	Lists the currently used configuration
show running-config	begin line vty	Pipes (sends) the command output to the **begin** command, which only lists output beginning with the first line that contains the text "line vty"
show dhcp lease	Lists any information the switch acquires as a DHCP client. This includes IP address, subnet mask, and default gateway information
show crypto key mypubkey rsa	Lists the public and shared key created for use with SSH using the **crypto key generate rsa** global configuration command
show ip ssh	Lists status information for the SSH server, including the SSH version
show ssh	Lists status information for current SSH connections into and out of the local switch
show interfaces vlan *number*	Lists the interface status, the switch's IPv4 address and mask, and much more
show ip default-gateway	Lists the switch's setting for its IPv4 default gateway
terminal history size *x*	Changes the length of the history buffer for the current user only, only for the current login to the switch
show history	Lists the commands in the current history buffer

CHAPTER 9

Configuring Switch Interfaces

This chapter covers the following exam topics:

2.0 LAN Switching Technologies

2.3 Troubleshoot interface and cable issues (collisions, errors, duplex, speed)

2.7 Configure, verify, and troubleshoot port security

    2.7.a Static

    2.7.b Dynamic

    2.7.c Sticky

    2.7.d Max MAC addresses

    2.7.e Violation actions

    2.7.f Err-disable recovery

This chapter completes Part II of the book. So far in this part, you have learned the skills to navigate the command-line interface (CLI) and use commands that configure and verify switch features. You learned about the primary purpose of a switch—forwarding Ethernet frames—and learned how to see that process in action by looking at the switch MAC address table. After learning about the switch data plane in Chapter 7, "Analyzing Ethernet LAN Switching," you learned a few management plane features in Chapter 8, "Configuring Basic Switch Management," like how to configure the switch to support Telnet and Secure Shell (SSH) by configuring IP address and login security.

In this final chapter of Part II, you pick up tools that loosely fit in the switch control plane. First, this chapter shows how you can configure and change the operation of switch interfaces: how to change the speed, duplex, or even disable the interface. The second half then shows how to add a security feature called port security, which monitors the source MAC address of incoming frames, deciding which frames are allowed and which cause a security violation.

"Do I Know This Already?" Quiz

Take the quiz (either here, or use the PCPT software) if you want to use the score to help you decide how much time to spend on this chapter. The answers are at the bottom of the page following the quiz, and the explanations are in DVD Appendix C and in the PCPT software.

Table 9-1 "Do I Know This Already?" Foundation Topics Section-to-Question Mapping

Foundation Topics Section	Questions
Configuring Switch Interfaces	1–3
Port Security	4–6

1. Which of the following describes a way to disable IEEE standard autonegotiation on a 10/100 port on a Cisco switch?

    a. Configure the **negotiate disable** interface subcommand

    b. Configure the **no negotiate** interface subcommand

    c. Configure the **speed 100** interface subcommand

    d. Configure the **duplex half** interface subcommand

    e. Configure the **duplex full** interface subcommand

    f. Configure the **speed 100** and **duplex full** interface subcommands

2. In which of the following modes of the CLI could you configure the duplex setting for interface Fast Ethernet 0/5?

    a. User mode

    b. Enable mode

    c. Global configuration mode

    d. VLAN mode

    e. Interface configuration mode

3. A Cisco Catalyst switch connects with its Gigabit0/1 port to an end user's PC. The end user, thinking the user is helping, manually sets the PC's OS to use a speed of 1000 Mbps and to use full duplex, and disables the use of autonegotiation. The switch's G0/1 port has default settings for speed and duplex. What speed and duplex settings will the switch decide to use? (Choose two answers.)

    a. Full duplex

    b. Half duplex

    c. 10 Mbps

    d. 1000 Mbps

4. Which of the following is required when configuring port security with sticky learning?

    a. Setting the maximum number of allowed MAC addresses on the interface with the **switchport port-security maximum** interface subcommand.

    b. Enabling port security with the **switchport port-security** interface subcommand.

    c. Defining the specific allowed MAC addresses using the **switchport port-security mac-address** interface subcommand.

    d. All the other answers list required commands.

5. A switch's port Gi0/1 has been correctly enabled with port security. The configuration sets the violation mode to restrict. A frame that violates the port security policy enters the interface, followed by a frame that does not. Which of the following answers correctly describe what happens in this scenario? (Choose two answers.)

   a. The switch puts the interface into an err-disabled state when the first frame arrives.

   b. The switch generates syslog messages about the violating traffic for the first frame.

   c. The switch increments the violation counter for Gi0/1 by 1.

   d. The switch discards both the first and second frame.

6. A Cisco Catalyst switch connects to what should be individual user PCs. Each port has the same port security configuration, configured as follows:

```
interface range gigabitethernet 0/1 - 24
 switchport mode access
 switchport port-security
 switchport port-security mac-address sticky
```

   Which of the following answers describe the result of the port security configuration created with these commands? (Choose two answers.)

   a. Prevents unknown devices with unknown MAC addresses from sending data through the switch ports.

   b. If a user connects a switch to the cable, prevents multiple devices from sending data through the port.

   c. Will allow any one device to connect to each port, and will save that device's MAC address into the startup-config.

   d. Will allow any one device to connect to each port, but *will not* save that device's MAC address into the startup-config.

Foundation Topics

Configuring Switch Interfaces

IOS uses the term *interface* to refer to physical ports used to forward data to and from other devices. Each interface can be configured with several settings, each of which might differ from interface to interface. IOS uses interface subcommands to configure these settings. Each of these settings may be different from one interface to the next, so you would first identify the specific interface, and then configure the specific setting.

This section begins with a discussion of three relatively basic per-interface settings: the port speed, duplex, and a text description. Following that, the text takes a short look at a pair of the most common interface subcommands: the **shutdown** and **no shutdown** commands, which administratively disable and enable the interface, respectively. This section ends with a discussion about autonegotiation concepts, which in turn dictates what settings a switch chooses to use when using autonegotiation.

Configuring Speed, Duplex, and Description

Switch interfaces that support multiple speeds (10/100 and 10/100/1000 interfaces), by default, will autonegotiate what speed to use. However, you can configure the speed and duplex settings with the **duplex {auto | full | half}** and **speed {auto | 10 | 100 | 1000}** interface subcommands. Simple enough.

Most of the time, using autonegotiation makes good sense, so when you set the duplex and speed, you typically have a good reason to do so. For instance, maybe you want to set the speed to the fastest possible on links between switches just to avoid the chance that autonegotiation chooses a slower speed.

The **description** text interface subcommand lets you add a text description to the interface. For instance, if you have good reason to configure the speed and duplex on a port, maybe add a description that says why you did. Example 9-1 shows how to configure **duplex** and **speed**, as well as the **description** command, which is simply a text description that can be configured by the administrator.

Example 9-1 *Configuring* speed, duplex, *and* description *on Switch Emma*

```
Emma# configure terminal
Enter configuration commands, one per line.  End with CNTL/Z.
Emma(config)# interface FastEthernet 0/1
Emma(config-if)# duplex full
Emma(config-if)# speed 100
Emma(config-if)# description Printer on 3rd floor, Preset to 100/full is connected
  here
Emma(config-if)# exit
Emma(config)# interface range FastEthernet 0/11 - 20
Emma(config-if-range)# description end-users connect here
Emma(config-if-range)# ^Z
Emma#
```

First, focus on the mechanics of moving around in configuration mode again by looking closely at the command prompts. The various **interface** commands move the user from global mode into interface configuration mode for a specific interface. For instance, the example configures the **duplex**, **speed**, and **description** commands all just after the **interface FastEthernet 0/1** command, which means that all three of those configuration settings apply to interface Fa0/1, and not to the other interfaces.

The **show interfaces status** command lists much of the detail configured in Example 9-1, even with only one line of output per interface. Example 9-2 shows an example, just after the configuration in Example 9-1 was added to the switch.

Answers to the "Do I Know This Already?" quiz:

1 F **2** E **3** A, D **4** B **5** B, C **6** B, D

Example 9-2 *Displaying Interface Status*

```
Emma# show interfaces status
Port      Name                  Status       Vlan     Duplex  Speed Type
Fa0/1     Printer on 3rd floo   notconnect   1        full     100  10/100BaseTX
Fa0/2                           notconnect   1        auto    auto  10/100BaseTX
Fa0/3                           notconnect   1        auto    auto  10/100BaseTX
Fa0/4                           connected    1        a-full  a-100 10/100BaseTX
Fa0/5                           notconnect   1        auto    auto  10/100BaseTX
Fa0/6                           connected    1        a-full  a-100 10/100BaseTX
Fa0/7                           notconnect   1        auto    auto  10/100BaseTX
Fa0/8                           notconnect   1        auto    auto  10/100BaseTX
Fa0/9                           notconnect   1        auto    auto  10/100BaseTX
Fa0/10                          notconnect   1        auto    auto  10/100BaseTX
Fa0/11    end-users connect     notconnect   1        auto    auto  10/100BaseTX
Fa0/12    end-users connect     notconnect   1        auto    auto  10/100BaseTX
Fa0/13    end-users connect     notconnect   1        auto    auto  10/100BaseTX
Fa0/14    end-users connect     notconnect   1        auto    auto  10/100BaseTX
Fa0/15    end-users connect     notconnect   1        auto    auto  10/100BaseTX
Fa0/16    end-users connect     notconnect   1        auto    auto  10/100BaseTX
Fa0/17    end-users connect     notconnect   1        auto    auto  10/100BaseTX
Fa0/18    end-users connect     notconnect   1        auto    auto  10/100BaseTX
Fa0/19    end-users connect     notconnect   1        auto    auto  10/100BaseTX
Fa0/20    end-users connect     notconnect   1        auto    auto  10/100BaseTX
Fa0/21                          notconnect   1        auto    auto  10/100BaseTX
Fa0/22                          notconnect   1        auto    auto  10/100BaseTX
Fa0/23                          notconnect   1        auto    auto  10/100BaseTX
Fa0/24                          notconnect   1        auto    auto  10/100BaseTX
Gi0/1                           notconnect   1        auto    auto  10/100/1000BaseTX
Gi0/2                           notconnect   1        auto    auto  10/100/1000BaseTX
```

Working through the output in the example:

FastEthernet 0/1 (Fa0/1): This output lists the first few characters of the configured description. It also lists the configured speed of 100 and duplex full per the **speed** and **duplex** commands in Example 9-1. However, it also states that Fa0/1 has a status of not-connect, meaning that the interface is not currently working. (That switch port did not have a cable connected when collecting this example, on purpose.)

FastEthernet 0/2 (Fa0/2): Example 9-1 did not configure this port at all. This port had all default configuration. Note that the "auto" text under the speed and duplex heading means that this port will attempt to autonegotiate both settings when the port comes up. However, this port also does not have a cable connected (again on purpose, for comparison).

FastEthernet 0/4 (Fa0/4): Like Fa0/2, this port has all default configuration, but was cabled to another working device to give yet another contrasting example. This device completed the autonegotiation process, so instead of "auto" under the speed and duplex headings, the output lists the negotiated speed and duplex (**a-full** and **a-100**). Note that the text includes the **a-** to mean that the listed speed and duplex values were autonegotiated.

Configuring Multiple Interfaces with the interface range Command

The bottom of the configuration in Example 9-1 shows a way to shorten your configuration work when making the same setting on multiple consecutive interfaces. To do so, use the **interface range** command. In the example, the **interface range FastEthernet 0/11 - 20** command tells IOS that the next subcommand(s) apply to interfaces Fa0/11 through Fa0/20. You can define a range as long as all interfaces are the same type and are numbered consecutively.

NOTE This book spells out all parameters fully to avoid confusion. However, most everyone abbreviates what they type in the CLI to the shortest unique abbreviation. For instance, the configuration commands **int f0/1** and **int ran f0/11 - 20** would also be acceptable.

IOS does not actually put the **interface range** command into the configuration. Instead, it acts as if you had typed the subcommand under every single interface in the specified range. Example 9-3 shows an excerpt from the **show running-config** command, listing the configuration of interfaces F0/11–12 from the configuration in Example 9-1. The example shows the same description command on both interfaces; to save space the example did not bother to show all 10 interfaces that have the same description text.

Example 9-3 *How IOS Expands the Subcommands Typed After* **interface range**

```
Emma# show running-config
! Lines omitted for brevity
interface FastEthernet0/11
 description end-users connect here
!
interface FastEthernet0/12
 description end-users connect here
! Lines omitted for brevity
```

Administratively Controlling Interface State with shutdown

As you might imagine, network engineers need a way to bring down an interface without having to travel to the switch and remove a cable. In short, we need to be able to decide which ports should be enabled, and which should be disabled.

In an odd turn of phrase, Cisco uses two interface subcommands to configure the idea of administratively enabling and disabling an interface: the **shutdown** command (to disable), and the **no shutdown** command (to enable). While the **no shutdown** command might seem like an odd command to enable an interface at first, you will use this command a lot in lab, and it will become second nature. (Most people in fact use the abbreviations **shut** and **no shut**.)

Example 9-4 shows an example of disabling an interface using the **shutdown** interface subcommand. In this case, switch SW1 has a working interface F0/1. The user connects at the console and disables the interface. IOS generates a log message each time an interface fails or recovers, and log messages appear at the console, as shown in the example.

Example 9-4 *Administratively Disabling an Interface with* **shutdown**

```
SW1# configure terminal
Enter configuration commands, one per line.  End with CNTL/Z.
```

```
SW1(config)# interface fastEthernet 0/1
SW1(config-if)# shutdown
SW1(config-if)#
*Mar  2 03:02:19.701: %LINK-5-CHANGED: Interface FastEthernet0/1, changed state to
  administratively down
*Mar  2 03:02:20.708: %LINEPROTO-5-UPDOWN: Line protocol on Interface FastEthernet0/1,
  changed state to down
```

To bring the interface back up again, all you have to do is follow the same process but use the **no shutdown** command instead.

Before leaving the simple but oddly named **shutdown/no shutdown** commands, take a look at two important show commands that list the status of a shutdown interface. The **show interfaces status** command lists one line of output per interface, and when shut down, lists the interface status as "disabled." That makes logical sense to most people. The **show interfaces** command (without the **status** keyword) lists many lines of output per interface, giving a much more detailed picture of interface status and statistics. With that command, the interface status comes in two parts, with one part using the phrase "administratively down," matching the highlighted log message in Example 9-4.

Example 9-5 shows an example of each of these commands. Note that both examples also use the F0/1 parameter (short for Fast Ethernet0/1), which limits the output to the messages about F0/1 only. Also note that F0/1 is still shut down at this point.

Example 9-5 *The Different Status Information About Shutdown in Two Different* show *Commands*

```
SW1# show interfaces f0/1 status


Port       Name               Status       Vlan       Duplex  Speed Type
Fa0/1                         disabled     1            auto   auto 10/100BaseTX


SW1# show interfaces f0/1
FastEthernet0/1 is administratively down, line protocol is down (disabled)
  Hardware is Fast Ethernet, address is 1833.9d7b.0e81 (bia 1833.9d7b.0e81)
  MTU 1500 bytes, BW 10000 Kbit/sec, DLY 1000 usec,
     reliability 255/255, txload 1/255, rxload 1/255
  Encapsulation ARPA, loopback not set
  Keepalive set (10 sec)
  Auto-duplex, Auto-speed, media type is 10/100BaseTX
  input flow-control is off, output flow-control is unsupported
  ARP type: ARPA, ARP Timeout 04:00:00
  Last input never, output 00:00:36, output hang never
  Last clearing of "show interface" counters never
  Input queue: 0/75/0/0 (size/max/drops/flushes); Total output drops: 0
  Queueing strategy: fifo
  Output queue: 0/40 (size/max)
  5 minute input rate 0 bits/sec, 0 packets/sec
  5 minute output rate 0 bits/sec, 0 packets/sec
```

```
      164 packets input, 13267 bytes, 0 no buffer
      Received 164 broadcasts (163 multicasts)
      0 runts, 0 giants, 0 throttles
      0 input errors, 0 CRC, 0 frame, 0 overrun, 0 ignored
      0 watchdog, 163 multicast, 0 pause input
      0 input packets with dribble condition detected
      66700 packets output, 5012302 bytes, 0 underruns
      0 output errors, 0 collisions, 1 interface resets
      0 unknown protocol drops
      0 babbles, 0 late collision, 0 deferred
      0 lost carrier, 0 no carrier, 0 pause output
      0 output buffer failures, 0 output buffers swapped out
```

Removing Configuration with the no Command

One purpose for the specific commands shown in Part II of the book is to teach you about that command. In some cases, the commands are not the end goal, and the text is attempting to teach you something about how the CLI works. This next short topic is more about the process than about the commands.

With some IOS configuration commands (but not all), you can revert to the default setting by issuing a **no** version of the command. What does that mean? Let me give you a few examples:

- If you earlier had configured **speed 100** on an interface, the **no speed** command on that same interface reverts to the default speed setting (which happens to be **speed auto**).

- Same idea with the **duplex** command: an earlier configuration of **duplex half** or **duplex full**, followed by **no duplex** on the same interface, reverts the configuration back to the default of duplex auto.

- If you had configured a **description** command with some text, to go back to the default state of having no **description** command at all for that interface, use the **no description** command.

Example 9-6 shows the process. In this case, switch SW1's F0/2 port has been configured with **speed 100**, **duplex half**, **description link to 2901-2**, and **shutdown**. You can see evidence of all four settings in the command that begins the example. (This command lists the running-config, but only the part for that one interface.) The example then shows the **no** versions of those commands, and closes with a confirmation that all the commands have reverted to default.

Example 9-6 *Removing Various Configuration Settings Using the* no *Command*

```
SW1# show running-config interface f0/2
Building configuration...

Current configuration : 95 bytes
!
interface FastEthernet0/2
 description link to 2901-2
```

```
  shutdown
  speed 100
  duplex half
  end


  SW1# configure terminal
  Enter configuration commands, one per line.  End with CNTL/Z.
  SW1(config)# interface fastEthernet 0/2
  SW1(config-if)# no speed
  SW1(config-if)# no duplex
  SW1(config-if)# no description
  SW1(config-if)# no shutdown
  SW1(config-if)# ^Z
  SW1#
  SW1# show running-config interface f0/2
  Building configuration...
  Current configuration : 33 bytes
  !
  interface FastEthernet0/2
  end
  SW1#
```

NOTE The **show running-config** and **show startup-config** commands typically do not display default configuration settings, so the absence of commands listed under interface F0/2 at the end of the example means that those commands now use default values.

Autonegotiation

For any 10/100 or 10/100/1000 interfaces—that is, interfaces that can run at different speeds—Cisco Catalyst switches default to a setting of **duplex auto** and **speed auto**. As a result, those interfaces attempt to automatically determine the speed and duplex setting to use. Alternatively, you can configure most devices, switch interfaces included, to use a specific speed and/or duplex.

In practice, using autonegotiation is easy: just leave the speed and duplex at the default setting, and let the switch port negotiate what settings to use on each port. However, problems can occur due to unfortunate combinations of configuration. Therefore, this next topic walks through more detail about the concepts behind autonegotiation, so you know better how to interpret the meaning of the switch **show** commands and when to choose to use a particular configuration setting.

Autonegotiation Under Working Conditions

Ethernet devices on the ends of a link must use the same standard or they cannot correctly send data. For example, a NIC cannot use 100BASE-T, which uses a two-pair UTP cable with a 100-Mbps speed, while the switch port on the other end of the link uses 1000BASE-T. Even if you used a cable that works with Gigabit Ethernet, the link would not work with one end trying to send at 100 Mbps while the other tried to receive the data at 1000 Mbps.

Upgrading to new and faster Ethernet standards becomes a problem because both ends have to use the same standard. For example, if you replace an old PC with a new one, the old one might have been using 100BASE-T while the new one uses 1000BASE-T. The switch port on the other end of the link needs to now use 1000BASE-T, so you upgrade the switch. If that switch had ports that would use only 1000BASE-T, you would need to upgrade all the other PCs connected to the switch. So, having both PC network interface cards (NIC) and switch ports that support multiple standards/speeds makes it much easier to migrate to the next better standard.

The IEEE autonegotiation protocol helps makes it much easier to operate a LAN when NICs and switch ports support multiple speeds. IEEE autonegotiation (IEEE standard 802.3u) defines a protocol that lets the two UTP-based Ethernet nodes on a link negotiate so that they each choose to use the same speed and duplex settings. The protocol messages flow outside the normal Ethernet electrical frequencies as out-of-band signals over the UTP cable. Basically, each node states what it can do, and then each node picks the best options that both nodes support: the fastest speed and the best duplex setting, with full duplex being better than half duplex.

NOTE Autonegotiation relies on the fact that the IEEE uses the same wiring pinouts for 10BASE-T and 100BASE-T, and that 1000BASE-T simply adds to those pinouts, adding two pairs.

Many networks use autonegotiation every day, particularly between user devices and the access layer LAN switches, as shown in Figure 9-1. The company installed four-pair cabling of the right quality to support 1000BASE-T, to be ready to support Gigabit Ethernet. As a result, the wiring supports 10-Mbps, 100-Mbps, and 1000-Mbps Ethernet options. Both nodes on each link send autonegotiation messages to each other. The switch in this case has all 10/100/1000 ports, while the PC NICs support different options.

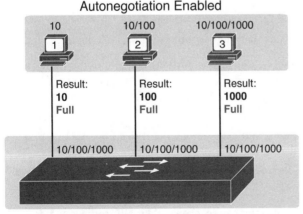

Figure 9-1 *IEEE Autonegotiation Results with Both Nodes Working Correctly*

The following list breaks down the logic, one PC at a time:

PC1: The switch port claims it can go as fast as 1000 Mbps, but PC1's NIC claims a top speed of 10 Mbps. Both the PC and switch choose the best speed both support (10 Mbps) and the best duplex (full).

PC2: PC2 claims a best speed of 100 Mbps, which means it can use 10BASE-T or 100BASE-T. The switch port and NIC negotiate to use the best speed of 100 Mbps and full duplex.

PC3: It uses a 10/100/1000 NIC, supporting all three speeds and standards, so both the NIC and switch port choose 1000 Mbps and full duplex.

Autonegotiation Results When Only One Node Uses Autonegotiation

Figure 9-1 shows the IEEE autonegotiation results when both nodes use the process. However, most Ethernet devices can disable autonegotiation, so it is just as important to know what happens when a node tries to use autonegotiation but the node gets no response.

Disabling autonegotiation is not always a bad idea. For instance, many network engineers disable autonegotiation on links between switches and simply configure the desired speed and duplex on both switches. However, mistakes can happen when one device on an Ethernet predefines speed and duplex (and disables autonegotiation), while the device on the other end attempts autonegotiation. In that case, the link might not work at all, or it might just work poorly.

> **NOTE**   Configuring both the speed and duplex on a Cisco switch interface disables autonegotiation.

IEEE autonegotiation defines some rules (defaults) that nodes should use as defaults when autonegotiation fails—that is, when a node tries to use autonegotiation but hears nothing from the device. The rules:

- **Speed:** Use your slowest supported speed (often 10 Mbps).
- **Duplex:** If your speed = 10 or 100, use half duplex; otherwise, use full duplex.

Cisco switches can make a better choice than that base IEEE logic, because Cisco switches can actually sense the speed used by other nodes, even without IEEE autonegotiation. As a result, Cisco switches use this slightly different logic to choose the speed when autonegotiation fails:

- **Speed:** Sense the speed (without using autonegotiation), but if that fails, use the IEEE default (slowest supported speed, often 10 Mbps).
- **Duplex:** Use the IEEE defaults: If speed = 10 or 100, use half duplex; otherwise, use full duplex.

Figure 9-2 shows three examples in which three users change their NIC settings and disable autonegotiation, while the switch (with all 10/100/1000 ports) attempts autonegotiation. That is, the switch ports all default to **speed auto** and **duplex auto**. The top of the figure shows the configured settings on each PC NIC, with the choices made by the switch listed next to each switch port.

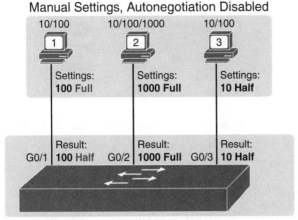

Figure 9-2 *IEEE Autonegotiation Results with Autonegotiation Disabled on One Side*

Reviewing each link, left to right:

■ **PC1:** The switch receives no autonegotiation messages, so it senses the electrical signal to learn that PC1 is sending data at 100 Mbps. The switch uses the IEEE default duplex based on the 100 Mbps speed (half duplex).

■ **PC2:** The switch uses the same steps and logic as with the link to PC1, except that the switch chooses to use full duplex because the speed is 1000 Mbps.

■ **PC3:** The user picks poorly, choosing the slower speed (10 Mbps) and the worse duplex setting (half). However, the Cisco switch senses the speed without using IEEE autonegotiation and then uses the IEEE duplex default for 10-Mbps links (half duplex).

PC1 shows a classic and unfortunately common end result: a *duplex mismatch*. The two nodes (PC1 and SW1's port G0/1) both use 100 Mbps, so they can send data. However, PC1, using full duplex, does not attempt to use carrier sense multiple access with collision detection (CSMA/CD) logic and sends frames at any time. Switch port G0/1, with half duplex, does use CSMA/CD. As a result, switch port G0/1 will believe collisions occur on the link, even if none physically occur. The switch port will stop transmitting, back off, resend frames, and so on. As a result, the link is up, but it performs poorly.

Autonegotiation and LAN Hubs

LAN hubs also impact how autonegotiation works. Basically, hubs do not react to autonegotiation messages, and they do not forward the messages. As a result, devices connected to a hub must use the IEEE rules for choosing default settings, which often results in the devices using 10 Mbps and half duplex.

Figure 9-3 shows an example of a small Ethernet LAN that uses a 20-year-old 10BASE-T hub. In this LAN, all devices and switch ports are 10/100/1000 ports. The hub supports only 10BASE-T.

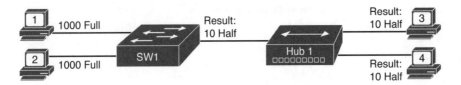

Figure 9-3 *IEEE Autonegotiation with a LAN Hub*

Note that the devices on the right need to use half duplex because the hub requires the use of the CSMA/CD algorithm to avoid collisions.

Port Security

If the network engineer knows what devices should be cabled and connected to particular interfaces on a switch, the engineer can use *port security* to restrict that interface so that only the expected devices can use it. This reduces exposure to attacks in which the attacker connects a laptop to some unused switch port. When that inappropriate device attempts to send frames to the switch interface, the switch can take different actions, ranging from simply issuing informational messages to effectively shutting down the interface.

Port security identifies devices based on the source MAC address of Ethernet frames the devices send. For example, in Figure 9-4, PC1 sends a frame, with PC1's MAC address as the source address. SW1's F0/1 interface can be configured with port security, and if so, SW1 would examine PC1's MAC address and decide whether PC1 was allowed to send frames into port F0/1.

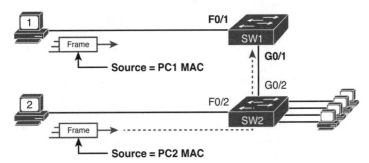

Figure 9-4 *Source MAC Addresses in Frames as They Enter a Switch*

Port security also has no restrictions on whether the frame came from a local device or was forwarded through other switches. For example, switch SW1 could use port security on its G0/1 interface, checking the source MAC address of the frame from PC2, when forwarded up to SW1 from SW2.

Port security has several flexible options, but all operate with the same core concepts. First, switches enable port security per port, with different settings available per port. Each port has a maximum number of allowed MAC addresses, meaning that for all frames entering that port, only that number of *different* source MAC addresses can be used in different incoming frames before port security thinks a violation has occurred. When a frame with a new source MAC address arrives, pushing the number of MAC addresses past the allowed maximum, a port security violation occurs. At that point, the switch takes action—by default, discarding all future incoming traffic on that port.

The following list summarizes these ideas common to all variations of port security:

- Define a maximum number of source MAC addresses allowed for all frames coming in the interface.

- Watch all incoming frames, and keep a list of all source MAC addresses, plus a counter of the number of different source MAC addresses.

- When adding a new source MAC address to the list, if the number of MAC addresses pushes past the configured maximum, a port security violation has occurred. The switch takes action (the default action is to shut down the interface).

Those rules define the basics, but port security allows other options as well, including letting you configure the specific MAC addresses allowed to send frames in an interface. For example, in Figure 9-4, switch SW1 connects through interface F0/1 to PC1, so the port security configuration could list PC1's MAC address as the specific allowed MAC address. But predefining MAC addresses for port security is optional: You can predefine all MAC addresses, none, or a subset of the MAC addresses.

You might like the idea of predefining the MAC addresses for port security, but finding the MAC address of each device can be a bother. Port security provides an easy way to discover the MAC addresses used off each port using a feature called *sticky secure MAC addresses*. With this feature, port security learns the MAC addresses off each port and stores them in the port security configuration (in the running-config file). This feature helps reduce the big effort of finding out the MAC address of each device.

As you can see, port security has a lot of detailed options. The next few sections walk you through these options to pull the ideas together.

Configuring Port Security

Port security configuration involves several steps. First, you need to disable the negotiation of a feature that is not discussed until Chapter 11, "Implementing Ethernet Virtual LANs," whether the port is an access or trunk port. For now, accept that port security requires a port to be configured to either be an access port or a trunking port. The rest of the commands enable port security, set the maximum allowed MAC addresses per port, and configure the actual MAC addresses, as detailed in this list:

Step 1.   Make the switch interface either a static access or trunk interface using the **switchport mode access** or the **switchport mode trunk** interface subcommands, respectively.

Step 2.   Enable port security using the **switchport port-security** interface subcommand.

Step 3.   (Optional) Override the default maximum number of allowed MAC addresses associated with the interface (1) by using the **switchport port-security maximum** *number* interface subcommand.

Step 4.   (Optional) Override the default action to take upon a security violation (shutdown) using the **switchport port-security violation** {protect | restrict | shutdown} interface subcommand.

9

Step 5. (Optional) Predefine any allowed source MAC addresses for this interface using the **switchport port-security mac-address** *mac-address* command. Use the command multiple times to define more than one MAC address.

Step 6. (Optional) Tell the switch to "sticky learn" dynamically learned MAC addresses with the **switchport port-security mac-address sticky** interface subcommand.

Figure 9-5 and Example 9-7 show four examples of port security. Three ports operate as access ports, while port F0/4, connected to another switch, operates as a trunk. Note that port security allows either a trunk or an access port, but requires that the port be statically set as one or the other.

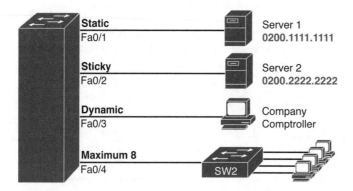

Figure 9-5 *Port Security Configuration Example*

Example 9-7 *Variations on Port Security Configuration*

```
SW1# show running-config
(Lines omitted for brevity)


interface FastEthernet0/1
 switchport mode access
 switchport port-security
 switchport port-security mac-address 0200.1111.1111
!
interface FastEthernet0/2
 switchport mode access
 switchport port-security
 switchport port-security mac-address sticky
!
interface FastEthernet0/3
 switchport mode access
 switchport port-security
!
interface FastEthernet0/4
 switchport mode trunk
 switchport port-security
 switchport port-security maximum 8
```

First, scan the configuration for all four interfaces in Example 9-7, focusing on the first two interface subcommands. Note that the first three interfaces in the example use the same first two interface subcommands, matching the first two configuration steps noted before Figure 9-5. The **switchport port-security** command enables port security, with all defaults, with the **switchport mode access** command meeting the requirement to configure the port as either an access or trunk port. The final port, F0/4, has a similar configuration, except that it has been configured as a trunk rather than as an access port.

Next, scan all four interfaces again, and note that the configuration differs on each interface after those first two interface subcommands. Each interface simply shows a different example for perspective.

The first interface, FastEthernet 0/1, adds one optional port security subcommand: **switchport port-security mac-address 0200.1111.1111**, which defines a specific source MAC address. With the default maximum source address setting of 1, only frames with source MAC 0200.1111.1111 will be allowed in this port. When a frame with a source other than 0200.1111.1111 enters F0/1, the switch will take the default violation action and disable the interface.

As a second example, FastEthernet 0/2 uses the same logic as FastEthernet 0/1, except that it uses the sticky learning feature. For port F0/2, the configuration the **switchport port-security mac-address sticky** command, which tells the switch to dynamically learn source MAC addresses and add **port-security** commands to the running-config. The end of upcoming Example 9-8 shows the running-config file that lists the sticky-learned MAC address in this case.

> **NOTE**   Port security does not save the configuration of the sticky addresses, so use the **copy running-config startup-config** command if desired.

The other two interfaces do not predefine MAC addresses, nor do they sticky-learn the MAC addresses. The only difference between these two interfaces' port security configuration is that FastEthernet 0/4 supports eight MAC addresses, because it connects to another switch and should receive frames with multiple source MAC addresses. Interface F0/3 uses the default maximum of one MAC address.

Verifying Port Security

Example 9-8 lists the output of two examples of the **show port-security interface** command. This command lists the configuration settings for port security on an interface, plus it lists several important facts about the current operation of port security, including information about any security violations. The two commands in the example show interfaces F0/1 and F0/2, based on Example 9-7's configuration.

Example 9-8   *Using Port Security to Define Correct MAC Addresses of Particular Interfaces*

```
SW1# show port-security interface fastEthernet 0/1
Port Security                  : Enabled
Port Status                    : Secure-shutdown
Violation Mode                 : Shutdown
Aging Time                     : 0 mins
```

```
Aging Type                : Absolute
SecureStatic Address Aging : Disabled
Maximum MAC Addresses     : 1
Total MAC Addresses       : 1
Configured MAC Addresses  : 1
Sticky MAC Addresses      : 0
Last Source Address:Vlan  : 0013.197b.5004:1
Security Violation Count  : 1


SW1# show port-security interface fastEthernet 0/2
Port Security             : Enabled
Port Status               : Secure-up
Violation Mode            : Shutdown
Aging Time                : 0 mins
Aging Type                : Absolute
SecureStatic Address Aging : Disabled
Maximum MAC Addresses     : 1
Total MAC Addresses       : 1
Configured MAC Addresses  : 1
Sticky MAC Addresses      : 1
Last Source Address:Vlan  : 0200.2222.2222:1
Security Violation Count  : 0


SW1# show running-config interface f0/2
Building configuration...
Current configuration : 188 bytes
!
interface FastEthernet0/2
 switchport mode access
 switchport port-security
 switchport port-security mac-address sticky
 switchport port-security mac-address sticky 0200.2222.2222
```

The first two commands in Example 9-8 confirm that a security violation has occurred on FastEthernet 0/1, but no violations have occurred on FastEthernet 0/2. The **show port-security interface fastethernet 0/1** command shows that the interface is in a *secure-shutdown* state, which means that the interface has been disabled because of port security. In this case, another device connected to port F0/1, sending a frame with a source MAC address other than 0200.1111.1111, is causing a violation. However, port Fa0/2, which used sticky learning, simply learned the MAC address used by Server 2.

The bottom of Example 9-8, as compared to the configuration in Example 9-7, shows the changes in the running-config because of sticky learning, with the **switchport port-security mac-address sticky 0200.2222.2222** interface subcommand.

Port Security Violation Actions

Finally, the switch can be configured to use one of three actions when a violation occurs. All three options cause the switch to discard the offending frame, but some of the options make the switch take additional actions. The actions include the sending of syslog messages to the console, sending SNMP trap messages to the network management station, and disabling the interface. Table 9-2 lists the options of the **switchport port-security violation** {**protect** | **restrict** | **shutdown**} command and their meanings.

Table 9-2   Actions When Port Security Violation Occurs

Option on the switchport port-security violation Command	Protect	Restrict	Shutdown*
Discards offending traffic	Yes	Yes	Yes
Sends log and SNMP messages	No	Yes	Yes
Increments the violation counter for each violating incoming frame	No	Yes	Yes
Disables the interface by putting it in an err-disabled state, discarding all traffic	No	No	Yes

*shutdown is the default setting.

Note that the shutdown option does not actually add the **shutdown** subcommand to the interface configuration. Instead, IOS puts the interface in an *error disabled* (err-disabled) state, which makes the switch stop all inbound and outbound frames. To recover from this state, someone must manually disable the interface with the **shutdown** interface command and then enable the interface with the **no shutdown** command.

Port Security MAC Addresses as Static and Secure but Not Dynamic

To complete this chapter, take a moment to think about Chapter 7's discussions about switching, along with all those examples of output from the **show mac address-table dynamic** EXEC command.

Once a switch port has been configured with port security, the switch no longer considers MAC addresses associated with that port as being dynamic entries as listed with the **show mac address-table dynamic** EXEC command. Even if the MAC addresses are dynamically learned, once port security has been enabled, you need to use one of these options to see the MAC table entries associated with ports using port security:

- **show mac address-table secure:** Lists MAC addresses associated with ports that use port security

- **show mac address-table static:** Lists MAC addresses associated with ports that use port security, as well as any other statically defined MAC addresses

Example 9-9 proves the point. It shows two commands about interface F0/2 from the port security example shown in Figure 9-5 and Example 9-7. In that example, port security was configured on F0/2 with sticky learning, so from a literal sense, the switch learned a MAC address off that port (0200.2222.2222). However, the **show mac address-table dynamic** command does not list the address and port, because IOS considers that MAC table entry to be a static entry. The **show mac address-table secure** command does list the address and port.

9

Example 9-9   *Using the* **secure** *Keyword to See MAC Table Entries When Using Port Security*

```
SW1# show mac address-table secure interface F0/2
          Mac Address Table
-------------------------------------------

Vlan    Mac Address      Type       Ports
----    -----------      --------   -----
   1    0200.2222.2222   STATIC     Fa0/2
Total Mac Addresses for this criterion: 1

SW1# show mac address-table dynamic interface f0/2
          Mac Address Table
-------------------------------------------

Vlan    Mac Address      Type       Ports
----    -----------      --------   -----
SW1#
```

Chapter Review

One key to doing well on the exams is to perform repetitive spaced review sessions. Review this chapter's material using either the tools in the book, DVD, or interactive tools for the same material found on the book's companion website. Refer to the "Your Study Plan" element section titled "Step 2: Build Your Study Habits Around the Chapter" for more details. Table 9-3 outlines the key review elements and where you can find them. To better track your study progress, record when you completed these activities in the second column.

Table 9-3   Chapter Review Tracking

Review Element	Review Date(s)	Resource Used
Review key topics		Book, DVD/website
Review key terms		Book, DVD/website
Repeat DIKTA questions		Book, PCPT
Review memory tables		Book, DVD/website
Review config checklists		Book, DVD/website
Do labs		Sim Lite, blog
Review command tables		Book

Review All the Key Topics

Table 9-4   Key Topics for Chapter 9

Key Topic Element	Description	Page Number
Example 9-1	Example of configuring **speed, duplex,** and **description**	193
Example 9-4	Example of disabling an interface using the **shutdown** command	195
List	Key decision rules for autonegotiation on Cisco switches when the other device does not participate	200
List	Summary of port security concepts	203
Table 9-2	Port security actions and the results of each action	207

Key Terms You Should Know

port security, autonegotiation, full duplex, half-duplex, 10/100, 10/100/1000

Do Labs

The Sim Lite software is a version of Pearson's full simulator learning product with a subset of the labs, included with this book for free. The subnet of labs all relate to this part. Take the time to try some of the labs. As always, also check the author's blog site pages for configuration exercises (Config Labs) at http://blog.certskills.com/ccent/.

Command References

Tables 9-5, 9-6, and 9-7 list configuration and verification commands used in this chapter. As an easy review exercise, cover the left column in a table, read the right column, and try to recall the command without looking. Then repeat the exercise, covering the right column, and try to recall what the command does.

Table 9-5   Switch Interface Configuration

Command	Mode/Purpose/Description
interface *type port-number*	Changes context to interface mode. The type is typically Fast Ethernet or Gigabit Ethernet. The possible port numbers vary depending on the model of switch—for example, Fa0/1, Fa0/2, and so on.
interface range *type port-number - end-port-number*	Changes the context to interface mode for a range of consecutively numbered interfaces. The subcommands that follow then apply to all interfaces in the range.
**shutdown	no shutdown**	Interface mode. Disables or enables the interface, respectively.
**speed {10	100	1000	auto}**	Interface mode. Manually sets the speed to the listed speed or, with the auto setting, automatically negotiates the speed.
**duplex {auto	full	half}**	Interface mode. Manually sets the duplex to half or full, or to autonegotiate the duplex setting.

9

Command	Mode/Purpose/Description
description *text*	Interface mode. Lists any information text that the engineer wants to track for the interface, such as the expected device on the other end of the cable.
no duplex no speed no description	Reverts to the default setting for each interface subcommand of **speed auto**, **duplex auto**, and the absence of a **description** command.

Table 9-6 Port Security Configuration

Command	Mode/Purpose/Description
switchport mode {access	trunk}	Interface configuration mode command that tells the switch to always be an access port, or always be a trunk port
switchport port-security mac-address *mac-address*	Interface configuration mode command that statically adds a specific MAC address as an allowed MAC address on the interface
switchport port-security mac-address sticky	Interface subcommand that tells the switch to learn MAC addresses on the interface and add them to the configuration for the interface as secure MAC addresses
switchport port-security maximum *value*	Interface subcommand that sets the maximum number of static secure MAC addresses that can be assigned to a single interface
switchport port-security violation {protect	restrict	shutdown}	Interface subcommand that tells the switch what to do if an inappropriate MAC address tries to access the network through a secure switch port

Table 9-7 Chapter 9 EXEC Command Reference

Command	Purpose
show running-config	Lists the currently used configuration
show running-config	interface *type number*	Displays the running-configuration excerpt of the listed interface and its subcommands only
show mac address-table dynamic [interface *type number*]	Lists the dynamically learned entries in the switch's address (forwarding) table
show mac address-table secure [interface *type number*]	Lists MAC addresses defined or learned on ports configured with port security
show mac address-table static [interface *type number*]	Lists static MAC addresses and MAC addresses learned or defined with port security

Command	Purpose
show interfaces [interface *type number*] status	Lists one output line per interface (or for only the listed interface if included), noting the description, operating state, and settings for duplex and speed on each interface
show interfaces [interface *type number*]	Lists detailed status and statistical information about all interfaces (or the listed interface only)
show port-security interface *type number*	Lists an interface's port security configuration settings and security operational status
show port-security	Lists one line per interface that summarizes the port security settings for any interface on which it is enabled

9

Part II Review

Keep track of your part review progress with the checklist shown in Table P2-1. Details on each task follow the table.

Table P2-1 Part II Part Review Checklist

Activity	1st Date Completed	2nd Date Completed
Repeat All DIKTA Questions		
Answer Part Review Questions		
Review Key Topics		
Create Terminology Mind Maps		
Create Command Mind Maps by Category		
Do Labs		

Repeat All DIKTA Questions

For this task, answer the "Do I Know This Already?" questions again for the chapters in this part of the book, using the PCPT software.

Answer Part Review Questions

For this task, answer the Part Review questions for this part of the book, using the PCPT software. Refer to the Introduction to this book, in the section "How to View Part Review Questions," for more details.

Review Key Topics

Review all key topics in all chapters in this part, either by browsing the chapters or by using the Key Topics application on the DVD or companion website.

Create Terminology Mind Maps

Similar to the exercise you did in the Part I review, without looking back at the chapters or your notes, create a mind map with all the terminology you can recall from Part II of the book. Your job is as follows:

- Think of every term that you can remember from Part II of the book.

- Organize the terms into two divisions: Ethernet terms and CLI terms. (Do not include CLI commands, just terms [for example, *enable mode*].)

- After you have written every term you can remember into one of the mind maps, review the Key Terms list at the end of Chapters 6 through 9. Add any terms you forgot to your mind maps.

Create Command Mind Maps by Category

Part II of this book introduced a large number of both configuration and EXEC commands. The sheer number of commands can be a bit overwhelming, so it helps to practice the process of remembering which commands exist and which ones work together for a particular feature. This mind map exercise focuses on that task.

Create one mind map for each of the categories of commands in this list:

Securing the console and Telnet with passwords, securing the console and Telnet with local usernames, SSH, switch IPv4 support, switch forwarding, port security, other switch admin, other interface subcommands

For each category, think of all configuration commands and all EXEC commands (mostly **show** commands). For each category, group the configuration commands separately from the EXEC commands. Figure P2-1 shows a sample for IPv4 commands on a switch.

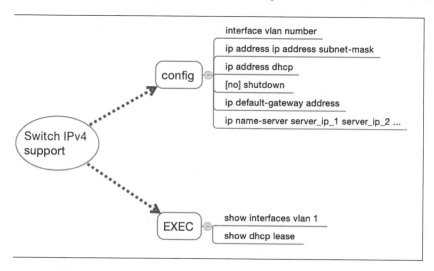

Figure P2-1 *Sample Mind Map from the Switch IPv4 Support Branch*

> **NOTE**   For more information on mind mapping, refer to the Introduction, in the section "About Mind Maps."

Finally, keep the following important points in mind when working on this project:

■   Most of the learning with this exercise happens when you do it. Reading some other mind map, or just rereading command tables, does not work as well for helping you remember for yourself.

■   Do this activity without notes and without looking at the book.

■   After you finish, review it and compare it against the command summary tables at the ends of the chapters, and note which commands you had originally forgotten.

■   Do not worry about every last parameter or the exact syntax; just write down the first few words of the command.

■   For later study, make a note about which commands you feel you truly understand and which ones about which you feel less confident.

■   Repeat this exercise when you have 10 spare minutes, as a way to see what you remember (again without your notes).

Appendix L, "Mind Map Solutions," lists a sample mind map answer.

Labs

This is the first book part with switch commands. If you have not done so, make your choices about what lab tools you intend to use and experiment with the commands in these chapters. Re-create examples in the chapters, and try all the **show** commands; the **show** commands are very important for answering SimLet questions:

Sim Lite: You can use the Pearson Network Simulator Lite included with this book to do some labs and get used to the CLI. All the labs in the ICND1 Sim Lite product are about topics in this part of the book, so make sure and work through those labs to start learning about the CLI.

Pearson Network Simulator: If you use the full Pearson ICND1 or CCNA simulator, focus more on the configuration scenario and troubleshooting scenario labs associated with the topics in this part of the book. These types of labs include a larger set of topics and work well as Part Review activities. (See the Introduction for some details about how to find which labs are about topics in this part of the book.)

Config Labs: In your idle moments, review and repeat any of the Config Labs for this book part in the author's blog; launch from blog.certskills.com/ccent and navigate to the Hands-on Config labs.

Part III of this book builds on the basics of implementing Ethernet in Part II by taking the concepts, configuration, and troubleshooting another step or two deeper.

Now that you know the basics of how to build a small Ethernet LAN with Cisco switches, Part III begins by looking at typical Ethernet LAN designs. Understanding how a small LAN with one or two switches works is a great place to start, but understanding why an experienced network engineer might build a larger LAN a particular way helps you understand how LANs work in real networks.

VLANs are one of the most powerful design tools for a network designer. VLANs also have a huge impact on how a switch works, which then impacts how you verify and troubleshoot the operation of a campus LAN. The second chapter in this part of the book shows the details of VLAN operation, along with VLAN trunking.

The final chapter in this part of the book ends the chapters that focus on Ethernet. The Ethernet troubleshooting chapter, of course, discusses many details of how to troubleshoot an Ethernet LAN after you have implemented it. From a learning perspective, it also serves as a great review of many of the topics in Parts II and III of the book.

Part III

Ethernet LANs: Design, VLANs, and Troubleshooting

CHAPTER 10

Analyzing Ethernet LAN Designs

This chapter covers the following exam topics:

1.0 Network Fundamentals

1.3 Describe the impact of infrastructure components in an enterprise network

  1.3.b Access points

  1.3.c Wireless controllers

1.4 Compare and contrast collapsed core and three-tier architectures

1.5 Compare and contrast network topologies

  1.5.a Star

  1.5.b Mesh

  1.5.c Hybrid

1.6 Select the appropriate cabling type based on implementation requirements

2.0 LAN Switching Technologies

2.3 Troubleshoot interface and cable issues (collisions, errors, duplex, speed)

Ethernet defines what happens on each Ethernet link, but the more interesting and more detailed work happens on the devices connected to those links: the network interface cards (NIC) inside devices and the LAN switches. This chapter takes the Ethernet LAN basics introduced in Chapter 2, "Fundamentals of Ethernet LANs," and dives deeply into many aspects of a modern Ethernet LAN, while focusing on the primary device used to create these LANs: LAN switches.

This chapter breaks down the discussion of Ethernet and LAN switching into two sections. The first major section looks at the logic used by LAN switches when forwarding Ethernet frames, along with the related terminology. The second section considers design and implementation issues, as if you were building a new Ethernet LAN in a building or campus. This second section considers design issues, including using switches for different purposes, when to choose different types of Ethernet links, and how to take advantage of Ethernet autonegotiation.

"Do I Know This Already?" Quiz

Take the quiz (either here, or use the PCPT software) if you want to use the score to help you decide how much time to spend on this chapter. The answers are at the bottom of the page following the quiz, and the explanations are in DVD Appendix C and in the PCPT software.

Table 10-1 "Do I Know This Already?" Foundation Topics Section-to-Question Mapping

Foundation Topics Section	Questions
Analyzing Collision Domains and Broadcast Domains	1–2
Analyzing Campus LAN Topologies	3–5
Analyzing LAN Physical Standard Choices	6

1. Which of the following devices would be in the same collision domain as PC1?

   a. PC2, which is separated from PC1 by an Ethernet hub

   b. PC3, which is separated from PC1 by a transparent bridge

   c. PC4, which is separated from PC1 by an Ethernet switch

   d. PC5, which is separated from PC1 by a router

2. Which of the following devices would be in the same broadcast domain as PC1? (Choose three answers.)

   a. PC2, which is separated from PC1 by an Ethernet hub

   b. PC3, which is separated from PC1 by a transparent bridge

   c. PC4, which is separated from PC1 by an Ethernet switch

   d. PC5, which is separated from PC1 by a router

3. In a two-tier campus LAN design, which of the following are typically true of the topology design? (Choose two answers.)

   a. The design uses a full mesh of links between access and distribution switches

   b. The design uses a partial mesh of links between access and distribution switches

   c. The design uses a partial mesh of links between the distribution and core switches

   d. The end user and server devices connect directly to access layer switches

4. In a three-tier campus LAN design, which of the following are typically true of the topology design? (Choose two answers.)

   a. The design uses a partial mesh of links between access and distribution switches

   b. The design uses a full mesh of links between access and distribution switches

   c. The design uses a partial mesh of links between the distribution and core switches

   d. The end user and server devices connect directly to distribution layer switches

5. Which one answer gives the strongest match between one part of a typical three-tier design with the idea behind the listed generic topology design term?

   a. The access layer looks like a partial mesh.

   b. The distribution layer looks like a full mesh.

   c. The distribution layer looks like a hybrid design.

   d. The access layer looks like a star design.

6. Which of the following Ethernet standards support a maximum cable length of longer than 100 meters? (Choose two answers.)

    a. 100BASE-T

    b. 1000BASE-SX

    c. 1000BASE-T

    d. 1000BASE-LX

Foundation Topics

Analyzing Collision Domains and Broadcast Domains

Ethernet devices, and the logic they use, have a big impact on why engineers design modern LANs in a certain way. Some of the terms used to describe key design features come from far back in the history of Ethernet, and because of their age, the meaning of each term may or may not be so obvious to someone learning Ethernet today. This first section of the chapter looks at two of these older terms in particular: collision domain and broadcast domain. And to understand these terms and apply them to modern Ethernet LANs, this section needs to work back through the history of Ethernet a bit, to put some perspective on the meaning behind these terms.

Ethernet Collision Domains

The term *collision domain* comes from the far back history of Ethernet LANs. To be honest, sometimes people new to Ethernet can get a little confused about what this term really means in the context of a modern Ethernet LAN, in part because modern Ethernet LANs, done properly, can completely prevent collisions. So to fully understand collision domains, we must first start with a bit of Ethernet history. This next section of the chapter looks at a few of the historical Ethernet devices, for the purpose of defining a collision domain, and then closing with some comments about how the term applies in a modern Ethernet LAN that uses switches.

10BASE-T with Hub

10BASE-T, introduced in 1990, significantly changed the design of Ethernet LANs, more like the designs seen today. 10BASE-T introduced the cabling model similar to today's Ethernet LANs, with each device connecting to a centralized device using an unshielded twisted-pair (UTP) cable. However, 10BASE-T did not originally use LAN switches; instead, the early 10BASE-T networks used a device called an *Ethernet hub*. (The technology required to build even a basic LAN switch was not yet available at that time.)

Although both a hub and a switch use the same cabling star topology, an Ethernet hub does not forward traffic like a switch. Ethernet hubs use physical layer processing to forward data. A hub does not interpret the incoming electrical signal as an Ethernet frame, look at the source and destination MAC address, and so on. Basically, a hub acts like a repeater, just with lots of ports. When a repeater receives an incoming electrical signal, it immediately *forwards a regenerated signal out all the other ports except the incoming port*. Physically, the hub just sends out a cleaner version of the same incoming electrical signal, as shown in Figure 10-1, with Larry's signal being repeated out the two ports on the right.

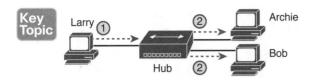

Figure 10-1 *10BASE-T (with a Hub): The Hub Repeats Out All Other Ports*

Because of the physical layer operation used by the hub, the devices attached to the network must use carrier sense multiple access with collision detection (CSMA/CD) to take turns (as introduced at the end of Chapter 2). Note that the hub itself does not use CSMA/CD logic; the hub always receives an electrical signal and starts repeating a (regenerated) signal out all other ports, with no thought of CSMA/CD. So, although a hub's logic works well to make sure all devices get a copy of the original frame, that same logic causes frames to collide. Figure 10-2 demonstrates that effect, when the two devices on the right side of the figure send a frame at the same time, and the hub physically transmits both electrical signals out the port to the left (toward Larry).

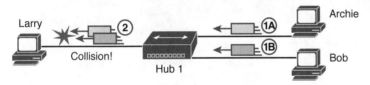

Figure 10-2 *Hub Operation Causing a Collision*

Because a hub makes no attempt to prevent collisions, the devices connected to it all sit within the same collision domain. A *collision domain* is the set of NICs and device ports for which if they sent a frame at the same time, the frames would collide. In Figures 10-1 and 10-2, all three PCs are in the same collision domain, as well as the hub. Summarizing the key points about hubs:

- The hub acts a multiport repeater, blindly regenerating and repeating any incoming electrical signal out all other ports, even ignoring CSMA/CD rules.

- When two or more devices send at the same time, the hub's actions cause an electrical collision, making both signals corrupt.

- The connected devices must take turns by using carrier sense multiple access with collision detection (CSMA/CD) logic, so the devices share the bandwidth.

- Hubs create a physical star topology.

Ethernet Transparent Bridges

From a design perspective, the introduction of 10BASE-T was a great improvement over the earlier types of Ethernet. It reduced cabling costs and cable installation costs, and improved the availability percentages of the network. But sitting here today, thinking of a LAN in which all devices basically have to wait their turn may seem like a performance issue, and it was. If Ethernet could be improved to allow multiple devices to send at the same time without causing a collision, Ethernet performance could be improved.

Answers to the "Do I Know This Already?" quiz:

1 A **2** A, B, C **3** B, D **4** A, C **5** D **6** B, D

The first method to allow multiple devices to send at the same time was Ethernet transparent bridges. Ethernet *transparent bridges*, or simply *bridges*, made these improvements:

- Bridges sat between hubs and divided the network into multiple *collision domains*.

- Bridges increase the capacity of the entire Ethernet, because each collision domain is basically a separate instance of CSMA/CD, so each collision domain can have one sender at a time.

Figure 10-3 shows the effect of building a LAN with two hubs, each separated by a bridge. The resulting two collision domains each support at most 10 Mbps of traffic each, compared to at most 10 Mbps if a single hub were used.

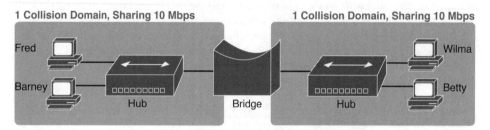

Figure 10-3 *Bridge Creates Two Collision Domains and Two Shared Ethernets*

Bridges create multiple collision domains as a side effect of their forwarding logic. A bridge makes forwarding decisions just like a modern LAN switch; in fact, bridges were the predecessors of the modern LAN switch. Like switches, bridges hold Ethernet frames in memory, waiting to send out the outgoing interface based on CSMA/CD rules. In other cases, the bridge does not even need to forward the frame. For instance, if Fred sends a frame destined to Barney's MAC address, then the bridge would never forward frames from the left to the right.

Ethernet Switches and Collision Domains

LAN switches perform the same basic core functions as bridges but at much faster speeds and with many enhanced features. Like bridges, switches segment a LAN into separate collision domains, each with its own capacity. And if the network does not have a hub, each single link in a modern LAN is considered its own collision domain, even if no collisions can actually occur in that case.

For example, Figure 10-4 shows a simple LAN with a switch and four PCs. The switch creates four collision domains, with the ability to send at 100 Mbps in this case on each of the four links. And with no hubs, each link can run at full duplex, doubling the capacity of each link.

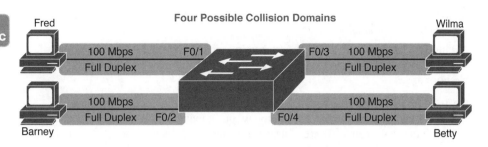

Figure 10-4 *Switch Creates Four Collision Domains and Four Ethernet Segments*

Now take a step back for a moment and think about some facts about modern Ethernet LANs. Today, you build Ethernet LANs with Ethernet switches, not with Ethernet hubs or bridges. The switches connect to each other. And every single link is a separate collision domain.

As strange as it sounds, each of those collision domains in a modern LAN may also never have a collision. Any link that uses full duplex—that is, both devices on the link use full duplex—does not have collisions. In fact, running with full duplex is basically this idea: No collisions can occur between a switch and a single device, so we can turn off CSMA/CD by running full duplex.

NOTE The routers in a network design also create separate collision domains, because frames entering or exiting one router LAN interface do not collide with frames on another of the router's LAN interfaces.

The Impact of Collisions on LAN Design

So, what is the useful takeaway from this discussion about collision domains? A long time ago, collisions were normal in Ethernet, so analyzing an Ethernet design to determine where the collision domains were was useful. On the other end of the spectrum, a modern campus LAN that uses only switches (and no hubs or transparent bridges), and full duplex on all links, has no collisions at all. So does the collision domain term still matter today? And do we need to think about collisions even still today?

In a word, the term collision domain still matters, and collisions still matter, in that network engineers need to be ready to understand and troubleshoot exceptions. Whenever a port that could use full duplex (therefore avoiding collisions) happens to use half duplex—by incorrect configuration, by the result of autonegotiation, or any other reason—collisions can now occur. In those cases, engineers need to be able identify the collision domain.

Summarizing the key points about collision domains:

- LAN switches place each separate interface into a separate collision domain.
- LAN bridges, which use the same logic as switches, placed each interface into a separate collision domain.
- Routers place each LAN interface into a separate collision domain. (The term collision domain does not apply to WAN interfaces.)
- LAN hubs do not place each interface into a separate collision domain.

■ A modern LAN, with all LAN switches and routers, with full duplex on each link, would not have collisions at all.

■ In a modern LAN with all switches and routers, even though full duplex removes collisions, think of each Ethernet link as a separate collision domain when the need to troubleshoot arises.

Figure 10-5 shows an example with a design that includes hubs, bridges, switches, and routers—a design that you would not use today, but it makes a good backdrop to remind us about which devices create separate collision domains.

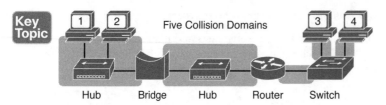

Hub   Bridge   Hub   Router   Switch

Figure 10-5 *Example of a Hub Not Creating Multiple Collision Domains, While Others Do*

Ethernet Broadcast Domains

Take any Ethernet LAN, and pick any device. Then think of that device sending an Ethernet broadcast. An Ethernet *broadcast domain* is the set of devices to which that broadcast is delivered.

To begin, think about a modern LAN for a moment, and where a broadcast frame flows. Imagine that all the switches still used the switch default to put each interface into VLAN 1. As a result, a broadcast sent by any one device would be flooded to all devices connected to all switches (except for the device that sent the original frame). For instance, in Figure 10-6, under the assumption that all ports are still assigned to VLAN 1, a broadcast would flow to all the devices shown in the figure.

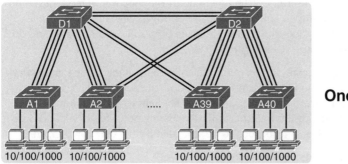

One VLAN!

Figure 10-6 *A Single Large Broadcast Domain*

Of all the common networking devices discussed in this book, only a router does not forward a LAN broadcast. Hubs of course forward broadcasts, because hubs do not even think about the electrical signal as an Ethernet frame. Bridges and switches use the same forwarding logic, flooding LAN broadcasts. Routers, as a side effect of their routing logic, do not forward Ethernet broadcast frames, so they separate a network into separate broadcast domains. Figure 10-7 collects those thoughts into a single example.

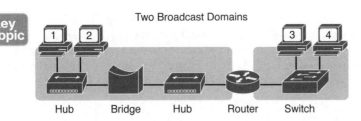

Figure 10-7   *Broadcast Domains Separated by a Router*

By definition, broadcasts sent by a device in one broadcast domain are not forwarded to devices in another broadcast domain. In this example, there are two broadcast domains. The router does not forward a LAN broadcast sent by a PC on the left to the network segment on the right.

Virtual LANs

Routers create multiple broadcast domains mostly as a side effect of how IP routing works. While a network designer might set about to use more router interfaces for the purpose of making a larger number of smaller broadcast domains, that plan quickly consumes router interfaces. But a better tool exists, one that is integrated into LAN switches and consumes no additional ports: virtual LANs (VLAN).

By far, VLANs give the network designer the best tool for designing the right number of broadcast domains, of the right size, with the right devices in each. To appreciate how VLANs do that, you must first think about one specific definition of what a LAN is:

A LAN consists of all devices in the same broadcast domain.

With VLANs, a switch configuration places each port into a specific VLAN. The switches create multiple broadcast domains by putting some interfaces into one VLAN and other interfaces into other VLANs. The switch forwarding logic does not forward frames from a port in one VLAN out a port into another VLAN—so the switch separates the LAN into separate broadcast domains. Instead, routers must forward packets between the VLANs by using routing logic. So, instead of all ports on a switch forming a single broadcast domain, the switch separates them into many, based on configuration.

For perspective, think about how you would create two different broadcast domains with switches if the switches had no concept of VLANs. Without any knowledge of VLANs, a switch would receive a frame on one port and flood it out all the rest of its ports. Therefore, to make two broadcast domains, two switches would be used—one for each broadcast domain, as shown in Figure 10-8.

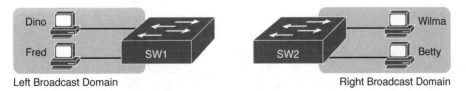

Figure 10-8   *Sample Network with Two Broadcast Domains and No VLANs*

Alternatively, with a switch that understands VLANs, you can create multiple broadcast domains using a single switch. All you do is put some ports in one VLAN and some in the other. (The Cisco Catalyst switch interface subcommand to do so is **switchport access vlan 2**, for instance, to place a port into VLAN 2.) Figure 10-9 shows the same two broadcast domains as in Figure 10-8, now implemented as two different VLANs on a single switch.

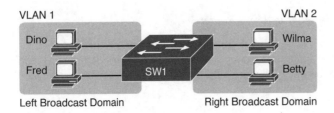

Figure 10-9 *Sample Network with Two VLANs Using One Switch*

This section briefly introduces the concept of VLANs, but Chapter 11, "Implementing Ethernet Virtual LANs," discusses VLANs in more depth, including the details of how to configure VLANs in campus LANs.

The Impact of Broadcast Domains on LAN Design

Modern LAN designs try to avoid collisions, because collisions make performance worse. There is no benefit to keeping collisions in the network. However, a LAN design cannot remove broadcasts, because broadcast frames play an important role in many protocols. So when thinking about broadcast domains, the choices are more about tradeoffs rather than designing to remove broadcasts.

For just one perspective, just think about the size of a broadcast domain—that is, the number of devices in the same broadcast domain. A small number of large broadcast domains can lead to poor performance for the devices in that broadcast domain. However, moving in the opposite direction, to making a large number of broadcast domains each with just a few devices, leads to other problems.

Consider the idea of a too-large broadcast domain for a moment. When a host receives a broadcast, the host must process the received frame. All hosts need to send some broadcasts to function properly, so when a broadcast arrives, the NIC must interrupt the computer's CPU to give the incoming message to the CPU. The CPU must spend time thinking about the received broadcast frame. (For example, IP Address Resolution Protocol [ARP] messages are LAN broadcasts, as mentioned in Chapter 4, "Fundamentals of IPv4 Addressing and Routing.") So, broadcasts happen, which is good, but broadcasts do require all the hosts to spend time processing each broadcast frame. The more devices in the same broadcast domain, the more unnecessary interruptions of each device's CPU.

This section of the book does not try to give a sweeping review of all VLAN design tradeoffs. Instead, you can see that the size of a VLAN should be considered, but many other factors come in to play as well. How big are the VLANs? How are the devices grouped? Do VLANs span across all switches or just a few? Is there any apparent consistency to the VLAN design, or is it somewhat haphazard? Answering these questions helps reveal what the designer was thinking, as well as what the realities of operating a network may have required.

> **NOTE**   If you would like more detail about Cisco recommendations about what to put in what VLAN, which impacts the size of VLANs, read the most recent Cisco document, "Campus LAN validated design" by searching on that phrase at Cisco.com.

Summarizing the main points about broadcast domains:

- Broadcasts exists, so be ready to analyze a design to define each broadcast domain, that is, each set of devices whose broadcasts reach the other devices in that domain.
- VLANs by definition are broadcast domains created though configuration.
- Routers, because they do not forward LAN broadcasts, create separate broadcast domains off their separate Ethernet interfaces.

Analyzing Campus LAN Topologies

The term *campus LAN* refers to the LAN created to support the devices in a building or in multiple buildings in somewhat close proximity to one another. For example, a company might lease office space in several buildings in the same office park. The network engineers can then build a campus LAN that includes switches in each building, plus Ethernet links between the switches in the buildings, to create a larger campus LAN.

When planning and designing a campus LAN, the engineers must consider the types of Ethernet available and the cabling lengths supported by each type. The engineers also need to choose the speeds required for each Ethernet segment. In addition, some thought needs to be given to the idea that some switches should be used to connect directly to end-user devices, whereas other switches might need to simply connect to a large number of these end-user switches. Finally, most projects require that the engineer consider the type of equipment that is already installed and whether an increase in speed on some segments is worth the cost of buying new equipment.

This second of three major sections of the chapter discusses the topology of a campus LAN design. Network designers do not just plug in devices to any port and connect switches to each other in an arbitrary way, like you might do with a few devices on the same table in a lab. Instead, there are known better ways to design the topology of a campus LAN, and this section introduces some of the key points and terms. The last major section of the chapter then looks at how to choose which Ethernet standard to use for each link in that campus LAN design, and why you might choose one versus another.

Two-Tier Campus Design (Collapsed Core)

To sift through all the requirements for a campus LAN, and then have a reasonable conversation about it with peers, most Cisco-oriented LAN designs use some common terminology to refer to the design. For this book's purposes, you should be aware of some of the key campus LAN design terminology.

The Two-Tier Campus Design

Figure 10-10 shows a typical design of a large campus LAN, with the terminology included in the figure. This LAN has around 1000 PCs connected to switches that support around 25 ports each. Explanations of the terminology follow the figure.

10

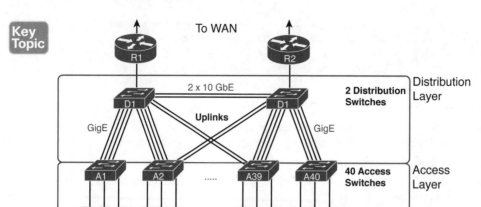

Figure 10-10 *Campus LAN with Design Terminology Listed*

Cisco uses three terms to describe the role of each switch in a campus design: *access*, *distribution*, and *core*. The roles differ based on whether the switch forwards traffic from user devices and the rest of the LAN (access), or whether the switch forwards traffic between other LAN switches (distribution and core).

Access switches connect directly to end users, providing user device access to the LAN. Access switches normally send traffic to and from the end-user devices to which they are connected and sit at the edge of the LAN.

Distribution switches provide a path through which the access switches can forward traffic to each other. By design, each of the access switches connects to at least one distribution switch, typically to two distribution switches for redundancy. The distribution switches provide the service of forwarding traffic to other parts of the LAN. Note that most designs use at least two uplinks to two different distribution switches (as shown in Figure 10-10) for redundancy.

The figure shows a two-tier design, with the tiers being the access tier (or layer) and the distribution tier (or layer). A two-tier design solves two major design needs:

- Provides a place to connect end-user devices (the access layer, with access switches)
- Connects the switches with a reasonable number of cables and switch ports by connecting all 40 access switches to two distribution switches

Topology Terminology Seen Within a Two-Tier Design

The exam topics happen to list a couple of terms about LAN and WAN topology and design, so this is a good place to pause to discuss those terms for a moment.

First, consider these more formal definitions of four topology terms:

Star: A design in which one central device connects to several others, so that if you drew the links out in all directions, the design would look like a star with light shining in all directions.

Full mesh: For any set of network nodes, a design that connects a link between each pair of nodes.

Partial mesh: For any set of network nodes, a design that connects a link between some pairs of nodes, but not all. In other words, a mesh that is not a full mesh.

Hybrid: A design that combines topology design concepts into a larger (typically more complex) design.

Armed with those formal definitions, note that the two-tier design is indeed a hybrid design that uses both a star topology at the access layer and a partial mesh at the distribution layer. To see why, consider Figure 10-11. It redraws a typical access layer switch, but instead of putting the PCs all below the switch, it spreads them around the switch. Then on the right, a similar version of the same drawing shows why the term star might be used—the topology looks a little like a child's drawing of a star.

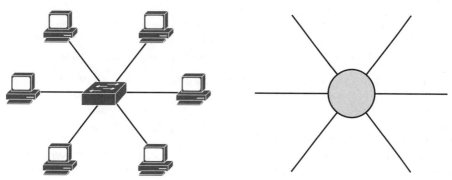

Figure 10-11   *The Star Topology Design Concept in Networking*

The distribution layer creates a partial mesh. If you view the access and distribution switches as nodes in a design, some nodes have a link between them, and some do not. Just refer to Figure 10-10 and note that, by design, none of the access layer switches connect to each other.

Finally, a design could use a full mesh. However, for a variety of reasons beyond the scope of the design discussion here, a campus design typically does not need to use the number of links and ports required by a full mesh design. However, just to make the point, first consider how many links and switch ports would be required for a single link between nodes in a full mesh, with six nodes, as shown in Figure 10-12.

10

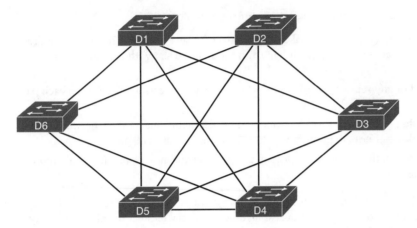

Figure 10-12   *Using a Full Mesh at the Distribution Layer, 6 Switches, 15 Links*

Even with only six switches, a full mesh would consume 15 links (and 30 switch ports—two per link).

Now think about a full mesh at the distribution layer for a design like Figure 10-10, with 40 access switches and two distribution switches. Rather than drawing it and counting it, the number of links is calculated with this old math formula from high school: $N(N − 1) / 2$, or in this case, $42 * 41 / 2 = 861$ links, and 1722 switch ports consumed among all switches.

For comparison's sake, the partial mesh design of Figure 10-10, with a pair of links from each access switch to each distribution switch, requires only 160 links and a total of 320 ports among all switches.

Three-Tier Campus Design (Core)

The two-tier design of Figure 10-10, with a partial mesh of links at the distribution layer, happens to be the most common campus LAN design. It also goes by two common names: a two-tier design (for obvious reasons), and a collapsed core (for less obvious reasons). The term *collapsed core* refers to the fact that the two-tier design does not have a third tier, the core tier. This next topic examines a three-tier design that does have a core, for perspective.

Imagine your campus has just two or three buildings. Each building has a two-tier design inside the building, with a pair of distribution switches in each building and access switches spread around the building as needed. How would you connect the LANs in each building? Well, with just a few buildings, it makes sense to simply cable the distribution switches together, as shown in Figure 10-13.

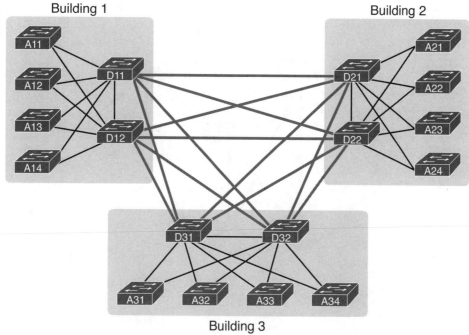

Figure 10-13   *Two-Tier Building Design, No Core, Three Buildings*

The design in Figure 10-13 works well, and many companies use this design. Sometimes the center of the network uses a full mesh, sometimes a partial mesh, depending on the availability of cables between the buildings.

However, a design with a third tier (a core tier) saves on switch ports and on cables in larger designs. And note that with the links between buildings, the cables run outside, are often more expensive to install, are almost always fiber cabling with more expensive switch ports, so conserving the number of cables used between buildings can help reduce costs.

A three-tier core design, unsurprisingly at this point, adds a few more switches (core switches), which provide one function: to connect the distribution switches. Figure 10-14 shows the migration of the Figure 10-13 collapsed core (that is, a design without a core) to a three-tier core design.

10

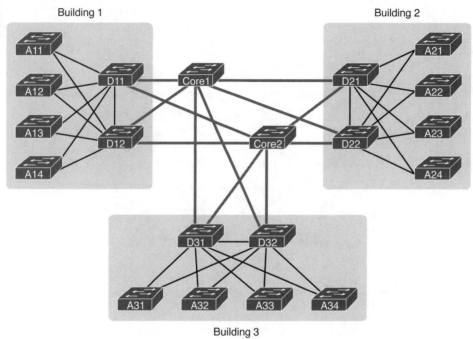

Figure 10-14 *Three-Tier Building Design (Core Design), Three Buildings*

> **NOTE** The core switches sit in the middle of the figure. In the physical world, they often sit in the same room as one of the distribution switches, rather than in some purpose-built room in the middle of the office park. The figure focuses more on the topology rather than the physical location.

By using a core design, with a partial mesh of links in the core, you still provide connectivity to all parts of the LAN, and to the routers that send packets over the WAN, just with fewer links between buildings.

The following list summarizes the terms that describe the roles of campus switches:

- **Access:** Provides a connection point (access) for end-user devices. Does not forward frames between two other access switches under normal circumstances.

- **Distribution:** Provides an aggregation point for access switches, providing connectivity to the rest of the devices in the LAN, forwarding frames between switches, but not connecting directly to end-user devices.

- **Core:** Aggregates distribution switches in very large campus LANs, providing very high forwarding rates for the larger volume of traffic due to the size of the network.

Topology Design Terminology

The ICND1 and CCNA exam topics specifically mention several network design terms related to topology. This next topic summarizes those key terms to connect the terms to the matching ideas.

First, consider Figure 10-15, which shows a few of the terms. First, on the left, drawings often show access switches with a series of cables, parallel to each other. However, an access switch and its access links is often called a *star topology*. Why? Look at the redrawn access switch in the center of the figure, with the cables radiating out from the center. It does not look like a real star, but it looks a little like a child's drawing of a star, hence the term star topology.

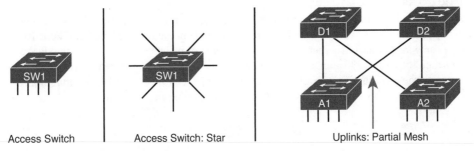

Access Switch | Access Switch: Star | Uplinks: Partial Mesh

Figure 10-15 *LAN Design Terminology*

The right side of the figure repeats a typical two-tier design, focusing on the mesh of links between the access and distribution switches. Any group of nodes that connect with more links than a star topology is typically called a *mesh*. In this case, the mesh is a *partial mesh*, because not all nodes have a direct link between each other. A design that connects all nodes with a link would be a *full mesh*.

Real networks make use of these topology ideas, but often a network combines the ideas together. For instance, the right side of Figure 10-14 combines the star topology of the access layer with the partial mesh of the distribution layer. So you might hear these designs that combine concepts called a *hybrid design*.

Analyzing LAN Physical Standard Choices

When you look at the design of a network designed by someone else, you can look at all the different types of cabling used, the different types of switch ports, and the Ethernet standards used in each case. Then ask yourself: Why did they choose a particular type of Ethernet link for each link in the network? Asking that question, and investigating the answer, starts to reveal much about building the physical campus LAN.

The IEEE has done an amazing job developing Ethernet standards that give network designers many options. Two themes in particular have helped Ethernet grow over the long term:

- The IEEE has developed many additional 802.3 standards for different types of cabling, different cable lengths, and for faster speeds.

- All the physical standards rely on the same consistent data-link details, with the same standard frame formats. That means that one Ethernet LAN can many types of physical links to meet distance, budget, and cabling needs.

For example, think about the access layer of the generic design drawings, but now think about cabling and Ethernet standards. In practice, access layer switches sit in a locked wiring closet somewhere on the same floor as the end user devices. Electricians have installed unshielded twisted-pair (UTP) cabling used at the access layer, running from that wiring closet to each wall plate at each office, cubicle, or any place where an Ethernet device might need to connect to the LAN. The type and quality of the cabling installed between the wiring closet and each Ethernet outlet dictate what Ethernet standards can be supported. Certainly, whoever designed the LAN at the time the cabling was installed thought about what type of cabling was needed to support the types of Ethernet physical standards that were going to be used in that LAN.

Ethernet Standards

Over time, the IEEE has continued to develop and release new Ethernet standards, for new faster speeds and to support new and different cabling types and cable lengths. Figure 10-16 shows some insight into Ethernet speed improvements over the years. The early standards up through the early 1990s ran at 10 Mbps, with steadily improving cabling and topologies. Then, with the introduction of Fast Ethernet (100 Mbps) in 1995, the IEEE began ramping up the speeds steadily over the next few decades, continuing even until today.

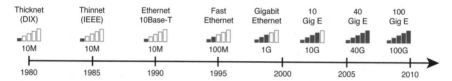

Figure 10-16 *Ethernet Standards Timeline*

NOTE Often, the IEEE first introduces support for the next higher speed using some forms of fiber optic cabling, and later, sometimes many years later, the IEEE completes the work to develop standards to support the same speed on UTP cabling. Figure 10-16 shows the earliest standards for each speed, no matter what cabling.

When the IEEE introduces support for a new type of cabling, or a faster speed, they create a new standard as part of 802.3. These new standards have a few letters behind the name. So, when speaking of the standards, sometimes you might refer to the standard name (with letters). For instance, the IEEE standardized Gigabit Ethernet support using inexpensive UTP cabling in standard 802.3ab. However, more often, engineers refer to that same standard as 1000BASE-T or simply Gigabit Ethernet. Table 10-2 lists some of the IEEE 802.3 physical layer standards and related names for perspective.

Table 10-2 IEEE Physical Layer Standards

Original IEEE Standard	Shorthand Name	Informal Names	Speed	Typical Cabling
802.3i	10BASE-T	Ethernet	10 Mbps	UTP
802.3u	100BASE-T	Fast Ethernet	100 Mbps	UTP
802.3z	1000BASE-X	Gigabit Ethernet, GigE	1000 Mbps (1 Gbps)	Fiber
802.3ab	1000BASE-T	Gigabit Ethernet, GigE	1000 Mbps (1 Gbps)	UTP
802.3ae	10GBASE-X	10 GigE	10 Gbps	Fiber
802.3an	10GBASE-T	10 GigE	10 Gbps	UTP
802.3ba	40GBASE-X	40 GigE	40 Gbps	Fiber
802.3ba	100GBASE-X	100 GigE	100 Gbps	Fiber

Choosing the Right Ethernet Standard for Each Link

When designing an Ethernet LAN, you can and should think about the topology, with an access layer, a distribution layer, and possibly a core layer. But thinking about the topology does not tell you which specific standards to follow for each link. Ultimately, you need to pick which Ethernet standard to use for each link, based on the following kinds of facts about each physical standard:

- The speed
- The maximum distance allowed between devices when using that standard/cabling
- The cost of the cabling and switch hardware
- The availability of that type of cabling already installed at your facilities

Consider the three most common types of Ethernet today (10BASE-T, 100BASE-T, and 1000BASE-T). They all have the same 100-meter UTP cable length restriction. They all use UTP cabling. However, not all UTP cabling meets the same quality standard, and as it turns out, the faster the Ethernet standard, the higher the required cable quality category needed to support that standard. As a result, some buildings might have better cabling that supports speeds up through Gigabit Ethernet, whereas some buildings may support only Fast Ethernet.

The Telecommunications Industry Association (TIA; tiaonline.org) defines Ethernet cabling quality standards. Each Ethernet UTP standard lists a TIA cabling quality (called a *category*) as the minimum category that the standard supports. For example, 10BASE-T allows for Category 3 (CAT3) cabling or better. 100BASE-T requires higher-quality CAT5 cabling, and 1000BASE-T requires even higher-quality CAT5e cabling. (The TIA standards follow a general "higher number is better cabling" in their numbering.) For instance, if an older facility had only CAT5 cabling installed between the wiring closets and each cubicle, the engineers would have to consider upgrading the cabling to fully support Gigabit Ethernet. Table 10-3 lists the more common types of Ethernet and their cable types and length limitations.

Table 10-3   Ethernet Types, Media, and Segment Lengths (Per IEEE)

Ethernet Type	Media	Maximum Segment Length
10BASE-T	TIA CAT3 or better, 2 pairs	100 m (328 feet)
100BASE-T	TIA CAT5 UTP or better, 2 pairs	100 m (328 feet)
1000BASE-T	TIA CAT5e UTP or better, 4 pairs	100 m (328 feet)
10GBASE-T	TIA CAT6a UTP or better, 4 pairs	100 m (328 feet)
10GBASE-T[1]	TIA CAT6 UTP or better, 4 pairs	38–55 m (127–180 feet)
1000BASE-SX	Multimode fiber	550 m (1800 feet)
1000BASE-LX	Multimode fiber	550 m (1800 feet)
1000BASE-LX	9-micron single-mode fiber	5 km (3.1 miles)

[1] The option for 10GBASE-T with slightly less quality CAT6 cabling, but at shorter distances, is an attempt to support 10Gig Ethernet for some installations with CAT6 installed cabling.

Ethernet defines standards for using fiber optic cables as well. Fiber optic cables include ultrathin strands of glass through which light can pass. To send bits, the switches can alternate between sending brighter and dimmer light to encode 0s and 1s on the cable.

10

Generally comparing optical cabling versus UTP cabling Ethernet standards, two obvious points stand out. Optical standards allow much longer cabling, while generally costing more for the cable and the switch hardware components. Optical cables experience much less interference from outside sources compared to copper cables, which allows for longer distances.

When considering optical Ethernet links, many standards exist, but with two general categories. Comparing the two, the cheaper options generally support distances into the hundreds of meters, using less expensive light-emitting diodes (LED) to transmit data. Other optical standards support much longer distances into multiple kilometers, using more expensive cabling and using lasers to transmit the data. The trade-off is basic: For a given link, how long does the cable need to run, what standards support that distance, and which is the least expensive to meet that need?

In reality, most engineers remember only the general facts from tables like Table 10-3: 100 meters for UTP, about 500 meters for multimode fiber, and about 5000 meters for some single mode fiber Ethernet standards. When it is time to get serious about designing the details of each link, the engineer must get into the details, calculating the length of each cable based on its path through the building, and so on.

Wireless LANs Combined with Wired Ethernet

Modern campus LANs include a large variety of wireless devices that connect to the access layer of the LAN. As it turns out, Cisco organizes wireless LANs into a separate certification track—CCNA, CCNP, and CCIE Wireless—so the CCNA R&S track has traditionally had only a little wireless LAN coverage. The current version of the exams are no different, with this one exam CCNA R&S topic mentioning wireless LANs:

> Describe the impact of infrastructure components in an enterprise network: Access points and wireless controllers

Do not let that small mention of wireless technology make you think that wireless is less important than Ethernet. In fact, there may be more wireless devices than wired at the access layer of today's enterprise networks. Both are important; Cisco just happens to keep the educational material for wireless in a separate certification track.

This last topic in the chapter examines that one exam topic that mentions two wireless terms.

Home Office Wireless LANs

First, the IEEE defines both Ethernet LANs and Wireless LANs. In case it was not obvious yet, all Ethernet standards use cables—that is, Ethernet defines wired LANs. The IEEE 802.11 working group defines Wireless LANs, also called Wi-Fi per a trademarked term from the Wi-Fi Alliance (wi-fi.org), a consortium that helps to encourage wireless LAN development in the marketplace.

Most of you have used Wi-Fi, and may use it daily. Some of you may have set it up at home, with a basic setup as shown in Figure 10-17. In a home, you probably used a single consumer device called a *wireless router*. One side of the device connects to the Internet, while the other side connects to the devices in the home. In the home, the devices can connect either with Wi-Fi or with a wired Ethernet cable.

SOHO

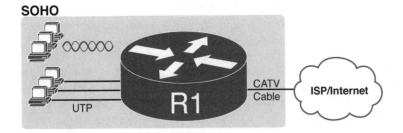

Figure 10-17 *A Typical Home Wired and Wireless LAN*

While the figure shows the hardware as a single router icon, internally, that one wireless router acts like three separate devices you would find in an enterprise campus:

■ An Ethernet switch, for the wired Ethernet connections

■ A wireless access point (AP), to communicate with the wireless devices and forward the frames to/from the wired network

■ A router, to route IP packets to/from the LAN and WAN (Internet) interfaces

Figure 10-18 repeats the previous figure, breaking out the internal components as if they were separate physical devices, just to make the point that a single consumer wireless router acts like several different devices.

SOHO

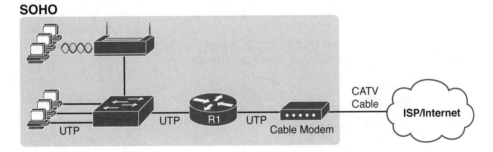

Figure 10-18 *A Representation of the Functions Inside a Consumer Wireless Routing Product*

In a small office/home office (SOHO) wireless LAN, the wireless AP acts autonomously, doing all the work required to create and control the wireless LAN (WLAN). (In most enterprise WLANs, the AP does not act autonomously.) In other words, the autonomous AP communicates with the various wireless devices using 802.11 protocols and radio waves. It uses Ethernet protocols on the wired side. It converts between the differences in header formats between 802.11 and 802.3 frames before forwarding to/from 802.3 Ethernet and 802.11 wireless frames.

Beyond those basic forwarding actions, the autonomous AP must perform a variety of control and management functions. The AP authenticates new devices, defines the name of the WLAN (called a service set ID, or SSID), and other details.

10

Enterprise Wireless LANs and Wireless LAN Controllers

If you connect to your WLAN at home from your tablet, phone, or laptop, and then walk down the street with that same device, you expect to lose your Wi-Fi connection at some point. You do not expect to somehow automatically connect to a neighbor's Wi-Fi network, particularly if they did the right thing and set up security functions on their AP to prevent others from accessing their home Wi-Fi network. The neighborhood does not create one WLAN supported by the devices in all the houses and apartments; instead, it has lots of little autonomous WLANs.

However, in an enterprise, the opposite needs to happen. We want people to be able to roam around the building and office campus and keep connected to the Wi-Fi network. This requires many APs, which work together rather than autonomously to create one wireless LAN.

First, think about the number of APs an enterprise might need. Each AP can cover only a certain amount of space, depending on a large number of conditions and the wireless standard. (The size varies, but the distances sit in the 100 to 200 feet range.) At the same time, you might have the opposite problem; you may just need lots of APs in a small space, just to add capacity to the WLAN. Much of the time spent designing WLANs revolves around deciding how many APs to place in each space, and of what types, to handle the traffic.

NOTE   If you have not paid attention before, start looking around the ceilings of any new buildings you enter, even retail stores, and look for their wireless APs.

Each AP must then connect to the wired LAN, because most of the destinations that wireless users need to communicate with sit in the wired part of the network. In fact, the APs typically sit close to where users sit, for obvious reasons, so the APs connect to the same access switches as the end users, as shown in Figure 10-19.

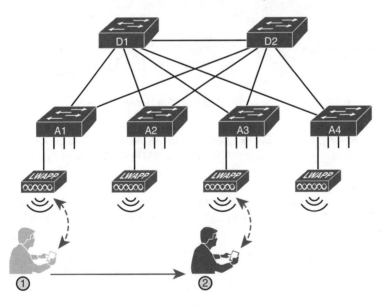

Figure 10-19 *Campus LAN, Multiple Lightweight APs, with Roaming*

Now imagine that is you at the bottom of the figure. Your smartphone has Wi-Fi enabled, so that when you walk into work, your phone automatically connects to the company WLAN. You roam around all day, going to meetings, lunch, and so on. All day long you stay connected to the company WLAN, but your phone connects to and uses many different APs.

Supporting roaming and other enterprise WLAN features by using autonomous APs can be difficult at best. You could imagine that if you had a dozen APs per floor, you might have hundreds of APs in a campus—all of which need to know about that one WLAN.

The solution: remove all the control and management features from the APs, and put them in one centralized place, called a Wireless Controller, or Wireless LAN Controller (WLC). The APs no longer act autonomously, but instead act as lightweight APs (LWAPs), just forwarding data between the wireless LAN and the WLC. All the logic to deal with roaming, defining WLANs (SSIDs), authentication, and so on happens in the centralized WLC rather than on each AP. Summarizing:

Wireless LAN controller: Controls and manages all AP functions (for example, roaming, defining WLANs, authentication)

Lightweight AP (LWAP): Forwards data between the wired and wireless LAN, and specifically forwarding data through the WLC using a protocol like Control And Provisioning of Wireless Access Points (CAPWAP)

With the WLC and LWAP design, the combined LWAPs and WLC can create one big wireless network, rather than creating a multitude of disjointed wireless networks. The key to making it all work is that all wireless traffic flows through the WLC, as shown in Figure 10-20. (The LWAPs commonly use a protocol called CAPWAP, by the way.)

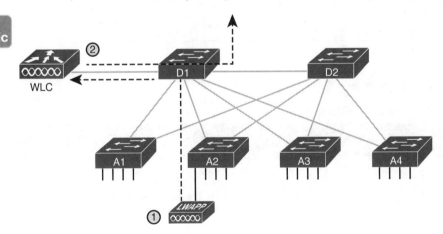

Figure 10-20 *Campus LAN, Multiple Lightweight APs, with Roaming*

By forwarding all the traffic through the WLC, the WLC can make the right decisions across the enterprise. For example, you might create a marketing WLAN, an engineering WLAN, and so on, and all the APs know about and support those multiple different WLANs. Users that connect to the engineering WLAN should use the same authentication rules regardless of which AP they use—and the WLC makes that possible. Or consider roaming for a moment. If at one instant a packet arrives for your phone, and you are associated with AP1, and when the next packet arrives over the wired network you are now connected to AP4, how could that packet be delivered through the network? Well, it always goes to the WLC, and because the WLC keeps in contact with the APs and knows that your phone just roamed to another AP, the WLC knows where to forward the packet.

Chapter Review

The "Your Study Plan" element, just before Chapter 1, "Introduction to TCP/IP Networking," discusses how you should study and practice the content and skills for each chapter before moving on to the next chapter. That element introduces the tools used here at the end of each chapter. If you haven't already done so, take a few minutes to read that section. Then come back here and do the useful work of reviewing the chapter to help lock into memory what you just read.

Review this chapter's material using either the tools in the book, DVD, or interactive tools for the same material found on the book's companion website. Table 10-4 outlines the key review elements and where you can find them. To better track your study progress, record when you completed these activities in the second column.

Table 10-4   Chapter Review Tracking

Review Element	Review Date(s)	Resource Used
Review key topics		Book, app
Review key terms		Book, app
Answer DIKTA questions		Book, PCPT
Review memory tables		Book, app

Review All the Key Topics

Table 10-5   Key Topics for Chapter 10

Key Topic Element	Description	Page Number
Figure 10-1	Effect of LAN hub repeating electrical signals	221
List	Key points about hubs	221
Figure 10-4	Switches create separate collision domains	223
List	Summary of points about collision domains	223
Figure 10-5	Collision domains example	224
Figure 10-7	Broadcast domain example	225
List	Summary of points about broadcast domains	227
Figure 10-10	Campus LAN design terms	228
List	Mesh topology terms	229
Figure 10-11	Star topology	229
Figure 10-13	A two-tier (collapsed core) LAN topology	231

Key Topic Element	Description	Page Number
Figure 10-14	A three-tier (core) LAN topology	232
List	Two key comparisons about Ethernet technology	233
Figure 10-20	The wireless LAN controller and lightweight access point terms in the context of a network diagram	239

Key Terms You Should Know

autonegotiation, broadcast domain, broadcast frame, collision domain, flooding, virtual LAN, access point, wireless LAN controller, star topology, full mesh, partial mesh, hub, transparent bridge, collapsed core design, core design, access layer, distribution layer, core layer

10

CHAPTER 11

Implementing Ethernet Virtual LANs

This chapter covers the following exam topics:

2.0 LAN Switching Technologies

2.1 Describe and verify switching concepts

> 2.1.a MAC learning and aging
>
> 2.1.b Frame switching
>
> 2.1.c Frame flooding
>
> 2.1.d MAC address table

2.4 Configure, verify, and troubleshoot VLANs (normal range) spanning multiple switches

> 2.4.a Access ports (data and voice)
>
> 2.4.b Default VLAN

2.5 Configure, verify, and troubleshoot inter-switch connectivity

> 2.5.a Trunk ports
>
> 2.5.b 802.1Q
>
> 2.5.c Native VLAN

At their heart, Ethernet switches receive Ethernet frames, make decisions, and then forward (switch) those Ethernet frames. That core logic revolves around MAC addresses, the interface in which the frame arrives, and the interfaces out which the switch forwards the frame. Several switch features have some impact on an individual switch's decisions about where to forward frames, but of all the topics in this book, virtual LANs (VLAN) easily have the biggest impact on those choices.

This chapter examines the concepts and configuration of VLANs. The first major section of the chapter explains the core concepts. These concepts include how VLANs work on a single switch, how to use VLAN trunking to create VLANs that span across multiple switches, and how to forward traffic between VLANs using a router. The second major section shows how to configure VLANs and VLAN trunks: how to statically assign interfaces to a VLAN.

"Do I Know This Already?" Quiz

Take the quiz (either here, or use the PCPT software) if you want to use the score to help you decide how much time to spend on this chapter. The answers are at the bottom of the page following the quiz, and the explanations are in DVD Appendix C and in the PCPT software.

Table 11-1 "Do I Know This Already?" Foundation Topics Section-to-Question Mapping

Foundation Topics Section	Questions
Virtual LAN Concepts	1–3
VLAN and VLAN Trunking Configuration and Verification	4–6

1. In a LAN, which of the following terms best equates to the term *VLAN*?

   a. Collision domain

   b. Broadcast domain

   c. Subnet

   d. Single switch

   e. Trunk

2. Imagine a switch with three configured VLANs. How many IP subnets are required, assuming that all hosts in all VLANs want to use TCP/IP?

   a. 0

   b. 1

   c. 2

   d. 3

   e. You cannot tell from the information provided.

3. Switch SW1 sends a frame to switch SW2 using 802.1Q trunking. Which of the answers describes how SW1 changes or adds to the Ethernet frame before forwarding the frame to SW2?

   a. Inserts a 4-byte header and does change the MAC addresses

   b. Inserts a 4-byte header and does not change the MAC addresses

   c. Encapsulates the original frame behind an entirely new Ethernet header

   d. None of the other answers are correct

4. Imagine that you are told that switch 1 is configured with the **dynamic auto** parameter for trunking on its Fa0/5 interface, which is connected to switch 2. You have to configure switch 2. Which of the following settings for trunking could allow trunking to work? (Choose two answers.)

   a. on

   b. dynamic auto

   c. dynamic desirable

   d. access

   e. None of the other answers are correct.

5. A switch has just arrived from Cisco. The switch has never been configured with any VLANs, but VTP has been disabled. An engineer gets into configuration mode and issues the **vlan 22** command, followed by the **name Hannahs-VLAN** command. Which of the following are true? (Choose two answers.)

    a. VLAN 22 is listed in the output of the **show vlan brief** command.

    b. VLAN 22 is listed in the output of the **show running-config** command.

    c. VLAN 22 is not created by this process.

    d. VLAN 22 does not exist in that switch until at least one interface is assigned to that VLAN.

6. Which of the following commands identify switch interfaces as being trunking interfaces: interfaces that currently operate as VLAN trunks? (Choose two answers.)

    a. show interfaces

    b. show interfaces switchport

    c. show interfaces trunk

    d. show trunks

Foundation Topics

Virtual LAN Concepts

Before understanding VLANs, you must first have a specific understanding of the definition of a LAN. For example, from one perspective, a LAN includes all the user devices, servers, switches, routers, cables, and wireless access points in one location. However, an alternative narrower definition of a LAN can help in understanding the concept of a virtual LAN:

> A LAN includes all devices in the same broadcast domain.

A broadcast domain includes the set of all LAN-connected devices, so that when any of the devices sends a broadcast frame, all the other devices get a copy of the frame. So, from one perspective, you can think of a LAN and a broadcast domain as being basically the same thing.

Without VLANs, a switch considers all its interfaces to be in the same broadcast domain. That is, for one switch, when a broadcast frame entered one switch port, the switch forwarded that broadcast frame out all other ports. With that logic, to create two different LAN broadcast domains, you had to buy two different Ethernet LAN switches, as shown in Figure 11-1.

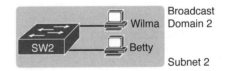

Figure 11-1   *Creating Two Broadcast Domains with Two Physical Switches and No VLANs*

With support for VLANs, a single switch can accomplish the same goals of the design in Figure 11-1—to create two broadcast domains—with a single switch. With VLANs, a switch can configure some interfaces into one broadcast domain and some into another, creating multiple broadcast domains. These individual broadcast domains created by the switch are called virtual LANs (VLAN).

For example, in Figure 11-2, the single switch creates two VLANs, treating the ports in each VLAN as being completely separate. The switch would never forward a frame sent by Dino (in VLAN 1) over to either Wilma or Betty (in VLAN 2).

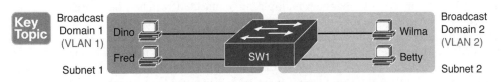

Figure 11-2 *Creating Two Broadcast Domains Using One Switch and VLANs*

Designing campus LANs to use more VLANs, each with a smaller number of devices, often helps improve the LAN in many ways. For example, a broadcast sent by one host in a VLAN will be received and processed by all the other hosts in the VLAN—but not by hosts in a different VLAN. Limiting the number of hosts that receive a single broadcast frame reduces the number of hosts that waste effort processing unneeded broadcasts. It also reduces security risks, because fewer hosts see frames sent by any one host. These are just a few reasons for separating hosts into different VLANs. The following list summarizes the most common reasons for choosing to create smaller broadcast domains (VLANs):

- To reduce CPU overhead on each device by reducing the number of devices that receive each broadcast frame

- To reduce security risks by reducing the number of hosts that receive copies of frames that the switches flood (broadcasts, multicasts, and unknown unicasts)

- To improve security for hosts that send sensitive data by keeping those hosts on a separate VLAN

- To create more flexible designs that group users by department, or by groups that work together, instead of by physical location

- To solve problems more quickly, because the failure domain for many problems is the same set of devices as those in the same broadcast domain

- To reduce the workload for the Spanning Tree Protocol (STP) by limiting a VLAN to a single access switch

This chapter does not examine all the reasons for VLANs in more depth. However, know that most enterprise networks use VLANs quite a bit. The rest of this chapter looks closely at the mechanics of how VLANs work across multiple Cisco switches, including the required configuration. To that end, the next section examines VLAN trunking, a feature required when installing a VLAN that exists on more than one LAN switch.

Creating Multiswitch VLANs Using Trunking

Configuring VLANs on a single switch requires only a little effort: You simply configure each port to tell it the VLAN number to which the port belongs. With multiple switches, you have to consider additional concepts about how to forward traffic between the switches.

When using VLANs in networks that have multiple interconnected switches, the switches need to use *VLAN trunking* on the links between the switches. VLAN trunking causes the switches to use a process called *VLAN tagging*, by which the sending switch adds another header to the frame before sending it over the trunk. This extra trunking header includes a *VLAN identifier* (VLAN ID) field so that the sending switch can associate the frame with a particular VLAN ID, and the receiving switch can then know in what VLAN each frame belongs.

Figure 11-3 shows an example that demonstrates VLANs that exist on multiple switches, but it does not use trunking. First, the design uses two VLANs: VLAN 10 and VLAN 20. Each switch has two ports assigned to each VLAN, so each VLAN exists in both switches. To forward traffic in VLAN 10 between the two switches, the design includes a link between switches, with that link fully inside VLAN 10. Likewise, to support VLAN 20 traffic between switches, the design uses a second link between switches, with that link inside VLAN 20.

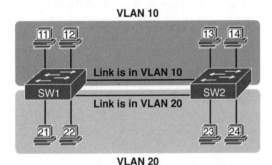

Figure 11-3 *Multiswitch VLAN Without VLAN Trunking*

The design in Figure 11-3 functions perfectly. For example, PC11 (in VLAN 10) can send a frame to PC14. The frame flows into SW1, over the top link (the one that is in VLAN 10) and over to SW2.

The design shown in Figure 11-3 works, but it simply does not scale very well. It requires one physical link between switches to support every VLAN. If a design needed 10 or 20 VLANs, you would need 10 or 20 links between switches, and you would use 10 or 20 switch ports (on each switch) for those links.

VLAN Tagging Concepts

VLAN trunking creates one link between switches that supports as many VLANs as you need. As a VLAN trunk, the switches treat the link as if it were a part of all the VLANs. At the same time, the trunk keeps the VLAN traffic separate, so frames in VLAN 10 would not go to devices in VLAN 20, and vice versa, because each frame is identified by VLAN number as it crosses the trunk. Figure 11-4 shows the idea, with a single physical link between the two switches.

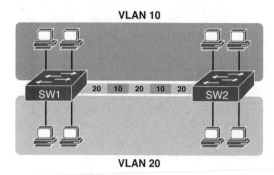

Figure 11-4 *Multiswitch VLAN with Trunking*

The use of trunking allows switches to pass frames from multiple VLANs over a single physical connection by adding a small header to the Ethernet frame. For example, Figure 11-5 shows PC11 sending a broadcast frame on interface Fa0/1 at Step 1. To flood the frame, switch SW1 needs to forward the broadcast frame to switch SW2. However, SW1 needs to let SW2 know that the frame is part of VLAN 10, so that after the frame is received, SW2 will flood the frame only into VLAN 10, and not into VLAN 20. So, as shown at Step 2, before sending the frame, SW1 adds a VLAN header to the original Ethernet frame, with the VLAN header listing a VLAN ID of 10 in this case.

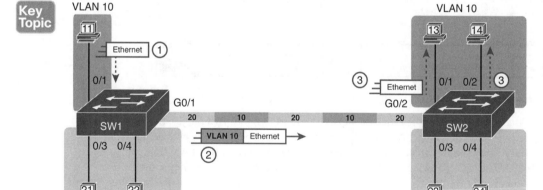

Figure 11-5 *VLAN Trunking Between Two Switches*

When SW2 receives the frame, it understands that the frame is in VLAN 10. SW2 then removes the VLAN header, forwarding the original frame out its interfaces in VLAN 10 (Step 3).

For another example, consider the case when PC21 (in VLAN 20) sends a broadcast. SW1 sends the broadcast out port Fa0/4 (because that port is in VLAN 20) and out Gi0/1 (because it is a trunk, meaning that it supports multiple different VLANs). SW1 adds a trunking header to the frame, listing a VLAN ID of 20. SW2 strips off the trunking header after determining that the frame is part of VLAN 20, so SW2 knows to forward the frame out only ports Fa0/3 and Fa0/4, because they are in VLAN 20, and not out ports Fa0/1 and Fa0/2, because they are in VLAN 10.

The 802.1Q and ISL VLAN Trunking Protocols

Cisco has supported two different trunking protocols over the years: Inter-Switch Link (ISL) and IEEE 802.1Q. Cisco created the ISL long before 802.1Q, in part because the IEEE had not yet defined a VLAN trunking standard. Years later, the IEEE completed work on the 802.1Q standard, which defines a different way to do trunking. Today, 802.1Q has become the more popular trunking protocol, with Cisco not even supporting ISL in some of its newer models of LAN switches, including the 2960 switches used in the examples in this book.

While both ISL and 802.1Q tag each frame with the VLAN ID, the details differ. 802.1Q inserts an extra 4-byte 802.1Q VLAN header into the original frame's Ethernet header, as shown at the top of Figure 11-6. As for the fields in the 802.1Q header, only the 12-bit VLAN ID field inside the 802.1Q header matters for topics discussed in this book. This 12-bit field supports a theoretical maximum of 2^{12} (4096) VLANs, but in practice it supports a maximum of 4094. (Both 802.1Q and ISL use 12 bits to tag the VLAN ID, with two reserved values [0 and 4095].)

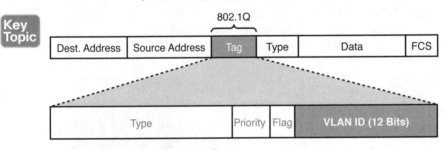

Figure 11-6 *802.1Q Trunking*

Cisco switches break the range of VLAN IDs (1–4094) into two ranges: the normal range and the extended range. All switches can use normal-range VLANs with values from 1 to 1005. Only some switches can use extended-range VLANs with VLAN IDs from 1006 to 4094. The rules for which switches can use extended-range VLANs depend on the configuration of the VLAN Trunking Protocol (VTP), which is discussed briefly in the section "VLAN Trunking Configuration," later in this chapter.

802.1Q also defines one special VLAN ID on each trunk as the *native VLAN* (defaulting to use VLAN 1). By definition, 802.1Q simply does not add an 802.1Q header to frames in the native VLAN. When the switch on the other side of the trunk receives a frame that does not have an 802.1Q header, the receiving switch knows that the frame is part of the native VLAN. Note that because of this behavior, both switches must agree on which VLAN is the native VLAN.

The 802.1Q native VLAN provides some interesting functions, mainly to support connections to devices that do not understand trunking. For example, a Cisco switch could be cabled to a switch that does not understand 802.1Q trunking. The Cisco switch could send frames in the native VLAN—meaning that the frame has no trunking header—so that the other switch would understand the frame. The native VLAN concept gives switches the capability of at least passing traffic in one VLAN (the native VLAN), which can allow some basic functions, like reachability to telnet into a switch.

Forwarding Data Between VLANs

If you create a campus LAN that contains many VLANs, you typically still need all devices to be able to send data to all other devices. This next topic discusses some concepts about how to route data between those VLANs.

First, it helps to know a few terms about some categories of LAN switches. All the Ethernet switch functions described in this book so far use the details and logic defined by OSI Layer 2 protocols. For example, Chapter 7, "Analyzing Ethernet LAN Switching," discussed how LAN switches receive Ethernet frames (a Layer 2 concept), look at the destination Ethernet MAC address (a Layer 2 address), and forward the Ethernet frame out some other interface. This chapter has already discussed the concept of VLANs as broadcast domains, which is yet another Layer 2 concept.

While some LAN switches work just as described so far in this book, some LAN switches have even more functions. LAN switches that forward data based on Layer 2 logic, as discussed so far in this book, often go by the name *Layer 2 switch*. However, some other switches can do some functions like a router, using additional logic defined by Layer 3 protocols. These switches go by the name *multilayer switch*, or *Layer 3 switch*. This section first discusses how to forward data between VLANs when using Layer 2 switches and ends with a brief discussion of how to use Layer 3 switches.

Routing Packets Between VLANs with a Router

When including VLANs in a campus LAN design, the devices in a VLAN need to be in the same subnet. Following the same design logic, devices in different VLANs need to be in different subnets. For example, in Figure 11-7, the two PCs on the left sit in VLAN 10, in subnet 10. The two PCs on the right sit in a different VLAN (20), with a different subnet (20).

Figure 11-7   *Layer 2 Switch Does Not Route Between the VLANs*

> **NOTE**   The figure refers to subnets somewhat generally, like "subnet 10," just so the subnet numbers do not distract. Also, note that the subnet numbers do not have to be the same number as the VLAN numbers.

Figure 11-7 shows the switch as if it were two switches broken in two to emphasize the point that Layer 2 switches will not forward data between two VLANs. When configured with some ports in VLAN 10 and others in VLAN 20, the switch acts like two separate switches in which it will forward traffic. In fact, one goal of VLANs is to separate traffic in one VLAN from another, preventing frames in one VLAN from leaking over to other

VLANs. For example, when Dino (in VLAN 10) sends any Ethernet frame, if SW1 is a Layer 2 switch, that switch will not forward the frame to the PCs on the right in VLAN 20.

The network as a whole needs to support traffic flowing into and out of each VLAN, even though the Layer 2 switch does not forward frames outside a VLAN. The job of forwarding data into and out of a VLAN falls to routers. Instead of switching Layer 2 Ethernet frames between the two VLANs, the network must route Layer 3 packets between the two subnets.

That previous paragraph has some very specific wording related to Layers 2 and 3, so take a moment to reread and reconsider it for a moment. The Layer 2 logic does not let the Layer 2 switch forward the Layer 2 protocol data unit (L2PDU), the Ethernet frame, between VLANs. However, routers can route Layer 3 PDUs (L3PDU) (packets) between subnets as their normal job in life.

For example, Figure 11-8 shows a router that can route packets between subnets 10 and 20. The figure shows the same Layer 2 switch as shown in Figure 11-7, with the same perspective of the switch being split into parts with two different VLANs, and with the same PCs in the same VLANs and subnets. Now Router R1 has one LAN physical interface connected to the switch and assigned to VLAN 10, and a second physical interface connected to the switch and assigned to VLAN 20. With an interface connected to each subnet, the Layer 2 switch can keep doing its job—forwarding frames inside a VLAN, while the router can do its job—routing IP packets between the subnets.

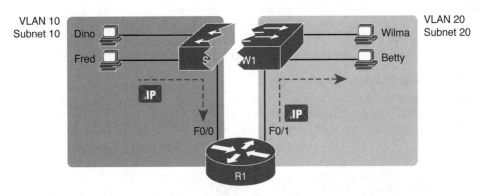

Figure 11-8   *Routing Between Two VLANs on Two Physical Interfaces*

The figure shows an IP packet being routed from Fred, which sits in one VLAN/subnet, to Betty, which sits in the other. The Layer 2 switch forwards two different Layer 2 Ethernet frames: one in VLAN 10, from Fred to R1's F0/0 interface, and the other in VLAN 20, from R1's F0/1 interface to Betty. From a Layer 3 perspective, Fred sends the IP packet to its default router (R1), and R1 routes the packet out another interface (F0/1) into another subnet where Betty resides.

While the design shown in Figure 11-8 works, it uses too many physical interfaces, one per VLAN. A much less expensive (and much preferred) option uses a VLAN trunk between the switch and router, requiring only one physical link between the router and switch, while supporting all VLANs. Trunking can work between any two devices that choose to support it: between two switches, between a router and a switch, or even between server hardware and a switch.

Figure 11-9 shows the same design idea as Figure 11-8, with the same packet being sent from Fred to Betty, except now R1 uses VLAN trunking instead of a separate link for each VLAN.

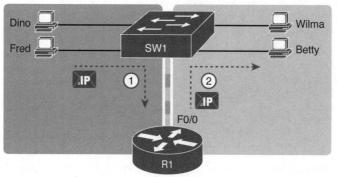

Figure 11-9 *Routing Between Two VLANs Using a Trunk on the Router*

> **NOTE** Because the router has a single physical link connected to the LAN switch, this design is sometimes called a *router-on-a-stick*.

As a brief aside about terminology, many people describe the concept in Figures 11-8 and 11-9 as "routing packets between VLANs." You can use that phrase, and people know what you mean. However, note that this phrase is not literally true, because it refers to routing packets (a Layer 3 concept) and VLANs (a Layer 2 concept). It just takes fewer words to say something like "routing between VLANs" rather than the literally true but long "routing Layer 3 packets between Layer 3 subnets, with those subnets each mapping to a Layer 2 VLAN."

Routing Packets with a Layer 3 Switch

Routing packets using a physical router, even with the VLAN trunk in the router-on-a-stick model shown in Figure 11-9, still has one significant problem: performance. The physical link puts an upper limit on how many bits can be routed, and less expensive routers tend to be less powerful, and might not be able to route a large enough number of packets per second (pps) to keep up with the traffic volumes.

The ultimate solution moves the routing functions inside the LAN switch hardware. Vendors long ago started combining the hardware and software features of their Layer 2 LAN switches, plus their Layer 3 routers, creating products called *Layer 3 switches* (also known as *multilayer switches*). Layer 3 switches can be configured to act only as a Layer 2 switch, or they can be configured to do both Layer 2 switching as well as Layer 3 routing.

Today, many medium- to large-sized enterprise campus LANs use Layer 3 switches to route packets between subnets (VLANs) in a campus.

In concept, a Layer 3 switch works a lot like the original two devices on which the Layer 3 switch is based: a Layer 2 LAN switch and a Layer 3 router. In fact, if you take the concepts and packet flow shown in Figure 11-8, with a separate Layer 2 switch and Layer 3 router, and then imagine all those features happening inside one device, you have the general idea of what a Layer 3 switch does. Figure 11-10 shows that exact concept, repeating many details of Figure 11-8, but with an overlay that shows the one Layer 3 switch doing the Layer 2 switch functions and the separate Layer 3 routing function.

11

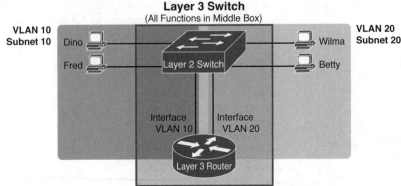

Figure 11-10 *Multilayer Switch: Layer 2 Switching with Layer 3 Routing in One Device*

This chapter introduces the core concepts of routing IP packets between VLANs (or more accurately, between the subnets on the VLANs). Chapter 18, "Configuring IPv4 Addresses and Static Routes," shows how to configure designs that use an external router with router-on-a-stick. This chapter now turns its attention to configuration and verification tasks for VLANs and VLAN trunks.

VLAN and VLAN Trunking Configuration and Verification

Cisco switches do not require any configuration to work. You can purchase Cisco switches, install devices with the correct cabling, turn on the switches, and they work. You would never need to configure the switch, and it would work fine, even if you interconnected switches, until you needed more than one VLAN. But if you want to use VLANs—and most enterprise networks do—you need to add some configuration.

This chapter separates the VLAN configuration details into two major sections. The first section looks at how to configure access interfaces, which are switch interfaces that do not use VLAN trunking. The second part shows how to configure interfaces that do use VLAN trunking.

Creating VLANs and Assigning Access VLANs to an Interface

This section shows how to create a VLAN, give the VLAN a name, and assign interfaces to a VLAN. To focus on these basic details, this section shows examples using a single switch, so VLAN trunking is not needed.

For a Cisco switch to forward frames in a particular VLAN, the switch must be configured to believe that the VLAN exists. In addition, the switch must have nontrunking interfaces (called *access interfaces*) assigned to the VLAN, and/or trunks that support the VLAN. The configuration steps for access interfaces are as follows, with the trunk configuration shown later in the section "VLAN Trunking Configuration":

Step 1. To configure a new VLAN, follow these steps:

　A. From configuration mode, use the **vlan** *vlan-id* command in global configuration mode to create the VLAN and to move the user into VLAN configuration mode.

　B. (Optional) Use the **name** *name* command in VLAN configuration mode to list a name for the VLAN. If not configured, the VLAN name is VLANZZZZ, where ZZZZ is the four-digit decimal VLAN ID.

Step 2. For each access interface (each interface that does not trunk, but instead belongs to a single VLAN), follow these steps:

　A. Use the **interface** *type number* command in global configuration mode to move into interface configuration mode for each desired interface.

　B. Use the **switchport access vlan** *id-number* command in interface configuration mode to specify the VLAN number associated with that interface.

　C. (Optional) Use the **switchport mode access** command in interface configuration mode to make this port always operate in access mode (that is, to not trunk).

While the list might look a little daunting, the process on a single switch is actually pretty simple. For example, if you want to put the switch's ports in three VLANs—11, 12, and 13—you just add three **vlan** commands: **vlan 11**, **vlan 12**, and **vlan 13**. Then, for each interface, add a **switchport access vlan 11** (or **12** or **13**) command to assign that interface to the proper VLAN.

NOTE The term *default VLAN* (as shown in the exam topics) refers to the default setting on the **switchport access vlan** *vlan-id* command, and that default is VLAN ID 1. In other words, by default, each port is assigned to access VLAN 1.

VLAN Configuration Example 1: Full VLAN Configuration

Example 11-1 shows the configuration process of adding a new VLAN and assigning access interfaces to that VLAN. Figure 11-11 shows the network used in the example, with one LAN switch (SW1) and two hosts in each of three VLANs (1, 2, and 3). The example shows the details of the two-step process for VLAN 2 and the interfaces in VLAN 2, with the configuration of VLAN 3 deferred until the next example.

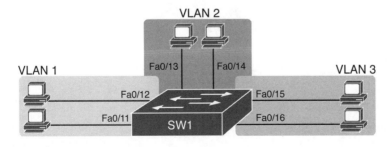

Figure 11-11 *Network with One Switch and Three VLANs*

Example 11-1 *Configuring VLANs and Assigning VLANs to Interfaces*

```
SW1# show vlan brief
VLAN Name                             Status    Ports
---- -------------------------------- --------- -------------------------------
1    default                          active    Fa0/1, Fa0/2, Fa0/3, Fa0/4
                                                Fa0/5, Fa0/6, Fa0/7, Fa0/8
                                                Fa0/9, Fa0/10, Fa0/11, Fa0/12
                                                Fa0/13, Fa0/14, Fa0/15, Fa0/16
                                                Fa0/17, Fa0/18, Fa0/19, Fa0/20
                                                Fa0/21, Fa0/22, Fa0/23, Fa0/24
                                                Gi0/1, Gi0/2
1002 fddi-default                     act/unsup
1003 token-ring-default               act/unsup
1004 fddinet-default                  act/unsup
1005 trnet-default                    act/unsup
! Above, VLANs 2 and 3 do not yet exist. Below, VLAN 2 is added, with name Freds-vlan,
! with two interfaces assigned to VLAN 2.

SW1# configure terminal
Enter configuration commands, one per line.  End with CNTL/Z.
SW1(config)# vlan 2
SW1(config-vlan)# name Freds-vlan
SW1(config-vlan)# exit
SW1(config)# interface range fastethernet 0/13 - 14
SW1(config-if)# switchport access vlan 2
SW1(config-if)# switchport mode access
SW1(config-if)# end

! Below, the show running-config command lists the interface subcommands on
! interfaces Fa0/13 and Fa0/14.
SW1# show running-config
! Many lines omitted for brevity
! Early in the output:
vlan 2
 name Freds-vlan
!
! more lines omitted for brevity
interface FastEthernet0/13
 switchport access vlan 2
 switchport mode access
!
interface FastEthernet0/14
 switchport access vlan 2
 switchport mode access
!
```

```
SW1# show vlan brief

VLAN Name                             Status    Ports
---- -------------------------------- --------- -------------------------------
1    default                          active    Fa0/1, Fa0/2, Fa0/3, Fa0/4
                                                Fa0/5, Fa0/6, Fa0/7, Fa0/8
                                                Fa0/9, Fa0/10, Fa0/11, Fa0/12
                                                Fa0/15, Fa0/16, Fa0/17, Fa0/18
                                                Fa0/19, Fa0/20, Fa0/21, Fa0/22
                                                Fa0/23, Fa0/24, Gi0/1, Gi0/2
2    Freds-vlan                       active    Fa0/13, Fa0/14
1002 fddi-default                     act/unsup
1003 token-ring-default               act/unsup
1004 fddinet-default                  act/unsup
1005 trnet-default                    act/unsup


SW1# show vlan id 2
VLAN Name                             Status    Ports
---- -------------------------------- --------- -------------------------------
2    Freds-vlan                       active    Fa0/13, Fa0/14

VLAN Type  SAID       MTU   Parent RingNo BridgeNo Stp  BrdgMode Trans1 Trans2
---- ----- ---------- ----- ------ ------ -------- ---- -------- ------ ------
2    enet  100010     1500  -      -      -        -    -        0      0

Remote SPAN VLAN
----------------
Disabled


Primary Secondary Type              Ports
------- --------- ----------------- -------------------------------------------
```

The example begins with the **show vlan brief** command, confirming the default settings of five nondeletable VLANs, with all interfaces assigned to VLAN 1. (VLAN 1 cannot be deleted, but can be used. VLANs 1002–1005 cannot be deleted and cannot be used as access VLANs today.) In particular, note that this 2960 switch has 24 Fast Ethernet ports (Fa0/1–Fa0/24) and two Gigabit Ethernet ports (Gi0/1 and Gi0/2), all of which are listed as being in VLAN 1 per that first command's output.

Next, the example shows the process of creating VLAN 2 and assigning interfaces Fa0/13 and Fa0/14 to VLAN 2. Note in particular that the example uses the **interface range** command, which causes the **switchport access vlan 2** interface subcommand to be applied to both interfaces in the range, as confirmed in the **show running-config** command output at the end of the example.

After the configuration has been added, to list the new VLAN, the example repeats the **show vlan brief** command. Note that this command lists VLAN 2, name Freds-vlan, and the interfaces assigned to that VLAN (Fa0/13 and Fa0/14). The **show vlan id 2** command that follows then confirms that ports Fa0/13 and Fa0/14 are assigned to VLAN 2.

11

The example surrounding Figure 11-11 uses six switch ports, all of which need to operate as access ports. That is, each port should not use trunking, but instead should be assigned to a single VLAN, as assigned by the **switchport access vlan** *vlan-id* command. However, as configured in Example 11-1, these interfaces could negotiate to later become trunk ports, because the switch defaults to allow the port to negotiate trunking and decide whether to act as an access interface or as a trunk interface.

For ports that should always act as access ports, add the optional interface subcommand **switchport mode access**. This command tells the switch to only allow the interface to be an access interface. The upcoming section "VLAN Trunking Configuration" discusses more details about the commands that allow a port to negotiate whether it should use trunking.

> **NOTE** The book includes a video that works through a different VLAN configuration example as well. You can find the video on the DVD and on the companion website.

VLAN Configuration Example 2: Shorter VLAN Configuration

Example 11-1 shows several of the optional configuration commands, with a side effect of being a bit longer than is required. Example 11-2 shows a much briefer alternative configuration, picking up the story where Example 11-1 ended and showing the addition of VLAN 3 (as shown in Figure 11-11). Note that SW1 does not know about VLAN 3 at the beginning of this example.

Example 11-2 *Shorter VLAN Configuration Example (VLAN 3)*

```
SW1# configure terminal
Enter configuration commands, one per line.  End with CNTL/Z.
SW1(config)# interface range Fastethernet 0/15 - 16
SW1(config-if-range)# switchport access vlan 3
% Access VLAN does not exist. Creating vlan 3
SW1(config-if-range)# ^Z


SW1# show vlan brief

VLAN Name                             Status    Ports
---- -------------------------------- --------- -------------------------------
1    default                          active    Fa0/1, Fa0/2, Fa0/3, Fa0/4
                                                Fa0/5, Fa0/6, Fa0/7, Fa0/8
                                                Fa0/9, Fa0/10, Fa0/11, Fa0/12
                                                Fa0/17, Fa0/18, Fa0/19, Fa0/20
                                                Fa0/21, Fa0/22, Fa0/23, Fa0/24
                                                Gi0/1, Gi0/2
2    Freds-vlan                       active    Fa0/13, Fa0/14
3    VLAN0003                         active    Fa0/15, Fa0/16
1002 fddi-default                     act/unsup
1003 token-ring-default               act/unsup
1004 fddinet-default                  act/unsup
1005 trnet-default                    act/unsup
```

Example 11-2 shows how a switch can dynamically create a VLAN—the equivalent of the **vlan** *vlan-id* global config command—when the **switchport access vlan** interface subcommand refers to a currently unconfigured VLAN. This example begins with SW1 not knowing about VLAN 3. When the **switchport access vlan 3** interface subcommand was used, the switch realized that VLAN 3 did not exist, and as noted in the shaded message in the example, the switch created VLAN 3, using a default name (VLAN0003). No other steps are required to create the VLAN. At the end of the process, VLAN 3 exists in the switch, and interfaces Fa0/15 and Fa0/16 are in VLAN 3, as noted in the shaded part of the **show vlan brief** command output.

VLAN Trunking Protocol

Before showing more configuration examples, you also need to know something about a Cisco protocol and tool called the VLAN Trunking Protocol (VTP). VTP is a Cisco proprietary tool on Cisco switches that advertises each VLAN configured in one switch (with the **vlan** *number* command) so that all the other switches in the campus learn about that VLAN. However, for various reasons, many enterprises choose not to use VTP.

This book does not discuss VTP as an end to itself. However, VTP has some small impact on how every Cisco Catalyst switch works, even if you do not try to use VTP. This brief section introduces enough details of VTP so that you can see these small differences in VTP that cannot be avoided.

This book attempts to ignore VTP as much as is possible. To that end, all examples in this book use switches that have either been set to use VTP transparent mode (with the **vtp mode transparent** global command) or to disable it (with the **vtp mode off** global command). Both options allow the administrator to configure both standard- and extended-range VLANs, and the switch lists the **vlan** commands in the running-config file.

Finally, on a practical note, if you happen to do lab exercises with real switches or with simulators, and you see unusual results with VLANs, check the VTP status with the **show vtp status** command. If your switch uses VTP server or client mode, you will find:

- The server switches can configure VLANs in the standard range only (1–1005).
- The client switches cannot configure VLANs.
- Both servers and clients may be learning new VLANs from other switches, and seeing their VLANs deleted by other switches, because of VTP.
- The **show running-config** command does not list any **vlan** commands.

If possible in lab, switch to VTP transparent mode and ignore VTP for your switch configuration practice until you are ready to focus on how VTP works when studying for the ICND2 exam topics.

11

NOTE Do not change VTP settings on any switch that also connects to the production network until you know how VTP works and you talk with experienced colleagues. If the switch you configure connects to other switches, which in turn connect to switches used in the production LAN, you could accidentally change the VLAN configuration in other switches with serious impact to the operation of the network. Be careful and never experiment with VTP settings on a switch unless it, and the other switches connected to it, have absolutely no physical links connected to the production LAN.

VLAN Trunking Configuration

Trunking configuration between two Cisco switches can be very simple if you just statically configure trunking. For example, if two Cisco 2960 switches connect to each other, they support only 802.1Q and not ISL. You could literally add one interface subcommand for the switch interface on each side of the link (**switchport mode trunk**), and you would create a VLAN trunk that supported all the VLANs known to each switch.

However, trunking configuration on Cisco switches includes many more options, including several options for dynamically negotiating various trunking settings. The configuration can either predefine different settings or tell the switch to negotiate the settings, as follows:

- **The type of trunking:** IEEE 802.1Q, ISL, or negotiate which one to use
- **The administrative mode:** Whether to always trunk, always not trunk, or negotiate

First, consider the type of trunking. Cisco switches that support ISL and 802.1Q can negotiate which type to use, using the Dynamic Trunking Protocol (DTP). If both switches support both protocols, they use ISL; otherwise, they use the protocol that both support. Today, many Cisco switches do not support the older ISL trunking protocol. Switches that support both types of trunking use the **switchport trunk encapsulation {dot1q | isl | negotiate}** interface subcommand to either configure the type or allow DTP to negotiate the type.

DTP can also negotiate whether the two devices on the link agree to trunk at all, as guided by the local switch port's administrative mode. The administrative mode refers to the configuration setting for whether trunking should be used. Each interface also has an *operational* mode, which refers to what is currently happening on the interface, and might have been chosen by DTP's negotiation with the other device. Cisco switches use the **switchport mode** interface subcommand to define the administrative trunking mode, as listed in Table 11-2.

Table 11-2   Trunking Administrative Mode Options with the **switchport mode** Command

Command Option	Description
access	Always act as an access (nontrunk) port
trunk	Always act as a trunk port
dynamic desirable	Initiates negotiation messages and responds to negotiation messages to dynamically choose whether to start using trunking
dynamic auto	Passively waits to receive trunk negotiation messages, at which point the switch will respond and negotiate whether to use trunking

For example, consider the two switches shown in Figure 11-12. This figure shows an expansion of the network of Figure 11-11, with a trunk to a new switch (SW2) and with parts of VLANs 1 and 3 on ports attached to SW2. The two switches use a Gigabit Ethernet link for the trunk. In this case, the trunk does not dynamically form by default, because both (2960) switches default to an administrative mode of *dynamic auto*, meaning that neither switch initiates the trunk negotiation process. By changing one switch to use *dynamic desirable* mode, which does initiate the negotiation, the switches negotiate to use trunking, specifically 802.1Q because the 2960s support only 802.1Q.

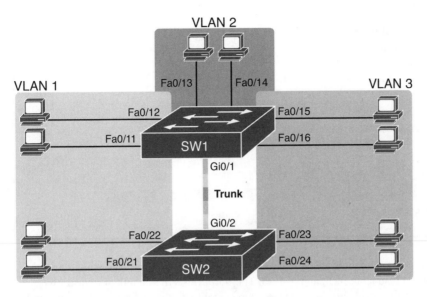

Figure 11-12 *Network with Two Switches and Three VLANs*

Example 11-3 begins by showing the two switches in Figure 11-12 with the default configuration so that the two switches do not trunk.

Example 11-3 *Initial (Default) State: Not Trunking Between SW1 and SW2*

```
SW1# show interfaces gigabit 0/1 switchport
Name: Gi0/1
Switchport: Enabled
Administrative Mode: dynamic auto
Operational Mode: static access
Administrative Trunking Encapsulation: dot1q
Operational Trunking Encapsulation: native
Negotiation of Trunking: On
Access Mode VLAN: 1 (default)
Trunking Native Mode VLAN: 1 (default)
Administrative Native VLAN tagging: enabled
Voice VLAN: none
Access Mode VLAN: 1 (default)
Trunking Native Mode VLAN: 1 (default)
Administrative Native VLAN tagging: enabled
Voice VLAN: none
Administrative private-vlan host-association: none
Administrative private-vlan mapping: none
Administrative private-vlan trunk native VLAN: none
Administrative private-vlan trunk Native VLAN tagging: enabled
Administrative private-vlan trunk encapsulation: dot1q
Administrative private-vlan trunk normal VLANs: none
Administrative private-vlan trunk private VLANs: none
```

11

```
Operational private-vlan: none
Trunking VLANs Enabled: ALL
Pruning VLANs Enabled: 2-1001
Capture Mode Disabled
Capture VLANs Allowed: ALL

Protected: false
Unknown unicast blocked: disabled
Unknown multicast blocked: disabled
Appliance trust: none

! Note that the next command results in a single empty line of output.
SW1# show interfaces trunk
SW1#
```

First, focus on the highlighted items from the output of the **show interfaces switchport** command at the beginning of Example 11-3. The output lists the default administrative mode setting of dynamic auto. Because SW2 also defaults to dynamic auto, the command lists SW1's operational status as "access," meaning that it is not trunking. ("Dynamic auto" tells both switches to sit there and wait on the other switch to start the negotiations.) The third shaded line points out the only supported type of trunking (802.1Q) on this 2960 switch. (On a switch that supports both ISL and 802.1Q, this value would by default list "negotiate," to mean that the type of encapsulation is negotiated.) Finally, the operational trunking type is listed as "native," which is a reference to the 802.1Q native VLAN.

The end of the example shows the output of the **show interfaces trunk** command, but with no output. This command lists information about all interfaces that currently operationally trunk; that is, it lists interfaces that currently use VLAN trunking. With no interfaces listed, this command also confirms that the link between switches is not trunking.

Next, consider Example 11-4, which shows the new configuration that enables trunking. In this case, SW1 is configured with the **switchport mode dynamic desirable** command, which asks the switch to both negotiate as well as to begin the negotiation process, rather than waiting on the other device. As soon as the command is issued, log messages appear showing that the interface goes down and then back up again, which happens when the interface transitions from access mode to trunk mode.

Example 11-4   *SW1 Changes from Dynamic Auto to Dynamic Desirable*

```
SW1# configure terminal
Enter configuration commands, one per line.  End with CNTL/Z.
SW1(config)# interface gigabit 0/1
SW1(config-if)# switchport mode dynamic desirable
SW1(config-if)# ^Z
SW1#
%LINEPROTO-5-UPDOWN: Line protocol on Interface GigabitEthernet0/1, changed state to
  down
%LINEPROTO-5-UPDOWN: Line protocol on Interface GigabitEthernet0/1, changed state to
  up
```

```
SW1# show interfaces gigabit 0/1 switchport
Name: Gi0/1
Switchport: Enabled
Administrative Mode: dynamic desirable
Operational Mode: trunk
Administrative Trunking Encapsulation: dot1q
Operational Trunking Encapsulation: dot1q
Negotiation of Trunking: On
Access Mode VLAN: 1 (default)
Trunking Native Mode VLAN: 1 (default)
! lines omitted for brevity


! The next command formerly listed a single empty line of output; now it lists
! information about the 1 operational trunk.
SW1# show interfaces trunk

Port          Mode         Encapsulation  Status        Native vlan
Gi0/1         desirable    802.1q         trunking      1


Port          Vlans allowed on trunk
Gi0/1         1-4094


Port          Vlans allowed and active in management domain
Gi0/1         1-3


Port          Vlans in spanning tree forwarding state and not pruned
Gi0/1         1-3


SW1# show vlan id 2
VLAN Name                             Status    Ports
---- -------------------------------- --------- -------------------------------
2    Freds-vlan                       active    Fa0/13, Fa0/14, G0/1


VLAN Type  SAID       MTU   Parent RingNo BridgeNo Stp  BrdgMode Trans1 Trans2
---- ----- ---------- ----- ------ ------ -------- ---- -------- ------ ------
2    enet  100010     1500  -      -      -        -    -        0      0


Remote SPAN VLAN
----------------
Disabled


Primary Secondary Type              Ports
------- --------- ----------------- -------------------------------------------
```

To verify whether trunking is working now, the middle of Example 11-4 lists the **show interfaces switchport** command. Note that the command still lists the administrative settings, which denote the configured values along with the operational settings, which list what the switch is currently doing. In this case, SW1 now claims to be in an operational mode of *trunk*, with an operational trunking encapsulation of dot1Q.

The end of the example shows the output of the **show interfaces trunk** command, which now lists G0/1, confirming that G0/1 is now operationally trunking. The next section discusses the meaning of the output of this command.

For the exams, you should be ready to interpret the output of the **show interfaces switchport** command, realize the administrative mode implied by the output, and know whether the link should operationally trunk based on those settings. Table 11-3 lists the combinations of the trunking administrative modes and the expected operational mode (trunk or access) resulting from the configured settings. The table lists the administrative mode used on one end of the link on the left, and the administrative mode on the switch on the other end of the link across the top of the table.

Table 11-3   Expected Trunking Operational Mode Based on the Configured Administrative Modes

Administrative Mode	Access	Dynamic Auto	Trunk	Dynamic Desirable
access	Access	Access	Do Not Use[1]	Access
dynamic auto	Access	Access	Trunk	Trunk
trunk	Do Not Use[1]	Trunk	Trunk	Trunk
dynamic desirable	Access	Trunk	Trunk	Trunk

[1] When two switches configure a mode of "access" on one end and "trunk" on the other, problems occur. Avoid this combination.

Finally, before leaving the discussion of configuring trunks, Cisco recommends disabling trunk negotiation on most ports for better security. The majority of switch ports on most switches will be used to connect to users. As a matter of habit, you can disable DTP negotiations altogether using the **switchport nonegotiate** interface subcommand.

Implementing Interfaces Connected to Phones

This next topic is a strange topic, at least in the context of access links and trunk links. In the world of IP telephony, telephones use Ethernet ports to connect to an Ethernet network so they can use IP to send and receive voice traffic sent via IP packets. To make that work, the switch's Ethernet port acts like an access port—but at the same time, the port acts like a trunk in some ways. This last topic of the chapter works through those main concepts.

Data and Voice VLAN Concepts

Before IP telephony, a PC could sit on the same desk as a phone. The phone happened to use UTP cabling, with that phone connected to some voice device (often called a *voice switch* or a *private branch exchange [PBX]*). The PC, of course, connected using a unshielded twisted-pair (UTP) cable to the usual LAN switch that sat in the wiring closet— sometimes in the same wiring closet as the voice switch. Figure 11-13 shows the idea.

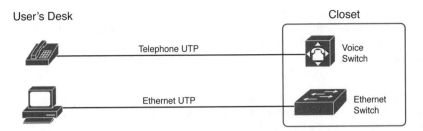

Figure 11-13 *Before IP Telephony: PC and Phone, One Cable Each, Connect to Two Different Devices*

The term *IP telephony* refers to the branch of networking in which the telephones use IP packets to send and receive voice as represented by the bits in the data portion of the IP packet. The phones connect to the network like most other end-user devices, using either Ethernet or Wi-Fi. These new IP phones did not connect via cable directly to a voice switch, instead connecting to the IP network using an Ethernet cable and an Ethernet port built in to the phone. The phones then communicated over the IP network with software that replaced the call setup and other functions of the PBX. (The current products from Cisco that perform this IP telephony control function are called *Cisco Unified Communication Manager*.)

The migration from using the already-installed telephone cabling, to these new IP phones that needed UTP cables that supported Ethernet, caused some problems in some offices. In particular:

- The older non-IP phones used a category of UTP cabling that often did not support 100-Mbps or 1000-Mbps Ethernet.

- Most offices had a single UTP cable running from the wiring closet to each desk, but now two devices (the PC and the new IP phone) both needed a cable from the desktop to the wiring closet.

- Installing a new cable to every desk would be expensive, plus you would need more switch ports.

To solve this problem, Cisco embedded small three-port switches into each phone.

IP telephones have included a small LAN switch, on the underside of the phone, since the earliest IP telephone products. Figure 11-14 shows the basic cabling, with the wiring closet cable connecting to one physical port on the embedded switch, the PC connecting with a short patch cable to the other physical port, and the phone's internal CPU connecting to an internal switch port.

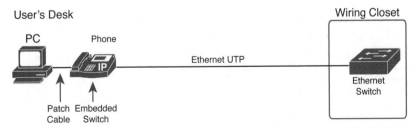

Figure 11-14 *Cabling with an IP Phone, a Single Cable, and an Integrated Switch*

Sites that use IP telephony, which includes most every company today, now have two devices off each access port. In addition, Cisco best practices for IP telephony design tell us to put the phones in one VLAN, and the PCs in a different VLAN. To make that happen, the switch port acts a little like an access link (for the PC's traffic), and a little like a trunk (for the phone's traffic). The configuration defines two VLANs on that port, as follows:

Data VLAN: Same idea and configuration as the access VLAN on an access port, but defined as the VLAN on that link for forwarding the traffic for the device connected to the phone on the desk (typically the user's PC).

Voice VLAN: The VLAN defined on the link for forwarding the phone's traffic. Traffic in this VLAN is typically tagged with an 802.1Q header.

Figure 11-15 illustrates this design with two VLANs on access ports that support IP telephones.

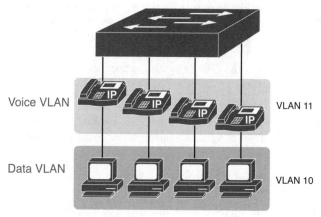

Figure 11-15 *A LAN Design, with Data in VLAN 10 and Phones in VLAN 11*

Data and Voice VLAN Configuration and Verification

Configuring a switch port to support IP phones, once you know the planned voice and data VLAN IDs, is easy. Making sense of the **show** commands once it is configured can be a challenge. The port acts like an access port in many ways. However, with most configuration options, the voice frames flow with an 802.1Q header, so that the link supports frames in both VLANs on the link. But that makes for some different **show** command output.

Example 11-5 shows an example. In this case, all four switch ports F0/1–F0/4 begin with default configuration. The configuration adds the new data and voice VLANs. The example then configures all four ports as access ports, and defines the access VLAN, which is also called the data VLAN when discussing IP telephony. Finally, the configuration includes the **switchport voice vlan 11** command, which defines the voice VLAN used on the port. The example matches Figure 11-15, using ports F0/1–F0/4.

Example 11-5 *Configuring the Voice and Data VLAN on Ports Connected to Phones*

```
SW1# configure terminal
Enter configuration commands, one per line.  End with CNTL/Z.
SW1(config)# vlan 10
SW1(config-vlan)# vlan 11
```

```
SW1(config-vlan)# interface range FastEthernet0/1 - 4
SW1(config-if)# switchport mode access
SW1(config-if)# switchport access vlan 10
SW1(config-if)# switchport voice vlan 11
SW1(config-if)#^Z
SW1#
```

NOTE   CDP, which is discussed in Chapter 33, "Device Management Protocols," must be enabled on an interface for a voice access port to work with Cisco IP Phones. CDP is enabled by default, so its configuration is not shown here.

The following list details the configuration steps for easier review and study:

Step 1.   Use the **vlan** *vlan-id* command in global configuration mode to create the data and voice VLANs if they do not already exist on the switch.

Step 2.   Configure the data VLAN like an access VLAN, as usual:

    A. Use the **interface** *type number* command global configuration mode to move into interface configuration mode.

    B. Use the **switchport access vlan** *id-number* command in interface configuration mode to define the data VLAN.

    C. Use the **switchport mode access** command in interface configuration mode to make this port always operate in access mode (that is, to not trunk).

Step 3.   Use the **switchport voice vlan** *id-number* command in interface configuration mode to set the voice VLAN ID.

Verifying the status of a switch port configured like Example 11-5 shows some different output compared to the pure access port and pure trunk port configurations seen earlier in this chapter. For example, the **show interfaces switchport** command shows details about the operation of an interface, including many details about access ports. Example 11-6 shows those details for port F0/4 after the configuration in Example 11-5 was added.

Example 11-6   *Verifying the Data VLAN (Access VLAN) and Voice VLAN*

```
SW1# show interfaces FastEthernet 0/4 switchport
Name: Fa0/4
Switchport: Enabled
Administrative Mode: static access
Operational Mode: static access
Administrative Trunking Encapsulation: dot1q
Operational Trunking Encapsulation: native
Negotiation of Trunking: Off
Access Mode VLAN: 10 (VLAN0010)
Trunking Native Mode VLAN: 1 (default)
Administrative Native VLAN tagging: enabled
Voice VLAN: 11 (VLAN0011)
! The rest of the output is omitted for brevity
```

Working through the first three highlighted lines in the output, all those details should look familiar for any access port. The **switchport mode access** configuration command statically configures the administrative mode to be an access port, so the port of course operates as an access port. Also, as shown in the third highlighted line, the **switchport access vlan 10** configuration command defined the access mode VLAN as highlighted here.

The fourth highlighted line shows the one small new piece of information: the voice VLAN ID, as set with the **switchport voice vlan 11** command in this case. This small line of output is the only piece of information in the output that differs from the earlier access port examples in this chapter.

These ports act more like access ports than trunk ports. In fact, the **show interfaces** *type number* **switchport** command boldly proclaims, "Operational Mode: static access." However, one other **show** command reveals just a little more about the underlying operation with 802.1Q tagging for the voice frames.

As mentioned earlier, the **show interfaces trunk** command—that is, the command that does not include a specific interface in the middle of the command—lists the operational trunks on a switch. With IP telephony ports, the ports do not show up in the list of trunks either—providing evidence that these links are *not* treated as trunks. Example 11-7 shows just such an example.

However, the **show interfaces trunk** command with the interface listed in the middle of the command, as is also shown in Example 11-7, does list some additional information. Note that in this case, the **show interfaces F0/4 trunk** command lists the status as not-trunking, but with VLANs 10 and 11 allowed on the trunk. (Normally, on an access port, only the access VLAN is listed in the "VLANs allowed on the trunk" list in the output of this command.)

Example 11-7 *Allowed VLAN List and the List of Active VLANs*

```
SW1# show interfaces trunk
SW1# show interfaces F0/4 trunk


Port         Mode              Encapsulation  Status        Native vlan
Fa0/4        off               802.1q         not-trunking  1


Port         Vlans allowed on trunk
Fa0/4        10-11


Port         Vlans allowed and active in management domain
Fa0/4        10-11


Port         Vlans in spanning tree forwarding state and not pruned
Fa0/4        10-11
```

Summary: IP Telephony Ports on Switches

It might seem like this short topic about IP telephony and switch configuration includes a lot of small twists and turns and trivia, and it does. The most important items to remember are as follows:

■ Configure these ports like a normal access port to begin: Configure it as a static access port and assign it an access VLAN.

■ Add one more command to define the voice VLAN (**switchport voice vlan** *vlan-id*).

■ Look for the mention of the voice VLAN ID, but no other new facts, in the output of the **show interfaces** *type number* **switchport** command.

■ Look for both the voice and data (access) VLAN IDs in the output of the **show interfaces** *type number* **trunk** command.

■ Do not expect to see the port listed in the list of operational trunks as listed by the **show interfaces trunk** command.

Chapter Review

One key to doing well on the exams is to perform repetitive spaced review sessions. Review this chapter's material using either the tools in the book, DVD, or interactive tools for the same material found on the book's companion website. Refer to the "Your Study Plan" element section titled "Step 2: Build Your Study Habits Around the Chapter" for more details. Table 11-4 outlines the key review elements and where you can find them. To better track your study progress, record when you completed these activities in the second column.

Table 11-4   Chapter Review Tracking

Review Element	Review Date(s)	Resource Used
Review key topics		Book, DVD/website
Review key terms		Book, DVD/website
Answer DIKTA questions		Book, PCPT
Do labs		Blog
Review memory tables		DVD/website
Review config checklists		Book, DVD/website
Review command tables		Book

Review All the Key Topics

Table 11-5   Key Topics for Chapter 11

Key Topic Element	Description	Page Number
Figure 11-2	Basic VLAN concept	245
List	Reasons for using VLANs	245
Figure 11-5	Diagram of VLAN trunking	247
Figure 11-6	802.1Q header	248
Figure 11-9	Routing between VLANs with router-on-a-stick	251
Figure 11-10	Routing between VLANs with Layer 3 switch	252

11

Key Topic Element	Description	Page Number
Table 11-2	Options of the **switchport mode** command	258
Table 11-3	Expected trunking results based on the configuration of the **switchport mode** command	262
List	Definitions of data VLAN and voice VLAN	264
List	Summary of data and voice VLAN concepts, configuration, and verification	267

Key Terms You Should Know

802.1Q, trunk, trunking administrative mode, trunking operational mode, VLAN, VTP, VTP transparent mode, Layer 3 switch, access interface, trunk interface, data VLAN, voice VLAN

Command References

Tables 11-6 and 11-7 list configuration and verification commands used in this chapter, respectively. As an easy review exercise, cover the left column in a table, read the right column, and try to recall the command without looking. Then repeat the exercise, covering the right column, and try to recall what the command does.

Table 11-6 Chapter 11 Configuration Command Reference

Command	Description
vlan *vlan-id*	Global config command that both creates the VLAN and puts the CLI into VLAN configuration mode
name *vlan-name*	VLAN subcommand that names the VLAN
[no] shutdown	VLAN mode subcommand that enables (**no shutdown**) or disables (**shutdown**) the VLAN
[no] shutdown vlan *vlan-id*	Global config command that has the same effect as the **[no] shutdown** VLAN mode subcommands
**vtp mode {server	client	transparent	off}**	Global config command that defines the VTP mode
**switchport mode {access	dynamic {auto	desirable}	trunk}**	Interface subcommand that configures the trunking administrative mode on the interface
switchport access vlan *vlan-id*	Interface subcommand that statically configures the interface into that one VLAN
**switchport trunk encapsulation {dot1q	isl	negotiate}**	Interface subcommand that defines which type of trunking to use, assuming that trunking is configured or negotiated
switchport trunk native vlan *vlan-id*	Interface subcommand that defines the native VLAN for a trunk port
switchport nonegotiate	Interface subcommand that disables the negotiation of VLAN trunking

Command	Description
switchport voice vlan *vlan-id*	Interface subcommand that defines the voice VLAN on a port, meaning that the switch uses 802.1Q tagging for frames in this VLAN
**switchport trunk allowed vlan {add	all	except	remove}** *vlan-list*	Interface subcommand that defines the list of allowed VLANs

Table 11-7   Chapter 11 EXEC Command Reference

Command	Description
show interfaces *interface-id* **switchport**	Lists information about any interface regarding administrative settings and operational state
show interfaces *interface-id* **trunk**	Lists information about all operational trunks (but no other interfaces), including the list of VLANs that can be forwarded over the trunk
**show vlan [brief	id** *vlan-id* **| name** *vlan-name* **| summary]**	Lists information about the VLAN
show vlan [*vlan***]**	Displays VLAN information
show vtp status	Lists VTP configuration and status information

11

CHAPTER 12

Troubleshooting Ethernet LANs

This chapter covers the following exam topics:

1.0 Network Fundamentals

1.7 Apply troubleshooting methodologies to resolve problems

    1.7.a Perform fault isolation and document

    1.7.b Resolve or escalate

    1.7.c Verify and monitor resolution

2.0 LAN Switching Technologies

2.1 Describe and verify switching concepts

    2.1.a MAC learning and aging

    2.1.b Frame switching

    2.1.c Frame flooding

    2.1.d MAC address table

2.3 Troubleshoot interface and cable issues (collisions, errors, duplex, speed)

2.4 Configure, verify, and troubleshoot VLANs (normal range) spanning multiple switches

    2.4.a Access ports (data and voice)

    2.4.b Default VLAN

2.5 Configure, verify, and troubleshoot inter-switch connectivity

    2.5.a Trunk ports

    2.5.b 802.1Q

    2.5.c Native VLAN

2.7 Configure, verify, and troubleshoot port security

    2.7.a Static

    2.7.b Dynamic

    2.7.c Sticky

    2.7.d Max MAC addresses

    2.7.e Violation actions

    2.7.f Err-disable recovery

This chapter focuses on the processes of verification and troubleshooting. *Verification* refers to the process of confirming whether a network is working as designed. *Trouble-shooting* refers to the follow-on process that occurs when the network is not working as designed, by trying to determine the real reason why the network is not working correctly, so that it can be fixed.

Sometimes, when people take their first Cisco exam, they are surprised at the number of verification and troubleshooting questions. Each of these questions requires you to apply networking knowledge to unique problems, rather than just being ready to answer questions about lists of facts that you've memorized. You need to have skills beyond simply remembering a lot of facts.

To help you prepare to answer troubleshooting questions, this book, as well as the ICND2 book, devotes different book elements to troubleshooting. These book elements do not just list the configuration, and they do not just list example output from different **show** commands. Instead, these elements discuss how to use different commands to verify what should be happening, and if not, how to find the root cause of the problem.

This chapter discusses a wide number of topics, many of which have already been discussed in Part II and the preceding chapters in Part III of the ICND1 book. First, this chapter begins with some perspectives on troubleshooting networking problems, because it is the first book element that focuses on troubleshooting, and because there is one exam topic that mentions the troubleshooting process and methods. At that point, this chapter looks at four key technical topics that matter to verifying and troubleshooting Ethernet LANs, as follows:

- Analyzing switch interfaces and cabling
- Predicting where switches will forward frames
- Troubleshooting port security
- Analyzing VLANs and VLAN trunks

"Do I Know This Already?" Quiz

Take the quiz (either here, or use the PCPT software) if you want to use the score to help you decide how much time to spend on this chapter. The answers are at the bottom of the page following the quiz, and the explanations are in DVD Appendix C and in the PCPT software.

Table 12-1   "Do I Know This Already?" Foundation Topics Section-to-Question Mapping

Foundation Topics Section	Questions
Perspectives on Applying Troubleshooting Methodologies	1
Analyzing Switch Interface Status and Statistics	2–4
Predicting Where Switches Will Forward Frames	5–6
Analyzing Port Security Operations on an Interface	7
Analyzing VLANs and VLAN Trunks	8

1. Which answers describe a good practice in applying good troubleshooting methodologies? (Choose two answers.)

   a. Perform problem isolation as fast as possible, including not slowing down to document your findings.

   b. The last step in a good troubleshooting process should be to take action to resolve the root cause of the problem.

   c. The last step in a good troubleshooting process should include monitoring the status to ensure that the problem is indeed solved and does not recur.

   d. Each worker should know and use the escalation process when they cannot resolve a particular problem.

2. The output of the **show interfaces status** command on a 2960 switch shows interface Fa0/1 in a "disabled" state. Which of the following is true about interface Fa0/1? (Choose three answers.)

   a. The interface is configured with the **shutdown** command.

   b. The **show interfaces fa0/1** command will list the interface with two status codes of administratively down and line protocol down.

   c. The **show interfaces fa0/1** command will list the interface with two status codes of up and down.

   d. The interface cannot currently be used to forward frames.

   e. The interface can currently be used to forward frames.

3. Switch SW1 uses its Gigabit 0/1 interface to connect to switch SW2's Gigabit 0/2 interface. SW2's Gi0/2 interface is configured with the **speed 1000** and **duplex full** commands. SW1 uses all defaults for interface configuration commands on its Gi0/1 interface. Which of the following are true about the link after it comes up? (Choose two answers.)

   a. The link works at 1000 Mbps (1 Gbps).

   b. SW1 attempts to run at 10 Mbps because SW2 has effectively disabled IEEE standard autonegotiation.

   c. The link runs at 1 Gbps, but SW1 uses half-duplex and SW2 uses full duplex.

   d. Both switches use full duplex.

4. In the following line taken from a **show interfaces fa0/1** command, which of the following are true about the interface? (Choose two answers.)

   ```
   Full-duplex, 100Mbps, media type is 10/100BaseTX
   ```

   a. The speed was definitely configured with the **speed 100** interface subcommand.

   b. The speed might have been configured with the **speed 100** interface subcommand.

   c. The duplex was definitely configured with the **duplex full** interface subcommand.

   d. The duplex might have been configured with the **duplex full** interface subcommand.

5. Which of the following commands list the MAC address table entries for MAC addresses configured by port security? (Choose two answers.)

   a. show mac address-table dynamic

   b. show mac address-table

   c. show mac address-table static

   d. show mac address-table port-security

6. On a Cisco Catalyst switch, you issue a **show mac address-table** command. Which of the following answers list information you would likely see in most lines of output? (Choose two answers.)

   a. A MAC address

   b. An IP address

   c. A VLAN ID

   d. Type (broadcast, multicast, or unicast)

7. The **show port-security interface f0/1** command lists a port status of secure-down. Which one of the following answers must be true about this interface at this time?

   a. The **show interface status** command lists the interface status as connected.

   b. The **show interface status** command lists the interface status as err-disabled.

   c. The **show port-security interface** command could list a mode of shutdown or restrict, but not protect.

   d. The **show port-security interface** command could list a violation counter value of 10.

8. The **show interfaces g0/1 switchport** command on SW1 shows the trunking status on a link connected to switch SW2. Based on the output, which of the following must be true on SW2's port connected to this link?

```
SW1# show interfaces gigabit0/1 switchport
Name: Gi0/1
Switchport: Enabled
Administrative Mode: trunk
Operational Mode: trunk
```

   a. The operational state per **show interfaces switchport** must be "trunk."

   b. The administrative state per **show interfaces switchport** must be "trunk."

   c. SW2 must use the **switchport mode trunk** configuration command on G0/2, or the link will not use trunking.

   d. SW2 can use the **switchport mode dynamic auto** configuration command as one option to make the link use trunking.

12

Foundation Topics

Perspectives on Applying Troubleshooting Methodologies

This first section of the chapter takes a brief diversion for one particular big idea: what troubleshooting processes could be used to resolve networking problems? Most of the CCENT and CCNA Routing and Switching exam topics list the word "troubleshoot" along with some technology, mostly with some feature that you configure on a switch or router. One exam topic makes mention of the troubleshooting process. This first section examines the troubleshooting process as an end to itself.

The first important perspective on the troubleshooting process is this: you can troubleshoot using any process or method that you want. However, all good methods have the same characteristics that result in faster resolution of the problem, and a better chance of avoiding that same problem in the future.

The one exam topic that mentions troubleshooting methods uses some pretty common terminology found in troubleshooting methods both inside IT and in other industries as well. The ideas make good common sense. From the exam topics:

Step 1.   **Problem isolation and documentation:** Problem isolation refers to the process of taking what you know about a possible issue, confirming that there is a problem, and determining which devices and cables could be part of the problem, and which ones are not part of the problem. This step also works best when the person troubleshooting the problem documents what they find, typically in a problem tracking system.

Step 2.   **Resolve or escalate:** Problem isolation should eventually uncover the root cause of the problem—that is, the cause which, if fixed, will resolve the problem. In short, resolving the problem means finding the root cause of the problem and fixing that problem. Of course, what do you do if you cannot find the root cause, or fix (resolve) that root cause once found? Escalate the problem. Most companies have a defined escalation process, with different levels of technical support and management support depending on whether the next step requires more technical expertise or management decision making.

Step 3.   **Verify or monitor:** You hear of a problem, you isolate the problem, document it, determine a possible root cause, and you try to resolve it. Now you need to verify that it really worked. In some cases, that may mean that you just do a few show commands. In other cases, you may need to keep an eye on it over a period of time, especially when you do not know what caused the root problem in the first place.

Like most real-life processes, the real troubleshooting process is seldom as neat as the three troubleshooting steps listed here. You move between them, you attempt to resolve the problem, it may or may not work, you work through the process over and over, get help from the escalation team as needed, and so on. But following these kinds of steps can help you resolve problems more consistently, more quickly, especially when the team must get involved in troubleshooting a problem

Troubleshooting on the Exams

The exams ask you questions that not only assess your knowledge, but they assess your troubleshooting skills. To do that, the exam does not require you to follow any particular troubleshooting methods. On the exam, you should focus on isolating the root cause of the problem, after which you will either (a) fix the problem or (b) answer a multichoice question about the symptoms and the root cause of the problem.

The exam uses two question types as the primary means to test troubleshooting skills. Sim questions begin with a broken configuration; your job is to find the configuration problem, and answer the question by fixing or completing the configuration. These are straightforward configuration troubleshooting questions, and you can recognize them on the exam when the exam tells you to answer the question by changing the configuration.

Simlet questions also give you a simulator where you access the command-line interface (CLI). However, instead of changing the configuration, these questions require you to verify the current operation of the network and then answer multichoice questions about the current operation. These questions make you do the same kinds of commands you would use when doing problem isolation and documentation, and then assess what you found by asking you several multichoice questions.

At some point, whether you stop now or sometime when you have 10 to 15 spare minutes, take the time to search Cisco.com for "exam tutorial." Cisco's exam tutorial shows all the question types, including Sim and Simlet types, and you can take over the user interface to get a better sense for how to navigate in the same user interface you will see on exam day.

A Deeper Look at Problem Isolation

On the exam, you may do 5–10 **show** commands in a Simlet question before finding all the answers to all the multichoice questions within that one Simlet question. So it sometimes helps to go through problem isolation like what you would do in a real network. In some questions, it may be obvious that the problem will be something to do with the switches or VLANs, but in others, you may have to do extra problem isolation work to even determine whether the problem is a WAN or LAN or routing problem, and which part of the network has the problem.

For example, consider the following problem based on the network in Figure 12-1. PC1 and PC2 supposedly sit in the same VLAN (10). At one time, the **ping 10.1.1.2** command on PC1 worked; now it does not.

VLAN10

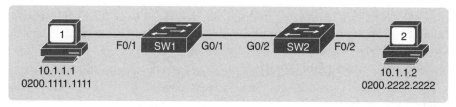

Figure 12-1 *Network with a Ping Problem*

NOTE This book covers two IP troubleshooting tools—ping and traceroute—in depth in Chapter 23, "IPv4 Troubleshooting Tools." For now, know that the **ping** command sends messages (inside IPv4 packets) that flow from one device to the other, and back, to test whether the IP network can deliver packets in both directions.

So, how do you attack this problem? If you doubt whether the figure is even correct, you could look at **show** command output to confirm the network topology. After it is confirmed, you could predict its normal working behavior based on your knowledge of LAN switching. As a result, you could predict where a frame sent by PC1 to PC2 should flow. To isolate the problem, you could look in the switch MAC tables to confirm the interfaces out which the frame should be forwarded, possibly then finding that the interface connected to PC2 has failed.

This first problem showed a relatively small network, with only two networking devices (two Layer 2 switches). As a result, you would probably guess that the exam question focused on either interface issues or VLAN issues or something you read in Part II and the previous chapters of Part III of this book.

Other Simlet questions might instead begin with a larger network, but they might still require you to do problem isolation about the Ethernet topics in Parts II and III. However, that problem isolation might need to start with Layer 3, just to decide where to begin looking for other problems.

For example, the user of PC1 in Figure 12-2 can usually connect to the web server on the right by entering www.example.com in PC1's web browser. However, that web-browsing attempt fails right now. The user calls the help desk, and the problem is assigned to a network engineer to solve.

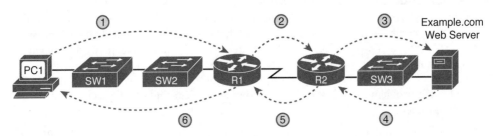

Figure 12-2 *Layer 3 Problem Isolation*

To begin the analysis, the network engineer can begin with the first tasks that would have to happen for a successful web-browsing session to occur. For example, the engineer would try to confirm that PC1 can resolve the hostname (www.example.com) to the correct IP address used by the server on the right. At that point, the Layer 3 IP problem isolation process can proceed, to determine which of the six routing steps shown in the figure has failed. The routing steps shown in Figure 12-2 are as follows:

Step 1. PC1 sends the packet to its default gateway (R1) because the destination IP address (of the web server) is in a different subnet.

Step 2. R1 forwards the packet to R2 based on R1's routing table.

Step 3. R2 forwards the packet to the web server based on R2's routing table.

Step 4. The web server sends a packet back toward PC1 based on the web server's default gateway setting (R2).

Step 5. R2 forwards the packet destined for PC1 by forwarding the packet to R1 according to R2's routing table.

Step 6. R1 forwards the packet to PC1 based on R1's routing table.

Many engineers break down network problems as in this list, analyzing the Layer 3 path through the network, hop by hop, in both directions. This process helps you take the first attempt at problem isolation. When the analysis shows which hop in the layer path fails, you can then look further at those details. And if in this case the Layer 3 problem isolation process discovers that Step 1, 3, 4, or 6 fails, the root cause might be related to Ethernet or other Layer 2 issues.

For example, imagine that the Layer 3 analysis determined that PC1 cannot even send a packet to its default gateway (R1), meaning that Step 1 in Figure 12-2 fails. To further isolate the problem and find the root causes, the engineer would need to determine the following:

- The MAC address of PC1 and of R1's LAN interface
- The switch interfaces used on SW1 and SW2
- The interface status of each switch interface
- The VLANs that should be used
- The expected forwarding behavior of a frame sent by PC1 to R1 as the destination MAC address

By gathering and analyzing these facts, the engineer can most likely isolate the problem's root cause and fix it.

Troubleshooting as Covered in This Book

All the exams related to CCENT and CCNA Routing and Switching include a variety of troubleshooting topics. In the current version of the ICND1 and ICND2 exam topics, Cisco lists around 30 specific major exam topics that include the word "troubleshoot." As a result, this book has three complete chapters devoted to troubleshooting, plus other smaller troubleshooting topics spread throughout different chapters. Plus, every concept, configuration, and verification topic helps you learn the background information required to troubleshoot that feature.

The rest of this chapter examines troubleshooting related to Ethernet LANs, with four major topics. All of the topics discuss familiar concepts, with familiar configuration and verification commands. However, in earlier configuration and verification discussions of these topics, the point was to show how to configure correctly and how to verify correct operation. In this case, the text takes a troubleshooting approach, looking for typical problems and how to isolate network problems by paying even more attention to the verification details.

The topics include the following:

- **Examining interface status and statistics:** Interfaces must be in a working state before a switch will forward frames on the interface. You must determine whether an interface is working, as well as determine the potential root causes for a failed switch interface.

12

■ **Analyzing where switches will forward frames:** You must know how to analyze a switch's MAC address table and how to then predict how a switch will forward a particular frame.

■ **Analyzing port security:** Port security can disable an interface if a violation occurs—but it can also filter frames while leaving the interface up. This section examines how to know what behavior will happen when a violation occurs, and how to know if it is happening right now or not.

■ **Analyzing VLANs and VLAN trunking:** Keeping a Layer 2 switch focus, this last section looks at what can go wrong with VLANs and VLAN trunks.

Analyzing Switch Interface Status and Statistics

This section makes the transition from the process focus of the previous section to the first of four technology-focused sections of this chapter. That process begins with finding out whether each switch interface works, and if working, whether any statistics reveal any additional problems. Unsurprisingly, Cisco switches do not use interfaces at all unless the interface is first considered to be in a functional or working state. In addition, the switch interface might be in a working state, but intermittent problems might still be occurring.

This section begins by looking at the Cisco switch interface status codes and what they mean so that you can know whether an interface is working. The rest of this section then looks at those more unusual cases in which the interface is working, but not working well, as revealed by different interface status codes and statistics.

Interface Status Codes and Reasons for Nonworking States

Cisco switches actually use two different sets of interface status codes—one set of two codes (words) that use the same conventions as do router interface status codes, and another set with a single code (word). Both sets of status codes can determine whether an interface is working.

The switch **show interfaces** and **show interfaces description** commands list the two-code status named the *line status* and *protocol status*. The line status *generally* refers to whether Layer 1 is working, with protocol status generally referring to whether Layer 2 is working.

> **NOTE** This book refers to these two status codes in shorthand by just listing the two codes with a slash between them, such as *up/up*.

The single-code interface status corresponds to different combinations of the traditional two-code interface status codes and can be easily correlated to those codes. For example, the **show interfaces status** command lists a connected state for working interfaces, with the same meaning as the up/up state seen with the **show interfaces** and **show interfaces description** commands. Table 12-2 lists the code combinations and some root causes that could have caused a particular interface status.

Table 12-2   LAN Switch Interface Status Codes

Line Status	Protocol Status	Interface Status	Typical Root Cause
administratively down	down	disabled	The **shutdown** command is configured on the interface.
down	down	notconnect	No cable; bad cable; wrong cable pinouts; speed mismatch; neighboring device is (a) powered off, (b) **shutdown**, or (c) error disabled.
up	down	notconnect	Not expected on LAN switch physical interfaces.
down	down (err-disabled)	err-disabled	Port security has disabled the interface.
up	up	connected	The interface is working.

Examining the notconnect state for a moment, note that this state has many causes that have been mentioned through this book. For example, using incorrect cabling pinouts, instead of the correct pinouts explained in Chapter 2, "Fundamentals of Ethernet LANs," causes a problem. However, one topic can be particularly difficult to troubleshoot—the possibility for both speed and duplex mismatches, as explained in the next section.

As you can see in the table, having a bad cable is just one of many reasons for the down/down state (or notconnect, per the **show interfaces status** command). Some examples of the root causes of cabling problems include the following:

- The installation of any equipment that uses electricity, even non-IT equipment, can interfere with the transmission on the cabling, and make the link fail.

- The cable could be damaged, for example, if it lies under carpet. If the user's chair keeps squashing the cable, eventually the electrical signal can degrade.

- Although optical cables do not suffer from electromagnetic interference (EMI), someone can try to be helpful and move a fiber-optic cable out of the way—bending it too much. A bend into too tight a shape can prevent the cable from transmitting bits (called *macrobending*).

For the other interface states listed in Table 12-2, only the up/up (connected) state needs more discussion. An interface can be in a working state, and it might really be working—or it might be working in a degraded state. The next few topics discuss how to examine an up/up (connected) interface to find out whether it is working well or having problems.

Interface Speed and Duplex Issues

Many unshielded twisted-pair (UTP)-based Ethernet interfaces support multiple speeds, either full or half duplex, and support IEEE standard autonegotiation (as discussed in Chapter 9, "Configuring Switch Interfaces," in the section "Autonegotiation"). These same interfaces can also be configured to use a specific speed using the **speed {10 | 100 | 1000}** interface subcommand, and a specific duplex using the **duplex {half | full}** interface subcommand. With both configured, a switch or router disables the IEEE-standard autonegotiation process on that interface.

12

The **show interfaces** and **show interfaces status** commands list both the actual speed and duplex settings on an interface, as demonstrated in Example 12-1.

Example 12-1 *Displaying Speed and Duplex Settings on Switch Interfaces*

```
SW1# show interfaces status

Port      Name             Status       Vlan       Duplex  Speed Type
Fa0/1                      notconnect   1            auto   auto 10/100BaseTX
Fa0/2                      notconnect   1            auto   auto 10/100BaseTX
Fa0/3                      notconnect   1            auto   auto 10/100BaseTX
Fa0/4                      connected    1          a-full  a-100 10/100BaseTX
Fa0/5                      connected    1          a-full  a-100 10/100BaseTX
Fa0/6                      notconnect   1            auto   auto 10/100BaseTX
Fa0/7                      notconnect   1            auto   auto 10/100BaseTX
Fa0/8                      notconnect   1            auto   auto 10/100BaseTX
Fa0/9                      notconnect   1            auto   auto 10/100BaseTX
Fa0/10                     notconnect   1            auto   auto 10/100BaseTX
Fa0/11                     connected    1          a-full     10 10/100BaseTX
Fa0/12                     connected    1            half    100 10/100BaseTX
Fa0/13                     connected    1          a-full  a-100 10/100BaseTX
Fa0/14                     disabled     1            auto   auto 10/100BaseTX
! Lines omitted for brevity


SW1# show interfaces fa0/13
FastEthernet0/13 is up, line protocol is up (connected)
  Hardware is Fast Ethernet, address is 0019.e86a.6f8d (bia 0019.e86a.6f8d)
  MTU 1500 bytes, BW 100000 Kbit, DLY 100 usec,
      reliability 255/255, txload 1/255, rxload 1/255
  Encapsulation ARPA, loopback not set
  Keepalive set (10 sec)
  Full-duplex, 100Mbps, media type is 10/100BaseTX
  input flow-control is off, output flow-control is unsupported
  ARP type: ARPA, ARP Timeout 04:00:00
  Last input 00:00:05, output 00:00:00, output hang never
  Last clearing of "show interface" counters never
  Input queue: 0/75/0/0 (size/max/drops/flushes); Total output drops: 0
  Queueing strategy: fifo
  Output queue: 0/40 (size/max)
  5 minute input rate 0 bits/sec, 0 packets/sec
  5 minute output rate 0 bits/sec, 0 packets/sec
     85022 packets input, 10008976 bytes, 0 no buffer
     Received 284 broadcasts (0 multicast)
     0 runts, 0 giants, 0 throttles
     0 input errors, 0 CRC, 0 frame, 0 overrun, 0 ignored
     0 watchdog, 281 multicast, 0 pause input
```

```
   0 input packets with dribble condition detected
   95226 packets output, 10849674 bytes, 0 underruns
   0 output errors, 0 collisions, 1 interface resets
   0 unknown protocol drops
   0 babbles, 0 late collision, 0 deferred
   0 lost carrier, 0 no carrier, 0 PAUSE output
   0 output buffer failures, 0 output buffers swapped out
```

Although both commands in the example can be useful, only the **show interfaces status** command implies how the switch determined the speed and duplex settings. The command output lists autonegotiated settings with a prefix of **a-**. For example, **a-full** means full duplex as autonegotiated, whereas **full** means full duplex but as manually configured. The example shades the command output that implies that the switch's Fa0/12 interface's speed and duplex were not found through autonegotiation, but Fa0/13 did use autonegotiation. Note that the **show interfaces fa0/13** command (without the **status** option) simply lists the speed and duplex for interface Fast Ethernet 0/13, with nothing implying that the values were learned through autonegotiation.

When the IEEE autonegotiation process works on both devices, both devices agree to the fastest speed supported by both devices. In addition, the devices use full duplex if it is supported by both devices, or half duplex if it is not. However, when one device has disabled autonegotiation, and the other device uses autonegotiation, the device using autonegotiation chooses the default duplex setting based on the current speed. The defaults are as follows:

- If the speed is not known through any means, use 10 Mbps, half duplex.
- If the switch successfully senses the speed without IEEE autonegotiation, by just looking at the signal on the cable:
  - If the speed is 10 or 100 Mbps, default to use half duplex.
  - If the speed is 1,000 Mbps, default to use full duplex.

> **NOTE** Ethernet interfaces using speeds faster than 1 Gbps always use full duplex.

While autonegotiation works well, these defaults allow for the possibility of a difficult-to-troubleshoot problem called a *duplex mismatch*. The "Autonegotiation" section in Chapter 9 explains how both devices could use the same speed, so the devices would consider the link to be up, but one side would use half-duplex and the other side would use full duplex.

The next example shows a specific case that causes a duplex mismatch. In Figure 12-3, imagine that SW2's Gi0/2 interface was configured with the **speed 100** and **duplex full** commands (these settings are not recommended on a Gigabit-capable interface, by the way). On Cisco switches, configuring both the **speed** and **duplex** commands disables IEEE auto-negotiation on that port. If SW1's Gi0/1 interface tries to use autonegotiation, SW1 would also use a speed of 100 Mbps, but default to use half duplex. Example 12-2 shows the results of this specific case on SW1.

12

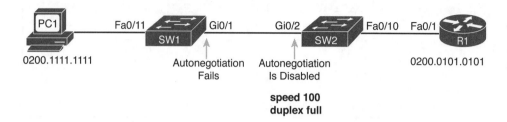

Figure 12-3 *Conditions to Create a Duplex Mismatch Between SW1 and SW2*

Example 12-2 *Confirming Duplex Mismatch on Switch SW1*

```
SW1# show interfaces gi0/1 status

Port      Name              Status       Vlan     Duplex  Speed Type
Gi0/1                       connected    trunk    a-half  a-100 10/100/1000BaseTX
```

First, focusing on the command output, the command confirms SW1's speed and duplex. It also lists a prefix of **a-** in the output, implying autonegotiation. Even with SW1 using autonegotiation defaults, the command still notes the values as being learned through autonegotiation.

Finding a duplex mismatch can be much more difficult than finding a speed mismatch, because *if the duplex settings do not match on the ends of an Ethernet segment, the switch interface will still be in a connected (up/up) state*. In this case, the interface works, but it might work poorly, with poor performance, and with symptoms of intermittent problems. The reason is that the device using half-duplex uses carrier sense multiple access collision detect (CSMA/CD) logic, waiting to send when receiving a frame, believing collisions occur when they physically do not—and actually stopping sending a frame because the switch thinks a collision occurred. With enough traffic load, the interface could be in a connect state, but it's extremely inefficient for passing traffic.

To identify duplex mismatch problems, check the duplex setting on each end of the link and watch for incrementing collision and late collision counters, as explained in the next section.

Common Layer 1 Problems on Working Interfaces

When the interface reaches the connect (up/up) state, the switch considers the interface to be working. The switch, of course, tries to use the interface, and at the same time, the switch keeps various interface counters. These interface counters can help identify problems that can occur even though the interface is in a connect state. This section explains some of the related concepts and a few of the most common problems.

Whenever the physical transmission has problems, the receiving device might receive a frame whose bits have changed values. These frames do not pass the error detection logic as implemented in the FCS field in the Ethernet trailer, as covered in Chapter 2. The receiving device discards the frame and counts it as some kind of *input error*. Cisco switches list this error as a CRC error, as highlighted in Example 12-3. (Cyclic redundancy check [CRC] is a term related to how the frame check sequence [FCS] math detects an error.)

Example 12-3 *Interface Counters for Layer 1 Problems*

```
SW1# show interfaces fa0/13
! lines omitted for brevity
     Received 284 broadcasts (0 multicast)
     0 runts, 0 giants, 0 throttles
     0 input errors, 0 CRC, 0 frame, 0 overrun, 0 ignored
     0 watchdog, 281 multicast, 0 pause input
     0 input packets with dribble condition detected
     95226 packets output, 10849674 bytes, 0 underruns
     0 output errors, 0 collisions, 1 interface resets
     0 unknown protocol drops
     0 babbles, 0 late collision, 0 deferred
     0 lost carrier, 0 no carrier, 0 PAUSE output
     0 output buffer failures, 0 output buffers swapped out
```

The number of input errors, and the number of CRC errors, are just a few of the counters in the output of the **show interfaces** command. The challenge is to decide which counters you need to think about, which ones show that a problem is happening, and which ones are normal and of no concern.

The example highlights several of the counters as examples so that you can start to understand which ones point to problems and which ones are just counting normal events that are not problems. The following list shows a short description of each highlighted counter, in the order shown in the example:

Runts: Frames that did not meet the minimum frame size requirement (64 bytes, including the 18-byte destination MAC, source MAC, type, and FCS). Can be caused by collisions.

Giants: Frames that exceed the maximum frame size requirement (1518 bytes, including the 18-byte destination MAC, source MAC, type, and FCS).

Input Errors: A total of many counters, including runts, giants, no buffer, CRC, frame, overrun, and ignored counts.

CRC: Received frames that did not pass the FCS math; can be caused by collisions.

Frame: Received frames that have an illegal format, for example, ending with a partial byte; can be caused by collisions.

Packets Output: Total number of packets (frames) forwarded out the interface.

Output Errors: Total number of packets (frames) that the switch port tried to transmit, but for which some problem occurred.

Collisions: Counter of all collisions that occur when the interface is transmitting a frame.

Late Collisions: The subset of all collisions that happen after the 64th byte of the frame has been transmitted. (In a properly working Ethernet LAN, collisions should occur within the first 64 bytes; late collisions today often point to a duplex mismatch.)

Note that many of these counters occur as part of the CSMA/CD process used when half duplex is enabled. Collisions occur as a normal part of the half-duplex logic imposed by CSMA/CD, so a switch interface with an increasing collisions counter might not even have a problem. However, one problem, called late collisions, points to the classic duplex mismatch problem.

If a LAN design follows cabling guidelines, all collisions should occur by the end of the 64th byte of any frame. When a switch has already sent 64 bytes of a frame, and the switch receives a frame on that same interface, the switch senses a collision. In this case, the collision is a late collision, and the switch increments the late collision counter in addition to the usual CSMA/CD actions to send a jam signal, wait a random time, and try again.

With a duplex mismatch, like the mismatch between SW1 and SW2 in Figure 12-3, the half-duplex interface will likely see the late collisions counter increment. Why? The half-duplex interface sends a frame (SW1), but the full duplex neighbor (SW2) sends at any time, even after the 64th byte of the frame sent by the half-duplex switch. So, just keep repeating the **show interfaces** command, and if you see the late collisions counter incrementing on a half-duplex interface, you might have a duplex mismatch problem.

A working interface (in an up/up state) can still suffer from issues related to the physical cabling as well. The cabling problems might not be bad enough to cause a complete failure, but the transmission failures result in some frames failing to pass successfully over the cable. For example, excessive interference on the cable can cause the various input error counters to keep growing larger, especially the CRC counter. In particular, if the CRC errors grow, but the collisions counters do not, the problem might simply be interference on the cable. (The switch counts each collided frame as one form of input error as well.)

Predicting Where Switches Will Forward Frames

This section begins the fourth of five major sections in this chapter. This section looks at a key part of the troubleshooting process for Ethernet LANs: predicting where frames should go in the LAN so that you can compare what should happen versus what is actually happening in a LAN.

Predicting the Contents of the MAC Address Table

As explained in Chapter 7, "Analyzing Ethernet LAN Switching," switches learn MAC addresses and then use the entries in the MAC address table to make a forwarding/filtering decision for each frame. To know exactly how a particular switch will forward an Ethernet frame, you need to examine the MAC address table on a Cisco switch.

The more formal troubleshooting process begins with a mental process where you predict where frames should flow in the LAN. As an exercise, review Figure 12-4 and try to create a MAC address table on paper for each switch. Include the MAC addresses for both PCs, as well as the Gi0/1 MAC address for R1. (Assume that all three are assigned to VLAN 10.) Then predict which interfaces would be used to forward a frame sent by Fred, Barney, and R1 to every other device.

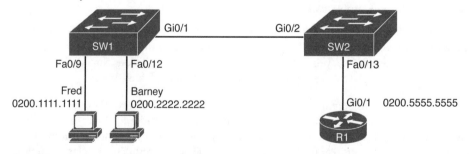

Figure 12-4 *Sample Network Used in Switch MAC Learning Examples*

The MAC table entries you predict in this case define where you think frames will flow. Even though this sample network in Figure 12-4 shows only one physical path through the Ethernet LAN, the exercise should be worthwhile, because it forces you to correlate what you'd expect to see in the MAC address table with how the switches forward frames. Figure 12-5 shows the resulting MAC table entries for PCs Fred and Barney, as well as for Router R1.

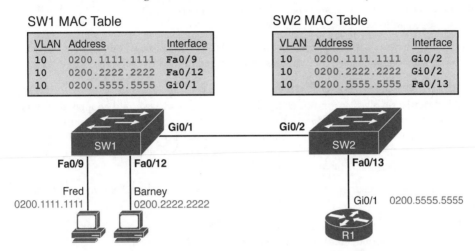

Figure 12-5 *Predictions for MAC Table Entries on SW1 and SW2*

While Figure 12-5 shows the concepts, Example 12-4 lists the same facts but in the form of the **show mac address-table dynamic** command on the switches. This command lists all dynamically learned MAC table entries on a switch, for all VLANs.

Example 12-4 *Examining SW1 and SW2 Dynamic MAC Address Table Entries*

```
SW1# show mac address-table dynamic
          Mac Address Table
-------------------------------------------


Vlan    Mac Address       Type        Ports
----    -----------       --------    -----
  10    0200.1111.1111    DYNAMIC     Fa0/9
  10    0200.2222.2222    DYNAMIC     Fa0/12
  10    0200.5555.5555    DYNAMIC     Gi0/1
SW2# show mac address-table dynamic
          Mac Address Table
-------------------------------------------


Vlan    Mac Address       Type        Ports
----    -----------       --------    -----
  10    0200.1111.1111    DYNAMIC     Gi0/2
  10    0200.2222.2222    DYNAMIC     Gi0/2
  10    0200.5555.5555    DYNAMIC     Fa0/13
```

12

When predicting the MAC address table entries, you need to imagine a frame sent by a device to another device on the other side of the LAN and then determine *which switch ports the frame would enter* as it passes through the LAN. For example, if Barney sends a frame to Router R1, the frame would enter SW1's Fa0/12 interface, so SW1 has a MAC table entry that lists Barney's 0200.2222.2222 MAC address with Fa0/12. SW1 would forward Barney's frame to SW2, arriving on SW2's Gi0/2 interface, so SW2's MAC table lists Barney's MAC address (0200.2222.2222) with interface Gi0/2.

After you predict the expected contents of the MAC address tables, you can then examine what is actually happening on the switches, as described in the next section.

Analyzing the Forwarding Path

Troubleshooting revolves around three big ideas: predicting what should happen, determining what is happening that is different than what should happen, and figuring out why that different behavior is happening. This next section discusses how to look at what is actually happening in a VLAN based on those MAC address tables, first using a summary of switch forwarding logic and then showing an example.

The following list summarizes switch forwarding logic including the LAN switching features discussed in this book:

Step 1. Process functions on the incoming interface, if the interface is currently in an up/up (connected) state, as follows:

   A. If configured, apply port security logic to filter the frame as appropriate.

   B. If the port is an access port, determine the interface's access VLAN.

   C. If the port is a trunk, determine the frame's tagged VLAN.

Step 2. Make a forwarding decision. Look for the frame's destination MAC address in the MAC address table, but only for entries in the VLAN identified in Step 1. If the destination MAC is...

   A. Found (unicast), forward the frame out the only interface listed in the matched address table entry.

   B. Not found (unicast), flood the frame out all other access ports (except the incoming port) in that same VLAN, plus out trunks that have not restricted the VLAN from that trunk (as discussed in Chapter 11, "Implementing Ethernet Virtual LANs," as related to the **show interfaces trunk** command).

   C. Broadcast, flood the frame, with the same rules as the previous step.

For an example of this process, consider a frame sent by Barney to its default gateway, R1 (0200.5555.5555). Using the steps just listed, the following occurs:

Step 1. Input interface processing:

   A. The port does not happen to have port security enabled.

   B. SW1 receives the frame on its Fa0/12 interface, an access port in VLAN 10.

Step 2. Make a forwarding decision: SW1 looks in its MAC address table for entries in VLAN 10:

   A. SW1 finds an entry (known unicast) for 0200.5555.5555, associated with VLAN 10, outgoing interface Gi0/1, so SW1 forwards the frame only out interface Gi0/1. (This link is a VLAN trunk, so SW1 adds a VLAN 10 tag to the 802.1Q trunking header.)

At this point, the frame with source 0200.2222.2222 (Barney) and destination 0200.5555.5555 (R1) is on its way to SW2. You can then apply the same logic for SW2, as follows:

Step 1.   Input interface processing:

   A. The port does not happen to have port security enabled.

   B. SW2 receives the frame on its Gi0/2 interface, a trunk; the frame lists a tag of VLAN 10. (SW2 will remove the 802.1Q header as well.)

Step 2.   Make a forwarding decision: SW2 looks for its MAC table for entries in VLAN 10:

   A. SW2 finds an entry (known unicast) for 0200.5555.5555, associated with VLAN 10, outgoing interface Fa0/13, so SW2 forwards the frame only out interface Fa0/13.

At this point, the frame should be on its way, over the Ethernet cable between SW2 and R1.

Analyzing Port Security Operations on an Interface

Generally speaking, any analysis of the forwarding process should consider any security features that might discard some frames or packets. For example, both routers and switches can be configured with access control lists (ACL) that examine the packets and frames being sent or received on an interface, with the router or switch discarding those packets/frames.

This book does not include coverage of switch ACLs, but the exams do cover a switch feature called port security. As covered in the ICND1 book's Chapter 9, "Configuring Switch Interfaces," the port security feature can be used to cause the switch to discard some frames sent into and out of an interface. Port security has three basic features with which it determines which frames to filter:

■ Limit which specific MAC addresses can send and receive frames on a switch interface, discarding frames to/from other MAC addresses

■ Limit the number of MAC addresses using the interface, discarding frames to/from MAC addresses learned after the maximum limit is reached

■ A combination of the previous two points

The first port security troubleshooting step should be to find which interfaces have port security enabled, followed by a determination as to whether any violations are currently occurring. The trickiest part relates to the differences in what the IOS does in reaction to violations based on the **switchport port-security violation** *violation-mode* interface subcommand, which tells the switch what to do when a violation occurs. The general process to find port security issues is as follows:

Step 1.   Identify all interfaces on which port security is enabled (**show running-config** or **show port-security**).

Step 2.   Determine whether a security violation is currently occurring based in part on the *violation mode* of the interface's port security configuration, as follows:

   A. shutdown: The interface will be in an err-disabled state, and the port security port status will be secure-down.

B. restrict: The interface will be in a connected state, the port security port status will be secure-up, but the **show port-security interface** command will show an incrementing violations counter.

C. protect: The interface will be in a connected state, and the **show port-security interface** command will not show an incrementing violations counter.

Step 3.   In all cases, compare the port security configuration to the diagram and to the Last Source Address field in the output of the **show port-security interface** command.

Because IOS reacts so differently with shutdown mode as compared to restrict and protect modes, the next few pages explain the differences—first for shutdown mode, then for the other two modes.

Troubleshooting Shutdown Mode and Err-disabled Recovery

Troubleshooting Step 2A refers to the interface err-disabled (error-disabled) state. This state verifies that the interface has been configured to use port security, that a violation has occurred, and that no traffic is allowed on the interface at the present time. This interface state implies that the shutdown violation mode is used, because it is the only one of the three port security modes that causes the interface to be disabled.

To recover from an err-disabled state, the interface must be shut down with the **shutdown** command, and then enabled with the **no shutdown** command. Example 12-5 lists an example in which the interface is in an err-disabled state.

Example 12-5 *Using Port Security to Define Correct MAC Addresses of Particular Interfaces*

```
! The first command lists all interfaces on which port security has been enabled,
! and the violation mode, under the heading "Security Action."
SW1# show port-security
Secure Port  MaxSecureAddr  CurrentAddr  SecurityViolation  Security Action
             (Count)        (Count)      (Count)
-----------------------------------------------------------------------------
    Fa0/13            1             1                 1           Shutdown
-----------------------------------------------------------------------------
Total Addresses in System (excluding one mac per port)    : 0
Max Addresses limit in System (excluding one mac per port) : 8192


!
! The next command shows the err-disabled state, implying a security violation.
SW1# show interfaces Fa0/13 status


Port       Name              Status        Vlan    Duplex  Speed Type
Fa0/13                       err-disabled  1               auto    auto 10/100BaseTX
!
! The next command's output has shading for several of the most important facts.
SW1# show port-security interface Fa0/13
```

```
Port Security              : Enabled
Port Status                : Secure-shutdown
Violation Mode             : Shutdown
Aging Time                 : 0 mins
Aging Type                 : Absolute
SecureStatic Address Aging : Disabled
Maximum MAC Addresses      : 1
Total MAC Addresses        : 1
Configured MAC Addresses   : 1
Sticky MAC Addresses       : 0
Last Source Address:Vlan   : 0200.3333.3333:2
Security Violation Count   : 1
```

The output of the **show port-security interface** command lists a couple of items helpful in the troubleshooting process. The port status of secure-shutdown means that the interface is disabled for all traffic as a result of a violation while in port security shutdown mode; this state is not used by the protect and restrict modes. The port security port status of secure-shutdown also means that the interface state should be err-disabled.

Note that in shutdown mode, the violations counter (at the bottom of the output) does not keep incrementing. Basically, once the first violating frame triggers IOS to move the port to an err-disabled state, IOS ignores any other incoming frames (not even counting them) until the engineer uses the **shutdown** and **no shutdown** commands on the interface, in succession. Note that the process of recovering the interface also resets the violation counter back to 0. Finally, note that the second-to-last line lists the source MAC address of the last frame received on the interface. This value can prove useful in identifying the MAC address of the device that caused the violation.

Figure 12-6 summarizes these behaviors, assuming the same scenario shown in the example.

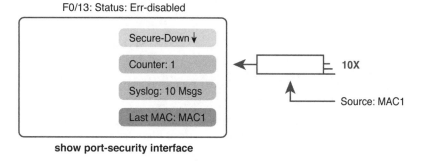

show port-security interface

Figure 12-6 *Summary of Actions: Port Security Violation Mode Shutdown*

Troubleshooting Restrict and Protect Modes

The restrict and protect violation modes take a much different approach to securing ports. These modes still discard offending traffic, but the interface remains in a connected (up/up) state, and in a port security state of secure-up. As a result, the port continues to forward good traffic and discard offending traffic.

Having a port in a seemingly good state that also discards traffic can be a challenge when troubleshooting. Basically, you have to know about this possible pitfall, and then know how to tell when port security is discarding some traffic on a port even though the interface status looks good.

The **show port-security interface** command reveals whether protect mode has discarded frames using the "last source address" item in the output. Example 12-6 shows a sample configuration and **show** command when using protect mode. In this case, the port is configured to allow Fa0/13 to receive frames sent by 0200.1111.1111 only. Ten frames have arrived, with a variety of source MAC addresses, with the last frame's source MAC address being 0200.3333.3333.

Example 12-6 *Port Security Using Protect Mode*

```
SW1# show running-config
! Lines omitted for brevity
interface FastEthernet0/13
 switchport mode access
 switchport port-security
 switchport port-security mac-address 0200.1111.1111
 switchport port-security violation protect
! Lines omitted for brevity


SW1# show port-security interface Fa0/13
Port Security               : Enabled
Port Status                 : Secure-up
Violation Mode              : Protect
Aging Time                  : 0 mins
Aging Type                  : Absolute
SecureStatic Address Aging  : Disabled
Maximum MAC Addresses       : 1
Total MAC Addresses         : 1
Configured MAC Addresses    : 1
Sticky MAC Addresses        : 0
Last Source Address:Vlan    : 0200.3333.3333:1
Security Violation Count    : 0
```

In protect mode, the **show port-security** interface command reveals practically nothing about whether the interfaces happen to be discarding traffic or not. For instance, in this case, this **show** command output was gathered after many frames had been sent by a PC with MAC address 0200.3333.3333, with all the frames being discarded by the switch because of port security. The command output shows the disallowed PC's 0200.3333.3333 MAC address as the last source MAC address in a received frame. However, if another frame with an allowed MAC address arrived (in this case, source MAC 0200.1111.1111), the next instance of the **show** command would list 0200.1111.1111 as the last source address. In particular, note that the interface remains in a secure-up state, and the violation counter does not increment.

Figure 12-7 summarizes the key points about the operation of Port Security protect mode, assuming a mix of frames with different source addresses. The figure emphasizes unpredict-ability of the last source MAC listed in the output, and the fact that the counter does not increment and that no syslog messages are generated for violating frames.

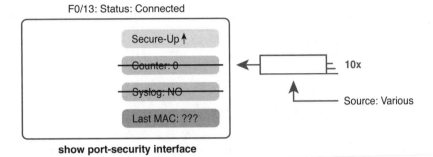

Figure 12-7   *Summary of Actions: Port Security Violation Mode Protect*

If this example had used violation mode restrict instead of protect, the port status would have also remained in a secure-up state; however, IOS would show some indication of port security activity, such as the incrementing violation counter as well as syslog messages. Example 12-7 shows an example of the violation counter and ends with an example port security syslog message. In this case, 97 incoming frames so far violated the rules, with the most recent frame having a source MAC address of 0200.3333.3333.

Example 12-7   *Port Security Using Violation Mode Restrict*

```
SW1# show port-security interface fa0/13
Port Security               : Enabled
Port Status                 : Secure-up
Violation Mode              : Restrict
Aging Time                  : 0 mins
Aging Type                  : Absolute
SecureStatic Address Aging  : Disabled
Maximum MAC Addresses       : 1
Total MAC Addresses         : 1
Configured MAC Addresses    : 1
Sticky MAC Addresses        : 0
Last Source Address:Vlan    : 0200.3333.3333:1
Security Violation Count    : 97
!
! The following log message also points to a port security issue.
!
01:46:58: %PORT_SECURITY-2-PSECURE_VIOLATION: Security violation occurred, caused by
MAC address 0200.3333.3333 on port FastEthernet0/13.
```

Figure 12-8 summarizes the key points about the restrict mode for port security. In this case, the figure matches the same scenario as the example again, with 97 total violating frames arriving so far, with the most recent being from source MAC MAC3.

12

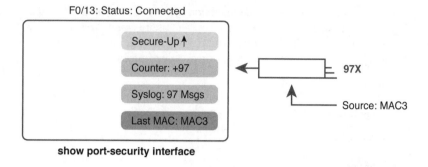

F0/13: Status: Connected

show port-security interface

Figure 12-8 *Summary of Actions: Port Security Violation Mode Restrict*

For the exams, a port security violation might not be a problem; it might be the exact function intended. The question text might well explicitly state what port security should be doing. In these cases, it can be quicker to just immediately look at the port security configuration. Then, compare the configuration to the MAC addresses of the devices connected to the interface. The most likely problem on the exams is that the MAC addresses have been misconfigured or that the maximum number of MAC addresses has been set too low.

Analyzing VLANs and VLAN Trunks

A switch's forwarding process, as discussed earlier in the section "Analyzing the Forwarding Path," depends in part on VLANs and VLAN trunking. Before a switch can forward frames in a particular VLAN, the switch must know about a VLAN and the VLAN must be active. And before a switch can forward a frame over a VLAN trunk, the trunk must currently allow that VLAN to pass over the trunk. This final of the five major sections in this chapter focuses on VLAN and VLAN trunking issues, specifically issues that impact the frame switching process. The four potential issues are as follows:

Step 1.	Identify all access interfaces and their assigned access VLANs and reassign into the correct VLANs as needed.
Step 2.	Determine whether the VLANs both exist (configured or learned with VTP) and are active on each switch. If not, configure and activate the VLANs to resolve problems as needed.
Step 3.	Check the allowed VLAN lists, on the switches on both ends of the trunk, and ensure that the lists of allowed VLANs are the same.
Step 4.	Check for incorrect configuration settings that result in one switch operating as a trunk, with the neighboring switch not operating as a trunk.

Ensuring That the Right Access Interfaces Are in the Right VLANs

To ensure that each access interface has been assigned to the correct VLAN, engineers simply need to determine which switch interfaces are access interfaces instead of trunk interfaces, determine the assigned access VLANs on each interface, and compare the information to the documentation. The **show** commands listed in Table 12-3 can be particularly helpful in this process.

Table 12-3   Commands That Can Find Access Ports and VLANs

EXEC Command	Description
show vlan brief show vlan	Lists each VLAN and all interfaces assigned to that VLAN (but does not include operational trunks)
show vlan id *num*	Lists both access and trunk ports in the VLAN
show interfaces *type number* switchport	Identifies the interface's access VLAN and voice VLAN, plus the configured and operational mode (access or trunk)
show mac address-table	Lists MAC table entries, including the associated VLAN

If possible, start this step with the **show vlan** and **show vlan brief** commands, because they list all the known VLANs and the access interfaces assigned to each VLAN. Be aware, however, that these two commands do not list operational trunks. The output does list all other interfaces (those not currently trunking), no matter whether the interface is in a working or nonworking state.

If the **show vlan** and **show interface switchport** commands are not available in a particular exam question, the **show mac address-table** command can also help identify the access VLAN. This command lists the MAC address table, with each entry including a MAC address, interface, and VLAN ID. If the exam question implies that a switch interface connects to a single device PC, you should only see one MAC table entry that lists that particular access interface; the VLAN ID listed for that same entry identifies the access VLAN. (You cannot make such assumptions for trunking interfaces.)

After you determine the access interfaces and associated VLANs, if the interface is assigned to the wrong VLAN, use the **switchport access vlan** *vlan-id* interface subcommand to assign the correct VLAN ID.

Access VLANs Not Being Defined

Switches do not forward frames for VLANs that are (a) not configured or (b) configured but disabled (shut down). This section summarizes the best ways to confirm that a switch knows that a particular VLAN exists, and if it exists, determines the state of the VLAN.

First, on the issue of whether a VLAN is defined, a VLAN can be defined to a switch in two ways: using the **vlan** *number* global configuration command, or it can be learned from another switch using VTP. This book purposefully ignores VTP as much as possible, so for this discussion, consider that the only way for a switch to know about a VLAN is to have a **vlan** command configured on the local switch.

Next, the **show vlan** command always lists all VLANs known to the switch, but the **show running-config** command does not. Switches configured as VTP servers and clients do not list the **vlan** commands in the running-config nor the startup-config file; on these switches, you must use the **show vlan** command. Switches configured to use VTP transparent mode, or that disable VTP, list the **vlan** configuration commands in the configuration files. (Use the **show vtp status** command to learn the current VTP mode of a switch.)

After you determine that a VLAN does not exist, the problem might be that the VLAN simply needs to be defined. If so, follow the VLAN configuration process as covered in detail in Chapter 11.

Access VLANs Being Disabled

For any existing VLANs, also verify whether the VLAN is active. The **show vlan** command should list one of two VLAN state values, depending on the current state: either *active* or *act/lshut*. The second of these states means that the VLAN is shut down. Shutting down a VLAN disables the VLAN on that switch only, so that *the switch will not forward frames in that VLAN*.

Switch IOS gives you two similar configuration methods with which to disable (**shutdown**) and enable (**no shutdown**) a VLAN. Example 12-8 shows how, first by using the global command [no] **shutdown vlan** *number* and then using the VLAN mode subcommand [no] **shutdown**. The example shows the global commands enabling and disabling VLANs 10 and 20, respectively, and using VLAN subcommands to enable and disable VLANs 30 and 40 (respectively).

Example 12-8 *Enabling and Disabling VLANs on a Switch*

```
SW2# show vlan brief

VLAN Name                             Status    Ports
---- -------------------------------- --------- -------------------------------
1    default                          active    Fa0/1, Fa0/2, Fa0/3, Fa0/4
                                                Fa0/5, Fa0/6, Fa0/7, Fa0/8
                                                Fa0/9, Fa0/10, Fa0/11, Fa0/12
                                                Fa0/14, Fa0/15, Fa0/16, Fa0/17
                                                Fa0/18, Fa0/19, Fa0/20, Fa0/21
                                                Fa0/22, Fa0/23, Fa0/24, Gi0/1
10   VLAN0010                         act/lshut Fa0/13
20   VLAN0020                         active
30   VLAN0030                         act/lshut
40   VLAN0040                         active
SW2# configure terminal
Enter configuration commands, one per line.  End with CNTL/Z.
SW2(config)# no shutdown vlan 10
SW2(config)# shutdown vlan 20
SW2(config)# vlan 30
SW2(config-vlan)# no shutdown
SW2(config-vlan)# vlan 40
SW2(config-vlan)# shutdown
SW2(config-vlan)#
```

Mismatched Trunking Operational States

Trunking can be configured correctly so that both switches forward frames for the same set of VLANs. However, trunks can also be misconfigured, with a couple of different results. In some cases, both switches conclude that their interfaces do not trunk. In other cases, one switch believes that its interface is correctly trunking, while the other switch does not.

The most common incorrect configuration—which results in both switches not trunking—is a configuration that uses the **switchport mode dynamic auto** command on both switches on the link. The word "auto" just makes us all want to think that the link would trunk automatically, but this command is both automatic and passive. As a result, both switches passively wait on the other device on the link to begin negotiations.

With this particular incorrect configuration, the **show interfaces switchport** command on both switches confirms both the administrative state (auto), as well as the fact that both switches operate as "static access" ports. Example 12-9 highlights those parts of the output from this command.

Example 12-9 *Operational Trunking State*

```
SW2# show interfaces gigabit0/2 switchport
Name: Gi0/2
Switchport: Enabled
Administrative Mode: dynamic auto
Operational Mode: static access
Administrative Trunking Encapsulation: dot1q
Operational Trunking Encapsulation: native
! lines omitted for brevity
```

A different incorrect trunking configuration results in one switch with an operational state of "trunk," while the other switch has an operational state of "static access." When this combination of events happens, the interface works a little. The status on each end will be up/up or connected. Traffic in the native VLAN will actually cross the link successfully. However, traffic in all the rest of the VLANs will not cross the link.

Figure 12-9 shows the incorrect configuration along with which side trunks and which does not. The side that trunks (SW1 in this case) enables trunking always, using the command **switchport mode trunk**. However, this command does not disable DTP negotiations. To cause this particular problem, SW1 also disables DTP negotiation using the **switchport nonegotiate** command. SW2's configuration also helps create the problem, by using a trunking option that relies on DTP. Because SW1 has disabled DTP, SW2's DTP negotiations fail, and SW2 does not trunk.

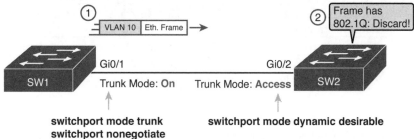

Figure 12-9 *Mismatched Trunking Operational States*

In this case, SW1 treats its G0/1 interface as a trunk, and SW2 treats its G0/2 interface as an access port (not a trunk). As shown in the figure at Step 1, SW1 could (for example) forward a frame in VLAN 10 (Step 1). However, SW2 would view any frame that arrives with an 802.1Q header as illegal, because SW2 treats its G0/2 port as an access port. So, SW2 discards any 802.1Q frames received on that port.

To deal with the possibility of this problem, always check the trunk's operational state on both sides of the trunk. The best commands to check trunking-related facts are **show interfaces trunk** and **show interfaces switchport**.

> **NOTE** Frankly, in real life, just avoid this kind of configuration. However, the switches do not prevent you from making these types of mistakes, so you need to be ready.

Chapter Review

One key to doing well on the exams is to perform repetitive spaced review sessions. Review this chapter's material using either the tools in the book, DVD, or interactive tools for the same material found on the book's companion website. Refer to the "Your Study Plan" element for more details. Table 12-4 outlines the key review elements and where you can find them. To better track your study progress, record when you completed these activities in the second column.

Table 12-4 Chapter Review Tracking

Review Element	Review Date(s)	Resource Used
Review key topics		Book, DVD/website
Review key terms		Book, DVD/website
Answer DIKTA questions		Book, PCPT
Review memory tables		Book, DVD/website
Review command tables		Book

Review All the Key Topics

Table 12-5 Key Topics for Chapter 12

Key Topic Element	Description	Page Number
List	Explanation of troubleshooting methodologies per exam topics	274
Table 12-2	Two types of interface state terms and their meanings	279
Example 12-1	Example that shows how to find the speed and duplex settings, as well as whether they were learned through autonegotiation	280
List	Defaults for IEEE autonegotiation	281
List	Explanations of different error statistics on switch interfaces	283
List	Summary of switch forwarding steps	286
List	Port security troubleshooting checklist	287
List	Potential issues to examine for VLANs and VLAN trunks	292
Table 12-3	Commands that identify access VLANs assigned to ports	293
Figure 12-9	How to poorly configure switches to reach a mismatched trunk operational state on the two ends of the trunk	295

Key Terms You Should Know

up and up, connected, error disabled, problem isolation, root cause, duplex mismatch, resolve, escalate

Command References

Tables 12-6 and 12-7 list configuration and verification commands used in this chapter, respectively. As an easy review exercise, cover the left column in a table, read the right column, and try to recall the command without looking. Then repeat the exercise, covering the right column, and try to recall what the command does.

Table 12-6   Commands for Catalyst Switch Configuration

Command	Description
shutdown no shutdown	Interface subcommands that administratively disable and enable an interface, respectively
switchport port-security violation {protect | restrict | shutdown}	Interface subcommand that tells the switch what to do if an inappropriate MAC address tries to access the network through a secure switch port
speed {auto | 10 | 100 | 1000}	Interface subcommand that manually sets the interface speed
duplex {auto | full | half}	Interface subcommand that manually sets the interface duplex

Table 12-7   Chapter 12 EXEC Command Reference

Command	Description
show mac address-table [dynamic | static] [address *hw-addr*] [interface *interface-id*] [vlan *vlan-id*]	Displays the MAC address table. The static option displays information about the restricted or static settings.
show port-security [interface *interface-id*] [address]	Displays information about security options configured on an interface.
show interfaces [*type number*]	Displays detailed information about interface status, settings, and counters.
show interfaces description	Displays one line of information per interface, with a two-item status (similar to the **show interfaces** command status), and includes any description that is configured on the interfaces.
show interfaces [*type number*] status	Displays summary information about interface status and settings, including actual speed and duplex, a single-item status code, and whether the interface was autonegotiated.
show interfaces [*type number*] switchport	Displays a large variety of configuration settings and current operational status, including VLAN trunking details, access and voice VLAN, and native VLAN.
show interfaces [*type number*] trunk	Lists information about the currently operational trunks (or just for the trunk listed in the command) and the VLANs supported on those trunks.
show vlan brief, show vlan	Lists each VLAN and all interfaces assigned to that VLAN but does not include trunks.
show vlan id *num*	Lists both access and trunk ports in the VLAN.
show vtp status	Lists the current VTP status, including the current mode.

12

Part III Review

Keep track of your part review progress with the checklist shown in Table P3-1. Details on each task follow the table.

Table P3-1   Part III Part Review Checklist

Activity	1st Date Completed	2nd Date Completed
Repeat All DIKTA Questions		
Answer Part Review Questions		
Review Key Topics		
Create Command Mind Maps by Category		
Do Labs		

Repeat All DIKTA Questions

For this task, answer the "Do I Know This Already?" questions again for the chapters in this part of the book, using the PCPT software.

Answer Part Review Questions

For this task, answer the Part Review questions for this part of the book, using the PCPT software.

Review Key Topics

Review all key topics in all chapters in this part, either by browsing the chapters or by using the Key Topics application on the DVD or companion website.

Create Terminology, Command, and Troubleshooting Causes Mind Maps

Part III of this book discusses the more advanced Ethernet concepts for this book, but from many directions: design, implementation, and troubleshooting. These next three mind maps help you collect and organize your thoughts from each direction.

Terminology: Start with a blank mind map, and create a map that organizes all the terms you can recall from this part, especially for Chapters 10 (design) and 11 (VLANs and trunking). After you have added all the terms you can recall, and organized which terms relate by connecting the terms into a hierarchy or other organization, go back to the Key Terms list at the end of each chapter. Add any terms you forgot to list in your map to this mind map.

Commands: Create a mind map that focuses on remembering the config and EXEC commands related to VLANs and trunking. Do not be worried about every single parameter on each command; this exercise is more about remembering the commands available to you for each feature. Once you do what you can from memory, go back and check your map against the Chapter 11 Command Reference tables at the end of the chapter, and add to your map.

Troubleshooting causes: Chapter 12 works through several issues that can cause problems for interfaces, port security, and VLANs and VLAN trunks. Create one mind map with branches for each of these, from memory, with the usual goal of exercising your memory and building more connectors in your brain. Then skim the chapter and add to your map.

Labs

Depending on your chosen lab tool, here are some suggestions for what to do in lab:

Pearson Network Simulator: If you use the full Pearson ICND1 or CCNA simulator, focus more on the configuration scenario and troubleshooting scenario labs associated with the topics in this part of the book. These types of labs include a larger set of topics, and work well as Part Review activities. (See the Introduction for some details about how to find which labs are about topics in this part of the book.)

Config Labs: In your idle moments, review and repeat any of the Config Labs for this book part in the author's blog; launch from blog.certskills.com/ccent and navigate to the Hands-on Config labs.

Other: If using other lab tools, as a few suggestions: make sure and experiment heavily with VLAN configuration and VLAN trunking configuration. Also, experiment with the combinations of port security settings detailed in Chapter 12, focusing on the output from the **show port-security** command. Finally, spend some time changing interface settings like **speed** and **duplex** on a link between two switches, to make sure that you understand which cases would result in a duplex mismatch.

The book makes a big transition at this point. Part I gave you a broad introduction to networking, and Parts II and III went into some detail about the dominant LAN technology today: Ethernet. Part IV transitions from Ethernet to the network layer details that sit above Ethernet and WAN technology, specifically IPv4. In fact, the next four parts of the book discuss IPv4-specific features, as shown in Figure P4-1.

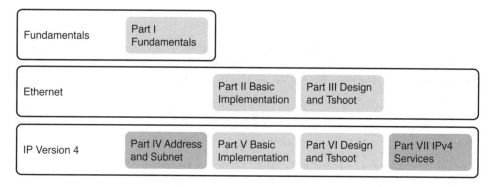

Figure P4-1 *Roadmap of Book Parts So Far*

Ethernet addressing, although important, did not require planning. The network engineer needs to understand MAC addresses, but MAC already exists on each Ethernet NIC, and switches learn the Ethernet MAC addresses dynamically without even needing to be configured to do so. Conversely, IP addressing requires planning, along with a much deeper understanding of the internal structure of the addresses. As a result, this book breaks down the addressing details into six separate chapters, spread across Parts IV and VI.

Part IV examines most of the basic details of IPv4 addressing and subnetting, mostly from the perspective of operating an IP network. Chapter 13 takes a grand tour of IPv4 addressing as implemented inside a typical enterprise network. Chapters 14, 15, and 16 look at some of the specific questions people must ask themselves when operating an IPv4 network. Note that Part VI also discusses other details related to IPv4 addressing, with those chapters taking more of a design approach to IP addressing.

Part IV

IP Version 4 Addressing and Subnetting

CHAPTER 13

Perspectives on IPv4 Subnetting

This chapter covers the following exam topics:

1.0 Network Fundamentals

1.8 Configure, verify, and troubleshoot IPv4 addressing and subnetting

1.9 Compare and contrast IPv4 address types

    1.9.a Unicast

1.10 Describe the need for private IPv4 addressing

Most entry-level networking jobs require you to operate and troubleshoot a network using a preexisting IP addressing and subnetting plan. The CCENT and CCNA Routing and Switching exams assess your readiness to use preexisting IP addressing and subnetting information to perform typical operations tasks, like monitoring the network, reacting to possible problems, and troubleshooting those problems.

However, you also need to understand how networks are designed and why. The thought processes used when monitoring any network continually ask the question, "Is the network working *as designed*?" If a problem exists, you must consider questions such as, "What happens when the network works normally, and what is different right now?" Both questions require you to understand the intended design of the network, including details of the IP addressing and subnetting design.

This chapter provides some perspectives and answers for the bigger issues in IPv4 addressing. What addresses can be used so that they work properly? What addresses should be used? When told to use certain numbers, what does that tell you about the choices made by some other network engineer? How do these choices impact the practical job of configuring switches, routers, hosts, and operating the network on a daily basis? This chapter hopes to answer these questions while revealing details of how IPv4 addresses work.

"Do I Know This Already?" Quiz

Take the quiz (either here, or use the PCPT software) if you want to use the score to help you decide how much time to spend on this chapter. The answers are at the bottom of the page following the quiz, and the explanations are in DVD Appendix C and in the PCPT software.

Table 13-1 "Do I Know This Already?" Foundation Topics Section-to-Question Mapping

Foundation Topics Section	Questions
Analyze Requirements	1–3
Make Design Choices	4–7

1. Host A is a PC, connected to switch SW1 and assigned to VLAN 1. Which of the following are typically assigned an IP address in the same subnet as host A? (Choose two answers.)

    a. The local router's WAN interface

    b. The local router's LAN interface

    c. All other hosts attached to the same switch

    d. Other hosts attached to the same switch and also in VLAN 1

2. Why does the formula for the number of hosts per subnet ($2^H - 2$) require the subtraction of two hosts?

    a. To reserve two addresses for redundant default gateways (routers)

    b. To reserve the two addresses required for DHCP operation

    c. To reserve addresses for the subnet ID and default gateway (router)

    d. To reserve addresses for the subnet broadcast address and subnet ID

3. A Class B network needs to be subnetted such that it supports 100 subnets and 100 hosts/subnet. Which of the following answers list a workable combination for the number of network, subnet, and host bits? (Choose two answers.)

    a. Network = 16, subnet = 7, host = 7

    b. Network = 16, subnet = 8, host = 8

    c. Network = 16, subnet = 9, host = 7

    d. Network = 8, subnet = 7, host = 17

4. Which of the following are private IP networks? (Choose two answers.)

    a. 172.31.0.0

    b. 172.32.0.0

    c. 192.168.255.0

    d. 192.1.168.0

    e. 11.0.0.0

5. Which of the following are public IP networks? (Choose three answers.)

    a. 9.0.0.0

    b. 172.30.0.0

    c. 192.168.255.0

    d. 192.1.168.0

    e. 1.0.0.0

6. Before Class B network 172.16.0.0 is subnetted by a network engineer, what parts of the structure of the IP addresses in this network already exist, with a specific size? (Choose two answers.)

   a. Network

   b. Subnet

   c. Host

   d. Broadcast

7. A network engineer spends time thinking about the entire Class B network 172.16.0.0, and how to subnet that network. He then chooses how to subnet this Class B network and creates an addressing and subnetting plan, on paper, showing his choices. If you compare his thoughts about this network before subnetting the network, to his thoughts about this network after mentally subnetting the network, which of the following occurred to the parts of the structure of addresses in this network?

   a. The subnet part got smaller.

   b. The host part got smaller.

   c. The network part got smaller.

   d. The host part was removed.

   e. The network part was removed.

Foundation Topics

Introduction to Subnetting

Say you just happened to be at the sandwich shop when they were selling the world's longest sandwich. You're pretty hungry, so you go for it. Now you have one sandwich, but at over 2 kilometers long, you realize it's a bit more than you need for lunch all by yourself. To make the sandwich more useful (and more portable), you chop the sandwich into meal-size pieces, and give the pieces to other folks around you, who are also ready for lunch.

Huh? Well, subnetting, at least the main concept, is similar to this sandwich story. You start with one network, but it is just one large network. As a single large entity, it might not be useful, and it is probably far too large. To make it useful, you chop it into smaller pieces, called subnets, and assign those subnets to be used in different parts of the enterprise internetwork.

This short section introduces IP subnetting. First, it shows the general ideas behind a completed subnet design that indeed chops (or subnets) one network into subnets. The rest of this section describes the many design steps that you would take to create just such a subnet design. By the end of this section, you should have the right context to then read through the subnetting design steps introduced throughout the rest of this chapter.

NOTE   This chapter, and in fact the rest of the chapters in this book up until Chapter 28, "Fundamentals of IP Version 6," focuses on IPv4 rather than IPv6. All references to *IP* refer to IPv4 unless otherwise stated.

Subnetting Defined Through a Simple Example

An IP network—in other words, a Class A, B, or C network—is simply a set of consecutively numbered IP addresses that follows some preset rules. These Class A, B, and C rules, first introduced back in section, "Class A, B, and C IP Networks," of Chapter 4, "Fundamentals of IPv4 Addressing and Routing," define that for a given network, all the addresses in the network have the same value in some of the octets of the addresses. For example, Class B network 172.16.0.0 consists of all IP addresses that begin with 172.16: 172.16.0.0, 172.16.0.1, 172.16.0.2, and so on, through 172.16.255.255. Another example: Class A network 10.0.0.0 includes all addresses that begin with 10.

An IP subnet is simply a subset of a Class A, B, or C network. If fact, the word *subnet* is a shortened version of the phrase *subdivided network*. For example, one subnet of Class B network 172.16.0.0 could be the set of all IP addresses that begin with 172.16.1, and would include 172.16.1.0, 172.16.1.1, 172.16.1.2, and so on, up through 172.16.1.255. Another subnet of that same Class B network could be all addresses that begin with 172.16.2.

To give you a general idea, Figure 13-1 shows some basic documentation from a completed subnet design that could be used when an engineer subnets Class B network 172.16.0.0.

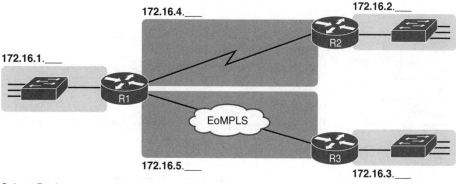

Subnet Design:

Class B 172.16.0.0
First 3 Octets are Equal

Figure 13-1   *Subnet Plan Document*

The design shows five subnets: one for each of the three LANs and one each for the two WAN links. The small text note shows the rationale used by the engineer for the subnets: Each subnet includes addresses that have the same value in the first three octets. For example, for the LAN on the left, the number shows 172.16.1.__, meaning "all addresses that begin with 172.16.1." Also, note that the design, as shown, does not use all the addresses in Class B network 172.16.0.0, so the engineer has left plenty of room for growth.

13

Operational View Versus Design View of Subnetting

Most IT jobs require you to work with subnetting from an operational view. That is, someone else, before you got the job, designed how IP addressing and subnetting would work for that particular enterprise network. You need to interpret what someone else has already chosen.

To fully understand IP addressing and subnetting, you need to think about subnetting from both a design and operational perspective. For example, Figure 13-1 simply states that in all these subnets, the first three octets must be equal. Why was that convention chosen? What alternatives exist? Would those alternatives be better for your internetwork today? All these questions relate more to subnetting design rather than to operation.

To help you see both perspectives, some chapters in this part of the book focus more on design issues, while others focus more on operations by interpreting some existing design. This current chapter happens to move through the entire design process for the purpose of introducing the bigger picture of IP subnetting. Following this chapter, the next three chapters each take one topic from this chapter and examine it more closely, either from an operational or design perspective.

The remaining three main sections of this chapter examine each of the steps listed in Figure 13-2, in sequence.

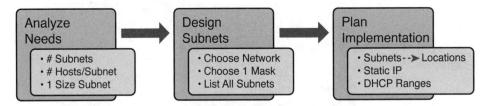

Figure 13-2   *Subnet Planning, Design, and Implementation Tasks*

Analyze Subnetting and Addressing Needs

This section discusses the meaning of four basic questions that can be used to analyze the addressing and subnetting needs for any new or changing enterprise network:

1. Which hosts should be grouped together into a subnet?
2. How many subnets does this network require?
3. How many host IP addresses does each subnet require?
4. Will we use a single subnet size for simplicity, or not?

Rules About Which Hosts Are in Which Subnet

Every device that connects to an IP internetwork needs to have an IP address. These devices include computers used by end users, servers, mobile phones, laptops, IP phones, tablets, and networking devices like routers, switches, and firewalls. In short, any device that uses IP to send and receive packets needs an IP address.

> **NOTE** When discussing IP addressing, the term *network* has specific meaning: a Class A, B, or C IP network. To avoid confusion with that use of the term *network*, this book uses the terms *internetwork* and *enterprise network* when referring to a collection of hosts, routers, switches, and so on.

The IP addresses must be assigned according to some basic rules, and for good reasons. To make routing work efficiently, IP addressing rules group addresses into groups called subnets. The rules are as follows:

- Addresses in the same subnet are not separated by a router.
- Addresses in different subnets are separated by at least one router.

Figure 13-3 shows the general concept, with hosts A and B in one subnet and host C in another. In particular, note that hosts A and B are not separated from each other by any routers. However, host C, separated from A and B by at least one router, must be in a different subnet.

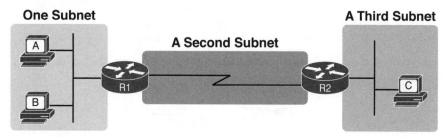

Figure 13-3 *PC A and B in One Subnet, and PC C in a Different Subnet*

The idea that hosts on the same link must be in the same subnet is much like the postal code concept. All mailing addresses in the same town use the same postal code (ZIP codes in the United States). Addresses in another town, whether relatively nearby or on the other side of the country, have a different postal code. The postal code gives the postal service a better ability to automatically sort the mail to deliver it to the right location. For the same general reasons, hosts on the same LAN are in the same subnet, and hosts in different LANs are in different subnets.

Note that the point-to-point WAN link in the figure also needs a subnet. Figure 13-3 shows Router R1 connected to the LAN subnet on the left and to a WAN subnet on the right. Router R2 connects to that same WAN subnet. To do so, both R1 and R2 will have IP addresses on their WAN interfaces, and the addresses will be in the same subnet. (An Ethernet over MPLS [EoMPLS] WAN link has the same IP addressing needs, with each of the two routers having an IP address in the same subnet.)

The Ethernet LANs in Figure 13-3 also show a slightly different style of drawing, using simple lines with no Ethernet switch. Drawings of Ethernet LANs when the details of the LAN switches do not matter simply show each device connected to the same line, as shown in Figure 13-3. (This kind of drawing mimics the original Ethernet cabling before switches and hubs existed.)

13

Finally, because the routers' main job is to forward packets from one subnet to another, routers typically connect to multiple subnets. For example, in this case, Router R1 connects to one LAN subnet on the left and one WAN subnet on the right. To do so, R1 will be configured with two different IP addresses, one per interface. These addresses will be in different subnets, because the interfaces connect the router to different subnets.

Determining the Number of Subnets

To determine the number of subnets required, the engineer must think about the internetwork as documented and count the locations that need a subnet. To do so, the engineer requires access to network diagrams, VLAN configuration details, and details about WAN links. For the types of links discussed in this book, you should plan for one subnet for every

- VLAN
- Point-to-point serial link
- Ethernet emulation WAN link (EoMPLS)

> **NOTE** WAN technologies like MPLS allow subnetting options other than one subnet per pair of routers on the WAN, but this book only uses WAN technologies that have one subnet for each point-to-point WAN connection between two routers.

For example, imagine that the network planner has only Figure 13-4 on which to base the subnet design.

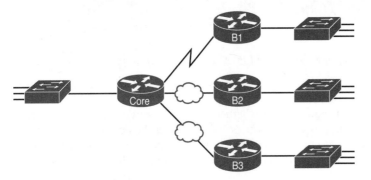

Figure 13-4 *Four-Site Internetwork with Small Central Site*

The number of subnets required cannot be fully predicted with only this figure. Certainly, three subnets will be needed for the WAN links, one per link. However, each LAN switch can be configured with a single VLAN, or with multiple VLANs. You can be certain that you need at least one subnet for the LAN at each site, but you might need more.

Next, consider the more detailed version of the same figure shown in Figure 13-5. In this case, the figure shows VLAN counts in addition to the same Layer 3 topology (the routers and the links connected to the routers). It also shows that the central site has many more switches, but the key fact on the left, regardless of how many switches exist, is that the central site has a total of 12 VLANs. Similarly, the figure lists each branch as having two VLANs. Along with the same three WAN subnets, this internetwork requires 21 subnets.

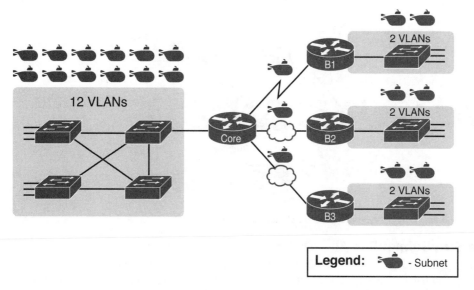

Figure 13-5 *Four-Site Internetwork with Larger Central Site*

Finally, in a real job, you would consider the needs today as well as how much growth you expect in the internetwork over time. Any subnetting plan should include a reasonable estimate of the number of subnets you need to meet future needs.

Determining the Number of Hosts per Subnet

Determining the number of hosts per subnet requires knowing a few simple concepts and then doing a lot of research and questioning. Every device that connects to a subnet needs an IP address. For a totally new network, you can look at business plans—numbers of people at the site, devices on order, and so on—to get some idea of the possible devices. When expanding an existing network to add new sites, you can use existing sites as a point of comparison, and then find out which sites will get bigger or smaller. And don't forget to count the router interface IP address in each subnet and the switch IP address used to remotely manage the switch.

Instead of gathering data for each and every site, planners often just use a few typical sites for planning purposes. For example, maybe you have some large sales offices and some small sales offices. You might dig in and learn a lot about only one large sales office and only one small sales office. Add that analysis to the fact that point-to-point links need a subnet with just two addresses, plus any analysis of more one-of-a-kind subnets, and you have enough information to plan the addressing and subnetting design.

For example, in Figure 13-6, the engineer has built a diagram that shows the number of hosts per LAN subnet in the largest branch, B1. For the two other branches, the engineer did not bother to dig to find out the number of required hosts. As long as the number of required IP addresses at sites B2 and B3 stays below the estimate of 50, based on larger site B1, the engineer can plan for 50 hosts in each branch LAN subnet and have plenty of addresses per subnet.

13

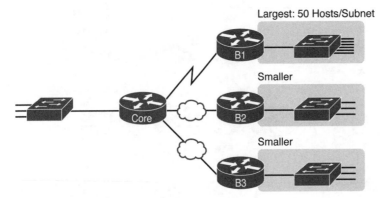

Figure 13-6   *Large Branch B1 with 50 Hosts/Subnet*

One Size Subnet Fits All—Or Not

The final choice in the initial planning step is to decide whether you will use a simpler design by using a one-size-subnet-fits-all philosophy. A subnet's size, or length, is simply the number of usable IP addresses in the subnet. A subnetting design can either use one size subnet, or varied sizes of subnets, with pros and cons for each choice.

Defining the Size of a Subnet

Before you finish this book, you will learn all the details of how to determine the size of the subnet. For now, you just need to know a few specific facts about the size of subnets. Chapter 14, "Analyzing Classful IPv4 Networks," and Chapter 15, "Analyzing Subnet Masks," give you a progressively deeper knowledge of the details.

The engineer assigns each subnet a *subnet mask*, and that mask, among other things, defines the size of that subnet. The mask sets aside a number of *host bits* whose purpose is to number different host IP addresses in that subnet. Because you can number 2^x things with x bits, if the mask defines H host bits, the subnet contains 2^H unique numeric values.

However, the subnet's size is not 2^H. It's $2^H - 2$, because two numbers in each subnet are reserved for other purposes. Each subnet reserves the numerically lowest value for the *subnet number* and the numerically highest value as the *subnet broadcast address*. As a result, the number of usable IP addresses per subnet is $2^H - 2$.

> **NOTE**   The terms *subnet number*, *subnet ID*, and *subnet address* all refer to the number that represents or identifies a subnet.

Figure 13-7 shows the general concept behind the three-part structure of an IP address, focusing on the host part and the resulting subnet size.

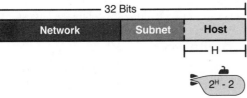

Figure 13-7 *Subnet Size Concepts*

One-Size Subnet Fits All

To choose to use a single-size subnet in an enterprise network, you must use the same mask for all subnets, because the mask defines the size of the subnet. But which mask?

One requirement to consider when choosing that one mask is this: That one mask must provide enough host IP addresses to support the largest subnet. To do so, the number of host bits (H) defined by the mask must be large enough so that $2^H - 2$ is larger than (or equal to) the number of host IP addresses required in the largest subnet.

For example, consider Figure 13-8. It shows the required number of hosts per LAN subnet. (The figure ignores the subnets on the WAN links, which require only two IP addresses each.) The branch LAN subnets require only 50 host addresses, but the main site LAN subnet requires 200 host addresses. To accommodate the largest subnet, you need at least 8 host bits. Seven host bits would not be enough, because $2^7 - 2 = 126$. Eight host bits would be enough, because $2^8 - 2 = 254$, which is more than enough to support 200 hosts in a subnet.

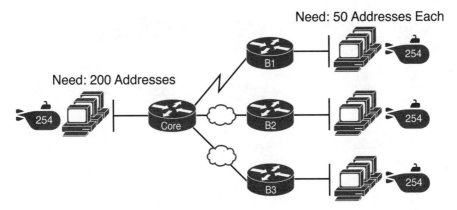

Figure 13-8 *Network Using One Subnet Size*

What's the big advantage when using a single-size subnet? Operational simplicity. In other words, keeping it simple. Everyone on the IT staff who has to work with networking can get used to working with one mask—and one mask only. They will be able to answer all subnetting questions more easily, because everyone gets used to doing subnetting math with that one mask.

The big disadvantage for using a single-size subnet is that it wastes IP addresses. For example, in Figure 13-8, all the branch LAN subnets support 254 addresses, while the largest branch subnet needs only 50 addresses. The WAN subnets only need two IP addresses, but each supports 254 addresses, again wasting more IP addresses.

The wasted IP addresses do not actually cause a problem in most cases, however. Most organizations use private IP networks in their enterprise internetworks, and a single Class A or Class B private network can supply plenty of IP addresses, even with the waste.

Multiple Subnet Sizes (Variable-Length Subnet Masks)

To create multiple sizes of subnets in one Class A, B, or C network, the engineer must create some subnets using one mask, some with another, and so on. Different masks mean different numbers of host bits, and a different number of hosts in some subnets based on the $2^H - 2$ formula.

For example, consider the requirements listed earlier in Figure 13-8. It showed one LAN subnet on the left that needs 200 host addresses, three branch subnets that need 50 addresses, and three WAN links that need two addresses. To meet those needs, but waste fewer IP addresses, three subnet masks could be used, creating subnets of three different sizes, as shown in Figure 13-9.

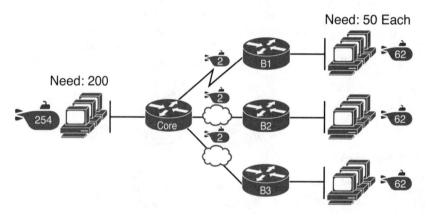

Figure 13-9 *Three Masks, Three Subnet Sizes*

The smaller subnets now waste fewer IP addresses compared to the design shown earlier in Figure 13-8. The subnets on the right that need 50 IP addresses have subnets with 6 host bits, for $2^6 - 2 = 62$ available addresses per subnet. The WAN links use masks with 2 host bits, for $2^2 - 2 = 2$ available addresses per subnet.

However, some are still wasted, because you cannot set the size of the subnet as some arbitrary size. All subnets will be a size based on the $2^H - 2$ formula, with H being the number of host bits defined by the mask for each subnet.

This Book: One-Size Subnet Fits All (Mostly)

For the most part, this book explains subnetting using designs that use a single mask, creating a single subnet size for all subnets. Why? First, it makes the process of learning subnetting easier. Second, some types of analysis that you can do about a network—specifically, calculating the number of subnets in the classful network—only make sense when a single mask is used.

However, you still need to be ready to work with variable-length subnet masks (VLSM), which is the practice of using different masks for different subnets in the same classful IP network. All of Chapter 22, "Variable-Length Subnet Masks," focuses on VLSM. However, all the examples and discussion up until that chapter purposefully avoid VLSM just to keep the discussion simpler, for the sake of learning to walk before you run.

Make Design Choices

Now that you know how to analyze the IP addressing and subnetting needs, the next major step examines how to apply the rules of IP addressing and subnetting to those needs and make some choices. In other words, now that you know how many subnets you need and how many host addresses you need in the largest subnet, how do you create a useful subnetting design that meets those requirements? The short answer is that you need to do the three tasks shown on the right side of Figure 13-10.

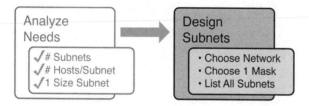

Figure 13-10   *Input to the Design Phase, and Design Questions to Answer*

Choose a Classful Network

In the original design for what we know of today as the Internet, companies used registered *public classful IP networks* when implementing TCP/IP inside the company. By the mid-1990s, an alternative became more popular: *private IP networks*. This section discusses the background behind these two choices, because it impacts the choice of what IP network a company will then subnet and implement in its enterprise internetwork.

Public IP Networks

The original design of the Internet required that any company that connected to the Internet had to use a *registered public IP network*. To do so, the company would complete some paperwork, describing the enterprise's internetwork and the number of hosts existing, plus plans for growth. After submitting the paperwork, the company would receive an assignment of either a Class A, B, or C network.

Public IP networks, and the administrative processes surrounding them, ensure that all the companies that connect to the Internet all use unique IP addresses. In particular, after a public IP network is assigned to a company, only that company should use the addresses in that network. That guarantee of uniqueness means that Internet routing can work well, because there are no duplicate public IP addresses.

For example, consider the example shown in Figure 13-11. Company 1 has been assigned public Class A network 1.0.0.0, and company 2 has been assigned public Class A network 2.0.0.0. Per the original intent for public addressing in the Internet, after these public network assignments have been made, no other companies can use addresses in Class A networks 1.0.0.0 or 2.0.0.0.

13

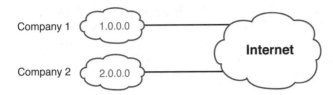

Figure 13-11 *Two Companies with Unique Public IP Networks*

This original address assignment process ensured unique IP addresses across the entire planet. The idea is much like the fact that your telephone number should be unique in the universe, your postal mailing address should also be unique, and your email address should also be unique. If someone calls you, your phone rings, but no one else's phone rings. Similarly, if company 1 is assigned Class A network 1.0.0.0, and it assigns address 1.1.1.1 to a particular PC, that address should be unique in the universe. A packet sent through the Internet to destination 1.1.1.1 should only arrive at this one PC inside company 1, instead of being delivered to some other host.

Growth Exhausts the Public IP Address Space

By the early 1990s, the world was running out of public IP networks that could be assigned. During most of the 1990s, the number of hosts newly connected to the Internet was growing at a double-digit pace, *per month*. Companies kept following the rules, asking for public IP networks, and it was clear that the current address-assignment scheme could not continue without some changes. Simply put, the number of Class A, B, and C networks supported by the 32-bit address in IP version 4 (IPv4) was not enough to support one public classful network per organization, while also providing enough IP addresses in each company.

NOTE The universe has run out of public IPv4 addresses in a couple of significant ways. IANA, which assigns public IPv4 address blocks to the five Regional Internet Registries (RIR) around the globe, assigned the last of the IPv4 address space in early 2011. By 2015, ARIN, the RIR for North America, exhausted its supply of IPv4 addresses, so that companies must return unused public IPv4 addresses to ARIN before they have more to assign to new companies. Try an online search for "ARIN depletion" to see pages about the current status of available IPv4 address space for just one RIR example.

The Internet community worked hard during the 1990s to solve this problem, coming up with several solutions, including the following:

- A new version of IP (IPv6), with much larger addresses (128 bit)
- Assigning a subset of a public IP network to each company, instead of an entire public IP network, to reduce waste
- Network Address Translation (NAT), which allows the use of private IP networks

These three solutions matter to real networks today. However, to stay focused on the topic of subnet design, this chapter focuses on the third option, and in particular, the private IP networks that can be used by an enterprise when also using NAT. Be aware that Part VIII gives more detail about the first bullet point, and Appendix N, "Classless Inter-Domain Routing," discusses the middle bullet in the list, and is optional reading for anyone interested in the topic.

Focusing on the third item in the bullet list, NAT (as detailed in Chapter 27, "Network Address Translation") allows multiple companies to use the exact same *private IP network*, using the same IP addresses as other companies while still connecting to the Internet. For example, Figure 13-12 shows the same two companies connecting to the Internet as in Figure 13-11, but now with both using the same private Class A network 10.0.0.0.

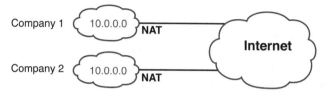

Figure 13-12   *Reusing the Same Private Network 10.0.0.0 with NAT*

Both companies use the same classful IP network (10.0.0.0). Both companies can implement their subnet design internal to their respective enterprise internetworks, without discussing their plans. The two companies can even use the exact same IP addresses inside network 10.0.0.0. And amazingly, at the same time, both companies can even communicate with each other through the Internet.

The technology called Network Address Translation makes it possible for companies to reuse the same IP networks, as shown in Figure 13-12. NAT does this by translating the IP addresses inside the packets as they go from the enterprise to the Internet, using a small number of public IP addresses to support tens of thousands of private IP addresses. That one bit of information is not enough to understand how NAT works; however, to keep the focus on subnetting, the book defers the discussion of how NAT works until Chapter 27. For now, accept that most companies use NAT, and therefore, they can use private IP networks for their internetworks.

Private IP Networks

Request For Comments (RFC) 1918 defines the set of private IP networks, as listed in Table 13-2. By definition, these private IP networks

- Will never be assigned to an organization as a public IP network
- Can be used by organizations that will use NAT when sending packets into the Internet
- Can also be used by organizations that never need to send packets into the Internet

So, when using NAT—and almost every organization that connects to the Internet uses NAT—the company can simply pick one or more of the private IP networks from the list of reserved private IP network numbers. RFC 1918 defines the list, which is summarized in Table 13-2.

Table 13-2   RFC 1918 Private Address Space

Class of Networks	Private IP Networks	Number of Networks
A	10.0.0.0	1
B	172.16.0.0 through 172.31.0.0	16
C	192.168.0.0 through 192.168.255.0	256

13

NOTE   According to an informal survey I ran on my blog a few years back, about half of the respondents said that their networks use private Class A network 10.0.0.0, as opposed to other private networks or public networks.

Choosing an IP Network During the Design Phase

Today, some organizations use private IP networks along with NAT, and some use public IP networks. Most new enterprise internetworks use private IP addresses throughout the network, along with NAT, as part of the connection to the Internet. Those organizations that already have registered public IP networks—often obtained before the addresses started running short in the early 1990s—can continue to use those public addresses throughout their enterprise networks.

After the choice to use a private IP network has been made, just pick one that has enough IP addresses. You can have a small internetwork and still choose to use private Class A network 10.0.0.0. It might seem wasteful to choose a Class A network that has over 16 million IP addresses, especially if you only need a few hundred. However, there's no penalty or problem with using a private network that is too large for your current or future needs.

For the purposes of this book, most examples use private IP network numbers. For the design step to choose a network number, just choose a private Class A, B, or C network from the list of RFC 1918 private networks.

Regardless, from a math and concept perspective, the methods to subnet a public IP network versus a private IP network are the same.

Choose the Mask

If a design engineer followed the topics in this chapter so far, in order, he would know the following:

■ The number of subnets required

■ The number of hosts/subnet required

■ That a choice was made to use only one mask for all subnets, so that all subnets are the same size (same number of hosts/subnet)

■ The classful IP network number that will be subnetted

This section completes the design process, at least the parts described in this chapter, by discussing how to choose that one mask to use for all subnets. First, this section examines default masks, used when a network is not subnetted, as a point of comparison. Next, the concept of borrowing host bits to create subnet bits is explored. Finally, this section ends with an example of how to create a subnet mask based on the analysis of the requirements.

Classful IP Networks Before Subnetting

Before an engineer subnets a classful network, the network is a single group of addresses. In other words, the engineer has not yet subdivided the network into many smaller subsets called *subnets*.

When thinking about an unsubnetted classful network, the addresses in a network have only two parts: the network part and host part. Comparing any two addresses in the classful network:

- The addresses have the same value in the network part.
- The addresses have different values in the host part.

The actual sizes of the network and host part of the addresses in a network can be easily predicted, as shown in Figure 13-13.

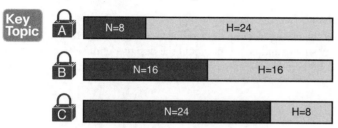

Figure 13-13 *Format of Unsubnetted Class A, B, and C Networks*

In Figure 13-13, N and H represent the number of network and host bits, respectively. Class rules define the number of network octets (1, 2, or 3) for Classes A, B, and C, respectively; the figure shows these values as a number of bits. The number of host octets is 3, 2, or 1, respectively.

Continuing the analysis of classful network before subnetting, the number of addresses in one classful IP network can be calculated with the same $2^H - 2$ formula previously discussed. In particular, the size of an unsubnetted Class A, B, or C network is as follows:

- **Class A:** $2^{24} - 2 = 16,777,214$
- **Class B:** $2^{16} - 2 = 65,534$
- **Class C:** $2^8 - 2 = 254$

Borrowing Host Bits to Create Subnet Bits

To subnet a network, the designer thinks about the network and host parts, as shown in Figure 13-13, and then the engineer adds a third part in the middle: the subnet part. However, the designer cannot change the size of the network part or the size of the entire address (32 bits). To create a subnet part of the address structure, the engineer borrows bits from the host part. Figure 13-14 shows the general idea.

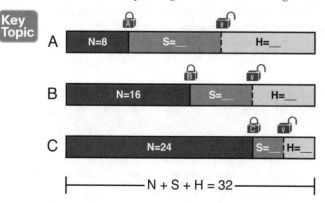

Figure 13-14 *Concept of Borrowing Host Bits*

Figure 13-14 shows a rectangle that represents the subnet mask. N, representing the number of network bits, remains locked at 8, 16, or 24, depending on the class. Conceptually, the designer moves a (dashed) dividing line into the host field, with subnet bits (S) between the network and host parts, and the remaining host bits (H) on the right. The three parts must add up to 32, because IPv4 addresses consist of 32 bits.

Choosing Enough Subnet and Host Bits

The design process requires a choice of where to place the dashed line shown in Figure 13-14. But what is the right choice? How many subnet and host bits should the designer choose? The answers hinge on the requirements gathered in the early stages of the planning process:

■ Number of subnets required

■ Number of hosts/subnet

The bits in the subnet part create a way to uniquely number the different subnets that the design engineer wants to create. With 1 subnet bit, you can number 2^1 or 2 subnets. With 2 bits, 2^2 or 4 subnets, with 3 bits, 2^3 or 8 subnets, and so on. The number of subnet bits must be large enough to uniquely number all the subnets, as determined during the planning process.

At the same time, the remaining number of host bits must also be large enough to number the host IP addresses in the largest subnet. Remember, in this chapter, we assume the use of a single mask for all subnets. This single mask must support both the required number of subnets and the required number of hosts in the largest subnet. Figure 13-15 shows the concept.

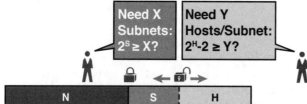

Figure 13-15 *Borrowing Enough Subnet and Host Bits*

Figure 13-15 shows the idea of the designer choosing a number of subnet (S) and host (H) bits and then checking the math. 2^S must be more than the number of required subnets, or the mask will not supply enough subnets in this IP network. Also, $2^H - 2$ must be more than the required number of hosts/subnet.

> **NOTE**   The idea of calculating the number of subnets as 2^S applies only in cases where a single mask is used for all subnets of a single classful network, as is being assumed in this chapter.

To effectively design masks, or to interpret masks that were chosen by someone else, you need a good working memory of the powers of 2. Appendix A, "Numeric Reference Tables," lists a table with powers of 2 up through 2^{32} for your reference.

Example Design: 172.16.0.0, 200 Subnets, 200 Hosts

To help make sense of the theoretical discussion so far, consider an example that focuses on the design choice for the subnet mask. In this case, the planning and design choices so far tell us the following:

- Use a single mask for all subnets.
- Plan for 200 subnets.
- Plan for 200 host IP addresses per subnet.
- Use private Class B network 172.16.0.0.

To choose the mask, the designer asks this question:

How many subnet (S) bits do I need to number 200 subnets?

From Table 13-3, you can see that S = 7 is not large enough (2^7 = 128), but S = 8 is enough (2^8 = 256). So, you need *at least* 8 subnet bits.

Next, the designer asks a similar question, based on the number of hosts per subnet:

How many host (H) bits do I need to number 200 hosts per subnet?

The math is basically the same, but the formula subtracts 2 when counting the number of hosts/subnet. From Table 13-3, you can see that H = 7 is not large enough ($2^7 - 2$ = 126), but H = 8 is enough ($2^8 - 2$ = 254).

Only one possible mask meets all the requirements in this case. First, the number of network bits (N) must be 16, because the design uses a Class B network. The requirements tell us that the mask needs at least 8 subnet bits, and at least 8 host bits. The mask only has 32 bits in it; Figure 13-16 shows the resulting mask.

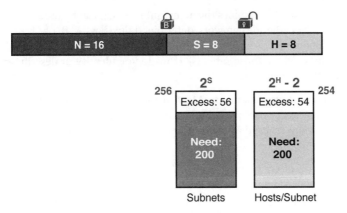

Figure 13-16   *Example Mask Choice, N = 16, S = 8, H = 8*

Masks and Mask Formats

Although engineers think about IP addresses in three parts when making design choices (network, subnet, and host), the subnet mask gives the engineer a way to communicate those design choices to all the devices in the subnet.

13

The subnet mask is a 32-bit binary number with a number of binary 1s on the left and with binary 0s on the right. By definition, the number of binary 0s equals the number of host bits; in fact, that is exactly how the mask communicates the idea of the size of the host part of the addresses in a subnet. The beginning bits in the mask equal binary 1, with those bit positions representing the combined network and subnet parts of the addresses in the subnet.

Because the network part always comes first, then the subnet part, and then the host part, the subnet mask, in binary form, cannot have interleaved 1s and 0s. Each subnet mask has one unbroken string of binary 1s on the left, with the rest of the bits as binary 0s.

After the engineer chooses the classful network and the number of subnet and host bits in a subnet, creating the binary subnet mask is easy. Just write down N 1s, S 1s, and then H 0s (assuming that N, S, and H represent the number of network, subnet, and host bits). Figure 13-17 shows the mask based on the previous example, which subnets a Class B network by creating 8 subnet bits, leaving 8 host bits.

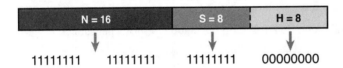

Figure 13-17 *Creating the Subnet Mask—Binary—Class B Network*

In addition to the binary mask shown in Figure 13-17, masks can also be written in two other formats: the familiar *dotted-decimal notation* (DDN) seen in IP addresses and an even briefer *prefix* notation. Chapter 15 discusses these formats and how to convert between the different formats.

Build a List of All Subnets

This final task of the subnet design step determines the actual subnets that can be used, based on all the earlier choices. The earlier design work determined the Class A, B, or C network to use, and the (one) subnet mask to use that supplies enough subnets and enough host IP addresses per subnet. But what are those subnets? How do you identify or describe a subnet? This section answers these questions.

A subnet consists of a group of consecutive numbers. Most of these numbers can be used as IP addresses by hosts. However, each subnet reserves the first and last numbers in the group, and these two numbers cannot be used as IP addresses. In particular, each subnet contains the following:

- **Subnet number:** Also called the *subnet ID* or *subnet address*, this number identifies the subnet. It is the numerically smallest number in the subnet. It cannot be used as an IP address by a host.

- **Subnet broadcast:** Also called the *subnet broadcast address* or *directed broadcast address*, this is the last (numerically highest) number in the subnet. It also cannot be used as an IP address by a host.

- **IP addresses:** All the numbers between the subnet ID and the subnet broadcast address can be used as a host IP address.

For example, consider the earlier case in which the design results were as follows:

Network   172.16.0.0 (Class B)

Mask   255.255.255.0 (for all subnets)

With some math, the facts about each subnet that exists in this Class B network can be calculated. In this case, Table 13-3 shows the first ten such subnets. It then skips many subnets and shows the last two (numerically largest) subnets.

Table 13-3   First Ten Subnets, Plus the Last Few, from 172.16.0.0, 255.255.255.0

Subnet Number	IP Addresses	Broadcast Address
172.16.0.0	172.16.0.1 – 172.16.0.254	172.16.0.255
172.16.1.0	172.16.1.1 – 172.16.1.254	172.16.1.255
172.16.2.0	172.16.2.1 – 172.16.2.254	172.16.2.255
172.16.3.0	172.16.3.1 – 172.16.3.254	172.16.3.255
172.16.4.0	172.16.4.1 – 172.16.4.254	172.16.4.255
172.16.5.0	172.16.5.1 – 172.16.5.254	172.16.5.255
172.16.6.0	172.16.6.1 – 172.16.6.254	172.16.6.255
172.16.7.0	172.16.7.1 – 172.16.7.254	172.16.7.255
172.16.8.0	172.16.8.1 – 172.16.8.254	172.16.8.255
172.16.9.0	172.16.9.1 – 172.16.9.254	172.16.9.255
Skipping many…		
172.16.254.0	172.16.254.1 – 172.16.254.254	172.16.254.255
172.16.255.0	172.16.255.1 – 172.16.255.254	172.16.255.255

After you have the network number and the mask, calculating the subnet IDs and other details for all subnets requires some math. In real life, most people use subnet calculators or subnet-planning tools. For the CCENT and CCNA Routing and Switching exams, you need to be ready to find this kind of information; in this book, Chapter 21, "Subnet Design," shows you how to find all the subnets of a given network.

Plan the Implementation

The next step, planning the implementation, is the last step before actually configuring the devices to create a subnet. The engineer first needs to choose where to use each subnet. For example, at a branch office in a particular city, which subnet from the subnet planning chart (Table 13-3) should be used for each VLAN at that site? Also, for any interfaces that require static IP addresses, which addresses should be used in each case? Finally, what range of IP addresses from inside each subnet should be configured in the DHCP server, to be dynamically leased to hosts for use as their IP address? Figure 13-18 summarizes the list of implementation planning tasks.

13

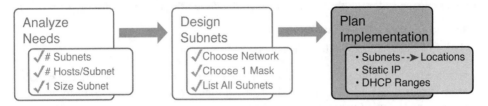

Figure 13-18 *Facts Supplied to the Plan Implementation Step*

Assigning Subnets to Different Locations

The job is simple: Look at your network diagram, identify each location that needs a subnet, and pick one from the table you made of all the possible subnets. Then, track it so that you know which ones you use where, using a spreadsheet or some other purpose-built subnet-planning tool. That's it! Figure 13-19 shows a sample of a completed design using Table 13-3, which happens to match the initial design sample shown way back in Figure 13-1.

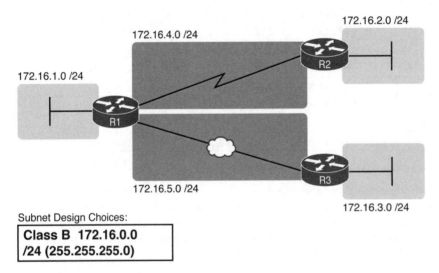

Figure 13-19 *Example of Subnets Assigned to Different Locations*

Although this design could have used any five subnets from Table 13-3, in real networks, engineers usually give more thought to some strategy for assigning subnets. For example, you might assign all LAN subnets lower numbers and WAN subnets higher numbers. Or you might slice off large ranges of subnets for different divisions of the company. Or you might follow that same strategy, but ignore organizational divisions in the company, paying more attention to geographies.

For example, for a U.S.-based company with a smaller presence in both Europe and Asia, you might plan to reserve ranges of subnets based on continent. This kind of choice is particularly useful when later trying to use a feature called route summarization.

NOTE   Although not discussed in this book, DVD Appendix O, "Route Summarization," provides content about route summarization from an earlier edition of this book, for those who are interested in further reading.

Figure 13-20 shows the general benefit of placing addressing in the network for easier route summarization, using the same subnets from Table 13-3 again.

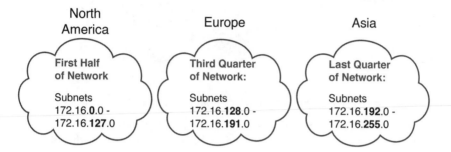

Figure 13-20   *Reserving 50 Percent of Subnets for North America and 25 Percent Each for Europe and Asia*

Choose Static and Dynamic Ranges per Subnet

Devices receive their IP address and mask assignment in one of two ways: dynamically by using Dynamic Host Configuration Protocol (DHCP) or statically through configuration. For DHCP to work, the network engineer must tell the DHCP server the subnets for which it must assign IP addresses. In addition, that configuration limits the DHCP server to only a subset of the addresses in the subnet. For static addresses, you simply configure the device to tell it what IP address and mask to use.

To keep things as simple as possible, most shops use a strategy to separate the static IP addresses on one end of each subnet, and the DHCP-assigned dynamic addresses on the other. It does not really matter whether the static addresses sit on the low end of the range of addresses or the high end.

For example, imagine that the engineer decides that, for the LAN subnets in Figure 13-19, the DHCP pool comes from the high end of the range, namely, addresses that end in .101 through .254. (The address that ends in .255 is, of course, reserved.) The engineer also assigns static addresses from the lower end, with addresses ending in .1 through .100. Figure 13-21 shows the idea.

13

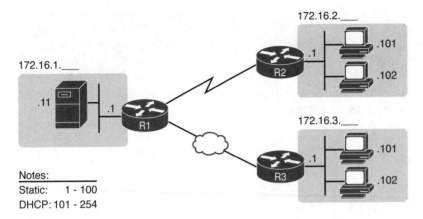

Figure 13-21 *Static from the Low End and DHCP from the High End*

Figure 13-21 shows all three routers with statically assigned IP addresses that end in .1. The only other static IP address in the figure is assigned to the server on the left, with address 172.16.1.11 (abbreviated simply as .11 in the figure).

On the right, each LAN has two PCs that use DHCP to dynamically lease their IP addresses. DHCP servers often begin by leasing the addresses at the bottom of the range of addresses, so in each LAN, the hosts have leased addresses that end in .101 and .102, which are at the low end of the range chosen by design.

Chapter Review

One key to doing well on the exams is to perform repetitive spaced review sessions. Review this chapter's material using either the tools in the book, DVD, or interactive tools for the same material found on the book's companion website. Refer to the "Your Study Plan" element for more details. Table 13-4 outlines the key review elements and where you can find them. To better track your study progress, record when you completed these activities in the second column.

Table 13-4 Chapter Review Tracking

Review Element	Review Date(s)	Resource Used
Review key topics		Book, DVD/website
Review key terms		Book, DVD/website
Answer DIKTA questions		Book, PCPT
Review memory tables		Book, DVD/website

Review All the Key Topics

Table 13-5   Key Topics for Chapter 13

Key Topic Element	Description	Page Number
List	Key facts about subnets	307
List	Rules about what places in a network topology need a subnet	308
Figure 13-7	Locations of the network, subnet, and host parts of an IPv4 address	311
List	Features that extended the life of IPv4	314
Figure 13-13	Formats of Class A, B, and C addresses when not subnetted	317
Figure 13-14	Formats of Class A, B, and C addresses when subnetted	317
Figure 13-15	General logic when choosing the size of the subnet and host parts of addresses in a subnet	318
List	Items that together define a subnet	320

Key Terms You Should Know

subnet, network, classful IP network, variable-length subnet masks (VLSM), network part, subnet part, host part, public IP network, private IP network, subnet mask

13

CHAPTER 14

Analyzing Classful IPv4 Networks

This chapter covers the following exam topics:

1.0 Network Fundamentals

1.8 Configure, verify, and troubleshoot IPv4 addressing and subnetting

1.9 Compare and contrast IPv4 address types

    1.9.a Unicast

    1.9.b Broadcast

When operating a network, you often start investigating a problem based on an IP address and mask. Based on the IP address alone, you should be able to determine several facts about the Class A, B, or C network in which the IP address resides. These facts can be useful when troubleshooting some networking problems.

This chapter lists the key facts about classful IP networks and explains how to discover these facts. Following that, this chapter lists some practice problems. Before moving to the next chapter, you should practice until you can consistently determine all these facts, quickly and confidently, based on an IP address.

"Do I Know This Already?" Quiz

Take the quiz (either here, or use the PCPT software) if you want to use the score to help you decide how much time to spend on this chapter. The answers are at the bottom of the page following the quiz, and the explanations are in DVD Appendix C and in the PCPT software.

Table 14-1 "Do I Know This Already?" Foundation Topics Section-to-Question Mapping

Foundation Topics Section	Questions
Classful Network Concepts	1–5

1. Which of the following are not valid Class A network IDs? (Choose two answers.)
   a. 1.0.0.0
   b. 130.0.0.0
   c. 127.0.0.0
   d. 9.0.0.0

2. Which of the following are not valid Class B network IDs?
   a. 130.0.0.0
   b. 191.255.0.0
   c. 128.0.0.0
   d. 150.255.0.0
   e. All are valid Class B network IDs.

3. Which of the following are true about IP address 172.16.99.45's IP network? (Choose two answers.)
   a. The network ID is 172.0.0.0.
   b. The network is a Class B network.
   c. The default mask for the network is 255.255.255.0.
   d. The number of host bits in the unsubnetted network is 16.

4. Which of the following are true about IP address 192.168.6.7's IP network? (Choose two answers.)
   a. The network ID is 192.168.6.0.
   b. The network is a Class B network.
   c. The default mask for the network is 255.255.255.0.
   d. The number of host bits in the unsubnetted network is 16.

5. Which of the following is a network broadcast address?
   a. 10.1.255.255
   b. 192.168.255.1
   c. 224.1.1.255
   d. 172.30.255.255

Foundation Topics

Classful Network Concepts

Imagine that you have a job interview for your first IT job. As part of the interview, you're given an IPv4 address and mask: 10.4.5.99, 255.255.255.0. What can you tell the interviewer about the classful network (in this case, the Class A network) in which the IP address resides?

This section, the first of two major sections in this chapter, reviews the concepts of *classful IP networks* (in other words, Class A, B, and C networks). In particular, this chapter examines how to begin with a single IP address and then determine the following facts:

- Class (A, B, or C)
- Default mask
- Number of network octets/bits
- Number of host octets/bits
- Number of host addresses in the network
- Network ID
- Network broadcast address
- First and last usable address in the network

IPv4 Network Classes and Related Facts

IP version 4 (IPv4) defines five address classes. Three of the classes, Classes A, B, and C, consist of unicast IP addresses. Unicast addresses identify a single host or interface so that the address uniquely identifies the device. Class D addresses serve as multicast addresses, so that one packet sent to a Class D multicast IPv4 address can actually be delivered to multiple hosts. Finally, Class E addresses were originally intended for experimentation, but were changed to simply be reserved for future use. The class can be identified based on the value of the first octet of the address, as shown in Table 14-2.

Table 14-2 IPv4 Address Classes Based on First Octet Values

Class	First Octet Values	Purpose
A	1–126	Unicast (large networks)
B	128–191	Unicast (medium-sized networks)
C	192–223	Unicast (small networks)
D	224–239	Multicast
E	240–255	Reserved (formerly experimental)

After you identify the class as either A, B, or C, many other related facts can be derived just through memorization. Table 14-3 lists that information for reference and later study; each of these concepts is described in this chapter.

Table 14-3   Key Facts for Classes A, B, and C

	Class A	Class B	Class C
First octet range	1 – 126	128 – 191	192 – 223
Valid network numbers	1.0.0.0 – 126.0.0.0	128.0.0.0 – 191.255.0.0	192.0.0.0 – 223.255.255.0
Total networks	$2^7 - 2 = 126$	$2^{14} = 16{,}384$	$2^{21} = 2{,}097{,}152$
Hosts per network	$2^{24} - 2$	$2^{16} - 2$	$2^8 - 2$
Octets (bits) in network part	1 (8)	2 (16)	3 (24)
Octets (bits) in host part	3 (24)	2 (16)	1 (8)
Default mask	255.0.0.0	255.255.0.0	255.255.255.0

At times, some people today look back and wonder, "Are there 128 class A networks, with two reserved networks, or are there truly only 126 class A networks?" Frankly, the difference is unimportant, and the wording is just two ways to state the same idea. The important fact to know is that Class A network 0.0.0.0 and network 127.0.0.0 are reserved. In fact, they have been reserved since the creation of Class A networks, as listed in RFC 791 (published in 1981).

Although it may be a bit of a tangent, what is more interesting today is that over time, other newer RFCs have also reserved small pieces of the Class A, B, and C address space. So, tables like Table 14-3, with the count of the numbers of Class A, B, and C networks, are a good place to get a sense of the size of the number; however, the number of reserved networks does change slightly over time (albeit slowly) based on these other reserved address ranges.

NOTE   If you are interested in seeing all the reserved IPv4 address ranges, just do an Internet search on "IANA IPv4 special-purpose address registry."

The Number and Size of the Class A, B, and C Networks

Table 14-3 lists the range of Class A, B, and C network numbers; however, some key points can be lost just referencing a table of information. This section examines the Class A, B, and C network numbers, focusing on the more important points and the exceptions and unusual cases.

First, the number of networks from each class significantly differs. Only 126 Class A networks exist: network 1.0.0.0, 2.0.0.0, 3.0.0.0, and so on, up through network 126.0.0.0. However, 16,384 Class B networks exist, with more than 2 million Class C networks.

Next, note that the size of networks from each class also significantly differs. Each Class A network is relatively large—over 16 million host IP addresses per network—so they were originally intended to be used by the largest companies and organizations. Class B networks are smaller, with over 65,000 hosts per network. Finally, Class C networks, intended for small organizations, have 254 hosts in each network. Figure 14-1 summarizes those facts.

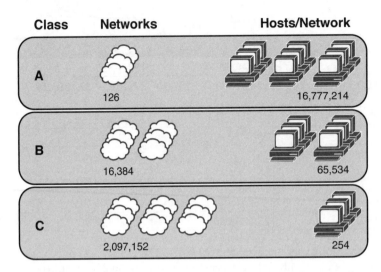

Figure 14-1 *Numbers and Sizes of Class A, B, and C Networks*

Address Formats

In some cases, an engineer might need to think about a Class A, B, or C network as if the network has not been subdivided through the subnetting process. In such a case, the addresses in the classful network have a structure with two parts: the *network part* (sometimes called the *prefix*) and the *host part*. Then, comparing any two IP addresses in one network, the following observations can be made:

> The addresses in the same network have the same values in the network part.
>
> The addresses in the same network have different values in the host part.

For example, in Class A network 10.0.0.0, by definition, the network part consists of the first octet. As a result, all addresses have an equal value in the network part, namely a 10 in the first octet. If you then compare any two addresses in the network, the addresses have a different value in the last three octets (the host octets). For example, IP addresses 10.1.1.1 and 10.1.1.2 have the same value (10) in the network part, but different values in the host part.

Figure 14-2 shows the format and sizes (in number of bits) of the network and host parts of IP addresses in Class A, B, and C networks, before any subnetting has been applied.

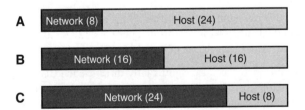

Figure 14-2 *Sizes (Bits) of the Network and Host Parts of Unsubnetted Classful Networks*

Default Masks

Although we humans can easily understand the concepts behind Figure 14-2, computers prefer numbers. To communicate those same ideas to computers, each network class has an associated *default mask* that defines the size of the network and host parts of an unsubnetted Class A, B, and C network. To do so, the mask lists binary 1s for the bits considered to be in the network part and binary 0s for the bits considered to be in the host part.

For example, Class A network 10.0.0.0 has a network part of the first single octet (8 bits) and a host part of last three octets (24 bits). As a result, the Class A default mask is 255.0.0.0, which in binary is

11111111 00000000 00000000 00000000

Figure 14-3 shows default masks for each network class, both in binary and dotted-decimal format.

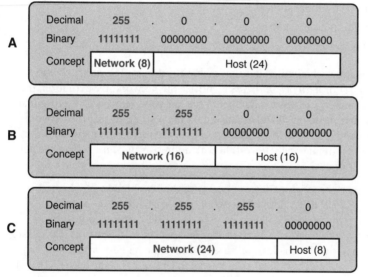

Figure 14-3   *Default Masks for Classes A, B, and C*

NOTE   Decimal 255 converts to the binary value 11111111. Decimal 0, converted to 8-bit binary, is 00000000. See Appendix A, "Numeric Reference Tables," for a conversion table.

Number of Hosts per Network

Calculating the number of hosts per network requires some basic binary math. First, consider a case where you have a single binary digit. How many unique values are there? There are, of course, two values: 0 and 1. With 2 bits, you can make four combinations: 00, 01, 10, and 11. As it turns out, the total combination of unique values you can make with N bits is 2^N.

Host addresses—the IP addresses assigned to hosts—must be unique. The host bits exist for the purpose of giving each host a unique IP address by virtue of having a different value in the host part of the addresses. So, with H host bits, 2^H unique combinations exist.

However, the number of hosts in a network is not 2^H; instead, it is $2^H - 2$. Each network reserves two numbers that would have otherwise been useful as host addresses, but have instead been reserved for special use: one for the network ID and one for the network broadcast address. As a result, the formula to calculate the number of host addresses per Class A, B, or C network is

$$2^H - 2$$

where H is the number of host bits.

Deriving the Network ID and Related Numbers

Each classful network has four key numbers that describe the network. You can derive these four numbers if you start with just one IP address in the network. The numbers are as follows:

- Network number
- First (numerically lowest) usable address
- Last (numerically highest) usable address
- Network broadcast address

First, consider both the network number and first usable IP address. The *network number*, also called the *network ID* or *network address*, identifies the network. By definition, the network number is the numerically lowest number in the network. However, to prevent any ambiguity, the people that made up IP addressing added the restriction that the network number cannot be assigned as an IP address. So, the lowest number in the network is the network ID. Then, the first (numerically lowest) host IP address is *one larger than* the network number.

Next, consider the network broadcast address along with the last (numerically highest) usable IP address. The TCP/IP RFCs define a network broadcast address as a special address in each network. This broadcast address could be used as the destination address in a packet, and the routers would forward a copy of that one packet to all hosts in that classful network. Numerically, a network broadcast address is always the highest (last) number in the network. As a result, the highest (last) number usable as an IP address is the address that is simply *one less than* the network broadcast address.

Simply put, if you can find the network number and network broadcast address, finding the first and last usable IP addresses in the network is easy. For the exam, you should be able to find all four values with ease; the process is as follows:

Step 1.   Determine the class (A, B, or C) based on the first octet.

Step 2.   Mentally divide the network and host octets based on the class.

Step 3.   To find the network number, change the IP address's host octets to 0.

Step 4.   To find the first address, add 1 to the fourth octet of the network ID.

Step 5.   To find the broadcast address, change the network ID's host octets to 255.

Step 6.   To find the last address, subtract 1 from the fourth octet of the network broadcast address.

The written process actually looks harder than it is. Figure 14-4 shows an example of the process, using Class A IP address 10.17.18.21, with the circled numbers matching the process.

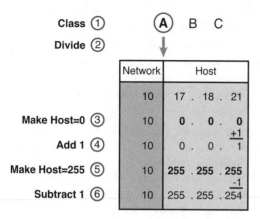

Figure 14-4   *Example of Deriving the Network ID and Other Values from 10.17.18.21*

Figure 14-4 shows the identification of the class as Class A (Step 1) and the number of network/host octets as 1 and 3, respectively. So, to find the network ID at Step 3, the figure copies only the first octet, setting the last three (host) octets to 0. At Step 4, just copy the network ID and add 1 to the fourth octet. Similarly, to find the broadcast address at Step 5, copy the network octets, but set the host octets to 255. Then, at Step 6, subtract 1 from the fourth octet to find the last (numerically highest) usable IP address.

Just to show an alternative example, consider IP address 172.16.8.9. Figure 14-5 shows the process applied to this IP address.

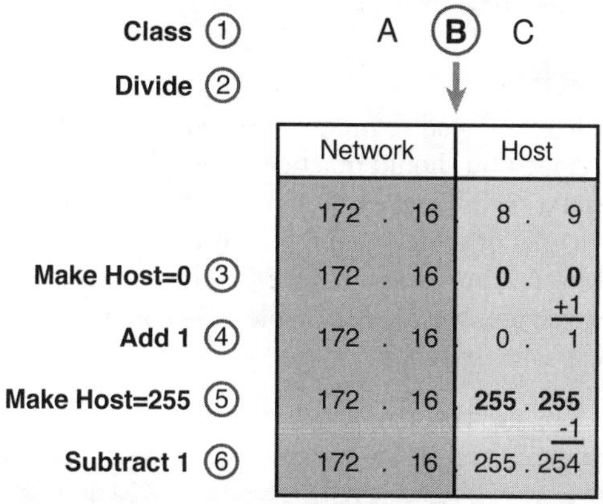

	Network	Host
Class ①	A **Ⓑ** C	
Divide ②		
	172 . 16	8 . 9
Make Host=0 ③	172 . 16	0 . 0
Add 1 ④	172 . 16	0 . 1
Make Host=255 ⑤	172 . 16	255 . 255
Subtract 1 ⑥	172 . 16	255 . 254

Figure 14-5   *Example Deriving the Network ID and Other Values from 172.16.8.9*

Figure 14-5 shows the identification of the class as Class B (Step 1) and the number of network/host octets as 2 and 2, respectively. So, to find the network ID at Step 3, the figure copies only the first two octets, setting the last two (host) octets to 0. Similarly, Step 5 shows the same action, but with the last two (host) octets being set to 255.

Unusual Network IDs and Network Broadcast Addresses

Some of the more unusual numbers in and around the range of Class A, B, and C network numbers can cause some confusion. This section lists some examples of numbers that make many people make the wrong assumptions about the meaning of the number.

For Class A, the first odd fact is that the range of values in the first octet omits the numbers 0 and 127. As it turns out, what would be Class A network 0.0.0.0 was originally reserved for some broadcasting requirements, so all addresses that begin with 0 in the first octet are reserved. What would be Class A network 127.0.0.0 is still reserved because of a special address used in software testing, called the loopback address (127.0.0.1).

For Class B (and C), some of the network numbers can look odd, particularly if you fall into a habit of thinking that 0s at the end means the number is a network ID, and 255s at the end means it's a network broadcast address. First, Class B network numbers range from 128.0.0.0 to 191.255.0.0, for a total of 2^{14} networks. However, even the very first (lowest number) Class B network number (128.0.0.0) looks a little like a Class A network number, because it ends with three 0s. However, the first octet is 128, making it a Class B network with a two-octet network part (128.0).

For another Class B example, the high end of the Class B range also might look strange at first glance (191.255.0.0), but this is indeed the numerically highest of the valid Class B network numbers. This network's broadcast address, 191.255.255.255, might look a little like a Class A broadcast address because of the three 255s at the end, but it is indeed the broadcast address of a Class B network.

Similarly to Class B networks, some of the valid Class C network numbers do look strange. For example, Class C network 192.0.0.0 looks a little like a Class A network because of the last three octets being 0, but because it is a Class C network, it consists of all addresses that begin with three octets equal to 192.0.0. Similarly, Class C network 223.255.255.0, another valid Class C network, consists of all addresses that begin with 223.255.255.

Practice with Classful Networks

As with all areas of IP addressing and subnetting, you need to practice to be ready for the CCENT and CCNA Routing and Switching exams. You should practice some while reading this chapter to make sure that you understand the processes. At that point, you can use your notes and this book as a reference, with a goal of understanding the process. After that, keep practicing this and all the other subnetting processes. Before you take the exam, you should be able to always get the right answer, and with speed. Table 14-4 summarizes the key concepts and suggestions for this two-phase approach.

Table 14-4 Keep-Reading and Take-Exam Goals for This Chapter's Topics

Time Frame	After Reading This Chapter	Before Taking the Exam
Focus on...	Learning how	Being correct and fast
Tools Allowed	All	Your brain and a notepad
Goal: Accuracy	90% correct	100% correct
Goal: Speed	Any speed	10 seconds

Practice Deriving Key Facts Based on an IP Address

Practice finding the various facts that can be derived from an IP address, as discussed throughout this chapter. To do so, complete Table 14-5.

Table 14-5   Practice Problems: Find the Network ID and Network Broadcast

	IP Address	Class	1, 2, or 3 Network Octets?	1, 2, or 3 Host Octets?	Network ID	Network Broadcast Address
1	1.1.1.1					
2	128.1.6.5					
3	200.1.2.3					
4	192.192.1.1					
5	126.5.4.3					
6	200.1.9.8					
7	192.0.0.1					
8	191.255.1.47					
9	223.223.0.1					

The answers are listed in the section "Answers to Earlier Practice Problems," later in this chapter.

Practice Remembering the Details of Address Classes

Tables 14-2 and 14-3, shown earlier in this chapter, summarized some key information about IPv4 address classes. Tables 14-6 and 14-7 show sparse versions of these same tables. To practice recalling those key facts, particularly the range of values in the first octet that identifies the address class, complete these tables. Then, refer to Tables 14-2 and 14-3 to check your answers. Repeat this process until you can recall all the information in the tables.

Table 14-6   Sparse Study Table Version of Table 14-2

Class	First Octet Values	Purpose
A		
B		
C		
D		
E		

Table 14-7   Sparse Study Table Version of Table 14-3

	Class A	Class B	Class C
First octet range			
Valid network numbers			
Total networks			
Hosts per network			
Octets (bits) in network part			
Octets (bits) in host part			
Default mask			

Chapter Review

One key to doing well on the exams is to perform repetitive spaced review sessions. Review this chapter's material using either the tools in the book, DVD, or interactive tools for the same material found on the book's companion website. Refer to the "Your Study Plan" element for more details. Table 14-8 outlines the key review elements and where you can find them. To better track your study progress, record when you completed these activities in the second column.

Table 14-8   Chapter Review Tracking

Review Element	Review Date(s)	Resource Used
Review key topics		Book, DVD/website
Review key terms		Book, DVD/website
Answer DIKTA questions		Book, PCPT
Review memory tables		Book, DVD/website
Practice analyzing classful IPv4 networks		DVD Appendix D, website

Review All the Key Topics

Table 14-9   Key Topics for Chapter 14

Key Topic Elements	Description	Page Number
Table 14-2	Address classes	328
Table 14-3	Key facts about Class A, B, and C networks	329
List	Comparisons of network and host parts of addresses in the same classful network	330
Figure 14-3	Default masks	331
Paragraph	Function to calculate the number of hosts per network	332
List	Steps to find information about a classful network	332

Key Terms You Should Know

network, classful IP network, network number, network ID, network address, network broadcast address, network part, host part, default mask

Additional Practice for This Chapter's Processes

For additional practice with analyzing classful networks, you may do the same set of practice problems using your choice of tools:

Application: Use the Analyzing Classful IPv4 Networks application on the DVD or companion website.

PDF: Alternatively, practice the same problems using DVD Appendix D, "Practice for Chapter 14: Analyzing Classful IPv4 Networks."

Answers to Earlier Practice Problems

Table 14-5, shown earlier, listed several practice problems. Table 14-10 lists the answers.

Table 14-10   Practice Problems: Find the Network ID and Network Broadcast

	IP Address	Class	Network Octets	Host Octets	Network ID	Network Broadcast
1	1.1.1.1	A	1	3	1.0.0.0	1.255.255.255
2	128.1.6.5	B	2	2	128.1.0.0	128.1.255.255
3	200.1.2.3	C	3	1	200.1.2.0	200.1.2.255
4	192.192.1.1	C	3	1	192.192.1.0	192.192.1.255
5	126.5.4.3	A	1	3	126.0.0.0	126.255.255.255
6	200.1.9.8	C	3	1	200.1.9.0	200.1.9.255
7	192.0.0.1	C	3	1	192.0.0.0	192.0.0.255
8	191.255.1.47	B	2	2	191.255.0.0	191.255.255.255
9	223.223.0.1	C	3	1	223.223.0.0	223.223.0.255

The class, number of network octets, and number of host octets all require you to look at the first octet of the IP address to determine the class. If a value is between 1 and 126, inclusive, the address is a Class A address, with one network and three host octets. If a value is between 128 and 191 inclusive, the address is a Class B address, with two network and two host octets. If a value is between 192 and 223, inclusive, it is a Class C address, with three network octets and one host octet.

The last two columns can be found based on Table 14-3, specifically the number of network and host octets along with the IP address. To find the network ID, copy the IP address, but change the host octets to 0. Similarly, to find the network broadcast address, copy the IP address, but change the host octets to 255.

The last three problems can be confusing, and were included on purpose so that you could see an example of these unusual cases, as follows.

Answers to Practice Problem 7 (from Table 14-5)

Consider IP address 192.0.0.1. First, 192 is on the lower edge of the first octet range for Class C; as such, this address has three network and one host octet. To find the network ID, copy the address, but change the single host octet (the fourth octet) to 0, for a network ID of 192.0.0.0. It looks strange, but it is indeed the network ID.

The network broadcast address choice for problem 7 can also look strange. To find the broadcast address, copy the IP address (192.0.0.1), but change the last octet (the only host octet) to 255, for a broadcast address of 192.0.0.255. In particular, if you decide that the broadcast should be 192.255.255.255, you might have fallen into the trap of logic, like "Change all 0s in the network ID to 255s," which is not the correct logic. Instead, change all host octets in the IP address (or network ID) to 255s.

Answers to Practice Problem 8 (from Table 14-5)

The first octet of problem 8 (191.255.1.47) sits on the upper edge of the Class B range for the first octet (128–191). As such, to find the network ID, change the last two octets (host octets) to 0, for a network ID of 191.255.0.0. This value sometimes gives people problems, because they are used to thinking that 255 somehow means the number is a broadcast address.

The broadcast address, found by changing the two host octets to 255, means that the broadcast address is 191.255.255.255. It looks more like a broadcast address for a Class A network, but it is actually the broadcast address for Class B network 191.255.0.0.

Answers to Practice Problem 9 (from Table 14-5)

Problem 9, with IP address 223.223.0.1, is near the high end of the Class C range. As a result, only the last (host) octet is changed to 0 to form the network ID 223.223.0.0. It looks a little like a Class B network number at first glance, because it ends in two octets of 0. However, it is indeed a Class C network ID (based on the value in the first octet).

CHAPTER 15

Analyzing Subnet Masks

This chapter covers the following exam topics:

1.0 Network Fundamentals

1.8 Configure, verify, and troubleshoot IPv4 addressing and subnetting

The subnet mask used in one or many subnets in an IP internetwork says a lot about the intent of the subnet design. First, the mask divides addresses into two parts: *prefix* and *host*, with the host part defining the size of the subnet. Then, the class (A, B, or C) further divides the structure of addresses in a subnet, breaking the prefix part into the *network* and *subnet* parts. The subnet part defines the number of subnets that could exist inside one classful IP network, assuming that one mask is used throughout the classful network.

The subnet mask holds the key to understanding several important subnetting design points. However, to analyze a subnet mask, you first need some basic math skills with masks. The math converts masks between the three different formats used to represent a mask:

- Binary
- Dotted-decimal notation (DDN)
- Prefix (also called classless interdomain routing [CIDR])

This chapter has two major sections. The first focuses totally on the mask formats and the math used to convert between the three formats. The second section explains how to take an IP address and its subnet mask and analyze those values. In particular, it shows how to determine the three-part format of the IPv4 address and describes the facts about the subnetting design that are implied by the mask.

"Do I Know This Already?" Quiz

Take the quiz (either here, or use the PCPT software) if you want to use the score to help you decide how much time to spend on this chapter. The answers are at the bottom of the page following the quiz, and the explanations are in DVD Appendix C and in the PCPT software.

Table 15-1 "Do I Know This Already?" Foundation Topics Section-to-Question Mapping

Foundation Topics Section	Questions
Subnet Mask Conversion	1–3
Defining the Format of IPv4 Addresses	4–7

1. Which of the following answers lists the prefix (CIDR) format equivalent of 255.255.254.0?

   a. /19

   b. /20

   c. /23

   d. /24

   e. /25

2. Which of the following answers lists the prefix (CIDR) format equivalent of 255.255.255.240?

   a. /26

   b. /28

   c. /27

   d. /30

   e. /29

3. Which of the following answers lists the dotted-decimal notation (DDN) equivalent of /30?

   a. 255.255.255.192

   b. 255.255.255.252

   c. 255.255.255.240

   d. 255.255.254.0

   e. 255.255.255.0

4. Working at the help desk, you receive a call and learn a user's PC IP address and mask (10.55.66.77, mask 255.255.255.0). When thinking about this using classful logic, you determine the number of network (N), subnet (S), and host (H) bits. Which of the following is true in this case?

   a. N=12

   b. S=12

   c. H=8

   d. S=8

   e. N=24

5. Working at the help desk, you receive a call and learn a user's PC IP address and mask (192.168.9.1/27). When thinking about this using classful logic, you determine the number of network (N), subnet (S), and host (H) bits. Which of the following is true in this case?

   a. N=24

   b. S=24

   c. H=8

   d. H=7

6. Which of the following statements is true about classless IP addressing concepts?

   a. Uses a 128-bit IP address

   b. Applies only for Class A and B networks

   c. Separates IP addresses into network, subnet, and host parts

   d. Ignores Class A, B, and C network rules

7. Which of the following masks, when used as the only mask within a Class B network, would supply enough subnet bits to support 100 subnets? (Choose two.)

   a. /24

   b. 255.255.255.252

   c. /20

   d. 255.255.252.0

Foundation Topics

Subnet Mask Conversion

This section describes how to convert between different formats for the subnet mask. You can then use these processes when you practice. If you already know how to convert from one format to the other, go ahead and move to the section "Practice Converting Subnet Masks," later in this chapter.

Three Mask Formats

Subnet masks can be written as 32-bit binary numbers, but not just any binary number. In particular, the binary subnet mask must follow these rules:

- The value must not interleave 1s and 0s.
- If 1s exist, they are on the left.
- If 0s exist, they are on the right.

For example, the following values would be illegal. The first is illegal because the value interleaves 0s and 1s, and the second is illegal because it lists 0s on the left and 1s on the right:

   10101010 01010101 11110000 00001111

   00000000 00000000 00000000 11111111

The following two binary values meet the requirements, in that they have all 1s on the left, followed by all 0s, with no interleaving of 1s and 0s:

   11111111 00000000 00000000 00000000

   11111111 11111111 11111111 00000000

Two alternative subnet mask formats exist so that we humans do not have to work with 32-bit binary numbers. One format, dotted-decimal notation (DDN), converts each set of 8 bits into the decimal equivalent. For example, the two previous binary masks would convert to the following DDN subnet masks, because binary 11111111 converts to decimal 255, and binary 00000000 converts to decimal 0:

255.0.0.0

255.255.255.0

Although the DDN format has been around since the beginning of IPv4 addressing, the third mask format was added later, in the early 1990s: the *prefix* format. This format takes advantage of the rule that the subnet mask starts with some number of 1s, and then the rest of the digits are 0s. Prefix format lists a slash (/) followed by the number of binary 1s in the binary mask. Using the same two examples as earlier in this section, the prefix format equivalent masks are as follows:

/8

/24

Note that although the terms *prefix* or *prefix mask* can be used, the terms *CIDR mask* or *slash mask* can also be used. This newer prefix style mask was created around the same time as the classless interdomain routing (CIDR) specification back in the early 1990s, and the acronym CIDR grew to be used for anything related to CIDR, including prefix-style masks. In addition, the term *slash mask* is sometimes used because the value includes a slash mark (/).

You need to get comfortable working with masks in different formats. The rest of this section examines how to convert between the three formats.

Converting Between Binary and Prefix Masks

Converting between binary and prefix masks should be relatively intuitive after you know that the prefix value is simply the number of binary 1s in the binary mask. For the sake of completeness, the processes to convert in each direction are

Binary to prefix: Count the number of binary 1s in the binary mask, and write the total, in decimal, after a /.

Prefix to binary: Write P binary 1s, where P is the prefix value, followed by as many binary 0s as required to create a 32-bit number.

Tables 15-2 and 15-3 show some examples.

Table 15-2   Example Conversions: Binary to Prefix

Binary Mask	Logic	Prefix Mask
11111111 11111111 11000000 00000000	Count 8 + 8 + 2 = 18 binary 1s	/18
11111111 11111111 11111111 11110000	Count 8 + 8 + 8 + 4 = 28 binary 1s	/28
11111111 11111000 00000000 00000000	Count 8 + 5 = 13 binary 1s	/13

Table 15-3   Example Conversions: Prefix to Binary

Prefix Mask	Logic	Binary Mask
/18	Write 18 1s, then 14 0s, total 32	11111111 11111111 11000000 00000000
/28	Write 28 1s, then 4 0s, total 32	11111111 11111111 11111111 11110000
/13	Write 13 1s, then 19 0s, total 32	11111111 11111000 00000000 00000000

Converting Between Binary and DDN Masks

By definition, a dotted-decimal number (DDN) used with IPv4 addressing contains four decimal numbers, separated by dots. Each decimal number represents 8 bits. So, a single DDN shows four decimal numbers that together represent some 32-bit binary number.

Conversion from a DDN mask to the binary equivalent is relatively simple to describe, but can be laborious to perform. First, to do the conversion, the process is as follows:

> For each octet, perform a decimal-to-binary conversion.

However, depending on your comfort level with doing decimal-to-binary conversions, that process can be difficult or time-consuming. If you want to think about masks in binary for the exam, consider picking one of the following methods to do the conversion and practicing until you can do it quickly and accurately:

- Do the decimal-binary conversions, but practice your decimal-binary conversions to get fast. If you choose this path, consider the Cisco Binary Game, which you can find by searching its name at the Cisco Learning Network (CLN) (http://learningnetwork.cisco.com).

- Use the decimal-binary conversion chart in Appendix A, "Numeric Reference Tables." This lets you find the answer more quickly now, but you cannot use the chart on exam day.

- Memorize the nine possible decimal values that can be in a decimal mask, and practice using a reference table with those values.

The third method, which is the method recommended in this book, takes advantage of the fact that any and every DDN mask octet must be one of only nine values. Why? Well, remember how a binary mask cannot interleave 1s and 0s, and the 0s must be on the right? It turns out that only nine different 8-bit binary numbers conform to these rules. Table 15-4 lists the values, along with other relevant information.

Table 15-4   Nine Possible Values in One Octet of a Subnet Mask

Binary Mask Octet	Decimal Equivalent	Number of Binary 1s
00000000	0	0
10000000	128	1
11000000	192	2
11100000	224	3
11110000	240	4
11111000	248	5

Binary Mask Octet	Decimal Equivalent	Number of Binary 1s
11111100	252	6
11111110	254	7
11111111	255	8

15

Many subnetting processes can be done with or without binary math. Some of those processes—mask conversion included—use the information in Table 15-4. You should plan to memorize the information in the table. I recommend making a copy of the table to keep handy while you practice. (You will likely memorize the contents of this table simply by practicing the conversion process enough to get both good and fast at the conversion.)

Using the table, the conversion processes in each direction with binary and decimal masks are as follows:

Binary to decimal: Organize the bits into four sets of eight. For each octet, find the binary value in the table and write down the corresponding decimal value.

Decimal to binary: For each octet, find the decimal value in the table and write down the corresponding 8-bit binary value.

Tables 15-5 and 15-6 show some examples.

Table 15-5   Conversion Example: Binary to Decimal

Binary Mask	Logic	Decimal Mask
11111111 11111111 11000000 00000000	11111111 maps to 255 11000000 maps to 192 00000000 maps to 0	255.255.192.0
11111111 11111111 11111111 11110000	11111111 maps to 255 11110000 maps to 240	255.255.255.240
11111111 11111000 00000000 00000000	11111111 maps to 255 11111000 maps to 248 00000000 maps to 0	255.248.0.0

Table 15-6   Conversion Examples: Decimal to Binary

Decimal Mask	Logic	Binary Mask
255.255.192.0	255 maps to 11111111 192 maps to 11000000 0 maps to 00000000	11111111 11111111 11000000 00000000
255.255.255.240	255 maps to 11111111 240 maps to 11110000	11111111 11111111 11111111 11110000
255.248.0.0	255 maps to 11111111 248 maps to 11111000 0 maps to 00000000	11111111 11111000 00000000 00000000

Converting Between Prefix and DDN Masks

When learning, the best way to convert between the prefix and decimal formats is to first convert to binary. For example, to move from decimal to prefix, first convert decimal to binary and then from binary to prefix.

For the exams, set a goal to master these conversions doing the math in your head. While learning, you will likely want to use paper. To train yourself to do all this without writing it down, instead of writing each octet of binary, just write the number of binary 1s in that octet.

Figure 15-1 shows an example with a prefix-to-decimal conversion. The left side shows the conversion to binary as an interim step. For comparison, the right side shows the binary interim step in shorthand that just lists the number of binary 1s in each octet of the binary mask.

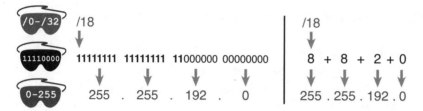

Figure 15-1 *Conversion from Prefix to Decimal: Full Binary Versus Shorthand*

Similarly, when converting from decimal to prefix, mentally convert to binary along the way, and as you improve, just think of the binary as the number of 1s in each octet. Figure 15-2 shows an example of such a conversion.

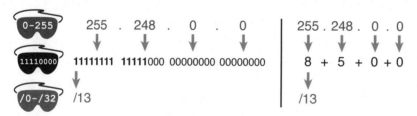

Figure 15-2 *Conversion from Decimal to Prefix: Full Binary Versus Shorthand*

Note that Appendix A has a table that lists all 33 legal subnet masks, with all three formats shown.

Practice Converting Subnet Masks

Before moving to the second half of this chapter, and thinking about what these subnet masks mean, first do some practice. Practice the processes discussed in this chapter until you get the right answer most of the time. Later, before taking the exam, practice more until you master the topics in this chapter and can move pretty fast, as outlined in the right column of Table 15-7.

Table 15-7   Keep-Reading and Take-Exam Goals for This Chapter's Topics

Time Frame	Before Moving to the Next Section	Before Taking the Exam
Focus On...	Learning how	Being correct and fast
Tools Allowed	All	Your brain and a notepad
Goal: Accuracy	90% correct	100% correct
Goal: Speed	Any speed	10 seconds

Table 15-8 lists eight practice problems. The table has three columns, one for each mask format. Each row lists one mask, in one format. Your job is to find the mask's value in the other two formats for each row. Table 15-12, located in the section "Answers to Earlier Practice Problems," later in this chapter, lists the answers.

Table 15-8   Practice Problems: Find the Mask Values in the Other Two Formats

Prefix	Binary Mask	Decimal
	11111111 11111111 11000000 00000000	
		255.255.255.252
/25		
/16		
		255.0.0.0
	11111111 11111111 11111100 00000000	
		255.254.0.0
/27		

Identifying Subnet Design Choices Using Masks

Subnet masks have many purposes. In fact, if ten experienced network engineers were independently asked, "What is the purpose of a subnet mask?" the engineers would likely give a variety of true answers. The subnet mask plays several roles.

This chapter focuses on one particular use of a subnet mask: defining the prefix part of the IP addresses in a subnet. The prefix part must be the same value for all addresses in a subnet. In fact, a single subnet can be defined as all IPv4 addresses that have the same value in the prefix part of their IPv4 addresses.

While the previous paragraph might sound a bit formal, the idea is relatively basic, as shown in Figure 15-3. The figure shows a network diagram, focusing on two subnets: a subnet of all addresses that begin with 172.16.2 and another subnet made of all addresses that begin with 172.16.3. In this example, the prefix—the part that has the same value in all the addresses in the subnet—is the first three octets.

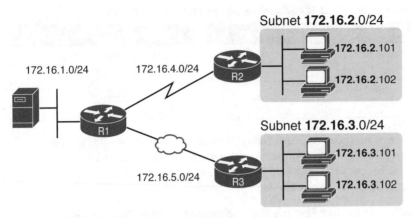

Figure 15-3 *Simple Subnet Design, with Mask /24*

While people can sit around a conference table and talk about how a prefix is three octets long, computers communicate that same concept using a subnet mask. In this case, the subnets use a subnet mask of /24, which means that the prefix part of the addresses is 24 bits (3 octets) long.

This section explains more about how to use a subnet mask to understand this concept of a prefix part of an IPv4 address, along with these other uses for a subnet mask. Note that this section discusses the first five items in the list.

- Defines the size of the prefix (combined network and subnet) part of the addresses in a subnet
- Defines the size of the host part of the addresses in the subnet
- Can be used to calculate the number of hosts in the subnet
- Provides a means for the network designer to communicate the design details—the number of subnet and host bits—to the devices in the network
- Under certain assumptions, can be used to calculate the number of subnets in the entire classful network
- Can be used in binary calculations of both the subnet ID and the subnet broadcast address

Masks Divide the Subnet's Addresses into Two Parts

The subnet mask subdivides the IP addresses in a subnet into two parts: the *prefix*, or *subnet part*, and the *host part*.

The prefix part identifies the addresses that reside in the same subnet, because all IP addresses in the same subnet have the same value in the prefix part of their addresses. The idea is much like the postal code (ZIP codes in the United States) in mailing addresses. All mailing addresses in the same town have the same postal code. Likewise, all IP addresses in the same subnet have identical values in the prefix part of their addresses.

The host part of an address identifies the host uniquely inside the subnet. If you compare any two IP addresses in the same subnet, their host parts will differ, even though the prefix parts of their addresses have the same value. To summarize these key comparisons:

Prefix (subnet) part: Equal in all addresses in the same subnet.

Host part: Different in all addresses in the same subnet.

For example, imagine a subnet that, in concept, includes all addresses whose first three octets are 10.1.1. So, the following list shows several addresses in this subnet:

10.1.1.**1**

10.1.1.**2**

10.1.1.**3**

In this list, the prefix or subnet part (the first three octets of 10.1.1) are equal. The host part (the last octet [in bold]) is different. So, the prefix or subnet part of the address identifies the group, and the host part identifies the specific member of the group.

The subnet mask defines the dividing line between the prefix and the host part. To do so, the mask creates a conceptual line between the binary 1s in the binary mask and the binary 0s in the mask. In short, if a mask has P binary 1s, the prefix part is P bits long and the rest of the bits are host bits. Figure 15-4 shows the general concept.

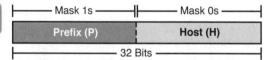

Figure 15-4 *Prefix (Subnet) and Host Parts Defined by Masks 1s and 0s*

The next figure, Figure 15-5, shows a specific example using mask 255.255.255.0. Mask 255.255.255.0 (/24) has 24 binary 1s, for a prefix length of 24 bits.

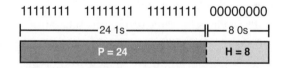

Figure 15-5 *Mask 255.255.255.0: P=24, H=8*

Masks and Class Divide Addresses into Three Parts

In addition to the two-part view of IPv4 addresses, you can also think about IPv4 addresses as having three parts. To do so, just apply Class A, B, and C rules to the address format to define the network part at the beginning of the address. This added logic divides the prefix into two parts: the *network* part and the *subnet* part. The class defines the length of the network part, with the subnet part simply being the rest of the prefix. Figure 15-6 shows the idea.

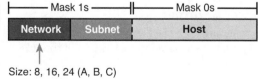

Figure 15-6 *Class Concepts Applied to Create Three Parts*

The combined network and subnet parts act like the prefix because all addresses in the same subnet must have identical values in the network and subnet parts. The size of the host part remains unchanged, whether viewing the addresses as having two parts or three parts.

To be complete, Figure 15-7 shows the same example as in the previous section, with the subnet of "all addresses that begin with 10.1.1." In that example, the subnet uses mask 255.255.255.0, and the addresses are all in Class A network 10.0.0.0. The class defines 8 network bits, and the mask defines 24 prefix bits, meaning that 24 – 8 = 16 subnet bits exist. The host part remains as 8 bits per the mask.

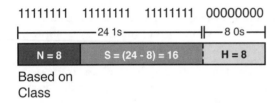

Figure 15-7   *Subnet 10.1.1.0, Mask 255.255.255.0: N=8, S=16, H=8*

Classless and Classful Addressing

The terms *classless addressing* and *classful addressing* refer to the two different ways to think about IPv4 addresses as described so far in this chapter. Classful addressing means that you think about Class A, B, and C rules, so the prefix is separated into the network and subnet parts, as shown in Figures 15-6 and 15-7. Classless addressing means that you ignore the Class A, B, and C rules and treat the prefix part as one part, as shown in Figures 15-4 and 15-5. The following more formal definitions are listed for reference and study:

Classless addressing: The concept that an IPv4 address has two parts—the prefix part plus the host part—as defined by the mask, with *no consideration of the class* (A, B, or C).

Classful addressing: The concept that an IPv4 address has three parts—network, subnet, and host—as defined by the mask *and Class A, B, and C rules*.

> **NOTE**   Unfortunately, the networking world uses the terms *classless* and *classful* in a couple of different ways. In addition to the classless and classful addressing described here, each routing protocol can be categorized as either a *classless routing protocol* or a *classful routing protocol*. In addition, the terms *classless routing* and *classful routing* refer to some details of how Cisco routers forward (route) packets using the default route in some cases. As a result, these terms can be easily confused and misused. So, when you see the words *classless* and *classful*, be careful to note the context: addressing, routing, or routing protocols.

Calculations Based on the IPv4 Address Format

After you know how to break an address down using both classless and classful addressing rules, you can easily calculate a couple of important facts using some basic math formulas.

First, for any subnet, after you know the number of host bits, you can calculate the number of host IP addresses in the subnet. Next, if you know the number of subnet bits (using classful addressing concepts) and you know that only one subnet mask is used throughout the network, you can also calculate the number of subnets in the network. The formulas just require that you know the powers of 2:

Hosts in the subnet: $2^H - 2$, where H is the number of host bits.

Subnets in the network: 2^S, where S is the number of subnet bits. Only use this formula if only one mask is used throughout the network.

> **NOTE** The section "Choose the Mask" in Chapter 13, "Perspectives on IPv4 Subnetting," details many concepts related to masks, including comments about this assumption of one mask throughout a single Class A, B, or C network.

The sizes of the parts of IPv4 addresses can also be calculated. The math is basic, but the concepts are important. Keeping in mind that IPv4 addresses are 32 bits long, the two parts with classless addressing must add up to 32 (P + H = 32), and with classful addressing, the three parts must add up to 32 (N + S + H = 32). Figure 15-8 shows the relationships.

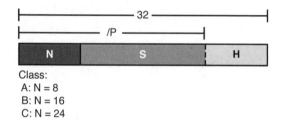

Class:
A: N = 8
B: N = 16
C: N = 24

Figure 15-8 *Relationship Between /P, N, S, and H*

You often begin with an IP address and mask, both when answering questions on the CCENT and CCNA Routing and Switching exams and when examining problems that occur in real networks. Based on the information in this chapter and earlier chapters, you should be able to find all the information in Figure 15-8 and then calculate the number of hosts/subnet and the number of subnets in the network. For reference, the following process spells out the steps:

Step 1. Convert the mask to prefix format (/P) as needed. (See the earlier section "Practice Converting Subnet Masks" for review.)

Step 2. Determine N based on the class. (See Chapter 14, "Analyzing Classful IPv4 Networks," for review.)

Step 3. Calculate S = P − N.

Step 4. Calculate H = 32 − P.

Step 5. Calculate hosts/subnet: $2^H - 2$.

Step 6. Calculate number of subnet: 2^S.

For example, consider the case of IP address 8.1.4.5 with mask 255.255.0.0. Following the process:

Step 1.   255.255.0.0 = /16, so P=16.

Step 2.   8.1.4.5 is in the range 1–126 in the first octet, so it is Class A; so N=8.

Step 3.   S = P – N = 16 – 8 = 8.

Step 4.   H = 32 – P = 32 – 16 = 16.

Step 5. $2^{16} - 2 = 65,534$ hosts/subnet.

Step 6. $2^{8} = 256$ subnets.

Figure 15-9 shows a visual analysis of the same problem.

Figure 15-9   *Visual Representation of Problem: 8.1.4.5, 255.255.0.0*

For another example, consider address 200.1.1.1, mask 255.255.255.252. Following the process:

Step 1.   255.255.255.252 = /30, so P=30.

Step 2.   200.1.1.1 is in the range 192–223 in the first octet, so it is Class C; so N=24.

Step 3.   S = P – N = 30 – 24 = 6.

Step 4.   H = 32 – P = 32 – 30 = 2.

Step 5. $2^{2} - 2 = 2$ hosts/subnet

Step 6. $2^{6} = 64$ subnets.

This example uses a popular mask for serial links, because serial links only require two host addresses, and the mask supports only two host addresses.

Practice Analyzing Subnet Masks

As with the other subnetting math in this book, using a two-phase approach may help. Take time now to practice until you feel like you understand the process. Then, before the exam, make sure you master the math. Table 15-9 summarizes the key concepts and suggestions for this two-phase approach.

Table 15-9   Keep-Reading and Take-Exam Goals for This Chapter's Topics

Time Frame	Before Moving to the Next Chapter	Before Taking the Exam
Focus On...	Learning how	Being correct and fast
Tools Allowed	All	Your brain and a notepad
Goal: Accuracy	90% correct	100% correct
Goal: Speed	Any speed	15 seconds

On a piece of scratch paper, answer the following questions. In each case:

- Determine the structure of the addresses in each subnet based on the class and mask, using classful IP addressing concepts. In other words, find the size of the network, subnet, and host parts of the addresses.
- Calculate the number of hosts in the subnet.
- Calculate the number of subnets in the network, assuming that the same mask is used throughout.

1. 8.1.4.5, 255.255.254.0
2. 130.4.102.1, 255.255.255.0
3. 199.1.1.100, 255.255.255.0
4. 130.4.102.1, 255.255.252.0
5. 199.1.1.100, 255.255.255.224

The answers are listed in the section "Answers to Earlier Practice Problems," later in this chapter.

Chapter Review

One key to doing well on the exams is to perform repetitive spaced review sessions. Review this chapter's material using either the tools in the book, DVD, or interactive tools for the same material found on the book's companion website. Refer to the "Your Study Plan" element for more details. Table 15-10 outlines the key review elements and where you can find them. To better track your study progress, record when you completed these activities in the second column.

Table 15-10   Chapter Review Tracking

Review Element	Review Date(s)	Resource Used
Review key topics		Book, DVD/website
Review key terms		Book, DVD/website
Answer DIKTA questions		Book, PCPT
Review memory tables		Book, DVD/website
Practice analyzing subnet masks		DVD Appendix E, DVD/website

Review All the Key Topics

Table 15-11 Key Topics for Chapter 15

Key Topic Element	Description	Page Number
List	Rules for binary subnet mask values	342
List	Rules to convert between binary and prefix masks	343
Table 15-4	Nine possible values in a decimal subnet mask	344
List	Rules to convert between binary and DDN masks	345
List	Some functions of a subnet mask	348
List	Comparisons of IP addresses in the same subnet	349
Figure 15-4	Two-part classless view of an IP address	349
Figure 15-6	Three-part classful view of an IP address	349
List	Definitions of classful addressing and classless addressing	350
List	Formal steps to analyze masks and calculate values	351

Key Terms You Should Know

binary mask, dotted-decimal notation (DDN), decimal mask, prefix mask, CIDR mask, classful addressing, classless addressing

Additional Practice for This Chapter's Processes

For additional practice with analyzing classful networks, you may do the same set of practice problems using your choice of tools:

Application: Use the Analyzing Subnet Masks application on the DVD or companion website.

PDF: Alternatively, practice the same problems found in both these apps using DVD Appendix E, "Practice for Chapter 15: Analyzing Subnet Masks."

Answers to Earlier Practice Problems

Table 15-8, shown earlier, listed several practice problems for converting subnet masks; Table 15-12 lists the answers.

Table 15-12 Answers to Problems in Table 15-8

Prefix	Binary Mask	Decimal
/18	11111111 11111111 11000000 00000000	255.255.192.0
/30	11111111 11111111 11111111 11111100	255.255.255.252
/25	11111111 11111111 11111111 10000000	255.255.255.128
/16	11111111 11111111 00000000 00000000	255.255.0.0
/8	11111111 00000000 00000000 00000000	255.0.0.0

Prefix	Binary Mask	Decimal
/22	11111111 11111111 11111100 00000000	255.255.252.0
/15	11111111 11111110 00000000 00000000	255.254.0.0
/27	11111111 11111111 11111111 11100000	255.255.255.224

Table 15-13 lists the answers to the practice problems from the earlier section "Practice Analyzing Subnet Masks."

Table 15-13 Answers to Problems from Earlier in the Chapter

	Problem	/P	Class	N	S	H	2^S	$2^H - 2$
1	8.1.4.5 255.255.254.0	23	A	8	15	9	32,768	510
2	130.4.102.1 255.255.255.0	24	B	16	8	8	256	254
3	199.1.1.100 255.255.255.0	24	C	24	0	8	N/A	254
4	130.4.102.1 255.255.252.0	22	B	16	6	10	64	1022
5	199.1.1.100 255.255.255.224	27	C	24	3	5	8	30

The following list reviews the problems:

1. For 8.1.4.5, the first octet (8) is in the 1–126 range, so it is a Class A address, with 8 network bits. Mask 255.255.254.0 converts to /23, so P – N = 15, for 15 subnet bits. H can be found by subtracting /P (23) from 32, for 9 host bits.

2. 130.4.102.1 is in the 128–191 range in the first octet, making it a Class B address, with N = 16 bits. 255.255.255.0 converts to /24, so the number of subnet bits is 24 – 16 = 8. With 24 prefix bits, the number of host bits is 32 – 24 = 8.

3. The third problem purposely shows a case where the mask does not create a subnet part of the address. The address, 199.1.1.100, has a first octet between 192 and 223, making it a Class C address with 24 network bits. The prefix version of the mask is /24, so the number of subnet bits is 24 – 24 = 0. The number of host bits is 32 minus the prefix length (24), for a total of 8 host bits. So in this case, the mask shows that the network engineer is using the default mask, which creates no subnet bits and no subnets.

4. With the same address as the second problem, 130.4.102.1 is a Class B address with N = 16 bits. This problem uses a different mask, 255.255.252.0, which converts to /22. This makes the number of subnet bits 22 – 16 = 6. With 22 prefix bits, the number of host bits is 32 – 22 = 10.

5. With the same address as the third problem, 199.1.1.100 is a Class C address with N = 24 bits. This problem uses a different mask, 255.255.255.224, which converts to /27. This makes the number of subnet bits 27 – 24 = 3. With 27 prefix bits, the number of host bits is 32 – 27 = 5.

CHAPTER 16

Analyzing Existing Subnets

This chapter covers the following exam topics:

1.0 Network Fundamentals

1.8 Configure, verify, and troubleshoot IPv4 addressing and subnetting

1.9 Compare and contrast IPv4 address types

   1.9.a Unicast

   1.9.b Broadcast

Often, a networking task begins with the discovery of the IP address and mask used by some host. Then, to understand how the internetwork routes packets to that host, you must find key pieces of information about the subnet, specifically the following:

- Subnet ID
- Subnet broadcast address
- Subnet's range of usable unicast IP addresses

This chapter discusses the concepts and math to take a known IP address and mask, and then fully describe a subnet by finding the values in this list. These specific tasks might well be the most important IP skills in the entire IP addressing and subnetting topics in this book, because these tasks might be the most commonly used tasks when operating and trouble-shooting real networks.

"Do I Know This Already?" Quiz

Take the quiz (either here, or use the PCPT software) if you want to use the score to help you decide how much time to spend on this chapter. The answers are at the bottom of the page following the quiz, and the explanations are in DVD Appendix C and in the PCPT software.

Table 16-1 "Do I Know This Already?" Foundation Topics Section-to-Question Mapping

Foundation Topics Section	Questions
Defining a Subnet	1
Analyzing Existing Subnets: Binary	2
Analyzing Existing Subnets: Decimal	3–6

1. When thinking about an IP address using classful addressing rules, an address can have three parts: network, subnet, and host. If you examined all the addresses in one subnet, in binary, which of the following answers correctly states which of the three parts of the addresses will be equal among all addresses? (Choose the best answer.)

   a. Network part only

   b. Subnet part only

   c. Host part only

   d. Network and subnet parts

   e. Subnet and host parts

2. Which of the following statements are true regarding the binary subnet ID, subnet broadcast address, and host IP address values in any single subnet? (Choose two answers.)

   a. The host part of the broadcast address is all binary 0s.

   b. The host part of the subnet ID is all binary 0s.

   c. The host part of a usable IP address can have all binary 1s.

   d. The host part of any usable IP address must not be all binary 0s.

3. Which of the following is the resident subnet ID for IP address 10.7.99.133/24?

   a. 10.0.0.0

   b. 10.7.0.0

   c. 10.7.99.0

   d. 10.7.99.128

4. Which of the following is the resident subnet for IP address 192.168.44.97/30?

   a. 192.168.44.0

   b. 192.168.44.64

   c. 192.168.44.96

   d. 192.168.44.128

5. Which of the following is the subnet broadcast address for the subnet in which IP address 172.31.77.201/27 resides?

   a. 172.31.201.255

   b. 172.31.255.255

   c. 172.31.77.223

   d. 172.31.77.207

6. A fellow engineer tells you to configure the DHCP server to lease the last 100 usable IP addresses in subnet 10.1.4.0/23. Which of the following IP addresses could be leased as a result of your new configuration?

  a. 10.1.4.156

  b. 10.1.4.254

  c. 10.1.5.200

  d. 10.1.7.200

  e. 10.1.255.200

Foundation Topics

Defining a Subnet

An IP subnet is a subset of a classful network, created by choice of some network engineer. However, that engineer cannot pick just any arbitrary subset of addresses; instead, the engineer must follow certain rules, such as the following:

- The subnet contains a set of consecutive numbers.

- The subnet holds 2^H numbers, where H is the number of host bits defined by the subnet mask.

- Two special numbers in the range cannot be used as IP addresses:

  - The first (lowest) number acts as an identifier for the subnet (*subnet ID*).

  - The last (highest) number acts as a *subnet broadcast address*.

- The remaining addresses, whose values sit between the subnet ID and subnet broadcast address, are used as *unicast IP addresses*.

This section reviews and expands the basic concepts of the subnet ID, subnet broadcast address, and range of addresses in a subnet.

An Example with Network 172.16.0.0 and Four Subnets

Imagine that you work at the customer support center, where you receive all initial calls from users who have problems with their computer. You coach the user through finding her IP address and mask: 172.16.150.41, mask 255.255.192.0. One of the first and most common tasks you will do based on that information is to find the subnet ID of the subnet in which that address resides. (In fact, this subnet ID is sometimes called the *resident subnet*, because the IP address exists in or resides in that subnet.)

Before getting into the math, examine the mask (255.255.192.0) and classful network (172.16.0.0) for a moment. From the mask, based on what you learned in Chapter 15, "Analyzing Subnet Masks," you can find the structure of the addresses in the subnet, including the number of host and subnet bits. That analysis tells you that two subnet bits exist, meaning that there should be four (2^2) subnets. Figure 16-1 shows the idea.

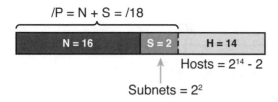

Figure 16-1   *Address Structure: Class B Network, /18 Mask*

16

> **NOTE**   This chapter, like the others in this part of the book, assumes that one mask is used throughout an entire classful network.

Because each subnet uses a single mask, all subnets of this single IP network must be the same size, because all subnets have the same structure. In this example, all four subnets will have the structure shown in the figure, so all four subnets will have $2^{14} - 2$ host addresses.

Next, consider the big picture of what happens with this example subnet design: The one Class B network now has four subnets of equal size. Conceptually, if you represent the entire Class B network as a number line, each subnet consumes one-fourth of the number line, as shown in Figure 16-2. Each subnet has a subnet ID—the numerically lowest number in the subnet—so it sits on the left of the subnet. And each subnet has a subnet broadcast address—the numerically highest number in the subnet—so it sits on the right side of the subnet.

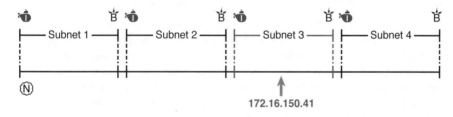

Legend:

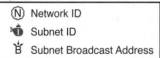

Figure 16-2   *Network 172.16.0.0, Divided into Four Equal Subnets*

The rest of this chapter focuses on how to take one IP address and mask and discover the details about that one subnet in which the address resides. In other words, you see how to find the resident subnet of an IP address. Again, using IP address 172.16.150.41 and mask 255.255.192.0 as an example, Figure 16-3 shows the resident subnet, along with the subnet ID and subnet broadcast address that bracket the subnet.

Answers to the "Do I Know This Already?" quiz:

1 D **2** B, D **3** C **4** C **5** C **6** C

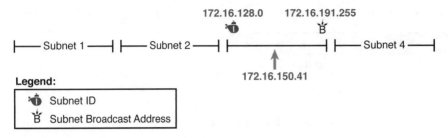

Figure 16-3   *Resident Subnet for 172.16.150.41, 255.255.192.0*

Subnet ID Concepts

A subnet ID is simply a number used to succinctly represent a subnet. When listed along with its matching subnet mask, the subnet ID identifies the subnet and can be used to derive the subnet broadcast address and range of addresses in the subnet. Rather than having to write down all these details about a subnet, you simply need to write down the subnet ID and mask, and you have enough information to fully describe the subnet.

The subnet ID appears in many places, but it is seen most often in IP routing tables. For example, when an engineer configures a router with its IP address and mask, the router calculates the subnet ID and puts a route into its routing table for that subnet. The router typically then advertises the subnet ID/mask combination to neighboring routers with some IP routing protocol. Eventually, all the routers in an enterprise learn about the subnet—again using the subnet ID and subnet mask combination—and display it in their routing tables. (You can display the contents of a router's IP routing table using the **show ip route** command.)

Unfortunately, the terminology related to subnets can sometimes cause problems. First, the terms *subnet ID*, *subnet number*, and *subnet address* are synonyms. In addition, people sometimes simply say *subnet* when referring to both the idea of a subnet and the number that is used as the subnet ID. When talking about routing, people sometimes use the term *prefix* instead of *subnet*. The term *prefix* refers to the same idea as *subnet*; it just uses terminology from the classless addressing way to describe IP addresses, as discussed in Chapter 15's section "Classless and Classful Addressing."

The biggest terminology confusion arises between the terms *network* and *subnet*. In the real world, people often use these terms synonymously, and that is perfectly reasonable in some cases. In other cases, the specific meaning of these terms, and their differences, matter to what is being discussed.

For example, people often might say, "What is the network ID?" when they really want to know the subnet ID. In another case, they might want to know the Class A, B, or C network ID. So, when one engineer asks something like, "What's the net ID for 172.16.150.41 slash 18?" use the context to figure out whether he wants the literal classful network ID (172.16.0.0, in this case) or the literal subnet ID (172.16.128.0, in this case).

For the exams, be ready to notice when the terms *subnet* and *network* are used, and then use the context to figure out the specific meaning of the term in that case.

Table 16-2 summarizes the key facts about the subnet ID, along with the possible synonyms, for easier review and study.

Table 16-2 Summary of Subnet ID Key Facts

Definition	Number that represents the subnet
Numeric Value	First (smallest) number in the subnet
Literal Synonyms	Subnet number, subnet address, prefix, resident subnet
Common-Use Synonyms	Network, network ID, network number, network address
Typically Seen In...	Routing tables, documentation

Subnet Broadcast Address

The subnet broadcast address has two main roles: to be used as a destination IP address for the purpose of sending packets to all hosts in the subnet, and as a means to find the high end of the range of addresses in a subnet.

The original purpose for the subnet broadcast address was to give hosts a way to send one packet to all hosts in a subnet, and to do so efficiently. For example, a host in subnet A could send a packet with a destination address of subnet B's subnet broadcast address. The routers would forward this one packet just like a packet sent to a host in subnet B. After the packet arrives at the router connected to subnet B, that last router would then forward the packet to all hosts in subnet B, typically by encapsulating the packet in a data link layer broadcast frame. As a result, all hosts in host B's subnet would receive a copy of the packet.

The subnet broadcast address also helps you find the range of addresses in a subnet, because the broadcast address is the last (highest) number in a subnet's range of addresses. To find the low end of the range, calculate the subnet ID; to find the high end of the range, calculate the subnet broadcast address.

Table 16-3 summarizes the key facts about the subnet broadcast address, along with the possible synonyms, for easier review and study.

Table 16-3 Summary of Subnet Broadcast Address Key Facts

Definition	A reserved number in each subnet that, when used as the destination address of a packet, causes the device to forward the packet to all hosts in that subnet
Numeric Value	Last (highest) number in the subnet
Literal Synonyms	Directed broadcast address
Broader-Use Synonyms	Network broadcast
Typically Seen In	In calculations of the range of addresses in a subnet

Range of Usable Addresses

The engineers implementing an IP internetwork need to know the range of unicast IP addresses in each subnet. Before you can plan which addresses to use as statically assigned IP addresses, which to configure to be leased by the DHCP server, and which to reserve for later use, you need to know the range of usable addresses.

To find the range of usable IP addresses in a subnet, first find the subnet ID and the subnet broadcast address. Then, just add 1 to the fourth octet of the subnet ID to get the first (lowest) usable address, and subtract 1 from the fourth octet of the subnet broadcast address to get the last (highest) usable address in the subnet.

16

For example, Figure 16-3 showed subnet ID 172.16.128.0, mask /18. The first usable address is simply one more than the subnet ID (in this case, 172.16.128.1). That same figure showed a subnet broadcast address of 172.16.191.255, so the last usable address is one less, or 172.16.191.254.

Now that this section has described the concepts behind the numbers that collectively define a subnet, the rest of this chapter focuses on the math used to find these values.

Analyzing Existing Subnets: Binary

What does it mean to "analyze a subnet"? For this book, it means that you should be able to start with an IP address and mask and then define key facts about the subnet in which that address resides. Specifically, that means discovering the subnet ID, subnet broadcast address, and range of addresses. The analysis can also include the calculation of the number of addresses in the subnet as discussed in Chapter 15, but this chapter does not review those concepts.

Many methods exist to calculate the details about a subnet based on the address/mask. This section begins by discussing some calculations that use binary math, with the next section showing alternatives that use only decimal math. Although many people prefer the decimal method for going fast on the exams, the binary calculations ultimately give you a better understanding of IPv4 addressing. In particular, if you plan to move on to attain Cisco certifications beyond CCNA Routing and Switching, you should take the time to understand the binary methods discussed in this section, even if you use the decimal methods for the exams.

Finding the Subnet ID: Binary

To start this section that uses binary, first consider a simple decimal math problem. The problem: Find the smallest three-digit decimal number that begins with 4. The answer, of course, is 400. And although most people would not have to break down the logic into steps, you know that 0 is the lowest-value digit you can use for any digit in a decimal number. You know that the first digit must be a 4, and the number is a three-digit number, so you just use the lowest value (0) for the last two digits, and find the answer: 400.

This same concept, applied to binary IP addresses, gives you the subnet ID. You have seen all the related concepts in other chapters, so if you already intuitively know how to find the subnet ID in binary, great! If not, the following key facts should help you see the logic:

All numbers in the subnet (subnet ID, subnet broadcast address, and all usable IP addresses) have the same value in the prefix part of the numbers.

The subnet ID is the lowest numeric value in the subnet, so its host part, in binary, is all 0s.

To find the subnet ID in binary, you take the IP address in binary and change all host bits to binary 0. To do so, you need to convert the IP address to binary. You also need to identify the prefix and host bits, which can be easily done by converting the mask (as needed) to prefix format. (Note that Appendix A, "Numeric Reference Tables," includes a decimal-binary conversion table.) Figure 16-4 shows the idea, using the same address/mask as in the earlier examples in this chapter: 172.16.150.41, mask /18.

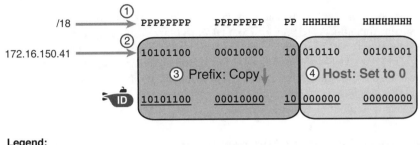

Legend:

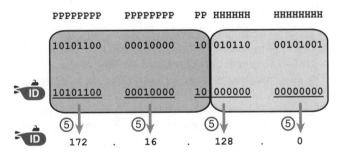

Subnet ID

Figure 16-4 *Binary Concept: Convert the IP Address to the Subnet ID*

Starting at the top of Figure 16-4, the format of the IP address is represented with 18 prefix (P) and 14 host (H) bits in the mask (Step 1). The second row (Step 2) shows the binary version of the IP address, converted from the dotted-decimal notation (DDN) value 172.16.150.41. (If you have not yet used the conversion table in Appendix A, it might be useful to double-check the conversion of all four octets based on the table.)

The next two steps show the action to copy the IP address's prefix bits (Step 3) and give the host bits a value of binary 0 (Step 4). This resulting number is the subnet ID (in binary).

The last step, not shown in Figure 16-4, is to convert the subnet ID from binary to decimal. This book shows that conversion as a separate step, in Figure 16-5, mainly because many people make a mistake at this step in the process. When converting a 32-bit number (like an IP address or IP subnet ID) back to an IPv4 DDN, you must follow this rule:

> Convert 8 bits at a time from binary to decimal, regardless of the line between the prefix and host parts of the number.

Figure 16-5 *Converting the Subnet ID from Binary to DDN*

Figure 16-5 shows this final step. Note that the third octet (the third set of 8 bits) has 2 bits in the prefix and 6 bits in the host part of the number, but the conversion occurs for all 8 bits.

NOTE   You can do the numeric conversions in Figures 16-4 and 16-5 by relying on the conversion table in Appendix A. To convert from DDN to binary, for each octet, find the decimal value in the table and then write down the 8-bit binary equivalent. To convert from binary back to DDN, for each octet of 8 bits, find the matching binary entry in the table and write down the corresponding decimal value. For example, 172 converts to binary 10101100, and 00010000 converts to decimal 16.

Finding the Subnet Broadcast Address: Binary

Finding the subnet broadcast address uses a similar process. To find the subnet broadcast address, use the same binary process used to find the subnet ID, but instead of setting all the host bits to the lowest value (all binary 0s), set the host part to the highest value (all binary 1s). Figure 16-6 shows the concept.

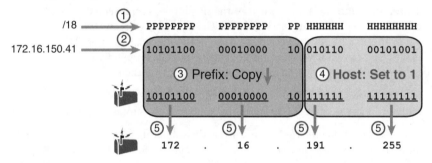

Legend:

Broadcast Address

Figure 16-6   *Finding a Subnet Broadcast Address: Binary*

The process in Figure 16-6 demonstrates the same first three steps shown in Figure 16-4. Specifically, it shows the identification of the prefix and host bits (Step 1), the results of converting the IP address 172.16.150.41 to binary (Step 2), and the copying of the prefix bits (first 18 bits, in this case). The difference occurs in the host bits on the right, changing all host bits (the last 14, in this case) to the largest possible value (all binary 1s). The final step converts the 32-bit subnet broadcast address to DDN format. Also, remember that with any conversion from DDN to binary or vice versa, the process always converts using 8 bits at a time. In particular, in this case, the entire third octet of binary 10111111 is converted back to decimal 191.

Binary Practice Problems

Figures 16-4 and 16-5 demonstrate a process to find the subnet ID using binary math. The following process summarizes those steps in written form for easier reference and practice:

Step 1.   Convert the mask to prefix format to find the length of the prefix (/P) and the length of the host part (32 – P).

Step 2.   Convert the IP address to its 32-bit binary equivalent.

Step 3.   Copy the prefix bits of the IP address.

Step 4.   Write down 0s for the host bits.

Step 5.   Convert the resulting 32-bit number, 8 bits at a time, back to decimal.

The process to find the subnet broadcast address is exactly the same, except in Step 4, you set the bits to 1s, as shown in Figure 16-6.

Take a few moments and run through the following five practice problems on scratch paper. In each case, find both the subnet ID and subnet broadcast address. Also, record the prefix style mask:

1. 8.1.4.5, 255.255.0.0
2. 130.4.102.1, 255.255.255.0
3. 199.1.1.100, 255.255.255.0
4. 130.4.102.1, 255.255.252.0
5. 199.1.1.100, 255.255.255.224

Tables 16-4 through 16-8 show the results for the five different examples. The tables show the host bits in bold, and they include the binary version of the address and mask and the binary version of the subnet ID and subnet broadcast address.

Table 16-4   Subnet Analysis for Subnet with Address 8.1.4.5, Mask 255.255.0.0

Prefix Length	/16	11111111 11111111 00000000 00000000
Address	8.1.4.5	00001000 00000001 **00000100 00000101**
Subnet ID	8.1.0.0	00001000 00000001 **00000000 00000000**
Broadcast Address	8.1.255.255	00001000 00000001 **11111111 11111111**

Table 16-5   Subnet Analysis for Subnet with Address 130.4.102.1, Mask 255.255.255.0

Prefix Length	/24	11111111 11111111 11111111 00000000
Address	130.4.102.1	10000010 00000100 01100110 **00000001**
Subnet ID	130.4.102.0	10000010 00000100 01100110 **00000000**
Broadcast Address	130.4.102.255	10000010 00000100 01100110 **11111111**

Table 16-6   Subnet Analysis for Subnet with Address 199.1.1.100, Mask 255.255.255.0

Prefix Length	/24	11111111 11111111 11111111 00000000
Address	199.1.1.100	11000111 00000001 00000001 **01100100**
Subnet ID	199.1.1.0	11000111 00000001 00000001 **00000000**
Broadcast Address	199.1.1.255	11000111 00000001 00000001 **11111111**

Table 16-7   Subnet Analysis for Subnet with Address 130.4.102.1, Mask 255.255.252.0

Prefix Length	/22	11111111 11111111 11111100 00000000
Address	130.4.102.1	10000010 00000100 011001**10 00000001**
Subnet ID	130.4.100.0	10000010 00000100 011001**00 00000000**
Broadcast Address	130.4.103.255	10000010 00000100 011001**11 11111111**

Table 16-8   Subnet Analysis for Subnet with Address 199.1.1.100, Mask 255.255.255.224

Prefix Length	/27	11111111 11111111 11111111 11100000
Address	199.1.1.100	11000111 00000001 00000001 01100100
Subnet ID	199.1.1.96	11000111 00000001 00000001 01100000
Broadcast Address	199.1.1.127	11000111 00000001 00000001 01111111

Shortcut for the Binary Process

The binary process described in this section so far requires that all four octets be converted to binary and then back to decimal. However, you can easily predict the results in at least three of the four octets, based on the DDN mask. You can then avoid the binary math in all but one octet and reduce the number of binary conversions you need to do.

First, consider an octet, and that octet only, whose DDN mask value is 255. The mask value of 255 converts to binary 11111111, which means that all 8 bits are prefix bits. Thinking through the steps in the process, at Step 2, you convert the address to some number. At Step 3, you copy the number. At Step 4, you convert the same 8-bit number back to decimal. All you did in those three steps, in this one octet, is convert from decimal to binary and convert the same number back to the same decimal value!

In short, the subnet ID (and subnet broadcast address) are equal to the IP address in octets for which the mask is 255.

For example, the resident subnet ID for 172.16.150.41, mask 255.255.192.0 is 172.16.128.0. The first two mask octets are 255. Rather than think about the binary math, you could just start by copying the address's value in those two octets: 172.16.

Another shortcut exists for octets whose DDN mask value is decimal 0, or binary 00000000. With a decimal mask value of 0, the math always results in a decimal 0 for the subnet ID, no matter the beginning value in the IP address. Specifically, just look at Steps 4 and 5 in this case: At Step 4, you would write down 8 binary 0s, and at Step 5, convert 00000000 back to decimal 0.

The following revised process steps take these two shortcuts into account. However, when the mask is neither 0 nor 255, the process requires the same conversions. At most, you have to do only one octet of the conversions. To find the subnet ID, apply the logic in these steps for each of the four octets:

Step 1.   If the mask = 255, copy the decimal IP address for that octet.

Step 2.   If the mask = 0, write down a decimal 0 for that octet.

Step 3.   If the mask is neither 0 nor 255 in this octet, use the same binary logic as shown in the section "Finding the Subnet ID: Binary," earlier in this chapter.

Figure 16-7 shows an example of this process, again using 172.16.150.41, 255.255.192.0.

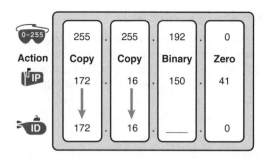

Legend:

Figure 16-7 *Binary Shortcut Example*

To find the subnet broadcast address, you can use a decimal shortcut similar to the one used to find the subnet ID: For DDN mask octets equal to decimal 0, set the decimal subnet broadcast address value to 255 instead of 0, as noted in the following list:

Step 1.   If the mask = 255, copy the decimal IP address for that octet.

Step 2.   If the mask = 0, write down a decimal 255 for that octet.

Step 3.   If the mask is neither 0 nor 255 in this octet, use the same binary logic as shown in the section "Finding the Subnet Broadcast Address: Binary," earlier in this chapter.

Brief Note About Boolean Math

So far, this chapter has described how humans can use binary math to find the subnet ID and subnet broadcast address. However, computers typically use an entirely different binary process to find the same values, using a branch of mathematics called *Boolean algebra*. Computers already store the IP address and mask in binary form, so they do not have to do any conversions to and from decimal. Then, certain Boolean operations allow the computers to calculate the subnet ID and subnet broadcast address with just a few CPU instructions.

You do not need to know Boolean math to have a good understanding of IP subnetting. However, in case you are interested, computers use the following Boolean logic to find the subnet ID and subnet broadcast address, respectively:

Perform a *Boolean AND* of the IP address and mask. This process converts all host bits to binary 0.

Invert the mask, and then perform a *Boolean OR* of the IP address and inverted subnet mask. This process converts all host bits to binary 1s.

Finding the Range of Addresses

Finding the range of usable addresses in a subnet, after you know the subnet ID and subnet broadcast address, requires only simple addition and subtraction. To find the first (lowest) usable IP address in the subnet, simply add 1 to the fourth octet of the subnet ID. To find the last (highest) usable IP address, simply subtract 1 from the fourth octet of the subnet broadcast address.

Analyzing Existing Subnets: Decimal

Analyzing existing subnets using the binary process works well. However, some of the math takes time for most people, particularly the decimal-binary conversions. And you need to do the math quickly for the Cisco CCENT and CCNA Routing and Switching exams. For the exams, you really should be able to take an IP address and mask, and calculate the subnet ID and range of usable addresses within about 15 seconds. When using binary methods, most people require a lot of practice to be able to find these answers, even when using the abbreviated binary process.

This section discusses how to find the subnet ID and subnet broadcast address using only decimal math. Most people can find the answers more quickly using this process, at least after a little practice, as compared with the binary process. However, the decimal process does not tell you anything about the meaning behind the math. So, if you have not read the earlier section "Analyzing Existing Subnets: Binary," it is worthwhile to read it for the sake of understanding subnetting. This section focuses on getting the right answer using a method that, after you have practiced, should be faster.

Analysis with Easy Masks

With three easy subnet masks in particular, finding the subnet ID and subnet broadcast address requires only easy logic and literally no math. Three easy masks exist:

255.0.0.0

255.255.0.0

255.255.255.0

These easy masks have only 255 and 0 in decimal. In comparison, difficult masks have one octet that has neither a 255 nor a 0 in the mask, which makes the logic more challenging.

NOTE The terms *easy mask* and *difficult mask* are terms created for use in this book to describe the masks and the level of difficulty when working with each.

When the problem uses an easy mask, you can quickly find the subnet ID based on the IP address and mask in DDN format. Just use the following process for each of the four octets to find the subnet ID:

Step 1.   If the mask octet = 255, copy the decimal IP address.

Step 2.   If the mask octet = 0, write a decimal 0.

A similar simple process exists to find the subnet broadcast address, as follows:

Step 1.   If the mask octet = 255, copy the decimal IP address.

Step 2.   If the mask octet = 0, write a decimal 255.

Before moving to the next section, take some time to fill in the blanks in Table 16-9. Check your answers against Table 16-15 in the section "Answers to Earlier Practice Problems," later in this chapter. Complete the table by listing the subnet ID and subnet broadcast address.

Table 16-9 Practice Problems: Find Subnet ID and Broadcast, Easy Masks

	IP Address	Mask	Subnet ID	Broadcast Address
1	10.77.55.3	255.255.255.0		
2	172.30.99.4	255.255.255.0		
3	192.168.6.54	255.255.255.0		
4	10.77.3.14	255.255.0.0		
5	172.22.55.77	255.255.0.0		
6	1.99.53.76	255.0.0.0		

Predictability in the Interesting Octet

Although three masks are easier to work with (255.0.0.0, 255.255.0.0, and 255.255.255.0), the rest make the decimal math a little more difficult, so we call these masks difficult masks. With difficult masks, one octet is neither a 0 nor a 255. The math in the other three octets is easy and boring, so this book calls the one octet with the more difficult math the *interesting octet*.

If you take some time to think about different problems and focus on the interesting octet, you will begin to see a pattern. This section takes you through that examination so that you can learn how to predict the pattern, in decimal, and find the subnet ID.

First, the subnet ID value has a predictable decimal value because of the assumption that a single subnet mask is used for all subnets of a single classful network. The chapters in this part of the book assume that, for a given classful network, the design engineer chooses to use a single subnet mask for all subnets. (See the section "One Size Subnet Fits All—Or Not" in Chapter 13, "Perspectives on IPv4 Subnetting," for more details.)

To see that predictability, consider some planning information written down by a network engineer, as shown in Figure 16-8. The figure shows four different masks the engineer is considering using in an IPv4 network, along with Class B network 172.16.0.0. The figure shows the third-octet values for the subnet IDs that would be created when using mask 255.255.128.0, 255.255.192.0, 255.255.224.0, and 255.255.240.0, from top to bottom in the figure.

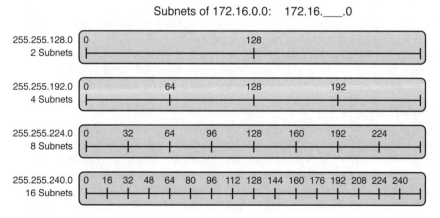

Figure 16-8 *Numeric Patterns in the Interesting Octet*

First, to explain the figure further, look at the top row of the figure. If the engineer uses 255.255.128.0 as the mask, the mask creates two subnets, with subnet IDs 172.16.0.0 and 172.16.128.0. If the engineer uses mask 255.255.192.0, the mask creates four subnets, with subnet IDs 172.16.0.0, 172.16.64.0, 172.16.128.0, and 172.16.192.0.

If you take the time to look at the figure, the patterns become obvious. In this case:

Mask: 255.255.128.0   Pattern: Multiples of 128

Mask: 255.255.192.0   Pattern: Multiples of 64

Mask: 255.255.224.0   Pattern: Multiples of 32

Mask: 255.255.240.0   Pattern: Multiples of 16

To find the subnet ID, you just need a way to figure out what the pattern is. If you start with an IP address and mask, just find the subnet ID closest to the IP address, without going over, as discussed in the next section.

Finding the Subnet ID: Difficult Masks

The following written process lists all the steps to find the subnet ID, using only decimal math. This process adds to the earlier process used with easy masks. For each octet:

Step 1.   If the mask octet = 255, copy the decimal IP address.

Step 2.   If the mask octet = 0, write a decimal 0.

Step 3.   If the mask is neither, refer to this octet as the *interesting octet*:

    A. Calculate the *magic number* as 256 – mask.

    B. Set the subnet ID's value to the multiple of the magic number that is closest to the IP address without going over.

The process uses two new terms created for this book: *magic number* and *interesting octet*. The term *interesting octet* refers to the octet identified at Step 3 in the process; in other words, it is the octet with the mask that is neither 255 nor 0. Step 3A then uses the term *magic number*, which is derived from the DDN mask. Conceptually, the magic number is the number you add to one subnet ID to get the next subnet ID in order, as shown in Figure 16-8. Numerically, it can be found by subtracting the DDN mask's value, in the interesting octet, from 256, as mentioned in Step 3A.

The best way to learn this process is to see it happen. In fact, if you can, stop reading now, use the DVD accompanying this book, and watch the videos about finding the subnet ID with a difficult mask. These videos demonstrate this process. You can also use the examples on the next few pages that show the process being used on paper. Then, follow the practice opportunities outlined in the section "Practice Analyzing Existing Subnets," later in this chapter.

Resident Subnet Example 1

For example, consider the requirement to find the resident subnet for IP address 130.4.102.1, mask 255.255.240.0. The process does not require you to think about prefix bits versus host bits, convert the mask, think about the mask in binary, or convert the IP address to and from binary. Instead, for each of the four octets, choose an action based on the value in the mask. Figure 16-9 shows the results; the circled numbers in the figure refer to the step numbers in the written process to find the subnet ID, as listed in the previous few pages.

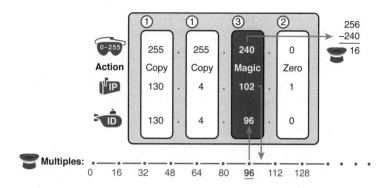

Figure 16-9 *Find the Subnet ID: 130.4.102.1, 255.255.240.0*

First, examine the three uninteresting octets (1, 2, and 4, in this example). The process keys on the mask, and the first two octets have a mask value of 255, so simply copy the IP address to the place where you intend to write down the subnet ID. The fourth octet has a mask value of 0, so write down a 0 for the fourth octet of the subnet ID.

The most challenging logic occurs in the interesting octet, which is the third octet in this example, because of the mask value 240 in that octet. For this octet, Step 3A asks you to calculate the magic number as 256 – mask. That means you take the mask's value in the interesting octet (240, in this case) and subtract it from 256: 256 – 240 = 16. The subnet ID's value in this octet must be a multiple of decimal 16, in this case.

Step 3B then asks you to find the multiples of the magic number (16, in this case) and choose the one closest to the IP address without going over. Specifically, that means that you should mentally calculate the multiples of the magic number, starting at 0. (Do not forget to start at 0!) Count, starting at 0: 0, 16, 32, 48, 64, 80, 96, 112, and so on. Then, find the multiple closest to the IP address value in this octet (102, in this case), without going over 102. So, as shown in Figure 16-9, you make the third octet's value 96 to complete the subnet ID of 130.4.96.0.

Resident Subnet Example 2

Consider another example: 192.168.5.77, mask 255.255.255.224. Figure 16-10 shows the results.

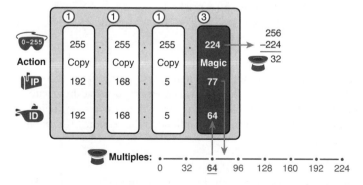

Figure 16-10 *Resident Subnet for 192.168.5.77, 255.255.255.224*

The three uninteresting octets (1, 2, and 3, in this case) require only a little thought. For each octet, each with a mask value of 255, just copy the IP address.

For the interesting octet, at Step 3A, the magic number is 256 – 224 = 32. The multiples of the magic number are 0, 32, 64, 96, and so on. Because the IP address value in the fourth octet is 77, in this case, the multiple must be the number closest to 77 without going over; therefore, the subnet ID ends with 64, for a value of 192.168.5.64.

Resident Subnet Practice Problems

Before moving to the next section, take some time to fill in the blanks in Table 16-10. Check your answers against Table 16-16 in the section "Answers to Earlier Practice Problems," later in this chapter. Complete the table by listing the subnet ID in each case. The text following Table 16-16 also lists explanations for each problem.

Table 16-10 Practice Problems: Find Subnet ID, Difficult Masks

Problem	IP Address	Mask	Subnet ID
1	10.77.55.3	255.248.0.0	
2	172.30.99.4	255.255.192.0	
3	192.168.6.54	255.255.255.252	
4	10.77.3.14	255.255.128.0	
5	172.22.55.77	255.255.254.0	
6	1.99.53.76	255.255.255.248	

Finding the Subnet Broadcast Address: Difficult Masks

To find a subnet's broadcast address, a similar process can be used. For simplicity, this process begins with the subnet ID, rather than the IP address. If you happen to start with an IP address instead, use the processes in this chapter to first find the subnet ID, and then use the following process to find the subnet broadcast address for that same subnet. For each octet:

Step 1. If the mask octet = 255, copy the subnet ID.

Step 2. If the mask octet = 0, write 255.

Step 3. If the mask is neither, identify this octet as the *interesting octet*:

    A. Calculate the *magic number* as 256 – mask.

    B. Take the subnet ID's value, add the magic number, and subtract 1 (ID + magic – 1).

As with the similar process used to find the subnet ID, you have several options for how to best learn and internalize the process. If you can, stop reading now, use the DVD accompanying this book, and watch the videos about finding the subnet broadcast address with a difficult mask. Also, look at the examples in this section, which show the process being used on paper. Then, follow the practice opportunities outlined in the section "Additional Practice for This Chapter's Processes."

Subnet Broadcast Example 1

The first example continues the first example from the section "Finding the Subnet ID: Difficult Masks," earlier in this chapter, as demonstrated in Figure 16-9. That example started with the IP address/mask of 130.4.102.1, 255.255.240.0, and showed how to find subnet ID 130.4.96.0. Figure 16-11 now begins with that subnet ID and the same mask.

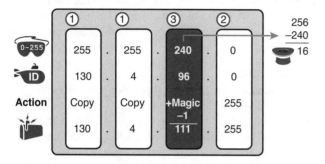

Figure 16-11 *Find the Subnet Broadcast: 130.4.96.0, 255.255.240.0*

First, examine the three uninteresting octets (1, 2, and 4). The process keys on the mask, and the first two octets have a mask value of 255, so simply copy the subnet ID to the place where you intend to write down the subnet broadcast address. The fourth octet has a mask value of 0, so write down a 255 for the fourth octet.

The logic related to the interesting octet occurs in the third octet in this example, because of the mask value 240. First, Step 3A asks you to calculate the magic number, as 256 – mask. (If you had already calculated the subnet ID using the decimal process in this book, you should already know the magic number.) At Step 3B, you take the subnet ID's value (96), add the magic number (16), and subtract 1, for a total of 111. That makes the subnet broadcast address 130.4.111.255.

Subnet Broadcast Example 2

Again, this example continues an earlier example, from the section "Resident Subnet Example 2," as demonstrated in Figure 16-10. That example started with the IP address/ mask of 192.168.5.77, mask 255.255.255.224 and showed how to find subnet ID 192.168.5.64. Figure 16-12 now begins with that subnet ID and the same mask.

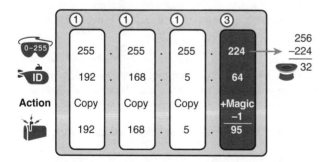

Figure 16-12 *Find the Subnet Broadcast: 192.168.5.64, 255.255.255.224*

First, examine the three uninteresting octets (1, 2, and 3). The process keys on the mask, and the first three octets have a mask value of 255, so simply copy the subnet ID to the place where you intend to write down the subnet broadcast address.

The interesting logic occurs in the interesting octet, the fourth octet in this example, because of the mask value 224. First, Step 3A asks you to calculate the magic number, as 256 − mask. (If you had already calculated the subnet ID, it is the same magic number, because the same mask is used.) At Step 3B, you take the subnet ID's value (64), add magic (32), and subtract 1, for a total of 95. That makes the subnet broadcast address 192.168.5.95.

Subnet Broadcast Address Practice Problems

Before moving to the next section, take some time to do several practice problems on a scratch piece of paper. Go back to Table 16-10, which lists IP addresses and masks, and practice by finding the subnet broadcast address for all the problems in that table. Then check your answers against Table 16-17 in the section "Answers to Earlier Practice Problems," later in this chapter.

Practice Analyzing Existing Subnets

As with the other subnetting math in this book, using a two-phase approach may help. Take time now to practice until you feel like you understand the process. Then, before the exam, make sure you master the math. Table 16-11 summarizes the key concepts and suggestions for this two-phase approach.

Table 16-11   Keep-Reading and Take-Exam Goals for This Chapter's Topics

Time Frame	Before Moving to the Next Chapter	Before Taking the Exam
Focus On...	Learning how	Being correct and fast
Tools Allowed	All	Your brain and a notepad
Goal: Accuracy	90% correct	100% correct
Goal: Speed	Any speed	20–30 seconds

A Choice: Memorize or Calculate

As described in this chapter, the decimal processes to find the subnet ID and subnet broadcast address do require some calculation, including the calculation of the magic number (256 − mask). The processes also use a DDN mask, so if an exam question gives you a prefix-style mask, you need to convert to DDN format before using the process in this book.

Over the years, some people have told me they prefer to memorize a table to find the magic number. These tables could list the magic number for different DDN masks and prefix masks, so you avoid converting from the prefix mask to DDN. Table 16-12 shows an example of such a table. Feel free to ignore this table, use it, or make your own.

Table 16-12   Reference Table: DDN Mask Values, Binary Equivalent, Magic Numbers, and Prefixes

Prefix, interesting octet 2	/9	/10	/11	/12	/13	/14	/15	/16
Prefix, interesting octet 3	/17	/18	/19	/20	/21	/22	/23	/24
Prefix, interesting octet 4	/25	/26	/27	/28	/29	/30		
Magic number	128	64	32	16	8	4	2	1
DDN mask in the interesting octet	128	192	224	240	248	252	254	255

Chapter Review

One key to doing well on the exams is to perform repetitive spaced review sessions. Review this chapter's material using either the tools in the book, DVD, or interactive tools for the same material found on the book's companion website. Refer to the "Your Study Plan" element for more details. Table 16-13 outlines the key review elements and where you can find them. To better track your study progress, record when you completed these activities in the second column.

Table 16-13 Chapter Review Tracking

Review Element	Review Date(s)	Resource Used
Review key topics		Book, DVD/website
Review key terms		Book, DVD/website
Answer DIKTA questions		Book, PCPT
Review memory tables		Book, DVD/website
Practice mask analysis		DVD Appendix F, DVD/website
Practice analyzing existing subnets		DVD Appendix F, DVD/website

Review All the Key Topics

Table 16-14 Key Topics for Chapter 16

Key Topic Element	Description	Page Number
List	Definition of a subnet's key numbers	358
Table 16-2	Key facts about the subnet ID	361
Table 16-3	Key facts about the subnet broadcast address	361
List	Steps to use binary math to find the subnet ID	364
List	General steps to use binary and decimal math to find the subnet ID	366
List	Steps to use decimal and binary math to find the subnet broadcast address	367
List	Steps to use only decimal math to find the subnet ID	370
List	Steps to use only decimal math to find the subnet broadcast address	372

Key Terms You Should Know

resident subnet, subnet ID, subnet number, subnet address, subnet broadcast address

Additional Practice for This Chapter's Processes

For additional practice with analyzing subnets, you may do the same set of practice problems using your choice of tools:

Application: Use the Analyzing Existing Subnets application on the DVD or companion website.

PDF: Alternatively, practice the same problems found in these apps using DVD Appendix F, "Practice for Chapter 16: Analyzing Existing Subnets."

Answers to Earlier Practice Problems

This chapter includes practice problems spread around different locations in the chapter. The answers are located in Tables 16-15, 16-16, and 16-17.

Table 16-15 Answers to Problems in Table 16-9

	IP Address	Mask	Subnet ID	Broadcast Address
1	10.77.55.3	255.255.255.0	10.77.55.0	10.77.55.255
2	172.30.99.4	255.255.255.0	172.30.99.0	172.30.99.255
3	192.168.6.54	255.255.255.0	192.168.6.0	192.168.6.255
4	10.77.3.14	255.255.0.0	10.77.0.0	10.77.255.255
5	172.22.55.77	255.255.0.0	172.22.0.0	172.22.255.255
6	1.99.53.76	255.0.0.0	1.0.0.0	1.255.255.255

Table 16-16 Answers to Problems in Table 16-10

	IP Address	Mask	Subnet ID
1	10.77.55.3	255.248.0.0	10.72.0.0
2	172.30.99.4	255.255.192.0	172.30.64.0
3	192.168.6.54	255.255.255.252	192.168.6.52
4	10.77.3.14	255.255.128.0	10.77.0.0
5	172.22.55.77	255.255.254.0	172.22.54.0
6	1.99.53.76	255.255.255.248	1.99.53.72

The following list explains the answers for Table 16-16:

1. The second octet is the interesting octet, with magic number 256 – 248 = 8. The multiples of 8 include 0, 8, 16, 24, ..., 64, 72, and 80. 72 is closest to the IP address value in that same octet (77) without going over, making the subnet ID 10.72.0.0.

2. The third octet is the interesting octet, with magic number 256 – 192 = 64. The multiples of 64 include 0, 64, 128, and 192. 64 is closest to the IP address value in that same octet (99) without going over, making the subnet ID 172.30.64.0.

3. The fourth octet is the interesting octet, with magic number 256 – 252 = 4. The multiples of 4 include 0, 4, 8, 12, 16, ..., 48, 52, and 56. 52 is the closest to the IP address value in that same octet (54) without going over, making the subnet ID 192.168.6.52.

4. The third octet is the interesting octet, with magic number 256 – 128 = 128. Only two multiples exist that matter: 0 and 128. 0 is the closest to the IP address value in that same octet (3) without going over, making the subnet ID 10.77.0.0.

5. The third octet is the interesting octet, with magic number 256 – 254 = 2. The multiples of 2 include 0, 2, 4, 6, 8, and so on—essentially all even numbers. 54 is closest to the IP address value in that same octet (55) without going over, making the subnet ID 172.22.54.0.

6. The fourth octet is the interesting octet, with magic number 256 − 248 = 8. The multiples of 8 include 0, 8, 16, 24, ..., 64, 72, and 80. 72 is closest to the IP address value in that same octet (76) without going over, making the subnet ID 1.99.53.72.

Table 16-17   Answers to Problems in the Section "Subnet Broadcast Address Practice Problems"

	Subnet ID	Mask	Broadcast Address
1	10.72.0.0	255.248.0.0	10.79.255.255
2	172.30.64.0	255.255.192.0	172.30.127.255
3	192.168.6.52	255.255.255.252	192.168.6.55
4	10.77.0.0	255.255.128.0	10.77.127.255
5	172.22.54.0	255.255.254.0	172.22.55.255
6	1.99.53.72	255.255.255.248	1.99.53.79

The following list explains the answers for Table 16-17:

1. The second octet is the interesting octet. Completing the three easy octets means that the broadcast address in the interesting octet will be 10.___.255.255. With magic number 256 − 248 = 8, the second octet will be 72 (from the subnet ID), plus 8, minus 1, or 79.

2. The third octet is the interesting octet. Completing the three easy octets means that the broadcast address in the interesting octet will be 172.30.___.255. With magic number 256 − 192 = 64, the interesting octet will be 64 (from the subnet ID), plus 64 (the magic number), minus 1, for 127.

3. The fourth octet is the interesting octet. Completing the three easy octets means that the broadcast address in the interesting octet will be 192.168.6.___. With magic number 256 − 252 = 4, the interesting octet will be 52 (the subnet ID value), plus 4 (the magic number), minus 1, or 55.

4. The third octet is the interesting octet. Completing the three easy octets means that the broadcast address will be 10.77.___.255. With magic number 256 − 128 = 128, the interesting octet will be 0 (the subnet ID value), plus 128 (the magic number), minus 1, or 127.

5. The third octet is the interesting octet. Completing the three easy octets means that the broadcast address will be 172.22.___.255. With magic number 256 − 254 = 2, the broadcast address in the interesting octet will be 54 (the subnet ID value), plus 2 (the magic number), minus 1, or 55.

6. The fourth octet is the interesting octet. Completing the three easy octets means that the broadcast address will be 1.99.53.___. With magic number 256 − 248 = 8, the broadcast address in the interesting octet will be 72 (the subnet ID value), plus 8 (the magic number), minus 1, or 79.

16

Part IV Review

Keep track of your part review progress with the checklist in Table P4-1. Details on each task follow the table.

Table P4-1 Part IV Part Review Checklist

Activity	1st Date Completed	2nd Date Completed
Repeat All DIKTA Questions		
Answer Part Review Questions		
Review Key Topics		
Create Subnet Terms Mind Map		
Subnetting Exercises		

Repeat All DIKTA Questions

For this task, use the PCPT software to answer the "Do I Know This Already?" questions again for the chapters in this part of the book.

Answer Part Review Questions

For this task, use PCPT to answer the Part Review questions for this part of the book.

Review Key Topics

Review all key topics in all chapters in this part, either by browsing the chapters or by using the Key Topics application on the DVD or companion website.

Create Terminology Mind Map

The topic of IPv4 addressing and subnetting happens to have many terms that are literal synonyms, many terms with similar meanings, along with terms that describe something about another term. So, create a mind map (call it map A) to organize all IP addressing and subnetting terms you remember. Use four main topic areas: IP addressing, IP networks, IP subnets, and masks. Inside these, subdivide terms as to whether they are either a synonym, a similar term, or a description.

Figure P4-1 shows the beginnings of one branch of the mind map to give you the general idea. For this branch, you would just remember any terms related to "IP address" and place them into one of these three categories. Your map can of course look different. As usual, first do this exercise without the book or your notes. Later, when you do look at the book again, make sure that you have at least included all the key terms from the ends of the chapters.

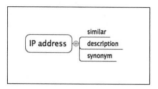

Figure P4-1 *Sample Beginning Point for Part IV Mind Map A*

NOTE For more information on mind mapping, refer to the Introduction, in the section "About Mind Maps."

If you do choose to use mind map software, record where you stored the file here in Table P4-2. Appendix L, "Mind Map Solutions," lists sample mind map answers, but as usual, your mind maps can and will look different.

Table P4-2 Configuration Mind Maps for Part IV Review

Map	Description	Where You Saved It
1	Mind Map: Subnetting Terms	

Subnetting Exercises

Chapter 14, "Analyzing Classful IPv4 Networks," Chapter 15, "Analyzing Subnet Masks," and Chapter 16, "Analyzing Existing Subnets," list some subnetting exercises, along with time and accuracy goals. Now is a good time to work on those goals. Some options include the following:

Practice from this book's DVD appendixes or DVD/web applications: The Chapter Review section of Chapters 14, 15, and 16 mention addressing and subnetting exercises included with this book. Find all the related applications in the Part IV Review section of the DVD or companion website, or open DVD Appendix D, "Practice for Chapter 14: Analyzing Classful IPv4 Networks," Appendix E, "Practice for Chapter 15: Analyzing Subnet Masks," and Appendix F, "Practice for Chapter 16: Analyzing Existing Subnets," for a simple PDF with the problems. Those exercises include activities such as analyzing classful networks, analyzing subnet masks, converting subnet masks, and analyzing existing subnets.

Pearson Network Simulator: The full Pearson ICND1 or CCNA simulator has subnetting math exercises that you can do by using CLI commands. Look for the labs with names "IP Address Rejection" and "Subnet ID Calculation" in their names.

Author's CCENT blog: I've written a few dozen subnetting exercises on the blog over the years—just look at the Questions category at the top of the page, and you will see a variety of IPv4 addressing and subnetting question types. Start at blog.certskills.com/ccent.

Part V of this book presents the foundations of what a Cisco router does and how to configure Cisco routers to implement those features. Much like Part II of this book introduced switch features, switch CLI, and all the common features most sites would use in Cisco switches, Part V walks through the most common features for Cisco routers.

Chapter 17 focuses on the basics of installing and operating a Cisco router. However, routers need some configuration before they can correctly route packets. So, Chapters 18 and 19 then show how routers learn the required IP addresses and subnets so that routers can do their jobs of routing IPv4 packets to all destinations. Chapter 18 first looks at configuring IP addresses, as well as static IP routes. Chapter 19 then shows how routers can dynamically learn about remote subnets using a routing protocol, in this case the Routing Information Protocol (RIP) Version 2.

Chapter 20 closes Part V with more of a host focus on the IPv4 network. This section walks through what happens when a host first connects to the network, first discovering its own IPv4 address with Dynamic Host Configuration Protocol (DHCP), resolving hostnames with Domain Name System (DNS), and then learning IP-MAC mapping information with Address Resolution Protocol (ARP).

Part V

Implementing IPv4

CHAPTER 17

Operating Cisco Routers

This chapter covers the following exam topics:

1.0 Network Fundamentals

1.6 Select the appropriate cabling type based on implementation requirements

1.8 Configure, verify, and troubleshoot IPv4 addressing and subnetting

5.0 Infrastructure Management

5.3 Configure and verify initial device configuration

Getting an IPv4 network up and working requires some basic steps: installing routers, configuring their IPv4 addresses, optionally configuring some static IPv4 routes, and then configuring a routing protocol to dynamically learn routes. This chapter focuses on Step 1: how to install an enterprise-class Cisco router, with just enough configuration to get the router working, ready for those next steps.

This chapter breaks the topics into two major headings. The first discusses the physical installation of an enterprise-class Cisco router. The second section looks at the command-line interface (CLI) on a Cisco router, which has the same look and feel as the Cisco switch CLI. This section first lists the similarities between a switch and router CLI, and then introduces the configuration required to make the router start forwarding IP packets on its interfaces.

"Do I Know This Already?" Quiz

Take the quiz (either here, or use the PCPT software) if you want to use the score to help you decide how much time to spend on this chapter. The answers are at the bottom of the page following the quiz, and the explanations are in DVD Appendix C and in the PCPT software.

Table 17-1 "Do I Know This Already?" Foundation Topics Section-to-Question Mapping

Foundation Topics Section	Questions
Installing Cisco Routers	1
Enabling IPv4 Support on Cisco Routers	2–6

1. Which of the following installation steps are more likely required on a Cisco router, but not typically required on a Cisco switch? (Choose two answers.)

   a. Connect Ethernet cables

   b. Connect serial cables

   c. Connect to the console port

   d. Connect the power cable

   e. Turn the on/off switch to "on"

2. Which of the following commands might you see associated with the router CLI, but not with the switch CLI?

   a. The **clock rate** command

   b. The **ip address** *address mask* command

   c. The **ip address dhcp** command

   d. The **interface vlan 1** command

3. You just bought two Cisco routers for use in a lab, connecting each router to a different LAN switch with their Fa0/0 interfaces. You also connected the two routers' serial interfaces using a back-to-back cable. Which of the following steps are not required to be able to forward IPv4 packets on both routers' interfaces? (Choose two answers.)

   a. Configuring an IP address on each router's Fast Ethernet and serial interfaces

   b. Configuring the **bandwidth** command on one router's serial interface

   c. Configuring the **clock rate** command on one router's serial interface

   d. Setting the interface **description** on both the Fast Ethernet and serial interface of each router

4. The output of the **show ip interface brief** command on R1 lists interface status codes of "down" and "down" for interface Serial 0/0. Which of the following could be true?

   a. The **shutdown** command is currently configured for that interface.

   b. R1's serial interface has been configured to use Frame Relay, but the router on the other end of the serial link has been configured to use PPP.

   c. R1's serial interface does not have a serial cable installed.

   d. Both routers have been cabled to a working serial link (CSU/DSUs included), but only one router has been configured with an IP address.

5. Which of the following commands do not list the IP address and mask of at least one interface? (Choose two answers.)

   a. **show running-config**

   b. **show protocols** *type number*

   c. **show ip interface brief**

   d. **show interfaces**

   e. **show version**

6. Which of the following is different on the Cisco switch CLI for a Layer 2 switch as compared with the Cisco router CLI?

   a. The commands used to configure simple password checking for the console

   b. The number of IP addresses configured

   c. The configuration of the device's hostname

   d. The configuration of an interface description

Foundation Topics

Installing Cisco Routers

Routers collectively provide the main feature of the network layer—the capability to forward packets end to end through a network. As introduced in Chapter 4, "Fundamentals of IPv4 Addressing and Routing," routers forward packets by connecting to various physical network links, like Ethernet, serial links, and Frame Relay, and then using Layer 3 routing logic to choose where to forward each packet. As a reminder, Chapter 2, "Fundamentals of Ethernet LANs," covered the details of making those physical connections to Ethernet networks, while Chapter 3, "Fundamentals of WANs," covered the basics of cabling with WAN links.

This section examines some of the details of router installation and cabling, first from the enterprise perspective and then from the perspective of connecting a typical small office/home office (SOHO) to an ISP using high-speed Internet.

Installing Enterprise Routers

A typical enterprise network has a few centralized sites as well as lots of smaller remote sites. To support devices at each site (the computers, IP phones, printers, and other devices), the network includes at least one LAN switch at each site. In addition, each site has a router, which connects to the LAN switch and to some WAN link. The WAN link provides connectivity from each remote site, back to the central site, and to other sites through the connection to the central site.

Figures 17-1 and 17-2 show contrasting ways to draw parts of an enterprise network. Both show a typical branch office on the left, with a router and some end-user PCs. The central site, on the right, has basically the same components, plus some servers. The sites connect using a point-to-point serial link connecting the two routers. The first figure omits many of the cabling details, making the figure more useful when you want to discuss general Layer 3 concepts; the second figure shows the cabling details.

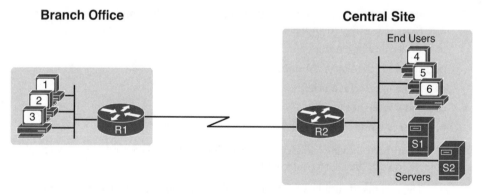

Figure 17-1 *Generic Enterprise Network Diagram*

Branch Office   **Central Site**

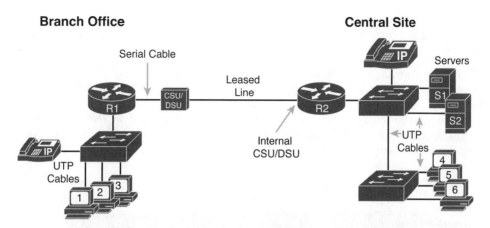

Figure 17-2   *More Detailed Cabling Diagram for the Same Enterprise Network*

The Ethernet cables in Figure 17-2 should be familiar. In particular, routers use the same Ethernet cabling pinouts as PCs, so each router uses a UTP cable with a straight-through pinout.

Next, consider the hardware on the ends of the serial link, in particular where the channel service unit/data service unit (CSU/DSU) hardware resides on each end of the serial link. It sits either outside the router as a separate device (as shown on the left) or integrated into the router's serial interface hardware (as shown on the right). Most new installations today include the CSU/DSU in the router's serial interface.

Finally, the serial link requires some cabling inside the same wiring closet or other space between where the telco serial line terminates and where the router sits on a shelf or in a rack. The WAN cable installed by the telco typically has an RJ-48 connector, which is the same size and shape as an RJ-45 connector. The telco cable with the RJ-48 connector inserts into the CSU/DSU. In the example of Figure 17-2, at the central site, the telco cable connects directly into the router's serial interface. At the branch office router, the cable connects to the external CSU/DSU, which then connects to the router serial interface using some other serial cable. (As a reminder, Chapter 3's section "Leased-Line Cabling" introduced the basics of this cabling.)

Cisco Integrated Services Routers

Product vendors, including Cisco, typically provide several different types of router hardware. Today, routers often do much more work than simply routing packets—in fact, they serve as a device or platform from which to provide many network services. Cisco even brands their enterprise routers not just as routers, but as "integrated services routers," emphasizing the multi-purpose nature of the products.

As an example, consider the networking functions needed at a typical branch office. A typical enterprise branch office needs a router for WAN/LAN connectivity, and a LAN switch to provide a high-performance local network and connectivity into the router and WAN. Many branches also need Voice over IP (VoIP) services to support IP phones, and several security services as well. Plus, it is hard to imagine a site with users that does not have Wi-Fi access today. So, rather than require multiple separate devices at one site, as shown in Figure 17-2, Cisco offers single devices that act as both router and switch, and provide other functions as well.

For the sake of learning and understanding the different functions, the CCENT and CCNA Routing and Switching exams focus on using a separate switch and separate router, which provides a much cleaner path for learning the basics.

Figure 17-3 shows a couple of pictures of the Cisco 4321 ISR, with some of the more important features highlighted. The top part of the figure shows a full view of the back of the router. This model comes with two built-in Gigabit Ethernet interfaces and two modular slots that allow you to add small cards called Network Interface Modules (NIMs). The bottom of the figure shows one example NIM (a NIM that provides two serial interfaces). The router has other items as well, including both an RJ-45 and USB console port.

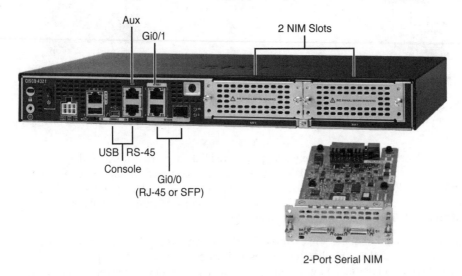

Figure 17-3 *Photos of a Model 4321 Cisco Integrated Services Router (ISR)*

Physical Installation

Armed with the cabling details in figures like Figure 17-2, and the router hardware details in figures like Figure 17-3, you can physically install a router. To install a router, follow these steps:

Step 1. Connect any LAN cables to the LAN ports.

Step 2. If using an external CSU/DSU, connect the router's serial interface to the CSU/DSU and the CSU/DSU to the line from the telco.

Step 3. If using an internal CSU/DSU, connect the router's serial interface to the line from the telco.

Step 4. Connect the router's console port to a PC (using a rollover cable), as needed, to configure the router.

Step 5. Connect a power cable from a power outlet to the power port on the router.

Step 6. Power on the router.

Note that the steps for router installation match those for a switch, except that Cisco enterprise routers typically have an on/off switch, while switches do not.

Installing Internet Access Routers

Routers play a key role in SOHO networks, connecting the LAN-attached end-user devices to a high-speed Internet access service. However, most SOHO products go by the name *router*, but happen to include many networking functions in a single device. Because of that, when learning about networking, it can be difficult to appreciate the different functions the device performs.

To help you understand the features of a router product used in a SOHO environment, Figure 17-4 first shows an example in which the SOHO network uses separate devices for each function. The first shows the devices and cabling, with a connection to the Internet using cable TV (CATV) as the high-speed Internet service.

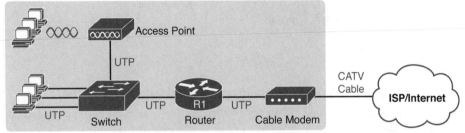

SOHO

17

Figure 17-4   *Devices in a SOHO Network with High-Speed CATV Internet*

This figure has many similarities to Figure 17-2, which shows a typical enterprise branch office. Some end-user PCs still connect with cabling to a switch, and the switch still connects to a router's Ethernet interface. Other end-user devices use a wireless LAN, with a wireless access point, that also connects to the Ethernet LAN. For both the wired and wireless devices, the router still provides routing services, forwarding IP packets.

The main differences between the SOHO connection in Figure 17-4 and the enterprise branch in Figure 17-2 relate to the connection into the Internet. An Internet connection that uses CATV or digital subscriber line (DSL) needs a device that converts between the Layer 1 and 2 standards used on the CATV cable or DSL line and the Ethernet used by the router. These devices, commonly called *cable modems* and *DSL modems*, respectively, convert between CATV Layer 1 and Layer 2 standards to Ethernet, and vice versa. Similarly, DSL modems convert between the DSL signals over a home telephone line and Ethernet.

To physically install a SOHO network with the devices shown in Figure 17-4, you basically need the correct UTP cables for the Ethernet connections, and either the CATV cable (for cable Internet services) or a phone line (for DSL services). Note that the router used in Figure 17-4 simply needs to have two Ethernet interfaces—one to connect to the LAN switch and one to connect to the cable modem.

Today, most new SOHO installations use an integrated device rather than the separate devices shown in Figure 17-4. Consumer-grade devices are often called cable routers or DSL routers, while in fact they do all the functions shown in Figure 17-4, including the roles of

- Router
- Switch

- Cable or DSL modem
- Wireless access point
- Hardware-enabled encryption

A newly installed high-speed SOHO Internet connection today probably looks more like Figure 17-5, with an integrated device.

SOHO

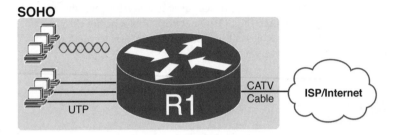

Figure 17-5   *SOHO Network, Using Cable Internet and an Integrated Device*

Enabling IPv4 Support on Cisco Router Interfaces

Routers support a relatively large number of features, with a large number of configuration and EXEC commands to support those features. You will learn about many of these features throughout the rest of this book.

> **NOTE**   For perspective, the Cisco router documentation includes a command reference, with an index to every single router command. A quick informal count of a recent IOS version listed around 5000 CLI commands.

This second section of the chapter focuses on commands related to router interfaces. To make routers work—that is, to route IPv4 packets—the interfaces must be configured. This section introduces the most common commands that configure interfaces, make them work, and give the interfaces IP addresses and masks.

Accessing the Router CLI

Accessing a router's command-line interface (CLI) works much like a switch. In fact, it works so much like accessing a Cisco switch CLI that this book relies on Chapter 6, "Using the Command-Line Interface," instead of repeating the same details here. If the details from Chapter 6 are not fresh in your memory, it might be worthwhile to spend a few minutes briefly reviewing Chapter 6 as well as Chapter 9, "Configuring Switch Interfaces," before reading further.

Cisco switches and routers share many of the same CLI navigation features, and many of the same configuration commands for management features. The following list mentions the highlights:

- User and Enable (privileged) mode
- Entering and exiting configuration mode, using the **configure terminal**, **end**, and **exit** commands and the Ctrl+Z key sequence

- Configuration of console, Telnet (vty), and enable secret passwords

- Configuration of Secure Shell (SSH) encryption keys and username/password login credentials

- Configuration of the hostname and interface description

- Configuration of Ethernet interfaces that can negotiate speed using the **speed** and **duplex** commands

- Configuration of an interface to be administratively disabled (**shutdown**) and administratively enabled (**no shutdown**)

- Navigation through different configuration mode contexts using commands like **line console 0** and **interface** *type number*

- CLI help, command editing, and command recall features

- The meaning and use of the startup-config (in NVRAM), running-config (in RAM), and external servers (like TFTP), along with how to use the **copy** command to copy the configuration files and IOS images

At first glance, this list seems to cover most everything covered in Chapter 8—and it does cover most of the details; however, a couple of topics covered in Chapter 8 do work differently with the router CLI as compared to the switch CLI, as follows:

- The configuration of IP addresses differs in some ways, with switches using a VLAN interface and routers using an IP address configured on each working interface.

- Many Cisco router models have an auxiliary (Aux) port, intended to be connected to an external modem and phone line to allow remote users to dial in to the router, and access the CLI, by making a phone call. Cisco switches do not have auxiliary ports.

- Router IOS defaults to disallow both Telnet and SSH into the router because of the default setting of **transport input none** in vty configuration mode. Chapter 8, "Configuring Basic Switch Management," already discussed the various options on this command to enable Telnet (**transport input telnet**), SSH (**transport input ssh**), or both (**transport input all** or **transport input telnet ssh**).

The router CLI also differs from a switch CLI just because switches and routers do different things. For example, Cisco Layer 2 switches support the **show mac address-table** command, but these Layer 2–only devices do not support the **show ip route** command, which routers use to list IPv4 routes. Some Cisco routers can do IP routing but not Layer 2 switching, so they support the **show ip route** command but not the **show mac address-table** command.

> **NOTE** The book includes a video that shows how to navigate the router CLI; you can find this video on the DVD and on the companion website.

Router Interfaces

One minor difference between Cisco switches and routers is that routers support a much wider variety of interfaces. Today, LAN switches support Ethernet LAN interfaces of various speeds. Routers support a variety of other types of interfaces, including serial interfaces, cable TV, DSL, 3G/4G wireless, and others not mentioned in this book.

Most Cisco routers have at least one Ethernet interface of some type. Many of those Ethernet interfaces support multiple speeds and use autonegotiation, so for consistency, the router IOS refers to these interfaces based on the fastest speed. For example, a 10-Mbps-only Ethernet interface would be configured with the **interface ethernet** *number* configuration command, a 10/100 interface with the **interface fastethernet** *number* command, and a 10/100/1000 interface with the **interface gigabitethernet** *number* command.

Some Cisco routers have serial interfaces. As you might recall from Chapter 3, Cisco routers use serial interfaces to connect to a serial link. Each point-to-point serial link can then use High-Level Data Link Control (HDLC, the default) or Point-to-Point Protocol (PPP).

Routers refer to interfaces in many commands, first by the type of interface (Ethernet, Fast Ethernet, Serial, and so on) and then with a unique number of that router. On routers, the interface numbers might be a single number, two numbers separated by a slash, or three numbers separated by slashes. For example, all three of the following configuration commands are correct on at least one model of Cisco router:

```
interface ethernet 0
interface fastEthernet 0/1
interface gigabitethernet 0/0
interface serial 1/0/1
```

Two of the most common commands to display the interfaces, and their status, are the **show ip interface brief** and **show interfaces** commands. The first of these commands displays a list with one line per interface, with some basic information, including the interface IP address and interface status. The second command lists the interfaces, but with a large amount of information per interface. Example 17-1 shows a sample of each command.

Example 17-1   *Listing the Interfaces in a Router*

```
R1# show ip interface brief
Interface                   IP-Address      OK? Method Status                Protocol
Embedded-Service-Engine0/0  unassigned      YES NVRAM  administratively down down
GigabitEthernet0/0          172.16.1.1      YES NVRAM  down                  down
GigabitEthernet0/1          unassigned      YES manual administratively down down
Serial0/0/0                 172.16.4.1      YES NVRAM  up                    up
Serial0/0/1                 172.16.5.1      YES NVRAM  up                    up
Serial0/1/0                 unassigned      YES NVRAM  up                    up
Serial0/1/1                 unassigned      YES NVRAM  administratively down down


R1# show interfaces serial 0/0/0
Serial0/0/0 is up, line protocol is up
  Hardware is WIC MBRD Serial
  Description: Link in lab to R2's S0/0/1
  Internet address is 172.16.4.1/24
  MTU 1500 bytes, BW 1544 Kbit/sec, DLY 20000 usec,
     reliability 255/255, txload 1/255, rxload 1/255
  Encapsulation HDLC, loopback not set
  Keepalive set (10 sec)
  Last input 00:00:03, output 00:00:06, output hang never
  Last clearing of "show interface" counters never
```

```
    Input queue: 0/75/0/0 (size/max/drops/flushes); Total output drops: 0
    Queueing strategy: fifo
    Output queue: 0/40 (size/max)
    5 minute input rate 0 bits/sec, 0 packets/sec
    5 minute output rate 0 bits/sec, 0 packets/sec
       42 packets input, 3584 bytes, 0 no buffer
       Received 42 broadcasts (0 IP multicasts)
       0 runts, 0 giants, 0 throttles
       0 input errors, 0 CRC, 0 frame, 0 overrun, 0 ignored, 0 abort
       41 packets output, 3481 bytes, 0 underruns
       0 output errors, 0 collisions, 4 interface resets
       3 unknown protocol drops
       0 output buffer failures, 0 output buffers swapped out
       0 carrier transitions
       DCD=up  DSR=up  DTR=up  RTS=up  CTS=up
```

17

NOTE Commands that refer to router interfaces can be significantly shortened by truncating the words. For example, **sh int fa0/0** can be used instead of **show interfaces fastethernet 0/0**. In fact, many network engineers, when looking over someone's shoulder, would say something like "just do a show int F-A-oh-oh command" in this case, rather than speaking the long version of the command.

Also, note that the **show interfaces** command lists a text interface description on about the third line, if configured. In this case, interface S0/0/0 had been previously configured with the **description Link in lab to R2's S0/0/1** command in interface configuration mode for interface S0/0/0. The **description** interface subcommand provides an easy way to keep small notes about what router interfaces connect to which neighboring devices, with the **show interfaces** command listing that information.

Interface Status Codes

Each interface has two *interface status codes*. To be usable, the two interface status codes must be in an "up" state. The first status code refers essentially to whether Layer 1 is working, and the second status code mainly (but not always) refers to whether the data link layer protocol is working. Table 17-2 summarizes these two status codes.

Table 17-2   Interface Status Codes and Their Meanings

Name	Location	General Meaning
Line status	First status code	Refers to the Layer 1 status. (For example, is the cable installed, is it the right/wrong cable, is the device on the other end powered on?)
Protocol status	Second status code	Refers generally to the Layer 2 status. It is always down if the line status is down. If the line status is up, a protocol status of down is usually caused by a mismatched data link layer configuration.

Several combinations of interface status codes exist, as summarized in Table 17-3. The table lists the status codes in order, from being disabled on purpose by the configuration to a fully working state.

Table 17-3 Typical Combinations of Interface Status Codes

Line Status	Protocol Status	Typical Reasons
Administratively down	Down	The interface has a **shutdown** command configured on it.
Down	Down	The interface is not **shutdown**, but the physical layer has a problem. For example, no cable has been attached to the interface, or with Ethernet, the switch interface on the other end of the cable is shut down or the switch is powered off.
Up	Down	Almost always refers to data link layer problems, most often configuration problems. For example, serial links have this combination when one router was configured to use PPP and the other defaults to use HDLC.
Up	Up	Layer 1 and Layer 2 of this interface are functioning.

For some examples, look back at Example 17-1's **show ip interface brief** command, to the three interfaces in the following list. The interfaces in this list each have a different combination of interface status codes; the list details the specific reasons for this status code in the lab used to create this example for the book.

G0/0: The interface is down/down, in this case because no cable was connected to the interface.

G0/1: The interface is administratively down/down, because the configuration includes the **shutdown** command under the G0/1 interface.

S0/0/0: The interface is up/up because a serial cable is installed, connected to another router in a lab, and is working.

Router Interface IP Addresses

Cisco enterprise routers require at least some configuration beyond the default configuration before they will do their primary job: routing IP packets. The following facts tell us that to make a router ready to route IPv4 packets on an interface, you need to enable the interface and assign it an IPv4 address:

■ Most Cisco router interfaces default to a disabled (**shutdown**) state and should be enabled with the **no shutdown** interface subcommand.

■ Cisco routers do not route IP packets in or out an interface until an IP address and mask have been configured; by default, no interfaces have an IP address and mask.

■ Cisco routers attempt to route IP packets for any interfaces that are in an up/up state and that have an IP address/mask assigned.

To configure the address and mask, simply use the **ip address** *address mask* interface subcommand. Figure 17-6 shows a simple IPv4 network, the same network used in several of the subnetting examples in Part IV of this book. The figure shows the IPv4 addresses on Router R1, with Example 17-2 showing the matching configuration.

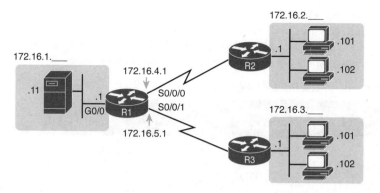

Figure 17-6 *IPv4 Addresses Used in Example 17-2*

Example 17-2 *Configuring IP Addresses on Cisco Routers*

```
R1# configure terminal
Enter configuration commands, one per line.  End with CNTL/Z.
R1config)# interface G0/0
R1(config-if)# ip address 172.16.1.1 255.255.255.0
R1(config-if)# no shutdown
R1(config-if)# interface S0/0/0
R1(config-if)# ip address 172.16.4.1 255.255.255.0
R1(config-if)# no shutdown
R1(config-if)# interface S0/0/1
R1(config-if)# ip address 172.16.5.1 255.255.255.0
R1(config-if)# no shutdown
R1(config-if)# ^Z
R1#
```

Example 17-3 shows the output of the **show protocols** command. This command confirms the state of each of the three R1 interfaces in Figure 17-6 and the IP address and mask configured on those same interfaces.

Example 17-3 *Verifying IP Addresses on Cisco Routers*

```
R1# show protocols
Global values:
  Internet Protocol routing is enabled
Embedded-Service-Engine0/0 is administratively down, line protocol is down
GigabitEthernet0/0 is up, line protocol is up
  Internet address is 172.16.1.1/24
GigabitEthernet0/1 is administratively down, line protocol is down
Serial0/0/0 is up, line protocol is up
  Internet address is 172.16.4.1/24
Serial0/0/1 is up, line protocol is up
  Internet address is 172.16.5.1/24
Serial0/1/0 is administratively down, line protocol is down
Serial0/1/1 is administratively down, line protocol is down
```

One of the first actions to take when verifying whether a router is working is to find the interfaces, check the interface status, and check to see whether the correct IP addresses and masks are used. Examples 17-1 and 17-3 showed samples of the key **show** commands, while Table 17-4 summarizes those commands and the types of information they display.

Table 17-4 Key Commands to List Router Interface Status

Command	Lines of Output per Interface	IP Configuration Listed	Interface Status Listed?
show ip interface brief	1	Address	Yes
show protocols [*type number*]	1 or 2	Address/mask	Yes
show interfaces [*type number*]	Many	Address/mask	Yes

Bandwidth and Clock Rate on Serial Interfaces

Cisco happens to place more of the WAN technologies in the ICND2 half of CCNA Routing and Switching exam content; however, you also need to be able to practice router configurations for ICND1 exam preparation, which could include using serial interfaces on any routers you buy or borrow for your lab. If you decide to build your own study lab with real gear, you need to know just a little more information about serial links. This last topic in the chapter discusses those details.

As mentioned back in Chapter 3, WAN serial links can run at a wide variety of speeds. To deal with the wide range of speeds, routers physically slave themselves to the speed as dictated by the CSU/DSU through a process called *clocking*. As a result, routers can use serial links without the need for additional configuration or autonegotiation to sense the serial link's speed. The CSU/DSU knows the speed, the CSU/DSU sends clock pulses over the cable to the router, and the router reacts to the clocking signal.

To build a serial link in a home lab, the routers can use serial interface cards that normally use an external CSU/DSU, and make a serial link, without requiring the expense of two CSU/DSUs. Chapter 3's Figure 3-5 introduced this concept, and it is repeated here as Figure 17-7. To make it work, the link uses two serial cables—one a DTE cable and the other a DCE cable—which swap the transmit and receive pair on the cables.

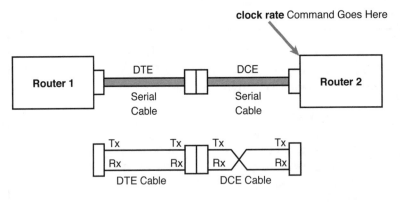

Figure 17-7 *Serial Link in Lab*

Using the correct cabling works, as long as you add one command: the **clock rate** interface subcommand. This command tells that router the speed at which to transmit bits on a serial link like the one shown in Figure 17-7. The **clock rate** command is not needed on real serial links, because the CSU/DSU provides the clocking. When you create a serial link in the lab using cables, without any real CSU/DSUs on the link, the router with the DCE cable must supply that clocking function, and the **clock rate** command tells the router to provide it.

> **NOTE** Newer router IOS versions automatically add a default **clock rate 2000000** command on serial interfaces that have a DCE cable connected to them. While helpful, this speed might be too high for some types of back-to-back serial cables, so consider using a lower speed in lab.

Example 17-4 shows the configuration of the **clock rate** command using the same Router R1 used in the earlier Example 17-2. The end of the example verifies that this router can use the **clock rate** command with the **show controllers** command. This command confirms that R1 has a V.35 DCE cable connected.

Example 17-4 *Router R1 Configuration with the* clock rate *Command*

```
R1# show running-config
! lines omitted for brevity
interface Serial0/0/0
 ip address 172.16.4.1 255.255.255.0
 clock rate 2000000
!
interface Serial0/0/1
 ip address 172.16.5.1 255.255.255.0
 clock rate 128000

! lines omitted for brevity


R1# show controllers serial 0/0/1
Interface Serial0
Hardware is PowerQUICC MPC860
DCE V.35, clock rate 128000
idb at 0x8169BB20, driver data structure at 0x816A35E4
! Lines omitted for brevity
```

> **NOTE** The **clock rate** command does not allow just any speed to be configured. However, the list of speeds does vary from router to router.

Some people confuse the router **bandwidth** command with the **clock rate** command. The **clock rate** command sets the actual Layer 1 speed used on the link, if no CSU/DSU is used, as just described. Conversely, every router interface has a bandwidth setting, either by default or configured. The bandwidth of the interface is the documented speed of the interface, which does not have to match the actual Layer 1 speed used on the interface.

17

That bandwidth setting does not impact how fast the interface transmits data. Instead, routers use the interface bandwidth setting as both documentation and as input to some other processes. For instance, the Open Shortest Path First (OSPF) and Enhanced Interior Gateway Routing Protocol (EIGRP) routing protocols, discussed in the ICND2 part of the CCNA Routing and Switching material, base their routing protocol metrics on the bandwidth by default.

Example 17-5 highlights the bandwidth setting on Router R1's S0/0/1 interface, as configured in the previous example. In that previous example, the **clock rate 128000** command sets the clock rate to 128 kbps, but it leaves the **bandwidth** command unset. As a result, IOS uses the default serial bandwidth setting of 1544, which means 1544 kbps—which is the speed of a T1 serial link.

Example 17-5   *Router Bandwidth Settings*

```
R1# show interfaces s0/0/1
Serial0/0/1 is up, line protocol is up
  Hardware is WIC MBRD Serial
  Description: link to R3
  Internet address is 10.1.13.1/24
  MTU 1500 bytes, BW 1544 Kbit/sec, DLY 20000 usec,
     reliability 255/255, txload 1/255, rxload 1/255
  Encapsulation HDLC, loopback not set
```

The common mistake people make is to know about clock rate, but mistakenly think that the bandwidth setting is just another term for "clock rate." It is not. Follow these rules to find these two interface settings:

To see the clock rate, look for the **clock rate** interface subcommand in the configuration, or use the **show controllers serial** *type number* command (as shown in Example 17-4.)

To see the bandwidth setting on an interface, look for the **bandwidth** interface subcommand in the configuration, or use the **show interfaces** [*type number*] command (as shown in Example 17-5).

Note that using default bandwidth settings on most router interfaces makes sense, with the exception of serial interfaces. IOS defaults to a bandwidth of 1544 (meaning 1544 kbps, or 1.544 Mbps) for serial interfaces, regardless of the speed dictated by the provider or by a **clock rate** command in the lab. Most engineers set the bandwidth to match the actual speed, for example, using the **bandwidth 128** interface subcommand on a link running at 128 kbps. On Ethernet 10/100 or 10/100/1000 interfaces, the router knows the speed used, and dynamically sets the Ethernet interface's bandwidth to match.

Router Auxiliary Port

Both routers and switches have a console port to allow administrative access, but most Cisco routers have an extra physical port called an auxiliary (Aux) port. The Aux port typically serves as a means to make a phone call to connect into the router to issue commands from the CLI.

The Aux port works like the console port, except that the Aux port is typically connected through a cable to an external analog modem, which in turn connects to a phone line. Then, the engineer uses a PC, terminal emulator, and modem to call the remote router. After being connected, the engineer can use the terminal emulator to access the router CLI, starting in user mode as usual.

Aux ports can be configured beginning with the **line aux 0** command to reach aux line configuration mode. From there, all the commands for the console line, covered mostly in Chapter 8, "Configuring Basic Switch Management," can be used. For example, the **login** and **password** *password* subcommands on the aux line could be used to set up simple password checking when a user dials in.

Chapter Review

One key to doing well on the exams is to perform repetitive spaced review sessions. Review this chapter's material using either the tools in the book, DVD, or interactive tools for the same material found on the book's companion website. Refer to the "Your Study Plan" element for more details. Table 17-5 outlines the key review elements and where you can find them. To better track your study progress, record when you completed these activities in the second column.

Table 17-5 Chapter Review Tracking

Review Element	Review Date(s)	Resource Used
Review key topics		Book, DVD/website
Review key terms		Book, DVD/website
Repeat DIKTA questions		Book, PCPT
Review memory tables		Book, DVD/website
Do labs		Blog
Review command tables		Book

Review All the Key Topics

Table 17-6 Key Topics for Chapter 17

Key Topic	Description	Page Number
List	Steps required to install a router	388
List	Similarities between a router CLI and a switch CLI	390
List	Items covered for switches in Chapters 6 and 8 that differ in some way on routers	391
Table 17-2	Router interface status codes and their meanings	393
Table 17-3	Combinations of the two interface status codes and the likely reasons for each combination	394
Table 17-4	Commands useful to display interface IPv4 addresses, masks, and interface status	396

Key Terms You Should Know

bandwidth, clock rate

Command References

Tables 17-7 and 17-8 list configuration and verification commands used in this chapter. As an easy review exercise, cover the left column in a table, read the right column, and try to recall the command without looking. Then repeat the exercise, covering the right column, and try to recall what the command does.

Table 17-7 Chapter 17 Configuration Command Reference

Command	Description
interface *type number*	Global command that moves the user into configuration mode of the named interface.
ip address *address mask*	Interface subcommand that sets the router's IPv4 address and mask.
[no] shutdown	Interface subcommand that enables (**no shutdown**) or disables (**shutdown**) the interface.
**duplex {full	half	auto}**	Interface command that sets the duplex, or sets the use of IEEE autonegotiation, for router LAN interfaces that support multiple speeds.
**speed {10	100	1000}**	Interface command for router Gigabit (10/100/1000) interfaces that sets the speed at which the router interface sends and receives data.
clock rate *rate-in-bps*	Interface command that sets the speed at which the router supplies a clocking signal, applicable only when the router has a DCE cable installed. The unit is bits/second.
description *text*	An interface subcommand with which you can type a string of text to document information about that particular interface.
bandwidth *rate-in-kbps*	Interface command that sets the speed at which the router considers the interface to operate, but does not dictate or control the actual speed. IOS then uses this setting for features that need some information about the speed of the interface (for example, some routing protocols use the information when calculating metrics). The unit is kilobits/second.

Table 17-8   Chapter 17 EXEC Command Reference

Command	Purpose
show interfaces [*type number*]	Lists a large set of informational messages about each interface, or about the one specifically listed interface.
show ip interface brief	Lists a single line of information about each interface, including the IP address, line and protocol status, and the method with which the address was configured (manual or Dynamic Host Configuration Protocol [DHCP]).
show protocols [*type number*]	Lists information about the listed interface (or all interfaces if the interface is omitted), including the IP address, mask, and line/protocol status.
show controllers [*type number*]	Lists many lines of information per interface, or for one interface, for the hardware controller of the interface. On serial interfaces, this command identifies the cable as either a DCE or DTE cable.

17

CHAPTER 18

Configuring IPv4 Addresses and Static Routes

This chapter covers the following exam topics:

Routers route IPv4 packets. That simple statement actually carries a lot of hidden meaning. For routers to route packets, routers follow a routing process. That routing process relies on information called IP routes. Each IP route lists a destination—an IP network, IP subnet, or some other group of IP addresses. Each route also lists instructions that tell the router where to forward packets sent to addresses in that IP network or subnet. For routers to do a good job of routing packets, routers need to have a detailed, accurate list of IP routes.

Routers use three methods to add IPv4 routes to their IPv4 routing tables. Routers first learn *connected routes*, which are routes for subnets attached to a router interface. Routers can also use *static routes*, which are routes created through a configuration command (**ip route**) that tells the router what route to put in the IPv4 routing table. And routers can use a routing protocol, in which routers tell each other about all their known routes, so that all routers can learn and build routes to all networks and subnets.

This chapter begins by reintroducing the IP routing process that relies on these routes. This IP routing discussion both reviews the concepts from Chapter 4, "Fundamentals of IPv4 Addressing and Routing," plus takes the concepts deeper, including showing information needed in a single IP route. Then, the second major heading in this chapter discusses connected routes, including variations of connected routes to VLANs connected to a router's VLAN trunk, and for connected routes on Layer 3 switches.

The final major section then looks at static routes, which let the engineer tell the router what route(s) to add to the router's IP routing table. The static route section also shows how to configure a static default route that is used when no other route matches an IP packet. Dynamic routing, using the Routing Information Protocol (RIP), awaits in Chapter 19, "Learning IPv4 Routes with RIPv2."

"Do I Know This Already?" Quiz

Take the quiz (either here, or use the PCPT software) if you want to use the score to help you decide how much time to spend on this chapter. The answers are at the bottom of the page following the quiz, and the explanations are in DVD Appendix C and in the PCPT software.

Table 18-1   "Do I Know This Already?" Foundation Topics Section-to-Question Mapping

Foundation Topics Section	Questions
IP Routing	1–2
Configuring Connected Routes	3–5
Configuring Static Routes	6–7

1. A PC user opens a command prompt and uses the **ipconfig** command to see that the PC's IP address and mask are 192.168.4.77 and 255.255.255.224. The user then runs a test using the **ping 192.168.4.117** command. Which of the following answers is the most likely to happen?

   a. The PC sends packets directly to the host with address 192.168.4.117.

   b. The PC sends packets to its default gateway.

   c. The PC sends a DNS query for 192.168.4.117.

   d. The PC sends an ARP looking for the MAC address of the DHCP server.

2. Router R1 lists a route in its routing table. Which of the following answers list a fact from a route that the router then compares to the packet's destination address? (Choose two answers.)

   a. Mask

   b. Next-hop router

   c. Subnet ID

   d. Outgoing interface

3. Router 1 has a Fast Ethernet interface 0/0 with IP address 10.1.1.1. The interface is connected to a switch. This connection is then migrated to use 802.1Q trunking. Which of the following commands could be part of a valid configuration for Router 1's Fa0/0 interface? (Choose two answers.)

   a. interface fastethernet 0/0.4

   b. dot1q enable

   c. dot1q enable 4

   d. trunking enable

   e. trunking enable 4

   f. encapsulation dot1q 4

4. A Layer 3 switch has been configured to route IP packets between VLANs 1, 2, and 3, which connect to subnets 172.20.1.0/25, 172.20.2.0/25, and 172.20.3.0/25, respectively. The engineer issues a **show ip route** command on the Layer 3 switch, listing the connected routes. Which of the following answers lists a piece of information that should be in at least one of the routes?

   a. Interface Gigabit Ethernet 0/0.3

   b. Next-hop router 172.20.4.1

   c. Interface VLAN 2

   d. Mask 255.255.255.0

5. An engineer configures a static IPv4 route on Router R1. Which of the following pieces of information should not be listed as a parameter in the configuration command that creates this static IPv4 route?

   a. The destination subnet's subnet ID

   b. The next-hop router's IP address

   c. The next-hop router's neighboring interface

   d. The subnet mask

6. Which of the following commands correctly configures a static route?

   a. ip route 10.1.3.0 255.255.255.0 10.1.130.253

   b. ip route 10.1.3.0 serial 0

   c. ip route 10.1.3.0 /24 10.1.130.253

   d. ip route 10.1.3.0 /24 serial 0

7. A network engineer configures the **ip route 10.1.1.0 255.255.255.0 s0/0/0** command on a router, and then issues a **show ip route** command from enable mode. No routes for subnet 10.1.1.0/24 appear in the output. Which of the following could be true?

a. The **ip route** command has incorrect syntax and was rejected in config mode.

b. interface s0/0/0 is down.

c. The router has no up/up interfaces in Class A network 10.0.0.0.

d. The **ip route** command is missing a next-hop router IP address.

Foundation Topics

IP Routing

IP routing—the process of forwarding IP packets—delivers packets across entire TCP/IP networks, from the device that originally builds the IP packet to the device that is supposed to receive the packet. In other words, IP routing delivers IP packets from the sending host to the destination host.

The complete end-to-end routing process relies on network layer logic on hosts and on routers. The sending host uses Layer 3 concepts to create an IP packet, forwarding the IP packet to the host's default gateway (default router). The process requires Layer 3 logic on the routers as well, by which the routers compare the destination address in the packet to their routing tables, to decide where to forward the IP packet next.

The routing process also relies on data-link and physical details at each link. IP routing relies on serial links, Ethernet LANs, wireless LANs, and many other networks that implement data link and physical layer standards. These lower-layer devices and protocols move the IP packets around the TCP/IP network by encapsulating and transmitting the packets inside data link layer frames.

Those previous two paragraphs summarize the key concepts about IP routing as introduced back in Chapter 4. Next, this section reviews IP routing, while taking the discussion another step or two deeper, taking advantage of the additional depth of knowledge discussed in Parts II and III of this book.

NOTE   Some references also incorrectly claim that the term *IP routing* includes the function of dynamically learning routes with IP routing protocols. IP routing protocols play an important role, but the term *IP routing* refers to the packet-forwarding process only.

IPv4 Routing Process Reference

Because you have already seen the basics back in Chapter 4, this section collects the routing process into steps for reference. The steps use many specific terms discussed in Parts II and III of this book. The upcoming descriptions and example then discuss these summaries of routing logic to make sure that each step is clear.

The routing process starts with the host that creates the IP packet. First, the host asks the question: Is the destination IP address of this new packet in my local subnet? The host uses its own IP address/mask to determine the range of addresses in the local subnet. Based on its own opinion of the range of addresses in the local subnet, a LAN-based host acts as follows:

Step 1. If the destination is local, send directly:

    A. Find the destination host's MAC address. Use the already-known Address Resolution Protocol (ARP) table entry, or use ARP messages to learn the information.

    B. Encapsulate the IP packet in a data-link frame, with the destination data-link address of the destination host.

Step 2. If the destination is not local, send to the default gateway:

    A. Find the default gateway's MAC address. Use the already-known Address Resolution Protocol (ARP) table entry, or use ARP messages to learn the information.

    B. Encapsulate the IP packet in a data-link frame, with the destination data-link address of the default gateway.

Figure 18-1 summarizes these same concepts. In the figure, host A sends a local packet directly to host D. However, for packets to host B, on the other side of a router and therefore in a different subnet, host A sends the packet to its default router (R1). (As a reminder, the terms *default gateway* and *default router* are synonyms.)

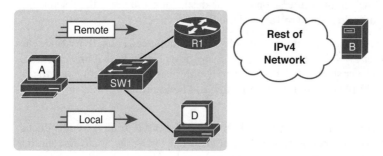

Figure 18-1 *Host Routing Logic Summary*

Routers have a little more routing work to do as compared with hosts. While the host logic began with an IP packet sitting in memory, a router has some work to do before getting to that point. With the following five-step summary of a router's routing logic, the router takes the first two steps just to receive the frame and extract the IP packet, before thinking about the packet's destination address at Step 3. The steps are as follows:

1. For each received data-link frame, choose whether or not to process the frame. Process it if

   A. The frame has no errors (per the data-link trailer Frame Check Sequence [FCS] field).

   B. The frame's destination data-link address is the router's address (or an appropriate multicast or broadcast address).

2. If choosing to process the frame at Step 1, de-encapsulate the packet from inside the data-link frame.

3. Make a routing decision. To do so, compare the packet's destination IP address to the routing table and find the route that matches the destination address. This route identifies the outgoing interface of the router and possibly the next-hop router.

4. Encapsulate the packet into a data-link frame appropriate for the outgoing interface. When forwarding out LAN interfaces, use ARP as needed to find the next device's MAC address.

5. Transmit the frame out the outgoing interface, as listed in the matched IP route.

This routing process summary lists many details, but sometimes you can think about the routing process in simpler terms. For example, leaving out some details, this paraphrase of the step list details the same big concepts:

> The router receives a frame, removes the packet from inside the frame, decides where to forward the packet, puts the packet into another frame, and sends the frame.

To give you a little more perspective on these steps, Figure 18-2 breaks down the same five-step routing process as a diagram. The figure shows a packet arriving from the left, entering a router Ethernet interface, with an IP destination of host C. The figure shows the packet arriving, encapsulated inside an Ethernet frame (both header and trailer).

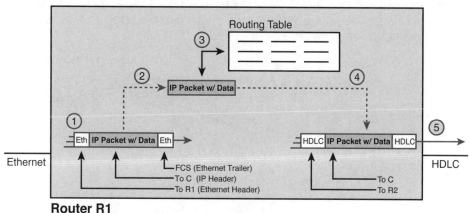

Figure 18-2 *Router Routing Logic Summary*

Router R1 processes the frame and packet as shown with the numbers in the figure, matching the same five-step process described just before the figure, as follows:

1. Router R1 notes that the received Ethernet frame passes the FCS check, and that the destination Ethernet MAC address is R1's MAC address, so R1 processes the frame.

2. R1 de-encapsulates the IP packet from inside the Ethernet frame's header and trailer.

3. R1 compares the IP packet's destination IP address to R1's IP routing table.

4. R1 encapsulates the IP packet inside a new data-link frame, in this case, inside a High-Level Data Link Control (HDLC) header and trailer.

5. R1 transmits the IP packet, inside the new HDLC frame, out the serial link on the right.

> **NOTE**   This chapter uses several figures that show an IP packet encapsulated inside a data link layer frame. These figures often show both the data-link header as well as the data-link trailer, with the IP packet in the middle. The IP packets all include the IP header, plus any encapsulated data.

An Example of IP Routing

The next several pages walk you through an example that discusses each routing step, in order, through multiple devices. That example uses a case in which host A (172.16.1.9) sends a packet to host B (172.16.2.9), with host routing logic and the five steps showing how R1 forwards the packet.

Figure 18-3 shows a typical IP addressing diagram for an IPv4 network with typical address abbreviations. The diagram can get a little too messy if it lists the full IP address for every router interface. When possible, these diagrams usually list the subnet, and then the last octet or two of the individual IP addresses—just enough so that you know the IP address, but with less clutter. For example, host A uses IP address 172.16.1.9, taking from subnet 172.16.1.0/24 (in which all addresses begin 172.16.1), and the .9 beside the host A icon. As another example, R1 uses address 172.16.1.1 on its LAN interface, 172.16.4.1 on one serial interface, and 172.16.5.1 on the other serial interface.

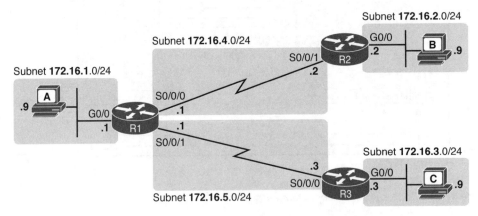

Figure 18-3   *IPv4 Network Used to Show Five-Step Routing Example*

Now on to the example, with host A (172.16.1.9) sending a packet to host B (172.16.2.9).

Host Forwards the IP Packet to the Default Router (Gateway)

In this example, host A uses some application that sends data to host B (172.16.2.9). After host A has the IP packet sitting in memory, host A's logic reduces to the following:

- My IP address/mask is 172.16.1.9/24, so my local subnet contains numbers 172.16.1.0–172.16.1.255 (including the subnet ID and subnet broadcast address).

- The destination address is 172.16.2.9, which is clearly not in my local subnet.

- Send the packet to my default gateway, which is set to 172.16.1.1.

- To send the packet, encapsulate it in an Ethernet frame. Make the destination MAC address be R1's G0/0 MAC address (host A's default gateway).

Figure 18-4 pulls these concepts together, showing the destination IP address and destination MAC address in the frame and packet sent by host A in this case. Note that the figure uses a common drawing convention in networking, showing an Ethernet as a few lines, hiding all the detail of the Layer 2 switches.

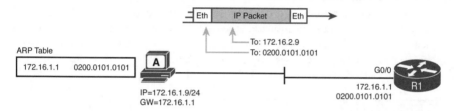

Figure 18-4 *Host A Sends Packet to Host B*

Routing Step 1: Decide Whether to Process the Incoming Frame

Routers receive many frames in an interface, particularly LAN interfaces. However, a router can and should ignore some of those frames. So, the first step in the routing process begins with a decision of whether a router should process the frame or silently discard (ignore) the frame.

First, the router does a simple but important check (Step 1A in the process summary) so that the router ignores all frames that had bit errors during transmission. The router uses the data-link trailer's FCS field to check the frame, and if errors occurred in transmission, the router discards the frame. (The router makes no attempt at error recovery; that is, the router does not ask the sender to retransmit the data.)

The router also checks the destination data-link address (Step 1B in the summary) to decide whether the frame is intended for the router. For example, frames sent to the router's unicast MAC address for that interface are clearly sent to that router. However, a router can actually receive a frame sent to some other unicast MAC address, and routers should ignore these frames.

For example, routers will receive some unicast frames sent to other devices in the VLAN just because of how LAN switches work. Think back to how LAN switches forward unknown unicast frames: frames for which the switch does not list the destination MAC address in the MAC address table. The LAN switch floods those frames. The result? Routers sometimes receive frames destined for some other device, with some other device's MAC address listed as the destination MAC address. Routers should ignore those frames.

In this example, host A sends a frame destined for R1's MAC address. So, after the frame is received, and after R1 confirms with the FCS that no errors occurred, R1 confirms that the frame is destined for R1's MAC address (0200.0101.0101 in this case). All checks have been passed, so R1 will process the frame, as shown in Figure 18-5. (Note that the large rectangle in the figure represents the internals of Router R1.)

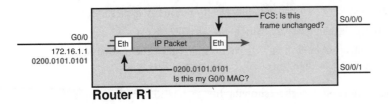

Figure 18-5   *Routing Step 1, on Router R1: Checking FCS and Destination MAC*

Routing Step 2: De-encapsulation of the IP Packet

After the router knows that it ought to process the received frame (per Step 1), the next step is a relatively simple step: de-encapsulating the packet. In router memory, the router no longer needs the original frame's data-link header and trailer, so the router removes and discards them, leaving the IP packet, as shown in Figure 18-6. Note that the destination IP address remains unchanged (172.16.2.9).

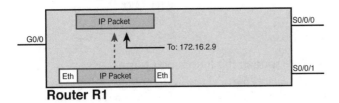

Figure 18-6   *Routing Step 2 on Router R1: De-encapsulating the Packet*

Routing Step 3: Choosing Where to Forward the Packet

While routing Step 2 required little thought, Step 3 requires the most thought of all the steps. At this point, the router needs to make a choice about where to forward the packet next. That process uses the router's IP routing table, with some matching logic to compare the packet's destination address with the table.

First, an IP routing table lists multiple routes. Each individual route contains several facts, which in turn can be grouped as shown in Figure 18-7. Part of each route is used to match the destination address of the packet, while the rest of the route lists forwarding instructions: where to send the packet next.

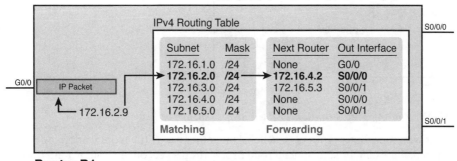

Router R1

Figure 18-7 *Routing Step 3 on Router R1: Matching the Routing Table*

Focus on the entire routing table for a moment, and notice the fact that it lists five routes. Earlier, Figure 18-3 showed the entire example network, with five subnets, so R1 has a route for each of the five subnets.

Next, look at the part of the five routes that Router R1 will use to match packets. To fully define each subnet, each route lists both the subnet ID and the subnet mask. When matching the IP packet's destination with the routing table, the router looks at the packet's destination IP address (172.16.2.9) and compares it to the range of addresses defined by each subnet. Specifically, the router looks at the subnet and mask information, which with a little math, the router can figure out in which of those subnets 172.16.2.9 resides (the route for subnet 172.16.2.0/24).

Finally, look to the right side of the figure, to the forwarding instructions for these five routes. After the router matches a specific route, the router uses the forwarding information in the route to tell the router where to send the packet next. In this case, the router matched the route for subnet 172.16.2.0/24, so R1 will forward the packet out its own interface S0/0/0, to Router R2 next, listed with its next-hop router IP address of 172.16.4.2.

> **NOTE** Routes for remote subnets typically list both an outgoing interface and next-hop router IP address. Routes for subnets that connect directly to the router list only the outgoing interface, because packets to these destinations do not need to be sent to another router.

Routing Step 4: Encapsulating the Packet in a New Frame

At this point, the router knows how it will forward the packet. However, routers cannot forward a packet without first wrapping a data-link header and trailer around it (encapsulation).

Encapsulating packets for serial links does not require a lot of thought, because of the simplicity of the HDLC and PPP protocols. As discussed back in Chapter 3, "Fundamentals of WANs," because serial links have only two devices on the link—the sender and the then-obvious receiver; the data-link addressing does not matter. In this example, R1 forwards the packet out S0/0/0, after encapsulating the packet inside an HDLC frame, as shown in Figure 18-8.

18

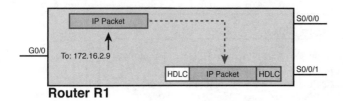

Figure 18-8   *Routing Step 4 on Router R1: Encapsulating the Packet*

Note that with some other types of data links, the router has a little more work to do at this routing step. For example, sometimes a router forwards packets out an Ethernet interface. To encapsulate the IP packet, the router would need to build an Ethernet header, and that Ethernet header's destination MAC address would need to list the correct value.

For example, consider this different sample network, with an Ethernet WAN link between Routers R1 and R2. R1 matches a route that tells R1 to forward the packet out R1's G0/1 Ethernet interface to 172.16.6.2 (R2) next. R1 needs to put R2's MAC address in the header, and to do that, R1 uses its IP ARP table information, as shown in Figure 18-9. If R1 did not have an ARP table entry for 172.16.6.2, R1 would first have to use ARP to learn the matching MAC address.

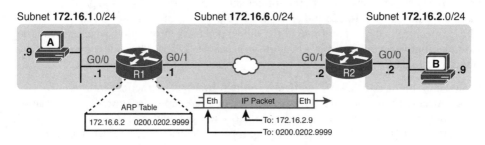

Figure 18-9   *Routing Step 4 on Router R1 with a LAN Outgoing Interface*

Routing Step 5: Transmitting the Frame

After the frame has been prepared, the router simply needs to transmit the frame. The router might have to wait, particularly if other frames are already waiting their turn to exit the interface.

Configuring IP Addresses and Connected Routes

Cisco routers enable IPv4 routing globally, by default. Then, to make the router be ready to route packets on a particular interface, the interface must be configured with an IP address and the interface must be configured such that it comes up, reaching a "line status up, line protocol up" state. Only at that point can routers route IP packets in and out a particular interface.

After a router can route IP packets out one or more interfaces, the router needs some routes. Routers can add routes to their routing tables through three methods:

Connected routes: Added because of the configuration of the **ip address** interface sub-command on the local router

Static routes: Added because of the configuration of the **ip route** global command on the local router

Routing protocols: Added as a function by configuration on all routers, resulting in a process by which routers dynamically tell each other about the network so that they all learn routes

This second of three sections discusses several variations on how to configure connected routes, while the last major section discusses static routes.

Connected Routes and the ip address Command

A Cisco router automatically adds a route to its routing table for the subnet connected to each interface, assuming that the following two facts are true:

- The interface is in a working state. In other words, the interface status in the **show interfaces** command lists a line status of up and a protocol status of up.

- The interface has an IP address assigned through the **ip address** interface subcommand.

The concept of connected routes is relatively basic. The router of course needs to know the subnet number connected to each of its interfaces, so the router can route packets to that subnet. The router does the math, taking the interface IP address and mask, and calculating the subnet ID. However, the router only needs that route when the interface is up and working, so the router includes a connected route in the routing table only when the interface is working.

Example 18-1 shows the connected routes on Router R1 in Figure 18-10. The first part of the example shows the configuration of IP addresses on all three of R1's interfaces. The end of the examples lists the output from the **show ip route** command, which lists these routes with a *c* as the route code, meaning *connected*.

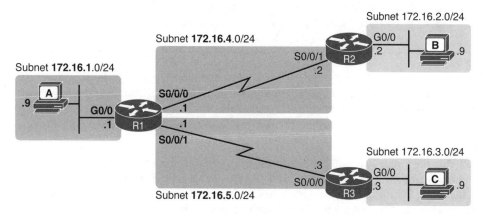

Figure 18-10 *Sample Network to Show Connected Routes*

Example 18-1   *Connected and Local Routes on Router R1*

```
! Excerpt from show running-config follows...
!
interface GigabitEthernet0/0
 ip address 172.16.1.1 255.255.255.0
!
interface Serial0/0/0
 ip address 172.16.4.1 255.255.255.0
!
interface Serial0/0/1
 ip address 172.16.5.1 255.255.255.0

R1# show ip route
Codes: L - local, C - connected, S - static, R - RIP, M - mobile, B - BGP
       D - EIGRP, EX - EIGRP external, O - OSPF, IA - OSPF inter area
       N1 - OSPF NSSA external type 1, N2 - OSPF NSSA external type 2
       E1 - OSPF external type 1, E2 - OSPF external type 2
       i - IS-IS, su - IS-IS summary, L1 - IS-IS level-1, L2 - IS-IS level-2
       ia - IS-IS inter area, * - candidate default, U - per-user static route
       o - ODR, P - periodic downloaded static route, H - NHRP, l - LISP
       + - replicated route, % - next hop override

Gateway of last resort is not set

      172.16.0.0/16 is variably subnetted, 6 subnets, 2 masks
C        172.16.1.0/24 is directly connected, GigabitEthernet0/0
L        172.16.1.1/32 is directly connected, GigabitEthernet0/0
C        172.16.4.0/24 is directly connected, Serial0/0/0
L        172.16.4.1/32 is directly connected, Serial0/0/0
C        172.16.5.0/24 is directly connected, Serial0/0/1
L        172.16.5.1/32 is directly connected, Serial0/0/1
```

Take a moment to look closely at each of the three highlighted routes in the output of **show ip route**. Each lists a C in the first column, and each has text that says "directly connected"; both identify the route as connected to the router. The early part of each route lists the matching parameters (subnet ID and mask), as shown in the earlier example in Figure 18-7. The end of each of these routes lists the outgoing interface.

Note that the router also automatically produces a different kind of route, called a *local route*. The local routes define a route for the one specific IP address configured on the router interface. Each local route has a /32 prefix length, defining a *host route*, which defines a route just for that one IP address. For example, the last local route, for 172.16.5.1/32, defines a route that matches only the IP address of 172.16.5.1. Routers use these local routes that list their own local IP addresses to more efficiently forward packets sent to the router itself.

The ARP Table on a Cisco Router

After a router has added these connected routes, the router can route IPv4 packets between those subnets. To do so, the router makes use of its IP ARP table.

The IPv4 ARP table lists the IPv4 address and matching MAC address of hosts connected to the same subnet as the router. When forwarding a packet to a host on the same subnet, the router encapsulates the packet, with a destination MAC address as found in the ARP table. If the router wants to forward a packet to an IP address on the same subnet as the router, but does not find an ARP table entry for that IP address, the router will use ARP messages to learn that device's MAC address.

Example 18-2 shows R1's ARP table based on the previous example. The output lists R1's own IP address of 172.16.1.1, with an age of -, meaning that this entry does not time out. Dynamically learned ARP table entries have an upward counter, like the 35-minute value for the ARP table entry for IP address 172.16.1.9. By default, IOS will timeout (remove) an ARP table entry after 240 minutes in which the entry is not used. (IOS resets the timer to 0 when an ARP table entry is used.) Note that to experiment in lab, you might want to empty all dynamic entries (or a single entry for one IP address) using the **clear ip arp** [*ip-address*] EXEC command.

Example 18-2 *Displaying a Router's IP ARP Table*

```
R2# show ip arp
Protocol  Address          Age (min)  Hardware Addr   Type   Interface
Internet  172.16.1.1             -     0200.2222.2222  ARPA   GigabitEthernet0/0
Internet  172.16.1.9            35     0200.3333.3333  ARPA   GigabitEthernet0/0
```

Thinking about how Router R1 forwards a packet to host A (172.16.1.9), over that final subnet, R1 does the following:

1. R1 looks in its ARP table for an entry for 172.16.1.9.

2. R1 encapsulates the IP packet in an Ethernet frame, adding destination 0200.3333.3333 to the Ethernet header (as taken from the ARP table).

3. R1 transmits the frame out interface G0/0.

Routing Between Subnets on VLANs

Almost all enterprise networks use VLANs. To route IP packets in and out of those VLANs—or more accurately, the subnets that sit on each of those VLANs—some router needs to have an IP address in each subnet and have a connected route to each of those subnets. Then the hosts in each subnet can use the router IP addresses as their default gateways, respectively.

Three options exist for connecting a router to each subnet on a VLAN. However, the first option requires too many interfaces and links, and is only mentioned to make the list complete:

■ Use a router, with one router LAN interface and cable connected to the switch for each and every VLAN (typically not used).

■ Use a router, with a VLAN trunk connecting to a LAN switch.

■ Use a Layer 3 switch.

Figure 18-11 shows an example network where the second and third options both happen to be used. The figure shows a central site campus LAN on the left, with 12 VLANs. At the central site, two of the switches act as Layer 3 switches, combining the functions of a router and a switch, routing between all 12 subnets/VLANs. The remote branch sites on the right side of the figure each use two VLANs; each router uses a VLAN trunk to connect to and route for both VLANs.

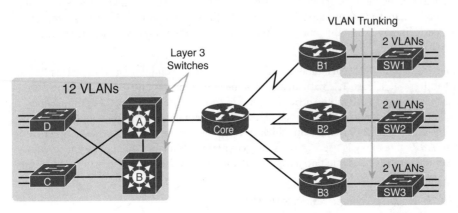

Figure 18-11   *Layer 3 Switching at the Central Site*

Note that Figure 18-11 just shows an example. The engineer could use Layer 3 switching at each site, or routers with VLAN trunking at each site. This chapter focuses more on the details of how to configure the features, as discussed in the next few pages.

Configuring Routing to VLANs Using 802.1Q on Routers

This next topic discusses how to route packets to subnets associated with VLANs connected to a router 802.1Q trunk. That long description can be a bit of a chore to repeat each time someone wants to discuss this feature, so over time, the networking world has instead settled on a shorter and more interesting name for this feature: router-on-a-stick (ROAS).

ROAS uses router VLAN trunking configuration to give the router a logical router interface connected to each VLAN, and therefore each subnet that sits on a separate VLAN. That trunking configuration revolves around subinterfaces. The router needs to have an IP address/mask associated with each VLAN on the trunk. However, the router uses only one physical interface on which to configure the **ip address** command. Cisco solves this problem by creating multiple virtual router interfaces, one associated with each VLAN on that trunk (at least for each VLAN that you want the trunk to support). Cisco calls these virtual interfaces *subinterfaces*.

The ROAS configuration creates a subinterface for each VLAN on the trunk, and the router then treats all frames tagged with that associated VLAN ID as if they came in or out of that subinterface. Figure 18-12 shows the concept with Router B1, one of the branch routers from Figure 18-11. Because this router needs to route between only two VLANs, the figure also shows two subinterfaces, named G0/0.10 and G0/0.20, which create a new place in the configuration where the per-VLAN configuration settings can be made. The router treats frames tagged with VLAN 10 as if they came in or out of G0/0.10, and frames tagged with VLAN 20 as if they came in or out G0/0.20.

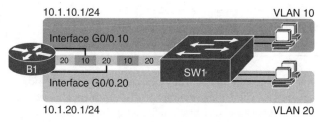

Figure 18-12 *Subinterfaces on Router B1*

In addition, most Cisco routers do not attempt to negotiate trunking, so in most cases, both the router and switch need to manually configure trunking. This chapter discusses the router side of that trunking configuration; the matching switch interface would need to be configured with the **switchport mode trunk** command.

Example 18-3 shows a full example of the 802.1Q trunking configuration required on Router B1 in the figure. More generally, these steps detail how to configure 802.1Q trunking on a router:

Step 1. Use the **interface** *type number.subint* command in global configuration mode to create a unique subinterface for each VLAN that needs to be routed.

Step 2. Use the **encapsulation dot1q** *vlan_id* command in subinterface configuration mode to enable 802.1Q and associate one specific VLAN with the subinterface.

Step 3. Use the **ip address** *address mask* command in subinterface configuration mode to configure IP settings (address and mask).

Example 18-3 *Router Configuration for the 802.1Q Encapsulation Shown in Figure 18-12*

```
B1# show running-config
! Only pertinent lines shown
interface gigabitethernet 0/0
! No IP address up here! No encapsulation up here!
!
interface gigabitethernet 0/0.10
 encapsulation dot1q 10
 ip address 10.1.10.1 255.255.255.0
!
interface gigabitethernet 0/0.20
 encapsulation dot1q 20
 ip address 10.1.20.1 255.255.255.0
!
B1# show ip route
Codes: L - local, C - connected, S - static, R - RIP, M - mobile, B - BGP
! Lines omitted for brevity

      10.0.0.0/8 is variably subnetted, 4 subnets, 2 masks
C        10.1.10.0/24 is directly connected, GigabitEthernet0/0.10
```

18

```
L        10.1.10.1/32 is directly connected, GigabitEthernet0/0.10
C        10.1.20.0/24 is directly connected, GigabitEthernet0/0.20
L        10.1.20.1/32 is directly connected, GigabitEthernet0/0.20
```

First, look at the subinterface numbers. The subinterface number begins with the period, like .10 and .20 in this case. These numbers can be any number from 1 up through a very large number (over 4 billion). The number just needs to be unique among all subinterfaces associated with this one physical interface. In fact, the subinterface number does not even have to match the associated VLAN ID. (The **encapsulation** command, and not the subinterface number, defines the VLAN ID associated with the subinterface.)

> **NOTE** Although not required, most sites do choose to make the subinterface number match the VLAN ID, as shown in Example 18-3, just to avoid confusion.

Each subinterface configuration lists two subcommands. One command (**encapsulation**) enables trunking and defines the VLAN whose frames are considered to be coming in and out of the subinterface. The **ip address** command works the same way it does on any other interface. Note that if the physical Ethernet interface reaches an up/up state, the subinterface should as well, which would then let the router add the connected routes shown at the bottom of the example.

Now that the router has a working interface, with IPv4 addresses configured, the router can route IPv4 packets on these subinterfaces. That is, the router treats these subinterfaces like any physical interface in terms of adding connected routes, matching those routes and forwarding packets to/from those connected subnets.

> **NOTE** As a brief aside, while Example 18-3 shows 802.1Q configuration, the Inter-Switch Link (ISL) configuration on the same router would be practically identical. Just substitute the keyword **isl** instead of **dot1q** in each case.

Example 18-3 shows one way to configure ROAS on a router, but that particular example avoids using the native VLAN. However, each 802.1Q trunk has one native VLAN, and when used, the configuration to use that native VLAN differs, with two options for the router side of the configuration:

- Configure the **ip address** command on the physical interface, but without an **encapsulation** command; the router considers this physical interface to be using the native VLAN.

- Configure the **ip address** command on a subinterface, and use the **encapsulation...native** subcommand.

Example 18-4 shows both configuration options with a small change to the same configuration in Example 18-3. In this case, VLAN 10 becomes the native VLAN. The top part of the example shows the option to configure the router to use native VLAN 10, assuming that the switch also has been configured to use native VLAN 10 as well. The second half of the example shows how to configure that same native VLAN on a subinterface.

Example 18-4 *Router Configuration Using Native VLAN 10 on Router B1*

```
! First option: put the native VLAN IP address on the physical interface
interface gigabitethernet 0/0
 ip address 10.1.10.1 255.255.255.0
!
interface gigabitethernet 0/0.20
 encapsulation dot1q 20
 ip address 10.1.20.1 255.255.255.0
```

```
! Second option: like normal, but add the native keyword
interface gigabitethernet 0/0.10
 encapsulation dot1q 10 native
 ip address 10.1.10.1 255.255.255.0
!
interface gigabitethernet 0/0.20
 encapsulation dot1q 20
 ip address 10.1.20.1 255.255.255.0
```

18

Besides just scanning the configuration, the **show vlans** command on a router spells out which router trunk interfaces use which VLANs, which VLAN is the native VLAN, plus some packet statistics. Example 18-5 shows a sample, based on the Router B1 configuration in Example 18-4 (bottom half), in which native VLAN 10 is configured on subinterface G0/0.10. Note that the output identifies VLAN 1 associated with the physical interface, VLAN 10 as the native VLAN associated with G0/0.10, and VLAN 20 associated with G0/0.20.

Example 18-5 *Sample* **show vlans** *Command to Match Sample Router Trunking Configuration*

```
R1# show vlans

Virtual LAN ID:  1 (IEEE 802.1Q Encapsulation)

   vLAN Trunk Interface:    GigabitEthernet0/0

   Protocols Configured:    Address:         Received:        Transmitted:
      Other                                  0                83

   69 packets, 20914 bytes input
   147 packets, 11841 bytes output

Virtual LAN ID:  10 (IEEE 802.1Q Encapsulation)

   vLAN Trunk Interface:    GigabitEthernet0/0.10

This is configured as native Vlan for the following interface(s) :
GigabitEthernet0/0
```

```
      Protocols Configured:     Address:          Received:          Transmitted:
             IP               10.1.10.1              2                   3
            Other                                    0                   1


      3 packets, 722 bytes input
      4 packets, 264 bytes output


 Virtual LAN ID:  20 (IEEE 802.1Q Encapsulation)


    vLAN Trunk Interface:     GigabitEthernet0/0.20


      Protocols Configured:     Address:          Received:          Transmitted:
             IP               10.1.20.1              0                  134
            Other                                    0                   1


      0 packets, 0 bytes input
      135 packets, 10498 bytes output
```

Configuring Routing to VLANs Using a Layer 3 Switch

The other option for routing traffic to VLANs uses a device called a Layer 3 switch or mul-
tilayer switch. As introduced back in Chapter 11, "Implementing Ethernet Virtual LANs," a
Layer 3 switch is one device that does two primary functions: Layer 2 LAN switching and
Layer 3 IP routing. The Layer 2 switch function forwards frames inside each VLAN, but it
will not forward frames between VLANs. The Layer 3 forwarding logic—routing—forwards
IP packets between VLANs.

The configuration of a Layer 3 switch mostly looks like the Layer 2 switching configuration shown back in Part II of this book, with a small bit of configuration added for the
Layer 3 functions. The Layer 3 switching function needs a virtual interface connected to
each VLAN internal to the switch. These *VLAN interfaces* act like router interfaces, with
an IP address and mask. The Layer 3 switch has an IP routing table, with connected routes
off each of these VLAN interfaces. (These interfaces are also referred to as switched virtual
interfaces [SVI].)

To show the concept, Figure 18-13 shows the design changes and configuration concept
for the same branch office used in Figures 18-11 and 18-12. The figure shows the Layer 3
switch function with a router icon inside the switch, to emphasize that the switch routes
the packets. The branch still has two user VLANs, so the Layer 3 switch needs one VLAN
interface for each VLAN. In addition, the traffic still needs to get to the router to access the
WAN, so the switch uses a third VLAN (VLAN 30 in this case) for the link to Router B1.
This link would not be a trunk, but would be an access link.

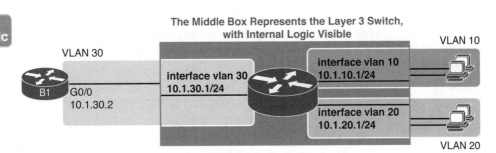

Figure 18-13 *Routing on VLAN Interfaces in a Layer 3 Switch*

The following steps show how to configure Layer 3 switching. Note that on some switches, like the 2960 switches used for the examples in this book, the ability to route IPv4 packets must be enabled first, with a **reload** of the switch required to enable the feature. The rest of the steps after Step 1 would apply to all models of Cisco switches that are capable of doing Layer 3 switching.

Step 1.   On some older models of switches, enable hardware support for IPv4 routing. For example, on 2960 switches, use the **sdm prefer lanbase-routing** in global configuration mode and **reload** the switch.

Step 2.   Use the **ip routing** command in global configuration mode to enable IPv4 routing on the switch.

Step 3.   Use the **interface vlan** *vlan_id* command in global configuration mode to create VLAN interfaces for each VLAN for which the Layer 3 switch is routing packets.

Step 4.   Use the **ip address** *address mask* command in interface configuration mode to configure an IP address and mask on the VLAN interface, enabling IPv4 on that VLAN interface.

Step 5.   Use the **no shutdown** command in interface configuration mode to enable the VLAN interface (if it is currently in a shutdown state).

Example 18-6 shows the configuration to match Figure 18-13. In this case, switch SW1, a 2960, has already used the **sdm prefer lanbase-routing** global command and been reloaded. The example shows the related configuration on all three VLAN interfaces.

Example 18-6 *VLAN Interface Configuration for Layer 3 Switching*

```
ip routing
!
interface vlan 10
 ip address 10.1.10.1 255.255.255.0
!
interface vlan 20
 ip address 10.1.20.1 255.255.255.0
!
interface vlan 30
 ip address 10.1.30.1 255.255.255.0
```

With the VLAN configuration shown here, the switch is ready to route packets between the VLANs as shown in Figure 18-13. To support the routing of packets, the switch adds connected IP routes, as shown in Example 18-7; note that each route is listed as being connected to a different VLAN interface.

Example 18-7   *Connected Routes on a Layer 3 Switch*

```
SW1# show ip route
! legend omitted for brevity


      10.0.0.0/8 is variably subnetted, 6 subnets, 2 masks
C        10.1.10.0/24 is directly connected, Vlan10
L        10.1.10.1/32 is directly connected, Vlan10
C        10.1.20.0/24 is directly connected, Vlan20
L        10.1.20.1/32 is directly connected, Vlan20
C        10.1.30.0/24 is directly connected, Vlan30
L        10.1.30.1/32 is directly connected, Vlan30
```

The switch would also need additional routes to the rest of the network shown in Figure 18-11, possibly using static routes as discussed in the final major section of this chapter.

Configuring Static Routes

All routers add connected routes, as discussed in the previous section. Then, most networks use dynamic routing protocols to cause each router to learn the rest of the routes in an internetwork. Networks use static routes—routes added to a routing table through direct configuration—much less often than dynamic routing. However, static routes can be useful at times, and they happen to be useful learning tools as well. This last of three major sections in the chapter discusses static routes.

Static Route Configuration

IOS allows the definition of individual static routes using the **ip route** global configuration command. Every **ip route** command defines a destination that can be matched, usually with a subnet ID and mask. The command also lists the forwarding instructions, typically listing either the outgoing interface or the next-hop router's IP address. IOS then takes that information and adds that route to the IP routing table.

As an example, Figure 18-14 shows a small IP network. The diagram actually holds a subset of Figure 18-3, from earlier in this chapter, with some of the unrelated details removed. The figure shows only the details related to a static route on R1, for subnet 172.16.2.0/24, which sits on the far right. To create that static route on R1, R1 will configure the subnet ID and mask, and either R1's outgoing interface (S0/0/0), or R2 as the next-hop router IP address (172.16.4.2).

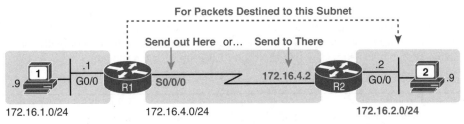

Figure 18-14 *Static Route Configuration Concept*

Example 18-8 shows the configuration of a couple of sample static routes. In particular, it shows routes on Router R1 in Figure 18-15, for the two subnets on the right side of the figure.

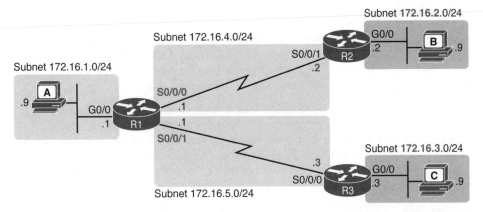

Figure 18-15 *Sample Network Used in Static Route Configuration Examples*

Example 18-8 *Static Routes Added to R1*

```
ip route 172.16.2.0 255.255.255.0 172.16.4.2
ip route 172.16.3.0 255.255.255.0 S0/0/1
```

The two example **ip route** commands show the two different styles. The first command shows subnet 172.16.2.0, mask 255.255.255.0, which sits on a LAN near Router R2. That same first command lists 172.16.4.2, R2's IP address, as the next-hop router. This route basically says this: To send packets to the subnet off Router R2, send them to R2.

The second route has the same kind of logic, but instead of identifying the next router by IP address, it lists the local router's outgoing interface. This route basically states: To send packets to the subnet off Router R3, send them out my own local S0/0/1 interface (which happens to connect to R3).

The routes created by these two **ip route** commands actually look a little different in the IP routing table. Both are static routes. However, the route that used the outgoing interface configuration is also noted as a connected route; this is just a quirk of the output of the **show ip route** command.

Example 18-9 lists these two routes using the **show ip route static** command. This command lists the details of static routes only, but it also lists a few statistics about all IPv4 routes. For example, the example shows two lines, for the two static routes configured in Example 18-8, but statistics state that this router has routes for ten subnets.

Example 18-9   *Static Routes Added to R1*

```
R1# show ip route static
Codes: L - local, C - connected, S - static, R - RIP, M - mobile, B - BGP
! lines omitted for brevity
Gateway of last resort is not set

      172.16.0.0/16 is variably subnetted, 10 subnets, 2 masks
S        172.16.2.0/24 [1/0] via 172.16.4.2
S        172.16.3.0/24 is directly connected, Serial0/0/1
```

IOS adds and removes these static routes dynamically over time, based on whether the outgoing interface is working or not. For example, in this case, if R1's S0/0/1 interface fails, R1 removes the static route to 172.16.3.0/24 from the IPv4 routing table. Later, when the interface comes up again, IOS adds the route back to the routing table.

Note that most sites use dynamic routing protocols to learn all the routes to remote subnets. However, when not using a dynamic routing protocol, the routers would need to configure static routes. For example, if the routers had only the configuration shown in the examples so far, PC A (from Figure 18-15) would not be able to receive packets back from PC B, because Router R2 does not have a route for PC A's subnet. R2 would need static routes for other subnets, as would R3.

> **NOTE**   The static routes shown so far in this chapter are called *network routes* or *subnet routes* because the command defines a route to an IP network or subnet, in comparison to a host route or default route, as explained in the next few pages.

Static Host Routes

Earlier, this chapter defined a host route as a route for a single host address, as noted with the IP address and a /32 mask. The earlier examples focused on the local routes added as a result of the **ip address** command; those routes are all host routes, with a /32 mask.

The **ip route** command can create static routes for remote hosts by using a mask of 255.255.255.255. This might make sense for cases in which redundant paths exist, and you want traffic to most of the hosts in the subnet to flow over one path, and traffic for one specific host to flow over the other path. For instance, you could define these two static routes for subnet 10.1.1.0/24 and host 10.1.1.9, with two different next-hop addresses, as follows:

```
ip route 10.1.1.0 255.255.255.0 10.2.2.2
ip route 10.1.1.9 255.255.255.255 10.9.9.9
```

Note that these two routes overlap: a packet sent to 10.1.1.9 that arrives at the router would match both routes. When that happens, routers use the most specific route (that is, the route with the longest prefix length). So, a packet sent to 10.1.1.9 would be forwarded to next-hop router 10.9.9.9, and packets sent to other destinations in subnet 10.1.1.0/24 would be sent to next-hop router 10.2.2.2.

Note that the section "IP Forwarding by Matching the Most Specific Route" in Chapter 24, "Troubleshooting IPv4 Routing," gets into this topic in more detail.

Static Routes with No Competing Routes

If the configured route has no competing routes, the router still checks a few rules before adding the route to its IP routing table. The router first checks for any competing routes (that is, whether there are any other routes for the exact same subnet). The other routes could be learned by a routing protocol, or be another static route.

Even if no competing routes exist, IOS also considers the following before adding the route to its routing table:

- For **ip route** commands that list an outgoing interface, that interface must be in an up/up state.
- For **ip route** commands that list a next-hop IP address, the local router must have a route to reach that next-hop address.

For example, earlier in Example 18-8, R1's command **ip route 172.16.2.0 255.255.255.0 172.16.4.2** defines a static route. Assume there were no competing routes and all links were working. Based on this route, R1 looks at its IP routing table and finds a route matching next-hop address 172.16.4.2 (R1's connected route for subnet 172.16.4.0/24). As a result, R1 adds the static route to subnet 172.16.2.0/24. Later, if R1's S0/0/0 were to fail, R1 would remove its connected route to 172.16.4.0/24, which would then cause R1 to remove its static route to 172.16.2.0/24.

You can also configure a static route so that IOS ignores these basic checks, always putting the IP route in the routing table. To do so, just use the **permanent** keyword on the **ip route** command. For example, by adding the **permanent** keyword to the end of the two commands in Example 18-8 as demonstrated in Example 18-10, R1 would now add these routes, regardless of whether the two WAN links were up.

Example 18-10 *Permanently Adding Static Routes to the IP Routing Table (Router R1)*

```
ip route 172.16.2.0 255.255.255.0 172.16.4.2 permanent
ip route 172.16.3.0 255.255.255.0 S0/0/1 permanent
```

Note that although the **permanent** keyword lets the router keep the route in the routing table without checking the outgoing interface or route to the next-hop address, it does not magically fix a broken route. For example, if the outgoing interface fails, the route will remain in the routing table, but the router cannot forward packets because the outgoing interface is down.

Static Routes with Competing Routes

Next, consider the case in which a static route competes with other static routes or routes learned by a routing protocol. That is, the **ip route** command defines a route to a subnet, but the router also knows of other static or dynamically learned routes to reach that same subnet. In these cases, the router must first decide which routing source has the better administrative distance, with lower being better, and then use the route learned from the better source.

To see how that works, consider the example illustrated in Figure 18-16, which shows a branch office with two WAN links: one very fast Gigabit Ethernet link and one rather slow (but cheap) T1. In this design, the network uses Open Shortest Path First Version 2 (OSPFv2) over the primary link, learning a route for subnet 172.16.2.0/24. R1 also defines a static route over the backup link to that exact same subnet, so R1 must choose whether to use the static route or the OSPF-learned route.

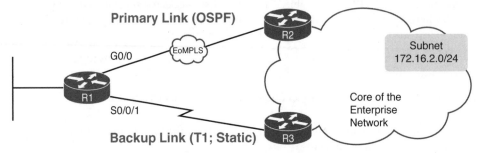

Figure 18-16 *Using a Floating Static Route to Key Subnet 172.16.2.0/24*

IOS considers static routes better than OSPF-learned routes. By default, IOS gives static routes an administrative distance of 1 and OSPF routes an administrative distance of 110. Using these defaults in Figure 18-16, R1 would use the lower path to reach subnet 172.16.2.0/24 in this case, which is not the intended design. Instead, the engineer prefers to use the OSPF-learned routes over the much-faster primary link, and use the static route over the backup link only as needed when the primary link fails.

To instead prefer the OSPF routes, the configuration would need to change the administrative distance settings and use what many networkers call a floating static route. A *floating static* route floats or moves into and out of the IP routing table depending on whether the better (lower) administrative distance route learned by the routing protocol happens to exist currently. Basically, the router ignores the static route during times when the better routing protocol route is known.

To implement a floating static route, just override the default administrative distance on the static route, making the value larger than the default administrative distance of the routing protocol. For example, the **ip route 172.16.2.0 255.255.255.0 172.16.5.3 130** command on R1 would do exactly that, setting the static route's administrative distance to 130. As long as the primary link stays up, and OSPF on R1 learns a route for 172.16.2.0/24, with administrative distance of 110, R1 ignores the static route.

Finally, note that while the **show ip route** command lists the administrative distance of most routes, as the first of two numbers inside two brackets, the **show ip route** *subnet* command plainly lists the administrative distance. Example 18-11 shows a sample, matching this most recent example.

Example 18-11 *Displaying the Administrative Distance of the Static Route*

```
R1# show ip route static
! Legend omitted for brevity

      172.16.0.0/16 is variably subnetted, 6 subnets, 2 masks
S        172.16.2.0/24 is directly connected, Serial0/0/1

R1# show ip route 172.16.2.0
Routing entry for 172.16.2.0/24
  Known via "static", distance 130, metric 0 (connected)
  Routing Descriptor Blocks:
  * directly connected, via Serial0/0/1
      Route metric is 0, traffic share count is 1
```

Static Default Routes

When a router tries to route a packet, the router might not match the packet's destination IP address with any route. When that happens, the router normally just discards the packet.

Routers can be configured so that they use either a statically configured or dynamically learned default route. The default route matches all packets, so that if a packet does not match any other more specific route in the routing table, the router can at least forward the packet based on the default route.

One classic example in which companies might use static default routes in their enterprise TCP/IP networks is when the company has many remote sites, each with a single, relatively slow WAN connection. Each remote site has only one possible physical route to use to send packets to the rest of the network. So, rather than use a routing protocol, which sends messages over the WAN and uses precious WAN bandwidth, each remote router might use a default route that sends all traffic to the central site, as shown in Figure 18-17.

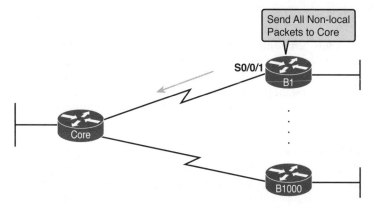

Figure 18-17 *Example Use of Static Default Routes at 1000 Low-Speed Remote Sites*

IOS allows the configuration of a static default route by using special values for the subnet and mask fields in the **ip route** command: 0.0.0.0 and 0.0.0.0. For example, the command

ip route 0.0.0.0 0.0.0.0 S0/0/1 creates a static default route on Router B1—a route that matches all IP packets—and sends those packets out interface S0/0/1.

Example 18-12 shows an example of a static default route, using Router R2 from Figure 18-16. Earlier, that figure, along with Example 18-10, showed R1 with static routes to the two subnets on the right side of the figure. Example 18-12 shows R2, on the right, using a static default route to route packets back to the left side of the figure.

Example 18-12 *Adding a Static Default Route on R2 (Figure 18-16)*

```
R2# configure terminal
Enter configuration commands, one per line.  End with CNTL/Z.
R2(config)# ip route 0.0.0.0 0.0.0.0 s0/0/1
R2(config)# ^Z
R2# show ip route
Codes: L - local, C - connected, S - static, R - RIP, M - mobile, B - BGP
       D - EIGRP, EX - EIGRP external, O - OSPF, IA - OSPF inter area
       N1 - OSPF NSSA external type 1, N2 - OSPF NSSA external type 2
       E1 - OSPF external type 1, E2 - OSPF external type 2
       i - IS-IS, su - IS-IS summary, L1 - IS-IS level-1, L2 - IS-IS level-2
       ia - IS-IS inter area, * - candidate default, U - per-user static route
       o - ODR, P - periodic downloaded static route, H - NHRP, l - LISP
       + - replicated route, % - next hop override


Gateway of last resort is 0.0.0.0 to network 0.0.0.0


S*    0.0.0.0/0 is directly connected, Serial0/0/1
      172.16.0.0/16 is variably subnetted, 4 subnets, 2 masks
C        172.16.2.0/24 is directly connected, GigabitEthernet0/0
L        172.16.2.2/32 is directly connected, GigabitEthernet0/0
C        172.16.4.0/24 is directly connected, Serial0/0/1
L        172.16.4.2/32 is directly connected, Serial0/0/1
```

The output of the **show ip route** command lists a few new and interesting facts. First, it lists the route with a code of S, meaning static, but also with a *, meaning it is a *candidate default route*. A router can learn about more than one default route, and the router then has to choose which one to use; the * means that it is at least a candidate to become the default route. Just above, the "Gateway of Last Resort" refers to the chosen default route, which in this case is the just-configured static route with outgoing interface S0/0/1.

Troubleshooting Static Routes

This entire section about static routes includes scattered comments that can help you troubleshoot static routes; however, the exam topics for this version of the exam happens to specifically mention troubleshooting for static routes. To that end, this final topic of the chapter summarizes the key points related to troubleshooting static routes, some already mentioned in this chapter, and some added here in this section.

This topic breaks static route troubleshooting into three perspectives: the route is in the routing table but is incorrect; the route is not in the routing table; the route is in the routing table, and is correct, but the packets do not arrive.

Troubleshooting Incorrect Static Routes that Appear in the IP Routing Table

This first troubleshooting item can be obvious, but it is worth pausing to think about. A static route is only as good as the input typed into the **ip route** command. IOS checks the syntax, and as mentioned earlier, makes a few other checks that this section reviews in the next heading. But once those checks are passed, IOS puts the route into the IP routing table, even if the route had poorly chosen parameters.

For instance, an exam question might show addresses 192.168.1.101 and .102, with mask /26, and you see a router with a command **ip route 192.168.1.64 255.255.255.224 192.168.1.65**. Did you see the problem immediately? The range of addresses in subnet 192.168.1.64, with mask 255.255.255.224, does not include the .101 and .102 addresses. So the **ip route** command has good syntax, but the engineer made a subnetting math mistake.

When you see an exam question that has static routes, and you see them in the output of **show ip route**, remember to check on these items:

- Is there a subnetting math error in the subnet ID and mask?
- Is the next-hop IP address correct, and referencing an IP address on a neighboring router?
- Is the outgoing interface correct, and referencing an interface on the local route (that is, the same router where the static route is configured)?

The Static Route Does Not Appear in the IP Routing Table

An **ip route** command can have correct syntax, accepted and added to the running-config file, and saved into the startup-config file, but never be placed into the IP routing table and seen in the output of the **show ip route** command. Why? Well, the earlier topics under headings "Static Routes with No Competing Routes" and "Static Routes with Competing Routes" explained the reasons.

For easier review and study, here are the reasons why an **ip route** command would be accepted when typed in the CLI, but the route would not appear in the IP routing table. Note that all three reasons can change over time; that is, the route may not appear right now, then conditions change, and then the route appears.

- The outgoing interface listed in the **ip route** command is not up/up.
- The next-hop router IP address listed in the **ip route** command is not reachable (that is, there is no route that matches the next-hop address).
- A better competing route (another route to the exact same subnet ID and mask) exists, and that competing route has a better (lower) administrative distance.

The Correct Static Route Appears but Works Poorly

This last section is a place to make two points, one mainstream, and one point to review a bit of trivia.

First, on the mainstream point, the static route can be perfect, but the packets from one host to the next still may not arrive. An incorrect static route is just one of many items to check when you're troubleshooting problems like "host A cannot connect to server B." The

18

root cause may be the static route, or it may be something else. Chapters 23 and 24 go into some depth about troubleshooting these types of problems.

On the more trivial point, you may recall the **permanent** keyword on the **ip route** command, as discussed earlier in the section titled "Static Routes with No Competing Routes." Basically, this keyword tells IOS to skip the checks of the current status of the outgoing interface and the check of a route for the next-hop router IP address. Any time you see an exam question with an **ip route** command with the **permanent** keyword, you need to do these checks yourself. IOS will put the route in the routing table, and if the interface is down or the next-hop address is unreachable, the router cannot possibly forward packets with that route.

Chapter Review

One key to doing well on the exams is to perform repetitive spaced review sessions. Review this chapter's material using either the tools in the book, DVD, or interactive tools for the same material found on the book's companion website. Refer to the "Your Study Plan" element for more details. Table 18-2 outlines the key review elements and where you can find them. To better track your study progress, record when you completed these activities in the second column.

Table 18-2   Chapter Review Tracking

Review Element	Review Date(s)	Resource Used
Review key topics		Book, DVD/website
Review key terms		Book, DVD/website
Repeat DIKTA questions		Book, PCPT
Review config checklists		Book, DVD/website
Do labs		Blog
Review command tables		Book

Review All the Key Topics

Table 18-3   Key Topics for Chapter 18

Key Topic Element	Description	Page Number
List	Steps taken by a host when forwarding IP packets	406
List	Steps taken by a router when forwarding IP packets	407
Figure 18-2	Diagram of five routing steps taken by a router	407
Figure 18-7	Breakdown of IP routing table with matching and forwarding details	411
List	Three common sources from which routers build IP routes	413
List	Rules regarding when a router creates a connected route	413
List	Three options for connecting a router to each VLAN	415
Figure 18-12	Concept of VLAN subinterfaces on a router	417

Key Topic Element	Description	Page Number
List	Two alternative methods to configure the native VLAN in a ROAS configuration	418
Figure 18-13	Layer 3 switching concept and configuration	421
Figure 18-14	Static route configuration concept	423
List	Troubleshooting checklist for routes that do appear in the IP routing table	429
List	Troubleshooting checklist for static routes that do not appear in the IP routing table	429

Key Terms You Should Know

default gateway/router, ARP table, routing table, next-hop router, outgoing interface, sub-interface, VLAN interface, Layer 3 switch, connected route, static route, default route, host route, floating static route, network route, administrative distance

Command References

Tables 18-4 and 18-5 list configuration and verification commands used in this chapter. As an easy review exercise, cover the left column in a table, read the right column, and try to recall the command without looking. Then repeat the exercise, covering the right column, and try to recall what the command does.

Table 18-4   Chapter 18 Configuration Command Reference

Command	Description
ip address *ip-address mask*	Interface subcommand that assigns the interface's IP address
interface *type number.subint*	Global command to create a subinterface and to enter configuration mode for that subinterface
encapsulation dot1q *vlan-id* [native]	A subinterface subcommand that tells the router to use 802.1Q trunking, for a particular VLAN, and with the **native** keyword, to not encapsulate in a trunking header
encapsulation isl *vlan-identifier*	A subinterface subcommand that tells the router to use ISL trunking for a particular VLAN
sdm prefer lanbase-routing	A command on Cisco switches that enables the switch to support IP routing if configured
[no] ip routing	Global command that enables (**ip routing**) or disables (**no ip routing**) the routing of IPv4 packets on a router or Layer 3 switch
interface vlan *vlan_id*	Global command on a Layer 3 switch to create a VLAN interface and to enter configuration mode for that VLAN interface
ip route *prefix mask* {*ip-address* | *interface-type interface-number*} [*distance*] [permanent]	Global configuration command that creates a static route

Table 18-5   Chapter 18 EXEC Command Reference

Command	Description
show ip route	Lists the router's entire routing table
show ip route [connected | static | rip]	Lists a subset of the IP routing table
show ip route *ip-address*	Lists detailed information about the route that a router matches for the listed IP address
show vlans	Lists VLAN configuration and statistics for VLAN trunks configured on routers
show arp, show ip arp	Lists the router's IPv4 ARP table
clear ip arp [*ip-address*]	Removes all dynamically learned ARP table entries, or if the command lists an IP address, removes the entry for that IP address only

CHAPTER 19

Learning IPv4 Routes with RIPv2

This chapter covers the following exam topics:

3.0 Routing Technologies

3.2 Interpret the components of routing table

   3.2.a Prefix

   3.2.b Network mask

   3.2.c Next hop

   3.2.d Routing protocol code

   3.2.e Administrative distance

   3.2.f Metric

   3.2.g Gateway of last resort

3.3 Describe how a routing table is populated by different routing information sources

   3.3.a Admin distance

3.5 Compare and contrast static routing and dynamic routing

3.7 Configure, verify, and troubleshoot RIPv2 for IPv4 (excluding authentication, filtering, manual summarization, redistribution)

Routers route IP packets. However, they cannot route packets without meaningful routes, routes for all destinations in the internetwork. And the most common way for routers to learn routes to remote subnets is to use a dynamic routing protocol.

Routing Information Protocol (RIP) Version 2 (RIPv2) is the only IP routing protocol discussed in depth in this book. The big idea is simple: An engineer enables RIPv2 on each router. RIPv2 then takes the connected routes it knows because of interface IP address configuration and then advertises them by sending messages to neighboring routers. Over time, as each router learns more routes, they advertise about those routes as well. By the end of the process, all routers know about all subnets, including details about redundant routes to reach each subnet. Each router can then put the best route for each subnet into its routing table, completing the goal of learning good routes to forward traffic to all subnets.

This chapter, one of the longer chapters in this book, takes RIPv2 and the topic of routing protocols from initial concept, into configuration and verifications, and ends with troubleshooting.

"Do I Know This Already?" Quiz

Take the quiz (either here, or use the PCPT software) if you want to use the score to help you decide how much time to spend on this chapter. The answers are at the bottom of the page following the quiz, and the explanations are in DVD Appendix C and in the PCPT software.

Table 19-1 "Do I Know This Already?" Foundation Topics Section-to-Question Mapping

Foundation Topics Section	Questions
RIP and Routing Protocol Concepts	1–2
Core RIPv2 Configuration and Verification	3–5
Optional RIPv2 Configuration and Verification	6
Troubleshooting RIPv2	7

1. Which of the following are features of RIPv2? (Choose two answers.)

   a. Uses a hop-count metric

   b. Sends update messages to broadcast address 255.255.255.255

   c. After convergence, only sends updates if a change occurs

   d. Uses split horizon as a loop prevention mechanism

2. Which of the following best describes the concept of the RIP hop count metric?

   a. The number of satellite links in a route.

   b. The number of routers between a router and a subnet, not counting that router.

   c. The number of routers between a router and a subnet, counting that router.

   d. The number of links between a router and a subnet, not counting the link where the subnet resides.

   e. The number of links between a router and a subnet, counting the link where the subnet resides.

3. Router R2 has interfaces with addresses/masks of 10.1.1.2/24 and 11.1.1.2/24. Which of the following commands would be part of a RIP Version 2 configuration on R2 that enables RIPv2 on both interfaces? (Choose three answers.)

   a. router rip

   b. router rip 3

   c. network 10.0.0.0

   d. network 10.1.1.1

   e. network 11.0.0.0

   f. network 11.1.1.2

4. Which of the following **network** commands, following a **router rip** command, would cause RIP to send updates out two interfaces whose IP addresses are 10.1.2.1 and 10.1.1.1, mask 255.255.255.0?

   a. network 10.0.0.0

   b. network 10.1.1.0 10.1.2.0

   c. network 10.1.1.1. 10.1.2.1

   d. network 10.1.0.0 255.255.0.0

   e. network 10

5. Review the snippet from a **show ip route** command on a router:

   ```
   R        10.1.2.0 [120/1] via 10.1.128.252, 00:00:13, Serial0/0/1
   ```

   Which of the following statements must be true regarding this output? (Choose two answers.)

   a. The administrative distance is 1.

   b. The administrative distance is 120.

   c. The metric is 1.

   d. The metric is not listed.

   e. The router added this route to the routing table 13 seconds ago.

   f. The router must wait 13 seconds before advertising this route again.

6. Review the snippet from a **show ip protocols** command on a router:

   ```
   Automatic network summarization is not in effect
   Maximum path: 5
   Routing for Networks:
     192.168.1.0
     192.168.5.0
   Passive Interface(s):
     GigabitEthernet0/1
   ```

   Which of the following commands would you expect the **show running-config** command to list in RIP configuration mode? (Choose two answers.)

   a. auto-summary

   b. network 192.168.5.1

   c. maximum-paths 5

   d. passive-interface gigabitethernet0/1

7. Routers R1 and R2 use RIPv2, and should exchange routes with each other. R1 and R2 connect on an Ethernet link, with both routers using their G0/0 interfaces. R2 learns routes from R1, but R1 does not learn routes from R2. Which of the following mistakes could result in this symptom?

   a. R2 has configured a **passive-interface gigabitethernet0/0** command.

   b. R1's and R2's IP address/mask values are 10.1.1.1/25 and 10.1.1.201/25, respectively.

   c. R1's has no RIP **network** command that matches R1's G0/0 interface IP address.

   d. R2 is missing a **no auto-summary** command.

Foundation Topics

RIP and Routing Protocol Concepts

Many IP routing protocols exist, in part due to the long history of IP. However, if you compare all the IP routing protocols, they all have some core features in common. Each routing protocol causes routers (and Layer 3 switches) to

1. Learn routing information about IP subnets from other neighboring routers

2. Advertise routing information about IP subnets to other neighboring routers

3. If a router learns of more than one route to reach one subnet, choose the best route based on that routing protocol's concept of a metric

4. React to changes when the network topology changes—for example, when a link fails, and converge to use a new choice of best route for each destination subnet

All the routing protocols do these same four functions, but the protocols differ in the details of how they accomplish these tasks. The rest of this chapter works through the details of how Routing Information Protocol Version 2 (RIPv2) accomplishes these tasks, with a few comments about other protocols sprinkled throughout.

History of Interior Gateway Protocols

Historically speaking, RIP Version 1 (RIPv1) was the first popularly used IP routing protocol, with the Cisco proprietary Interior Gateway Routing Protocol (IGRP) being introduced a little later, as shown as the first wave in Figure 19-1.

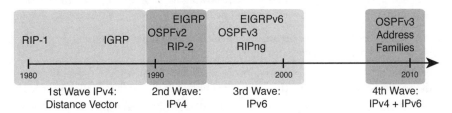

Figure 19-1 *Timeline for IP IGPs*

By the early 1990s, business and technical factors pushed the IPv4 world toward a second wave of better routing protocols. That second wave includes RIP Version 2 (RIPv2), OSPF Version 2 (OSPFv2), and Enhanced Interior Gateway Routing Protocol (EIGRP), all protocols found in use today for IPv4.

The first and second wave of routing protocols worked with IPv4 but not IPv6. IPv6 emerged in the mid-1990s as a long-term solution to IPv4 growth issues in the Internet. These new IPv6 routing protocols included EIGRP for IPv6 (sometimes called EIGRPv6), OSPF Version 3 (OSPFv3), and RIP next generation (RIPng). (Yes, RIPng was named after the *Star Trek* series.)

The fourth wave shown in Figure 19-1 is there mainly to overcome a bit of history with OSPF and is listed here just to be fully correct. When OSPFv3 was created, it supported advertising IPv6 routes only. So, for many years, OSPFv2 implied IPv4-only, and OSPFv3 implied IPv6-only. Around 2010, OSPFv3 was improved to advertise both IPv4 and IPv6 routes using a feature called address families.

Comparing IGPs

Today, you would most likely see the second- and third-wave routing protocols in most networks. In fact, Cisco considers IGRP to be so old that it does not even include IGRP in its more recent IOS versions. EIGRP and OSPFv2 are easily the most popular IPv4 routing protocols, with RIPv2 used much less. However, RIPv2 is listed in the ICND1 exam topics, and it has one huge advantage versus EIGRP and OSPFv2: RIPv2 is easier to learn.

What is an IGP in the first place? All the routing protocols mentioned so far in this chapter happen to be categorized as interior gateway protocols (IGP) rather than as an exterior gateway protocols (EGP). These two terms use the word *gateway* instead of *router* because routers were called gateways in the earliest days of IP routing. The designers of some routing protocols intended the routing protocol for use inside one company or organization (IGP), with other routing protocols intended for use between companies and between Internet service providers (ISP) in the Internet (EGPs).

This chapter falls back to using the term IGP when talking about all the routing protocols mentioned in this chapter.

Any time an engineer thinks about what routing protocol to use, he can make some basic comparisons between the routing protocols. The following list describes four of the major comparison points when comparing these routing protocols:

- **The underlying routing protocol algorithm:** Specifically, whether the routing protocol uses logic referenced as distance vector (DV) or link state (LS).

- **The usefulness of the metric:** The routing protocol chooses which route is best based on its metric; so the better the metric, the better the choices made by that routing protocol.

- **The speed of convergence:** How long does it take all the routers to learn about a change in the network and update their IPv4 routing tables? That concept, called *convergence time*, varies depending on the routing protocol.

- **Whether the protocol is a public standard or a vendor-proprietary function:** RIP and OSPF happen to be standards, defined by RFCs. EIGRP happens to be defined by Cisco, and until 2013, was kept private.

RIP's *hop count* metric treats each router as a hop, so the hop count is the number of other routers between a router and some remote subnet. RIP's hop-count metric means that RIP picks the route with the smallest number of links and routers. However, that shortest route may have the slowest links. In fact, Figure 19-2 shows just such a case on the left, with RIP choosing the one-hop route from Router B to subnet 10.1.1.0, even though it crosses the slower 100-Mbps link instead of the two-hop route over two 1-Gbps links.

A routing protocol whose metric was based (at least in part) on link bandwidth might be a better choice in the topology shown in Figure 19-2. For example, EIGRP does base its metric in part on link bandwidth. EIGRP, on the right side of the figure, chooses the route that happens to have more links through the network (and more hops), but both links have a faster bandwidth of 1 Gbps on each link.

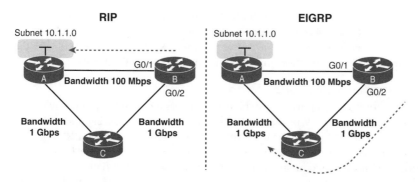

Figure 19-2 *EIGRP Choosing the Longer but Better Route to Subnet 10.1.1.0*

Distance Vector Basics

Each IGP can be categorized based on its internal logic, either distance vector (used by RIP) or link state. The next few pages explain more about how a DV protocol actually exchanges routing information, using RIPv2 as an example. The ICND2 book's chapters about OSPF describe link state logic, and the ICND2 book's chapters on EIGRP get into more detail about some advanced distance vector features.

The Concept of a Distance and a Vector

The term *distance vector* describes what a router knows about each route. When a router learns about a route to a subnet, the routers learn three important facts related to each route: the destination subnet, the distance (that is, the routing protocol metric), and the vector (that is, the link and next-hop router to use as part of that route).

Figure 19-3 begins to develop that concept showing RIP updates in the small boxes on the left. That is, Router R1 receives RIP updates from three neighboring routers. Each update describes a different route for subnet X, with a different metric. The fact that a particular router sends the RIP message identifies the next-hop router for the route. In this case, the three RIP updates advertise the following routes:

■ The four-hop route (distance) through R2 (vector) for subnet X

■ The three-hop route (distance) through R5 (vector) for subnet X

■ The two-hop route (distance) through R7 (vector) for subnet X

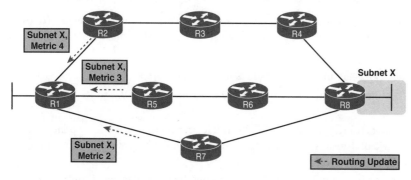

Figure 19-3 *Information Learned Using DV Protocols*

Taking Figure 19-3 a step further, imagine if R1 had learned only one route to subnet X, say the route learned from R2. R1 would use that route because it is the only route R1 knows for subnet X. However, having learned three routes to subnet X, R1 picks the route with the best (lowest) metric, in this case the two-hop route through next-hop Router R7.

Full Update Messages and Split Horizon

While Figure 19-3 shows a conceptual figure, Figure 19-4 gets more specific about what RIPv2 actually does. Like many DV protocols, RIPv2 sends a periodic routing update based on a relatively short timer. The periodic part of the term refers to the fact that RIP repeats the same update over and over on a timed basis even if nothing changes. Figure 19-4 illustrates this concept, with a detailed breakdown of the steps following the figure.

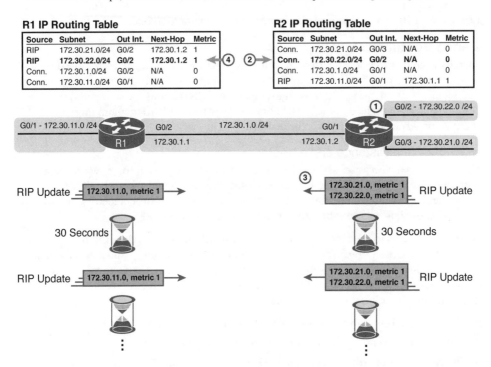

Figure 19-4 *Normal Steady-State RIP Operations: Full Update with Split Horizon*

This figure shows a lot of information, so take the time to work through the details, following the numbers in the figure versus the following list. For example, consider what router R1 learns for subnet 172.30.22.0/24, which is the subnet connected to R2's G0/2 interface:

1. R2 interface G0/2 has an IP address and is in an up/up state.

2. R2 adds a connected route for 172.30.22.0/24, off interface G0/2, to R2's routing table.

3. R2 advertises its route for 172.30.22.0/24 to R1, with metric 1, in a RIP update sent to R1. The metric of 1 means that R1's metric to reach this subnet will be metric 1 (hop count 1).

4. R1 adds a route for subnet 172.30.22.0/24, listing it as a RIP learned route with metric 1.

Also, take a moment to focus more on the route learned at Step 4: The bold route in R1's routing table. This route is for 172.30.22.0/24, as learned from R2. It lists R1's local G0/2 interface as the outgoing interface because R1 received the update on R1's G0/2 interface. R1's route also lists R2's IP address of 172.30.1.2 as next-hop router because that's the IP address from which R1 learned the route. Think of R1's outgoing interface and next-hop router information as the forwarding instructions for this route.

Split Horizon

Figure 19-4 also shows a common DV feature called *split horizon*. Note that both routers list all four subnets in their IP routing tables. However, the RIP update messages do not list four subnets. The reason? Split horizon.

Split horizon is a DV feature that tells a router to omit some routes from an update sent out an interface. Which routes are omitted from an update sent out interface X? The routes that would use interface X as the outgoing interface. Those routes that are not advertised on an interface usually include the routes learned in routing updates received on that interface.

Split horizon is difficult to learn by reading words, and much easier to learn by seeing an example. Figure 19-5 continues the same example as Figure 19-4, but focusing on R1's RIP update sent out R1's G0/2 interface to R2. Figure 19-5 shows R1's routing table with three light-colored routes, all of which list G0/2 as the outgoing interface. When building the RIP update to send out that same G0/2 interface, split horizon rules tell R1 to ignore those light-colored routes. Only the bold route, which does not have G0/2 as an outgoing interface, can be included in R1's RIP update sent out G0/2.

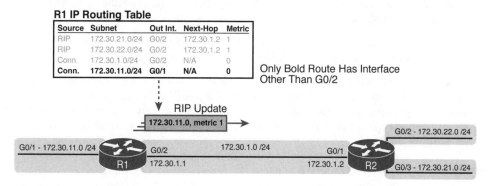

Figure 19-5 *R1 Does Not Advertise Three Routes Due to Split Horizon*

Route Poisoning

DV protocols help prevent routing loops by ensuring that every router learns that the route has failed, through every means possible, as quickly as possible. A routing loop occurs when the routes for some destination, on a set of routers, would cause a packet sent to that destination to keep looping between those routers and never arrive at the destination. Routing protocols attempt to prevent any routing loop. One of these features, *route poisoning*, helps all routers know for sure that a route has failed.

Route poisoning refers to the practice of advertising a failed route, but with a special metric value called *infinity*. Routers consider routes advertised with an infinite metric to have failed.

Figure 19-6 shows an example of route poisoning with RIP, with R2's G0/2 interface failing, meaning that R2's route for 172.30.22.0/24 has failed. RIP defines infinity as 16.

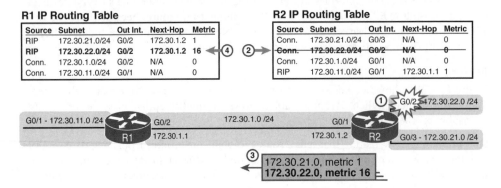

Figure 19-6 *Route Poisoning*

Figure 19-6 shows the following process, again following the numbers in the figure:

1. R2's G0/2 interface fails.

2. R2 removes its connected route for 172.30.22.0/24 from its routing table.

3. R2 advertises 172.30.22.0 with an infinite metric (which for RIP is 16).

4. R1 realizes that the route to 172.30.22.0/24 no longer works. Depending on conditions not discussed here, R1 either removes the route from its routing table or marks the route as unusable (with an infinite metric) for a few minutes before removing the route.

By the end of this process, Router R1 knows for sure that its old route for subnet 172.30.22.0/24 has failed, which helps R1 avoid introducing looping IP routes.

Note that all routing protocols have mechanisms to use to mark routes as expired in some way, in some cases using an infinite metric value similar to RIP. RIP uses 16 per the RIP protocol definition; as a result, a route with hop count 15 is the longest valid route that can be used in a RIP network, because advertising a route with hop count 16 would be considered a poison route.

Summarizing RIPv2 Features

This final section briefly mentions a few more features of RIPv2, and collects those features into a table for easier review and study.

Of course, RIPv2 adds features beyond RIPv1. For instance, RIPv2 supports authentication, which is a feature by which routers can use a password-like mechanism to make sure they exchange routes only with authentic other routers. RIPv2 also supports manual route summarization, which allows an engineer to plan and reduce the size of routing tables. (The DVD Appendix O, "Route Summarization," copied from a previous edition of this book, provides more detail if you are interested.) However, this book does not get into details about these features beyond this brief mention.

For another difference, RIPv2 sends its update message—the message that lists routing information—to the 224.0.0.9 multicast IP address. RIPv1 used the local subnet broadcast address of 255.255.255.255. Using the multicast address is more efficient and causes less impact to other hosts.

Finally, RIPv2 adds support for variable-length subnet masks (VLSM). Chapter 22, "Variable Length Subnet Masks," goes into detail about VLSM. To review, VLSM means that inside one classful network (one Class A, B, or C network), more than one subnet mask is used. For instance, the network in Figure 19-7 uses VLSM because all the subnets are from Class A network 10.0.0.0, but some subnets use a /24 mask whereas others use a /30 mask.

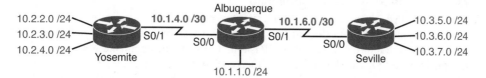

Figure 19-7   *An Example of VLSM*

Table 19-2 lists the features comparing RIPv1 and RIPv2. However, note that the list of features in the table is more about emphasizing the features of RIPv2 than stressing the differences between the two versions.

Table 19-2   Key Features of RIPv1 and RIPv2

Feature	RIPv1	RIPv2
Hop-count metric	Yes	Yes
Sets 15 as the largest metric for a working route	Yes	Yes
Sends full routing updates	Yes	Yes
Uses split horizon	Yes	Yes
Uses route poisoning, with metric 16 to mean "infinite"	Yes	Yes
Sends mask in routing update, thereby supporting VLSM	No	Yes
Supports manual route summarization	No	Yes
Sends updates to 224.0.0.9 multicast address	No	Yes
Supports authentication	No	Yes

Core RIPv2 Configuration and Verification

RIPv2 requires three basic configuration commands, with just a couple of **show** commands to check RIPv2 status. This second of four major sections of this chapter focuses on that core configuration and verification.

Configuring Core RIPv2 Features

RIPv2 configuration is simple compared to the concepts related to routing protocols. The configuration process uses three required commands, with only one command, the **network** command, requiring any real thought. You should also know the more popular **show** commands for helping you analyze and troubleshoot routing protocols.

The RIPv2 configuration process takes only the following three required steps, with the possibility that the third step might need to be repeated several times on the same router:

Step 1. Use the **router rip** command in global configuration mode to move into RIP configuration mode.

Step 2. Use the **version 2** command in RIP configuration mode to tell the router to use RIP Version 2 exclusively.

Step 3. Use one or more **network** *net-number* commands in RIP configuration mode to enable RIP on the correct interfaces.

Understanding the RIP network Command

To configure RIPv2, always start with those first two commands in the configuration checklist, and then think hard about the third step, the **network** command. The RIP **network** indirectly identifies the interfaces on which RIP is then enabled. The command has one parameter: some classful IP network number. IOS then compares each interface IP address of each interface on the local router with the IP network in the **network** command. IOS enables RIP on each interface whose IP address is in that same classful network.

For example, in Figure 19-8, the configuration on the left uses two **network** commands. The first **network** command happens to match one interface IP address of the four interfaces on the right, because one of the interfaces is in classful network 10.0.0.0. The second command matches two interfaces, because both are in classful network 172.16.0.0. Neither of the two **network** commands match the fourth interface, which is in classful network 192.168.1.0.

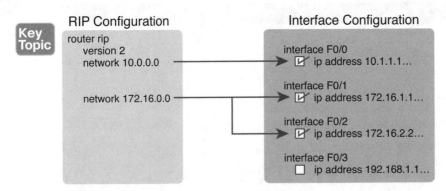

Figure 19-8 *RIP Network Command Enabling RIP Per-Interface Logic*

So, what does RIPv2 do on an interface once enabled? Well, RIP takes three separate actions once enabled on an interface. So rather than think of enabling RIP on an interface as one idea, break it into these three actions, which will help when you think about some later configuration and troubleshooting topics. The following are the three actions:

- The router sends routing updates out the interface.
- The router listens for and processes incoming updates on that same interface.
- The router advertises about the subnet connected to the interface.

Note that with the **version 2** command configured, the updates sent and received per this list are RIP version 2 updates.

RIP Configuration Example, with Many IP Networks

Keeping these facts in mind, now consider how to configure RIP on a single router. Examine Figure 19-9 for a moment and try to apply the first three configuration steps to this router and anticipate the configuration required on the router to enable RIP on all interfaces.

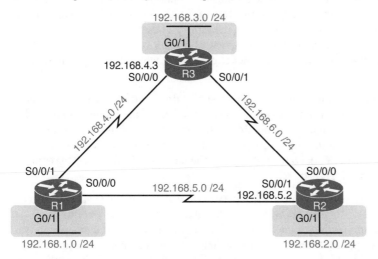

Figure 19-9   *RIPv2 Configuration: Three Routers, Each Connected to Three Networks*

Take a close look at the IP subnets listed in the figure. All links use an entire Class C network. I chose to use different Class C networks on each link on purpose so that each router connects to multiple classful networks. For instance, R2 will need **network** commands for networks 192.168.2.0, 192.168.5.0, and 192.168.6.0. Example 19-1 shows the configuration for all three routers.

Example 19-1   *R1, R2, and R3 RIPv2 Configuration, for Figure 19-9*

```
! Router R1 configuration
router rip
 version 2
 network 192.168.1.0
 network 192.168.4.0
 network 192.168.5.0
! Router R2 configuration
router rip
 version 2
 network 192.168.2.0
 network 192.168.5.0
 network 192.168.6.0
! Router R3 configuration
router rip
 version 2
 network 192.168.3.0
 network 192.168.4.0
 network 192.168.6.0
```

19

First, focus on meeting the primary goals. All three routers have the **router rip** and **version 2** commands, which together enable RIPv2, but without enabling RIPv2 on any interfaces.

Next, focus on the three **network** commands on each router. Each router has three **network** commands in this example because each router connects to three different classful networks. For example, R1 lists IP network 192.168.1.0, 192.168.4.0, and 192.168.5.0 in its three **network** commands, because according to the figure, R1 connects directly to those three IP networks. Those three commands enable RIPv2 on R1's G0/1, S0/0/0, and S0/0/1 interfaces. The **network** commands on the other two routers enable RIPv2 on their interfaces, respectively.

This particular example configuration gives us a good backdrop to discuss a common question about RIPv2 configuration and **network** commands. First, no one router has **network** commands for all six classful IP network numbers. The **network** command does not predefine all classful networks in the entire topology. Instead, it triggers local logic on that one router, matching the **network** commands against the interface IP addresses on that one router, as shown earlier in Figure 19-8.

Finally, on a complete side note about the RIP **network** command: IOS will actually accept a parameter besides a classful network number. IOS will not even issue an error message. However, IOS, knowing that the parameter must be a classful network number, interprets the IP address and changes the number to the matching network number. For example, if you were to type **network 10.1.2.3** in RIP configuration mode, IOS would accept the command, with no error message, and change what you typed so that the configuration has a **network 10.0.0.0** command. Your original **network 10.1.2.3** command would disappear.

RIP Configuration Example, with One IP Network

Figure 19-9, used in the first RIP configuration example, purposefully used many IP networks so that the configuration required several RIPv2 **network** commands. However, often a design will use subnets of one classful network, as shown in Figure 19-10. In this case, all six subnets are subnets of Class A network 10.0.0.0. Note that Figures 19-9 and 19-10 are identical other than the IPv4 subnets used.

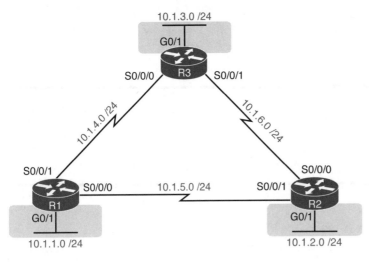

Figure 19-10 *Three Routers, Each Connected to Subnets of Class A Network 10.0.0.0*

To enable RIPv2 on all interfaces, each router needs only one **network** command: the
network 10.0.0.0 command. That one command on a router matches all three interfaces.
Example 19-2 shows the identical configuration used by all three routers.

Example 19-2 *The Identical RIPv2 Configuration Used for R1, R2, R3 for Figure 19-10*

```
router rip
 version 2
 network 10.0.0.0
```

RIPv2 Verification

IOS includes three primary **show** commands that are helpful to confirm how well RIPv2 is
working. Table 19-3 lists the commands and their main purpose.

Table 19-3 RIP Operational Commands

Command	Purpose
show ip route [rip]	Routes: This command lists IPv4 routes as learned by RIP. The **show ip route** command lists all IPv4 routes, and the **show ip route rip** command lists RIP-learned routes only.
show ip protocols	Configuration: This command lists information about the RIP configuration, plus the IP addresses of neighboring RIP routers from which the local router has learned routes.
show ip rip database	Best routes: This command lists the prefix/length of all best routes known to RIP on this router, including routes learned from neighbors and connected routes for interfaces on which RIP has been enabled.

Examining RIP Routes in the IP Routing Table

To begin, consider Router R1's routing table, based on Figure 19-9 and the configuration
in Example 19-1. That is the sample with six different Class C networks in the three-router
design. Example 19-3 shows the full IP routing table, as well as just the RIP-learned routes.

Example 19-3 *The* **show ip route** *Command*

```
R1# show ip route
Codes: L - local, C - connected, S - static, R - RIP, M - mobile, B - BGP
       D - EIGRP, EX - EIGRP external, O - OSPF, IA - OSPF inter area
       N1 - OSPF NSSA external type 1, N2 - OSPF NSSA external type 2
       E1 - OSPF external type 1, E2 - OSPF external type 2
       i - IS-IS, su - IS-IS summary, L1 - IS-IS level-1, L2 - IS-IS level-2
       ia - IS-IS inter area, * - candidate default, U - per-user static route
       o - ODR, P - periodic downloaded static route, H - NHRP, l - LISP
       a - application route
       + - replicated route, % - next hop override

Gateway of last resort is not set

      192.168.1.0/24 is variably subnetted, 2 subnets, 2 masks
C        192.168.1.0/24 is directly connected, GigabitEthernet0/1
L        192.168.1.1/32 is directly connected, GigabitEthernet0/1
```

19

```
R       192.168.2.0/24 [120/1] via 192.168.5.2, 00:00:21, Serial0/0/0
R       192.168.3.0/24 [120/1] via 192.168.4.3, 00:00:05, Serial0/0/1
        192.168.4.0/24 is variably subnetted, 2 subnets, 2 masks
C          192.168.4.0/24 is directly connected, Serial0/0/1
L          192.168.4.1/32 is directly connected, Serial0/0/1
        192.168.5.0/24 is variably subnetted, 2 subnets, 2 masks
C          192.168.5.0/24 is directly connected, Serial0/0/0
L          192.168.5.1/32 is directly connected, Serial0/0/0
R       192.168.6.0/24 [120/1] via 192.168.5.2, 00:00:21, Serial0/0/0
                       [120/1] via 192.168.4.3, 00:00:05, Serial0/0/1
R1# show ip route rip
! The same lines of legend show up here - removed for brevity

R       192.168.2.0/24 [120/1] via 192.168.5.2, 00:00:21, Serial0/0/0
R       192.168.3.0/24 [120/1] via 192.168.4.3, 00:00:05, Serial0/0/1
R       192.168.6.0/24 [120/1] via 192.168.5.2, 00:00:21, Serial0/0/0
                       [120/1] via 192.168.4.3, 00:00:05, Serial0/0/1
```

First, scan around all the detail in the **show ip route** command. Notice the legend at the top—about 10 lines of output—which are the same for every **show ip route** command. The legend lists the routing codes, which are short codes that identify the source from which a route is learned. In this case, Router R1 IPv4 routes with three codes—C, L, and R—meaning connected, local, and RIP.

Scan farther down in the output to see the individual routes. The routes list the subnet and then mask in prefix format, followed by other details. Ignoring the detail for another moment, notice the three highlighted RIP-learned routes, both in the output of the **show ip route** command and in the **show ip route rip** command at the end of the example. The highlighted lines show the same routes, but the **show ip route rip** command lists only the RIP routes, and not the connected and local routes.

Each line in the output of these commands reveals many details about a route. Using R1's route to 192.168.2.0/24 as an example, the details are as follows:

- The network number and mask are listed, 192.168.2.0 and /24 in this case. (In some cases, the mask is on a heading line just above the route.)
- The next-hop router's IP address is 192.168.5.2 in this case.
- The outgoing interface is Serial0/0/0 in this case.
- The update RIP timer that measures how long it has been since R1 has last heard about this route in a periodic RIP update is 21 seconds ago in this case.
- The RIP metric for this route (1 in this case), is listed as the second number in the square brackets. For example, between R1 and subnet 192.168.2.0/24, one other router (R2) exists, so it is a one-hop route.
- The administrative distance of the route is 120 in this case; the first number in brackets.

Take the time now to review the other two RIP routes, noting the values for these various items in those routes.

To better understand RIP metrics, think for a moment what would happen in this three-router topology of Figure 19-9 if R1's S0/0/0 interface failed. R1's one-hop route to 192.168.2.0/24 uses that outgoing interface, but if it were to fail, R1 would converge to use the two-hop route that runs through R3 next. Example 19-4 shows the RIP routes on R1 again after that failure.

Example 19-4 *The* **show ip route** *Command with New Metric 2 for Subnet 192.168.2.0*

```
R1# show ip route rip
! The same lines of legend show up here - removed for brevity


R     192.168.2.0/24 [120/2] via 192.168.4.3, 00:00:01, Serial0/0/1
R     192.168.3.0/24 [120/1] via 192.168.4.3, 00:00:01, Serial0/0/1
R     192.168.6.0/24 [120/1] via 192.168.4.3, 00:00:01, Serial0/0/1
```

NOTE   In lab, all you have to do to re-create the link failure in this example is to issue a **shutdown** command under R1's S0/0/0 interface.

Examine the highlighted route in detail, and compare it to R1's route for 192.168.2.0 from the previous example. In this case, the network, mask, and administrative distance remain the same. However, the metric is now 2, because this route goes through R3 and then R2, for two hops. It also lists forwarding directions of going through 192.168.4.3 (R3's S0/0/0 IP address) and going out R1's S0/0/1 interface.

Comparing Routing Sources with Administrative Distance

As you just examined, when an internetwork has redundant links and uses a single routing protocol, each router may learn multiple routes to reach a particular subnet. That one routing protocol then uses a metric to choose the best route, and the router adds that route to its routing table. For instance, R1 uses the metric 1 route for 192.168.2.0/24 when all links were working, and then the metric 2 route for 192.168.2.0/24 when a link in that better route failed.

However, some enterprises use multiple IP routing protocols. One router might learn of multiple routes to a particular subnet using different routing protocols. In these cases, the metric does not help the router choose which route is best, because each routing protocol uses a metric unique to that routing protocol. For example, RIP uses the hop count as the metric, but EIGRP uses a math formula with bandwidth and delay as inputs. A route with RIP metric 1 might need to be compared to an EIGRP route, to the same subnet, but with metric 4,132,768. (Yes, EIGRP metrics tend to be large numbers.) Because the numbers have different meanings, there is no real way to compare the metrics.

The router still needs to choose the best route even between routes learned by different routing protocols, or between routing protocols and static routes. IOS solves this problem by assigning a numeric value to each routing protocol. IOS then chooses the route whose routing protocol has the lower number. This number is called the administrative distance (AD). For example, EIGRP defaults to use an AD of 90, and RIP defaults to use the value of 120, as shown in the routes in Example 19-3 and 19-4. Given the lower-is-better logic used with administrative distance, an EIGRP route to a subnet would be chosen instead of a competing RIP route.

19

Table 19-4 lists the AD values for the most common sources of routing information.

Table 19-4 IOS Defaults for Administrative Distance

Route Source	Administrative Distance
Connected routes	0
Static routes	1
EIGRP	90
OSPF	110
RIP (v1 and v2)	120
DHCP default route	254
Unknown or unbelievable	255

NOTE You might recall a brief mention of administrative distance in Chapter 18, "Configuring IPv4 Addresses and Static Routes." That chapter explained how to configure a floating static route that was used only when the routing protocol did not learn a route for a given subnet, using administrative distance as the key mechanism.

Revealing RIP Configuration with the show ip protocols Command

The **show ip route** command shows the end result of RIP's work, but the **show ip protocols** command tells us something about how RIP works and about the RIP configuration. Example 19-5 lists the output of this command, taken from Router R1 in Figure 19-9, again based on the configuration in Example 19-1.

Example 19-5 *The* **show ip protocols** *Command Based on Example 19-1 Configuration*

```
R1# show ip protocols
Routing Protocol is "rip"
  Outgoing update filter list for all interfaces is not set
  Incoming update filter list for all interfaces is not set
  Sending updates every 30 seconds, next due in 23 seconds
  Invalid after 180 seconds, hold down 180, flushed after 240
  Redistributing: rip
  Default version control: send version 2, receive version 2
    Interface          Send  Recv  Triggered RIP  Key-chain
    GigabitEthernet0/1   2     2
    Serial0/0/0          2     2
    Serial0/0/1          2     2
  Automatic network summarization is in effect
  Maximum path: 4
  Routing for Networks:
    192.168.1.0
    192.168.4.0
    192.168.5.0
  Routing Information Sources:
```

```
    Gateway          Distance      Last Update
    192.168.4.3           120      00:00:18
    192.168.5.2           120      00:00:05
Distance: (default is 120)
```

The example highlights the configuration information that can be gleaned from the output, at least for configuration commands mentioned in this chapter, as follows:

■ The **version 2** RIP subcommand configured R1 to send version 2 updates only and to process received version 2 updates only as well.

■ Automatic summarization (per the default **auto-summary** command) is enabled.

■ The **maximum-paths** command is set to 4 (also the default).

■ The "Routing for Networks" section re-lists the configuration of **network** commands, listing the network numbers in those commands. In this case, it implies three RIP subcommands: **network 192.168.1.0**, **network 192.168.4.0**, and **network 192.168.5.0**.

The output also lists RIP status information. For instance, look at the bottom of the example, to the "Routing Information Sources" section (not highlighted). It lists two gateways (that is, routers) by IP address. This list is the list of IP addresses of neighboring routers from which R1 has heard RIP updates. (If you look back to Figure 19-9, you will see these two IP addresses as addresses on R3 and R2, respectively.) The last update timer lists the time since R1 last heard from the neighbor; remember, RIP relies on the periodic receipt of RIP updates to know that the neighbor still exists. In short, this list shows that R1 is learning RIP routes from these two routers.

Examining the Best RIP Routes Using RIP Database

One more command can reveal some important details about RIP operation on a router: the **show ip rip database** command. This command lists the prefix/length of each subnet known to the local router's RIP process. This command lists the local router's best route to each known subnet. In particular, this command lists

■ Routes for subnets learned from other RIP routers

■ Routes for connected subnets for which RIP is enabled on interfaces due to the RIP **network** command(s)

The fact that the **show ip rip database** command lists both learned routes and connected routes for RIP-enabled interfaces makes this command unique. In comparison, Examples 19-3 and 19-4 show samples of the **show ip route** command from R1 in Figure 19-10, listing RIP-learned routes. However, you cannot tell for sure on which interfaces RIP has been enabled based on this output. Example 19-5 shows how the **show ip protocols** command identifies the interfaces on which RIP is enabled, with three interfaces on that same Router R1. However, this command does not identify any RIP-learned routes.

As shown in Example 19-6, the **show ip rip database** command lists both connected and RIP-learned routes. The sample is again taken from Router R1 in Figure 19-10, with all interfaces working. The output identifies the same three RIP-learned routes listed in Example 19-4, with the hop-count metrics in brackets and the next-hop router IP addresses listed (R2, address 10.1.5.2, and R3, 10.1.4.3). The output also lists the connected subnets, identifying the interfaces on which RIP has been enabled.

Example 19-6 *The* show ip rip database *Command on Router R1 (Figure 19-10)*

```
R1# show ip rip database
10.0.0.0/8      auto-summary
10.1.1.0/24     directly connected, GigabitEthernet0/1
10.1.2.0/24
    [1] via 10.1.5.2, 00:00:00, Serial0/0/0
10.1.3.0/24
    [1] via 10.1.4.3, 00:00:08, Serial0/0/1
10.1.4.0/24     directly connected, Serial0/0/1
10.1.5.0/24     directly connected, Serial0/0/0
10.1.6.0/24
    [1] via 10.1.5.2, 00:00:00, Serial0/0/0
    [1] via 10.1.4.3, 00:00:08, Serial0/0/1
```

Optional RIPv2 Configuration and Verification

This next major section, the third of four major sections in this chapter, introduces a few optional RIPv2 features. The features are passive interfaces, maximum (routing) paths, automatic route summarization, and discontiguous networks.

Controlling RIP Updates with the passive-interface Command

In some cases, you want to enable RIP on an interface so that you can advertise about the connected subnet, but you do not need to advertise routes on that interface. This is typically true for any router LAN interface for which that router interface is the only interface connected to the LAN. No other routers connect to the LAN, so the router does not need to send updates onto the LAN.

The RIPv2 **passive-interface** command can be used to stop all RIPv2 updates from being sent out the interface that is matched by a **network** command. By making an interface passive to RIP, the RIP process no longer sends RIP updates out that interface. RIP will still process any received updates and will still advertise about the connected subnet.

IOS gives us two configuration methods to make interfaces passive. The first is the most obvious: use the **passive-interface** *type number* RIP subcommand for each interface that you want to make passive to RIP.

Example 19-7 shows a revised version of the Router R1 configuration first shown in Example 19-2. In that example, all three routers (from Figure 19-10) connect to subnets of network 10.0.0.0. All three routers also have a G0/1 LAN interface that connects to a LAN that has no other routers connected to it. Example 19-7 shows the original configuration from Example 19-2, with the addition of the **passive-interface** command to make the LAN interface passive.

Example 19-7 *Directing RIPv2 to Not Send Advertisements with* **passive-interface**

```
router rip
 version 2
 network 10.0.0.0
 passive-interface G0/1
```

The second configuration method flips the logic: Make all interfaces passive by default, with the **passive-interface default** RIP subcommand, and then selectively make interfaces not be passive, with the **no passive-interface** *type number* RIP subcommand. Using this method makes sense when a router has mostly passive interfaces and only a few nonpassive interfaces. However, just to show the configuration, Example 19-8 converts the configuration of Example 19-7 to this alternate style, under the assumption that R1 has three interfaces enabled for RIP: S0/0/0 and S0/0/1 (which should not be passive), and G0/1 (which should be passive).

Example 19-8   *Using the* **passive-interface default** *Command Option*

```
router rip
 version 2
 network 10.0.0.0
 passive-interface default
 no passive-interface s0/0/0
 no passive-interface s0/0/1
```

Supporting Multiple Equal-Cost Routes with Maximum Paths

What should a router do when it learns multiple routes for the same subnet but the metrics tie? Routing protocols use their metrics to choose the best route to each destination subnet, but with RIP's hop-count metric, ties can easily happen. So RIP needs options for how to deal with a tie.

RIP's default behavior when it learns more than one route that ties is to put multiple routes into the routing table and use them all. Once in the routing table, the router's forwarding logic balances the packets across those equal-metric routes.

For instance, consider Figure 19-11. R1 will learn two different 2-hop routes to subnet 10.1.4.0 (a router with R3 as the next-hop router and a route with R2 as the next-hop router). R1 will then place both routes in its routing table, with equal metric (2). When R1 needs to forward a packet to subnet 10.1.4.0, R1 can send some packets over one route and some over the other, balancing the load.

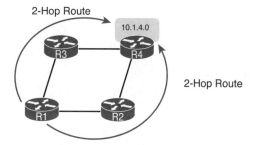

Figure 19-11   *Equal-Cost Routes with RIP*

Cisco refers to this feature of using multiple equal-metric routes to the same destination as *equal-cost load balancing*. RIP controls this behavior with the **maximum-paths** *number-of-paths* RIP subcommand, whose default setting of 4 means that RIP will use the feature by default, with up to 4 equal cost routes for each subnet. This command can be set larger (the maximum setting is dependent on the route model and IOS version), and it can be set as low

19

as 1. Setting the value to 1 disables the feature, so that RIP places the first-learned equal-metric route into the routing table.

Understanding Autosummarization and Discontiguous Classful Networks

Older routing protocols, namely RIPv1 and IGRP, were classified as *classful routing protocols*. These older classful routing protocols had to use a more careful and cautious subnet design plan to avoid a problem called a *discontiguous classful network*. These simpler old routing protocols just got confused when a classful network became discontiguous, because of a required feature of classful routing protocols called autosummarization.

Today, most enterprises use OSPF or EIGRP, or in a few cases, RIPv2. All these protocols are classless routing protocols. These classless routing protocols either do not have a problem with discontiguous classful networks or can be configured so they do not have a problem. In fact, when using RIPv2, if you simply configure the **no auto-summary** RIP subcommand on every router, you can avoid the problem altogether. But of course, it helps to understand what the problem is as well, so this section looks at both autosummarization and the discontiguous network problem.

A routing protocol that uses autosummarization automatically creates a summary route under certain conditions. That automatic process happens when

■ That one router connects to subnets of multiple different classful networks

■ That router uses a routing protocol that uses the autosummary feature. (Note that classful routing protocols had to use this feature and could not disable it.)

To see specifically what that means, consider Figure 19-12, which shows one router (R3) that connects to several subnets of network 10.0.0.0 on the right and to a serial link in network 172.16.0.0 on the left. In other words, R3 meets the first criteria in the list. If using a routing protocol with the autosummarization feature, R3, when advertising a route to the left toward R2, would automatically create a summary route: a route for the entire Class A network 10.0.0.0, as shown in the figure.

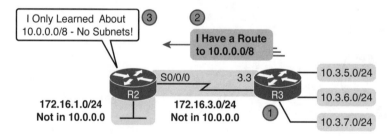

Figure 19-12 *Autosummarization Example*

Following the steps in the figure:

1. R3 has autosummary enabled, with the RIPv2 **auto-summary** router subcommand.
2. R3 advertises a route for all of Class A network 10.0.0.0, instead of advertising routes for each subnet inside network 10.0.0.0, because the link to R2 is a link in another network (172.16.0.0).

3. R2 learns one route in network 10.0.0.0: a route to 10.0.0.0/8, which represents all of network 10.0.0.0, with R3 as the next-hop router.

Autosummarization is not necessarily bad by itself, but when combined with a design that creates a discontiguous classful network, the combination is bad. Which of course begs the question of what is a discontiguous classful network. First, more formally:

Contiguous network: A network topology in which subnets of network X are not separated by subnets of any other classful network

Discontiguous network: A network topology in which subnets of network X are separated by subnets of some other classful network

Figure 19-13 makes the idea more obvious. First, look to the far left and right and see the subnet IDs for several subnets of network 10.0.0.0. Then look in the center, and see subnets of network 172.16.0.0. The subnets of network 10.0.0.0 are separated by subnets of another network, so network 10.0.0.0 is discontiguous.

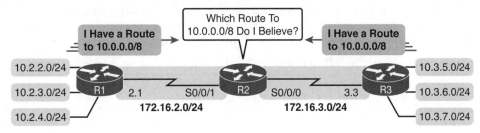

Figure 19-13 *Discontiguous Network 10.0.0.0*

The figure also points out the issue when combining autosummarization and discontiguous networks. With autosummarization on both R1 and R3, R1 declares with its routing update "All of network 10.0.0.0 is over here." R3 does the same. R2, in the middle, is confused and does not even realize that it is confused. If R2 sends all packets destined for network 10.0.0.0 to the left, the hosts in the subnets on the right will be unreachable, and vice versa. If R2 balances the traffic over the two routes to network 10.0.0.0, sending some to the left and some to the right, then it appears that random hosts work for short periods of time.

This problem has two solutions. The old-fashioned solution is to create IP addressing plans that do not create discontiguous classful networks. In other words, keep all subnets of each classful network together in a design. For instance, in this case, use subnets of network 10.0.0.0 for those links in the middle of the figure, or use subnets of a third classful network instead of the 172.16.0.0 subnets on the left.

The other solution solves the problem by disabling autosummarization with the **no auto-summary** RIPv2 subcommand. This command is needed on the router that connects to both classful networks (Routers R1 and R3 in Figure 19-13), because those are the routers that automatically create summary routes. Figure 19-14 shows the results with this solution: R1 and R3 advertise about all their subnets to R2, and R2 knows specific routes for each subnet, solving the problem.

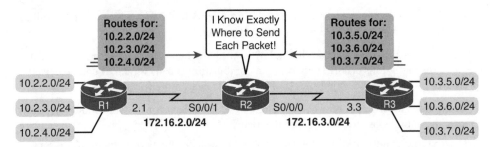

Figure 19-14 *The Effect of* **no auto-summary** *on the Network from Figure 19-13*

Verifying Optional RIP Features

All the configuration settings for these optional features can be seen in the output of the **show ip protocols** command. Example 19-9 shows a sample from Router R1, based on the original Figure 19-9 and Example 19-1. (That is the example with six different IP networks, with each router needing three different **network** commands.) The RIP configuration is listed at the top of the example for perspective, with each of these optional settings changed from their default values to make it more obvious in the output of the example.

Example 19-9 *Verifying RIPv2 Optional Configuration in* **show ip protocols** *Output*

```
R2# show running-config
! Lines other than the RIP configuration are omitted
router rip
 version 2
 network 192.168.1.0
 network 192.168.4.0
 network 192.168.5.0
 no auto-summary
 maximum-paths 3
 passive-interface gigabitethernet0/1


R1# show ip protocols
Routing Protocol is "rip"
  Outgoing update filter list for all interfaces is not set
  Incoming update filter list for all interfaces is not set
  Sending updates every 30 seconds, next due in 23 seconds
  Invalid after 180 seconds, hold down 180, flushed after 240
  Redistributing: rip
  Default version control: send version 2, receive version 2
    Interface           Send  Recv  Triggered RIP  Key-chain
    Serial0/0/0         2     2
    Serial0/0/1         2     2
  Automatic network summarization is not in effect
  Maximum path: 3
  Routing for Networks:
    192.168.1.0
    192.168.4.0
```

```
        192.168.5.0
 Passive Interface(s):
    GigabitEthernet0/1
 Routing Information Sources:
    Gateway          Distance      Last Update
    192.168.4.3          120       00:00:03
    192.168.5.2          120       00:00:09
 Distance: (default is 120)
```

On a final note regarding the passive interfaces, note that the **show ip protocols** output lists an interface either in the primary list of interfaces (those that are not passive) or in the list of passive interfaces, but not both. For instance, interface G0/1 is in the list under the heading "Passive Interface(s):" but is not under the heading "Interface."

Example 19-10 closes this section by showing an example in which a router has learned multiple equal-cost routes. In this case, R1 has learned two 1-hop routes to subnet 192.168.6.0/24, just as was shown in Figure 19-11. Note that the **show ip route** command lists the subnet ID on one line, with two different sets of forwarding instructions (outgoing interface and next-hop IP address) listed on the two lines.

Example 19-10 *Evidence of Equal-Cost Load Balancing*

```
R1# show ip route rip
! Legend omitted for brevity

      192.168.1.0/24 is variably subnetted, 2 subnets, 2 masks
C        192.168.1.0/24 is directly connected, GigabitEthernet0/1
L        192.168.1.1/32 is directly connected, GigabitEthernet0/1
R      192.168.2.0/24 [120/1] via 192.168.5.2, 00:00:21, Serial0/0/0
R      192.168.3.0/24 [120/1] via 192.168.4.3, 00:00:05, Serial0/0/1
      192.168.4.0/24 is variably subnetted, 2 subnets, 2 masks
C        192.168.4.0/24 is directly connected, Serial0/0/1
L        192.168.4.1/32 is directly connected, Serial0/0/1
      192.168.5.0/24 is variably subnetted, 2 subnets, 2 masks
C        192.168.5.0/24 is directly connected, Serial0/0/0
L        192.168.5.1/32 is directly connected, Serial0/0/0
R      192.168.6.0/24 [120/1] via 192.168.5.2, 00:00:21, Serial0/0/0
                      [120/1] via 192.168.4.3, 00:00:05, Serial0/0/1
```

That concludes this chapter's examination of a few optional RIPv2 features. The following list summarizes these options and their configuration:

Step 1.   Disable RIP sent updates on some interfaces as follows:

    A. Use the **passive-interface** *type number* command in RIP configuration mode to make RIP not send RIP updates out that RIP-enabled interface.

    B. Use the **passive-interface default** command in RIP configuration mode to make RIP not send RIP updates out all interfaces by default, and then selectively use the **no passive-interface** *type number* command in RIP configuration mode to enable RIP sent updates on some interfaces.

Step 2.   Use the **no auto-summary** command in RIP configuration mode to disable automatic summarization on routers that connect to multiple classful networks, as needed.

Step 3.   Use the **maximum-paths** *number* command in RIP configuration mode to set the number of equal-metric routes for a single destination subnet to add to the IP routing table.

RIPv2 Default Routes

In network designs that use a single router at a remote site, the remote router can use a default route rather than using a routing protocol. The section "Static Default Routes" in Chapter 18 shows that exact scenario, with branch offices, each with a single router. Each branch office router could use a static default route that forwards packets over the single WAN link toward the core of the enterprise network.

In some designs, the network engineer might want to use the default route concept, except that multiple routers may exist in that part of the network. All the routers in that part of the network would need to forward their packets to the one router that has a WAN link connected to another part of the enterprise or to the Internet.

Figure 19-15 shows an example, with enterprise routers R1, B01, and B02 all wanting to use the one link to the Internet that is connected to R1. To make that work, R1 uses a default route that points directly over that link to the Internet. Routers B01 and B02 have default routes that forward packets to R1, so R1 will then forward packets by default to the Internet. (The figure shows the default routes on each router as arrow lines.)

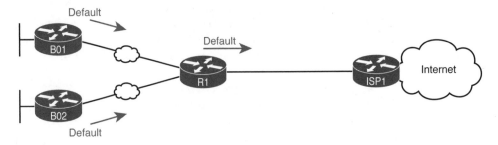

Figure 19-15 *Branch Routers with Default Route to R1; R1 with Default Route to Internet*

Learning Default Routes Using Static Routes and RIPv2

The enterprise routers in this design could each use a static default route, but RIPv2 provides an alternative that uses a static default route on only one router. One router, directly connected to the link of the true default route, configures a static default route as normal. That router then uses RIPv2 to advertise a default route—a route to 0.0.0.0, mask /0—to the other routers. Basically, the remote routers learn default routes like those shown for routers B01 and B02 in Figure 19-15, pointing to the router that originally advertised the default route.

Figure 19-16 shows the basic idea of what happens on the router on which the static default route is configured. R1 configures a static route to the Internet at Step 1, and then advertises that static route to the other routers with RIPv2 at Step 2.

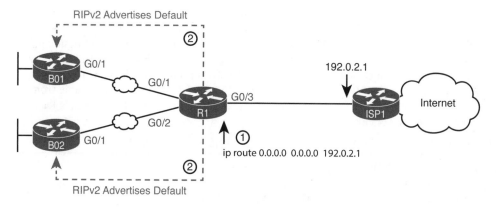

Figure 19-16 *A Scenario for RIPv2 to Advertise Default Routes*

The key to making the process work is the addition of the **default-information originate** command to the RIP configuration on the router where the static default route is configured, as demonstrated in Example 19-11. This new RIP subcommand tells the router simply this:

If the IPv4 routing table has a default route in it, advertise a default route with RIP, with this local router as the eventual destination of those default routes.

Note that only the router that originally advertises the default route—Router R1 in the example shown in the figure—needs the **default-information originate** command. Other RIPv2 routers, like B01 and B02 in the example, learn the default route like any other RIP-learned route.

Example 19-11 *Configuring Router R1 to Advertise a Default Route with RIPv2*

```
R1# configure terminal
R1(config)# ip route 0.0.0.0 0.0.0.0 192.0.2.1
R1(config)# router rip
R1(config-router)# default-information originate
R1(config-router)# end
R1#
```

To verify the configuration, first check on the static default route. The configuration and verification of the static default route on Router R1 looks the same as it did in the "Static Default Routes" section in Chapter 18. Example 19-12 shows a sample from Router R1; note the static route to prefix/length 0.0.0.0/0 and the Gateway of Last Resort set to the next-hop address of 192.0.2.1.

Example 19-12 *Displaying the Static Default Route Configured on Router R1*

```
R1# show ip route static
! Legend omitted
Gateway of last resort is 192.0.2.1 to network 0.0.0.0

S*    0.0.0.0/0 [1/0] via 192.0.2.1
```

The other routers list default routes in their routing table, but of course the routes show up as RIP-learned routes instead of static routes. Note that the route for 0.0.0.0/0 shows up with a code of R, meaning that it is a RIP-learned route. The route also has an * beside it, meaning that this route is a candidate to be the default route for this router. The Gateway of Last Resort (which is the chosen default route for this router) lists the same next-hop IP address listed in the RIP-learned default route. Example 19-13 shows an example from router B01, which will use a default route with next-hop address 10.1.12.1, which is R1's IP address on the WAN link.

Example 19-13 *Router B01 with Default Route Learned Using RIPv2*

```
B01# show ip route rip
! Legend omitted
Gateway of last resort is 10.1.12.1 to network 0.0.0.0

R*      0.0.0.0/0 [120/1] via 10.1.12.1, 00:00:06, GigabitEthernet0/1
```

Learning a Default Route Using DHCP

Chapter 20, "DHCP and IP Networking on Hosts," discusses how Dynamic Host Configuration Protocol (DHCP) can be used by hosts to learn their IP addresses. Hosts can also learn other important details using DHCP, like the subnet mask to use, the DNS server IP addresses, and the IP address of the router on the subnet to use as the default gateway.

Routers that connect to the Internet can use DHCP as well. In particular, a router with a link to the Internet can dynamically learn the interface IPv4 address it should use. Additionally, DHCP announces the IP address of the ISP's router on the other end of the Internet connection, listed as the default gateway in the DHCP messages. And that default gateway IP address is the address the enterprise router would normally use as the next-hop address on its default route to the Internet.

To pull those ideas together, examine the details in Figure 19-17. The figure repeats the same design shown in the previous two figures, with one change. In this case, enterprise Router R1 uses DHCP to learn its IP address (192.0.2.2). The DHCP process also lists a default gateway, 192.0.2.1, which in this case identifies the ISP router's IP address on the link.

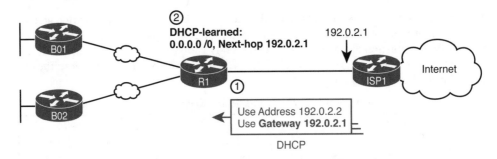

Figure 19-17 *Enterprise Router Building and Advertising Default Routes with DHCP Client*

By dynamically learning the IP address of the ISP router, Router R1 can dynamically add a default route to its routing table. R1's new default route will use the default gateway IP address from the DHCP message—which is the ISP router's IP address—as the next-hop address. Then, using the same RIPv2 methods and the **default-information originate** RIP subcommand configured on Router R1, R1 will advertise a default route to the other routers.

Example 19-14 shows the configuration on Router R1. Note that it begins with R1 configuring its G0/1 interface to use DHCP to learn the IP address to use on the interface, using the **ip address dhcp** command.

Example 19-14 *Learning an Address and Default Static Route with DHCP*

```
R1# configure terminal
R1(config)# interface gigabitethernet0/1
R1(config-if)# ip address dhcp
R1(config-if)# end
R1#
R1# show ip route static
! Legend omitted
Gateway of last resort is 192.0.2.1 to network 0.0.0.0

S*    0.0.0.0/0 [254/0] via 192.0.2.1
```

The end of the example shows the default route added to R1's routing table as a result of learning a default gateway address of 192.0.2.1 from DHCP. Oddly, the route shows this route as a static route, although the route is learned dynamically. In fact, the only difference in the output of the **show ip route static** command in this case, versus the case with the static route as configured with the **ip route** command, is the administrative distance of 254. IOS uses a default administrative distance of 1 for static routes configured with the **ip route** configuration command (as seen in Example 19-12). When adding a route to the default gateway, as learned with DHCP, IOS uses a default administrative distance of 254, as shown here in Example 19-14.

Finally, not shown in the example, the remote routers still learn the route, so R1 also needs the default-information originate RIP subcommand. On those remote routers like B01 and B02, there is no difference in the show command output for the default routes.

Troubleshooting RIPv2

Welcome to this fourth and final major section of this chapter, a section that focuses on troubleshooting RIPv2.

Troubleshooting on the ICND1, ICND2, and CCNA R&S exams requires thinking about question types. First, Sim questions typically begin with a broken configuration, and to answer the question, you must reconfigure one or more devices to fix the configuration. To prepare for Sim questions, you need to master the art of correct configuration so that you quickly recognize the incorrect configuration. The earlier topics have already covered configuration in some depth.

However, Simlet questions make you exercise your verification and troubleshooting skills, and this final section hopes to focus more on those skills. With Simlet questions, you do see a Simulator where you can issue commands. The lab may or may not be configured correctly, and you may or may not be able to see the configuration.

To be ready for these types of questions, you must be ready to predict what different symptoms would be when a network was misconfigured in a particular way, and what the available **show** commands would look like. With RIPv2, that primarily means that you have to think about the output of the **show ip route** and **show ip protocols** commands, in cases of misconfiguration, which is the focus of this section.

This section examines the most common misconfiguration items with the RIP settings included in this chapter, with a discussion of typical symptoms. The end of the section summarizes these common issues for easier review and study.

All the examples in this section use the same small sample topology, specifically chosen as a good backdrop to discuss the issues in this section. Figure 19-18 shows the topology, interfaces, and IP subnets, and Example 19-15 that follows shows the correct configuration on both routers.

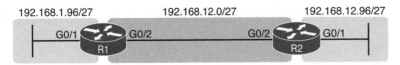

192.168.1.96/27   192.168.12.0/27   192.168.12.96/27

Figure 19-18 *Sample Network for Troubleshooting Examples*

Example 19-15 *R1 and R2 Correct RIPv2 Configuration*

```
! Configuration on router R1
interface G0/1
 ip address 192.168.1.101 255.255.255.224
interface G0/2
 ip address 192.168.12.1 255.255.255.224
!
router rip
 version 2
 no auto-summary
 network 192.168.1.0
 network 192.168.12.0
! Configuration on router R2
interface G0/1
 ip address 192.168.12.102 255.255.255.224
interface G0/2
 ip address 192.168.12.2 255.255.255.224
!
router rip
 version 2
 network 192.168.12.0
```

Symptoms with Missing and Incorrect network Commands

As a first example, think about the symptoms that should occur when a router is missing a **network** command, or the command was incorrect so that it does not match an interface or interfaces. Basically, two things happen:

- The router does not advertise about the subnets on those interfaces.

- The router does not exchange routing information with other routers on those interfaces.

Imagine that the engineer left out either of the **network** commands on Router R1 in Example 19-15. Can you imagine the results? Can you predict the output of the **show ip protocols** command—the one command that reveals RIPv2 configuration details other than the **show running-config** command?

Consider the omission of the **network 192.168.12.0** command from R1 first. Per the figure, that means that R1 would not enable RIPv2 on the link between R1 and R2, so that R1 and R2 would not exchange RIPv2 routes at all. The **show ip protocols** command on R1 would not list R2 as an information source, and that output on R1 would omit R1's G0/2 interface in the list of interfaces. Example 19-16 shows those facts with R1's **show ip protocols** command output for just this example with a missing **network 192.168.12.0** command.

Example 19-16   show ip protocols *on R1 with Missing* network 192.168.12.0 *Command*

```
R1# show ip protocols
Routing Protocol is "rip"
  Outgoing update filter list for all interfaces is not set
  Incoming update filter list for all interfaces is not set
  Sending updates every 30 seconds, next due in 4 seconds
  Invalid after 180 seconds, hold down 180, flushed after 240
  Redistributing: rip
  Default version control: send version 2, receive version 2
    Interface              Send  Recv  Triggered RIP  Key-chain
    GigabitEthernet0/1     2     2
  Automatic network summarization is not in effect
  Maximum path: 4
  Routing for Networks:
    192.168.1.0
  Routing Information Sources:
    Gateway         Distance      Last Update
  Distance: (default is 120)
```

In particular, note that R1 lists only one interface in its list of interfaces (G0/1) and no information sources, per the highlighted sections. It also lists only one network under the heading "Routing for Networks," which is the section that lists the networks in the configured **network** commands.

Now think about the opposite case, in which the configuration of Example 19-17 omits the **network 192.168.1.0** command but includes the **network 192.168.12.0** command. In that case, R1 and R2 will communicate with RIP. But what symptoms might you expect to see? In this case, R1 will not advertise about the subnet off R1's G0/1 interface, 192.168.1.96/27, because there is no **network** command matching that interface. As a result, R2 will not list

19

192.168.1.96/27 in its IP routing table, and R1 will not list its interface G0/1 in the list of enabled interfaces in the output of the **show ip protocols** command. Example 19-17 shows the output from **show ip protocols** on R1 in this case.

Example 19-17 show ip protocols *on R1 with Missing* network 192.168.1.0 *Command*

```
R1# show ip protocols
Routing Protocol is "rip"
  Outgoing update filter list for all interfaces is not set
  Incoming update filter list for all interfaces is not set
  Sending updates every 30 seconds, next due in 4 seconds
  Invalid after 180 seconds, hold down 180, flushed after 240
  Redistributing: rip
  Default version control: send version 2, receive version 2
    Interface             Send  Recv  Triggered RIP  Key-chain
    GigabitEthernet0/2    2     2
  Automatic network summarization is not in effect
  Maximum path: 4
  Routing for Networks:
    192.168.12.0
  Routing Information Sources:
    Gateway        Distance      Last Update
    192.168.12.2       120       00:00:12
  Distance: (default is 120)
```

Again, this example provides another chance to practice an important troubleshooting skill: to re-create the RIP configuration's **network** commands based on the output of the **show ip protocols** command. The section with the heading "Routing for Networks" in Example 19-17 lists only 192.168.12.0, meaning that only the **network 192.168.12.0** command exists. Earlier, Example 19-16 lists only 192.168.1.0, meaning only the **network 192.168.1.0** command exists in that case.

Issues Related to Passive Interfaces

The **passive-interface** command has a basic and useful function, but when used incorrectly, not only does it cause problems but the problem has an odd symptom. The passive interface feature should never be used on an interface that connects to another RIP router. However, if one router is incorrectly configured to be passive, whereas a neighboring router is not, the passive router still hears RIP updates, while the correctly configured router does not hear updates.

For example, imagine you start with the correct configuration shown in Example 19-15 again. Then imagine that the engineer misreads the figure and adds a **passive-interface g0/2** command to R1, instead of a **passive-interface g0/1** command (which would make sense). Figure 19-19 shows the results: R1 quits sending RIP updates to R2, but R2 keeps sending them to R1. R1 has the incorrect configuration but R2 suffers.

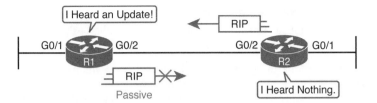

Figure 19-19 *One-Way Exchange of Routes with Incorrect Passive Interface*

Anytime you see a RIP problem in which routes are not being learned, make sure to check for passive interfaces in the configuration and with **show ip protocols.**

Issues Related to auto-summary

The earlier section "Understanding Autosummarization and Discontiguous Classful Networks" discussed when a network needs to disable the use of autosummarization. But when you do need to disable automatic summarization, there is one common mistake: to put the **no auto-summary** command on the wrong router.

As noted earlier, the **auto-summary** and **no auto-summary** setting only impacts routers that connect directly to multiple classful networks. In the small network topology used in this troubleshooting section (Figure 19-18), R1 directly connects to subnets of two different classful networks, so a **no auto-summary** command would affect its operation. R2 does not connect to subnets of two different classful networks, so a **no auto-summary** command on R2 would have no effect.

First, the original configuration in Example 19-15 lists a **no auto-summary** command on Router R1. As a result, R1 does not perform automatic summarization, instead advertising a route for 192.168.1.96/27 to R2. Example 19-18 shows that route on Router R2 in the top half of the example.

Example 19-18   show ip route rip *on R2 with Different* auto-summary *Settings on R1*

```
! R2's RIP route with no auto-summary configured on R1 (per Example 19-12)
R2# show ip route | section 192.168.1.0
! lines omitted for brevity
     192.168.1.0/27 is subnetted, 1 subnets
R       192.168.1.96 [120/1] via 192.168.12.1, 00:00:16, GigabitEthernet0/2
! R2's RIP route with auto-summary configured on R1
R2# show ip route rip
! lines omitted for brevity
R    192.168.1.0/24 [120/1] via 192.168.12.1, 00:00:03, GigabitEthernet0/2
```

Now consider the mistake of putting the **no auto-summary** command on R2 in this case and leaving R1 with a default setting of **auto-summary.** In this case, the design does not create a discontiguous classful network, so no real problem exists. However, changing R1 to use the **auto-summary** setting would cause R2 to learn a different route: R1 would advertise a route for Class C network 192.168.1.0/24 to R2, instead of a route for subnet 192.168.1.96/27. The second half of Example 19-18 shows that route, after that change to the configurations of R1 and R2.

19

RIP Issues Caused by Other Router Features

RIP could be configured perfectly but still not work due to other issues. This last part of the troubleshooting section takes a brief look at these other features.

First, RIP operates only on working interfaces; that is, interfaces that are in an up and up status per the **show interfaces** and **show ip interfaces** commands. Chapter 17, "Operating Cisco Routers," and Chapter 24, "Troubleshooting IPv4 Routing," go into more detail about issues that can cause an interface to fail.

RIP requires that all neighbors on a link be in the same subnet. That makes good sense from an IP design perspective, but it is the kind of error that can be easily created for an exam question. For instance, Example 19-15—the correct configuration to go along with Figure 19-15 and the examples in this troubleshooting section—shows R1 and R2 with addresses 192.168.12.1 and 192.168.12.2, both with mask /27 on their shared Ethernet link. If R2 had been misconfigured with 192.168.12.202/27, R1's 192.168.12.1/27 address/mask would be in a different subnet, and R1 and R2 would ignore the RIP updates received from each other.

Finally, you have not yet gotten to the chapters about access control lists (ACL) yet (Chapter 25, "Basic IPv4 Access Control Lists," and Chapter 26, "Advanced IPv4 Access Control Lists," cover ACLs), but ACLs act as packet filters. The router can watch packets as they pass through the router, match the packet header, and decide to filter some packets based on those matches. The ACL configuration could inadvertently match and discard RIP messages. As it turns out, the RIP uses UDP as a transport protocol, with well-known UDP port 520. Any ACL that matches and discards these packets cause the symptom in which the RIP configuration is correct but the routers do not hear from each other.

Summary of RIP Troubleshooting Issues

Summarizing the troubleshooting issues mentioned in this section, for easier review and study:

Step 1. The RIP **network** command controls where RIP operates. If a missing **network** command fails to enable RIP on an interface:

 A. RIP will not advertise about that connected subnet.

 B. RIP will not send advertisements out that interface or process received advertisements in that interface.

Step 2. The **passive-interface** command should not be used for interfaces that connect to other routers. If configured, the passive router does not advertise routes to neighboring routers, even though the passive router can still learn RIP routes from RIP messages entering that interface.

Step 3. The **no auto-summary** command has an impact only on routers that directly connect to more than one classful network. However, the command is needed only if a discontiguous classful network exists.

Step 4. Some non-RIP features impact RIP operation, namely

 A. Interfaces must be working for RIPv2 to use the interfaces.

 B. Two routers on the same link must have IP addresses in the same subnet for RIPv2 to exchange routing information.

 C. Note that ACLs can filter RIP update messages and therefore break RIP.

Chapter Review

One key to doing well on the exams is to perform repetitive spaced review sessions. Review this chapter's material using either the tools in the book, DVD, or interactive tools for the same material found on the book's companion website. Refer to the "Your Study Plan" element for more details. Table 19-5 outlines the key review elements and where you can find them. To better track your study progress, record when you completed these activities in the second column.

Table 19-5   Chapter Review Tracking

Review Element	Review Date(s)	Resource Used
Review key topics		Book, DVD/website
Review key terms		Book, DVD/website
Repeat DIKTA questions		Book, PCPT
Review memory tables		Book, DVD/website
Review config checklists		Book, DVD/website
Do labs		Blog
Review command tables		Book

19

Review All the Key Topics

Table 19-6   Key Topics for Chapter 19

Key Topic Element	Description	Page Number
List	Comparisons of IGPs	438
Table 19-2	A list of RIPv2 features in comparison to RIPv1	443
Figure 19-8	Matching logic on one router with the RIP **network** command	444
List	The three actions RIP takes when enabled on an interface	444
Table 19-3	RIP verification commands	447
List	Analysis of the contents of a single IP route in the output of the **show ip route** command	448
Table 19-4	List of administrative distance values	450
List	Common troubleshooting issues	466

Key Terms You Should Know

administrative distance, distance vector, exterior gateway protocol (EGP), interior gateway protocol (IGP), metric, routing update, contiguous network, discontiguous network, auto-summarization, passive interface, IP routing table, hop count

Command References

Tables 19-7 and 19-8 list configuration and verification commands used in this chapter. As an easy review exercise, cover the left column in a table, read the right column, and try to recall the command without looking. Then repeat the exercise, covering the right column, and try to recall what the command does.

Table 19-7 Chapter 19 Configuration Command Reference

Command	Description
router rip	Global command that moves the user into RIP configuration mode
network *network-number*	RIP subcommand that lists a classful network number, enabling RIP on all of that router's interfaces in that classful network
version 2	RIP subcommand that sets the RIP version
passive-interface {*interface-type interface-number*}	RIP subcommand that tells RIP to no longer advertise RIP updates on the listed interface
passive-interface default	RIP subcommand that changes the default setting on RIP-enabled interfaces to be passive instead of not passive
no passive-interface {*interface-type interface-number*}	RIP subcommand that overrides a default passive setting per the **passive-interface default** command for the listed interface
[no] auto-sunmmary	RIP subcommand that toggles on (**auto-summary**) and off (**no auto-summary**) the autosummarization feature of RIP
maximum-paths *number*	RIP subcommand that sets the number of equal-metric routes for the same subnet that RIP will add to the IP routing table
default-information originate	RIP subcommand that causes RIP to advertise a default route—a route for prefix 0.0.0.0, mask 0.0.0.0—if the local router has a default route in its routing table already
ip address dhcp	Interface subcommand that causes a router to act as a DHCP client, learning the IPv4 address to use on the interface and dynamically learning a default route that uses the DHCP-announced default gateway address as the next-hop IP address in a static route

Table 19-8 Chapter 19 EXEC Command Reference

Command	Lists information about all routes known by the local RIP process, including those not added to the local router's routing table.
show ip interface brief	Lists one line per router interface, including the IP address and interface status; an interface must have an IP address and be in an "up and up" status before RIP begins to work on the interface
show ip route [rip]	Lists the routing table, including RIP-learned routes, and optionally just RIP-learned routes
show ip route *ip-address*	Lists details about the route the router would match for a packet sent to the listed IP address
show ip protocols	Lists information about the RIP configuration, plus the IP addresses of neighboring RIP routers from which the local router has learned routes
show ip rip database	Lists information about all routes known by the local RIP process, including those not added to the local router's routing table.

CHAPTER 20

DHCP and IP Networking on Hosts

This chapter covers the following exam topics:

1.0 Network Fundamentals

1.8 Configure, verify, and troubleshoot IPv4 addressing and subnetting

1.9 Compare and contrast IPv4 address types

    1.9.a Unicast

    1.9.b Broadcast

    1.9.c Multicast

4.0 Infrastructure Services

4.1 Describe DNS lookup operation

4.3 Configure and verify DHCP on a router (excluding static reservations)

    4.3.a Server

    4.3.b Relay

    4.3.c Client

    4.3.d TFTP, DNS, and gateway options

4.4 Troubleshoot client- and router-based DHCP connectivity issues

In the world of TCP/IP, the word *host* refers to any device with an IP address: your phone, your tablet, a PC, a router, a switch—any device that uses IP to provide a service or just needs an IP address to be managed. The term *host* includes some less-obvious devices as well: the electronic advertising video screen at the mall, your electrical power meter that uses the same technology as mobile phones to submit your electrical usage information for billing, your new car.

No matter the type of host, any host that uses IPv4 needs four IPv4 settings to work properly:

- IP address
- Subnet mask
- Default routers
- DNS server IP addresses

This last chapter in this part of the book completes the discussion of how to build a basic IPv4 network by focusing on the IPv4 settings on hosts. In particular, this chapter begins by discussing how a host can dynamically learn these four settings using the Dynamic Host Configuration Protocol (DHCP). The middle section of the chapter then discusses some tips for how to verify that a host has all four of these IPv4 settings. The third and final section takes a brief tangent to summarize and further explain the differences in the three main types of IPv4 addresses: unicast, broadcast, and multicast.

"Do I Know This Already?" Quiz

Take the quiz (either here, or use the PCPT software) if you want to use the score to help you decide how much time to spend on this chapter. The answers are at the bottom of the page following the quiz, and the explanations are in DVD Appendix C and in the PCPT software.

Table 20-1 "Do I Know This Already?" Foundation Topics Section-to-Question Mapping

Foundation Topics Section	Questions
Configuring Routers to Support DHCP	1–3
Verifying Host IPv4 Settings	4
IPv4 Address Types	5–6

1. A PC connects to a LAN and uses DHCP to lease an IP address for the first time. Of the usual four DHCP messages that flow between the PC and the DHCP server, which ones do the client send? (Choose two answers.)

    a. Acknowledgment

    b. Discover

    c. Offer

    d. Request

2. An enterprise puts the DHCP and DNS servers on VLAN 10/subnet 10 in Atlanta, using IP address 10.1.10.1 for the DHCP server and 10.1.10.2 for the DNS server. A remote router sits in Boston, with devices on the Boston LAN using the DHCP and DNS servers in Atlanta. Which of the following needs to be configured in the routers in this enterprise to support DHCP and DNS?

    a. The **ip helper-address 10.1.10.1** command in the Atlanta router

    b. The **ip helper-address 10.1.10.2** command in the Boston router

    c. The **ip name-server 10.1.10.2** command in the Atlanta router

    d. The **ip dhcp-server 10.1.10.1** command in the Boston router

    e. None of the other answers are correct.

3. Fred decides to migrate from an old DHCP server platform to use a Cisco router at the headquarters building. This DHCP server, created with configuration in IOS on a Cisco router, supports 200 remote subnets. Which of the following settings are made outside of a per-subnet pool of addresses?

   a. Client IP address

   b. Addresses in that subnet excluded from being leased by the server

   c. Default router

   d. DNS server

   e. Length of address lease

4. PC1, a new PC, just booted for the first time when connected to an enterprise network. PC1 used DHCP to lease IP address 10.1.1.1, learning mask 255.255.255.0, DNS server 10.9.9.9, and default gateway 10.1.1.2, with a lease time of 7 days. Assume that the PC has sent nothing else over the network because the DHCP process completed. The user then opens a web browser and types www.ciscopress.com. Which of the following actions happens next?

   a. PC1 sends an ARP request to find the web server's MAC address.

   b. PC1 sends an ARP request to find the default gateway's (10.1.1.2) MAC address.

   c. PC1 sends a DNS request about www.ciscopress.com to the DNS server (10.9.9.9).

   d. PC1 sends an IP packet to the www.ciscopress.com web server IP address.

5. A packet is sent to a destination address. That single packet is routed through the network to the final router, which then sends the packet to all hosts connected to that one subnet. Which of the following IP address types was used as the destination IP address?

   a. A unicast address

   b. A network broadcast address

   c. A subnet broadcast address

   d. A multicast address

6. A packet is sent to a destination address. That single packet is replicated by a few routers based on the routers' knowledge of hosts that had earlier registered to receive packets sent to that destination address. The routers do not forward copies of the packet onto subnets where no hosts have registered, and do forward copies of the packet onto subnets where at least one host has registered to receive those packets. Which of the following IP address types was used as the destination IP address?

   a. A unicast address

   b. A network broadcast address

   c. A subnet broadcast address

   d. A multicast address

Foundation Topics

Implementing and Troubleshooting DHCP

Dynamic Host Configuration Protocol (DHCP) is one of the most commonly used protocols in a TCP/IP network. The vast majority of hosts in a TCP/IP network are user devices, and the vast majority of user devices learn their IPv4 settings using DHCP.

Using DHCP has several advantages over the other option of manually configuring IPv4 settings. The configuration of host IP settings sits in a DHCP server, with each client learning these settings using DHCP messages. As a result, the host IP configuration is controlled by the IT staff, rather than on local configuration on each host, resulting in fewer user errors. DHCP allows both the permanent assignment of host addresses, but more commonly, DHCP assigns a temporary lease of IP addresses. With these leases, the DHCP server can reclaim IP addresses when a device is removed from the network, making better use of the available addresses.

DHCP also enables mobility. For example, every time a user moves to a new location with a tablet computer—to a coffee shop, a client location, or back at the office—the user's device can connect to another wireless LAN, use DHCP to lease a new IP address in that LAN, and begin working on the new network. Without DHCP, the user would have to ask for information about the local network and configure settings manually, with more than a few users making mistakes.

Although DHCP works automatically for user hosts, it does require some preparation from the network, with some configuration on routers. In some enterprise networks, that router configuration can be a single command on many of the router's LAN interfaces (**ip helper-address** *server-ip*), which identifies the DHCP server by its IP address. In other cases, the router acts as the DHCP server. Regardless, the routers have some role to play.

This first major section of the chapter takes a complete tour of DHCP, from concept, to router configuration, verification, and troubleshooting.

DHCP Concepts

Sit back for a moment, and think about the role of DHCP for a host computer. The host acts as a DHCP client. As a DHCP client, the host begins with no IPv4 settings: no IPv4 address, no mask, no default router, and no DNS server IP addresses. But a DHCP client does have knowledge of the DHCP protocol, so the client can use that protocol to (a) discover a DHCP server and (b) request to lease an IPv4 address.

The DHCP process to lease an IP address uses the following four messages between the client and server. (Also, as a way to help remember the messages, note that the first letters spell DORA):

20

Discover: Sent by the DHCP client to find a willing DHCP server

Offer: Sent by a DHCP server to offer to lease to that client a specific IP address (and inform the client of its other parameters)

Request: Sent by the DHCP client to ask the server to lease the IPv4 address listed in the Offer message.

Acknowledgment: Sent by the DHCP server to assign the address, and to list the mask, default router, and DNS server IP addresses

DHCP clients, however, have a somewhat unique problem: they do not have an IP address yet, but they need to send IP packets. To make that work, DHCP messages make use of two special IPv4 addresses that allow a host that has no IP address to still be able to send and receive messages on the local subnet:

0.0.0.0: An address reserved for use as a source IPv4 address for hosts that do not yet have an IP address.

255.255.255.255: The local broadcast IP address. Packets sent to this destination address are broadcast on the local data link, but routers do not forward them.

To see how these addresses work, Figure 20-1 shows an example of the IP addresses used between a host (A) and a DHCP server on the same LAN. Host A, a client, sends a Discover message, with source IP address of 0.0.0.0 because host A does not have an IP address to use yet. Host A sends the packet to destination 255.255.255.255, which is sent in a LAN broadcast frame, reaching all hosts in the subnet. The client hopes that there is a DHCP server on the local subnet. Why? Packets sent to 255.255.255.255 only go to hosts in the local subnet; Router R1 will not forward this packet.

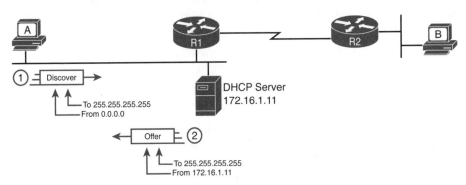

Figure 20-1 *DHCP Discover and Offer*

> **NOTE** Figure 20-1 shows one example of the addresses that can be used in a DHCP Request. This example shows details assuming the DHCP client chooses to use a DHCP option called the *broadcast flag*; all examples in this book assume the broadcast flag is used.

Now look at the Offer message sent back by the DHCP server. The server sets the destination IP address to 255.255.255.255 again. Why? Host A still does not have an IP address, so the server cannot send a packet directly to host A. So, the server sends the packet to "all local hosts in the subnet" address (255.255.255.255). (The packet is also encapsulated in an Ethernet broadcast frame.)

Note that all hosts in the subnet receive the Offer message. However, the original Discover message lists a number called the client ID, typically based on the host's MAC address, that identifies the original host (host A in this case). As a result, host A knows that the Offer message is meant for host A. The rest of the hosts will receive the Offer message, but notice that the message lists another device's DHCP client ID, so the rest of the hosts ignore the Offer message.

Supporting DHCP for Remote Subnets with DHCP Relay

Network engineers have a major design choice to make with DHCP: Do they put a DHCP server in every LAN subnet, or locate a DHCP server in a central site? The question is legitimate. Cisco routers can act as the DHCP server, so a distributed design could use the router at each site as the DHCP server. With a DHCP server in every subnet, as shown in Figure 20-1, the protocol flows stay local to each LAN.

However, a centralized DHCP server approach has advantages as well. In fact, some Cisco design documents suggest a centralized design as a best practice, in part because it allows for centralized control and configuration of all the IPv4 addresses assigned throughout the enterprise.

With a centralized DHCP server, those DHCP messages that flowed only on the local subnet in Figure 20-1 somehow need to flow over the IP network to the centralized DHCP server and back. To make that work, the routers connected to the remote LAN subnets need an interface subcommand: the **ip helper-address** *server-ip* command.

The **ip helper-address** *server-ip* subcommand tells the router to do the following for the messages coming in an interface, from a DHCP client:

1. Watch for incoming DHCP messages, with destination IP address 255.255.255.255.
2. Change that packet's source IP address to the router's incoming interface IP address.
3. Change that packet's destination IP address to the address of the DHCP server (as configured in the **ip helper-address** command).
4. Route the packet to the DHCP server.

This command gets around the "do not route packets sent to 255.255.255.255" rule by changing the destination IP address. Once the destination has been set to match the DHCP server's IP address, the network can route the packet to the server.

> **NOTE** This feature, by which a router relays DHCP messages by changing the IP addresses in the packet header, is called *DHCP Relay*.

Figure 20-2 shows an example of the process. Host A sits on the left, as a DHCP client. The DHCP server (172.16.2.11) sits on the right. R1 has an **ip helper-address 172.16.2.11** command configured, under its G0/0 interface. At Step 1, Router R1 notices the incoming DHCP packet destined for 255.255.255.255. Step 2 shows the results of changing both the source and destination IP address, with R1 routing the packet.

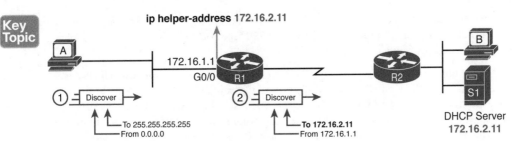

Figure 20-2 *IP Helper Address Effect*

The router uses a similar process for the return DHCP messages from the server. First, for the return packet from the DHCP server, the server simply reverses the source and destination IP address of the packet received from the router (relay agent). For example, in Figure 20-2, the Discover message lists source IP address 172.16.1.1, so the server sends the Offer message back to destination IP address 172.16.1.1.

When a router receives a DHCP message, addressed to one of the router's own IP addresses, the router realizes the packet might be part of the DHCP relay feature. When that happens, the DHCP relay agent (Router R1) needs to change the destination IP address, so that the real DHCP client (host A), which does not have an IP address yet, can receive and process the packet. Figure 20-3 shows one example of how these addresses work, when R1 receives the DHCP Offer message sent to R1's own 172.16.1.1 address. R1 changes the packet's destination to 255.255.255.255, and forwards it out G0/0, because the packet was destined to G0/0's 172.16.1.1 IP address. As a result, all hosts in that LAN (including the DHCP client A) will receive the message.

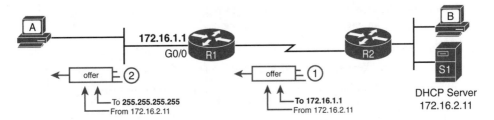

Figure 20-3 *IP Helper Address for the Offer Message Returned from the DHCP Server*

Many enterprise networks use a centralized DHCP server, so the normal router configuration includes an **ip helper-address** command on every LAN interface/subinterface. With that standard configuration, user hosts off any router LAN interface can always reach the DHCP server and lease an IP address.

Information Stored at the DHCP Server

A DHCP server might sound like some large piece of hardware, sitting in a big locked room with lots of air conditioning to keep the hardware cool. However, like most servers, the server is actually software, running on some server OS. The DHCP server could be a piece of software downloaded for free and installed on an old PC. However, because the server needs to be available all the time, to support new DHCP clients, most companies install the software on a very stable and highly available data center, but the DHCP service is still created by software.

To be ready to answer DHCP clients, and to supply them with an IPv4 address and other information, the DHCP server (software) needs configuration. DHCP servers typically organize these IPv4 settings per subnet, because the information the server tells the client is usually the same for all hosts in the same subnet, but slightly different for different subnets. For example, IP addressing rules tell us that all hosts on the same subnet should use the same mask, but hosts in different subnets would have a different default gateway setting.

The following list shows the types of settings the DHCP server needs to know to support DHCP clients:

Subnet ID and mask: The DHCP server can use this information to know all addresses in the subnet. (The DHCP server knows to not lease the subnet ID or subnet broadcast address.)

Reserved (excluded) addresses: The server needs to know which addresses in the subnet to *not* lease. This list allows the engineer to reserve addresses to be used as static IP addresses. For example, most router and switch IP addresses, server addresses, and addresses of most anything other than user devices use a statically assigned IP address. Most of the time, engineers use the same convention for all subnets, either reserving the lowest IP addresses in all subnets, or reserving the highest IP addresses in all subnets.

Default router(s): This is the IP address of the router on that subnet.

DNS IP address(es): This is a list of DNS server IP addresses.

Figure 20-4 shows the concept behind the preconfiguration on a DHCP server for two LAN-based subnets, 172.16.1.0/24 and 172.16.2.0/24. The DHCP server sits on the right. For each subnet, the server defines all the items in the list. In this case, the configuration reserves the lowest IP addresses in the subnet to be used as static addresses.

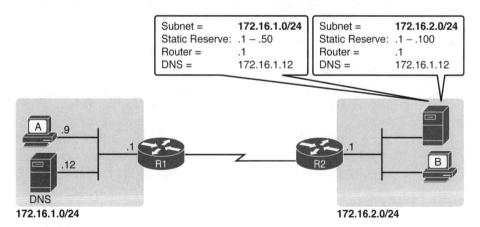

Figure 20-4 *Preconfiguration on a DHCP Server*

The configuration can list other parameters as well. For example, it can set the time limit for leasing an IP address. The server leases an address for a time (usually a number of days), and then the client can ask to renew the lease. If the client does not renew, the server can reclaim the IP address and put it back in the pool of available IP addresses. The server configuration sets the maximum time for the lease.

DHCP uses three allocation modes, based on small differences in the configuration at the DHCP server. *Dynamic allocation* refers to the DHCP mechanisms and configuration described throughout this chapter. Another method, *automatic allocation*, sets the DHCP lease time to infinite. As a result, once the server chooses an address from the pool and assigns the IP address to a client, the IP address remains with that same client indefinitely. A third mode, *static allocation*, preconfigures the specific IP address for a client based on the client's MAC address. That specific client is the only client that then uses the IP address. (Note that this chapter shows examples and configuration for dynamic allocation only.)

Of note, the exam topics mention one other configuration DHCP server setting for a value that can be passed to DHCP clients—the IP address of a Trivial File Transfer Protocol (TFTP) server. TFTP servers provide a basic means of storing files that can then be transferred to a client host. As it turns out, Cisco IP phones rely on TFTP to retrieve several configuration files when the phone initializes. DHCP plays a key role by supplying the IP address of the TFTP server that the phones should use.

DHCP Server Configuration on Routers

A quick Google search on "DHCP server products" reveals that many companies offer DHCP server software. Cisco routers (and some Cisco switches) can also act as a DHCP server with just a little added configuration.

Configuring a Cisco router to act as a DHCP server uses a new configuration concept, one per subnet, called a *DHCP pool*. All the per-subnet settings go into a per-subnet DHCP pool. The only DHCP command that sits outside the pool is the command that defines the list of addresses excluded from being leased by DHCP. The Cisco IOS DHCP server configuration steps are as follows:

Step 1. Use the **ip dhcp excluded-address** *first last* command in global configuration mode to list addresses that should be excluded (that is, not leased by DHCP).

Step 2. Use the **ip dhcp pool** *name* command in global configuration mode to both create a DHCP pool for a subnet and to navigate into DHCP pool configuration mode. Then also:

> **A.** Use the **network** *subnet-ID mask* or **network** *subnet-ID prefix-length* command in DHCP pool configuration mode to define the subnet for this pool.

> **B.** Use the **default-router** *address1 address2...* command in DHCP pool configuration mode to define default router IP address(es) in that subnet.

> **C.** Use the **dns-server** *address1 address2...* command in DHCP pool configuration mode to define the list of DNS server IP addresses used by hosts in this subnet.

> **D.** Use the **lease** *days hours minutes* command in DHCP pool configuration mode to define the length of the lease, in days, hours, and minutes

> **E.** Use the **domain-name** *name* command in DHCP pool configuration mode to define the DNS domain name.

> **F.** Use the **next-server** *ip-address* command in DHCP pool configuration mode to define the TFTP server IP address used by any hosts (like phones) that need a TFTP server.

Of course, an example can help, particularly with so many configuration commands required. Figure 20-5 shows the organization of the configuration, while sticking to pseudocode rather than the specific configuration commands. (Upcoming Example 20-1 shows a matching configuration.) Note that for each of the two LAN subnets, there is a global command to exclude addresses, and then a group of settings for each of two different DHCP pools.

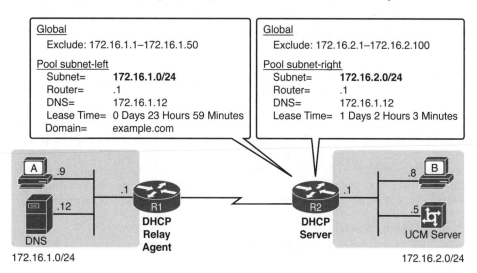

Figure 20-5 *DHCP Server Configuration Pseudocode*

Example 20-1 *R2 as a DHCP Server Per the Concepts in Figure 20-5*

```
ip dhcp excluded-address 172.16.1.1 172.16.1.50
ip dhcp excluded-address 172.16.2.1 172.16.2.100
!
ip dhcp pool subnet-left
 network 172.16.1.0 255.255.255.0
 dns-server 172.16.1.12
 default-router 172.16.1.1
 lease 0 23 59
 domain-name example.com
 next-server 172.16.2.5
!
ip dhcp pool subnet-right
 network 172.16.2.0 /24
 dns-server 172.16.1.12
 default-router 172.16.2.1
 lease 1 2 3
 next-server 172.16.2.5
```

Focus on subnet 172.16.1.0/24 for a moment: the subnet configured as pool subnet-left. The subnet ID and mask match the subnet ID chosen for that subnet. Then, the global **ip dhcp excluded-address** command, just above, reserves 172.16.1.1 through 172.16.1.50, so that this DHCP server will not lease these addresses. The server will automatically exclude the subnet ID (172.16.1.0) as well, so this DHCP server will begin leasing IP addresses starting with the .51 address.

Now look at the details for subnet-right. It uses a DHCP pool **network** command with a prefix style mask. It defines the same DNS server, as does the pool for the other subnet, but a different default router setting, because, of course, the default router in each subnet is different. This pool includes a lease time of 1:02:03 (1 day, 2 hours, and 3 minutes) just as an example.

Also note that both subnets list a TFTP server IP address of the Unified Communications Manager (UCM) server with the **next-server** command. In most cases, you would find this setting in the pools for subnets in which phones reside.

Finally, note that configuring a router as a DHCP server does not remove the need for the **ip helper-address** command. If DHCP clients still exist on LANs that do not have a DHCP server, then the routers connected to those LANs still need the **ip helper-address** command. For example, in Figure 20-5, R1 would still need the **ip helper-address** command on its LAN interface. R2 would not need the command on its LAN interface, because R2 could service those requests, rather than needing to forward the DHCP messages to some other server.

IOS DHCP Server Verification

The IOS DHCP server function has several different **show** commands. These three commands list most of the details:

show ip dhcp binding: Lists state information about each IP address currently leased to a client

show ip dhcp pool [*poolname*]: Lists the configured range of IP addresses, plus statistics for the number of currently leased addresses and the high-water mark for leases from each pool

show ip dhcp server statistics: Lists DHCP server statistics

Example 20-2 shows sample output from two of these commands, based on the configuration from Figure 20-5 and Example 20-1. In this case, the DHCP server leased one IP address from each of the pools, one for host A, and one for host B, as shown in the highlighted portions of the output.

Example 20-2 *Verifying Current Operation of a Router-Based DHCP Server*

```
R2# show ip dhcp binding
Bindings from all pools not associated with VRF:
IP address          Client-ID/              Lease expiration        Type
                    Hardware address/
                    User name
172.16.1.51         0063.6973.636f.2d30.    Oct 12 2012 02:56 AM    Automatic
                    3230.302e.3131.3131.
                    2e31.3131.312d.4661.
                    302f.30
172.16.2.101        0063.6973.636f.2d30.    Oct 12 2012 04:59 AM    Automatic
                    3230.302e.3232.3232.
```

```
                        2e32.3232.322d.4769.
                        302f.30
R2# show ip dhcp pool subnet-right
Pool subnet-right :
 Utilization mark (high/low)      : 100 / 0
 Subnet size (first/next)         : 0 / 0
 Total addresses                  : 254
 Leased addresses                 : 1
 Pending event                    : none
 1 subnet is currently in the pool :
 Current index       IP address range                Leased addresses
 172.16.2.102        172.16.2.1     - 172.16.2.254    1
```

Note that the output in Example 20-2 does not happen to list the excluded addresses, but it does show the effects. The addresses assigned to the clients end with .51 (host A, subnet 172.16.1.0) and .101 (host B, subnet 172.16.2.0), proving that the server did exclude the addresses as shown in the configuration in Example 20-1. The server avoided the .1 through .50 addresses in subnet 172.16.1.0, and the .1 through .100 addresses in subnet 172.16.2.0.

> **NOTE**   The DHCP server keeps status (state) information about each DHCP client that leases an address. Specifically, it remembers the DHCP client ID, and the IP address leased to the client. As a result, an IPv4 DHCP server can be considered to be a stateful DHCP server. This description will be useful when reading about DHCP for IPv6 in Chapter 31, "Implementing IPv6 Addressing on Hosts."

20

Troubleshooting DHCP Services

Chapter 19, "Learning IPv4 Routes with RIPv2," closed with a section about troubleshooting RIPv2. That section makes the point that to be ready for Simlet questions in particular, you have to be ready to predict what symptoms would occur when the network was misconfigured in particular ways. This next section takes a similar approach, pointing out the most typical issues that could be introduced through incorrect or missing configuration, and then discussing what symptoms should happen and how to recognize those problems.

This section begins with a typical look at configuration mistakes and the symptoms that occur with those mistakes. In particular, this section looks at problems with the relay agent's helper address as well as the IOS DHCP server configuration. This section then looks at non-DHCP problems related to that data plane, breaking the problem into issues between the client and relay agent, and between the relay agent and DHCP server. The final section takes a short look at how a DHCP server prevents duplicate IP addresses between hosts that use static IP addresses and those that use DHCP.

DHCP Relay Agent Configuration Mistakes and Symptoms

One configuration mistake that prevents DHCP client from leasing an IP address is the misconfiguration or the omission of the **ip helper-address** interface subcommand on the router acting as the DHCP relay agent. The relay agent takes the incoming DHCP message, changes the destination address of the packet to be the address on the **ip helper-address** *address* command, and forwards the packet to that address. If the command is missing, the router does not attempt to forward the DHCP messages at all; if it is incorrect, the relay agent forwards the DHCP packets, but they never arrive at the actual DHCP server.

The main problem symptom in this case is the failure of a DHCP client to lease an address. If you can identify a client that has a problem, and you know what VLAN or subnet in which that host resides, you can then work to identify any routers connected to that subnet, to find and correct the **ip helper-address** subcommands.

Beyond that step, this list summarizes a few other related points.

■ The DHCP relay agent feature is needed on interfaces only if the DHCP server is on a different subnet; it is not needed if the DHCP server is on the same subnet as the client.

■ On routers with VLAN trunks (with a router-on-a-stick [ROAS] subinterface configuration), the subinterfaces also need an **ip helper-address** command (assuming they meet the first criteria in this list).

■ If an exam question does not allow you to look at the configuration, use the **show ip interface** [*type number*] command to view the **ip helper-address** setting on an interface.

About that last point, Example 20-3 shows an example of the **show ip interface g0/0** command. In this case, the interface has been configured with the **ip helper-address 172.16.2.11** command; the **show** command output basically restates that fact. (The configuration matches the earlier examples surrounding Figures 20-2 and 20-3 for Router R1.) Note that if there were no **ip helper-address** configured on the interface, the text would instead read "Helper address is not set."

Example 20-3 *Listing the Current Helper Address Setting with* **show ip interface**

```
R1# show ip interface g0/0
GigabitEthernet0/0 is up, line protocol is up
  Internet address is 182.16.1.1/24
  Broadcast address is 255.255.255.255
  Address determined by non-volatile memory
  MTU is 1500 bytes
  Helper address is 172.16.2.11
! Lines omitted for brevity (about 20 lines)
```

IOS DHCP Server Configuration Mistakes and Symptoms

When using an IOS DHCP server, from a troubleshooting perspective, break issues into two broad categories: those that prevent DHCP clients from leasing an address, and those that allow the lease but provide incorrect settings to the client.

First, the primary configuration mistake that causes a failure in the DHCP lease process is the misconfiguration of the **network** command. The problem revolves around these key facts:

■ The packet from the relay agent to the DHCP server uses the relay agent's interface IP address as the source IP address in the forwarded DHCP message. (See Figure 20-2 for a reminder.)

■ The DHCP server compares that source IP address in the received DHCP packet to the **network** commands in its DHCP pools to find the right pool.

- Each **network** *subnet mask* command implies a range of addresses, just like any other IP network or subnet shown with a subnet mask.

- If the source IP address of the packet is not in the range of addresses implied by any **network** command in all the pools, the DHCP server has no pool to use for that request. The DHCP server does not know how to respond, so it does not reply at all.

As an example of that failure, consider the configuration shown in Figure 20-6. The left side shows the configuration on R1, a DHCP relay agent that has two interfaces configured with the **ip helper-address 172.16.2.11** command. The DHCP server configuration on the right lists two pools, intended as one pool for each subnet off Router R1. However, the **network 172.16.3.0 /25** command implies an address range of 172.16.3.0 to 172.16.3.127, and the relay agent's interface address of 172.16.3.254 is not within that range of numbers. The solution would be to correct the DHCP server's **network** command to use a /24 mask.

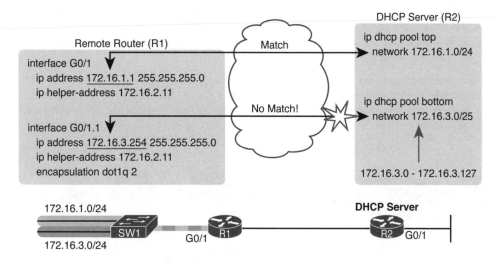

Figure 20-6 *An Example Misconfiguration of a DHCP Pool* **network** *Command*

> **NOTE** The **ip helper-address** configuration on the left is correct. The figure uses a ROAS configuration here just to reinforce the comment in the earlier section that ROAS subinterfaces also need an **ip helper-address** subcommand.

While you ultimately need to find this kind of problem and fix the configuration, on the exam you need to be ready to discover the root cause based on symptoms and **show** commands as well. So, when troubleshooting DHCP issues, and the client fails to lease an address, look at the IOS DHCP server's **network** commands. Calculate the range of IP addresses as if that command were defining a subnet. Then compare that range of addresses by the **network** command in each pool to the interface addresses on the DHCP relay agent routers. Every relay agent interface (that is, every interface with an **ip helper-address** command configured) should be included in a pool defined at the IOS DHCP server.

The DHCP server can also be misconfigured in a way that allows the lease of an address, but then causes other problems. If the lease process works, but the rest of the parameters given to the client are incorrect or missing, the client could operate, but operate poorly. This list summarizes the kinds of mistakes and the resulting symptoms:

■ With the DNS server IP addresses incorrectly configured on the server (or omitted), hosts would fail to resolve hostnames into their associated IP addresses.

■ With the default gateway IP address incorrectly configured on the server (or omitted), hosts could not communicate outside the local subnet.

■ With the TFTP server IP address incorrectly configured (or omitted), an IP phone would fail to correctly load its configuration.

Chapter 24, "Troubleshooting IPv4 Routing," discusses host troubleshooting in more depth, including these issues.

IP Connectivity from DHCP Relay Agent to DHCP Server

For the DHCP process to work with a centralized server, IP broadcast packets must flow between the client and relay agent, and IP unicast packets must flow between the relay agent and the DHCP server. Any problem that prevents the flow of these packets also prevents DHCP from working.

For perspective, consider the topology in Figure 20-7, which again shows the relay agent on the left and the DHCP server on the right. The server uses IP address 172.16.2.11, and the relay agent uses interface address 172.16.1.1. Any failure that prevents the flow of IP packets between those two IP addresses would prevent host A from leasing an IP address.

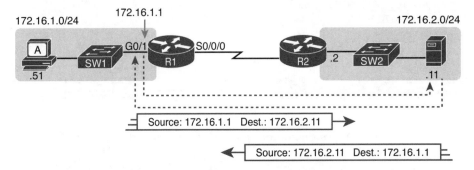

Figure 20-7 *Addresses Used between Relay Agent and Server*

This chapter does not attempt to work through IP troubleshooting. However, two upcoming chapters explain two useful tools (extended **ping** and **traceroute** commands, Chapter 23, "IPv4 Troubleshooting Tools,") and then describe how to troubleshoot DHCP connectivity in particular ("DHCP Issues" in Chapter 24. For now, remember the IP addresses used on the packets between the relay agent and server, and know that you may need to troubleshoot IP routing to ensure those packets can be delivered.

LAN Connectivity Between the DHCP Client and Relay Agent

Back in Figures 20-1, 20-2, and 20-3, you saw that the DHCP messages on the same LAN as the DHCP client all showed a destination IP address of 255.255.255.255. What does that really mean? When a packet uses this 255.255.255.255 address:

- The address is called the *local broadcast address*.
- Packets sent to this address are not forwarded as-is by routers.
- On a LAN, the sender of an IP local broadcast packet encapsulates these IP packets in an Ethernet frame with an Ethernet broadcast destination address (FFFF.FFFF.FFFF), so the LAN broadcasts the frame.

As a result of the logic in these steps, the broadcast DHCP messages can easily flow between the client and router, as long as the LAN works. Chapter 12, "Troubleshooting Ethernet LANs," discusses how to troubleshoot the LAN.

Summary of DHCP Troubleshooting

In summary, as a study tool, the following list summarizes the key troubleshooting ideas from this chapter:

Step 1. If using a centralized DHCP server, at least one router on each remote subnet that has DHCP clients must act as DHCP relay agent, and have a correctly configured **ip helper-address** *address* subcommand on the interface connected to that subnet.

Step 2. If using a centralized IOS DHCP server, make sure the DHCP pools' **network** commands match the entire network's list of router interfaces that have an **ip helper-address** command pointing to this DHCP server.

Step 3. Troubleshoot for any IP connectivity issues between the DHCP relay agent and the DHCP server, using the relay agent interface IP address and the server IP address as the source and destination of the packets.

Step 4. Troubleshoot for any LAN issues between the DHCP client and the DHCP relay agent.

Also, as one final note about DHCP in the real world, DHCP might seem dangerous at this point, with all the focus on potential problems in this section, combined with the importance of DHCP and its use by most end user devices. However, DHCP has some great availability features. First, most DHCP servers set their lease times for at least a few days, often a week, or maybe longer. Combined with that, the DHCP protocol has several processes through which the client reconfirms the existing lease with the server, and releases the same IP address in advance of the expiration of the lease. Clients do not simply wait until the moment the lease would expire to then contact the DHCP server, hoping it is available. So the network can have outages, and DHCP clients that have already leased an address can continue to work without any problem.

Detecting Conflicts with Offered Versus Used Addresses

Beyond troubleshooting the types of problems that would prevent DHCP from working, the IOS DHCP server tries to prevent another type of problem: assigning IP addresses with DHCP when another host tries to statically configure that same IP address. Although the DHCP server configuration clearly lists the addresses in the pool, plus those to be excluded from the pool, hosts can still statically configure addresses from the range inside the DHCP pool. In other words, no protocols prevent a host from statically configuring and using an IP address from within the range of addresses used by the DHCP server.

Knowing that some host might have statically configured an address from within the range of addresses in the DHCP pool, both DHCP servers and clients try to detect such problems, called *conflicts*, before the client uses a newly leased address.

DHCP servers detect conflicts by using pings. Before offering a new IP address to a client, the DHCP server first pings the address. If the server receives a response to the ping, some other host must already be using the address, which lets the server know a conflict exists. The server notes that particular address as being in conflict, and the server does not offer the address, moving on to the next address in the pool.

The DHCP client can also detect conflicts, but instead of using ping, it uses ARP. In the client case, when the DHCP client receives from the DHCP server an offer to use a particular IP address, the client sends an Address Resolution Protocol (ARP) request for that address. If another host replies, the DHCP client has found a conflict.

Example 20-4 lists output from the router-based DHCP server on R2, after host B detected a conflict using ARP. Behind the scenes, host B used DHCP to request a lease, with the process working normally until host B used ARP and found some other device already used 172.16.2.102. At that point, host B then sent a DHCP message back to the server, rejecting the use of address 172.16.2.102. The example shows the router's log message related to host B's discovery of the conflict, and a **show** command that lists all conflicted addresses.

Example 20-4   *Displaying Information About DHCP Conflicts in IOS*

```
*Oct 16 19:28:59.220: %DHCPD-4-DECLINE_CONFLICT: DHCP address conflict:
  client 0063.6973.636f.2d30.3230.302e.3034.3034.2e30.3430.342d.4769.302f.30
    declined 172.16.2.102.
R2# show ip dhcp conflict

IP address         Detection method   Detection time            VRF
172.16.2.102       Gratuitous ARP     Oct 16 2012 07:28 PM
```

The **show ip dhcp conflict** command lists the method through which the server added each address to the conflict list: either gratuitous ARP, as detected by the client, or ping, as detected by the server. The server avoids offering these conflicted addresses to any future clients, until the engineer uses the **clear ip dhcp conflict** command to clear the list.

Verifying Host IPv4 Settings

Some hosts use DHCP to learn their IPv4 settings. Others manually set all their settings. Other hosts actually allow you to make some settings manually, and learn other settings with DHCP.

Regardless of how a given host builds its IPv4 configuration, that host will either work, or have problems. And if it has problems, someone needs to be ready and able to jump in and help solve the problem. On hosts, that means someone needs to be able to find the IPv4 settings, make sure they are correct, and troubleshoot problems related to the host IP settings.

This short section brushes the surface of how to verify IPv4 settings on hosts. This section touches on each of the settings, showing some host commands used to confirm each setting, as well as giving a few related hints on how to confirm if it is working or not.

IP Address and Mask Configuration

Most every OS in the world—certainly the more common OSs people work with every day—have a fairly easy-to-reach window that lists most if not all the IPv4 settings in one place. For example, Figure 20-8 shows the Network configuration screen from a user host OS (Mac OS X in this case), with all the IPv4 settings. This particular example shows the big four settings: address, mask, router, and DNS.

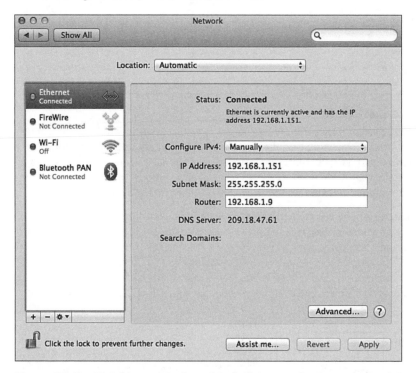

Figure 20-8 *IP Address, Mask, and Default Router Settings on Mac OS*

However, beyond these windows into the graphical user interface (GUI) of any OS, most OSs have a variety of networking commands available from a command line. Interestingly, some of the commands are the same across many different OSs, even between Microsoft Windows versions and other OSs.

For example, to verify the IP address, mask, default router, and other settings, OSs typically support either the **ipconfig** (Windows) or **ifconfig** (Linux and Mac OS) commands. Both commands have several options that can be seen by adding a -? to the end. Example 20-5 shows a sample from a Windows PC.

Example 20-5 ipconfig /all *(Windows)*

```
C:\DOCUME1\OWNER> ipconfig /all
Windows IP Configuration


Ethernet adapter Wireless Network Connection 3:


        Connection-specific DNS Suffix  . : Belkin
```

```
Description . . . . . . . . . . . : Linksys WUSB600N Dual-Band Wireless-N USB
   Network Adapter
Physical Address. . . . . . . . . : 00-1E-E5-D8-CB-E4
Dhcp Enabled. . . . . . . . . . . : Yes
Autoconfiguration Enabled . . . . : Yes
IP Address. . . . . . . . . . . . : 192.168.2.13
Subnet Mask . . . . . . . . . . . : 255.255.255.0
Default Gateway . . . . . . . . . : 192.168.2.1
DHCP Server . . . . . . . . . . . : 192.168.2.1
DNS Servers . . . . . . . . . . . : 192.168.2.1
Lease Obtained. . . . . . . . . . : Wednesday, October 10, 2012 3:25:00AM
Lease Expires . . . . . . . . . . : Monday, January 18, 2013 11:14:07 PM
```

Name Resolution with DNS

The Domain Name System (DNS) defines a protocol as well as a worldwide system of servers that use DNS. While incredibly useful—it might be one of the single most important protocols in the world of TCP/IP—DNS does not require attention from the routers and switches between the user devices and the DNS servers. This short section explains why, but shows you a few router commands related to DNS that might be handy anyway.

Inside a single enterprise, the company uses a couple of redundant DNS servers, each of which can resolve any host names for any hosts inside the company. Figure 20-9 shows an example using a single company, with a client on the left using the DNS server at the top of the figure. Step 1 shows the DNS Request message, asking the DNS server to resolve name "Server1" into its corresponding IP address. The DNS server sends back a DNS Reply, listing the IP address. Finally, at Step 3, the client can send a packet to 10.1.2.3, the address used by Server1.

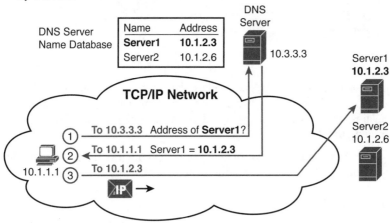

Figure 20-9 *Host Resolves Name to IP Address Before Sending Packet to Server1*

Now stop for a moment, and focus on the To: part of the three messages. Each packet has a known unicast destination address. The routers in the TCP/IP network can simply forward those packets. No need for any special configuration, no need for a command and function like the **ip helper-address** command used with DHCP. In short, the routers and switches have no extra work to do, and no extra configuration required, to support DNS between a host and the DNS servers.

Default Routers

As discussed in some detail back in Chapter 18, IPv4 host routing logic reduces to a basic two-part choice. For packets destined for a host in the same subnet, the local host sends the packet directly, ignoring any routers. For packets destined for a host in a different subnet, the local host next sends the packet to its default gateway (also known as the default router), expecting that router to forward the packet.

Interestingly, a couple of simple errors can occur between any LAN-based host and their default router. For a LAN-based host's default router setting to work, the following must be true:

- The host link to the LAN and the default router link to the LAN must be in the same VLAN.

- The host and default router IP addresses must be in the same subnet.

- The host default router setting must refer to the same IP address configured on the router. (In other words, if the host claims the default router is 10.1.1.1, make sure the router interface IP address is not 10.1.1.2.)

- The LAN switches must not discard the frame because of the port security configuration.

All of the preceding settings and choices can be mismatched between a host and the default router. On the router, the settings can be checked with the usual CLI commands: **show interfaces**, **show ip interface brief**, **show protocols**, and **show running-config**. On the switch, to check the VLAN assignments, use **show interfaces status**, **show vlan**, and **show interfaces switchport**.

On the host, the methods to check the default router setting of course differ depending on the OS. A look at the settings using the GUI simply lists the default router. However, a common command on most user host OSs is the **netstat -rn** command, which lists the default gateway as the route for either destination 0.0.0.0 or as default. Example 20-6 shows a **netstat -rn** command from a Mac, with the default router setting highlighted.

Example 20-6   netstat -rn *Command (Mac OS X)*

```
Wendell-Odoms-iMac:~ wendellodom$ netstat -rn
Routing tables


Internet:
Destination        Gateway            Flags      Refs       Use   Netif Expire
default            192.168.1.1        UGSc         45         0     en0
127                127.0.0.1          UCS           0         0     lo0
127.0.0.1          127.0.0.1          UH           36   9143335     lo0
169.254            link#4             UCS           0         0     en0
192.168.1          link#4             UCS           4         0     en0
192.168.1.1/32     link#4             UCS           1         0     en0
192.168.1.1        5c:d9:98:59:b3:fc  UHLWIir      44       553     en0   1190
192.168.1.150/32   link#4             UCS           0         0     en0
192.168.1.255      ff:ff:ff:ff:ff:ff  UHLWbI        0         5     en0
```

Another good step to take to verify the default router is to find out whether ARP works for the default router. For example, host A in Figure 20-10, when sending packets to host D, in the same subnet, will send the packet directly to host D. So, host A will first need an ARP entry for host D. Similarly, before sending a packet to server B, which sits on another subnet, host A will need an ARP entry for R1's MAC address.

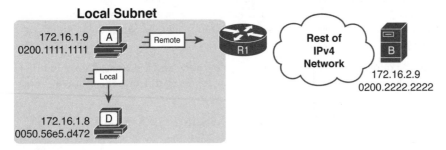

Figure 20-10 *Host IP and MAC Addresses in the Next Two ARP Examples*

The **arp -a** command happens to be another common command on many user OSs. Example 20-7 shows host A's ARP table after host A successfully sent a packet to both server B and host D. Note that server B's IP address of 172.16.2.9 is not listed, because the ARP table lists IP addresses for IP addresses on the same subnet, and not those on remote subnets.

Example 20-7 *ARP Table on Host A (Windows)*

```
C:\Users\wodom> arp -a

Interface: 172.16.1.9 --- 0xa
  Internet Address      Physical Address      Type
    172.16.1.1          02-00-01-01-01-01     dynamic
    172.16.1.8          00-50-56-e5-d4-72     dynamic
```

Routers also need to keep an ARP table, so they can encapsulate IP packets into LAN frames. Example 20-8 shows the output of the **show arp** command on Router R1, which lists an entry for host A (172.16.1.9), and for the router itself (172.16.1.1). (Note that hosts typically do not list their own IP addresses in their own ARP cache, but the Cisco router ARP cache does.)

Example 20-8 *ARP Table on Router R1*

```
R1# show arp
Protocol  Address          Age (min)  Hardware Addr   Type   Interface
Internet  172.16.1.1            -      0200.0101.0101  ARPA   GigabitEthernet0/0
Internet  172.16.1.9            2      0200.1111.1111  ARPA   GigabitEthernet0/0
```

IPv4 Address Types

The IPv4 address space includes three major categories of addresses: unicast, broadcast, and multicast. For the current exam, Cisco lists one exam topic that asks you to compare and contrast these address types. To help you make those comparisons, this section explains multicast addressing, while pulling together the key ideas about unicast and broadcast IP addresses that have already been introduced, to pull the ideas together.

You may be wondering why this topic about IPv4 address types sits at the end of a chapter about DHCP and IP networking on hosts. Honestly, I could have put this topic in several chapters. The main reason it is here is that you have already seen the IP broadcast addresses in action, including the 255.255.255.255 local broadcast as shown in this chapter.

Review of Unicast (Class A, B, and C) IP Addresses

Unicast IP addresses are those Class A, B, and C IP addresses assigned to hosts, router interfaces, and other networking devices. Because most discussions about IP addressing refer to unicast IP addresses, most of us just refer to them as IP addresses, and leave out the word *unicast*.

Just to be complete and define the concept, unicast addresses identify one interface on one device to IP. Just like your postal address gives the post office an address to use to send letters to your one specific house or apartment, a unicast IP address gives the IP network an address to use to send packets to one specific host. However, with IP, instead of addressing the device, unicast addresses identify individual interfaces. For example:

- A router with four LAN interfaces, and two WAN interfaces, has six unicast addresses, each in a different subnet, one for each interface.

- A PC with both an Ethernet network interface card (NIC) and a wireless NIC would have two unicast IPv4 addresses, one for each interface.

IP Broadcast Addresses

Broadcast IPv4 addresses give IP a way to send one packet that the network delivers to multiple hosts. IPv4 defines several types of broadcast addresses, with each type being used to reach a different set of hosts. These different broadcast IP addresses give different overhead protocols like DHCP the ability to efficiently reach all hosts in a specific part of the network. The following list reviews the three IP broadcast address types:

Local broadcast address: 255.255.255.255. Used to send a packet on a local subnet, knowing that routers will not forward the packet as is. Also called a *limited broadcast*.

Subnet broadcast address: One reserved address for each subnet, namely the numerically highest number in the subnet, as discussed in Chapter 15, "Analyzing Subnet Masks." A packet sent to a subnet broadcast address can be routed to the router connected to that subnet, and then sent as a data link broadcast to all hosts in that one subnet. Also called an *all-hosts broadcast* to emphasize that all hosts in a subnet are reached, and also called a *directed broadcast*.

Network broadcast address: One reserved address for each classful network, namely the numerically highest number in the network. Used to send one packet to all hosts in that one network. Also called an *all-subnets broadcast*, referring to the fact that the packet reaches all subnets in a network.

This chapter has already shown how a local broadcast works, sending the message over the same subnet in which it was first transmitted, but no further. However, the other two types are a little more interesting.

Subnet and network broadcasts provide a way to send packets to all hosts in a subnet or network (respectively) while reducing waste. For instance, with a subnet broadcast, routers forward the packet just like any other IP packet going to that subnet. When that packet arrives at the router connected to that subnet, the last router then encapsulates the packet in a LAN broadcast, so that all hosts receive a copy. Figure 20-11 shows the idea.

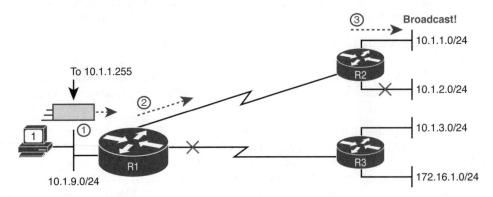

Figure 20-11   *Example of a Subnet Broadcast to 10.1.1.255*

The figure shows two key points. R1 does not flood or broadcast the frame to all other routers, instead routing it to the next router (R2 in this case) so that the packet reaches subnet 10.1.1.0/24. R2, connected to subnet 10.1.1.0/24, forwards the packet onto the LAN, but encapsulates the packet in an Ethernet broadcast frame, so that it reaches all hosts in the subnet.

The figure shows the intended use of the subnet broadcast address; however, it presents a security issue today. Many attacks start with a ping to subnet broadcast addresses, hoping to get many hosts to reply. Cisco changed the IOS default many years ago to disable the forwarding of subnet broadcasts onto a connected subnet (that is, it disables Step 3 in Figure 20-11). That default setting is based on the **no ip directed-broadcast** interface subcommand.

A network broadcast packet (a packet with a network broadcast address as the destination) works in a similar way. To reach all subnets, however, the routers create copies of the packet and flood it so it reaches all subnets inside the classful network. On any LAN interfaces, the packet is forwarded in a LAN broadcast, just as shown in Step 3 of Figure 20-11.

IPv4 Multicast Addresses (Class D Addresses)

Multicast IP addresses and the related protocols help solve a similar problem as compared to broadcast addresses, but mainly for applications, and without the same security issues experienced by broadcast addresses. To see how it works, consider this example. A video application may be designed to show live video feeds. If 10 people at the same remote site in the same subnet want to watch the same video at the same time, the application could be designed so that the application sent the same video data 10 times, once to each client in the same subnet. An application designed to use Class D multicast addresses could send 1 packet, which the routers would route across the WAN, and then deliver a copy to all 10 hosts in the destination subnet.

When using multicast, all the hosts still use their individual unicast IP address for their normal traffic, while also using the same multicast IPv4 address for the multicast application. Any server or client that happens to use an application designed to take advantage of IP multicast then also uses the Class D multicast addresses that the application chooses to use. You can think of a Class D address more as a multicast group—in fact, it is often called that—because hosts join the group so that they can receive the packets sent by the multicast application.

Class D addresses begin with a first octet of between 224 and 239, with some ranges reserved for various purposes. Much of the Class D address space is set aside for a company to deploy one of these multicast applications, and then pick an address from the Class D range, and configure it to be used by a multicast application.

As an example, imagine the video application uses Class D address 226.1.1.1. Figure 20-12 illustrates the process by which the application at the server on the left sends one multicast packet with destination address 226.1.1.1. Note that for this process to work, the hosts with * beside them registered with their local routers to notify the routers that the host wants to receive packets destined to multicast address 226.1.1.1. When the action in this figure begins, the routers collectively know which subnets have hosts that want a copy of multi- casts sent to 226.1.1.1, and which subnets do not.

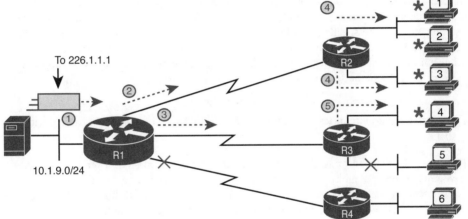

Figure 20-12   *Example of a Multicast Packet Flow for Three Registered Hosts*

Following the steps in the figure:

1. The server on the left generates and sends a multicast packet.

2. Router R1 replicates the packet to send a copy to both R2...

3. ...and to R3. R1 does not replicate and send a copy to R4, because there are no hosts near R4 listening for packets sent to 226.1.1.1.

4. R2 processes the multicast packet received from R1, and because of the earlier host registration process, R2 knows that at least one host off both its LAN interfaces are listening for packets sent to 226.1.1.1. R2 therefore forwards a copy of the packet out each of its LAN interfaces.

5. R3 receives the multicast packet from R1, and uses the same kind of logic as R2. However, R3 knows from the earlier host registration process that only one of its LAN interfaces connects to a subnet with hosts listening for packets sent to 226.1.1.1, so R3 forwards a copy of the packet out that one interface only.

As you can see from this example, the server sent one packet and the routers replicated the packet so it reached all the correct locations in the network.

As another comparison between unicast and multicast addresses, note that multicast addresses may be used as destination IP addresses only, whereas unicast addresses may be used as both the destination and source address. For instance, consider the packets in the example shown in Figure 20-12. All those packets flow from one host, so the packet uses a unicast IP address of that host's unicast IP address.

Finally, to complete one more comparison between unicast IP addressing and multicast IP addressing, think about that last hop router in the example shown in Figure 20-11. If a router such as R2 or R3 had forwarded a unicast IP packet, the router would look in its ARP cache to find the unicast IP address for the destination in that connected subnets, and the associated unicast MAC address. That will not work when forwarding a multicast packet with a multicast (Class D) destination IP address.

To encapsulate a multicast IP packet over an Ethernet LAN, IP multicast calculates the destination MAC address with a simple process. The process copies the last 23 bits of the IP address behind a reserved 25-bit prefix to form the 48-bit destination MAC address. The resulting MAC address, called a multicast MAC address, begins with hex 01005E. So, the multicast IP packet, encapsulated in the multicast Ethernet frame, is forwarded out the router interface onto the LAN. At that point, the switches take one of the following approaches to forwarding the frame so that all hosts who want a copy of the frame get a copy:

■ Flood the multicast frame as if it were a broadcast

■ Use other Ethernet multicast features that flood the frame only to those same devices that registered to receive a copy

If you feel like these few pages probably left out some detail; indeed, several books have been written about IP multicast all to itself. The topic is indeed large. For this book's purposes, know the main comparison points with unicast addressing. Multicast addressing gives applications that need to communicate the same data at the same time to multiple hosts a much more efficient way to do that. If the application is written to make use of IP multicast, the application can consume much less traffic in the network, as compared to using unicast IP addresses and sending every host a copy of the packet.

Comparing and Contrasting IP Address Types

The last few pages reviewed unicast and broadcast addresses, and explained the core concepts behind IP multicast addresses. Table 20-2 summarizes the key comparison points mentioned throughout this section for convenient study.

Table 20-2 Comparisons of Unicast, Broadcast, and Multicast IP Addresses

	Unicast	Broadcast	Multicast
Primarily used for data sent by the most common user apps (web, email, chat, and so on)	Yes	No	No
Assigned to hosts with DHCP	Yes	No	No
Uses Class A, B, and C addresses	Yes	No	No
Primarily used by overhead protocols (DHCP, ARP) to send one message to more than one device	No	Yes	No
Used as destination IP address only	No	Yes	Yes
Primarily used by applications that send the same data at the same time to multiple clients	No	No	Yes
Uses Class D addresses	No	No	Yes

Chapter Review

One key to doing well on the exams is to perform repetitive spaced review sessions. Review this chapter's material using either the tools in the book, DVD, or interactive tools for the same material found on the book's companion website. Refer to the "Your Study Plan" element for more details. Table 20-3 outlines the key review elements and where you can find them. To better track your study progress, record when you completed these activities in the second column.

20

Table 20-3 Chapter Review Tracking

Review Element	Review Date(s)	Resource Used
Review key topics		Book, DVD/website
Review key terms		Book, DVD/website
Repeat DIKTA questions		Book, PCPT
Review memory table		Book, DVD/website
Review config checklist		Book, DVD/website
Do labs		Blog
Review command tables		Book

Review All the Key Topics

Table 20-4 Key Topics for Chapter 20

Key Topic Element	Description	Page Number
List	Definitions of special IPv4 addresses 0.0.0.0 and 255.255.255.255	474
List	Four logic steps created by the **ip helper-address** command	475
Figure 20-2	What the **ip helper-address** command changes in a DHCP Discover message	476
List	DHCP verification commands	480
Checklist	DHCP troubleshooting checklist	485
Checklist	Verification checklist for comparing host IPv4 settings with default router IPv4 settings	489
List	Descriptions of three different types of IPv4 broadcast addresses	491
Figure 20-12	Example of the flow of an IPv4 multicast message	493
Table 20-2	Points of comparison for unicast, broadcast, and multicast IP addresses	495

Key Terms You Should Know

DHCP client, DHCP server, DHCP relay agent, local broadcast IP address, subnet broadcast IP address, network broadcast IP address, multicast IP address, DNS Request, DNS Reply

Command References

Tables 20-5, 20-6, and 20-7 list configuration and verification commands used in this chapter. As an easy review exercise, cover the left column in a table, read the right column, and try to recall the command without looking. Then repeat the exercise, covering the right column, and try to recall what the command does.

Table 20-5 Chapter 20 Configuration Command Reference

Command	Description
ip dhcp excluded-address *first last*	A global command that reserves an inclusive range of addresses, so that the DHCP server function does not lease out these addresses.
ip dhcp pool *pool-name*	A global command that creates a pool, by name, and moves the user to DHCP server pool configuration mode.
network *subnet-id {ddn-mask	/prefix-length}*	A DHCP pool mode subcommand that defines a network or subnet causing the DHCP server to lease out IP addresses in that subnet.
default-router *address1 address2...*	A DHCP pool mode subcommand that defines one or more routers as default routers, with that information passed for clients served by this pool.
dns-server *address1 address2...*	A DHCP pool mode subcommand that defines the list of DNS servers that the DHCP server will list for clients served by this pool.

Command	Description
lease {*days* [*hours* [*minutes*]] | **infinite**}	A DHCP pool mode subcommand that defines the length of time for a DHCP lease, for clients served by this pool.
ip helper-address *IP-address*	An interface subcommand that tells the router to notice local subnet broadcasts (to 255.255.255.255) that use UDP, and change the source and destination IP address, enabling DHCP servers to sit on a remote subnet.

Table 20-6   Chapter 20 EXEC Command Reference

Command	Description
show arp, show ip arp	Lists the router's IPv4 ARP table
show ip dhcp binding	Lists the currently leased IP addresses on a DHCP server, along with the client identifier and lease time information
show ip dhcp pool *name*	Lists the configured range of addresses in the pool, along with usage statistics and utilization high/low-water marks
show ip dhcp server statistics	Lists statistics about the requests served by the DHCP server
show ip dhcp conflict	Lists IP addresses that the DHCP server found were already in use when the server tried to lease the address to a host
clear ip dhcp conflict	Removes all entries from the DHCP server's conflict list

20

Table 20-7   Chapter 20 Generic Host Networking Command Reference

Command	Description
ipconfig, ifconfig	Lists IP settings for the interface (NIC)
netstat -rn	Lists the hosts routing table, often listing the default router with a route to 0.0.0.0
arp -a	Lists the host's ARP table

Part V Review

Keep track of your part review progress with the checklist in Table P5-1. Details on each task follow the table.

Table P5-1 Part V Part Review Checklist

Activity	1st Date Completed	2nd Date Completed
Repeat All DIKTA Questions		
Answer Part Review Questions		
Review Key Topics		
Create Command Mind Map by Category		
Do Labs		

Repeat All DIKTA Questions

For this task, answer the "Do I Know This Already?" questions again for the chapters in this part of the book, using the PCPT software.

Answer Part Review Questions

For this task, use PCPT to answer the Part Review questions for this part of the book.

Review Key Topics

Review all key topics in all chapters in this part, either by browsing the chapters or by using the Key Topics application on the DVD or companion website.

Create Command Mind Map by Category

Like Parts II and III of this book, Part V introduced more than a few CLI commands, this time on routers. The sheer number of commands can be a bit overwhelming, so it helps to take a step back from the details and let your brain sift through what you remember, and what it thinks go together, so that you can then realize which commands you need to review so that you remember them better.

The goal with this mind map exercise is to help you remember the commands. This exercise does not focus on the details, every single parameter of every command, or even their meaning. The goal is to help you organize the commands internally so that you know which commands to consider when faced with a real-life problem or an exam question.

Similar to Part II's mind map, create a mind map with the following categories of commands from this part of the book:

Router interface commands that affect Layers 1 and 2, IP addressing, static and default routing, router trunking and Layer 3 switching, RIPv2, DHCP server, host networking commands, and miscellaneous

In this mind map, for each category, think of all configuration commands and all EXEC commands (mostly **show** commands). For each category, group the configuration commands separately from the EXEC commands. Figure P5-1 shows a sample for the switch IPv4 commands.

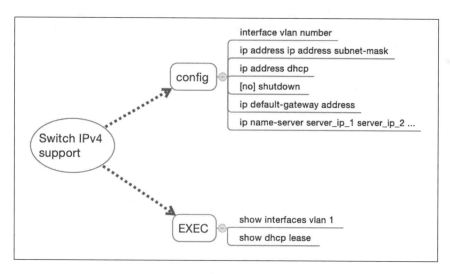

Figure P5-1 *Sample Mind Map from the Switch IPv4 Branch*

> **NOTE** For more information on mind mapping, refer to the Introduction, in the section "About Mind Maps."

If you do choose to use mind map software rather than paper, you might want to remember where you stored your mind map files. Table P5-2 lists the mind maps for this part review and a place to record those filenames.

Table P5-2 Configuration Mind Maps for Part V Review

Map	Description	Where You Saved It
1	Commands Mind Map	

Labs

Depending on your chosen lab tool, here are some suggestions for what to do in lab:

Pearson Network Simulator: If you use the full Pearson ICND1 or CCNA simulator, focus more on the configuration scenario and troubleshooting scenario labs associated with the topics in this part of the book. These types of labs include a larger set of topics and work well as Part Review activities. (See the Introduction for some details about how to find which labs are about topics in this part of the book.)

Config Labs: In your idle moments, review and repeat any of the Config Labs for this book part in the author's blog; launch from blog.certskills.com/ccent/ and navigate to the Hands-on Config labs.

Other: If using other lab tools, here are a few suggestions: Make sure and experiment heavily with IPv4 addressing, static routing, and RIPv2. Also experiment with DHCP server and client configuration. To test, you can make a LAN switch or another router act as a DHCP client with the **ip address dhcp** command, which tells the device to use DHCP to lease an address. Make sure to spend time with key commands such as **show ip route** and **show ip protocols**.

Implementing IPv4 means planning for IPv4 addressing and subnetting, and then configuring the addresses and masks on hosts and routers. To help you learn to do that, Part IV introduced the basics of IPv4 addressing, and Part V then showed how to implement addressing and IPv4 routing on routers and hosts.

Part VI continues with those same topics, but with a deeper look. This part begins with two more chapters about subnetting, both of which require you to think about design. Instead of focusing on one mask, one address, or one subnet, the work looks at the entire enterprise network. What subnets could be used? Which ones are currently in use or planned for use? Which other subnets could be used? Chapter 21 looks at those questions while still using a single mask throughout the design, and Chapter 22 looks at those questions (and the common mistakes) when using different masks with different subnets.

The next two chapters continue the theme of taking a deeper look at IPv4, but instead of design, these chapters focus on troubleshooting. Chapter 23 shows how to use the most common tools to troubleshoot IPv4 routing problems, namely ping and traceroute. Chapter 24 then shows applied IPv4 troubleshooting. That final chapter in this part discusses a variety of IPv4 issues, with explanations of the symptoms as well as lists of the possible root causes.

Part VI

IPv4 Design and Troubleshooting

CHAPTER 21

Subnet Design

This chapter covers the following exam topics:

1.0 Network Fundamentals

1.8 Configure, verify and troubleshoot IPv4 addressing and subnetting

So far in this book, most of the discussion about IPv4 used examples with the addresses and masks already given. This book has shown many examples already, but the examples so far do not ask you to pick the IP address or pick the mask. Instead, as discussed back in Chapter 13, "Perspectives on IPv4 Subnetting," this book so far has assumed that someone else designed the IP addressing and subnetting plan, and this book shows how to implement it.

This chapter turns that model around. It goes back to the progression of building and implementing IPv4, as discussed in Chapter 13, as shown in Figure 21-1. This chapter picks up the story right after some network engineer has chosen a Class A, B, or C network to use for the enterprise's IPv4 network. And then this chapter discusses the design choices related to picking one subnet mask to use for all subnets (the first major section) and what subnet IDs that choice creates (the second major section).

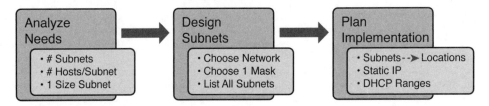

Figure 21-1 *Subnet Design and Implementation Process from Chapter 13*

Note that Chapter 22, "Variable-Length Subnet Masks," then changes the design choice of using a single mask, instead allowing any mask for each subnet through the use of variable-length subnet masks (VLSM).

"Do I Know This Already?" Quiz

Take the quiz (either here, or use the PCPT software) if you want to use the score to help you decide how much time to spend on this chapter. The answers are at the bottom of the page following the quiz, and the explanations are in DVD Appendix C and in the PCPT software.

Table 21-1 "Do I Know This Already?" Foundation Topics Section-to-Question Mapping

Foundation Topics Section	Questions
Choosing the Mask(s) to Meet Requirements	1–3
Finding All Subnet IDs	4–6

1. An IP subnetting design effort is under way at a company. So far, the senior engineer has decided to use Class B network 172.23.0.0. The design calls for 100 subnets, with the largest subnet needing 500 hosts. Management requires that the design accommodate 50 percent growth in the number of subnets and the size of the largest subnet. The requirements also state that a single mask must be used throughout the Class B network. How many masks meet the requirements?

   a. 0

   b. 1

   c. 2

   d. 3+

2. An IP subnetting design requires 200 subnets and 120 hosts/subnet for the largest subnets, and requires that a single mask be used throughout the one private IP network that will be used. The design also requires planning for 20 percent growth in the number of subnets and number of hosts/subnet in the largest subnet. Which of the following answers lists a private IP network and mask that, if chosen, would meet the requirements?

   a. 10.0.0.0/25

   b. 10.0.0.0/22

   c. 172.16.0.0/23

   d. 192.168.7.0/24

3. An engineer has planned to use Class B network 172.19.0.0 and a single subnet mask throughout the network. The answers list the masks considered by the engineer. Choose the mask that, among the answers, supplies the largest number of hosts per subnet, while also supplying enough subnet bits to support 1000 subnets.

   a. 255.255.255.0

   b. /26

   c. 255.255.252.0

   d. /28

4. An engineer has calculated the list of subnet IDs, in consecutive order, for network 172.30.0.0, assuming that the /22 mask is used throughout the network. Which of the following are true? (Choose two answers.)

   a. Any two consecutive subnet IDs differ by a value of 22 in the third octet.

   b. Any two consecutive subnet IDs differ by a value of 16 in the fourth octet.

   c. The list contains 64 subnet IDs.

   d. The last subnet ID is 172.30.252.0.

5. Which of the following are valid subnet IDs for network 192.168.9.0 using mask /29, assuming that mask /29 is used throughout the network?

   a. 192.168.9.144

   b. 192.168.9.58

   c. 192.168.9.242

   d. 192.168.9.9

6. Which of the following is not a valid subnet ID for network 172.19.0.0 using mask /24, assuming that mask /24 is used throughout the network?

   a. 172.19.0.0

   b. 172.19.1.0

   c. 172.19.255.0

   d. 172.19.0.16

Foundation Topics

Choosing the Mask(s) to Meet Requirements

This first major section examines how to find all the masks that meet the stated requirements for the number of subnets and the number of hosts per subnet. To that end, the text assumes that the designer has already determined these requirements and has chosen the network number to be subnetted. The designer has also made the choice to use a single subnet mask value throughout the classful network.

Armed with the information in this chapter, you can answer questions such as the following, a question that matters both for real engineering jobs and the Cisco exams:

You are using Class B network 172.16.0.0. You need 200 subnets and 200 hosts/subnet. Which of the following subnet mask(s) meet the requirements? (This question is then followed by several answers that list different subnet masks.)

To begin, this section reviews the concepts in Chapter 13's section "Choose the Mask." That section introduced the main concepts about how an engineer, when designing subnet conventions, must choose the mask based on the requirements.

After reviewing the related concepts from Chapter 13, this section examines this topic in more depth. In particular, this chapter looks at three general cases:

- No masks meet the requirements.
- One and only one mask meets the requirements.
- Multiple masks meet the requirements.

For this last case, the text discusses how to determine all masks that meet the requirements and the trade-offs related to choosing which one mask to use.

Review: Choosing the Minimum Number of Subnet and Host Bits

The network designer must examine the requirements for the number of subnets and number of hosts/subnet, and then choose a mask. As discussed in detail in Chapter 15, "Analyzing Subnet Masks," a classful view of IP addresses defines the three-part structure of an IP address: network, subnet, and host. The network designer must choose the mask so that the number of subnet and host bits (S and H, respectively, in Figure 21-2) meet the requirements.

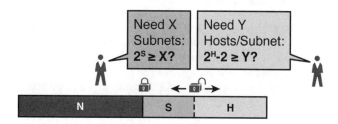

Figure 21-2 *Choosing the Number of Subnet and Host Bits*

Basically, the designer must choose S subnet bits so that the number of subnets that can be uniquely numbered with S bits (2^S) is at least as large as the required number of subnets. The designer applies similar logic to the number of host bits H, while noting that the formula is $2^H - 2$, because of the two reserved numbers in each subnet. So, keeping the powers of 2 handy, as shown in Table 21-2, will be useful when working through these problems.

Table 21-2 Powers of 2 Reference for Designing Masks

Number of Bits	2^X	Number of Bits	2^X	Number of Bits	2^X	Number of Bits	2^X
1	2	5	32	9	512	13	8192
2	4	6	64	10	1024	14	16,384
3	8	7	128	11	2048	15	32,768
4	16	8	256	12	4096	16	65,536

Answers to the "Do I Know This Already?" quiz:

1 A **2** B **3** B **4** C, D **5** A **6** D

More formally, the process must determine the minimum values for both S and H that meet the requirements. The following list summarizes the initial steps to choose the mask:

Step 1. Determine the number of network bits (N) based on the class.

Step 2. Determine the smallest value of S, so that $2^S => X$, where X represents the required number of subnets.

Step 3. Determine the smallest value of H, so that $2^H - 2 => Y$, where Y represents the required number of hosts/subnet.

The next three sections examine how to use these initial steps to choose a subnet mask.

No Masks Meet Requirements

After you determine the required number of subnet and host bits, those bits might not fit into a 32-bit IPv4 subnet mask. Remember, the mask always has a total of 32 bits, with binary 1s in the network and subnet parts and binary 0s in the host part. For the exam, a question might provide a set of requirements that simply cannot be met with 32 total bits.

For example, consider the following sample exam question:

A network engineer is planning a subnet design. The engineer plans to use Class B network 172.16.0.0. The network has a need for 300 subnets and 280 hosts per subnet. Which of the following masks could the engineer choose?

The three-step process shown in the previous section shows that these requirements mean that a total of 34 bits will be needed, so no mask meets the requirements. First, as a Class B network, 16 network bits exist, with 16 host bits from which to create the subnet part and to leave enough host bits to number the hosts in each subnet. For the number of subnet bits, S=8 does not work, because $2^8 = 256 < 300$. However, S=9 works, because $2^9 = 512 => 300$. Similarly, because $2^8 - 2 = 254$, which is less than 300, 8 host bits are not enough but 9 host bits ($2^9 - 2 = 510$) are just enough.

These requirements do not leave enough space to number all the hosts and subnet, because the network, subnet, and host parts add up to more than 32:

N=16, because as a Class B network, 16 network bits exist.

The minimum S=9, because S=8 provides too few subnets ($2^8 = 256 < 300$) but S=9 provides $2^9 = 512$ subnets.

The minimum H=9, because H=8 provides too few hosts ($2^8 - 2 = 254 < 280$) but H=9 provides $2^9 - 2 = 510$ hosts/subnet.

Figure 21-3 shows the resulting format for the IP addresses in this subnet, after the engineer has allocated 9 subnet bits on paper. Only 7 host bits remain, but the engineer needs 9 host bits.

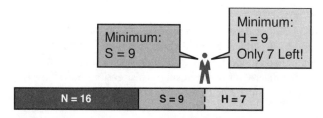

Figure 21-3   *Too Few Bits for the Host Part, Given the Requirements*

One Mask Meets Requirements

The process discussed in this chapter in part focuses on finding the smallest number of subnet bits and the smallest number of host bits to meet the requirements. If the engineer tries to use these minimum values, and the combined network, subnet, and host parts add up to exactly 32 bits, exactly one mask meets the requirements.

For example, consider a revised version of the example in the previous section, with smaller numbers of subnet and hosts, as follows:

> A network engineer is planning a subnet design. The engineer plans to use Class B network 172.16.0.0. The network has a need for 200 subnets and 180 hosts per subnet. Which of the following masks could the engineer choose?

The three-step process to determine the numbers of network, minimum subnet, and minimum host bits results in a need for 16, 8, and 8 bits, respectively. As before, with a Class B network, 16 network bits exist. With a need for only 200 subnets, S=8 does work, because $2^8 = 256 => 200$; 7 subnet bits would not supply enough subnets ($2^7 = 128$). Similarly, because $2^8 - 2 = 254 => 180$, 8 host bits meet the requirements; 7 host bits (for 126 total hosts/subnet) would not be enough.

Figure 21-4 shows the resulting format for the IP addresses in this subnet.

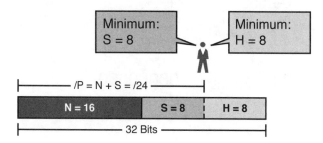

Figure 21-4   *One Mask That Meets Requirements*

Figure 21-4 shows the mask conceptually. To find the actual mask value, simply record the mask in prefix format (/P), where P = N + S or, in this case, /24.

Multiple Masks Meet Requirements

Depending on the requirements and choice of network, several masks might meet the requirements for the numbers of subnets and hosts/subnet. In these cases, you need to find all the masks that could be used. Then, you have a choice, but what should you consider when choosing one mask among all those that meet your requirements? This section shows how to find all the masks, as well as the facts to consider when choosing one mask from the list.

Finding All the Masks: Concepts

To help you better understand how to find all the subnet masks in binary, this section uses two major steps. In the first major step, you build the 32-bit binary subnet mask on paper. You write down binary 1s for the network bits, binary 1s for the subnet bits, and binary 0s for the host bits, just as always. However, you will use the minimum values for S and H. And when you write down these bits, you will not have 32 bits yet!

For example, consider the following problem, similar to the earlier examples in this chapter but with some changes in the requirements:

A network engineer is planning a subnet design. The engineer plans to use Class B network 172.16.0.0. The network has a need for 50 subnets and 180 hosts per subnet. Which of the following masks could the engineer choose?

This example is similar to an earlier example, except that only 50 subnets are needed in this case. Again, the engineer is using private IP network 172.16.0.0, meaning 16 network bits. The design requires only 6 subnet bits in this case, because $2^6 = 64 => 50$, and with only 5 subnet bits, $2^5 = 32 < 50$. The design then requires a minimum of 8 host bits.

One way to discuss the concepts and find all the masks that meet these requirements is to write down the bits in the subnet mask: binary 1s for the network and subnet parts and binary 0s for the host part. However, think of the 32-bit mask as 32-bit positions, and when writing the binary 0s, *write them on the far right*. Figure 21-5 shows the general idea.

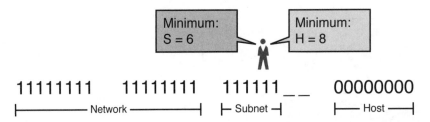

Figure 21-5 *Incomplete Mask with N=16, S=6, and H=8*

Figure 21-5 shows 30 bits of the mask, but the mask must have 32 bits. The 2 remaining bits might become subnet bits, being set to binary 1. Alternatively, these 2 bits could be made host bits, being set to binary 0. The engineer simply needs to choose based on whether he would like more subnet bits, to number more subnets, or more host bits, to number more hosts/subnet.

Regardless of the requirements, when choosing any IPv4 subnet mask, you must always follow this rule:

A subnet mask begins with all binary 1s, followed by all binary 0s, with no interleaving of 1s and 0s.

With the example shown in Figure 21-5, with 2 open bits, one value (binary 01) breaks this rule. However, the other three combinations of 2 bits (00, 10, and 11) do not break the rule. As a result, three masks meet the requirements in this example, as shown in Figure 21-6.

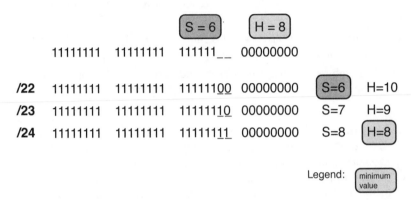

Figure 21-6 *Three Masks That Meet the Requirements*

In the three masks, the first has the least number of subnet bits among the three masks, but therefore has the most number of host bits. So, the first mask maximizes the number of hosts/subnet. The last mask uses the minimum value for the number of host bits, therefore using the most number of subnet bits allowed while still meeting the requirements. As a result, the last mask maximizes the number of subnets allowed.

Finding All the Masks: Math

Although the concepts related to the example shown in Figures 21-5 and 21-6 are important, you can find the range of masks that meets the requirements more easily just using some simple math. The process to find the masks just requires a few steps, after you know N and the minimum values of S and H. The process finds the value of /P when using the least number of subnet bits, and when using the least number of host bits, as follows:

Step 1.   Calculate the shortest prefix mask (/P) based on the *minimum value of S*, where P = N + S.

Step 2.   Calculate the longest prefix mask (/P) based on the *minimum value of H*, where P = 32 − H.

Step 3.   The range of valid masks includes all /P values between the two values calculated in the previous steps.

For example, in the example shown in Figure 21-6, N = 16, the minimum S = 6, and the minimum H = 8. The first step identifies the shortest prefix mask (the /P with the smallest value of P) of /22 by adding N and S (16 + 6). The second step identifies the longest prefix mask that meets the requirements by subtracting the smallest possible value for H (8, in this

21

case) from 32, for a mask of /24. The third step reminds us that the range is from /22 to /24, meaning that /23 is also an option.

Choosing the Best Mask

When multiple possible masks meet the stated requirements, the engineer has a choice of masks. That, of course, begs some questions: Which mask should you choose? Why would one mask be better than the other? The reasons can be summarized into three main options:

To maximize the number of hosts/subnet: To make this choice, use the shortest prefix mask (that is, the mask with the smallest /P value), because this mask has the largest host part.

To maximize the number of subnets: To make this choice, use the longest prefix mask (that is, the mask with the largest /P value), because this mask has the largest subnet part.

To increase both the numbers of supported subnets and hosts: To make this choice, choose a mask in the middle of the range, which gives you both more subnet bits and more host bits.

For example, in Figure 21-6, the range of masks that meet the requirements is /22 – /24. The shortest mask, /22, has the least subnet bits but the largest number of host bits (10) of the three answers, maximizing the number of hosts/subnet. The longest mask, /24, maximizes the number of subnet bits (8), maximizing the number of subnets, at least among the options that meet the original requirements. The mask in the middle, /23, provides some growth in both subnets and hosts/subnet.

The Formal Process

Although this chapter has explained various steps in finding a subnet mask to meet the design requirements, it has not yet collected these concepts into a list for the entire process. The following list collects all these steps into one place for reference. Note that this list does not introduce any new concepts compared to the rest of this chapter; it just puts all the ideas in one place.

Step 1. Find the number of network bits (N) per class rules.

Step 2. Calculate the minimum number of subnet bits (S) so that $2^S =>$ the number of required subnets.

Step 3. Calculate the minimum number of host bits (H) so that $2^H - 2 =>$ the number of required hosts/subnet.

Step 4. If $N + S + H > 32$, no mask meets the need.

Step 5. If $N + S + H = 32$, one mask meets the need. Calculate the mask as /P, where $P = N + S$.

Step 6. If $N + S + H < 32$, multiple masks meet the need:

    A. Calculate mask /P based on the minimum value of S, where $P = N + S$. This mask maximizes the number of hosts/subnet.

    B. Calculate mask /P based on the minimum value of H, where $P = 32 - H$. This mask maximizes the number of possible subnets.

    C. Note that the complete range of masks includes all prefix lengths between the two values calculated in Steps 6A and 6B.

Practice Choosing Subnet Masks

Take the usual two-phase approach to learning new subnetting math and processes. Take the time now to practice to make sure you understand the fundamentals, using the book and notes as needed. Then, sometime before taking the exam, practice until you can reach the goals in the right column of Table 21-3.

Table 21-3   Keep-Reading and Take-Exam Goals for Choosing a Subnet Mask

Time Frame	Before Moving to the Next Chapter	Before Taking the Exam
Focus On	Learning how	Being correct and fast
Tools Allowed	All	Your brain and a notepad
Goal: Accuracy	90% correct	100% correct
Goal: Speed	Any speed	15 seconds

Practice Problems for Choosing a Subnet Mask

The following list shows three separate problems, each with a classful network number and a required number of subnets and hosts/subnet. For each problem, determine the minimum number of subnet and host bits that meet the requirements. If more than one mask exists, note which mask maximizes the number of hosts/subnet and which maximizes the number of subnets. If only one mask meets the requirements, simply list that mask. List the masks in prefix format:

1. Network 10.0.0.0, need 1500 subnets, need 300 hosts/subnet

2. Network 172.25.0.0, need 130 subnets, need 127 hosts/subnet

3. Network 192.168.83.0, need 8 subnets, need 8 hosts/subnet

Table 21-8, found in the later section "Answers to Earlier Practice Problems," lists the answers.

Finding All Subnet IDs

After the person designing the IP subnetting plan has chosen the one mask to use throughout the Class A, B, or C network, he will soon need to start assigning specific subnet IDs for use in specific VLANs, serial links, and other places in the internetwork that need a subnet. But what are those subnet IDs? As it turns out, after the network ID and one subnet mask for all subnets have been chosen, finding all the subnet IDs just requires doing a little math. This second major section of this chapter focuses on that math, which focuses on a single question:

Given a single Class A, B, or C network, and the single subnet mask to use for all subnets, what are all the subnet IDs?

When learning how to answer this question, you can think about the problem in either binary or decimal. This chapter approaches the problem using decimal. Although the process itself requires only simple math, the process requires practice before most people can confidently answer this question.

The decimal process begins by identifying the first, or numerically lowest, subnet ID. After that, the process identifies a pattern in all subnet IDs for a given subnet mask so that you can find each successive subnet ID through simple addition. This section examines the key ideas behind this process first; then you are given a formal definition of the process.

> **NOTE**   Some videos included on the accompanying DVD describe the same fundamental processes to find all subnet IDs. You can view those videos before or after reading this section, or even instead of reading this section, as long as you learn how to independently find all subnet IDs. The process step numbering in the videos might not match the steps shown in this edition of the book.

First Subnet ID: The Zero Subnet

The first step in finding all subnet IDs of one network is incredibly simple: Copy the network ID. That is, take the Class A, B, or C network ID—in other words, the classful network ID—and write it down as the first subnet ID. No matter what Class A, B, or C network you use, and no matter what subnet mask you use, the first (numerically lowest) subnet ID is equal to the network ID.

For example, if you begin with classful network 172.20.0.0, no matter what the mask is, the first subnet ID is 172.20.0.0.

This first subnet ID in each network goes by two special names: either *subnet zero* or the *zero subnet*. The origin of these names is related to the fact that a network's zero subnet, when viewed in binary, has a subnet part of all binary 0s. In decimal, the zero subnet can be easily identified, because the zero subnet always has the exact same numeric value as the network ID itself.

In the past, engineers avoided using zero subnets because of the ambiguity with one number that could represent the entire classful network or it could represent one subnet inside the classful network. To help control that, IOS has a global command that can be set one of two ways:

ip subnet-zero, which allows the configuration of addresses in the zero subnet.

no ip subnet-zero, which prevents the configuration of addresses in the zero subnet.

Although most sites use the default setting to allow zero subnets, you can use the **no ip subnet-zero** command to prevent configuring addresses that are part of a zero subnet. Example 21-1 shows how a router rejects an **ip address** command after changing to use **no ip subnet-zero**. Note that the error message does not mention the zero subnet, instead simply stating "bad mask."

Example 21-1   *Effects of* [no] ip subnet-zero *on a Local Router*

```
R1# configure terminal
Enter configuration commands, one per line.    End with CNTL/Z.
R1(config)# no ip subnet-zero
R1(config)# interface g0/1
R1(config-if)# ip address 10.0.0.1 255.255.255.0
Bad mask /24 for address 10.0.0.1
```

Note that the **no ip subnet-zero** command affects the local router's **ip address** commands, as well as the local router's **ip route** commands (which define static routes). However, it does not affect the local router's routes as learned with a routing protocol.

Finding the Pattern Using the Magic Number

Subnet IDs follow a predictable pattern, at least when using our assumption of a single subnet mask for all subnets of a network. The pattern uses the *magic number*, as discussed in Chapter 16, "Analyzing Existing Subnets." To review, the magic number is 256, minus the mask's decimal value, in a particular octet that this book refers to as the *interesting octet*.

Figure 21-7 shows four examples of these patterns with four different masks. For example, just look at the top of the figure to start. It lists mask 255.255.128.0 on the left. The third octet is the interesting octet, with a mask value other than 0 or 255 in that octet. The left side shows a magic number calculated as 256 – 128 = 128. So, the pattern of subnet IDs is shown in the highlighted number line; that is, the subnet IDs when using this mask will have either a 0 or 128 in the third octet. For example, if using network 172.16.0.0, the subnet IDs would be 172.16.0.0 and 172.16.128.0.

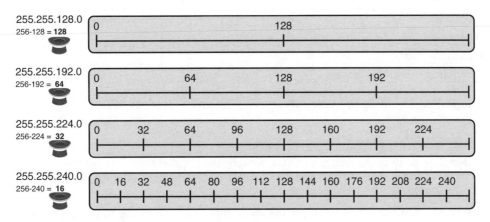

Figure 21-7 *Patterns with Magic Numbers for Masks /17 – /20*

Now focus on the second row, with another example, with mask 255.255.192.0. This row shows a magic number of 64 (256 – 192 = 64), so the subnet IDs will use a value of 0, 64, 128, or 192 (multiples of 64) in the third octet. For example, if used with network 172.16.0.0, the subnet IDs would be 172.16.0.0, 172.16.64.0, 172.16.128.0, and 172.16.192.0.

Looking at the third row/example, the mask is 255.255.224.0, with a magic number of 256 – 224 = 32. So, as shown in the center of the figure, the subnet ID values will be multiples of 32. For example, if used with network 172.16.0.0 again, this mask would tell us that the subnet IDs are 172.16.0.0, 172.16.32.0, 172.16.64.0, 172.16.96.0, and so on.

Finally, for the bottom example, mask 255.255.240.0 makes the magic number, in the third octet, be 16. So, all the subnet IDs will be a multiple of 16 in the third octet, with those values shown in the middle of the figure.

A Formal Process with Less Than 8 Subnet Bits

Although it can be easy to see the patterns in Figure 21-7, it might not be as obvious exactly how to apply those concepts to find all the subnet IDs in every case. This section outlines a specific process to find all the subnet IDs.

21

To simplify the explanations, this section assumes that less than 8 subnet bits exist. Later, the section "Finding All Subnets with More Than 8 Subnet Bits," describes the full process that can be used in all cases.

First, to organize your thoughts, you might want to organize the data into a table like Table 21-4. This book refers to this chart as the list-all-subnets chart.

Table 21-4 Generic List-All-Subnets Chart

Octet	1	2	3	4
Mask				
Magic Number				
Network Number/Zero Subnet				
Next Subnet				
Next Subnet				
Next Subnet				
Broadcast Subnet				
Out of Range—Used by Process				

A formal process to find all subnet IDs, given a network and a single subnet mask, is as follows:

Step 1. Write down the subnet mask, in decimal, in the first empty row of the table.

Step 2. Identify the interesting octet, which is the one octet of the mask with a value other than 255 or 0. Draw a rectangle around the column of the interesting octet.

Step 3. Calculate and write down the magic number by subtracting the *subnet mask's interesting octet* from 256.

Step 4. Write down the classful network number, which is the same number as the zero subnet, in the next empty row of the list-all-subnets chart.

Step 5. To find each successive subnet number:

A. For the three uninteresting octets, copy the previous subnet number's values.

B. For the interesting octet, add the magic number to the previous subnet number's interesting octet.

Step 6. When the sum calculated in Step 5B reaches 256, stop the process. The number with the 256 in it is out of range, and the previous subnet number is the broadcast subnet.

Although the written process is long, with practice, most people can find the answers much more quickly with this decimal-based process than by using binary math. As usual, most people learn this process best by seeing it in action, exercising it, and then practicing it. To that end, review the two following examples and watch any videos that came with this book that show additional examples.

Example 1: Network 172.16.0.0, Mask 255.255.240.0

To begin this example, focus on the first four of the six steps, when subnetting network 172.16.0.0 using mask 255.255.240.0. Figure 21-8 shows the results of these first four steps:

Step 1. Record mask 255.255.240.0, which was given as part of the problem statement. (Figure 21-8 also shows the network ID, 172.16.0.0, for easy reference.)

Step 2. The mask's third octet is neither 0 nor 255, which makes the third octet interesting.

Step 3. Because the mask's value in the third octet is 240, the magic number = 256 − 240 = 16.

Step 4. Because the network ID is 172.16.0.0, the first subnet ID, the zero subnet, is also 172.16.0.0.

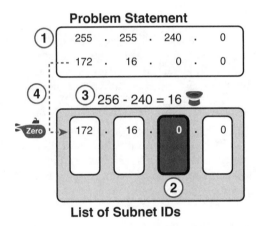

Figure 21-8 *Results of First Four Steps: 172.16.0.0, 255.255.240.0.*

These first four steps discover the first subnet (the zero subnet) and get you ready to do the remaining steps by identifying the interesting octet and the magic number. Step 5 in the process tells you to copy the three boring octets and add the magic number (16, in this case) in the interesting octet (octet 3, in this case). Keep repeating this step until the interesting octet value equals 256 (per Step 6). When the total is 256, you have listed all the subnet IDs, and the line with 256 on it is not a correct subnet ID. Figure 21-9 shows the results of the Step 5 actions.

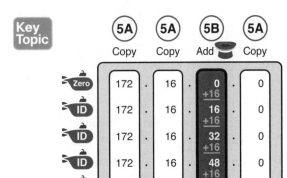

Figure 21-9   *List of Subnet IDs: 172.16.0.0, 255.255.240.0*

> **NOTE**   In any list of all the subnet IDs of a network, the numerically highest subnet ID is called the *broadcast subnet*. Decades ago, engineers avoided using the broadcast subnet. However, using the broadcast subnet causes no problems. The term *broadcast subnet* has its origins in the fact that if you determine the subnet broadcast address inside the broadcast subnet, it has the same numeric value as the network-wide broadcast address.

> **NOTE**   People sometimes confuse the terms *broadcast subnet* and *subnet broadcast address*. The *broadcast subnet* is one subnet, namely the numerically highest subnet; only one such subnet exists per network. The term *subnet broadcast address* refers to the one number in each and every subnet that is the numerically highest number in that subnet.

Example 2: Network 192.168.1.0, Mask 255.255.255.224

With a Class C network and a mask of 255.255.255.224, this example makes the fourth octet the interesting octet. However, the process works the same, with the same logic, just with the interesting logic applied in a different octet. As with the previous example, the following list outlines the first four steps, with Figure 21-10 showing the results of the first four steps:

Step 1.   Record mask 255.255.255.224, which was given as part of the problem statement, and optionally record the network number (192.168.1.0).

Step 2.   The mask's fourth octet is neither 0 nor 255, which makes the fourth octet interesting.

Step 3.   Because the mask's value in the fourth octet is 224, the magic number = 256 – 224 = 32.

Step 4.   Because the network ID is 192.168.1.0, the first subnet ID, the zero subnet, is also 192.168.1.0.

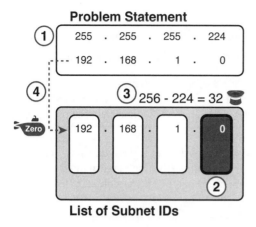

Figure 21-10 *Results of First Four Steps: 192.168.1.0, 255.255.255.224*

From this point, Step 5 in the process tells you to copy the values in the first three octets and then add the magic number (32, in this case) in the interesting octet (octet 4, in this case). Keep doing so until the interesting octet value equals 256 (per Step 6). When the total is 256, you have listed all the subnet IDs, and the line with 256 on it is not a correct subnet ID. Figure 21-11 shows the results of these steps.

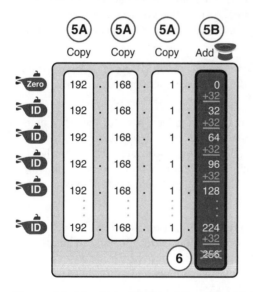

Figure 21-11 *List of Subnet IDs: 192.168.1.0, 255.255.255.224*

Finding All Subnets with Exactly 8 Subnet Bits

The formal process in the earlier section "A Formal Process with Less Than 8 Subnet Bits" identified the interesting octet as the octet whose mask value is neither a 255 nor a 0. If the mask defines exactly 8 subnet bits, you must use a different logic to identify the interesting octet; otherwise, the same process can be used. In fact, the actual subnet IDs can be a little more intuitive.

Only two cases exist with exactly 8 subnet bits:

A Class A network with mask 255.255.0.0; the entire second octet contains subnet bits.

A Class B network with mask 255.255.255.0; the entire third octet contains subnet bits.

In each case, use the same process as with less than 8 subnet bits, but identify the interesting octet as the one octet that contains subnet bits. Also, because the mask's value is 255, the magic number will be 256 – 255 = 1, so the subnet IDs are each 1 larger than the previous subnet ID.

For example, for 172.16.0.0, mask 255.255.255.0, the third octet is the interesting octet and the magic number is 256 – 255 = 1. You start with the zero subnet, equal in value to network number 172.16.0.0, and then add 1 in the third octet. For example, the first four subnets are as follows:

172.16.0.0 (zero subnet)

172.16.1.0

172.16.2.0

172.16.3.0

Finding All Subnets with More Than 8 Subnet Bits

Earlier, the section "A Formal Process with Less Than 8 Subnet Bits" assumed less than 8 subnet bits for the purpose of simplifying the discussions while you learn. In real life, you need to be able to find all subnet IDs with any valid mask, so you cannot assume less than 8 subnet bits.

The examples that have at least 9 subnet bits have a minimum of 512 subnet IDs, so writing down such a list would take a lot of time. To conserve space, the examples will use short-hand rather than list hundreds or thousands of subnet IDs.

The process with less than 8 subnet bits told you to count in increments of the magic number in one octet. With more than 8 subnet bits, the new expanded process must tell you how to count in multiple octets. So, this section breaks down two general cases: (a) when 9–16 subnet bits exist, which means that the subnet field exists in only two octets, and (b) cases with 17 or more subnet bits, which means that the subnet field exists in three octets.

Process with 9–16 Subnet Bits

To understand the process, you need to know a few terms that the process will use. Figure 21-12 shows the details, with an example that uses Class B network 130.4.0.0 and mask 255.255.255.192. The lower part of the figure details the structure of the addresses per the mask: a network part of two octets because it is a Class B address, a 10-bit subnet part per the mask (/26), and 6 host bits.

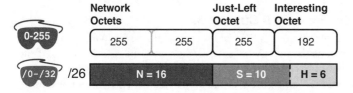

Figure 21-12 *Fundamental Concepts and Terms for the >8 Subnet Bit Process*

In this case, subnet bits exist in two octets: octets 3 and 4. For the purposes of the process, the rightmost of these octets is the interesting octet, and the octet just to the left is the cleverly named *just-left* octet.

The updated process, which makes adjustments for cases in which the subnet field is longer than 1 octet, tells you to count in increments of the magic number in the interesting octet, but count by 1s in the just-left octet. Formally:

Step 1. Calculate subnet IDs using the 8-subnet-bits-or-less process. However, when the total adds up to 256, move to the next step; consider the subnet IDs listed so far as a *subnet block*.

Step 2. Copy the previous subnet block, but add 1 to the just-left octet in all subnet IDs in the new block.

Step 3. Repeat Step 2 until you create the block with a just-left octet of 255, but go no further.

To be honest, the formal concept can cause you problems until you work through some examples, so even if the process remains a bit unclear in your mind, you should work through the following examples instead of rereading the formal process.

First, consider an example based on Figure 21-12, with network 130.4.0.0 and mask 255.255.255.192. Figure 21-12 already showed the structure, and Figure 21-13 shows the subnet ID block created at Step 1.

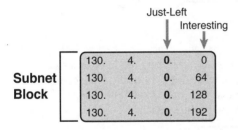

Figure 21-13   *Step 1: Listing the First Subnet ID Block*

The logic at Step 1, to create this subnet ID block of four subnet IDs, follows the same magic number process seen before. The first subnet ID, 130.4.0.0, is the zero subnet. The next three subnet IDs are each 64 bigger, because the magic number, in this case, is 256 − 192 = 64.

Steps 2 and 3 from the formal process tell you how to create 256 subnet blocks, and by doing so, you will list all 1024 subnet IDs. To do so, create 256 total subnet blocks: one with a 0 in the just-left octet, one with a 1 in the just-left octet, and another with a 2 in the just-left octet, up through 255. The process continues through the step at which you create the subnet block with 255 in the just-left octet (third octet, in this case). Figure 21-14 shows the idea, with the addition of the first few subnet blocks.

21

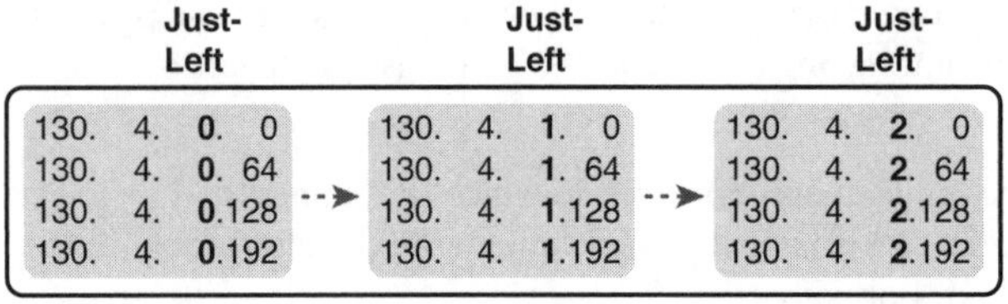

Figure 21-14   *Step 2: Replicating the Subnet Block with +1 in the Just-Left Octet*

This example, with 10 total subnet bits, creates 256 blocks of four subnets each, for a total of 1024 subnets. This math matches the usual method of counting subnets, because $2^{10} = 1024$.

Process with 17 or More Subnet Bits

To create a subnet design that allows 17 or more subnet bits to exist, the design must use a Class A network. In addition, the subnet part will consist of the entire second and third octets, plus part of the fourth octet. That means a lot of subnet IDs: at least 2^{17} (or 131,072) subnets. Figure 21-15 shows an example of just such a structure, with a Class A network and a /26 mask.

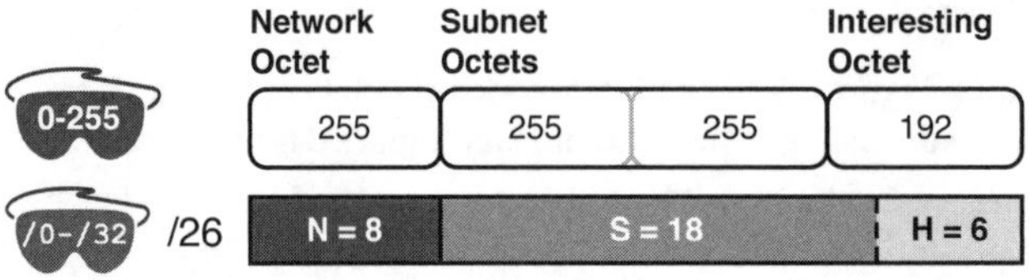

Figure 21-15   *Address Structure with 18 Subnet Bits*

To find all the subnet IDs in this example, you use the same general process as with 9–16 subnet bits, but with many more subnet blocks to create. In effect, you have to create a subnet block for all combinations of values (0–255, inclusive) in both the second and third octet. Figure 21-16 shows the general idea. Note that with only 2 subnet bits in the fourth octet in this example, the subnet blocks will have four subnets each.

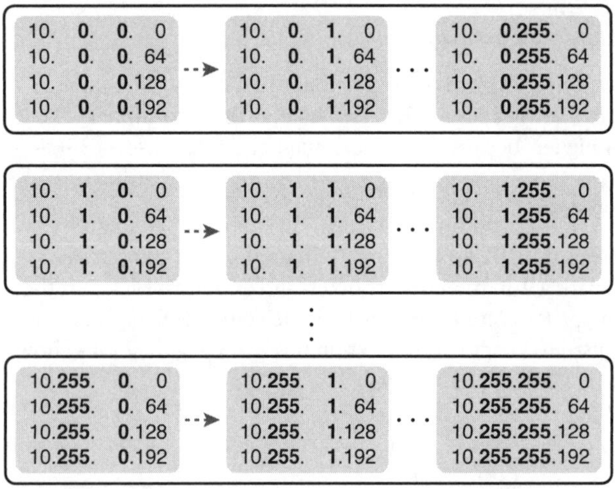

Figure 21-16   *256 Times 256 Subnet Blocks of Four Subnets*

Practice Finding All Subnet IDs

Before moving to the next chapter, practice until you get the right answer most of the time—but use any tools you want and take all the time you need. Then, you can move on with your reading. *Before taking the exam*, practice until you reach the goals in the right column of Table 21-5, which summarizes the key concepts and suggestions for this two-phase approach.

Table 21-5 Keep-Reading and Take-Exam Goals for This Chapter's Topics

Time Frame	Before Moving to the Next Chapter	Before Taking the Exam
Focus On	Learning how	Being correct and fast
Tools Allowed	All	Your brain and a notepad
Goal: Accuracy	90% correct	100% correct
Goal: Speed	Any speed	45 seconds

Practice Problems for Finding All Subnet IDs

The following list shows three separate problems, each with a classful network number and prefix-style mask. Find all subnet IDs for each problem:

1. 192.168.9.0/27
2. 172.30.0.0/20
3. 10.0.0.0/17

The section "Answers to Earlier Practice Problems," later in this chapter, lists the answers.

Chapter Review

One key to doing well on the exams is to perform repetitive spaced review sessions. Review this chapter's material using either the tools in the book, DVD, or interactive tools for the same material found on the book's companion website. Refer to the "Your Study Plan" element for more details. Table 21-6 outlines the key review elements and where you can find them. To better track your study progress, record when you completed these activities in the second column.

Table 21-6 Chapter Review Tracking

Review Element	Review Date(s)	Resource Used
Review key topics		Book, DVD/website
Review key terms		Book, DVD/website
Answer DIKTA questions		Book, PCPT
Practice subnet design		DVD Appendix G, DVD/website

Review All the Key Topics

Table 21-7 Key Topics for Chapter 21

Key Topic Element	Description	Page Number
Definition	Facts about binary values in subnet masks	511
List	The shorter three-step process to find all prefix masks that meet certain requirements	511
List	Reasons to choose one subnet mask versus another	512
Step list	The complete process for finding and choosing masks to meet certain requirements	512
Step list	Formal steps to find all subnet IDs when less than 8 subnet bits exist	516
Figure 21-9	An example of adding the magic number in the interesting octet to find all subnet IDs	518
Step list	Formal steps to find all subnet IDs when more than 8 subnet bits exist	521

Key Terms You Should Know

zero subnet, subnet zero, broadcast subnet

Additional Practice for This Chapter's Processes

For additional practice with subnet mask design and finding all subnet IDs, you may do the same set of practice problems using your choice of tools:

Application: Use the Subnet Design application on the DVD or companion website.

PDF: Alternatively, practice the same problems found in both these apps using DVD Appendix G, "Practice for Chapter 21: Subnet Design."

Answers to Earlier Practice Problems

Answers to Practice Choosing Subnet Masks

The earlier section "Practice Choosing Subnet Masks" listed three practice problems. The answers are listed here so that the answers are nearby but not visible from the list of problems. Table 21-8 lists the answers, with notes related to each problem following the table.

Table 21-8   Practice Problems: Find the Masks That Meet Requirements

Problem	Class	Minimum Subnet Bits	Minimum Host Bits	Prefix Range	Prefix to Maximize Subnets	Prefix to Maximize Hosts
1	A	11	9	/19 – /23	/23	/19
2	B	8	8	/24	—	—
3	C	3	4	/27 – /28	/28	/27

1. N=8, because the problem lists Class A network 10.0.0.0. With a need for 1500 subnets, 10 subnet bits supply only 1024 subnets (per Table 21-2), but 11 subnet bits (S) would provide 2048 subnets—more than the required 1500. Similarly, the smallest number of host bits would be 9, because $2^8 - 2 = 254$, and the design requires 300 hosts/subnet. The shortest prefix mask would then be /19, found by adding N (8) and the smallest usable number of subnet bits S (11). Similarly, with a minimum H value of 9, the longest prefix mask, maximizing the number of subnets, is 32 – H = /23.

2. N=16, because the problem lists Class B network 172.25.0.0. With a need for 130 subnets, 7 subnet bits supply only 128 subnets (per Table 21-2), but 8 subnet bits (S) would provide 256 subnets—more than the required 130. Similarly, the smallest number of host bits would be 8, because $2^7 - 2 = 126$—close to the required 127, but not quite enough, making H = 8 the smallest number of host bits that meets requirements. Note that the network, minimum subnet bits, and minimum host bits add up to 32, so only one mask meets the requirements, namely /24, found by adding the number of network bits (16) to the minimum number of subnet bits (8).

3. N=24, because the problem lists Class C network 192.168.83.0. With a need for eight subnets, 3 subnet bits supply enough, but just barely. The smallest number of host bits would be 4, because $2^3 - 2 = 6$, and the design requires 8 hosts/subnet. The shortest prefix mask would then be /27, found by adding N (24) and the smallest usable number of subnet bits S (3). Similarly, with a minimum H value of 4, the longest prefix mask, maximizing the number of subnets, is 32 – H = /28.

Answers to Practice Finding All Subnet IDs

The earlier section "Practice Finding All Subnet IDs" listed three practice problems. The answers are listed here so that they are not visible from the same page as the list of problems.

Answer, Practice Problem 1

Problem 1 lists network 192.168.9.0, mask /27. The mask converts to DDN mask 255.255.255.224. When used with a Class C network, which has 24 network bits, only 3 subnet bits exist, and they all sit in the fourth octet. So, this problem is a case of less than 8 subnet bits, with the fourth octet as the interesting octet.

To get started listing subnets, first write down the zero subnet and then start adding the magic number in the interesting octet. The zero subnet equals the network ID (192.168.9.0, in this case). The magic number, calculated as 256 – 224 = 32, should be added to the previous subnet ID's interesting octet. Table 21-9 lists the results.

21

Table 21-9   List-All-Subnets Chart: 192.168.9.0/27

Octet	1	2	3	4
Mask	255	255	255	224
Magic Number	—	—	—	32
Classful Network/Subnet Zero	192	168	9	0
First Nonzero Subnet	192	168	9	32
Next Subnet	192	168	9	64
Next Subnet	192	168	9	96
Next Subnet	192	168	9	128
Next Subnet	192	168	9	160
Next Subnet	192	168	9	192
Broadcast Subnet	192	168	9	224
Invalid—Used by Process	192	168	9	256

Answer, Practice Problem 2

Problem 2 lists network 172.30.0.0, mask /20. The mask converts to DDN mask 255.255.240.0. When used with a Class B network, which has 16 network bits, only 4 subnet bits exist, and they all sit in the third octet. So, this problem is a case of less than 8 subnet bits, with the third octet as the interesting octet.

To get started listing subnets, first write down the zero subnet and then start adding the magic number in the interesting octet. The zero subnet equals the network ID (or 172.30.0.0, in this case). The magic number, calculated as 256 – 240 = 16, should be added to the previous subnet ID's interesting octet. Table 21-10 lists the results.

Table 21-10   List-All-Subnets Chart: 172.30.0.0/20

Octet	1	2	3	4
Mask	255	255	240	0
Magic Number	—	—	16	—
Classful Network/Subnet Zero	172	30	0	0
First Nonzero Subnet	172	30	16	0
Next Subnet	172	30	32	0
Next Subnet	172	30	Skipping...	0
Next Subnet	172	30	224	0
Broadcast Subnet	172	30	240	0
Invalid—Used by Process	172	30	256	0

Answer, Practice Problem 3

Problem 3 lists network 10.0.0.0, mask /17. The mask converts to DDN mask 255.255.128.0. When used with a Class A network, which has 8 network bits, 9 subnet bits exist. Using the terms unique to this chapter, octet 3 is the interesting octet, with only 1 subnet bit in that octet, and octet 2 is the just-left octet, with 8 subnet bits.

In this case, begin by finding the first subnet block. The magic number is 256 – 128 = 128. The first subnet (zero subnet) equals the network ID. So, the first subnet ID block includes the following:

10.0.0.0

10.0.128.0

Then, you create a subnet block for all 256 possible values in the just-left octet, or octet 2 in this case. The following list shows the first three subnet ID blocks, plus the last subnet ID block, rather than listing page upon page of subnet IDs:

10.0.0.0 (zero subnet)

10.0.128.0

10.1.0.0

10.1.128.0

10.2.0.0

10.2.128.0

…

10.255.0.0

10.255.128.0 (broadcast subnet)

21

CHAPTER 22

Variable-Length Subnet Masks

This chapter covers the following exam topics:

1.0 Network Fundamentals

1.8 Configure, verify, and troubleshoot IPv4 addressing and subnetting

IPv4 addressing and subnetting use a lot of terms, a lot of small math steps, and a lot of concepts that fit together. While learning those concepts, it helps to keep things as simple as possible. One way this book has kept the discussion simpler so far was to show examples that use one mask only inside a single Class A, B, or C network.

This chapter removes that restriction by introducing variable-length subnet masks (VLSM). VLSM simply means that the subnet design uses more than one mask in the same classful network. VLSM has some advantages and disadvantages, but when learning, the main challenge is that a subnetting design that uses VLSM requires more math, and it requires that you think about some other issues as well. This chapter walks you through the concepts, the issues, and the math.

"Do I Know This Already?" Quiz

Take the quiz (either here, or use the PCPT software) if you want to use the score to help you decide how much time to spend on this chapter. The answers are at the bottom of the page following the quiz, and the explanations are in DVD Appendix C and in the PCPT software.

Table 22-1 "Do I Know This Already?" Foundation Topics Section-to-Question Mapping

Foundation Topics Section	Questions
VLSM Concepts and Configuration	1–2
Finding VLSM Overlaps	3–4
Adding a New Subnet to an Existing VLSM Design	5

1. Which of the following routing protocols support VLSM? (Choose three answers.)

   a. RIPv1

   b. RIPv2

   c. EIGRP

   d. OSPF

2. What does the acronym VLSM stand for?

   a. Variable-length subnet mask

   b. Very long subnet mask

   c. Vociferous longitudinal subnet mask

   d. Vector-length subnet mask

   e. Vector loop subnet mask

3. R1 has configured interface Fa0/0 with the **ip address 10.5.48.1 255.255.240.0** command. Which of the following subnets, when configured on another interface on R1, would not be considered an overlapping VLSM subnet?

   a. 10.5.0.0 255.255.240.0

   b. 10.4.0.0 255.254.0.0

   c. 10.5.32.0 255.255.224.0

   d. 10.5.0.0 255.255.128.0

4. R4 has a connected route for 172.16.8.0/22. Which of the following answers lists a subnet that overlaps with this subnet?

   a. 172.16.0.0/21

   b. 172.16.6.0/23

   c. 172.16.16.0/20

   d. 172.16.11.0/25

5. A design already includes subnets 192.168.1.0/26, 192.168.1.128/30, and 192.168.1.160/29. Which of the following subnets is the numerically lowest subnet ID that could be added to the design, if you wanted to add a subnet that uses a /28 mask?

   a. 192.168.1.144/28

   b. 192.168.1.112/28

   c. 192.168.1.64/28

   d. 192.168.1.80/28

   e. 192.168.1.96/28

Foundation Topics

VLSM Concepts and Configuration

VLSM occurs when an internetwork uses more than one mask for different subnets of a single Class A, B, or C network. Figure 22-1 shows an example of VLSM used in Class A network 10.0.0.0.

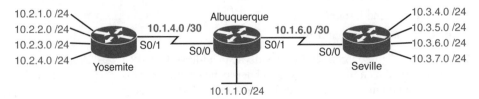

Figure 22-1 *VLSM in Network 10.0.0.0: Masks /24 and /30*

Figure 22-1 shows a typical choice of using a /30 prefix (mask 255.255.255.252) on point-to-point serial links, with mask /24 (255.255.255.0) on the LAN subnets. All subnets are of Class A network 10.0.0.0, with two masks being used, therefore meeting the definition of VLSM.

Oddly enough, a common mistake occurs when people think that VLSM means "using more than one mask in some internetwork" rather than "using more than one mask *in a single classful network*." For example, if in one internetwork diagram, all subnets of network 10.0.0.0 use a 255.255.240.0 mask, and all subnets of network 11.0.0.0 use a 255.255.255.0 mask, the design uses two different masks. However, Class A network 10.0.0.0 uses only one mask, and Class A network 11.0.0.0 uses only one mask. In that case, the design does not use VLSM.

VLSM provides many benefits for real networks, mainly related to how you allocate and use your IP address space. Because a mask defines the size of the subnet (the number of host addresses in the subnet), VLSM allows engineers to better match the need for addresses with the size of the subnet. For example, for subnets that need fewer addresses, the engineer uses a mask with fewer host bits, so the subnet has fewer host IP addresses. This flexibility reduces the number of wasted IP addresses in each subnet. By wasting fewer addresses, more space remains to allocate more subnets.

VLSM can be helpful for both public and private IP addresses, but the benefits are more dramatic with public networks. With public networks, the address savings help engineers avoid having to obtain another registered IP network number from regional IP address assignment authorities. With private networks, as defined in RFC 1918, running out of addresses is not as big a negative, because you can always grab another private network from RFC 1918 if you run out.

Classless and Classful Routing Protocols

Before you can deploy a VLSM design, you must first use a routing protocol that supports VLSM. To support VLSM, the routing protocol must advertise the mask along with each subnet. Without mask information, the router receiving the update would be confused.

Answers to the "Do I Know This Already?" quiz:

1 B, C, D   **2** A   **3** A   **4** D   **5** C

For example, if a router learned a route for 10.1.8.0, but with no mask information, what does that mean? Is that subnet 10.1.8.0/24? 10.1.8.0/23? 10.1.8.0/30? The dotted-decimal number 10.1.8.0 happens to be a valid subnet number with a variety of masks, and because multiple masks can be used with VLSM, the router has no good way to make an educated guess. To effectively support VLSM, the routing protocol needs to advertise the correct mask along with each subnet so that the receiving router knows the exact subnet that is being advertised.

By definition, *classless routing protocols* advertise the mask with each advertised route, and *classful routing protocols* do not. The classless routing protocols, as noted in Table 22-2, are the newer, more advanced routing protocols. Not only do these more advanced classless routing protocols support VLSM, but they also support manual route summarization, which allows a routing protocol to advertise one route for a larger subnet instead of multiple routes for smaller subnets.

Table 22-2   Classless and Classful Interior IP Routing Protocols

Routing Protocol	Is It Classless?	Sends Mask in Updates?	Supports VLSM?	Supports Manual Route Summarization?
RIPv1	No	No	No	No
RIPv2	Yes	Yes	Yes	Yes
EIGRP	Yes	Yes	Yes	Yes
OSPF	Yes	Yes	Yes	Yes

Beyond VLSM itself, the routing protocols do not have to be configured to support VLSM or to be classless. There is no command to enable or disable the fact that classless routing protocols include the mask with each route. The only configuration choice you must make is to use a classless routing protocol.

VLSM Configuration and Verification

Cisco routers do not configure VLSM, enable or disable it, or need any configuration to use it. From a configuration perspective, VLSM is simply a side effect of using the **ip address** interface subcommand. Routers collectively configure VLSM by virtue of having IP addresses in the same classful network but with different masks.

For example, Example 22-1 shows two of the interfaces from router Yosemite from Figure 22-1. The example shows the IP address assignments on two interfaces, one with a /24 mask and one with a /30 mask, both with IP addresses in Class A network 10.0.0.0.

Example 22-1   *Configuring Two Interfaces on Yosemite, Resulting in VLSM*

```
Yosemite# configure terminal
Yosemite(config)# interface Fa0/0
Yosemite(config-if)# ip address 10.2.1.1 255.255.255.0
Yosemite(config-if)# interface S0/1
Yosemite(config-if)# ip address 10.1.4.1 255.255.255.252
```

The use of VLSM can also be detected by a detailed look at the output of the **show ip route** command. This command lists routes in groups, by classful network, so that you see all the subnets of a single Class A, B, or C network all in a row. Just look down the list, and

22

look to see, if any, how many different masks are listed. For example, Example 22-2 lists the routing table on Albuquerque from Figure 22-1; Albuquerque uses masks /24 and /30 inside network 10.0.0.0, as noted in the highlighted line in the example.

Example 22-2 *Albuquerque Routing Table with VLSM*

```
Albuquerque# show ip route
! Legend omitted for brevity

     10.0.0.0/8 is variably subnetted, 14 subnets, 3 masks
D       10.2.1.0/24 [90/2172416] via 10.1.4.1, 00:00:34, Serial0/0
D       10.2.2.0/24 [90/2172416] via 10.1.4.1, 00:00:34, Serial0/0
D       10.2.3.0/24 [90/2172416] via 10.1.4.1, 00:00:34, Serial0/0
D       10.2.4.0/24 [90/2172416] via 10.1.4.1, 00:00:34, Serial0/0
D       10.3.4.0/24 [90/2172416] via 10.1.6.2, 00:00:56, Serial0/1
D       10.3.5.0/24 [90/2172416] via 10.1.6.2, 00:00:56, Serial0/1
D       10.3.6.0/24 [90/2172416] via 10.1.6.2, 00:00:56, Serial0/1
D       10.3.7.0/24 [90/2172416] via 10.1.6.2, 00:00:56, Serial0/1
C       10.1.1.0/24 is directly connected, FastEthernet0/0
L       10.1.1.1/32 is directly connected, FastEthernet0/0
C       10.1.6.0/30 is directly connected, Serial0/1
L       10.1.6.1/32 is directly connected, Serial0/1
C       10.1.4.0/30 is directly connected, Serial0/0
L       10.1.4.1/32 is directly connected, Serial0/0
```

NOTE For the purposes of understanding whether a design uses VLSM, ignore the /32 "local" routes that a router automatically creates for its own interface IP addresses.

So ends the discussion of VLSM as an end to itself. This chapter is devoted to VLSM, but it took a mere three to four pages to fully describe it. Why the entire VLSM chapter? Well, to work with VLSM, to find problems with it, to add subnets to an existing design, and to design using VLSM from scratch—in other words, to apply VLSM to real networks—takes skill and practice. To do these same tasks on the exam requires skill and practice. The rest of this chapter examines the skills to apply VLSM and provides some practice for these two key areas:

■ Finding VLSM overlaps

■ Adding new VLSM subnets without overlaps

Finding VLSM Overlaps

Regardless of whether a design uses VLSM, the subnets used in any IP internetwork design should not overlap their address ranges. When subnets in different locations overlap their addresses, a router's routing table entries overlap. As a result, hosts in different locations can be assigned the same IP address. Routers clearly cannot route packets correctly in these cases. In short, a design that uses overlapping subnets is considered to be an incorrect design and should not be used.

This section begins with a short discussion about VLSM design, to drive home the ideas behind VLSM overlaps. It then gets into an operational and troubleshooting approach to the topic, by looking at existing designs and trying to find any existing overlaps.

Designing Subnetting Plans with VLSM

When creating a subnetting plan using VLSM, you have to be much more careful in choosing what subnets to use. First, whatever masks you use in a VLSM design, each subnet ID must be a valid subnet ID given the mask that you use for that subnet.

For example, consider a subnet plan for Class B network 172.16.0.0. To create a subnet with a /24 mask, the subnet ID must be a subnet ID that you could choose if you subnetted the whole Class B network with that same mask. Chapter 21, "Subnet Design," discusses how to find those subnets in depth, but with a Class B network and a /24 mask, the possible subnet IDs should be easy to calculate by now: 172.16.0.0 (the zero subnet), then 172.16.1.0, 172.16.2.0, 172.16.3.0, 172.16.4.0, and so on, up through 172.16.255.0.

> **NOTE**   Subnet IDs must always follow this important binary rule as noted back in Chapter 16, "Analyzing Existing Subnets": In binary, each subnet ID has a host field of all binary 0s. If you use the math and processes to find all subnet IDs per Chapter 21, all those subnet IDs happen to have binary 0s in the host fields.

Now expand your thinking about subnet IDs to a VLSM design. To begin, you would decide that you need some subnets with one mask, other subnets with another mask, and so on, to meet the requirements for different sizes of different subnets. For instance, imagine you start with a brand-new VLSM design, with Class B network 172.16.0.0. You plan to have some subnets with /22 masks, some with /23, and some with /24. You might develop then a planning diagram, or at least draw the ideas, with something like Figure 22-2.

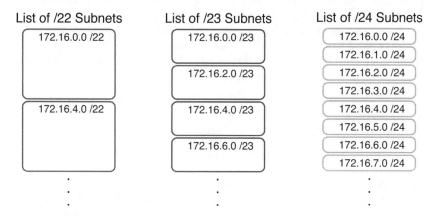

Figure 22-2   *Possible Subnet IDs of Network 172.16.0.0, with /22, /23, and /24 Masks*

The drawing shows the first few subnet IDs available with each mask, but you cannot use all subnets from all three lists in a design. As soon as you choose to use one subnet from any column, you remove some subnets from the other lists because subnets cannot overlap. Overlapping subnets are subnets whose range of addresses include some of the same addresses.

As an example, Figure 22-3 shows the same list of the first few possible /22, /23, and /24 subnets of Class B network 172.16.0.0. However, it shows a check mark beside two subnets that have been allocated for use; that is, on paper, the person making the subnetting plan has decided to use these two subnets somewhere in the network. The subnets with a dark gray shading and an X in them can no longer be used because they have some overlapping addresses with the subnets that have check marks (172.16.3.0/24 and 172.16.4.0/22).

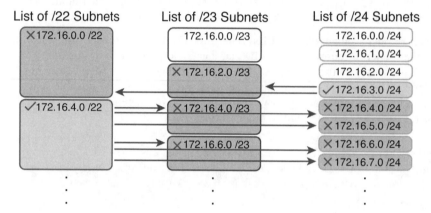

Figure 22-3 *Selecting Two Subnets Disallows Other Subnets in Different Columns*

Just to complete the example, first look at subnet 172.16.4.0 on the lower left. That subnet includes addresses from the subnet ID of 172.16.4.0 through the subnet broadcast address of 172.16.7.255. As you can see just by looking at the subnet IDs to the right, all the subnets referenced with the arrowed lines are within that same range of addresses.

Now look to the upper right of the figure, to subnet 172.16.3.0/24. The subnet has a range of 172.16.3.0–172.16.3.255 including the subnet ID and subnet broadcast address. That subnet overlaps with the two subnets referenced to the left. For instance, subnet 172.16.0.0/22 includes the range from 172.16.0.0–172.16.3.255. But because there is some overlap, once the design has allocated the 172.16.3.0/24 subnet, the 172.16.2.0/23 and 172.16.0.0/22 subnets could not be used without causing problems, because:

A subnetting design, whether using VLSM or not, should not allow subnets whose address ranges overlap. If overlapping subnets are implemented, routing problems occur and some hosts simply cannot communicate outside their subnets.

These address overlaps are easier to see when not using VLSM. When not using VLSM, overlapped subnets have identical subnet IDs, so to find overlaps, you just have to look at the subnet IDs. With VLSM, overlapped subnets may not have the same subnet ID, as was the case in this most recent example with the subnets across the top of Figure 22-3. To find these overlaps, you have to look at the entire range of addresses in each subnet, from subnet ID to subnet broadcast address, and compare the range to the other subnets in the design.

An Example of Finding a VLSM Overlap

For example, imagine that a practice question for the CCENT exam shows Figure 22-4. It uses a single Class B network (172.16.0.0), with VLSM, because it uses three different masks: /23, /24, and /30.

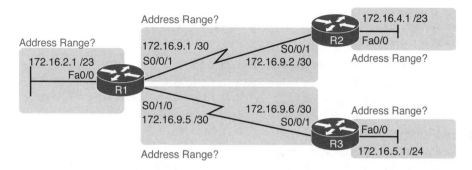

Figure 22-4 *VLSM Design with Possible Overlap*

Now imagine that the exam question shows you the figure, and either directly or indirectly asks whether overlapping subnets exist. This type of question might simply tell you that some hosts cannot ping each other, or it might not even mention that the root cause could be that some of the subnets overlap. To answer such a question, you could follow this simple but possibly laborious process:

Step 1. Calculate the subnet ID and subnet broadcast address of each subnet, which gives you the range of addresses in that subnet.

Step 2. List the subnet IDs in numerical order (along with their subnet broadcast addresses).

Step 3. Scan the list from top to bottom, comparing each pair of adjacent entries, to see whether their range of addresses overlaps.

For example, Table 22-3 completes the first two steps based on Figure 22-4, listing the subnet IDs and subnet broadcast addresses, in numerical order based on the subnet IDs.

Table 22-3 Subnet IDs and Broadcast Addresses, in Numerical Order, from Figure 22-4

Subnet	Subnet Number	Broadcast Address
R1 LAN	172.16.2.0	172.16.3.255
R2 LAN	172.16.4.0	172.16.5.255
R3 LAN	172.16.5.0	172.16.5.255
R1-R2 serial	172.16.9.0	172.16.9.3
R1-R3 serial	172.16.9.4	172.16.9.7

The VLSM design is invalid in this case because of the overlap between R2's LAN subnet and R3's LAN subnet. As for the process, Step 3 states the somewhat obvious step of comparing the address ranges to see whether any overlaps occur. Note that, in this case, none of the subnet numbers are identical, but two entries (highlighted) do overlap. The design is invalid because of the overlap, and one of these two subnets would need to be changed.

As far as the three-step process works, note that if two adjacent entries in the list overlap, compare three entries at the next step. The two subnets already marked as overlapped can overlap with the next subnet in the list. For example, the three subnets in the following list overlap in that the first subnet overlaps with the second and third subnets in the list. If you followed the process shown here, you would have first noticed the overlap between the first two subnets in the list, so you would then also need to check the next subnet in the list to find out if it overlapped.

10.1.0.0/16 (subnet ID 10.1.0.0, broadcast 10.1.255.255)

10.1.200.0/24 (subnet ID 10.1.200.0, broadcast 10.1.200.255)

10.1.250.0/24 (subnet ID 10.1.250.0, broadcast 10.1.250.255)

Practice Finding VLSM Overlaps

As typical of anything to with applying IP addressing and subnetting, practice helps. To that end, Table 22-4 lists three practice problems. Just start with the five IP addresses listed in a single column, and then follow the three-step process outlined in the previous section to find any VLSM overlaps. The answers can be found near the end of this chapter, in the section "Answers to Earlier Practice Problems."

Table 22-4 VLSM Overlap Practice Problems

Problem 1	Problem 2	Problem 3
10.1.34.9/22	172.16.126.151/22	192.168.1.253/30
10.1.29.101/23	172.16.122.57/27	192.168.1.113/28
10.1.23.254/22	172.16.122.33/30	192.168.1.245/29
10.1.17.1/21	172.16.122.1/30	192.168.1.125/30
10.1.1.1/20	172.16.128.151/20	192.168.1.122/30

Adding a New Subnet to an Existing VLSM Design

The task described in this section happens frequently in real networks: choosing new subnets to add to an existing design. In real life, you can use IP Address Management (IPAM) tools that help you choose a new subnet so that you do not cause an overlap. However, for both real life and for the CCENT and CCNA Routing and Switching exams, you need to be ready to do the mental process and math of choosing a subnet that does not create an overlapped VLSM subnet condition. In other words, you need to pick a new subnet and not make a mistake!

For example, consider the internetwork shown earlier in Figure 22-2, with classful network 172.16.0.0. An exam question might suggest that a new subnet, with a /23 prefix length, needs to be added to the design. The question might also say, "Pick the numerically lowest subnet number that can be used for the new subnet." In other words, if both 172.16.4.0 and 172.16.6.0 would work, use 172.16.4.0.

So, you really have a couple of tasks: To find all the subnet IDs that could be used, rule out the ones that would cause an overlap, and then check to see whether the question guides you to pick either the numerically lowest (or highest) subnet ID. This list outlines the specific steps:

Step 1. Pick the subnet mask (prefix length) for the new subnet, based on the design requirements (if not already listed as part of the question).

Step 2. Calculate all possible subnet numbers of the classful network using the mask from Step 1, along with the subnet broadcast addresses.

Step 3.   Make a list of existing subnet IDs and matching subnet broadcast addresses.

Step 4.   Compare the existing subnets to the candidate new subnets to rule out overlapping new subnets.

Step 5.   Choose the new subnet ID from the remaining subnets identified at Step 4, paying attention to whether the question asks for the numerically lowest or numerically highest subnet ID.

An Example of Adding a New VLSM Subnet

For example, Figure 22-5 shows an existing internetwork that uses VLSM. (The figure uses the same IP addresses as shown in Figure 22-4, but with R3's LAN IP address changed to fix the VLSM overlap shown in Figure 22-4.) In this case, you need to add a new subnet to support 300 hosts. Imagine that the question tells you to use the smallest subnet (least number of hosts) to meet that requirement. You use some math and logic you learned earlier in your study to choose mask /23, which gives you 9 host bits, for $2^9 - 2 = 510$ hosts in the subnet.

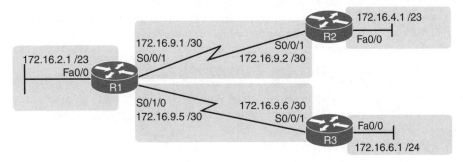

Figure 22-5   *Internetwork to Which You Need to Add a /23 Subnet, Network 172.16.0.0*

At this point, just follow the steps listed before Figure 22-5. For Step 1, you have already been given the mask (/23). For Step 2, you need to list all the subnet numbers and broadcast addresses of 172.16.0.0, assuming the /23 mask. You will not use all these subnets, but you need the list for comparison to the existing subnets. Table 22-5 shows the results, at least for the first five possible /23 subnets.

Table 22-5   First Five Possible /23 Subnets

Subnet	Subnet Number	Subnet Broadcast Address
First (zero)	172.16.0.0	172.16.1.255
Second	172.16.2.0	172.16.3.255
Third	172.16.4.0	172.16.5.255
Fourth	172.16.6.0	172.16.7.255
Fifth	172.16.8.0	172.16.9.255

Next, at Step 3, list the existing subnet numbers and broadcast addresses, as shown earlier in Figure 22-5. To do so, do the usual math to take an IP address/mask to then find the subnet ID and subnet broadcast address. Table 22-6 summarizes that information, including the locations, subnet numbers, and subnet broadcast addresses.

22

Table 22-6   Existing Subnet IDs and Broadcast Addresses from Figure 22-5

Subnet	Subnet Number	Subnet Broadcast Address
R1 LAN	172.16.2.0	172.16.3.255
R2 LAN	172.16.4.0	172.16.5.255
R3 LAN	172.16.6.0	172.16.6.255
R1-R2 serial	172.16.9.0	172.16.9.3
R1-R3 serial	172.16.9.4	172.16.9.7

At this point, you have all the information you need to look for the overlap at Step 4. Simply compare the range of numbers for the subnets in the previous two tables. Which of the possible new /23 subnets (Table 22-5) overlap with the existing subnets (Table 22-6)? In this case, the second through fifth subnets in Table 22-5 overlap, so rule those out as candidates to be used. (Table 22-5 denotes those subnets with gray highlights.)

Step 5 has more to do with the exam than with real network design, but it is still worth listing as a separate step. Multiple-choice questions sometimes need to force you into a single answer, and asking for the numerically lowest or highest subnet does that. This particular example asks for the numerically lowest subnet number, which in this case is 172.16.0.0/23.

NOTE   The answer, 172.16.0.0/23, happens to be a zero subnet. For the exam, the zero subnet should be avoided if (a) the question implies the use of classful routing protocols or (b) the routers are configured with the **no ip subnet-zero** global configuration command. Otherwise, assume that the zero subnet can be used.

Chapter Review

One key to doing well on the exams is to perform repetitive spaced review sessions. Review this chapter's material using either the tools in the book, DVD, or interactive tools for the same material found on the book's companion website. Refer to the "Your Study Plan" element for more details. Table 22-7 outlines the key review elements and where you can find them. To better track your study progress, record when you completed these activities in the second column.

Table 22-7   Chapter Review Tracking

Review Element	Review Date(s)	Resource Used
Review key topics		Book, DVD/website
Review key terms		Book, DVD/website
Repeat DIKTA questions		Book, PCPT
Review memory tables		Book, DVD/website
Practice finding VLSM overlaps		DVD Appendix H, DVD/website
Practice adding new VLSM subnets		DVD Appendix H, DVD/website

Review All the Key Topics

Table 22-8 Key Topics for Chapter 22

Key Topic Element	Description	Page Number
Table 22-2	Classless and classful routing protocols listed and compared	531
Text	Rule about subnetting designs cannot allow subnets to overlap	532
List	Steps to analyze an existing design to discover any VLSM overlaps	535
List	Steps to follow when adding a new subnet to an existing VLSM design	536

Key Terms You Should Know

classful routing protocol, classless routing protocol, overlapping subnets, variable-length subnet masks (VLSM)

Additional Practice for This Chapter's Processes

For additional practice with finding VLSM overlaps and adding a new subnet to a VLSM design, you may do the same set of practice problems using your choice of tools:

Application: Use the Variable-Length Subnet Masks application on the DVD or companion website.

PDF: Alternatively, practice the same problems found in both these apps using DVD Appendix H, "Practice for Chapter 22: Variable-Length Subnet Masks."

Answers to Earlier Practice Problems

22

Answers to Practice Finding VLSM Overlaps

This section lists the answers to the three practice problems in the section "Practice Finding VLSM Overlaps," as listed earlier in Table 22-4. Note that the tables that list details of the answer reordered the subnets as part of the process.

In Problem 1, the second and third subnet IDs listed in Table 22-9 happen to overlap. The second subnet's range completely includes the range of addresses in the third subnet.

Table 22-9 VLSM Overlap Problem 1 Answers (Overlaps Highlighted)

Reference	Original Address and Mask	Subnet ID	Broadcast Address
1	10.1.1.1/20	10.1.0.0	10.1.15.255
2	10.1.17.1/21	10.1.16.0	10.1.23.255
3	10.1.23.254/22	10.1.20.0	10.1.23.255
4	10.1.29.101/23	10.1.28.0	10.1.29.255
5	10.1.34.9/22	10.1.32.0	10.1.35.255

In Problem 2, again the second and third subnet IDs (listed in Table 22-10) happen to overlap, and again, the second subnet's range completely includes the range of addresses in the third subnet. Also, the second and third subnet IDs are the same value, so the overlap is more obvious.

Table 22-10   VLSM Overlap Problem 2 Answers (Overlaps Highlighted)

Reference	Original Address and Mask	Subnet ID	Broadcast Address
1	172.16.122.1/30	172.16.122.0	172.16.122.3
2	172.16.122.57/27	172.16.122.32	172.16.122.63
3	172.16.122.33/30	172.16.122.32	172.16.122.35
4	172.16.126.151/22	172.16.124.0	172.16.127.255
5	172.16.128.151/20	172.16.128.0	172.16.143.255

In Problem 3, three subnets overlap. Subnet 1's range completely includes the range of addresses in the second and third subnets, as shown in Table 22-11. Note that the second and third subnets do not overlap with each other, so for the process in this book to find all the overlaps, after you find that the first two subnets overlap, you should compare the next entry in the table (3) with both of the two known-to-overlap entries (1 and 2).

Table 22-11   VLSM Overlap Problem 3 Answers (Overlaps Highlighted)

Reference	Original Address and Mask	Subnet ID	Broadcast Address
1	192.168.1.113/28	192.168.1.112	192.168.1.127
2	192.168.1.122/30	192.168.1.120	192.168.1.123
3	192.168.1.125/30	192.168.1.124	192.168.1.127
4	192.168.1.245/29	192.168.1.240	192.168.1.247
5	192.168.1.253/30	192.168.1.252	192.168.1.255

CHAPTER 23

IPv4 Troubleshooting Tools

This chapter covers the following exam topics:

1.0 Network Fundamentals

1.8 Configure, verify, and troubleshoot IPv4 addressing and subnetting

4.0 Infrastructure Services

4.1 Describe DNS lookup operation

4.2 Troubleshoot client connectivity issues involving DNS

5.0 Infrastructure Management

5.6 Use Cisco IOS tools to troubleshoot and resolve problems

   5.6.a Ping and traceroute with extended option

The first two chapters here in Part VI of the book made us think more about the entire enterprise IPv4 network. Chapter 21, "Subnet Design," examined all the subnets in a subnetting plan, so you could look at an enterprise network and know which subnets could be used, beyond what subnets were already in use. Chapter 22, "Variable-Length Subnet Masks," took that a step further, looking at the entire enterprise IPv4 network when using variable-length subnet masks (VLSM), thinking about what subnets do exist and which ones could exist within the rules of VLSM.

This chapter and the next keep that approach toward the entire enterprise network. However, the topic moves from subnetting design to troubleshooting. How do you troubleshoot an IPv4 network? How do you verify correct operation, identify root causes, and fix those for various IP routing features? How do you do that in the presence of an IP addressing and subnetting plan, requiring you to apply all that subnetting math from Part IV of this book and from the last few chapters? This chapter and the next start to answer some of those questions.

In particular, this chapter focuses on IP troubleshooting tools, with two in particular: ping and traceroute. Both tools test the IPv4 data plane; that is, the ability of each networking device to route or forward IPv4 packets. A problem with routing is often a symptom but not a root cause, with the root cause then being other problems, like interface failures, routing protocol issues, misconfiguration of various features, and the like.

The chapter ends with a short discussion of two other router tools that can also be useful for troubleshooting: Telnet and Secure Shell (SSH).

"Do I Know This Already?" Quiz

The troubleshooting chapters of this book pull in concepts from many other chapters. In fact, troubleshooting IPv4 may be one of the most important topics to learn for both the CCENT and CCNA R&S certifications. So, it is useful to read this chapter (and the next chapter, also about troubleshooting IPv4 networks) regardless of your current knowledge level. For these reasons, some troubleshooting chapters do not include a "Do I Know This Already?" quiz.

Foundation Topics

Problem Isolation Using the ping Command

Someone sends you an email or text, or a phone message, asking you to look into a user's network problem. You Secure Shell (SSH) to a router and issue a **ping** command that works. What does that result rule out as a possible reason for the problem? What does it rule in as still being a possible root cause?

Then you issue another **ping** to another address, and this time the ping fails. Again, what does the failure of that **ping** command tell you? What parts of IPv4 routing may still be a problem, and what parts do you now know are not a problem?

The **ping** command gives us one of the most common network troubleshooting tools. When the **ping** command succeeds, it confirms many individual parts of how IP routing works, ruling out some possible causes of the current problem. When a **ping** command fails, it often helps narrow down where in the internetwork the root cause of the problem may be happening, further isolating the problem.

This section begins with a brief explanation of how ping works. It then moves on to some suggestions and analysis of how to use the **ping** command to isolate problems by removing some items from consideration.

Ping Command Basics

The **ping** command tests connectivity by sending packets to an IP address, expecting the device at that address to send packets back. The command sends packets that mean "if you receive this packet, and it is addressed to you, send a reply back." Each time the **ping** command sends one of these packets and receives back the message sent back by the other host, the **ping** command knows a packet made it from the source host to the destination and back.

More formally, the **ping** command uses the Internet Control Message Protocol (ICMP), specifically the ICMP echo request and ICMP echo reply messages. ICMP defines many other messages as well, but these two messages were made specifically for connectivity testing by commands like ping. As a protocol, ICMP does not rely on TCP or UDP, and it does not use any application layer protocol. It exists as a protocol used to assist IP by helping manage the IP network functions.

Figure 23-1 shows the ICMP messages, with IP headers, in an example. In this case, the user at host A opens a command prompt and issues the **ping 172.16.2.101** command, testing connectivity to host B. The command sends one echo request, and waits (Step 1); host B receives the messages, and sends back an echo reply (Step 2).

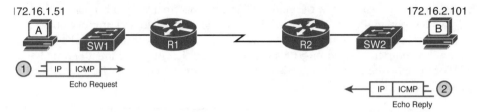

Figure 23-1   *Concept Behind ping 172.16.2.101 on Host A*

The **ping** command is supported on many different devices and many common operating systems. The command has many options: the name or IP address of the destination, how many times the command should send an echo request, how long the command should wait (timeout) for an echo reply, how big to make the packets, and many other options. Example 23-1 shows a sample from host A, with the same command that matches the concept in Figure 23-1: a **ping 172.16.2.101** command on host A.

Example 23-1   *Sample Output from Host A's **ping 172.16.2.101** Command*

```
Wendell-Odoms-iMac:~ wendellodom$ ping 172.16.2.101
PING 172.16.2.101 (172.16.2.101): 56 data bytes
64 bytes from 172.16.2.101: icmp_seq=0 ttl=64 time=1.112 ms
64 bytes from 172.16.2.101: icmp_seq=1 ttl=64 time=0.673 ms
64 bytes from 172.16.2.101: icmp_seq=2 ttl=64 time=0.631 ms
64 bytes from 172.16.2.101: icmp_seq=3 ttl=64 time=0.674 ms
64 bytes from 172.16.2.101: icmp_seq=4 ttl=64 time=0.642 ms
64 bytes from 172.16.2.101: icmp_seq=5 ttl=64 time=0.656 ms
^C
--- 172.16.2.101 ping statistics ---
6 packets transmitted, 6 packets received, 0.0% packet loss
round-trip min/avg/max/stddev = 0.631/0.731/1.112/0.171 ms
```

Strategies and Results When Testing with the ping Command

Often, the person handling initial calls from users about problems (often called a customer support rep, or CSR) cannot issue **ping** commands from the user's device. In some cases, talking users through typing the right commands and making the right clicks on their machines can be a problem. Or, the user just might not be available. As an alternative, using different **ping** commands from different routers can help isolate the problem.

The problem with using **ping** commands from routers, instead of from the host that has the problem, is that no single router **ping** command can exactly replicate a **ping** command done from the user's device. However, each different **ping** command can help isolate a problem further. The rest of this section of **ping** commands discusses troubleshooting IPv4 routing by using various **ping** commands from the command-line interface (CLI) of a router.

Testing Longer Routes from Near the Source of the Problem

Most problems begin with some idea like "host X cannot communicate with host Y." A great first troubleshooting step is to issue a **ping** command from X for host Y's IP address. However, assuming the engineer does not have access to host X, the next best test is to ping host X's IP address from the router nearest the host that has the problem.

For instance, in Figure 23-1, imagine that the user of host A had called IT support with a problem related to sending packets to host B. A **ping 172.16.2.101** command on host A would be a great first troubleshooting step, but the CSR cannot access host A or get in touch with the user of host A. So, the CSR telnets to Router R1, and pings host B from there, as shown in Example 23-2.

Example 23-2   *Router R2 Pings Host B (Two Commands)*

```
R1# ping 172.16.2.101
Type escape sequence to abort.
Sending 5, 100-byte ICMP Echos to 172.16.2.101, timeout is 2 seconds:
.!!!!
Success rate is 80 percent (4/5), round-trip min/avg/max = 1/2/4 ms
R1# ping 172.16.2.101
Type escape sequence to abort.
Sending 5, 100-byte ICMP Echos to 172.16.2.101, timeout is 2 seconds:
!!!!!
Success rate is 100 percent (5/5), round-trip min/avg/max = 1/2/4 ms
```

First, take a moment to review the output of the first IOS **ping** command. By default, the Cisco IOS **ping** command sends five echo messages, with a timeout of 2 seconds. If the command does not receive an echo reply within 2 seconds, the command considers that message to be a failure, and the command lists a period. If a successful reply is received within 2 seconds, the command displays an exclamation point. So, in this first command, the first echo reply timed out, whereas the other four received a matching echo reply within 2 seconds.

As a quick aside, the example shows a common and normal behavior with **ping** commands: the first **ping** command shows one failure to start, but then the rest of the messages work. This usually happens because some device in the end-to-end route is missing an ARP table entry.

Now think about troubleshooting and what a working **ping** command tells us about the current behavior of this internetwork. First, focus on the big picture for a moment:

- R1 can send ICMP echo request messages to host B (172.16.2.101).
- R1 sends these messages from its outgoing interface's IP address (by default), 172.16.4.1 in this case.
- Host B can send ICMP echo reply messages to R1's 172.16.4.1 IP address (hosts send echo reply messages to the IP address from which the echo request was received).

23

Figure 23-2 shows the packet flow.

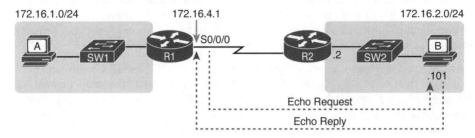

Figure 23-2 *Standard ping 172.6.2.101 Command Using the Source Interface IP Address*

Next, think about IPv4 routing. In the forward direction, R1 must have a route that matches host B's address (172.16.2.101); this route will be either a static route or one learned with a routing protocol. R2 also needs a route for host B's address, in this case a connected route to B's subnet (172.16.2.0/24), as shown in the top arrow lines in Figure 23-3.

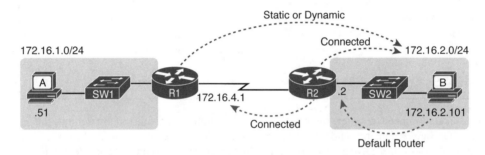

Figure 23-3 *Layer 3 Routes Needed for R1's Ping 172.16.2.101 to Work*

The arrow lines on the bottom of Figure 23-3 show the routes needed to forward the ICMP echo reply message back to Router R1's 172.16.4.1 interface. First, host B must have a valid default router setting because 172.16.4.1 sits in a different subnet than host B. R2 must also have a route that matches destination 172.16.4.1 (in this case, likely to be a connected route).

The working **ping** commands in Example 23-2 also require the data link and physical layer details to be working. The serial link must be working: The router interfaces must be up/up, which typically indicates that the link can pass data. On the LAN, R2's LAN interface must be in an up/up state. In addition, everything discussed about Ethernet LANs must be working because the **ping** confirmed that the packets went all the way from R1 to host B and back. In particular

■ The switch interfaces in use are in a connected (up/up) state.

■ Port security does not filter frames sent by R2 or host B.

■ STP has placed the right ports into a forwarding state.

NOTE The ICND2 book discusses STP in depth, but the need to consider STP port state is mentioned here for completeness for those planning to achieve CCNA R&S certification.

The **ping 172.16.2.101** command in Example 23-2 also confirms that IP access control lists (ACL) did not filter the ICMP messages. As a reminder, an ACL on a router does not filter packets created on that same router, so R1 would not have filtered its own ICMP echo request message. The rest of the ICMP messages could have been filtered entering or exiting the router interfaces. Figure 23-4 shows the locations where an IP ACL could have filtered the messages generated as a result of R1's **ping 172.16.2.101** command.

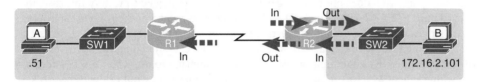

Figure 23-4 *Locations Where IP ACLs Could Have Filtered the Ping Messages*

Finally, the working **ping 172.16.2.101** command on R1 can also be used to reasonably predict that ARP worked on R2 and host B and that switch SW2 learned MAC addresses for its MAC address table. R2 and host B need to know each other's MAC addresses so that they can encapsulate the IP packet inside an Ethernet frame, which means both must have a matching ARP table entry. The switch learns the MAC address used by R2 and by host B when it sends the ARP messages or when it sends the frames that hold the IP packets. Figure 23-5 shows the type of information expected in those tables.

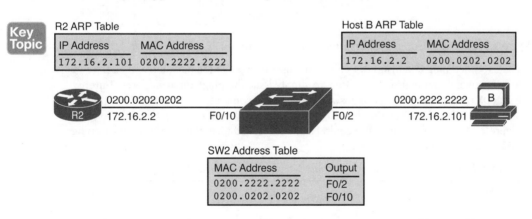

Figure 23-5 *Router and Host ARP Tables, with the Switch MAC Address Table*

As you can see from the last few pages, a strategy of using a **ping** command from near the source of the problem can rule out a lot of possible root causes of any problems between two hosts—assuming the **ping** command succeeds. However, this **ping** command does not act exactly like the same **ping** command on the actual host. To overcome some of what is missing in the **ping** command from a nearby router, the next several examples show some strategies for testing other parts of the path between the two hosts that may have a current problem.

Using Extended Ping to Test the Reverse Route

Pinging from the default router, as discussed in the past few pages, misses an opportunity to test IP routes more fully. In particular, it does not test the reverse route back toward the original host.

For instance, referring to the internetwork in Figure 23-2 again, note that the reverse routes do not point to an address in host A's subnet. When R1 processes the **ping 172.16.2.101** command, R1 has to pick a source IP address to use for the echo request, and routers choose the *IP address of the outgoing interface.* The echo request from R1 to host B flows with source IP address 172.16.4.1 (R1's S0/0/0 IP address). The echo reply flows back to that same address (172.16.4.1).

A standard ping often does not test the reverse route that you need to test. In this case, the standard **ping 172.16.2.101** command on R1 does not test whether the routers can route back to subnet 172.16.1.0/24, instead testing their routes for subnet172.16.4.0. A better ping test would test the route back to host A's subnet; an extended ping from R1 can cause that test to happen. Extended ping allows R1's **ping** command to use R1's LAN IP address from within subnet 172.16.1.0/24. Then, the echo reply messages would flow to host A's subnet, as shown in Figure 23-6.

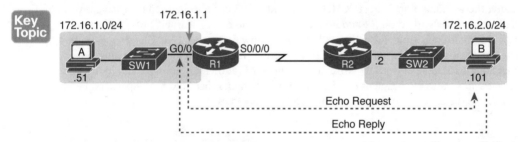

Figure 23-6 *Extended Ping Command Tests the Route to 172.16.1.51 (Host A)*

The extended **ping** command does allow the user to type all the parameters on a potentially long command, but it also allows users to simply issue the **ping** command, press **Enter**, with IOS then asking the user to answer questions to complete the command, as shown in Example 23-3. The example shows the **ping** command on R1 that matches the logic in Figure 23-6. This same command could have been issued from the command line as **ping 172.16.2.101 source 172.16.1.1**.

Example 23-3 *Testing the Reverse Route Using the Extended Ping*

```
R1# ping
Protocol [ip]:
Target IP address: 172.16.2.101
Repeat count [5]:
Datagram size [100]:
Timeout in seconds [2]:
Extended commands [n]: y
Source address or interface: 172.16.1.1
Type of service [0]:
Set DF bit in IP header? [no]:
Validate reply data? [no]:
Data pattern [0xABCD]:
```

```
Loose, Strict, Record, Timestamp, Verbose[none]:
Sweep range of sizes [n]:
Type escape sequence to abort.
Sending 5, 100-byte ICMP Echos to 172.16.2.101, timeout is 2 seconds:
Packet sent with a source address of 172.16.1.1
!!!!!
Success rate is 100 percent (5/5), round-trip min/avg/max = 1/2/4 ms
```

This particular extended **ping** command tests the same routes for the echo request going to the right, but it forces a better test of routes pointing back to the left for the ICMP echo reply. For that direction, R2 needs a route that matches address 172.16.1.1, which is likely to be a route for subnet 172.16.1.0/24—the same subnet in which host A resides.

From a troubleshooting perspective, using both standard and extended **ping** commands can be useful. However, neither can exactly mimic a **ping** command created on the host itself because the routers cannot send packets with the host's IP address. For instance, the extended **ping** in Example 23-3 uses source IP address 172.16.1.1, which is not host A's IP address. As a result, neither the standard or extended **ping** commands in these two examples so far in this chapter can test for some kinds of problems, such as the following:

- ACLs that discard packets based on host A's IP address, while that same ACL permits packets matched on the router's IP address

- LAN switch port security issues that filter A's packets (based on A's MAC address)

- IP routes on routers that happen to match host A's 172.16.1.51 address, with different routes that match R1's 172.16.1.1 address

- Problems with host A's default router setting

> **NOTE**   ACLs are covered in ICND1 Chapter 25, "Basic IPv4 Access Control Lists," and Chapter 26, "Advanced IPv4 Access Control Lists." For now, know that a router can look at packets as they enter or exit an interface, make comparisons to the header fields, and if matched, make a choice to either discard the packet or let it through. ACLs act as a packet filter based on criteria the network engineer configures on the router.

23

Testing LAN Neighbors with Standard Ping

Testing using a **ping** of another device on the LAN can quickly confirm whether the LAN can pass packets and frames. Specifically, a working **ping** rules out many possible root causes of a problem. For instance, Figure 23-7 shows the ICMP messages that occur if R1 issues the command **ping 172.16.1.51**, pinging host A, which sits on the same VLAN as R1.

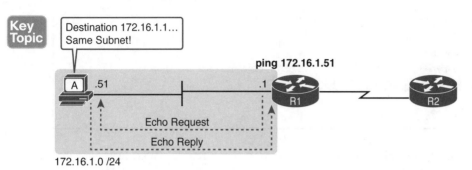

Figure 23-7 *Standard* ping *Command Confirms That the LAN Works*

If the ping works, it confirms the following, which rules out some potential issues:

- The host with address 172.16.1.51 replied.

- The LAN can pass unicast frames from R1 to host 172.16.1.51 and vice versa.

- You can reasonably assume that the switches learned the MAC addresses of the router and the host, adding those to the MAC address tables.

- Host A and Router R1 completed the ARP process and list each other in their respective Address Resolution Protocol (ARP) tables.

The failure of a ping, even with two devices on the same subnet, can point to a variety of problems, like those mentioned in this list. For instance, if the **ping 172.16.1.51** on R1 fails (Figure 23-7), that result points to this list of potential root causes:

- **IP addressing problem:** Host A could be statically configured with the wrong IP address.

- **DHCP problems:** If you are using Dynamic Host Configuration Protocol (DHCP), many problems could exist: Host A could be using a different IP address than 172.16.1.51, the DHCP configuration could be wrong, the routers may be missing the DHCP relay configuration and so host A never got its IPv4 address lease, and so on.

- **VLAN trunking problems:** The router could be configured for 802.1Q trunking, when the switch is not (or vice versa).

- **LAN problems:** Any LAN problem discussed in Parts II and III of the ICND1 book, and Part I of the ICND2 book.

So, whether the ping works or fails, simply pinging a LAN host from a router can help further isolate the problem.

Testing LAN Neighbors with Extended Ping

A standard ping of a LAN host from a router does not test that host's default router setting. However, an extended ping can test the host's default router setting. Both tests can be useful, especially for problem isolation, because

- If a standard ping of a local LAN host works…

- But an extended ping of the same LAN host fails…

- The problem likely relates somehow to the host's default router setting.

First, to understand why the standard and extended ping results have different effects, consider first the standard **ping 172.16.1.51** command on R1, as shown previously in Figure 23-7. As a standard **ping** command, R1 used its LAN interface IP address (172.16.1.1) as the source of the ICMP Echo. So, when the host (A) sent back its ICMP echo reply, host A considered the destination of 172.16.1.1 as being on the same subnet. Host A's ICMP echo reply message, sent back to 172.16.1.1, would work even if host A did not have a default router setting at all!

In comparison, Figure 23-8 shows the difference when using an extended ping on Router R1. An extended ping from local Router R1, using R1's S0/0/0 IP address of 172.16.4.1 as the source of the ICMP echo request, means that host A's ICMP echo reply will flow to an address in another subnet, which makes host A use its default router setting.

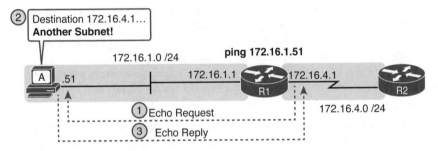

Figure 23-8 *Extended **ping** Command Does Test Host A's Default Router Setting*

The comparison between the previous two figures shows one of the most classic mistakes when troubleshooting networks. Sometimes, the temptation is to connect to a router and ping the host on the attached LAN, and it works. So, the engineer moves on, thinking that the network layer issues between the router and host work fine, when the problem still exists with the host's default router setting.

Testing WAN Neighbors with Standard Ping

As with a standard ping test across a LAN, a standard ping test between routers over a serial WAN link tests whether the link can pass IPv4 packets. With a properly designed IPv4 addressing plan, two routers on the same serial link should have IP addresses in the same subnet. A ping from one router to the serial IP address of the other router confirms that an IP packet can be sent over the link and back, as shown in the **ping 172.16.4.2** command on R1 in Figure 23-9.

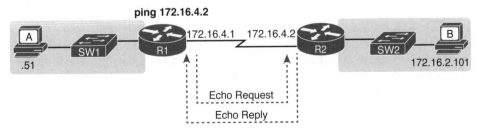

Figure 23-9 *Pinging Across a WAN Link*

A successful ping of the IP address on the other end of a serial link that sits between two routers confirms several specific facts, such as the following:

- Both router's serial interfaces are in an up/up state.
- The Layer 1 and 2 features of the link work.
- The routers believe that the neighboring router's IP address is in the same subnet.
- Inbound ACLs on both routers do not filter the incoming packets, respectively.
- The remote router is configured with the expected IP address (172.16.4.2 in this case).

Note that troubleshooting serial links poses a bit of a sequencing issue in these books, because Cisco places almost all WAN topics into the ICND2 part of the CCNA R&S exam topics, so the WAN details sit in the ICND2 book. In fact, this book includes some WAN topics to support the discussion of other features within ICND1, like ping and traceroute. For now, ICND1 readers who plan to move on to ICND2 and to get their CCNA R&S certification can wait until you get into the WAN topics in the ICND2 book. If you just want to get into the detail now, I put a copy of the ICND2 book's chapter "Implementing Point-to-Point WANs," on the DVD of the ICND1 book, just for you. Feel free to use that DVD chapter (on the DVD as DVD-only Appendix P) if you do not happen to have a copy of the ICND2 book.

Testing by pinging the other neighboring router does not test many other features, though. For instance, pinging the neighboring router's serial IP address only tests one route on each router: the connected route to the subnet on the serial link. This ping does not test any routes for subnets on LANs. Also, neither the source or destination IP address matches the two hosts that have the original problem, so this test does not do much to help find issues with ACLs. However, although the test is limited in scope, it does let you rule out WAN links as having a Layer 1 or 2 problem, and it rules out some basic Layer 3 addressing problems.

Using Ping with Names and with IP Addresses

All the ping examples so far in this chapter show a ping of an IP address. However, the **ping** command can use hostnames, and pinging a hostname allows the network engineer to further test whether the Domain Name System (DNS) process works.

First, most every TCP/IP application today uses hostnames rather than IP addresses to identify the other device. No one opens a web browser and types in http://72.163.4.161/. Instead, they type in a web address, like www.cisco.com, which includes the hostname www.cisco.com. Then, before a host can send data to a specific IP address, the host must first ask a DNS server to resolve that hostname into the matching IP address.

For example, in the small internetwork used for several examples in this chapter, a **ping B** command on host A tests A's DNS settings, as shown in Figure 23-10. When host A sees the use of a hostname (B), it first looks in its local DNS name cache to find out whether it has already resolved the name B. If not, host A first asks the DNS to supply (resolve) the name into its matching IP address (Step 1 in the figure). Only then does host A send a packet to 172.16.2.101, host B's IP address (Step 2).

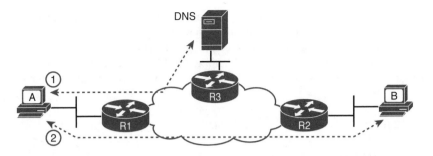

Figure 23-10 *DNS Name Resolution by Host A*

When troubleshooting, testing from the host by pinging using a hostname can be very help-ful. The command, of course, tests the host's own DNS client settings. For instance, a classic comparison is to first ping the destination host using the hostname, which requires a DNS request. Then, repeat the same test, but use the destination host's IP address instead of its name, which does not require the DNS request. If the ping of the hostname fails but the ping of the IP address works, the problem usually has something to do with DNS.

Problem Isolation Using the traceroute Command

Like **ping**, the **traceroute** command helps network engineers isolate problems. Here is a comparison of the two:

- Both send messages in the network to test connectivity.
- Both rely on other devices to send back a reply.
- Both have wide support on many different operating systems.
- Both can use a hostname or an IP address to identify the destination.
- On routers, both have a standard and extended version, allowing better testing of the reverse route.

The biggest differences relate to the more detailed results in the output of the **traceroute** command and the extra time and effort it takes **traceroute** to build that output. This third of three major sections examines how traceroute works, plus some suggestions of how to use this more detailed information to more quickly isolate IP routing problems.

traceroute Basics

Imagine some network engineer or CSR starts to troubleshoot some problem. They **ping** from the user's host, **ping** from a nearby router, and after a few commands, convince them-selves that the host can indeed send and receive IP packets. The problem might not be solved yet, but the problem does not appear to be a network problem.

Now imagine the next problem comes along, and this time the **ping** command fails. It appears that some problem does exist in the IP network. Where is the problem? Where should the engineer look more closely? Although **ping** can prove helpful in isolating the source of the problem, the **traceroute** command may be a better option. The **traceroute** command systematically helps pinpoint routing problems by showing how far a packet goes through an IP network before being discarded.

23

The **traceroute** command identifies the routers in the path from source host to destination host. Specifically, it lists the next-hop IP address of each router that would be in each of the individual routes. For instance, a **traceroute 172.16.2.101** command on host A in Figure 23-11 would identify an IP address on Router R1, another on Router R2, and then host B, as shown in the figure. Example 23-4 that follows lists the output of the command, taken from host A.

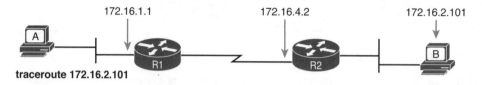

Figure 23-11   *IP Addresses Identified by a Successful* **traceroute 172.16.2.101** *Command*

Example 23-4   *Output from* **traceroute 172.16.2.101** *on Host A*

```
Wendell-Odoms-iMac:~ wendellodom$ traceroute 172.16.2.101
traceroute to 172.16.2.101, 64 hops max, 52 byte packets
 1  172.16.1.1 (172.16.1.1)  0.870 ms  0.520 ms  0.496 ms
 2  172.16.4.2 (172.16.4.2) 8.263 ms  7.518 ms  9.319 ms
 3  172.16.2.101 (172.16.2.101) 16.770 ms  9.819 ms  9.830 ms
```

How the traceroute Command Works

The **traceroute** command gathers information by generating packets that trigger error messages from routers; these messages identify the routers, letting the **traceroute** command list the routers' IP addresses in the output of the command. That error message is the ICMP Time-to-Live Exceeded (TTL Exceeded) message, originally meant to notify hosts when a packet had been looping around a network.

Ignoring traceroute for a moment, and focusing on IP routing, IPv4 routers defeat routing loops in part by discarding looping IP packets. To do so, the IPv4 header holds a field called Time To Live (TTL). The original host that creates the packet sets an initial TTL value. Then, each router that forwards the packet decrements the TTL value by 1. When a router decrements the TTL to 0, the router perceives the packet is looping, and the router discards the packet. The router also notifies the host that sent the discarded packet by sending an ICMP TTL Exceeded message.

Now back to traceroute. Traceroute sends messages with low TTL values to make the routers send back a TTL Exceeded message. Specifically, a **traceroute** command begins by sending several packets (usually three), each with the header TTL field equal to 1. When that packet arrives at the next router—host A's default Router R1 in the example of Figure 23-12—the router decrements TTL to 0 and discards the packet. The router then sends host A the TTL Exceeded message, which identifies the router's IP address to the **traceroute** command.

Standard and Extended traceroute

The standard and extended options for the **traceroute** command give you many of the same options as the **ping** command. For instance, Example 23-5 lists the output of a standard **traceroute** command on Router R1. Like the standard **ping** command, a standard **traceroute** command chooses an IP address based on the outgoing interface for the packet sent by the command. So, in this example, the packets sent by R1 come from source IP address 172.16.4.1, R1's S0/0/0 IP address.

Example 23-5 *Standard* **traceroute** *Command on R1*

```
R1# traceroute 172.16.2.101
Type escape sequence to abort.
Tracing the route to 172.16.2.101
VRF info: (vrf in name/id, vrf out name/id)
  1 172.16.4.2 0 msec 0 msec 0 msec
  2 172.16.2.101 0 msec 0 msec *
```

The extended **traceroute** command, as shown in Example 23-6, follows the same basic command structure as the extended **ping** command. The user can type all the parameters on one command line, but it is much easier to just type **traceroute**, press **Enter**, and let IOS prompt for all the parameters, including the source IP address of the packets (172.16.1.1 in this example).

Example 23-6 *Extended* **traceroute** *Command on R1*

```
R1# traceroute
Protocol [ip]:
Target IP address: 172.16.2.101
Source address: 172.16.1.1
Numeric display [n]:
Timeout in seconds [3]:
Probe count [3]:
Minimum Time to Live [1]:
Maximum Time to Live [30]:
Port Number [33434]:
Loose, Strict, Record, Timestamp, Verbose[none]:
Type escape sequence to abort.
Tracing the route to 172.16.2.101
VRF info: (vrf in name/id, vrf out name/id)
  1 172.16.4.2 0 msec 0 msec 0 msec
  2 172.16.2.101 0 msec 0 msec *
```

Both the **ping** and **traceroute** commands exist on most operating systems, including Cisco IOS. However, some operating systems use a slightly different syntax for **traceroute**. For example, most Windows operating systems support **tracert** and **pathping**, and not **traceroute**. Linux and OS X support the **traceroute** command.

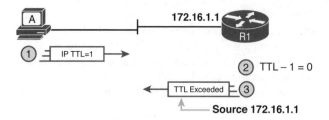

Figure 23-12   *How* **traceroute** *Identifies the First Router in the Route*

The **traceroute** command sends several TTL=1 packets, checking them to see whether the TTL Exceeded messages flow from the same router, based on the source IP address of the TTL Exceeded message. Assuming the messages come from the same router, the **traceroute** command lists that IP address as the next line of output on the command.

To find all the routers in the path, and finally confirm that packets flow all the way to the destination host, the **traceroute** command sends a packet with TTL=1, TTL=2, then 3, 4, and so on, until the destination host replies. Figure 23-13 shows the packet from the second set with a TTL=2. In this case, one router (R1) actually forwards the packet, while another router (R2) happens to decrement the TTL to 0, causing a TTL Exceeded message being sent back to host A.

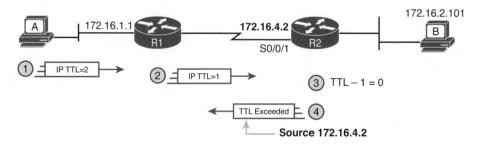

Figure 23-13   *TTL=2 Message Sent by* **traceroute**

The figure shows these four steps:

1. The **traceroute** command sends a packet from the second set with TTL=2.
2. Router R1 processes the packet and decrements TTL to 1. R1 forwards the packet.
3. Router R2 processes the packet and decrements TTL to 0. R2 discards the packet.
4. R2 notifies the sending host of the discarded packet by sending a TTL Exceeded ICMP message. The source IP address of that message is 172.16.4.2.

Finally, the choice of source IP address to use on the time-exceeded message returned by routers has a big impact on the output of the **traceroute** command. Most routers use simpler logic that also makes command output like **traceroute** more consistent and meaningful. That logic: choose the TTL Exceeded message's source IP address based on the source interface of the original message that was discarded due to TTL. In the example in Figure 23-13, the original message at Step 2 arrived on R2's S0/0/1 interface, so at Step 3, R2 uses S0/0/1's IP address as the source IP address of the TTL exceeded message, and as the interface out which to send the message.

> **NOTE**   Host OS **traceroute** commands usually create ICMP echo requests. The Cisco IOS **traceroute** command instead creates IP packets with a UDP header. This bit of information may seem trivial at this point. However, note that an ACL may actually filter the traffic from a host's **traceroute** messages but not the router **traceroute** command, or vice versa.

Using traceroute to Isolate the Problem to Two Routers

One of the best features of the **traceroute** command, as compared to ping, is that when it does not complete it gives an immediate clue as to where to look next. With ping, when the ping fails, the next step is usually to use more **ping** commands. With traceroute, it tells you what router to try to connect and look at the routes and in which direction.

> **NOTE**   As a reminder, this book uses the term *forward route* for routes that send the packets sent by the **ping** or **traceroute** command, and *reverse route* for the packets sent back.

When a problem exists, a **traceroute** command results in a partial list of routers. Then the command either finishes with an incomplete list or it runs until the user must stop the command. In either case, the output does not list all routers in the end-to-end route, because of the underlying problem.

> **NOTE**   In addition, the **traceroute** command may not finish even though the network has no problems. Routers and firewalls may filter the messages sent by the **traceroute** command, or the TTL Exceeded messages, which would prevent the display of portions or all or part of the path.

The last router listed in the output of a **traceroute** command's output tells us where to look next to isolate the problem, as follows:

- Connect to the CLI of the last router listed, to look at forward route issues.
- Connect to the CLI of the next router that should have been listed, to look for reverse route issues.

To see why, consider an example based on the internetwork in Figure 23-14. In this case, R1 uses an extended traceroute to host 5.5.5.5, with source IP address 1.1.1.1. This command's output lists router 2.2.2.2, then 3.3.3.3, and then the command cannot complete.

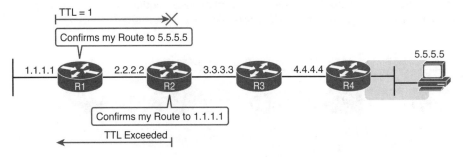

Figure 23-14   *Messages That Cause the* **traceroute** *Command to List 2.2.2.2*

First, Figure 23-14 focuses on the first line of output: the line that lists first-hop router 2.2.2.2.

The figure shows the TTL=1 message at the top and the TTL Exceeded message back on the bottom. This first pair of messages in the figure must have worked, because without them, the **traceroute** command on R1 cannot have learned about a router with address 2.2.2.2. The first (top) message required R1 to have a route for 5.5.5.5, which sent the packets to R2 next. The TTL Exceeded message required that R2 have a route that matched address 1.1.1.1, to send the packets back to R1's LAN IP address.

Next, Figure 23-15 focuses on the messages that allow the second line of output on R1's sample **traceroute** command: the line that correctly lists 3.3.3.3 as the next router in the route.

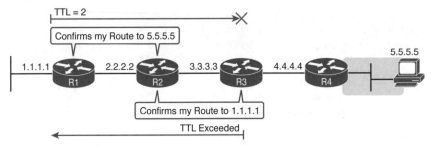

Figure 23-15 *Messages That Cause the* **traceroute** *Command to List 3.3.3.3*

Following the same logic, the traceroute output lists 3.3.3.3 because the messages in Figure 23-15 must have worked. For these messages to flow, the routes listed in Figure 23-14 must exist, plus new routes listed in Figure 23-15. Specifically, the TTL=2 packet at the top requires R2 to have a route for 5.5.5.5, which sends the packets to R3 next. The TTL Exceeded message requires that R3 have a route that matches address 1.1.1.1, to send the packets back toward R1's LAN IP address.

In this example, the **traceroute 5.5.5.5** command does not list any routers beyond 2.2.2.2 and 3.3.3.3 However, based on the figures, it is clear that 4.4.4.4 should be the next IP address listed. To help isolate the problem further, why might the next messages—the message with TTL=3 and the response—fail?

Figure 23-16 points out the routing issues that can cause this command to not be able to list 4.4.4.4 as the next router. First, R3 must have a forward route matching destination 5.5.5.5 and forwarding the packet to Router R4. The return message requires a reverse route matching destination 1.1.1.1 and forwarding the packet back to Router R3.

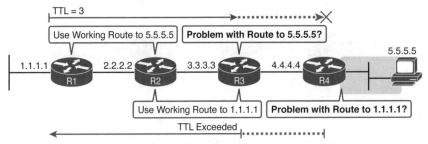

Figure 23-16 *Issues That Could Prevent* **traceroute** *from Listing 4.4.4.4*

In conclusion, for this example, if a routing problem prevents the **traceroute** command from working, the problem exists in one of two places: the forward route to 5.5.5.5 on Router R3, or the reverse route to 1.1.1.1 on R4.

Telnet and SSH

The **ping** and **traceroute** commands do give networkers two great tools to begin isolating the cause of an IP routing problem. However, these two commands tell us nothing about the operation state inside the various network devices. Once you begin to get an idea of the kinds of problems and the possible locations of the problems using **ping** and **traceroute**, the next step is to look at the status of various router and switch features. One way to do that is to use Telnet or Secure Shell (SSH) to log in to the devices.

Common Reasons to Use the IOS Telnet and SSH Client

Normally, a network engineer would log in to the remote device using a Telnet or SSH client on their PC, tablet, or any other user device. In fact, often times, the same software package does both Telnet and SSH. However, in some cases, you may want to take advantage of the Telnet and SSH client built in to IOS on the routers and switches, to Telnet/SSH from one Cisco device to the next.

To understand why, consider the example shown in Figure 23-17. The figure shows arrowed lines to three separate IP addresses on three separate Cisco routers. PC1 has attempted to Telnet to each address from a different tab in PC1's Telnet/SSH client. However, R2 happens to have an error in its routing protocol configuration, so R1, R2, and R3 fail to learn any routes from each other. As a result, PC1's Telnet attempt to both 10.1.2.2 (R2) and 10.1.3.2 (R3) fails.

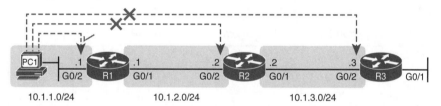

Figure 23-17   *Telnet Works from PC1 to R1 but Not to R2 or R3*

In some cases, like this one, a Telnet or SSH login from the network engineer's device can fail, while you could still find a way to log in using the **telnet** and **ssh** commands to use the Telnet and SSH clients on the routers or switches. With this particular scenario, all the individual data links work; the problem is with the routing protocol exchanging routes. PC1 can ping R1's 10.1.1.1 IP address, R1 can ping R2's 10.1.2.2 address, and R2 can ping R3's 10.1.3.3 address. Because each link works, and each router can send and receive packets with its neighbor on the shared data link, you could Telnet/SSH to each successive device.

Figure 23-18 shows the idea. On the left, PC1 begins with either a Telnet/SSH or a console connection into Router R1, as shown on the left. Then the user issues the **telnet 10.1.2.2** command from R1 to Telnet to R2. Once logged into R2, the user can issue commands on R2. Then from R2, the user could issue the **telnet 10.1.3.3** command to Telnet to R3, from which the user could issue commands on R3.

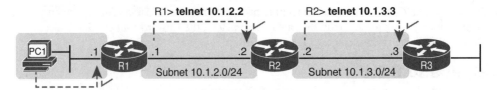

Figure 23-18 *Successive Telnet Connections: PC1 to R1, R1 to R2, and R2 to R3*

The Telnet connections shown in Figure 23-18 work because each Telnet in this case uses source and destination addresses in the same subnet. For example, R1's **telnet 10.1.2.2** command uses 10.1.2.2 as the destination of course. R1 uses the outgoing interface IP address used to send packets to 10.1.2.2, 10.1.2.1 in this case. Because each of these **telnet** commands connects to an IP address in a connected subnet, the routing protocol could be completely misconfigured, and you could still Telnet/SSH to each successive device to troubleshoot and fix the problem.

Network engineers also use the IOS Telnet and SSH client just for preference. For instance, if you need to log in to several Cisco devices, you could open several windows and tabs on your PC, and log in from your PC (assuming the network was not having problems). Or, you could log in from your PC to some nearby Cisco router or switch, and from there Telnet or SSH to other Cisco devices.

IOS Telnet and SSH Examples

Using the IOS Telnet client via the **telnet** *host* command is pretty simple. Just use the IP address or hostname to identify the host to which you want to connect, and press **Enter**. Example 23-7 shows an example based on Figure 23-18, with R1 using Telnet to connect to 10.1.2.2 (R2).

Example 23-7 *Telnet from R1 to R2 to View Interface Status on R2*

```
R1# telnet 10.1.2.2
Trying 10.1.2.2 ... Open


User Access Verification


Username: wendell
Password:
R2>
R2> show ip interface brief
Interface               IP-Address      OK? Method Status                Protocol
GigabitEthernet0/0      unassigned      YES unset  administratively down down
GigabitEthernet0/1      10.1.3.2        YES manual up                    up
GigabitEthernet0/2      10.1.2.2        YES manual up                    up
GigabitEthernet0/3      unassigned      YES unset  administratively down down
```

Take the time to pay close attention to the command prompts. The example begins with the user logged in to Router R1, with the R1# command prompt. The first command confirms the IP addresses and interfaces shown for Router R1 in Figure 23-17 and Figure 23-18.

After issuing the **telnet 10.1.2.2** command, R2 asks the user for both a username and password, because Router R2 uses local username authentication, which requires those credentials. The **show ip interfaces brief** command at the end of the output shows Router R2's interfaces and IP addresses again per Figure 23-17 and Figure 23-18.

The **ssh -l** *username host* command in Example 23-8 follows the same basic ideas as the **telnet** *host* command, but with an SSH client. The **-l** flag means that the next parameter is the login username. In this case, the user begins logged in to Router R1, and then uses the **ssh -l wendell 10.1.2.2** command to SSH to Router R2. R2 expects a username/password of wendell/odom, with wendell supplied in the command, and odom supplied when R2 prompts the user.

Example 23-8 *SSH Client from R1 to R2 to View Interface Status on R2*

```
R1# ssh -l wendell 10.1.2.2


Password:


R2>
R2> show ip interface brief
Interface              IP-Address      OK? Method Status                Protocol
GigabitEthernet0/0     unassigned      YES unset  administratively down down
GigabitEthernet0/1     10.1.3.2        YES manual up                    up
GigabitEthernet0/2     10.1.2.2        YES manual up                    up
GigabitEthernet0/3     unassigned      YES unset  administratively down down
```

When you have finished using the other router, you can log out from your Telnet or SSH connection using the **exit** or **quit** command.

Finally, note that IOS supports a mechanism to use hotkeys to move between multiple Telnet or SSH sessions from the CLI. Basically, starting at one router, you could telnet or SSH to a router, do some commands, and instead of using the exit command to end your connection, you could keep the connection open while still moving back to the command prompt of the original router. For instance, if starting at Router R1, you could Telnet to R2, R3, and R4, suspending but not exiting those Telnet connections. Then you could easily move between the sessions to issue new commands with a few keystrokes.

23

Chapter Review

One key to doing well on the exams is to perform repetitive spaced review sessions. Review this chapter's material using either the tools in the book, DVD, or interactive tools for the same material found on the book's companion website. Refer to the "Your Study Plan" element for more details. Table 23-1 outlines the key review elements and where you can find them. To better track your study progress, record when you completed these activities in the second column.

Table 23-1   Chapter Review Tracking

Review Element	Review Date(s)	Resource Used
Review key topics		Book, DVD/website
Review key terms		Book, DVD/website

Review All the Key Topics

Table 23-2   Key Topics for Chapter 23

Key Topic Element	Description	Page Number
Figure 23-5	ARP tables on Layer 3 hosts, with MAC address tables on Layer 2 switch	547
Figure 23-6	How extended ping in IOS performs a better test of the reverse route	548
List	Types of root causes of host connectivity problems that cannot be found by router **ping** commands	549
Figure 23-7	Why a standard ping over a LAN does not exercise a host's default router logic	550
List	Network layer problems that could cause a ping to fail between a router and host on the same LAN subnet	550
List	Testing a host's default router setting using extended ping	550
List	Comparisons between the **ping** and **traceroute** commands	553
List	The two places to look for routing problems when a **traceroute** command does not complete	557

Key Terms You Should Know

ping, traceroute, ICMP echo request, ICMP echo reply, extended ping, forward route, reverse route, DNS

CHAPTER 24

Troubleshooting IPv4 Routing

This chapter covers the following exam topics:

1.0 Network Fundamentals

1.8 Configure, verify, and troubleshoot IPv4 addressing and subnetting

3.0 Routing Technologies

3.2 Interpret the components of routing table

    3.2.a Prefix

    3.2.b Network mask

    3.2.c Next hop

    3.2.d Routing protocol code

4.0 Infrastructure Services

4.2 Troubleshoot client connectivity issues involving DNS

4.4 Troubleshoot client- and router-based DHCP connectivity issues

5.0 Infrastructure Management

5.6 Use Cisco IOS tools to troubleshoot and resolve problems

    5.6.a Ping and traceroute with extended option

By this point in the book, you have learned a lot about IPv4 addressing, subnetting, and routing. The four chapters in Part IV explained the basics of IPv4 addressing. Then Part V showed how to implement simple IPv4 networks with routers, showing how to configure the control plane so that routers learned the correct routes. That part also linked in how hosts work along with their nearby default router. And now Part VI has added more detail to your knowledge, with more advanced IP addressing and subnetting topics, and with troubleshooting tools in the previous chapter.

This chapter has one obvious goal and one not-so-obvious goal. The obvious goal is to discuss troubleshooting of how IPv4 routing works. This chapter pulls together the ideas about the IPv4 data plane that have already been discussed in Parts IV, V, and VI. However, this chapter takes a troubleshooting approach, discussing what could go wrong and what the symptoms would be if they did go wrong.

This chapter also reviews several topics related to the IPv4 data plane all in one chapter. This book contains a lot of content about IPv4, and reading through the content in this chapter can help you realize which topics you already understand well, and which topics you did not quite master yet. To that end, this chapter's second big goal is to give you a chance to identify weaker areas and to strengthen your understanding, before moving on to the final third or so of this book.

This chapter breaks the topics into two major sections. The first major section focuses on issues between a host and its default router. The second major section then looks at issues that prevent routers from forwarding packets.

"Do I Know This Already?" Quiz

A few of the troubleshooting chapters in this book serve both to discuss troubleshooting of the topics, and to serve as a tool to summarize and review some important topics. This chapter is one of those chapters. As a result, it is useful to read these chapters regardless of your current knowledge level; so this chapter does not include a "Do I Know This Already?" quiz. However, if you feel particularly confident about troubleshooting IPv4 routing features covered in this book, feel free to move to the "Chapter Review" section near the end of this chapter to bypass the majority of the chapter.

Foundation Topics

Problems Between the Host and the Default Router

Imagine that you work as a customer support representative (CSR) fielding calls from users about problems. A user left a message stating that he couldn't connect to a server. You could not reach him when you called back, so you did a series of pings from that host's default router. At the end of those pings, you think the problem exists somewhere between the user's device and the default router—for instance, between Router R1 and host A, as shown in Figure 24-1.

Problem Domain

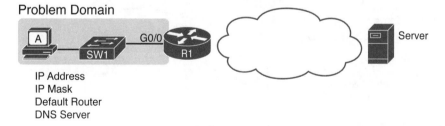

Figure 24-1 *Focus of the Discussions in This Section of the Chapter*

This first major section of the chapter focuses on problems that can occur on hosts, their default routers, and between the two. To begin, this section looks at the host itself, and its four IPv4 settings, as listed in the figure. Following that, the discussion moves to the default router, with focus on the LAN interface, and the settings that must work for the router to serve as a host's default router.

Root Causes Based on a Host's IPv4 Settings

A typical IPv4 host gets its four key IPv4 settings in one of two ways: either through static configuration or by using Dynamic Host Configuration Protocol (DHCP). In both cases, the settings can actually be incorrect. Clearly, any static settings can be set to a wrong number just through human error when typing the values. More surprising is the fact that the DHCP can set the wrong values: The DHCP process can work, but with incorrect values configured at the DHCP server, the host can actually learn some incorrect IPv4 settings.

This section first reviews the settings on the host, and what they should match, followed by a discussion of typical issues.

Ensure IPv4 Settings Correctly Match

Once an engineer thinks that a problem exists somewhere between a host and its default router, the engineer should review the host's IPv4 settings versus the intended settings. That process begins by guiding the user through the graphical user interface (GUI) of the host operating system or by using command-line commands native to host operating systems, such as **ipconfig** and **ifconfig**. This process should uncover obvious issues, like completely missing parameters, or if using DHCP, the complete failure of DHCP to learn any of the IPv4 settings.

If the host has all its settings, the next step is to check the values to match them with the rest of the internetwork. The Domain Name System (DNS) server IP address—usually a list of at least two addresses—should match the DNS server addresses actually used in the internetwork. The rest of the settings should be compared to the correct LAN interface on the router that is used as this host's default router. Figure 24-2 collects all the pieces that should match, with some explanation to follow.

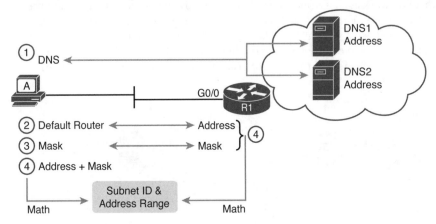

Figure 24-2 *Host IPv4 Settings Compared to What the Settings Should Match*

As numbered in the figure, these steps should be followed to check the host's IPv4 settings:

Step 1.   Check the host's list of DNS server addresses against the actual addresses used by those servers.

Step 2.   Check the host's default router settings against the router's LAN interface configuration, for the **ip address** command.

Step 3.   Check the subnet mask used by the router and the host; if they use a different mask, the subnets will not exactly match, which will cause problems for some host addresses.

Step 4.   The host and router should attach to the exact same subnet—same subnet ID and same range of IP addresses. So, use both the router's and host's IP address and mask, calculate the subnet ID and range of addresses, and confirm they are in the same subnet as the subnet implied by the address/mask of the router's **ip address** command.

If an IPv4 host configuration setting is missing, or simply wrong, checking these settings can quickly uncover the root cause. For instance, if you can log in to the router and do a **show interfaces G0/0** command, and then ask the user to issue an **ipconfig /all** (or similar) command and read the output to you, you can compare all the settings in Figure 24-2.

However, although checking the host settings is indeed very useful, some problems related to hosts are not so easy to spot. The next few topics walk through some example problems to show some symptoms that occur when some of these less obvious problems occur.

Mismatched Masks Impact Route to Reach Subnet

A host and its default router should agree about the range of addresses in the subnet. Sometimes, people are tempted to skip over this check, ignoring the mask either on the host or the router and assuming that the mask used on one device must be the same mask as on the other device. However, if the host and router have different subnet mask values, and therefore each calculates a different range of addresses in the subnet, problems happen.

To see one such example, consider the network in Figure 24-3. Host A has IP address/mask 10.1.1.9/24, with default router 10.1.1.150. Some quick math puts 10.1.1.150—the default router address—inside host A's subnet, right? Indeed it does, and it should. Host A's math for this subnet reveals subnet ID 10.1.1.0, with a range of addresses from 10.1.1.1 through 10.1.1.254, and subnet broadcast address 10.1.1.255.

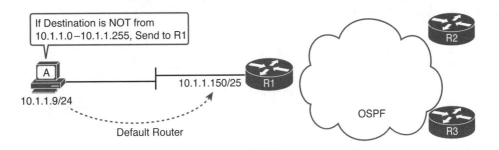

Figure 24-3   *Mismatched Subnet Calculations Appear to Work*

In this case, the host routing of packets, to destinations outside the subnet, works well. However, the reverse direction, from the rest of the network back toward the host, does not. A quick check of Router R1's configuration reveals the IP address/mask as shown in Figure 24-3, which results in the connected route for subnet 10.1.1.128/25, as shown in Example 24-1.

Example 24-1   *R1's IP Address, Mask, Plus the Connected Subnet That Omits Host A's*
Address

```
R1# show running-config interface g0/0
Building configuration...

Current configuration: 185 bytes
!
interface GigabitEthernet0/0
 description LAN at Site 1
 mac-address 0200.0101.0101
 ip address 10.1.1.150 255.255.255.128
 ip helper-address 10.1.2.130
 duplex auto
 speed auto
end


R1# show ip route connected
! Legend omitted for brevity


      10.0.0.0/8 is variably subnetted, 9 subnets, 4 masks
C        10.1.1.128/25 is directly connected, GigabitEthernet0/0
L        10.1.1.150/32 is directly connected, GigabitEthernet0/0
! Other routes omitted for brevity
```

Because of this particular mismatch, R1's view of the subnet puts host A (10.1.1.9) outside
R1's view of the subnet (10.1.1.128/25, range 10.1.1.129 to 10.1.1.254). R1 adds a connected route for subnet 10.1.1.128/25 into R1's routing table, and even advertises this route
(with Open Shortest Path First [OSPF] in this case) to the other routers in the network, as
shown in Figure 24-4. All the routers know how to route packets to subnet 10.1.1.128/25,
but unfortunately that route does not include host A's 10.1.1.9 IP address.

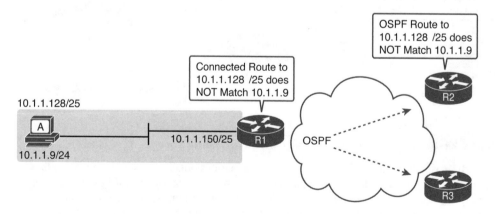

Figure 24-4   *Routers Have No Route That Matches Host A's 10.1.1.9 Address*

Hosts should use the same subnet mask as the default router, and the two devices should agree as to what subnet exists on their common LAN. Otherwise, problems may exist immediately, as in this example, or they might not exist until other hosts are added later.

Typical Root Causes of DNS Problems

When a host lists the wrong IP addresses for the DNS servers, the symptoms are somewhat obvious: Any user actions that require name resolution fail. Assuming that the only problem is the incorrect DNS setting, any network testing with commands like **ping** and **traceroute** fails when using names, but it works when using IP addresses instead of names.

When a ping of another host's hostname fails, but a ping of that same host's IP address works, some problem exists with DNS. For example, imagine a user calls the help desk complaining that he cannot connect to Server1. The CSR issues a **ping server1** command from the CSR's own PC, which both works and identifies the IP address of Server1 as 1.1.1.1. Then the CSR asks the user to try two commands from the user's PC: both a **ping Server1** command (which fails), and a **ping 1.1.1.1** command (which works). Clearly, the DNS name resolution process on the user's PC is having some sort of problem.

This book does not go into much detail about how DNS truly works behind the scenes, but even with a basic analysis, two major types of potential DNS issues are obvious:

- A user host (DNS client) that has an incorrect setting for the DNS server IP address(es)
- An IP connectivity problem between the user's host and the correct DNS server

Although the first problem may be more obvious, note that it can happen both with static settings on the host and with DHCP. If a host lists the wrong DNS server IP address, and the setting is static, just change the setting. If the wrong DNS server address is learned with DHCP, you need to examine the DHCP server configuration. (If using the IOS DHCP server feature, you make this setting with the **dns-server** *server-address* command in DHCP pool mode.)

The second bullet point brings up an important issue for troubleshooting any real-world networking problem. Most every real user application uses names, not addresses, and most hosts use DNS to resolve names. So, every connection to a new application involves two sets of packets: packets that flow between the host and the DNS server, and packets that flow between the host and the real server, as shown in Figure 24-5.

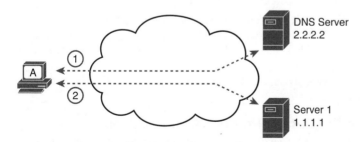

Figure 24-5 *DNS Name Resolution Packets Flow First; Then Packets to the Real Server*

Finally, before leaving the topic of name resolution, note that the router can be configured with the IP addresses of the DNS servers, so that router commands will attempt to resolve names. For instance, a user of the router command-line interface (CLI) could issue a command **ping server1** and rely on a DNS request to resolve server1 into its matching IP address. To configure a router to use a DNS for name resolution, the router needs the **ip name-server** *dns1-address dns2-address...* global command. It also needs the **ip domain-lookup** global command, which is enabled by default.

For troubleshooting, it can be helpful to set a router or switch DNS settings to match that of the local hosts. However, note that these settings have no impact on the user DNS requests.

> **NOTE**   On a practical note, IOS defaults with the **ip domain-lookup** command, but with no DNS IP address known. Most network engineers either add the configuration to point to the DNS servers or disable DNS using the **no ip domain-lookup** command.

Wrong Default Router IP Address Setting

Clearly, having a host that lists the wrong IP address as its default router causes problems. Hosts rely on the default router when sending packets to other subnets, and if a host lists the wrong default router setting, the host may not be able to send packets to a different subnet.

Figure 24-6 shows just such an example. In this case, hosts A and B both misconfigure 10.1.3.4 as the default router due to the same piece of bad documentation. Router R3 uses IP address 10.1.3.3. (For the sake of discussion, assume that no other host or router in this subnet currently uses address 10.1.3.4.)

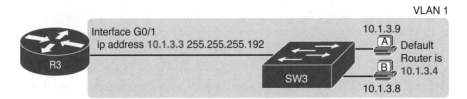

Figure 24-6   *Incorrect Default Router Setting on Hosts A and B*

In this case, several functions do work. For instance, hosts A and B can send packets to other hosts on the same LAN. The CSR at the router CLI can issue a **ping 10.1.3.9** and **ping 10.1.3.8** command, and both work. As a result of those two working pings, R3 would list the MAC address of the two PCs in the output of the **show arp** command. Similarly, the hosts would list R3's 10.1.3.3 IP address (and matching MAC address) in their ARP caches (usually displayed with the **arp –a** command). The one big problem in this case happens when the hosts try to send packets off-subnet. In that case, try to send the packets to IP address 10.1.3.4 next, which fails.

Root Causes Based on the Default Router's Configuration

Hosts must have correct IPv4 settings to work properly, but having correct settings does not guarantee that a LAN-based host can successfully send a packet to the default router. The LAN between the host and the router must work. In addition, the router itself must be working correctly, based on the design of the internetwork.

This next topic looks at problems between hosts and their default router, focusing on two problem areas. First, the text examines typical DHCP issues, followed by a discussion of router interfaces and what causes that interface to fail.

DHCP Issues

Hosts that use DHCP to lease an IP address, and learn other settings, rely on the network to pass the DHCP messages. In particular, if the internetwork uses a centralized DHCP server, with many remote LAN subnets using the centralized DHCP server, the routers have to enable a feature called *DHCP Relay* to make DHCP work. Without DHCP Relay, DHCP requests from hosts never leave the local LAN subnet.

Figure 24-7 shows some of the big ideas behind how DHCP Relay works. In this example, a DHCP client (Host A) sits on the left, with the DHCP server (172.16.2.11) on the right. The client begins the DHCP lease process by sending a DHCP Discover message, one that would flow only across the local LAN without DHCP Relay configured on Router R1. To be ready to forward the Discover message, R1 enables DHCP Relay with the **ip helper-address 172.16.2.11** command configured under its G0/0 interface.

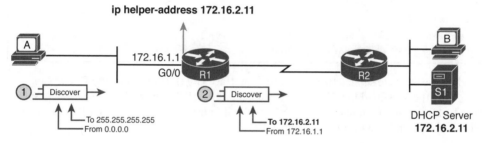

Figure 24-7 *IP Helper Address Effect*

The steps in the figure point out the need for DHCP Relay. At Step 1, host A sends a message, with destination IP and L2 broadcast address of 255.255.255.255 and ff:ff:ff:ff:ff:ff, respectively. Packets sent to this IP address, the "local subnet broadcast address," should never be forwarded past the router. All devices on the subnet receive and process the frame. In addition, because of the **ip helper-address** command configured on R1, Router R1 will continue to de-encapsulate the frame and packet to identify that it is a DHCP request and take action. Step 2 shows the results of DHCP Relay, where R1 changes both the source and destination IP address, with R1 routing the packet to the address listed in the command: 172.16.2.11.

The following troubleshooting checklist gives us a place to start when troubleshooting DHCP-related issues:

Step 1.   If using a centralized DHCP server, at least one router on each remote subnet that has DHCP clients must act as DHCP relay agent, and have a correctly configured **ip helper-address** *address* subcommand on the interface connected to that subnet.

Step 2.   Troubleshoot for any IP connectivity issues between the DHCP relay agent and the DHCP server, using the relay agent interface IP address and the server IP address as the source and destination of the packets.

Step 3. Whether using a local DHCP server or centralized server, troubleshoot for any LAN issues between the DHCP client and the DHCP relay agent.

Step 4. Troubleshoot incorrect server configuration.

Also, if the configuration includes the **ip helper-address** command but lists the wrong DHCP server IP address, again DHCP fails completely.

For instance, Example 24-2 shows an updated configuration for ROAS on Router R3, based on the same scenario as in Figure 24-6. The router configuration works fine for supporting IPv4 and making the router reachable. However, only one subinterface happens to list an **ip helper-address** command.

Example 24-2 *Forgetting to Support DHCP Relay on a ROAS Subinterface*

```
interface GigabitEthernet0/1
 ip address 10.1.3.3 255.255.255.192
 ip helper-address 10.1.2.130
!
interface GigabitEthernet0/1.2
 encapsulation dot1q 2
 ip address 10.1.3.65 255.255.255.192
! There is no ip helper-address command on this subinterface!
```

In this case, hosts in subnet 10.1.3.0/26 (off interface G0/1) that want to use DHCP can, assuming the host at address 10.1.2.130 is indeed the DHCP server. However, hosts in subnet 10.1.3.64/26 (off subinterface G0/1.2) will fail to learn settings with DHCP because of the lack of an **ip helper-address** command.

The second step in the checklist begs for the use of an extended **ping** or extended **traceroute** command. Remember, the DHCP relay agent changes the source and destination IP address of the original DHCP request, using the relay agent interface IP address as the source. Figure 24-8 shows an example, with the DHCP relay agent interface as 172.16.1.1 and the server at 172.16.2.11. From the relay agent router's CLI (Router R1), an extended ping of 172.16.2.11, using R1's G0/1 IP address of 172.16.1.1 as the source addresses, would use those exact same IP addresses.

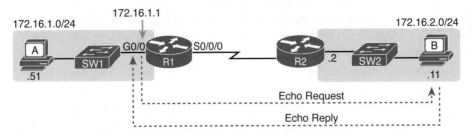

Figure 24-8 *IP Helper Address Effect*

As for Steps 3 and 4 in the list of DHCP relay agent troubleshooting tips, the next topic looks at the issues related to Step 3, focusing on interfaces on the local LAN. As for Step 4, which focuses on DHCP server misconfiguration, the ICND1 book's Chapter 20, "DHCP and IP Networking on Hosts," discusses server configuration issues in depth.

Router LAN Interface and LAN Issues

At some point, the problem isolation process may show that a host cannot ping its default router and vice versa. That is, neither device can send an IP packet to the other device on the same subnet. This basic test tells the engineer that the router, host, and LAN between them, for whatever reasons, cannot pass the packet encapsulated in an Ethernet frame between the two devices.

The root causes for this basic LAN connectivity issue fall into two categories:

■ Problems that cause the router LAN interface to fail

■ Problems with the LAN itself

A router's LAN interface must be in a working state before the router will attempt to send packets out that interface (or receive packets in that interface). Specifically, the router LAN interface must be in an up/up state; if in any other state, the router will not use the interface for packet forwarding. So, if a ping from the router to a LAN host fails (or vice versa), check the interface status, and if not up, find the root cause for the router interface to not be up.

Alternatively, the router interface can be in an up/up state, but problems can exist in the LAN itself. In this case, every topic related to Ethernet LANs may be a root cause. In particular, LAN details such as Ethernet cable pinouts, port security, and even Spanning Tree Protocol, may be root causes of LAN issues.

For instance, in Figure 24-9, Router R3 connects to a LAN with four switches. R3's LAN interface (G0/1) can reach an up/up state if the link from R3 to SW1 works. However, many other problems could prevent R3 from successfully sending an IP packet, encapsulated in an Ethernet frame, to the hosts attached to switches SW3 and SW4.

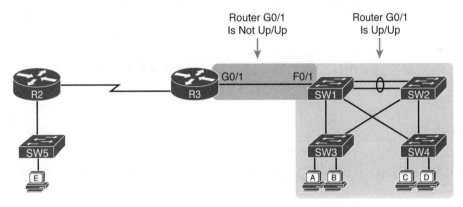

Figure 24-9 *Where to Look for Problems Based on Router LAN Interface Status*

> **NOTE** This book leaves the discussion of LAN issues, as shown on the right side of Figure 24-9, to the various LAN-focused chapters of the ICND1 and ICND2 books.

Router LAN interfaces can fail to reach a working up/up state for several reasons, including the common reasons listed in Table 24-1.

Table 24-1 Common Reasons Why Router LAN Interfaces Are Not Up/Up

Reason	Description	Router Interface State
Speed mismatch	The router and switch can both use the **speed** interface subcommand to set the speed, but to different speeds.	Down/down
Shutdown at router	The router interface has been configured with the **shutdown** interface subcommand.	Admin down/down
Shutdown at switch	The neighboring switch interface has been configured with the **shutdown** interface subcommand, while the router interface is **no shutdown**.	Down/down
Err-disabled switch	The neighboring switch port uses port security, which has put the port in an err-disabled state.	Down/down
No cable/bad cable	The router has no cable installed, or the cable pinouts are incorrect.*	Down/down

* Cisco switches use a feature called auto-mdix, which automatically detects some incorrect cabling pinouts and internally changes the pin logic to allow the cable to be used. As a result, not all incorrect cable pinouts result in an interface failing.

Using the speed mismatch root cause as an example, you could configure Figure 24-9's R3's G0/1 with the **speed 1000** command and SW1's F0/1 interface with the **speed 100** command. The link simply cannot work at these different speeds, so the router and switch interfaces both fall to a down/down state. Example 24-3 shows the resulting state, this time with the **show interfaces description** command, which lists one line of output per interface.

Example 24-3 show interfaces description *Command with Speed Mismatch*

```
R3# show interfaces description
Interface                      Status         Protocol Description
Gi0/0                          up             up
Gi0/1                          down           down       link to campus LAN
Se0/0/0                        admin down     down
Se0/0/1                        up             up
Se0/1/0                        up             up
Se0/1/1                        admin down     down
```

Problems with Routing Packets Between Routers

The first half of this chapter focused on the first hop that an IPv4 packet takes when passing over a network. This second major section now looks at issues related to how routers forward the packet from the default router to the final host.

In particular, this section begins by looking at the IP routing logic inside a single router. These topics review how to understand what a router currently does. Following that, the discussion expands to look at some common root causes of routing problems, causes that come from incorrect IP addressing, particularly when the addressing design uses variable-length subnet masks (VLSM).

The end of this section turns away from the core IP forwarding logic, looking at other issues that impact packet forwarding, including issues related to router interface status (which needs to be up/up) and how IPv4 access control lists (ACL) can filter IPv4 traffic.

IP Forwarding by Matching the Most Specific Route

Any router's IP routing process requires that the router compare the destination IP address of each packet with the existing contents of that router's IP routing table. Often, only one route matches a particular destination address. However, in some cases, a particular destination address matches more than one of the router's routes.

The following router features can create overlapping subnets:

- Autosummarization
- Manual route summarization
- Static routes
- Incorrectly designed subnetting plans that cause subnets to overlap their address ranges

In some cases, overlapping routes cause a problem; in other cases, the overlapping routes are just a normal result of using some feature. This section focuses on how a router chooses which of the overlapping routes to use, for now ignoring whether the overlapping routes are a problem. The section "Routing Problems Caused by Incorrect Addressing Plans," later in this chapter, discusses some of the problem cases.

Now on to how a router matches the routing table, even with overlapping routes in its routing table. If only one route matches a given packet, the router uses that one route. However, when more than one route matches a packet's destination address, the router uses the "best" route, defined as follows:

When a particular destination IP address matches more than one route in a router's IPv4 routing table, the router uses the most specific route—in other words, the route with the longest prefix length mask.

Using show ip route and Subnet Math to Find the Best Route

We humans have a couple of ways to figure out what choice a router makes for choosing the best route. One way uses the **show ip route** command, plus some subnetting math, to decide the route the router will choose. To let you see how to use this option, Example 24-4 shows a series of overlapping routes.

Example 24-4   **show ip route** *Command with Overlapping Routes*

```
R1# show ip route ospf
Codes: L - local, C - connected, S - static, R - RIP, M - mobile, B - BGP
       D - EIGRP, EX - EIGRP external, O - OSPF, IA - OSPF inter area
       N1 - OSPF NSSA external type 1, N2 - OSPF NSSA external type 2
       E1 - OSPF external type 1, E2 - OSPF external type 2
       i - IS-IS, su - IS-IS summary, L1 - IS-IS level-1, L2 - IS-IS level-2
       ia - IS-IS inter area, * - candidate default, U - per-user static route
       o - ODR, P - periodic downloaded static route, H - NHRP, l - LISP
       + - replicated route, % - next hop override
```

```
Gateway of last resort is 172.16.25.129 to network 0.0.0.0


      172.16.0.0/16 is variably subnetted, 9 subnets, 5 masks
O        172.16.1.1/32 [110/50] via 172.16.25.2, 00:00:04, Serial0/1/1
O        172.16.1.0/24 [110/100] via 172.16.25.129, 00:00:09, Serial0/1/0
O        172.16.0.0/22 [110/65] via 172.16.25.2, 00:00:04, Serial0/1/1
O        172.16.0.0/16 [110/65] via 172.16.25.129, 00:00:09, Serial0/1/0
O        0.0.0.0/0 [110/129] via 172.16.25.129, 00:00:09, Serial0/1/0
!
```

NOTE   As an aside, the **show ip route ospf** command lists only OSPF-learned routes, but the statistics for numbers of subnets and masks (9 and 5 in the example, respectively) are for all routes, not just OSPF-learned routes.

To predict which of its routes a router will match, two pieces of information are required: the destination IP address of the packet and the contents of the router's routing table. The subnet ID and mask listed for a route define the range of addresses matched by that route. With a little subnetting math, a network engineer can find the range of addresses matched by each route. For instance, Table 24-2 lists the five subnets listed in Example 24-4 and the address ranges implied by each.

Table 24-2   Analysis of Address Ranges for the Subnets in Example 24-4

Subnet/Prefix	Address Range
172.16.1.1/32	172.16.1.1 (just this one address)
172.16.1.0/24	172.16.1.0–172.16.1.255
172.16.0.0/22	172.16.0.0–172.16.3.255
172.16.0.0/16	172.16.0.0–172.16.255.255
0.0.0.0/0	0.0.0.0–255.255.255.255 (all addresses)

NOTE   The route listed as 0.0.0.0/0 is the default route.

As you can see from these ranges, several of the routes' address ranges overlap. When matching more than one route, the route with the longer prefix length is used. That is, a route with /16 is better than a route with /10; a route with a /25 prefix is better than a route with a /20 prefix; and so on.

For example, a packet sent to 172.16.1.1 actually matches all five routes listed in the routing table in Example 24-4. The various prefix lengths range from /0 to /32. The longest prefix (largest /P value, meaning the best and most specific route) is /32. So, a packet sent to 172.16.1.1 uses the route to 172.16.1.1/32, and not the other routes.

The following list gives some examples of destination IP addresses. For each address, the list describes the routes from Table 24-2 that the router would match, and which specific route the router would use.

172.16.1.1: Matches all five routes; the longest prefix is /32, the route to 172.16.1.1/32.

172.16.1.2: Matches last four routes; the longest prefix is /24, the route to 172.16.1.0/24.

172.16.2.3: Matches last three routes; the longest prefix is /22, the route to 172.16.0.0/22.

172.16.4.3: Matches the last two routes; the longest prefix is /16, the route to 172.16.0.0/16.

Using show ip route *address* to Find the Best Route

A second way to identify the route a router will use, one that does not require any subnetting math, is the **show ip route** *address* command. The last parameter on this command is the IP address of an assumed IP packet. The router replies by listing the route it would use to route a packet sent to that address.

For example, Example 24-5 lists the output of the **show ip route 172.16.4.3** command on the same router used in Example 24-4. The first line of (highlighted) output lists the matched route: the route to 172.16.0.0/16. The rest of the output lists the details of that particular route, like the outgoing interface of S0/1/0 and the next-hop router of 172.16.25.129.

Example 24-5   show ip route *Command with Overlapping Routes*

```
R1# show ip route 172.16.4.3
Routing entry for 172.16.0.0/16
  Known via "ospf 1", distance 110, metric 65, type intra area
  Last update from 10.2.2.5 on Serial0/1/0, 14:22:06 ago
  Routing Descriptor Blocks:
  * 172.16.25.129, from 172.16.25.129, 14:22:05 ago, via Serial0/1/0
      Route metric is 65, traffic share count is 1
```

Certainly, if you have an option, just using a command to check what the router actually chooses is a much quicker option than doing the subnetting math.

show ip route Reference

The **show ip route** command plays a huge role in troubleshooting IP routing and IP routing protocol problems. Many chapters in both the ICND1 and ICND2 books mention various facts about this command. This section pulls the concepts together in one place for easier reference and study.

Figure 24-10 shows the output of a sample **show ip route** command. The figure numbers various parts of the command output for easier reference, with Table 24-3 describing the output noted by each number.

24

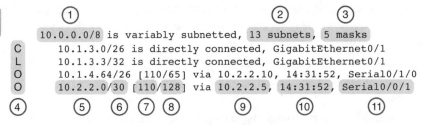

Figure 24-10 show ip route *Command Output Reference*

Table 24-3 Descriptions of the **show ip route** Command Output

Item	Idea	Value in the Figure	Description
1	Classful network	10.0.0.0/8	The routing table is organized by classful network. This line is the heading line for classful network 10.0.0.0; it lists the default mask for Class A networks (/8).
2	Number of subnets	13 subnets	Lists the number of routes for subnets of the classful network known to this router, from all sources, including local routes—the /32 routes that match each router interface IP address.
3	Number of masks	5 masks	The number of different masks used in all routes known to this router inside this classful network.
4	Legend code	C, L, O	A short code that identifies the source of the routing information. *O* is for OSPF, *D* for EIGRP, *C* for Connected, *S* for static, and *L* for local. (See Example 24-4 for a sample of the legend.)
5	Subnet ID	10.2.2.0	The subnet number of this particular route.
6	Prefix length	/30	The prefix mask used with this subnet.
7	Administrative distance	110	If a router learns routes for the listed subnet from more than one source of routing information, the router uses the source with the lowest administrative distance (AD).
8	Metric	128	The metric for this route.
9	Next-hop router	10.2.2.5	For packets matching this route, the IP address of the next router to which the packet should be forwarded.
10	Timer	14:31:52	For OSPF and EIGRP routes, this is the time since the route was first learned.
11	Outgoing interface	Serial0/0/1	For packets matching this route, the interface out which the packet should be forwarded.

Routing Problems Caused by Incorrect Addressing Plans

The existence of overlapping routes in a router's routing table does not necessarily mean a problem exists. Both automatic and manual route summarization result in overlapping routes on some routers, with those overlaps not causing problems. However, some overlaps, particularly those related to addressing mistakes, can cause problems for user traffic. So, when troubleshooting, if overlapping routes exist, the engineer should also look for the specific reasons for overlaps that actually cause a problem.

Simple mistakes in either the IP addressing plan or the implementation of that plan can cause overlaps that also cause problems. In these cases, one router claims to be connected to a subnet with one address range, while another router claims to be connected to another subnet with an overlapping range, breaking IP addressing rules. The symptoms are that the routers sometimes forward the packets to the right host, but sometimes not.

This problem can occur whether or not VLSM is used. However, the problem is much harder to find when VLSM is used. This section reviews VLSM, shows examples of the problem both with and without VLSM, and discusses the configuration and verification commands related to these problems.

Recognizing When VLSM Is Used or Not

An internetwork is considered to be using VLSM when multiple subnet masks are used for different subnets of *a single classful network*. For example, if in one internetwork all subnets come from network 10.0.0.0, and masks /24, /26, and /30 are used, the internetwork uses VLSM.

Sometimes people fall into the trap of thinking that any internetwork that uses more than one mask must be using VLSM, but that is not always the case. For instance, if an internetwork uses subnets of network 10.0.0.0, all of which use mask 255.255.240.0, and subnets of network 172.16.0.0, all of which use a 255.255.255.0 mask, the design does not use VLSM. Two different masks are used, but only one mask is used in any single classful network. The design must use more than one mask for subnets of a single classful network to be using VLSM.

Only classless routing protocols can support VLSM. The three IPv4 IGP routing protocols included in the current CCNA Routing and Switching certification (RIPv2, OSPF, and EIGRP) are all classless routing protocols.

Overlaps When Not Using VLSM

Even when you are not using VLSM, addressing mistakes that create overlapping subnets can occur. For instance, Figure 24-11 shows a sample network with router LAN IP address/mask information. An overlap exists, but it might not be obvious at first glance.

24

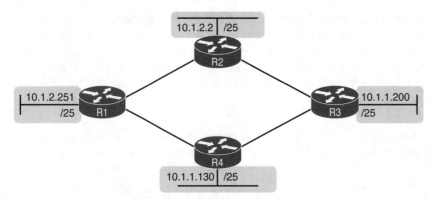

Figure 24-11 *IP Addresses on LAN Interfaces, with One Mask (/25) in Network 10.0.0.0*

If an overlap exists when all subnets use the same mask, the overlapping subnets have the exact same subnet ID, and the exact same range of IP addresses in the subnet. To find the overlap, all you have to do is calculate the subnet ID of each subnet and compare the numbers. For instance, Figure 24-12 shows an updated version of Figure 24-11, with subnet IDs shown and with identical subnet IDs for the LANs off R3 and R4.

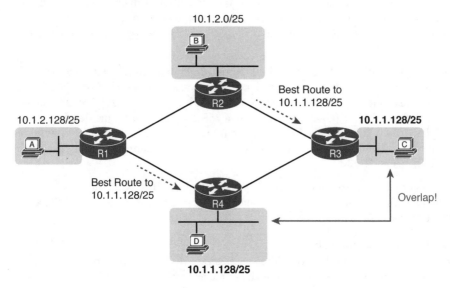

Figure 24-12 *Subnet IDs Calculated from Figure 24-11*

Using the same subnet in two different places (as is done in Figure 24-12) breaks the rules of IPv4 addressing because the routers get confused about where to send packets. In this case, for packets sent to subnet 10.1.1.128/25, some routers send packets so they arrive at R3, whereas others think the best route points toward R4. Assuming all routers use a routing protocol, such as OSPF, both R3 and R4 advertise a route for 10.1.1.128/25.

In this case, R1 and R2 will likely send packets to two different instances of subnet 10.1.1.128/25. With these routes, hosts near R1 will be able to communicate with 10.1.1.128/25 hosts off R4's LAN, but not those off R3's LAN, and vice versa.

Finally, although the symptoms point to some kind of routing issues, the root cause is an invalid IP addressing plan. No IP addressing plan should use the same subnet on two different LANs, as was done in this case. The solution: Change R3 or R4 to use a different, non-overlapping subnet on its LAN interface.

Overlaps When Using VLSM

When using VLSM, the same kinds of addressing mistakes can lead to overlapping subnets; they just may be more difficult to notice.

First, overlaps between subnets that have different masks will cause only a partial overlap. That is, two overlapping subnets will have different sizes and possibly different subnet IDs. The overlap occurs between all the addresses of the smaller subnet, but with only part of the larger subnet. Second, the problems between hosts only occur for some destinations (specifically the subset of addresses in the overlapped ranges), making it even tougher to characterize the problem.

For instance, Figure 24-13 shows an example with a VLSM overlap. The figure shows only the IP address/mask pairs of router and host interfaces. First, look at the example and try to find the overlap by looking at the IP addresses.

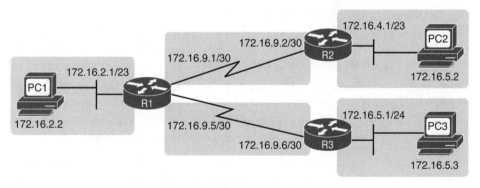

Figure 24-13 *VLSM IP Addressing Plan in Network 172.16.0.0*

To find the overlap, the person troubleshooting the problem needs to analyze each subnet, finding not only the subnet ID but also the subnet broadcast address and the range of addresses in the subnet. If the analysis stops with just looking at the subnet ID, the overlap may not be noticed (as is the case in this example).

Figure 24-14 shows the beginning analysis of each subnet, with only the subnet ID listed. Note that the two overlapping subnets have different subnet IDs, but the lower-right subnet (172.16.5.0/24) completely overlaps with part of the upper-right subnet (172.16.4.0/23). (Subnet 172.16.4.0/23 has a subnet broadcast address of 172.16.5.255, and subnet 172.16.5.0/24 has a subnet broadcast address of 172.16.5.255.)

24

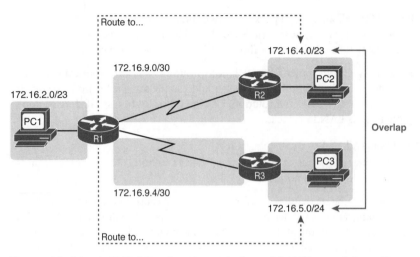

Figure 24-14 *A VLSM Overlap Example, but with Different Subnet IDs*

To be clear, the design with actual subnets whose address ranges overlap is incorrect and should be changed. However, once implemented, the symptoms show up as routing problems, like the similar case without VLSM. **ping** commands fail, and **traceroute** commands do complete for only certain hosts (but not all).

Configuring Overlapping VLSM Subnets

IP subnetting rules require that the address ranges in the subnets used in an internetwork should not overlap. IOS sometimes can recognize when a new **ip address** command creates an overlapping subnet, but sometimes not, as follows:

Preventing the overlap on a single router: IOS detects the overlap when the **ip address** command implies an overlap with another **ip address** command *on the same router*.

Allowing the overlap on different routers: IOS cannot detect an overlap when an **ip address** command overlaps with an **ip address** command on another router.

The router shown in Example 24-6 prevents the configuration of an overlapping VLSM subnet. The example shows Router R3 configuring Fa0/0 with IP address 172.16.5.1/24 and attempting to configure Fa0/1 with 172.16.5.193/26. The ranges of addresses in each subnet are as follows:

Subnet 172.16.5.0/24:   172.16.5.1–172.16.5.254

Subnet 172.16.5.192/26: 172.16.5.193–172.16.5.254

Example 24-6 *Single Router Rejects Overlapped Subnets*

```
R3# configure terminal
R3(config)# interface Fa0/0
R3(config-if)# ip address 172.16.5.1 255.255.255.0
R3(config-if)# interface Fa0/1
R3(config-if)# ip address 172.16.5.193 255.255.255.192
% 172.16.5.192 overlaps with FastEthernet0/0
R3(config-if)#
```

IOS knows that it is illegal to overlap the ranges of addresses implied by a subnet. In this case, because both subnets would be connected subnets, this single router knows that these two subnets should not coexist because that would break subnetting rules, so IOS rejects the second command.

As an aside of how IOS handles these errors, IOS only performs the subnet overlap check for interfaces that are not in a shutdown state. When configuring an interface in shutdown state, IOS actually accepts the **ip address** command that would cause the overlap. Later, when the **no shutdown** command is issued, IOS checks for the subnet overlap and issues the same error message shown in Example 24-6. IOS leaves the interface in the shutdown state until the overlap condition has been resolved.

IOS cannot detect the configuration of overlapping subnets on different routers, as shown in Example 24-7. The example shows the configuration of the two overlapping subnets on R2 and R3 from Figure 24-13.

Example 24-7 *Two Routers Accept Overlapped Subnets*

```
! First, on router R2
R2# configure terminal
R2(config)# interface G0/0
R2(config-if)# ip address 172.16.4.1 255.255.254.0
! Next, on router R3
R3# configure terminal
R3(config)# interface G0/0
R3(config-if)# ip address 172.16.5.1 255.255.255.0
```

Pointers to Related Troubleshooting Topics

A router's data plane may fail due to features beyond those mentioned in this chapter or in this book. However, other chapters of the ICND1 and ICND2 books explain troubleshooting of a couple of other features that directly impact a router's forwarding logic. This short section references those other topics for completeness, even though the details sit in other chapters.

Router WAN Interface Status

One of the steps in the IP routing troubleshooting process described earlier, in the "Router LAN Interface and LAN Issues" section, says to check the interface status, ensuring that the required interface is working. For a router interface to be working, the two interface status codes must both be listed as up, with engineers usually saying the interface is "up and up."

So far, the ICND1 book has explored only basic information about how serial links work, leaving that detail for the ICND2 book. For this book, know that for a serial link, both routers must have working serial interfaces in an up/up state before they can send IPv4 packets to each other. The two routers should also have serial IP addresses in the same subnet.

24

> **NOTE** If you would like to pause here and learn more about WAN links now, the ICND2 book chapter "Implementing Point-to-Point WANs" is included on the DVD as a resource as Appendix P for those of you who have bought only the ICND1 book so far.

Filtering Packets with Access Lists

Practically every networking device used today has some ability to filter traffic at the data plane. That is, the device can monitor packets during the forwarding process, compare those packets to a list of rules, and discard (filter) some packets based on those rules. Cisco IOS calls this feature *access control lists* (ACL), and it is the topic of the next two chapters of the book.

Any troubleshooting checklist related to the data plane could include a line item for "...the packet is filtered by an ACL." However, in this book, the ACL chapters come after this chapter. So make sure to review the ACL troubleshooting details in Chapter 26, "Advanced IPv4 Access Control Lists." That chapter includes some details about how ACLs filter packets, and how ACLs impact the **ping** command.

Chapter Review

One key to doing well on the exams is to perform repetitive spaced review sessions. Review this chapter's material using either the tools in the book, DVD, or interactive tools for the same material found on the book's companion website. Refer to the "Your Study Plan" element for more details. Table 24-4 outlines the key review elements and where you can find them. To better track your study progress, record when you completed these activities in the second column.

Table 24-4 Chapter Review Tracking

Review Element	Review Date(s)	Resource Used
Review key topics		Book, DVD/website
Review memory tables		Book, DVD/website

Review All the Key Topics

Table 24-5 Key Topics for Chapter 24

Key Topic Element	Description	Page Number
Figure 24-2, checklist	A checklist of how to troubleshoot issues between the IPv4 settings on a host and its default router	566
List	Two root causes of DNS problems	569
List	Conditions that must be true for DHCP messages to be able to flow from a client to a DHCP server	571
Table 24-1	Common reasons why router LAN interfaces are not up/up	574
Definition	When more than one route matches a packet's destination address, the router uses the "best" (most specific) route	575
Figure 24-10, Table 24-3	**show ip route** field reference and explanations	578
List	Types of overlapping IP address configuration issues that IOS can and cannot recognize	582

Part VI Review

Keep track of your part review progress with the checklist in Table P6-1. Details on each task follow the table.

Table P6-1 Part VI Part Review Checklist

Activity	1st Date Completed	2nd Date Completed
Repeat All DIKTA Questions		
Answer Part Review Questions		
Review Key Topics		
Create Process Mind Map		
Do Labs		

Repeat All DIKTA Questions

For this task, use the PCPT software to answer the "Do I Know This Already?" questions again for the chapters in this part of the book.

Answer Part Review Questions

For this task, use PCPT to answer the Part Review questions for this part of the book.

Review Key Topics

Review all key topics in all chapters in this part, either by browsing the chapters or by using the Key Topics application on the DVD or companion website.

Create Process Mind Map

This book part explains several types of problems that can be solved by following a process outlined in the chapter. The next mind map exercise helps to review the big ideas of what each type of problem does. This review does not focus on the details of how to find the answer to any one problem, leaving that for all the other practice suggestions included near the end of Chapter 21, "Subnet Design," and Chapter 22, "Variable-Length Subnet Masks."

Those chapters discussed the following types of problems that can be solved with some arithmetic:

■ **Choosing subnet masks:** Based on design requirements, choose one mask to use throughout a classful IP network.

■ **Finding all subnet IDs:** Calculate all subnet IDs of a network.

■ **Finding VLSM overlaps:** Discovering mistakes in a design in which two or more subnets' address ranges overlap.

■ **Adding new subnets to an existing VLSM design:** Discovering an open slot in the existing subnet design into which a new VLSM subnet can be added.

Create a mind map with a branch for each topic in the list. For each branch, begin with the core concept and branch into three subtopics, as shown in this list and in Figure P6-1:

■ **Given:** The information you have and the assumptions you make to start the problem.

■ **Process:** The information or terms used during the process. Do not write the specific steps of the process; the goal here is just to make memory connections so that you know it is this process, and not some other process.

■ **Result:** The facts you determine by doing the problem.

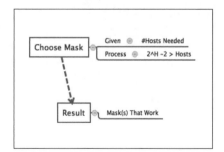

Figure P6-1 *Sample Mind Map for Part VI Mind Map*

If you do choose to use mind map software rather than paper, you might want to remember where you stored your mind map files. Table P6-2 lists the mind maps for this part review and a place to record those filenames.

Table P6-2   Configuration Mind Maps for Part VI Review

Map	Description	Where You Saved It
1	Mind Map: Process Reminders	

Appendix L, "Mind Map Solutions," lists a sample mind map answer, but as usual, your mind map can and will look different.

Labs

Depending on your chosen lab tool, here are some suggestions for what to do in lab:

Pearson Network Simulator: If you use the full Pearson ICND1 or CCNA simulator, focus more on the configuration scenario and troubleshooting scenario labs associated with the topics in this part of the book. These types of labs include a larger set of topics and work well as Part Review activities. (See the Introduction for some details about how to find which labs are about topics in this part of the book.)

Other: If using other lab tools, as a few suggestions: build any IPv4 network and experiment with standard and extended ping and traceroute, as well as with the Telnet and SSH client commands. Also scan Chapter 24, "Troubleshooting IPv4 Routing," for the types of root causes, and try to re-create some of those in the lab.

Part VII completes this book's topics on IPv4 networks by looking at a couple of services that help secure enterprise networks as well as create useful addressing options when connecting to the Internet.

Chapter 25 and 26 discuss the basics and more advanced features of IPv4 access control lists (ACL). ACLs are IPv4 packet filters that can be programmed to look at IPv4 packet headers, make choices, and either allow a packet through or discard the packet. Chapters 25 and 26 discuss these topics in depth, for several types of IPv4 ACLs, from configuration to verification and troubleshooting.

Chapter 27, the last chapter in this part, discusses Network Address Translation (NAT). NAT helps solve a big problem with IPv4 addressing in the Internet, and is used by almost every enterprise and home user of the Internet.

Part VII

IPv4 Services: ACLs and NAT

CHAPTER 25

Basic IPv4 Access Control Lists

This chapter covers the following exam topics:

4.0 Infrastructure Services

4.6 Configure, verify, and troubleshoot IPv4 standard numbered and named access list for routed interfaces

Almost every other topic in the scope of CCENT and CCNA R&S focuses on achieving a core goal of any TCP/IP network: delivering IPv4 packets from the source host to the destination host. This chapter, along with the next chapter, focuses instead on preventing some of those packets from being allowed to reach their destinations, by using IPv4 access control lists (ACL).

IPv4 ACLs have many uses, but the CCENT and CCNA R&S certifications focus on their most commonly known use: as packet filters. You want hosts in one subnet to be able to communicate throughout your corporate network, but maybe there is a pocket of servers with sensitive data that must be protected. Maybe government privacy rules require you to further secure and protect access, not just with usernames and login, but even to protect the ability to deliver a packet to the protected host or server. IP ACLs provide a useful solution to achieve those goals.

IPv4 ACLs give network engineers the ability to program a filter into a router. Each router, on each interface, for both the inbound and outbound direction, can enable a different ACL with different rules. Each ACL's rules tell the router which packets to discard, and which to allow through.

This chapter discusses the basics of IPv4 ACLs, and in particular, one type of IP ACL: standard numbered IP ACLs. Chapter 26, "Advanced IPv4 Access Control Lists," completes the discussion by describing other types of IP ACLs.

"Do I Know This Already?" Quiz

Take the quiz (either here, or use the PCPT software) if you want to use the score to help you decide how much time to spend on this chapter. The answers are at the bottom of the page following the quiz, and the explanations are in DVD Appendix C and in the PCPT software.

Table 25-1 "Do I Know This Already?" Foundation Topics Section-to-Question Mapping

Foundation Topics Section	Questions
IP Access Control List Basics	1
Standard Numbered IPv4 ACLs	2–5
Practice Applying Standard IP ACLs	6

1. Barney is a host with IP address 10.1.1.1 in subnet 10.1.1.0/24. Which of the following are things that a standard IP ACL could be configured to do? (Choose two answers.)

   a. Match the exact source IP address.

   b. Match IP addresses 10.1.1.1 through 10.1.1.4 with one **access-list** command without matching other IP addresses.

   c. Match all IP addresses in Barney's subnet with one **access-list** command without matching other IP addresses.

   d. Match only the packet's destination IP address.

2. Which of the following answers list a valid number that can be used with standard numbered IP ACLs? (Choose two answers.)

   a. 1987

   b. 2187

   c. 187

   d. 87

3. Which of the following wildcard masks is most useful for matching all IP packets in subnet 10.1.128.0, mask 255.255.255.0?

   a. 0.0.0.0

   b. 0.0.0.31

   c. 0.0.0.240

   d. 0.0.0.255

   e. 0.0.15.0

   f. 0.0.248.255

4. Which of the following wildcard masks is most useful for matching all IP packets in subnet 10.1.128.0, mask 255.255.240.0?

   a. 0.0.0.0

   b. 0.0.0.31

   c. 0.0.0.240

   d. 0.0.0.255

   e. 0.0.15.255

   f. 0.0.248.255

5. ACL 1 has three statements, in the following order, with address and wildcard mask values as follows: 1.0.0.0 0.255.255.255, 1.1.0.0 0.0.255.255, and 1.1.1.0 0.0.0.255. If a router tried to match a packet sourced from IP address 1.1.1.1 using this ACL, which ACL statement does a router consider the packet to have matched?

  a. First

  b. Second

  c. Third

  d. Implied deny at the end of the ACL

6. Which of the following **access-list** commands matches all packets sent from hosts in subnet 172.16.4.0/23?

  a. access-list 1 permit 172.16.0.5 0.0.255.0

  b. access-list 1 permit 172.16.4.0 0.0.1.255

  c. access-list 1 permit 172.16.5.0

  d. access-list 1 permit 172.16.5.0 0.0.0.127

Foundation Topics

IPv4 Access Control List Basics

IPv4 access control lists (IP ACL) give network engineers a way to identify different types of packets. To do so, the ACL configuration lists values that the router can see in the IP, TCP, UDP, and other headers. For example, an ACL can match packets whose source IP address is 1.1.1.1, or packets whose destination IP address is some address in subnet 10.1.1.0/24, or packets with a destination port of TCP port 23 (Telnet).

IPv4 ACLs perform many functions in Cisco routers, with the most common use as a packet filter. Engineers can enable ACLs on a router so that the ACL sits in the forwarding path of packets as they pass through the router. After it is enabled, the router considers whether each IP packet will either be discarded or allowed to continue as if the ACL did not exist.

However, ACLs can be used for many other IOS features as well. As an example, ACLs can be used to match packets for applying quality of service (QoS) features. QoS allows a router to give some packets better service, and other packets worse service. For example, packets that hold digitized voice need to have very low delay, so ACLs can match voice packets, with QoS logic in turn forwarding voice packets more quickly than data packets.

This first section introduces IP ACLs as used for packet filtering, focusing on these aspects of ACLs: the locations and direction in which to enable ACLs, matching packets by examining headers, and taking action after a packet has been matched.

ACL Location and Direction

Cisco routers can apply ACL logic to packets at the point at which the IP packets enter an interface, or the point at which they exit an interface. In other words, the ACL becomes associated with an interface and for a direction of packet flow (either in or out). That is, the ACL can be applied inbound to the router, before the router makes its forwarding (routing) decision, or outbound, after the router makes its forwarding decision and has determined the exit interface to use.

The arrows in Figure 25-1 show the locations at which you could filter packets flowing left to right in the topology. For example, imagine that you wanted to allow packets sent by host A to server S1, but to discard packets sent by host B to server S1. Each arrowed line represents a location and direction at which a router could apply an ACL, filtering the packets sent by host B.

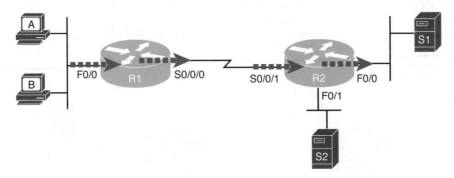

Figure 25-1 *Locations to Filter Packets from Hosts A and B Going Toward Server S1*

The four arrowed lines in the figure point out the location and direction for the router interfaces used to forward the packet from host B to server S1. In this particular example, those interfaces and direction are inbound on R1's F0/0 interface, outbound on R1's S0/0/0 interface, inbound on R2's S0/0/1 interface, and outbound on R2's F0/0 interface. If, for example, you enabled an ACL on R2's F0/1 interface, in either direction, that ACL could not possibly filter the packet sent from host B to server S1, because R2's F0/1 interface is not part of the route from B to S1.

In short, to filter a packet, you must enable an ACL on an interface that processes the packet, in the same direction the packet flows through that interface.

When enabled, the router then processes every inbound or outbound IP packet using that ACL. For example, if enabled on R1 for packets inbound on interface F0/0, R1 would compare every inbound IP packet on F0/0 to the ACL to decide that packet's fate: to continue unchanged, or to be discarded.

Matching Packets

When you think about the location and direction for an ACL, you must already be thinking about what packets you plan to filter (discard), and which ones you want to allow through. To tell the router those same ideas, you must configure the router with an IP ACL that matches packets. *Matching packets* refers to how to configure the ACL commands to look at each packet, listing how to identify which packets should be discarded, and which should be allowed through.

25

Each IP ACL consists of one or more configuration commands, with each command listing details about values to look for inside a packet's headers. Generally, an ACL command uses logic like "look for these values in the packet header, and if found, discard the packet." (The action could instead be to allow the packet, rather than discard.) Specifically, the ACL looks for header fields you should already know well, including the source and destination IP addresses, plus TCP and UDP port numbers.

For example, consider an example with Figure 25-2, in which you want to allow packets from host A to server S1, but to discard packets from host B going to that same server. The hosts all now have IP addresses, and the figure shows pseudocode for an ACL on R2. Figure 25-2 also shows the chosen location to enable the ACL: inbound on R2's S0/0/1 interface.

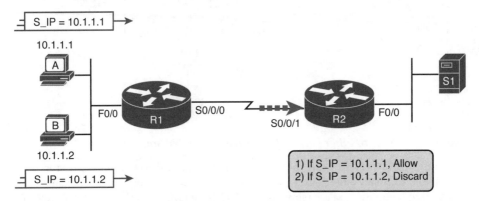

Figure 25-2 *Pseudocode to Demonstrate ACL Command-Matching Logic*

Figure 25-2 shows a two-line ACL in a rectangle at the bottom, with simple matching logic: both statements just look to match the source IP address in the packet. When enabled, R2 looks at every inbound IP packet on that interface and compares each packet to those two ACL commands. Packets sent by host A (source IP address 10.1.1.1) are allowed through, and those sourced by host B (source IP address 10.1.1.2) are discarded.

Taking Action When a Match Occurs

When using IP ACLs to filter packets, only one of two actions can be chosen. The configuration commands use keywords **deny** and **permit**, and they mean (respectively) to discard the packet or to allow it to keep going as if the ACL did not exist.

This book focuses on using ACLs to filter packets, but IOS uses ACLs for many more features. Those features typically use the same matching logic. However, in other cases, the **deny** or **permit** keywords imply some other action. For example, Chapter 27, "Network Address Translation," uses ACLs to match packets, but matching with a **permit** keyword tells the router to apply NAT functions that translate the IP addresses.

Types of IP ACLs

Cisco IOS has supported IP ACLs since the early days of Cisco routers. Beginning with the original standard numbered IP ACLs in the early days of IOS, which could enable the logic shown earlier around Figure 25-2, Cisco has added many ACL features, including the following:

- Standard numbered ACLs (1–99)
- Extended numbered ACLs (100–199)
- Additional ACL numbers (1300–1999 standard, 2000–2699 extended)
- Named ACLs
- Improved editing with sequence numbers

This chapter focuses solely on standard numbered IP ACLs, while the next chapter discusses the other three primary categories of IP ACLs. Briefly, IP ACLs will be either numbered or named in that the configuration identifies the ACL either using a number or a name. ACLs will also be either standard or extended, with extended ACLs having much more robust abilities in matching packets. Figure 25-3 summarizes the big ideas related to categories of IP ACLs.

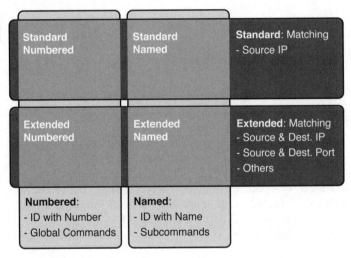

Figure 25-3 *Comparisons of IP ACL Types*

Standard Numbered IPv4 ACLs

The title of this section serves as a great introduction, if you can decode what Cisco means by each specific word. This section is about a type of Cisco filter (ACL) that matches only the source IP address of the packet (*standard*), is configured to identify the ACL using numbers rather than names (*numbered*), and looks at IPv4 packets.

This section examines the particulars of standard numbered IP ACLs. First, it examines the idea that one ACL is a list, and what logic that list uses. Following that, the text closely looks at how to match the source IP address field in the packet header, including the syntax of the commands. This section ends with a complete look at the configuration and verification commands to implement standard ACLs.

25

List Logic with IP ACLs

A single ACL is both a single entity and, at the same time, a list of one or more configuration commands. As a single entity, the configuration enables the entire ACL on an interface, in a specific direction, as shown earlier in Figure 25-1. As a list of commands, each command has different matching logic that the router must apply to each packet when filtering using that ACL.

When doing ACL processing, the router processes the packet, compared to the ACL, as follows:

ACLs use first-match logic. Once a packet matches one line in the ACL, the router takes the action listed in that line of the ACL, and stops looking further in the ACL.

To see exactly what that means, consider the example built around Figure 25-4. The figure shows an example ACL 1 with three lines of pseudocode. This example applies ACL 1 on R2's S0/0/1 interface, inbound (the same location as in earlier Figure 25-2).

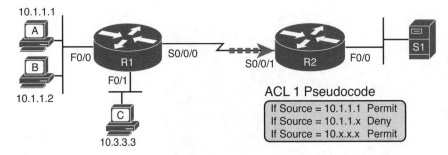

Figure 25-4 *Backdrop for Discussion of List Process with IP ACLs*

Consider the first-match ACL logic for a packet sent by host A to server S1. The source IP address will be 10.1.1.1, and it will be routed so that it enters R2's S0/0/1 interface, driving R2's ACL 1 logic. R2 compares this packet to the ACL, matching the first item in the list with a permit action. So this packet should be allowed through, as shown in Figure 25-5, on the left.

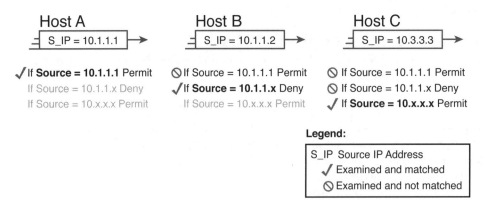

Figure 25-5 *ACL Items Compared for Packets from Hosts A, B, and C in Figure 25-4*

Next, consider a packet sent by host B, source IP address 10.1.1.2. When the packet enters R2's S0/0/1 interface, R2 compares the packet to ACL 1's first statement, and does not make a match (10.1.1.1 is not equal to 10.1.1.2). R2 then moves to the second statement, which requires some clarification. The ACL pseudocode, back in Figure 25-4, shows 10.1.1.x, which is meant to be shorthand that any value can exist in the last octet. Comparing only the first three octets, R2 decides that this latest packet does have a source IP address that begins with first three octets 10.1.1, so R2 considers that to be a match on the second statement. R2 takes the listed action (deny), discarding the packet. R2 also stops ACL processing on the packet, ignoring the third line in the ACL.

Finally, consider a packet sent by host C, again to server S1. The packet has source IP address 10.3.3.3, so when it enters R2's S0/0/1 interface, and drives ACL processing on R2, R2 looks at the first command in ACL 1. R2 does not match the first ACL command (10.1.1.1 in the command is not equal to the packet's 10.3.3.3). R2 looks at the second command, compares the first three octets (10.1.1) to the packet source IP address (10.3.3), still no match. R2 then looks at the third command. In this case, the wildcard means ignore the last three octets, and just compare the first octet (10), so the packet matches. R2 then takes the listed action (permit), allowing the packet to keep going.

This sequence of processing an ACL as a list happens for any type of IOS ACL: IP, other protocols, standard or extended, named or numbered.

Finally, if a packet does not match any of the items in the ACL, the packet is discarded. The reason is that every IP ACL has a *deny all* statement implied at the end of the ACL. It does not exist in the configuration, but if a router keeps searching the list, and no match is made by the end of the list, IOS considers the packet to have matched an entry that has a **deny** action.

Matching Logic and Command Syntax

Standard numbered IP ACLs use the following global command:

```
access-list {1-99 | 1300-1999} {permit | deny} matching-parameters
```

Each standard numbered ACL has one or more **access-list** commands with the same number, any number from the ranges shown in the preceding line of syntax. (One number is no better than the other.)

Besides the ACL number, each **access-list** command also lists the action (**permit** or **deny**), plus the matching logic. The rest of this section examines how to configure the matching parameters, which for standard ACLs, means that you can only match the source IP address, or portions of the source IP address using something called an ACL wildcard mask.

Matching the Exact IP Address

To match a specific source IP address, the entire IP address, all you have to do is type that IP address at the end of the command. For example, the previous example uses pseudocode for "permit if source = 10.1.1.1." The following command configures that logic with correct syntax using ACL number 1:

```
access-list 1 permit 10.1.1.1
```

Matching the exact full IP address is that simple.

In earlier IOS versions, the syntax included a **host** keyword. Instead of simply typing the full IP address, you first typed the **host** keyword, and then the IP address. Note that in later

25

IOS versions, if you use the **host** keyword, IOS accepts the command, but then removes the keyword.

```
access-list 1 permit host 10.1.1.1
```

Matching a Subset of the Address with Wildcards

Often, the business goals you want to implement with an ACL do not match a single particular IP address, but rather a range of IP addresses. Maybe you want to match all IP addresses in a subnet. Maybe you want to match all IP addresses in a range of subnets. Regardless, you want to check for more than one IP address in a range of addresses.

IOS allows standard ACLs to match a range of addresses using a tool called a *wildcard mask*. Note that this is not a subnet mask. The wildcard mask (which this book abbreviates as *WC mask*) gives the engineer a way to tell IOS to ignore parts of the address when making comparisons, essentially treating those parts as wildcards, as if they already matched.

You can think about WC masks in decimal and in binary, and both have their uses. To begin, think about WC masks in decimal, using these rules:

Decimal 0: The router must compare this octet as normal.

Decimal 255: The router ignores this octet, considering it to already match.

Keeping these two rules in mind, consider Figure 25-6, which demonstrates this logic using three different but popular WC masks: one that tells the router to ignore the last octet, one that tells the router to ignore the last two octets, and one that tells the router to ignore the last three octets.

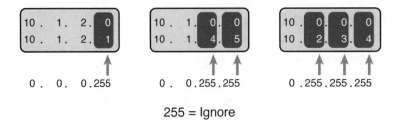

Figure 25-6   *Logic for WC Masks 0.0.0.255, 0.0.255.255, and 0.255.255.255*

All three examples in the boxes of Figure 25-6 show two numbers that are clearly different. The WC mask causes IOS to compare only some of the octets, while ignoring other octets. All three examples result in a match, because each wildcard mask tells IOS to ignore some octets. The example on the left shows WC mask 0.0.0.255, which tells the router to treat the last octet as a wildcard, essentially ignoring that octet for the comparison. Similarly, the middle example shows WC mask 0.0.255.255, which tells the router to ignore the two octets on the right. The rightmost case shows WC mask 0.255.255.255, telling the router to ignore the last three octets when comparing values.

To see the WC mask in action, think back to the earlier example related to Figure 25-4 and Figure 25-5. The pseudocode ACL in those two figures used logic that can be created using a WC mask. As a reminder, the logic in the pseudocode ACL in those two figures included the following:

Line 1: Match and permit all packets with a source address of exactly 10.1.1.1.

Line 2: Match and deny all packets with source addresses with first three octets 10.1.1.

Line 3: Match and permit all addresses with first single octet 10.

Figure 25-7 shows the updated version of Figure 25-4, but with the completed, correct syntax, including the WC masks. In particular, note the use of WC mask 0.0.0.255 in the second command, telling R2 to ignore the last octet of the number 10.1.1.0, and the WC mask 0.255.255.255 in the third command, telling R2 to ignore the last three octets in the value 10.0.0.0.

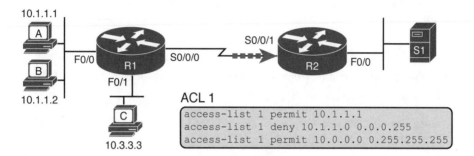

Figure 25-7 *Syntactically Correct ACL Replaces Pseudocode from Figure 25-4*

Finally, note that when using a WC mask, the **access-list** command's loosely defined *source* parameter should be a 0 in any octets where the WC mask is a 255. IOS will specify a source address to be 0 for the parts that will be ignored, even if nonzero values were configured.

Binary Wildcard Masks

Wildcard masks, as dotted-decimal number (DDN) values, actually represent a 32-bit binary number. As a 32-bit number, the WC mask actually directs the router's logic bit by bit. In short, a WC mask bit of 0 means the comparison should be done as normal, but a binary 1 means that the bit is a wildcard, and can be ignored when comparing the numbers.

Thankfully, for the purposes of CCENT and CCNA R&S study, and for most real-world applications, you can ignore the binary WC mask. Why? Well, we generally want to match a range of addresses that can be easily identified by a subnet number and mask, whether it be a real subnet, or a summary route that groups subnets together. (See DVD Appendix O, "Route Summarization," for more on summary routes.) If you can describe the range of addresses with a subnet number and mask, you can find the numbers to use in your ACL with some simple decimal math, as discussed next.

NOTE If you really want to know the binary mask logic, take the two DDN numbers the ACL will compare (one from the **access-list** command, and the other from the packet header) and convert both to binary. Then, also convert the WC mask to binary. Compare the first two binary numbers bit by bit, but also ignore any bits for which the WC mask happens to list a binary 1, because that tells you to ignore the bit. If all the bits you checked are equal, it's a match!

25

Finding the Right Wildcard Mask to Match a Subnet

In many cases, an ACL needs to match all hosts in a particular subnet. To match a subnet with an ACL, you can use the following shortcut:

- Use the subnet number as the source value in the **access-list** command.
- Use a wildcard mask found by subtracting the subnet mask from 255.255.255.255.

For example, for subnet 172.16.8.0 255.255.252.0, use the subnet number (172.16.8.0) as the address parameter, and then do the following math to find the wildcard mask:

$$
\begin{array}{r}
255.255.255.255 \\
-255.255.252.0 \\
\hline
0.\quad 0.\quad 3.255
\end{array}
$$

Continuing this example, a completed command for this same subnet would be as follows:

```
access-list 1 permit 172.16.8.0 0.0.3.255
```

The upcoming section, "Practice Applying Standard IP ACLs," gives you a chance to practice matching subnets when configuring ACLs.

Matching Any/All Addresses

In some cases, you will want one ACL command to match any and all packets that reach that point in the ACL. First, you have to know the (simple) way to match all packets using the **any** keyword. More importantly, you need to think about when to match any and all packets.

First, to match any and all packets with an ACL command, just use the **any** keyword for the address. For example, to permit all packets:

```
access-list 1 permit any
```

So, when and where should you use such a command? Remember, all Cisco IP ACLs end with an implicit deny any concept at the end of each ACL. That is, if a router compares a packet to the ACL, and the packet matches none of the configured statements, the router discards the packet. Want to override that default behavior? Configure a **permit any** at the end of the ACL.

You might also want to explicitly configure a command to deny all traffic (for example, **access-list 1 deny any**) at the end of an ACL. Why, when the same logic already sits at the end of the ACL anyway? Well, the ACL **show** commands list counters for the number of packets matched by each command in the ACL, but there is no counter for that implicit deny any concept at the end of the ACL. So, if you want to see counters for how many packets are matched by the deny any logic at the end of the ACL, configure an explicit **deny any**.

Implementing Standard IP ACLs

This chapter has already introduced all the configuration steps in bits and pieces. This section summarizes those pieces as a configuration process. The process also refers to the **access-list** command, whose generic syntax is repeated here for reference:

```
access-list access-list-number {deny | permit} source [source-wildcard]
```

Step 1. Plan the location (router and interface) and direction (in or out) on that interface:

A. Standard ACLs should be placed near to the destination of the packets so that they do not unintentionally discard packets that should not be discarded.

B. Because standard ACLs can only match a packet's source IP address, identify the source IP addresses of packets as they go in the direction that the ACL is examining.

Step 2. Configure one or more **access-list** global configuration commands to create the ACL, keeping the following in mind:

A. The list is searched sequentially, using first-match logic.

B. The default action, if a packet does not match any of the **access-list** commands, is to **deny** (discard) the packet.

Step 3. Enable the ACL on the chosen router interface, in the correct direction, using the **ip access-group** *number* {**in** | **out**} interface subcommand.

The rest of this section shows a couple of examples.

Standard Numbered ACL Example 1

The first example shows the configuration for the same requirements demonstrated with Figure 25-4 and Figure 25-5. Restated, the requirements for this ACL are as follows:

1. Enable the ACL inbound on R2's S0/0/1 interface.

2. Permit packets coming from host A.

3. Deny packets coming from other hosts in host A's subnet.

4. Permit packets coming from any other address in Class A network 10.0.0.0.

5. The original example made no comment about what to do by default, so simply deny all other traffic.

Example 25-1 shows a completed correct configuration, starting with the configuration process, followed by output from the **show running-config** command.

Example 25-1 *Standard Numbered ACL Example 1 Configuration*

```
R2# configure terminal
Enter configuration commands, one per line.  End with CNTL/Z.
R2(config)# access-list 1 permit 10.1.1.1
R2(config)# access-list 1 deny 10.1.1.0 0.0.0.255
R2(config)# access-list 1 permit 10.0.0.0 0.255.255.255
R2(config)# interface S0/0/1
R2(config-if)# ip access-group 1 in
R2(config-if)# ^Z
R2# show running-config
! Lines omitted for brevity

access-list 1 permit 10.1.1.1
access-list 1 deny 10.1.1.0 0.0.0.255
access-list 1 permit 10.0.0.0 0.255.255.255
```

25

First, pay close attention to the configuration process at the top of the example. Note that the **access-list** command does not change the command prompt from the global configuration mode prompt, because the **access-list** command is a global configuration command. Then, compare that to the output of the **show running-config** command: the details are identical compared to the commands that were added in configuration mode. Finally, make sure to note the **ip access-group 1 in** command, under R2's S0/0/1 interface, which enables the ACL logic (both location and direction).

Example 25-2 lists some output from Router R2 that shows information about this ACL. The **show ip access-lists** command lists details about IPv4 ACLs only, while the **show access-lists** command lists details about IPv4 ACLs plus any other types of ACLs that are currently configured, for example, IPv6 ACLs.

Example 25-2   *ACL* **show** *Commands on R2*

```
R2# show ip access-lists
Standard IP access list 1
     10 permit 10.1.1.1 (107 matches)
     20 deny   10.1.1.0, wildcard bits 0.0.0.255 (4 matches)
     30 permit 10.0.0.0, wildcard bits 0.255.255.255 (10 matches)
R2# show access-lists
Standard IP access list 1
     10 permit 10.1.1.1 (107 matches)
     20 deny   10.1.1.0, wildcard bits 0.0.0.255 (4 matches)
     30 permit 10.0.0.0, wildcard bits 0.255.255.255 (10 matches)
R2# show ip interface s0/0/1
Serial0/0/1 is up, line protocol is up
  Internet address is 10.1.2.2/24
  Broadcast address is 255.255.255.255
  Address determined by setup command
  MTU is 1500 bytes
  Helper address is not set
  Directed broadcast forwarding is disabled
  Multicast reserved groups joined: 224.0.0.9
  Outgoing access list is not set
  Inbound  access list is 1
! Lines omitted for brevity
```

The output of these commands shows two items of note. The first line of output in this case notes the type (standard), and the number. If more than one ACL existed, you would see multiple stanzas of output, one per ACL, each with a heading line like this one. Next, these commands list packet counts for the number of packets that the router has matched with each command. For example, 107 packets so far have matched the first line in the ACL.

Finally, the end of the example lists the **show ip interface** command output. This command lists, among many other items, the number or name of any IP ACL enabled on the interface per the **ip access-group** interface subcommand.

Standard Numbered ACL Example 2

For the second example, use Figure 25-8, and imagine your boss gave you some requirements hurriedly in the hall. At first, he tells you he wants to filter packets going from the servers on the right toward the clients on the left. Then, he says he wants you to allow access for hosts A, B, and other hosts in their same subnet to server S1, but deny access to that server to the hosts in host C's subnet. Then, he tells you that, additionally, hosts in host A's subnet should be denied access to server S2, but hosts in host C's subnet should be allowed access to server S2. All by filtering packets going right to left only, and then he tells you: put the ACL inbound on R2's F0/0 interface.

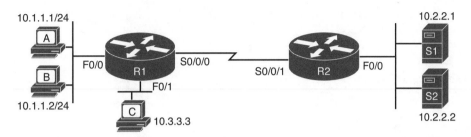

Figure 25-8   *Standard Numbered ACL Example 2*

If you cull through all the boss's comments, the requirements might reduce to the following:

1. Enable the ACL inbound on R2's F0/0 interface.

2. Permit packets from server S1 going to hosts in A's subnet.

3. Deny packets from server S1 going to hosts in C's subnet.

4. Permit packets from server S2 going to hosts in C's subnet.

5. Deny packets from server S2 going to hosts in A's subnet.

6. (There was no comment about what to do by default; use the implied **deny all** default.)

As it turns out, you cannot do everything your boss asked with a standard ACL. For example, consider the obvious command for requirement number 2: **access-list 2 permit 10.2.2.1**. That permits all traffic whose source IP is 10.2.2.1 (server S1). The very next requirement asks you to filter (deny) packets sourced from that same IP address! Even if you added another command that checked for source IP address 10.2.2.1, the router would never get to it, because routers use first-match logic when searching the ACL. You cannot check both the destination and source IP address, because standard ACLs cannot check the destination IP address.

To solve this problem, you should get a new boss! No, seriously, you have to rethink the problem and change the rules. In real life, you would probably use an extended ACL instead, which lets you check both the source and destination IP address.

For the sake of practicing another standard ACL, imagine your boss lets you change the requirements. First, you will use two outbound ACLs, both on Router R1. Each ACL will permit traffic from a single server to be forwarded onto that connected LAN, with the following modified requirements:

1. Using an outbound ACL on R1's F0/0 interface, permit packets from server S1, and deny all other packets.

2. Using an outbound ACL on R1's F0/1 interface, permit packets from server S2, and deny all other packets.

25

Example 25-3 shows the configuration that completes these requirements.

Example 25-3   *Alternative Configuration in Router R1*

```
access-list 2 remark This ACL permits server S1 traffic to host A's subnet
access-list 2 permit 10.2.2.1
!
access-list 3 remark This ACL permits server S2 traffic to host C's subnet
access-list 3 permit 10.2.2.2
!
interface F0/0
 ip access-group 2 out
!
interface F0/1
 ip access-group 3 out
```

As highlighted in the example, the solution with ACL number 2 permits all traffic from server S1, with that logic enabled for packets exiting R1's F0/0 interface. All other traffic will be discarded because of the implied deny all at the end of the ACL. In addition, ACL 3 permits traffic from server S2, which is then permitted to exit R1's F0/1 interface. Also, note that the solution shows the use of the **access-list remark** parameter, which allows you to leave text documentation that stays with the ACL.

NOTE When routers apply an ACL to filter packets in the outbound direction, as shown in Example 25-3, the router checks packets that it routes against the ACL. However, a router does not filter packets that the router itself creates with an outbound ACL. Examples of those packets include routing protocol messages, and packets sent by the **ping** and **traceroute** commands on that router.

Troubleshooting and Verification Tips

Troubleshooting IPv4 ACLs requires some attention to detail. In particular, you have to be ready to look at the address and wildcard mask and confidently predict the addresses matched by those two combined parameters. The upcoming practice problems a little later in this chapter can help prepare you for that part of the work. But a few other tips can help you verify and troubleshoot ACL problems on the exams as well.

First, you can tell if the router is matching packets or not with a couple of tools. Example 25-2 already showed that IOS keeps statistics about the packets matched by each line of an ACL. In addition, if you add the **log** keyword to the end of an **access-list** command, IOS then issues log messages with occasional statistics about matches of that particular line of the ACL. Both the statistics and the log messages can be helpful in deciding which line in the ACL is being matched by a packet.

For example, Example 25-4 shows an updated version of ACL 2 from Example 25-3, this time with the **log** keyword added. The bottom of the example then shows a typical log message, this one showing the resulting match based on a packet with source IP address 10.2.2.1 (as matched with the ACL), to destination address 10.1.1.1.

Example 25-4   *Creating Log Messages for ACL Statistics*

```
R1# show running-config
! lines removed for brevity
access-list 2 remark This ACL permits server S1 traffic to host A's subnet
access-list 2 permit 10.2.2.1 log
!
interface F0/0
 ip access-group 2 out

R1#
Feb  4 18:30:24.082: %SEC-6-IPACCESSLOGNP: list 2 permitted 0 10.2.2.1 -> 10.1.1.1, 1
  packet
```

Anytime you troubleshoot an ACL for the first time, before getting into the details of the matching logic, take the time to think about both the interface on which the ACL is enabled, and the direction of packet flow. Sometimes, the matching logic is perfect—but the ACL has been enabled on the wrong interface, or for the wrong direction, to match the packets as configured for the ACL.

For example, Figure 25-9 repeats the same ACL shown earlier in Figure 25-7. The first line of that ACL matches the specific host address 10.1.1.1. If that ACL exists on Router R2, placing that ACL as an inbound ACL on R2's S0/0/1 interface can work, because packets sent by host 10.1.1.1—on the left side of the figure—can enter R2's S0/0/1 interface. However, if R2 enables ACL 1 on its F0/0 interface, for inbound packets, the ACL will never match a packet with source IP address 10.1.1.1, because packets sent by host 10.1.1.1 will never enter that interface. Packets sent by 10.1.1.1 will exit R2's F0/0 interface, but never enter it, just because of the network topology.

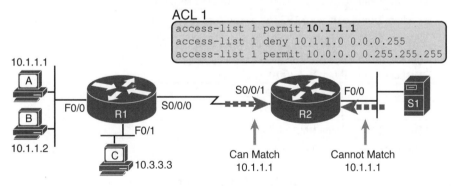

Figure 25-9   *Example of Checking the Interface and Direction for an ACL*

25

Practice Applying Standard IP ACLs

Some CCENT and CCNA R&S topics, like ACLs, simply require more drills and practice than others. ACLs require you to think of parameters to match ranges of numbers, and that of course requires some use of math, and some use of processes.

This section provides some practice problems and tips, from two perspectives. First, this section asks you to build one-line standard ACLs to match some packets. Second, this section asks you to interpret existing ACL commands to describe what packets the ACL will match. Both skills are useful for the exams.

Practice Building access-list Commands

In this section, practice getting comfortable with the syntax of the **access-list** command, particularly with choosing the correct matching logic. These skills will be helpful when reading about extended and named ACLs in the next chapter.

First, the following list summarizes some important tips to consider when choosing matching parameters to any **access-list** command:

- To match a specific address, just list the address.
- To match any and all addresses, use the **any** keyword.
- To match based only on the first one, two, or three octets of an address, use the 0.255.255.255, 0.0.255.255, and 0.0.0.255 WC masks, respectively. Also, make the source (address) parameter have 0s in the wildcard octets (those octets with 255 in the wildcard mask).
- To match a subnet, use the subnet ID as the source, and find the WC mask by subtracting the DDN subnet mask from 255.255.255.255.

Table 25-2 lists the criteria for several practice problems. Your job: Create a one-line standard ACL that matches the packets. The answers are listed in the section, "Answers to Earlier Practice Problems," later in this chapter.

Table 25-2 Building One-Line Standard ACLs: Practice

Problem	Criteria
1	Packets from 172.16.5.4
2	Packets from hosts with 192.168.6 as the first three octets
3	Packets from hosts with 192.168 as the first two octets
4	Packets from any host
5	Packets from subnet 10.1.200.0/21
6	Packets from subnet 10.1.200.0/27
7	Packets from subnet 172.20.112.0/23
8	Packets from subnet 172.20.112.0/26
9	Packets from subnet 192.168.9.64/28
10	Packets from subnet 192.168.9.64/30

Reverse Engineering from ACL to Address Range

In some cases, you may not be creating your own ACL. Instead, you may need to interpret some existing **access-list** commands. To answer these types of questions on the exams, you need to determine the range of IP addresses matched by a particular address/wildcard mask combination in each ACL statement.

Under certain assumptions that are reasonable for CCENT and CCNA R&S certifications, calculating the range of addresses matched by an ACL can be relatively simple. Basically, the range of addresses begins with the address configured in the ACL command. The range of addresses ends with the sum of the address field and the wildcard mask. That's it.

For example, with the command **access-list 1 permit 172.16.200.0 0.0.7.255**, the low end of the range is simply 172.16.200.0, taken directly from the command itself. Then, to find the high end of the range, just add this number to the WC mask, as follows:

$$\begin{array}{r} 172.16.200.0 \\ + \ 0. \ \ 0. \ \ \ \ 7.255 \\ \hline 172.16.207.255 \end{array}$$

For this last bit of practice, look at the existing **access-list** commands in Table 25-3. In each case, make a notation about the exact IP address, or range of IP addresses, matched by the command.

Table 25-3   Finding IP Addresses/Ranges Matching by Existing ACLs

Problem	Commands for Which to Predict the Source Address Range
1	access-list 1 permit 10.7.6.5
2	access-list 2 permit 192.168.4.0 0.0.0.127
3	access-list 3 permit 192.168.6.0 0.0.0.31
4	access-list 4 permit 172.30.96.0 0.0.3.255
5	access-list 5 permit 172.30.96.0 0.0.0.63
6	access-list 6 permit 10.1.192.0 0.0.0.31
7	access-list 7 permit 10.1.192.0 0.0.1.255
8	access-list 8 permit 10.1.192.0 0.0.63.255

Interestingly, IOS lets the CLI user type an **access-list** command in configuration mode, and IOS will potentially change the address parameter before placing the command into the running-config file. This process of just finding the range of addresses matched by the **access-list** command expects that the **access-list** command came from the router, so that any such changes were complete.

The change IOS can make with an **access-list** command is to convert to 0 any octet of an address for which the wildcard mask's octet is 255. For example, with a wildcard mask of 0.0.255.255, IOS ignores the last two octets. IOS expects the address field to end with two 0s. If not, IOS still accepts the **access-list** command, but IOS changes the last two octets of the address to 0s. Example 25-5 shows an example, where the configuration shows address 10.1.1.1, but wildcard mask 0.0.255.255.

Example 25-5   *IOS Changing the Address Field in an* access-list *Command*

```
R2# configure terminal
Enter configuration commands, one per line.  End with CNTL/Z.
R2(config)# access-list 21 permit 10.1.1.1 0.0.255.255
R2(config)# ^Z
R2#
R2# show ip access-lists
Standard IP access list 21
    10 permit 10.1.0.0, wildcard bits 0.0.255.255
```

25

The math to find the range of addresses relies on the fact that either the command is fully correct, or that IOS has already set these address octets to 0, as shown in the example.

> **NOTE** The most useful WC masks, in binary, do not interleave 0s and 1s. This book assumes the use of only these types of WC masks. However, Cisco IOS allows WC masks that interleave 0s and 1s, but using these WC masks break the simple method of calculating the range of addresses. As you progress through to CCIE studies, be ready to dig deeper to learn how to determine what an ACL matches.

Chapter Review

One key to doing well on the exams is to perform repetitive spaced review sessions. Review this chapter's material using either the tools in the book, DVD, or interactive tools for the same material found on the book's companion website. Refer to the "Your Study Plan" element for more details. Table 25-4 outlines the key review elements and where you can find them. To better track your study progress, record when you completed these activities in the second column.

Table 25-4 Chapter Review Tracking

Review Element	Review Date(s)	Resource Used
Review key topics		Book, DVD/website
Review key terms		Book, DVD/website
Repeat DIKTA questions		Book, PCPT
Review command tables		Book

Review All the Key Topics

Table 25-5 Key Topics for Chapter 25

Key Topic Element	Description	Page Number
Paragraph	Summary of the general rule of the location and direction for an ACL	595
Figure 25-3	Summary of four main categories of IPv4 ACLs in Cisco IOS	597
Paragraph	Summary of first-match logic used by all ACLs	598
List	Wildcard mask logic for decimal 0 and 255	600
List	Wildcard mask logic to match a subnet	602
List	Steps to plan and implement a standard IP ACL	603
List	Tips for creating matching logic for the source address field in the **access-list** command	608

Key Terms You Should Know

standard access list, wildcard mask

Additional Practice for This Chapter's Processes

For additional practice with analyzing subnets, you may do the same set of practice problems using your choice of tools:

Application: Use the Basic IPv4 Access Control Lists application on the DVD or companion website.

PDF: Alternatively, practice the same problems found in these apps using DVD Appendix I, "Practice for Chapter 25: Basic IPv4 Access Control Lists."

Command References

Tables 25-6 and 25-7 list configuration and verification commands used in this chapter. As an easy review exercise, cover the left column in a table, read the right column, and try to recall the command without looking. Then repeat the exercise, covering the right column, and try to recall what the command does.

Table 25-6   Chapter 25 Configuration Command Reference

Command	Description
access-list *access-list-number* {deny | permit} *source* [*source-wildcard*] [log]	Global command for standard numbered access lists. Use a number between 1 and 99 or 1300 and 1999, inclusive
access-list *access-list-number* remark *text*	Defines a remark that helps you remember what the ACL is supposed to do
ip access-group *number* {in | out}	Interface subcommand to enable access lists

Table 25-7   Chapter 25 EXEC Command Reference

Command	Description
show ip interface [*type number*]	Includes a reference to the access lists enabled on the interface
show access-lists [*access-list-number* | *access-list-name*]	Shows details of configured access lists for all protocols
show ip access-lists [*access-list-number* | *access-list-name*]	Shows IP access lists

25

Answers to Earlier Practice Problems

Table 25-8 lists the answers to the problems listed earlier in Table 25-2.

Table 25-8   Building One-Line Standard ACLs: Answers

Problem	Answers
1	access-list 1 permit 172.16.5.4
2	access-list 2 permit 192.168.6.0 0.0.0.255
3	access-list 3 permit 192.168.0.0 0.0.255.255
4	access-list 4 permit any
5	access-list 5 permit 10.1.200.0 0.0.7.255
6	access-list 6 permit 10.1.200.0 0.0.0.31
7	access-list 7 permit 172.20.112.0 0.0.1.255
8	access-list 8 permit 172.20.112.0 0.0.0.63
9	access-list 9 permit 192.168.9.64 0.0.0.15
10	access-list 10 permit 192.168.9.64 0.0.0.3

Table 25-9 lists the answers to the problems listed earlier in Table 25-3.

Table 25-9   Address Ranges for Problems in Table 25-3: Answers

Problem	Address Range
1	One address: 10.7.6.5
2	192.168.4.0 – 192.168.4.127
3	192.168.6.0 – 192.168.6.31
4	172.30.96.0 – 172.30.99.255
5	172.30.96.0 – 172.30.96.63
6	10.1.192.0 – 10.1.192.31
7	10.1.192.0 – 10.1.193.255
8	10.1.192.0 – 10.1.255.255

CHAPTER 26

Advanced IPv4 Access Control Lists

This chapter covers the following exam topics:

4.0 Infrastructure Services

4.6 Configure, verify, and troubleshoot IPv4 standard numbered and named access list for routed interfaces

Cisco routers use IPv4 access control lists (ACL) for many different applications: to match packets to make filtering decisions, to match packets for Network Address Translation (NAT), to match packets to make quality of service (QoS) decisions, and for several other reasons.

IPv4 ACLs are either standard or extended ACLs, with standard ACLs matching only the source IP address, and extended matching a variety of packet header fields. At the same time, IP ACLs are either numbered or named. Figure 26-1 shows the categories, and the main features of each, as introduced in the previous chapter.

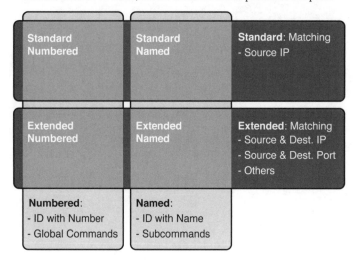

Figure 26-1 *Comparisons of IP ACL Types*

This chapter discusses the other three categories of ACLs beyond standard numbered IP ACLs, and ends with a few miscellaneous features to secure Cisco routers and switches.

"Do I Know This Already?" Quiz

Take the quiz (either here, or use the PCPT software) if you want to use the score to help you decide how much time to spend on this chapter. The answers are at the bottom of the page following the quiz, and the explanations are in DVD Appendix C and in the PCPT software.

Table 26-1 "Do I Know This Already?" Foundation Topics Section-to-Question Mapping

Foundation Topics Section	Questions
Extended IP Access Control Lists	1–3
Named ACLs and ACL Editing	4
Troubleshooting with IPv4 ACLs	5–6

1. Which of the following fields cannot be compared based on an extended IP ACL? (Choose two answers.)

    a. Protocol

    b. Source IP address

    c. Destination IP address

    d. TOS byte

    e. URL

    f. Filename for FTP transfers

2. Which of the following **access-list** commands permit packets going from host 10.1.1.1 to all web servers whose IP addresses begin with 172.16.5? (Choose two answers.)

    a. access-list 101 permit tcp host 10.1.1.1 172.16.5.0 0.0.0.255 eq www

    b. access-list 1951 permit ip host 10.1.1.1 172.16.5.0 0.0.0.255 eq www

    c. access-list 2523 permit ip host 10.1.1.1 eq www 172.16.5.0 0.0.0.255

    d. access-list 2523 permit tcp host 10.1.1.1 eq www 172.16.5.0 0.0.0.255

    e. access-list 2523 permit tcp host 10.1.1.1 172.16.5.0 0.0.0.255 eq www

3. Which of the following **access-list** commands permits packets going to any web client from all web servers whose IP addresses begin with 172.16.5?

    a. access-list 101 permit tcp host 10.1.1.1 172.16.5.0 0.0.0.255 eq www

    b. access-list 1951 permit ip host 10.1.1.1 172.16.5.0 0.0.0.255 eq www

    c. access-list 2523 permit tcp any eq www 172.16.5.0 0.0.0.255

    d. access-list 2523 permit tcp 172.16.5.0 0.0.0.255 eq www 172.16.5.0 0.0.0.255

    e. access-list 2523 permit tcp 172.16.5.0 0.0.0.255 eq www any

4. In a router running a recent IOS version (at least version 15.0), an engineer needs to delete the second line in ACL 101, which currently has four commands configured. Which of the following options could be used? (Choose two answers.)

   a. Delete the entire ACL and reconfigure the three ACL statements that should remain in the ACL.

   b. Delete one line from the ACL using the **no access-list...** global command.

   c. Delete one line from the ACL by entering ACL configuration mode for the ACL and then deleting only the second line based on its sequence number.

   d. Delete the last three lines from the ACL from global configuration mode, and then add the last two statements back into the ACL.

5. An engineer is considering configuring an ACL on Router R1. The engineer could use ACL A which would be enabled with the **ip access-group A out** command on interface G0/1, or ACL B, which would be enabled with the **ip access-group B in** command on that same interface. R1's G0/1 interface uses IPv4 address 1.1.1.1. Which of the answers is true when comparing these options? (Choose two answers.)

   a. ACL A creates more risk of filtering important overhead traffic than ACL B.

   b. ACL B creates more risk of filtering important overhead traffic than ACL A.

   c. A **ping 1.1.1.1** command on R1 would bypass ACL A even if enabled.

   d. A **ping 1.1.1.1** command on R1 would bypass ACL B even if enabled.

6. An engineer configures an ACL but forgets to save the configuration. At that point, which of the following commands displays the configuration of an IPv4 ACL, including line numbers? (Choose two answers.)

   a. **show running-config**

   b. **show startup-config**

   c. **show ip access-lists**

   d. **show access-lists**

Foundation Topics

Extended Numbered IP Access Control Lists

Extended IP access lists have many similarities compared to the standard numbered IP ACLs discussed in the previous chapter. Just like standard IP ACLs, you enable extended access lists on interfaces for packets either entering or exiting the interface. IOS searches the list sequentially. Extended ACLs also use first-match logic, because the router stops the search through the list as soon as the first statement is matched, taking the action defined in the first-matched statement. All these features are also true of standard numbered access lists (and named ACLs).

Extended ACLs differ from standard ACLs mostly because of the larger variety of packet header fields that can be used to match a packet. One extended ACL statement can examine multiple parts of the packet headers, requiring that all the parameters be matched correctly to match that one ACL statement. That powerful matching logic makes extended access lists both more useful and more complex than standard IP ACLs.

Matching the Protocol, Source IP, and Destination IP

Like standard numbered IP ACLs, extended numbered IP ACLs also use the **access-list** global command. The syntax is identical, at least up through the **permit** or **deny** keyword. At that point, the command lists matching parameters, and those differ, of course. In particular, the extended ACL **access-list** command requires three matching parameters: the IP protocol type, the source IP address, and the destination IP address.

The IP header's Protocol field identifies the header that follows the IP header. Figure 26-2 shows the location of the IP Protocol field, the concept of it pointing to the type of header that follows, along with some details of the IP header for reference.

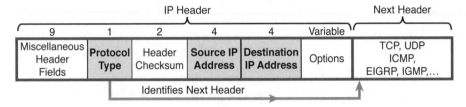

Figure 26-2 *IP Header, with Focus on Required Fields in Extended IP ACLs*

IOS requires that you configure parameters for the three highlighted parts of Figure 26-2. For the protocol type, you simply use a keyword, such as **tcp**, **udp**, or **icmp**, matching IP packets that happen to have a TCP, UDP, or ICMP header, respectively, following the IP header. Or you can use the keyword **ip**, which means "all IPv4 packets." You also must configure some values for the source and destination IP address fields that follow; these fields use the same syntax and options for matching the IP addresses as discussed in Chapter 25, "Basic IPv4 Access Control Lists." Figure 26-3 shows the syntax.

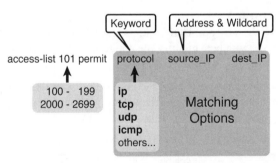

Figure 26-3 *Extended ACL Syntax, with Required Fields*

> **NOTE** When matching IP addresses in the source and destination fields, there is one difference with standard ACLs: When matching a specific IP address, the extended ACL requires the use of the **host** keyword. You cannot simply list the IP address alone.

26

Table 26-2 lists several sample **access-list** commands that use only the required matching parameters. Feel free to cover the right side and use the table for an exercise, or just review the explanations to get an idea for the logic in some sample commands.

Table 26-2 Extended **access-list** Commands and Logic Explanations

access-list Statement	What It Matches
access-list 101 deny tcp any any	Any IP packet that has a TCP header
access-list 101 deny udp any any	Any IP packet that has a UDP header
access-list 101 deny icmp any any	Any IP packet that has an ICMP header
access-list 101 deny ip host 1.1.1.1 host 2.2.2.2	All IP packets from host 1.1.1.1 going to host 2.2.2.2, regardless of the header after the IP header
access-list 101 deny udp 1.1.1.0 0.0.0.255 any	All IP packets that have a UDP header following the IP header, from subnet 1.1.1.0/24, and going to any destination

The last entry in Table 26-2 helps make an important point about how IOS processes extended ACLs:

In an extended ACL **access-list** command, all the matching parameters must match the packet for the packet to match the command.

For example, in that last example from Table 26-2, the command checks for UDP, a source IP address from subnet 1.1.1.0/24, and any destination IP address. If a packet with source IP address 1.1.1.1 were examined, it would match the source IP address check, but if it had a TCP header instead of UDP, it would not match this **access-list** command. All parameters must match.

Matching TCP and UDP Port Numbers

Extended ACLs can also examine parts of the TCP and UDP headers, particularly the source and destination port number fields. The port numbers identify the application that sends or receives the data.

The most useful ports to check are the well-known ports used by servers. For example, web servers use well-known port 80 by default. Figure 26-4 shows the location of the port numbers in the TCP header, following the IP header.

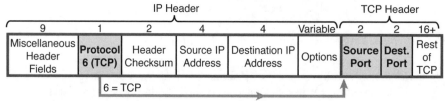

Figure 26-4 *IP Header, Followed by a TCP Header and Port Number Fields*

When an extended ACL command includes either the **tcp** or **udp** keyword, that command can optionally reference the source and/or destination port. To make these comparisons, the syntax uses keywords for equal, not equal, less than, greater than, and for a range of port numbers. In addition, the command can use either the literal decimal port numbers, or more convenient keywords for some well-known application ports. Figure 26-5 shows the positions of the source and destination port fields in the **access-list** command and these port number keywords.

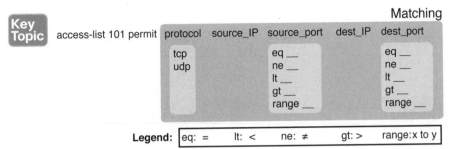

Figure 26-5 *Extended ACL Syntax with TCP and UDP Port Numbers Enabled*

For example, consider the simple network shown in Figure 26-6. The FTP server sits on the right, with the client on the left. The figure shows the syntax of an ACL that matches the following:

■ Packets that include a TCP header

■ Packets sent from the client subnet

■ Packets sent to the server subnet

■ Packets with TCP destination port 21 (FTP server control port)

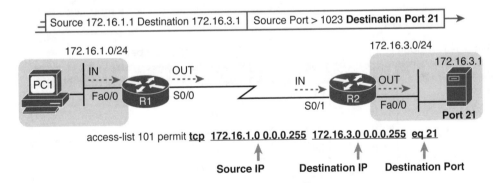

Figure 26-6 *Filtering Packets Based on Destination Port*

To fully appreciate the matching of the destination port with the **eq 21** parameters, consider packets moving from left to right, from PC1 to the server. Assuming the server uses well-known port 21 (FTP control port), the packet's TCP header has a destination port value of 21. The ACL syntax includes the **eq 21** parameters after the destination IP address. The position after the destination address parameters is important: That position identifies the fact that the **eq 21** parameters should be compared to the packet's destination port. As a result, the ACL statement shown in Figure 26-6 would match this packet, and the destination port of 21, if used in any of the four locations implied by the four dashed arrowed lines in the figure.

26

Conversely, Figure 26-7 shows the reverse flow, with a packet sent by the server back toward PC1. In this case, the packet's TCP header has a source port of 21, so the ACL must check the source port value of 21, and the ACL must be located on different interfaces. In this case, the **eq 21** parameters follow the source address field, but come before the destination address field.

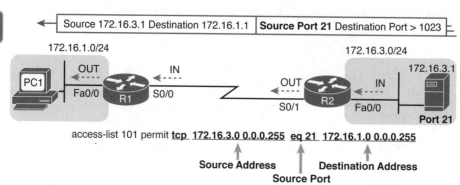

Figure 26-7   *Filtering Packets Based on Source Port*

When examining ACLs that match port numbers, first consider the location and direction in which the ACL will be applied. That direction determines whether the packet is being sent to the server, or from the server. At that point, you can decide whether you need to check the source or destination port in the packet. For reference, Table 26-3 lists many of the popular port numbers and their transport layer protocols and applications. Note that the syntax of the **access-list** commands accepts both the port numbers and a shorthand version of the application name.

Table 26-3   Popular Applications and Their Well-Known Port Numbers

Port Number(s)	Protocol	Application	access-list Command Keyword
20	TCP	FTP data	ftp-data
21	TCP	FTP control	ftp
22	TCP	SSH	—
23	TCP	Telnet	telnet
25	TCP	SMTP	smtp
53	UDP, TCP	DNS	domain
67	UDP	DHCP Server	bootps
68	UDP	DHCP Client	bootpc
69	UDP	TFTP	tftp
80	TCP	HTTP (WWW)	www
110	TCP	POP3	pop3
161	UDP	SNMP	snmp
443	TCP	SSL	—
514	UDP	Syslog	—
16,384 – 32,767	UDP	RTP (voice, video)	—

Table 26-4 lists several example **access-list** commands that match based on port numbers. Cover the right side of the table, and try to characterize the packets matched by each command. Then, check the right side of the table to see if you agree with the assessment.

Table 26-4   Extended **access-list** Command Examples and Logic Explanations

access-list Statement	What It Matches
access-list 101 deny tcp any gt 1023 host 10.1.1.1 eq 23	Packets with a TCP header, any source IP address, with a source port greater than (gt) 1023, a destination IP address of exactly 10.1.1.1, and a destination port equal to (eq) 23.
access-list 101 deny tcp any host 10.1.1.1 eq 23	The same as the preceding example, but any source port matches, because that parameter is omitted in this case.
access-list 101 deny tcp any host 10.1.1.1 eq telnet	The same as the preceding example. The **telnet** keyword is used instead of port 23.
access-list 101 deny udp 1.0.0.0 0.255.255.255 lt 1023 any	A packet with a source in network 1.0.0.0/8, using UDP with a source port less than (lt) 1023, with any destination IP address.

Extended IP ACL Configuration

Because extended ACLs can match so many different fields in the various headers in an IP packet, the command syntax cannot be easily summarized in a single generic command. However, the two commands in Table 26-5 summarize the syntax options as covered in this book.

Table 26-5   Extended IP Access List Configuration Commands

Command	Configuration Mode and Description
access-list *access-list-number* {**deny** | **permit**} *protocol source source-wildcard destination destination-wildcard* [**log** | **log-input**]	Global command for extended numbered **access lists**. Use a number between 100 and 199 or 2000 and 2699, inclusive
access-list *access-list-number* {**deny** | **permit**} {**tcp** | **udp**} *source source-wildcard* [*operator* [*port*]] *destination destination-wildcard* [*operator* [*port*]] [**established**] [**log**]	A version of the **access-list** command with parameters specific to TCP and/or UDP

The configuration process for extended ACLs mostly matches the same process used for standard ACLs. You must choose the location and direction in which to enable the ACL, particularly the direction, so that you can characterize whether certain addresses and ports will be either the source or destination. Configure the ACL using **access-list** commands, and when complete, then enable the ACL using the same **ip access-group** command used with standard ACLs. All these steps mirror what you do with standard ACLs; however, when configuring, keep the following differences in mind:

■ Place extended ACLs as close as possible to the source of the packets that will be filtered. Filtering close to the source of the packets saves some bandwidth.

26

- Remember that all fields in one **access-list** command must match a packet for the packet to be considered to match that **access-list** statement.

- Use numbers of 100–199 and 2000–2699 on the **access-list** commands; no one number is inherently better than another.

Extended IP Access Lists: Example 1

This example focuses on understanding basic syntax. In this case, the ACL denies Bob access to all FTP servers on R1's Ethernet, and it denies Larry access to server1's web server. Figure 26-8 shows the network topology; Example 26-1 shows the configuration on R1.

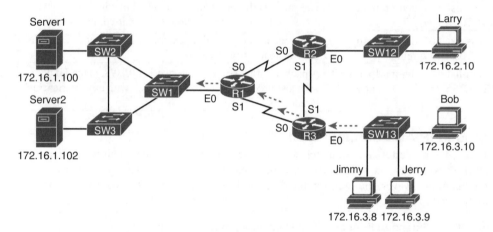

Figure 26-8 *Network Diagram for Extended Access List Example 1*

Example 26-1 *R1's Extended Access List: Example 1*

```
interface Serial0
 ip address 172.16.12.1 255.255.255.0
 ip access-group 101 in
!
interface Serial1
 ip address 172.16.13.1 255.255.255.0
 ip access-group 101 in
!
access-list 101 remark Stop Bob to FTP servers, and Larry to Server1 web
access-list 101 deny tcp host 172.16.3.10 172.16.1.0 0.0.0.255 eq ftp
access-list 101 deny tcp host 172.16.2.10 host 172.16.1.100 eq www
access-list 101 permit ip any any
```

The first ACL statement prevents Bob's access to FTP servers in subnet 172.16.1.0. The second statement prevents Larry's access to web services on Server1. The final statement permits all other traffic.

Focusing on the syntax for a moment, there are several new items to review. First, the access-list number for extended access lists falls in the range of 100 to 199 or 2000 to 2699. Following the **permit** or **deny** action, the *protocol* parameter defines whether you want to check for all IP packets or specific headers, such as TCP or UDP headers. When you check for TCP or UDP port numbers, you must specify the TCP or UDP protocol. Both FTP and web use TCP.

This example uses the **eq** parameter, meaning "equals," to check the destination port numbers for FTP control (keyword **ftp**) and HTTP traffic (keyword **www**). You can use the numeric values—or, for the more popular options, a more obvious text version is valid. (If you were to type **eq 80**, the config would show **eq www**.)

This example enables the ACL in two places on R1: inbound on each serial interface. These locations achieve the goal of the ACL. However, that initial placement was made to make the point that Cisco suggests that you locate them as close as possible to the source of the packet. Therefore, Example 26-2 achieves the same goal as Example 26-1 of stopping Bob's access to FTP servers at the main site, and it does so with an ACL on R3.

Example 26-2 *R3's Extended Access List Stopping Bob from Reaching FTP Servers Near R1*

```
interface Ethernet0
 ip address 172.16.3.1 255.255.255.0
 ip access-group 103 in

access-list 103 remark deny Bob to FTP servers in subnet 172.16.1.0/24
access-list 103 deny tcp host 172.16.3.10 172.16.1.0 0.0.0.255 eq ftp
access-list 103 permit ip any any
```

The new configuration on R3 meets the goals to filter Bob's traffic, while also meeting the overarching design goal of keeping the ACL close to the source of the packets. ACL 103 on R3 looks a lot like ACL 101 on R1 from Example 26-1, but this time, the ACL does not bother to check for the criteria to match Larry's traffic, because Larry's traffic will never enter R3's Ethernet 0 interface. ACL 103 filters Bob's FTP traffic to destinations in subnet 172.16.1.0/24, with all other traffic entering R3's E0 interface making it into the network.

Extended IP Access Lists: Example 2

Example 26-3, based on the network shown in Figure 26-9, shows another example of how to use extended IP access lists. This example uses the following criteria:

- Sam is not allowed access to the subnet of Bugs or Daffy.
- Hosts on the Seville Ethernet are not allowed access to hosts on the Yosemite Ethernet.
- All other combinations are allowed.

26

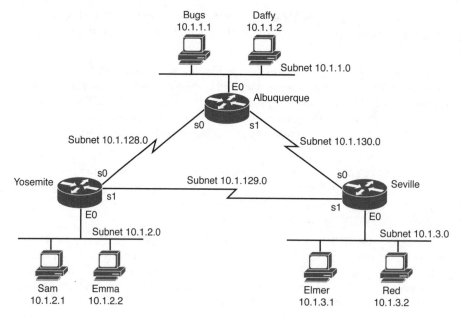

Figure 26-9   *Network Diagram for Extended Access List Example 2*

Example 26-3   *Yosemite Configuration for Extended Access List Example*

```
interface ethernet 0
 ip access-group 110 in
!
access-list 110 deny ip host 10.1.2.1 10.1.1.0 0.0.0.255
access-list 110 deny ip 10.1.2.0 0.0.0.255 10.1.3.0 0.0.0.255
access-list 110 permit ip any any
```

This configuration solves the problem with few statements while keeping to the Cisco design guideline of placing extended ACLs as close as possible to the source of the traffic. The ACL filters packets that enter Yosemite's E0 interface, which is the first router interface that packets sent by Sam enter. If the route between Yosemite and the other subnets changes over time, the ACL still applies. Also, the filtering mandated by the second requirement (to disallow Seville's LAN hosts from accessing Yosemite's) is met by the second **access-list** statement. Stopping packet flow from Yosemite's LAN subnet to Seville's LAN subnet stops effective communication between the two subnets. Alternatively, the opposite logic could have been configured at Seville.

Practice Building access-list Commands

Table 26-6 supplies a practice exercise to help you get comfortable with the syntax of the extended **access-list** command, particularly with choosing the correct matching logic. Your job: create a one-line extended ACL that matches the packets. The answers are in the section, "Answers to Earlier Practice Problems," later in this chapter. Note that if the criteria mentions a particular application protocol, for example, "web client," that means to specifically match for that application protocol.

Table 26-6 Building One-Line Extended ACLs: Practice

Problem	Criteria
1	From web client 10.1.1.1, sent to a web server in subnet 10.1.2.0/24.
2	From Telnet client 172.16.4.3/25, sent to a Telnet server in subnet 172.16.3.0/25. Match all hosts in the client's subnet as well.
3	ICMP messages from the subnet in which 192.168.7.200/26 resides to all hosts in the subnet where 192.168.7.14/29 resides.
4	From web server 10.2.3.4/23's subnet to clients in the same subnet as host 10.4.5.6/22.
5	From Telnet server 172.20.1.0/24's subnet, sent to any host in the same subnet as host 172.20.44.1/23.
6	From web client 192.168.99.99/28, sent to a web server in subnet 192.168.176.0/28. Match all hosts in the client's subnet as well.
7	ICMP messages from the subnet in which 10.55.66.77/25 resides to all hosts in the subnet where 10.66.55.44/26 resides.
8	Any and every IPv4 packet.

Named ACLs and ACL Editing

Now that you have a good understanding of the core concepts in IOS IP ACLs, this section examines a few enhancements to IOS support for ACLs: named ACLs and ACL editing with sequence numbers. Although both features are useful and important, neither adds any function as to what a router can and cannot filter. Instead, named ACLs and ACL sequence numbers make it easier to remember ACL names and edit existing ACLs when an ACL needs to change.

Named IP Access Lists

Named IP ACLs have many similarities with numbered IP ACLs. They can be used for filtering packets, plus for many other purposes. They can match the same fields as well: Standard numbered ACLs can match the same fields as a standard named ACL, and extended numbered ACLs can match the same fields as an extended named ACL.

Of course, there are differences between named and numbered ACLs. Named ACLs originally had three big differences compared to numbered ACLs:

- Using names instead of numbers to identify the ACL, making it easier to remember the reason for the ACL
- Using ACL subcommands, not global commands, to define the action and matching parameters
- Using ACL editing features that allow the CLI user to delete individual lines from the ACL and insert new lines

You can easily learn named ACL configuration by just converting numbered ACLs to use the equivalent named ACL configuration. Figure 26-10 shows just such a conversion, using a simple three-line standard ACL number 1. To create the three **permit** subcommands for the named ACL, you literally copy parts of the three numbered ACL commands, beginning with the **permit** keyword.

26

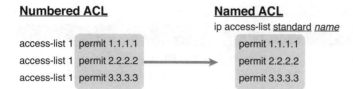

Numbered ACL

access-list 1 permit 1.1.1.1
access-list 1 permit 2.2.2.2
access-list 1 permit 3.3.3.3

Named ACL

ip access-list standard *name*

permit 1.1.1.1
permit 2.2.2.2
permit 3.3.3.3

Figure 26-10 *Named ACL Versus Numbered ACL Configuration*

The only truly new part of the named ACL configuration is the **ip access-list** global configuration command. This command defines whether an ACL is a standard or extended ACL, and defines the name. It also moves the user to ACL configuration mode, as shown in upcoming Example 26-4. Once in ACL configuration mode, you configure **permit**, **deny**, and **remark** commands that mirror the syntax of numbered ACL **access-list** commands. If you're configuring a standard named ACL, these commands match the syntax of standard numbered ACLs; if you're configuring extended named ACLs, they match the syntax of extended numbered ACLs.

Example 26-4 shows the configuration of a named extended ACL. Pay particular attention to the configuration mode prompts, which show ACL configuration mode.

Example 26-4 *Named Access List Configuration*

```
Router# configure terminal
Enter configuration commands, one per line.  End with Ctrl-Z.
Router(config)# ip access-list extended barney
Router(config-ext-nacl)# permit tcp host 10.1.1.2 eq www any
Router(config-ext-nacl)# deny udp host 10.1.1.1 10.1.2.0 0.0.0.255
Router(config-ext-nacl)# deny ip 10.1.3.0 0.0.0.255 10.1.2.0 0.0.0.255
Router(config-ext-nacl)# deny ip 10.1.2.0 0.0.0.255 10.2.3.0 0.0.0.255
Router(config-ext-nacl)# permit ip any any
Router(config-ext-nacl)# interface serial1
Router(config-if)# ip access-group barney out
Router(config-if)# ^Z
Router# show running-config
Building configuration...


Current configuration:


! lines omitted for brevity


interface serial 1
 ip access-group barney out
!
ip access-list extended barney
 permit tcp host 10.1.1.2 eq www any
 deny    udp host 10.1.1.1 10.1.2.0 0.0.0.255
 deny    ip 10.1.3.0 0.0.0.255 10.1.2.0 0.0.0.255
 deny    ip 10.1.2.0 0.0.0.255 10.2.3.0 0.0.0.255
 permit ip any any
```

Example 26-4 begins with the creation of an ACL named barney. The **ip access-list extended barney** command creates the ACL, naming it barney and placing the user in ACL configuration mode. This command also tells the IOS that barney is an extended ACL. Next, five different **permit** and **deny** statements define the matching logic and action to be taken upon a match. The **show running-config** command output lists the named ACL configuration before the single entry is deleted.

Named ACLs allow the user to delete and add new lines to the ACL from within ACL configuration mode. Example 26-5 shows how, with the **no deny ip . . .** command deleting a single entry from the ACL. Notice that the output of the **show access-list** command at the end of the example still lists the ACL, with four **permit** and **deny** commands instead of five.

Example 26-5 *Removing One Command from a Named ACL*

```
Router# configure terminal
Enter configuration commands, one per line.  End with Ctrl-Z.
Router(config)# ip access-list extended barney
Router(config-ext-nacl)# no deny ip 10.1.2.0 0.0.0.255 10.2.3.0 0.0.0.255
Router(config-ext-nacl)# ^Z
Router# show access-list

Extended IP access list barney
    10 permit tcp host 10.1.1.2 eq www any
    20 deny   udp host 10.1.1.1 10.1.2.0 0.0.0.255
    30 deny   ip 10.1.3.0 0.0.0.255 10.1.2.0 0.0.0.255
    50 permit ip any any
```

Editing ACLs Using Sequence Numbers

Numbered ACLs have existed in IOS since the early days of Cisco routers and IOS; however, for many years, through many IOS versions, the ability to edit a numbered IP ACL was poor. For example, to simply delete a line from the ACL, the user had to delete the entire ACL and then reconfigure it.

The ACL editing feature uses an ACL sequence number that is added to each ACL **permit** or **deny** statement, with the numbers representing the sequence of statements in the ACL. ACL sequence numbers provide the following features for both numbered and named ACLs:

New configuration style for numbered: Numbered ACLs use a configuration style like named ACLs, as well as the traditional style, for the same ACL; the new style is required to perform advanced ACL editing.

Deleting single lines: An individual ACL **permit** or **deny** statement can be deleted with a **no** *sequence-number* subcommand.

Inserting new lines: Newly added **permit** and **deny** commands can be configured with a sequence number before the **deny** or **permit** command, dictating the location of the statement within the ACL.

Automatic sequence numbering: IOS adds sequence numbers to commands as you configure them, even if you do not include the sequence numbers.

26

To take advantage of the ability to delete and insert lines in an ACL, both numbered and named ACLs must use the same overall configuration style and commands used for named ACLs. The only difference in syntax is whether a name or number is used. Example 26-6 shows the configuration of a standard numbered IP ACL, using this alternative configuration style. The example shows the power of the ACL sequence number for editing. In this example, the following occurs:

Step 1. Numbered ACL 24 is configured using this new-style configuration, with three **permit** commands.

Step 2. The **show ip access-lists** command shows the three permit commands with sequence numbers 10, 20, and 30.

Step 3. The engineer deletes only the second **permit** command using the **no 20** ACL subcommand, which simply refers to sequence number 20.

Step 4. The **show ip access-lists** command confirms that the ACL now has only two lines (sequence numbers 10 and 30).

Step 5. The engineer adds a new **deny** command to the beginning of the ACL, using the **5 deny 10.1.1.1** ACL subcommand.

Step 6. The **show ip access-lists** command again confirms the changes, this time listing three commands, sequence numbers 5, 10, and 30.

> **NOTE** For this example, note that the user does not leave configuration mode, instead using the **do** command to tell IOS to issue the **show ip access-lists** EXEC command from configuration mode.

Example 26-6 *Editing ACLs Using Sequence Numbers*

```
! Step 1: The 3-line Standard Numbered IP ACL is configured.
R1# configure terminal
Enter configuration commands, one per line.  End with Ctrl-Z.
R1(config)# ip access-list standard 24
R1(config-std-nacl)# permit 10.1.1.0 0.0.0.255
R1(config-std-nacl)# permit 10.1.2.0 0.0.0.255
R1(config-std-nacl)# permit 10.1.3.0 0.0.0.255


! Step 2: Displaying the ACL's contents, without leaving configuration mode.
R1(config-std-nacl)# do show ip access-lists 24
Standard IP access list 24
    10 permit 10.1.1.0, wildcard bits 0.0.0.255
    20 permit 10.1.2.0, wildcard bits 0.0.0.255
    30 permit 10.1.3.0, wildcard bits 0.0.0.255


! Step 3: Still in ACL 24 configuration mode, the line with sequence number 20 is
  deleted.
R1(config-std-nacl)# no 20


! Step 4: Displaying the ACL's contents again, without leaving configuration mode.
```

```
! Note that line number 20 is no longer listed.
R1(config-std-nacl)#do show ip access-lists 24
Standard IP access list 24
    10 permit 10.1.1.0, wildcard bits 0.0.0.255
    30 permit 10.1.3.0, wildcard bits 0.0.0.255


! Step 5: Inserting a new first line in the ACL.
R1(config-std-nacl)# 5 deny 10.1.1.1


! Step 6: Displaying the ACL's contents one last time, with the new statement
!(sequence number 5) listed first.
R1(config-std-nacl)# do show ip access-lists 24
Standard IP access list 24
    5 deny    10.1.1.1
    10 permit 10.1.1.0, wildcard bits 0.0.0.255
    30 permit 10.1.3.0, wildcard bits 0.0.0.255
```

Note that although Example 26-6 uses a numbered ACL, named ACLs use the same process to edit (add and remove) entries.

Numbered ACL Configuration Versus Named ACL Configuration

As a brief aside about numbered ACLs, note that IOS actually allows two ways to configure numbered ACLs in the more recent versions of IOS. First, IOS supports the traditional method, using the **access-list** global commands shown earlier in Examples 26-1, 26-2, and 26-3. IOS also supports the numbered ACL configuration with commands just like named ACLs, as shown in Example 26-6.

Oddly, IOS always stores numbered ACLs with the original style of configuration, as global **access-list** commands, no matter which method is used to configure the ACL. Example 26-7 demonstrates these facts, picking up where Example 26-6 ended, with the following additional steps:

Step 7.   The engineer lists the configuration (**show running-config**), which lists the old-style configuration commands—even though the ACL was created with the new-style commands.

Step 8.   The engineer adds a new statement to the end of the ACL using the old-style **access-list 24 permit 10.1.4.0 0.0.0.255** global configuration command.

Step 9.   The **show ip access-lists** command confirms that the old-style **access-list** command from the previous step followed the rule of being added only to the end of the ACL.

Step 10.   The engineer displays the configuration to confirm that the parts of ACL 24 configured with both new-style commands and old-style commands are all listed in the same old-style ACL (**show running-config**).

Example 26-7   *Adding to and Displaying a Numbered ACL Configuration*

```
! Step 7: A configuration snippet for ACL 24.
R1# show running-config
```

26

```
! The only lines shown are the lines from ACL 24
access-list 24 deny    10.1.1.1
access-list 24 permit 10.1.1.0 0.0.0.255
access-list 24 permit 10.1.3.0 0.0.0.255


! Step 8: Adding a new access-list 24 global command
R1# configure terminal
Enter configuration commands, one per line.  End with CNTL/Z.
R1(config)# access-list 24 permit 10.1.4.0 0.0.0.255
R1(config)# ^Z


! Step 9: Displaying the ACL's contents again, with sequence numbers. Note that even
! the new statement has been automatically assigned a sequence number.
R1# show ip access-lists 24
Standard IP access list 24
    5 deny    10.1.1.1
    10 permit 10.1.1.0, wildcard bits 0.0.0.255
    30 permit 10.1.3.0, wildcard bits 0.0.0.255
    40 permit 10.1.4.0, wildcard bits 0.0.0.255


! Step 10: The numbered ACL configuration remains in old-style configuration commands.
R1# show running-config
! The only lines shown are the lines from ACL 24
access-list 24 deny    10.1.1.1
access-list 24 permit 10.1.1.0 0.0.0.255
access-list 24 permit 10.1.3.0 0.0.0.255
access-list 24 permit 10.1.4.0 0.0.0.255
```

ACL Implementation Considerations

ACLs can be a great tool to enhance the security of a network, but engineers should think about some broader issues before simply configuring an ACL to fix a problem. To help, Cisco makes the following general recommendations in the courses on which the CCNA R&S exams are based:

- Place extended ACLs as close as possible to the source of the packet. This strategy allows ACLs to discard the packets early.

- Place standard ACLs as close as possible to the destination of the packet. This strategy avoids the mistake with standard ACLs (which match the source IPv4 address only) of unintentionally discarding packets that did not need to be discarded.

- Place more specific statements early in the ACL.

- Disable an ACL from its interface (using the **no ip access-group** interface subcommand) before making changes to the ACL.

The first point deals with the concept of where to locate your ACLs. If you intend to filter a packet, filtering closer to the packet's source means that the packet takes up less bandwidth in the network, which seems to be more efficient—and it is. Therefore, Cisco suggests locating extended ACLs as close to the source as possible.

However, the second point seems to contradict the first point, at least for standard ACLs, to locate them close to the destination. Why? Well, because standard ACLs look only at the source IP address, they tend to filter more than you want filtered when placed close to the source. For example, imagine that Fred and Barney are separated by four routers. If you filter Barney's traffic sent to Fred on the first router, Barney can't reach any hosts near the other three routers. So, the Cisco courses make a blanket recommendation to locate standard ACLs closer to the destination to avoid filtering traffic you do not mean to filter.

For the third item in the list, by placing more specific matching parameters early in each list, you are less likely to make mistakes in the ACL. For example, imagine that the ACL first listed a command that permitted traffic going to 10.1.1.0/24, and the second command denied traffic going to host 10.1.1.1. Packets sent to host 10.1.1.1 would match the first command, and never match the more specific second command. Note that later IOS versions prevent this mistake during configuration in some cases, as shown later in this chapter in Example 26-11.

Finally, Cisco recommends that you disable the ACLs on the interfaces before you change the statements in the list. By doing so, you avoid issues with the ACL during an interim state. First, if you delete an entire ACL, and leave the IP ACL enabled on an interface with the **ip access-group** command, IOS does not filter any packets (that was not always the case in far earlier IOS versions)! As soon as you add one ACL command to that enabled ACL, however, IOS starts filtering packets based on that ACL. Those interim ACL configurations could cause problems.

For example, suppose you have ACL 101 enabled on S0/0/0 for output packets. You delete list 101 so that all packets are allowed through. Then, you enter a single **access-list 101** command. As soon as you press Enter, the list exists, and the router filters all packets exiting S0/0/0 based on the one-line list. If you want to enter a long ACL, you might temporarily filter packets you don't want to filter! Therefore, the better way is to disable the list from the interface, make the changes to the list, and then reenable it on the interface.

Troubleshooting with IPv4 ACLs

The use of IPv4 ACLs makes troubleshooting IPv4 routing more difficult. Any data plane troubleshooting process can include a catchall phrase to include checking for ACLs. A network can have all hosts working, DHCP settings correct, all LANs working, all router interfaces working, and all routers having learned all routes to all subnets—and ACLs can still filter packets. Although ACLs provide that important service of filtering some packets, ACLs can make the troubleshooting process that much more difficult.

This third of the three major sections of this chapter focuses on troubleshooting in the presence of IPv4 ACLs. It breaks the discussion into two parts. The first part gives advice about common problems you might see on the exam, and how to find those with **show** commands and some analysis. The second part then looks at how ACLs impact the **ping** command.

Analyzing ACL Behavior in a Network

ACLs cause some of the biggest challenges when troubleshooting problems in real networking jobs. The packets created by commands like **ping** and **traceroute** do not exactly match the fields in packets created by end users. The ACLs sometimes filter the **ping** and **traceroute** traffic, making the network engineer think some other kind of problems exists when no problems exist at all. Or, the problem with the end-user traffic really is caused by the ACL, but the ping and traceroute traffic works fine, because the ACL matches the end user traffic with a **deny** action but matches the ping and traceroute traffic with a **permit** action.

As a result, much of ACL troubleshooting requires thinking about ACL configuration versus the packets that flow in a network, rather that using a couple of IOS commands that identify the root cause of the problem. The **show** commands that help are those that give you the configuration of the ACL, and on what interfaces the ACL is enabled. You can also see statistics about which ACL statements have been matched. And using pings and traceroutes can help—as long as you remember that ACLs may apply different actions to those packets versus the end user traffic.

The following list phrases the ACL troubleshooting steps into a list for easier study. The list also expands on the idea of analyzing each ACL in Step 3. None of the ideas in the list are new compared to this chapter and the previous chapter, but it acts more as a summary of the common issues:

Step 1. Determine on which interfaces ACLs are enabled, and in which direction (**show running-config, show ip interfaces**).

Step 2. Find the configuration of each ACL (**show access-lists, show ip access-lists, show running-config**).

Step 3. Analyze the ACLs to predict which packets should match the ACL, focusing on the following points:

   A. Misordered ACLs: Look for misordered ACL statements. IOS uses first-match logic when searching an ACL.

   B. Reversed source/destination addresses: Analyze the router interface, the direction in which the ACL is enabled, compared to the location of the IP address ranges matched by the ACL statements. Make sure the source IP address field could match packets with that source IP address, rather than the destination, and vice versa for the destination IP address field.

   C. Reversed source/destination ports: For extended ACLs that reference UDP or TCP port numbers, continue to analyze the location and direction of the ACL versus the hosts, focusing on which host acts as the server using a well-known port. Ensure that the ACL statement matches the correct source or destination port depending on whether the server sent or will receive the packet.

   D. Syntax: Remember that extended ACL commands must use the **tcp** and **udp** keywords if the command needs to check the port numbers.

   E. Syntax: Note that ICMP packets do not use UDP or TCP; ICMP is considered to be another protocol matchable with the **icmp** keyword (instead of **tcp** or **udp**).

   F. Explicit deny any: Instead of using the implicit **deny any** at the end of each ACL, use an explicit configuration command to deny all traffic at the end of the ACL so that the **show** command counters increment when that action is taken.

   G. Dangerous inbound ACLs: Watch for inbound ACLs, especially those with deny all logic at the end of the ACL. These ACLs may discard incoming overhead protocols, like routing protocol messages.

H. **Standard ACL location:** Standard ACLs enabled close to the source of matched addresses can discard the packets as intended, but also discard packets that should be allowed through. Always pay close attention to the requirements of the ACL in these cases.

This chapter (and the previous) have already discussed the details of Step 3. The first two steps are important for Simlet questions in case you are not allowed to look at the configuration; you can use other **show** commands to determine all the relevant ACL configuration. The next few pages show some of the related commands and how they can uncover some of the issues described in the just-completed ACL troubleshooting checklist.

ACL Troubleshooting Commands

If you suspect ACLs are causing a problem, the first problem-isolation step is to find the location and direction of the ACLs. The fastest way to do this is to look at the output of the **show running-config** command and to look for **ip access-group** commands under each interface. However, in some cases, enable mode access may not be allowed, and **show** commands are required. Instead, use the **show ip interfaces** command to find which ACLs are enabled on which interfaces, as shown in Example 26-8.

Example 26-8   *Sample* show ip interface *Command*

```
R1> show ip interface s0/0/1
Serial0/0/1 is up, line protocol is up
  Internet address is 10.1.2.1/24
  Broadcast address is 255.255.255.255
  Address determined by setup command
  MTU is 1500 bytes
  Helper address is not set
  Directed broadcast forwarding is disabled
  Multicast reserved groups joined: 224.0.0.9
  Outgoing access list is not set
  Inbound  access list is 102
! roughly 26 more lines omitted for brevity
```

Note that the command output lists whether an ACL is enabled, in both directions, and which ACL it is. The example shows an abbreviated version of the **show ip interface S0/0/1** command, which lists messages for just this one interface. The **show ip interface** command would list the same messages for every interface in the router.

Step 2 of the ACL troubleshooting checklist then says that the contents of the ACL must be found. Again, the quickest way to look at the ACL is to use the **show running-config** command. If not available, the **show access-lists** and **show ip access-lists** commands list the same details shown in the configuration. These commands also list a useful counter that lists the number of packets that have matched each line in the ACL. Example 26-9 shows an example.

Example 26-9   show ip access-lists *Command Example*

```
R1# show ip access-lists
Extended IP access list 102
    10 permit ip 10.1.2.0 0.0.0.255 10.1.4.0 0.0.1.255 (15 matches)
```

26

The counter can be very useful for troubleshooting. If you can generate traffic that you think should match a particular line in an ACL, then you should see the matches increment on that counter. If you keep generating traffic that should match, but that line's counter never goes up, then those packets do not match that line in that ACL. Those packets could be matching an earlier line in the same ACL, or might not even be reaching that router (for any reason).

After the locations, directions, and configuration details of the various ACLs have been discovered in Steps 1 and 2, the hard part begins—analyzing what the ACL really does. For example, one of the most common tasks you will do is to look at the address fields and decide the range of addresses matched by that field. Remember, for an ACL that sits in a router configuration, you can easily find the address range. The low end of the range is the address (the first number), and the high end of the range is the sum of the address and wildcard mask. For instance, with ACL 102 in Example 26-9, which is obviously con-figured in some router, the ranges are as follows:

Source 10.1.2.0, wildcard 0.0.0.255: Matches from 10.1.2.0 through 10.1.2.255

Destination 10.1.4.0, wildcard 0.0.1.255: Matches from 10.1.4.0 through 10.1.5.255

The next few pages work through some analysis of a few of the items from Step 3 in the troubleshooting checklist.

Example Issue: Reversed Source/Destination IP Addresses

IOS cannot recognize a case in which you attempt to match the wrong addresses in the source or destination address field. So, be ready to analyze the enabled ACLs and their direction versus the location of different subnets in the network. Then ask yourself about the packets that drive that ACL: what could the source and destination addresses of those packets be? And does the ACL match the correct address ranges, or not?

For example, consider Figure 26-11, a figure that will be used in several troubleshooting examples in this chapter. The requirements for the next ACL follow the figure.

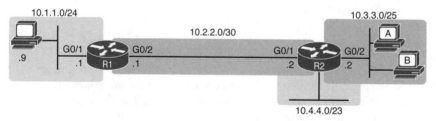

Figure 26-11   *Example Network Used in IPv4 ACL Troubleshooting Examples*

For this next ACL, the requirements ask that you allow and prevent various flows, as follows:

- Allow hosts in subnet 10.3.3.0/25 and subnet 10.1.1.0/24 to communicate
- Prevent hosts in subnet 10.4.4.0/23 and subnet 10.1.1.0/24 from communicating
- Allow all other communications between hosts in network 10.0.0.0
- Prevent all other communications

Example 26-10 shows the ACL used in this case on R2. At first glance, it meets all those requirements straight down the list.

Example 26-10 *Troubleshooting Example 2 per Step 3B: Source and Destination Mismatch*

```
R2# show ip access-lists
Standard IP access list Step3B
 10 permit 10.3.3.0 0.0.0.127
 20 deny 10.4.4.0 0.0.1.255
 30 permit 10.0.0.0 0.255.255.255 (12 matches)
R2#
R2# show ip interface G0/1 | include Inbound
 Inbound access list is Step3B
```

The problem in this case is that the ACL has been enabled on R2's G0/1 interface, inbound. Per the figure, packets coming from a source address in subnets 10.3.3.0/25 and 10.4.4.0/23 should be forwarded out R2's G0/1 interface, rather than coming in that interface. So, do not let the matching logic in the ACL that perfectly mirrors the requirements fool you; make sure and check the location of the ACL, direction, and the location of the IP addresses.

Note that Step 3C suggests a similar issue regarding matching well-known ports with TCP and UDP. The earlier section in this chapter titled "Matching TCP and UDP Port Numbers" has already discussed those ideas in plenty of detail. Just make sure to check where the server sits versus the location and direction of the ACL.

Steps 3D and 3E: Common Syntax Mistakes

Steps 3D and 3E describe a couple of common syntax mistakes. First, to match a TCP port in an ACL statement, you must use a **tcp** protocol keyword instead of **ip** or any other value. Otherwise, IOS rejects the command as having incorrect syntax. Same issue with trying to match UDP ports: a **udp** protocol keyword is required.

To match ICMP, IOS includes an **icmp** protocol keyword to use instead of **tcp** or **udp**. In fact, the main conceptual mistake is to think of ICMP as an application protocol that uses either UDP or TCP; it uses neither. To match all ICMP messages, for instance, use the **permit icmp any any** command in an extended named ACL.

Example Issue: Inbound ACL Filters Routing Protocol Packets

A router bypasses outbound ACL logic for packets the router itself generates. That might sound like common sense, but it is important to stop and think about that fact in context. A router can have an outgoing ACL, and that ACL can and will discard packets that the router receives in one interface and then tries to forward out some other interface. But if the router creates the packet, for instance, for a routing protocol message, the router bypasses the outbound ACL logic for that packet.

However, a router does not bypass inbound ACL logic. If an ACL has an inbound ACL enabled, and a packet arrives in that interface, the router checks the ACL. Any and all IPv4 packets are considered by the ACL—including important overhead packets like routing protocol updates.

For example, consider a seemingly good ACL on a router, like the Step3G ACL in Example 26-11. That ACL lists a couple of **permit** commands, and has an implicit deny any at the end of the list. At first, it looks like any other reasonable ACL.

26

Example 26-11   *Troubleshooting Example 2 per Step 3G: Filtering RIP by Accident*

```
R1# show ip access-lists
Standard IP access list Step3G
 10 permit host 10.4.4.1
 20 permit 10.3.3.0 0.0.0.127 (12 matches)
! using the implicit deny to match everything else
R1#
! On router R1:
R1# show ip interface G0/2 | include Inbound
    Inbound access list is Step3G
```

Now look at the location and direction (inbound on R1, on R1's G0/2) and consider that location versus the topology Figure 26-11 for a moment. None of those **permit** statements match the RIP updates sent by R2, sent out R2's G0/1 interface toward R1. RIP messages use UDP (well-known port 520), and R2's G0/1 interface is 10.2.2.2 per the figure. R1 would match incoming RIP messages with the implicit deny all at the end of the list. The symptoms in this case, assuming only that one ACL exists, would be that R1 would not learn routes from R2, but R2 could still learn RIP routes from R1.

Of the three routing protocols discussed in the ICND1 and ICND2 books, RIPv2 uses UDP as a transport, while OSPF and EIGRP do not even use a transport protocol. As a result, to match RIPv2 packets with an ACL, you need the **udp** keyword and you need to match well-known port 520. OSPF and EIGRP can be matched with special keywords as noted in Table 26-7. The table also list the addresses used by each protocol.

Table 26-7   Key Fields for Matching Routing Protocol Messages

Protocol	Source IP Address	Destination IP Addresses	ACL Protocol Keyword
RIPv2	Source interface	224.0.0.9	**udp** (port 520)
OSPF	Source interface	224.0.0.5, 224.0.0.6	**ospf**
EIGRP	Source interface	224.0.0.10	**eigrp**

Example 26-12 shows a sample ACL with three lines, one to match each routing protocol, just to show the syntax. Note that in this case, the ACL matches the address fields with the **any** keyword. You could include lines like these in any inbound ACL to ensure that routing protocol packets would be permitted.

Example 26-12   *Example ACL that Matches all RIPv2, OSPF, and EIGRP with a Permit*

```
R1# show ip access-lists
ip access-list extended RoutingProtocolExample
 10 permit udp any any eq 520
 20 permit ospf any any
 30 permit eigrp any any
 remark a complete ACL would also need more statements here
R1#
```

ACL Interactions with Router-Generated Packets

Routers bypass outbound ACL logic for packets generated by that same router. This logic helps avoid cases in which a router discards its own overhead traffic. This logic applies to packets that a router creates for overhead processes like routing protocols, as well as for commands, like **ping** and **traceroute**. This section adds a few perspectives about how ACLs impact troubleshooting, and how this exception to outbound ACL logic applies, particularly commands used from the router CLI.

Local ACLs and a Ping from a Router

For the first scenario, think about a ping command issued by a router. The command generates packets, and the router sends those packets (holding the ICMP echo request messages) out one of the router interfaces, and typically some ICMP echo reply messages are received back. As it turns out, not all ACLs will attempt to filter those packets.

As a backdrop to discuss what happens, Figure 26-12 illustrates a simple network topology with two routers connected to a serial link. Note that in this figure four IP ACLs exist, named A, B, C, and D, as noted by the thick arrows in the drawing. That is, ACL A is an outbound ACL on R1's S0/0/0, ACL B is an inbound ACL on R2's S0/0/1, and so on.

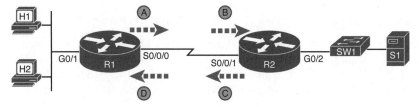

Figure 26-12 *Sample Network with IP ACLs in Four Locations*

As an example, consider a **ping** command issued from R1's CLI (after a user connects to R1's CLI using SSH). The **ping** command pings server S1's IP address. The IPv4 packets with the ICMP messages flow from R1 to S1 and back again. Which of those four ACLs could possibly filter the ICMP Echo Request toward S1, and the ICMP Echo Reply back toward R1?

Routers bypass their own outbound ACLs for packets generated by the router, as shown in Figure 26-13. Even though ACL A exists as an outgoing ACL on Router R1, R1 bypasses its own outgoing ACL logic of ACL A for the ICMP Echo Requests generated by R1.

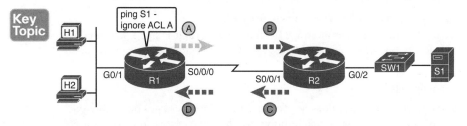

Figure 26-13 *R1 Ignores Outgoing ACL for Packets Created by Its Own* **ping** *Command*

Router Self-Ping of a Serial Interface IPv4 Address

The previous example uses a router's ping command when pinging a host. However, network engineers often need to ping router IP addresses, including using a self-ping. The term *self-ping* refers to a ping of a device's own IPv4 address. And for point-to-point serial links, a self-ping actually sends packets over the serial link, which causes some interested effects with ACLs.

When a user issues a self-ping for that local router's serial IP address, the router actually sends the ICMP echo request out the link to the other router. The neighboring router then receives the packet and routes the packet with the ICMP echo request back to the original router. Figure 26-14 shows an example of a self-ping (**ping 172.16.4.1**) of Router R1's own IP address on a point-to-point serial link, with the ICMP echo request out the link to Router R2. At Step 2, R2 treats it like any other packet not destined for one of R2's own IPv4 addresses: R2 routes the packet. Where? Right back to Router R1, as shown in the figure.

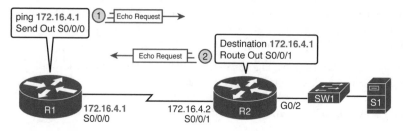

Figure 26-14   *The First Steps in a Self-Ping on R1, for R1's S0/0/0 IP Address*

Now think about those four ACLs in the earlier figures compared to Figure 26-14. R1 generates the ICMP echo request, so R1 bypasses outbound ACL A. ACLs B, C, and D could filter the packet. Note that the packet sent by R2 back to R1 is not generated by R2 in this case; R2 is just routing R1's original packet back to R1.

A self-ping of a serial interface actually tests many parts of a point-to-point serial link, as follows:

■ The link must work at Layers 1, 2, and 3. Specifically, both routers must have a working (up/up) serial interface, with correct IPv4 addresses configured.

■ ACLs B, C, and D must permit the ICMP echo request and reply packets.

So, when troubleshooting, if you choose to use self-pings and they fail, but the serial interfaces are in an up/up state, do not forget to check to see whether the ACLs have filtered the Internet Control Management Protocol (ICMP) traffic.

Router Self-Ping of an Ethernet Interface IPv4 Address

A self-ping of a router's own Ethernet interface IP address works a little like a self-ping of a router's serial IP address, but with a couple of twists:

■ Like with serial interface, the local router interface must be working (in an up/up state); otherwise, the ping fails.

■ Unlike serial interfaces, the router does not forward the ICMP messages physically out the interface, so security features on neighboring switches (like port security) or routers (like ACLs) cannot possibly filter the messages used by the **ping** command.

■ Like serial interfaces, an incoming IP ACL on the local router does process the router self-ping of an Ethernet-based IP address.

Figure 26-15 walks through an example. In this case, R2 issues a **ping 172.16.2.2** command to ping its own G0/2 IP address. Just like with a self-ping on serial links, R2 creates the

ICMP echo request. However, R2 basically processes the ping down its own TCP/IP stack and back up again, with the ICMP echo never leaving the router's Ethernet interface. R2 does check the Ethernet interface status, showing a failure if the interface is not up/up. R2 does not apply outbound ACL logic to the packet, because R2 created the packet, but R2 will apply inbound ACL logic to the packet, as if the packet had been physically received on the interface.

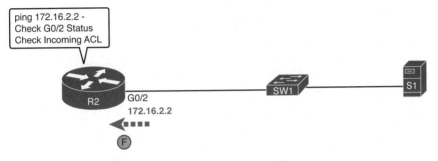

Figure 26-15 *Self-Ping of a Router's Ethernet Address*

Chapter Review

One key to doing well on the exams is to perform repetitive spaced review sessions. Review this chapter's material using either the tools in the book, DVD, or interactive tools for the same material found on the book's companion website. Refer to the "Your Study Plan" element for more details. Table 26-8 outlines the key review elements and where you can find them. To better track your study progress, record when you completed these activities in the second column.

Table 26-8 Chapter Review Tracking

Review Element	Review Date(s)	Resource Used
Review key topics		Book, DVD/website
Review key terms		Book, DVD/website
Repeat DIKTA questions		Book, PCPT
Review memory tables		Book, DVD/website
Review command tables		Book

Review All the Key Topics

Table 26-9 Key Topics for Chapter 26

Key Topic Element	Description	Page Number
Figure 26-3	Syntax and notes about the three required matching fields in the extended ACL **access-list** command	617
Paragraph	Summary of extended ACL logic that all parameters must match in a single **access-list** statement for a match to occur	618

Key Topic Element	Description	Page Number
Figure 26-4	Drawing of the IP header followed by a TCP header	618
Figure 26-5	Syntax and notes about matching TCP and UDP ports with extended ACL **access-list** commands	619
Figure 26-7	Logic and syntax to match TCP source ports	620
List	Guidelines for using extended numbered IP ACLs	621
List	Differences between named and numbered ACLs when named ACLs introduced	625
List	Features enabled by IOS 12.3 ACL sequence numbers	627
List	ACL implementation recommendations	630
Checklist	ACL troubleshooting checklist	632
Figure 26-13	Example of a router bypassing its outbound ACL logic for packets the router generates	637

Key Terms You Should Know

extended access list, named access list

Command References

Tables 26-10 and 26-11 list configuration and verification commands used in this chapter. As an easy review exercise, cover the left column in a table, read the right column, and try to recall the command without looking. Then repeat the exercise, covering the right column, and try to recall what the command does.

Table 26-10 Chapter 26 ACL Configuration Command Reference

Command	Description
access-list *access-list-number* {**deny** | **permit**} *protocol source source-wildcard destination destination-wildcard* [**log**]	Global command for extended numbered **access lists.** Use a number between 100 and 199 or 2000 and 2699, inclusive.
access-list *access-list-number* {**deny** | **permit**} **tcp** *source source-wildcard* [*operator* [*port*]] *destination destination-wildcard* [*operator* [*port*]] [**log**]	A version of the **access-list** command with TCP-specific parameters.
access-list *access-list-number* **remark** *text*	Defines a remark that helps you remember what the ACL is supposed to do.
ip access-group {*number* | *name* [**in** | **out**]}	Interface subcommand to enable access lists.
access-class *number* | *name* [**in** | **out**]	Line subcommand to enable either standard or extended access lists on vty lines.
ip access-list {**standard** | **extended**} *name*	Global command to configure a named standard or extended ACL and enter ACL configuration mode.
{**deny** | **permit**} *source* [*source wildcard*] [**log**]	ACL mode subcommand to configure the matching details and action for a standard named ACL.

Command	Description
{deny | permit} *protocol source source-wildcard destination destination-wildcard* [log]	ACL mode subcommand to configure the matching details and action for an extended named ACL.
{deny | permit} tcp *source source-wildcard* [*operator* [*port*]] *destination destination-wildcard* [*operator* [*port*]] [log]	ACL mode subcommand to configure the matching details and action for a named ACL that matches TCP segments.
remark *text*	ACL mode subcommand to configure a description of a named ACL.

Table 26-11   Chapter 26 EXEC Command Reference

Command	Description
show ip *interface* [*type number*]	Includes a reference to the access lists enabled on the interface
show access-lists [*access-list-number* | *access-list-name*]	Shows details of configured access lists for all protocols
show ip access-lists [*access-list-number* | *access-list-name*]	Shows IP access lists

Answers to Earlier Practice Problems

Table 26-12 lists the answers to the practice problems listed in Table 26-6. Note that for any question that references a client, you might have chosen to match port numbers greater than 1023. The answers in this table mostly ignore that option, but just to show one sample, the answer to the first problem lists one with a reference to client ports greater than 1023 and one without. The remaining answers simply omit this part of the logic.

Table 26-12   Building One-Line Extended ACLs: Answers

	Criteria
1	access-list 101 permit tcp host 10.1.1.1 10.1.2.0 0.0.0.255 eq www
	or
	access-list 101 permit tcp host 10.1.1.1 gt 1023 10.1.2.0 0.0.0.255 eq www
2	access-list 102 permit tcp 172.16.4.0 0.0.0.127 172.16.3.0 0.0.0.127 eq telnet
3	access-list 103 permit icmp 192.168.7.192 0.0.0.63 192.168.7.8 0.0.0.7
4	access-list 104 permit tcp 10.2.2.0 0.0.1.255 eq www 10.4.4.0 0.0.3.255
5	access-list 105 permit tcp 172.20.1.0 0.0.0.255 eq 23 172.20.44.0 0.0.1.255
6	access-list 106 permit tcp 192.168.99.96 0.0.0.15 192.168.176.0 0.0.0.15 eq www
7	access-list 107 permit icmp 10.55.66.0 0.0.0.127 10.66.55.0 0.0.0.63
8	access-list 108 permit ip any any

26

CHAPTER 27

Network Address Translation

This chapter covers the following exam topics:

1.0 Network Fundamentals

1.10 Describe the need for private IPv4 addressing

4.0 Infrastructure Services

4.7 Configure, verify, and troubleshoot inside source NAT

    4.7.a Static

    4.7.b Pool

    4.7.c PAT

This last of the chapters about IPv4 topics looks at a very popular and very important part of both enterprise and small office/home office (SOHO) networks: Network Address Translation, or NAT. NAT helped solve a big problem with IPv4: The IPv4 address space would have been completely consumed by the mid-1990s. After it was consumed, the Internet could not continue to grow, which would have significantly slowed the development of the Internet.

This chapter actually discusses two short-term solutions to the IPv4 address exhaustion issue, which also serves as a good lead-in to IP version 6 (IPv6). NAT, along with classless interdomain routing (CIDR), helped extend the life of IPv4 as the network layer protocol of the Internet from the 1990s into the 2010s. Part VIII of this book discusses the long-term solution that will become the standard for the Internet: IP version 6 (IPv6).

This chapter breaks the topics into three major sections. The first section explains the challenges to the IPv4 address space caused by the Internet revolution of the 1990s. The second section explains the basic concept behind NAT, how several variations of NAT work, and how the Port Address Translation (PAT) option conserves the IPv4 address space. The final section shows how to configure NAT from the Cisco IOS Software command-line interface (CLI), and how to troubleshoot NAT.

"Do I Know This Already?" Quiz

Take the quiz (either here, or use the PCPT software) if you want to use the score to help you decide how much time to spend on this chapter. The answers are at the bottom of the page following the quiz, and the explanations are in DVD Appendix C and in the PCPT software.

Table 27-1 "Do I Know This Already?" Foundation Topics Section-to-Question Mapping

Foundation Topics Section	Questions
Perspectives on IPv4 Address Scalability	1–2
Network Address Translation Concepts	3–4
NAT Configuration and Troubleshooting	5–7

1. Which of the following summarized subnets represent routes that could have been created for CIDR's goal to reduce the size of Internet routing tables?

   a. 10.0.0.0 255.255.255.0

   b. 10.1.0.0 255.255.0.0

   c. 200.1.1.0 255.255.255.0

   d. 200.1.0.0 255.255.0.0

2. Which of the following are not private addresses according to RFC 1918? (Choose two answers.)

   a. 172.31.1.1

   b. 172.33.1.1

   c. 10.255.1.1

   d. 10.1.255.1

   e. 191.168.1.1

3. With static NAT, performing translation for inside addresses only, what causes NAT table entries to be created?

   a. The first packet from the inside network to the outside network

   b. The first packet from the outside network to the inside network

   c. Configuration using the **ip nat inside source** command

   d. Configuration using the **ip nat outside source** command

4. With dynamic NAT, performing translation for inside addresses only, what causes NAT table entries to be created?

   a. The first packet from the inside network to the outside network

   b. The first packet from the outside network to the inside network

   c. Configuration using the **ip nat inside source** command

   d. Configuration using the **ip nat outside source** command

5. NAT has been configured to translate source addresses of packets for the inside part of the network, but only for some hosts as identified by an access control list. Which of the following commands indirectly identifies the hosts?

   a. ip nat inside source list 1 pool barney

   b. ip nat pool barney 200.1.1.1 200.1.1.254 netmask 255.255.255.0

   c. ip nat inside

   d. ip nat inside 200.1.1.1 200.1.1.2

6. Examine the following configuration commands:

```
interface Ethernet0/0
 ip address 10.1.1.1 255.255.255.0
 ip nat inside
interface Serial0/0
 ip address 200.1.1.249 255.255.255.252
ip nat inside source list 1 interface Serial0/0
access-list 1 permit 10.1.1.0 0.0.0.255
```

If the configuration is intended to enable source NAT overload, which of the following commands could be useful to complete the configuration? (Choose two answers.)

   a. The **ip nat outside** command

   b. The **ip nat pat** command

   c. The **overload** keyword

   d. The **ip nat pool** command

7. Examine the following **show** command output on a router configured for dynamic NAT:

```
-- Inside Source
access-list 1 pool fred refcount 2288
 pool fred: netmask 255.255.255.240
    start 200.1.1.1 end 200.1.1.7
    type generic, total addresses 7, allocated 7 (100%), misses 965
```

Users are complaining about not being able to reach the Internet. Which of the following is the most likely cause?

   a. The problem is not related to NAT, based on the information in the command output.

   b. The NAT pool does not have enough entries to satisfy all requests.

   c. Standard ACL 1 cannot be used; an extended ACL must be used.

   d. The command output does not supply enough information to identify the problem.

Foundation Topics

Perspectives on IPv4 Address Scalability

The original design for the Internet required every organization to ask for, and receive, one or more registered classful IPv4 network numbers. The people administering the program ensured that none of the IP networks were reused. As long as every organization used only IP addresses inside its own registered network numbers, IP addresses would never be duplicated, and IP routing could work well.

Connecting to the Internet using only a registered network number, or several registered network numbers, worked well for a while. In the early to mid-1990s, it became apparent that the Internet was growing so fast that all IP network numbers would be assigned by the mid-1990s! Concern arose that the available networks would be completely assigned, and some organizations would not be able to connect to the Internet.

The main long-term solution to the IPv4 address scalability problem was to increase the size of the IP address. This one fact was the most compelling reason for the advent of IP version 6 (IPv6). (Version 5 was defined much earlier, but was never deployed, so the next attempt was labeled as version 6.) IPv6 uses a 128-bit address, instead of the 32-bit address in IPv4. With the same or improved process of assigning unique address ranges to every organization connected to the Internet, IPv6 can easily support every organization and individual on the planet, with the number of IPv6 addresses theoretically reaching above 10^{38}.

Many short-term solutions to the addressing problem were suggested, but three standards worked together to solve the problem. Two of the standards work closely together: Network Address Translation (NAT) and private addressing. These features together allow many organizations to use the same unregistered IPv4 network numbers internally—and still communicate well with the Internet. The third standard, classless interdomain routing (CIDR), allows ISPs to reduce the wasting of IPv4 addresses by assigning a company a subset of a network number rather than the entire network. CIDR also can allow Internet service providers (ISP) to summarize routes such that multiple Class A, B, or C networks match a single route, which helps reduce the size of Internet routing tables.

NOTE   These tools have worked well. Estimates in the early 1990s predicted that the world would run out of IPv4 addresses by the mid-1990s, but IANA did not exhaust the IPv4 address space until February 2011, and ARIN (the RIR for North America) did not exhaust its supply of public IPv4 addresses until September 2015.

CIDR

CIDR is a global address assignment convention that defines how the Internet Assigned Numbers Authority (IANA), its member agencies, and ISPs should assign the globally unique IPv4 address space to individual organizations.

Answers to the "Do I Know This Already?" quiz:

1 D **2** B, E **3** C **4** A **5** A **6** A, C **7** B

CIDR, defined in RFC 4632, has two main goals. First, CIDR defines a way to assign public IP addresses, worldwide, to allow route aggregation or route summarization. These route summaries greatly reduce the size of routing tables in Internet routers.

Figure 27-1 shows a typical case of CIDR route aggregation, and how CIDR could be used to replace over 65,000 routes with one route. First, imagine that ISP 1 owns Class C networks 198.0.0.0 through 198.255.255.0—not by accident, but by purposeful and thoughtful design to make this route aggregation example possible. In other words, IANA allocated all addresses that begin with 198 to one of the five Regional Internet Registries (RIR), and that RIR assigned this entire range to one big ISP in that part of the world.

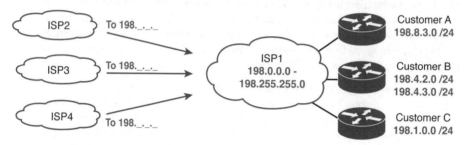

Figure 27-1 *Typical Use of CIDR*

The assignment of all addresses that begin with 198 to one ISP lets other ISPs use one route—a route for 198.0.0.0/8—to match all those addresses, forwarding packets for those addresses to ISP1. Figure 27-1 shows the ISPs on the left each with one route to 198.0.0.0/8—in other words, a route to all hosts whose IP address begins with 198. 65,536 Class C IP networks begin with 198, and this one summary route represents all those IP networks.

The second major CIDR feature allows RIRs and ISPs to reduce waste by assigning a subset of a classful network to a single customer. For example, imagine that ISP1's customer A needs only 10 IP addresses and that customer C needs 25 IP addresses. ISP1 does something like this:

- Assign customer A CIDR block 198.8.3.16/28, with 14 assignable addresses 198.8.3.17 to 198.8.3.30.

- Assign customer B CIDR block 198.8.3.32/27, with 30 assignable addresses (198.8.3.33 to 198.8.3.62).

These *CIDR blocks* act very much like a public IP network, in particular, they give each company a consecutive set of public IPv4 addresses to use. The public address assignment process has much less waste than before as well. In fact, most public address assignments for the last 20 years have been a CIDR block rather than an entire class A, B, or C network.

Note that Appendix N, "Classless Inter-domain Routing" provides a more detailed explanation of the terms, process, and math related to CIDR block assignment.

Private Addressing

Some computers might never be connected to the Internet. These computers' IP addresses could be duplicates of registered IP addresses in the Internet. When designing the IP addressing convention for such a network, an organization could pick and use any network number(s) it wanted, and all would be well. For example, you can buy a few routers, connect them in your office, and configure IP addresses in network 1.0.0.0, and it would work. The IP addresses you use might be duplicates of real IP addresses in the Internet, but if all you want to do is learn on the lab in your office, everything will be fine.

When building a private network that will have no Internet connectivity, you can use IP network numbers called *private internets*, as defined in RFC 1918, *Address Allocation for Private Internets*. This RFC defines a set of networks that will never be assigned to any organization as a registered network number. Instead of using someone else's registered network numbers, you can use numbers in a range that are not used by anyone else in the public Internet. Table 27-2 shows the private address space defined by RFC 1918.

Table 27-2   RFC 1918 Private Address Space

Range of IP Addresses	Network(s)	Class of Networks	Number of Networks
10.0.0.0 to 10.255.255.255	10.0.0.0	A	1
172.16.0.0 to 172.31.255.255	172.16.0.0 – 172.31.0.0	B	16
192.168.0.0 to 192.168.255.255	192.168.0.0 – 192.168.255.0	C	256

In other words, any organization can use these network numbers. However, no organization is allowed to advertise these networks using a routing protocol on the Internet.

Network Address Translation Concepts

NAT, defined in RFC 3022, allows a host that does not have a valid, registered, globally unique IP address to communicate with other hosts through the Internet. The hosts might be using private addresses or addresses assigned to another organization. In either case, NAT allows these addresses that are not Internet ready to continue to be used and still allows communication with hosts across the Internet.

NAT achieves its goal by using a valid registered IP address to represent the private address to the rest of the Internet. The NAT function changes the private IP addresses to publicly registered IP addresses inside each IP packet, as shown in Figure 27-2.

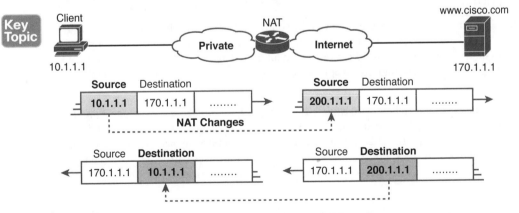

Figure 27-2   *NAT IP Address Swapping: Private Addressing*

Notice that the router, performing NAT, changes the packet's source IP address when the packet leaves the private organization. The router performing NAT also changes the destination address in each packet that is forwarded back into the private network. (Network 200.1.1.0 is a registered network in Figure 27-2.) The NAT feature, configured in the router labeled NAT, performs the translation.

This book discusses *source NAT*, which is the type of NAT that allows enterprises to use private addresses and still communicate with hosts in the Internet. Within source NAT, Cisco IOS supports several different ways to configure NAT. The next few pages cover the concepts behind several of these variations.

Static NAT

Static NAT works just like the example shown in Figure 27-2, but with the IP addresses statically mapped to each other. To help you understand the implications of static NAT and to explain several key terms, Figure 27-3 shows a similar example with more information.

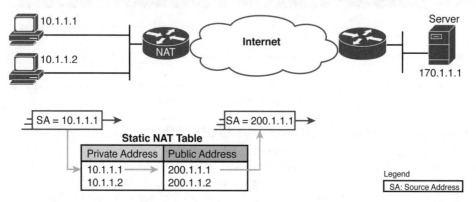

Figure 27-3   *Static NAT Showing Inside Local and Global Addresses*

First, the concepts: The company's ISP has assigned it registered network 200.1.1.0. Therefore, the NAT router must make the private IP addresses look like they are in network 200.1.1.0. To do so, the NAT router changes the source IP addresses in the packets going from left to right in the figure.

In this example, the NAT router changes the source address (SA in the figure) of 10.1.1.1 to 200.1.1.1. With static NAT, the NAT router simply configures a one-to-one mapping between the private address and the registered address that is used on its behalf. The NAT router has statically configured a mapping between private address 10.1.1.1 and public, registered address 200.1.1.1.

Supporting a second IP host with static NAT requires a second static one-to-one mapping using a second IP address in the public address range. For example, to support 10.1.1.2, the router statically maps 10.1.1.2 to 200.1.1.2. Because the enterprise has a single registered Class C network, it can support at most 254 private IP addresses with NAT, with the usual two reserved numbers (the network number and network broadcast address).

The terminology used with NAT, particularly with configuration, can be a little confusing. Notice in Figure 27-3 that the NAT table lists the private IP addresses as "private" and the public, registered addresses from network 200.1.1.0 as "public." Cisco uses the term *inside local* for the private IP addresses in this example and *inside global* for the public IP addresses.

Using NAT terminology, the enterprise network that uses private addresses, and therefore needs NAT, is the "inside" part of the network. The Internet side of the NAT function is the "outside" part of the network. A host that needs NAT (such as 10.1.1.1 in the example) has the IP address it uses inside the network, and it needs an IP address to represent it in the outside network. So, because the host essentially needs two different addresses to represent it, you need two terms. Cisco calls the private IP address used in the inside network the *inside local* address and the address used to represent the host to the rest of the Internet the *inside global* address. Figure 27-4 repeats the same example, with some of the terminology shown.

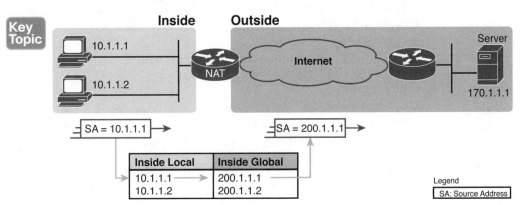

Figure 27-4 *Static NAT Terminology*

Source NAT changes only the IP address of inside hosts. Therefore, the current NAT table shown in Figure 27-4 shows the inside local and corresponding inside global registered addresses. The term *inside local* refers to the address used for the host inside the enterprise, the address used locally versus globally, which means in the enterprise instead of the global Internet. Conversely, the term *inside global* still refers to an address used for the host inside the enterprise, but it is the global address used while the packet flows through the Internet.

Note that the NAT feature destination NAT, not covered in this book, uses similar terms *outside local* and *outside global*. However, with source NAT, one of the terms, *outside global*, is used. This term refers to the host that resides outside the enterprise. Because source NAT does not change that address, the term outside global applies at all times.

Table 27-3 summarizes these four similar terms, and refers to the IPv4 addresses used as samples in the last three figures as examples.

Table 27-3 NAT Addressing Terms

Term	Values in Figures	Meaning
Inside local	10.1.1.1	**Inside:** Refers to the permanent location of the host, from the enterprise's perspective: it is inside the enterprise. **Local:** Means not global; that is, local. It is the address used for that host while the packet flows in the local enterprise rather than the global Internet. **Alternative:** Think of it as inside private, because this address is typically a private address.
Inside global	200.1.1.1	**Inside:** Refers to the permanent location of the host, from the enterprise's perspective. **Global:** Means global as in the global Internet. It is the address used for that host while the packet flows in the Internet. **Alternative:** Think of it as inside public, because the address is typically a public IPv4 address.
Outside global	170.1.1.1	With source NAT, the one address used by the host that resides outside the enterprise, which NAT does not change, so there is no need for a contrasting term. **Alternative:** Think of it as outside public, because the address is typically a public IPv4 address.
Outside local	—	This term is not used with source NAT. With destination NAT, the address would represent a host that resides outside the enterprise, but the address used to represent that host as packets pass through the local enterprise.

Dynamic NAT

Dynamic NAT has some similarities and differences compared to static NAT. Like static NAT, the NAT router creates a one-to-one mapping between an inside local and inside global address, and changes the IP addresses in packets as they exit and enter the inside network. However, the mapping of an inside local address to an inside global address happens dynamically.

Dynamic NAT sets up a pool of possible inside global addresses and defines matching criteria to determine which inside local IP addresses should be translated with NAT. For example, in Figure 27-5, a pool of five inside global IP addresses has been established: 200.1.1.1 through 200.1.1.5. NAT has also been configured to translate any inside local addresses that start with 10.1.1.

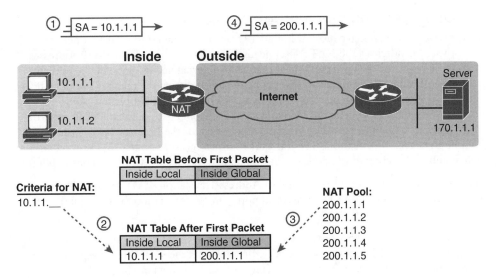

Figure 27-5 *Dynamic NAT*

The numbers 1, 2, 3, and 4 in the figure refer to the following sequence of events:

1. Host 10.1.1.1 sends its first packet to the server at 170.1.1.1.

2. As the packet enters the NAT router, the router applies some matching logic to decide whether the packet should have NAT applied. Because the logic has been configured to match source IP addresses that begin with 10.1.1, the router adds an entry in the NAT table for 10.1.1.1 as an inside local address.

3. The NAT router needs to allocate an IP address from the pool of valid inside global addresses. It picks the first one available (200.1.1.1, in this case) and adds it to the NAT table to complete the entry.

4. The NAT router translates the source IP address and forwards the packet.

The dynamic entry stays in the table as long as traffic flows occasionally. You can configure a timeout value that defines how long the router should wait, having not translated any packets with that address, before removing the dynamic entry. You can also manually clear the dynamic entries from the table using the **clear ip nat translation** * command.

NAT can be configured with more IP addresses in the inside local address list than in the inside global address pool. The router allocates addresses from the pool until all are allocated. If a new packet arrives from yet another inside host, and it needs a NAT entry, but all the pooled IP addresses are in use, the router simply discards the packet. The user must try again until a NAT entry times out, at which point the NAT function works for the next host that sends a packet. Essentially, the inside global pool of addresses needs to be as large as the maximum number of concurrent hosts that need to use the Internet at the same time—unless you use PAT, as is explained in the next section.

Overloading NAT with Port Address Translation

Some networks need to have most, if not all, IP hosts reach the Internet. If that network uses private IP addresses, the NAT router needs a very large set of registered IP addresses. With static NAT, for each private IP host that needs Internet access, you need a publicly registered IP address, completely defeating the goal of reducing the number of public IPv4 addresses needed for that organization. Dynamic NAT lessens the problem to some degree, because every single host in an internetwork should seldom need to communicate with the Internet at the same time. However, if a large percentage of the IP hosts in a network will need Internet access throughout that company's normal business hours, NAT still requires a large number of registered IP addresses, again failing to reduce IPv4 address consumption.

The NAT Overload feature, also called Port Address Translation (PAT), solves this problem. Overloading allows NAT to scale to support many clients with only a few public IP addresses.

The key to understanding how overloading works is to recall how hosts use TCP and User Datagram Protocol (UDP) ports. To see why, first consider the idea of three separate TCP connections to a web server, from three different hosts, as shown in Figure 27-6.

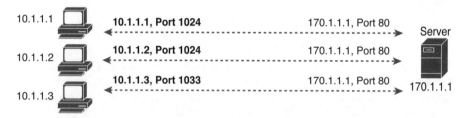

Figure 27-6   *Three TCP Connections from Three PCs*

Next, compare those three TCP connections in Figure 27-6 to three similar TCP connections, now with all three TCP connections from one client, as shown in Figure 27-7. The server does realize a difference, because the server sees the IP address and TCP port number used by the clients in both figures. However, the server really does not care whether the TCP connections come from different hosts, or the same host; the server just sends and receives data over each connection.

Figure 27-7   *Three TCP Connections from One PC*

NAT takes advantage of the fact that, from a transport layer perspective, the server doesn't care whether it has one connection each to three different hosts or three connections to a single host IP address. NAT overload (PAT) translates not only the address, but the port number when necessary, making what looks like many TCP or UDP flows from different hosts look like the same number of flows from one host. Figure 27-8 outlines the logic.

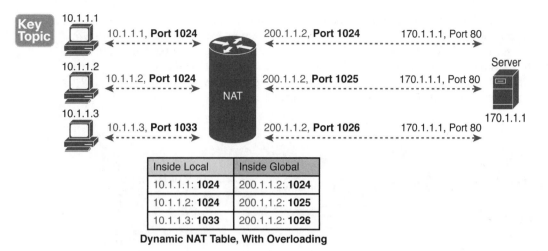

Dynamic NAT Table, With Overloading

Figure 27-8 *NAT Overload (PAT)*

When PAT creates the dynamic mapping, it selects not only an inside global IP address but also a unique port number to use with that address. The NAT router keeps a NAT table entry for every unique combination of inside local IP address and port, with translation to the inside global address and a unique port number associated with the inside global address. And because the port number field has 16 bits, NAT overload can use more than 65,000 port numbers, allowing it to scale well without needing many registered IP addresses—in many cases, needing only one inside global IP address.

Of the three types of NAT covered in this chapter so far, PAT is by far the most popular option. Static NAT and Dynamic NAT both require a one-to-one mapping from the inside local to the inside global address. PAT significantly reduces the number of required registered IP addresses compared to these other NAT alternatives.

NAT Configuration and Troubleshooting

In the following sections, you read about how to configure the three most common variations of NAT: static NAT, dynamic NAT, and PAT, along with the **show** and **debug** commands used to troubleshoot NAT.

Static NAT Configuration

Static NAT configuration requires only a few configuration steps. Each static mapping between a local (private) address and a global (public) address must be configured. In addition, because NAT may be used on a subset of interraces, the router must be told on which interfaces it should use NAT. Those same interface subcommands tell NAT whether the interface is inside or outside. The specific steps are as follows:

Step 1. Use the **ip nat inside** command in interface configuration mode to configure interfaces to be in the inside part of the NAT design.

Step 2. Use the **ip nat outside** command in interface configuration mode to configure interfaces to be in the outside part of the NAT design.

Step 3. Use the **ip nat inside source static** *inside-local inside-global* in global configuration mode to configure the static mappings.

Figure 27-9 shows the familiar network used in the description of static NAT earlier in this chapter, which is also used for the first several configuration examples. In Figure 27-9, you can see that Certskills has obtained Class C network 200.1.1.0 as a registered network number. That entire network, with mask 255.255.255.0, is configured on the serial link between Certskills and the Internet. With a point-to-point serial link, only two of the 254 valid IP addresses in that network are consumed, leaving 252 addresses.

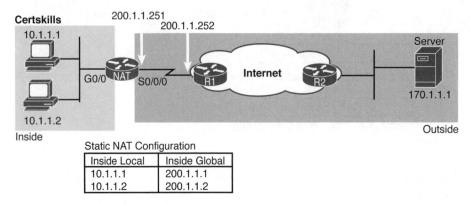

Figure 27-9   *Sample Network for NAT Examples, with Public Class C 200.1.1.0/24*

When planning a NAT configuration, you must find some IP addresses to use as inside global IP addresses. Because these addresses must be part of some registered IP address range, it is common to use the extra addresses in the subnet connecting the enterprise to the Internet—for example, the extra 252 IP addresses in network 200.1.1.0 in this case. The router can also be configured with a loopback interface and assigned an IP address that is part of a globally unique range of registered IP addresses.

Example 27-1 lists the NAT configuration, using 200.1.1.1 and 200.1.1.2 for the two static NAT mappings.

Example 27-1   *Static NAT Configuration*

```
NAT# show running-config
!
! Lines omitted for brevity
!
interface GigabitEthernet0/0
 ip address 10.1.1.3 255.255.255.0
 ip nat inside
!
interface Serial0/0/0
 ip address 200.1.1.251 255.255.255.0
 ip nat outside
!
ip nat inside source static 10.1.1.2 200.1.1.2
ip nat inside source static 10.1.1.1 200.1.1.1
```

```
NAT# show ip nat translations
Pro Inside global        Inside local      Outside local      Outside global
--- 200.1.1.1            10.1.1.1          ---                ---
--- 200.1.1.2            10.1.1.2          ---                ---


NAT# show ip nat statistics
Total active translations: 2 (2 static, 0 dynamic; 0 extended)
Outside interfaces:
  Serial0/0/0
Inside interfaces:
  GigabitEthernet0/0
Hits: 100  Misses: 0
Expired translations: 0
Dynamic mappings:
```

The static mappings are created using the **ip nat inside source static** command. The **inside** keyword means that NAT translates addresses for hosts on the inside part of the network. The **source** keyword means that NAT translates the source IP address of packets coming into its inside interfaces. The **static** keyword means that the parameters define a static entry, which should never be removed from the NAT table because of timeout. Because the design calls for two hosts, 10.1.1.1 and 10.1.1.2, to have Internet access, two **ip nat inside** commands are needed.

After creating the static NAT entries, the router needs to know which interfaces are "inside" and which are "outside." The **ip nat inside** and **ip nat outside** interface subcommands identify each interface appropriately.

A couple of **show** commands list the most important information about NAT. The **show ip nat translations** command lists the two static NAT entries created in the configuration. The **show ip nat statistics** command lists statistics, listing things such as the number of currently active translation table entries. The statistics also include the number of hits, which increments for every packet for which NAT must translate addresses.

Dynamic NAT Configuration

As you might imagine, dynamic NAT configuration differs in some ways from static NAT, but it has some similarities as well. Dynamic NAT still requires that each interface be identified as either an inside or outside interface, and of course static mapping is no longer required. Dynamic NAT uses an access control list (ACL) to identify which inside local (private) IP addresses need to have their addresses translated, and it defines a pool of registered public IP addresses to allocate. The specific steps are as follows:

Step 1. Use the **ip nat inside** command in interface configuration mode to configure interfaces to be in the inside part of the NAT design (just like with static NAT).

Step 2. Use the **ip nat outside** command in interface configuration mode to configure interfaces to be in the outside part of the NAT design (just like with static NAT).

Step 3. Configure an ACL that matches the packets entering inside interfaces for which NAT should be performed.

Step 4. Use the **ip nat pool** *name first-address last-address* **netmask** *subnet-mask* command in global configuration mode to configure the pool of public registered IP addresses.

Step 5. Use the **ip nat inside source list** *acl-number* **pool** *pool-name* command in global configuration mode to enable dynamic NAT. Note the command references the ACL (Step 3) and pool (Step 4) per previous steps.

The next example shows a sample dynamic NAT configuration using the same network topology as the previous example (see Figure 27-9). In this case, the same two inside local addresses, 10.1.1.1 and 10.1.1.2, need translation. However, unlike the previous static NAT example, the configuration in Example 27-2 places the public IP addresses (200.1.1.1 and 200.1.1.2) into a pool of dynamically assignable inside global addresses.

Example 27-2 *Dynamic NAT Configuration*

```
NAT# show running-config
!
! Lines omitted for brevity
!
interface GigabitEthernet0/0
 ip address 10.1.1.3 255.255.255.0
 ip nat inside
!
interface Serial0/0/0
 ip address 200.1.1.251 255.255.255.0
 ip nat outside
!
ip nat pool fred 200.1.1.1 200.1.1.2 netmask 255.255.255.252
ip nat inside source list 1 pool fred
!
access-list 1 permit 10.1.1.2
access-list 1 permit 10.1.1.1
```

Dynamic NAT configures the pool of public (global) addresses with the **ip nat pool** command listing the first and last numbers in an inclusive range of inside global addresses. For example, if the pool needed ten addresses, the command might have listed 200.1.1.1 and 200.1.1.10, which means that NAT can use 200.1.1.1 through 200.1.1.10.

Dynamic NAT also performs a verification check on the **ip nat pool** command with the required **netmask** parameter. If the address range would not be in the same subnet, assuming the configured **netmask** was used on the addresses in the configured range, then IOS will reject the **ip nat pool** command. For example, as configured with the low end of 200.1.1.1, high end of 200.1.1.2, and a mask of 255.255.255.252, IOS would use the following checks, to ensure that both calculations put 200.1.1.1 and 200.1.1.2 in the same subnet:

■ 200.1.1.1 with mask 255.255.255.252 implies subnet 200.1.1.0, broadcast address 200.1.1.3.

■ 200.1.1.2 with mask 255.255.255.252 implies subnet 200.1.1.0, broadcast address 200.1.1.3.

If the command had instead showed a low and high end value of 200.1.1.1 and 200.1.1.6, again with mask 255.255.255.252, IOS would reject the command. IOS would do the math spelled out in the following list, realizing that the numbers were in different subnets:

■ 200.1.1.1 with mask 255.255.255.252 implies subnet 200.1.1.0, broadcast address 200.1.1.3.

■ 200.1.1.6 with mask 255.255.255.252 implies subnet 200.1.1.4, broadcast address 200.1.1.7.

One other big difference between the dynamic NAT and static NAT configuration in Example 27-1 has to do with two options in the **ip nat inside source** command. The dynamic NAT version of this command refers to the name of the NAT pool it wants to use for inside global addresses—in this case, fred. It also refers to an IP ACL, which defines the matching logic for inside local IP addresses. So, the logic for the **ip nat inside source list 1 pool fred** command in this example is as follows:

Create NAT table entries that map between hosts matched by ACL 1, for packets entering any inside interface, allocating an inside global address from the pool called fred.

Dynamic NAT Verification

Examples 27-3 and 27-4 show the evidence that dynamic NAT begins with no NAT table entries, but the router reacts after user traffic correctly drives the NAT function. Example 27-3 shows the output of the **show ip nat translations** and **show ip nat statistics** commands before any users generate traffic that makes NAT do some work. The **show ip nat translations** command, which lists the NAT table entries, lists a blank line; the **show ip nat statistics** command, which shows how many times NAT has created a NAT table entry, shows 0 active translations.

Example 27-3 *Dynamic NAT Verifications Before Generating Traffic*

```
! The next command lists one empty line because no entries have been dynamically
! created yet.
NAT# show ip nat translations

NAT# show ip nat statistics
Total active translations: 0 (0 static, 0 dynamic; 0 extended)
Peak translations: 8, occurred 00:02:44 ago
Outside interfaces:
  Serial0/0
Inside interfaces:
  Ethernet0/0
Hits: 0  Misses: 0
CEF Translated packets: 0, CEF Punted packets: 0
Expired translations: 0
Dynamic mappings:
-- Inside Source
[id 1] access-list 1 pool fred refcount 0
 pool fred: netmask 255.255.255.252
    start 200.1.1.1 end 200.1.1.2
```

```
      type generic, total addresses 2, allocated 0 (0%), misses 0


Total doors: 0
Appl doors: 0
Normal doors: 0
Queued Packets: 0
```

The **show ip nat statistics** command at the end of the example lists some particularly interesting troubleshooting information with two different counters labeled "misses," as highlighted in the example. The first occurrence of this counter counts the number of times a
new packet comes along, needing a NAT entry, and not finding one. At that point, dynamic
NAT reacts and builds an entry. The second misses counter toward the end of the command
output lists the number of misses in the pool. This counter only increments when dynamic
NAT tries to allocate a new NAT table entry and finds no available addresses, so the packet
cannot be translated—probably resulting in an end user not getting to the application.

Next, Example 27-4 updates the output of both commands after the user of host at 10.1.1.1
telnets to host 170.1.1.1.

Example 27-4   *Dynamic NAT Verifications After Generating Traffic*

```
NAT# show ip nat translations
Pro Inside global      Inside local      Outside local      Outside global
--- 200.1.1.1          10.1.1.1          ---                ---


NAT# show ip nat statistics
Total active translations: 1 (0 static, 1 dynamic; 0 extended)
Peak translations: 11, occurred 00:04:32 ago
Outside interfaces:
  Serial0/0
Inside interfaces:
  Ethernet0/0
Hits: 69  Misses: 1
Expired translations: 0
Dynamic mappings:
-- Inside Source
access-list 1 pool fred refcount 1
[eml fred: netmask 255.255.255.252
    start 200.1.1.1 end 200.1.1.2
    type generic, total addresses 2, allocated 1 (50%), misses 0
```

The example begins with host 10.1.1.1 telnetting to 170.1.1.1 (not shown), with the NAT
router creating a NAT entry. The NAT table shows a single entry, mapping 10.1.1.1 to
200.1.1.1. And, the first line in the output of the **show ip nat statistics** command lists a
counter for 1 active translation, as shown in the NAT table at the top of the example.

Take an extra moment to consider the highlighted line, where the **show ip nat statistics**
command lists 1 miss and 69 hits. The first miss counter, now at 1, means that one packet
arrived that needed NAT but there was no NAT table entry. NAT reacted and added a NAT

table entry, so the hit counter of 69 means that the next 69 packets used the newly added NAT table entry. The second misses counter, still at 0, did not increment because the NAT pool had enough available inside global IP addresses to use to allocate the new NAT table entry. Also note that the last line lists statistics on the number of pool members allocated (1) and the percentage of the pool currently in use (50%).

The dynamic NAT table entries time out after a period of inactivity, putting those inside global addresses back in the pool for future use. Example 27-5 shows a sequence in which two different hosts make use of inside global address 200.1.1.1. Host 10.1.1.1 uses inside global address 200.1.1.1 at the beginning of the example. Then, instead of just waiting on the NAT entry to time out, the example clears the NAT table entry with the **clear ip nat translation** * command. At that point, the user at 10.1.1.2 telnets to 170.1.1.1, and the new NAT table entry appears, using the same 200.1.1.1 inside global address.

Example 27-5   *Example of Reuse of a Dynamic Inside Global IP Address*

```
! Host 10.1.1.1 currently uses inside global 200.1.1.1
NAT# show ip nat translations
Pro Inside global       Inside local        Outside local      Outside global
--- 200.1.1.1           10.1.1.1            ---                ---
NAT# clear ip nat translation *

!
! telnet from 10.1.1.2 to 170.1.1.1 happened next; not shown
!
! Now host 10.1.1.2 uses inside global 200.1.1.1

NAT# show ip nat translations
Pro Inside global       Inside local        Outside local      Outside global
--- 200.1.1.1           10.1.1.2            ---                ---
!
! Telnet from 10.1.1.1 to 170.1.1.1 happened next; not shown
!
NAT# debug ip nat
IP NAT debugging is on

Oct 20 19:23:03.263: NAT*: s=10.1.1.1->200.1.1.2, d=170.1.1.1 [348]
Oct 20 19:23:03.267: NAT*: s=170.1.1.1, d=200.1.1.2->10.1.1.1 [348]
Oct 20 19:23:03.464: NAT*: s=10.1.1.1->200.1.1.2, d=170.1.1.1 [349]
Oct 20 19:23:03.568: NAT*: s=170.1.1.1, d=200.1.1.2->10.1.1.1 [349]
```

Finally, at the end of Example 27-5, you see that host 10.1.1.1 has telnetted to another host in the Internet, plus the output from the **debug ip nat** command. This **debug** command causes the router to issue a message every time a packet has its address translated for NAT. You generate the output results by entering a few lines from the Telnet connection from 10.1.1.1 to 170.1.1.1. The debug output tells us that host 10.1.1.1 now uses inside global address 200.1.1.2 for this new connection.

NAT Overload (PAT) Configuration

The static and dynamic NAT configurations matter, but the NAT overload (PAT) configuration in this section matters more. This is the feature that saves public IPv4 addresses and prolonged IPv4's life.

NAT overload, as mentioned earlier, allows NAT to support many inside local IP addresses with only one or a few inside global IP addresses. By essentially translating the private IP address and port number to a single inside global address, but with a unique port number, NAT can support many (over 65,000) private hosts with only a single public, global address.

Two variations of PAT configuration exist in IOS. If PAT uses a pool of inside global addresses, the configuration looks exactly like dynamic NAT, except the **ip nat inside source list** global command has an **overload** keyword added to the end. If PAT just needs to use one inside global IP address, the router can use one of its interface IP addresses. Because NAT can support over 65,000 concurrent flows with a single inside global address, a single public IP address can support an entire organization's NAT needs.

The following statement details the configuration difference between NAT overload and 1:1 NAT when using a NAT pool:

Use the same steps for configuring dynamic NAT, as outlined in the previous section, but include the **overload** keyword at the end of the **ip nat inside source list** global command.

The following checklist details the configuration when using an interface IP address as the sole inside global IP address:

Step 1.   As with dynamic and static NAT, configure inside interfaces with the **ip nat inside** interface subcommand.

Step 2.   As with dynamic and static NAT, configure outside interfaces with the **ip nat outside** interface subcommand.

Step 3.   As with dynamic NAT, configure an ACL that matches the packets entering inside interfaces.

Step 4.   Configure the **ip nat inside source list** *acl-number* **interface** *type/number* **overload** global configuration command, referring to the ACL created in Step 3 and to the interface whose IP address will be used for translations.

Example 27-2 demonstrated a dynamic NAT configuration. To convert it to a PAT configuration, the **ip nat inside source list 1 pool fred overload** command would be used instead, simply adding the **overload** keyword.

The next example shows PAT configuration using a single interface IP address. Figure 27-10 shows the same familiar network, with a few changes. In this case, the ISP has given Certskills a subset of network 200.1.1.0: CIDR subnet 200.1.1.248/30. In other words, this subnet has two usable addresses: 200.1.1.249 and 200.1.1.250. These addresses are used on either end of the serial link between Certskills and its ISP. The NAT feature on the Certskills router translates all NAT addresses to its serial IP address, 200.1.1.249.

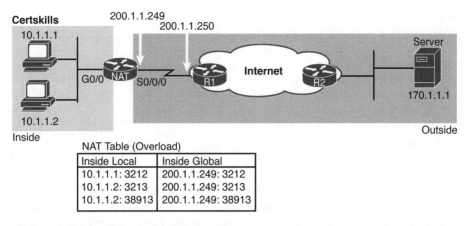

Figure 27-10 *NAT Overload and PAT*

In Example 27-6, which shows the NAT overload configuration, NAT translates using inside global address 200.1.1.249 only, so the NAT pool is not required. In the example, host 10.1.1.2 creates two Telnet connections, and host 10.1.1.1 creates one Telnet connection, causing three dynamic NAT entries, each using inside global address 200.1.1.249, but each with a unique port number.

Example 27-6 *NAT Overload Configuration*

```
NAT# show running-config
!
! Lines Omitted for Brevity
!
interface GigabitEthernet0/0
 ip address 10.1.1.3 255.255.255.0
 ip nat inside
!
interface Serial0/0/0
 ip address 200.1.1.249 255.255.255.252
 ip nat outside
!
ip nat inside source list 1 interface Serial0/0/0 overload
!
access-list 1 permit 10.1.1.2
access-list 1 permit 10.1.1.1
!

NAT# show ip nat translations
Pro Inside global      Inside local      Outside local      Outside global
tcp 200.1.1.249:3212   10.1.1.1:3212     170.1.1.1:23       170.1.1.1:23
tcp 200.1.1.249:3213   10.1.1.2:3213     170.1.1.1:23       170.1.1.1:23
tcp 200.1.1.249:38913  10.1.1.2:38913    170.1.1.1:23       170.1.1.1:23
NAT# show ip nat statistics
```

```
Total active translations: 3 (0 static, 3 dynamic; 3 extended)
Peak translations: 12, occurred 00:01:11 ago
Outside interfaces:
  Serial0/0/0
Inside interfaces:
  GigabitEthernet0/0
Hits: 103  Misses: 3
Expired translations: 0
Dynamic mappings:
-- Inside Source
access-list 1 interface Serial0/0/0 refcount 3
```

The **ip nat inside source list 1 interface serial 0/0/0 overload** command has several parameters, but if you understand the dynamic NAT configuration, the new parameters shouldn't
be too hard to grasp. The **list 1** parameter means the same thing as it does for dynamic
NAT: Inside local IP addresses matching ACL 1 have their addresses translated. The **interface serial 0/0/0** parameter means that the only inside global IP address available is the IP
address of the NAT router's interface serial 0/0/0. Finally, the **overload** parameter means
that overload is enabled. Without this parameter, the router does not perform overload, just
dynamic NAT.

As you can see in the output of the **show ip nat translations** command, three translations
have been added to the NAT table. Before this command, host 10.1.1.1 creates one Telnet
connection to 170.1.1.1, and host 10.1.1.2 creates two Telnet connections. The router creates one NAT table entry for each unique combination of inside local IP address and port.

NAT Troubleshooting

The majority of NAT troubleshooting issues relate to getting the configuration correct.
Source NAT has several configuration options—static, dynamic, PAT—with several configuration commands for each. So work hard at building skills with the configuration so you can
quickly recognize configuration mistakes. The following troubleshooting checklist summarizes the most common source NAT issues, most of which relate to incorrect configuration.

Reversed inside and outside: Ensure that the configuration includes the **ip nat inside**
and **ip nat outside** interface subcommands, and that the commands are not reversed (the
ip nat inside command on outside interfaces, and vice versa). With source NAT, only the
inside interface triggers IOS to add new translations, so designating the correct inside
interfaces is particularly important.

Static NAT: Check the **ip nat inside source static** command to ensure it lists the inside
local address first, and the inside global IP address second.

Dynamic NAT (ACL): Ensure that the ACL configured to match packets sent by the
inside hosts match that host's packets, before any NAT translation has occurred. For
example, if an inside local address of 10.1.1.1 should be translated to 200.1.1.1, ensure
that the ACL matches source address 10.1.1.1, not 200.1.1.1.

Dynamic NAT (pool): For dynamic NAT without PAT, ensure that the pool has enough
IP addresses. When not using PAT, each inside host consumes one IP address from the
pool. A large or growing value in the second misses counter in the **show ip nat statistics**
command output can indicate this problem. Also, compare the configured pool to the

list of addresses in the NAT translation table (**show ip nat translations**). Finally, if the pool is small, the problem may be that the configuration intended to use PAT, and is missing the **overload** keyword (see next item).

PAT: It is easy to forget to add the **overload** option on the end of **ip nat inside source list** command. PAT configuration is identical to a valid dynamic NAT configuration except that PAT requires the **overload** keyword. Without it, dynamic NAT works, but the pool of addresses is typically consumed very quickly. The NAT router will not translate nor forward traffic for hosts if there is not an available pool IP address for their traffic, so some hosts experience an outage.

ACL: As mentioned in Chapter 26, "Advanced IPv4 Access Control Lists," you can always add a check for ACLs that cause a problem. Perhaps NAT has been configured correctly, but an ACL exists on one of the interfaces, discarding the packets. Note that the order of operations inside the router matters in this case. For packets entering an interface, IOS processes ACLs before NAT. For packets exiting an interface, IOS processes any outbound ACL after translating the addresses with NAT.

User traffic required: NAT reacts to user traffic. If you configure NAT in a lab, NAT does not act to create translations (**show ip nat translations**) until some user traffic enters the NAT router on an inside interface, triggering NAT to do a translation. The NAT configuration can be perfect, but if no inbound traffic occurs that matches the NAT configuration, NAT does nothing.

IPv4 routing: IPv4 routing could prevent packets from arriving on either side of the NAT router. Note that the routing must work for the destination IP addresses used in the packets.

With source NAT, the user sits at some user device like a PC. They attempt to connect to some server, using that server's DNS name. After DNS resolution, the client (the inside host) sends an IP packet with a destination address of the server. For instance, as shown in Figure 27-11, PC1 sends an IP packet with destination IP address 170.1.1.1, some server in the Internet. PC1 is an inside host, the server is an outside host, and 170.1.1.1 is the outside global address. (Note that these addresses match the previous example, which referenced Figure 27-10.)

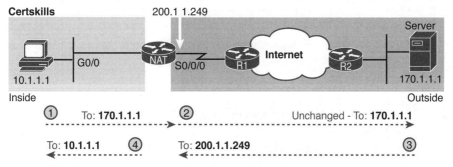

Figure 27-11 *Destination Address Changes on Outside to Inside (Only) with Source NAT*

Note that with source NAT in what should be a familiar design, the destination IP address of the packet does not change during the entire trip. So, troubleshooting of IPv4 routing toward the outside network will be based on the same IP address throughout.

Now look at Steps 3 and 4 in the figure, which reminds us that the return packet will first flow to the NAT inside global address (200.1.1.249 in this case) as shown at Step 3. Then NAT converts the destination address to 10.1.1.1 in this case. So, to troubleshoot packets flowing right to left in this case, you have to troubleshoot based on two different destination IP addresses.

Chapter Review

One key to doing well on the exams is to perform repetitive spaced review sessions. Review this chapter's material using either the tools in the book, DVD, or interactive tools for the same material found on the book's companion website. Refer to the "Your Study Plan" element for more details. Table 27-4 outlines the key review elements and where you can find them. To better track your study progress, record when you completed these activities in the second column.

Table 27-4 Chapter Review Tracking

Review Element	Review Date(s)	Resource Used
Review key topics		Book, DVD/website
Review key terms		Book, DVD/website
Repeat DIKTA questions		Book, PCPT
Review memory tables		Book, DVD/website
Review command tables		Book

Review All the Key Topics

Table 27-5 Key Topics for Chapter 27

Key Topic Element	Description	Page Number
Table 27-2	List of private IP network numbers	647
Figure 27-2	Main concept of NAT translating private IP addresses into publicly unique global addresses	647
Figure 27-4	Typical NAT network diagram with key NAT terms listed	649
Table 27-3	List of four key NAT terms and their meanings	650
Figure 27-8	Concepts behind address conservation achieved by NAT overload (PAT)	653
Paragraph	Summary of differences between dynamic NAT configuration and PAT using a pool	660
List	NAT troubleshooting checklist	662

Key Terms You Should Know

CIDR, inside global, inside local, NAT overload, outside global, Port Address Translation, private IP network, source NAT

Command References

Tables 27-6 and 27-7 list configuration and verification commands used in this chapter. As an easy review exercise, cover the left column in a table, read the right column, and try to recall the command without looking. Then repeat the exercise, covering the right column, and try to recall what the command does.

Table 27-6   Chapter 27 Configuration Command Reference

Command	Description
ip nat {inside | outside}	Interface subcommand to enable NAT and identify whether the interface is in the inside or outside of the network
ip nat inside source {list {*access-list-number* | *access-list-name*}} {interface *type number* | pool *pool-name*} [overload]	Global command that enables NAT globally, referencing the ACL that defines which source addresses to NAT, and the interface or pool from which to find global addresses
ip nat pool *name start-ip end-ip* {netmask *netmask* | prefix-length *prefix-length*}	Global command to define a pool of NAT addresses
ip nat inside source static *inside-local inside-global*	Global command that lists the inside and outside address (or, an outside interface whose IP address should be used) to be paired and added to the NAT translation table

Table 27-7   Chapter 27 EXEC Command Reference

Command	Description
show ip nat statistics	Lists counters for packets and NAT table entries, as well as basic configuration information
show ip nat translations [verbose]	Displays the NAT table
clear ip nat translation {* | [inside *global-ip local-ip*] [outside *local-ip global-ip*]}	Clears all or some of the dynamic entries in the NAT table, depending on which parameters are used
clear ip nat translation *protocol* inside *global-ip global-port local-ip local-port* [outside *local-ip global-ip*]	Clears some of the dynamic entries in the NAT table, depending on which parameters are used
debug ip nat	Issues a log message describing each packet whose IP address is translated with NAT

Part VII Review

Keep track of your part review progress with the checklist in Table P7-1. Details on each task follow the table.

Table P7-1   Part VII Part Review Checklist

Activity	1st Date Completed	2nd Date Completed
Repeat All DIKTA Questions		
Answer Part Review Questions		
Review Key Topics		
Create Command Mind Map by Category		
Do Labs		

Repeat All DIKTA Questions

For this task, use the PCPT software to answer the "Do I Know This Already?" questions again for the chapters in this part of the book.

Answer Part Review Questions

For this task, use PCPT to answer the Part Review questions for this part of the book.

Review Key Topics

Review all key topics in all chapters in this part, either by browsing the chapters or by using the Key Topics application on the DVD or companion website.

Create Command Mind Map by Category

Create a command mind map to help you remember the commands. This exercise does not focus on every single parameter of every command, or even their meaning. The goal is to help you organize the commands internally so that you know which commands to consider when faced with a real-life problem or an exam question. Create a mind map with the following categories of commands from this part of the book:

Numbered standard IPv4 ACLs, numbered extended IPv4 ACLs, named IPv4 ACLs, and NAT

In this mind map, for each category, think of all configuration commands and all EXEC commands (mostly **show** commands). For each category, group the configuration commands separately from the EXEC commands. Figure P7-1 shows an example of the organization.

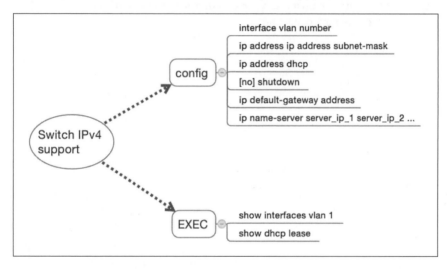

Figure P7-1 *Sample Mind Map from the Switch IPv4 Branch*

Appendix L, "Mind Map Solutions," lists a sample mind map answer, but as usual, your mind map can and will look different.

If you do choose to use mind map software rather than paper, you might want to remember where you stored your mind map files. Table P7-2 lists the mind maps for this part review and a place to record those filenames.

Table P7-2 Configuration Mind Maps for Part VII Review

Map	Description	Where You Saved It
1	Commands Mind Map	

Do Labs

Depending on your chosen lab tool, here are some suggestions for what to do in lab:

Pearson Network Simulator: If you use the full Pearson ICND1 or CCNA simulator, focus more on the configuration scenario and troubleshooting scenario labs associated with the topics in this part of the book. These types of labs include a larger set of topics and work well as Part Review activities. (See the Introduction for some details about how to find which labs are about topics in this part of the book.)

Config Labs: In your idle moments, review and repeat any of the Config Labs for this book part in the author's blog; launch from blog.certskills.com/ccent and navigate to the Hands-on Config labs.

Other: If using other lab tools, here are a few suggestions: When building ACL labs, you can test with Telnet (port 23), SSH (port 22), ping (ICMP), and traceroute (UDP) traffic as generated from an extra router. So, do not just configure the ACL; make an ACL that can match these types of traffic, denying some and permitting others, and then test. For NAT, you can also test with the **ping** command.

So far, this book has mostly ignored IP version 6 (IPv6). This part reverses the trend, collecting all the specific IPv6 topics into five chapters.

The chapters in this part of the book walk you through the same topics discussed throughout this book for IPv4, often using IPv4 as a point of comparison. Certainly, many details differ when comparing IPv4 and IPv6. However, many core concepts about IP addressing, subnetting, routing, and routing protocols remain the same. The chapters in this part build on those foundational concepts, adding the specific details about how IPv6 forwards IPv6 packets from one host to another.

Part VIII

IP Version 6

CHAPTER 28

Fundamentals of IP Version 6

This chapter covers the following exam topics:

1.0 Network Fundamentals

1.12 Configure, verify, and troubleshoot IPv6 addressing

IPv4 has been a solid and highly useful part of the growth of TCP/IP and the Internet. For most of the long history of the Internet, and for most corporate networks that use TCP/IP, IPv4 is the core protocol that defines addressing and routing. However, even though IPv4 has many great qualities, it does have some shortcomings, creating the need for a replacement protocol: IP version 6 (IPv6).

IPv6 defines the same general functions as IPv4, but with different methods of implementing those functions. For example, both IPv4 and IPv6 define addressing, the concepts of subnetting larger groups of addresses into smaller groups, headers used to create an IPv4 or IPv6 packet, and the rules for routing those packets. At the same time, IPv6 handles the details differently; for example, using a 128-bit IPv6 address rather than the 32-bit IPv4 address.

This chapter focuses on the core network layer functions of addressing and routing. The first section of this chapter looks at the big concepts, while the second section looks at the specifics of how to write and type IPv6 addresses.

"Do I Know This Already?" Quiz

Take the quiz (either here, or use the PCPT software) if you want to use the score to help you decide how much time to spend on this chapter. The answers are at the bottom of the page following the quiz, and the explanations are in DVD Appendix C and in the PCPT software.

Table 28-1 "Do I Know This Already?" Foundation Topics Section-to-Question Mapping

Foundation Topics Section	Questions
Introduction to IPv6	1–2
IPv6 Addressing Formats and Conventions	3–6

1. Which of the following was a short-term solution to the IPv4 address exhaustion problem?

   a. IP version 6

   b. IP version 5

   c. NAT/PAT

   d. ARP

2. A router receives an Ethernet frame that holds an IPv6 packet. The router then makes a decision to route the packet out a serial link. Which of the following statements is true about how a router forwards an IPv6 packet?

   a. The router discards the Ethernet data-link header and trailer of the received frame.

   b. The router makes the forwarding decision based on the packet's source IPv6 address.

   c. The router keeps the Ethernet header, encapsulating the entire frame inside a new IPv6 packet before sending it over the serial link.

   d. The router uses the IPv4 routing table when choosing where to forward the packet.

3. Which of the following is the shortest valid abbreviation for FE80:0000:0000:0100:0000:0000:0000:0123?

   a. FE80::100::123

   b. FE8::1::123

   c. FE80::100:0:0:0:123:4567

   d. FE80:0:0:100::123

4. Which of the following is the shortest valid abbreviation for 2000:0300:0040:0005:6000:0700:0080:0009?

   a. 2:3:4:5:6:7:8:9

   b. 2000:300:40:5:6000:700:80:9

   c. 2000:300:4:5:6000:700:8:9

   d. 2000:3:4:5:6:7:8:9

5. Which of the following is the unabbreviated version of IPv6 address 2001:DB8::200:28?

   a. 2001:0DB8:0000:0000:0000:0000:0200:0028

   b. 2001:0DB8::0200:0028

   c. 2001:0DB8:0:0:0:0:0200:0028

   d. 2001:0DB8:0000:0000:0000:0000:200:0028

6. Which of the following is the prefix for address 2000:0000:0000:0005:6000:0700:0080:0009, assuming a mask of /64?

   a. 2000::5::/64

   b. 2000::5:0:0:0:0/64

   c. 2000:0:0:5::/64

   d. 2000:0:0:5:0:0:0:0/64

Foundation Topics

Introduction to IPv6

IP version 6 (IPv6) serves as the replacement protocol for IP version 4 (IPv4).

Unfortunately, that one bold statement creates more questions than it answers. Why does IPv4 need to be replaced? If IPv4 needs to be replaced, when will that happen—and will it happen quickly? What exactly happens when a company or the Internet replaces IPv4 with IPv6? And the list goes on.

While this introductory chapter cannot get into every detail of why IPv4 needs to eventually be replaced by IPv6, the clearest and most obvious reason for migrating TCP/IP networks to use IPv6 is growth. IPv4 uses a 32-bit address, which totals to a few billion addresses. Interestingly, that seemingly large number of addresses is too small. IPv6 increases the address to 128 bits in length. For perspective, IPv6 supplies more than 10,000,000,000,000,000,000,000,000,000,000 times as many addresses as IPv4.

The fact that IPv6 uses a different size address field, with some different addressing rules, means that many other protocols and functions change as well. For example, IPv4 routing—in other words, the packet-forwarding process—relies on an understanding of IPv4 addresses. To support IPv6 routing, routers must understand IPv6 addresses and routing. To dynamically learn routes for IPv6 subnets, routing protocols must support these different IPv6 addressing rules, including rules about how IPv6 creates subnets. As a result, the migration from IPv4 to IPv6 is much more than changing one protocol (IP), but it impacts many protocols.

This first section of the chapter discusses some of the reasons for the change from IPv4 to IPv6, along with the protocols that must change as a result.

The Historical Reasons for IPv6

In the last 40+ years, the Internet has gone from its infancy to being a huge influence in the world. It first grew through research at universities, from the ARPANET beginnings of the Internet in the late 1960s into the 1970s. The Internet kept growing fast in the 1980s, with the Internet's fast growth still primarily driven by research and the universities that joined in that research. By the early 1990s, the Internet began to transform to allow commerce, allowing people to sell services and products over the Internet, which drove yet another steep spike upward in the growth of the Internet. Eventually, fixed Internet access (primarily through dial, digital subscriber line [DSL], and cable) became common, followed by the pervasive use of the Internet from mobile devices like smartphones. Figure 28-1 shows some of these major milestones with general dates.

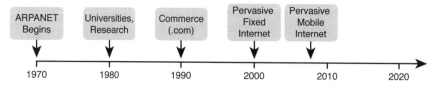

Figure 28-1 *Some Major Events in the Growth of the Internet*

The incredible growth of the Internet over a fairly long time created a big problem for public IPv4 addresses: the world was running out of addresses. For instance, in 2011, IANA allocated the final /8 address blocks (the same size as a class A network), allocating one final /8 block to each of the five Regional Internet Registries (RIR). At that point, RIRs could no longer receive new allocations of public addresses from IANA to then turn around and assign smaller address blocks to companies or ISPs.

At that point in 2011, each of the five RIRs still had public addresses to allocate or assign. However, over the years after 2011, the RIRs have each gradually reached the point of also exhausting their supply of addresses. For example, in late 2015, ARIN, the RIR for North America, announced that it had exhausted its supply, and was now managing requests for new address blocks with a waiting list.

These events are significant in that the day has finally come in which new companies can attempt to connect to the Internet, but they can no longer simply use IPv4, ignoring IPv6. Their only option will be IPv6, because IPv4 has no public addresses left.

NOTE   You can track ARIN's progress through this interesting transition in the history of the Internet at its IPv4 address depletion site: http://teamarin.net/category/ipv4-depletion/.

Even though the press has rightfully made a big deal about running out of IPv4 addresses, those who care about the Internet knew about this potential problem since the late 1980s. The problem, generally called the *IPv4 address exhaustion* problem, could literally have caused the huge growth of the Internet in the 1990s to have come to a screeching halt! Something had to be done.

The IETF came up with several short-term solutions to make IPv4 addresses last longer, and one long-term solution: IPv6. NAT and CIDR, the short-term solutions discussed in Chapter 27, "Network Address Translation," helped extend IPv4's life another couple of decades. IPv6 creates a more permanent and long-lasting solution, replacing IPv4, with a new IPv6 header and new IPv6 addresses. The address size supports a huge number of addresses, solving the address shortage problem for generations (we hope). Figure 28-2 shows some of the major address exhaustion timing.

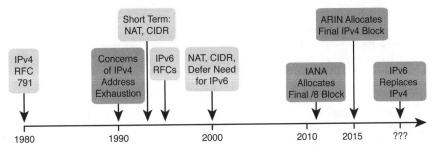

Figure 28-2   *Timeline for IPv4 Address Exhaustion and Short-/Long-Term Solutions*

NOTE   The website www.potaroo.net, by Geoff Huston, shows many interesting statistics about the growth of the Internet, including IPv4 address exhaustion.

The rest of this first section examines IPv6, comparing it to IPv4, focusing on the common features of the two protocols. In particular, this section compares the protocols (including addresses), routing, routing protocols, and miscellaneous other related topics.

NOTE   You might wonder why the next version of IP is not called IP version 5. There was an earlier effort to create a new version of IP, and it was numbered version 5. IPv5 did not progress to the standards stage. However, to prevent any issues, because version 5 had been used in some documents, the next effort to update IP was numbered as version 6.

The IPv6 Protocols

The primary purpose of the core IPv6 protocol mirrors the same purpose of the IPv4 protocol. That core IPv6 protocol, as defined in RFC 2460, defines a packet concept, addresses for those packets, and the role of hosts and routers. These rules allow the devices to forward packets sourced by hosts, through multiple routers, so that they arrive at the correct destination host. (IPv4 defines those same concepts for IPv4 back in RFC 791.)

However, because IPv6 impacts so many other functions in a TCP/IP network, many more RFCs must define details of IPv6. Some other RFCs define how to migrate from IPv4 to IPv6. Others define new versions of familiar protocols, or replace old protocols with new ones. For example:

Older OSPF Version 2 Upgraded to OSPF Version 3: The older Open Shortest Path First (OSPF) version 2 works for IPv4, but not for IPv6, so a newer version, OSPF version 3, was created to support IPv6. (Note: OSPFv3 was later upgraded to support advertising both IPv4 and IPv6 routes.)

ICMP Upgraded to ICMP Version 6: Internet Control Message Protocol (ICMP) worked well with IPv4, but needed to be changed to support IPv6. The new name is ICMPv6.

ARP Replaced by Neighbor Discovery Protocol: For IPv4, Address Resolution Protocol (ARP) discovers the MAC address used by neighbors. IPv6 replaces ARP with a more general Neighbor Discovery Protocol (NDP).

NOTE   If you go to any website that lists the RFCs, like http://www.rfc-editor.org, you can find almost 300 RFCs that have IPv6 in the title.

Although the term IPv6, when used broadly, includes many protocols, the one specific protocol called IPv6 defines the new 128-bit IPv6 address. Of course, writing these addresses in binary would be a problem—they probably would not even fit on the width of a piece of paper! IPv6 defines a shorter hexadecimal format, requiring at most 32 hexadecimal digits (one hex digit per 4 bits), with methods to abbreviate the hexadecimal addresses as well.

For example, all of the following are IPv6 addresses, each with 32 or less hex digits.

2345:1111:2222:3333:4444:5555:6666:AAAA

2000:1:2:3:4:5:6:A

FE80::1

The upcoming section "IPv6 Addressing Formats and Conventions" discusses the specifics of how to represent IPv6 addresses, including how to legally abbreviate the hex address values.

Like IPv4, IPv6 defines a header, with places to hold both the source and destination address fields. Compared to IPv4, the IPv6 header does make some other changes besides simply making the address fields larger. However, even though the IPv6 header is larger than an IPv4 header, the IPv6 header is actually simpler (on purpose), to reduce the work done each time a router must route an IPv6 packet. Figure 28-3 shows the required 40-byte part of the IPv6 header.

28

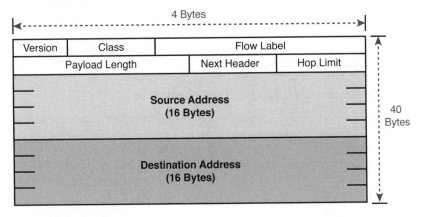

Figure 28-3 *IPv6 Header*

IPv6 Routing

As with many functions of IPv6, IPv6 routing looks just like IPv4 routing from a general perspective, with the differences being clear only once you look at the specifics. Keeping the discussion general for now, IPv6 uses these ideas the same way as IPv4:

■ To be able to build and send IPv6 packets out an interface, end-user devices need an IPv6 address on that interface.

■ End-user hosts need to know the IPv6 address of a default router, to which the host sends IPv6 packets if the host is in a different subnet.

■ IPv6 routers de-encapsulate and re-encapsulate each IPv6 packet when routing the packet.

■ IPv6 routers make routing decisions by comparing the IPv6 packet's destination address to the router's IPv6 routing table; the matched route lists directions of where to send the IPv6 packet next.

NOTE You could take the preceding list, and replace every instance of IPv6 with IPv4, and all the statements would be true of IPv4 as well.

While the list shows some concepts that should be familiar from IPv4, the next few figures show the concepts with an example. First, Figure 28-4 shows a few settings on a host. The host (PC1) has an address of 2345::1. PC1 also knows its default gateway of 2345::2. (Both values are valid abbreviations for real IPv6 addresses.) To send an IPv6 packet to host PC2, on another IPv6 subnet, PC1 creates an IPv6 packet and sends it to R1, PC1's default gateway.

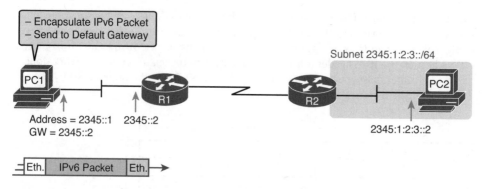

Figure 28-4   *IPv6 Host Building and Sending an IPv6 Packet*

The router (R1) has many small tasks to do when forwarding this IPv6 packet, but for now, focus on the work R1 does related to encapsulation. As seen in Step 1 of Figure 28-5, R1 receives the incoming data-link frame, and extracts (de-encapsulates) the IPv6 packet from inside the frame, discarding the original data-link header and trailer. At Step 2, once R1 knows to forward the IPv6 packet to R2, R1 adds a correct outgoing data-link header and trailer to the IPv6 packet, encapsulating the IPv6 packet.

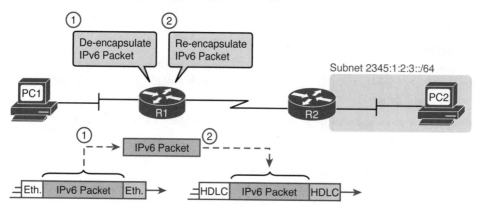

Figure 28-5   *IPv6 Router Performing Routine Encapsulation Tasks When Routing IPv6*

When a router like R1 de-encapsulates the packet from the data-link frame, it must also decide what type of packet sits inside the frame. To do so, the router must look at a proto-col type field in the data-link header, which identifies the type of packet inside the data-link frame. Today, most data-link frames carry either an IPv4 packet or an IPv6 packet.

To route an IPv6 packet, a router must use its IPv6 routing table instead of the IPv4 rout-ing table. The router must look at the packet's destination IPv6 address and compare that address to the router's current IPv6 routing table. The router uses the forwarding instruc-tions in the matched IPv6 route to forward the IPv6 packet. Figure 28-6 shows the overall process.

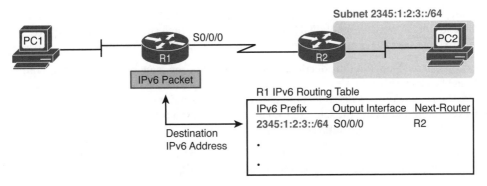

Figure 28-6   *Comparing an IPv6 Packet to R1's IPv6 Routing Table*

Note that again, the process works like IPv4, except that the IPv6 packet lists IPv6 addresses, and the IPv6 routing table lists routing information for IPv6 subnets (called prefixes).

Finally, in most enterprise networks, the routers will route both IPv4 and IPv6 packets at the same time. That is, your company will not decide to adopt IPv6, and then late one weekend night turn off all IPv4 and enable IPv6 on every device. Instead, IPv6 allows for a slow migration, during which some or all routers forward both IPv4 and IPv6 packets. (The migration strategy of running both IPv4 and IPv6 is called *dual stack*.) All you have to do is configure the router to route IPv6 packets, in addition to the existing configuration for routing IPv4 packets.

IPv6 Routing Protocols

IPv6 routers need to learn routes for all the possible IPv6 prefixes (subnets). Just like with IPv4, IPv6 routers use routing protocols, with familiar names, and generally speaking, with familiar functions.

None of the IPv4 routing protocols could be used to advertise IPv6 routes originally. They all required some kind of update to add messages, protocols, and rules to support IPv6. Over time, Routing Information Protocol (RIP), Open Shortest Path First (OSPF), Enhanced Interior Gateway Routing Protocol (EIGRP), and Border Gateway Protocol (BGP) were all updated to support IPv6. Table 28-2 lists the names of these routing protocols, with a few comments.

Table 28-2   IPv6 Routing Protocols

Routing Protocol	Defined By	Notes
RIPng (RIP next generation)	RFC	The "next generation" is a reference to a TV series, *Star Trek: the Next Generation*.
OSPFv3 (OSPF version 3)	RFC	The OSPF you have worked with for IPv4 is actually OSPF version 2, so the new version for IPv6 is OSPFv3.
EIGRPv6 (EIGRP for IPv6)	Cisco	Cisco owns the rights to the EIGRP protocol, but Cisco also now publishes EIGRP as an informational RFC.
MP BGP-4 (Multiprotocol BGP version 4)	RFC	BGP version 4 was created to be highly extendable; IPv6 support was added to BGP version 4 through one such enhancement, MP BGP-4.

In addition, these routing protocols also follow the same interior gateway protocol (IGP) and exterior gateway protocol (EGP) conventions as their IPv4 cousins. RIPng, EIGRPv6, and OSPFv3 act as interior gateway protocols, advertising IPv6 routes inside an enterprise.

As you can see from this introduction, IPv6 uses many of the same big ideas as IPv4. Both define headers with a source and destination address. Both define the routing of packets, with the routing process discarding old data-link headers and trailers when forwarding the packets. And routers use the same general process to make a routing decision, comparing the packet's destination IP address to the routing table.

The big differences between IPv4 and IPv6 revolve around the bigger IPv6 addresses. The next topic begins looking at the specifics of these IPv6 addresses.

IPv6 Addressing Formats and Conventions

The CCENT and CCNA R&S exams require some fundamental skills in working with IPv4 addresses. For example, you need to be able to interpret IPv4 addresses, like 172.21.73.14. You need to be able to work with prefix-style masks, like /25, and interpret what that means when used with a particular IPv4 address. And you need to be able to take an address and mask, like 172.21.73.14/25, and find the subnet ID.

This second major section of this chapter discusses these same ideas for IPv6 addresses. In particular, this section looks at

■ How to write and interpret unabbreviated 32-digit IPv6 addresses

■ How to abbreviate IPv6 addresses, and how to interpret abbreviated addresses

■ How to interpret the IPv6 prefix length mask

■ How to find the IPv6 prefix (subnet ID), based on an address and prefix length mask

The biggest challenge with these tasks lies in the sheer size of the numbers. Thankfully, the math to find the subnet ID—often a challenge for IPv4—is easier for IPv6, at least to the depth discussed in this book.

Representing Full (Unabbreviated) IPv6 Addresses

IPv6 uses a convenient hexadecimal (hex) format for addresses. To make it more readable, IPv6 uses a format with eight sets of four hex digits, with each set of four digits separated by a colon. For example:

2340:1111:AAAA:0001:1234:5678:9ABC:1234

NOTE   For convenience, the author uses the term *quartet* for one set of four hex digits, with eight quartets in each IPv6 address. Note that the IPv6 RFCs do not use the term *quartet*.

IPv6 addresses also have a binary format as well, but thankfully, most of the time you do not need to look at the binary version of the addresses. However, in those cases, converting from hex to binary is relatively easy. Just change each hex digit to the equivalent 4-bit value listed in Table 28-3.

Table 28-3   Hexadecimal/Binary Conversion Chart

Hex	Binary	Hex	Binary
0	0000	8	1000
1	0001	9	1001
2	0010	A	1010
3	0011	B	1011
4	0100	C	1100
5	0101	D	1101
6	0110	E	1110
7	0111	F	1111

Abbreviating and Expanding IPv6 Addresses

IPv6 also defines ways to abbreviate or shorten how you write or type an IPv6 address. Why? Although using a 32-digit hex number works much better than working with a 128-bit binary number, 32 hex digits is still a lot of digits to remember, recognize in command output, and type on a command line. The IPv6 address abbreviation rules let you shorten these numbers.

Computers and routers typically use the shortest abbreviation, even if you type all 32 hex digits of the address. So even if you would prefer to use the longer unabbreviated version of the IPv6 address, you need to be ready to interpret the meaning of an abbreviated IPv6 address as listed by a router or host. This section first looks at abbreviating addresses, and then at expanding addresses.

Abbreviating IPv6 Addresses

Two basic rules let you, or any computer, shorten or abbreviate an IPv6 address:

1. Inside each quartet of four hex digits, remove the leading 0s (0s on the left side of the quartet) in the three positions on the left. (Note: at this step, a quartet of 0000 will leave a single 0.)

2. Find any string of two or more consecutive quartets of all hex 0s, and replace that set of quartets with a double colon (::). The :: means "two or more quartets of all 0s." However, you can only use :: once in a single address, because otherwise the exact IPv6 might not be clear.

For example, consider the following IPv6 address. The bold digits represent digits in which the address could be abbreviated.

FE00:**0000:0000:000**1:**0000:0000:0000:00**56

Applying the first rule, you would look at all eight quartets independently. In each, remove all the leading 0s. Note that five of the quartets have four 0s, so for these, only remove three 0s, leaving the following value:

FE00:0:0:1:0:0:0:56

While this abbreviation is valid, the address can be abbreviated more, using the second rule. In this case, two instances exist where more than one quartet in a row has only a 0. Pick the longest such sequence, and replace it with ::, giving you the shortest legal abbreviation:

FE00:0:0:1::56

While FE00:0:0:1::56 is indeed the shortest abbreviation, this example happens to make it easier to see the two most common mistakes when abbreviating IPv6 addresses. First, never remove trailing 0s in a quartet (0s on the right side of the quartet). In this case, the first quartet of FE00 cannot be shortened at all, because the two 0s trail. So, the following address, which begins now with only FE in the first quartet, is not a correct abbreviation of the original IPv6 address:

FE:0:0:1::56

The second common mistake is to replace all series of all 0 quartets with a double colon. For example, the following abbreviation would be incorrect for the original IPv6 address listed in this topic:

FE00::1::56

The reason this abbreviation is incorrect is because now you do not know how many quartets of all 0s to substitute into each :: to find the original unabbreviated address.

Expanding Abbreviated IPv6 Addresses

To expand an IPv6 address back into its full unabbreviated 32-digit number, use two similar rules. The rules basically reverse the logic of the previous two rules:

1. In each quartet, add leading 0s as needed until the quartet has four hex digits.
2. If a double colon (::) exists, count the quartets currently shown; the total should be less than 8. Replace the :: with multiple quartets of 0000 so that eight total quartets exist.

The best way to get comfortable with these addresses and abbreviations is to do some yourself. Table 28-4 lists some practice problems, with the full 32-digit IPv6 address on the left, and the best abbreviation on the right. The table gives you either the expanded or abbreviated address, and you need to supply the opposite value. The answers sit at the end of the chapter, in the section "Answers to Earlier Practice Problems."

Table 28-4   IPv6 Address Abbreviation and Expansion Practice

Full	Abbreviation
2340:0000:0010:0100:1000:ABCD:0101:1010	
	30A0:ABCD:EF12:3456:ABC:B0B0:9999:9009
2222:3333:4444:5555:0000:0000:6060:0707	
	3210::
210F:0000:0000:0000:CCCC:0000:0000:000D	
	34BA:B:B::20
FE80:0000:0000:0000:DEAD:BEFF:FEEF:CAFE	
	FE80::FACE:BAFF:FEBE:CAFE

Representing the Prefix Length of an Address

IPv6 uses a mask concept, called the *prefix length*, similar to IPv4 subnet masks. Similar to the IPv4 prefix-style mask, the IPv6 prefix length is written as a /, followed by a decimal number. The prefix length defines how many bits of the IPv6 address define the IPv6 prefix, which is basically the same concept as the IPv4 subnet ID.

When writing IPv6 addresses, if the prefix length matters, the prefix length follows the IPv6 address. When writing documentation, you can leave a space between the address and the /, but when typing the values into a Cisco router, you might need to configure with or without the space. For example, use either of these for an address with a 64-bit prefix length:

2222:1111:0:1:A:B:C:D/64

2222:1111:0:1:A:B:C:D /64

Finally, note that the prefix length is a number of bits, so with IPv6, the legal value range is from 0 through 128, inclusive.

Calculating the IPv6 Prefix (Subnet ID)

With IPv4, you can take an IP address and the associated subnet mask, and calculate the subnet ID. With IPv6 subnetting, you can take an IPv6 address and the associated prefix length, and calculate the IPv6 equivalent of the subnet ID: an *IPv6 prefix*.

Like with different IPv4 subnet masks, some IPv6 prefix lengths make for an easy math problem to find the IPv6 prefix, while some prefix lengths make the math more difficult. This section looks at the easier cases, mainly because the size of the IPv6 address space lets us all choose to use IPv6 prefix lengths that make the math much easier.

Finding the IPv6 Prefix

In IPv6, a prefix represents a group of IPv6 addresses. For now, this section focuses on the math, and only the math, for finding the number that represents that prefix. Chapter 29, "IPv6 Addressing and Subnetting," then starts putting more meaning behind the actual numbers.

Each IPv6 prefix, or subnet if you prefer, has a number that represents the group. Per the IPv6 RFCs, the number itself is also called the prefix, but many people just call it a subnet number or subnet ID, using the same terms as IPv4.

Like IPv4, you can start with an IPv6 address and prefix length, and find the prefix, with the same general rules that you use in IPv4. If the prefix length is /P, use these rules:

1. Copy the first P bits.
2. Change the rest of the bits to 0.

When using a prefix length that happens to be a multiple of 4, you do not have to think in terms of bits, but in terms of hex digits. A prefix length that is a multiple of 4 means that each hex digit is either copied, or changed to 0. Just for completeness, if the prefix length is indeed a multiple of 4, the process becomes

1. Identify the number of hex digits in the prefix by dividing the prefix length (which is in bits) by 4.
2. Copy the hex digits determined to be in the prefix per the first step.
3. Change the rest of the hex digits to 0.

Figure 28-7 shows an example, with a prefix length of 64. In this case, Step 1 looks at the /64 prefix length, and calculates that the prefix has 16 hex digits. Step 2 copies the first 16 digits of the IPv6 address, while Step 3 records hex 0s for the rest of the digits.

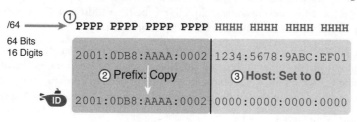

Legend:

 Subnet ID

Figure 28-7 *Creating the IPv6 Prefix from an Address/Length*

After you find the IPv6 prefix, you should also be ready to abbreviate the IPv6 prefix using the same rules you use to abbreviate IPv6 addresses. However, you should pay extra attention to the end of the prefix, because it often has several octets of all 0 values. As a result, the abbreviation typically ends with two colons (::).

For example, consider the following IPv6 address that is assigned to a host on a LAN:

2000:1234:5678:9ABC:1234:5678:9ABC:1111/64

This example shows an IPv6 address that itself cannot be abbreviated. After you calculate the prefix for the subnet in which the address resides, by zeroing out the last 64 bits (16 digits) of the address, you find the following prefix value:

2000:1234:5678:9ABC:**0000:0000:0000:0000**/64

This value can be abbreviated, with four quartets of all 0s at the end, as follows:

2000:1234:5678:9ABC::/64

To get better at the math, take some time to work through finding the prefix for several practice problems, as listed in Table 28-5. The answers sit at the end of the chapter, in the section "Answers to Earlier Practice Problems."

Table 28-5 Finding the IPv6 Prefix from an Address/Length Value

Address/Length	Prefix
2340:0:10:100:1000:ABCD:101:1010/64	
30A0:ABCD:EF12:3456:ABC:B0B0:9999:9009/64	
2222:3333:4444:5555::6060:707/64	
3210::ABCD:101:1010/64	
210F::CCCC:B0B0:9999:9009/64	
34BA:B:B:0:5555:0:6060:707/64	
3124::DEAD:CAFE:FF:FE00:1/64	
2BCD::FACE:BEFF:FEBE:CAFE/64	

Working with More-Difficult IPv6 Prefix Lengths

Some prefix lengths make the math to find the prefix very easy, some mostly easy, and some require you to work in binary. If the prefix length is a multiple of 16, the process of copying part of the address copies entire quartets. If the prefix length is not a multiple of 16, but is a multiple of 4, at least the boundary sits at the edge of a hex digit, so you can avoid working in binary.

Although the /64 prefix length is by far the most common prefix length, you should be ready to find the prefix when using a prefix length that is any multiple of 4. For example, consider the following IPv6 address and prefix length:

2000:1234:5678:9ABC:1234:5678:9ABC:1111/56

Because this example uses a /56 prefix length, the prefix includes the first 56 bits, or first 14 complete hex digits, of the address. The rest of the hex digits will be 0, resulting in the following prefix:

2000:1234:5678:9A00:0000:0000:0000:0000/56

This value can be abbreviated, with four quartets of all 0s at the end, as follows:

2000:1234:5678:9A00::/56

This example shows an easy place to make a mistake. Sometimes, people look at the /56 and think of that as the first 14 hex digits, which is correct. However, they then copy the first 14 hex digits, and add a double colon, showing the following:

2000:1234:5678:9A::/56

This abbreviation is not correct, because it removed the trailing "00" at the end of the fourth quartet. So, be careful when abbreviating when the boundary is not at the edge of a quartet.

Once again, some extra practice can help. Table 28-6 uses examples that have a prefix length that is a multiple of 4, but is not on a quartet boundary, just to get some extra practice. The answers sit at the end of the chapter, in the section "Answers to Earlier Practice Problems."

Table 28-6   Finding the IPv6 Prefix from an Address/Length Value

Address/Length	Prefix
34BA:B:B:0:5555:0:6060:707/80	
3124::DEAD:CAFE:FF:FE00:1/80	
2BCD::FACE:BEFF:FEBE:CAFE/48	
3FED:F:E0:D00:FACE:BAFF:FE00:0/48	
210F:A:B:C:CCCC:B0B0:9999:9009/40	
34BA:B:B:0:5555:0:6060:707/36	
3124::DEAD:CAFE:FF:FE00:1/60	
2BCD::FACE:1:BEFF:FEBE:CAFE/56	

Chapter Review

One key to doing well on the exams is to perform repetitive spaced review sessions. Review this chapter's material using either the tools in the book, DVD, or interactive tools for the same material found on the book's companion website. Refer to the "Your Study Plan" element for more details. Table 28-7 outlines the key review elements and where you can find them. To better track your study progress, record when you completed these activities in the second column.

Table 28-7   Chapter Review Tracking

Review Element	Review Date(s)	Resource Used
Review key topics		Book, DVD/website
Review key terms		Book, DVD/website
Repeat DIKTA questions		Book, PCPT
Review memory table		Book, DVD/website
Review command tables		Book

Review All the Key Topics

Table 28-8   Key Topics for Chapter 28

Key Topic Element	Description	Page Number
List	Similarities between IPv4 and IPv6	677
List	Rules for abbreviating IPv6 addresses	681
List	Rules for expanding an abbreviated IPv6 address	682
List	Process steps to find an IPv6 prefix, based on the IPv6 address and prefix length	683

Key Terms You Should Know

IPv4 address exhaustion, IP version 6 (IPv6), OSPF version 3 (OSPFv3), EIGRP version 6 (EIGRPv6), prefix, prefix length, quartet

Additional Practice for This Chapter's Processes

For additional practice with IPv6 abbreviations, you may do the same set of practice problems using your choice of tools:

Application: Use the Fundamentals of IP Version 6 application on the DVD or companion website.

PDF: Alternatively, practice the same problems found in these apps using DVD Appendix J, "Practice for Chapter 28: Fundamentals of IP Version 6."

Answers to Earlier Practice Problems

This chapter includes practice problems spread around different locations in the chapter. The answers are located in Tables 28-9, 28-10, and 28-11.

Table 28-9   Answers to Questions in the Earlier Table 28-4

Full	Abbreviation
2340:0000:0010:0100:1000:ABCD:0101:1010	2340:0:10:100:1000:ABCD:101:1010
30A0:ABCD:EF12:3456:0ABC:B0B0:9999:9009	30A0:ABCD:EF12:3456:ABC:B0B0:9999:9009
2222:3333:4444:5555:0000:0000:6060:0707	2222:3333:4444:5555::6060:707
3210:0000:0000:0000:0000:0000:0000:0000	3210::
210F:0000:0000:0000:CCCC:0000:0000:000D	210F::CCCC:0:0:D
34BA:000B:000B:0000:0000:0000:0000:0020	34BA:B:B::20
FE80:0000:0000:0000:DEAD:BEFF:FEEF:CAFE	FE80::DEAD:BEFF:FEEF:CAFE
FE80:0000:0000:0000:FACE:BAFF:FEBE:CAFE	FE80::FACE:BAFF:FEBE:CAFE

Table 28-10   Answers to Questions in the Earlier Table 28-5

Address/Length	Prefix
2340:0:10:100:1000:ABCD:101:1010/64	2340:0:10:100::/64
30A0:ABCD:EF12:3456:ABC:B0B0:9999:9009/64	30A0:ABCD:EF12:3456::/64
2222:3333:4444:5555::6060:707/64	2222:3333:4444:5555::/64
3210::ABCD:101:1010/64	3210::/64
210F::CCCC:B0B0:9999:9009/64	210F::/64
34BA:B:B:0:5555:0:6060:707/64	34BA:B:B::/64
3124::DEAD:CAFE:FF:FE00:1/64	3124:0:0:DEAD::/64
2BCD::FACE:BEFF:FEBE:CAFE/64	2BCD::/64

Table 28-11   Answers to Questions in the Earlier Table 28-6

Address/Length	Prefix
34BA:B:B:0:5555:0:6060:707/80	34BA:B:B:0:5555::/80
3124::DEAD:CAFE:FF:FE00:1/80	3124:0:0:DEAD:CAFE::/80
2BCD::FACE:BEFF:FEBE:CAFE/48	2BCD::/48
3FED:F:E0:D00:FACE:BAFF:FE00:0/48	3FED:F:E0::/48
210F:A:B:C:CCCC:B0B0:9999:9009/40	210F:A::/40
34BA:B:B:0:5555:0:6060:707/36	34BA:B::/36
3124::DEAD:CAFE:FF:FE00:1/60	3124:0:0:DEA0::/60
2BCD::FACE:1:BEFF:FEBE:CAFE/56	2BCD:0:0:FA00::/56

CHAPTER 29

IPv6 Addressing and Subnetting

This chapter covers the following exam topics:

1.0 Network Fundamentals

1.11 Identify the appropriate IPv6 addressing scheme to satisfy addressing requirements in a LAN/WAN environment

1.12 Configure, verify, and troubleshoot IPv6 addressing

1.14 Compare and contrast IPv6 address types

  1.14.a Global unicast

  1.14.b Unique local

IPv4 organizes the address space in a couple of ways. First, IPv4 splits addresses by class, with Classes A, B, and C defining unicast IPv4 addresses. (The term *unicast* refers to the fact that each address is used by only one interface.) Then, within the Class A, B, and C address range, the Internet Assigned Numbers Authority (IANA) and the Internet Corporation for Assigned Names and Numbers (ICANN) reserve most of the addresses as public IPv4 addresses, with a few reserved as private IPv4 addresses.

IPv6 does not use any concept like the classful network concept used by IPv4. However, IANA does still reserve some IPv6 address ranges for specific purposes, even with some address ranges that serve as both public IPv6 addresses and private IPv6 addresses. IANA also attempts to take a practical approach to reserving ranges of the entire IPv6 address space for different purposes, using the wisdom gained from several decades of fast growth in the IPv4 Internet.

This chapter has two major sections. The first examines *global unicast addresses*, which serve as public IPv6 addresses. The second major section looks at *unique local addresses*, which serve as private IPv6 addresses.

"Do I Know This Already?" Quiz

Take the quiz (either here, or use the PCPT software) if you want to use the score to help you decide how much time to spend on this chapter. The answers are at the bottom of the page following the quiz, and the explanations are in DVD Appendix C and in the PCPT software.

Table 29-1 "Do I Know This Already?" Foundation Topics Section-to-Question Mapping

Foundation Topics Section	Questions
Global Unicast Addressing Concepts	1–4
Unique Local Unicast Addresses	5

1. Which of the following IPv6 addresses appears to be a unique local unicast address, based on its first few hex digits?

   a. 3123:1:3:5::1

   b. FE80::1234:56FF:FE78:9ABC

   c. FDAD::1

   d. FF00::5

2. Which of the following IPv6 addresses appears to be a global unicast address, based on its first few hex digits?

   a. 3123:1:3:5::1

   b. FE80::1234:56FF:FE78:9ABC

   c. FDAD::1

   d. FF00::5

3. When subnetting an IPv6 address block, an engineer shows a drawing that breaks the address structure into three pieces. Comparing this concept to a three-part IPv4 address structure, which part of the IPv6 address structure is most like the IPv4 network part of the address?

   a. Subnet

   b. Interface ID

   c. Network

   d. Global routing prefix

   e. Subnet router anycast

4. When subnetting an IPv6 address block, an engineer shows a drawing that breaks the address structure into three pieces. Assuming that all subnets use the same prefix length, which of the following answers lists the name of the field on the far right side of the address?

   a. Subnet

   b. Interface ID

   c. Network

   d. Global routing prefix

   e. Subnet router anycast

5. For the IPv6 address FD00:1234:5678:9ABC:DEF1:2345:6789:ABCD, which part of the address is considered the global ID of the unique local address?

   a. None; this address has no global ID.

   b. 00:1234:5678:9ABC

   c. DEF1:2345:6789:ABCD

   d. 00:1234:5678

   e. FD00

Foundation Topics

Global Unicast Addressing Concepts

This first major section of the chapter focuses on one type of unicast IPv6 addresses: global unicast addresses. As it turns out, many of the general concepts and processes behind these global unicast IPv6 addresses follow the original intent for public IPv4 addresses. So, this section begins with a review of some IPv4 concepts, followed by the details of how a company can use global unicast addresses.

This first section also discusses IPv6 subnetting, and the entire process of taking a block of global unicast addresses and creating subnets for one company. This process takes a globally unique global routing prefix, creates IPv6 subnets, and assigns IPv6 addresses from within each subnet, much like with IPv4.

A Brief Review of Public and Private IPv4 Addresses

In the history of IPv4 addressing, the world started out with a plan that gave every single host a globally unique public IPv4 address. However, as discussed in several places already, the IPv4 address space had too few addresses. So, in the 1990s, companies started using addresses from the private IPv4 address range, as defined in RFC 1918. These companies either simply did not connect to the Internet, or to connect to the Internet, they used Network Address Translation (NAT), sharing a few public globally unique IPv4 addresses for all host connections into the Internet.

The next few pages briefly review some of the major concepts behind using public and private addresses in IPv4, as a comparison to the equivalent addresses in IPv6.

Review of Public IPv4 Addressing Concepts

In the original design for the IPv4 Internet, the Internet relied on every IPv4 host using a unicast address that was unique in the universe. To make that happen, three major steps in planning had to occur so that each unicast address was unique:

■ The company or organization asked for and received the rights to the exclusive use of a public Class A, B, or C IPv4 network number.

■ The engineers at that company subdivided that classful network into smaller subnets, making sure to use each subnet in only one place in the company.

■ The engineers chose individual IPv4 addresses from within each subnet, making sure to use each address for only one host interface.

Figure 29-1 shows a conceptual view of the breakdown of a classful IPv4 network into subnets, with each subnet holding individual unicast IPv4 addresses. The figure represents the entire public Class A, B, or C network with the largest rectangle, and each individual unicast IPv4 address using a mailbox icon.

One Public Class A, B, or C Network

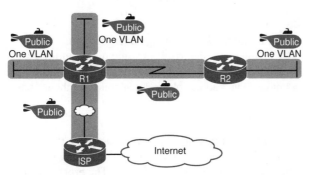

Figure 29-1 *Unique IP Network, Unique Subnets, and Unique Addresses Per Subnet*

Figure 29-1 shows some of the general concepts behind how an enterprise could take a classful IPv4 network and subdivide it into subnets, but the network engineer must also plan where to use subnets in the enterprise internetwork. By now, the ideas should be relatively familiar, but for review, the following each need a separate IPv4 subnet:

- VLAN
- Point-to-point serial link
- Ethernet emulation WAN link (EoMPLS)

For example, in the enterprise internetwork shown in Figure 29-2, the enterprise network engineer plans for five subnets. In this example, each router LAN interface connects to a LAN that uses a single VLAN, for a total of three subnets for the three VLANs. The serial and Ethernet WAN links each need a subnet as well. (Subnets for the Internet will be assigned by the various Internet service providers [ISP].)

Figure 29-2 *Example Internetwork with Five IPv4 Subnets with Public Addresses*

Answers to the "Do I Know This Already?" quiz:

1 C **2** A **3** D **4** B **5** D

Review of Private IPv4 Addressing Concepts

Frankly, today, most companies do not use public IPv4 addresses throughout their enter-prise internetworks. The world starting running out of IPv4 addresses, and this IPv4 address exhaustion problem required some changes.

Today, most enterprise internetworks use private IPv4 addresses for most hosts. The rea-son being that using private IPv4 addresses (per RFC 1918), along with Network Address Translation / Port Address Translation (NAT/PAT), significantly reduces the number of public IPv4 addresses needed by that organization. Using private IPv4 addresses, with NAT/PAT, allowed one public IPv4 address to support a fairly large enterprise internetwork, putting off the day when the world would run out of public IPv4 addresses. (See the section, "The Historical Reasons for IPv6" in Chapter 28, "Fundamentals of IP Version 6," for a review of some of the events that drove the need for private IPv4 addresses and NAT/PAT.)

For comparison, Figure 29-3 repeats the same enterprise internetwork design shown in Figure 29-2. However, in this case, the enterprise uses private IPv4 addresses in most of the network, with Router R1 performing NAT/PAT, reducing the number of required public IPv4 addresses.

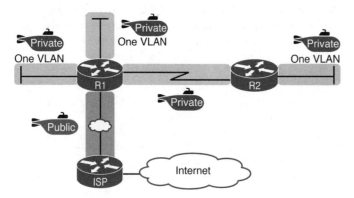

Figure 29-3 *Example Internetwork with Four Private Subnets*

Public and Private IPv6 Addresses

IPv6 allows two similar options for unicast addressing, beginning with *global unicast* addressing. These addresses work like the original design for IPv4 using public addresses. Similar to public IPv4 addresses, IPv6 global unicast addresses rely on an administrative process that assigns each company a unique IPv6 address block. Each company then subnets this IPv6 address block, and only uses addresses from within that block. The result: That company uses addresses that are unique across the globe as well.

The second IPv6 option uses *unique local* IPv6 addresses, which work more like the IPv4 private addresses. Companies that do not plan to connect to the Internet, and companies that plan to use IPv6 NAT, can use these private unique local addresses. The process also works similarly to IPv4: The engineer can read the details in an RFC, pick some numbers, and start assigning IPv6 addresses, without having to register with IANA or any other authority.

The following lists summarizes the comparisons between global unicast addresses and unique local addresses:

Global unicast: Addresses that work like public IPv4 addresses. The organization that needs IPv6 addresses asks for a registered IPv6 address block, which is assigned as a global routing prefix. After that, only that organization uses the addresses inside that block of addresses; that is, the addresses that begin with the assigned prefix.

Unique local: Works somewhat like private IPv4 addresses, with the possibility that multiple organizations use the exact same addresses, and with no requirement for registering with any numbering authority.

The rest of this first major section of the chapter examines global unicast addresses in more detail, while the second major section of the chapter examines unique local addresses.

> **NOTE** Just for completeness sake, note that you might also find documentation about another range of addresses called *site local*. These addresses, defined by prefix FEC0::/10 (so that they begin with FEC, FED, FEE, or FEF), were originally intended to be used like IPv4 private addresses. They have now been removed from the IPv6 standards.

The IPv6 Global Routing Prefix

IPv6 global unicast addresses allow IPv6 to work more like the original design of the IPv4 Internet. In other words, each organization asks for a block of IPv6 addresses, which no one else can use. That organization further subdivides the address block into smaller chunks, called *subnets*. Finally, to choose what IPv6 address to use for any host, the engineer chooses an address from the right subnet.

That reserved block of IPv6 addresses—a set of addresses that only one company can use—is called a *global routing prefix*. Each organization that wants to connect to the Internet, and use IPv6 global unicast addresses, should ask for and receive a global routing prefix. Very generally, you can think of the global routing prefix like an IPv4 Class A, B, or C network number from the range of public IPv4 addresses.

The term *global routing prefix* might not make you think of a block of IPv6 addresses at first. The term actually refers to the idea that Internet routers can have one route that refers to all the addresses inside the address block, without a need to have routes for smaller parts of that block. For example, Figure 29-4 shows three companies, with three different IPv6 global routing prefixes; the router on the right (R4) has one IPv6 route for each global routing prefix.

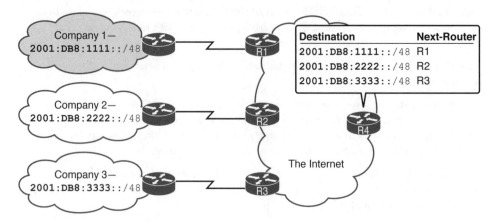

Figure 29-4 *Three Global Routing Prefixes, with One Route per Prefix*

The global routing prefix sets those IPv6 addresses apart for use by that one company, just like a public IPv4 network or CIDR address block does in IPv4. All IPv6 addresses inside that company should begin with that global routing prefix, to avoid using other companies' IPv6 addresses. No other companies should use IPv6 addresses with that same prefix. And thankfully, IPv6 has plenty of space to allow all companies to have a global routing prefix, with plenty of addresses.

Both the IPv6 and IPv4 address assignment process rely on the same organizations: IANA (along with ICANN), the Regional Internet Registries (RIR), and ISPs. For example, an imaginary company, Company1, received the assignment of a global routing prefix. The prefix means "All addresses whose first 12 hex digits are 2001:0DB8:1111," as represented by prefix 2001:0DB8:1111::/48. To receive that assignment, the process shown in Figure 29-5 happened.

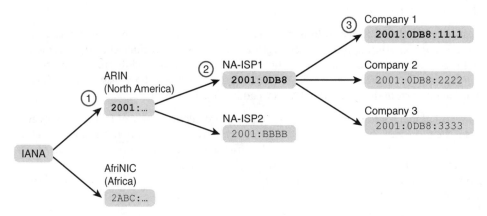

Figure 29-5 *Prefix Assignment with IANA, RIRs, and ISPs*

The event timeline in the figure uses a left-to-right flow; in other words, the event on the far left must happen first. Following the flow from left to right in the figure:

1. **IANA gives ARIN prefix 2001::/16:** ARIN (the RIR for North America) asks IANA for the assignment of a large block of addresses. In this imaginary example, IANA gives ARIN a prefix of "all addresses that begin 2001," or 2001::/16.

2. **ARIN gives NA-ISP1 prefix 2001:0DB8::/32:** NA-ISP1, an imaginary ISP based in North America, asks ARIN for a new IPv6 prefix. ARIN takes a subset of its 2001::/16 prefix, specifically all addresses that begin with the 32 bits (8 hex digits) 2001:0DB8, and gives it to the ISP.

3. **NA-ISP1 gives Company 1 2001:0DB8:1111::/48:** Company 1 decides to start supporting IPv6, so it goes to its ISP, NA-ISP1, to ask for a block of global unicast addresses. NA-ISP1 gives Company 1 a "small" piece of NA-ISP1's address block, in this case the addresses that begin with the 48 bits (12 hex digits) of 2001:0DB8:1111 (2001:0DB8:1111::/48).

> **NOTE** If you do not plan to connect to the Internet using IPv6 for a while, and just want to experiment, you do not need to ask for an IPv6 global routing prefix to be assigned. Just make up IPv6 addresses and configure your devices.

Address Ranges for Global Unicast Addresses

Global unicast addresses make up the majority of the IPv6 address space. However, unlike IPv4, the rules for which IPv6 address fall into which category are purposefully more flexible than they were with IPv4 and the rules for IPv4 Classes A, B, C, D, and E.

Originally, IANA reserved all IPv6 addresses that begin with hex 2 or 3 as global unicast addresses. (This address range can be written succinctly as prefix 2000::/3.)

Later RFCs made the global unicast address range wider, basically to include all IPv6 addresses not otherwise allocated for other purposes. For example, the unique local unicast addresses, discussed later in this chapter, all start with hex FD. So, while global unicast addresses would not include any addresses that begin with FD, any address ranges that are not specifically reserved, for now, are considered to be global unicast addresses.

Finally, just because an amazingly enormous number of addresses sit within the global unicast address range, IANA does not assign prefixes from all over the address range. IPv4 has survived well for more than 30 years with an admittedly too-small address size. By making smart and practical choices in assigning IPv6 addresses, the IPv6 address space could last much longer than IPv4.

Table 29-2 lists the address prefixes discussed in this book, and their purpose.

Table 29-2   Some Types of IPv6 Addresses and Their First Hex Digit(s)

Address Type	First Hex Digits
Global unicast	2 or 3 (originally); all not otherwise reserved (today)
Unique local	FD
Multicast	FF
Link local	FE80

IPv6 Subnetting Using Global Unicast Addresses

After an enterprise has a block of reserved global unicast addresses—in other words, a global routing prefix—the company needs to subdivide that large address block into subnets.

Subnetting IPv6 addresses works generally like IPv4, but with mostly simpler math (hoorah!). Because of the absolutely large number of addresses available, most everyone uses the easiest possible IPv6 prefix length: /64. Using /64 as the prefix length for all subnets makes the IPv6 subnetting math just as easy as using a /24 mask for all IPv4 subnets. In addition, the dynamic IPv6 address assignment process works better with a /64 prefix length as well; so in practice, and in this book, expect IPv6 designs to use a /64 prefix length.

This section does walk you through the different parts of IPv6 subnetting, while mostly using examples that use a /64 prefix length. The discussion defines the rules about which addresses should be in the same subnet, and which addresses need to be in different subnets. Plus this section looks at how to analyze the global routing prefix and associated prefix length to find all the IPv6 prefixes (subnet IDs) and the addresses in each subnet.

> **NOTE**   If the IPv4 subnetting concepts are a little vague, you might want to reread Chapter 13, "Perspectives on IPv4 Subnetting," which discusses the subnetting concepts for IPv4.

Deciding Where IPv6 Subnets Are Needed

First, IPv6 and IPv4 both use the same concepts about where a subnet is needed: one for each VLAN and one for each point-to-point WAN connection (serial and EoMPLS). Figure 29-6 shows an example of the idea, using the small enterprise internetwork of Company 1. Company 1 has two LANs, with a point-to-point serial link connecting the sites. It also has an Ethernet WAN link connected to an ISP. Using the same logic you would use for IPv4, Company 1 needs four IPv6 subnets.

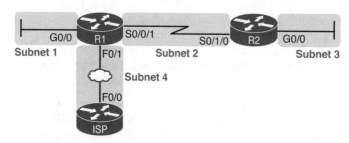

Figure 29-6 *Locations for IPv6 Subnets*

The Mechanics of Subnetting IPv6 Global Unicast Addresses

To understand how to subnet your one large block of IPv6 addresses, you need to understand some of the theory and mechanisms IPv6 uses. To learn those details, it can help to compare IPv6 with some similar concepts from IPv4.

With IPv4, without subnetting, an address has two parts: a network part and a host part. Class A, B, and C rules define the length of the network part, with the host part making up the rest of the 32-bit IPv4 address, as shown in Figure 29-7.

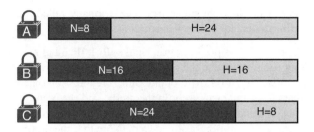

Figure 29-7   *Classful View of Unsubnetted IPv4 Networks*

To subnet an IPv4 Class A, B, or C network, the network engineer for the enterprise makes some choices. Conceptually, the engineer creates a three-part view of the addresses, adding a subnet field in the center, while shortening the host field. (Many people call this "borrowing host bits.") The size of the network part stays locked per the Class A, B, and C rules, with the line between the subnet and host part being flexible, based on the choice of subnet mask. Figure 29-8 shows the idea, for a subnetted Class B network.

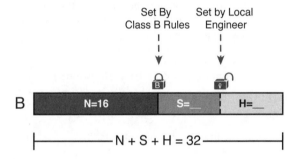

Figure 29-8   *Classful View of Subnetted IPv4 Networks*

IPv6 uses a similar concept, with the details in Figure 29-9. The structure shows three major parts, beginning with the global routing prefix, which is the initial value that must be the same in all IPv6 addresses inside the enterprise. The address ends with the interface ID, which acts like the IPv4 host field. The subnet field sits between the two other fields, used as a way to number and identify subnets, much like the subnet field in IPv4 addresses.

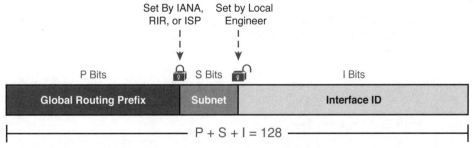

Figure 29-9   *Structure of Subnetted IPv6 Global Unicast Addresses*

First, just think about the general idea with IPv6, comparing Figure 29-9 to Figure 29-8. The IPv6 global routing prefix acts like the IPv4 network part of the address structure. The IPv6 subnet part acts like the IPv4 subnet part. And the right side of the IPv6, formally called the *interface ID* (short for interface identifier), acts like the IPv4 host field.

Now focus on the IPv6 global routing prefix and its prefix length. Unlike IPv4, IPv6 has no concept of address classes, so no preset rules determine the prefix length of the global routing prefix. However, when a company applies to an ISP, RIR, or any other organization that can allocate a global routing prefix, that allocation includes both the prefix, and the prefix length. After a company receives a global routing prefix and that prefix length, the length of the prefix typically does not change over time, and is basically locked. (Note that the prefix length of the global routing prefix is often between /32 and /48, or possibly as long as /56.)

Next, look to the right side of Figure 29-9 to the interface ID field. For several reasons that become more obvious the more you learn about IPv6, this field is often 64 bits long. Does it have to be 64 bits long? No. However, using a 64-bit interface ID field works well in real networks, and there are no reasons to avoid using a 64-bit interface ID field.

Finally, look to the center of Figure 29-9, and the subnet field. Similar to IPv4, this field creates a place with which to number IPv6 subnets. The length of the subnet field is based on the other two facts: the length of the global routing prefix and the length of the interface ID. And with the commonly used 64-bit interface ID field, the subnet field is typically 64−P bits, with P being the length of the global routing prefix.

Next, consider the structure of a specific global unicast IPv6 address, 2001:0DB8:1111:0001:0000:0000:0000:0001, as seen in Figure 29-10. In this case:

■ The company was assigned prefix 2001:0DB8:1111, with prefix length /48.

■ The company uses the usual 64-bit interface ID.

■ The company has a subnet field of 16 bits, allowing for 2^{16} IPv6 subnets.

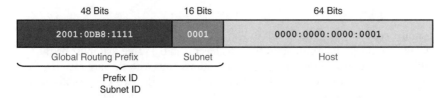

Figure 29-10 *Address Structure for Company 1 Example*

The example in Figure 29-10, along with a little math, shows one reason why so many companies use a /64 prefix length for all subnets. With this structure, Company 1 can support 2^{16} possible subnets (65,536). Few companies need that many subnets. Then, each subnet supports over 10^{18} addresses per subnet (2^{64}, minus some reserved values). So, for both subnets and hosts, the address structure supports far more than are needed. Plus, the /64 prefix length for all subnets makes the math simple, because it cuts the 128-bit IPv6 address in half.

Listing the IPv6 Subnet Identifier

Like with IPv4, IPv6 needs to identify each IPv6 subnet with some kind of a subnet identifier, or subnet ID. Figure 29-10 lists the informal names for this number (subnet ID), and the more formal name (prefix ID). Routers then list the IPv6 subnet ID in routing tables, along with the prefix length.

Chapter 28, "Fundamentals of IP Version 6," has already discussed how to find the subnet ID, given an IPv6 address and prefix length. The math works the same way when working with global unicasts, as well as the unique local addresses discussed later in the chapter. Because Chapter 28 has already discussed the math, this chapter does not repeat the math. However, for completeness, the example in Figure 29-10, the subnet ID would be

2001:DB8:1111:1::/64

List All IPv6 Subnets

With IPv4, if you choose to use a single subnet mask for all subnets, you can sit and write down all the subnets of a Class A, B, or C network using that one subnet mask. With IPv6, the same ideas apply. If you plan to use a single prefix length for all subnets, you can start with the global routing prefix and write down all the IPv6 subnet IDs as well.

To find all the subnet IDs, you simply need to find all the unique values that will fit inside the subnet part of the IPv6 address, basically following these rules:

- All subnet IDs begin with the global routing prefix.
- Use a different value in the subnet field to identify each different subnet.
- All subnet IDs have all 0s in the interface ID.

As an example, take the IPv6 design shown in Figure 29-10, and think about all the subnet IDs. First, all subnets will use the commonly used /64 prefix length. This company uses a global routing prefix of 2001:0DB8:1111::/48, which defines the first 12 hex digits of all the subnet IDs. To find all the possible IPv6 subnet IDs, think of all the combinations of unique values in the fourth quartet, and then represent the last four quartets of all 0s with a :: symbol. Figure 29-11 shows the beginning of just such a list.

```
  2001:0DB8:1111:0000::      2001:0DB8:1111:0008::
✓ 2001:0DB8:1111:0001::      2001:0DB8:1111:0009::
✓ 2001:0DB8:1111:0002::      2001:0DB8:1111:000A::
✓ 2001:0DB8:1111:0003::      2001:0DB8:1111:000B::
✓ 2001:0DB8:1111:0004::      2001:0DB8:1111:000C::
  2001:0DB8:1111:0005::      2001:0DB8:1111:000D::
  2001:0DB8:1111:0006::      2001:0DB8:1111:000E::
  2001:0DB8:1111:0007::      2001:0DB8:1111:000F::
```
Global Routing Prefix   Subnet   Global Routing Prefix   Subnet

Figure 29-11 *First 16 Possible Subnets with a 16-bit Subnet Field in This Example*

The example allows for 65,536 subnets, so clearly the example will not list all the possible subnets. However, in that fourth quartet, all combinations of hex values would be allowed.

NOTE The IPv6 subnet ID, more formally called the *subnet router anycast address*, is reserved, and should not be used as an IPv6 address for any host.

Assign Subnets to the Internetwork Topology

After an engineer lists all the possible subnet IDs (based on the subnet design), the next step is to choose which subnet ID to use for each link that needs an IPv6 subnet. Just like with

IPv4, each VLAN, each serial link, each EoMPLS link, and many other data link instances need an IPv6 subnet.

Figure 29-12 shows an example using Company 1 again. The figure uses the four subnets from Figure 29-11 that have check marks beside them. The check marks are just a reminder to not use those four subnets in other locations.

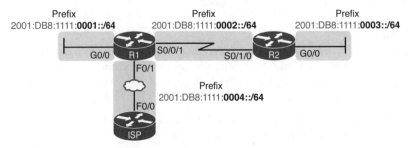

Figure 29-12 *Subnets in Company 1, with Global Routing Prefix of 2001:0DB8:1111::/48*

Assigning Addresses to Hosts in a Subnet

Now that the engineer has planned which IPv6 subnet will be used in each location, the individual IPv6 addressing can be planned and implemented. Each address must be unique, in that no other host interface uses the same IPv6 address. Also, the hosts cannot use the subnet ID itself.

The process of assigning IPv6 addresses to interfaces works similarly to IPv4. Addresses can be configured statically, along with the prefix length, default router, and Domain Name System (DNS) IPv6 addresses. Alternatively, hosts can learn these same settings dynamically, using either Dynamic Host Configuration Protocol (DHCP) or a built-in IPv6 mechanism called Stateless Address Autoconfiguration (SLAAC).

For example, Figure 29-13 shows some static IP addresses that could be chosen for the router interfaces based on the subnet choices shown in Figure 29-12. In each case, the router interfaces use an interface ID that is a relatively low number, easily remembered.

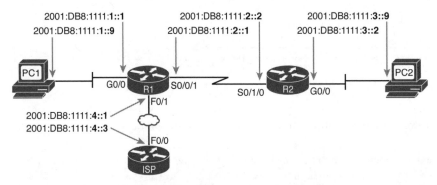

Figure 29-13 *Example Static IPv6 Addresses Based on the Subnet Design of Figure 29-12*

This chapter puts off the details of how to configure the IPv6 addresses until the next two chapters. Chapter 30, "Implementing IPv6 Addressing on Routers," looks at how to configure IPv6 addresses on routers, with both static configuration and dynamic configuration.

Chapter 31, "Implementing IPv6 Addressing on Hosts," examines how to configure hosts with IPv6 addresses, with more focus on the dynamic methods and the related protocols.

Unique Local Unicast Addresses

Unique local unicast addresses act as private IPv6 addresses. These addresses have many similarities with global unicast addresses, particularly in how to subnet. The biggest difference lies in the literal number (unique local addresses begin with hex FD), and with the administrative process: The unique local prefixes are not registered with any numbering authority, and can be used by multiple organizations.

Although the network engineer creates unique local addresses without any registration or assignment process, the addresses still need to follow some rules, as follows:

- Use FD as the first two hex digits.
- Choose a unique 40-bit global ID.
- Append the global ID to FD to create a 48-bit prefix, used as the prefix for all your addresses.
- Use the next 16 bits as a subnet field.
- Note that the structure leaves a convenient 64-bit interface ID field.

Figure 29-14 shows the format of these unique local unicast addresses.

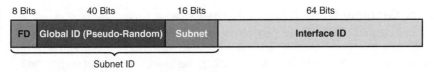

Figure 29-14 *IPv6 Unique Local Unicast Address Format*

> **NOTE** Just to be completely exact, IANA actually reserves prefix FC00::/7, and not FD00::/8, for these addresses. FC00::/7 includes all addresses that begin with hex FC and FD. However, an RFC (4193) requires the eighth bit of these addresses to be set to 1; so in practice today, the unique local addresses all begin with their first two digits as FD.

Subnetting with Unique Local IPv6 Addresses

Subnetting using unique local addresses works just like subnetting with global unicast addresses with a 48-bit global routing prefix. The only difference is that with global unicasts, you start by asking for a global routing prefix to be assigned to your company, and that global routing prefix might or might not have a /48 prefix length. With unique local, you create that prefix locally, and the prefix begins with /48, with the first 8 bits set and the next 40 bits randomly chosen.

The process can be as simple as choosing a 40-bit value as your global ID. 40 bits requires 10 hex digits, so you can even avoid thinking in binary, and just make up a unique 10-hex-digit value. For example, imagine you chose a 40-bit global ID of 00 0001 0001. Your addresses must begin with the two hex digits FD, making the entire prefix be FD00:0001:0001::/48, or FD00:1:1::/48 when abbreviated.

To create subnets, just as you did in the earlier examples with a 48-bit global routing prefix, treat the entire fourth quartet as a subnet field, as shown in Figure 29-14.

Figure 29-15 shows an example subnetting plan using unique local addresses. The example repeats the same topology shown earlier in Figure 29-12; that figure showed subnetting with a global unicast prefix. This example uses the exact same numbers for the fourth quartet's subnet field, simply replacing the 48-bit global unicast prefix with this new local unique prefix of FD00:1:1.

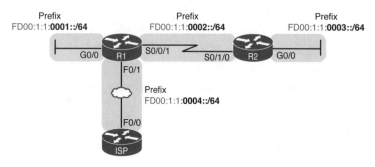

Figure 29-15   *Subnetting Using Unique Local Addresses*

The Need for Globally Unique Local Addresses

The example in Figure 29-15 shows an easy-to-remember prefix of FD00:1:1::/48. Clearly, I made up the easy-to-remember global ID in this example. What global ID would you choose for your company? Would you pick a number that you could not abbreviate, and make it shorter? If you had to pick the IPv6 prefix for you unique local addresses from the options in the following list, which would you pick for your company?

■ FDE9:81BE:A059::/48

■ FDF0:E1D2:C3B4::/48

■ FD00:1:1::/48

Given freedom to choose, most people would pick an easy-to-remember, short-to-type prefix, like FD00:1:1::/48. And in a lab or other small network used for testing, making up an easy to use number is reasonable. However, for use in real corporate networks, you should not just make up any global ID you like—you should try to follow the unique local address rules that strive to help make your addresses unique in the universe—even without registering a prefix with an ISP or RIR.

RFC 4193 defines unique local addresses. Part of that RFC stresses the importance of choosing your global ID in a way to make it statistically unlikely to be used by other companies. What is the result of unique global IDs at every company? Making all these unique local addresses unique across the globe. So if you do plan on using unique local addresses in a real network, plan on using the random number generator logic listed in RFC 4193 to create your prefix.

One of the big reasons to attempt to use a unique prefix, rather than everyone using the same easy-to-remember prefixes, is to be ready for the day that your company merges with or buys another company. Today, with IPv4, a high percentage of companies use private IPv4 network 10.0.0.0. When they merge their networks, the fact that both use network 10.0.0.0 makes the network merger more painful than if the companies had used different private IPv4 networks. With IPv6 unique local addresses, if both companies did the right thing, and randomly chose a prefix, they will most likely be using completely different prefixes, making the merger much simpler. However, companies that take the seemingly easy way out, and choose an easy-to-remember prefix like FD00:1:1, greatly increase their risk of requiring extra effort when merging with another company that also chose to use that same prefix.

Chapter Review

One key to doing well on the exams is to perform repetitive spaced review sessions. Review this chapter's material using either the tools in the book, DVD, or interactive tools for the same material found on the book's companion website. Refer to the "Your Study Plan" element for more details. Table 29-3 outlines the key review elements and where you can find them. To better track your study progress, record when you completed these activities in the second column.

Table 29-3   Chapter Review Tracking

Review Element	Review Date(s)	Resource Used
Review key topics		Book, DVD/website
Review key terms		Book, DVD/website
Repeat DIKTA questions		Book, PCPT
Review memory table		Book, DVD/website

Review All the Key Topics

Table 29-4   Key Topics for Chapter 29

Key Topic Element	Description	Page Number
List	Network links that need an IPv6 subnet	691
List	Two types of IPv6 unicast addresses	693
Table 29-2	Values of the initial hex digits of IPv6 addresses, and the address type implied by each	695
Figure 29-9	Subnetting concepts for IPv6 global unicast addresses	697
List	Rules for how to find all IPv6 subnet IDs, given the global routing prefix, and prefix length used for all subnets	699
List	Rules for building unique local unicast addresses	701
Figure 29-14	Subnetting concepts for IPv6 unique local addresses	701

Key Terms You Should Know

global unicast address, global routing prefix, unique local address, subnet ID (prefix ID), subnet router anycast address

CHAPTER 30

Implementing IPv6 Addressing on Routers

This chapter covers the following exam topics:

1.0 Network Fundamentals

1.12 Configure, verify, and troubleshoot IPv6 addressing

1.13 Configure and verify IPv6 Stateless Address Auto Configuration

1.14 Compare and contrast IPv6 address types

    1.14.a Global unicast

    1.14.b Unique local

    1.14.c Link local

    1.14.d Multicast

    1.14.e Modified EUI 64

    1.14.f Autoconfiguration

    1.14.g Anycast

With IPv4 addressing, some devices, like servers and routers, typically use static predefined IPv4 addresses. End-user devices do not mind if their address changes from time to time, and they typically learn an IPv4 address dynamically using DHCP. IPv6 uses the same general mode, with servers, routers, and other devices in the control of the IT group often using predefined IPv6 addresses, and with end-user devices using dynamically learned IPv6 addresses.

This chapter focuses on the addresses configured on routers, while Chapter 31, "Implementing IPv6 Addressing on Hosts," focuses on the addresses learned by IPv6 hosts.

Routers require unicast IPv6 addresses on their interfaces. At the same time, routers use a variety of other IPv6 addresses to participate in many of the protocols and roles required of a router. This chapter begins with the more obvious IPv6 addressing configuration, with features that mirror IPv4 features, showing how to configure interfaces with IPv6 addresses and view that configuration with **show** commands. The second half of the chapter introduces new IPv6 addressing concepts, showing some other addresses used by routers when doing different tasks.

"Do I Know This Already?" Quiz

Take the quiz (either here, or use the PCPT software) if you want to use the score to help you decide how much time to spend on this chapter. The answers are at the bottom of the page following the quiz, and the explanations are in DVD Appendix C and in the PCPT software.

Table 30-1 "Do I Know This Already?" Foundation Topics Section-to-Question Mapping

Foundation Topics Section	Questions
Implementing Unicast IPv6 Addresses on Routers	1–3
Special Addresses Used by Routers	4–5

1. Router R1 has an interface named Gigabit Ethernet 0/1, whose MAC address has been set to 0200.0001.000A. Which of the following commands, added in R1's Gigabit Ethernet 0/1 configuration mode, gives this router's G0/1 interface a unicast IPv6 address of 2001:1:1:1:1:200:1:A, with a /64 prefix length?

   a. ipv6 address 2001:1:1:1:1:200:1:A/64

   b. ipv6 address 2001:1:1:1:1:200:1:A/64 eui-64

   c. ipv6 address 2001:1:1:1:1:200:1:A /64 eui-64

   d. ipv6 address 2001:1:1:1:1:200:1:A /64

   e. None of the other answers are correct.

2. Router R1 has an interface named Gigabit Ethernet 0/1, whose MAC address has been set to 5055.4444.3333. This interface has been configured with the **ipv6 address 2000:1:1:1::/64 eui-64** subcommand. What unicast address will this interface use?

   a. 2000:1:1:1:52FF:FE55:4444:3333

   b. 2000:1:1:1:5255:44FF:FE44:3333

   c. 2000:1:1:1:5255:4444:33FF:FE33

   d. 2000:1:1:1:200:FF:FE00:0

3. Router R1 currently supports IPv4, routing packets in and out all its interfaces. R1's configuration needs to be migrated to support dual-stack operation, routing both IPv4 and IPv6. Which of the following tasks must be performed before the router can also support routing IPv6 packets? (Choose two answers.)

   a. Enable IPv6 on each interface using an **ipv6 address** interface subcommand.

   b. Enable support for both versions with the **ip versions 4 6** global command.

   c. Additionally enable IPv6 routing using the **ipv6 unicast-routing** global command.

   d. Migrate to dual-stack routing using the **ip routing dual-stack** global command.

4. Router R1 has an interface named Gigabit Ethernet 0/1, whose MAC address has been set to 0200.0001.000A. The interface is then configured with the **ipv6 address 2001:1:1:1:200:FF:FE01:B/64** interface subcommand; no other **ipv6 address** commands are configured on the interface. Which of the following answers lists the link local address used on the interface?

   a. FE80::FF:FE01:A

   b. FE80::FF:FE01:B

   c. FE80::200:FF:FE01:A

   d. FE80::200:FF:FE01:B

5. Which of the following multicast addresses is defined as the address for sending packets to only the IPv6 routers on the local link?

   a. FF02::1

   b. FF02::2

   c. FF02::5

   d. FF02::A

Foundation Topics

Implementing Unicast IPv6 Addresses on Routers

Every company bases its enterprise network on one or more protocol models, or protocol stacks. In the earlier days of networking, enterprise networks used one or more protocol stacks from different vendors, as shown on the left of Figure 30-1. Over time, companies added TCP/IP (based on IPv4) to the mix. Eventually, companies migrated fully to TCP/IP as the only protocol stack in use.

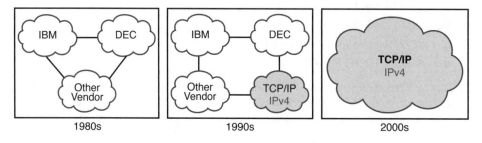

Figure 30-1 *Migration of Enterprise Networks to Use TCP/IP Stack Only, IPv4*

The emergence of IPv6 requires that IPv6 be implemented in end-user hosts, servers, routers, and other devices. However, corporations cannot just migrate all devices from IPv4 to IPv6 over one weekend. Instead, what will likely occur is some kind of long-term migration and coexistence, in which for a large number of years, most corporate networks again use multiple protocol stacks: one based on IPv4 and one based on IPv6.

Eventually, over time, we might all see the day when enterprise networks run only IPv6, without any IPv4 remaining, but that day might take awhile. Figure 30-2 shows the progression, just to make the point, but who knows how long it will take?

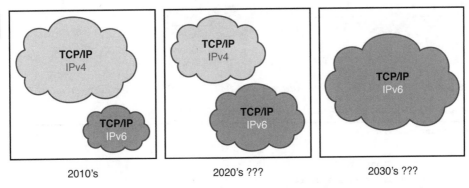

Figure 30-2 *Possible Path Through Dual-Stack (IPv4 and IPv6) over a Long Period*

One way to add IPv6 support to an established IPv4-based enterprise internetwork is to implement a dual-stack strategy. To do so, the routers can be configured to route IPv6 packets, with IPv6 addresses on their interfaces, with a similar model to how routers support IPv4. Then hosts can implement IPv6 when ready, running both IPv4 and IPv6 (dual stacks). The first major section of this chapter shows how to configure and verify unicast IPv6 addresses on routers.

Static Unicast Address Configuration

Cisco routers give us two options for static configuration of IPv6 addresses. In one case, you configure the full 128-bit address, while in the other, you configure a 64-bit prefix and let the router derive the second half of the address (the interface ID). The next few pages show how to configure both options and how the router chooses the second half of the IPv6 address.

Configuring the Full 128-Bit Address

To statically configure the full 128-bit unicast address—either global unicast or unique local—the router needs an **ipv6 address** *address/prefix-length* interface subcommand on each interface. The address can be an abbreviated IPv6 address or the full 32-digit hex address. The command includes the prefix length value, at the end, with no space between the address and prefix length.

The configuration of the router interface IPv6 address really is that simple. Figure 30-3, along with Examples 30-1 and 30-2, shows a basic example. The figure shows the global unicast IPv6 address used by two different routers, on two interfaces each. As usual, all subnets use a /64 prefix length.

Answers to the "Do I Know This Already?" quiz:

1 A **2** B **3** A, C **4** A **5** B

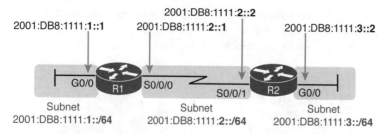

Figure 30-3 *Sample 128-bit IPv6 Addresses to Be Configured on Cisco Router Interfaces*

Example 30-1 *Configuring Static IPv6 Addresses on R1*

```
ipv6 unicast-routing
!
interface GigabitEthernet0/0
 ipv6 address 2001:DB8:1111:1::1/64
!
interface Serial0/0/0
 ipv6 address 2001:0db8:1111:0002:0000:0000:0000:0001/64
```

Example 30-2 *Configuring Static IPv6 Addresses on R2*

```
ipv6 unicast-routing
!
interface GigabitEthernet0/0
 ipv6 address 2001:DB8:1111:3::2/64
!
interface Serial0/0/1
 ipv6 address 2001:db8:1111:2::2/64
```

NOTE The configuration on R1 in Example 30-1 uses both abbreviated and unabbreviated addresses, and both lowercase and uppercase hex digits, showing that all are allowed. Router **show** commands list the abbreviated value with uppercase hex digits.

Enabling IPv6 Routing

While the configurations shown in Examples 30-1 and 30-2 focus on the IPv6 address configuration, they also include an important but often overlooked step when configuring IPv6 on Cisco routers: IPv6 routing needs to be enabled.

Before routers can route (forward) IPv6 packets, IPv6 routing must be enabled. On Cisco routers, IPv4 routing is enabled by default, but IPv6 routing is not enabled by default. The solution takes only a single command—**ipv6 unicast-routing**—which enables IPv6 routing on the router.

Note that a router must enable IPv6 globally (**ipv6 unicast-routing**) and enable IPv6 on the interface (**ipv6 address**) before the router will attempt to route packets in and out an interface. (If the router happens to omit the **ipv6 unicast-routing** command, it can still be configured with interface IPv6 addresses, but the router acts like an IPv6 host and does not route IPv6 packets.)

Verifying the IPv6 Address Configuration

IPv6 uses many **show** commands that mimic the syntax of IPv4 **show** commands. For example:

- The **show ipv6 interface brief** command gives you interface IPv6 address info, but not prefix length info, similar to the IPv4 **show ip interface brief** command.

- The **show ipv6 interface** command gives the details of IPv6 interface settings, much like the **show ip interface** command does for IPv4.

The one notable difference in the most common commands is that the **show interfaces** command still lists the IPv4 address and mask but tells us nothing about IPv6. So, to see IPv6 interface addresses, use commands that begin with **show ipv6**. Example 30-3 lists a few samples from Router R1, with the explanations following.

Example 30-3   *Verifying Static IPv6 Addresses on Router R1*

```
! The first interface is in subnet 1
R1# show ipv6 interface GigabitEthernet 0/0
GigabitEthernet0/0 is up, line protocol is up
  IPv6 is enabled, link-local address is FE80::1FF:FE01:101
  No Virtual link-local address(es):
  Description: LAN at Site 1
  Global unicast address(es):
    2001:DB8:1111:1::1, subnet is 2001:DB8:1111:1::/64
  Joined group address(es):
    FF02::1
    FF02::2
    FF02::A
    FF02::1:FF00:1
    FF02::1:FF01:101
  MTU is 1500 bytes
  ICMP error messages limited to one every 100 milliseconds
  ICMP redirects are enabled
  ICMP unreachables are sent
  ND DAD is enabled, number of DAD attempts: 1
  ND reachable time is 30000 milliseconds (using 30000)
  ND advertised reachable time is 0 (unspecified)
  ND advertised retransmit interval is 0 (unspecified)
  ND router advertisements are sent every 200 seconds
  ND router advertisements live for 1800 seconds
  ND advertised default router preference is Medium
  Hosts use stateless autoconfig for addresses.

R1# show ipv6 interface S0/0/0
Serial0/0/0 is up, line protocol is up
  IPv6 is enabled, link-local address is FE80::1FF:FE01:101
  No Virtual link-local address(es):
  Description: link to R2
```

30

```
   Global unicast address(es):
     2001:DB8:1111:2::1, subnet is 2001:DB8:1111:2::/64
   Joined group address(es):
     FF02::1
     FF02::2
     FF02::A
     FF02::1:FF00:1
     FF02::1:FF01:101
   MTU is 1500 bytes
! Lines omitted for brevity


R1# show ipv6 interface brief
GigabitEthernet0/0      [up/up]
     FE80::1FF:FE01:101
     2001:DB8:1111:1::1
GigabitEthernet0/1      [administratively down/down]
     unassigned
Serial0/0/0             [up/up]
     FE80::1FF:FE01:101
     2001:DB8:1111:2::1
Serial0/0/1             [administratively down/down]
     unassigned
```

First, focus on the output of the two **show ipv6 interface** commands that make up most of the output in Example 30-3. The first command lists interface G0/0, showing output about that interface only. Note that the output lists the configured IPv6 address and prefix length, as well as the IPv6 subnet (2001:DB8:1111:1::/64), which the router calculated based on the IPv6 address. The second **show ipv6 interface** command shows similar details for interface S0/0/0, with some of the volume of output omitted.

The end of the example lists the output of the **show ipv6 interface brief** command. Similar to the IPv4-focused **show ip interface brief** command, this command lists IPv6 addresses, but not the prefix length or prefixes. This command also lists all interfaces on the router, whether or not IPv6 is enabled on the interfaces. For example, in this case, the only two interfaces on R1 that have an IPv6 address are G0/0 and S0/0/0, as configured earlier in Example 30-1.

Beyond the IPv6 addresses on the interfaces, the router also adds IPv6 connected routes to the IPv6 routing table off each interface. Just as with IPv4, the router keeps these connected routes in the IPv6 routing table only when the interface is in a working (up/up) state. But if the interface has an IPv6 unicast address configured, and the interface is working, the router adds the connected routes. Example 30-4 shows the connected IPv6 on Router R1 from Figure 30-3.

Example 30-4 *Displaying Connected IPv6 Routes on Router R1*

```
R1# show ipv6 route connected
IPv6 Routing Table - default - 5 entries
Codes: C - Connected, L - Local, S - Static, U - Per-user Static route
```

```
        B - BGP, R - RIP, I1 - ISIS L1, I2 - ISIS L2
        IA - ISIS interarea, IS - ISIS summary, D - EIGRP, EX - EIGRP external
        ND - ND Default, NDp - ND Prefix, DCE - Destination, NDr - Redirect
        O - OSPF Intra, OI - OSPF Inter, OE1 - OSPF ext 1, OE2 - OSPF ext 2
        ON1 - OSPF NSSA ext 1, ON2 - OSPF NSSA ext 2
C    2001:DB8:1111:1::/64 [0/0]
      via GigabitEthernet0/0, directly connected
C    2001:DB8:1111:2::/64 [0/0]
      via Serial0/0/0, directly connected
```

Generating a Unique Interface ID Using Modified EUI-64

IPv6 follows the same general model as IPv4 regarding which types of devices typically use static, predefined addresses and which use dynamically learned address. For example, routers inside an enterprise use static IPv4 addresses, while end-user devices typically learn their IPv4 address using DHCP. With IPv6, routers also typically use static IPv6 addresses, while user devices use DHCP or Stateless Address Auto Configuration (SLAAC) to dynamically learn their IPv6 address.

Interestingly, routers have two options for configuring a stable and predictable IPv6 interface address that does not change. One method, discussed already in this chapter, uses the **ipv6 address** command to define the entire 128-bit address, as shown in Examples 30-1 and 30-2. The other method uses this same **ipv6 address** command to configure only the 64-bit IPv6 prefix for the interface and lets the router automatically generate a unique interface ID.

This second method uses rules called modified EUI-64 (extended unique identifier). Often, in the context of IPv6 addressing, people refer to modified EUI-64 as just EUI-64; there is no other term or concept about EUI-64 that you need to know for IPv6. The configuration that uses EUI-64 includes a keyword to tell the router to use EUI-64 rules, along with the 64-bit prefix. The router then uses EUI-64 rules to create the interface ID part of the address, as follows:

1. Split the 6-byte (12-hex-digit) MAC address in two halves (6 hex digits each).

2. Insert FFFE in between the two, making the interface ID now have a total of 16 hex digits (64 bits).

3. Invert the seventh bit of the interface ID.

Figure 30-4 shows the major pieces of how the address is formed.

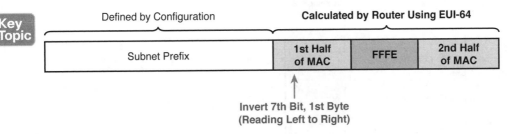

Figure 30-4 *IPv6 Address Format with Interface ID and EUI-64*

Although this process might seem a bit convoluted, it works. Also, with a little practice, you can look at an IPv6 address and quickly notice the FFFE in the middle of the interface ID and then easily find the two halves of the corresponding interface's MAC address. But you need to be ready to do the same math, in this case to predict the EUI-64 formatted IPv6 address on an interface.

For example, if you ignore the final step of inverting the seventh bit, the rest of the steps just require that you move the pieces around. Figure 30-5 shows two examples, just so you see the process.

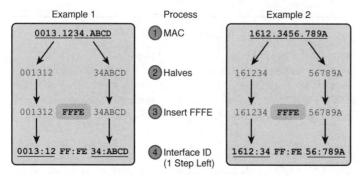

Figure 30-5 *Two Examples of Most of the EUI-64 Interface ID Process*

Both examples follow the same process. Each starts with the MAC address, breaking it into two halves (Step 2). The third step inserts FFFE in the middle, and the fourth step inserts a colon every four hex digits, keeping with IPv6 conventions.

While the examples in Figure 30-5 show most of the steps, they omit the final step. The final step requires that you convert the first byte (first two hex digits) from hex to binary, invert the seventh of the 8 bits, and convert the bits back to hex. Inverting a bit means that if the bit is a 0, make it a 1; if it is a 1, make it a 0. Most of the time, with IPv6 addresses, the original bit will be 0 and will be inverted to a 1.

For example, Figure 30-6 completes the two examples from Figure 30-5, focusing only on the first two hex digits. The examples show each pair of hex digits (Step 1) and the binary equivalent (Step 2). Step 3 shows a copy of those same 8 bits, except the seventh bit is inverted; the example on the left inverts from 0 to 1, and the example on the right inverts from 1 to 0. Finally, the bits are converted back to hex at Step 4.

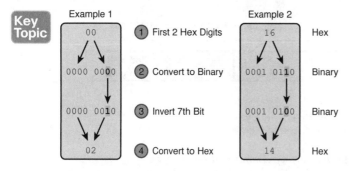

Figure 30-6 *Inverting the Seventh Bit of an EUI-64 Interface ID Field*

NOTE If you do not remember how to do hex to binary conversions, take a few moments to review the process. If you memorize the 16 hex values for digits 0 through F, with the corresponding binary values, the conversion can be easy. If you do not have those handy in your memory, take a few moments to look at Table A-2 in Appendix A, "Numeric Reference Tables."

For those of you who prefer the decimal shortcuts, with a little memorization you can do the bit-flip math without doing any hex-binary conversions. First, note that the process to invert the seventh bit, when working with a hexadecimal IPv6 address, flips the third of 4 bits in a single hex digit. With only 16 single hex digits, you could memorize what each hex digit becomes if its third bit is inverted, and you can easily memorize those values with a visual process.

If you want to try to memorize the values, it helps to work through the following process a few times, so grab a piece of scratch paper. Then write the 16 single hex digits as shown on the left side of Figure 30-7. That is, write them in eight rows of two numbers each, with the spacing as directed in the figure.

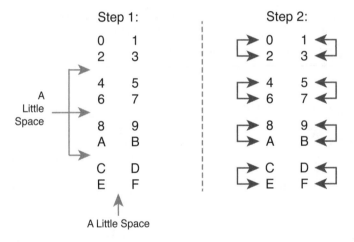

Figure 30-7 *A Mnemonic Device to Help Memorize Bit Inversion Shortcut*

Next, start at the top of the lists, and draw arrow lines between two numbers in the same column on the top left (0 and 2). Then move down the left-side column, connecting the next two digits (4 and 6) with an arrow line, then 8 and A, and then C and E. Repeat the process on the right, re-creating the right side of Figure 30-7.

The figure you drew (and the right side of Figure 30-7) shows the hex digits which, when you invert their third bit, converts to the other. That is, 0 converts to 2; 2 converts to 0; 1 converts to 3; 3 converts to 1; 4 converts to 6; 6 converts to 4; and so on. So, on the exam, if you can remember the pattern to redraw Figure 30-7, you could avoid doing binary/hexadecimal conversion. Use whichever approach makes you more comfortable.

As usual, the best way to get comfortable with forming these EUI-64 interface IDs is to calculate some yourself. Table 30-2 lists some practice problems, with an IPv6 64-bit prefix in the first column and the MAC address in the second column. Your job is to calculate the full (unabbreviated) IPv6 address using EUI-64 rules. The answers are at the end of the chapter, in the section "Answers to Earlier Practice Problems."

Table 30-2   IPv6 EUI-64 Address Creation Practice

Prefix	MAC Address	Unabbreviated IPv6 Address
2001:DB8:1:1::/64	0013.ABAB.1001	
2001:DB8:1:1::/64	AA13.ABAB.1001	
2001:DB8:1:1::/64	000C.BEEF.CAFE	
2001:DB8:1:1::/64	B80C.BEEF.CAFE	
2001:DB8:FE:FE::/64	0C0C.ABAC.CABA	
2001:DB8:FE:FE::/64	0A0C.ABAC.CABA	

Configuring a router interface to use the EUI-64 format uses the **ipv6 address** *address/prefix-length* **eui-64** interface subcommand. The **eui-64** keyword tells the router to find the interface MAC address and do the EUI-64 conversion math to find the interface ID.

Example 30-5 shows a revised configuration on Router R1, as compared to the earlier Example 30-1. In this case, R1 uses EUI-64 formatting for its IPv6 addresses.

Example 30-5   *Configuring R1's IPv6 Interfaces Using EUI-64*

```
ipv6 unicast-routing
!
! The ipv6 address command now lists a prefix, not the full address
interface GigabitEthernet0/0
 ipv6 address 2001:DB8:1111:1::/64 eui-64
!
interface Serial0/0/0
 ipv6 address 2001:DB8:1111:2::/64 eui-64


R1# show ipv6 interface brief
GigabitEthernet0/0      [up/up]
    FE80::1FF:FE01:101
    2001:DB8:1111:1:0:1FF:FE01:101
GigabitEthernet0/1      [administratively down/down]
    unassigned
Serial0/0/0             [up/up]
    FE80::1FF:FE01:101
    2001:DB8:1111:2:0:1FF:FE01:101
Serial0/0/1             [administratively down/down]
    unassigned
```

Note that the example shows EUI-64 being used on a serial interface, which does not have an associated MAC address. For interfaces that do not have a MAC address, the router chooses the MAC of the lowest-numbered router interface that does have a MAC. In this example, R1 uses its G0/0 interface MAC to form the EUI-64 interface ID for all the serial interfaces.

> **NOTE**   When you use EUI-64, the address value in the **ipv6 address** command should be the prefix, not the full 128-bit IPv6 address. However, if you mistakenly type the full address and still use the **eui-64** keyword, IOS accepts the command and converts the address to the matching prefix before putting the command into the running config file. For example, IOS converts **ipv6 address 2000:1:1:1::1/64 eui-64** to **ipv6 address 2000:1:1:1::/64 eui-64**.

Dynamic Unicast Address Configuration

In most cases, network engineers will configure the IPv6 addresses of router interfaces so that the addresses do not change until the engineer changes the router configuration. However, routers can be configured to use dynamically learned IPv6 addresses. These can be useful for routers connecting to the Internet through some types of Internet access technologies, like DSL and cable modems.

Cisco routers support two ways for the router interface to dynamically learn an IPv6 address to use:

- Stateful DHCP
- Stateless Address Autoconfiguration (SLAAC)

Both methods use the familiar **ipv6 address** command. Of course, neither option configures the actual IPv6 address; instead, the commands configure a keyword that tells the router which method to use to learn its IPv6 address. Example 30-6 shows the configuration, with one interface using stateful DHCP and one using SLAAC.

Example 30-6   *Router Configuration to Learn IPv6 Addresses with DHCP and SLAAC*

```
! This interface uses DHCP to learn its IPv6 address
interface FastEthernet0/0
 ipv6 address dhcp
!
! This interface uses SLAAC to learn its IPv6 address
interface FastEthernet0/1
 ipv6 address autoconfig
```

Cisco routers also have to be ready to play a role with DHCP and SLAAC on behalf of other IPv6 devices in the network. Chapter 31, which focuses on implementing IPv6 on hosts, discusses the protocols and the responsibilities of the routers.

Special Addresses Used by Routers

IPv6 configuration on a router begins with the simple steps discussed in the first part of this chapter. After you configure the **ipv6 unicast-routing** global configuration command, to enable the function of IPv6 routing, the addition of a unicast IPv6 address on an interface causes the router to do the following:

- Gives the interface a unicast IPv6 address
- Enables the routing of IPv6 packets in/out that interface
- Defines the IPv6 prefix (subnet) that exists off that interface
- Tells the router to add a connected IPv6 route for that prefix, to the IPv6 routing table, when that interface is up/up

> **NOTE**   In fact, if you pause and look at the list again, the same ideas happen for IPv4 when you configure an IPv4 address on a router interface.

While all the IPv6 features in this list work much like similar features in IPv4, IPv6 also has a number of additional functions not seen in IPv4. Often, these additional functions use other IPv6 addresses, many of which are multicast addresses. This second major section of the chapter examines the additional IPv6 addresses seen on routers, with a brief description of how they are used.

Link-Local Addresses

IPv6 uses link-local addresses as a special kind of unicast IPv6 address. These addresses are not used for normal IPv6 packet flows that contain data for applications. Instead, these addresses are used by some overhead protocols and for routing. This next topic first looks at how IPv6 uses link-local addresses and then how routers create link-local addresses.

Link-Local Address Concepts

Each IPv6 host (routers included) uses an additional unicast address called a link-local address. Packets sent to a link-local address do not leave the IPv6 subnet because routers do not forward packets sent to a link-local address.

IPv6 uses link-local addresses for a variety of protocols. Many IPv6 protocols that need to send messages inside a single subnet typically use link-local addresses, rather than the host's global unicast or unique local address. For example, Neighbor Discovery Protocol (NDP), which replaces the functions of IPv4's ARP, uses link-local addresses.

Routers also use link-local addresses as the next-hop IP addresses in IPv6 routes, as shown in Figure 30-8. IPv6 hosts also use a default router (default gateway) concept, like IPv4, but instead of the router address being in the same subnet, hosts refer to the router's link-local address. The **show ipv6 route** command lists the link-local address of the neighboring router, and not the global unicast or unique local unicast address.

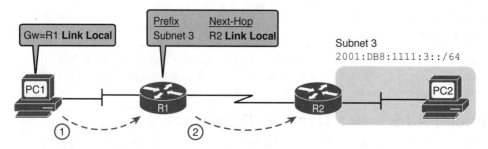

Figure 30-8   *IPv6 Using Link-Local Addresses as the Next-Hop Address*

Following are some key facts about link-local addresses:

Unicast (not multicast): Link-local addresses represent a single host, and packets sent to a link-local address should be processed by only that one IPv6 host.

Forwarding scope is the local link only: Packets sent to a link-local address do not leave the local data link because routers do not forward packets with link-local destination addresses.

Automatically generated: Every IPv6 host interface (and router interface) can create its own link-local address automatically, solving some initialization problems for hosts before they learn a dynamically learned global unicast address.

Common uses: Link-local addresses are used for some overhead protocols that stay local to one subnet and as the next-hop address for IPv6 routes.

Creating Link-Local Addresses on Routers

IPv6 hosts and routers can calculate their own link-local address, for each interface, using some basic rules. First, all link-local addresses start with the same prefix, as shown on the left side of Figure 30-9. By definition, the first 10 bits must match prefix FE80::/10, meaning that the first three hex digits will be either FE8, FE9, FEA, or FEB. However, when following the RFC, the next 54 bits should be binary 0, so the link-local address should always start with FE80:0000:0000:0000 as the first four unabbreviated quartets.

Figure 30-9 *Link-Local Address Format*

The second half of the link-local address, in practice, can be formed with different rules. Cisco routers use the EUI-64 format to create the interface ID (see the earlier section "Generating a Unique Interface ID Using Modified EUI-64"). As a result, a router's complete link-local address should be unique because the MAC address that feeds into the EUI-64 process should be unique. Other OSs randomly generate the interface ID. For example, Microsoft OSs use a somewhat random process to choose the interface ID, and change it over time, in an attempt to prevent some forms of attacks. Finally, link-local addresses can simply be configured.

IOS creates a link-local address for any interface that has configured at least one other unicast address using the **ipv6 address** command (global unicast or unique local). To see the link-local address, just use the usual commands that also list the unicast IPv6 address: **show ipv6 interface** and **show ipv6 interface brief**. Example 30-7 shows an example from Router R1.

Example 30-7 *Comparing Link-Local Addresses with EUI-Generated Unicast Addresses*

```
R1# show ipv6 interface brief
GigabitEthernet0/0     [up/up]
    FE80::1FF:FE01:101
    2001:DB8:1111:1:0:1FF:FE01:101
GigabitEthernet0/1     [administratively down/down]
    unassigned
Serial0/0/0            [up/up]
    FE80::1FF:FE01:101
    2001:DB8:1111:2:0:1FF:FE01:101
Serial0/0/1            [administratively down/down]
    unassigned
```

First, examine the two pairs of highlighted entries in the example. For each of the two interfaces that have a global unicast address (G0/0 and S0/0/0), the output lists the global unicast, which happens to begin with 2001 in this case. At the same time, the output also lists the link-local address for each interface, beginning with FE80.

Next, focus on the two addresses listed under interface G0/0. If you look closely at the second half of the two addresses listed for interface G0/0, you will see that both addresses have the same interface ID value. The global unicast address was configured in this case with the **ipv6 address 2001:DB8:1111:1::/64 eui-64** command, so the router used EUI-64 logic to form both the global unicast address and the link-local address. The interface MAC address in this case is 0200.0101.0101, so the router calculates an interface ID portion of both addresses as 0000:01FF:FE01:0101 (unabbreviated). After abbreviation, Router R1's link-local address on interface G0/0 becomes FE80::1FF:FE01:101.

IOS can either automatically create the link-local address, or it can be configured. IOS chooses the link-local address for the interface based on the following rules:

- If configured, the router uses the value in the **ipv6 address** *address* **link-local** interface subcommand. Note that the configured link-local address must be from the correct address range for link-local addresses; that is, an address from prefix FE80::/10. In other words, the address must begin with FE8, FE9, FEA, or FEB.

- If not configured, the IOS calculates the link-local address using EUI-64 rules, as discussed and demonstrated in and around Example 30-7. The calculation uses EUI-64 rules even if the interface unicast address does not use EUI-64.

Routing IPv6 with Only Link-Local Addresses on an Interface

Also, note that Cisco routers can enable IPv6 on an interface without using a global unicast address at all using the **ipv6 enable** command. Most of the time, the **ipv6 address** *address prefix* interface subcommand both enables IPv6 on an interface and defines a global unicast address for that interface. The **ipv6 enable** interface subcommand simply enables IPv6 on the interface.

The **ipv6 enable** interface subcommand makes a router interface relatively functional in some cases. It always causes the router to create a link-local address, and to be ready to process IPv6 packets on that interface. In some cases, that is all the router needs for IPv6 addressing on the interface.

Router WAN links often do not need to use subnets of global unicast addresses. For example, consider the simple IPv6 network in Figure 30-10. The LAN on the left and right, where IPv6 hosts exist, needs a global unicast subnet to use so that the hosts can have a unique IPv6 address. However, the two routers connected to the WAN link do not need global unicast addresses. As discussed earlier around Figure 30-8, the next-hop router in an IPv6 route is the neighbor's link-local address. So, link-local addressing in the center network provides all the IPv6 addressing that R1 and R2 need to forward packets between each other.

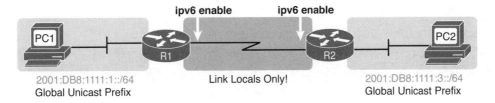

ipv6 enable   **ipv6 enable**

2001:DB8:1111:1::/64   Link Locals Only!   2001:DB8:1111:3::/64
Global Unicast Prefix   Global Unicast Prefix

Figure 30-10   *Typical Use of the* **ipv6 enable** *Command*

IPv6 Multicast Addresses

IPv6 uses multicast IPv6 addresses for several purposes. Like IPv4, IPv6 includes a range of multicast addresses that can be used by applications, with many of the same fundamental concepts as IPv4 multicasts (as discussed back in Chapter 20). For instance, an enterprise could use IPv6 addresses that begin with FF08::/16 (that is, the first 4 hex digits being FF08) as addresses to support multicast applications.

This next section focuses on two uses of IPv6 multicast addresses as used for overhead protocols. The first, link-local multicast addresses, are multicast addresses useful for communicating over a single link. The other type is a special overhead multicast address calculated for each host, called the solicited-node multicast address.

Local Scope Multicast Addresses

Stop for a moment and think about some of the control plane protocols discussed throughout this book so far. Some of those IPv4 control plane protocols used IPv4 broadcasts, which were then sent as Ethernet broadcast frames, destined to the Ethernet broadcast address of FFFF.FFFF.FFFF. While useful, those broadcasts required every host in the VLAN to process the broadcast frame, even if only one other device needed to think about the message.

IPv6 makes extensive use of IPv6 multicast addresses that allow any IPv6 node to use control plane protocols without the same negative impact on the hosts in a VLAN that do not care about that particular control plane protocol. For instance, each IPv6 routing protocol has a unique multicast address, so that packets sent to that address can be ignored by all IPv6 hosts and even ignored by routers that do not run that routing protocol.

IPv6 also defines a scope for multicast packets; that is, IPv6 defines how far into the network a multicast packet should be forwarded. Multicast addresses that begin FF08 (FF02::/16) have a link-local scope, meaning that routers will not forward these packets outside the local subnet—which is good. Many control plane protocols need to send messages that stay on the local subnet, so these link-local multicasts play an important role. In comparison, the addresses that begin FF08 (Ff08::/16), typically used for a multicast application with users throughout the enterprise, have an organization-local scope, meaning that packets sent to these addresses are forwarded throughout the organization but not out into the Internet.

The best way to get a sense of these link-local multicast addresses is to look at popular addresses and their use. For instance, IPv6 reserves an address used to communicate with all IPv6 devices in a subnet, or all routers in a subnet, or all OSPF routers in a subnet, and so on.

30

Table 30-3 lists the most common local-scope IPv6 multicast addresses.

Table 30-3   Key IPv6 Local-Scope Multicast Addresses

Short Name	Multicast Address	Meaning	IPv4 Equivalent
All-nodes	FF02::1	All-nodes (all interfaces that use IPv6 that are on the link)	A subnet broadcast address
All-routers	FF02::2	All-routers (all IPv6 router interfaces on the link)	None
All-OSPF, All-OSPF-DR	FF02::5, FF02::6	All OSPF routers and all OSPF-designated routers, respectively	224.0.0.5, 224.0.0.6
RIPng Routers	FF02::9	All RIPng routers	224.0.0.9
EIGRPv6 Routers	FF02::A	All routers using EIGRP for IPv6 (EIGRPv6)	224.0.0.10
DHCP Relay Agent	FF02::1:2	All routers acting as a DHCPv6 relay agent	None

Example 30-8 repeats the output of the **show ipv6 interface** command to show the multicast addresses used by Router R1 on its G0/0 interface. In this case, the highlighted lines show the all-nodes address (FF02::1), all-routers (FF02::2), and EIGRPv6 (FF02::A).

Example 30-8   *Verifying Static IPv6 Addresses on Router R1*

```
R1# show ipv6 interface GigabitEthernet 0/0
GigabitEthernet0/0 is up, line protocol is up
  IPv6 is enabled, link-local address is FE80::1FF:FE01:101
  No Virtual link-local address(es):
  Description: LAN at Site 1
  Global unicast address(es):
    2001:DB8:1111:1::1, subnet is 2001:DB8:1111:1::/64
  Joined group address(es):
    FF02::1
    FF02::2
    FF02::A
    FF02::1:FF00:1
    FF02::1:FF01:101
  ! Lines omitted for brevity
```

Solicited-Node Multicast Addresses

Many of the multicast addresses that protocols use are simply numbers reserved by an RFC. You just need to remember the numbers and notice them in **show** commands. However, one particular type of multicast address, called the solicited-node multicast address, varies from host to host, so its value is not preset. This last topic of the chapter briefly describes this type of multicast address.

Every interface has a solicited-node multicast address in addition to the usual unicast addresses, but the purpose of this multicast address is hard to explain with a short set of words. Instead, start with this list, which breaks down the concepts that effectively define what the solicited-node multicast address is for a particular host interface:

- **Multicast:** The address is a multicast address (not a unicast address)
- **Link-local:** The scope is link-local, meaning routers do not forward messages sent to this address
- **Calculated:** The address is calculated based on the unicast IPv6 address of the host, specifically based only on the last six hex digits of the unicast address
- **Operation:** Each host interface must listen for packets sent to its solicited-node multicast address.
- **Overlap:** Because of the calculation, some hosts might have the same solicited-node multicast address.

This last bullet item gets to the key function of these solicited-node multicast addresses. Packets sent to a particular solicited-node multicast address might be processed by just one host, or it might be processed by multiple hosts. If more than one host in a subnet happens to have equal values in the last six hex digits of its unicast addresses, they calculate and use the same solicited-node multicast address. And some protocols want this kind of logic of sending one multicast packet to all hosts that happen to have these similar unicast IPv6 addresses. As a result, the solicited-node multicast address was born.

All IPv6 hosts must listen for messages sent to their solicited-node multicast address(es). So, for each interface and for each unicast address on each interface, the device must determine its solicited-node multicast address(es) and listen for packets sent to those addresses.

The logic to find a solicited-node multicast address, after you know the unicast address, is simple. Start with the predefined /104 prefix shown in Figure 30-11. In other words, all the solicited-node multicast addresses begin with the abbreviated FF02::1:FF. In the last 24 bits (6 hex digits), copy the unicast address into the solicited-node address.

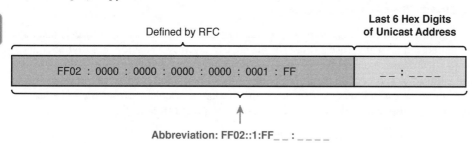

Figure 30-11 *Solicited-Node Multicast Address Format*

To see samples of these addresses on a router, look back to Example 30-8. The last two lines of command output show the solicited-node multicast addresses for Router R1's G0/0 interface: FF02::1:FF00:1 and FF02::1:FF01:101. Note that in this case, the reason R1's G0/0 has two such addresses is that one matches the router's global unicast address on that interface, whereas the other matches the link-local (unicast) address.

Anycast Addresses

Imagine that routers collectively need to implement some service. Rather than have one router supply that service, that service works best when implemented on several routers. But the hosts that use the service need to contact only the nearest such service, and the network wants to hide all these details from the hosts. Hosts can send just one packet to an IPv6 address, and the routers will forward the packet to the nearest router that supports that service by virtue of supporting that destination IPv6 address.

IPv6 anycast addresses provide that exact function. The *any* part of the name refers to the fact that any of the instances of the service can be used. Figure 30-12 shows this big concept, with two major steps:

Step 1. Two routers configure the exact same IPv6 address, designated as an anycast address, to support some service.

Step 2. In the future, when any router receives a packet for that anycast address, the other routers simply route the packet to the nearest of the routers that support the address.

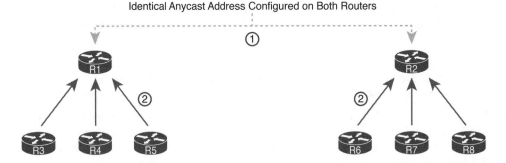

Figure 30-12 *IPv6 Anycast Addresses*

To make this anycast process work, the routers implementing the anycast address must be configured and then advertise a route for the anycast address. The addresses do not come from a special reserved range of addresses; instead, they are from the unicast address range. Often, the address is configured with a /128 prefix so that the routers advertise a host route for that one anycast address. At that point, the routing protocol advertises the route just like any other IPv6 route; the other routers cannot tell the difference.

Example 30-9 shows a sample configuration on a router. Note that the actual address (2001:1:1:2::99) looks like any other unicast address; the value can be chosen like any other IPv6 unicast addresses. However, note the different **anycast** keyword on the **ipv6 address** command, telling the local router that the address has a special purpose as an anycast address. Finally, note that the **show ipv6 interface** command does identify the address as an anycast address, but the **show ipv6 interface brief** command does not.

Example 30-9 *Configuring and Verifying IPv6 Anycast Addresses*

```
R1# configure terminal
Enter configuration commands, one per line.  End with CNTL/Z.
R1(config)# interface gigabitEthernet 0/0
R1(config-if)# ipv6 address 2001:1:1:1::1/64
```

```
R1(config-if)# ipv6 address 2001:1:1:2::99/128 anycast
R1(config-if)# ^Z
R1#
R1# show ipv6 interface g0/0
GigabitEthernet0/0 is up, line protocol is up
  IPv6 is enabled, link-local address is FE80::11FF:FE11:1111
  No Virtual link-local address(es):
  Global unicast address(es):
    2001:1:1:1::1, subnet is 2001:1:1:1::/64
    2001:1:1:2::99, subnet is 2001:1:1:2::99/128 [ANY]
  ! Lines omitted for brevity
R1# show ipv6 interface brief g0/0
GigabitEthernet0/0      [up/up]
    FE80::11FF:FE11:1111
    2001:1:1:1::1
    2001:1:1:2::99
```

NOTE The *subnet router anycast address* is one special anycast address in each subnet. It is reserved for use by routers as a way to send a packet to any router on the subnet. The address's value in each subnet is the same number as the subnet ID; that is, the address has the same prefix value as the other addresses and all binary 0s in the interface ID.

Miscellaneous IPv6 Addresses

Together, this chapter and the preceding chapter have introduced most of the IPv6 addressing concepts included in this book. This short topic mentions a few remaining IPv6 addressing ideas and summarizes the topics for easy study.

First, all IPv6 hosts can use two additional special addresses:

- The unknown (unspecified) IPv6 address, ::, or all 0s
- The loopback IPv6 address, ::1, or 127 binary 0s with a single 1

A host can use the unknown address (::) when its own IPv6 address is not yet known, or when the host wonders if its own IPv6 address might have problems. For example, hosts use the unknown address during the early stages of dynamically discovering their IPv6 address. When a host does not yet know what IPv6 address to use, it can use the :: address as its source IPv6 address.

The IPv6 loopback address gives each IPv6 host a way to test its own protocol stack. Just like the IPv4 127.0.0.1 loopback address, packets sent to ::1 do not leave the host but are instead simply delivered down the stack to IPv6 and back up the stack to the application on the local host.

IPv6 Addressing Configuration Summary

This chapter completes the discussion of various IPv6 address types, while showing how to enable IPv6 on interfaces. Many implementations will use the **ipv6 address** command on each router LAN interface, and either that same command or the **ipv6 enable** command on the WAN interfaces. For exam prep, Table 30-4 summarizes the various commands and the automatically generated IPv6 addresses in one place for review and study.

Table 30-4 Summary of IPv6 Address Types and the Commands That Create Them

Type	Prefix/Address Notes	Enabled with What Interface Subcommand
Global unicast	Many prefixes	**ipv6 address** *address/prefix-length*
		ipv6 address *prefix/prefix-length* **eui-64**
Other type	FD00::/8	**ipv6 address** *prefix/prefix-length* **eui-64**
Link local	FE80::/10	**ipv6 address** *address* **link-local**
		Autogenerated by all **ipv6 address** commands
		Autogenerated by the **ipv6 enable** command
All hosts multicast	FF02::1	Autogenerated by all **ipv6 address** commands
All routers multicast	FF02::2	Autogenerated by all **ipv6 address** commands
Routing protocol multicasts	Various	Added to the interface when the corresponding routing protocol is enabled on the interface
Solicited-node multicast	FF02::1:FF /104	Autogenerated by all **ipv6 address** commands
Anycast	Any unicast address	**ipv6 address** *address/prefix-length* **anycast**

Chapter Review

One key to doing well on the exams is to perform repetitive spaced review sessions. Review this chapter's material using either the tools in the book, DVD, or interactive tools for the same material found on the book's companion website. Refer to the "Your Study Plan" element for more details. Table 30-5 outlines the key review elements and where you can find them. To better track your study progress, record when you completed these activities in the second column.

Table 30-5 Chapter Review Tracking

Review Element	Review Date(s)	Resource Used
Review key topics		Book, DVD/website
Review key terms		Book, DVD/website
Repeat DIKTA questions		Book, PCPT
Do labs		Blog
Review command tables		Book

Review All the Key Topics

Table 30-6   Key Topics for Chapter 30

Key Topic Element	Description	Page Number
Figure 30-2	Concept drawing about the need for dual stacks for the foreseeable future	707
List	Rules for creating an IPv6 address using EUI-64 rules	711
Figure 30-4	Conceptual drawing of how to create an IPv6 address using EUI-64 rules	711
Figure 30-6	Example of performing the bit inversion when using EUI-64	712
List	Functions IOS enables when an IPv6 is configured on a working interface	715
List	Key facts about IPv6 link-local addresses	716
Figure 30-11	Conceptual drawing of how to make a solicited-node multicast address	721
List	Other special IPv6 addresses	723
Table 30-4	IPv6 address summary with the commands that enable each address type	724

Key Terms You Should Know

dual stacks, EUI-64, link-local address, link-local scope, solicited-node multicast address, all-nodes multicast address, all-routers multicast address, anycast address, subnet-router anycast address

Additional Practice for This Chapter's Processes

For additional practice with IPv6 abbreviations, you may do the same set of practice problems using your choice of tools:

Application: Use the Fundamentals of IP Version 6 application on the DVD or companion website.

PDF: Alternatively, practice the same problems found in these apps using DVD Appendix K, "Practice for Chapter 30: Implementing IPv6 Addressing on Routers."

Create your own problems using any real router or simulator: Get into the router CLI, into configuration mode, and configure the **mac-address** *address* and **ipv6 address** *prefix*/**64 eui-64** command. Then predict the IPv6 unicast address, link-local address, and solicited-node multicast address; finally, check your predictions against the **show ipv6 interface** command.

Command References

Tables 30-7 and 30-8 list configuration and verification commands used in this chapter. As an easy review exercise, cover the left column in a table, read the right column, and try to recall the command without looking. Then repeat the exercise, covering the right column, and try to recall what the command does.

Table 30-7   Chapter 30 Configuration Command Reference

Command	Description
ipv6 unicast-routing	Global command that enables IPv6 routing on the router.
ipv6 address *ipv6-address/ prefix-length* [eui-64]	Interface subcommand that manually configures either the entire interface IP address, or a /64 prefix with the router building the EUI-64 format interface ID automatically.
ipv6 address *ipv6-address/ prefix-length* [anycast]	Interface subcommand that manually configures an address to be used as an anycast address.
ipv6 enable	Enables IPv6 on an interface and generates a link-local address.
ipv6 address dhcp	Interface subcommand that enables IPv6 on an interface, causes the router to use DHCP client processes to try to lease an IPv6 address, and creates a link-local address for the interface.

Table 30-8   Chapter 30 EXEC Command Reference

Command	Description
show ipv6 route [connected] [local]	Lists IPv6 routes, or just the connected routes, or just the local routes.
show ipv6 interface [*type number*]	Lists IPv6 settings on an interface, including link-local and other unicast IP addresses (or for the listed interface).
show ipv6 interface brief [*type number*]	Lists interface status and IPv6 addresses for each interface (or for the listed interface).

Answers to Earlier Practice Problems

Table 30-2, earlier in this chapter, listed several practice problems in which you needed to calculate the IPv6 address based on EUI-64 rules. Table 30-9 lists the answers to those problems.

Table 30-9   Answers to IPv6 EUI-64 Address Creation Practice

Prefix	MAC Address	IPv6 Address, Last Half Unabbreviated
2001:DB8:1:1::/64	0013.ABAB.1001	2001:DB8:1:1:0213:ABFF:FEAB:1001
2001:DB8:1:1::/64	AA13.ABAB.1001	2001:DB8:1:1:A813:ABFF:FEAB:1001
2001:DB8:1:1::/64	000C.BEEF.CAFE	2001:DB8:1:1:020C:BEFF:FEEF:CAFE
2001:DB8:1:1::/64	B80C.BEEF.CAFE	2001:DB8:1:1:BA0C:BEFF:FEEF:CAFE
2001:DB8:FE:FE::/64	0C0C.ABAC.CABA	2001:DB8:FE:FE:0E0C:ABFF:FEAC:CABA
2001:DB8:FE:FE::/64	0A0C.ABAC.CABA	2001:DB8:FE:FE:080C:ABFF:FEAC:CABA

CHAPTER 31

Implementing IPv6 Addressing on Hosts

This chapter covers the following exam topics:

1.0 Network Fundamentals

1.12 Configure, verify, and troubleshoot IPv6 addressing

1.13 Configure and verify IPv6 Stateless Address Auto Configuration

1.14 Compare and contrast IPv6 address types

    1.14.f Autoconfiguration

IPv6 hosts act like IPv4 hosts in many ways, using similar ideas, similar protocols, and even similar or identical commands for the same purpose. At the same time, IPv6 sometimes takes a much different approach than does IPv4, using a much different solution with a new protocol or command. For example:

- Similar to IPv4, IPv6 hosts use a unicast address, prefix length (mask), default router, and DNS server.

- Similar to IPv4, IPv6 uses a protocol to dynamically learn the MAC address of other hosts in the same LAN-based subnet.

- Unlike IPv4, IPv6 hosts use the Neighbor Discovery Protocol (NDP) for many functions, including the functions done by IPv4's ARP.

- Similar to IPv4, IPv6 hosts can use DHCP to learn their four primary IPv6 settings.

- Unlike IPv4, IPv6 supports a dynamic address assignment process other than DHCP, called Stateless Address Auto Configuration (SLAAC).

This chapter focuses on the four primary IPv6 settings on hosts: the address, prefix length, default router address, and DNS server address. However, to understand how hosts dynamically learn those addresses, this chapter begins its first major section devoted to NDP, which plays a key role in several IPv6 processes. The middle section of the chapter then focuses on how hosts dynamically learn their IPv6 settings, with both DHCP and SLAAC. The final major section of this chapter looks at the tools to verify a host's IPv6 settings, many of which use the same commands used for IPv4.

"Do I Know This Already?" Quiz

Take the quiz (either here, or use the PCPT software) if you want to use the score to help you decide how much time to spend on this chapter. The answers are at the bottom of the page following the quiz, and the explanations are in DVD Appendix C and in the PCPT software.

Table 31-1 "Do I Know This Already?" Foundation Topics Section-to-Question Mapping

Foundation Topics Section	Questions
The Neighbor Discovery Protocol	1–3
Dynamic Configuration of Host IPv6 Settings	4–5
Troubleshooting IPv6 Addressing	6

1. PC1, PC2, and Router R1 all connect to the same VLAN and IPv6 subnet. PC1 wants to send its first IPv6 packet to PC2. What protocol or message will PC1 use to discover the MAC address to which PC1 should send the Ethernet frame that encapsulates this IPv6 packet?

   a. ARP

   b. NDP NS

   c. NDP RS

   d. SLAAC

2. PC1 and Router R1 connect to the same VLAN and IPv6 subnet. The user of PC1 pings the IPv6 address of a host that sits at a remote site, so that the packets flow through R1, PC1's default router. PC1 does not statically configure its default router setting. Which of the following answers lists a protocol or message that PC1 could have used when trying to learn what IPv6 address to use as its default router?

   a. EUI-64

   b. NDP NS

   c. DAD

   d. NDP RS

3. Which of the following pieces of information does a router supply in an NDP Router Advertisement (RA) message? (Choose two answers.)

   a. Router IPv6 address

   b. Host name of the router

   c. IPv6 prefix(es) on the link

   d. IPv6 address of DHCP server

4. Host PC1 dynamically learns its IPv6 settings using Stateless Address Auto Configuration (SLAAC). Which one of PC1's settings is most likely to be learned from the stateless DHCPv6 server?

   a. Host address

   b. Prefix length

   c. Default router address

   d. DNS server address(es)

5. Host PC1 dynamically learns its IPv6 settings using Stateless Address Auto Configuration (SLAAC). Think about the host's unicast address as two parts: the prefix and the interface ID. Which of the answers list a way that SLAAC learns or builds the value of the interface ID portion of the host's address? (Choose two answers.)

   a. Learned from a DHCPv6 server

   b. Built by the host using EUI-64 rules

   c. Learned from a router using NDP RS/RA messages

   d. Built by the host using a random value

6. Three routers connect to the same VLAN and IPv6 subnet. All three routers have sent NDP RA messages, in reply to various IPv6 hosts' NDP RS messages, asking to learn about the available IPv6 routers in the subnet. A network engineer issues the **show ipv6 neighbors** command on R1. Which of the answers best describes the kind of NDP information held in this output?

   a. IPv6 neighbors (both routers and hosts) plus their MAC addresses, without noting which are routers

   b. IPv6 neighbors (both routers and hosts) plus their MAC addresses, and also noting which are routers

   c. IPv6 routers, with no information about nonrouters, with no MAC address info

   d. IPv6 routers, with no information about nonrouters, with MAC address info

Foundation Topics

The Neighbor Discovery Protocol

IPv6 hosts need to know several important IPv6 settings that mirror the settings needed on IPv4 hosts: an address, the associated prefix length (mask equivalent), the default router address, and the DNS server address(es). Figure 31-1 shows those four concepts for PC1 on the left.

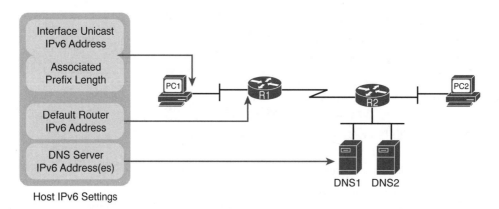

Figure 31-1 *IPv6 Settings Needed on Hosts*

Note that of the four settings, three are unicast IPv6 addresses. The PC's own IPv6 address is typically a global unicast or unique local unicast, as are the PC's references to the DNS servers. However, because the default router must be locally reachable, the default router setting typically refers to the router's link-local address.

Neighbor Discovery Protocol (NDP) defines several different functions related to IPv6 addressing, as follows:

SLAAC: When using Stateless Address Auto Configuration (SLAAC), the host uses NDP messages to learn the first part of its address, plus the prefix length.

Router Discovery: Hosts learn the IPv6 addresses of the available IPv6 routers in the same subnet using NDP messages.

Duplicate Address Detection: No matter how a host sets or learns its IPv6 address, the host waits to use the address until the host knows that no other host uses the same address. How does a host detect this problem? Using NDP messages, of course, through a process called Duplicate Address Detection (DAD).

Neighbor MAC Discovery: After a host has passed the DAD process and uses its IPv6 address, a LAN-based host will need to learn the MAC address of other hosts in the same subnet. NDP replaces IPv4's ARP, providing messages that replace the ARP Request and Reply messages.

The rest of this section steps through each of these four functions to varying degrees. Note that this section defers most of the discussion of the SLAAC process until later in the chapter, focusing more on the core NDP functions in this section.

Discovering Routers with NDP RS and RA

For IPv6, ICMPv6 replaces the ICMP protocol. As with ICMP for IPv4, ICMPv6 includes a Request and Echo Reply message for use by the **ping** command. ICMPv6 also includes all the NDP messages, like the two messages in this list. These two messages enable routers to learn addressing and subnet information from any routers in the subnet.

Router Solicitation (RS): This message is sent to the "all-IPv6-routers" local-scope multicast address of FF02::2 so that the message asks all routers, on the local link only, to identify themselves.

Router Advertisement (RA): This message, sent by the router, lists many facts, including the link-local IPv6 address of the router. When unsolicited, it is sent to the all-IPv6-hosts local-scope multicast address of FF02::1. When sent in response to an RS message, it flows back to either the unicast address of the host that sent the RS or to the all-IPv6-hosts address FF02::1.

For example, Figure 31-2 shows how host PC1 can learn R1's link-local address. The process is indeed simple, with PC1 first asking and R1 replying.

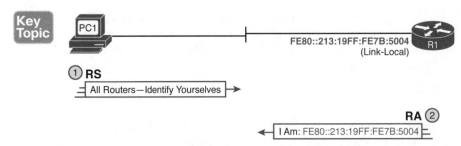

Figure 31-2 *Example NDP RS/RA Process to Find the Default Routers*

> **NOTE** IPv6 allows multiple prefixes and multiple default routers to be listed in the RA message; Figure 31-2 just shows one of each for simplicity's sake.

IPv6 does not use broadcasts, but it does use multicasts. In this case, the RS message flows to the all-routers multicast address (FF02::2) so that all routers will receive the message. It has the same good effect as a broadcast with IPv4, without the negatives of a broadcast. In this case, only IPv6 routers will spend any CPU cycles processing the RS message. The RA message can flow either to the unicast IPv6 address of PC1 or to the all-nodes FF02::1 address.

Note that while Figure 31-2 shows how a host can ask to learn about any routers, routers also periodically send unsolicited RA messages, even without an incoming RS. When routers send these periodic RA messages, they basically advertise details about IPv6 on the link. In this case, the RA messages flow to the FF02::1 all-nodes IPv6 multicast address.

Discovering Addressing Info for SLAAC with NDP RS and RA

The NDP RS and RA messages give hosts a means to ask routers to supply information; they also give routers a means to supply that information to hosts. In short, RS/RA can act as a basic query/response protocol (or solicitation/advertisement, if you prefer the words from the RS and RA acronyms).

What could an IPv6 router know that an IPv6 host might want to learn? Figure 31-2 shows one fact learned through the RS and RA messages—namely, the IPv6 address of the IPv6 router. Another useful fact is the prefix and prefix length used on the local link. Routers know the prefix and prefix length because of the typical **ipv6 address** command on each interface; that command lists the prefix length and enough information for the router to calculate the associated IPv6 prefix. A host can learn these details using the RS and RA message exchange, as shown in Figure 31-3.

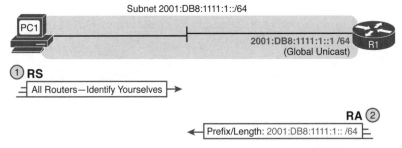

Figure 31-3 *Using NDP RS/RA to Discover the Prefix/Length on the LAN*

As it turns out, the SLAAC process, used by hosts to dynamically learn an IPv6 address, uses the prefix/prefix length information learned from the router using RS and RA messages. The later section "Using Stateless Address Auto Configuration" discusses the entire process.

Discovering Neighbor Link Addresses with NDP NS and NA

NDP defines a second pair of matched solicitation and advertisement messages: the Neighbor Solicitation (NS) and Neighbor Advertisement (NA) messages. Basically, the NS acts like an IPv4 ARP request, asking the host with a particular unicast IPv6 address to send back a reply. The NA message acts like an IPv4 ARP Reply, listing that host's MAC address.

The process of sending the NS and NA messages follows the same general process as RS and RA: The NS message asks for information, and the NA supplies the information. The most obvious difference is that while RS/RA focuses on information held by routers, NS/NA focuses on information that could be held by any IPv6 host.

Neighbor Solicitation (NS): This message asks a host with a particular IPv6 address (the target address) to send back an NA with its MAC address listed. The NS message is sent to the solicited-node multicast address associated with the target address, so the message is processed only by hosts whose last six hex digits match the address that is being queried.

Neighbor Advertisement (NA): This message lists the sender's address as the target address, along with the matching MAC address. It is sent back to the unicast address of the host that sent the original NS message. In some cases, a host sends an unsolicited NA, in which case the message is sent to the all-IPv6-hosts local-scope multicast address FF02::1.

> **NOTE** With NDP, the word *neighbor* refers to the fact that the devices will be on the same data link; for example, the same VLAN.

Figure 31-4 shows an example of how a host (PC1) uses an NS message to learn the MAC address used by another host. The NDP NS and NA messages replace the IPv4 ARP proto-col in that it lets hosts discover the link-layer address of other IPv6 hosts on the same data link. (IPv6 refers to hosts on the same data link as simply *on-link*.) The NS message lists a target IPv6 unicast address, with the implied question: "What is your link address?" The NA message, in this example sent back to the original host that asked the question, lists that link address. Figure 31-4 shows an example.

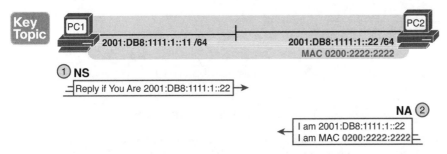

Figure 31-4 *Example NDP NS/NA Process to Find the Neighbor's Link Addresses*

At Step 1 of this particular example, PC1 sends the solicitation to find PC2's MAC address. PC1 first looks in its NDP neighbor table, the equivalent of the IPv4 ARP cache, and does not find the MAC address for IPv6 address 2001:DB8:1111:1::22. So, at Step 1, PC1 sends the NDP NS message to the matching solicited-node multicast address for 2001:DB8:1111:1::22 or FF02::1:FF00:22. Only IPv6 hosts whose address ends with 00:0022 will listen for this solicited-node multicast address. As a result, only a small subset of hosts on this link will process the received NDP NS message.

At Step 2, PC2 reacts to the received NS message. PC2 sends back an NA message in reply, listing PC2's MAC address. PC1 records PC2's MAC address in PC1's NDP neighbor table.

NOTE To view a host's NDP neighbor table, use these commands: (Windows) **netsh interface ipv6 show neighbors;** (Linux) **ip -6 neighbor show;** (Mac OS) **ndp -an.**

Discovering Duplicate Addresses Using NDP NS and NA

The NDP NS/NA messages also require hosts to do an important check to avoid using duplicate IPv6 addresses. IPv6 uses the Duplicate Address Detection (DAD) process before using a unicast address to make sure that no other node on that link is already using the address. If another host already uses that address, the first host simply does not use the address until the problem is resolved.

The term *DAD* refers to the function, but the function uses NDP NS and NA messages. Basically, a host sends an NS message, but it lists the address the host wants to use as the target address. If no duplicate exists, no other host should reply with an NA. However, if another host already uses that address, that host will reply with an NA, identifying a duplicate use of the address. Figure 31-5 shows an example in which a duplicate is detected.

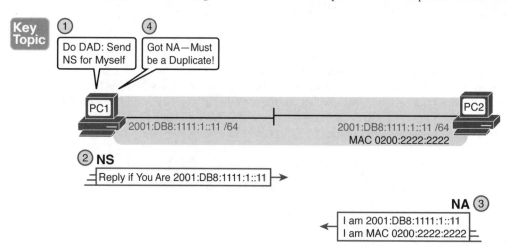

Figure 31-5 *Example Duplicate Address Detection (DAD) with NDP NS/NA*

Figure 31-5 shows an example in which both PC1 and PC2 attempt to use the same IPv6 address. PC2 is already using the address, and PC1 uses DAD before using the address. The figure shows the following steps:

1. PC1, before using address 2001:DB8:1111:1::11, must use DAD.

2. PC1 sends an NS message, listing the address PC1 now wants to use (2001:DB8:1111:1::11) as the target.

3. PC2 receives the NS, sees what PC2 already uses as its own address, and sends back an NA.

4. PC1, on receiving the NA message for its own IPv6 address, realizes a duplicate address exists.

Hosts do the DAD check for each of their unicast addresses, link-local addresses included, both when the address is first used and each time the host's interface comes up.

NDP Summary

This chapter explains some of the more important functions performed by NDP. NDP does more than what is listed in this chapter, and the protocol allows for addition of other functions, so NDP might continue to grow. For now, use Table 31-2 as a study reference for the four NDP features discussed here.

Table 31-2 NDP Function Summary

Function	Protocol Messages	Who Discovers Info	Who Supplies Info	Info Supplied
Router discovery	RS and RA	Any IPv6 host	Any IPv6 router	Link-local IPv6 address of router
Prefix/length discovery	RS and RA	Any IPv6 host	Any IPv6 router	Prefix(es) and associated prefix lengths used on local link
Neighbor discovery	NS and NA	Any IPv6 host	Any IPv6 host	Link-layer address (for example, MAC address) used by a neighbor
Duplicate Address Detection	NS and NA	Any IPv6 host	Any IPv6 host	Simple confirmation whether a unicast address is already in use

Dynamic Configuration of Host IPv6 Settings

By the time IPv6 was created back in the early to mid-1990s, the world had a decade or two of experience with IPv4. That experience with IPv4 had already shown the need for hosts to dynamically learn their IPv4 settings, including the host's IPv4 address. By the time IPv6 was being created, DHCP for IPv4 had already become the preferred IPv4 solution to allow hosts to dynamically learn their IPv4 address and other settings.

DHCP worked well for IPv4, so creating a version of DHCP for IPv6 (DHCPv6) made perfect sense. However, while DHCP has many advantages, one possible disadvantage is that DHCP requires a server that keeps information about each host (client) and its address. The designers of IPv6 wanted an alternative dynamic address assignment tool, one that did not require a server. The answer? SLAAC.

This second major section of the chapter first looks at DHCPv6, followed by SLAAC.

Dynamic Configuration Using Stateful DHCP and NDP

DHCP for IPv6 (DHCPv6) gives an IPv6 host a way to learn host IPv6 configuration settings, using the same general concepts as DHCP for IPv4. The host exchanges messages with a DHCP server, and the server supplies the host with configuration information, including a lease of an IPv6 address, along with prefix length and DNS server address information.

> **NOTE**   The DHCP version is not actually version 6; the name just ends in "v6" in reference to the support for IPv6.

More specifically, stateful DHCPv6 works like the more familiar DHCP for IPv4 in many other general ways, as follows:

- DHCP clients on a LAN send messages that flow only on the local LAN, hoping to find a DHCP server.

- If the DHCP server sits on the same LAN as the client, the client and server can exchange DHCP messages directly, without needing help from a router.

- If the DHCP server sits on another link as compared to the client, the client and server rely on a router to forward the DHCP messages.

- The router that forwards messages from one link to a server in a remote subnet must be configured as a DHCP Relay Agent, with knowledge of the DHCP server's IPv6 address.

- Servers have configuration that lists pools of addresses for each subnet from which the server allocates addresses.

- Servers offer a lease of an IP address to a client, from the pool of addresses for the client's subnet; the lease lasts a set time period (usually days or weeks).

- The server tracks state information, specifically a client identifier (often based on the MAC address), along with the address that is currently leased to that client.

DHCPv6 has two major branches of how it can be used: stateful DHCPv6 and stateless DHCPv6. Stateful DHCPv6 works more like the DHCPv4 model, especially related to that last item in the list. A stateful DHCPv6 server tracks information about which client has a lease for what IPv6 address; the fact that the server knows information about a specific client is called state information, making the DHCP server a stateful DHCP server.

Stateless DHCP servers do not track any per-client information. The upcoming section "Using Stateless Address Auto Configuration" discusses how stateless DHCPv6 servers have an important role when a company decides to use SLAAC.

Differences Between DHCPv6 and DHCPv4

While stateful DHCPv6 has many similarities to DHCPv4, many particulars differ as well. Figure 31-6 shows one key difference: Stateful DHCPv6 does not supply default router information to the client. Instead, the client host uses the built-in NDP protocol to learn the routers' IPv6 addresses directly from the local routers.

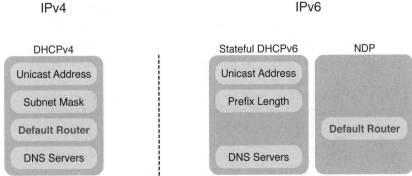

Figure 31-6 *Sources of Specific IPv6 Settings When Using Stateful DHCP*

DHCPv6 also updates the protocol messages to use IPv6 packets instead of IPv4 packets, with new messages and fields as well. For example, Figure 31-7 shows the names of the DHCPv6 messages, which replace the DHCPv4 Discover, Offer, Request, and Acknowledgment (DORA) messages. Instead, DHCPv6 uses the Solicit, Advertise, Request, and Reply messages.

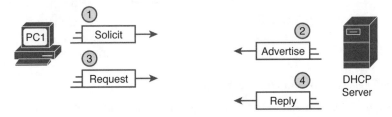

Figure 31-7 *Four Stateful DHCPv6 Messages Between Client and Server*

The four DHCPv6 messages work in two matched pairs with the same general flow as the similar DHCPv4 messages. The Solicit and Advertise messages complete the process of the client searching for the IPv6 address of a DHCPv6 server (the Solicit message) and the server advertising an address (and other configuration settings) for the client to possibly use (the Advertise message). The Request and Reply messages let the client ask to lease the address, with the server confirming the lease in the Reply message.

DHCPv6 Relay Agents

For enterprises that choose to use stateful DHCPv6, often the DHCP server sits at a central site, far away from many of the clients that use the DHCPv6 server. In those cases, the local router at each site must act as a DHCP relay agent.

The concepts of DHCPv6 relay work like DHCPv4 relay, as discussed in the section "Supporting DHCP for Remote Subnets with DHCP Relay," in Chapter 20, "DHCP and IP Networking on Hosts." The client sends a message that only flows inside the local LAN. The router then changes the source and destination IP address, forwarding the packet to the DHCP server. When the server sends a reply, it actually flows to an address on the router (the relay agent), which changes the addresses in that packet as well.

The differences for IPv6 become more obvious when you look at some of the IPv6 address-es used in DHCPv6 messages, like the Solicit message used to lead off a DHCPv6 flow. As shown in Figure 31-8, the client uses the following addresses in the solicit message:

Source of link-local: The client uses its own link-local address as the source address of the packet.

Destination address of "all-DHCP-agents" FF02::1:2: This link-local scope multicast address is used to send packets to two types of devices: DHCP servers and routers acting as DHCP relay agents.

With a link-local scope multicast destination address, the Solicit message sent by a host would flow only on the local LAN. Figure 31-8 shows some of the particulars of how R1, acting as a DHCPv6 relay agent, assists DHCPv6 clients like host A to deliver DHCPv6 packets to the DHCPv6 server.

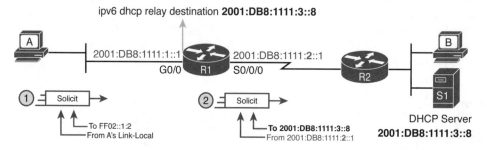

Figure 31-8 *DHCPv6 Relay Agent and DHCP IPv6 Addresses*

Focus first on Step 1, in which host A, the DHCPv6 client, builds and sends its DHCPv6 Solicit message. The message flows from host A's link-local address to the all-DHCP-agents multicast address FF02::1:2. With a link-local scope multicast destination address, the Solicit message sent by a host would flow only on the local LAN.

Step 2 shows the results of R1's work as the DHCPv6 relay agent. R1 listens for incoming DHCPv6 messages sent to FF02::1:2, and processes the message sent by host A. R1 changes the destination IPv6 address of the packet to match the DHCPv6 server on the right. R1 also changes the source IPv6 address to be one of R1's IPv6 addresses. With DHCPv6, by default R1 uses the address of its outgoing interface (S0/0/0) as the source IPv6 address, which is slightly different from the DHCPv4 relay agent. R1 then forwards the Solicit mes-sage to the server.

The return DHCPv6 messages from the server to the client (not shown in the figure) flow first to the relay agent router's IPv6 address—in other words, to 2001:DB8:1111:2::1 in this case. The relay agent then converts the destination address of those messages as well and forwards the DHCPv6 messages to the client's link-local address.

Example 31-1 shows the DHCPv6 relay agent configuration for R1 in Figure 31-8. The top of the example shows the **ipv6 dhcp relay** interface subcommand, with reference to the IPv6 address of the DHCPv6 server. The bottom of the figure shows the output of the **show ipv6 interface** command, which confirms that R1 is now listening for multicasts sent to the all-DHCP-agents multicast address FF02::1:2.

Example 31-1 *Configuring Router R1 to Support Remote DHCPv6 Server*

```
interface GigabitEthernet0/0
 ipv6 dhcp relay destination 2001:DB8:1111:3::8


R1# show ipv6 interface g0/0
GigabitEthernet0/0 is up, line protocol is up
  IPv6 is enabled, link-local address is FE80::FF:FE00:1
  No Virtual link-local address(es):
  Description: to SW1 port F0/1
  Global unicast address(es):
    2001:DB8:1111:1::1, subnet is 2001:DB8:1111:1::/64 [EUI]
  Joined group address(es):
    FF02::1
    FF02::2
    FF02::A
    FF02::1:2
    FF02::1:FF00:1
! Lines omitted for brevity
```

Using Stateless Address Auto Configuration

The stateful nature of DHCPv4, as well as its newer cousin stateful DHCPv6, causes some challenges. Someone has to configure, administer, and manage the DHCP server(s). The configuration includes ranges of IP addresses for every subnet. Then, when a host (client) leases the address, the server notes which client is using which address. All these functions work, and work well, but the reliance on a stateful DHCP server requires some thought and attention from the IT staff.

IPv6's SLAAC provides an alternative method for dynamic IPv6 address assignment—without needing a stateful server. In other words, SLAAC does not require a server to assign or lease the IPv6 address, does not require the IT staff to preconfigure data per subnet, and does not require the server to track which device uses which IPv6 address.

The term *SLAAC* refers to both a specific part of how a host learns one IPv6 setting—its IPv6 address—plus the overall process of learning all four key host IPv6 settings (address, prefix length, default router, and DNS server addresses). This next topic begins by looking at the tasks done by SLAAC related to the IPv6 address. Then the text looks at the overall process that uses SLAAC to find all four host settings—a process that uses NDP as well as stateless DHCP.

Building an IPv6 Address Using SLAAC

When using SLAAC, a host does not lease its IPv6 address, or even learn its IPv6 address. Instead, the host learns part of the address—the prefix—and then makes up the rest of its own IPv6 address. Specifically, a host using SLAAC to choose its own IPv6 address uses the following steps:

1. Learn the IPv6 prefix used on the link, from any router, using NDP RS/RA messages.

2. Choose its own IPv6 address by making up the interface ID value to follow the just-learned IPv6 prefix.

3. Before using the address, first use DAD to make sure that no other host is already using the same address.

Figure 31-9 summarizes the first two steps, while noting the two most common ways a host completes the address. Hosts can use EUI-64 rules, as discussed in Chapter 30's section "Generating a Unique Interface ID Using Modified EUI-64." Alternatively, the host can use a process to choose a random number.

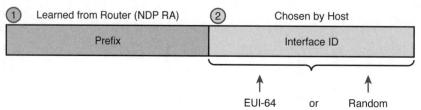

Figure 31-9   *Host IPv6 Address Formation Using SLAAC*

Combining SLAAC with NDP and Stateless DHCP

When using SLAAC, a host actually makes use of three different tools to find its four IPv6 settings, as noted in Figure 31-10. SLAAC itself focuses on the IPv6 address only. The host then uses NDP messages to learn both the prefix length and the IPv6 addresses of the available routers on the link. Finally, the host makes use of stateless DHCP to learn the IPv6 addresses of any DNS servers.

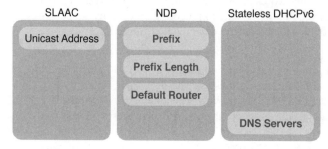

Figure 31-10   *Sources of Specific IPv6 Settings When Using SLAAC*

Stateless DHCP solves the last piece of this puzzle when also using SLAAC. The host needs to know the DNS servers' IPv6 addresses. The solution? Use DHCPv6. However, the host, acting as the DHCPv6 client, asks the server for only the DNS server addresses, and not for a lease of an IPv6 address.

So, why does the world need to call this service *stateless DHCPv6*? The DHCP server with stateless DHCPv6 has far less work to do, and the network engineer has far less administrative work to do. With stateless DHCPv6, the DHCPv6 server

- Needs simple configuration only, specifically a small number of addresses for the DNS servers, but nothing else
- Needs no per-subnet configuration: no subnet list, no per-subnet address pools, no list of excluded addresses per subnet, and no per-subnet prefix lengths
- Has no need to track state information about DHCP leases—that is, which devices lease which IPv6 address—because the server does not lease addresses to any clients

Table 31-3 summarizes the key comparison points between stateless DHCP and stateful DHCP.

Table 31-3   Comparison of Stateless and Stateful DHCPv6 Services

Feature	Stateful DHCP	Stateless DHCP
Remembers IPv6 address (state information) of clients	Yes	No
Leases IPv6 address to client	Yes	No
Supplies list of DNS server addresses	Yes	Yes
Commonly used with SLAAC	No	Yes

Troubleshooting IPv6 Addressing

This third and final major section of the chapter examines a few commands to verify and troubleshoot IPv6 addressing configuration on hosts. Specifically, this section examines the host's IPv6 settings and then looks at the usual commands to test whether a host can send packets: **ping** and **traceroute**.

Note that this section lists some commands on different host OSs. As usual, the goal of listing host commands is to give a general idea of the information that can be viewed on a host. However, keep in mind that this and other chapters do not attempt to show each variation of every networking command on every OS; instead, the goal is to reinforce the ideas discussed earlier in the chapter.

Verifying Host IPv6 Connectivity from Hosts

Most end-user OSs support a convenient way to look at IPv6 settings from the graphical user interface. In some cases, all four of the key IPv6 host settings can be on the same window, whereas in other cases, seeing all the settings might require navigation to multiple windows or tabs in the same window.

As an example, Figure 31-11 shows a window from Mac OS X, which lists three of the four IPv6 host settings. The one missing setting, the DNS server setting, is in another tab (as shown near the top of the image).

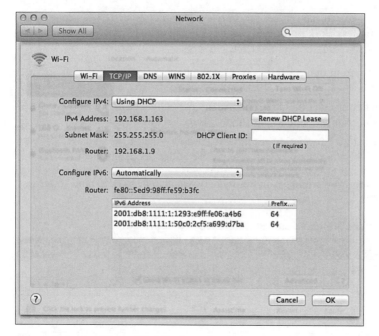

Figure 31-11   *Three IPv6 Settings for Dynamic Address Assignment on Mac OS X*

Take a moment to look at the details in Figure 31-11's image. The image shows the IPv4 settings at the top, as being learned with DHCP. The lower half of the window shows the IPv6 settings as having been learned "Automatically," which means that the host will use either stateful DHCP or SLAAC. In this case, the host used SLAAC to give itself two IPv6 addresses inside the same 2001:DB8:1111:1::/64 subnet—one using EUI-64 rules and one with a random interface ID. (Note that IPv6 host logic includes many details not discussed in this chapter, including the reasons why a host might use two addresses rather than one.)

Hosts also support a range of commands to check the same information. For IPv6 settings, many OSs use familiar commands: **ipconfig** on Windows OSs and **ifconfig** on Linux and Mac OS. Example 31-2 shows an **ifconfig** command from the same Mac used to create Figure 31-11 for comparison. In particular, if you look at the two highlighted fields, you can see the EUI-64 interface ID that resulted from using this host's MAC address.

Example 31-2   *Sample ifconfig Command from a Mac*

```
WOair$ ifconfig en0
en0: flags=8863<UP,BROADCAST,SMART,RUNNING,SIMPLEX,MULTICAST> mtu 1500
        ether 10:93:e9:06:a4:b6
        inet6 fe80::1293:e9ff:fe06:a4b6%en0 prefixlen 64 scopeid 0x4
        inet 192.168.1.163 netmask 0xffffff00 broadcast 192.168.1.255
        inet6 2001:db8:1111:1:1293:e9ff:fe06:a4b6 prefixlen 64 autoconf
        inet6 2001:db8:1111:1:50c0:2cf5:a699:d7ba prefixlen 64 autoconf temporary
        media: autoselect
        status: active
```

Beyond simply checking the four key IPv6 settings on the host, testing the installation of a new host also requires testing whether the host has connectivity to the rest of the internetwork, using the usual tools: the **ping** and **traceroute** commands.

As for the commands themselves, some OSs (notably Microsoft Windows variants and Cisco routers and switches) let you use the same **ping** and **traceroute** commands used with IPv4. Some other OSs require a different command, like the **ping6** and **traceroute6** commands used with Mac OS and Linux. (The upcoming examples show both variations.)

As for the output of the **ping** and **traceroute** commands, most people who understand the IPv4 version of these commands need no coaching whatsoever to understand the IPv6 version. The output is mostly unchanged compared to the IPv4 equivalents, other than the obvious differences with listing IPv6 addresses. For comparison, upcoming Examples 31-3 and 31-4 show sample output, using the internetwork displayed in Figure 31-12.

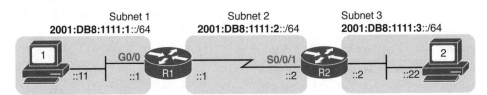

Figure 31-12 *IPv6 Internetwork for* ping *and* traceroute *Examples*

Example 31-3 shows three **ping** commands, taken from PC1, a Linux host. (Linux happens to replace the older commands with the **ping6** and **traceroute6** commands.) The first two commands show IPv6 pings, the first to R1's LAN IPv6 address, followed by PC1 pinging PC2's IPv6 address. The final command shows an IPv4 ping for comparison.

Example 31-3 *The* ping6 *Command from PC1, for R1 and PC2*

```
Master@PC1:$ ping6 2001:db8:1111:1::1
PING 2001:db8:1111:1::1 (2001:db8:1111:1::1) 56 data bytes
64 bytes from 2001:db8:1111:1::1: icmp_seq=1 ttl=64 time=1.26 ms
64 bytes from 2001:db8:1111:1::1: icmp_seq=2 ttl=64 time=1.15 ms
^C
--- 2001:db8:1111:1::1 ping statistics ---
2 packets transmitted, 2 received, 0% packet loss, time 1001 ms
rtt min/avg/max/mdev = 1.156/1.210/1.263/0.062 ms


Master@PC1:$ ping6 2001:db8:1111:3::22
PING 2001:db8:1111:3::22 (2001:db8:1111:3::22) 56 data bytes
64 bytes from 2001:db8:1111:3::22: icmp_seq=1 ttl=64 time=2.33 ms
64 bytes from 2001:db8:1111:3::22: icmp_seq=2 ttl=64 time=2.59 ms
64 bytes from 2001:db8:1111:3::22: icmp_seq=3 ttl=64 time=2.03 ms
^C
--- 2001:db8:1111:3::22 ping statistics ---
3 packets transmitted, 3 received, 0% packet loss, time 2003 ms
rtt min/avg/max/mdev = 2.039/2.321/2.591/0.225 ms
```

```
! An IPv4 ping next, for comparison - ping of PC2 from PC1
Master@PC1:$ ping 10.1.3.22
PING 10.1.3.22 (10.1.3.22) 56 data bytes
64 bytes from 10.1.3.22: icmp_seq=1 ttl=64 time=2.45 ms
64 bytes from 10.1.3.22: icmp_seq=2 ttl=64 time=2.55 ms
64 bytes from 10.1.3.22: icmp_seq=3 ttl=64 time=2.14 ms
^C
--- 10.1.3.22 ping statistics ---
3 packets transmitted, 3 received, 0% packet loss, time 2014 ms
rtt min/avg/max/mdev = 2.04/2.318/2.604/0.224 ms
```

Example 31-4 shows a **traceroute6** command on PC1, finding the route to PC2. The output mirrors the style of output for most IPv4 **traceroute** commands, other than the obvious difference of listing IPv6 addresses. Note that the output lists R1's G0/0 IPv6 address, then R2's S0/0/1 IPv6 address, and then finally PC2's address to end the output.

Example 31-4   *The* traceroute6 *Command from PC1, for PC2*

```
Master@PC1:$ traceroute6 2001:db8:1111:3::22
traceroute to 2001:db8:1111:3::22 (2001:db8:1111:3::22) from 2001:db8:1111:1::11,
   30 hops max, 24 byte packets
1  2001:db8:1111:1::1  (2001:db8:1111:1::1)   0.794 ms  0.648 ms  0.604 ms
2  2001:db8:1111:2::2  (2001:db8:1111:2::2)   1.606 ms  1.49 ms  1.497 ms
3  2001:db8:1111:3::22 (2001:db8:1111:3::22)  2.038 ms  1.911 ms  1.899 ms
```

Verifying Host Connectivity from Nearby Routers

For router verification commands for IPv6, some IPv6 features use the exact same command as with IPv4, but some substitute "ipv6" for "ip." And in some cases, particularly with functions that do not exist in IPv4 or have changed quite a bit, routers support brand-new commands. This section looks at a couple of router commands useful to verify IPv6 host connectivity, some old and some new for IPv6.

First, for the more familiar commands. Cisco routers and switches support the **ping** and **traceroute** commands with the same basic features for IPv6 as with IPv4. For the standard version of the commands, the commands accept either an IPv4 or an IPv6 address as input. For the extended versions of these commands, the first prompt question asks for the protocol. Just type **ipv6**, instead of using the default of **ip**, and answer the rest of the questions.

Of course, an example helps, particularly for the extended commands. Example 31-5 begins with an extended IPv6 **ping**, from R1 to PC2, using R1's G0/0 interface as the source of the packets. The second command shows a standard IPv6 **traceroute** from R1 to PC2.

Example 31-5   *Extended* ping *and Standard* traceroute *for IPv6 from Router R1*

```
R1# ping
Protocol [ip]: ipv6
Target IPv6 address: 2001:db8:1111:3::22
Repeat count [5]:
Datagram size [100]:
```

```
Timeout in seconds [2]:
Extended commands? [no]: yes
Source address or interface: GigabitEthernet0/0
UDP protocol? [no]:
Verbose? [no]:
Precedence [0]:
DSCP [0]:
Include hop by hop option? [no]:
Include destination option? [no]:
Sweep range of sizes? [no]:
Type escape sequence to abort.
Sending 5, 100-byte ICMP Echos to 2001:DB8:1111:3::22, timeout is 2 seconds:
Packet sent with a source address of 2001:DB8:1111:1::1
!!!!!
Success rate is 100 percent (5/5), round-trip min/avg/max = 0/1/4 ms


R1# traceroute 2001:db8:1111:3::22
Type escape sequence to abort.
Tracing the route to 2001:DB8:1111:3::22


  1 2001:DB8:1111:2::2 4 msec 0 msec 0 msec
  2 2001:DB8:1111:3::22 0 msec 4 msec 0 msec
```

Another way to verify host settings from a router is to look at the router's neighbor table. All IPv6 hosts, routers included, keep an IPv6 neighbor table: a list of all neighboring IPv6 addresses and matching MAC addresses. Basically, this table replaces the IPv4 ARP table, and it contains the content learned with NDP NS and NA messages.

One way to verify whether a neighboring host is responsive is to find out whether it will send back an NDP NA when the router sends it an NDP NS (to discover the host's MAC address). To do so, the router could clear its neighbor table (**clear ipv6 neighbor**) and then ping a host on some connected interface. The router will first need to send an NDP NS, and the host must send an NDP NA back. If the router shows that host's MAC address in the neighbor table, the host must have just replied with an NDP NA. Example 31-6 shows a sample of an IPv6 neighbor table, from Router R2 in upcoming Figure 31-13, using the **show ipv6 neighbors** command.

Example 31-6 *The* **show ipv6 neighbors** *Command on Router R2*

```
R2# show ipv6 neighbors
IPv6 Address                       Age Link-layer Addr State Interface
FE80::11FF:FE11:1111                  0 0200.1111.1111  STALE Gi0/0
FE80::22FF:FE22:2222                  1 0200.2222.2222  STALE Gi0/0
2001:DB8:1111:3::22                   0 0200.2222.2222  REACH Gi0/0
FE80::FF:FE00:3333                     1 0200.0000.3333  DELAY Gi0/0
2001:DB8:1111:3::33                    0 0200.1111.1111  REACH Gi0/0
2001:DB8:1111:3::3                     0 0200.0000.3333  REACH Gi0/0
```

Finally, routers can also list information about the available routers on a LAN subnet, which impacts the connectivity available to hosts. As a reminder, routers send NDP RA messages to announce their willingness to act as an IPv6 router on a particular LAN subnet. Cisco routers watch for RA messages received from other routers (routers send periodic unsolicited RA messages, by the way). The **show ipv6 routers** command lists any other routers, but not the local router.

As an example, consider the topology shown in Figure 31-13. R1 is the only IPv6 router on the LAN on the left, so R1 does not hear any RA messages from other routers on that LAN subnet. However, R2 and R3, connected to the same subnet, hear NDP RAs from each other. Example 31-7 lists the output of the **show ipv6 routers** command on R1 (with no routers listed) and R2 (with one router listed) for comparison's sake.

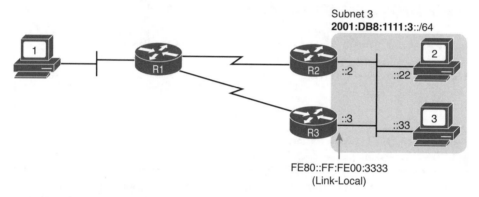

Figure 31-13 *Sample IPv6 Internetwork with Two Routers on the Same Link (VLAN)*

Example 31-7 *Listing All Routers with the* show ipv6 routers *Command*

```
! No routers listed by this command on R1
R1# show ipv6 routers
R1#
! The next command happens on R2 - one router (R3) listed
R2# show ipv6 routers
Router FE80::FF:FE00:3333 on GigabitEthernet0/0, last update 0 min
  Hops 64, Lifetime 1800 sec, AddrFlag=0, OtherFlag=0, MTU=1500
  HomeAgentFlag=0, Preference=Medium
  Reachable time 0 (unspecified), Retransmit time 0 (unspecified)
  Prefix 2001:DB8:1111:3::/64 onlink autoconfig
    Valid lifetime 2592000, preferred lifetime 604800
```

Finally, one last thought related to commands on hosts themselves: The host can, of course, list its own NDP information. Interestingly, most hosts list the neighbor table and then just flag which entries also happen to be routers (the ones that also sent an NDP RA at some point).

Example 31-8 shows an example, this time from a host using Mac OS. Of the two highlighted entries, the first, with the flags field ("Flgs") listing an "R," is a router that formerly sent an RA to announce itself. The second highlighted entry is for a host, so the letter "R" is not listed under the "Flgs" (flags) heading.

Example 31-8 *Example NDP Neighbor Table, Mac OS X*

```
WOAir$ ndp -an
Neighbor                          Linklayer Address  Netif Expire   St Flgs Prbs
::1                               (incomplete)       lo0 permanent  R
2001:db8:1111:1::1                5c:d9:98:59:b3:fc  en0 1s         D  R
2001:db8:1111:1:1293:e9ff:fe06:a4b6 10:93:e9:6:a4:b6 en0 5s           R
```

Chapter Review

One key to doing well on the exams is to perform repetitive spaced review sessions. Review this chapter's material using either the tools in the book, DVD, or interactive tools for the same material found on the book's companion website. Refer to the "Your Study Plan" element for more details. Table 31-4 outlines the key review elements and where you can find them. To better track your study progress, record when you completed these activities in the second column.

31

Table 31-4   Chapter Review Tracking

Review Element	Review Date(s)	Resource Used
Review key topics		Book, DVD/website
Review key terms		Book, DVD/website
Repeat DIKTA questions		Book, PCPT
Review memory table		Book, DVD/website
Review command tables		Book

Review All the Key Topics

Table 31-5   Key Topics for Chapter 31

Key Topic Element	Description	Page Number
List	Four functions for which NDP plays a major role	731
List	Descriptions of the NDP RS and RA messages	731
Figure 31-2	Example use of NDP RS and RA	732
List	Descriptions of the NDP NS and NA messages	733
Figure 31-4	Example use of NDP NS and NA	733
Figure 31-5	Example use of NDP for Duplicate Address Detection (DAD)	734
Table 31-2	Summary of NDP functions discussed in this chapter	735
List	Similarities between DHCP for IPv4 and stateful DHCP for IPv6	736
Figure 31-6	Key difference between DHCPv4 and stateful DHCPv6	737
List	Steps a host takes to build its IPv6 address when using SLAAC	740
Figure 31-9	SLAAC address creation concepts	740
Example 31-3	Examples of the **ping6** command	743

Key Terms You Should Know

Neighbor Discovery Protocol (NDP), Router Solicitation (RS), Router Advertisement (RA), Neighbor Solicitation (NS), Neighbor Advertisement (NA), Stateless Address Auto Configuration (SLAAC), Duplicate Address Detection (DAD), stateful DHCPv6, stateless DHCPv6, IPv6 neighbor table

Command References

Tables 31-6, 31-7, and 31-8 list configuration and verification commands used in this chapter, respectively. As an easy review exercise, cover the left column in a table, read the right column, and try to recall the command without looking. Then repeat the exercise, covering the right column, and try to recall what the command does.

Table 31-6   Chapter 31 Configuration Command Reference

Command	Description
ipv6 dhcp relay destination *server-address*	Interface subcommand that enables the IPv6 DHCP relay agent.

Table 31-7   Chapter 31 EXEC Command Reference

Command	Description
ping {*host-name* | *ipv6-address*}	Tests IPv6 routes by sending an ICMP packet to the destination host.
traceroute {*host-name* | *ipv6-address*}	Tests IPv6 routes by discovering the IP addresses of the routes between a router and the listed destination.
show ipv6 neighbors	Lists the router's IPv6 neighbor table.
show ipv6 routers	Lists any neighboring routers that advertised themselves through an NDP RA message.

Table 31-8   Chapter 31 Host Command Reference

Command (Microsoft, Apple, Linux)	Description
ipconfig / ifconfig / ifconfig	Lists interface settings, including IPv4 and IPv6 addresses.
ping / ping6 / ping6	Tests IP routes by sending an ICMPv6 packet to the destination host.
tracert / traceroute6 / traceroute6	Tests IP routes by discovering the IPv6 addresses of the routes between a router and the listed destination.
netsh interface ipv6 show neighbors / ndp -an / ip -6 neighbor show	Lists a host's IPv6 neighbor table.

CHAPTER 32

Implementing IPv6 Routing

This chapter covers the following exam topics:

3.0 Routing Technologies

3.6 Configure, verify, and troubleshoot IPv4 and IPv6 static routing

3.6.a Default route

3.6.b Network route

3.6.c Host route

3.6.d Floating static

The one remaining piece of the IPv6 story for this book is how routers learn IPv6 routes. Interestingly, Cisco chose to keep IPv6 routing protocols in the ICND2 half of the CCNA R&S exam, leaving only static IPv6 routes for discussion in the ICND1 half. So this chapter discusses the simplest and most straightforward ways for a router to create IPv6 routes: connected, local, and static routes.

The chapter breaks the topics into two main sections. The first section of this chapter walks you through the details of how IPv6, similar to IPv4, adds both connected and local routes based on each interface IPv6 address. The second major section of this chapter then looks at how to configure static IPv6 routes by typing in commands, in this case using the **ipv6 route** command instead of IPv4's **ip route** command.

"Do I Know This Already?" Quiz

Take the quiz (either here, or use the PCPT software) if you want to use the score to help you decide how much time to spend on this chapter. The answers are at the bottom of the page following the quiz, and the explanations are in DVD Appendix C and in the PCPT software.

Table 32-1 "Do I Know This Already?" Foundation Topics Section-to-Question Mapping

Foundation Topics Section	Questions
Connected and Local IPv6 Routes	1–2
Static IPv6 Routes	3–6

Refer to the following figure for questions 1, 3, and 4.

1. A router has been configured with the **ipv6 address 2000:1:2:3::1/64** command on its G0/1 interface as shown in the figure. The router creates a link-local address of FE80::FF:FE00:1 as well. The interface is working. Which of the following routes will the router add to its IPv6 routing table? (Choose two answers.)

   a. A route for 2000:1:2:3::/64

   b. A route for FE80::FF:FE00:1/64

   c. A route for 2000:1:2:3::1/128

   d. A route for FE80::FF:FE00:1/128

2. A router has been configured with the **ipv6 address 3111:1:1:1::1/64** command on its G0/1 interface and **ipv6 address 3222:2:2:2::1/64** on its G0/2 interface. Both interfaces are working. Which of the following routes would you expect to see in the output of the **show ip route connected** command? (Choose two answers.)

   a. A route for 3111:1:1:1::/64

   b. A route for 3111:1:1:1::1/64

   c. A route for 3222:2:2:2::/64

   d. A route for 3222:2:2:2::2/128

3. An engineer needs to add a static IPv6 route for prefix 2000:1:2:3::/64 to Router R5's configuration, in the figure shown with question 1. Which of the following answers shows a valid static IPv6 route for that subnet, on Router R5?

   a. **ipv6 route 2000:1:2:3::/64 S0/1/1**

   b. **ipv6 route 2000:1:2:3::/64 S0/1/0**

   c. **ip route 2000:1:2:3::/64 S0/1/1**

   d. **ip route 2000:1:2:3::/64 S0/1/0**

4. An engineer needs to add a static IPv6 route for prefix 2000:1:2:3::/64 to Router R5 in the figure shown with question 1. Which of the following answers shows a valid static IPv6 route for that subnet on Router R5?

   a. **ipv6 route 2000:1:2:3::/64 2000:1:2:56::5**

   b. **ipv6 route 2000:1:2:3::/64 2000:1:2:56::6**

   c. **ipv6 route 2000:1:2:3::/64 FE80::FF:FE00:5**

   d. **ipv6 route 2000:1:2:3::/64 FE80::FF:FE00:6**

5. An engineer types the command **ipv6 route 2001:DB8:8:8::/64 2001:DB8:9:9::9 129** in configuration mode of Router R1 and presses **Enter**. Later, a **show ipv6 route** command does not list any route for subnet 2001:DB8:8:8::/64. Which of the following could have caused the route to not be in the IPv6 routing table?

   a. The command should be using a next-hop link-local address instead of a global unicast.

   b. The command is missing an outgoing interface parameter, so IOS rejected the **ipv6 route** command.

   c. The router has no routes that match 2001:DB8:9:9::9.

   d. A route for 2001:DB8:8:8::/64 with administrative distance 110 already exists.

6. The command output shows two routes from the longer output of the **show ipv6 route** command. Which answers are true about the output? (Choose two answers.)

```
R1# show ipv6 route static
! Legend omitted for brevity
S    2001:DB8:2:2::/64 [1/0]
       via 2001:DB8:4:4::4
S    ::/0 [1/0]
       via Serial0/0/1, directly connected
```

   a. The route to ::/0 is added because of an **ipv6 route** global command.

   b. The administrative distance of the route to 2001:DB8:2:2::/64 is 1.

   c. The route to ::/0 is added because of an **ipv6 address** interface subcommand.

   d. The route to 2001:DB8:2:2::/64 is added because of an IPv6 routing protocol.

Foundation Topics

Connected and Local IPv6 Routes

A Cisco router adds IPv6 routes to its IPv6 routing table for several reasons. Many of you could predict those reasons at this point in your reading, in part because the logic mirrors the logic routers use for IPv4. Specifically, a router adds IPv6 routes based on the following:

■ The configuration of IPv6 addresses on working interfaces (connected and local routes)

■ The direct configuration of a static route (static routes)

■ The configuration of a routing protocol, like OSPFv3, on routers that share the same data link (dynamic routes)

This chapter examines the first of these two topics.

> **NOTE**   Cisco leaves all IPv6 routing protocols until the ICND2 half of the CCNA R&S exam topics, so Part VI of that book discusses IPv6 routing protocols. If you do not have the ICND2 book and want a little background info about IPv6 routing protocols, check Appendix Q in this book (on the DVD), for the section titled "Dynamic Routes with OSPFv3," for OSPFv3 material from an earlier edition of this book.

Rules for Connected and Local Routes

Routers add and remove connected routes and local routes, based on the interface configuration and the interface state. First, the router looks for any configured unicast addresses on any interfaces by looking for the **ipv6 address** command. Then, if the interface is working—if the interface has a "line status is up, protocol status is up" notice in the output of the **show interfaces** command—the router adds both a connected and local route.

> **NOTE** Routers do not create IPv6 routes for link-local addresses.

The connected and local routes themselves follow the same general logic as with IPv4. The connected route represents the subnet connected to the interface, whereas the local route is a host route for only the specific IPv6 address configured on the interface.

As an example, consider a router, with a working interface, configured with the **ipv6 address 2000:1:1:1::1/64** command. The router will calculate the subnet ID based on this address and prefix list, and it will place a connected route for that subnet (2000:1:1:1::/64) into the routing table. The router also takes the listed IPv6 address and creates a host route for that address, with a /128 prefix length. (With IPv4, host routes have a /32 prefix length, while IPv6 uses a /128 prefix length, meaning "exactly this one address.")

The following list summarizes the rules about how routers create routes based on the configuration of an interface IPv6 unicast address, for easier review and study:

Key Topic

1. Routers create IPv6 routes based on each unicast IPv6 address on an interface, as configured with the **ipv6 address** command, as follows:

    A. The router creates a route for the subnet (a connected route).

    B. The router creates a host route (/128 prefix length) for the router IPv6 address (a local route).

2. Routers do not create routes based on the link-local addresses associated with the interface.

3. Routers remove the connected and local routes for an interface if the interface fails, and they re-add these routes when the interface is again in a working (up/up) state.

Example of Connected IPv6 Routes

While the concept of connected and local IPv6 routes works much like IPv4 routes, seeing a few examples can certainly help. To show some sample routes, Figure 32-1 gives the details of one sample internetwork used in this chapter. The figure shows the IPv6 subnet IDs. The upcoming examples focus on the connected and local routes on Router R1.

Answers to the "Do I Know This Already?" quiz:

1 A, C **2** A, C **3** A **4** B **5** C **6** A, B

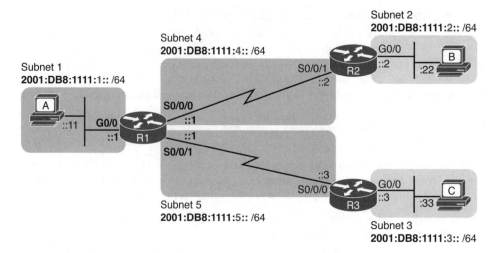

Figure 32-1   *Sample Network Used to Show Connected and Local Routes*

To clarify the notes in Figure 32-1, note that the figure shows IPv6 prefixes (subnets), with a shorthand notation for the interface IPv6 addresses. The figure shows only the abbreviated interface ID portion of each interface address near each interface. For example, R1's G0/0 interface address would begin with subnet ID value 2001:DB8:1111:1, added to ::1, for 2001:DB8:1111:1::1.

Now on to the example of connected routes. To begin, consider the configuration of Router R1 from Figure 32-1, as shown in Example 32-1. The excerpt from the **show running-config** command on R1 shows three interfaces, all of which are working. Also note that no static route or routing protocol configuration exists.

Example 32-1   *IPv6 Addressing Configuration on Router R1*

```
ipv6 unicast-routing
!
interface serial0/0/0
  ipv6 address 2001:db8:1111:4::1/64
!
interface serial0/0/1
  ipv6 address 2001:db8:1111:5::1/64
!
interface gigabitethernet0/0
  ipv6 address 2001:db8:1111:1::1/64
```

Based on Figure 32-1 and Example 32-1, R1 should have three connected IPv6 routes, as highlighted in Example 32-2.

Example 32-2   *Routes on Router R1 Before Adding Static Routes or Routing Protocols*

```
R1# show ipv6 route
IPv6 Routing Table - default - 7 entries
Codes: C - Connected, L - Local, S - Static, U - Per-user Static route
```

```
            B - BGP, R - RIP, I1 - ISIS L1, I2 - ISIS L2
            IA - ISIS interarea, IS - ISIS summary, D - EIGRP, EX - EIGRP external
            ND - Neighbor Discovery, l - LISP
            O - OSPF Intra, OI - OSPF Inter, OE1 - OSPF ext 1, OE2 - OSPF ext 2
            ON1 - OSPF NSSA ext 1, ON2 - OSPF NSSA ext 2
C    2001:DB8:1111:1::/64 [0/0]
       via GigabitEthernet0/0, directly connected
L    2001:DB8:1111:1::1/128 [0/0]
       via GigabitEthernet0/0, receive
C    2001:DB8:1111:4::/64 [0/0]
       via Serial0/0/0, directly connected
L    2001:DB8:1111:4::1/128 [0/0]
       via Serial0/0/0, receive
C    2001:DB8:1111:5::/64 [0/0]
       via Serial0/0/1, directly connected
L    2001:DB8:1111:5::1/128 [0/0]
       via Serial0/0/1, receive
L    FF00::/8 [0/0]
       via Null0, receive
```

All three highlighted routes show the same basic kinds of information, so for discussion, focus on the first pair of highlighted lines, which detail the connected route for subnet 2001:DB8:1111:1::/64. The first pair of highlighted lines state: The route is a "directly connected" route; the interface ID is GigabitEthernet0/0; and the prefix/length is 2001:DB8:1111:1::/64. At the far left, the code letter "C" identifies the route as a connected route (per the legend above). Also note that the numbers in brackets mirror the same ideas as IPv4's **show ip route** command: The first number represents the administrative distance, and the second is the metric.

Examples of Local IPv6 Routes

Continuing this same example, three local routes should exist on R1 for the same three interfaces as the connected routes. Indeed, that is the case, with one extra local route for other purposes. Example 32-3 shows only the local routes, as listed by the **show ipv6 route local** command, with highlights of one particular local route for discussion.

Example 32-3 *Local IPv6 Routes on Router R1*

```
R1# show ipv6 route local
! Legend omitted for brevity

L    2001:DB8:1111:1::1/128 [0/0]
       via GigabitEthernet0/0, receive
L    2001:DB8:1111:4::1/128 [0/0]
       via Serial0/0/0, receive
L    2001:DB8:1111:5::1/128 [0/0]
       via Serial0/0/1, receive
L    FF00::/8 [0/0]
       via Null0, receive
```

For the highlighted local route, look for a couple of quick facts. First, look back to R1's configuration in Example 32-1, and note R1's IPv6 address on its G0/0 interface. This local route lists the exact same address. Also note the /128 prefix length, meaning this route matches packets sent to that address (2001:DB8:1111:1::1), and only that address.

> **NOTE** While the **show ipv6 route local** command shows all local IPv6 routes, the **show ipv6 route connected** command shows all connected routes.

Static IPv6 Routes

While routers automatically add connected and local routes based on the interface configuration, static routes require direct configuration with the **ipv6 route** command. Simply put, someone configures the command, and the router places the details from the command into a route in the IPv6 routing table.

The **ipv6 route** command follows the same general logic as does IPv4's **ip route** command, as discussed in Chapter 18, "Configuring IPv4 Addresses and Static Routes." For IPv4, the **ip route** command starts by listing the subnet ID and mask, so for IPv6, the **ipv6 route** command begins with the prefix and prefix length. Then the respective commands list the directions of how this router should forward packets toward that destination subnet or prefix by listing the outgoing interface or the address of the next-hop router.

Figure 32-2 shows the concepts behind a single **ipv6 route** command, demonstrating the concepts behind a static route on Router R1 for the subnet on the right (subnet 2, or 2001:DB8:1111:2::/64). A static route on R1, for this subnet, will begin with **ipv6 route 2001:DB8:1111:2::/64**, followed by either the outgoing interface (S0/0/0) or the next-hop IPv6 address, or both.

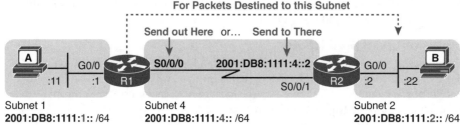

Figure 32-2 *Logic Behind IPv6 Static Route Commands (IPv6 Route)*

Now that you understand the big ideas with IPv6 static routes, the next few pages walk you through a series of examples. In particular, the examples look at configuring static routes with an outgoing interface, then with a next-hop global unicast address, and then with a next-hop link-local address. This section ends with a discussion of static IPv6 default routes.

Static Routes Using the Outgoing Interface

This first IPv6 static route example uses the outgoing interface option. As a reminder, for both IPv4 and IPv6 static routes, when the command references an interface, the interface is a local interface. That is, it is an interface on the router where the command is added. In this case, as shown in Figure 32-2, R1's **ipv6 route** command would use interface S0/0/0, as shown in Example 32-4.

Example 32-4 *Static IPv6 Routes on Router R1*

```
! Static route on router R1
R1(config)# ipv6 route 2001:db8:1111:2::/64 s0/0/0
```

While Example 32-4 shows the correct syntax of the route, if using static routes throughout this internetwork, more static routes are needed. For example, to support traffic between hosts A and B, R1 is now prepared. Host A will forward all its IPv6 packets to its default router (R1), and R1 can now route those packets out S0/0/0 to R2 next. However, Router R2 does not yet have a route back to host A's subnet, subnet 1 (2001:DB8:1111:1::/64), so a complete solution requires more routes.

Example 32-5 solves this problem by giving Router R2 a static route for subnet 1 (2001:DB8:1111:1::/64). After adding this route, hosts A and B should be able to ping each other.

Example 32-5 *Static IPv6 Routes on Router R2*

```
! Static route on router R2
R2(config)# ipv6 route 2001:db8:1111:1::/64 s0/0/1
```

Many options exist for verifying the existence of the static route and testing whether hosts can use the route. **ping** and **traceroute**, as discussed in Chapter 31, "Implementing IPv6 Addressing on Hosts," can test connectivity. From the router command line, the **show ipv6 route** command will list all the IPv6 routes. The shorter output of the **show ipv6 route static** command, which lists only static routes, could also be used; Example 32-6 shows that output, with the legend omitted.

Example 32-6 *Verification of Static Routes Only on R1*

```
R1# show ipv6 route static
! Legend omitted for brevity
S   2001:DB8:1111:2::/64 [1/0]
      via Serial0/0/0, directly connected
```

This command lists many facts about the one static route on R1. First, the code "S" in the left column does identify the route as a static route. (However, the later phrase "directly connected" might mislead you to think this is a connected route; trust the "S" code.) Note that the prefix (2001:DB8:1111:2::/64) matches the configuration (in Example 32-4), as does the outgoing interface (S0/0/0).

While this command lists basic information about each static route, it does not state whether this route would be used when forwarding packets to a particular destination. For example, if host A sent an IPv6 packet to host B (2001:DB8:1111:2::22), would R1 use this static route? As it turns out, R1 would use that route, as confirmed by the **show ipv6 route 2001:DB8:1111:2::22** command. This command asks the router to list the route the router would use when forwarding packets to that particular address. Example 32-7 shows an example.

Example 32-7 *Displaying the Route R1 Uses to Forward to Host B*

```
R1# show ipv6 route 2001:db8:1111:2::22
Routing entry for 2001:DB8:1111:2::/64
```

32

```
 Known via "static", distance 1, metric 0
 Route count is 1/1, share count 0
 Routing paths:
   directly connected via Serial0/0/0
     Last updated 00:01:29 ago
```

Static Routes Using Next-Hop IPv6 Address

Static IPv6 routes that refer to a next-hop address have two options: the unicast address on the neighboring router (global unicast or unique local) or the link-local address of that same neighboring router. Figure 32-3 spells out those two options with an updated version of Figure 32-2, this time showing Router R2's global unicast as well as R2's link-local address.

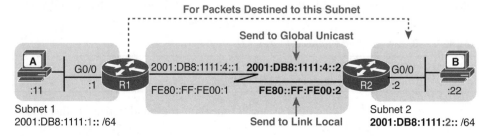

Figure 32-3 *Using Unicast or Link-Local as the Next-Hop Address for Static Routes*

The next few pages walk you through examples, first with a global unicast as a next-hop and then with a link-local as a next-hop.

Example Static Route with a Global Unicast Next-Hop Address

This example uses the internetwork shown in Figure 32-3, but with the earlier static routes removed. That is, both routers have only connected and local routes to begin the example.

In Example 32-8, both R1 and R2 add static routes that refer to the neighbor's global unicast address. R1 adds a route for subnet 2 (on the right), while R2 adds a route for subnet 1 (on the left). Note that the example shows routes in both directions so that the two hosts can send packets to each other.

Example 32-8 *Static IPv6 Routes Using Global Unicast Addresses*

```
! The first command is on router R1, listing R2's global unicast address
R1(config)# ipv6 route 2001:db8:1111:2::/64 2001:DB8:1111:4::2
! The next command is on router R2, listing R1's global unicast address
R2(config)# ipv6 route 2001:db8:1111:1::/64 2001:db8:1111:4::1
```

The **ipv6 route** command itself is relatively straightforward. Focus on R1's route, which matches the logic shown in Figure 32-3. The command lists subnet 2 (2001:DB8:1111:2::/64). It then lists R2's global unicast address (ending in 4::2).

The verification commands on R1, as shown in Example 32-9, list the usual information. Example 32-9 shows two commands, first listing R1's only static route (the one configured in Example 32-8). The end of the example lists the **show ipv6 route 2001:DB8:1111:2::22** command, which lists the route R1 uses when forwarding packets to Host B, proving that R1 uses this new static route when forwarding packets to that host.

Example 32-9 *Verification of Static Routes to a Next-Hop Global Unicast Address*

```
R1# show ipv6 route static
! Legend omitted for brevity
S   2001:DB8:1111:2::/64 [1/0]
     via 2001:DB8:1111:4::2


R1# show ipv6 route 2001:db8:1111:2::22/64
Routing entry for 2001:DB8:1111:2::/64
  Known via "static", distance 1, metric 0
  Backup from "ospf 1 [110]"
  Route count is 1/1, share count 0
  Routing paths:
    2001:DB8:1111:4::2
      Last updated 00:07:43 ago
```

Example Static Route with a Link-Local Next-Hop Address

Static routes that refer to a neighbor's link-local address work a little like both of the preceding two styles of static routes. First, the **ipv6 route** command refers to a next-hop address, namely a link-local address. However, the command must also refer to the router's local outgoing interface. Why both? The **ipv6 route** command cannot simply refer to a link-local next-hop address by itself, because the link-local address does not, by itself, tell the local router which outgoing interface to use.

Interestingly, when the **ipv6 route** command refers to a global unicast next-hop address, the router can deduce the outgoing interface. For example, the earlier example on R1, as shown in Example 32-8, shows R1 with a static IPv6 route with a next-hop IPv6 address of 2001:DB8:1111:4::2. R1 can look at its IPv6 routing table, see its connected route that includes this 2001:DB8:1111:4::2 address, and see a connected route off R1's S0/0/0. As a result, with a next-hop global unicast address, R1 can deduce the correct outgoing interface (R1's S0/0/0).

With a link-local next-hop address, a router cannot work through this same logic, so the outgoing interface must also be configured. Example 32-10 shows the configuration of static routes on R1 and R2, replacements for the two routes previously configured in Example 32-8.

Example 32-10 *Static IPv6 Routes Using Link-Local Neighbor Addresses*

```
! The first command is on router R1, listing R2's link-local address
R1(config)# ipv6 route 2001:db8:1111:2::/64 S0/0/0 FE80::FF:FE00:2
! The next command is on router R2, listing R1's link-local address
R2(config)# ipv6 route 2001:db8:1111:1::/64 S0/0/1 FE80::FF:FE00:1
```

Example 32-11 verifies the configuration in Example 32-10 by repeating the **show ipv6 route static** and **show ipv6 route 2001:DB8:1111:2::22** commands used in Example 32-9. Note that the output from both commands differs slightly in regard to the forwarding details. Because the new commands list both the next-hop address and outgoing interface, the **show** commands also list both the next-hop (link-local) address and the outgoing interface. If you refer back to Example 32-9, you will see only a next-hop address listed.

Example 32-11   *Verification of Static Routes to a Next-Hop Link-Local Address*

```
R1# show ipv6 route static
! Legend omitted for brevity


S    2001:DB8:1111:2::/64 [1/0]
     via FE80::FF:FE00:2, Serial0/0/0


R1# show ipv6 route 2001:db8:1111:2::22
Routing entry for 2001:DB8:1111:2::/64
  Known via "static", distance 1, metric 0
  Backup from "ospf 1 [110]"
  Route count is 1/1, share count 0
  Routing paths:
    FE80::FF:FE00:2, Serial0/0/0
        Last updated 00:08:10 ago
```

Static Default Routes

IPv6 supports a default route concept, similar to IPv4. The default route tells the router what to do with an IPv6 packet when the packet matches no other IPv6 route. The logic is pretty basic:

- With no default route, the router discards the IPv6 packet.
- With a default route, the router forwards the IPv6 packet based on the default route.

Default routes can be particularly useful in a couple of network design cases. For example, with an enterprise network design that uses a single router at each branch office, with one WAN link to each branch, the branch routers have only one possible path over which to forward packets. In a large network, when using a routing protocol, the branch router could learn thousands of routes—all of which point back toward the core of the network over that one WAN link.

Branch routers could use default routes instead of a routing protocol. The branch router would forward all traffic to the core of the network. Figure 32-4 shows just such an example, with two sample branch routers on the right and a core site router on the left.

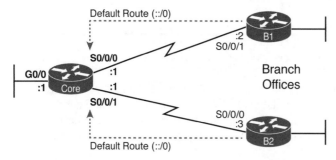

Figure 32-4   *Using Static Default Routes at Branches to Forward Back to the Core*

To configure a static default route, use the same rules already discussed in this section of the chapter, but use a specific value to note the route as a default route: ::/0. Taken literally, the double colon (::) is the IPv6 abbreviation for all 0s, and the /0 means the prefix length is 0. This idea mirrors the IPv4 convention to refer to the default route as 0.0.0.0/0. Otherwise, just configure the **ipv6 route** command as normal.

Example 32-12 shows one such sample static default route on Router B1 from Figure 32-4. This example uses the outgoing interface option.

Example 32-12   *Static Default Route for Branch Router B1*

```
!Forward out B1's S0/0/1 local interface...
B1(config)# ipv6 route ::/0 S0/0/1
```

With IPv6, the router displays the default a little more cleanly than with IPv4. The **show ipv6 route** command simply includes the route in the output of the command, along with the other routes. Example 32-13 shows an example, with "::/0" listed to denote this route as the default route.

Example 32-13   *Router B1's Static Default Route (Using Outgoing Interface)*

```
B1# show ipv6 route static
IPv6 Routing Table - default - 10 entries
Codes: C - Connected, L - Local, S - Static, U - Per-user Static route
       B - BGP, R - RIP, I1 - ISIS L1, I2 - ISIS L2
       IA - ISIS interarea, IS - ISIS summary, D - EIGRP, EX - EIGRP external
       ND - ND Default, NDp - ND Prefix, DCE - Destination, NDr - Redirect
       O - OSPF Intra, OI - OSPF Inter, OE1 - OSPF ext 1, OE2 - OSPF ext 2
       ON1 - OSPF NSSA ext 1, ON2 - OSPF NSSA ext 2
S   ::/0 [1/0]
     via Serial0/0/1, directly connected
```

Static IPv6 Host Routes

Both IPv4 and IPv6 allow the definition of static host routes; that is, a route to a single host IP address. With IPv4, those routes use a /32 mask, which identifies a single IPv4 address in the **ip route** command; with IPv6, a /128 mask identifies that single host in the **ipv6 route** command.

A host route follows the same rules as a route for any other IPv6 subnet. For instance, in Figure 32-3, host B sits on the right side of the figure. Earlier examples showed R1's static routes for the subnet in which host B resides; for example, the routes for Router R1 in Examples 32-8 and 32-10. To create a host route on R1, referring to host B's specific IPv6 address, just change those commands to refer to host B's entire IPv6 address (2001:DB8:1111:2::22), with prefix length /128.

Example 32-14 shows two sample host routes. Both define a host route to host B's IPv6 address on Router R1 in Figure 32-3. One uses Router R2's link-local address as the next-hop address, and one uses R2's global unicast address as the next-hop address.

Example 32-14 *Static Host IPv6 Routes on R1, for Host B*

```
! The first command lists host B's address, prefix length /128,
! with R2's link-local address as next-hop, with an outgoing interface.
R1(config)# ipv6 route 2001:db8:1111:2::22/128 S0/0/0 FE80::FF:FE00:2
! The next command also lists host B's address, prefix length /128,
! but with R2's global unicast address as next-hop, and no outgoing interface.
R1(config)# ipv6 route 2001:db8:1111:2::22/128 2001:DB8:1111:4::2
```

Floating Static IPv6 Routes

Next, consider the case in which a static route competes with other static routes or routes learned by a routing protocol. For example, consider the topology shown in Figure 32-5, which shows a branch office with two WAN links: one very fast Gigabit Ethernet link and one rather slow (but cheap) T1. In this design, the network uses OSPFv3 to learn IPv6 routes over the primary link, learning a route for subnet 2001:DB8:1111:7::/64. R1 also defines a static route over the backup link to that exact same subnet, so R1 must choose whether to use the static route or the OSPF-learned route.

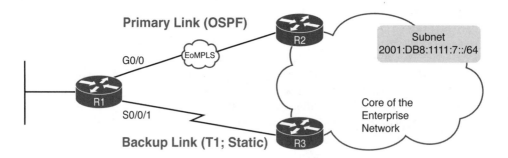

Figure 32-5 *Using a Floating Static Route to Key Subnet 172.16.2.0/24*

IOS considers static routes better than OSPF-learned routes by default due to administrative distance. IOS uses the same administrative distance concept and default values for IPv6 as it does for IPv4. As a result, a static IPv6 over the lower route would be given an administrative distance of 1, and an OSPFv3-learned route over the top path would be given an administrative distance of 110. R1 would use the lower path to reach subnet 2001:DB8:1111:7::/64 in this case, which is not the intended design. Instead, the engineer prefers to use the OSPF-learned routes over the much-faster primary link and use the static route over the backup link only as needed when the primary link fails.

To instead prefer the OSPF routes, the configuration would need to change the administrative distance settings and use what many networkers call a floating static route. Like an IPv4 floating static route, an IPv6 *floating static* route floats or moves into and out of the IPv6 routing table depending on whether the better (lower) administrative distance route learned by the routing protocol happens to exist currently. Basically, the router ignores the static route during times when the better routing protocol route is known.

To implement an IPv6 floating static route, just override the default administrative distance on the static route, making the value larger than the default administrative distance of the routing protocol. For example, the **ipv6 route 3444:4:4:4::/64 3444:2:2:2::2 130** command on R1 would do exactly that, setting the static route's administrative distance to 130. As long as the primary link (G0/0) stays up, and OSPFv3 on R1 learns a route for 3444:4:4:4::/64 with OSPF's default administrative distance of 110, R1 ignores the static route whose administrative distance is explicitly configured as 130.

Finally, note that both the **show ipv6 route** and **show ipv6 route 3444:4:4:4::/64** command list the administrative distance. Example 32-15 shows a sample matching this most recent example. Note that in this case, the static route is in use in the IPv6 routing table.

Example 32-15   *Displaying the Administrative Distance of the Static Route*

```
R1# show ipv6 route static
! Legend omitted for brevity
S    3444:4:4:4::/64 [130/0]
     via 3444:2:2:2::2


R1# show ipv6 route 3444:4:4:4::/64
Routing entry for 3444:4:4:4::/64
  Known via "static", distance 130, metric 0
  Route count is 1/1, share count 0
  Routing paths:
    3444:2:2:2::2
      Last updated 00:00:58 ago
```

Table 32-2 lists some of the default administrative distance values used with IPv6.

Table 32-2   IOS Defaults for Administrative Distance

Route Source	Administrative Distance
Connected routes	0
Static routes	1
NDP	2
EIGRP	90
OSPF	110
RIP	120
Unknown or unbelievable	255

Default Routes with SLAAC on Router Interfaces

The section, "Learning a Default Route Using DHCP" in Chapter 19 discusses how routers can use DHCP on their own interface and learn their IP address, mask, and even a default IPv4 route. In particular, that process can be useful on a router that connects to the Internet. The enterprise router uses DHCP as a client, learning its own IPv4 address with DHCP and adding a default route pointing to the ISP's router as the next-hop IPv4 address.

Routers can accomplish the same goals with IPv6, just with a few different protocols and methods. As with IPv4, the IPv6 enterprise router can dynamically learn its IPv6 address and dynamically create a default IPv6 route to the ISP's router. This section shows the details, with the enterprise router using SLAAC to learn its address and the information needed to create a default route.

32

First, the enterprise router that connects to the ISP, like Router R1 in Figure 32-6, requires the configuration of the interface subcommand **ipv6 address autoconfig default**. This command tells the router that, on that interface, use SLAAC to build its own IPv6 address. R1 would act like any host that uses SLAAC, as shown in Step 2 of the figure, and send an NDP RS message over the link. As noted at Step 3, the ISP router would send back an RA message, announcing router ISP1's IPv6 address and the IPv6 prefix used on the link.

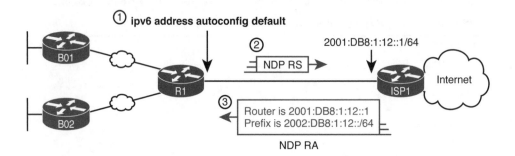

Figure 32-6   *Enterprise Router Using SLAAC to Build IPv6 Address and Default IPv6 Route*

When R1 receives the NDP RA message, it does the following:

Interface address: Builds its own interface IPv6 address using the SLAAC process, based on the prefix in the RA.

Local /128 Route: Adds a local (/128) IPv6 route for the address, as it would for any interface IPv6 address.

Connected Route for Prefix: Adds a connected (/64) route for the prefix learned in the NDP RA message.

Default route: R1 adds a default route, to destination ::/0, with the next-hop address of ISP1's address of 2001:DB8:1:12::1, as learned in the RA sent by router ISP1.

Note that the router can be configured to add this default route or not. As shown in the figure, the router builds a default route. Using the **ipv6 address autoconfig** subcommand without the **default** keyword causes the router to build its address with SLAAC but not add a default route.

Example 32-16 shows the three IPv6 routes on Router R1 just mentioned in the list. In particular, note the codes for the connected route and the default route; both codes begin with ND, meaning the route was learned with NDP. In particular, as highlighted in the legend part of the output, *ND* refers to an NDP-learned default route, and *NDp* refers to an NDP-learned prefix (as listed in the NDP RA message in Figure 32-6 in this case). Note also that these same two routes have an administrative distance of 2, which is the default administrative distance of IPv6 routes learned with NDP.

Example 32-16   *Learning an Address and Default Static Route with DHCP*

```
R1# show ipv6 route
IPv6 Routing Table - default - 4 entries
Codes: C - Connected, L - Local, S - Static, U - Per-user Static route
```

```
       B - BGP, HA - Home Agent, MR - Mobile Router, R - RIP
       H - NHRP, I1 - ISIS L1, I2 - ISIS L2, IA - ISIS interarea
       IS - ISIS summary, D - EIGRP, EX - EIGRP external, NM - NEMO
       ND - ND Default, NDp - ND Prefix, DCE - Destination, NDr - Redirect
       O - OSPF Intra, OI - OSPF Inter, OE1 - OSPF ext 1, OE2 - OSPF ext 2
       ON1 - OSPF NSSA ext 1, ON2 - OSPF NSSA ext 2, la - LISP alt
       lr - LISP site-registrations, ld - LISP dyn-eid, a - Application
ND    ::/0 [2/0]
      via FE80::22FF:FE22:2222, Serial0/0/0
NDp 2001:DB8:1:12::/64 [2/0]
      via Serial0/0/0, directly connected
L    2001:DB8:1:12:32F7:DFF:FE29:8560/128 [0/0]
      via Serial0/0/0, receive
! lines omitted for brevity
```

Troubleshooting Static IPv6 Routes

The current set of CCENT and CCNA R&S exam topics includes troubleshooting of both IPv4 and IPv6 static routes. Chapter 18 already discussed how to troubleshoot IPv4 static routes, and many of those same concepts apply to IPv6 static routes. However, IPv6 static routes do have a few small differences. This last part of the chapter looks at troubleshooting IPv6 static routes, reviewing many of the same troubleshooting rules applied to IPv4 static routes, while focusing on the details specific to IPv6.

This topic breaks static route troubleshooting into two perspectives: the route is in the routing table but is incorrect and cases in which the route is not in the routing table.

Troubleshooting Incorrect Static Routes That Appear in the IPv6 Routing Table

A static route is only as good as the input typed into the **ipv6 route** command. IOS checks the syntax of the command, of course. However, IOS cannot tell if you choose the incorrect outgoing interface, incorrect next-hop address, or incorrect prefix/prefix-length in a static route. If the parameters pass the syntax checks, IOS places the **ipv6 route** command into the running-config file. Then, if no other problem exists (as discussed at the next heading), IOS puts the route into the IP routing table—even though the route may not work because of the poorly chosen parameters.

For instance, an exam question might show a figure with Router R1 having an address of 2001:1:1:1::1 and neighboring Router R2 with an address of 2001:1:1:1::2. If R1 lists a static route with the command **ipv6 route 3333::/64 2001:1:1:1::1**, the command would be accepted by IOS with correct syntax, but it would not be effective as a route. R1 cannot use its own IPv6 address as a next-hop address. IOS does not prevent the configuration of the command, however; it allows the command and adds the route to the IPv6 routing table, but the route cannot possibly forward packets correctly.

When you see an exam question that has static routes, and you see them in the output of **show ipv6 route**, remember that the routes may have incorrect parameters. Check for these types of mistakes:

Step 1. Prefix/Length: Does the **ipv6 route** command reference the correct subnet ID (prefix) and mask (prefix length)?

Step 2. If using a next-hop IPv6 address that is a link-local address:

A. Is the link-local address an address on the correct neighboring router? (It should be an address on another router on a shared link.)

B. Does the **ipv6 route** command also refer to the correct outgoing interface on the local router?

Step 3. If using a next-hop IPv6 address that is a global unicast or unique local address, is the address the correct unicast address of the neighboring router?

Step 4. If referencing an outgoing interface, does the **ipv6 route** command reference the interface on the local router (that is, the same router where the static route is configured)?

This troubleshooting checklist works through the various cases in which IOS would accept the configuration of the static IPv6 route, but the route would not work because of the incorrect parameters in context. It helps to see a few examples. Figure 32-7 shows a sample network to use for the examples; all the examples focus on routes added to Router R1, for the subnet on the far right.

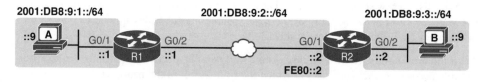

Figure 32-7 *Sample Topology for Incorrect IPv6 Route Examples*

Example 32-17 shows five **ipv6 route** commands. All have correct syntax, but all have one incorrect value; that is, the route will not work because of the types of problems in the troubleshooting checklist. Look for the short comment at the end of each configuration command to see why each is incorrect.

Example 32-17 ipv6 route *Commands with Correct Syntax but Incorrect Ideas*

```
ipv6 route 2001:DB8:9:33::/64 2001:DB8:9:2::2    ! Step 1: Wrong prefix
ipv6 route 2001:DB8:9:3::/64 G0/2 FE80::AAA9     ! Step 2A: Wrong neighbor link local
ipv6 route 2001:DB8:9:3::/64 FE80::2             ! Step 2B: Missing outgoing interface
ipv6 route 2001:DB8:9:3::/64 2001:DB8:9:2::1     ! Step 3: Wrong neighbor address
ipv6 route 2001:DB8:9:3::/64 G0/1 FE80::2        ! Step 4: Wrong interface on R1
```

All these incorrect examples have correct syntax and would be added to R1's IPv6 routing table if configured on R1. However, all have flaws. Working through the examples in order:

Step 1. The prefix (2001:DB8:9:33::) has a typo in the fourth quartet (33 instead of 3).

Step 2A. The figure shows R2's G0/1 with link-local address FE80::2, but the command uses FE80::AAA9.

Step 2B. The command uses the correct link-local address on R2's address on the common link (FE80::2 per the figure), but it omits the outgoing interface of R1's G0/2 interface. (See the next example for more detail.)

Step 3.   The figure shows the subnet in the center as 2001:DB8:9:2::/64, with R1 using the ::1 address and R2 using ::2. For the fourth command, R1's command should use R2's address 2001:DB8:9:2::2, but it uses R1's own 2001:DB8:9:2::1 address instead.

Step 4.   As a command on R1, the outgoing interface references R1's own interfaces. R1's G0/1 is the interface on the left, whereas R1 should use its G0/2 interface on the right when forwarding packets to subnet 2001:DB8:9:3::/64.

The key takeaway for this section is to know that a route in the IPv6 routing table may be incorrect due to poor choices for the parameters. The parameters should always include the neighboring router's IPv6 addresses, but the local router's interface type/number, and in all cases, the correct prefix/length. The fact that a route is in the IPv6 routing table, particularly a static route, does not mean it is a correct route.

Note that of the five example commands in Example 32-17, IOS would accept all of them except the third one. IOS can notice the case of omitting the outgoing interface if the next-hop address is a link-local address. Example 32-18 shows a sample of the error message from IOS.

Example 32-18 *IOS Rejects the* **ipv6 route** *Command with Link-Local and No Outgoing Interface*

```
R1# configure terminal
Enter configuration commands, one per line.  End with CNTL/Z.
R1(config)# ipv6 route 2001:DB8:9:3::/64 FE80::2
% Interface has to be specified for a link-local nexthop
R1(config)# ^Z
R1#
R1# show running-config | include ipv6 route
R1#
```

The Static Route Does Not Appear in the IPv6 Routing Table

The preceding few pages focused on IPv6 static routes that show up in the IPv6 routing table but unfortunately have incorrect parameters. The next page looks at IPv6 routes that have correct parameters, but IOS does not place them into the IPv6 routing table.

When you add an **ipv6 route** command to the configuration, and the syntax is correct, IOS considers that route to be added to the IPv6 routing table. IOS makes the following checks before adding the route; note that IOS uses this same kind of logic for IPv4 static routes:

- For **ipv6 route** commands that list an outgoing interface, that interface must be in an up/up state.

- For **ipv6 route** commands that list a global unicast or unique local next-hop IP address (that is, not a link-local address), the local router must have a route to reach that next-hop address.

- If another IPv6 route exists for that exact same prefix/prefix-length, the static route must have a better (lower) administrative distance.

For example, Router R1, again from Figure 32-3, has been configured with IPv6 addresses. Example 32-19 shows the addition of an **ipv6 route** command for remote subnet 2001:DB8:9:3::/64, but with incorrect next-hop address 2001:DB8:9:3::2. That address is on R2, but it is the address on the far side of R2, on R2's G0/2 interface.

Example 32-19 *No Route for Next-Hop IPv6 Address in Static Route*

```
R1# configure terminal
Enter configuration commands, one per line.  End with CNTL/Z.
R1(config)# ipv6 route 2001:DB8:9:3::/64 2001:DB8:9:3::2
R1(config)# ^Z
R1# show ipv6 route
IPv6 Routing Table - default - 5 entries
Codes: C - Connected, L - Local, S - Static, U - Per-user Static route
       B - BGP, HA - Home Agent, MR - Mobile Router, R - RIP
       H - NHRP, I1 - ISIS L1, I2 - ISIS L2, IA - ISIS interarea
       IS - ISIS summary, D - EIGRP, EX - EIGRP external, NM - NEMO
       ND - ND Default, NDp - ND Prefix, DCE - Destination, NDr - Redirect
       RL - RPL, O - OSPF Intra, OI - OSPF Inter, OE1 - OSPF ext 1
       OE2 - OSPF ext 2, ON1 - OSPF NSSA ext 1, ON2 - OSPF NSSA ext 2
       la - LISP alt, lr - LISP site-registrations, ld - LISP dyn-eid
       a - Application
C   2001:DB8:9:1::/64 [0/0]
     via GigabitEthernet0/1, directly connected
L   2001:DB8:9:1::1/128 [0/0]
     via GigabitEthernet0/1, receive
C   2001:DB8:9:2::/64 [0/0]
     via GigabitEthernet0/2, directly connected
L   2001:DB8:9:2::1/128 [0/0]
     via GigabitEthernet0/2, receive
L   FF00::/8 [0/0]
     via Null0, receive
```

Chapter Review

One key to doing well on the exams is to perform repetitive spaced review sessions. Review this chapter's material using either the tools in the book, DVD, or interactive tools for the same material found on the book's companion website. Refer to the "Your Study Plan" element for more details. Table 32-3 outlines the key review elements and where you can find them. To better track your study progress, record when you completed these activities in the second column.

Table 32-3   Chapter Review Tracking

Review Element	Review Date(s)	Resource Used
Review key topics		Book, DVD/website
Answer DIKTA questions		Book, PCPT
Review memory tables		Book, DVD/website
Do labs		Blog
Review command tables		Book

Review All the Key Topics

Table 32-4   Key Topics for Chapter 32

Key Topic Element	Description	Page Number
List	Methods by which a router can build IPv6 routes	752
List	Rules for IPv6 connected and local routes	753
Figure 32-2	IPv6 static route concepts	756
Checklist	Items to check on **ipv6 route** command that cause problems with IPv6 static routes	766
Checklist	Items to check other than the **ipv6 route** command that cause problems with IPv6 static routes	767

Command References

Tables 32-5 and 32-6 list configuration and verification commands used in this chapter. As an easy review exercise, cover the left column in a table, read the right column, and try to recall the command without looking. Then repeat the exercise, covering the right column, and try to recall what the command does.

Table 32-5   Chapter 32 Configuration Command Reference

Command	Description
ipv6 route *prefix/length next-hop-address*	Global command to define an IPv6 static route to a next-hop router IPv6 address.
ipv6 route *prefix/length outgoing-interface*	Global command to define an IPv6 static route, with packets forwarded out the local router interface listed in the command.
ipv6 route *prefix/length next-hop-address outgoing-interface*	Global command to define an IPv6 static route, with both the next-hop address and local router outgoing interface listed.
ipv6 route *::/0 {[next-hop-address] [outgoing-interface]}*	Global command to define a default IPv6 static route.

Command	Description
ipv6 address autoconfig [default]	Interface subcommand that tells the router to use SLAAC to find/build its own interface IPv6 address, and with the **default** parameter, to add a default route with a next hop of the router that responds with the RA message.

Table 32-6   Chapter 32 EXEC Command Reference

Command	Description
show ipv6 route [connected | local | static]	Lists routes in the routing table.
show ipv6 route *address*	Displays detailed information about the route this router uses to forward packets to the IPv6 address listed in the command.

Part VIII Review

Keep track of your part review progress with the checklist in Table P8-1. Details on each task follow the table.

Table P8-1   Part VIII Part Review Checklist

Activity	1st Date Completed	2nd Date Completed
Repeat All DIKTA Questions		
Answer Part Review Questions		
Review Key Topics		
Create IPv6 Addressing Mind Map		
Create IPv6 Configuration and Verification Command Mind Map		
Do Labs		

Repeat All DIKTA Questions

For this task, use the PCPT software to answer the "Do I Know This Already?" questions again for the chapters in this part of the book.

Answer Part Review Questions

For this task, use PCPT to answer the Part Review questions for this part of the book.

Review Key Topics

Review all key topics in all chapters in this part, either by browsing the chapters or using the Key Topics application on the DVD or companion website.

Create IPv6 Addressing Mind Map

Addressing is the biggest difference between IPv4 and IPv6. Think about IPv6 addresses for a few moments—the terms, the structure, the types, and anything related to addressing. Then make a mind map that collects all the addressing concepts and terms into one mind map.

When thinking about addressing, try to organize the information to your liking. There is no one right answer. However, if you want some guidance on how to organize the information, some of the concepts and terms can be organized by type of address. For instance, link-local addresses are one type. In that part of the mind map, you could list all terms and facts about link-local addresses, as shown in Figure P8-1.

Figure P8-1 *Sample Mind Map for the Link-Local Branch*

Chapter 28, "Fundamentals of IP Version 6," through Chapter 30, "Implementing IPv6 Addressing on Routers," contain most of the IPv6 addressing concepts in this book. Try to fit all the addressing terms from the "Key Terms" sections of those chapters into the map, along with all IPv6 addressing concepts and the values that identify an address as being a particular type of IPv6 address.

Create IPv6 Configuration and Verification Command Mind Map

Create a command mind map for IPv6 router commands. Break it into two major sections: addressing and static routes. Inside each, break the commands into configuration and verification commands.

Appendix L, "Mind Map Solutions," lists sample mind map answers, but as usual, your mind map can and will look different.

Table P8-2 Configuration Mind Maps for Part VIII Review

Map	Description	Where You Saved It
1	IPv6 Addressing Mind Map	
2	IPv6 Commands Mind Map	

Do Labs

Depending on your chosen lab tool, here are some suggestions for what to do in lab:

Pearson Network Simulator: The full Pearson ICND1 or CCNA simulator has practice for the usual types of activities, as well as a special type of lab that lets you practice IPv6 addressing math processes by using commands in the lab. Check out all the IPv6 labs, but make sure to use the IPv6 Subnet ID Calculation and IPv6 EUI-64 Calculation labs as well. And as always in Part Review, use the configuration scenario and troubleshooting scenario labs.

Config Labs: As always, take advantage of the Config Labs for this book part in the author's blog; launch from blog.certskills.com/ccent/ and navigate to the Hands-on Config labs.

Other: If using other lab tools, as a few suggestions: Getting used to IPv6 addresses takes some time. Do more than a few repetitions of configuring different IPv6 addresses in a small topology. Then use all the IPv6 **show** commands, and pay close attention to all the special IPv6 addresses created on each interface. Then add static IPv6 routes to match your subnets.

Part IX is the final part with new technical content in this book—hooray!

This final part moves through a wide variety of small topics. Many of the topics apply equally to both routers and switches, particularly the topics in Chapters 33 and 34. Chapters 35 and 36 focus a little more on routers. However, for all features, the discussion centers on managing the devices in the network.

Part IX

Network Device Management

CHAPTER 33

Device Management Protocols

This chapter covers the following exam topics:

2.0 LAN Switching Technologies

2.6 Configure and verify Layer 2 Protocols

    2.6.a Cisco Discovery Protocol

    2.6.b LLDP

4.0 Infrastructure Services

4.5 Configure and verify NTP operating in a client/server mode

5.0 Infrastructure Management

5.1 Configure and verify device-monitoring using syslog

5.2 Configure and verify device management

    5.2.b Using Cisco Discovery Protocol and LLDP for device discovery

    5.2.d Logging

    5.2.e Timezone

    5.2.f Loopback

5.6 Use Cisco IOS tools to troubleshoot and resolve problems

    5.6.b Terminal Monitor

    5.6.c Log events

This chapter begins Part IX with a discussion of the concepts, configuration, and verification of three functions found on Cisco routers and switches. These functions focus more on managing the network devices themselves than on managing the network that devices create.

Most computing devices have a need to notify the administrator of any significant issue; generally, across the world of computing, messages of this type are called log messages. Cisco devices generate log messages as well. The first section shows how a Cisco device handles those messages and how you can configure routers and switches to ignore the messages or save them in different ways.

Next, different router and switch functions benefit from synchronizing their time-of-day clocks. Like most every computing device, routers and switches have an internal clock function to keep time. Network Time Protocol (NTP) provides a means for devices to synchronize their time, as discussed in the second section.

The final major section focuses on two protocols that do the same kinds of work: Cisco Discovery Protocol (CDP) and Link Layer Discovery Protocol (LLDP). Both provide a means for network devices to learn about neighboring devices, without requiring the IPv4 or IPv6 be working at the time.

"Do I Know This Already?" Quiz

Take the quiz (either here, or use the PCPT software) if you want to use the score to help you decide how much time to spend on this chapter. The answers are at the bottom of the page following the quiz, and the explanations are in DVD Appendix C and in the PCPT software.

Table 33-1 "Do I Know This Already?" Foundation Topics Section-to-Question Mapping

Foundation Topics Section	Questions
System Message Logging (Syslog)	1–2
Network Time Protocol (NTP)	3–4
Analyzing Topology Using CDP and LLDP	5–6

1. What level of logging to the console is the default for a Cisco device?

   a. Informational

   b. Errors

   c. Warnings

   d. Debugging

2. What command limits the messages sent to a syslog server to levels 4 through 0?

   a. **logging trap 0-4**

   b. **logging trap 0,1,2,3,4**

   c. **logging trap 4**

   d. **logging trap through 4**

3. Which of the following is accurate about the NTP client function on a Cisco router?

   a. The client synchronizes its time-of-day clock based on the NTP server.

   b. It counts CPU cycles of the local router CPU to more accurately keep time.

   c. The client synchronizes its serial line clock rate based on the NTP server.

   d. The client must be connected to the same subnet as an NTP server.

4. Router R2 uses NTP in client/server mode. Which of the following correctly describes the use of the NTP configuration commands on Router R2? (Choose two answers.)

   a. The **ntp server** command enables R2's NTP server function but not the client function.

   b. The **ntp server** command enables R2's NTP server and client functions.

   c. The **ntp master** command enables R2's NTP server function.

   d. The **ntp master** command enables R2's client function and references the server.

5. Imagine that a switch connects through an Ethernet cable to a router, and the router's host name is Hannah. Which of the following commands could tell you information about the IOS version on Hannah without establishing a Telnet connection to Hannah? (Choose two answers.)

  a. show neighbors Hannah

  b. show cdp

  c. show cdp neighbors

  d. show cdp neighbors Hannah

  e. show cdp entry Hannah

  f. show cdp neighbors detail

6. A switch is cabled to a router whose host name is Hannah. Which of the following LLDP commands could identify Hannah's model of hardware? (Choose two answers.)

  a. show neighbors

  b. show neighbors Hannah

  c. show lldp

  d. show lldp interface

  e. show lldp neighbors

  f. show lldp entry Hannah

Foundation Topics

System Message Logging (Syslog)

It is amazing just how helpful Cisco devices try to be to their administrators. When major (and even not-so-major) events take place, these Cisco devices attempt to notify administrators with detailed system messages. As you learn in this section, these messages vary from the very mundane to those that are incredibly important. Thankfully, administrators have a large variety of options for storing these messages and being alerted to those that could have the largest impact on the network infrastructure.

When an event happens that the device's OS thinks is interesting, how does the OS notify us humans? Cisco IOS can send the messages to anyone currently logged in to the device. It can also store the message so that a user can later look at the messages. The next few pages examine both topics.

Sending Messages in Real Time to Current Users

Cisco IOS running on a device at least tries to allow current users to see log messages when they happen. Not every router or switch may have users connected, but if some user is logged in, the router or switch benefits by making the network engineer aware of any issues.

By default, IOS shows log messages to console users for all severity levels of messages. That default happens because of the default **logging console** global configuration command. In fact, if you have been using a console port throughout your time reading this book, you likely have already noticed many syslog messages, like messages about interfaces coming up or going down.

For other users (that is, Telnet and SSH users), the device requires a two-step process before the user sees the messages. First, IOS has another global configuration setting—**logging monitor**—that tells IOS to enable the sending of log messages to all logged users. However, that default configuration is not enough to allow the user to see the log messages. The user must also issue the **terminal monitor** EXEC command during the login session, which tells IOS that this terminal session would like to receive log messages.

Figure 33-1 summarizes these key points about how IOS on a Cisco router or switch processes log messages for currently connected users. In the figure, user A sits at the console, and always receives log messages. On the right, the fact that user B sees messages (because user B issued the **terminal monitor** command after login), and user C does not, shows that each user can control whether or not she receives log messages.

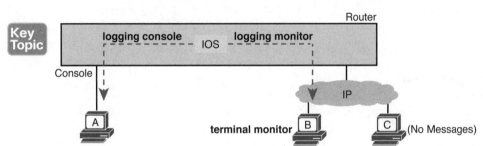

Figure 33-1 *IOS Processing for Log Messages to Current Users*

Storing Log Messages for Later Review

With logging to the console and to terminals, an event happens, IOS sends the messages to the console and terminal sessions, and then IOS can discard the message. However, clearly, it would be useful to keep a copy of the log messages for later review, so IOS provides two primary means to keep a copy.

IOS can store copies of the log messages in RAM by virtue of the **logging buffered** global configuration command. Then any user can come back later and see the old log messages by using the **show logging** EXEC command.

As a second option—an option used frequently in production networks—all devices store their log messages centrally to a syslog server. RFC 5424 defines the Syslog protocol, which provides the means by which a device like a switch or router can use a UDP protocol to send messages to a syslog server for storage. All devices can send their log messages to the server. Later, a user can connect to the server (typically with a graphical user interface) and browse the log messages from various devices. To configure a router or switch to send log messages to a syslog server, add the **logging** {*address*|*hostname*} global command, referencing the IP address or hostname of the syslog server.

Figure 33-2 shows the ideas behind the buffered logging and syslog logging.

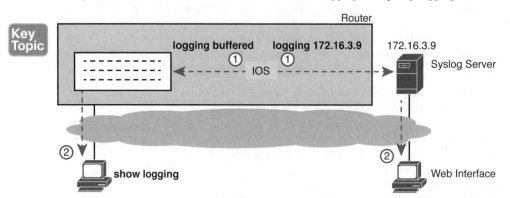

Figure 33-2   *IOS Storing Log Messages for Later View: Buffered and Syslog Server*

Log Message Format

IOS defines the format of log messages. The message begins with some data fields about the message, followed by some text more easily read by humans. For example, take a close look at this sample message:

```
*Dec 18 17:10:15.079: %LINEPROTO-5-UPDOWN: Line protocol on Interface
  FastEthernet0/0, changed state to down
```

Notice that by default on this particular device, we see the following:

A timestamp: *Dec 18 17:10:15.079

The facility on the router that generated the message: %LINEPROTO

The severity level: 5

A mnemonic for the message: UPDOWN

The description of the message: Line protocol on Interface FastEthernet0/0, changed state to down

IOS dictates most of the contents of the messages, but you can at least toggle on and off the use of the timestamp (which is included by default) and a log message sequence number (which is not enabled by default). Example 33-1 reverses those defaults by turning off time-stamps and turning on sequence numbers.

Example 33-1   *Disabling Timestamps and Enabling Sequence Numbers in Log Messages*

```
R1(config)# no service timestamps
R1(config)# service sequence-numbers
R1(config)# end
R1#
000011: %SYS-5-CONFIG_I: Configured from console by console
```

To see the change in format, look at the log message at the end of the example. As usual, when you exit configuration mode, the device issues yet another log message. Comparing this message to the previous example, you can see it now no longer lists the time of day but does list a sequence number.

Log Message Severity Levels

Log messages may just tell you about some mundane event, or they may tell you of some critical event. To help you make sense of the importance of each message, IOS assigns each message a severity level (as noted in the same messages in the preceding page or so). Figure 33-3 shows the severity levels: the lower the number, the more severe the event that caused the message. (Note that the values on the left and center are used in IOS commands.)

Keyword	Numeral	Description	
Alert	1	Immediate action required	Severe
Emergency	0	System unusable	
Critical	2	Critical Event (Highest of 3)	
Error	3	Error Event (Middle of 3)	Impactful
Warning	4	Warning Event (Lowest of 3)	
Notification	5	Normal, More Important	Normal
Informational	6	Normal, Less Important	
Debug	7	Requested by User Debug	Debug

Figure 33-3 *Syslog Message Severity Levels by Keyword and Numeral*

Figure 33-3 breaks the eight severity levels into four sections just to make a little more sense of the meaning. The two top levels in the figure are the most severe. Messages from this level mean a serious and immediate issue exists. The next three levels, called Critical, Error, and Warning, also tell about events that impact the device, but they are not as immediate and severe. For instance, one common log message about an interface failing to a physically down state shows as a severity level 3 message.

Continuing down the figure, IOS uses the next two levels (5 and 6) for messages that are more about notifying the user rather than errors. Finally, the last level in the figure is used for messages requested by the **debug** command, as shown in an example later in this chapter.

Table 33-2 summarizes the configuration commands used to enable logging and to set the severity level for each type. When the severity level is set, IOS will send that service messages of that severity level and more severe. For example, the command **logging console 4** causes IOS to send severity level 0–4 messages to the console. Also, note that the command to disable each service is the **no** version of the command, with *no* in front of the command (**no logging console**, **no logging monitor**, and so on).

Table 33-2 How to Configure Logging Message Levels for Each Log Service

Service	To Enable Logging	To Set Message Levels
Console	**logging console**	**logging console** *level-name*	*level-number*
Monitor	**logging monitor**	**logging monitor** *level-name*	*level-number*
Buffered	**logging buffered**	**logging buffered** *level-name*	*level-number*
Syslog	**logging host** *address*	*hostname*	**logging trap** *level-name*	*level-number*

Configuring and Verifying System Logging

With the information in Table 33-2, configuring syslog in a Cisco IOS router or switch should be relatively straightforward. Example 33-2 shows a sample, based on Figure 33-4. The figure shows a syslog server at IP address 172.16.3.9. Both switches and both routers will use the same configuration shown in Example 33-2, although the example shows the configuration process on a single device, Router R1.

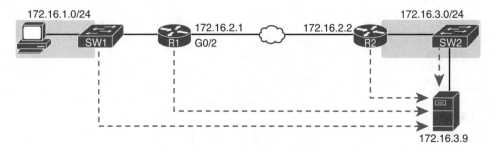

Figure 33-4　*Sample Network Used in Logging Examples*

Example 33-2　*Syslog Configuration on R1*

```
logging console 7
logging monitor debug
logging buffered 4
logging host 172.16.3.9
logging trap warning
```

First, note that the example configures the same message level at the console and for terminal monitoring (level 7, or debug), and the same level for both buffered and logging to the syslog server (level 4, or warning). The levels may be set using the numeric severity level or the name as shown earlier in Figure 33-3.

The **show logging** command confirms those same configuration settings and also lists the log messages per the logging buffered configuration. Example 33-3 shows a sample, with the configuration settings to match Example 33-2 highlighted in gray.

Example 33-3　*Viewing the Configured Log Settings per the Earlier Example*

```
R1# show logging
Syslog logging: enabled (0 messages dropped, 3 messages rate-limited, 0 flushes, 0
  overruns, xml disabled, filtering disabled)


No Active Message Discriminator.


No Inactive Message Discriminator.


    Console logging: level debugging, 45 messages logged, xml disabled,
                   filtering disabled
    Monitor logging: level debugging, 0 messages logged, xml disabled,
                   filtering disabled
```

```
    Buffer logging:  level warnings, 0 messages logged, xml disabled,
                     filtering disabled
    Exception Logging: size (8192 bytes)
    Count and timestamp logging messages: disabled
    Persistent logging: disabled

No active filter modules.

    Trap logging: level warnings, 0 message lines logged
        Logging to 172.16.3.9  (udp port 514, audit disabled,
            link up),
            0 message lines logged,
            0 message lines rate-limited,
            0 message lines dropped-by-MD,
            xml disabled, sequence number disabled
            filtering disabled
        Logging Source-Interface:      VRF Name:

Log Buffer (8192 bytes):
```

You might notice by now that knowing the names of all eight log message levels can be handy if you want to understand the output of the commands. Most of the **show** commands list the log message levels by name, not by number. As you can see in the gray highlights in this example, two levels list "debug," and two list "warning," even though some of the configuration commands referred to those levels by number.

Also, you cannot know this from the output, but in Example 33-3, Router R1 has no buffered log messages. (Note the counter value of 0 for buffered logging messages.) If any log messages had been buffered, the actual log messages would be listed at the end of the command. In this case, I had just booted the router, and no messages had been buffered yet. (You could also clear out the old messages from the log with the **clear logging** EXEC command.)

The next example shows the difference between the current severity levels. This example shows the user disabling interface G0/1 on R1 with the **shutdown** command and then re-enabling it with the **no shutdown** command. If you look closely at the highlighted messages, you will see several severity 5 messages and one severity 3 message. The **logging buffered 4** global configuration command on R1 (see Example 33-2) means that R1 will not buffer the severity level 5 log messages, but it will buffer the severity level 3 message. Example 33-4 ends by showing that log message at the end of the output of the **show logging** command.

Example 33-4 *Seeing Severity 3 and 5 Messages at the Console, and Severity 3 Only in the Buffer*

```
R1# configure terminal
Enter configuration commands, one per line.  End with CNTL/Z.
R1(config)# interface g0/1
R1(config-if)# shutdown
R1(config-if)#
```

```
*Oct 21 20:07:07.244: %LINK-5-CHANGED: Interface GigabitEthernet0/1, changed state to
  administratively down
*Oct 21 20:07:08.244: %LINEPROTO-5-UPDOWN: Line protocol on Interface
  GigabitEthernet0/1, changed state to down
R1(config-if)# no shutdown
R1(config-if)#
*Oct 21 20:07:24.312: %LINK-3-UPDOWN: Interface GigabitEthernet0/1, changed state to
  up
*Oct 21 20:07:25.312: %LINEPROTO-5-UPDOWN: Line protocol on Interface
  GigabitEthernet0/1, changed state to up
R1(config-if)# ^Z
R1#
*Oct 21 20:07:36.546: %SYS-5-CONFIG_I: Configured from console by console
R1# show logging
! Skipping about 20 lines, the same lines in Example 33-3, until the last few lines


Log Buffer (8192 bytes):


*Oct 21 20:07:24.312: %LINK-3-UPDOWN: Interface GigabitEthernet0/1, changed state to
  up
```

The debug Command and Log Messages

Of the eight log message severity levels, one level, debug level (7), has a special purpose: for
messages generated as a result of a user logged in to the router or switch who issues a **debug**
command.

The **debug** EXEC command gives the network engineer a way to ask IOS to monitor for
certain internal events, with that monitoring process continuing over time, so that IOS can
issue log messages when those events occur. The engineer can log in, issue the **debug** command, and move on to other work. The user can even log out of the device, and the debug
remains enabled. IOS continues to monitor the request in that **debug** command and generate log messages about any related events. The debug remains active until some user issues
the **no debug** command with the same parameters, disabling the debug.

> **NOTE**   While the **debug** command is just one command, it has a huge number of options,
> much like the **show** command may be one command, but it also has many, many options.

The best way to see how the **debug** command works, and how it uses log messages, is to
see an example. Figure 33-4 shows a small network with two routers, both of which happen to use RIPv2. RIPv2 sends periodic updates every 30 seconds. In the design shown
in Figure 33-4, focus on R2's advertisement to R1, in which R2 will advertise its route for
172.16.3.0/24 to R1. Example 33-5 shows what happens from the console of R1 after issuing the **debug ip rip** EXEC command.

Example 33-5   *Using* debug ip rip *from R1's Console*

```
R1# debug ip rip
RIP protocol debugging is on
R1#
```

```
*Oct 21 20:26:55.316: RIP: received v2 update from 172.16.2.2 on GigabitEthernet0/2
*Oct 21 20:26:55.317:         172.16.3.0/24 via 0.0.0.0 in 1 hops
*Oct 21 20:27:14.200: RIP: sending v2 update to 224.0.0.9 via GigabitEthernet0/2
  (172.16.2.1)
*Oct 21 20:27:14.200: RIP: build update entries
*Oct 21 20:27:14.201:   172.16.1.0/24 via 0.0.0.0, metric 1, tag 0
R1# no debug ip rip
RIP protocol debugging is off
R1#
```

The console user sees the log messages created on behalf of that **debug** command after the debug command completes. Per the earlier configuration in Example 33-2, R1's **logging console 7** command tells us that the console user will receive severity levels 0–7, which includes level 7 debug messages. Note that with the current settings, these debug messages would not be in the local log message buffer (because of the level in the **logging buffered warning** command), nor would they be sent to the syslog server (because of the level in the **logging trap 4** command).

Note that the console user automatically sees the log messages as shown in Example 33-4. However, as noted in the text describing Figure 33-1, a user who connects to R1 would need to also issue the **terminal monitor** command to see those debug messages. For instance, anyone logged in with SSH at the time Example 33-4's output was gathered would not have seen the output, even with the **logging monitor debug** command configured on Router R1, without first issuing a **terminal monitor** command.

Note that all enabled debug options use router CPU, which can cause problems for the router. You can monitor CPU use with the **show process cpu** command, but you should use caution when using **debug** commands carefully on production devices. Also, note the more CLI users that receive debug messages, the more CPU that is consumed. So, some installations choose to not include debug-level log messages for console and terminal logging, requiring users to look at the logging buffer or syslog for those messages, just to reduce router CPU load.

Network Time Protocol (NTP)

Each networking device has some concept of a date and a time-of-day clock. For instance, the log messages discussed in the first major section of this chapter had a timestamp with the date and time of day listed. Now imagine looking at all the log messages from all routers and switches stored at a syslog server. All those messages have a date and timestamp, but how do we make sure the timestamps are consistent? How do we make sure that all devices synchronize their time-of-day clocks so that you can make sense of all the log messages at the syslog server? How could you make sense of the messages for an event that impacted devices in three different time zones?

For example, consider the messages on two routers, R1 and R2, as shown in Example 33-6. Routers R1 and R2 do not synchronize their clocks. A problem keeps happening on the serial link between the two routers. A network engineer looks at all the log messages as stored on the syslog server. However, when the engineer sees some messages from R1, at 13:38:39 (around 1:40 p.m.), he does not think to look for messages from R2 that have a timestamp of around 9:45 a.m.

Example 33-6   *Log Messages from Two Routers, Compared*

```
*Oct 19 13:38:37.568: %OSPF-5-ADJCHG: Process 1, Nbr 2.2.2.2 on Serial0/0/0 from FULL
   to DOWN, Neighbor Down: Interface down or detached
*Oct 19 13:38:40.568: %LINEPROTO-5-UPDOWN: Line protocol on Interface Serial0/0/0,
   changed state to down
! These messages happened on router R2
Oct 19 09:44:09.027: %LINK-3-UPDOWN: Interface Serial0/0/1, changed state to down
Oct 19 09:44:09.027: %OSPF-5-ADJCHG: Process 1, Nbr 1.1.1.1 on Serial0/0/1 from FULL
   to DOWN, Neighbor Down: Interface down or detached
```

In reality, the messages in both parts of Example 33-6 happened within 0.5 seconds of each other because I issued a **shutdown** command on one of the routers. However, the two routers' time-of-day clocks were not synchronized, which makes the messages on the two routers look unrelated. With synchronized clocks, the two routers would have listed practically identical timestamps of almost the exact same time when these messages occurred, making it much easier to read and correlate messages.

Routers, switches, other networking devices, and pretty much every device known in the IT world has a time-of-day clock. For a variety of reasons, it makes sense to synchronize those clocks so that all devices have the same time of day, other than differences in time zone. The Network Time Protocol (NTP) provides the means to do just that.

NTP gives any device a way to synchronize their time-of-day clocks. NTP provides protocol messages that devices use to learn the timestamp of other devices. Devices send timestamps to each other with NTP messages, continually exchanging messages, with one device changing its clock to match the other, eventually synchronizing the clocks. As a result, actions that benefit from synchronized timing, like the timestamps on log messages, work much better.

Setting the Time and Timezone

NTP's job is to synchronize clocks, but NTP works best if you set the device clock to a reasonably close time before enabling the NTP client function with the **ntp server** command. For instance, my wristwatch says 8:52 p.m. right now. Before starting NTP on a new router or switch so that it synchronizes with another device, I should set the time to 8:52 p.m., set the correct date and timezone, and even tell the device to adjust for daylight savings time—and then enable NTP. Setting the time correctly gives NTP a good start toward synchronizing.

Example 33-7 shows how to set the date, time, timezone, and daylight savings time. Oddly, it uses two configuration commands (for the timezone and daylight savings time), and one EXEC command to set the date and time on the router.

Example 33-7   *Setting the Date/Time with* **clock set**, *Plus Timezone/DST*

```
R1# configure terminal
Enter configuration commands, one per line.  End with CNTL/Z.
R1(config)# clock timezone EST -5
R1(config)# clock summer-time EDT recurring
R1(config)# ^Z
R1#
R1# clock set 20:52:49 21 October 2015
```

```
*Oct 21 20:52:49.000: %SYS-6-CLOCKUPDATE: System clock has been updated from 00:36:38
 UTC Thu Oct 22 2015 to 20:52:49 UTC Wed Oct 21 2015, configured from console by
 console.
R1# show clock
20:52:55.051 EDT Wed Oct 21 2015
```

Focus on the two configuration commands first. You should set the first two commands before setting the time of day with the **clock set** EXEC command because the two configuration commands impact the time that is set. In the first command, the **clock timezone** part defines the command and a keyword. The next parameter, "EST" in this case, is any value you choose, but choose the name of the timezone of the device. This value shows up in **show** commands, so although you make up the value, the value needs to be meaningful to all. I chose EST, the acronym for US Eastern Standard Time. The "-5" parameter means that this device is 5 hours behind Universal Time Coordinated (UTC).

The **clock summer-time** part of the second command defines what to do, again with the "EDT" being a field in which you could have used any value. However, you should use a meaningful value. This is the value shown with the time in **show** commands when daylight savings time is in effect, so I chose EDT because it is the acronym for daylight savings time in that same EST time zone. Finally, the **recurring** keyword tells the router to spring forward an hour and fall back an hour automatically over the years.

The **clock set** EXEC command then sets the time, day of the month, month, and year. However, note that IOS interprets the time as typed in the command in the context of the time zone and daylight savings time. In the example, the **clock set** command lists a time of 20:52:49 (the command uses a time syntax with a 24-hour format, not with a 12-hour format plus a.m./p.m.). As a result of that time plus the two earlier configuration commands, the **show clock** command (issued seconds later) lists that time, but also notes the time as EDT, rather than UTC time.

Implementing NTP Clients, Servers, and Client/Server Mode

With NTP, servers supply information about the time of day to clients, and clients react by adjusting their clocks to match. The process requires repeated small adjustments over time to maintain that synchronization. The configuration itself can be simple (to the extent covered in this book), or it can be extensive once you add security configuration and redundancy.

As an example, just to show the basic syntax and **show** commands, consider Figure 33-5. It has three routers, all of which will use NTP. R1 will act as an NTP client, R3 as an NTP server, but R2 will be in client/server mode.

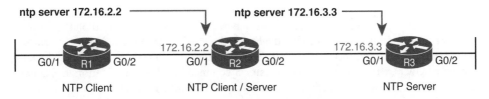

Figure 33-5 *R1 as NTP Client, R2 as Client/Server, R3 as Server*

In a real network that had only these few devices, you would probably make one device act as an NTP server and have all other devices act as an NTP client. However, Figure 33-5 shows R2 acting as an NTP client/server router just to explain what that means because the exam topics mention the term. In particular:

- NTP clients adjust their own time based on what they hear from an NTP server.
- NTP servers supply time information to clients but do not adjust their time as a result.
- NTP clients/servers play both roles. As a client, the device connects to an NTP server to synchronize its time, and as a server, it supplies time information to other devices.

Example 33-8 shows the basic configuration for all three devices in the figure to act in each role. Note that to act as an NTP client, the device configures the **ntp server address | hostname** command. This command performs two related functions:

- It tells the router to act as an NTP client, referencing the NTP server's IP address or hostname.
- It tells the router to also act as an NTP server after that router has synchronized its time with some reliable source (such as the NTP server listed in the command).

In this example, which matches the NTP design in Figure 33-5, R1 refers to R2 (172.16.2.2) as server, and R2 refers to R3 (172.16.3.3) as server.

Example 33-8 *NTP Client/Server Configuration*

```
! Configuration on R1:
ntp server 172.16.2.2
! Configuration on R2:
ntp server 172.16.3.3
! Configuration on R3:
ntp master 2
```

To work correctly, at least one NTP server must also be a trusted *clock source*. If using purpose-built NTP servers (that is, when not using routers and switches as NTP servers), those servers would typically be good clock sources. In that case, all the routers and switches could use the **ntp server** command to refer to those NTP servers. However, in lab with only Cisco routers and switches using NTP, to make NTP work, you must set up at least one router or switch as a clock source using the **ntp master** command. The **ntp master** command tells the router to act as an NTP server and trust its internal clock as a good clock source.

The configuration in Example 33-8 works, but in many cases, routers might have multiple **ntp server** commands configured for redundancy. The goal is to have at least one usable clock source (servers per multiple **ntp server** commands, or internal clock as per the **ntp master** command). The router then chooses the best NTP clock source based on the *stratum level*. The stratum level defines the quality of the clock source; the lower the stratum, the better the source. For instance, with R3's **ntp master 2** command (defining R3's clock as a stratum 2 clock), R2 could add an **ntp master 5** command to the configuration in Example 33-8. As a result, R2 would synchronize and use the time learned from R3 (with the better stratum) under normal conditions, but be ready to rely on its internal clock if connectivity to R3 failed.

Example 33-9 shows verification commands per the configuration as shown in Example 33-8.

Example 33-9   *Verifying NTP Client Status on R1 and R2*

```
R1# show ntp associations

  address         ref clock      st   when  poll reach delay offset   disp
*~172.16.2.2      10.1.3.3        3    50    64   377   1.223  0.090  4.469
 * sys.peer, # selected, + candidate, - outlyer, x falseticker, ~ configured


R1# show ntp status
Clock is synchronized, stratum 4, reference is 172.16.2.2
nominal freq is 250.0000 Hz, actual freq is 250.0000 Hz, precision is 2**21
ntp uptime is 1553800 (1/100 of seconds), resolution is 4000
reference time is DA5E7147.56CADEA7 (19:54:31.339 EST Thu Feb 4 2016)
clock offset is 0.0986 msec, root delay is 2.46 msec
root dispersion is 22.19 msec, peer dispersion is 5.33 msec
loopfilter state is 'CTRL' (Normal Controlled Loop), drift is 0.000000009 s/s
system poll interval is 64, last update was 530 sec ago.
R2# show ntp associations
! This output is taken from router R2, acting in client/server mode
  address         ref clock      st   when  poll reach delay offset   disp
*~172.16.3.3      127.127.1.1     2    49    64   377   1.220  -7.758  3.695
 * sys.peer, # selected, + candidate, - outlyer, x falseticker, ~ configured
```

First, look at the **show ntp associations** command output on R1. It lists the IP address of R2, as configured in the **ntp server 172.16.2.2** command on R1. The * means that R1 has peered with 172.16.2.2 with NTP, and that R1 has one such association. Now look down to the bottom, to this same command on R2. R2 lists 172.16.3.3, which is R3, because of R2's **ntp server 172.16.3.3** command.

The command in the middle, **show ntp status**, on R1, lists many NTP-specific details. Of particular note is the first line that states whether it has synchronized with some other NTP server. In this case, R1 has synchronized. Any router acting as an NTP client will list "unsynchronized" in that first line until the NTP synchronization process completes with at least one server. Note that a router acting solely as an NTP server (like R3), and not attempting to synchronize its time, will always show "unsynchronized" in that first line of command output.

NTP Using a Loopback Interface for Better Availability

An NTP server will accept NTP messages arriving to any of its IPv4 addresses by default. However, the clients reference a specific IP address on the NTP server. That creates an availability issue.

For instance, consider the topology in Figure 33-6, with Router R4 on the right acting as NTP server and the other routers acting as clients. R4 has three IP addresses that the clients could put in their **ntp server** *address* commands. Now consider what happens when one interface on R4 fails, but only one. No matter which of the three interfaces fails, that IP address on that interface cannot be used to send and receive packets. In that case, for any NTP clients that had referred to that specific IP address

33

■ There would likely still be a route to reach R4 itself.

■ The NTP client would not be able to send packets to the configured address because that interface is down.

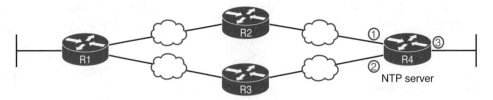

Figure 33-6 *The Availability Issue of Referencing an NTP Server's Physical Interface IP Address*

What is needed is a way to send a packet to R4, a way that is not tied to the state of any one interface. That is, as long as there is some path to send packets to R4 itself, allow NTP to keep working. The goal is to avoid the case in which a single interface failure on Router R4 also causes NTP to fail.

Cisco uses the router loopback interface to meet that exact need. Loopback interfaces are virtual interfaces internal to Cisco IOS, created via the command **interface loopback** *number*, where the number is an integer. Once configured, that loopback interface exists inside that router and is not tied to any physical interface. A loopback interface can be assigned an IP address, routing protocols can advertise about the subnet, and you can ping/traceroute to that address. It acts like other physical interfaces in many ways, but once configured, it remains in an up/up state as long as

■ The router remains up

■ You do not issue a **shutdown** command on that loopback interface

> **NOTE** This discussion is not about the special IPv4 loopback address 127.0.0.1. The loopback interface discussed in this section is a different concept altogether.

Example 33-10 shows the small configuration change that adds the loopback interface to the NTP configuration, which is based on Figure 33-5. In this case, the Example 33-10 configuration changes slightly the configuration shown earlier in Example 33-8. R1, still acting as client, now points to R2's new loopback interface IP address of 172.16.9.9. R2 now has configuration for a new loopback interface (loopback 0). R2 also has a command that tells it to use that loopback 0 interface's IP address as the source address when sending NTP packets.

Example 33-10 *NTP Client/Server Configuration on R1 and R2 Using a Loopback Interface*

```
! Configuration on R1, a client
ntp server 172.16.9.9
! Configuration on R2 for its server function
interface loopback 0
 ip address 172.16.9.9 255.255.255.0
!
```

```
ntp master 4
ntp source loopback 0
! Verification on router R2
R2# show interfaces loopback 0
Loopback0 is up, line protocol is up
  Hardware is Loopback
   Internet address is 172.16.9.9/24
! lines omitted for brevity
```

Loopback interfaces have a wide range of uses across IOS features. They are mentioned here with NTP because NTP is a feature that can benefit from using loopback interfaces. The ICND2 book shows how to use loopback interfaces with OSPF configuration for a completely different purpose.

Analyzing Topology Using CDP and LLDP

The first two major sections of this chapter showed two features—Syslog and NTP—that work the same way on both routers and switches. This final section shows yet another feature common to both routers and switches, with two similar protocols: the Cisco Discovery Protocol (CDP) and the Link Layer Discovery Protocol (LLDP). This section focuses on CDP, followed by LLDP.

Examining Information Learned by CDP

CDP discovers basic information about neighboring routers and switches without needing to know the passwords for the neighboring devices. To discover information, routers and switches send CDP messages out each of their interfaces. The messages essentially announce information about the device that sent the CDP message. Devices that support CDP learn information about others by listening for the advertisements sent by other devices.

CDP discovers several useful details from the neighboring Cisco devices:

Device identifier: Typically the host name

Address list: Network and data link addresses

Port identifier: The interface on the remote router or switch on the other end of the link that sent the CDP advertisement

Capabilities list: Information on what type of device it is (for example, a router or a switch)

Platform: The model and OS level running on the device

CDP plays two general roles: to provide information to the devices to support some function and to provide information to the network engineers that manage the devices. For example, Cisco IP Phones use CDP to learn the data and voice VLAN IDs as configured on the access switch (as discussed in "Data and Voice VLAN Concepts" in Chapter 11, "Implementing Ethernet Virtual LANs"). For that second role, CDP has **show** commands that list information about neighboring devices, as well as information about how CDP is working. Table 33-3 describes the three **show** commands that list the most important CDP information.

33

Key Topic

Table 33-3   **show cdp** Commands That List Information About Neighbors

Command	Description
show cdp neighbors [*type number*]	Lists one summary line of information about each neighbor or just the neighbor found on a specific interface if an interface was listed.
show cdp neighbors detail	Lists one large set (approximately 15 lines) of information, one set for every neighbor.
show cdp entry *name*	Lists the same information as the **show cdp neighbors detail** command, but only for the named neighbor (case sensitive).

NOTE   Cisco routers and switches support the same CDP commands, with the same parameters and same types of output.

The next example shows the power of the information in CDP commands. The example uses the network shown in Figure 33-7, with Example 33-11 listing the output of several **show cdp** commands.

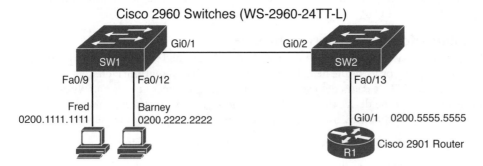

Figure 33-7   *Small Network Used in CDP Examples*

Example 33-11   show cdp *Command Examples: SW2*

```
SW2# show cdp neighbors
Capability Codes: R - Router, T - Trans Bridge, B - Source Route Bridge
                  S - Switch, H - Host, I - IGMP, r - Repeater, P - Phone,
                  D - Remote, C - CVTA, M - Two-port Mac Relay


Device ID        Local Intrfce     Holdtme    Capability  Platform  Port ID
SW1              Gig 0/2           170               S I  WS-C2960- Gig 0/1
R1               Fas 0/13          136             R S I  CISCO2901 Gig 0/1
```

The **show cdp neighbors** command lists one line per neighbor. (Look for the Device ID column, and the list that includes SW1 and R1.) Each of those two lines lists the most important topology information about each neighbor: the neighbor's host name (Device ID), the local device's interface, and the neighboring device's interface (under the Port heading).

Pay close attention to the local device's interface and the neighboring device's interface, comparing the example to the figure. For example, SW2's **show cdp neighbors** command lists an entry for SW1, with SW2's local interface of Gi0/2 and SW1's interface of Gi0/1 under the heading "Port ID."

This command also lists the platform, identifying the specific model of the neighboring router or switch. So, even using this basic information, you could either construct a figure like Figure 33-7 or confirm that the details in the figure are correct.

Next, consider the **show cdp neighbors detail** command as shown in Example 33-12, again taken from switch SW2. This command lists more detail, as you might have guessed. The detail lists the full name of the switch model (WS-2960-24TT-L) and the IP address configured on the neighboring device. You have to look closely, but the example has one long group of messages for each of the two neighbors; the example includes one comment line with gray highlight to help you find the dividing point between groups of messages.

Example 33-12   show cdp neighbors detail *Command on SW2*

```
SW2# show cdp neighbors detail
-------------------------
Device ID: SW1
Entry address(es):
  IP address: 172.16.1.1
Platform: cisco WS-C2960-24TT-L,  Capabilities: Switch IGMP
Interface: GigabitEthernet0/2,  Port ID (outgoing port): GigabitEthernet0/1
Holdtime : 161 sec

Version :
Cisco IOS Software, C2960 Software (C2960-LANBASEK9-M), Version 15.0(1)SE3, RELEASE
  SOFTWARE (fc1)
Technical Support: http://www.cisco.com/techsupport
Copyright (c) 1986-2012 by Cisco Systems, Inc.
Compiled Wed 30-May-12 14:26 by prod_rel_team

advertisement version: 2
Protocol Hello:  OUI=0x00000C, Protocol ID=0x0112; payload len=27,
  value=00000000FFFFFFFF010221FF00000000000018339D7B0E80FF0000
VTP Management Domain: ''
Native VLAN: 1
Duplex: full
Management address(es):
  IP address: 172.16.1.1

! This is a comment from the author: next lines are about R1.
-------------------------
Device ID: R1
Entry address(es):
  IP address: 10.1.1.9
Platform: Cisco CISCO2901/K9,  Capabilities: Router Switch IGMP
```

33

```
Interface: FastEthernet0/13,   Port ID (outgoing port): GigabitEthernet0/1
Holdtime : 127 sec


Version :
Cisco IOS Software, C2900 Software (C2900-UNIVERSALK9-M), Version 15.2(4)M1, RELEASE
   SOFTWARE (fc1)
Technical Support: http://www.cisco.com/techsupport
Copyright (c) 1986-2012 by Cisco Systems, Inc.
Compiled Thu 26-Jul-12 20:54 by prod_rel_team


advertisement version: 2
VTP Management Domain: ''
Duplex: full
Management address(es):
```

NOTE   The **show cdp entry** *name* command lists the exact same details shown in the output of the **show cdp neighbors detail** command, but for only the one neighbor listed in the command.

As you can see, you can sit on one device and discover a lot of information about a neighboring device—a fact that actually creates a security exposure. Cisco recommends that CDP be disabled on any interface that might not have a need for CDP. For switches, any switch port connected to another switch, a router, or to an IP phone should use CDP.

Finally, note that CDP shows information about directly connected neighbors. For instance, **show cdp neighbors** on SW1 would list an entry for SW2 in this case, but not R1, because R1 is not directly connected to SW1.

Configuring and Verifying CDP Itself

Most of the work you do with CDP relates to what CDP can tell you with **show** commands. However, it is an IOS feature, so you can configure CDP and use some **show** commands to examine the status of CDP itself.

IOS typically enables CDP globally and on each interface by default. You can then disable CDP per interface with the **no cdp enable** interface subcommand and later re-enable it with the **cdp enable** interface subcommand. To disable and re-enable CDP globally on the device, use the **no cdp run** and **cdp run** global commands, respectively.

To examine the status of CDP itself, use the commands in Table 33-4.

Table 33-4   Commands Used to Verify CDP Operations

Command	Description
show cdp	States whether CDP is enabled globally, and lists the default update and holdtime timers.
show cdp interface [*type number*]	States whether CDP is enabled on each interface, or a single interface if the interface is listed, and states update and holdtime timers on those interfaces.
show cdp traffic	Lists global statistics for the number of CDP advertisements sent and received.

Example 33-13 lists sample output from each of the commands in Table 33-4, based on switch SW2 in Figure 33-7.

Example 33-13   show cdp *Commands That Show CDP Status*

```
SW2# show cdp
Global CDP information:
    Sending CDP packets every 60 seconds
    Sending a holdtime value of 180 seconds
    Sending CDPv2 advertisements is enabled


SW2# show cdp interface FastEthernet0/13
FastEthernet0/13 is up, line protocol is up
  Encapsulation ARPA
  Sending CDP packets every 60 seconds
  Holdtime is 180 seconds
SW2# show cdp traffic
CDP counters :
    Total packets output: 304, Input: 305
    Hdr syntax: 0, Chksum error: 0, Encaps failed: 0
    No memory: 0, Invalid packet: 0,
    CDP version 1 advertisements output: 0, Input: 0
    CDP version 2 advertisements output: 304, Input: 305
```

Implementing Link Layer Discovery Protocol

Cisco created the Cisco-proprietary CDP before any standard existed for a similar protocol. CDP has many benefits. As a Layer 2 protocol, sitting on top of Ethernet, it does not rely on a working Layer 3 protocol. It provides device information that can be useful in a variety of ways. Cisco had a need but did not see a standard that met the need, so Cisco made up a protocol, as has been the case many times over history with many companies and protocols.

Link Layer Discovery Protocol (LLDP), defined in IEEE standard 802.1AB, provides a standardized protocol that provides the same general features as CDP. LLDP has similar configuration and practically identical **show** commands as compared with CDP. For example, scan the output in Example 33-14. It shows LLDP output from switch SW2, taken once LLDP was enabled in the same network used in the CDP examples. You should see similar information in the command output, but also some differences in formatting and small differences in the information provided.

Example 33-14   show lldp *Commands on SW2*

```
SW2# show lldp neighbors
Capability codes:
    (R) Router, (B) Bridge, (T) Telephone, (C) DOCSIS Cable Device
    (W) WLAN Access Point, (P) Repeater, (S) Station, (O) Other


Device ID          Local Intf    Hold-time   Capability   Port ID
SW1                Gi0/2         105         B            Gi0/1
R2                 Fa0/13        91          R            Gi0/1


Total entries displayed: 2


SW2# show lldp entry R2


Capability codes:
    (R) Router, (B) Bridge, (T) Telephone, (C) DOCSIS Cable Device
    (W) WLAN Access Point, (P) Repeater, (S) Station, (O) Other
------------------------------------------------
Chassis id: 0200.2222.2222
Port id: Gi0/1
Port Description: GigabitEthernet0/1
System Name: R2


System Description:
Cisco IOS Software, C2900 Software (C2900-UNIVERSALK9-M), Version 15.4(3)M3, RELEASE
  SOFTWARE (fc2)
Technical Support: http://www.cisco.com/techsupport
Copyright (c) 1986-2015 by Cisco Systems, Inc.
Compiled Fri 05-Jun-15 13:24 by prod_rel_team


Time remaining: 100 seconds
System Capabilities: B,R
Enabled Capabilities: R
Management Addresses:
    IP: 10.1.1.9
Auto Negotiation - not supported
Physical media capabilities - not advertised
Media Attachment Unit type - not advertised
Vlan ID: - not advertised



Total entries displayed: 1
```

The most important take-away from the output is the consistency between CDP and LLDP in how they refer to the interfaces. Both the **show cdp neighbors** and **show lldp neighbors** commands have "local intf" (interface) and "port ID" columns. These columns refer to the local device's interface and the neighboring device's interface, respectively.

LLDP typically requires configuration, but with similar structure to CDP configuration. To enable LLDP global, use the **lldp run** global command. Then, to enable it on each desired interface, you need to add two commands: **lldp transmit** and **lldp receive**. (You can configure LLDP to only send or only receive messages by configuring only one of the options.)

Finally, checking LLDP status uses the exact same commands as CDP as listed in Table 33-4, other than the fact that you use the **lldp** keyword instead of **cdp**. For instance, **show lldp interface** lists the interfaces on which LLDP is enabled.

Chapter Review

One key to doing well on the exams is to perform repetitive spaced review sessions. Review this chapter's material using either the tools in the book, DVD, or interactive tools for the same material found on the book's companion website. Refer to the "Your Study Plan" element for more details. Table 33-5 outlines the key review elements and where you can find them. To better track your study progress, record when you completed these activities in the second column.

Table 33-5 Chapter Review Tracking

Review Element	Review Date(s)	Resource Used
Review key topics		Book, DVD/website
Review key terms		Book, DVD/website
Answer DIKTA questions		Book, PCPT
Review memory tables		Book, App
Do labs		Blog
Review command references		Book

Review All the Key Topics

Table 33-6 Key Topics for Chapter 33

Key Topic Element	Description	Page Number
Figure 33-1	Logging to console and terminal	781
Figure 33-2	Logging to syslog and buffer	782
Figure 33-3	Log message levels	783
Table 33-2	Logging configuration commands	783
List	Roles of NTP clients, servers, and client/servers	790
List	Key facts about loopback interfaces	792
List	Information gathered by CDP	793
Table 33-3	Three CDP **show** commands that list information about neighbors	794

Key Terms You Should Know

log message, syslog server, Network Time Protocol (NTP), NTP client, NTP Client/Server Mode, NTP Server, NTP synchronization, CDP, LLDP

Command References

Tables 33-7 and 33-8 list configuration and verification commands used in this chapter. As an easy review exercise, cover the left column in a table, read the right column, and try to recall the command without looking. Then repeat the exercise, covering the right column, and try to recall what the command does.

Table 33-7 Configuration Command Reference

Command	Description
[no] logging console	Enables (or disables with the **no** option) logging to the console device.
[no] logging monitor	Enables (or disables with the **no** option) logging to users connected to the device with SSH or Telnet.
[no] logging buffered	Enables (or disables with the **no** option) logging to an internal buffer.
logging [host] *ip-address* | *hostname*	Enables logging to a syslog server.
logging console *level-name* | *level-number*	Sets the log message level for console log messages.
logging monitor *level-name* | *level-number*	Sets the log message level for log messages sent to SSH and Telnet users.
logging buffered *level-name* | *level-number*	Sets the log message level for buffered log messages displayed later by the **show logging** command.
logging trap *level-name* | *level-number*	Sets the log message level for messages sent to syslog servers.
[no] service sequence-numbers	Global command to enable or disable (with the **no** option) the use of sequence numbers in log messages.
clock timezone *name* *+−number*	Global command that names a timezone and defines the +/− offset versus UTC.
clock summertime *name* recurring	Global command that names a daylight savings time for a timezone and tells IOS to adjust the clock automatically.
ntp server *address* | *hostname*	Global command that configures the device as an NTP client by referring to the address or name of an NTP server.
ntp master *stratum-level*	Global command that configures the device as an NTP server and assigns its local clock stratum level.
ntp source *name/number*	Global command that tells NTP to use the listed interface (by name/number) for the source IP address for NTP messages.
interface loopback *number*	Global command that, at first use, creates a loopback interface. At all uses, it also moves the user into interface configuration mode for that interface.

Command	Description
[no] cdp run	Global command that enables and disables (with the **no** option) CDP for the entire switch or router.
[no] cdp enable	Interface subcommand to enable and disable (with the **no** option) CDP for a particular interface.
[no] lldp run	Global command to enable and disable (with the **no** option) LLDP for the entire switch or router.
[no] lldp transmit	Interface subcommand to enable and disable (with the **no** option) the transmission of LLDP messages on the interface.
[no] lldp receive	Interface subcommand to enable and disable (with the **no** option) the processing of received LLDP messages on the interface.

Table 33-8   Chapter 33 EXEC Command Reference

Command	Description
show logging	Lists the current logging configuration, and lists buffered log messages at the end.
terminal monitor terminal no monitor	For a user (SSH or Telnet) session, toggles on (**terminal monitor**) or off (**terminal no monitor**) the receipt of log messages, for that one session, if **logging monitor** is also configured.
[no] debug {*various*}	EXEC command to enable or disable (with the **no** option) one of a multitude of debug options.
show clock	Lists the time-of-day and the date per the local device.
show ntp associations	Shows all NTP clients and servers with which the local device is attempting to synchronize with NTP.
show ntp status	Shows current NTP client status in detail.
show interfaces loopback *number*	Shows the current status of the listed loopback interface.
show cdp | lldp neighbors [*type number*]	Lists one summary line of information about each neighbor; optionally, lists neighbors off the listed interface.
show cdp | lldp neighbors detail	Lists one large set of information (approximately 15 lines) for every neighbor.
show cdp | lldp entry *name*	Displays the same information as **show cdp|lldp neighbors detail** but only for the named neighbor.
show cdp | lldp	States whether CDP or LLDP is enabled globally, and lists the default update and holdtime timers.
show cdp | lldp interface [*type number*]	States whether CDP or LDP is enabled on each interface, or a single interface if the interface is listed.
show cdp | lldp traffic	Displays global statistics for the number of CDP or LDP advertisements sent and received.

33

CHAPTER 34

Device Security Features

This chapter covers the following exam topics:

1.0 Network Fundamentals

1.3 Describe the impact of infrastructure components in an enterprise network

1.3.a Firewalls

5.0 Infrastructure Management

5.4 Configure, verify, and troubleshoot basic device hardening

5.4.a Local authentication

5.4.b Secure password

5.4.c Access to device

5.4.c.1 Source address

5.4.c.2 Telnet/SSH

5.4.d Login banner

This chapter is all about preventing the wrong people from gaining access to your routers and switches. The focus here is not on the network itself, but the devices.

The first half of the chapter focuses on passwords. Earlier chapters introduced many of the configuration concepts related to login security. This chapter revisits those topics and takes the discussion a little deeper, particularly about how to create the most secure passwords possible.

The second half of the chapter discusses a wide variety of tools with the theme of keeping out the people who should not be in the router or switch. This section includes login banners, which should be set to tell unauthorized personnel to go away; preventing common methods of attack by disabling ports and services; and using ACLs to filter the address of the devices that attempt to log in to the router or switch.

"Do I Know This Already?" Quiz

Take the quiz (either here, or use the PCPT software) if you want to use the score to help you decide how much time to spend on this chapter. The answers are at the bottom of the page following the quiz, and the explanations are in DVD Appendix C and in the PCPT software.

Table 34-1 "Do I Know This Already?" Foundation Topics Section-to-Question Mapping

Foundation Topics Section	Questions
Securing IOS Passwords	1–3
Cisco Device Hardening	4–5

1. Imagine that you have configured the **enable secret** command, followed by the **enable password** command, from the console. You log out of the switch and log back in at the console. Which command defines the password that you had to enter to access privileged mode?

   a. enable password

   b. enable secret

   c. Neither

   d. The **password** command, if it's configured

2. Some IOS commands store passwords as clear text, but you can then encrypt the passwords with the **service password-encryption** global command. By comparison, other commands store a computed hash of the password, rather than storing the password. Comparing the two options, which one answer is the *most accurate* about why one method is better than the other?

   a. Using hashes is preferred because encrypted IOS passwords can be easily decrypted.

   b. Using hashes is preferred because of the large CPU effort required for encryption.

   c. Using encryption is preferred because it provides stronger password protection.

   d. Using encryption is preferred because of the large CPU effort required for hashes.

3. A network engineer issues a **show running-config** command and sees only one line of output that mentions the **enable secret** command, as follows:

   ```
   enable secret 5 $1$ZGMA$e8cmvkz4UjiJhVp7.maLE1
   ```

   Which of the following is true about users of this router?

   a. A user must type 1ZGMA$e8cmvkz4UjiJhVp7.maLE1 to reach enable mode.

   b. The router will hash the clear-text password that the user types to compare to the hashed password.

   c. A **no service password-encryption** configuration command would decrypt this password.

   d. The router will decrypt the password in the configuration to compare to the clear-text password typed by the user.

4. The following command was copied and pasted into configuration mode when a user was telnetted into a Cisco switch:

   ```
   banner login this is the login banner
   ```

   Which of the following is true about what occurs the next time a user logs in from the console?

   a. No banner text is displayed.

   b. The banner text "his is " is displayed.

   c. The banner text "this is the login banner" is displayed.

   d. The banner text "Login banner configured, no text defined" is displayed.

5. A single-line ACL has been added to a router configuration using the command **ip access-list 1 permit 172.16.4.0 0.0.1.255**. The configuration also includes the **ip access-class 1 in** command in VTY configuration mode. Which answer accurately describes how the router uses ACL 1?

   a. Hosts in subnet 172.16.4.0/23 alone can telnet into the router.

   b. CLI users cannot telnet from the router to hosts in subnet 172.16.4.0/23 alone.

   c. Hosts in subnet 172.16.4.0/23 alone can log in but cannot reach enable mode of the router.

   d. The router will only forward packets with source addresses in subnet 172.16.4.0/23.

Foundation Topics

Securing IOS Passwords

The ultimate way to protect passwords in Cisco IOS devices is to not store passwords in IOS devices. That is, for any functions that can use an external Authentication, Authorization, and Accounting (AAA) server, use it. However, it is common to store some passwords in a router or switch configuration, and this first section of the chapter discusses some of the ways to protect those passwords.

As a brief review, Figure 34-1 summarizes some typical login security configuration on a router or switch. On the lower left, you see Telnet support configured, with the use of a password only (no username required). On the right, the configuration adds support for login with both username and password, supporting both Telnet and SSH users. The upper left shows the one command required to define an enable password in a secure manner.

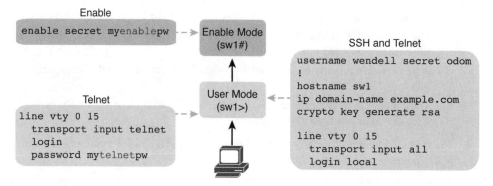

Figure 34-1 *Example Login Security Configuration*

The rest of this first section of the chapter discusses how to make these passwords secure. In particular, this section looks at ways to avoid keeping clear-text passwords in the configuration and storing the passwords in ways that make it difficult for attackers to learn the password.

Encrypting Older IOS Passwords with service password-encryption

Some older-style IOS passwords create a security exposure because the passwords exist in the configuration file as clear-text. These clear-text passwords might be seen in printed versions of the configuration files, in a backup copy of the configuration file stored on a server, or as displayed on a network engineer's display.

Cisco attempted to solve this clear-text problem by adding a command to encrypt those passwords: the **service password-encryption** global configuration command. This command encrypts passwords that are normally held as clear text, specifically the passwords for these commands:

password *password* (console or vty mode)

username *name* **password** *password* (global)

enable *name* **password** *password* (global)

To see how it works, Example 34-1 shows how the **service password-encryption** command encrypts the clear-text console password. The example uses the **show running-config | section line con 0** command both before and after the encryption; this command lists only the section of the configuration about the console.

Example 34-1   *Encryption and the* service password-encryption *Command*

```
Switch3# show running-config | section line con 0
line con 0
 password cisco
 login


Switch3# configure terminal
Enter configuration commands, one per line.   End with CNTL/Z.
Switch3(config)# service password-encryption
Switch3(config)# ^Z


Switch3# show running-config | section line con 0
line con 0
 password 7 070C285F4D06
 login
```

A close examination of the before and after **show running-config** command output reveals both the obvious effect and a new concept. The encryption process now hides the original clear-text password. Also, IOS needs a way to signal that the value in the **password** command lists an encrypted password, rather than the clear text. IOS adds the encryption or encoding type of "7" to the command, which specifically refers to passwords encrypted with the **service password-encryption** command. (IOS considers the clear-text passwords to be type 0; some commands list the 0, and some do not.)

Answers to the "Do I Know This Already?" quiz:

1 B **2** A **3** B **4** B **5** A

While the **service password-encryption** global command encrypts passwords, the **no service password-encryption** global command does not immediately decrypt the passwords back to their clear-text state. Instead, the process works as shown in Figure 34-2. Basically, after you enter the **no service password-encryption** command, the passwords remain encrypted until you change a password.

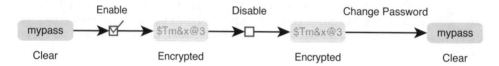

Figure 34-2 *Encryption is Immediate, Decryption Awaits Next Password Change*

Unfortunately, the **service password-encryption** command does not protect the passwords very well. Armed with the encrypted value, you can search the Internet and find sites with tools to decrypt these passwords. In fact, you can take the encrypted password from this example, plug it into one of these sites, and it decrypts to "cisco." So, the **service password-encryption** command will slow down the curious, but it will not stop a knowledgeable attacker.

Encoding the Enable Passwords with Hashes

In the earliest days of IOS, Cisco used the **enable password** *password* global command to define the password that users had to use to reach enable mode (after using the **enable** EXEC command). However, as just noted, the **enable password** *password* command stored the password as clear text, or was encrypted in a way that was easily decrypted.

Cisco solved the problem of only weak ways to store the password of the **enable password** *password* global command by making a more secure replacement: the **enable secret** *password* global command. However, both these commands exist in IOS even today. The next few pages look at these two commands from a couple of angles, including interactions between these two commands, why the **enable secret** command is more secure, along with a note about some advancements in how IOS secures the **enable secret** password.

Interactions Between Enable Password and Enable Secret

First, for real life: use the **enable secret** *password* global command, and ignore the **enable password** *password* global command. That has been true for around 20 years.

However, to be complete, Cisco has never removed the much weaker **enable password** command from IOS. So, on a single switch (or router), you can configure one or the other, both, or neither. What then does the switch expect us to type as the password to reach enable mode? It boils down to these rules:

Both commands configured: Users must use the password in the **enable secret** *password* command (and ignore the **enable password** *password* command).

Only one command configured: Use the password in that one command.

Neither command configured (default): Console users move directly to enable mode without a password prompt; Telnet and SSH users are rejected with no option to supply an enable password.

Making the Enable Secret Truly Secret with a Hash

Cisco's **enable secret** command protects the password value by never even storing the clear-text password in the configuration. However, that one sentence may cause you a bit of confusion: If the router or switch does not remember the clear-text password, how can the switch know that the user typed the right password after using the **enable** command? This section works through a few basics to show you how and appreciate why the password's value is secret.

First, by default, IOS uses a hash function called Message Digest 5 (MD5) to store an alternative value in the configuration, rather than the clear-text password. Think of MD5 as a rather complex mathematical formula. In addition, this formula is chosen so that even if you know the exact result of the formula—that is, the result after feeding the clear-text password through the formula as input—it is computationally difficult to compute the original clear-text password. Figure 34-3 shows the main ideas:

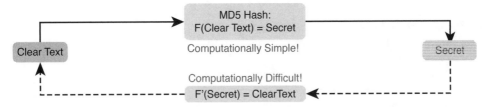

Figure 34-3   *One-Way Nature of MD5 Hash to Create Secret*

> **NOTE**   "Computationally difficult" is almost a code phrase, meaning that the designers of the function hope that no one is willing to take the time to compute the original clear text.

34

So, if the original clear-text password cannot be re-created, how can a switch or router use it to compare to the clear-text password typed by the user? The answer depends on another fact about these security hashes like MD5: Each clear-text input results in a unique result from the math formula.

The **enable secret fred** command generates an MD5 hash. If a user types "fred" when trying to enter enable mode, IOS will run MD5 against that value and get the same MD5 hash as is listed in the **enable secret** command, so IOS allows the user to access enable mode. If the user typed any other value besides "fred", IOS would compute a different MD5 hash than the value stored with the **enable secret** command, and IOS would reject that user's attempt to reach enable mode.

Knowing that fact, the switch can make a comparison when a user types a password after using the **enable** EXEC command as follows:

Step 1.   IOS computes the MD5 hash of the password in the **enable secret** command and stores the hash of the password in the configuration.

Step 2.   When the user types the **enable** command to reach enable mode, a password that needs to be checked against that configuration command, IOS hashes the clear-text password as typed by the user.

Step 3.   IOS compares the two hashed values: If they are the same, the user-typed password must be the same as the configured password.

As a result, IOS can store the hash of the password but never store the clear-text password; however, it can still determine whether the user typed the same password.

Switches and routers already use the logic described here, but you can see the evidence by looking at the switch configuration. Example 34-2 shows the creation of the **enable secret** command, with a few related details. This example shows the stored (hashed) value as revealed in the **show running-configuration** command output. That output also shows that IOS changed the **enable secret fred** command to list the encryption type 5 (which means the listed password is actually an MD5 hash of the clear-text password). The gobbledygook long text string is the hash, preventing others from reading the password.

Example 34-2   *Cisco IOS Encoding Password "cisco" as Type 5 (MD5)*

```
Switch3(config)# enable secret fred
Switch3(config)# ^Z
Switch3# show running-config | include enable secret

enable secret 5 $1$ZGMA$e8cmvkz4UjiJhVp7.maLE1

Switch3# configure terminal
Enter configuration commands, one per line.    End with CNTL/Z.
Switch3(config)# no enable secret
Switch3(config)# ^Z
```

The end of the example also shows an important side point about deleting the **enable secret** password: After you are in enable mode, you can delete the enable secret password using the **no enable secret** command, without even having to enter the password value. You can also overwrite the old password by just repeating the **enable secret** command. But you cannot view the original clear-text password.

NOTE   Example 34-2 shows another shortcut illustrating how to work through long **show** command output, this time using the pipe to the **include** command. The **| include enable secret** part of the command processes the output from **show running-config** to include only the lines with the case-sensitive text "enable secret."

Improved Hashes for Cisco's Enable Secret

The use of any hash function to encode passwords relies on several key features of the particular hash function. In particular, every possible input value must result in a single hashed value, so that when users type a password, only one password value matches each hashed value. Also, the hash algorithm must be computationally difficult (in other words, a pain in the neck) to compute the clear-text password based on the hashed value to discourage attackers.

As of the publication of this book in 2016, the MD5 hash algorithm has been around about 25 years. Over those years, computers have gotten much faster, and researchers have found creative ways to attack the MD5 algorithm, making MD5 less challenging to crack. That is, someone who saw your running configuration would have an easier time re-creating your clear-text secret passwords.

These facts are not meant to say that MD5 was bad, but like many cryptographic functions before MD5, progress was made, and new functions were needed. (In fact, the **enable secret** command's use of MD5 as its only hash algorithm spanned over 15 years.) Cisco has begun to improve the way that it encodes secret passwords in IOS. At press time, Cisco has added two newer security hashes for passwords to router IOS images, as noted in Figure 34-4.

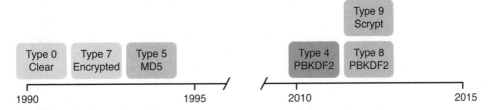

Figure 34-4 *Timeline of Encryptions/Hashes of Cisco IOS Passwords*

IOS now supports two alternative algorithm types in the more recent router IOS images. Both use an SHA-256 hash instead of MD5, but with some differences in the particulars of how each algorithm uses SHA-256. Table 34-2 shows the configuration of all three algorithm types on the **enable secret** command.

Table 34-2 Commands and Encoding Types for the **enable secret** Command

Command	Type	Algorithm
enable [algorithm-type md5] secret *password*	5	MD5
enable algorithm-type sha-256 secret *password*	8	SHA-256
enable algorithm-type scrypt secret *password*	9	SHA-256

Example 34-3 shows the **enable secret** being changed from MD5 to the scrypt algorithm. Of note, the example shows that only one **enable secret** command should exist between those three commands in Table 34-2. Basically, if you configure another **enable secret** command with a different algorithm type, that command replaces any existing **enable secret** command.

Example 34-3 *Cisco IOS Encoding Password "mypass1" as Type 9 (SHA-256)*

```
R1# show running-config | include enable
enable secret 5 $1$ZSYj$725dBZmLUJ0nx8gFPTtTv0
R1# configure terminal
Enter configuration commands, one per line.  End with CNTL/Z.
R1(config)# enable algorithm-type scrypt secret mypass1
R1(config)# ^Z
R1#
R1# show running-config | include enable
enable secret 9 $9$II/EeKiRW91uxE$fwYuOE5EHoii16AWv2wSywkLJ/KNeGj8uK/24B0TVU6
R1#
```

Following the process shown in the example, the first command confirms that the current **enable secret** command uses encoding type 5, meaning it uses MD5. Second, the user configures the password using algorithm type scrypt. The last command confirms that only one **enable secret** command exists in the configuration, now with encoding type 9.

34

Hiding the Passwords for Local Usernames

Cisco added the **enable secret** command back in the 1990s to overcome the problems with the **enable password** command. The **username password** and **username secret** commands have a similar history. Originally, IOS supported the **username** *user* **password** *password* command—a command that had those same issues of being a clear-text password or a poorly encrypted value. Many years later, Cisco added the **username** *user* **secret** *password* global command.

Today, the **username secret** command is preferred over the **username password** command; however, IOS does not use the same logic for the **username** command as it does for allowing both the **enable secret** plus **enable password** commands to exist in the same configuration. IOS allows

- Only one **username** command for a given username—either a **username** *name* **password** *password* command or a **username** *name* **secret** *password* command
- A mix of commands (**username password** and **username secret**) in the same router or switch

You should use the **username secret** command instead of the **username password** command when possible. However, the ICND2 book happens to include one case in which you still need to use the **username password** command because the router needs to know the clear-text password for a function of performing authentication over serial links.

Cisco Device Hardening

The term *device hardening* refers to making it more difficult for attackers to gain access to the device or to cause problems for the device. This section does not attempt to mention all such details, but it does touch on a few items. (Note that the CCNA Security certification gets into much more detail about router and switch device security.)

In particular, this second major section of the chapter begins by showing how to set some login banner message text for users. The next two topics look at how to secure items unused in the device—unused switch ports on switches and unused software services in both routers and switches. The final section examines how to secure login access based on filtering which user IP addresses can be used to log in to the switch or router using ACLs.

Configuring Login Banners

Cisco switches and routers can display a variety of banners to a new user when logging in to the switch or router. A banner is simply some text that appears on the screen for the user. You can configure a router or switch to display multiple banners, some before login and some after.

IOS supports three banners based on the first keyword in the **banner** command. Table 34-3 lists the three most popular banners and their typical use.

Table 34-3 Banners and Their Typical Use

Banner	Typical Use
Message of the Day (MOTD)	Used for temporary messages that can change from time to time, such as "Router1 down for maintenance at midnight."
Login	Because it is always shown before the user logs in, this message is often used to show warning messages, like "Unauthorized Access Prohibited."
Exec	Because this banner always appears after login, it typically lists device information that outsiders should not see but that internal staff might want to know, for example, the exact location of the device.

In what may seem like trivia, the banners actually appear in different places based on a couple of conditions. Figure 34-5 summarizes when the user sees each of these banners, reading from top to bottom. Console and Telnet users see the banners in the order shown on the left, and SSH users see the banners in the order on the right.

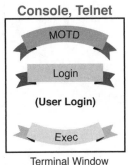
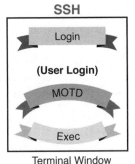

Figure 34-5 *Banner Sequence Compared: Console/Telnet Versus SSH (Blue Ribbon Set © Grounder)*

NOTE If using SSH, and the switch or router uses only SSHv1, the login banner is not shown to the SSH user.

The **banner** global configuration command can be used to configure all three types of these banners. In each case, the type of banner is listed as the first parameter, with **motd** being the default option. The first nonblank character after the banner type is called a beginning delimiter character. When a delimiter character is used, the banner text can span several lines, with the CLI user pressing Enter at the end of each line. The CLI knows that the banner has been configured as soon as the user enters the same delimiter character again.

Example 34-4 shows the configuration process for all three types of banners from Table 34-3, followed by a sample user login session from the console that shows the banners in use. The first configured banner in the example, the MOTD banner, omits the banner type in the **banner** command as a reminder that **motd** is the default banner type. The first two **banner** commands use a # as the delimiter character. The third **banner** command uses a Z as the delimiter, just to show that any character can be used. Also, the last **banner** command shows multiple lines of banner text.

Example 34-4 *Banner Configuration*

```
! Below, the three banners are created in configuration mode. Note that any
! delimiter can be used, as long as the character is not part of the message
! text.

SW1(config)# banner #
Enter TEXT message.    End with the character '#'.
(MOTD) Switch down for maintenance at 11PM Today #
SW1(config)# banner login #
Enter TEXT message.    End with the character '#'.
(Login) Unauthorized Access Prohibited!!!!
#
SW1(config)# banner exec Z
Enter TEXT message.    End with the character 'Z'.
(Exec) Company picnic at the park on Saturday.
 Don't tell outsiders!
Z
SW1(config)# end

! Below, the user of this router quits the console connection, and logs
! back in, seeing the motd and login banners, then the password prompt,
! and then the exec banner.

SW1# quit

SW1 con0 is now available

Press RETURN to get started.

(MOTD) Switch down for maintenance at 11PM Today
(Login) Unauthorized Access Prohibited!!!!

User Access Verification

Username: fred
Password:
(Exec) Company picnic at the park on Saturday.
 Don't tell outsiders!
SW1>
```

Securing Unused Switch Interfaces

The default settings on Cisco switches work great if you want to buy a switch, unbox it, plug it in, and have it immediately work without any other effort. Those same defaults have an unfortunate side effect for security, however. With all default configuration, an attacker might use unused interfaces to gain access to the LAN. So, Cisco makes some general recommendations to override the default interface settings to make the unused ports more secure, as follows:

- Administratively disable the interface using the **shutdown** interface subcommand.

- Prevent VLAN trunking by making the port a nontrunking interface using the **switchport mode access** interface subcommand.

- Assign the port to an unused VLAN using the **switchport access vlan** *number* interface subcommand.

- Set the native VLAN so that it is not VLAN 1 but instead is an unused VLAN, using the **switchport trunk native vlan** *vlan-id* interface subcommand. (Chapter 9, "Configuring Switch Interfaces," discusses the native VLAN in more detail.)

Frankly, if you just shut down the interface, the security exposure goes away, but the other tasks prevent any immediate problems if someone else comes around and enables the interface by configuring a **no shutdown** command.

Controlling Telnet and SSH Access with ACLs

When an external user connects to a router or switch using Telnet or SSH, IOS uses a vty line to represent that user connection. IOS can apply an ACL to those inbound connections by applying an ACL to the vty line, filtering the addresses from which IPv4 hosts can telnet or SSH into the router or switch.

For example, imagine that all the network engineering staff's devices connect into subnet 10.1.1.0/24. The security policy states that only the network engineering staff should be allowed to telnet or SSH into any of the Cisco routers in a network. In such a case, the configuration shown in Example 34-5 could be used on each router to deny access from IP addresses not in that subnet.

34

Example 34-5 *vty Access Control Using the* **access-class** *Command*

```
line vty 0 4
 login
 password cisco
 access-class 3 in
!
! Next command is a global command that matches IPv4 packets with
! a source address that begins with 10.1.1.
 access-list 3 permit 10.1.1.0 0.0.0.255
```

The **access-class** command refers to the matching logic in **access-list 3**. The keyword **in** refers to Telnet and SSH connections into this router—in other words, people telnetting into this router. As configured, ACL 3 checks the source IP address of packets for incoming Telnet connections.

IOS also supports using ACLs to filter outbound Telnet and SSH connections. For example, consider a user who first uses telnet or SSH to connect to the CLI, and now sits in user or enable mode. With an outbound vty filter, IOS will apply ACL logic if the user tries the **telnet** or **ssh** commands to connect *out of the local device* to another device.

To configure an outbound VTY ACL, use the **access-class** *acl* **out** command in VTY configuration mode. Once configured, the router filters attempts by current vty users to use the **telnet** and **ssh** commands to initiate new connections to other devices.

Of the two options—to protect inbound and outbound connections—protecting inbound connections is by far the more important and more common. However, to be complete, outbound VTY ACLs have a surprisingly odd feature in how they use the ACL. When the **out** keyword is used, the standard IP ACL listed in the **access-class** command actually looks at the *destination IP address*, and not the source. That is, it filters based on the device to which the **telnet** or **ssh** command is trying to connect.

Firewalls

Up to this point, this chapter has focused on securing the routers and switches used to build networks. The final few pages of this chapter examine one additional networking device— the firewall—explaining the basic function of a firewall and its role in an enterprise network.

Typical Location and Uses of Firewalls

Traditionally, a firewall sits in the forwarding path of all packets so that the firewall can then choose which packets to discard and which to allow through. By doing so, the firewall protects the network from different kinds of issues by allowing only the intended types of traffic to flow in and out of the network. In fact, in its most basic form, firewalls do the same kinds of work that routers do with ACLs, but firewalls can perform that packet-filtering function with many more options, as well as perform other security tasks.

Figure 34-6 shows a typical network design for a site that uses a physical firewall. The figure shows a firewall, like the Cisco Adaptive Security Appliance (ASA) firewall, connected to a Cisco router, which in turn connects to the Internet. All enterprise traffic going to or from the Internet would be sent through the firewall. The firewall would consider its rules and make a choice for each packet, whether the packet should be allowed through.

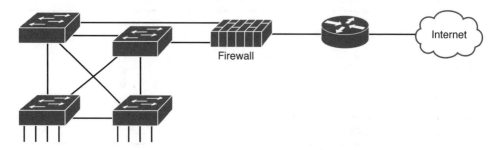

Figure 34-6 *Firewall as Positioned in the Packet Forwarding Path*

Although firewalls have some router-like features (such as packet forwarding and packet filtering), they provide much more advanced security features than a traditional router. For example, most firewalls can use the following kinds of logic to make the choice of whether to discard or allow a packet:

- Like router IP ACLs, match the source and destination IP addresses
- Like router IP ACLs, identify applications by matching their static well-known TCP and UDP ports

- Watch application-layer flows to know what additional TCP and UDP ports are used by a particular flow, and filter based on those ports

- Match the text in the URI of an HTTP request—that is, look at and compare the contents of what is often called the web address—and match patterns to decide whether to allow or deny the download of the web page identified by that URI

- Keep state information by storing information about each packet, and make decisions about filtering future packets based on the historical state information (called *stateful inspection*, or being a stateful firewall)

The stateful firewall feature provides the means to prevent a variety of attacks and is one of the more obvious differences between the ACL processing of a router versus security filtering by a firewall. Routers must spend as little time as possible processing each packet so that the packets experience little delay passing through the router. The router cannot take the time to gather information about a packet, and then for future packets, consider some saved state information about earlier packets when making a filtering decision. Because they focus on network security, firewalls do save some information about packets and can consider that information for future filtering decisions.

As an example of the benefits of using a stateful firewall, consider a simple denial of service (DoS) attack. An attacker can make this type of attack against a web server by using tools that create (or start to create) a large volume of TCP connections to the server. The firewall might allow TCP connections to that server normally, but imagine that the server might typically receive 10 new TCP connections per second under normal conditions and 100 per second at the busiest times. A DoS attack might attempt thousands or more TCP connections per second, driving up CPU and RAM use on the server and eventually overloading the server to the point that it cannot serve legitimate users.

A stateful firewall could be tracking the number of TCP connections per second—that is, recording state information based on earlier packets—including the number of TCP connection requests from each client IP address to each server address. The stateful firewall could notice a large number of TCP connections, check its state information, and then notice that the number of requests is very large from a small number of clients to that particular server, which is typical of some kinds of DoS attacks. The stateful firewall could then start filtering those packets, helping the web server survive the attack, whereas a stateless firewall or a router ACL would not have had the historical state information to realize that a DoS attack was occurring.

Security Zones

Firewalls not only filter packets, they also pay close attention to which host initiates communications. That concept is most obvious with TCP as the transport layer protocol, where the client initiates the TCP connection by sending a TCP segment that sets the SYN bit only (as seen in Figure 5-5 in Chapter 5, "Fundamentals of TCP/IP Transport and Applications").

Firewalls use logic that considers which host initiated a TCP connection by watching these initial TCP segments. To see the importance of who initiates the connections, think about a typical enterprise network with a connection to the Internet, as shown in Figure 34-7. The company has users inside the company who open web browsers, initiating connections to web servers across the Internet. However, by having a working Internet connection, that same company opens up the possibility that an attacker might try to create a TCP connection to the company's internal web servers used for payroll processing. Of course, the company does not want random Internet users or attackers to be able to connect to their payroll server.

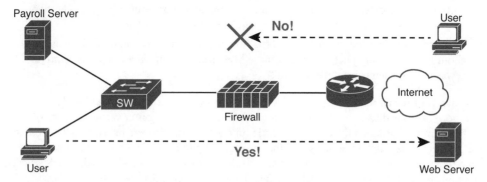

Figure 34-7 *Allowing Outbound Connections and Preventing Inbound Connections*

Firewalls use the concept of *security zones* (also called a *zone* for short) when defining which hosts can initiate new connections. The firewall has rules, and those rules define which host can initiate connections from one zone to another zone. Also, by using zones, a firewall can place multiple interfaces into the same zone, in cases for which multiple interfaces should have the same security rules applied. Figure 34-8 depicts the idea with the inside part of the enterprise considered to be in a separate zone compared to the interfaces connected toward the Internet.

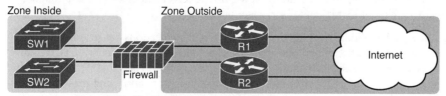

Figure 34-8 *Using Security Zones with Firewalls*

The most basic firewall rule when using two zones like Figure 34-8 reduces to this logic:

> Allow hosts from zone inside to initiate connections to hosts in zone outside, for a pre-defined set of safe well-known ports (like HTTP port 80, for instance).

Note that with this one simple rule, the correct traffic is allowed while filtering the unwant-ed traffic by default. Firewalls typically disallow all traffic unless a rule specifically allows the packet. So, with this simple rule to allow inside users to initiate connections to the out-side zone, and that alone, the firewall also prevents outside users from initiating connections to inside hosts.

Most companies have an inside and outside zone, as well as a special zone called the *demili-tarized zone (DMZ)*. Although the DMZ name comes from the real world, it has been used in IT for decades to refer to a firewall security zone used to place servers that need to be available for use by users in the public Internet. For example, Figure 34-9 shows a typical

Internet edge design, with the addition of a couple of web servers in its DMZ connected through the firewall. The firewall then needs another rule that enables users in the zone outside—that is, users in the Internet—to initiate connections to those web servers in the DMZ. By separating those web servers into the DMZ, away from the rest of the enterprise, the enterprise can prevent Internet users from attempting to connect to the internal devices in the inside zone, preventing many types of attacks.

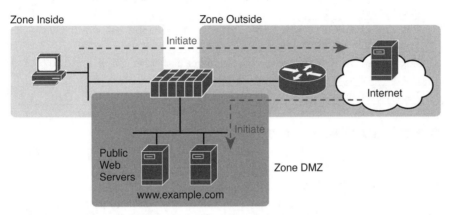

Figure 34-9   *Using a DMZ for Enterprise Servers That Need to Be Accessible from the Internet*

Chapter Review

One key to doing well on the exams is to perform repetitive spaced review sessions. Review this chapter's material using either the tools in the book, DVD, or interactive tools for the same material found on the book's companion website. Refer to the "Your Study Plan" element for more details. Table 34-4 outlines the key review elements and where you can find them. To better track your study progress, record when you completed these activities in the second column.

Table 34-4   Chapter Review Tracking

Review Element	Review Date(s)	Resource Used
Review key topics		Book, DVD/website
Review key terms		Book, DVD/website
Repeat DIKTA questions		Book, PCPT
Review memory tables		Book, DVD/website
Do labs		Blog
Review command tables		Book

Review All the Key Topics

Table 34-5   Key Topics for Chapter 34

Key Topic Element	Description	Page Number
List	Commands whose passwords are encrypted by **service password-encryption**	805
List	Rules for when IOS uses the password set with the **enable password** versus **enable secret** commands	806
List	Logic by which IOS can use the **enable secret** hash when a user types a clear-text password to reach enable mode	807
Figure 34-5	Banner messages	811

Key Terms You Should Know

Telnet, SSH, local username, login banner, message of the day, MD5 hash, device hardening

Command References

Tables 34-6, 34-7, and 34-8 list configuration and verification commands used in this chapter. As an easy review exercise, cover the left column in a table, read the right column, and try to recall the command without looking. Then repeat the exercise, covering the right column, and try to recall what the command does.

Table 34-6   Login Security Configuration Commands

Command	Mode/Purpose/Description
line console 0	Changes the context to console configuration mode.
line vty *1st-vty last-vty*	Changes the context to vty configuration mode for the range of vty lines listed in the command.
login	Console and vty configuration mode. Tells IOS to prompt for a password.
password *pass-value*	Console and vty configuration mode. Lists the password required if the **login** command is configured.
login local	Console and vty configuration mode. Tells IOS to prompt for a username and password, to be checked against locally configured **username** global configuration commands.
username *name* **secret** *pass-value*	Global command. Defines one of possibly multiple usernames and associated passwords, stored as a hashed value.
username *name* **password** *pass-value*	Global command. Defines a username and password, stored in clear text in the configuration by default.
crypto key generate rsa [modulus 512 | 768 | 1024]	Global command. Creates and stores (in a hidden location in flash memory) the keys required by SSH.
transport input {telnet | ssh | all | none}	vty line configuration mode. Defines whether Telnet and/or SSH access is allowed into this switch.

Command	Mode/Purpose/Description
[no] service password-encryption	Global command that encrypts all clear-text passwords in the running-config. The **no** version of the command disables the encryption of passwords when the password is set.
enable secret *pass-value*	Global command to create the enable password, stored as a hashed value instead of clear text.
enable password *pass-value*	Global command to create the enable password, stored as a clear text instead of a hashed value.
enable [algorithm-type md5 | sha-256 | scrypt] secret *pass-value*	Global command to create the enable password, stored as a hashed value instead of clear text, with the hash defined by the algorithm type.
no enable secret no enable password	Global command to delete the **enable secret** or **enable password** commands, respectively.

Table 34-7   Device Hardening Configuration Commands

Command	Mode/Purpose/Description
banner [motd | exec | login] *delimiter banner-text delimiter*	Global command that defines a banner that is displayed at different times when users log in to the switch or router.
shutdown	Interface subcommand that disables the interface.
switchport mode access	Interface subcommand on switches that makes the switch act as an access port and not act as a trunk port.
switchport access vlan *number*	Interface subcommand on switches that defines the access VLAN ID.
switchport trunk native vlan *number*	Interface subcommand on switches that defines the native VLAN ID used when trunking.
no cdp enable	Interface subcommand that disables CDP on that interface.
no cdp run	Global command that disables CDP globally.
access-class *number* | *name* in	A vty mode command that enables inbound ACL checks against Telnet and SSH clients connecting to the router.

Table 34-8   Chapter 34 EXEC Command Reference

Command	Purpose
show running-config | section vty	Lists the vty lines and subcommands from the configuration.
show running-config | section con	Lists the console and subcommands from the configuration.
show running-config | include enable	Lists all lines in the configuration with the word "enable."

34

CHAPTER 35

Managing IOS Files

This chapter covers the following exam topics:

5.0 Infrastructure Management

5.2 Configure and verify device management

    5.2.a Backup and restore device configuration

5.3 Configure and verify initial device configuration

5.5 Perform device maintenance

    5.5.a Cisco IOS upgrades and recovery (SCP, FTP, TFTP, and MD5 verify)

    5.5.b Password recovery and configuration register

    5.5.c File system management

Cisco has a wide and complex product catalog. The CCENT and CCNA R&S exams focus on two major branches of the product line: routers that run Cisco IOS software as the operating system (OS) and Catalyst LAN switches that also run IOS. While the IOS for each type of device has some differences, just because routers and switches perform different functions, IOS that runs on these switches and routers has many similarities. Within the exams, Cisco attempts to be generic in that the exam does not ask you to make distinctions between different models of routers and switches.

This chapter looks at some topics that again apply to IOS that runs in both Cisco routers and Cisco Catalyst switches. In particular, this chapter looks at the IOS itself: the file systems where the IOS stores files, how to upgrade IOS, and what happens when you reboot the router or switch to upgrade the IOS. This chapter also looks at how to manage configuration files beyond simply keeping them inside router or switch memory in the startup-config file. This chapter also includes a brief discussion about how to recover if you lose the password for a router or switch.

Note that this chapter focuses on features on Cisco routers. However, many of the same features work either exactly the same, or in a very similar way, on Cisco Catalyst switches.

"Do I Know This Already?" Quiz

Take the quiz (either here, or use the PCPT software) if you want to use the score to help you decide how much time to spend on this chapter. The answers are at the bottom of the page following the quiz, and the explanations are in DVD Appendix C and in the PCPT software.

Table 35-1 "Do I Know This Already?" Foundation Topics Section-to-Question Mapping

Foundation Topics Section	Questions
Managing Cisco IOS Images and Upgrades	1–4
Password Recovery	5
Managing Configuration Files	6–7

1. An engineer needs to put a new IOS image into a router's flash memory as part of an IOS upgrade. Which of the following could the engineer do to move files into the router?

   a. Use the **copy ftp flash** command to copy files into flash using FTP.

   b. Use the **copy flash tftp** command to copy files using TFTP into flash.

   c. Use the **copy scp flash** command to copy files into flash using SCP.

   d. Use the **ios restore** command to copy files into flash from the file archive.

2. What is the first step a typical Cisco router takes during the boot process when attempting to locate an operating system to load?

   a. The router looks for an image on a TFTP server.

   b. The router checks its configuration register boot field.

   c. The router boots to ROMMON.

   d. The router looks in flash memory for a Cisco IOS image file.

3. After your Cisco router boots, what is a simple way to verify the Cisco IOS image that was loaded and the location from which it was copied into RAM?

   a. **show running-config**

   b. **show boot**

   c. **show cisco ios**

   d. **show version**

4. Which value in the configuration register controls how the router boots?

   a. The third hexadecimal character

   b. The second hexadecimal character

   c. The first hexadecimal character

   d. The last hexadecimal character

5. You have forgotten your privileged mode password and cannot access global configuration mode. During the password recovery process, how can you change the configuration register if you cannot remember enough passwords to get into configuration mode of the router?

    a. Using ROMMON mode

    b. Using the Setup Utility

    c. Using the GUI for configuring the device

    d. Using password reset mode

6. What type of router memory is used to store the configuration used by the router when it is up and working?

    a. RAM

    b. ROM

    c. Flash

    d. NVRAM

7. An engineer has made dozens of configuration changes to a router's configuration in the previous hour. The engineer wants to revert back to a configuration that he had previously saved to an external FTP server. Which facilities would allow the engineer to go back to using the exact same running configuration that the router had an hour ago without reloading the router?

    a. Use the **copy ftp running-config** command

    b. Use the **copy ftp startup-config** command

    c. Use the **archive restore ftp** command

    d. Use the **config replace** command

Foundation Topics

Managing Cisco IOS Images and Upgrades

IOS exists as a file—a single file—that the router then loads into RAM to use as its operating system (OS). This first major section of the chapter works through the story of how to upgrade to a new version of IOS.

This first section has one primary purpose but many secondary purposes. Primarily, this section shows how to upgrade IOS on a router. As a secondary goal, this section works through a variety of small IOS features that engineers use during that upgrade process—features not covered in any detail until this point in the book. This section explains these topics, in order:

1. The IOS File System

2. Upgrading IOS Images

3. The Cisco IOS Boot Sequence

The IOS File System

Every OS creates file systems to store files. A computer needs some type of permanent storage, but it needs more than just a place to store bytes. The OS organizes the storage into a file system, which includes directories, structure, and filenames, with the associated rules.

By using a file system, the OS can keep data organized so the user and the applications can find the data later.

Every OS defines its own file system conventions. Windows OSs, for instance, use a left-leaning slash (\) in directory structures, like \Desktop\Applications. Linux and OS X use a right-leaning slash, for example, /Desktop. Each OS refers to physical disks slightly differently as well, and IOS is no different.

As for the physical storage, Cisco routers typically use flash memory, with no hard disk drive. Flash memory is rewriteable, permanent storage, which is ideal for storing files that need to be retained when the router loses power. Cisco purposefully uses flash memory rather than hard disk drives in its products because there are no moving parts in flash memory, so there is a smaller chance of failure as compared with disk drives. Some routers have flash memory on the motherboard. Others have flash memory slots that allow easy removal and replacement of the flash card, but with the intent that the card remain in the device most of the time. Also, many devices have USB slots that support USB flash drives.

For each physical memory device in the router, IOS creates a simple IOS file system (IFS) and gives that device a name. Example 35-1 lists the surprisingly long list of IOS file systems. Note that the entries of type *disk* and *usbflash* are the physical storage devices in that router. In this case, the router has one of two of the 2901's compact flash slots populated with a 256 MB flash card, and one of the two USB flash slots populated with an 8 GB USB flash drive. Look at the size column and prefixes column in the output to find these devices, based on their types as *disk* and *usbflash*.

Example 35-1   *Cisco IOS File Systems on a Router*

```
R2# show file systems
File Systems:


      Size(b)       Free(b)        Type  Flags  Prefixes
            -             -      opaque     rw   archive:
            -             -      opaque     rw   system:
            -             -      opaque     rw   tmpsys:
            -             -      opaque     rw   null:
            -             -     network     rw   tftp:
*   256487424      49238016        disk     rw   flash0: flash:#
            -             -        disk     rw   flash1:
       262136        253220       nvram     rw   nvram:
            -             -      opaque     wo   syslog:
            -             -      opaque     rw   xmodem:
            -             -      opaque     rw   ymodem:
            -             -     network     rw   rcp:
            -             -     network     rw   pram:
            -             -     network     rw   http:
            -             -     network     rw   ftp:
```

35

```
         -              -    network    rw    scp:
         -              -     opaque    ro    tar:
         -              -    network    rw    https:
         -              -     opaque    ro    cns:
   7794737152     7483719680  usbflash   rw    usbflash0:
74503236 bytes copied in 187.876 secs (396555 bytes/sec)
```

The example lists 20 different IOS file systems in this case, but the router does not have 20 different physical storage devices. Instead, IOS uses these file systems for other purposes as well, with these types:

- **Opaque:** To represent logical internal file systems for the convenience of internal functions and commands
- **Network:** To represent external file systems found on different types of servers for the convenience of reference in different IOS commands
- **Disk:** For flash
- **Usbflash:** For USB flash
- **NVRAM:** A special type for NVRAM memory, the default location of the startup-config file

Many IOS commands refer to files in an IFS, but only some commands refer directly to the files by their formal names. The formal names use the prefix as seen in the far right column of Example 35-1. For instance, the command **more flash0:/wotemp/fred** would display the contents of file *fred* in directory */wotemp* in the first flash memory slot in the router. (The **more** command itself displays the contents of a file.) However, many commands use a keyword that indirectly refers to a formal filename, to reduce typing. For example:

- **show running-config** command: Refers to file system:running-config
- **show startup-config** command: Refers to file nvram:startup-config
- **show flash** command: Refers to default flash IFS (usually flash0:)

Upgrading IOS Images

One of the first steps to upgrade a router's IOS to a new version is to obtain the new IOS image and put it in the right location. Typically, Cisco routers have their IOS in one of the local physical file systems, most often in permanent flash. The only requirement is that the IOS be in some reachable file system—even if the file sits on an external server and the device loads the OS over the network. However, the best practice is to store each device's IOS file in flash that will remain with the device permanently.

Figure 35-1 illustrates the process to upgrade an IOS image into flash memory, using the following steps:

Step 1.   Obtain the IOS image from Cisco, usually by downloading the IOS image from cisco.com using HTTP or FTP.

Step 2.   Place the IOS image someplace that the router can reach. Locations include TFTP or FTP servers in the network or a USB flash drive that is then inserted into the router.

Step 3.   Issue the **copy** command from the router, copying the file into the flash memory that usually remains with the router on a permanent basis. (Routers usually cannot boot from the IOS image in a USB flash drive.)

Figure 35-1   *Copying IOS Image as Part of the Cisco IOS Software Upgrade Process*

Copying a New IOS Image to a Local IOS File System Using TFTP

Example 35-2 provides an example of Step 3 from the figure, copying the IOS image into flash memory. In this case, Router R2, a 2901, copies an IOS image from a TFTP server at IP address 2.2.2.1.

Example 35-2   **copy tftp flash** *Command Copies the IOS Image to Flash Memory*

```
R2# copy tftp flash
Address or name of remote host []? 2.2.2.1
Source filename []? c2900-universalk9-mz.SPA.152-4.M1.bin
Destination filename [c2900-universalk9-mz.SPA.152-4.M1.bin ]?
Accessing tftp://2.2.2.1/c2900-universalk9-mz.SPA.152-4.M1.bin ...
Loading c2900-universalk9-mz.SPA.152-4.M1.bin from 2.2.2.1 (via GigabitEthernet0/1):
!!!!!!!!!!!!!!!!!!!!!!!!!!!!!!!!!!!!!!!!!!!!!!!!!!!!!!!!!!!!!!!!!!!!!!!!!!!!!!!!!!!!!!!!
!!!!!!!!!!!!!!!!!!!!!!!!!!!!!!!!!!!!!!!!!!!!!!!!!!!!!!!!!!!!!!!!!!!!!!!!!!!!!!!!!!!!!!!!
!!!!!!!!!!!!!!!!!!!!!!!!!!!!!!!!!!!!!!!!!!!!!!!!!!!!!!!!!!!!!!!!!!!!!!!!!!!!!!!!!!!!!!!!
!!!!!!!!!!!!!!!!!!!!!!!!!!!!!!!!!!!!!!!
[OK - 97794040 bytes]

97794040 bytes copied in 187.876 secs (396555 bytes/sec)
R2#
```

35

The **copy** command does a simple task—copy a file—but the command also has several small items to check. It needs a few pieces of information from the user, so the command prompts the user for that information by showing the user some text and waiting for the user's input. The bold items in the example show the user's input. The router then has to check to make sure the copy will work. The command works through these kinds of questions:

1. What is the IP address or host name of the TFTP server?

2. What is the name of the file?

3. Ask the server to learn the size of the file, and then check the local router's flash to ask whether enough space is available for this file in flash memory.

4. Does the server actually have a file by that name?

5. Do you want the router to erase any old files in flash?

The router prompts you for answers to some of these questions, as necessary. For each question, you should either type an answer or press **Enter** if the default answer (shown in square brackets at the end of the question) is acceptable. Afterward, the router erases flash memory if directed, copies the file, and then verifies that the checksum for the file shows that no errors occurred in transmission.

> **NOTE**   Most people use the IOS filenames that Cisco supplies because these names embed information about the IOS image, like the version. Also, if you want to use the same destination filename as the source, avoid the mistake of typing "y" or "yes" to confirm the selection; instead, you would be setting the destination filename to "y" or "yes." Simply press **Enter** to confirm the selection listed in brackets.

You can view the contents of the flash file system to see the IOS file that was just copied by using a couple of commands. The **show flash** command shows the files in the default flash file system (flash0:), as seen at the top of Example 35-3. Below it, the more general **dir flash0:** command lists the contents of that same file system, with similar information. (You can use the **dir** command to display the contents of any local IFS.)

Example 35-3   *Command Copies the IOS Image to Flash Memory*

```
R4# show flash
-#- --length-- -----date/time------ path
1    104193476 Jul 21 2015 13:38:06 +00:00 c2900-universalk9-mz.SPA.154-3.M3.bin
3      3000320 Jul 10 2012 00:05:44 +00:00 cpexpress.tar
4         1038 Jul 10 2012 00:05:52 +00:00 home.shtml
5       122880 Jul 10 2012 00:06:02 +00:00 home.tar
6      1697952 Jul 10 2012 00:06:16 +00:00 securedesktop-ios-3.1.1.45-k9.pkg
7       415956 Jul 10 2012 00:06:28 +00:00 sslclient-win-1.1.4.176.pkg
8         1153 Aug 16 2012 18:20:56 +00:00 wo-lic-1
9     97794040 Oct 10 2014 21:06:38 +00:00 c2900-universalk9-mz.SPA.152-4.M1.bin

49238016 bytes available (207249408 bytes used)


R4# dir flash0:
Directory of flash0:/

    1  -rw-   104193476  Jul 21 2015 13:38:06 +00:00 c2900-universalk9-mz.SPA.154-3.
                                                     M3.bin
    3  -rw-     3000320  Jul 10 2012 00:05:44 +00:00 cpexpress.tar
    4  -rw-        1038  Jul 10 2012 00:05:52 +00:00 home.shtml
    5  -rw-      122880  Jul 10 2012 00:06:02 +00:00 home.tar
    6  -rw-     1697952  Jul 10 2012 00:06:16 +00:00 securedesktop-ios-3.1.1.45-k9.
                                                     pkg
    7  -rw-      415956  Jul 10 2012 00:06:28 +00:00 sslclient-win-1.1.4.176.pkg
    8  -rw-        1153  Aug 16 2012 18:20:56 +00:00 wo-lic-1
    9  -rw-    97794040  Oct 10 2014 21:06:38 +00:00 c2900-universalk9-mz.SPA.152-4.
                                                     M1.bin

256487424 bytes total (49238016 bytes free)
```

Pay close attention to the memory usage per file and for the IFS as shown in the example. The output lists the size in bytes for each file. Note that the IOS file is about 104 MB.

Note that the size of the IOS file matches the size shown earlier in the TFTP transfer in Example 35-2. The end of each of the commands then lists the amount of space available for new files to be added to flash (one lists it as "bytes available"; the other as "bytes free"). However, that same ending line of each command shows slightly different information about usage: **show flash** lists the bytes used, whereas the **dir** command lists the total bytes (bytes used plus bytes free). Play around with the numbers in this example to make sure you know which command lists which particular total.

Verifying IOS Code Integrity with MD5

You download the IOS from Cisco, copy it to your router, and run it. Is it really the code from Cisco? Or did some nefarious attacker somehow get you to download a fake IOS that has a virus?

Cisco provides a means to check the integrity of the IOS file to prevent this type of problem. Figure 35-2 shows the basic mechanics of the process. First, when Cisco builds a new IOS image, it calculates and publishes an MD5 hash value for that specific IOS file. That is, Cisco uses as input the IOS file itself, runs the MD5 math algorithm against that file, producing a hex code. Cisco places that code at the download site for all to see. Then, you run that same MD5 math on your router against the IOS file on the router, using the IOS **verify** command. That command will list the MD5 hash as recalculated on your router. If both MD5 hashes are equal, the file has not changed.

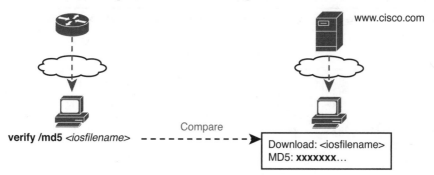

Figure 35-2 *MD5 Verification of IOS Images—Concepts*

The **verify /md5** command generates the MD5 hash on your router, as shown in Example 35-4. Note that you can include the hash value computed by Cisco as the last parameter (as shown in the example), or leave it off. If you include it, IOS will tell you if the locally computed value matches what you copied into the command. If you leave it out, the **verify** command lists the locally computed MD5 hash, and you have to do the picky character-by-character check of the values yourself.

Example 35-4 *Verifying Flash Memory Contents with the* **show flash** *Command*

```
R2# verify /md5 flash0:c2900-universalk9-mz.SPA.154-3.M3.bin a79e325e6c498b70829d4d
  b0afba5041
.........................................................................................
.........................................................................................
.....MD5 of flash0:c2900-universalk9-mz.SPA.154-3.M3.bin Done!
Verified (flash0:c2900-universalk9-mz.SPA.154-3.M3.bin) = a79e325e6c498b70829d4d
  b0afba5041
```

Copying Images with FTP

The networking world has many options for file transfer, several of which IOS supports for the transfer of files into and out of the IOS file systems that reside on the router. TFTP and FTP have been supported for the longest time, with more recent support added for protocols like SCP. Table 35-2 lists some of the names of file transfer protocols that you might come across when working with routers.

Table 35-2 Common Methods to Copy Files Outside a Router

Method	Method (Full Name)	Router's Role	Encrypted?
TFTP	Trivial File Transfer Protocol	Client	No
FTP	File Transfer Protocol	Client	No
SCP	Secure Copy Protocol	Server	Yes

To copy files with FTP, you follow the same kind of process you use with TFTP (see Example 35-5). You can follow the interactive prompts after using an EXEC command like **copy ftp flash**. However, the **copy** command allows you to use a URI for the source and/or destination, which lets you put most or all of the information in the command line itself. Each URI refers to the formal name of a file in the IFS.

Example 35-5 *Installing a New IOS with FTP*

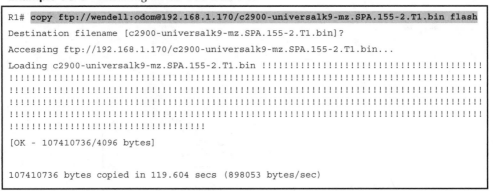

```
R1# copy ftp://wendell:odom@192.168.1.170/c2900-universalk9-mz.SPA.155-2.T1.bin flash
Destination filename [c2900-universalk9-mz.SPA.155-2.T1.bin]?
Accessing ftp://192.168.1.170/c2900-universalk9-mz.SPA.155-2.T1.bin...
Loading c2900-universalk9-mz.SPA.155-2.T1.bin !!!!!!!!!!!!!!!!!!!!!!!!!!!!!!!!!!!!!!!!
!!!!!!!!!!!!!!!!!!!!!!!!!!!!!!!!!!!!!!!!!!!!!!!!!!!!!!!!!!!!!!!!!!!!!!!!!!!!!!!!!!!!!!!!!!
!!!!!!!!!!!!!!!!!!!!!!!!!!!!!!!!!!!!!!!!!!!!!!!!!!!!!!!!!!!!!!!!!!!!!!!!!!!!!!!!!!!!!!!!!!
!!!!!!!!!!!!!!!!!!!!!!!!!!!!!!!!!!!!!!!!!!!!!!!!!!!!!!!!!!!!!!!!!!!!!!!!!!!!!!!!!!!!!!!!!!
!!!!!!!!!!!!!!!!!!!!!!!!!!!!!!!!!!!!!!!!!!!!!!!!!!!!!!!!!!!!!!!!!!!!!!!!!!!!!!!!!!!!!!!!!!
!!!!!!!!!!!!!!!!!!!!!!!!!!!!!!!!!!!!!!
[OK - 107410736/4096 bytes]

107410736 bytes copied in 119.604 secs (898053 bytes/sec)
```

First, take a close look at the long URI in the command that begins with "ftp". The "ftp" part identifies the protocol, of course. After the //, the text references the username (wendell) and password (odom), as well as the FTP server's IP address. After the single / comes the filename on the server.

Although the command is long, it has only two parameters, with the long first parameter and the short keyword **flash** as the second parameter. The **copy** command lists the source location as the first parameter and the destination as the second. The destination in this case, **flash**, is a keyword that refers to the default flash, typically flash0:, but it does not identify a specific filename. As a result, IOS prompts the user for a specific destination filename, with a default (in brackets) to keep the source filename. In this case, the user just pressed Enter to accept the default. To avoid being prompted at all, the command could have listed **flash:c2900-universalk9-mz.SPA.155-2.T1.bin** as that second parameter, fully defining the destination file.

Finally, with another twist, you can configure the FTP username and password on the router so that you do not have to include them in the **copy** command. For instance, the global configuration commands **ip ftp username wendell** and **ip ftp password odom** would have configured those values. Then the **copy** command would have begun with **copy ftp://192.168.1.170/...**, omitting the username:password in the command, without needing to then prompt the user for the username and password.

Copying Images with SCP

SSH Copy Protocol (SCP) provides a secure way to transfer files, but with a small twist as compared to other methods mentioned in this chapter: the router acts as the server, and you do not use the **copy** command on the router. Instead, you configure the router to act as an SCP server and then use an SCP client command or application on a desktop computer to transfer the files.

SCP uses SSH for two key parts of the work to securely transfer files: to authenticate the user and to encrypt all data transfer. SSH already does those tasks anyway, so SCP, defined after SSH was well established, simply relies on SSH to do those tasks. SCP then defines a method to transfer files.

To make SCP work on a router, the router first needs configuration to support SSH login as normal, as discussed in detail back in Chapter 8, "Configuring Basic Switch Management." Then you just need to change one command plus add another, as follows:

- Give the SSH user direct access to privileged mode by adding parameters to the **username** command, for example, **username fred privilege-level 15 password barney**.
- Enable the SCP server with the **ip scp server enable** global command.

> **NOTE** While this book does not go into details about IOS privilege levels, enable mode is considered to be privilege level 15. The **username privilege 15** command means that the user would be granted enable mode access at login, without first being placed into user mode.

Then to use SCP to transfer files, the network engineer must use an SCP client on some computer that has network connectivity to the router. You can search the web for SCP clients, many of which are integrated as part of SSH clients. However, for the purpose of transferring files with Cisco devices, a command-line SCP client may actually be the best choice.

Example 35-6 shows an SCP file copy with a router, using the Mac OS X built-in **scp** command. The command again copies an IOS file from the computer to the router, like the earlier examples. Note that it uses the full URI of the destination, with the username (wendell), router IP address (192.168.1.9), and IOS filename. The command then prompts the user for the password and begins transferring the file.

Example 35-6 *SCP Client IOS Copy from a Mac to a Router*

```
WO-iMac:Desktop wendellodom$ scp c2900-universalk9-mz.SPA.155-2.T1.bin
wendell@192.168.1.9:flash0:c2900-universalk9-mz.SPA.155-2.T1.bin
 Password:
c2900-universalk9-mz.SPA.155-2.T1.bin                100%  102MB 322.8KB/s
  05:25
```

35

Once you copy the IOS file into a local IOS file system on the router, you must **reload** the router to start using the new IOS. The next topic looks at the entire IOS boot process, including how to make a router start using the new version of IOS.

The Cisco IOS Software Boot Sequence

Cisco routers perform the same types of tasks that a typical computer performs when you power it on or reboot (reload) it. However, most end-user computers have a single instance of the OS installed, so the computer does not have to choose which OS to load. In contrast, a router can have multiple IOS images available both in flash memory and on external servers, so the router needs a process to pick which IOS image to load into RAM and use. This section examines the entire boot process, with extra emphasis on the options that impact a router's choice of what IOS image to load.

> **NOTE** Routers can load IOS or a special-purpose OS called ROMMON. ROMMON is used for special purposes like password recovery. ROMMON can be used to send and receive IP packets to load a new IOS, but it does not route packets. A third very old special-purpose OS, called RXBOOT, is no longer included in this book because it applies only to very old routers models.

When a router first powers on, it follows these four steps:

Step 1. The router performs a power-on self-test (POST) process to discover the hardware components and verify that all components work properly.

Step 2. The router copies a bootstrap program from ROM into RAM and runs the bootstrap program.

Step 3. The bootstrap program decides which IOS image (or the ROMMON OS) to load into RAM, and then the bootstrap program loads the OS. After loading the chosen OS image, the bootstrap program hands over control of the router hardware to the newly loaded OS.

Step 4. If the bootstrap program happened to load IOS, once IOS is running, it finds the startup-config file and loads it into RAM as the running-config.

All routers attempt all four steps each time the router is powered on or reloaded. The first two steps do not have any options to choose; either both of these steps succeed or the initialization fails. If it fails, you might need to call the Cisco Technical Assistance Center (TAC) for support. However, Steps 3 and 4 have several configurable options that tell the router what to do next, as noted in Figure 35-3.

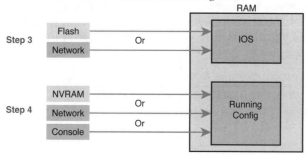

Figure 35-3 *Loading IOS and Initial Configuration*

As you can see, the router has options at both Steps 3 and 4 in the figure. However, at Step 4, routers almost always load the configuration from NVRAM (the startup-config file), when it exists. There is no real advantage to storing the initial configuration anywhere else except NVRAM, so this chapter does not look further into the options of Step 4. But there are reasonable motivations for keeping IOS images in flash and on servers in the network, so the rest of this section examines Step 3 in more detail.

The Configuration Register

A router's configuration register has an impact on a router's choice of which OS to load.

Routers use a *configuration register* to find some configuration settings at boot time, before the router has loaded IOS and read the startup-config file. The 16 bits (4 hex digits) in the configuration register set a variety of different parameters. For example, the console runs at a speed of 9600 bps by default, but that console speed is based on the default settings of a couple of bits in the configuration register. By changing specific bits in the configuration register, the next time the router boots, you can change the speed of the console line.

You can set the configuration register value with the **config-register** global configuration command. Engineers set the configuration register to different values for many reasons, but the most common are to help tell the router what IOS image to load, as explained in the next few pages, and in the password recovery process. For example, the global configuration command **config-register 0x2100** sets the value to hexadecimal 2100, which causes the router to load the ROMMON OS rather than IOS the next time the router is reloaded.

Interestingly, Cisco routers automatically save the new configuration register value when you press **Enter** at the end of the **config-register** command; you do not need to use the **copy running-config startup-config** command after changing the configuration register. However, the configuration register's new value has no effect until the next time the router is reloaded.

NOTE   On most Cisco routers, the default configuration register setting is hexadecimal 2102, which leaves the console speed at 9600 bps and tells the router to load an IOS image.

How a Router Chooses Which OS to Load

A router chooses the OS to load based on two factors:

- The last hex digit in the configuration register (called the *boot field*)
- Any **boot system** global configuration commands in the startup-config file

The boot field, the fourth hex digit in the configuration register, tells the router the initial instructions about what OS to try to load. The router looks at the boot field's value when the router is powered on or when reloaded. The boot field's value then tells the router how to proceed with choosing which OS to load.

NOTE   Cisco represents hexadecimal values by preceding the hex digits with 0x; for example, 0xA would mean a single hex digit A.

The process to choose which OS to load on modern Cisco routers happens as follows:

1. If boot field = 0, use the ROMMON OS.

2. If boot field = 1, load the first IOS file found in flash memory.

3. If boot field = 2-F:

   A. Try each **boot system** command in the startup-config file, in order, until one works.

   B. If none of the **boot system** commands work, load the first IOS file found in flash memory.

4. If all other attempts fail, load ROMMON, from which you can perform further steps to recover by copying a new IOS image into flash.

> **NOTE**   The actual step numbers are not important; the list is just numbered for easier reference.

The first two steps are pretty straightforward, but Step 3 then tells the router to look to the second major method to tell the router which IOS to load: the **boot system** global configuration command. This command can be configured multiple times on one router, with each new **boot system** command being added to the end of a list of **boot system** commands. Each command can point to different files in flash memory, and filenames and IP addresses of servers, telling the router where to look for an IOS image to load. The router tries to load the IOS images in the order of the configured **boot system** commands.

Both Step 2 and Step 3B refer to a concept of the "first" IOS file, a concept that needs a little more explanation. Routers number the files stored in flash memory, with each new file usually getting a higher and higher number. When a router tries Step 2 or Step 3B from the preceding list, the router looks in flash memory, starting with file number 1, and then file number 2, and so on, until it finds the lowest numbered file that happens to be an IOS image. The router then loads that file.

Interestingly, most routers end up using Step 3B to find their IOS image. From the factory, Cisco routers do not have any **boot system** commands configured; in fact, they do not have any configuration in the startup-config file at all. Cisco loads flash memory with a single IOS when it builds and tests the router, and the configuration register value is set to 0x2102, meaning a boot field of 0x2. With all these settings, the process tries Step 3 (because boot = 2), finds no **boot system** commands (because the startup-config is empty), and then looks for the first file in flash memory at Step 3B.

> **NOTE**   Routers do not search all flash file systems for an IOS image. The details vary depending on the router model, but routers consider one flash file system to be the default IOS file system to look for IOS images.

Figure 35-4 summarizes the key concepts behind how a router chooses the OS to load.

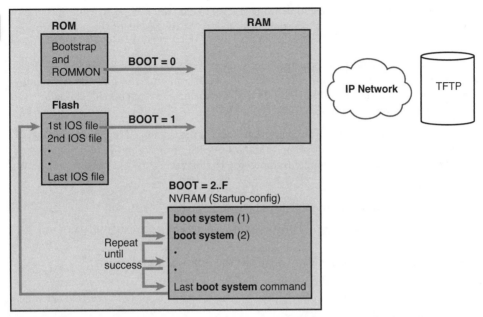

Figure 35-4 *Choices for Choosing the OS at Boot Time: Modern Cisco Router*

The **boot system** commands need to refer to the exact file that the router should load. Table 35-3 shows several examples of the commands.

Table 35-3 Sample **boot system** Commands

Boot System Command	Result
boot system flash	The first file from system flash memory is loaded.
boot system flash *filename*	IOS with the name *filename* is loaded from system flash memory.
boot system tftp *filename* **10.1.1.1**	IOS with the name *filename* is loaded from the TFTP server at address 10.1.1.1.

Finally, remember the process of upgrading the IOS? The whole point of the **boot system** commands and boot field of the configuration register is to control which IOS loads. Once a new IOS has been copied into flash memory on the router, the upgrade process has a few more steps. Add a **boot system** command to refer to the correct new file, save the configuration, and reload the router. The router will now go through the boot sequence discussed in this section, load the new IOS image, and the IOS upgrade is complete. For instance, Example 35-2 showed a router copying an IOS image into flash; that router would then also need a **boot system flash:c2900-universalk9-mz.SPA.152-4.M1.bin** command saved into the startup-config.

Verifying the IOS Image Using the show version Command

Once it is upgraded, you should verify the new IOS has loaded using the **show version** command. This command lists not only the version of software but also the source from which the router found the IOS image and the time since it loaded the IOS. As a result, the **show version** command actually identifies some key facts about the results of the previous boot process.

The **show version** command lists many other facts as well, as shown in Example 35-7. The example shows output from Router R2, which has been configured with the **boot system flash:c2900-universalk9-mz.SPA.152-4.M1.bin** command and been reloaded, migrating to use the new Version 15.2(4) IOS.

To help point out some of the many important facts in this command, the example shows many highlighted items. The following list describes each of the items in the output in the same order as they are shown in the example, top to bottom:

1. The IOS version

2. The uptime (the length of time that has passed since the last reload)

3. The reason for the last reload of IOS (reload command, power off/on, software failure)

4. The time of the last loading of IOS (if the router's clock has been set)

5. The source from which the router loaded the current IOS

6. The amount of RAM memory

7. The number and types of interfaces

8. The amount of NVRAM memory

9. The amount of flash memory

10. The configuration register's current and future setting (if different)

Key Topic

Example 35-7 show version *Command Output*

```
R2# show version
Cisco IOS Software, C2900 Software (C2900-UNIVERSALK9-M), Version 15.2(4)M1, RELEASE
  SOFTWARE (fc1)
Technical Support: http://www.cisco.com/techsupport
Copyright  1986-2012 by Cisco Systems, Inc.
Compiled Thu 26-Jul-12 20:54 by prod_rel_team

ROM: System Bootstrap, Version 15.0(1r)M15, RELEASE SOFTWARE (fc1)

R2 uptime is 44 minutes
System returned to ROM by reload at 19:44:01 UTC Tue Feb 12 2013
System restarted at 19:45:53 UTC Tue Feb 12 2013
System image file is "flash:c2900-universalk9-mz.SPA.152-4.M1.bin"
Last reload type: Normal Reload
Last reload reason: Reload Command

This product contains cryptographic features and is subject to United
States and local country laws governing import, export, transfer and

! Rest of legal disclaimer omitted
```

```
Cisco CISCO2901/K9 (revision 1.0) with 483328K/40960K bytes of memory.
Processor board ID FTX1628837T
2 Gigabit Ethernet interfaces
4 Serial(sync/async) interfaces
1 terminal line
DRAM configuration is 64 bits wide with parity enabled.
255K bytes of non-volatile configuration memory.
3425968K bytes of USB Flash usbflash1 (Read/Write)
250880K bytes of ATA System CompactFlash 0 (Read/Write)


License Info:

License UDI:

-------------------------------------------------
Device#    PID                      SN
-------------------------------------------------
*0         CISCO2901/K9             FTX1628837T


Technology Package License Information for Module:'c2900'
-----------------------------------------------------------------
Technology     Technology-package           Technology-package
               Current      Type            Next reboot
-----------------------------------------------------------------
ipbase         ipbasek9     Permanent       ipbasek9
security       None         None            None
uc             None         None            None
data           None         None            None

Configuration register is 0x2102
```

Password Recovery

Suppose that you are sitting at your desk and you try to Secure Shell (SSH) or Telnet to a router. However, you cannot log in. Or, you can get into user mode but not into enable mode because you forgot the **enable secret** password. You want to recover, or at least reset the passwords, so you can get into the router and change the configuration. What can you do?

Cisco provides a way to reset the passwords on a router when sitting beside the router. With access to the router console and the ability to power the router off and back on, anyone can reset all the passwords on the router to new values.

The details differ from router model to router model. However, if you go to www.cisco.com and search for "password recovery," within the first few hits you should see a master password recovery page. This page lists instructions on how to perform password recovery (actually password reset) for almost any model of Cisco product.

> **NOTE**   Cisco generally refers to the topic in this section as password recovery, but you do not actually recover and learn the password that you forgot. Instead, you change the password to a new value.

The General Ideas Behind Cisco Password Recovery/Reset

Although the details differ from model to model, all the password recovery procedures follow the same general principles. First, the end goal of the process is to make the router boot IOS while ignoring the startup-config file. Of course, this startup configuration holds all the passwords. Once the router boots while ignoring the initial configuration, the router has no passwords at all, so you can log in at the console with no password restrictions and reconfigure all the passwords.

One config-register bit holds the key: the ignore configuration bit. (The bit is the second bit in the third nibble, reading left to right.) When set to binary 1, the router will ignore the startup-config file the next time the router is loaded. To set that value, the default configuration register value of 0x2102 can be changed to 0x2142.

Unfortunately, under normal circumstances, you need to remember the enable password to reach the mode to configure the configuration register's value. When you need to do password recovery, you clearly do not know the passwords, so how can you change the configuration register? The solution is to use ROMMON mode.

ROMMON enables you to set the configuration register. ROMMON contains a small and different set of CLI commands as compared to IOS, with the commands varying from router model to router model. However, each router's ROMMON software supports some command, usually the **confreg** command, that lets you set the configuration register. For instance, the ROMMON command **confreg 0x2142** would set the correct bit to tell the router to ignore the startup-config file at reload.

So, how do you get the router to boot in ROMMON mode? Older routers require you to press the break key at the console during boot of the router. Some newer routers happen to have all removable flash memory—on those, just remove the flash (so there is no IOS available), and turn the router off and back on, and the router has no IOS to load—so it loads ROMMON. (Put the flash back in once ROMMON loads.)

In summary, the big ideas behind password recovery are as follows:

Step 1.   Boot ROMMON, either by breaking into the boot process from the console or by first removing all the flash memory.

Step 2.   Set the configuration register to ignore the startup-config file (for example, confreg 0x2142).

Step 3.   Boot the router with an IOS. The router boots with no configuration. Now you can reach enable mode from the console without needing any passwords.

A Specific Password Reset Example

Example 35-8 shows a sample password recovery/reset process on a 2901 router. The example begins with Router R1 powered on and the user connected at the console. These 2901 routers use compact flash slots for the primary flash memory; in this example, I removed the flash memory and rebooted the router so that the normal boot process caused ROMMON to load. Look at the highlighted steps in the example for the specific action that resets the password.

Example 35-8   *A Password Recovery/Reset Example*

```
! 1) User walks to the router and powers off the router


! 2) User removes all flash memory


! 3) User turns router back on again


System Bootstrap, Version 15.0(1r)M15, RELEASE SOFTWARE (fc1)
Technical Support: http://www.cisco.com/techsupport
Copyright  2011 by cisco Systems, Inc.


! 4) Several lines of messages omitted: ROMMON is initializing


Readonly ROMMON initialized

rommon 1> confreg 0x2142

You must reset or power cycle for new config to take effect
rommon 2 >
! 5) Just above, user sets the config register to ignore the startup-config.

! 6) User powers off router and then safely plugs the flash back in.

! 7) User powers on router, so that the router now boots IOS.


System Bootstrap, Version 15.0(1r)M15, RELEASE SOFTWARE (fc1)
Technical Support: http://www.cisco.com/techsupport
Copyright  2011 by cisco Systems, Inc.


! Lots of IOS initialization messages omitted; watch for these next messages



        --- System Configuration Dialog ---


Would you like to enter the initial configuration dialog? [yes/no]: no
```

35

```
Press RETURN to get started!


! 8) Just above, IOS asked the user if they wanted to do the initial config dialogue.
! That happens when a router boots with no startup config. That confirms the router
! booted and ignored startup-config. The user answered no, to avoid using setup.


! 9) Below, the console user logs in with no passwords required to reach enable mode.


Router>
Router>enable
Router#


! 10) Next, user copies the starting config to make the router do its normal job
Router# copy startup-config running-config
Destination filename [running-config]?
3297 bytes copied in 0.492 secs (6701 bytes/sec)


! 11) User changes the forgotten enable secret password, and sets config register back
! to the default setting of 0x2102
R1# configure terminal
Enter configuration commands, one per line.  End with CNTL/Z.
R1(config)# enable secret cisco
R1(config)# config-reg 0x2102
R1(config)# ^Z
R1#


! 12) User saves his changes to the password
R1# copy running-config startup-config
Destination filename [startup-config]?
3297 bytes copied in 0.492 secs (6701 bytes/sec)
R1#
```

Note that those last few steps are pretty important. Remember, this process makes the router boot with no initial configuration, so it is clearly disruptive to the normal working state of the router, even beyond the time required to work through the process. The **copy startup-config running-config** command makes up for the fact that the router ignored the startup-config file when it booted IOS. Also, to be ready for the next time the router reloads, put the configuration register value back to its normal permanent value, usually hex 2102.

> **NOTE**   When using this process, at the end, take the time to check the interface state of the router interfaces. The **copy running-config startup-config** command could result in some of the interfaces remaining in a shutdown state, depending on the current state of the cabling and the state of the connected devices. So, make sure to check and enable any interfaces with the **no shutdown** interface subcommand.

Managing Configuration Files

Cisco routers and switches happen to use two different configuration files: a startup-config file to save the configuration to use each time the device boots, and the running-config file that holds the currently used configuration for current use inside RAM. Chapter 6, "Using the Command-Line Interface," introduced those ideas, and by now, you should be used to changing the running-config file using configuration mode and saving the running-config using the **copy running-config startup-config** command.

This last of three major sections of the chapter takes the discussion of configuration files much further. It begins with a look at the traditional methods to copy configuration files outside the router or switch. It then examines more recent options to archive and restore the configuration. This section ends with a brief example of the setup process by which the router can build an initial configuration file.

Copying and Erasing Configuration Files

A good operational plan includes regular backup of the configuration files. The startup and running-config files reside in the router only, and that poses a risk. If the router configuration is never backed up to an external site and the router fails, then even after you replace the router hardware, you may have difficulty piecing a correct router configuration together based on old project notes.

The IOS **copy** command gives you a way to make a copy of the configuration, and has been around for a long time. This command lets you use any of the IFS references to network protocols, including TFTP, FTP, and SCP.

You can also just copy files to and from removable USB flash memory in the router. The USB slots on most recent models of Cisco routers allow you to insert and remove the USB flash drives with IOS running. For instance, a Cisco 2901 router has two USB flash drive slots (usbflash0: and usbflash1:). As demonstrated in Example 35-9, an engineer could easily copy the running-config file to flash.

Example 35-9   *Copying a File to USB Flash*

```
R1# copy running-config usbflash1:temp-copy-of-config
Destination filename [temp-copy-of-config]?
3159 bytes copied in 0.944 secs (3346 bytes/sec)


R1# dir usbflash1:
Directory of usbflash1:/

! lines listing other files omitted for brevity.
   74  -rw-        3159  Feb 12 2013 22:17:00 +00:00   temp-copy-of-config


7783804928 bytes total (7685111808 bytes free)
R1#
```

While useful in a lab, using USB flash to back up configuration files does not work well with thousands of devices spread around many sites. More than likely, you would back up the files to a more centralized server over the network. The next topic looks at the overall backup and restore plan for systematically backing up configurations.

Traditional Configuration Backup and Restore with the copy Command

One primary motivation of copying the configuration to an external server is to then later restore the configuration if a problem occurs. Like any backup and restore process, the configuration restore process is just as important as backing up the configuration. However, the IOS **copy** command, which has been in IOS for a long time, has an odd behavior when copying files to the running config file to restore the configuration. That odd behavior impacts how to restore the configuration rather than how to back up the configuration.

The **copy** command does not replace the running-config file when copying a configuration into RAM. Effectively, any copy into the running-config file works just as if you entered the commands in the "from" configuration file while in configuration mode. In some cases, adding the new commands does actually replace the old command; for instance, the **ip address** interface subcommand would simply replace the old value. However, with other commands, the command would not replace the old configuration but add to it instead (for instance, with IP **access-list** commands), creating a different configuration.

To drive the point home with a few examples, Figure 35-5 shows the cases that result in a replacement of the configuration versus an addition to the configuration. The figure shows commands to copy to and from a TFTP server. Note that the two commands with an asterisk beside them are the ones that effectively add the configuration.

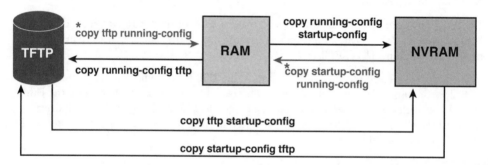

Figure 35-5   *Copy into RAM (running-config) Adds Configuration Instead of Replacing*

Because of the effect of copying configurations into the running-config file, the restore process basically avoids using the **copy** command to copy a backup configuration file into running-config. The complete process, using the **copy** command, to both back up and restore configurations, works like this:

Step 1.   To back up: Copy the running-config file to some external server; for instance, **copy running-config tftp**.

Step 2.   To restore:

  A. Copy the backup configuration into the startup-configuration file using the **copy** command, which replaces the startup-config file; for instance, **copy tftp startup-config**.

  B. Issue the **reload** command, which reloads, or reboots, the router. That process erases all running config in RAM and then copies the startup-config into RAM as part of the reload process.

Alternatives for Configuration Backup and Restore

Cisco has improved the backup and restore process over the years beyond the basic capabilities of the IOS **copy** command. Two improvements stand out as compared to the use of the **copy** command:

- Create backup configurations, called *archives*, based on the use of the **archive** EXEC command. Archives can be created by command, based on a configured timer, or automatically created each time someone saves the configuration.

- Perform a restore of the archived configuration to the running-config file without requiring a reload by using the **configure replace** command.

The archival process revolves around an IOS file system called the archive. The router just needs to know where to store these configuration files. The router also needs to know whether or not to save the configuration archives automatically. Those rules define the archive—when to automatically save the configuration and where to save them. Example 35-10 shows a sample archive configuration, in which the router defines an FTP server at address 192.168.1.170 as the place to store the configurations, with username wendell and password odom. It also defines automatic backup every 1,440 minutes (that is, daily) and stores a copy of the configuration every time the configuration is saved (per the **write-memory** subcommand).

Example 35-10 *Creating a Configuration Archive*

```
R1# configure terminal
Enter configuration commands, one per line.  End with CNTL/Z.
R1(config)# archive
R1(config-archive)# path ftp://wendell:odom@192.168.1.170/
R1(config-archive)# time-period 1440
R1(config-archive)# write-memory
R1(config-archive)# ^Z
R1#
```

35

NOTE IOS originally used the **write memory** EXEC command to save the configuration; that command was replaced by the **copy running-config startup-config** command. The **archive** feature's **write-memory** command appears to refer to this old EXEC command.

The configuration in the example makes a great improvement over using the **copy** command. First, it improves backups by backing up the configuration automatically. It also improves the restore process because of the **configure replace** command. Basically, the **configure replace** command allows you to copy a configuration archive into the running-config file, so it completely replaces the running-config without requiring a reload of the router. Basically, the router analyzes all the configuration, does a series of comparisons, and determines what sequence of configuration commands would be required to change the configuration correctly—all without reloading the router.

To show the process, Example 35-11 shows a sequence in which a router does not have an ACL (141) at the time the archive is made. Then the user changes the configuration to add an ACL 141. Next, the **configure replace** command is used to restore the earlier archived configuration (which doesn't have ACL 141). Because the restore should replace the running-config file, the running-config should no longer have ACL 141 at the end of the process. The example also shows the hostname being changed as a more obvious confirmation that the **configure replace** command changed the configuration.

Example 35-11 *Replacing the Running-config with the* **configure replace** *Command*

```
R1# archive config
Writing -Oct-24-09-46-43.165-2
R1# show archive
The maximum archive configurations allowed is 10.
The next archive file will be named ftp://wendell:odom@192.168.1.170/-<timestamp>-3
 Archive #  Name
    1          ftp://wendell:odom@192.168.1.170/-Oct-24-09-21-38.865-0
    2          ftp://wendell:odom@192.168.1.170/-Oct-24-09-22-22.561-1
    3          ftp://wendell:odom@192.168.1.170/-Oct-24-09-46-43.165-2 <- Most Recent

R1# configure terminal
Enter configuration commands, one per line.  End with CNTL/Z.
R1(config)# hostname ridiculousname
ridiculousname(config)# access-list 141 permit ip host 2.2.2.2 host 3.3.3.3
ridiculousname(config)# ^Z
ridiculousname#
*Oct 24 09:47:57.189: %SYS-5-CONFIG_I: Configured from console by console

ridiculousname# configure replace ftp://wendell:odom@192.168.1.170/
  -Oct-24-09-46-43.165-2
This will apply all necessary additions and deletions
to replace the current running configuration with the
contents of the specified configuration file, which is
assumed to be a complete configuration, not a partial
configuration. Enter Y if you are sure you want to proceed. ? [no]: y
Loading -Oct-24-09-46-43.165-2 !
[OK - 6498/4096 bytes]

Loading -Oct-24-09-46-43.165-2 !
Total number of passes: 1
Rollback Done

R1# show access-list 141
R1#
```

Note that by the end of the example, the hostname has reverted back to the original name (R1) and ACL 141 is no longer configured, as expected.

Erasing Configuration Files

IOS supports three different commands to erase the startup-config file in NVRAM. The **write erase** and **erase startup-config** commands are older, whereas the **erase nvram:** command is the more recent, and recommended, command.

Note that Cisco IOS does not have a command that erases the contents of the running-config file. To clear out the running-config file, simply erase the startup-config file; then **reload** the router so that the router loads an empty startup-config file into the running-config.

Initial Configuration (Setup Mode)

Cisco IOS software supports two primary methods of giving a router or switch an initial basic configuration: configuration mode and setup mode. Setup mode leads a switch administrator through a basic configuration by using questions that prompt the administrator. Because configuration mode is required for most configuration tasks, most networking personnel quickly get comfortable with configuration mode and do not use setup at all. However, new users sometimes like to use setup mode, particularly until they become more familiar with the CLI configuration mode.

Just so you know how to get to setup mode, an engineer can get into setup mode in two ways. Figure 35-6 shows one of the methods that occurs during the boot process: If the router boots, with no initial configuration, the router asks if the user wants to enter the "initial configuration dialogue," also known simply as setup mode. You can also enter setup mode by using the **setup** command from privileged mode.

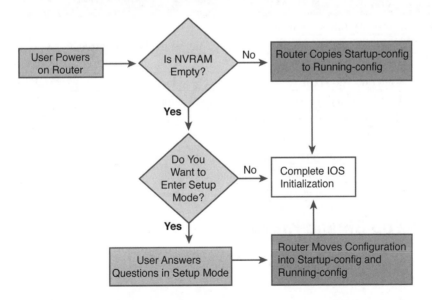

Figure 35-6 *Logic and Decisions for Entering Setup Mode After Reload*

35

> **NOTE** Example 35-8, earlier in this chapter, showed the password recovery process. That process caused a router to boot while ignoring the initial configuration, causing the router to ask the user the question shown in Figure 35-6.

Chapter Review

One key to doing well on the exams is to perform repetitive spaced review sessions. Review this chapter's material using either the tools in the book, DVD, or interactive tools for the same material found on the book's companion website. Refer to the "Your Study Plan" element for more details. Table 35-4 outlines the key review elements and where you can find them. To better track your study progress, record when you completed these activities in the second column.

Table 35-4 Chapter Review Tracking

Review Element	Review Date(s)	Resource Used
Review key topics		Book, DVD/website
Review key terms		Book, DVD/website
Repeat DIKTA questions		Book, PCPT
Review memory tables		Book, DVD/website
Review command tables		Book

Review All the Key Topics

Table 35-5 Key Topics for Chapter 35

Key Topic	Description	Page
Example 35-4	The **verify /md5** command	827
List	Additional configuration beyond SSH support to also support SCP	829
List	Router boot process steps	830
List	Router decision process to choose the OS to load	832
Figure 35-4	Router OS load decision process in graphical form	833
Example 35-7	The **show version** command and its many key facts	834
List	General password reset process	836
List	Traditional configuration backup and restore steps	840
List	Newer IOS configuration backup and restore steps	841
Example 35-11	Sample use of the newer IOS backup and restore process	842

Key Terms You Should Know

boot field, configuration register, IOS image, ROMMON, startup-config file, running-config file, setup mode, IOS, ROM, flash memory, NVRAM, IOS File System, code integrity, configuration archive, SCP

Command References

Tables 35-6 and 35-7 list configuration and verification commands used in this chapter. As an easy review exercise, cover the left column in a table, read the right column, and try to recall the command without looking. Then repeat the exercise, covering the right column, and try to recall what the command does.

Table 35-6   Chapter 35 Configuration Commands

Command	Mode and Purpose
config-register *value*	Global command that sets the hexadecimal value of the configuration register.
boot system {*file-uri* | *filename*}	Global command that identifies an externally located IOS image using a URI.
boot system flash [*flash-fs*:] [*filename*]	Global command that identifies the location of an IOS image in flash memory.
boot system {tftp | ftp} *filename* [*ip-address*]	Global command that identifies an external server, protocol, and filename to use to load an IOS from an external server.
archive	Global command that moves the user into archive mode.
write-memory	Archive mode command to tell the router to archive the configuration each time the configuration is saved to startup-config.
time-period *minutes*	Archive mode command to define the time between the automatic creation of a new configuration archive.
path *uri*	Archive mode command that defines where to store configurations.
ip ftp username *name*	Global command to define the username used when referencing the **ftp:** IOS file system but not supplying a username.
ip ftp password *pass*	Global command to define the password used when referencing the **ftp:** IOS file system but not supplying a password.
username *name* privilege-level 15 secret *pass*	Global command to define a username useful to SCP with a privilege level that enables SCP file transfers.

35

Table 35-7   Chapter 35 EXEC Command Reference

Command	Purpose
reload	Enable mode EXEC command that reboots the switch or router.
copy *from-location to-location*	Enable mode EXEC command that copies files from one file location to another. Locations include the startup-config and running-config files, files on TFTP and RPC servers, and flash memory.
copy running-config startup-config	Enable mode EXEC command that saves the active config, replacing the startup-config file used when the switch initializes.
copy startup-config running-config	Enable mode EXEC command that merges the startup-config file with the currently active config file in RAM.
show running-config	Lists the contents of the running-config file.
write erase erase startup-config erase nvram:	Each one of the three enable mode EXEC commands erases the startup-config file.
setup	Enable mode EXEC command that places the user in setup mode, in which Cisco IOS asks the user for input on simple switch configurations.
show flash	Lists the names and size of the files in flash memory, as well as noting the amount of flash memory consumed and available.
dir *filesystem:* dir *filesystem:directory*	Lists the files in the referenced file system, or file system directory.
verify /md5 *filesystem:name* *[MD5-hash]*	Performs an MD5 hash of the referenced file and displays the results. If listed, the command compares the MD5 hash in the command with the results of performing MD5 on the local file.
archive config	Creates a copy of the running-config file in the archive.
configure replace *filesystem:name*	Copies the referenced file into running-config, replacing the running-config, without reloading the router.

CHAPTER 36

IOS License Management

This chapter covers the following exam topics:

5.0 Infrastructure Management

5.2 Configure and verify device management

5.2.c Licensing

Over its long history, Cisco has used a few different strategies with how it manages licenses for its router and switch products. This chapter focuses on the most commonly used methods for the Cisco installed base of products at the time that Cisco released the current exams. This license method is often called PAK licensing because the licensing process uses a value called a product authorization key (PAK). This chapter also briefly introduces the earlier licensing methods and the new emerging licensing method that will replace PAK licensing over time, just for perspective.

This chapter also guides you through the process of verifying your current licensing on a router, installing a new license, activating a license code, and backing up and uninstalling licensing from a device.

"Do I Know This Already?" Quiz

Take the quiz (either here, or use the PCPT software) if you want to use the score to help you decide how much time to spend on this chapter. The answers are at the bottom of the page following the quiz, and the explanations are in DVD Appendix C and in the PCPT software.

Table 36-1 "Do I Know This Already?" Foundation Topics Section-to-Question Mapping

Foundation Topics Section	Questions
IOS Packaging	1
IOS Software Activation with Universal Images	2–5

1. Imagine a Cisco router model X. Cisco produced IOS software for this model of router such that its customer could pay for baseline features, additional data features, additional voice features, and additional security features. With this traditional method of software production from Cisco, for a single IOS version, how many IOS images would be available for this one router model X?

   a. 1

   b. 2

   c. 3

   d. >3

2. What is the name of the new Cisco IOS image file that provides access to all major IOS features?

   a. Universal

   b. Full

   c. Complete

   d. Enhanced

3. What command enables you to show the UDI of your Cisco router?

   a. show udi

   b. show license udi

   c. show base udi

   d. show udi base

4. Which of the following answers lists a CLI command on a router that is useful when installing a paid-for technology package license onto a 2901 router that uses Cisco IOS licensing and an IOS universal image?

   a. license boot module c2900 technology-package *technology-package*

   b. license boot module technology-package *technology-package* install

   c. license install *url technology-package*

   d. license install *url*

5. Which of the following answers lists a CLI command on a router that is useful when installing a right-to-use license onto a 2901 router that uses Cisco IOS licensing and an IOS universal image?

   a. license boot module c2900 technology-package *technology-package*

   b. license boot module technology-package *technology-package* install

   c. license install *url technology-package*

   d. license install *url*

Foundation Topics

IOS Packaging

Cisco builds the Cisco Internetwork Operating System (IOS) software as a single file. Using a single file makes installation of a new IOS simple: You download the one file from Cisco, copy it to flash memory on the router, and then take steps to make sure the router boots the next time using the new IOS image.

Cisco continues to build the IOS as a single file today but has changed what it includes in the IOS image files. This section looks at both the old and new methodologies for constructing images. This chapter also covers the new IOS licensing features that enable a router to use different parts of the IOS.

IOS Images per Model, Series, and per Software Version/Release

Since the early days of Cisco, back in the 1980s, through about the first 10 years of this century, Cisco created each IOS image for a particular router model, version and release, and feature set.

First, Cisco needed different IOS images for different router models, or at least for different router families, because of hardware differences. A low-end router with limited physical interfaces needed different software to support its interfaces than a high-end router that supported many different types of interface cards. Also, different router models often used different processors, so Cisco compiled different IOS images for use on those different processors.

Second, Cisco needed different IOS images for each new version or release of Cisco IOS software. Cisco identifies major revisions to Cisco IOS software using the term *version*, with smaller changes to IOS being called a *release*. However, Cisco did not use a model in which you install the IOS as one file and then add bug fixes as separate files. Instead, to add a bug fix, to move to a new release, or to move to a new version, you had to get a whole new IOS file from Cisco and then install and use the file on your routers. While this process is not necessarily difficult (as you learned in Chapter 35, "Managing IOS Files"), it does provide administrative overhead as it needs to be planned for carefully.

Figure 36-1 shows a conceptual view of how Cisco ended up with many IOS images for each router. Routers had different IOS images for each router model or model series and, within each model series, different IOS files for each version of the software. For instance, the Cisco 2800 series had one set of IOS images for the 2801 router and another set for the other three routers in that series. For the 2801, for each new release, Cisco created and made available a whole new IOS file, posted for download at Cisco.com.

Answers to the "Do I Know This Already?" quiz:

1 D **2** A **3** B **4** D **5** A

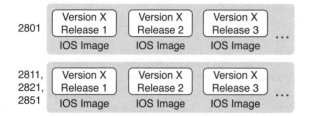

Figure 36-1 *IOS Images per Model or Model Series, per Version/Release*

Original Packaging: One IOS Image per Feature Set Combination

In addition, Cisco created one image for each combination of IOS feature sets that was allowed on a router. A *feature set* is a group of related IOS features. For instance, voice features in a router would be in one feature set, whereas security features, like an intrusion prevention system (IPS), would be in a security feature set.

The feature set concept has a very basic business motivation: pricing. Customers who want fewer features want to pay less. Cisco desired more flexible pricing depending on the needs of a customer.

Using feature sets means that Cisco has to build even more IOS images. Not only did Cisco need one IOS image per model (or model series), per IOS version and even for each release, Cisco needed a different image per combination of feature sets.

To understand the point, Figure 36-2 shows a conceptual view of seven IOS images. Each is for the same model of router for the same software version/release. All the images have the same basic IP functions. Some have additional feature sets as well. And although the figure shows seven options to make the point, the number of combinations in the figure is far smaller than the real number of feature set combinations for a typical router model.

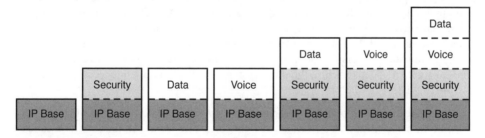

Figure 36-2 *Old IOS Image Packaging: Different Images with Different Feature Sets*

For example, suppose you want to use a particular security feature that requires the Security feature set. You could choose to purchase any of the four IOS images with the highlighted Security feature set. If you did not want any advanced IP features, or voice features, you could avoid the IOS images on the right, which would be a little more expensive because of the number of feature sets included.

New IOS Packaging: One Universal Image with All Feature Sets

Cisco changed around 2008 or so (with a long transition) to use a different IOS packaging model, a model that uses a universal image. The term *universal image* means "all feature sets." Basically, instead of the old model of one image per feature set combination, as in

Figure 36-2, Cisco builds one universal image with all feature sets. There would still be a different universal image per router model or model series, per version/release, just not a different image for different feature sets.

For example, if a router supported the IP Base features, plus Voice, Security, and an advanced IP feature set, Cisco would produce one universal image with all those features for each router model/series and for each version/release. Figure 36-3 shows an example of one image containing the IP Base, Security, Voice, Data, and Video features.

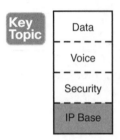

Figure 36-3 *Universal Image: One Image Holds All Features*

IOS Software Activation with Universal Images

From the beginning of Cisco as a company in the late 1980s, until the late 2000s, Cisco permitted anyone to download any IOS image for any Cisco router. This download process required you to click that you agree with the company's terms of use. However, anyone could get the IOS images, and the images worked on real Cisco gear. There was no mechanism to confirm that the person installing the IOS file into the router had the right to do so.

Cisco policies worked well for trustworthy customers, but as you would probably guess, it opened up the possibility of people misusing Cisco IOS software. For instance, companies could buy used Cisco hardware, download the latest Cisco IOS software, and use it—in spite of that usage breaking the Cisco terms of use and in spite of not having paid Cisco anything for the use of the software. Or, customers could choose to avoid paying for the rights to download new versions of Cisco IOS versions, through a Cisco service agreement (often called SMARTnet), because the older system allowed most anyone to download newer software.

Around the late 2000s Cisco introduced a new process that verified the rights of the user to download the software and also verified the right for the device to run the software (called software licensing). Cisco introduced these features in routers around the time Cisco introduced the 1900, 2900, and 3900 series of Cisco routers (called Integrated Services Routers Generation 2, or ISR G2 routers).

First, to protect software downloads, Cisco checks users' rights when they try to download the software. An individual user's profile lists a company, and if that company has paid for a current service agreement that allows software downloads for a particular model of device, the user can indeed download the software. Otherwise, the Cisco download site rejects the attempt to download the software.

Second, the devices need to activate the software to allow long-term use of the IOS image. This idea is simple: To use the feature sets embedded in the universal image, you must unlock the feature set using a software activation process defined by Cisco. The universal image already has all the feature sets in it. The software activation process achieves three major goals:

- **Automatically enables the IP Base:** The router arrives from Cisco with the IP base feature set already enabled and activated, without any additional action required.

- **Enables other feature sets:** The network engineer must enable (activate) any additional desired feature sets on the router (see Figure 36-2). Without software activation, the feature does not work, and the related commands are not recognized by the CLI.

- **Verifies legal rights:** The process checks and confirms that the Cisco customer has paid for the right to use that feature set on that router.

For instance, a customer could buy a new current model of Cisco router that uses a universal image and the Cisco software activation process. All such routers come with the most basic feature set (IP Base) enabled already, with a license key for that feature already installed on the router. That is, the user does not have to do anything to start using the router and get IPv4 routing to work. Later, the customer could choose to use software activation to enable the Security feature set—a process that requires the installation of a license key for the Security feature set, as shown in Figure 36-4.

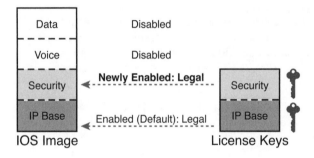

Figure 36-4 *License Keys Inside a Router That Enable IOS Features*

Cisco has a variety of different types of features and licenses that can be enabled. Cisco calls the feature sets with the most significant set of features technology packages. Table 36-2 provides the technology package licenses that are available on the 4400 series routers, which are popular Cisco branch routers at the time of publication of the book.

Table 36-2 Some Technology Package Licenses

Technology Package License	Features
IP Base	Entry-level IOS functionality
Application Experience	Performance routing (PfR), WAAS, NBAR2
Unified Communications	VoIP, IP Telephony
Security	IOS firewall, IPsec, DMVPN, VPN

NOTE   The IP Base license is a prerequisite for installing the other licenses.

The Future: Cisco ONE Licensing

Changing how an OS performs licensing activities upon itself can be a challenge for any software vendor. For instance, IOS today has features to support the licensing as introduced in the preceding pages. However, can you imagine if Cisco wanted to use a completely different method to manage and enforce licensing on its routers, switches, and other products? Making that kind of change requires much more than adding support for a few new commands to IOS; it takes serious planning for the architecture of products, systems to check for license rights, and updates to IOS, and other considerations as well.

And even once the vendor implements a new plan, it is almost impossible to apply that plan to the current installed base; so many years must pass while the customer base slowly moves through a technology refresh cycle and replaces routers, switches, and the associated software.

At the time Cisco began working on this latest version of the CCNA R&S exams (100-105, 200-105, and 200-125), Cisco was already in the middle of a migration to a new software licensing method called Cisco ONE Licensing. This new method promises to be an improvement on many levels. It removes the per-device effort to add and remove licenses. Instead, if you are a company using X routers with feature set Y, the process just checks to see that you have those rights, without requiring the engineer to touch every router. It also performs some licensing independently from the device—for instance, if you license a security feature set for a router and later upgrade to a new router model, you still have the rights to use the security feature set. With the licensing as described in this chapter, the license is tied to the hardware, so when you upgrade hardware, the license to use software on that hardware has no value.

So, for your real job, keep a watch for newer Cisco products that may use Cisco ONE licensing. The rest of this chapter now focuses on the processes for Cisco licensing that exists in most of the installed base.

Managing Software Activation with Cisco License Manager

Cisco customers can purchase feature sets when ordering the router or add them later. If they are purchased when ordering the router, Cisco adds the licenses to the router at the factory, and the customer has no additional work to add licenses. Alternatively, the customer can later purchase a license for a feature set and then follow the software activation process to enable that feature set on the router.

Most larger companies will likely manage Cisco licenses using an application called the Cisco License Manager (CLM). This free software package can be installed on many Windows client and server operating systems, as well as on Sun Solaris and Red Hat Linux. The CLM

- Communicates with Cisco's Product License Registration Portal over the Internet
- Takes as input information about feature licenses purchased from any Cisco reseller
- Communicates with the company's routers and switches to install license keys, enabling features on the correct devices

Figure 36-5 shows the central location of CLM in the Cisco licensing process.

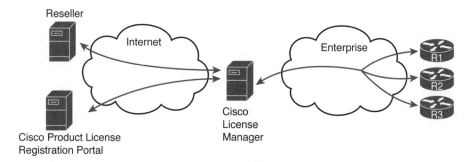

Figure 36-5 *Location of Cisco License Manager in Software Activation*

If you use CLM, you need to know only the big ideas of what needs to be done with licensing, while ignoring many details of how licensing happens. Instead, CLM tracks the information. You can purchase the licenses from any Cisco reseller. The application lets you see what you have purchased and see the licenses that have already been assigned for use on specific devices. You can also choose specific devices to receive new rights to use new feature sets and enable those features through an easy-to-use graphical user interface.

Manually Activating Software Using Licenses

CLM gives you an easier way to manage the entire Cisco software activation process, but you can also use a completely manual process. The manual process requires you to web browse to the Cisco Product License Registration Portal (www.cisco.com/go/license) and also do some CLI commands on your router. Plus, you must follow a multistep process to put all the pieces together. Basically, you do all the work that CLM does for you. This next topic looks at the cleanest version of the process, without going into any of the options.

First, each of the same router models that supports software licensing has a unique identifying number named the *unique device identifier* (UDI). The UDI has two main components: the product ID (PID) and the serial number (SN). The following example shows the output from the **show license udi** command. In Example 36-1, you can clearly see the product ID, serial number, and UDI of the router.

Example 36-1 *Examining the UDI on a Cisco Router*

```
R1# show license udi
Device#    PID                    SN              UDI

-----------------------------------------------------------------------

*0         CISCO2901/K9           FTX162883H0     CISCO2901/K9:FTX162883H0
```

Next, the process requires proof that you paid for a license to use a particular feature on a particular model of router. The real world uses paper receipts to show that you bought something at a store; for software feature sets, the receipt is called a product authorization key, or PAK. The PAK acts as a receipt; plus, it has another unique number on it, which Cisco can find in a database to confirm what feature set license you actually bought.

The next step connects the license, which you can use on any router of that same model, to a specific router. To do so, you walk through a process that marries the PAK (the generic rights to a license) to the UDI (that identifies a specific router) to create a license key. To do so, you open a web browser and copy the PAK and UDI numbers onto a web page at the Cisco Product License Registration Portal. Cisco checks out the details: that the UDI is for a real router, that the PAK is real, that you have not already used that one PAK to enable this feature on another router, and any other checks to prevent fraud. If it all checks out, Cisco emails you with the license key file attached (also available for download).

Figure 36-6 summarizes these first three steps, with Figure 36-7 showing the later steps:

Step 1. At the Cisco Product License Registration Portal (which you can reach from www.cisco.com/go/license), input the UDI of the router, as gathered using the **show license udi** command.

Step 2. At that same portal, type in the PAK for the license you purchased, as learned from your reseller or directly from Cisco.

Step 3. Copy the license key file (download or email) when prompted at Cisco's Product License Registration Portal website.

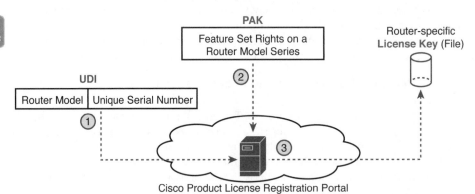

Figure 36-6 *PAK and UDI Needed to Get Unique License Key File from Cisco.com*

NOTE As of the time of this writing, the landing page for the Cisco Product License Registration Portal (www.cisco.com/go/license) included videos about how to do the steps in Figure 36-6 plus the rest of the process of how to work with Cisco licenses. The videos call the process in Steps 1 and 2 "fulfilling a PAK."

After the three steps shown in Figure 36-6, the router still does not have the feature set enabled. At this point, the license key exists as a file after Step 3. That license key unlocks that one feature set on one router: the router whose UDI was used to create the key. The rest of the process enables the license on that one router, by moving the license key file into that one router and reloading the router.

The next step can use any supported method to make the license key file available to the router, with a couple of commands to follow. In a lab, the simplest way is to just copy the file to a USB flash drive and move the flash drive to the router's USB slot. For remote routers, just copy the file to a known TFTP, FTP, or HTTP server. The steps, picking up with Step 4 as a continuation of the previous list, are as follows:

Step 4.   Make the file available to the router via USB or some network server.

Step 5.   From the router CLI, issue the **license install** *url* command to install the license key file into the router. (The URL points to the file.)

Step 6.   Reload the router to pick up the changes.

Figure 36-7 shows these next three steps.

Figure 36-7   *Copying and Installing the License on a Router*

Example of Manually Activating a License

To bring the concept from the general to the specific, the next few pages show an example of the installation of a Data license on a model 2901 router. The example begins by showing the current state of the licenses in a sample router and then shows how to change the licenses.

Showing the Current License Status

The example begins with Router R1, with only the IP Base feature enabled. No other licenses have been enabled on this router. Example 36-2 shows the status of the available features, with the enabled IP Base highlighted and the three technology package licenses highlighted, as well: Security, Voice, and Data.

NOTE   This example uses a 2901 router, which has a "Data" feature set, named datak9, instead of the "Application Experience" feature set in the 4400 series routers as mentioned in Table 36-2.

Example 36-2   *Initial License Status on Router R1*

```
R1# show license
Index 1 Feature: ipbasek9
        Period left: Life time
        License Type: Permanent
        License State: Active, In Use
        License Count: Non-Counted
        License Priority: Medium
Index 2 Feature: securityk9
        Period left: Not Activated
        Period Used: 0  minute  0  second
        License Type: EvalRightToUse
        License State: Not in Use, EULA not accepted
        License Count: Non-Counted
        License Priority: None
```

36

```
Index 3 Feature: uck9
         Period left: Not Activated
         Period Used: 0  minute  0  second
         License Type: EvalRightToUse
         License State: Not in Use, EULA not accepted
         License Count: Non-Counted
         License Priority: None
Index 4 Feature: datak9
         Period left: Not Activated
         Period Used: 0  minute  0  second
         License Type: Permanent
         License State: Active, Not in Use
         License Count: Non-Counted
         License Priority: Medium
! Lines omitted for brevity; 8 more feature licenses available
```

The highlighted lines spell out the current state. The first highlight refers to the IP Base feature set, with an unlimited lifetime. (Note that Cisco enables the IP Base feature set on all routers, with the other feature sets being optional upgrades.) The next three highlighted sections list the Security, Voice (Unified Communications, or UC), and Data licenses, respectively, all listed as Not Activated. Also, note that the output of the **show license** command on a 2901 includes several additional feature licenses omitted from the example for the sake of space.

The **show license** command shows several lines of status information per feature, but as shown in Example 36-3, the **show version** and **show license feature** commands list shorter status information. The **show license feature** command lists one line of output, with the Enabled column on the right showing the current status. The **show version** command lists license information for the main technology feature packages at the end of the output.

Example 36-3 *Initial License Status on Router R1*

```
R1# show license feature


Feature name      Enforcement   Evaluation   Subscription   Enabled   RightToUse
ipbasek9          no            no           no             yes       no
securityk9        yes           yes          no             no        yes
uck9              yes           yes          no             no        yes
datak9            yes           yes          no             no        yes
gatekeeper        yes           yes          no             no        yes
SSL_VPN           yes           yes          no             no        yes
ios-ips-update    yes           yes          yes            no        yes
SNASw             yes           yes          no             no        yes
hseck9            yes           no           no             no        no
cme-srst          yes           yes          no             no        yes
WAAS_Express      yes           yes          no             no        yes
UCVideo           yes           yes          no             no        yes
```

```
R1# show version
Cisco IOS Software, C2900 Software (C2900-UNIVERSALK9-M), Version 15.1(4)M4, RELEASE
  SOFTWARE (fc1)


! Lines omitted for brevity


License UDI:
--------------------------------------------------


Device#     PID                    SN
--------------------------------------------------
*0          CISCO2901/K9           FTX1628838P



Technology Package License Information for Module:'c2900'


-----------------------------------------------------------------
Tecnology    Technology-package          Technology-package
             Current      Type           Next reboot
-----------------------------------------------------------------
ipbase       ipbasek9     Permanent      ipbasek9
security     None         None           None
uc           None         None           None
data         None         None           None


Configuration register is 0x2102
```

Adding a Permanent Technology Package License

Next, Example 36-4 shows the engineer installing the license on router R1 for the Data feature set. The engineer has already followed the steps to get the license file from the Cisco Product License Registration Portal, with the file placed onto a USB drive and plugged into R1. That is, from Figures 36-6 and 36-7, the engineer has completed Steps 1 through 4.

Example 36-4 shows the final steps to install the license file on router R1. The example shows the contents of the USB flash drive, with the license file highlighted. It then shows the command to change the licensing on the router.

Example 36-4   *Installing a License on the Cisco Router*

```
R1# dir usbflash1:
Directory of usbflash1:/
    1  -rw-        4096  Feb 11 2013 17:17:00  FTX1628838P_201302111432454180.lic


7783804928 bytes total (7782912000 bytes free)


R1# license install usbflash1:FTX1628838P_201302111432454180.lic
```

```
Installing...Feature:datak9...Successful:Supported
1/1 licenses were successfully installed
0/1 licenses were existing licenses
0/1 licenses were failed to install

R1#
Feb 11 22:35:20.786: %LICENSE-6-INSTALL: Feature datak9 1.0 was installed in this
  device. UDI=CISCO2901/K9:FTX1628838P; StoreIndex=1:Primary License Storage

Feb 11 22:35:21.038: %IOS_LICENSE_IMAGE_APPLICATION-6-LICENSE_LEVEL: Module name =
  c2900 Next reboot level = datak9 and License = datak9
```

After a **reload** (not shown), the router now supports the features in the Data feature set.
Example 36-5 confirms the change in the licensing status, with the Data license now mirror-
ing the status for the IP Base feature set.

Example 36-5   *Verifying the Installed License on a Router*

```
R1# show license
Index 1 Feature: ipbasek9
        Period left: Life time
        License Type: Permanent
        License State: Active, In Use
        License Count: Non-Counted
        License Priority: Medium
!
! Omitted section for security and UC feature sets - output is unchanged vs.
  Example 36-3
!
Index 4 Feature: datak9
        Period left: Life time
        License Type: Permanent
        License State: Active, In Use
        License Count: Non-Counted
        License Priority: Medium
! Lines omitted for brevity
```

You can also verify the installed license using the **show version** command, as shown in
Example 36-6.

Example 36-6   *Using* **show version** *to Verify Licensing Information*

```
R1# show version | begin Technology Package
Technology Package License Information for Module:'c2900'

----------------------------------------------------------------
Technology    Technology-package              Technology-package
              Current         Type            Next reboot
```

```
--------------------------------------------------------------
ipbase      ipbasek9     Permanent     ipbasek9

security    securityk9   None          None

uc          None         None          None

data        datak9       Permanent     datak9


Configuration register is 0x2102
```

Right-to-Use Licenses

Although a software licensing model may work well in some cases for legitimate Cisco customers, it might not work well in other cases. For instance, when legitimate Cisco customers want to test a router feature before they decide to purchase licenses for all their routers, Cisco does not want the mechanics of licensing to get in the way of making that sale. So, Cisco makes the licensing flexible enough to allow use of the licensing without purchasing a PAK. These customers can simply enable most features, without paying for a PAK, for a 60-day evaluation period. After that? The feature stays enabled, with no time limit. The software licensing works on an honor system, asking people to not take advantage.

Cisco allows the use of these features today, without a PAK, using a *right-to-use* license. To enable a feature license as a right-to-use license, the engineer needs to use the **license boot module** command, with a reload to allow the router to start using the feature. For instance, Example 36-7 shows how to add the Security feature set to router R1 as a right-to-use evaluation license.

Example 36-7   *Activating an Evaluation Right-to-Use License*

```
R1(config)# license boot module c2900 technology-package securityk9


PLEASE READ THE  FOLLOWING TERMS  CAREFULLY. INSTALLING THE LICENSE OR

LICENSE KEY  PROVIDED FOR  ANY CISCO  PRODUCT  FEATURE  OR  USING SUCH

PRODUCT  FEATURE  CONSTITUTES  YOUR  FULL ACCEPTANCE OF THE FOLLOWING

TERMS. YOU MUST NOT PROCEED FURTHER IF YOU ARE NOT WILLING TO BE BOUND

BY ALL THE TERMS SET FORTH HEREIN.


! The rest of the EULA is omitted...


Activation of the  software command line interface will be evidence of

your acceptance of this agreement.



ACCEPT? [yes/no]: yes

% use 'write' command to make license boot config take effect on next boot


Feb 12 01:35:45.060: %IOS_LICENSE_IMAGE_APPLICATION-6-LICENSE_LEVEL: Module name =
  c2900 Next reboot level = securityk9 and License = securityk9

Feb 12 01:35:45.524: %LICENSE-6-EULA_ACCEPTED: EULA for feature securityk9 1.0 has
  been accepted. UDI=CISCO2901/K9:FTX1628838P; StoreIndex=0:Built-In License Storage

R1(config)# ^Z
```

36

Once the router is reloaded, the feature set is available, and works just as well as if you had purchased a PAK and downloaded a license file from Cisco.com. Example 36-8 lists the output of the **show license** command again, to show the differences in how the command lists the results of the installation of a right-to-use license.

Example 36-8 *Activating an Evaluation Right-to-Use License*

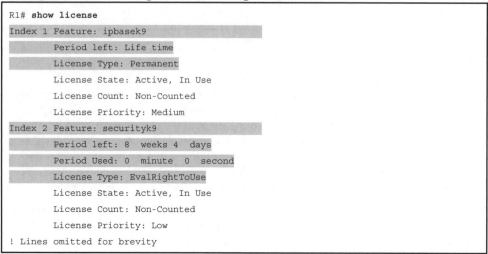

```
R1# show license
Index 1 Feature: ipbasek9
        Period left: Life time
        License Type: Permanent
        License State: Active, In Use
        License Count: Non-Counted
        License Priority: Medium
Index 2 Feature: securityk9
        Period left: 8  weeks 4  days
        Period Used: 0  minute  0  second
        License Type: EvalRightToUse
        License State: Active, In Use
        License Count: Non-Counted
        License Priority: Low
! Lines omitted for brevity
```

In this example, the IP Base and Data licenses are permanent, but the right-to-use license appears to have only 60 days left (8 weeks, 4 days). The first 60 days is considered an evaluation period. The output continues over time to count downward toward 0 days left, at which point, it converts to a lifetime time period.

Chapter Review

One key to doing well on the exams is to perform repetitive spaced review sessions. Review this chapter's material using either the tools in the book, DVD, or interactive tools for the same material found on the book's companion website. Refer to the "Your Study Plan" element for more details. Table 36-3 outlines the key review elements and where you can find them. To better track your study progress, record when you completed these activities in the second column.

Table 36-3 Chapter Review Tracking

Review Element	Review Date(s)	Resource Used
Review key topics		Book, DVD/website
Review key terms		Book, DVD/website
Repeat DIKTA questions		Book, PCPT
Review memory tables		Book, DVD/website
Review command tables		Book

Review All the Key Topics

Table 36-4   Key Topics for Chapter 36

Key Topic Element	Description	Page Number
Figure 36-3	The new Cisco universal image	852
Table 36-2	Some Cisco technology package licenses	853
Figure 36-6	Three steps to manually add software licenses to a Cisco router	856

Key Terms You Should Know

IOS feature set, universal image, product authorization key (PAK), universal device identifier (UDI)

Command References

Tables 36-5 and 36-6 list configuration and verification commands used in this chapter. As an easy review exercise, cover the left column in a table, read the right column, and try to recall the command without looking. Then repeat the exercise, covering the right column, and try to recall what the command does.

Table 36-5   Chapter 36 Configuration Command Reference

Command	Description
license boot module c2900 technology-package *package-name*	Global command used to add a right-to-use license to a router.

Table 36-6   Chapter 36 EXEC Command Reference

Command	Description
show license	Displays a group of lines for each feature in the currently running IOS image, along with several status variables related to software activation and licensing, whether or not it is in use or activated.
show license feature	Displays one line for each feature in the currently running IOS image, along with several status variables related to software activation and licensing, whether or not it is in use or activated.
show license udi	Displays the UDI of the router.
dir *filesystem*	Displays the files inside the listed file system. For instance, **dir usbflash1:** lists the files in one of the USB slots on a 2901 router.
show version	Displays various information about the current IOS version, including the licensing details at the end of the command's output.
license install *url*	Installs a license key file into a router.

36

Part IX Review

Keep track of your part review progress with the checklist in Table P9-1. Details on each task follow the table.

Table P9-1 Part IX Part Review Checklist

Activity	1st Date Completed	2nd Date Completed
Repeat All DIKTA Questions		
Answer Part Review Questions		
Review Key Topics		
Create Command Mind Maps		
Do Labs		

Repeat All DIKTA Questions

For this task, use the PCPT software to answer the "Do I Know This Already?" questions again for the chapters in this part of the book.

Answer Part Review Questions

For this task, use PCPT to answer the Part Review questions for this part of the book.

Review Key Topics

Review all key topics in all chapters in this part, either by browsing the chapters or using the Key Topics application on the DVD or companion website.

Create Command Mind Maps by Category

Part IX of this book contains a wide variety of topics, some of which use several configuration commands, and some of which use many EXEC commands. Create the usual style of command mind map for the main topics in the chapters for this book. As usual, focus more on remembering the commands and which commands work together, rather than worrying about every single parameter on each command.

Create one mind map for each of these categories. Note that the categories match many of the major headings in the chapters in this part of the book. Make your mind map without using your notes and the book first, and when you cannot do more, then refer to your notes and the book.

syslog, NTP, CDP & LLDP, passwords and login, device hardening, managing IOS upgrades, managing configuration files, managing IOS licensing

Appendix L, "Mind Map Solutions," lists sample mind map answers, but as usual, your mind map can and will look different.

Table P9-2 Configuration Mind Maps for Part IX Review

Map	Description	Where You Saved It
1	Part IX Command Mind Map(s)	

Do Labs

Depending on your chosen lab tool, here are some suggestions for what to do in lab:

Pearson Network Simulator: Once NetSim has been updated for the 100-105, 200-105, and 200-125 exams, you will see labs for all these topics that are easily found in the "Sort by Chapter" tab of the Sim. Do those labs. If you are using the older version of the Simulator (for the 100-101, 200-101, or 200-120 exams), the labs are spread across the ICND1 and ICND2 halves of that product. You may find them most easily by just searching on key terms, like NTP, syslog, and so on.

Config Labs: In your idle moments, review and repeat any of the Config Labs for this book part in the author's blog; launch from blog.certskills.com/ccent/configlab.

Other: If using other lab tools, here are a few suggestions. Most of the topics in this part use a short configuration with a few EXEC commands, and you can do meaningful labs with just two devices plus a laptop. This might be a great place to borrow some gear, or if you have been meaning to own a few used routers or switches, buy those and try labs on the topics in this part of the book.

Part X

Final Review

Chapter 37: Final Review

Final Review

Congratulations! You made it through the book, and now it's time to finish getting ready for the exam. This chapter helps you get ready to take and pass the exam in two ways.

This chapter begins by talking about the exam itself. You know the content and topics. Now you need to think about what happens during the exam, and what you need to do in these last few weeks before taking the exam. At this point, everything you do should be focused on getting you ready to pass so that you can finish up this hefty task.

The second section of this chapter gives you some exam review tasks as your final preparation for your ICND1, ICND2, or CCNA exam.

Advice About the Exam Event

Now that you have finished the bulk of this book, you could just register for your Cisco ICND1, ICND2, or CCNA R&S exam; show up; and take the exam. However, if you spend a little time thinking about the exam event itself, learning more about the user interface of the real Cisco exams, and the environment at the Vue testing centers, you will be better prepared, particularly if this is your first Cisco exam. This first of three major sections in this chapter gives some advice about the Cisco exams and the exam event itself.

Learn the Question Types Using the Cisco Certification Exam Tutorial

In the weeks leading up to your exam, you should think more about the different types of exam questions and have a plan for how to approach those questions. One of the best ways to learn about the exam questions is to use the Cisco Certification Exam Tutorial.

To find the Cisco Certification Exam Tutorial, go to www.cisco.com and search for "exam tutorial." The tutorial sits inside a web page with a Flash presentation of the exam user interface. The tutorial even lets you take control as if you were taking the exam. When using the tutorial, make sure that you take control and try the following:

- Try to click next on the multichoice, single-answer question without clicking an answer, and see that the testing software tells you that you have too few answers.

- On the multichoice, multianswer question, select too few answers and click Next to again see how the user interface responds.

- In the drag-and-drop questions, drag the answers to the obvious answer locations, but then drag them back to the original location. (You can do this on the real exam if you change your mind when answering a question.)

- On the simulation question, first just make sure that you can get to the command-line interface (CLI) on one of the routers. To do so, you have to click the PC icon for a PC connected to the router console; the console cable appears as a dashed line, whereas network cables are solid lines.

- Still on the Sim question, make sure that you look at the scroll areas at the top, at the side, and in the terminal emulator window. These scroll bars let you view the entire question and scenario.

- Still on the Sim question, make sure that you can toggle between the topology window and the terminal emulator window by clicking "Show topology" and "Hide topology." Hang out here and click around until you are completely comfortable navigating—and do it again tomorrow and the next day.

- On the Testlet question, answer one multichoice question, move to the second and answer it, and then move back to the first question, confirming that inside a Testlet, you can move around between questions.

- Again on the Testlet question, click the Next button to see the pop-up window that Cisco uses as a prompt to ask whether you want to move on. (Testlets might actually allow you to give too few answers and still move on, so make extra sure that you answer with the correct number of answers in each Testlet question.) After you click to move past the Testlet, you cannot go back to change your answer for any of these questions.

Think About Your Time Budget Versus Number of Questions

On exam day, you need to keep an eye on your speed. Going too slowly hurts you because you might not have time to answer all the questions. Going too fast can be hurtful if you are rushing because you are fearful about running out of time. So, you need to be able to somehow know whether you are moving quickly enough to answer all the questions, while not rushing.

The exam user interface shows some useful information, namely a countdown timer as well as upward question counter. The question counter shows a question number for the question you are answering, and it shows the total number of questions on your exam.

Unfortunately, some questions require lots more time than others, and for this and other reasons, time estimating can be a challenge.

First, before you show up to take the exam, you only know a range of the number of questions for the exam; for example, the Cisco website might list the CCNA R&S exam as having from 50 to 60 questions. But you do not know how many questions are on your exam until the exam begins, when you go through the screens that lead up to the point where you click "Start exam," which starts your timed exam.

Next, some questions (call them *time burners*) clearly take a lot more time to answer:

> **Normal-time questions:** Multichoice and drag-and-drop, approximately 1 minute each
>
> **Time burners:** Sims, Simlets, and Testlets, approximately 6–8 minutes each

Finally, in the count of 50–60 questions on a single exam, even though Testlet and Simlet questions contain several multichoice questions, the exam software counts each Testlet and Simlet question as one question in the question counter. For example, if a Testlet question has four embedded multiple-choice questions, in the exam software's question counter, that counts as one question. So when you start the exam, you might see that you will have 50 questions, but you don't know how many of those are time burners.

NOTE   While Cisco does not tell us why you might get 50 questions whereas someone else taking the same exam might get 60 questions, it seems reasonable to think that the person with 50 questions might have a few more of the time burners, making the two exams equivalent.

You need a plan for how you will check your time, a plan that does not distract you from the exam. You can ponder the facts listed here and come up with your own plan. If you want a little more guidance, the next topic shows one way to check your time that uses some simple math so it does not take much time away from the test.

A Suggested Time-Check Method

You can use the following math to do your time check in a way that weights the time based on those time-burner questions. You do not have to use this method. But this math uses only addition of whole numbers, to keep it simple. It gives you a pretty close time estimate, in my opinion.

The concept is simple. Just do a simple calculation that estimates the time you should have used so far. Here's the math:

Number of Questions Answered So Far + 7 Per Time Burner answered so far

Then you check the timer to figure out how much time you have spent:

- You have used exactly that much time, or a little more time: Your timing is perfect.
- You have used less time: You are ahead of schedule.
- You have used noticeably more time: You are behind schedule.

For example, if you have already finished 17 questions, 2 of which were time burners, your time estimate is 17 + 7 + 7 = 31 minutes. If your actual time is also 31 minutes, or maybe 32 or 33 minutes, you are right on schedule. If you have spent less than 31 minutes, you are ahead of schedule.

So, the math is pretty easy: Questions answered, plus 7 per time burner, is the guesstimate of how long you should have taken so far if you are right on time.

NOTE   This math is an estimate; I make no guarantees that the math will be an accurate predictor on every exam.

Miscellaneous Pre-Exam Suggestions

Here are just a few more suggestions for things to think about before exam day arrives:

- Get some earplugs. Testing centers often have some, but if you do not want to chance it, come prepared with your own. (They will not let you bring your own noise-canceling headphones into the room if they follow the rules disallowing any user electronic devices in the room, so think low-tech disposable, or even bring a cotton ball.) The testing center is typically one room at a company that does something else as well, oftentimes a training center, and almost certainly you will share the room with other test takers coming and going. So, there are people talking in nearby rooms and other office noises. Earplugs can help.

- Some people like to spend the first minute of the exam writing down some notes for reference, before actually starting the exam. For example, maybe you want to write down the table of magic numbers for finding IPv4 subnet IDs. If you plan to do that, practice making those notes. Before each practice exam, transcribe those lists, just like you expect to do at the real exam.

- Plan your travel to the testing center with enough time so that you will not be rushing to make it just in time.

- If you tend to be nervous before exams, practice your favorite relaxation techniques for a few minutes before each practice exam, just to be ready to use them.

Exam-Day Advice

I hope the exam goes well for you. Certainly, the better prepared you are, the better chances you have on the exam. But these small tips can help you do your best on exam day:

- Rest the night before the exam, rather than staying up late to study. Clarity of thought is more important than one extra fact, especially because the exam requires so much analysis and thinking rather than just remembering facts.

- If you did not bring earplugs, ask the testing center for some, even if you cannot imagine you would use them. You never know whether they might help.

- You can bring personal effects into the building and testing company's space, but not into the actual room in which you take the exam. So, save a little stress and bring as little extra stuff with you as possible. If you have a safe place to leave briefcases, purses, electronics, and so on, leave them there. However, the testing center should have a place to store your things as well. Simply put, the less you bring, the less you have to worry about storing. (For example, I have been asked to remove even my analog wristwatch on more than one occasion.)

- The exam center will give you a laminated sheet and pen, as a place to take notes. (Test center personnel typically do not let you bring paper and pen into the room, even if supplied by the testing center.) I always ask for a second pen as well.

- If they're available, grab a few tissues from the box in the room, for two reasons. One: Avoid having to get up in the middle of the exam. Two: If you need to erase your laminated sheet, doing that with a tissue paper rather than your hand helps prevent the oil from your hand making the pen stop working well.

- Leave for the testing center with extra time, so you do not have to rush.

- Plan on finding a restroom before going into the testing center. If you cannot find one, of course you can use one in the testing center, and test personnel will direct you and give you time before your exam starts.

- Do not drink a 64-ounce caffeinated drink on the trip to the testing center. After the exam starts, the exam timer will not stop while you go to the restroom.

- On exam day, use any relaxation techniques that you have practiced to help get your mind focused while you wait for the exam.

Reserve the Hour After the Exam in Case You Fail

Some people pass these exams on the first attempt, and some do not. The exams are not easy. If you fail to pass the exam that day, you will likely be disappointed. And that is understandable. But it is not a reason to give up. In fact, I added this short topic to give you a big advantage in case you do fail.

The most important study hour for your next exam attempt is the hour just after your failed attempt.

Prepare to fail before you take the exam. That is, prepare your schedule to give yourself an hour, or at least a half an hour, immediately after the exam attempt, in case you fail. Then follow these suggestions:

- Bring pen and paper, preferably a notebook you can write in if you have to write standing up or sitting somewhere inconvenient.

- Make sure you know where pen and paper are so that you can take notes immediately after the exam. Keep these items in your backpack if using the train or bus, or on the car seat in the car.

- Install an audio recording app on your phone, and be prepared to start talking into your app when you leave the testing center.

- Before the exam, scout the testing center, and plan the place where you will sit and take your notes, preferably somewhere quiet.

- Write down anything in particular that you can recall from any question.

- Write down details of questions you know you got right as well, because doing so may help trigger a memory of another question.

- Draw the figures that you can remember.

- Most importantly, write down any tidbit that might have confused you: terms, config commands, show commands, scenarios, topology drawings, anything.

- Take at least three passes at remembering. That is, you will hit a wall where you do not remember more. So, start on your way back to the next place, and then find a place to pause and take more notes. And do it again.

- When you have sucked your memory dry, take one more pass while thinking of the major topics in the book, to see if that triggers any other memory of a question.

Once collected, *you cannot share the information with anyone*, because doing so would break Cisco's nondisclosure agreement (NDA). Cisco is serious about cheating and would consider the fact that you would share this kind of info publicly. But you can use your information to study for your next attempt. Remember, anything that uncovers what you do not know is valuable when studying for your next attempt. See the section "Study Suggestions After You Failed to Pass" in this chapter for the rest of the story.

Exam Review

This exam review completes the Study Plan materials as suggested by this book. At this point, you have read the other chapters of the book, and you have done the Chapter Review and Part Review tasks. Now you need to do the final study and review activities before taking the exam, as detailed in this section.

The Exam Review section suggests some new activities and repeats some old. However, whether new or old, the activities all focus on filling in your knowledge gaps, finishing off your skills, and completing the study process. While repeating some tasks you did at Chapter Review and Part Review can help, you need to be ready to take an exam, so the Exam Review asks you to spend a lot of time answering exam questions.

The Exam Review walks you through suggestions for several types of tasks and gives you some tracking tables for each activity. The main categories are

- Practicing for speed
- Taking practice exams
- Finding what you do not know well yet (knowledge gaps)
- Configuring and verifying functions from the CLI
- Repeating the Chapter and Part Review tasks

Practice Subnetting and Other Math-Related Skills

Like it or not, some of the questions on the Cisco ICND1, ICND2, and CCNA R&S exams require you to do some math. To pass, you have to be good at the math. You also need to know when to use each process.

The Cisco exams also have a timer. Some of the math crops up often enough so that, if you go slow with the math, or if you have to write down all the details of how you compute the answers, you might well run out of time to answer all the questions. (The two biggest reasons I hear about why people do not finish on time are these: slow speed with the math-related work and slow speed when doing simulator questions using the CLI.)

However, look at the time crunch as a positive instead of a negative. Right now, before the exam, you know about the time pressure. You know that if you keep practicing subnetting and other math, you will keep getting faster and better. As exam day approaches, if you have spare minutes, try more practice with anything to do with subnetting in particular. Look at it as a way to prepare now so that you do not have to worry about time pressure so much on the day of the exam.

Table 37-1 lists the topics in this chapter that both require math and require speed. Table 37-2 lists items for which the math or process is important, but speed is probably less important. By this point in your study, you should already be confident at finding the right answer to these kinds of problems. Now is the time to finish off your skills at getting the right answers, plus getting faster so that you reduce your time pressure on the exams.

NOTE The time goals in the table are goals I chose to give you an idea of a good time. If you happen to be a little slower on a few tasks, that does not mean you cannot do well on the test. But if you take much more time for almost every task, know that the math-related work can cause you some time problems.

37

Table 37-1   ICND1 Math-Related Activities That Benefit from Speed Practice

Chapter	Activity	Book's Excellent Speed Goal (Seconds)	Self-Check: Date/Time	Self-Check: Date/Time
14	From a unicast IPv4 address, find key facts about its classful network.	10		
15	From one mask in any format, convert to the other two mask formats.	10		

Chapter	Activity	Book's Excellent Speed Goal (Seconds)	Self-Check: Date/Time	Self-Check: Date/Time
15	Given an IPv4 address and mask, find the number of network, subnet, and host bits, plus the number of hosts/subnet and number of subnets.	15		
16	Given an IPv4 address and mask, find the resident subnet, subnet broadcast address, and range of usable addresses.	20–30		
21	Given a set of mask requirements, choose the best subnet mask.	15		
21	Given a classful network and one mask, find all subnet IDs.	45		

Table 37-2 ICND1 Math-Related Activities That Can Be Less Time Sensitive

Chapter	Activity	Self-Check: Date/Time	Self-Check: Date/Time
22	Find VLSM overlaps, with problems that contain 5–6 subnets.		
22	Add VLSM subnets, with problems that contain 5–6 subnets.		
25	Build an ACL command to match a subnet's addresses.		
25	List the addresses matched by one existing ACL command.		
28	Find the best abbreviation for one IPv6 address.		
30	Find the IPv6 address of one router interface when using EUI-64.		

You can practice the math with some practice apps or matching DVD appendixes that come with this book. All the chapters listed in Tables 37-1 and 37-2 have matching DVD appendixes with additional practice, and the apps located both on the DVD and the book's companion website let you practice those same problems. Finally, the author's blogs include extra practice problems that were created just to give you another source from which to practice.

Take Practice Exams

One day soon, you need to pass a real Cisco exam at a Vue testing center. So, it's time to practice the real event as much as possible.

A practice exam using the Pearson IT Certification Practice Test (PCPT) exam software lets you experience many of the same issues as when taking a real Cisco exam. The software gives you a number of questions, with a countdown timer shown in the window. After you answer a question, you cannot go back to it (yes, that's true on Cisco exams). If you run out of time, the questions you did not answer count as incorrect.

The process of taking the timed practice exams helps you prepare in three key ways:

■ To practice the exam event itself, including time pressure, the need to read carefully, with a need to concentrate for long periods

■ To build your analysis and critical thinking skills when examining the network scenario built into many questions

■ To discover the gaps in your networking knowledge so that you can study those topics before the real exam

As much as possible, treat the practice exam events as if you were taking the real Cisco exam at a Vue testing center. The following list gives some advice on how to make your practice exam more meaningful, rather than just one more thing to do before exam day rolls around:

■ Set aside two hours for taking the 90-minute timed practice exam.

■ Make a list of what you expect to do for the 10 minutes before the real exam event. Then visualize yourself doing those things. Before taking each practice exam, practice those final 10 minutes before your exam timer starts. (The earlier section "Exam-Day Advice" lists some suggestions about what to do in those last 10 minutes.)

■ You cannot bring anything with you into the Vue exam room, so remove all notes and help materials from your work area before taking a practice exam. You can use blank paper, a pen, and your brain only. Do not use calculators, notes, web browsers, or any other app on your computer.

■ Real life can get in the way, but if at all possible, ask anyone around you to leave you alone for the time you will practice. If you must do your practice exam in a distracting environment, wear headphones or earplugs to reduce distractions.

■ Do not guess, hoping to improve your score. Answer only when you have confidence in the answer. Then, if you get the question wrong, you can go back and think more about the question in a later study session.

Practicing Taking the ICND1 Exam

To take an ICND1 practice exam, you need to select one or both of the ICND1 exams from PCPT. If you followed the study plan in this book, you will not have seen any of the questions in these two exam databases before now. After you select one of these two exams, you simply need to choose the Practice Exam option in the upper right and start the exam.

You should plan to take between one and three ICND1 practice exams with these two exam databases. Even people who are already well prepared should do at least one practice exam, just to experience the time pressure and the need for prolonged concentration.

Table 37-3 gives you a checklist to record your different practice exam events. Note that recording both the date and the score is helpful for some other work you will do, so note both. Also, in the Time Notes section, if you finish on time, note how much extra time you had; if you run out of time, note how many questions you did not have time to answer.

37

Table 37-3   ICND1 Practice Exam Checklist

Exam	Date	Score	Time Notes
ICND1			
ICND1			
ICND1			

Advice on How to Answer Exam Questions

Open a web browser. Yes, take a break and open a web browser on any device. Do a quick search on a fun topic. Then, before you click a link, get ready to think where your eyes go for the first 5–10 seconds after you click the link. Now, click a link and look at the page. Where did your eyes go?

Interestingly, web browsers and the content on those web pages have trained us all to scan. Web page designers actually design content expecting certain scan patterns. Regardless of the pattern, when reading a web page, almost no one reads sequentially, and no one reads entire sentences. People scan for the interesting graphics and the big words, and then scan the space around those noticeable items.

Other parts of our electronic culture have also changed how the average person reads. For example, many of you grew up using texting and social media, sifting through hundreds or thousands of messages—but each message barely fills an entire sentence. (In fact, that previous sentence would not fit in a tweet, being longer than 140 characters.)

Those everyday habits have changed how we all read and think in front of a screen. Unfortunately, those same habits often hurt our scores when taking computer-based exams.

If you scan exam questions like you read web pages, texts, and tweets, you will probably make some mistakes because you missed a key fact in the question, answer, or exhibits. It helps to start at the beginning and read all the words—a process that is amazingly unnatural for many people today.

NOTE I have talked to many college professors, in multiple disciplines, and Cisco Networking Academy instructors, and they consistently tell me that the number-one test-taking issue today is that people do not read the question well enough to understand the details.

When you are taking the practice exams and answering individual questions, let me make two suggestions. First, before the practice exam, think about your own personal strategy for how you will read a question. Make your approach to multiple-choice questions in particular be a conscious decision on your part. Second, if you want some suggestions on how to read an exam question, use the following strategy:

Step 1.   Read the question itself, thoroughly, from start to finish.

Step 2.   Scan any exhibit (usually command output) or figure.

Step 3.   Scan the answers to look for the types of information. (Numeric? Terms? Single words? Phrases?)

Step 4.   Reread the question thoroughly, from start to finish, to make sure that you understand it.

Step 5.   Read each answer thoroughly, while referring to the figure/exhibit as needed. After reading each answer, before reading the next answer:

   A. If correct, select as correct.

   B. If for sure it is incorrect, mentally rule it out.

   C. If unsure, mentally note it as a possible correct answer.

> **NOTE**   Cisco exams will tell you the number of correct answers. The exam software also helps you finish the question with the right number of answers noted. For example, the software prevents you from selecting too many answers. Also, if you try to move on to the next question but have too few answers noted, the exam software asks if you truly want to move on. And you should guess when unsure on the actual exam—there is no penalty for guessing.

Use the practice exams as a place to practice your approach to reading. Every time you click to the next question, try to read the question following your approach. If you are feeling time pressure, that is the perfect time to keep practicing your approach, to reduce and eliminate questions you miss because of scanning the question instead of reading thoroughly.

Taking Other Practice Exams

Many people add other practice exams and questions other than those that come with this book. Frankly, using other practice exams in addition to the questions that come with this book can be a good idea, for many reasons. The other exam questions can use different terms in different ways, emphasize different topics, and show different scenarios that make you rethink some topics.

Note that the publisher does sell products that include additional test questions. The *CCENT/CCNA ICND1 100-105 Official Cert Guide Premium Edition eBook and Practice Test* product is basically the publisher's eBook version of this book. It includes a soft copy of the book, in formats you can read on your computer or on the most common book readers and tablets. The product includes all the content you would normally get with the DVD that comes with the print book, including all the question databases mentioned in this chapter. Additionally, this product includes two more ICND1 exam databases.

> **NOTE**   In addition to getting the extra questions, the Premium editions have links to every test question, including those in the print book, to the specific section of the book for further reference. This is a great learning tool if you need more detail than what you find in the question explanations. You can purchase the eBooks and additional practice exams at 70 percent off the list price using the coupon on the back of the activation code card in the DVD sleeve, making the Premium editions the best and most cost-efficient way to get more practice questions.

Find Knowledge Gaps Through Question Review

You just took a number of practice exams. You probably learned a lot, gained some exam-taking skills, and improved your networking knowledge and skills. But if you go back and look at all the questions you missed, you might be able to find a few small gaps in your knowledge.

37

One of the hardest things to find when doing your final exam preparation is to discover gaps in your knowledge and skills. In other words, what topics and skills do you need to know that you do not know? Or what topics do you think you know, but you misunderstand about some important fact? Finding gaps in your knowledge at this late stage requires more than just your gut feel about your strengths and weaknesses.

This next task uses a feature of PCPT to help you find those gaps. The PCPT software tracks each practice exam you take, remembering your answer for every question, and whether you got it wrong. You can view the results and move back and forth between seeing the question and seeing the results page. To find gaps in your knowledge, follow these steps:

Step 1.   Pick and review one of your practice exams.

Step 2.   Review each incorrect question until you are happy that you understand the question.

Step 3.   When finished with your review for a question, mark the question.

Step 4.   Review all incorrect questions from your exam until all are marked.

Step 5.   Move on to the next practice exam.

Figure 37-1 shows a sample "Question Review" page, in which all the questions were answered incorrectly. The results list a "Correct" column, with no check mark meaning that the answer was incorrect.

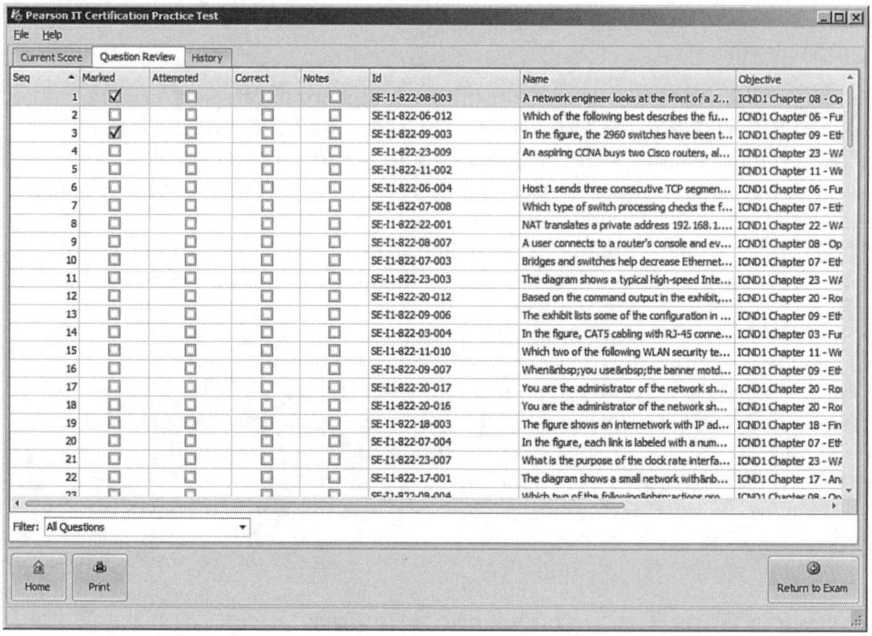

Figure 37-1   *PCPT Grading Results Page*

To perform the process of reviewing questions and marking them as complete, you can move between this Question Review page and the individual questions. Just double-click a question to move back to that question. From the question, you can click "Grade Exam" to move back to the grading results and to the Question Review page shown in Figure 37-1.

The question window also shows the place to mark the question, in the upper left, as shown in Figure 37-2.

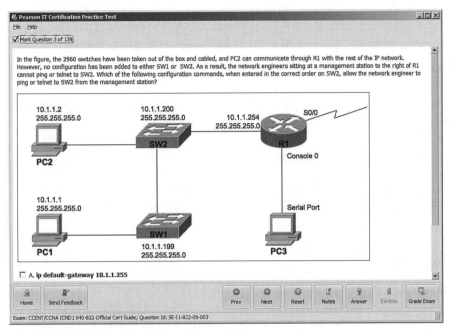

Figure 37-2 *Reviewing a Question, with Mark Feature in Upper Left*

If you want to come back later to look through the questions you missed from an earlier exam, start at the PCPT home screen. From there, instead of clicking the Start button to start a new exam, click the View Grade History button to see your earlier exam attempts and work through any missed questions.

Track your progress through your gap review in Table 37-4. PCPT lists your previous practice exams by date and score, so it helps to note those values in the table for comparison to the PCPT menu.

Table 37-4 Tracking Checklist for Gap Review of Practice Exams

Exam (ICND1, ICND2, or CCNA)	Original Practice Exam Date	Original Exam Score	Date Gap Review Was Completed

Practice Hands-On CLI Skills

To do well on Sim and Simlet questions, you need to be comfortable with many Cisco router and switch commands, as well as how to use them from a Cisco CLI. As described in the introduction to this book, Sim questions require you to decide what configuration command(s) need to be configured to fix a problem or to complete a working configuration. Simlet questions require you to answer multichoice questions by first using the CLI to issue **show** commands to look at the status of routers and switches in a small network.

To be ready for the exam, you need to know the following kinds of information:

CLI navigation: Basic CLI mechanics of moving into and out of user, enable, and configuration modes

Individual configuration: The meaning of the parameters of each configuration command

Feature configuration: The set of configuration commands, both required and optional, for each feature

Verification of configuration: The **show** commands that directly identify the configuration settings

Verification of status: The **show** commands that list current status values, and the ability to decide incorrect configuration or other problem causes of less-than-optimal status values

To help remember and review all this knowledge and skill, you can do the tasks listed in the next several pages.

Review Mind Maps from Part Review

During Part Review, you created different mind maps with both configuration and verification commands. To remember the specific mind maps, flip back to each part's Part Review section.

Do Labs

Whatever method you chose for building hands-on CLI skills, take some time to review and do some labs to practice the commands. At this point, you should have thought about configuration quite a bit, whether in a Simulator, on real gear, or even just as paper exercises. While it might be impractical to repeat every lab, make it a point to practice any commands and features for which you feel a little unsure about the topics from your review of the mind maps.

First, make it a point to review labs for the major configuration topics in the chapter as listed in Table 37-5.

Table 37-5 Lab Topic Checklist

Topic	Chapter	Date You Finished Lab Review
Switch IPv4	8	
Switch port security	9	
VLANs	11	
VLAN trunking	11	
Router IPv4 addresses and static routes	18	
RIPv2	19	
DHCP Relay and Server	20	
Standard ACLs	25	

Topic	Chapter	Date You Finished Lab Review
Extended and named ACLs	26	
NAT	27	
IPv6 addressing on routers	30	
IPv6 static routes	32	
Syslog, NTP, CDP, and LLDP	33	
Banners	34	
Telnet and SSH Access ACLs	34	

One great way to practice is to use the Pearson Network Simulator (the Sim) at www.pearsonitcertification.com/networksimulator.

Second, use the Config checklist app available from the book DVD or companion website. Working through all the configuration checklists, you should also see most of those topics in Table 37-5. Make sure you remember all the required and optional configuration commands.

Third, you should be able to repeat any or all of the Config Labs found on my blog site. When you are truly prepared for the exam, you should be able to do these labs without much reference to your notes. The launch site for all CCENT (ICND1) Config Labs is blog.certskills.com/ccent. From there, navigate to the Hands On… Config Lab category from the site menus.

Assess Whether You Are Ready to Pass (and the Fallacy of Exam Scores)

When you take a practice exam with PCPT, PCPT gives you a score, on a scale from 300 to 1000. Why? Cisco gives a score of between 300 and 1000 as well. But the similarities end there.

With PCPT, the score is a basic percentage but expressed as a number from 0 to 1000. For example, answer 80 percent correct, and the score is 800; get 90 percent correct, and the score is 900. If you start a practice exam and click through it without answering a single question, you get a 0.

However, Cisco does not score exams in the same way. The following is what we do know about Cisco exam scoring:

- Cisco uses a scoring scale from 300 to 1000.
- It tells us that it gives partial credit but provides no further details.

So, what does an 800 or a 900 mean on the actual Cisco exams? Many people think those scores mean 80 percent or 90 percent, but we don't know. Cisco doesn't reveal the details of scoring to us. It doesn't reveal the details of partial credit. It seems reasonable to expect a Sim question to be worth more points than a multichoice single-answer question, but we do not know.

The reason I mention all these facts to you is this:

Do not rely too much on your PCPT practice exam scores to assess whether you are ready to pass. Those scores are a general indicator, in that if you make a 700 one time and a 900 a week later, you are probably now better prepared. But that 900 on your PCPT

37

practice exam does not mean you will likely make a 900 on the actual exam—because we do not know how Cisco scores the exam.

So, what can you use as a way to assess whether you are ready to pass? Unfortunately, the answer requires some extra effort, and the answer will not be some nice convenient number that looks like an exam score. But you can self-assess your skills as follows:

1. When you do take an exam with PCPT, you should understand the terms used in the questions and answers.

2. You should be able to look at the list of key topics from each chapter and explain each topic in a sentence or two to a friend.

3. You should be able to do subnetting math at around the suggested speeds shown in this chapter in Table 37-1.

4. You should be able to do all the Config Labs, or labs of similar challenge level, and get them right consistently.

5. For chapters with **show** commands, you should understand the fields highlighted in gray in the examples spread about the book, and when looking at those examples, you should know which values show configuration settings and which show status information.

6. For the key topics that list various troubleshooting root causes, when you review those lists, you should remember and understand the concept behind each item in the list without needing to look further at the chapter.

Study Suggestions After Failing to Pass

None of us wants to take and fail any exam, but some of you will. And even if you pass the ICND1 100-105 exam on your first try, if you keep going with Cisco certifications, you will probably fail some exams along the way. I mention failing an exam not to focus on the negative, but to help prepare you for how to pass the next attempt after failing an earlier attempt. This section collects some of the advice I have given to readers over the years who have contacted me after a failed attempt, asking for help about what to do next.

The single most important bit of advice is to change your mindset about Cisco exams. Cisco exams are not like high school or college exams where your failing grade matters. Instead, a Cisco exam is more like a event on the road to completing an impressive major accomplishment, one that most people have to try a few times to achieve.

For instance, achieving a Cisco certification is more like training to run a marathon in under 4 hours. The first time running a marathon, you may not even finish, or you may finish at 4:15 rather than under 4:00. But finishing a marathon in 4:15 means that you have prepared and are getting pretty close to your goal. Or maybe it is more like training to complete an obstacle course (any Ninja Warrior fans out there? www.nbc.com/american-ninja-warrior). Maybe you got past the first three obstacles today, but you couldn't climb over the 14-foot high warped wall. That just means you need to practice on that wall a little more.

So change your mindset. You're a marathon runner looking to improve your time or a Ninja Warrior looking to complete the obstacle course. And you are getting better skills every time you study, which helps you compete in the market.

With that attitude and analogy in mind, the rest of this section lists specific study steps that can help:

First, study the notes you took about your failed attempt. (See the earlier section "Reserve the Hour After the Exam in Case You Fail.") Do not share that information with others, but use it to study. Before you take the exam again, you should be able to answer every actual exam question you can remember from the last attempt. Even if you never see the exact same question again, you will still get a good return for your effort.

Second, spend more time on activities that uncover your weaknesses. When doing that, you have to slow down and be more self-aware. For instance, answer practice questions in study mode, and *do not guess*. Do not click on to the next question, but pause and ask yourself if you are really sure about both the wrong and correct answers. If unsure, fantastic! You just discovered a topic to go back and dig in to learn it more deeply. Or when you do a lab, you may refer to your notes without thinking, so now think about it when you turn to your notes because that tells you where you are unsure. That might be a reminder that you have not mastered those commands yet.

Third, think about your time spent on the exam. Did you run out of time? Go too fast? Too slow? If too slow, were you slow on subnetting, or Sims, or something else? Then make a written plan as to how you will approach time on the next attempt and how you will track time use. And if you ran out of time, practice for the things that slowed you down.

Fourth, if you failed the CCNA R&S 200-125 exam, reconsider your choice for the one-exam path rather than the two-exam path. Think about the ICND1 topics on the CCNA exam. Did you know those pretty well? If so, you may be ready to pass ICND1 now. That's another step closer, and then you can focus on the ICND2 exam.

(For perspective, the original *CCNA Official Cert Guide* was 500 pages long. The combined ICND1 and ICND2 books have grown to over 1,600 pages of technology chapters, for three times as much content as the original CCNA exam. It's just a lot of content.)

Other Study Tasks

If you got to this point and still feel the need to prepare some more, this last topic gives you three suggestions.

First, the Chapter Review and Part Review sections give you some useful study tasks.

Second, use more exam questions from other sources. You can always get more questions in the *Cisco Press Premium Edition eBook and Practice Test* products, which include an eBook copy of this book plus additional questions in additional PCPT exam banks. However, you can search the Internet for questions from many sources and review those questions as well.

37

NOTE   Some vendors claim to sell practice exams that contain the literal exam questions from the exam. These exams, called "brain dumps," are against the Cisco testing policies. Cisco strongly discourages using any such tools for study.

Finally, join in the discussions on the Cisco Learning Network. Try to answer questions asked by other learners; the process of answering makes you think much harder about the topic. When someone posts an answer with which you disagree, think about why and talk about it online. This is a great way to both learn more and build confidence.

Final Thoughts

You have studied quite a bit, worked hard, and sacrificed time and money to be ready for the exam. I hope your exam goes well, that you pass, and that you pass because you really know your stuff and will do well in your IT and networking career.

I encourage you to celebrate when you pass and ask advice when you do not. The Cisco Learning Network is a great place to make posts to celebrate and to ask advice for the next time around. I personally would love to hear about your progress through Twitter (@wendellodom) or my Facebook page (facebook.com/wendellodom). I wish you well, and congratulations for working through the entire book!

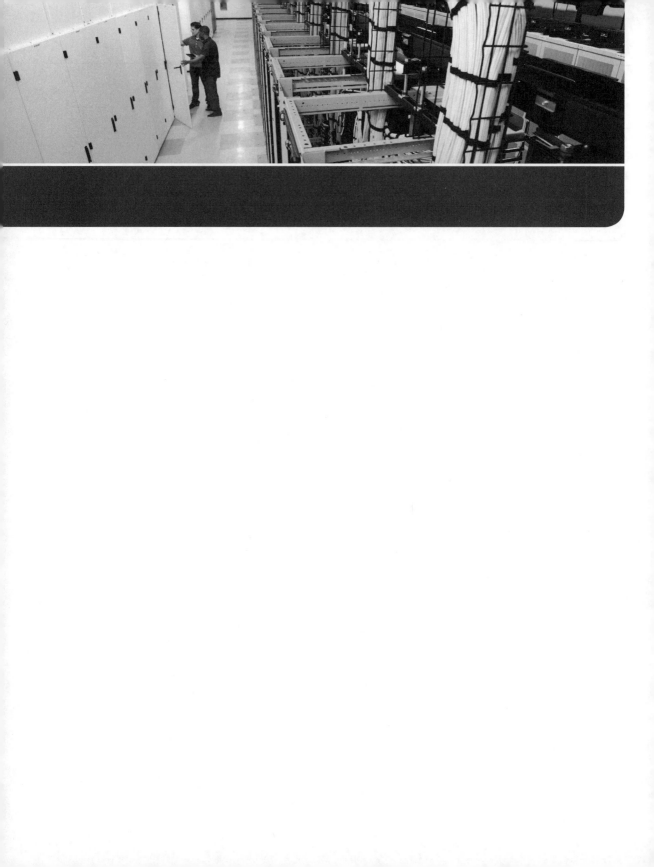

Part XI

Appendixes

Numeric Reference Tables

This appendix provides several useful reference tables that list numbers used throughout this book. Specifically:

Table A-1: A decimal-binary cross reference, useful when converting from decimal to binary and vice versa.

Table A-1   Decimal-Binary Cross Reference, Decimal Values 0–255

Decimal Value	Binary Value	Decimal Value	Binary Value	Decimal Value	Binary Value	Decimal Value	Binary Value
0	00000000	32	00100000	64	01000000	96	01100000
1	00000001	33	00100001	65	01000001	97	01100001
2	00000010	34	00100010	66	01000010	98	01100010
3	00000011	35	00100011	67	01000011	99	01100011
4	00000100	36	00100100	68	01000100	100	01100100
5	00000101	37	00100101	69	01000101	101	01100101
6	00000110	38	00100110	70	01000110	102	01100110
7	00000111	39	00100111	71	01000111	103	01100111
8	00001000	40	00101000	72	01001000	104	01101000
9	00001001	41	00101001	73	01001001	105	01101001
10	00001010	42	00101010	74	01001010	106	01101010
11	00001011	43	00101011	75	01001011	107	01101011
12	00001100	44	00101100	76	01001100	108	01101100
13	00001101	45	00101101	77	01001101	109	01101101
14	00001110	46	00101110	78	01001110	110	01101110
15	00001111	47	00101111	79	01001111	111	01101111
16	00010000	48	00110000	80	01010000	112	01110000
17	00010001	49	00110001	81	01010001	113	01110001
18	00010010	50	00110010	82	01010010	114	01110010
19	00010011	51	00110011	83	01010011	115	01110011
20	00010100	52	00110100	84	01010100	116	01110100
21	00010101	53	00110101	85	01010101	117	01110101
22	00010110	54	00110110	86	01010110	118	01110110
23	00010111	55	00110111	87	01010111	119	01110111
24	00011000	56	00111000	88	01011000	120	01111000
25	00011001	57	00111001	89	01011001	121	01111001
26	00011010	58	00111010	90	01011010	122	01111010
27	00011011	59	00111011	91	01011011	123	01111011
28	00011100	60	00111100	92	01011100	124	01111100
29	00011101	61	00111101	93	01011101	125	01111101
30	00011110	62	00111110	94	01011110	126	01111110
31	00011111	63	00111111	95	01011111	127	01111111

Table A-1   Decimal-Binary Cross Reference, Decimal Values 0–255

Decimal Value	Binary Value	Decimal Value	Binary Value	Decimal Value	Binary Value	Decimal Value	Binary Value
128	10000000	160	10100000	192	11000000	224	11100000
129	10000001	161	10100001	193	11000001	225	11100001
130	10000010	162	10100010	194	11000010	226	11100010
131	10000011	163	10100011	195	11000011	227	11100011
132	10000100	164	10100100	196	11000100	228	11100100
133	10000101	165	10100101	197	11000101	229	11100101
134	10000110	166	10100110	198	11000110	230	11100110
135	10000111	167	10100111	199	11000111	231	11100111
136	10001000	168	10101000	200	11001000	232	11101000
137	10001001	169	10101001	201	11001001	233	11101001
138	10001010	170	10101010	202	11001010	234	11101010
139	10001011	171	10101011	203	11001011	235	11101011
140	10001100	172	10101100	204	11001100	236	11101100
141	10001101	173	10101101	205	11001101	237	11101101
142	10001110	174	10101110	206	11001110	238	11101110
143	10001111	175	10101111	207	11001111	239	11101111
144	10010000	176	10110000	208	11010000	240	11110000
145	10010001	177	10110001	209	11010001	241	11110001
146	10010010	178	10110010	210	11010010	242	11110010
147	10010011	179	10110011	211	11010011	243	11110011
148	10010100	180	10110100	212	11010100	244	11110100
149	10010101	181	10110101	213	11010101	245	11110101
150	10010110	182	10110110	214	11010110	246	11110110
151	10010111	183	10110111	215	11010111	247	11110111
152	10011000	184	10111000	216	11011000	248	11111000
153	10011001	185	10111001	217	11011001	249	11111001
154	10011010	186	10111010	218	11011010	250	11111010
155	10011011	187	10111011	219	11011011	251	11111011
156	10011100	188	10111100	220	11011100	252	11111100
157	10011101	189	10111101	221	11011101	253	11111101
158	10011110	190	10111110	222	11011110	254	11111110
159	10011111	191	10111111	223	11011111	255	11111111

A

Table A-2: A hexadecimal-binary cross reference, useful when converting from hex to binary and vice versa.

Table A-2 Hex-Binary Cross Reference

Hex	4-Bit Binary
0	0000
1	0001
2	0010
3	0011
4	0100
5	0101
6	0110
7	0111
8	1000
9	1001
A	1010
B	1011
C	1100
D	1101
E	1110
F	1111

Table A-3: Powers of 2, from 2^1 through 2^{32}.

Table A-3   Powers of 2

X	2^X	X	2^X
1	2	17	131,072
2	4	18	262,144
3	8	19	524,288
4	16	20	1,048,576
5	32	21	2,097,152
6	64	22	4,194,304
7	128	23	8,388,608
8	256	24	16,777,216
9	512	25	33,554,432
10	1024	26	67,108,864
11	2048	27	134,217,728
12	4096	28	268,435,456
13	8192	29	536,870,912
14	16,384	30	1,073,741,824
15	32,768	31	2,147,483,648
16	65,536	32	4,294,967,296

A

Table A-4: Table of all 33 possible subnet masks, in all three formats.

Table A-4 All Subnet Masks

Decimal	Prefix	Binary			
0.0.0.0	/0	00000000	00000000	00000000	00000000
128.0.0.0	/1	10000000	00000000	00000000	00000000
192.0.0.0	/2	11000000	00000000	00000000	00000000
224.0.0.0	/3	11100000	00000000	00000000	00000000
240.0.0.0	/4	11110000	00000000	00000000	00000000
248.0.0.0	/5	11111000	00000000	00000000	00000000
252.0.0.0	/6	11111100	00000000	00000000	00000000
254.0.0.0	/7	11111110	00000000	00000000	00000000
255.0.0.0	/8	11111111	00000000	00000000	00000000
255.128.0.0	/9	11111111	10000000	00000000	00000000
255.192.0.0	/10	11111111	11000000	00000000	00000000
255.224.0.0	/11	11111111	11100000	00000000	00000000
255.240.0.0	/12	11111111	11110000	00000000	00000000
255.248.0.0	/13	11111111	11111000	00000000	00000000
255.252.0.0	/14	11111111	11111100	00000000	00000000
255.254.0.0	/15	11111111	11111110	00000000	00000000
255.255.0.0	/16	11111111	11111111	00000000	00000000
255.255.128.0	/17	11111111	11111111	10000000	00000000
255.255.192.0	/18	11111111	11111111	11000000	00000000
255.255.224.0	/19	11111111	11111111	11100000	00000000
255.255.240.0	/20	11111111	11111111	11110000	00000000
255.255.248.0	/21	11111111	11111111	11111000	00000000
255.255.252.0	/22	11111111	11111111	11111100	00000000
255.255.254.0	/23	11111111	11111111	11111110	00000000
255.255.255.0	/24	11111111	11111111	11111111	00000000
255.255.255.128	/25	11111111	11111111	11111111	10000000
255.255.255.192	/26	11111111	11111111	11111111	11000000
255.255.255.224	/27	11111111	11111111	11111111	11100000
255.255.255.240	/28	11111111	11111111	11111111	11110000
255.255.255.248	/29	11111111	11111111	11111111	11111000
255.255.255.252	/30	11111111	11111111	11111111	11111100
255.255.255.254	/31	11111111	11111111	11111111	11111110
255.255.255.255	/32	11111111	11111111	11111111	11111111

CCENT/CCNA ICND1 100-105 Exam Updates

Over time, reader feedback allows Pearson to gauge which topics give our readers the most problems when taking the exams. To assist readers with those topics, the authors create new materials clarifying and expanding on those troublesome exam topics. As mentioned in the Introduction, the additional content about the exam is contained in a PDF on this book's companion website, at http://www.ciscopress.com/title/9781587205804.

This appendix is intended to provide you with updated information if Cisco makes minor modifications to the exam upon which this book is based. When Cisco releases an entirely new exam, the changes are usually too extensive to provide in a simple update appendix. In those cases, you might need to consult the new edition of the book for the updated content.

This appendix attempts to fill the void that occurs with any print book. In particular, this appendix does the following:

- Mentions technical items that might not have been mentioned elsewhere in the book
- Covers new topics if Cisco adds new content to the exam over time
- Provides a way to get up-to-the-minute current information about content for the exam

Always Get the Latest at the Book's Product Page

You are reading the version of this appendix that was available when your book was printed. However, given that the main purpose of this appendix is to be a living, changing document, it is important that you look for the latest version online at the book's companion website. To do so, follow these steps:

Step 1.   Browse to www.ciscopress.com/title/9781587205804.

Step 2.   Click the **Updates** tab.

Step 3.   If there is a new Appendix B document on the page, download the latest Appendix B document.

> **NOTE**   The downloaded document has a version number. Comparing the version of the print Appendix B (Version 1.0) with the latest online version of this appendix, you should do the following:
>
> ■   **Same version:** Ignore the PDF that you downloaded from the companion website.
>
> ■   **Website has a later version:** Ignore this Appendix B in your book and read only the latest version that you downloaded from the companion website.

Technical Content

The current Version 1.0 of this appendix does not contain additional technical coverage.

10/100   A short reference to an Ethernet NIC or switch port that supports speed of 10 Mbps and 100 Mbps.

10/100/1000   A short reference to an Ethernet NIC or switch port that supports speeds of 10 Mbps, 100 Mbps, and 1000 Mbps (that is, 1 Gbps).

10BASE-T   The 10-Mbps baseband Ethernet specification using two pairs of twisted-pair cabling (Categories 3, 4, or 5): One pair transmits data and the other receives data. 10BASE-T, which is part of the IEEE 802.3 specification, has a distance limit of approximately 100 m (328 feet) per segment.

100BASE-T   A name for the IEEE Fast Ethernet standard that uses two-pair copper cabling, a speed of 100 Mbps, and a maximum cable length of 100 meters.

1000BASE-T   A name for the IEEE Gigabit Ethernet standard that uses four-pair copper cabling, a speed of 1000 Mbps (1 Gbps), and a maximum cable length of 100 meters.

802.1Q   The IEEE standardized protocol for VLAN trunking.

802.11a   The IEEE standard for wireless LANs using the U-NII spectrum, OFDM encoding, and speeds of up to 54 Mbps.

802.11b   The IEEE standard for wireless LANs using the ISM spectrum, DSSS encoding, and speeds of up to 11 Mbps.

802.11g   The IEEE standard for wireless LANs using the ISM spectrum, OFDM or DSSS encoding, and speeds of up to 54 Mbps.

802.11n   The IEEE standard for wireless LANs using the ISM spectrum, OFDM encoding, and multiple antennas for single-stream speeds up to 150 Mbps.

A

AAA   Authentication, authorization, and accounting. Authentication confirms the identity of the user or device. Authorization determines what the user or device is allowed to do. Accounting records information about access attempts, including inappropriate requests.

AAA server   A server that holds security information and provides services related to user login, particularly authentication (is the user who they say they are), authorization (once authenticated, what do we allow the user to do), and accounting (tracking the user).

access interface   A LAN network design term that refers to a switch interface connected to end-user devices, configured so that it does not use VLAN trunking.

access layer   In a campus LAN design, the switches that connect directly to endpoint devices (servers, user devices), and also connect into the distribution layer switches.

access link   In Frame Relay, the physical serial link that connects a Frame Relay DTE device, usually a router, to a Frame Relay switch. The access link uses the same physical layer standards as do point-to-point leased lines.

access point   A wireless LAN device that provides a means for wireless clients to send data to each other and to the rest of a wired network, with the AP connecting to both the wireless LAN and the wired Ethernet LAN.

accounting   In security, the recording of access attempts. *See* AAA.

address block   A set of consecutive IPv4 addresses. The term is most often used for a class-less prefix as defined by CIDR, but can also refer to any subnet or IPv4 network.

adjacent-layer interaction   The general topic of how on one computer, two adjacent layers in a networking architectural model work together, with the lower layer providing services to the higher layer.

administrative distance   In Cisco routers, a means for one router to choose between multiple routes to reach the same subnet when those routes were learned by different routing protocols. The lower the administrative distance, the better the source of the routing information.

ADSL   Asymmetric digital subscriber line. One of many DSL technologies, ADSL is designed to deliver more bandwidth downstream (from the central office to the customer site) than upstream.

all-nodes multicast address   A specific IPv6 multicast address, FF02::1, with link-local scope, used to send packets to all devices on the link that support IPv6.

all-routers multicast address   A specific IPv6 multicast address, FF02::2, with link-local scope, used to send packets to all devices that act as IPv6 routers on the local link.

anycast address   An address shared by two or more hosts that exist in different parts of the network, so that by design, the routers will forward packets to the nearest of the two servers, allowing clients to communicate with the nearest such server, not caring which particular server with which the client communicates.

ARP   Address Resolution Protocol. An Internet protocol used to map an IP address to a MAC address. Defined in RFC 826.

ARP table   A list of IP addresses of neighbors on the same VLAN, along with their MAC addresses, as kept in memory by hosts and routers.

ARPANET   The first packet-switched network, first created around 1970, which served as the predecessor to the Internet.

asymmetric   A feature of many Internet access technologies, including DSL, cable, and modems, in which the downstream transmission rate is higher than the upstream transmission rate.

asynchronous   The lack of an imposed time ordering on a bit stream. Practically, both sides agree to the same speed, but there is no check or adjustment of the rates if they are slightly different. However, because only 1 byte per transfer is sent, slight differences in clock speed are not an issue.

authentication   In security, the verification of the identity of a person or a process. *See* AAA.

authorization   In security, the determination of the rights allowed for a particular user or device. *See* AAA.

autonegotiation   An IEEE standard mechanism (802.3u) with which two nodes can exchange messages for the purpose of choosing to use the same Ethernet standards on both ends of the link, ensuring that the link functions and functions well.

autonomous system   An internetwork in the administrative control of one organization, company, or governmental agency, inside which that organization typically runs an interior gateway protocol (IGP).

autosummarization   A routing protocol feature in which the a router that sits at the boundary between different classful networks will automatically advertise a route for one entire classful network into the other classful network, and vice versa.

auxiliary port   A physical connector on a router that is designed to be used to allow a remote terminal, or PC with a terminal emulator, to access a router using an analog modem.

B

back-to-back link   A serial link between two routers, created without CSU/DSUs, by connecting a DTE cable to one router and a DCE cable to the other. Typically used in labs to build serial links without the expense of an actual leased line from the telco.

bandwidth   A reference to the speed of a networking link. Its origins come from earlier communications technology in which the range, or width, of the frequency band dictated how fast communications could occur.

basic service set (BSS)   In wireless LANs, a WLAN with a single access point.

binary mask   An IPv4 subnet mask written as a 32-bit binary number.

bitwise Boolean AND   A Boolean AND between two numbers of the same length in which the first bit in each number is ANDed, and then the second bit in each number, and then the third, and so on.

Boolean AND   A math operation performed on a pair of one-digit binary numbers. The result is another one-digit binary number. 1 AND 1 yields 1; all other combinations yield a 0.

boot field   The low-order 4 bits of the configuration register in a Cisco router. The value in the boot field in part tells the router where to look for a Cisco IOS image to load.

broadcast address   Generally, any address that represents all devices, and can be used to send one message to all devices. In Ethernet, the MAC address of all binary 1s, or FFFF.FFFF. FFFF in hex. For IPv4, *see* subnet broadcast address.

broadcast domain   A set of all devices that receive broadcast frames originating from any device within the set. Devices in the same VLAN are in the same broadcast domain.

broadcast frame   An Ethernet frame sent to destination address FFFF.FFFF.FFFF, meaning that the frame should be delivered to all hosts on that LAN.

broadcast subnet   When subnetting a Class A, B, or C network, the one subnet in each classful network for which all subnet bits have a value of binary 1. The subnet broadcast address in this subnet has the same numeric value as the classful network's network-wide broadcast address.

bus   A common physical signal path composed of wires or other media across which signals can be sent from one part of a computer to another.

C

cable Internet   An Internet access technology that uses a cable TV (CATV) cable, normally used for video, to send and receive data.

CDP   Cisco Discovery Protocol. A media- and protocol-independent device-discovery protocol that runs on most Cisco-manufactured equipment, including routers, access servers, and switches. Using CDP, a device can advertise its existence to other devices and receive information about other devices on the same LAN or on the remote side of a WAN.

CDP neighbor   A device on the other end of some communications cable that is advertising CDP updates.

CIDR   Classless inter-domain routing. An RFC-standard tool for global IP address range assignment. CIDR reduces the size of Internet routers' IP routing tables, helping deal with the rapid growth of the Internet. The term *classless* refers to the fact that the summarized groups of networks represent a group of addresses that do not conform to IPv4 classful (Class A, B, and C) grouping rules.

CIDR mask   Another term for a prefix mask, one that uses prefix or CIDR notation, in which the mask is represented by a slash (/) followed by a decimal number.

CIDR notation   *See* prefix notation.

circuit switching   A generic reference to network services, typically WAN services, in which the provider sets up a (Layer 1) circuit between two devices, and the provider makes no attempt to interpret the meaning of the bits. *See also* packet switching.

classful addressing   A concept in IPv4 addressing that defines a subnetted IP address as having three parts: network, subnet, and host.

classful IP network   An IPv4 Class A, B, or C network; called a classful network because these networks are defined by the class rules for IPv4 addressing.

classful routing protocol   Does not transmit the mask information along with the subnet number, and therefore must consider Class A, B, and C network boundaries and perform auto-summarization at those boundaries. Does not support VLSM.

classless addressing   A concept in IPv4 addressing that defines a subnetted IP address as having two parts: a prefix (or subnet) and a host.

classless inter-domain routing   The name of an RFC that defines several important features related to public IPv4 addressing: a global address assignment strategy to keep the size of IPv4 routing tables smaller, and the ability to assign public IPv4 addresses in sizes based on any prefix length.

classless prefix   A range of public IPv4 addresses as defined by with CIDR.

classless prefix length   The mask (prefix length) used when defining a classless prefix.

classless routing protocol   An inherent characteristic of a routing protocol, specifically that the routing protocol does send subnet masks in its routing updates, thereby removing any need to make assumptions about the addresses in a particular subnet or network, making it able to support VLSM and manual route summarization.

CLI   Command-line interface. An interface that enables the user to interact with the operating system by entering commands and optional arguments.

clock rate   The speed at which a serial link encodes bits on the transmission medium.

clock source   The device to which the other devices on the link adjust their speed when using synchronous links.

clocking   The process of supplying a signal over a cable, either on a separate pin on a serial cable or as part of the signal transitions in the transmitted signal, so that the receiving device can keep synchronization with the sending device.

code integrity   A software security term that refers to how likely that the software (code) being used is the software supplied by the vendor, unchanged, with no viruses or other changes made to the software.

codec   Coder-decoder. An integrated circuit device that transforms analog voice signals into a digital bit stream and then transforms digital signals back into analog voice signals.

collapsed core design   A campus LAN design in which the design does not use a separate set of core switches in addition to the distribution switches—in effect collapsing the core into the distribution switches.

collision domain   A set of network interface cards (NIC) for which a frame sent by one NIC could result in a collision with a frame sent by any other NIC in the same collision domain.

command-line interface   *See* CLI.

configuration archive   An IOS concept by which some IOS file system is defined as a place to store configuration archives of a Cisco router or switch, allowing automatic and manual archive, and easier restore.

configuration mode   A part of the Cisco IOS Software CLI in which the user can type configuration commands that are then added to the device's currently used configuration file (running-config).

configuration register   In Cisco routers, a 16-bit, user-configurable value that determines how the router functions during initialization. In software, the bit position is set by specifying a hexadecimal value using configuration commands.

connected   The single-item status code listed by a switch **show interfaces status** command, with this status referring to a working interface.

connected route   On a router, an IP route added to the routing table when the router interface is both up and has an IP address configured. The route is for the subnet that can be calculated based on the configured IP address and mask.

connection establishment   The process by which a connection-oriented protocol creates a connection. With TCP, a connection is established by a three-way transmission of TCP segments.

console port   A physical socket on a router or switch to which a cable can be connected between a computer and the router/switch, for the purpose of allowing the computer to use a terminal emulator and use the CLI to configure, verify, and troubleshoot the router/switch.

contiguous network   A network topology in which subnets of network X are not separated by subnets of any other classful network.

convergence   The time required for routing protocols to react to changes in the network, removing bad routes and adding new, better routes so that the current best routes are in all the routers' routing tables.

core design   A campus LAN design that connects each access switch to distribution switches, and distribution switches into core switches, to provide a path between all LAN devices.

core layer   In a campus LAN design, the switches that connect the distribution layer switches, and to each other, to provide connectivity between the various distribution layer switches.

CPE   Customer premises equipment. Any equipment related to communications that is located at the customer site, as opposed to inside the telephone company's network.

crossover cable   An Ethernet cable that swaps the pair used for transmission on one device to a pair used for receiving on the device on the opposite end of the cable. In 10BASE-T and 100BASE-TX networks, this cable swaps the pair at pins 1,2 to pins 3,6 on the other end of the cable, and the pair at pins 3,6 to pins 1,2 as well.

CSMA/CD   Carrier sense multiple access with collision detection. A media-access mechanism in which devices ready to transmit data first check the channel for a carrier. If no carrier is sensed for a specific period of time, a device can transmit. If two devices transmit at once, a collision occurs and is detected by all colliding devices. This collision subsequently delays retransmissions from those devices for some random length of time.

CSU/DSU   Channel service unit/data service unit. A device that understands the Layer 1 details of serial links installed by a telco and how to use a serial cable to communicate with networking equipment such as routers.

D

data VLAN   A VLAN used by typical data devices connected to an Ethernet, like PCs and servers. Used in comparison to a Voice VLAN.

DCE Data communications equipment. From a physical layer perspective, the device providing the clocking on a WAN link, typically a CSU/DSU, is the DCE. From a packet-switching perspective, the service provider's switch, to which a router might connect, is considered the DCE.

decimal mask An IPv4 subnet mask written in dotted decimal notation; for example, 255.255.255.0.

de-encapsulation On a computer that receives data over a network, the process in which the device interprets the lower-layer headers and, when finished with each header, removes the header, revealing the next-higher-layer PDU.

default gateway/default router On an IP host, the IP address of some router to which the host sends packets when the packet's destination address is on a subnet other than the local subnet.

default mask The mask used in a Class A, B, or C network that does not create any subnets; specifically, mask 255.0.0.0 for Class A networks, 255.255.0.0 for Class B networks, and 255.255.255.0 for Class C networks.

default route On a router, the route that is considered to match all packets that are not otherwise matched by some more specific route.

demarc The legal term for the demarcation or separation point between the telco's equipment and the customer's equipment.

denial of service (DoS) A type of attack whose goal is to cause problems by preventing legitimate users from being able to access services, thereby preventing the normal operation of computers and networks.

device hardening A security term referring to whatever activities one might do to secure a device or type of device, for instance, by securing login access to a router or switch, and using ACLs to limit what users can login to a router or switch.

DHCP Dynamic Host Configuration Protocol. A protocol used by hosts to dynamically discover and lease an IP address, and learn the correct subnet mask, default gateway, and DNS server IP addresses.

DHCP client Any device that uses DHCP protocols to ask to lease an IP address from a DHCP server, or to learn any IP settings from that server.

DHCP relay agent The name of the router IOS feature that forwards DHCP messages from client to servers by changing the destination IP address from 255.255.255.255 to the IP address of the DHCP server.

DHCP server Software that waits for DHCP clients to request to lease IP addresses, with the server assigning a lease of an IP address as well as listing other important IP settings for the client.

directed broadcast address *See* subnet broadcast address.

discontiguous network A network topology in which a subnets of network X are separated by subnets of some other classful network.

distance vector The logic behind the behavior of some interior routing protocols, such as RIP. Distance vector routing algorithms call for each router to send its entire routing table in each update, but only to its neighbors. Distance vector routing algorithms can be prone to routing loops but are computationally simpler than link-state routing algorithms.

distribution layer In a campus LAN design, the switches that connect to access layer switches as the most efficient means to provide connectivity from the access layer into the other parts of the LAN.

DNS Domain Name System. An application layer protocol used throughout the Internet for translating host names into their associated IP addresses.

DNS Reply In the Domain Name System (DNS), a message sent by a DNS server to a DNS client in response to a DNS Request, identifying the IP address assigned to a particular hostname or fully qualified domain name (FQDN).

DNS Request In the Domain Name System (DNS), a message sent by a DNS client to a DNS server, listing a hostname or fully qualified domain name (FQDN), asking the server to discover and reply with the IP address associated with that hostname or FQDN.

dotted-decimal notation (DDN) The format used for IP version 4 addresses, in which four decimal values are used, separated by periods (dots).

DSL Digital subscriber line. Public network technology that delivers high bandwidth over conventional telco local-loop copper wiring at limited distances. Typically used as an Internet access technology, connecting a user to an ISP.

DSL modem A device that connects to a telephone line, using DSL standards, to transmit and receive data to/from a telco using DSL.

DTE Data terminal equipment. From a Layer 1 perspective, the DTE synchronizes its clock based on the clock sent by the DCE. From a packet-switching perspective, the DTE is the device outside the service provider's network, typically a router.

dual stack A mode of operation in which a host or router runs both IPv4 and IPv6.

duplex mismatch On opposite ends of any Ethernet link, the condition in which one of the two devices uses full-duplex logic and the other uses half-duplex logic, resulting in unnecessary frame discards and retransmissions on the link.

duplicate address detection (DAD) A term used in IPv6 to refer to how hosts first check whether another host is using a unicast address before the first host uses that address.

E

E1 Similar to a T1, but used in Europe. It uses a rate of 2.048 Mbps and 32 64-kbps channels, with 1 channel reserved for framing and other overhead.

EIGRP Enhanced Interior Gateway Routing Protocol. An advanced version of IGRP developed by Cisco. Provides superior convergence properties and operating efficiency and combines the advantages of link-state protocols with those of distance vector protocols.

EIGRP version 6   The version of the EIGRP routing protocol that supports IPv6, and not IPv4.

enable mode   A part of the Cisco IOS CLI in which the user can use the most powerful and potentially disruptive commands on a router or switch, including the ability to then reach configuration mode and reconfigure the router.

encapsulation   The placement of data from a higher-layer protocol behind the header (and in some cases, between a header and trailer) of the next-lower-layer protocol. For example, an IP packet could be encapsulated in an Ethernet header and trailer before being sent over an Ethernet.

encryption   Applying a specific algorithm to data to alter the appearance of the data, making it incomprehensible to those who are not authorized to see the information.

error detection   The process of discovering whether a data link level frame was changed during transmission. This process typically uses a Frame Check Sequence (FCS) field in the data link trailer.

error disabled   An interface state on LAN switches that can be the result of one of many security violations.

error recovery   The process of noticing when some transmitted data was not successfully received and resending the data until it is successfully received.

escalate   In the context of troubleshooting methods, a defined business process by which the person assigned to troubleshoot a problem can move the problem on to another worker, in cases in which the original worker cannot solve the problem, or the problem has a large impact and needs more attention.

Ethernet   A series of LAN standards defined by the IEEE, originally invented by Xerox Corporation and developed jointly by Xerox, Intel, and Digital Equipment Corporation.

Ethernet address   A 48-bit (6-byte) binary number, usually written as a 12-digit hexadecimal number, used to identify Ethernet nodes in an Ethernet network. Ethernet frame headers list a destination and source address field, used by the Ethernet devices to deliver Ethernet frames to the correct destination.

Ethernet frame   A term referring to an Ethernet data link header and trailer, plus the data encapsulated between the header and trailer.

Ethernet link   A generic term for any physical link between two Ethernet nodes, no matter what type of cabling is used.

Ethernet over MPLS (EoMPLS)   A term referring specifically to how a service provider can create an Ethernet WAN service using an MPLS network. More generally, a term referring to Ethernet WAN services.

Ethernet port   A generic term for the opening on the side of any Ethernet node, typically in an Ethernet NIC or LAN switch, into which an Ethernet cable can be connected.

EtherType   Jargon that shortens the term *Ethernet Type*, which refers to the Type field in the Ethernet header. The Type field identifies the type of packet encapsulated inside an Ethernet frame.

EUI-64   Literally, a standard for an extended unique identifier that is 64 bits long. Specifically for IPv6, a set of rules for forming the a 64-bit identifier, used as the interface ID in IPv6 addresses, by starting with a 48-bit MAC address, inserting FFFE (hex) in the middle, and inverting the seventh bit.

extended access list   A list of IOS **access-list** global configuration commands that can match multiple parts of an IP packet, including the source and destination IP address and TCP/UDP ports, for the purpose of deciding which packets to discard and which to allow through the router.

extended ping   An IOS command in which the **ping** command accepts many other options besides just the destination IP address.

exterior gateway protocol (EGP)   A routing protocol that was designed to exchange routing information between different autonomous systems.

F

Fast Ethernet   The common name for all the IEEE standards that send data at 100 megabits per second.

filter   Generally, a process or a device that screens network traffic for certain characteristics, such as source address, destination address, or protocol, and determines whether to forward or discard that traffic based on the established criteria.

firewall   A device that forwards packets between the less secure and more secure parts of the network, applying rules that determine which packets are allowed to pass, and which are not.

flash memory   A type of read/write permanent memory that retains its contents even with no power applied to the memory, and uses no moving parts, making the memory less likely to fail over time.

floating static route   A static IP route that uses a higher administrative distance that other routes, typically routes learned by a routing protocol. As a result, the router will not use the static route if the routing protocol route has been learned, but then use the static route if the routing protocol fails to learn the route.

flood/flooding   The result of the LAN switch forwarding process for broadcasts and unknown unicast frames. Switches forward these frames out all interfaces, except the interface in which the frame arrived. Switches also flood multicasts by default, although this behavior can be changed.

flow control   The process of regulating the amount of data sent by a sending computer toward a receiving computer. Several flow control mechanisms exist, including TCP flow control, which uses windowing.

forward   To send a frame received in one interface out another interface, toward its ultimate destination.

forward acknowledgment   A process used by protocols that do error recovery, in which the number that acknowledges data lists the next data that should be sent, not the last data that was successfully received.

forward route   From one host's perspective, the route over which a packet travels from that host to some other host.

four-wire circuit   A line from the telco with four wires, composed of two twisted-pair wires. Each pair is used to send in one direction, so a four-wire circuit allows full-duplex communication.

frame   A term referring to a data link header and trailer, plus the data encapsulated between the header and trailer.

Frame Check Sequence   A field in many data link trailers used as part of the error-detection process.

Frame Relay   An international standard data link protocol that defines the capabilities to create a frame-switched (packet-switched) service, allowing DTE devices (typically routers) to send data to many other devices using a single physical connection to the Frame Relay service.

full duplex   Generically, any communication in which two communicating devices can concurrently send and receive data. In Ethernet LANs, the allowance for both devices to send and receive at the same time, allowed when both devices disable their CSMA/CD logic.

full mesh   A network topology in which more than two devices can physically communicate and, by choice, all pairs of devices are allowed to communicate directly.

G

Gigabit Ethernet   The common name for all the IEEE standards that send data at 1 gigabit per second.

global routing prefix   An IPv6 prefix that defines an IPv6 address block made up of global unicast addresses, assigned to one organization, so that the organization has a block of globally unique IPv6 addresses to use in its network.

global unicast address   A type of unicast IPv6 address that has been allocated from a range of public globally unique IP addresses, as registered through IANA/ICANN, its member agencies, and other registries or ISPs.

H

half duplex   Generically, any communication in which only one device at a time can send data. In Ethernet LANs, the normal result of the CSMA/CD algorithm that enforces the rule that only one device should send at any point in time.

HDLC   High-Level Data Link Control. A bit-oriented synchronous data link layer protocol developed by the International Organization for Standardization (ISO).

head end   The upstream, transmit end of a cable TV (CATV) installation.

header   In computer networking, a set of bytes placed in front of some other data, encapsulating that data, as defined by a particular protocol.

history buffer   In a Cisco router or switch, the function by which IOS keeps a list of commands that the user has used in this login session, both in EXEC mode and configuration mode. The user can then recall these commands for easier repeating or making small edits and issuing similar commands.

hop count   The metric used by the RIP routing protocol. Each router in an IP route is considered a hop, so for example, if two other routers sit between a router and some subnet, that router would have a hop count of two for that route.

host   Any device that uses an IP address.

host address   The IP address assigned to a network card on a computer.

hostname   The alphanumeric name of an IP host.

host part   A term used to describe a part of an IPv4 address that is used to uniquely identify a host inside a subnet. The host part is identified by the bits of value 0 in the subnet mask.

host route   A route with a /32 mask, which by virtue of this mask represents a route to a single host IP address.

HTML   Hypertext Markup Language. A simple document-formatting language that uses tags to indicate how a given part of a document should be interpreted by a viewing application, such as a web browser.

HTTP   Hypertext Transfer Protocol. The protocol used by web browsers and web servers to transfer files, such as text and graphic files.

hub   A LAN device that provides a centralized connection point for LAN cabling, repeating any received electrical signal out all other ports, thereby creating a logical bus. Hubs do not interpret the electrical signals as a frame of bits, so hubs are considered to be Layer 1 devices.

I

IANA   The Internet Assigned Numbers Authority (IANA). An organization that owns the rights to assign many operating numbers and facts about how the global Internet works, including public IPv4 and IPv6 addresses. *See also* ICANN.

ICANN   The Internet Corporation for Assigned Names and Numbers. An organization appointed by IANA to oversee the distributed process of assigning public IPv4 and IPv6 addresses across the globe.

ICMP   Internet Control Message Protocol. A TCP/IP network layer protocol that reports errors and provides other information relevant to IP packet processing.

ICMP echo reply   One type of ICMP message, created specifically to be used as the message sent by the **ping** command to test connectivity in a network. The **ping** command expects to receive these messages from other hosts, after the **ping** command first sends an ICMP echo request message to the host.

ICMP echo request   One type of ICMP message, created specifically to be used as the message sent by the **ping** command to test connectivity in a network. The **ping** command sends these messages to other hosts, expecting the other host to reply with an ICMP echo reply message.

IEEE   Institute of Electrical and Electronics Engineers. A professional organization that develops communications and network standards, among other activities.

IEEE 802.11   The IEEE base standard for wireless LANs.

IEEE 802.1Q   The IEEE-standard VLAN trunking protocol. 802.1Q includes the concept of a native VLAN, for which no VLAN header is added, and a 4-byte VLAN header is inserted after the original frame's Type/Length field.

IEEE 802.2   An IEEE LAN protocol that specifies an implementation of the LLC sublayer of the data link layer.

IEEE 802.3   A set of IEEE LAN protocols that specifies the many variations of what is known today as an Ethernet LAN.

IETF   The Internet Engineering Task Force. The IETF serves as the primary organization that works directly to create new TCP/IP standards.

inactivity timer   For switch MAC address tables, a timer associated with each entry that counts time upward from 0 and is reset to 0 each time a switch receives a frame with the same MAC address. The entries with the largest timers can be removed to make space for additional MAC address table entries.

inside global   For packets sent to and from a host that resides inside the trusted part of a network that uses NAT, a term referring to the IP address used in the headers of those packets when those packets traverse the global (public) Internet.

inside local   For packets sent to and from a host that resides inside the trusted part of a network that uses NAT, a term referring to the IP address used in the headers of those packets when those packets traverse the enterprise (private) part of the network.

interior gateway protocol (IGP)   *See* interior routing protocol.

interior routing protocol   A routing protocol designed for use within a single organization.

Internetwork Operating System   The operating system (OS) of Cisco routers and switches, which provides the majority of a router's or switch's features, with the hardware providing the remaining features.

intrusion detection system (IDS)   A security function that examines more complex traffic patterns against a list of both known attack signatures and general characteristics of how attacks can be carried out, rating each perceived threat and reporting the threats.

intrusion prevention system (IPS)   A security function that examines more complex traffic patterns against a list of both known attack signatures and general characteristics of how attacks can be carried out, rating each perceived threat, and reacting to prevent the more significant threats.

IOS Cisco Internetwork Operating System Software that provides the majority of a router's or switch's features, with the hardware providing the remaining features.

IOS feature set A set of related features that can be enabled on a router to enable certain functionality. For example, the Security feature set would enable the capability to have the router act as a firewall in the network.

IOS File System (IFS) A file system created by a Cisco device that uses IOS.

IOS image A file that contains the IOS.

IP Internet Protocol. The network layer protocol in the TCP/IP stack, providing routing and logical addressing standards and services.

IP address (IP version 4) In IP version 4 (IPv4), a 32-bit address assigned to hosts using TCP/IP. Each address consists of a network number, an optional subnetwork number, and a host number. The network and subnetwork numbers together are used for routing, and the host number is used to address an individual host within the network or subnetwork.

IP address (IP version 6) In IP version 6 (IPv6), a 128-bit address assigned to hosts using TCP/IP. Addresses use different formats, commonly using a routing prefix, subnet, and interface ID, corresponding to the IPv4 network, subnet, and host parts of an address.

IP network *See* classful IP network.

IP packet An IP header, followed by the data encapsulated after the IP header, but specifically not including any headers and trailers for layers below the network layer.

IP routing table *See* routing table.

IP subnet Subdivisions of a Class A, B, or C network, as configured by a network administrator. Subnets allow a single Class A, B, or C network to be used instead of multiple networks, and still allow for a large number of groups of IP addresses, as is required for efficient IP routing.

IP version 4 Literally, the version of the Internet Protocol defined in an old RFC 791, standardized in 1980, and used as the basis of TCP/IP networks and the Internet for over 30 years.

IP version 6 A newer version of the Internet Protocol defined in RFC 2460, as well as many other RFCs, whose creation was motivated by the need to avoid the IPv4 address exhaustion problem.

IPv4 address exhaustion The process by which the public IPv4 addresses, available to create the Internet, were consumed through the 1980s until today, with the expectation that eventually the world would run out of available IPv4 addresses.

IPv6 neighbor table The IPv6 equivalent of the ARP table. A table that lists IPv6 addresses of other hosts on the same link, along with their matching MAC addresses, as typically learned using Neighbor Discovery Protocol (NDP).

ISL Inter-Switch Link. A Cisco-proprietary protocol that maintains VLAN information as traffic flows between switches and routers.

ISO   International Organization for Standardization. An international organization that is responsible for a wide range of standards, including many standards relevant to networking. The ISO developed the OSI reference model, a popular networking reference model.

K

keepalive   A proprietary feature of Cisco routers in which the router sends messages on a periodic basis as a means of letting the neighboring router know that the first router is still alive and well.

known unicast frame   An Ethernet frame whose destination MAC address is listed in a switch's MAC address table, so the switch will forward the frame out the one port associated with that entry in the MAC address table.

L

L2PDU   Layer 2 protocol data unit. Often called a frame. The data compiled by a Layer 2 protocol, including Layer 2 header, encapsulated high-layer data, and Layer 2 trailer.

L3PDU   Layer 3 protocol data unit. Often called a packet. The data compiled by a Layer 3 protocol, including Layer 3 headers and the encapsulated high-layer data, but not including lower-layer headers and trailers.

L4PDU   Layer 4 protocol data unit. Often called a segment. The data compiled by a Layer 4 protocol, including Layer 4 headers and encapsulated high-layer data, but not including lower-layer headers and trailers.

Layer 3 protocol   A protocol that has characteristics like OSI Layer 3, which defines logical addressing and routing. IPv4 and IPv6 are Layer 3 protocols.

Layer 3 switch   *See* multilayer switch.

learning   The process used by switches for discovering MAC addresses, and their relative location, by looking at the source MAC address of all frames received by a bridge or switch.

leased line   A serial communications circuit between two points, provided by some service provider, typically a telephone company (telco). Because the telco does not sell a physical cable between the two endpoints, instead charging a monthly fee for the ability to send bits between the two sites, the service is considered to be a leased service.

lightweight access point   A wireless AP that communicates with wireless clients but must rely on and communicate through a wireless LAN controller into the wired part of the network.

link-local address   A type of unicast IPv6 address that represents an interface on a single data link. Packets sent to a link-local address cross only that particular link and are never forwarded to other subnets by a router. Used for communications that do not need to leave the local link.

link-local scope   With IPv6 multicasts, a term that refers to the parts (scope) of the network to which a multicast packet can flow, with link-local referring to the fact that the packet stays on the subnet in which it originated.

link state   A classification of the underlying algorithm used in some routing protocols. Link-state protocols build a detailed database that lists links (subnets) and their state (up, down), from which the best routes can then be calculated.

link-state advertisement (LSA)   In OSPF, the name of the data structure that resides inside the LSDB and describes in detail the various components in a network, including routers and links (subnets).

link-state database (LSDB)   In OSPF, the data structure in RAM of a router that holds the various LSAs, with the collective LSAs representing the entire topology of the network.

LLC   Logical Link Control. The higher of the two data link layer sublayers defined by the IEEE. Synonymous with IEEE 802.2.

LLDP   Link Layer Discovery Protocol. An IEEE standard protocol (IEEE 802.1AB) that defines messages, encapsulated directly in Ethernet frames so they do not rely on a work-ing IPv4 or IPv6 network, for the purpose of giving devices a means of announcing basic device information to other devices on the LAN. It is a standardized protocol similar to Cisco Discovery Protocol (CDP).

local broadcast IP address   IPv4 address 255.255.255.255. A packet sent to this address is sent as a data link broadcast, but only flows to hosts in the subnet into which it was originally sent. Routers do not forward these packets.

local loop   A line from the premises of a telephone subscriber to the telephone company CO.

local username   A username (with matching password), configured on a router or switch. It is considered local because it exists on the router or switch, and not on a remote server.

log message   A message generated by any computer, but including Cisco routers and switch-es, for which the device OS wants to notify the owner or administrator of the device about some event.

logical address   A generic reference to addresses as defined by Layer 3 protocols that do not have to be concerned with the physical details of the underlying physical media. Used mainly to contrast these addresses with data link addresses, which are generically considered to be physical addresses because they differ based on the type of physical medium.

login banner   In a Cisco router or switch, a text message that the router/switch displays for the user during the login process.

M

MAC   Media Access Control. The lower of the two sublayers of the data link layer defined by the IEEE. Synonymous with IEEE 802.3 for Ethernet LANs.

MAC address   A standardized data link layer address that is required for every device that connects to a LAN. Ethernet MAC addresses are 6 bytes long and are controlled by the IEEE. Also known as a *hardware address*, a *MAC layer address*, and a *physical address*.

MAC address table   A table of forwarding information held by a Layer 2 switch, built dynamically by listening to incoming frames and used by the switch to match frames to make decisions about where to forward the frame.

MD5 hash   A specific mathematical algorithm intended for use in various security protocols. In the context of Cisco routers and switches, the devices store the MD5 hash of certain passwords, rather than the passwords themselves, in an effort to make the device more secure.

message of the day   One type of login banner that can be defined on a Cisco router or switch.

metric   A unit of measure used by routing protocol algorithms to determine the best route for traffic to use to reach a particular destination.

microsegmentation   The process in LAN design by which every switch port connects to a single device, with no hubs connected to the switch ports, creating a separate collision domain per interface. The term's origin relates to the fact that one definition for the word "segment" is "collision domain," with a switch separating each switch port into a separate collision domain or segment.

modem   Modulator-demodulator. A device that converts between digital and analog signals so that a computer can send data to another computer using analog telephone lines. At the source, a modem converts digital signals to a form suitable for transmission over analog communication facilities. At the destination, the analog signals are returned to their digital form.

Modified EUI-64   *See* EUI-64.

multicast IP address   A class D IPv4 address. When used as a destination address in a packet, the routers collectively work to deliver copies of the one original packet to all hosts who have previously registered to receive packets sent to that particular multicast address.

multilayer switch   A LAN switch that can also perform Layer 3 routing functions. The name comes from the fact that this device makes forwarding decisions based on logic from multiple OSI layers (Layers 2 and 3).

multimode   A type of fiber-optic cabling with a larger core than single-mode cabling, allowing light to enter at multiple angles. Such cabling has lower bandwidth than single-mode fiber but requires a typically cheaper light source, such as an LED rather than a laser.

N

name resolution   The process by which an IP host discovers the IP address associated with a hostname, often involving sending a DNS request to a DNS server, with the server supplying the IP address used by a host with the listed hostname.

name server   A server connected to a network that resolves network names into network addresses.

named access list   An ACL that identifies the various statements in the ACL based on a name, rather than a number.

NAT   Network Address Translation. A mechanism for reducing the need for globally unique IP addresses. NAT allows an organization with addresses that are not globally unique to connect to the Internet, by translating those addresses into public addresses in the globally routable address space.

NAT overload   Another term for Port Address Translation (PAT). One of several methods of configuring NAT, in this case translating TCP and UDP flows based on port numbers in addition to using one or only a few inside global addresses.

neighbor   In routing protocols, another router with which a router decides to exchange routing information.

Neighbor Advertisement (NA)   A message defined by the IPv6 Neighbor Discovery Protocol (NDP), used to declare to other neighbors a host's MAC address. Sometimes sent in response to a previously received NDP Neighbor Solicitation (NS) message.

Neighbor Discovery Protocol (NDP)   A protocol that is part of the IPv6 protocol suite, used to discover and exchange information about devices on the same subnet (neighbors). In particular, it replaces the IPv4 ARP protocol.

Neighbor Solicitation (NS)   A message defined by the IPv6 Neighbor Discovery Protocol (NDP), used to ask a neighbor to reply with a Neighbor Advertisement, which lists the neighbor's MAC address.

network   A collection of computers, printers, routers, switches, and other devices that can communicate with each other over some transmission medium.

network address   *See* network number.

network broadcast address   In IPv4, a special address in each classful network that can be used to broadcast a packet to all hosts in that same classful network. Numerically, the address has the same value as the network number in the network part of the address and all 255s in the host octets—for example, 10.255.255.255 is the network broadcast address for classful network 10.0.0.0.

network ID   A number that identifies an IPv4 network, using a number in dotted-decimal notation (like IP addresses); a number that represents any single Class A, B, or C IP network.

network interface card (NIC)   A computer card, sometimes an expansion card and sometimes integrated into the motherboard of the computer, that provides the electronics and other functions to connect to a computer network. Today, most NICs are specifically Ethernet NICs, and most have an RJ-45 port, the most common type of Ethernet port.

network number   A number that uses dotted-decimal notation like IP addresses, but the number itself represents all hosts in a single Class A, B, or C IP network.

network part   The portion of an IPv4 address that is either 1, 2, or 3 octets/bytes long, based on whether the address is in a Class A, B, or C network.

network route   A route for a classful network.

Network Time Protocol (NTP)   A protocol used to synchronize time-of-day clocks so that multiple devices use the same time of day, which allows log messages to be more easily matched based on their timestamps.

networking model   A generic term referring to any set of protocols and standards collected into a comprehensive grouping that, when followed by the devices in a network, allows all the devices to communicate. Examples include TCP/IP and OSI.

next-hop router   In an IP route in a routing table, part of a routing table entry that refers to the next IP router (by IP address) that should receive packets that match the route.

NIC   *See* network interface card.

NTP client   Any device that attempts to use the Network Time Protocol (NTP) to synchronize its time by adjusting the local device's time based on NTP messages received from a server.

NTP client/server mode   A mode of operation with the Network Time Protocol (NTP) in which the device acts as both an NTP client, synchronizing its time with some servers, and as an NTP server, supplying time information to clients.

NTP server   Any device that uses Network Time Protocol (NTP) to help synchronize time-of-day clocks for other devices by telling other devices its current time.

NTP synchronization   The process with the Network Time Protocol (NTP) by which different devices send messages, exchanging the devices' current time-of-day clock information and other data, so that some devices adjust their clocks to the point that the time-of-day clocks list the same time (often accurate to at least the same second).

NVRAM   Nonvolatile RAM. A type of random-access memory (RAM) that retains its contents when a unit is powered off.

O

ordered data transfer   A networking function, included in TCP, in which the protocol defines how the sending host should number the data transmitted, defines how the receiving device should attempt to reorder the data if it arrives out of order, and specifies to discard the data if it cannot be delivered in order.

OSI   Open System Interconnection reference model. A network architectural model developed by the ISO. The model consists of seven layers, each of which specifies particular network functions, such as addressing, flow control, error control, encapsulation, and reliable message transfer.

OSPF   Open Shortest Path First. A popular link-state IGP that uses a link-state database and the Shortest Path First (SPF) algorithm to calculate the best routes to reach each known subnet.

OSPF version 2   The version of the OSPF routing protocol that supports IPv4, and not IPv6, and has been commonly used for over 20 years.

OSPF version 3   The version of the OSPF routing protocol that originally supported only IPv6, and not IPv4, but now supports IPv4 through the use of address family configuration.

outgoing interface   In an IP route in a routing table, part of a routing table entry that refers to the local interface out which the local router should forward packets that match the route.

outside global   With source NAT, the one address used by the host that resides outside the enterprise, which NAT does not change, so there is no need for a contrasting term.

overlapping subnets   An (incorrect) IP subnet design condition in which one subnet's range of addresses includes addresses in the range of another subnet.

P

packet   A logical grouping of bytes that includes the network layer header and encapsulated data, but specifically does not include any headers and trailers below the network layer.

packet switching   A generic reference to network services, typically WAN services, in which the service examines the contents of the transmitted data to make some type of forwarding decision. This term is mainly used to contrast with the WAN term *circuit switching*, in which the provider sets up a (Layer 1) circuit between two devices and the provider makes no attempt to interpret the meaning of the bits.

partial mesh   A network topology in which more than two devices could physically communicate but, by choice, only a subset of the pairs of devices connected to the network is allowed to communicate directly.

passive interface   With a routing protocol, a router interface for which the routing protocol is enabled on the interface, but for which the routing protocol does not send routing protocol messages out that interface.

patch cable   An Ethernet cable, usually short, that connects from a device's Ethernet port to a wall plate or switch. With wiring inside a building, electricians prewire from the wiring closet to each cubicle or other location, with a patch cable connecting the short distance from the wall plate to the user device.

PDU   Protocol data unit. An OSI term to refer generically to a grouping of information by a particular layer of the OSI model. More specifically, an LxPDU would imply the data and headers as defined by Layer x.

periodic update   With routing protocols, the concept that the routing protocol advertises routes in a routing update on a regular periodic basis. This is typical of distance vector routing protocols.

ping   An Internet Control Message Protocol (ICMP) echo message and its reply; ping often is used in IP networks to test the reachability of a network device.

pinout   The documentation and implementation of which wires inside a cable connect to each pin position in any connector.

port   In TCP and UDP, a number that is used to uniquely identify the application process that either sent (source port) or should receive (destination port) data. In LAN switching, another term for switch interface.

Port Address Translation (PAT)   A NAT feature in which one inside global IP address supports over 65,000 concurrent TCP and UDP connections.

port number   A field in a TCP or UDP header that identifies the application that either sent (source port) or should receive (destination port) the data inside the data segment.

port security   A Cisco switch feature in which the switch watches Ethernet frames that come in an interface (a port), tracks the source MAC addresses of all such frames, and takes a security action if the number of different such MAC addresses is exceeded.

PPP   Point-to-Point Protocol. A protocol that provides router-to-router and host-to-network connections over synchronous point-to-point and asynchronous point-to-point circuits.

prefix   In IPv6, this term refers to the number that identifies a group of IPv6 addresses. An IPv6 subnet identifier.

prefix length   In IPv6, the number of bits in an IPv6 prefix.

prefix mask   A term to describe an IPv4 subnet mask when represented as a slash (/) followed by a decimal number. The decimal number is the number of binary 1s in the mask.

prefix notation (IP version 4)   A shorter way to write a subnet mask in which the number of binary 1s in the mask is simply written in decimal. For example, /24 denotes the subnet mask with 24 binary 1 bits in the subnet mask. The number of bits of value binary 1 in the mask is considered to be the prefix length.

private addresses   IP addresses in several Class A, B, and C networks that are set aside for use inside private organizations. These addresses, as defined in RFC 1918, are not routable through the Internet.

private IP network   Any of the IPv4 Class A, B, or C networks as defined by RFC 1918, intended for use inside a company but not used as public IP networks.

problem isolation   The part of the troubleshooting process in which the engineer attempts to rule out possible causes of the problem until the root cause of the problem can be identified.

product authorization key (PAK)   During the IOS licensing process, the number that Cisco assigns a customer giving the customer the right to enable an IOS feature set on one of that customer's routers of a particular model series (chosen at the time the PAK was purchased).

protocol data unit (PDU)   A generic term referring to the header defined by some layer of a networking model, and the data encapsulated by the header (and possibly trailer) of that layer, but specifically not including any lower-layer headers and trailers.

Protocol Type field   A field in a LAN header that identifies the type of header that follows the LAN header. Includes the DIX Ethernet Type field, the IEEE 802.2 DSAP field, and the SNAP protocol Type field.

PSTN   Public switched telephone network. A general term referring to the variety of telephone networks and services in place worldwide. Sometimes called *POTS*, or *plain old telephone service*.

PTT   Post, telephone, and telegraph. A government agency that provides telephone services. PTTs exist in some areas outside of North America and provide both local and long-distance telephone services.

public IP address   An IP address that is part of a registered network number, as assigned by an Internet Assigned Numbers Authority (IANA) member agency, so that only the organization to which the address is registered is allowed to use the address. Routers in the Internet should have routes allowing them to forward packets to all the publicly registered IP addresses.

public IP network   Any IPv4 Class A, B, or C network assigned for use by one organization only, so that the addresses in the network are unique across the Internet, allowing packets to be sent through the public Internet using the addresses.

Q

quartet   A term used in this book, but not in other references, to refer to a set of four hex digits in an IPv6 address.

R

RAM   Random-access memory. A type of volatile memory that can be read and written by a microprocessor.

Regional Internet Registry   An organization (five globally) that receives allocations of public IPv4 addresses from IANA, and then manages that address space in their major geographic region, performing public address allocations to ISPs and assignments directly to companies that use the addresses.

resident subnet   Each IP subnet contains a number of unicast IP addresses; that subnet is the resident subnet for each of those addresses; that is, the subnet in which those addresses reside.

resolve   In the context of troubleshooting methods, the part of the process by which you fix the root cause of a problem so that the problem no longer exists.

reverse route   From one host's perspective, for packets sent back to the host from another host, the route over which the packet travels.

RFC   Request For Comments. A document used as the primary means for communicating information about the TCP/IP protocols. Some RFCs are designated by the Internet Architecture Board (IAB) as Internet standards, and others are informational. RFCs are available online from numerous sources, including http://www.rfc-editor.org.

RIP   Routing Information Protocol. An interior gateway protocol (IGP) that uses distance vector logic and router hop count as the metric. RIP version 2 (RIPv2) replaced the older RIP version 1 (RIPv1), with RIPv2 providing more features, including support for VLSM.

RIR   *See* Regional Internet Registry.

RJ-45   A popular type of cabling connector used for Ethernet cabling. It is similar to the RJ-11 connector used for telephone wiring in homes in the United States. RJ-45 allows the connection of eight wires.

ROM   Read-only memory. A type of nonvolatile memory that can be read but not written to by the microprocessor.

ROMMON   A shorter name for ROM Monitor, which is a low-level operating system that can be loaded into Cisco routers for several seldom-needed maintenance tasks, including password recovery and loading a new IOS when flash memory has been corrupted.

root cause   A troubleshooting term that refers to the reason why a problem exists, specifically a reason for which, if changed, the problem would either be solved or changed to a different problem.

routed protocol   A protocol that defines packets that can be routed by a router. Examples of routed protocols include IPv4 and IPv6.

Router Advertisement (RA)   A message defined by the IPv6 Neighbor Discovery Protocol (NDP), used by routers to announce their willingness to act as an IPv6 router on a link. These can be sent in response to a previously received NDP Router Solicitation (RS) message.

router ID (RID)   In OSPF, a 32-bit number, written in dotted-decimal notation, that uniquely identifies each router.

Router Solicitation (RS)   A message defined by the IPv6 Neighbor Discovery Protocol (NDP), used to ask any routers on the link to reply, identifying the router, plus other configuration settings (prefixes and prefix lengths).

routing protocol   A set of messages and processes with which routers can exchange information about routes to reach subnets in a particular network. Examples of routing protocols include the Enhanced Interior Gateway Routing Protocol (EIGRP), the Open Shortest Path First (OSPF) protocol, and the Routing Information Protocol (RIP).

routing table   A list of routes in a router, with each route listing the destination subnet and mask, the router interface out which to forward packets destined to that subnet, and as needed, the next-hop router's IP address.

routing update   A generic reference to any routing protocol's messages in which it sends routing information to a neighbor.

running-config file   In Cisco IOS switches and routers, the name of the file that resides in RAM memory, holding the device's currently used configuration.

S

same-layer interaction   The communication between two networking devices for the purposes of the functions defined at a particular layer of a networking model, with that communication happening by using a header defined by that layer of the model. The two devices set values in the header, send the header and encapsulated data, with the receiving devices interpreting the header to decide what action to take.

SCP   Secure Copy Protocol. A method to securely copy files that uses the authentication and encryption services of SSH; can be used to copy files to/from Cisco devices.

Secure Shell (SSH)   A TCP/IP application layer protocol that supports terminal emulation between a client and server, using dynamic key exchange and encryption to keep the communications private.

segment   In TCP, a term used to describe a TCP header and its encapsulated data (also called an *L4PDU*). Also in TCP, the process of accepting a large chunk of data from the application layer and breaking it into smaller pieces that fit into TCP segments. In Ethernet, a segment is either a single Ethernet cable or a single collision domain (no matter how many cables are used).

segmentation   The process of breaking a large piece of data from an application into pieces appropriate in size to be sent through the network.

serial cable   A type of cable with many different styles of connectors used to connect a router to an external CSU/DSU on a leased-line installation.

serial interface   A type of interface on a router, used to connect to some types of WAN links, particularly leased lines and Frame Relay access links.

setup mode   An option on Cisco IOS switches and routers that prompts the user for basic configuration information, resulting in new running-config and startup-config files.

SFTP   SSH File Transfer Protocol. A file transfer protocol that assumes a secure channel, such as an encrypted SSH connection, which then provides the means to transfer files over the secure channel.

shared Ethernet   An Ethernet that uses a hub, or even the original coaxial cabling, that results in the devices having to take turns sending data, sharing the available bandwidth.

shortest path first (SPF) algorithm   The name of the algorithm used by link-state routing protocols to analyze the LSDB and find the least-cost routes from that router to each subnet.

single mode   A type of fiber-optic cabling with a narrow core that allows light to enter only at a single angle. Such cabling has a higher bandwidth than multimode fiber but requires a light source with a narrow spectral width (such as a laser).

sliding windows   For protocols such as TCP that allow the receiving device to dictate the amount of data the sender can send before receiving an acknowledgment—a concept called a *window*—a reference to the fact that the mechanism to grant future windows is typically just a number that grows upward slowly after each acknowledgment, sliding upward.

solicited-node multicast address   A type of IPv6 multicast address, with link-local scope, used to send packets to all hosts in the subnet that share the same value in the last six hex digits of their unicast IPv6 addresses. Begins with FF02::1:FF00:0/104.

Source NAT   The type of Network Address Translation (NAT) used most commonly in networks (as compared to destination NAT), in which the source IP address of packets entering an inside interface is translated.

Spanning Tree Protocol (STP)   A protocol that uses the Spanning Tree algorithm, allowing a switch to dynamically work around loops in a network topology by creating a spanning tree. Switches exchange bridge protocol data unit (BPDU) messages with other switches to detect loops and then remove the loops by blocking selected switch interfaces.

standard access list   A list of IOS global configuration commands that can match only a packet's source IP address, for the purpose of deciding which packets to discard and which to allow through the router.

star topology   A network topology in which endpoints on a network are connected to a common central device by point-to-point links.

startup-config file   In Cisco IOS switches and routers, the name of the file that resides in NVRAM memory, holding the device's configuration that will be loaded into RAM as the running-config file when the device is next reloaded or powered on.

stateful DHCPv6   A term used in IPv6 to contrast with stateless DHCP. Stateful DHCP keeps track of which clients have been assigned which IPv6 addresses (state information).

stateless address autoconfiguration (SLAAC)   A feature of IPv6 in which a host or router can be assigned an IPv6 unicast address without the need for a stateful DHCP server.

stateless DHCPv6   A term used in IPv6 to contrast with stateful DHCP. Stateless DHCP servers don't lease IPv6 addresses to clients. Instead, they supply other useful information, such as DNS server IP addresses, but with no need to track information about the clients (state information).

static route   An IP route on a router created by the user configuring the details of the route on the local router.

STP   Shielded twisted-pair. This type of cabling has a layer of shielded insulation to reduce electromagnetic interference (EMI).

straight-through cable   In Ethernet, a cable that connects the wire on pin 1 on one end of the cable to pin 1 on the other end of the cable, pin 2 on one end to pin 2 on the other end, and so on.

subinterface   One of the virtual interfaces on a single physical interface.

subnet   Subdivisions of a Class A, B, or C network, as configured by a network administrator. Subnets allow a single Class A, B, or C network to be used instead of multiple networks, and still allow for a large number of groups of IP addresses, as is required for efficient IP routing.

subnet address   *See* subnet number.

subnet broadcast address   A special address in each IPv4 subnet, specifically the largest numeric address in the subnet, designed so that packets sent to this address should be delivered to all hosts in that subnet.

subnet ID (IPv4)   *See* subnet number.

subnet ID (IPv6)   The number that represents the IPv6 subnet. Also known as the IPv6 prefix, or more formally as the subnet router anycast address.

subnet ID (prefix ID)   *See* subnet number

subnet mask   A 32-bit number that numerically describes the format of an IP address, by representing the combined network and subnet bits in the address with mask bit values of 1, and representing the host bits in the address with mask bit values of 0.

subnet number   In IPv4, a dotted-decimal number that represents all addresses in a single subnet. Numerically, the smallest value in the range of numbers in a subnet, reserved so that it cannot be used as a unicast IP address by a host.

subnet part   In a subnetted IPv4 address, interpreted with classful addressing rules, one of three parts of the structure of an IP address, with the subnet part uniquely identifying different subnets of a classful IP network.

subnet router anycast address   A special anycast address in each IPv6 subnet, reserved for use by routers as a way to send a packet to any router on the subnet. The address's value in each subnet is the same number as the subnet ID.

subnet zero   An alternative term for zero subnet. *See* zero subnet.

subnetting   The process of subdividing a Class A, B, or C network into smaller groups called subnets.

switch   A network device that filters, forwards, and floods Ethernet frames based on the destination address of each frame.

switched Ethernet   An Ethernet that uses a switch, and particularly not a hub, so that the devices connected to one switch port do not have to contend to use the bandwidth available on another port. This term contrasts with *shared Ethernet*, in which the devices must share bandwidth, whereas switched Ethernet provides much more capacity, as the devices do not have to share the available bandwidth.

symmetric   A feature of many Internet access technologies in which the downstream transmission rate is the same as the upstream transmission rate.

synchronous   The imposition of time ordering on a bit stream. Practically, a device will try to use the same speed as another device on the other end of a serial link. However, by examining transitions between voltage states on the link, the device can notice slight variations in the speed on each end and can adjust its speed accordingly.

syslog   A syslog server takes system messages from network devices and stores these messages in a database. The syslog server also provides reporting capabilities on these system messages. Some can even respond to select system messages with certain actions such as emailing and paging.

syslog server   A server application that collects syslog messages from many devices over the network, and provides a user interface so that IT administrators can view the log messages to troubleshoot problems.

T

T1   A line from the telco that allows transmission of data at 1.544 Mbps, with the ability to treat the line as 24 different 64-kbps DS0 channels (plus 8 kbps of overhead).

TCP   Transmission Control Protocol. A connection-oriented transport layer TCP/IP protocol that provides reliable data transmission.

TCP/IP   Transmission Control Protocol/Internet Protocol. A common name for the suite of protocols developed by the U.S. Department of Defense in the 1970s to support the construction of worldwide internetworks. TCP and IP are the two best-known protocols in the suite.

telco   A common abbreviation for telephone company.

Telnet   The standard terminal-emulation application layer protocol in the TCP/IP protocol stack. Telnet is used for remote terminal connection, enabling users to log in to remote systems and use resources as if they were connected to a local system. Telnet is defined in RFC 854.

TFTP   Trivial File Transfer Protocol. An application protocol that allows files to be transferred from one computer to another over a network, but with only a few features, making the software require little storage space.

three-tier design   *See* core design.

trace   Short for traceroute. A program available on many systems that traces the path that a packet takes to a destination. It is used mostly to troubleshoot routing problems between hosts.

traceroute   A program available on many systems that traces the path that a packet takes to a destination. It is used mostly to debug routing problems between hosts.

trailer   In computer networking, a set of bytes placed behind some other data, encapsulating that data, as defined by a particular protocol. Typically, only data link layer protocols define trailers.

transparent bridge   The name of a networking device that was a precursor to modern LAN switches. Bridges forward frames between LAN segments based on the destination MAC address. Transparent bridging is so named because the presence of bridges is transparent to network end nodes.

trunk   In campus LANs, an Ethernet segment over which the devices add a VLAN header that identifies the VLAN in which the frame exists.

trunk interface   A switch interface configured so that it operates using VLAN trunking (either 802.1Q or ISL).

trunking   Also called VLAN trunking. A method (using either the Cisco ISL protocol or the IEEE 802.1Q protocol) to support multiple VLANs, allowing traffic from those VLANs to cross a single link.

trunking administrative mode   The configured trunking setting on a Cisco switch interface, as configured with the **switchport mode** command.

trunking operational mode   The current behavior of a Cisco switch interface for VLAN trunking.

twisted-pair   Transmission medium consisting of two insulated wires, with the wires twisted around each other in a spiral. An electrical circuit flows over the wire pair, with the current in opposite directions on each wire, which significantly reduces the interference between the two wires.

two-tier design   *See* collapsed core design.

U

UDP   User Datagram Protocol. Connectionless transport layer protocol in the TCP/IP protocol stack. UDP is a simple protocol that exchanges datagrams without acknowledgments or guaranteed delivery.

unicast address   Generally, any address in networking that represents a single device or interface, instead of a group of addresses (as would be represented by a multicast or broadcast address).

unicast IP address   An IP address that represents a single interface. In IPv4, these addresses come from the Class A, B, and C ranges.

unique local address   A type of IPv6 unicast address meant as a replacement for IPv4 private addresses.

universal device identifier (UDI)   A number that Cisco assigns to each router to uniquely identify the router's type and unique serial number, for the purpose of enabling the IOS software licensing process to work.

universal image   The Cisco IOS universal image contains all feature sets for the specific device for which it was made. The administrator just needs to license and enable the specific features he or she desires.

unknown unicast frame   An Ethernet frame whose destination MAC address is not listed in a switch's MAC address table, so the switch must flood the frame.

up and up   Jargon referring to the two interface states on a Cisco IOS router or switch (line status and protocol status), with the first "up" referring to the line status and the second "up" referring to the protocol status. An interface in this state should be able to pass data link frames.

update timer   The time interval that regulates how often a routing protocol sends its next periodic routing updates. Distance vector routing protocols send full routing updates every update interval.

URI   Uniform Resource Identifier. The formal and correct term for the formatted text used to refer to objects in an IP network. This text is commonly called a URL or a web address. For example, http://www.certskills.com/blog is a URI that identifies the protocol (HTTP), hostname (www.certskills.com), and web page (blog).

URL   Uniform Resource Locator. The widely popular terms for the formatted text used to refer to objects in an IP network. For example, http://www.certskills.com/blog is a URL that identifies the protocol (HTTP), host name (www.certskills.com), and web page (blog).

user mode A mode of the user interface to a router or switch in which the user can type only nondisruptive EXEC commands, generally just to look at the current status, but not to change any operational settings.

UTP Unshielded twisted-pair. A type of cabling, standardized by the Telecommunications Industry Association (TIA), that holds twisted pairs of copper wires (typically four pair) and does not contain any shielding from outside interference.

V

variable-length subnet mask (VLSM) The capability to specify a different subnet mask for the same Class A, B, or C network number on different subnets. VLSM can help optimize available address space.

virtual circuit (VC) In packet-switched services like Frame Relay, VC refers to the ability of two DTE devices (typically routers) to send and receive data directly to each other, which supplies the same function as a physical leased line (leased circuit), but doing so without a physical circuit. This term is meant as a contrast with a leased line or leased circuit.

virtual LAN (VLAN) A group of devices, connected to one or more switches, with the devices grouped into a single broadcast domain through switch configuration. VLANs allow switch administrators to separate the devices connected to the switches into separate VLANs without requiring separate physical switches, gaining design advantages of separating the traffic without the expense of buying additional hardware.

virtual private network (VPN) The process of securing communication between two devices whose packets pass over some public and unsecured network, typically the Internet. VPNs encrypt packets so that the communication is private, and authenticate the identity of the endpoints.

VLAN *See* virtual LAN.

VLAN configuration database The name of the collective configuration of VLAN IDs and names on a Cisco switch.

VLAN interface A configuration concept inside Cisco switches, used as an interface between IOS running on the switch and a VLAN supported inside the switch, so that the switch can assign an IP address and send IP packets into that VLAN.

VLAN Trunking Protocol (VTP) A Cisco-proprietary messaging protocol used between Cisco switches to communicate configuration information about the existence of VLANs, including the VLAN ID and VLAN name.

voice VLAN A VLAN defined for use by IP Phones, with the Cisco switch notifying the phone about the voice VLAN ID so that the phone can use 802.1Q frames to support traffic for the phone and the attached PC (which uses a data VLAN).

VoIP Voice over IP. The transport of voice traffic inside IP packets over an IP network.

VTP *See* VLAN Trunking Protocol.

VTP client mode   One of three VTP operational modes for a switch with which switches learn about VLAN numbers and names from other switches, but which does not allow the switch to be directly configured with VLAN information.

VTP server mode   One of three VTP operational modes. Switches in server mode can configure VLANs, tell other switches about the changes, and learn about VLAN changes from other switches.

VTP transparent mode   One of three VTP operational modes. Switches in transparent mode can configure VLANs, but they do not tell other switches about the changes, and they do not learn about VLAN changes from other switches.

W

web server   Software, running on a computer, that stores web pages and sends those web pages to web clients (web browsers) that request the web pages.

well-known port   A TCP or UDP port number reserved for use by a particular application. The use of well-known ports allows a client to send a TCP or UDP segment to a server, to the correct destination port for that application.

Wi-Fi Alliance   An organization formed by many companies in the wireless industry (an industry association) for the purpose of getting multivendor certified-compatible wireless products to market in a more timely fashion than would be possible by simply relying on standardization processes.

wide-area network (WAN)   A part of a larger network that implements mostly OSI Layer 1 and 2 technology, connects sites that typically sit far apart, and uses a business model in which a consumer (individual or business) must lease the WAN from a service provider (often a telco).

wildcard mask   The mask used in Cisco IOS ACL commands and OSPF and EIGRP **network** commands.

window   Represents the number of bytes that can be sent without receiving an acknowledgment.

wired LAN   A local-area network (LAN) that physically transmits bits using cables, often the wires inside cables. A term for local-area networks that use cables, emphasizing the fact that the LAN transmits data using wires (in cables) instead of wireless radio waves. *See also* wireless LAN.

wireless LAN   A local-area network (LAN) that physically transmits bits using radio waves. The name "wireless" compares these LANs to more traditional "wired" LANs, which are LANs that use cables (which often have copper wires inside).

wireless LAN Controller (WLC)   A device that cooperates with wireless lightweight access points (LWAP) to create a wireless LAN by performing some control functions for each LWAP and forwarding data between each LWAP and the wired LAN.

WLAN client   A wireless device that wants to gain access to a wireless access point for the purpose of communicating with other wireless devices or other devices connected to the wired internetwork.

Z

zero subnet   For every classful IPv4 network that is subnetted, the one subnet whose subnet number has all binary 0s in the subnet part of the number. In decimal, the zero subnet can be easily identified because it is the same number as the classful network number.

Index

Symbols

A

B

H

I

O

Q-R

S

W-X-Y-Z

REGISTER YOUR PRODUCT at CiscoPress.com/register

Access Additional Benefits and SAVE 35% on Your Next Purchase

- Download available product updates.
- Access bonus material when applicable.
- Receive exclusive offers on new editions and related products.
  (Just check the box to hear from us when setting up your account.)
- Get a coupon for 35% for your next purchase, valid for 30 days.
  Your code will be available in your Cisco Press cart. (You will also find
  it in the Manage Codes section of your account page.)

Registration benefits vary by product. Benefits will be listed on your account page
under Registered Products.

CiscoPress.com – Learning Solutions for Self-Paced Study, Enterprise, and the Classroom
Cisco Press is the Cisco Systems authorized book publisher of Cisco networking technology,
Cisco certification self-study, and Cisco Networking Academy Program materials.

At **CiscoPress.com** you can
- Shop our books, eBooks, software, and video training.
- Take advantage of our special offers and promotions (ciscopress.com/promotions).
- Sign up for special offers and content newsletters (ciscopress.com/newsletters).
- Read free articles, exam profiles, and blogs by information technology experts.
- Access thousands of free chapters and video lessons.

Connect with Cisco Press – Visit CiscoPress.com/community
Learn about Cisco Press community events and programs.

Cisco Press